WELCOME TO *The World* IS A TEXT
THIRD EDITION

Writing, Reading, and Thinking About Visual and Popular Culture

JONATHAN SILVERMAN

University of Massachusetts Lowell

DEAN RADER

University of San Francisco

PEARSON

Prentice Hall

Upper Saddle River, New Jersey 07458

Library of Congress Cataloging-in-Publication Data

Silverman, Jonathan.
    The world is a text : writing, reading and thinking about visual and
popular culture / Jonathan Silverman, Dean Rader. -- 3rd ed.
        p. cm.
    Includes bibliographical references and index.
    ISBN-13: 978-0-13-603345-5
    ISBN-10: 0-13-603345-8
    1. English language--Rhetoric. 2. Culture--Problems, exercises, etc. 3.
Readers--Culture. 4. Critical thinking. 5. College readers. 6. Report
writing. 7. Semiotics. I. Rader, Dean. II. Title.
    PE1408.S48785 2008
    808'.0427--dc22

                                2008021636

VP/Editorial Director: Leah Jewell	**Manager, Cover Visual Research and**
Editor-in-Chief: Craig Campanella	**Permissions:** Karen Sanatar
Senior Editor: Brad Potthoff	**Manager, Rights and Permissions:** Zina Arabia
Editorial Assistant: Tracy Clough	**Manager, Visual Research:** Beth Brenzel
Marketing Director: Brandy Dawson	**Image Coordinator:** Fran Toepfer
Marketing Manager: Sandra McGuire	**Full-Service Production and**
Marketing Assistant: Adam Mertin	**Composition:** Aptara®, Inc.
Text Permission Specialist: Kathleen Karcher	**Full-Service Project Management:** Kelly Ricci
Senior Operations Supervisor: Sherry Lewis	**Printer/Binder:** Courier Companies
Project Manager: Maureen Benicasa	**Cover art:** Beathan/CORBIS-NY
Senior Art Director: Nancy Wells	(*front* and *back*)
Interior & Cover Design: Ilze Lemesis	**Cover Printer:** Phoenix Color Corp.
Director, Image Resource Center: Melinda Reo	

This book was set in 10/12 Minion.
Credits and acknowledgments borrowed from other sources and reproduced, with permission, in this textbook appear on page 707.

Pearson Education LTD., London   Pearson Education North Asia Ltd
Pearson Education Singapore, Pte. Ltd   Pearson Educación de Mexico, S.A. de C.V.
Pearson Education, Canada, Ltd   Pearson Education Malaysia, Pte. Ltd
Pearson Education–Japan   Pearson Education, Upper Saddle River,
Pearson Education Australia PTY, Limited   New Jersey

10 9 8 7 6 5 4
ISBN-13: 978-0-13-603345-5
ISBN-10: 0-13-603345-8

WELCOME TO *The World* IS A TEXT

THIRD EDITION

Writing, Reading, and Thinking
About Visual and Popular Culture

Contents

v

SECTION TWO–THE WORLD IS A TEXT: READING   73

1. Reading and Writing About the World Around You   74

2. Reading and Writing About Television   118

The Reality TV Suite

3. Reading and Writing About Visual Art   194

The "Is It Art?" Suite

4. Reading and Writing About Race and Ethnicity   266

The Native American Mascot Suite

6. Reading and Writing About Gender   426

7. Reading and Writing About Public and Private Space   478

8. Reading and Writing About Advertising, Journalism, and the Media   538

9. Reading and Writing About Relationships   606

10. Reading and Writing About Music   652

11. Reading and Writing About Technology   704

Alternative Table of Contents

Below are the readings in *The World Is a Text* grouped according to subject matter, genre, or style of writing. They offer cross-chapter ways of reading individual works.

African American Issues

Arab and Arab American Issues

Asian American Issues

Argumentative/Persuasive Essays

Comparison/Contrast

Definitional Essays

Fun!

Images, Visual Culture & Non-Traditional Texts

Literature (Fiction, Literary Non-Fiction, and Poetry)

Native American Issues

Personal (Uses First Person)

Race/Ethnicity

Researched Essays (Works with Citations)

Young Adults/Teenagers/Children

Preface

Welcome to the 3rd edition of *The World Is a Text*. We have done a great deal of revising for this edition, and we hope you like what you see. As in the previous editions, we continue to foreground visual and cultural rhetoric along with a pedagogy of writing that encourages this facility in students.

As always, *The World Is a Text* continues to be about process, a trend that never fails to engage educators across the country. In recent months, Harvard University released a document that proposed changes in its curriculum in an attempt to make it more process-oriented (in fact, one of the authors of this book published an op-ed piece on what Harvard's new core means for higher education). As English professors—especially professors who teach composition and writing—we endorse such a change. It dovetails nicely with the emphasis on process most writing teachers endorse. And it specifically links with our book, which is about learning to read cultural texts. Indeed, one of the goals of the new curriculum, according to this task force, is that "students also should know how to 'read' cultural and aesthetic expressions." Without question, this interpretive process is a driving force of *The World Is a Text*.

Although we do not want to overstate the connection between this new trend in education and our book, it does bear noting that to live in the world today means being able to be engaged with and cognizant of the many different types of texts surrounding us. These texts beg for intelligent decoding. Such work requires a visual literacy, but more importantly a commitment to making connections between texts and experiences, to view culture with a skeptical eye, and perhaps most importantly, to be able to communicate those ideas clearly and thoughtfully.

Our first edition came out of these ideas, combined with a fruitless search for a textbook that did the work we wanted it to do. Although there are many popular culture readers out there—good ones, in fact—we never found quite the book we wanted; one that focused on the classroom experience and the writing situation. We think the classroom should be a dynamic place, and we believe writing and discussion are crucial to learning how to think. In that regard, *The World Is a Text* is as much a book for teachers as it is for students. We hope that our questions, introductions, and exercises give professors the tools they need to teach students how to write with clarity and intelligence, to read more actively and astutely, and to engage the world more actively. Whereas all three missions are crucial, the first two are clearly more aimed at academic achievement. The last mission is critical as teachers. We believe students who read their worlds more actively are not only better students, but also better citizens of the world.

In this edition, as in the last two, *The World Is a Text* relies on a modified semiotic approach as its pedagogical theory; it is based on the assumption that reading occurs at all times and places. It also relies on traditional critical skills used by literary scholars and the generally contextual approach employed by cultural studies scholars. The book also features a sophisticated way of thinking about texts, writing, and the rhetorical moment. In fact, one of our guiding concepts is Kenneth Burke's notion of rhetoric as the "use of language as a symbolic means of inducing cooperation in beings that by nature respond to symbols." *The World Is a Text* considers how various texts enact rhetorical strategies and how students might begin not only to recognize these strategies, but also use those strategies for their own writing. Textual analysis (reading) and textual formation (writing) jointly contribute to the larger process of knowledge making. Thus, *The World Is a Text* is interested in helping students to ask not simply *what* something means, but *how* something means.

And because knowledge making requires knowledge of how we make arguments and sentences and theses and assertions, this book goes one step further than similar readers. In our experience, writing remains a secondary concern for most similar books. One of our goals is to make the writing experience a vital part of the entire book from the introduction, to the section on writing, to each individual reading. For instance, Section I, *The World Is a Text: Writing*, is a comprehensive approach to the various stages of the writing process. We walk students through selecting a topic, brainstorming, outlining, developing a thesis, and revising. We offer help with research and citation. We even provide a unique section on making the transition from high school to college writing. One of our goals is to help students make these connections between reading and writing, thinking and writing, revising and re-visioning. In this edition, we respond to instructors who liked the section on semiotics but want more on rhetoric. We added additional material on process writing and research writing, as well as more strategies for approaching writing assignments, particularly those involving nontraditional texts. In addition, we provide more student essays; each chapter has one or more examples of student responses to nontraditional texts. In addition, a new and improved website also reinforces the emphasis on *writing*, not just reading. We also bolstered the rhetorical material, including new sections on claims, synthesis, and visual and cultural persuasion.

The World Is a Text also focuses on encountering media and texts in general. Each chapter has questions that encourage students to respond not only to readings, but to the texts and media themselves. Every chapter has an introduction that focuses on reading media and individual texts (not the readings themselves). In the readings that follow, each piece features questions geared toward both reading and writing. And its general apparatus in the form of worksheets and classroom exercises encourages students to use the readings as a starting point for their own explorations of television, race, movies, art, and the other media and texts we include here.

On a more theoretical level, we show how language in text and context functions to produce meaning. And we talk about how writing is fundamentally linked to other aspects of critical inquiry like reading, listening, thinking, and speaking. Just as Burke argues that all literature is a piece of rhetoric, we suggest that all texts are rhetoric, and that every moment is a potential moment for reading—and therefore for writing.

Features of *The World Is a Text*—Edition *Trois*

If you are familiar with editions *un et deux*, you will find much that is familiar here. You will also encounter quite a bit that is new. We didn't make these changes because we were unhappy with the previous editions (although we were mortified by some typos that made it into the printed version), but rather that academic and popular culture changes so rapidly, we always feel like we need to update our book accordingly. So, there are a number of new readings, instructional matter, and illustrations that we hope benefit (and enlighten) professors and students alike. For example, we added more readings on social networking services, television, and the importance of blogs. We also augmented our emphasis on visual rhetoric by including more images and photographs. Chapter 3, on Visual Arts, has been greatly expanded.

In addition to new content, we made many structural changes as well. The technology chapter migrated *entirely* to the Internet, and with it, many more readings, related not only to technology, but to all the chapters in the book. Think of the site as a portal to a very large *World (Is a Text)*. We have also added many new suites—"Is It Art?" "Reading Photographs," "The Iraq War," and "Authenticity" to name a few. We have also updated some readings in current suites.

Our biggest revision was the difficult decision to excise our literature chapter. However, in its stead is an innovative Chapter 1 that we are very excited about called "Reading and Writing about the World around You," which is a collection of original commissioned essays designed to serve as entrees to the rest of the book's chapters. We asked colleagues, friends, other writers, and students to "read" anything they wanted, and they came up with a variety of topics—everything from essays about biology labs to fashion to *Family Guy*. Although we miss the poems, we are optimistic about this change, in part because it more fully establishes the book as a visual and cultural rhetoric grounded in semiotics.

Overall, our goals for this edition remain consonant with the previous edition. We hope *The World Is a Text* will help students bridge culture and text. However, we present material in a way that provides context, direction, and structure. In that sense, the book is traditional; however, the expanded nature of what a text is makes our approach innovative. We hope that, in turn, this will allow students to expand their idea of reading and therefore expand their critical relationship to the world. In an academic setting, where "accountability" and "practicality" are watchwords, giving students a more interpretative way of looking at and writing about the world seems especially appropriate.

Acknowledgments

We would like to acknowledge more people than can comfortably fit, but here's a start. First, we want to express our gratitude to everyone at Prentice Hall, especially our editor, Brad Potthoff, and his helpful assistant, Tracy Clough. We also want to thank Leah Jewell, Brandy Dawson, and Corey Good (our first editor on this project). We thank Kelly Ricci and everyone at Aptara Inc., as well as Kathleen Karcher for copyright help. We also thank our copy editor, Mercy Heston, who caught many errors. Thanks go out to the various authors who wrote original pieces for the book, gave us the rights to reprint things at a reduced rate, and made helpful suggestions. We also appreciate the impressive feedback from professors and students who used the book. We really aren't joking; please email us if you have questions or suggestions.

We are also grateful for the advice, critiques, and suggestions from the people who graciously agreed to review and comment on *The World Is a Text* in manuscript: Lauren Ingraham, University of Tennessee; Steven Bidlake, Central Oregon Community College; Kelly Sassi, University of Michigan; Greg Barnhisel, Duquesne University; Pat Tyrer, West Texas A&M University; Adrienne Bliss, Ball State University; Jason Walker, San Francisco State; Mitra Ganley, San Francisco State; Loren Barroca, San Mateo Community College; Denise Cummings, Rollins College; Leslie Taylor Collins, University of Tennessee at Chattanooga; Linsey Cuti, Kankakee Community College; Karen Gardiner, University of Alabama; Amy Lawlor, Pasadena City College; David Moutray, Kankakee Community College; Patricia Webb, Arizona State University; and Lynn Wright, Pasadena City College. We also thank Cherelyn Willet, who composed a great poem entirely of passages from *The World Is a Text*. We are now convinced she knows the book better than we do.

We are appreciative of the many scholars who read and commented on the first and second editions of the book but who are not mentioned here. We also thank all who used or posted *The World Is a Text* bumper stickers that were floating around the CCCC convention in San Antonio. We're hoping for bowling shirts for this edition. We also thank Johnny Cash, Beck, Nirvana, Radiohead, Cat Power, Aimee Mann, Lyle Lovett, The Fountains of Wayne, De La Soul, Cornershop, Sufjan Stevens, Badly Drawn Boy, Bonnie "Prince" Billy, The Last Town Chorus, and Loop!Station (a fantastic San Francisco band Dean is obsessed with) who, unknowingly, provided the soundtrack for the writing process of this new edition. Of course, we thank our students at VCU, USF, and Pace for giving us feedback and providing constant inspiration.

For their valuable assistance in manuscript preparation, we thank Jennifer Bede, Danielle Atwood, and Erin Schietinger. For their help with the reading gender chapter, we thank Rachel Crawford, Nicole Raeburn, and Jill Ramsey; for the reading race and ethnicity chapter, Katherine Clay Bassard; for reading the technology chapter, Michael Keller; and for the introduction, Patty Strong. We also thank Miles McCrimmon for reading an early version of the proposal and for his work on the instructor's manuals.

A big thank you goes to Ecco Coffee Shop and the bar at the St. Francis Hotel, both of Santa Fe, New Mexico, where we did most of the writing for this edition.

Lisa Mahar, author of *American Signs*, was of great help, as was Svetlana Mintcheva, director of the Arts Program of the National Coalition against Censorship. We're still grateful to Rigo of San Francisco for his murals. We also thank all of the authors in Chapter 1 who contributed original pieces. We also thank Steve Grody for his special introduction to the images of graffiti. Thanks, too, to the students who submitted and contributed their work.

In areas of institutional and collegial support, the following were of special help: Catherine Ingrassia, Marcel Cornis-Pope, Richard Fine, Margret Vopel Schluer, Sharon Call Laslie, Ginny Schmitz, Bill Tester, Tom De Haven, Laura Browder, David Latane, Nick Sharp, Elizabeth Savage, Randy Lewis, Emily Roderer, Pat Perry, Elizabeth Cooper, Elizabeth Hodges, Bill Griffin, James Kinney, Marguerite Harkness, Michael Keller, Leslie Shiel, Nick Frankel, Faye Prichard, Angier Brock Caudle, Traci Wood, Walter Srebnick, Carol Dollison, Geoff Brackett, Jeannie Chiu, Kristin di Gennaro, Martha Driver, Steven Goldleaf, Tom Henthorne, Todd Heyden, Eugene Richie, Mark Hussey, Karla Jay, Helane Levine-Keating, Amy Martin, Sid Ray, Walter Raubicheck, William Sievert, Michael Roberts, Nira Herrmann, Katie Henninger, Kathie Tovo, Frank Goodyear, Anne Collins, Jan Lisiak, Teresa Genaro, Suzanne Forgarty, Michael Tanner, Dan Marano, Elisabeth Piedmont-Marton, Jeffrey Meikle, Mark Smith, Greg Barnhisel, Fouzia Baber, Anne Darby, Matt Compton, Matt King, Carlease Briggs, Virginia Colwell, Rita Botts, Sarah Hawkins, Whitney Black, Tracy Seeley, Eileen Chia-Ching Fung, Alan Heinemann, Patricia Hill, Carolyn Brown, Carolyn Webber, Sean Michaelson, John Pinelli, Robert Bednar, Wendy McCredie, Leonard Schulze, Jean-Pierre Metereau, Steven Vrooman, Beth Barry, Amy Randolph, T. Paul Hernandez, Chris Haven, Brian Clements, George McCoy, Michael Strysick, Brian Brennan, Mike Henry, LeAnne Howe, Brian Dempster, Cary Cordova, Monica Chiu, Andrew Macalister, Aranzazu Borrachero, Cecilia Santos, Vamsee Juluri, Jeff Paris, Christopher Kamrath, Susan Steinberg, Susan Paik, Peter Novak, Heather Barkley, Colleen Stevens, Freddie Wiant, Mark Merrit, Brian Dempster, Zachary White, Marika Brussel, Loren Barroca, Michael Bloch, T-Bone Needham, Jonathan Hunt, and Brandon Brown. We gratefully acknowledge the reviewers for this edition: Leslie Taylor Collins, University of Tennessee at Chattanooga; Linsey Cuti, Kankakee Community College; Karen Gardiner, University of Alabama; Amy Lawlor, Pasadena City College; David Moutray, Kankakee Community College; Patricia Webb, Arizona State University; and Lynn Wright, Pasadena City College. A good friend and loyal user of *The World Is a Text*, Jason Walker, passed away during the preparation of this third edition. He and his partner Mitra Ganley-Walker used *The World Is a Text* in innovative ways in their service learning class. As this book goes to press, Jason's inspirational ideas and his dedication to his students are with us.

In addition, we thank the English Department at Pace University, the Henry Birnbaum Library at Pace University, English Department at Virginia Commonwealth University, the VCU James Branch Cabell Library, the Andover Summer Session, and the Department of English and the Dean's Office of the University of San Francisco, particularly Dean Jennifer Turpin and the excellent staff of the Dean's Office in the College of Arts and Sciences. A special nod goes out to John Pinelli and his staff.

Finally, we thank Melvin Silverman, Beverly Silverman, Joel Silverman, Alba Estanoz, Jason Silverman, Christian Leahy, Ginger Rader, Gary Rader, Barbara Glenn, Amy Rader Kice, Adam Kice, and Isabella Kice. Dean is also particularly grateful to Jill Ramsey for marrying him only a couple of weeks before this very edition went to press.

We are most grateful to all of you who adopted this book for your classes, and a particularly hearty thank you to all of the students who made, for better or worse, this text a part of your world.

Jonathan Silverman
University of Massachusetts Lowell

Dean Rader
University of San Francisco
Email us at:
World.Text@Gmail.com

About the Authors

Jonathan Silverman and Dean Rader conceived the idea of *The World is a Text* while commuting to their job outside Austin, Texas. Frustrated with the textbook they were using in their freshman composition courses, they set out to write a book that merged rhetoric and writing with popular and visual culture. Jonathan is an assistant professor of English at University of Massachusetts at Lowell, where he teaches composition, journalism, and literature. As this book goes to press, he is serving as a Fulbright Roving Scholar in Norway. As a rover, he visits high schools all over Norway and talks about American culture, including such topics as electronic journalism, Brooklyn, New York, and the legendary Johnny Cash, about which he has just completed a manuscript titled *Nine Choices: Johnny Cash and American Culture*. Dean has published widely in the fields of American Indian Studies, American poetry, and composition studies. He is also an award-winning poet. His newest book, *Engaged Resistance: American Indian Art, Literature, and Film* is forthcoming from

Jonathan Silverman   **Dean Rader**

The University of Texas Press. Dean is an associate professor of English at the University of San Francisco, where he recently completed a four-year tenure as the Associate Dean for Arts & Humanities. He also curates the arts and culture blog, *The Weekly Rader*. In 2008, he and Jonathan also began *SemiObama,* a blog that uses the concepts laid out in this book to offer "Readings" of Barack Obama in popular culture through the lens of semiotics.

THE WORLD IS A TEXT THE WORLD IS A

TEXT THE WORLD IS A TEXT THE WORLD IS

A TEXT THE WORLD IS A TEXT THE WORLD

IS A TEXT THE WORLD IS A TEXT

introduction

THE WORLD IS A TEXT THE WORLD IS A

TEXT THE WORLD IS A TEXT THE WORLD IS

A TEXT THE WORLD IS A TEXT THE WORLD

IS A TEXT THE WORLD IS A TEXT THE

The World Is a *Really Big* Text at the Unisphere, Queens, New York.

READING, WRITING, CULTURE, AND TEXTS: AN INTRODUCTION TO THE INTRODUCTION

WE ARE BORN READERS. FROM AN EARLY AGE, WE MAKE SENSE OF EVERYTHING BY DRAWING CONCLUSIONS BASED ON OUR EXPERIENCES—SIMILAR TO THE PROCESS WE UNDERTAKE WHEN WE NOW READ A BOOK FOR SCHOOL OR PLEASURE. WE READ FOR THE FIRST TIME WHEN WE, AS BABIES, EXPRESS RECOGNITION OF OUR PARENTS. THIS CONTINUES THROUGHOUT CHILDHOOD, ADOLESCENCE, AND ADULTHOOD. WE BECOME BETTER AT READING TRADITIONAL TEXTS SUCH AS SHORT STORIES, NOVELS, AND POEMS (WHAT WE CALL "FORMAL READING") THROUGH OUR SCHOOLING, AND NONTRADITIONAL TEXTS SUCH AS TELEVISION, ARCHITECTURE, AND PEOPLE THROUGH OUR EXPERIENCE ("INFORMAL READING"), ALTHOUGH OFTEN IT IS A PARALLEL AND INTERSECTING PROCESS. IN BOTH FORMS OF READING, WE LEARN HOW TO UNDERSTAND WHAT SYMBOLS MEAN AND FIGURE OUT WHAT THE AUTHOR IS "SAYING" AS WE TRY TO UNDERSTAND OUR COMPLICATED RELATIONSHIPS WITH OTHER PEOPLE AND PLACES; WE LEARN WHAT A "NICE" NEIGHBORHOOD LOOKS LIKE, OR HOW TO DETERMINE WHEN A POTENTIAL MATE "LIKES" US.

Over the course of our lives, we arrive at, question, and revise millions of different beliefs based on our own readings, our own acts of interpretation (of which there are dozens every day). We perform these acts of informal reading when encountering popular culture and the media. When we attempt to make sense of a movie, a television show or a news report, to put it in perspective with our experiences, we are reading and interpreting. Of course, this kind of reading may not be exactly the same type of interpretation we do with the short stories and poems we are assigned in English classes, but making sense of people, images, ideas, and places remains a significant form of interpretation nonetheless. Because this reading is so important, and because we do so much of it, we should think of our entire world as something that can and should be read. In short, we can think of the world as a text.

How and what we read in this text that is our world is important—we make decisions about who we spend time with, where we live, where we eat, what we wear, and other important considerations based on informal reading. We also construct a worldview based on these readings and the readings of other people. We influence other people's readings, and they influence ours. A comment or even a physical reaction from a parent, teacher, or friend can guide our responses to a text. Sometimes these influences are harmless—not liking a particular band or television show because a friend does not is no big deal. But often these influences can have consequences that go beyond simple dislike or like; we can learn to read the world in limiting, prejudicial ways that affect not only our lives, but also the lives of our fellow citizens. If we imitate our parents' (or friend's or neighbor's or teacher's) negative reaction to people of particular ethnicities or accept abusive behavior by friends or family toward a certain gender, we have incorporated someone else's negative reading into our own worldview, much like we might accept a *Cliff's Notes* view of *The Great Gatsby* as our own. But for better or worse, our readings are not permanent. As we grow older and become more adept at reading our world, we constantly rewrite our worldview. That's where this book comes in.

Our goal is to help you take **texts** (movies, pieces of art, experiences, people, places, ideas, traditions, advertisements, etc.), both familiar and unfamiliar, and *read* them much the same way you read a written text. Many of these texts are visual or have visual elements, and past tendencies probably have been to "see" them rather than "read" them—that is, you likely simply regarded them rather than *interpreted* them. In this book, however, instead of looking through texts by not actively interpreting, we ask you to look *at* them—to slow down and decode texts in ways you may not have previously. In addition, we want you to try formalizing this reading process. What we mean by "formal" here is the process we undertake when analyzing literature (or, depending on your training, math formulas, a painting, or research data). One of the primary elements of formal reading is the breaking down of a text into smaller elements and interpreting them. Analyzing a short story for themes, character development, and figurative language (symbols, metaphors, etc.) is formal reading, as is the process of pouring over a Supreme Court decision. Explicating a poem is a classic example of formal "decoding." Looking at a poem's rhyme, meter, symbolism, tone, structure, and design is a formal process that involves posing questions about what the poem is trying to do and how it does it. Although it may feel natural to think of reading or decoding poems in this way, approaching an advertisement or a television show or a gender may feel a bit foreign at first. Over the course of reading this book, we hope that this process ceases to feel alien and begins to seem natural, especially as you become more familiar with analyzing the elements associated with these cultural and visual texts.

To sum up, the traditional analytical "work" you have done in English classes is something we want to imitate here. We believe that texts, including those that are nontraditional such as public spaces, songs, and advertisements, have meanings that can be uncovered through the exploration of their elements. You may know a public space seems ugly—but we want you to understand *why*. You may already sense that advertisements use sex to sell products, but we want you to understand *how*. The idea is not only to slow the interpretive process down, but also to make more conscious your meaning-making, a process you undertake all the time—whether you intend to or not.

SEMIOTICS: THE STUDY OF SIGNS (AND TEXTS)

All reading we do, perhaps anything we do, is backed up by various ideas or theories—from the simple idea that the acts we undertake have consequences both good and bad, to the more complex theories about relativity and gravity. In this book, we rely on a theory that the world itself is open to interpretation—that we can make meaning out of just about anything. The notion that the world is a text open to interpretation is itself a theory, which has a strong connection to **semiotics**, the study of signs. In this part of the introduction, we elaborate on the idea of semiotics as a way of having you understand some of the assumptions we made when writing this book. You can use the rest of the book without focusing too much on the theory.

In semiotics, the main idea is that everything is a sign. You already know what signs are, because you encounter them everywhere. There are traffic signs, signs telling whether something is open or closed, signs in your classroom urging you not to smoke, or cheat, or informing you where the exit is. You do very little work in trying to understand these signs, which seemingly need no interpretation. Once you understand what "stop" means, or that red in fact means "stop," or that green means "go," or that yellow means "slow down" or "caution," there is little need to stop, think, and interpret these signs each time you see them. Of course, you did not always know what these signs meant; at some point in your childhood, you picked up the ideas behind these signs and now take them for granted. The important thing to realize, however, is that our culture has come to a common understanding that a number of random signs and symbols—a cross, a red octagon, a round green light, a stick figure with the outline of a skirt—stand in for or symbolize specific concepts.

We have a broader idea of signs (or texts) in this book, although how we talk about signs here is based on the most rudimentary cultural symbols. A *sign* is an object or idea or combination of the two that refers to something besides itself, and it depends on others to recognize that it's a sign. The red octagon and the letters S–T–O–P mean "Stop" to most of us through the combination of the shape, color, and letters; a blue diamond with "HALT" on it would catch our attention, but we would not treat it in the same way, despite the fact that *halt* and *stop* are synonyms, or that a blue diamond is a perfectly fine combination of color and shape. The stop sign as we now know it carries a meaning beyond a simple combination of word, color, and shape. It carries the weight and force of history, law, and ubiquity.

Another example: We know an "Open" sign at a store means the store is transacting business. But "Open" itself is an arbitrary sign, unique to English-speaking cultures. The symbols O–P–E–N are characters English speakers have identified as "letters," and those letters, when put together in a certain way, create "words." If we were to put these symbols together, "Δ•≠»" and hang them on the door of a coffee shop, we would just confuse people because our culture has not assigned specific meanings for these symbols. But, what if we came across this sign: ABIERTO—In Spanish, "abierto" means "open." So, if we read Spanish, then we can decode the sign. Or, if we live, say, in San Diego, and we've grown up knowing these seven letters mean "open" in Spanish, then we can also decode it. And in some places, a sign contains both *abierto* and *open* to indicate that it's signifying to two different sets of clientele. "Open" and "abierto" can both be signs, but so can their presence together be a sign. If we saw an abierto and an open sign in one place, we might draw conclusions about

where we were (a neighborhood where English and Spanish are spoken), who owned the restaurant or store (bilingual owners?), and who their audience was (primarily speakers of Spanish and English). In other words, the presence of both signs is itself a sign—taken together they create meaning.

Semioticians ("sign-studiers") have a more formal way of referring to signs. Ferdinand de Saussure, a Swiss linguist working in the nineteenth and twentieth centuries, believed that signs contained two elements: the **signifier** and the **signified,** which, when taken together, often create meaning. The *signifier* is the object that exists, and the *signified* is what it means. In other words, the letters O–P–E–N are the signifier, and the message that a place is open for business is the signified, and the external reality is that the store or restaurant is open for business. Similarly, using our stop sign example, the actual red sign with the STOP written in white letters is the signifier. The signified is the message that you must bring your car to a complete halt when you approach this sign.

SYSTEMS OF READING: MAKING SENSE OF CULTURAL TEXTS

Sometimes the same signifiers (physical signs) can have different signifieds (meanings). For instance, what do you think of when you see the word "pan"? Most of you probably imagine an item for cooking. Or, you might think of a critic "panning" or criticizing a bad movie. However, a Spanish speaker who saw the word *pan* in our bilingual store would most likely imagine bread. The signifier "pan" in Spanish cultures refers not to an item for cooking, but to what English speakers think of when they see the signifier "bread." Thus, people from both cultures would experience the same signifier, but what is signified would be entirely different.

However, we don't even need other languages for there to be various signified meanings for the same signifier. Photographers may think of a pan or wide-angle shot. Scholars of Greek mythology may think of the Greek god who is half goat and half man. The letters p–a–n remain the same, but the meanings change; the sign—the word—"pan" has different meanings. We also can have the same signified but with different signifiers. For example, "soda," "pop," or "Coke" are all different signifiers that different people from different parts of the country use to refer to a flavored carbonated drink.

So when we talk about signs, we are not talking only about physical signs but also about a system of reading. In this system, we can interpret images, words whose letters are arbitrarily assigned meaning, and experiences—really just about anything. Sometimes we make these interpretations with little or no effort and sometimes with a lot of work. Many semioticians believe that everything is a sign, including the way we are writing this introduction. The words are signs, and so is the way you are reading them (it's simply a more complex way of saying that everything is a text).

And more complex signs of course do not reveal themselves so easily. For example, let's consider a very famous sign (or text)—the *Mona Lisa.* Its power in some part comes from its simplicity and its unreadability. We don't know why she is smiling, we only have a vague idea of who she is, and we will likely never know. That smile, or half-smile, has become so famous that its life as a sign has transcended even its power as an image. The painting is a signifier, but its signified is ambiguous and difficult to determine. If we look at the various images of the *Mona Lisa* on shirts, mousepads, posters, even variations of the original (we like the version where Mona Lisa has a big black moustache), we can agree that the *Mona Lisa* has become a symbol of something 1) traditional, 2) artistic, 3) commercial, and yet 4) universal, and perhaps 5) modern. We can agree that something about its power has not diminished despite or because of its age. But our signified—our mental concept of what *"Mona Lisa*–ness" is—depends on what perspective we bring to the reality of this artwork. Does it signify our definition of a masterpiece? A commodity? A self-portrait by the artist?

We don't know exactly (but people guess all the time). And that's why sometimes sign reading is so frustrating. Some signs are easier to read and understand, so easy that we don't even know that we are reading. Others, like paintings—and more importantly, human relationships—are more difficult. One of the most complex components of reading texts is suspending judgments about a text's values. In your initial semiotic analysis—your initial reading of a text—try to consider all aspects of a text before applying a label like "good" or "bad" (or "interesting" or "boring"). Such labels can come only after a thorough reading of the text under question. Later, if you want to argue that a text has problems, then you would use the details, the information you gleaned from your reading, to support these assertions in your papers. In attacking the *Mona Lisa*, for example, it would be acceptable to most professors for you to guess about what you thought da Vinci meant in painting her if you can defend your guess. Reading

Source: Leonardo da Vinci (1452–1519). *Mona Lisa,* oil on canvas, 77 × 53 cm. Inv. 779. Photo: R. G. Ojeda. Louvre, Paris. Reunion des Muses Nationaux/Art Resource, NY.

visually, in fact, often means such guessing is a natural part of doing any sort of paper.

Overall, the basic idea behind semiotics should not be foreign to you—on a fundamental level, it simply means reading and interpreting nontraditional objects like you would a short story or a poem.

THE "SEMIOTIC SITUATION" (OR THE "MOVING TEXT")

As you may have guessed, you do this type of work all the time. You read people and relationships every day, having developed this skill over your years of reading the world. For instance, let's say you are walking down Wall Street in New York City. You see a man dressed in a suit, talking on a cell phone, carrying a copy of *The Wall Street Journal,* and yelling "Sell Microsoft at 42! Sell! Sell! Sell!" What would you assume his profession is? He could be a lawyer. He could be a banker. But given the context (where you are, Wall Street), what he's talking about (stocks), and how he's dressed (a suit), the best interpretation of this text might be that he is a stockbroker. You could be wrong, but based on the clues of the text, that's a pretty good reading.

We perform this work constantly. For example, on first dates we try to read the other person for cues of attraction and enjoyment; quarterbacks read a defense before every play and pass; we read a classroom when we enter it; we read a friend's house, and especially his or her room, by scanning posters, its cleanliness, its odor, and its collection of books and music. These moments are what we call **semiotic situations.** They are moments in which we try to make sense of our surroundings or interpret one aspect of our surroundings based on the signs or texts of our situation. The copy of *The Wall Street Journal*, the cell phone, the man's comments—all are signs that represent a text that can be read. But when we read these signs together, they help us make sense of the larger text (the man) and the larger text than that (Wall Street) and an even larger text than that (America). As you may have guessed by now, this act of reading can even help you make sense of the largest text of all—the world—in both literal and mythical ways.

Because we are always trying to make sense of the world, because we are always reading, we often find ourselves in semiotic situations. This book builds on your own methods of reading and tries to sharpen them so that you become more critical and thoughtful readers of the complex text that is our world. We keep returning to the reading metaphor because it aptly describes the process of making sense of our surroundings. When we read a poem or a short story, we pay attention to detail: we look for symbols, metaphors, and hidden themes. We "read between the lines," meaning that we read not only what's there, but also what's *not* there. We do this frequently as well; we "read into things." Beer commercials never come right out and suggest that attractive, straight, single women will immediately become attracted to straight men if the men drink a certain kind of beer, but that is implied in almost every ad. People we are interested in dating may not tell us what kind of people they are, where they come from, what kind of music they like or what their political leanings are, but by paying attention to the clothes they wear or the comments they make, or the bumper stickers on their cars, we may be able to begin to piece together a better interpretation of the text that is this person. In other words, we already know how to read books and poems, and we also know how to read the world itself. This book will help you merge your experiences from formal and informal, as well as conscious and unconscious reading.

TEXTS, THE WORLD, YOU, AND YOUR PAPERS

We hope by now that you understand what we mean by *reading the world as a text*, and that this notion seems both comfortable and interesting to you. However, you are probably wondering how any of this figures into your writing course. As you have no doubt figured out by this time in your academic career, writing is fundamentally connected to reading and thinking. In fact, the great British novelist E. M. Forster (*A Room with a View* and *Howard's End*) once wrote, "How can I tell what I think till I see what I've said?" To our knowledge, there has never been a great writer who was not also a great thinker. What's more, to be a great thinker and a great writer, we must also be great readers. Writing is so intimately tied to thinking and thinking so intimately tied to the act of *reading* the world and one's surroundings, that the three form a kind of trinity of articulation and expression:

Of course, by "reading" we mean not only reading books and newspapers and magazines, but also the semiotic situation or the nontraditional text, the practice of reading the world. Writing, thinking, and reading are a symbiotic process, a cycle in which they feed off and influence each other. Thus, if we are reading and thinking, then the chances are we will be better prepared to do good writing.

RHETORIC: WRITING'S SOUNDTRACK

Good writing is also grounded on solid *rhetorical* principles, as is good reading (as we have broadly defined *reading* so far). **Rhetoric** comes from the Greek word *rhetorik*, whose literal definition means speech or speaking. In English, "rhetoric" has come to refer to the art of speaking or writing effectively—usually with an emphasis on persuasion. This book considers rhetoric broadly, exploring how it works not only in cultural and visual texts but also how you can apply rhetorical principles and strategies to your writing to make your papers more effective.

The history of rhetoric is a long and complicated one, and it is worth knowing a little about its background. Generally, scholars link the birth of rhetoric with the Sophists (Greek thinkers from the 5th century B.C.E.), who first began studying and theorizing the concept of public speech. Later, rhetoric became one of the three pillars of the liberal arts and a foundation for classical education. The great Greek philosopher Plato (437–347 B.C.E.) had issues with rhetoric being considered an art; for him it was more of a cheap skill—essentially, fancy flattery. He considered medicine a true art and compared rhetoric to cooking. Given the current popularity of *Top Chef*, that's not so bad, but at the time, it was a bit of an insult. Ultimately, Plato argued that rhetoric could never be an art, because it had no subject; it had nothing to ground it. Thus, when you hear a pundit describe a political speech as "all rhetoric," the pundit is using rhetoric in much the same way Plato saw it—as empty, content-free verbiage.

However, Aristotle (384–322 B.C.E.), also a famous Greek philosopher and Plato's student, argued that rhetoric was one of the great arts and that its subject was *all* things. In fact, Aristotle found the subject of medicine and warfare rather narrow, whereas, in his mind, rhetoric had no bounds. For him, rhetoric cast the widest net and because it could encompass so much, it was worthy of study. In fact, in his famous study *On Rhetoric*, Aristotle advances a concept of rhetoric ("the art of finding the possible means of persuasion in reference to any given situation") that informs current rhetorical theory and much of this book.

Indeed, with the advent of the modern media, advertising, and visual culture, rhetoric has grown to encompass all persuasive techniques, strategies, and approaches beyond mere speaking and writing. One of the main goals of our book is to help you to detect various strategies of persuasion in any situation, whether it is an advertisement, a movie, a building, or fashion. To that end, *The World Is a Text* is interested in both cultural and visual rhetoric—how cultural and visual texts make arguments. As you will see, we discuss the "rhetorical moment" or the "rhetorical situation" a great deal. By this, we mean the many different situations Aristotle refers to that will require you to use new interpretive skills. You cannot read all texts the same way–you must adjust your reading to meet the signs of the text. For example, commercials for heart medication may make different arguments than those for Match.com. Beer ads in *Maxim* rely on an entirely different set of images, codes, and associations than those for Diet Coke in *Cosmopolitan*. Thus, the rhetorical tools advertisers use and that readers (like you) employ can change dramatically in any given situation.

In addition, the study of rhetoric carries with it a sense of the *polis* (Greek for *city* or *public*) that the authors of this book find utterly appealing. Originally linked to public oratory, rhetoric now subsumes under its umbrella political speeches, public art, television shows, commercials, billboards, and now, the Internet. Plato and Aristotle could never have imagined the degree to which rhetoric has been stretched. Nevertheless, rhetorical approaches help make sense of everything from grafitti to buildings to video games to movies to clothing. In short, any text designed to make meaning or have an effect incorporates some aspect of rhetoric. An awareness of the history, reach, and goals of rhetoric make you better readers of the world. Ultimately, rhetoric is about civic engagement.

The World Is a Text is a visual and cultural rhetoric, meaning that this book is a kind of treatise, a playbook, a how-to manual of rhetorical principles, with emphases on texts and approaches that make meaning in both cultural and visual realms. We offer strategies for decoding cultural texts; we provide various strategies for reading and writing; and we offer step-by-step instructions on both reading and writing. Later in this introduction, we discuss various ways of making arguments and provide strategies for identifying how other texts make arguments with the ultimate goal of rounding out your vocabulary and your facility in regard to persuasion in discourse. One of the most famous scholars of rhetoric, Kenneth Burke, describes *rhetoric* as the "use of language as a symbolic means of inducing cooperation in beings that by nature respond to symbols." Burke's emphasis on symbols point to the importance of signs, signifiers, and the visual language on which so much of the communication in our world relies. His interest in cooperation reveals the degree to which rhetoric is woven into the fabric of a culture, part of the garment that humans wear in the world. The visual and cultural implications of rhetoric and their importance for undergraduate education and writing undergird the larger scope of this book.

FROM RHETORIC TO WRITING

As you have no doubt gleaned by now, our goal is to help you learn to see the rhetorical strategies of various texts and also to get you started writing your own. We are firm believers that textual analysis (reading) and textual formation (writing) jointly contribute to the larger process of knowledge making. Thus, we are interested in helping you to ask not simply *what* something means but *how* something means. This is why reading will help your writing: it teaches you how to be savvy consumers and producers of texts. You'll get to know texts from the inside out, so that when it comes to writing your essay, you will know from the inside how arguments work. Most mechanics agree that the best way to build an engine is to take one apart so that you can see its inner workings. Similarly, the best way to learn to write essays and make arguments is to take essays and arguments apart and look at their various components.

Here is also where our instructions about reading and your assignments for writing intersect, because learning to identify rhetoric in cultural and visual texts better enables you to use rhetoric in your papers.

In fact, writing is itself an important component of interpretation. Writers and thinkers have long seen writing as a means of helping us arrive at ideas. When we think abstractly, we tend to gloss over ideas so fast that we don't slow down and articulate them. They are more sensations than thoughts. To put them down on paper, to compose them into sentences, ideas, and reasons, is harder than thinking. Indeed, if you have done freewriting exercises, you may have had no idea what you thought about something until you wrote it down. It's no surprise that journaling or keeping a diary is vitally important to writers. The act of writing can often be an act of unlocking: the door opens and ideas, reactions, fears, and hopes walk right out of your head and on to the page and say, "Here I am!" Sometimes, we wish they had stayed inside, but this is where the interesting work happens, and here is where learning to read the world as a text can help you as you learn to write on a college level. Learning to write well allows us to move into the world of ideas, interaction, and exchange. And learning to read outside our traditional ideas of what it means to read will expand your mind even further.

Writing about the world as a text may not only facilitate writing and thinking, but also writing and feeling. Although we certainly do not want to diminish the logical aspect of writing, we want to pay attention to a component of writing that is often overlooked, and that is the emotional component. Franz Kafka, Emily Dickinson, Pablo Neruda, and dozens of other writers turned and continue to turn to writing because it helps them get a handle on the world and relieves anxiety. Writing is or can be rewarding, refreshing, rejuvenating. In part, writing means sharing, participating in a community of language and ideas. We learn about others and ourselves through writing because writing is simultaneously self-exploration and self-examination. We see ourselves in a larger context. Of course, we may not always like what we discover (perhaps traces of sexism or racism or classism), but uncovering those elements of our personality and understanding them is an extremely rewarding experience. Writing that is honest, candid, and reflective attracts us, because those are traits we value.

At the same time, we do not want to neglect the idea that writing is a difficult process to master. Between us, we have authored thousands of papers, articles, handouts, tests, reports, and now, this book. In almost every case, we went through multiple drafts, stared at the computer screen, cursed whatever picture was on the wall for its interference, and struggled at various points along the way. In fact, this very introduction went through between fifteen and twenty drafts. In some ways, writing is very much like exercising: It doesn't always feel great when you are doing it, but when you are finished, it is both rewarding and good for you. We are *drafters* by nature—we believe that whereas writing is a form of thinking, several drafts are often needed to convert that thinking into something worth showing the public.

By now, you should be beginning to see some direct connections between writing and reading. Only by reading well can you write well. A good essay makes sense of a topic using detail, insight, and purpose—the same traits one uses to read. We believe that the readings and questions in this book are a good springboard for that writing process. Some of the essays may anger you, but that's okay. Some will make you laugh, some will confuse you, and some will make you see a movie or a place or a gender in ways you never have before. We hope that these readings and images not only show you what writing can do, but also that the texts in this book spark your imagination and push you toward the writing process so that your own work will be as vigorous and as provocative as the texts presented here.

In the next section, we provide you with some hands-on examples of visual and cultural rhetorical readings so that you can see first hand how you might make the transition from the act of *reading* to the act of *writing*.

READING THE WORLD AS A TEXT: WRITING'S OVERTURE. THREE CASE STUDIES

In this section, we walk you through the act of interpretation, of reading semiotically; that is, we help you read certain texts in ways that you may find unfamiliar. However, as stated earlier, we believe that living critically in the world means living as an informed, questioning, and engaged person. Learning to read the world as a text is a good way to begin.

CASE STUDY 1 Reading Public Space: Starbucks

One of the most familiar places in our modern world is the coffee shop, and in particular, Starbucks. As a ubiquitous presence, it could make for an interesting "read"—many ideas about the world could come from reading a Starbucks. With this in mind, we sat down one morning in a Starbucks and did a reading. We began with note taking, just writing down what we saw and thought. This is a transcribed version.

Note taking: brown, green, red, brown patterned carpet.

Green

Lighting non-fluorescent

Curves

Wood—metal

Tables different types

Products art—decoration

Logo "coffee-related art" photos

Baby chairs, modern garbage cans

Advertisements, baskets, games, "Cranium" wood

Handicapped bathrooms—*The New York Times,* windows, mahogany, metal door handles, pull to get in, push

Music: "cool," varied

With this information, we can begin to construct a series of observations that could develop into ideas:

Starbucks relies on moderate earth tones for decoration.

Their seating places are made of durable materials.

Their artwork is a mix of coffee photographs and advertisements.

There is lots of light. The lighting they use is bright but not harsh, avoiding fluorescent light.

Their advertisements are prominent within the store. Their products are geared to the middle and upper classes both by design and content. (Oops—an argument slipped in!)

As you can see by the last statement, in the process of writing down observations, arguments about the text itself may present themselves, which is what we were hoping for. In this case, the idea that Starbucks is geared toward a particular target audience is an argument, and potentially one that you might pursue in a paper. How could you make this a paper? You could expand the idea of a target audience into multiple paragraphs: one about products, another about décor, maybe one about music, and perhaps another about the location of the particular Starbucks you are in.

If we were going to construct a thesis statement, it might sound like this: Starbucks appeals to the middle and upper classes through a combination of its décor, music, products, and location.

Well, that thesis statement is okay and would work to organize a paper, but it is still pretty vague. We could ask why Starbucks wants to sell its wares to a particular demographic through its design. We know the answer to this already—they are a commercial venture. But the question of "how" still raises itself—we can see the target audience and the tools, but how they are using them is a different story. Maybe another question is this: What is Starbucks trying to sell *besides* coffee? What experience can someone hope to get by entering Starbucks? We would argue that Starbucks is trying to sell an idea of "cool" or "hip" to its customers. And for its target audience of middle- and upper-class people, cool is something these people may feel they need to buy. So a new thesis could be: "Starbucks tries to sell its idea of cool to the middle and upper classes through its hip music; sturdy, smooth décor; and its sleek and streamlined products."

This could still improve, but notice that this thesis gives you an automatic organization of paragraphs about décor, music, merchandise, and location. From here, you could work on incorporating the details of your observations as evidence for the points you are making. For example, you could describe in some detail the nature of the furnishings, the various songs that play over the loudspeaker, and the general location of this particular Starbucks. If you wanted to, you might research how companies use these elements to make their businesses more profitable.

We hope, through this example, that you can see how this sort of thing might work. We began with a trip to Starbucks and ended up talking about demographics and public space. Not all such experiences could end up as papers, but you would be surprised how many can.

CASE STUDY 2 Reading Fonts: How Type Can Say a Lot About Type

Although you are only a few words into this section, the shift in font has already altered your reading experience. We associate many things with certain fonts; more than we might expect. Even though you know this is a book for a class, the simple change of font may have made you think of *Throne of Blood II* or some older European manuscript, although no reference to either appeared until just now. **If we were to ask you what fliers written in this font were advertising, what would you say? Even if you have never been to a jazz concert or a Broadway play, you would likely guess one of those two options.** *Similarly, if an invitation appeared in your mailbox engraved in this script, what would you think? Does this font suggest a luau? An American Idol watch party? Probably not. In fact, we are willing to bet that your attitude, your general happiness, even your basic anxiety level has altered a bit simply through an alteration of font.* For example, those of you who have relied on Courier to make your essays appear longer may be visited with a sense of joy, nostalgia, or anxiety at seeing it here, in a textbook, where it's just not supposed to be.

In truth, we had several conversations about the most appropriate font for *The World Is a Text*. We wanted to express seriousness and scholarly competence, but at the same time, we hoped for a font that would convey a sort of contemporary edginess that we thought the book embodied. THAT FONT PROBABLY WOULD HAVE LOOKED MORE LIKE THIS THAN WHAT WE SETTLED ON, BUT ULTIMATELY, WE DECIDED THAT THIS IS A FONT FOR ADVERTISING OR MENUS—NOT A BOOK. PLUS, THE ALL-CAPS SITUATION MAKES IT LOOK LIKE WE ARE YELLING AT THE READER. That something as small as font can carry so many associations, hang-ups, and biases speaks to the unspoken power of semiotics and the importance of visual rhetoric.

Fonts tell us how the designers of a text want to be seen. Retailers, advertisers, designers, t-shirt manufacturers, sports franchises, and alcohol producers take full advantage of fonts to influence the public. For example, what if the Oakland Raiders began the 2008 football season with the same famous black and silver pirate logo, but with all the lettering on the uniforms, helmets, and memorabilia in this font:

The Oakland Raiders

Or, if The Raider Nation, considered by sports aficionados to be the craziest, rowdiest fans of any professional American franchise, suddenly changed their promotional and Web font to

THE RAIDER NATION
Win, Lose or Tie, Raiders til We Die!!!

In both cases, the groups would lose all credibility—even if the play of the team or the insanity of the fans remained the same—because neither of these fonts suggest dominance, fear, or aggression. The first evokes silliness; the second, old-school cursive or cross-stitch.

These two examples reveal yet another truism about semiotics—signs are almost never value free. This is certainly the case for fonts. Every font carries associations and assumptions. Take the examples used previously. One reason they seem so ludicrous is that both are somewhat stereotypically *feminine*. The humor comes in the gap between the values we associate with professional football and the values we associate with curly font. **THE OAKLAND RAIDERS AND THE RAIDER NATION** might work, because we tend to associate this Stencil font with the military, and we tend to associate the military with masculinity, force, power, strength, and victory. THE OAKLAND RAIDERS AND THE RAIDER NATION probably would not work because this Desdemona font calls up art déco, France, and all kinds of associations that are antithetical to the image of American football. Thus, how serious we take a font is often related to its perceived femininity or masculinity. Consider what traits in font we might link with femininity and which we might consider masculine. Pay attention to flourishes, curls, and fat and wide lines.

Just as fonts often carry gender values, they also frequently carry cultural values as well. For example, why would this sign seem incorrect?

Jean Luc's
French Bistro

For better or worse, when we see this font, we tent to think of one kind of cuisine, but when we think of French food, we never consider this font as even a remote possibility for an effective medium of communication. Similarly, we may also carry prejudices toward cultures without even knowing it. To some, an odd juxtaposition of appearance and content can come off not simply as discordant, but offensive as well.

God Bless the United States of America

Even though the sentiment may be genuine and completely in line with traditional American Christian values, the Arabic font–a source of fear and anxiety to some Americans–somehow sends a different message than if the same phrase appeared in a less loaded font:

God Bless the United States of America

or

God Bless the United States of America

If both of these last two examples feel more appropriate than the Arabic-influenced font, it might be useful to examine how and why this might be.

In the introduction, we distinguish between the signified and the signifier, and the font/message equation is a perfect example of this complex linguistic and visual coding. If fonts carry positive or negative associations, it is because, over time, a culture has imbued them with meaning—a kind of stereotyping. Our culture would like to think of words and language in nonvisual terms, but the font issue points to ways in which even the written word sends messages.

One final example. Let's say there is a restaurant called "Beverly's." Based on the font used in the sign in front of the restaurant, think about what kind of food and ambiance is suggested by each sign:

BEVERLY'S

Beverly's

BEVERLYS

Ⓑⓔⓥⓔⓡⓛⓨ'Ⓢ

Beverly's

BEVERLY'S

Guessing what kind of place the various fonts evoke is relatively easy and fun, but the harder part is figuring out why a certain font sends the message it does. The Beverly's signs are another instance when cultural and visual rhetorics merge. For your papers, if you decide to read an advertisement or a commercial or a movie poster or a building, remember that a font is not merely a means of delivering the written message, it is also a visual cue along with photographs, logos, brands, and illustrations that underscores the larger argument the text is making.

CASE STUDY 3 Can We Laugh? Reading Art and Humor in Geico Commercials

Geico is funny. From the talking gecko with the undetermined British accent (Cockney?) to the celebrity "interpreters," to the caveman series, Geico has made viewers laugh perhaps harder than any other advertiser in recent memory.

But...

Geico is a commercial enterprise that makes us laugh only to sell us something. Is there anything wrong with this? And more importantly, how might we write about such a phenomenon? Thinking about the Geico ads raises all sorts of questions about art, entertainment, and commerce, not to mention the nature of humor.

In sitting down to write this, we thought about how we might take this reaction to Geico's commercials and convert it into an argument for an essay. We already know that the commercials engage topics that are popular targets of semiotic analysis—art and advertising. A number of influential writers have "read" billboards, ads in magazines, and television commercials—especially those broadcast during the Super Bowl—in an attempt to make sense of corporate strategies, cultural mores, and common assumptions about race and gender. But the Geico ads complicate these lenses. In fact, the Caveman ads have very little to say about Geico at all; so selecting the right lens for reading these commercials is important. To help you make sense of the Geico ads, we've provided a sample semiotic reading, taking as our point of departure their most obvious trait—humor.

One way of beginning a reading of the Geico commercials might be to inquire into why these commercials are funny, and to do that, we should determine what types of humor they use. In this situation, as in any such reading, we begin with the obvious. In this case, it's the gecko. The gecko himself has made it clear that he's a pitchman for the company solely because of the similar name. "Because Geico sounds like gecko—that's the only reason I'm here," he says in one commercial. From the start, then, the commercial is asking to be read through a lens of comedy. Despite their charm, geckos don't know anything about car insurance. They can't even drive. The gecko doesn't provide price quotes or reliability statistics; Geico's use of the gecko is merely for humor's sake. What makes this interesting is that the Geico commercials derive their humor from the fact that they are commercials about commercials. In other words, the commercials in many ways are advertising themselves with only a secondary hook to the product of insurance.

So part of the humor is *meta-commentary*, or what is often referred to as "going meta." *Meta-ness* simply means acknowledging the subject of what you are talking about as you are talking about it. When the gecko refers to his role in the commercial *during the commercial*, it is a form of a meta-commentary. Part of the humor here has to do with the way we perceive advertising, as something that is supposed to be forced on us to pay for the television we are watching or the periodical we're reading.[1] Instead, Geico lets us know that we are indeed watching a commercial, and that the commercial may not tell us anything *useful* about the product.

In turn, this suggests that Geico is not trying to deceive the customer. You might ask yourself whether this is actually true, or whether it matters, or whether Geico is really being "honest"—or even whether this question matters in trying to evaluate the commercials. To do this, you should consider what kind of *appeal* the commercial makes. In the language of rhetoric, one might argue that Geico appeals to both our *ethos*—our common sense, our sense of ethics, or the credibility of the company itself—as well as our *pathos*, our emotions—it's making us laugh. The *logos*, or logic, of the appeal is less apparent; indeed, what we are doing here is trying to decode the logos, so one could argue that its appeal is minimal if we cannot readily perceive it. (We talk more about ethos, pathos, and logos later in this

---

[1] Which is why some people are outraged at the commercial ads shown before movies—we have already paid for the movie!

introduction—**"How Do I Argue About Popular Culture Texts? A Guide for Building Good Arguments"** [Part IV].)

The commercials' ethos appeal builds through a cumulative trust of a company that so willingly makes light of itself. Such an appeal thirty years ago might not have been as effective, because these commercials might have conveyed the idea that a company that jokes about itself cannot be taken seriously, but to increasingly savvy consumers, such an approach punctures our usual resistance to companies that do nothing but brag about their products (almost *all* car companies' commercials use this appeal). Geico trusts its viewer to understand the commercials on multiple levels.

Then you might ask why it is important to laugh at insurance commercials. To do that, inquire into the cultural associations surrounding insurance. How are insurance salesmen and insurance companies perceived? That's right: negatively. Not only that, but insurance generally is associated with misfortune; no one calls an insurance company unless something terrible happens. So, when anything insurance-related makes us laugh, the company has already broken down some viewer resistance because so little about insurance is positive, funny, or engaging.

Let's get more into a closer reading of these commercials, which show other humorous appeals. The "celebrity interpreter" commercials pair a celebrity with a "Geico customer," who is labeled on screen as a "real person," whereas the celebrity is labeled as an "actor," or in the case of Burt Bacharach, a "celebrity." This is funny, because it implies Burt Bacharach is not a real person, and it's also funny because it entertains the notion that celebrities are somehow more equipped to endorse products rather than real users. Note again—why should a commercial for insurance even play with this idea? It has little to do with insurance. Of course, in these commercials, celebrities are silly—Bacharach's second line is the hilarious, but nonsensical, "Lizard licks his eyeball," which is, again, a meta-commentary, as it refers to previous Geico commercials when the gecko does, in fact, appear to lick his eyeball. And other celebrities are similarly of no help in validating Geico's competency as an insurance company, like Charo, Little Richard, and Don La Fontaine, the famous announcer for action movie trailers. And yet, we still laugh. To round out your reading of this commercial, you should ask yourself what effect this form of humor has on the viewer, and why Geico invests in these kinds of commercials.

Finally, think about Geico ads as a larger project. Here is where some research is useful. Watch past commercials on YouTube. Track down Geico sales numbers. Read articles about their ad campaigns. From this perspective, it is clear that Geico has established a reputation through humor—the reality show parody (*Tiny House*), the gecko himself, and the Caveman series, all of which emphasize branding over information. Geico likely hopes humor, a form of absurdity, will emphasize the importance of consumers for the company, but it's also mainly designed to help emphasize the Geico name, building brand awareness. The messages can be somewhat contradictory—does Geico want its customers to laugh or purchase? Is humor consonant with good insurance service? In a business sense, the Geico ads have paid off, adding two million customers from 2002 to 2006, for a total of seven million.[2]

We know why Geico made these commercials, but why do we laugh—and buy? And should we be laughing at something that is so explicitly commercial? In writing a paper, you

---

[2]Theresa Howard, "Gecko Wasn't First Choice for Geico," *USA Today,* July 16, 2006, http://www.usatoday.com/money/advertising/adtrack/2006-07-16-geico_x.htm (accessed July 23, 2007).

could argue either side pretty convincingly. On the negative side, you could argue that you should be skeptical of the motives of a producer of art that means to sell you something—it means that the art is not "pure." This is a variation of an argument that has been made many times over the years. Some even argue that the Geico ads are not art but commerce. That, then, raises even more complicated questions about the interplay between commerce and entertainment. What if the Geico commercials are substantially more fun than the tedious reruns of *King of Queens*?

However, you could point to the fact that people like one of the co-authors—who does not drive—have no financial stake in the ads, and so the ads are really just entertainment for those viewers. Others could argue that most, if not all, art does not have a pure basis, and that to be entertained is a primary consideration in terms of whether to evaluate a piece of art. In the suite appropriately titled "Is It Art?" we tackle this question in more depth.

READING THIS TEXT AS A TEXT: TIPS ON USING THIS BOOK

As you can see, the process of writing a paper involves posing a number of questions about the text you are writing, looking closely at your paper, and trying to organize and arrange an argument. Of course, this process is the same for reading a text; both involve thinking and, in particular, explorative thinking. We hope that you see the necessary connections between reading and writing, writing and reading, and that you understand how the processes of each facilitates the other. Learning to read with care, insight, knowledge, and openness helps you write with those same qualities.

We hope that our book is written with insight, knowledge, and openness, just as we hope that you read it with such. To augment this, we are going to give you a brief overview of the rest of the book, so that you can become a particularly good reader of the text that is *The World Is a Text*. To that end, we arranged the book to help you with the writing and the reading processes. We begin with an overview of the writing section.

The World Is a Text: Writing

This section begins on page 23 and provides numerous strategies for writing, drafting, researching, and persuading. Let us be clear at the outset that we designed our section on writing as an introduction to the writing process. By no means should you consider this section a comprehensive guide to constructing papers. Our section here is merely an overture to the symphony that is your paper. Virtually no other book of this kind discusses the difficult process of transitioning from high school writing to college writing. *The World Is a Text* is unique in this regard, as we begin our section on writing with a short explanation of how college essays differ from high school essays. The segment entitled "How Do I Write a Text for College? Making the Transition from High School Writing," by guest author Patty Strong, is not so much a nuts-and-bolts essay as it is a description of how your thinking (and therefore your writing) process must change to do college-level writing. We think you'll find this segment very helpful, and we recommend that you read it first.

One of the most difficult challenges facing beginning college writers is figuring out what they want to say in their papers. Actually settling on a thesis can be frustrating. Sadly, there is no guaranteed remedy for the malady of the elusive thesis; however, we provide some steps that should make the thesis process slightly less anxiety provoking in the next segment. Our new **"From Semiotics to Lenses: Finding an Approach for Your Essays"** and our considerably expanded **"How Do I Write About Popular Culture Texts? A Tour through the Writing Process"** walk you through the entire paper-writing process, from thinking about ways to approach your topic, to understanding the assignment, to freewriting, to outlining, to building your opening paragraph. We also added information on constructing a good thesis and on making and building arguments. Finally, we include an annotated student paper in which we walk you through what a student writer does well in an actual undergraduate writing assignment.

We say this throughout *The World Is a Text*, but we will restate it here—always listen to your professors in regard to your assignments. Their patterns and requirements may differ from our recommendations. Although you should feel free to use this book, you should first and foremost follow your professor's advice—even if it is different from ours.

It is quite common for instructors to assign a personal essay as the first major assignment in a first-year writing class. To help you with this assignment, we provide an overview of the personal essay. **"How Am I a Text? On Writing Personal Essays"** suggests the ways in which you are a text, worthy and ready to be read. You have a wealth of experiences and a mind full of ideas. This segment offers some very solid advice that should facilitate the move from private topic to public writing.

Finally, we end this segment with some information on researching popular-culture texts. If you are assigned a research paper in your course, pay very close attention to this segment. The simple act of going to the library and figuring out how and where to look can be intimidating, but we break it down into a manageable process.

Even though we think this section provides a good entrée into the book as a whole, there is a wealth of information out there. Online writing labs like those at Purdue University and the University of Texas are accessible on the Internet and have more detailed information than we can provide here. For more complete descriptions of writing, rhetoric, and the construction of papers, consult our sister publication, *Strategies for Successful Writing: A Rhetoric, Research Guide, Reader, and Handbook,* edited by James A. Reinking, Andrew W. Hart, and Robert von der Osten (also published by Prentice Hall).

The World Is a Text: Reading

This section begins with Chapter 1 on page 74. Of course, it is the most important section of the book—the part where you will spend most of your time. To make navigation of these chapters easy for you, we designed each chapter the same way, so you should have no trouble maneuvering through the readings, the worksheets, or the questions. You will find the following in each chapter:

I. Introduction
II. Worksheet
III. Readings
    a. Chapter Readings
        1. Questions (This Text: Reading/Your Text: Writing)
    b. Suite of readings
        1. Questions (This Text: Reading/Your Text: Writing)

IV. Reading Outside the Lines
   a. Classroom exercises
   b. Essay ideas

We have several goals in this book. We want to help you become a better reader of the world generally and a better reader of texts like television and movies specifically. We also want to make you a better reader of essays about those topics. We remain confident that your increased abilities as a reader translate into better writing.

To help with these missions, the book focuses both on the texts like public space and art, and readings about these texts. Our introductions orient you to the text being read and to some basic questions and issues surrounding these areas of study. Following the introduction in each chapter is a worksheet that focuses on both the readings in the chapter and interpretation of the general text (such as gender or public space). Read these worksheets closely before you read the rest of the chapter.

Each chapter contains essays that focus on different aspects of texts, such as television and race, and then a group of texts about a particular topic—called "suites"—such as reality television (television) or censorship (visual arts). These grouped essays are to show the different ways you might approach a topic, with the hope that you can use some of these ideas in approaching your own interpretation of television shows or paintings. In analyzing these essays, you will develop a better sense of how writers write.

As you read, your primary objective is to identify the author's main points, the argument or arguments she or he tries to make. This is called the author's "rhetorical strategy," and deciphering a rhetorical strategy is just like reading any other kind of text. Pay attention to the evidence that the author uses to make his or her point. Does the author use statistics, personal experience, research, rumor, or the experiences of others? Read each entry at least twice. On the first reading, make notes. If there is a word you don't recognize or an idea that puzzles you, underline or highlight it. Try to find the author's thesis, and mark that. Underline other important points throughout the piece. On your second read, take your level of analysis one step further by asking questions about the passages you underlined. This process will help your transition into writing.

After each entry there are two sets of questions. The first set, called **"This Text: Reading,"** is designed to help you understand the text you just read. The second set, entitled **"Your Text: Writing,"** will help get you started writing about the text (public space, music, race, etc.) or the article itself.

Following the texts are some supplemental items that should help with class discussion and will assist you in thinking about a paper topic. In many of the chapters, we've also included a sample student paper (or two). These are papers actually written by our students on the same topics and texts as you, so that you can see how someone in a similar semiotic situation might turn a text to read into a text to be written. We are not suggesting that you mimic these papers; we want to give you an idea of how such a paper might look. Not all are examples of stellar writing, but if you and your instructors go over them in class, they will help you visualize your own papers.

Finally, because you worked your way through this rather long introduction to reading texts, we thought it might be useful for you if we read our own text. We like this book a lot; in fact, we feel very strongly about its premise: that you can become a better writer, a better student, that you can *be* in the world more fully if you are a critical, thoughtful, insightful reader of the world around you.

Our book relies on the premise that we are always reading and interpreting consciously or not. *The World Is a Text*'s goals are primarily to help you understand the relationship between reading traditional texts such as novels, short stories, and poems, as well as other less-traditional texts such as movies, the Internet, art works, and television. Equally important, we also want you to discover that perhaps the most valuable way of learning about the world is through writing about it. Finally, and perhaps most important, we want you to learn to read your surroundings actively. The first two premises are geared more toward academic achievement; the third is oriented toward helping you become a better citizen of the world and a more active participant in the world in which you live.

Some of you may take exception to specific aspects of this book. Particular images, individual essays, or even parts of our introductions may make you mad, they may upset you, and they may challenge some of your most secure assumptions. We think that is good. We believe critical inquiry is part of the college experience. Another kind of problem that you or your instructor may have with our book is what is not in it. We understand that there are many texts we could have included in these chapters. It pains us to think of all the great stories, essays, poems, and art works that we had to leave out. There are also many different texts we could have read, such as sports, video games, cars, business, and families. But we wanted to leave some things out there for you to explore on your own. Such is the nature of textbooks.

In this edition, we expanded the possibilities for reading by including a special opening chapter constructed entirely of original commissioned essays written especially for this edition of *The World Is a Text*. In addition, we provide links to additional readings as part of our completely online technology chapter.

SO, THE WORLD IS A TEXT: WHAT CAN YOU DO WITH IT?

Although digesting the book's contents is a lifetime project, a project the authors still regularly undertake and refine, our hope is that after reading this book and writing your papers that you engage the world more actively. Doing so will make you more of an actor in your own show and enable you to understand your role in the world.

We are not saying the book will have immediate and measurable effects, but the more you engage the world as a text, the more you will see subtleties as well as potential forms of manipulation. You may notice the beauty of a public courtyard or the ugliness of a building. You may find yourself arguing with film directors, questioning the structure of a sitcom, and raising objections about a political ad. But engaging the world need not be a grim, political task. You may also find that you are able to see the subtle beauty in a house in your neighborhood, or the amusing effectiveness of an ad, or the cleverness of a lyric. Developing higher critical faculties also allows you more control of them. Students sometimes complain that English teachers "read too much" into things, or that we're "taking the fun out of watching television." If we do these things, it has to do with our ability to turn our critical abilities on and off; thinking almost becomes a new toy once you realize you can understand the world better and in different ways. Don't get us wrong—we watch dumb movies just as you do. However, if we want to engage that dumb movie—to better examine its particular dumbness—we can do that too.

We want you to have the same abilities; more than the particular skill of watching movies, we want you to engage the world more actively. In doing so, you may enhance, in all sorts of ways, the text that is your life.

A note on format: This book is formatted in Modern Language Association style, known by most scholars and teachers as "MLA style." Throughout the book, however, you will see several other styles of formatting, including American Psychological Association (APA), Chicago or Turabian, and Associated Press (AP) style. Each discipline, such as English or history or psychology, has its own preferred form. Because the book covers so many different types of texts and crosses disciplines, and our readers come from many disciplines, we decided to keep to the original style of the article or book portion we are reprinting whenever possible.

THE WORLD IS A TEXT THE WORLD IS A

TEXT THE WORLD IS A TEXT THE WORLD IS

A TEXT THE WORLD IS A TEXT THE WORLD

IS A TEXT THE WORLD IS A TEXT

writing

THE WORLD IS A TEXT THE WORLD IS A

TEXT THE WORLD IS A TEXT THE WORLD IS

A TEXT THE WORLD IS A TEXT THE WORLD

IS A TEXT THE WORLD IS A TEXT THE

A SHORT GUIDE TO *THE WORLD IS A TEXT:* WRITING

This section provides a number of resources specifically designed to help you with the actual paper-writing process. If you have been in any large bookstore, you have probably seen the dozens, even hundreds, of books devoted to writing, which suggests that there are many different approaches to writing. Not surprisingly, these approaches have changed over time, and it is possible that in the future our suggestions here will seem outdated. That said, you should feel reassured that there is a lot of overlap among those who both teach and write about writing concerning the most effective ways to teach writing. And although every professor is different and every assignment has its own quirks, we are confident that the information here will be of use to you in many ways.

- **Part I** of the writing section, **"How Do I Write a Text for College? Making the Transition from High School Writing,"** by contributor Patty Strong, guides the new college-level writer through some basic transitional steps so that the adjustment from high school writing to college writing will not be so difficult. Just as you make an intellectual leap in math classes from high school to college, so does your writing make a big leap. This section will aid you in that transition.

- **Part II, "From Semiotics to Lenses: Finding an Approach for Your Essays,"** helps usher you into the writing process by providing an overview of the many different approaches available to you before you start typing away. It provides both vocabulary and infrastructure to help you envision a means of addressing your topic so that you start off on the right path.

- **Part III** of this section is the largest, and perhaps, the most important. **"How Do I Write about Popular Culture Texts? A Tour through the Writing Process"** walks you through the actual writing process, beginning with how to understand the assignment and working through brainstorming, outlining, drafting, editing, and revising. We also added a section that looks closely at the opening paragraph of student essays. This section features some good strategies for developing that important first paragraph.

- **"How Do I Argue about Popular Culture Texts? A Guide for Building Good Arguments"** (**Part IV**) focuses on the argumentation process. Also expanded, this section explains such concepts as logos, pathos, and ethos, and offers some guidance not simply on how to make good arguments, but also how not to fall into faulty arguments and argumentative fallacies.

- **Part V, "How Do I Get Info on Songs? Researching Popular Culture Texts,"** offers advice on how to research nontraditional texts, such as buildings, cars, movies, television shows, and public space. Many of your classes—regardless of topic—will require some kind of researched paper. This segment helps you get started with your research.

- **Part VI** should prove one of the most useful for you. **"How Do I Know What a Good Paper Looks Like? An Annotated Student Essay"** features an actual student paper that we have annotated. If you are a freshman, you may have no idea what a good college-level essay looks like. Here is an example of one, with explanations as to what this author does well.

- **Part VII, "How Do I Cite This Car? Guidelines for Citing Popular Culture Texts,"** shows you how to cite all of that good research you've just done. Putting together a Bibliography or a Works Cited page is an important component of any research project. This section provides examples for citing unusual texts.

- Many instructors ask their students to write personal essays, especially in the first semester of composition courses, so in the final section we include a short guide to this process in **Part VIII**'s cleverly entitled **"How Am I a Text? Writing Personal Essays."** You should always adhere to the guidelines your professor provides, but this short section should supplement what you discuss in class.

Although this section might not be as compelling as essays on *The Simpsons* or *Seinfeld,* it is important nonetheless. Reading and writing feed each other in complex ways, so try to give both your attention.

PART I. HOW DO I WRITE A TEXT FOR COLLEGE? MAKING THE TRANSITION FROM HIGH SCHOOL WRITING

by Patty Strong

Writing is thinking. This is what we teachers of college writing believe. Hidden inside that tiny suitcase of a phrase is my whole response to the topic assigned me by my colleague, Jonathan Silverman, one of the authors of the textbook you are currently reading. Knowing my background as a former teacher of high school English, Dr. Silverman asked me to write a piece for students on the differences between writing in high school and writing in college. I have had some time to ponder my answer, and it is this: Writing is thinking. Now that's not very satisfactory, is it? I must unpack that suitcase of a phrase. I will open it up for you, pull out a few well-traveled and wearable ideas, ideas that you may want to try on yourself as you journey through your college writing assignments.

Writing is thinking. I suggest that this idea encompasses the differences between high school writing and the writing expected from students on a college level, not because high school teachers don't expect their students to think, but rather that most students themselves do not approach the writing as an *opportunity to think.* Students might construct many other kinds of sentences with writing as subject: Writing is hard. Writing is a duty. Writing is something I do to prove that I know something.

When I taught high school English, I certainly assigned writing in order to find out what my students knew. Did they, for example, know what I had taught them about the light and dark symbolism in Chapter 18 of *The Scarlet Letter*? Did they know precisely what Huck Finn said after he reconsidered his letter to Miss Watson ("All right, then, I'll *go* to hell!") and did they know what I, their teacher, had told them those words meant in terms of Huck's moral development? Could my students spit this information back at me in neat, tidy sentences? That's not to say I didn't encourage originality and creativity in my students' writing, but those were a sort of bonus to the bottom line knowledge I was expecting them to be able to reproduce.

College writing is different precisely because it moves beyond the limited conception that writing is writing what we already know. In college, students write to discover what they don't know, to uncover what they didn't know they knew. Students in college should not worry about not having anything to write, because it is the physical and intellectual act of writing, of moving that pen across the page (or tapping the keyboard) that produces the thoughts that become what you have to write. The act of writing will produce the thinking. This thinking need not produce ideas you already know to be true, but should explore meanings and attitude and questions, which are the things that we all wonder and care about.

My discussion of these matters has so far been fairly abstract, caught up in the wind of ideas. Practical matters are of importance here, too, so I will address some points that as a college student you should know. First, your professors are not responsible for your education—you are. While your teachers may in fact care very much that you learn and do well in your course-work, it is not their responsibility to see that you are successful. Your college teacher may not do things you took for granted like reminding you of assignments and tests and paper dead-lines. They probably won't accept your illness or the illness of a loved one or a fight with a girl-friend as legitimate excuses for late work. Sloppy work, late work, thoughtless work, tardiness, absences from class—these things are the student's problems. Successful college students ac-cept responsibility for their problems. They expect that consequences will be meted out. Suc-cessful students do not offer excuses, lame or otherwise, although they may offer appropriate resolutions. Successful students understand that their education is something they are privi-leged to own, and as with a dear possession, they must be responsible for managing it. If you wrecked your beloved car, would you find fault with the person who taught you how to drive?

On to the writing task at hand. You will want to write well in college. You probably want to write better and more maturely than you have in the past. To do this, you must be will-ing to take thinking risks, which are writing risks. I read an interesting quote the other day that I shared with my writing students because I believed it to be true and pretty profound. The American writer Alvin Toffler wrote that "The illiterate of the twenty-first century will not be those who cannot read and write, but those who cannot learn, unlearn, and relearn." And so it's true that when you come to the university for your "higher education," you must be willing to unlearn some old things and relearn them in new ways. That's probably true for just about every academic subject you will explore during your university career, and it is certainly true about the writing courses you will take.

Writing is thinking. Writing will lead you toward thought. Your college writing teach-ers will expect more of your thinking, thinking you have come to through the process of writing and rewriting. In order to get where you need to be, you must relearn what writing is. You must see that writing is not duty, obligation, and regurgitation, but opportunity, ex-ploration, and discovery. The realization that writing is thinking and that thinking *leads* to writing is the main idea behind this book—the simple notion that the world is a text to be thought and written about. The successful college writer understands that he or she writes not just for the teacher, not just to prove something to the teacher in order to get a grade, but to uncover unarticulated pathways to knowledge and understanding.

PART II. FROM SEMIOTICS TO LENSES: FINDING AN APPROACH FOR YOUR ESSAYS

by Dean Rader and Jonathan Silverman

In the first eight pages of this book, we talk a great deal about semiotics as that pathway to knowledge and understanding. Formal and informal decoding of cultural and visual cues can be pretty interesting stuff, but you may be wondering what bearing this has on college, grades, and your class. You are going to have to write some papers for this course, and these concepts will help you land on a topic for your paper. Your next step, however, is to select an approach for that paper. Only rarely can essays be simply observational; most of the time you have to turn those observations into arguments. Thus, in order to make an argument, you have to have an approach, or what talk show host Jim Rome might call a "take." There are any number of **approaches** or **lenses** when writing about nontraditional/popular culture/visual texts. We began with **semiotics** as it explains how texts make meaning through signification and connotation. But there are other ways of thinking about texts beyond their theoretical components. In the second part of this introduction, we devote a great number of pages to helping you with the *micro* aspects of your arguments, but the following paragraphs give you a broad introduction to the *macro* aspects of your papers by providing some of the language you need in order to approach these texts.

The main approaches we consider here are those of lenses, microscopes, and windows; language and elements of literary interpretation; context, historical and otherwise; social and political approaches, such as race, class, gender, sexual orientation, region, age—and more; and finally, academic disciplines.

Lenses, Microscopes, and Windows

The idea of a lens is a metaphor for "putting on" a particular point of view in order to think, read, and write about it, in much the same way you might put on sunglasses or reading glasses to see the world in a different way. Aside from the major lenses of race and gender, which we address later, there are other lenses you may put on when reading texts, such as college student or consumer; Democrat or Republican (or Independent); rural, urban, or suburban; Western or Eastern European or Asian; queer (as in Katherine Gantz's essay about *Seinfeld* in Chapter 2 (pp. 134–151), and so on. By thinking either with or through your own perspective or someone else's, you can put into words the point of view you may have already been using.

A microscope takes something small and makes it bigger. In much the same way, you might take a portion of a text or short contained text, examine it closely, and reveal some larger truths. For example, one might examine a particular image, such as the couch at Central Perk in *Friends,* or Lisa Simpson's pearls in *The Simpsons,* or the gargoyle on a building and write about how they represent a particular idea of the creator—such an approach can be part of a larger paper or an examination of its own. For instance, one could write an entire paper on the border of the beach and the forest as a means of understanding the complexities, fears, and tensions of *Lost.*

A window allows one to look outward from a particular perspective, also as a way of exploring a larger truth. One could look at a television show as a way of writing about race or ethnicity or politics. You might, for example, use cable news as a window for the way Americans view politics, a popular album as a window for a way young people view gender attitudes, or a new shopping mall as a window for how Americans currently view consumption. Later in this introduction, we talk about the movie *Office Space* as a window onto the mind-numbing corporate job.

Your professor may point out that these approaches overlap with some of the ones we discuss further—that's true. But we find that sometimes we as scholars and students get untracked when trying to apply the language of traditional interpretation to nontraditional texts.

Language and Elements of Literary Interpretation

In a sense, each text has an argument and narrative that invites interpretation, whether it's a movie, an advertisement, or a building. One way of thinking about this is to figure out the "grammar" of whatever the text is. If stories are made up of words, buildings are made up of materials, which are almost always chosen deliberately for effect. Movies are made up of scenes, advertisements of discrete images, specific editing choices, camera angles, and soundtracks that when taken together, create a kind of cinematic grammar. Now, think about what a particular element of a building could mean. For example, what effect does a new building constructed entirely of brick have on the viewer? What connotations or meanings do bricks have? Why might a designer put in columns? Why build a new building to look like an old warehouse? When a movie character wears a cowboy hat, what does it mean? A critic in *Rolling Stone* makes the argument that the trumpets in Sufjan Stevens' "Casmir Pulaski Day"—an ode to a dead childhood friend—signal Stevens' displeasure with God. For the critic, that a particular sound—the blast of trumpets, which are mentioned in the Bible—is similar to a way a writer might use a description of landscape to make a larger point in a novel or short story.

Metaphor remains one of the most popular approaches to any text. A metaphor is a part of a narrative or text that can be taken for the whole of the text itself or as a small indicator of a larger trend. For example, commentators often describe reality shows as metaphors for the decline in quality television (some suggest such shows reflect a culture's lack of interest in *story* in favor of spectacle) or as metaphors for the postmodern world we live in (everything is edited, everything is performance). Some argue that *Lost* is a metaphor for the sense of directionlessness and entrapment felt by young people today. In the '90s, grunge music became a metaphor for Generation X's need for controlled catharsis. Metaphors can be tricky, because sometimes they lead an author to read too much into a text or to over-interpret, but metaphor can be an excellent lens for making sense of a popular text.

Context, Historical and Otherwise

Reading a work through the lens of context is another way of making sense of a text and of establishing an argument about that text. For instance, understanding the historical situation of the Old South, slavery, and black/white relations helps make sense of *The Adventures of Huckleberry Finn*. Knowing a bit about William Randolph Hearst and the newspaper business in the '20s, '30s, and '40s makes viewing *Citizen Kane* more meaningful. To place something in context means in essence to put something in perspective, often through comparison. If you were writing about *The Cosby Show*, you could put the show into any number of contexts: family sitcoms, comedies that featured African American characters, the 1980s generally, sitcoms, working-parent shows, comedies that featured former stand-up comedians, and so on. The reason you put nontraditional texts, or all texts for that matter, into context is to gain perspective by looking at similar items. Typically, we think of context in historical or temporal terms—comparing a building to others built in the same era, for example—but *context* could also mean comparing all baseball stadiums in terms of their playability, seating, and vistas. Finally, *context* can also refer to genre—the "kind" of text it is. For instance, if you want to write about Metallica, you probably would not compare them to Kronos Quartet, Iron and Wine, or Celine Dion, because those acts are all operating in different genres. For the purposes of your paper, it would be most fruitful to place Metallica in context—perhaps reading them alongside AC/DC, Nirvana, or Linkin Park.

Race, Class, Gender, Sexual Orientation, Region, Age—and More

One's experiences affect one's perspective. As we see in Chapter 4, about race and ethnicity, and Chapter 6, concerning gender people often write from the larger perspective of these groups, who have been historically discriminated against. But discrimination does not need to drive one's group perspective. One such example is bell hooks' examination of *Waiting to Exhale* (pp. 374–379), done as a close reading of the movie through the perspective of African-American thought, and even more specifically, African American feminism. As a college student, you probably see things differently from your professor; if you come from a working-class background, you may see things from a different perspective than someone from a more wealthy background. In a famous essay on economic class, critic Michael Parenti reads *Pretty Woman* through the lens of class, arguing that the movie upholds traditional upper-class patriarchal values. On the opposite end, the wonderful British comedy *The Full Monty* can be read as a celebration of working-class men and women. You will see such readings throughout this book, both in the gender and race chapters but in other chapters as well. One of the funniest essays in *The World Is a Text* is Gantz's piece on *Seinfeld,* in which she reads the popular sitcom through the lens of queer theory.

Academic Disciplines

This book might be part of a course called "Writing Across the Disciplines." Although there are different definitions of what that means, generally it signals that your professor or department wants you to learn to write in your chosen discipline or major. Social scientists read texts differently than artists. Scientists approach information in a distinct way, as do semioticians, literary scholars, and cultural critics. In Chapter 1, physicist Brandon Brown reads a science lab. His lens is informed by an entirely different set of criteria than if an architect were reading the same lab or if the reader were an insurance adjuster. The accoutrement of disciplinary readings is vocabulary, prose style, and citation. Sometimes this simply means that you need to be attuned to the citation style of your discipline; English departments, for example, use the Modern Language Association style, known as MLA, whereas psychology departments use the American Psychology Association style, or APA. History departments often use Chicago (or Turabian), whereas other disciplines may have their own styles.

Disciplinary approaches can also affect issues of subjectivity and objectivity. For example, in literary studies, film studies, and media studies, writers often ground their writing in argument, interpretation, and insight. But, in many social sciences, soft sciences, and the hard sciences, scholars rely on data and objective proof. Thus, a scientist, a film scholar, and a political scientist would each read Al Gore's movie *An Inconvenient Truth* through three very different lenses, because they work in three utterly distinct disciplines.

But this might also mean a larger issue than of writing style or content. This book contains writing more focused on English-related subjects, but throughout, you find writings done in other disciplines as well. *The World Is a Text* is proud to offer a mix of various disciplinary readings, each reflecting the format of the field.

Landing on an Approach: An Entrée to the Essay Itself

Your professor may have a specific approach in mind for you, but he or she may not. In general, the approach you take will probably mirror your own lenses. If you were raised on a farm in Ohio, you will likely always, in some way or another, look at people, places, and things through the Ohio-rural-farm lens. Thus, you may read a movie like *Field of Dreams* (even though it is set in Iowa) quite differently than a baseball player who grew up in Puerto Rico. As you try to land on an approach for your essay, think about what sort of lenses you tend to look through on a daily basis.

But we would also be lax if we did not suggest that such essential perspectives can be changed. For example, most people who live or work in Manhattan will tell you that New York has transformed them, has made them look at the world differently—even if they came from small towns in the Midwest. Perhaps more important is your willingness to try on approaches or lenses. One of the foremost experiences one of your authors had was learning about others' developed, theoretical perspectives on the world around them; fellow graduate students were feminists, or had race-oriented perspectives, or were highly political, or had completely absorbed even more obscure perspectives. By trying to understand others' perspectives, both through reading and discussion, one can become a better reader of texts.

PART III. HOW DO I WRITE ABOUT POPULAR AND VISUAL CULTURE TEXTS? A TOUR THROUGH THE WRITING PROCESS

We begin by underscoring how important being a good reader is for the writing process. Both processes are about discovery, insight, ordering, and argument. The process of writing, however, differs from the product of writing. When we say *product,* we mean the produced or finished version—the completed paper that you submit to your instructor. The writing *process* is the always complex, sometimes arduous, often frustrating, and frequently rushed series of events that eventually lead you to the finished product. There are a lot of theories about writing, so we will not bore you with an overview of all of them. Chances are, your instructor or your institution's writing center has a series of handouts or guidelines that will help you along the way, but we thought we would take you on a quick tour of what we see as the highlights of the writing process, with an added emphasis on building a good first paragraph and building sound arguments.

But first, you need to understand the assignment.

Understanding the Assignment

This is usually the easiest part of the writing process, but it, too, is important. And because you are learning how to be savvy readers of various texts, this task should be easy for you. First, you should read the assignment for the paper as you would read a poem or an advertisement. Look for textual clues that seem particularly important. In fact, we recommend making a list of questions about the assignment itself, such as:

- What questions do I have to answer in order to complete or answer the assignment? Do I have a research or writing question that my paper must answer?
- Does my assignment contain any code words, such as "compare," "analyze," "research," "unpack," or "explore"? If so, what do these terms mean?
- What text or texts am I supposed to write about? Do I understand these texts?
- What is my audience? For whom am I writing?
- What are the parameters of the assignment? What can I do? What can I not do? Is there anything I don't understand before beginning?

One of the biggest mistakes students make is paying too little attention to the assignment. Like any text, it contains textual cues to help you understand it.

Freewriting and Brainstorming

Freewriting and brainstorming are crucial to the writing process because they generally produce your topic. Freewriting involves the random and uncensored act of writing down anything that comes into your mind on a particular topic. There are any number of ways to freewrite; some teachers and students like visually oriented methods, whereas others prefer a straightforward "Write all you can down in five minutes" approach. Some of our students set a stopwatch at two minutes, and within that two minutes, write down anything and everything that pops into their heads. When the two minutes are up, they review the list to see if any pattern or ideas emerge. From this list of random stuff, you can generally narrow down a topic. Let's say your assignment is to analyze the film *The Return of the King,* and you see that you jotted down several things that have to do with the way the movie looks. From that, you could decide that you want to write on the innovative "look" of the movie.

At this point, you can move on to brainstorming. Here, you take a blank piece of paper, or sit down in front of a blank computer screen, and write the topic of your paper across the top: The "look" of *The Return of the King.* Now, write down everything that pops into your head about the look of *The Return of the King.* See if you can come up with 10 to 20 ideas, observations, or questions. When you are done, look closely at your list. Does a pattern emerge? Are there certain questions or ideas that seem to fit together? Let's say you've written "cool effects," "lots of action," "scary creatures," "mythical overtones," "religious symbols," "good vs. evil," "darkness vs. light," "beautiful scenery," "the camera angles were very unique," "very serious," "it felt like fantasy," and "good wins, evil loses." Based on these observations, it looks like you could write a paper about good versus evil, or perhaps certain symbols in the film, like light and dark or white and black. Or, you could take things in a different direction and talk about how the "look" of the movie (camera angles, the setting, the colors, and the effects) make a certain argument or contribute to the theme in some way. Yet another possibility is to combine these observations into a paper that looks at the theme *and* the form.

The goal here is to try to hone in on your topic—the overall subject of your paper. At this point, your topic does not have to be perfectly formulated, but you should be getting an idea of how you might narrow your topic down to something that you can feasibly write a paper about. It's possible—even likely—that as you start plotting an outline, a more defined topic will emerge.

Outlining

Once you have your topic, you need to organize your paper. Outlines are helpful because they provide a visual map of your paper so that you can see where you're going and where you've been. An outline is also useful in helping you see if your ideas fit together, if the paper is coherent, and if the paper is equally distributed among your various points. If you find yourself getting stuck or suffering from writer's block, an outline might help push you along. In addition, an outline presents your ideas in a logical format, and it shows the relationship among the various components of your paper.

The truth is that deciding on these various components is a process of trial and error. We change our minds all the time. So, as authors of this text, we are reluctant to say that one approach is better than another. Writing is always an organic process—that is, it grows at its own pace in its own way, and as a writer, you will likely need to adjust to accommodate where your ideas want to go.

No doubt, your instructor will talk a great deal about developing a **thesis** (which is the main argument or focus of your essay—what you *argue* about your topic), and he or she may encourage you to make this thesis part of your outline. This is a common strategy. The only problem is that you may make an outline with an idea of a thesis, finish the outline, and decide you need to change your thesis. At that point, you should make yet another outline.

During the writing process, you may hone your thesis yet again, at which point, you will probably want to draft another outline so that you stay on course given your new thesis. Our point here is that there is no clearcut process when you are talking about the very fuzzy beginning stages of writing a paper. You should do whatever works for you—whatever leads to the most organized product.

Unlike most other books, we decided to combine a section on outlining and thesis-making because for us, the two go hand in hand. Most books suggest that writers figure out a thesis *before* doing an outline. Our experience, however, tells us that arriving at a thesis is often hard, and we don't always know *exactly* what we want to say about our topic until we get a visual map of the paper. Just remember that the first outline you make doesn't have to be the last outline—you can and should change it as you see fit.

Now, to that visual map. Traditionally, an outline states your topic (maybe states your thesis), enumerates your main points and supporting arguments in Roman numerals and, beneath the Roman numerals, lists your evidence in letters. For an essay with two main points, an outline might look something like this:

THE TITLE OF MY ESSAY
    I. Introduction (1–2 paragraphs)
        Thesis: This is my thesis statement, if I have one at this point
    II. My first point (2–4 paragraphs)
        a. My supporting evidence
        b. My supporting evidence
    III. My second point (2–6 paragraphs)
        a. My supporting evidence
            1. Further evidence, graphs, statistics, perhaps
        b. My supporting evidence
            1. Further evidence
    IV. My smart conclusion (1–2 paragraphs)

Notice how the outline helps flesh out an organizing idea, even if it is in the most general way. The final outline almost never matches up with the first version, but an outline can help you see the strengths and weaknesses of your organization, and it can help you think in an organized way.

Still, outlining in this manner may not suit everyone. Some students (and professors) do not like outlining, because they do not refer to the outline when writing, and they feel like the whole process is a waste of time. Others like to outline at various stages of writing; some outline after they have written a draft to make sure they have covered everything they wanted to cover. Those approaches are okay as well; so is writing an outline that is less formal in nature. At various times, we have written outlines that are barely outlines—just a mere list of points. Other times, we have written outlines with topic sentences of every one of our paragraphs. The approach you take will depend not only on class requirements, but also on the topic of your paper, your knowledge of the topic, and the amount of research required.

The reason we are committed to outlining is that it separates to some degree the thinking and composing stages of writing; if you know to some degree what you want to say before you start the actual putting words on paper, the more likely you are to write a clear and thoughtful draft, one that needs less extensive revision. The thinking aspect of outlining is why it is at once so difficult and eventually rewarding.

Constructing a Good Thesis

Now that you have an idea of the work an outline can do, we move on to helping you construct a **thesis.** As stated earlier, a thesis is the *argument that you make* about your topic. It is the main point, the assertion, you set forth in your essay.

We should say at the outset that the term "thesis" is only one possible term for the paper's argument. Some instructors like the term "claim," some like "focus," still others like "controlling idea." Regardless of what term you use, the concept is the same. The thesis is the idea you propose in your paper—it is not a statement of fact, but rather a claim, an assertion.

The most important first step is to distinguish among a **topic,** a **thesis,** and a **thesis statement.** One of the great mistakes students make is that they assume a topic is a thesis. A topic is merely the avenue to the freeway that is the thesis, the appetizer to the main course. Let's say you are writing a paper about Affirmative Action. The topic is what you write about, which is Affirmative Action. Your thesis is the argument you make about Affirmative Action. Your thesis statement is the actual articulation, the statement or statements in which you unpack or explain your thesis. Now, a thesis statement does not have to be (nor should it be) one simplified sentence; in fact, it could and probably should be two or three sentences, or even a full paragraph. (A book can have a thesis statement that goes on for pages.)

We might break down these three components as follows:

Topic: What you are writing about (Affirmative Action)

Thesis: What you argue about your topic (Affirmative Action is a necessary law)

Thesis statement: The reason or explanation of your overall thesis—this usually appears in the first or second paragraph of your essay. For example: Affirmative Action is a necessary law because it prevents discriminatory hiring practices. Minorities, women, people with disabilities, and gay and lesbian workers have suffered discrimination for decades. Affirmative Action not only redresses past wrongs, but also sets a level playing field for all job applicants. In short, it ensures democracy.)

Generally, the topic causes you the least anxiety. Your instructor will help you with your topic and may even provide one for you. In any case, you cannot start a paper without a topic.

The real task is figuring out your **thesis.** Many students worry about not having a thesis when they begin the writing process, but that's normal, and in a way preferable in the quest to find a thesis that is truly an argument. Sometimes it's enough to have what we might refer to as a **thesis question**—a question that when answered through writing and research, actually reveals to you your thesis. Or you might have what we call a "working thesis," one that is too broad for a final paper, but is specific enough to guide you through the writing process. Often you must write a first draft of your essay before a thesis finally emerges. Remember that writing is exploration and discovery, so it may take some freewriting, brainstorming, outlining, and drafting before you land on a thesis. But stay with the process—you will eventually find an argument.

Perhaps the most confusing aspect of the thesis for students is the realization that a good thesis means you might be wrong. In fact, you know you are on the road to a good thesis if you think someone might be able to argue against your point. Writing is grounded in rhetoric, which, as we discussed earlier, is the art of persuasion. Your goal in your papers is not necessarily to change your audience's mind, but to get them to consider your ideas. Thus, your thesis needs to be something manageable, something reasonable that you can argue about with confidence and clarity.

The most effective strategy we found with helping our students understand a thesis is to use the example of the *hypothesis*. As most of you know, a *hypothesis* is an educated guess. A thesis is the same thing. In Greek, *thesis* means "a proposition" or "an idea"; *hypo* is Greek for "under" or "beneath." So, literally, a *hypothesis* is a "proposition laid down." Your thesis is the same thing. It is not a fact; it is not a statement. It is an idea, a proposition that you lay down on paper and then set out to support. You are not absolutely sure that Affirmative Action is a necessary law, but you believe it is. You are pretty confident in your stance, but you also know that someone could write an essay arguing why Affirmative Action should be abolished. This possibility of disagreement is how you know you have a good thesis, because you must provide sound reasons and convincing examples to support your assertion about the necessity for Affirmative Action.

Why must a thesis be an educated guess? Because if a thesis is a statement of fact, there is literally nothing to argue. If your thesis is "Affirmative Action is a law that was designed to prevent discrimination," you have simply stated a fact. There is nothing at stake, nothing to debate. Even a thesis like "Affirmative Action is an important law" is rather weak. Virtually no one would suggest that Affirmative Action is not important. It has been extraordinarily important in American culture. So, again, that is not the best thesis you could come up with, although it remains better than our first example. However, arguing that it is a *necessary* law makes your thesis more provocative, more risky. Therefore, it is likely to draw interest and get people excited. Readers will want to see your reasons and think about the examples you provide.

Let's break it down even further, using an example from this book. Let's say you are writing about visual art. Your topic is censorship and the *Sensation* exhibit—our book features a reproduction of the painting exhibited at the Brooklyn Museum that prompted Mayor Rudolph Giuliani to threaten to shut down the exhibit—Chris Ofili's *Holy Virgin Mary*. We also print Diana Mack's discussion of the exhibition in the "Is It Art?" suite. Here are some sample theses for that topic.

Weak thesis: The *Sensation* exhibit in New York raised a lot of questions about censorship and public money.

This is a weak thesis statement because it is a statement of fact. No one would debate this point.

Better thesis: The *Sensation* exhibit in New York deserved to run its course despite public opinion.

This is a better thesis statement because it proposes something a bit controversial. Many people, including the mayor of New York at the time, could argue against this thesis. That tells you that you are on the right track.

Even better thesis: It is important that the *Sensation* exhibit in New York was allowed to happen without being censored, despite political opposition to the content of some of the pieces. Freedom of speech and freedom of expression are critical parts of American ideas of liberty, and silencing works of art meant for public consumption is in violation of our most basic rights.

This thesis statement is even better because it provides a bit more precision, and it gives a reason for the author's stance. It is easier, then, for this writer to prove the thesis because the reason is already articulated. Honing in on a good thesis is the foundation for building a good paragraph—which, in turn, is the foundation for building a good essay.

Building an Opening Paragraph: A Case Study

The opening paragraph for your essay does a great deal of work, both for your essay and for your audience. For your audience, it sets up your argument and informs them what is going to happen in the remaining pages. In the paper, it functions as the road map, pointing readers down certain avenues, and telling them to avoid others. If your reader is confused after the first paragraph, she may remain confused for a good bit of your essay, and that's never what you want.

An opening paragraph should do a number of things—it should engage the reader's interest with an entertaining or provocative opening sentence, and it should provide the road map for the rest of the paper. In addition, your opening paragraph is typically the home for your thesis statement (although some professors might have different preferences on whether your thesis must go in the first paragraph). It is also the face for your paper, so it should be extremely well organized, moving from a general observation to the more-specific thesis statement (think of an upside down pyramid—broad going down to narrow). For the writer, the opening paragraph is critical because it provides the formula for working through the issues of the essay itself. A vague opener provides too little direction; a paragraph that tries to argue three or four different topics never gets on the right track; and a paragraph that does not make an argument has a tendency to go nowhere, because it keeps restating facts instead of staking out a position and making an argument.

The purpose of this section is to avoid these pitfalls. Here, we give you some models of opening paragraphs before and after revision to show you how a thorough revising process can improve your opening paragraph, strengthen your thesis, and provide a good entrée into your essay.

Let's say you are writing about the movie *Office Space*. You know that you like the movie. You think it's funny, and all of your friends think it's funny. During parties and over lunch, you trade lines with each other. You all agree that the movie speaks to your generation in some odd way, but you are having trouble figuring out *exactly* what you want to say about it. You decide (wisely) to make a list of all possible arguments and some questions about those arguments:

- *Office Space* speaks to people of my generation. (Why is this important?)
- *Office Space* is funny. (But that's not an argument). *Office Space* is the funniest movie of the last 5 years. (But how would I prove that?)
- *Office Space* makes a connection with college students like no other movie. (Is this true? What about *Lord of the Rings* or *Caddyshack*?)
- *Office Space* was not a huge box office hit, but it is wildly popular among college students. (Maybe its biggest audience is college students?)
- We like *Office Space* because it's funny.
- We like *Office Space* because it's about rebellion.
- It's anti-establishment, anti-corporate.
- Maybe we identify because it's also anti-institution, like school or college.
- *Office Space* appeals to college students because they can identify with the anti-institution theme. (But we are all part of institutions—school, jobs.)
- We like *Office Space* because it's anti-institution and yet not. (It's kind of subversive, but not *really*. The people in it are kind of lazy.)

This is a pretty good list. We can likely get some kind of argument from it.

The trick is finding something that is truly an argument. Saying that *Office Space* is funny is not much of an argument. Most would agree with this, and really, who cares if it's funny or not? That doesn't help us understand the movie any better. Also, arguing that college students like it is also overstating the obvious. The key is to explain *why* this particular movie appeals to college students at this particular time. Of course, one could talk about the fantasy of stealing a million dollars or getting a date with Jennifer Aniston, or the bigger fantasy of enjoying working construction over being in a cubicle, but those kinds of ideas occur in other movies. What sets this movie apart is the idea of being subversive (sort of) in an institutional setting. You want your paper to be unique, and you want it to tell your readers something they might actually find compelling. Readers can usually tell after an opening paragraph if there is anything in there for them, so as you craft your essay, ask yourself—Am I giving pertinent information? Is my argument interesting? Will people like this?

So, the first try at an opening paragraph might look like this:

> *Office Space,* directed by Mike Judge, has become a classic movie for college students. It's funny plot, it's witty dialogue and stance on corporate life appeals to students across disciplines and states. One might wonder why a movie that was not a box-office sensation has become a cult sensation among college students, but it's clear that *Office Space* appeals to students in a number of ways. Perhaps the biggest way is the movie's theme of rebellion. Students can identify with the movie's anti-corporate message.

Okay, so what do we see here? On a micro level, there are some problems with the prose: the rogue apostrophe in *it's* (second sentence) has to go; the phrase "across disciplines and states" is vague and not really helpful; "box-office sensation" is a cliché and also vague; "number of ways" also doesn't do much work. Still, there is also a great deal of information here to work with. The beginnings of our thesis probably rest in the last two sentences—it's there that we make our argument. On closer examination, however, it would appear that the last sentence isn't *really* an argument. Almost no one would disagree with that statement, so *proving* it would be easy but, ultimately, pointless. Essays that merely sum up what everyone agrees with do little to further our understanding of the issue or topic at hand. From an entertainment perspective, a good opening paragraph needs to give us reasons to keep reading, so the next version should incorporate some reasons why the movie appeals to students. It should also be a bit more sophisticated and precise. So, in the next version, list some reasons the movie appeals to college students, and give the date of the film, for starters. Also, do a bit of research and see what you can come up with.

Draft two might come out like this:

> *Office Space* (1999), directed by Mike Judge of *Beavis and Butthead* fame, has become an underground classic among American college students. It is not uncommon to overhear students quoting entire passages from the movie, and there is even an *Office Space* drinking game. Though the movie features a couple of funny subplots involving dating and stealing a million dollars, the real draw of the movie lies in the fact that it is rather anti-establishment. The main character of the film doesn't simply quit his job—he actually stops working. What's more, he gets rewarded for it through a promotion. Thus, *Office Space* sends a message to college students that when they enter the same corporate environment, they too can be rewarded for rebelling against the corporate mindset.

Wow, what happened here? On one hand, the paragraph is much stronger. Notice the increased specificity: American college students, examples of how students enjoy the movie, more active verbs instead of being verbs (is, are); even some details from the movie itself. But, beyond all that, the thesis has gone off in a different direction! Our argument was that students relate to the movie's theme of rebellion; now, it would appear that we are arguing that students like the movie because they will get rewarded for rebelling. Is that what we want to argue? Is that the reason students like the movie? Does the appeal of the movie lie in the fact that students relate to it, or that it gives them hope? What if it's both? Is there a way to work both into the thesis? Generally, the more precise you are, and the more thorough your thesis is, the better; however, yours has gone off in a different direction! In truth, probably both things appeal to students, so why not strengthen the thesis and the essay by making arguments about both?

The resulting third draft:

Mike Judge took slacking to new heights with his hilarious cartoon *Beavis and Butthead*, which chronicled the lives of two under-achieving teen-age boys who had a great deal of fun doing a great deal of nothing. Judge's first movie involving real humans is also about doing nothing, but this time it's recent college graduates who find themselves working in cubicles for a mind-numbing corporation. Despite the fact that *Office Space* (1999) was not a huge hit at the box office, it has become an underground classic across university campuses. Students quote entire scenes to each other from memory, *Office Space* t-shirts abound, and there is even an *Office Space* drinking game. One might wonder why a movie with no real stars except for Jennifer Aniston has made such an impact on this generation of students. Though there are some funny subplots involving dating and stealing a million dollars from a corporation, the main action of the movie comes when the main character, Peter, decides to stop working, but winds up getting a promotion. Thus, the movie appeals to students not simply because it champions rebelling against the man, but it suggests one might get rewarded for doing so. On one hand, students identify with the desire to completely stop working, and they like the idea that things might turn out better for them if they do. Ultimately, students are drawn to *Office Space* because it tells them they can be anti-establishment and successful at the same time.

This version is better not because it is longer, but because it provides detail, it is precise, and it features a thorough three-sentence thesis statement. Readers know from this opening paragraph that we are going to read an essay that 1) makes an argument and 2) makes an argument about the two ways/reasons the movie appeals to college students.

Because we have a focused thesis, we can now go into a lot of detail in the rest of our paper about how and why students related to specific scenes and concepts, and we can also make some interesting observations about "safe rebellion" and rewards. From here on, the writing process involves "proving" and elaborating on the thesis.

A note here on opening paragraphs: One of the authors believes that writing the opening paragraph should come closer to the end of the composing process rather than the beginning. Although getting a thesis early is important, writing an opening paragraph before you know what you want to say might mean you must extensively revise the paragraph or scrap it altogether. Some writers, however, need to "begin with beginning"—they can't go on until they know exactly what their argument is going to be. Ultimately, your preference regarding the writing process is less important that the finished product.

Finally, avoid writing a clichéd introduction. Do not use phrases like "since the beginning of time," which is much too general and tells us little. Also, resist using a dictionary definition of an important word. These two strategies should almost never be used in college writing. If you want to use a time construction, confine it to specific knowable time, such as "the recent past" or "in the 1990s." If you find yourself drifting toward a dictionary definition, try defining it yourself, looking in a more specialized source such as a book about the subject (but be careful to cite), or engaging the definition you find by arguing with it or refining it. *Never* write: "The dictionary defines [your subject here] as . . ." —there are many different dictionaries, all of which define words differently.

If you take your opening paragraph seriously, use it as a method of organization, and make it interesting, you will be off to a good start with your paper.

Building Good Paragraphs

Building a good paper is relatively simple, once you understand the formula. By *formula,* we do *not* necessarily mean a standard five-paragraph essay. Instead of thinking of your paper in terms of numbers of paragraphs, think in terms of **points** or **reasons**. By "points," we mean ideas, concepts, observations, or reasons that support the argument you make in your thesis. The units that help you organize these points are the paragraphs themselves. This section helps you get a handle on how to structure your paragraphs so that you make the most of your supporting points.

For a typical undergraduate paper, you do not want too many or too few points. If you are arguing about Affirmative Action, how many reasons do you want to include in your paper to support your thesis? Do you want seven? No, that's too many. One? That's too few. Generally, we suggest two to four points or reasons for a standard three- to six-page paper. For a longer paper, like a research paper, you may want four or five points to drive home your argument. But the danger of including too many points in your paper is that, unless you can supply ample evidence for each point, an overabundance of points winds up having the opposite of the intended effect. Rather than bolstering your argument by the sheer number of reasons, you tend to weaken your argument because you dilute your points through an overabundance of reasons and a lack of evidence. In other words, it's better to write three or four paragraphs for one or two points than to write five paragraphs for five points. Write more about less as, opposed to less about more.

The key to making and supporting your assertions is the paragraph. Paragraphs are the infrastructure of your essay; they frame and support the arguments you make. Every paragraph is like a mini-essay. Just as your essay has a thesis statement, so does your paragraph have a **topic sentence**—a sentence in which you lay out the main idea for that paragraph. Once you write your topic sentence, then you have to provide evidence to support the claim you've made in your topic sentence. Each paragraph has its own topic and its own mini-assertion, and when taken together, all of these paragraphs work together to support the overall thesis of the entire essay.

Topic sentences should establish the mini-argument of your paragraph. Try to make them assertive and focused, because they serve as a small map to the theme of your paragraph. Some examples:

> *Weak topic sentence:* This is a plan one finds in the library.
> *Weak topic sentence:* *Family Guy* first aired in 2002.

These are weak topic sentences because they simply state facts rather than advance an argument. Note the topic sentence of the previous two paragraphs. Neither are over-the-top in terms of making an argument, but notice how both sentences make assertions. Following are topic sentences from a freshman essay on the overuse of medication in the United States:

- The increasing over-use of medication has been made possible by the "quick-fix" mentality that has become prevalent in our society.
- A big factor leading to the increasing amount of over-medication is the rampant advertising of new drugs by the pharmaceutical companies.

- In addition to our desire for quick and easy solutions, America's preoccupation with youth and physical perfection is also to blame in the overflow of drug consumption in our society.

This last example is particularly good because it includes a **transition** ("in addition to our desire for quick and easy solutions") in the topic sentence. The topic of the preceding paragraph focuses on America's desire for quick and easy solutions, and the author used the topic sentence not only to advance her idea about youth and physical perfection, but she also reminded the reader of her previous topic, making her overall argument feel connected, part of a piece. Remember—make assertions in your topic sentences.

Once you have a clear, focused topic sentence, it is time to move on to the rest of your paragraph. For instance, let's say your topic sentence is: "The *Sensation* exhibit was an important test for American culture because First Amendment rights were at stake." What might be your next move? You should probably quote the First Amendment, or at least part of it. Then, explain how the *Sensation* exhibit was protected by the First Amendment. Give examples of specific pieces from the show that are pertinent to this discussion. This is also the right time to bring in quotes from other people that support your assertions. If you quote from another source, or if you quote from a primary text, be sure you explain how the passage you quote supports your thesis. (And, of course, cite the quote's origin.) The quote cannot explain itself—you must tell your audience why that quote is important, why and how the statistics you include are evidence the reader should pay attention to.

Finally, and this is very important, end your paragraphs well. The most common mistake students make when writing paragraphs is that they tend to trail off. Make that last sentence a kind of connector—make it tie everything in the paragraph back to the topic sentence. Also, when possible, reinforce the fact that your paragraphs are working together by writing transition sentences from one paragraph to the next. For example, a good transition in the essay on the *Sensation* exhibit would acknowledge the topic of the preceding paragraph and lead into the topic for the paragraph at hand. Such a sentence might look like this: "Not only did the *Sensation* exhibit reinforce First Amendment rights of the artists, it underscored the right of viewers and museum-goers to enjoy art their tax dollars helped support." Note how this sentence refers to the subject of the previous paragraph (artistic freedom) and also how it informs us of the topic we are about to engage (publicly funded art).

Start on your next paragraph with the same model. Keep doing this until you have built yourself a paper. Then go back and revise and edit, revise and edit, revise and edit. The key to building good paragraphs is using them to make arguments. The next section walks you through that process.

Drafting the Whole Essay

Although we spend a great deal of energy explaining various strategies for composing a paper, it still comes down to the actual work of thinking about a topic, doing your own method of prewriting (outlining, brainstorming, etc.), and putting the words on paper. In other words, you still have to write that first draft.

Sentence by sentence, and paragraph by paragraph, you start building your paper. Remember to give as much detail as possible. Include examples from the text you are writing about, and try to avoid plot summary or unnecessary description. Remember: *Analyze, don't summarize.* In other words, do not simply provide information—make sense of information for us.

Once you finish your first draft, you may discover that buried somewhere in your closing paragraph is the very good articulation of the thesis you've been trying to prove for several pages. This happens because, as we've said, writing is a discovery process. So by working through your ideas, your arguments, your textual examples, you start to focus on what you've been trying to say all along.

Now that you have a better idea of what you want to say, it's time for the real work—editing and revising.

Editing and Revising, Editing and Revising, Editing and Revising

The single biggest mistake student writers make is turning in their first draft. The first draft is often little more than a blueprint—it's merely an experiment. In the editing and revising stage, you convert the process of writing into the written product. Here, you turn a bad paper into a decent one, or a good paper into a great one. You can clear up confusing sentences, focus your argument, correct bad grammar, and, most important, make your paper clearer and more thorough. Students think that they are good writers if papers come easily. This is the biggest myth in writing. A good paper happens through several stabs at editing and revising. For instance, this very introduction has gone through somewhere between fifteen and twenty revisions.

There are a number of strategies for editing and revising, so we'll give you a couple of our favorites. First, when you are ready to edit and revise, **read your paper through backward.** Start at the very end, and read it backward, one sentence at a time. This forces you to slow down and see the sentence as its own entity. It's probably the most useful strategy for correcting your own writing. Even more helpful is getting a peer to read your paper. Another person can point out errors, inconsistencies, or vague statements that you may miss because you are too close to the process. An often painful but very effective way of editing is reading your paper out loud. The authors often do this, especially when presenting their work to other people.

Finally, we also recommend that **although you may write hot, you should edit cold.** What we mean by this is that you need to step back from your paper when you edit. Look at it objectively. Try not to get caught up in your prose or your argument. Work on being succinct and clear. Practically, this means not working on your paper for a period of time, even if that period is hours, not days. As professors, we are well aware that you may wait until the last minute to write a paper. Although we are not endorsing this way of composing, you still need to find a way to step away from the paper and come back to it to get some perspective on what you have written.

This is also the time go to back over the arguments you made. (Here we introduce some terms that you see again in the upcoming "A Guide for Building Arguments" section.) Look at your **logos** and **pathos**—are they appropriate? Have you made argumentative errors? Are you guilty of using fallacies? Do you supply enough good evidence to support your assertions? Do you end your paragraphs well?

It may take several drafts (in fact, it should) before you feel comfortable with your paper. So, we recommend at least three different passes at editing and revising before turning in your paper. We advocate going back over and looking at your language one last time. Do not use words that are not part of your vocabulary; try to avoid stating the obvious. Be original, be honest, and be engaged. We urge you, above all else, to think complexly, but write simply. A note here from one of the authors: In writing a recent book, he has, conservatively, rewritten his introduction to a chapter more than thirty times. Revising is often a great deal of work, and sometimes rewriting takes multiple drafts.

Finally, we want to reiterate here that writing is not easy or simple for anyone. Although you may think that you are not a strong writer, and that others write more easily and naturally, the truth is that all "good" writers spend a significant amount of time revising their work. In fact, most good writers enjoy this part of the composing process, because it's the time when they see their writing actually turn into something worth sharing with someone else.

Turning in the Finished Product

The most enjoyable part of the process! Doublecheck spelling and grammar issues. If you did a research paper, check your citations and go over your Bibliography or Works Cited pages. Confirm you did *not* plagiarize.

Turn in the paper and go celebrate!

SOME FINAL TIPS—A RECAP

- Distinguish between a topic and a thesis.
- Your thesis doesn't have to be one concise sentence; it can be several sentences, perhaps even an entire paragraph. It might even be helpful to think of your thesis as your focus, your idea that you are trying to support.
- "Thesis" comes from "hypothesis." A *hypothesis* is an educated guess. So is your thesis. It's an educated guess, an idea that you are trying to support. You don't have to develop an over-the-top airtight argument; you simply want your reader to consider your point of view.
- Writing is conversation; it is dialogue. Keep asking questions of yourself, your writing and your topic. Ask yourself, "Why is this so?" Make sure you answer. Be specific; be thorough.
- Consider your audience. You should never assume they have read the text you are writing about, so don't toss around names or scenes without explaining them a little. It's called "giving context." There is a big difference between giving context (valuable information) and summarizing the plot (regurgitation).
- Make good arguments. Use logos, pathos, and ethos appropriately. Try to avoid fallacies.

FIVE STEPS TO WRITING A GOOD PAPER

1. Formulate a good, supportable thesis.
2. Then, set out to explain or prove your thesis in well-constructed paragraphs, using your own interpretation and details from the text to support your points.
3. Build sound, solid arguments that support your thesis.
4. Quote from other sources or provide details from the primary text, and explain why the passage you quote is important to your overall thesis.
5. Keep working through your paper in the same way.

PART IV. HOW DO I ARGUE ABOUT POPULAR CULTURE TEXTS? A GUIDE FOR BUILDING GOOD ARGUMENTS

Knowing Your Arguments

As we suggest in the previous section, building a good paper is dependent on making good **arguments** and supporting them with solid evidence. In contemporary American culture, "argument" tends to carry negative connotations. Few like getting into arguments, and no one wants to be seen as an argumentative person. However, in writing, "argument" has a slightly different meaning. When we talk about arguments or argumentation, what we mean is staking out a position or taking a stance. In writing and rhetoric, "to argue" means to put forth an assertion or a proposition, and to support that position with evidence. If you are using this book, then most of the writing you do in your class involves making an argument and backing it up. So, in your regular, nonwriting life, feel free to go on avoiding arguments; but in your writing life, we urge you to think positively about the prospect of making a compelling argument.

Before we go into specific kinds of arguments, it might be useful to think about why we make arguments. In academic settings, it is important to be able to argue a specific point because almost all information is debatable, particularly in the arts, humanities, and social sciences. Should welfare be abolished? Is capital punishment moral? Is Picasso's *Guernica* transgressive? Is there a relationship between Christianity and Buddhism? Should we discount the poetry of Ezra Pound, T. S. Eliot, and e. e. cummings because of some anti-Semitic passages? These are important questions with no clear answers. Accordingly, you need to be able to justify or explain your opinions on these issues. Holding an opinion and backing up that opinion is argument, and we engage in this kind of argumentation all the time. What is the best album of the '90s? What is the best horror movie? What five books would you take to a desert island, and why? These are fun arguments, and perhaps mostly intellectual exercises, but down the road, being able to argue persuasively might be important in a job ("Here is why we should choose Bob's marketing strategy"), a relationship ("Honey, I know you think I should get an MBA, but let me tell you why an MFA in creative writing is better for me and the kids"), to making purchases ("Let me give you seven reasons why we don't need an SUV"). In fact, in putting this book together the co-authors had daily (but friendly and funny) arguments over what readings to publish, the tone of this very chapter, and what should go on the cover. Finally, knowing how arguments work also helps you discover more fully your own stance on a particular issue. Often, understanding how you feel about a topic is difficult if you do not write or talk about it.

The question is, *how* does one make an effective argument? There are two ways to look at this question. The first is to approach it from the perspective of the argument; the other is to approach it from the perspective of the audience. When we think of arguments, we tend to break them down into two types—logical and emotional. Arguments that appeal to our sense of logic are arguments of **logos** (Greek for "word" or "reason"); those that cater to our emotions are arguments of **pathos** (Greek for "suffering" and "feeling"). Both are effective forms of persuasion, but they function in different ways and sometimes serve different purposes. Although you should use both in your essays, your main focus should be on building an argument based on **logos.**

Arguments of logos appeal to our sense of reason and logic. They tend to rely on facts, statistics, specific examples, and authoritative statements. Your supporting evidence for these kinds of arguments is critical. It must be accurate, valid, truthful, and specific. For instance, while looking over essays we thought might be useful for the new chapter on relationships, we came across a study arguing that long-distance romantic relationships among college students generally didn't last very long. Based on this description, what kinds of evidence do you think the authors of the study relied on? Rumor and innuendo? A survey of people who graduated from college in 1979? A close examination of TV shows about college students? A review of the film *Animal House?* Of course not. The authors were sociologists who surveyed hundreds of college students who were or had been involved in long-distance relationships. They provided almost six pages of statistics; they allowed for differences in age, race, gender, and location; and they did their survey over a respectable amount of time. In short, they relied on objective data, scientific reasoning, and sound survey practices to help make their argument that long distance relationships in college tend not to work out. For a nice example of an argument grounded in logos, see the essay by E. G. Chrichton, "Is the NAMES Quilt Art?" in Chapter 3.

Think about what kinds of information would persuade you in certain situations. What would make you buy an iPod over some other MP3 player? Or, more importantly, what would convince you to buy a Volvo over a Hyundai for driving around your newborn twins? If you were going to write a paper on fire safety, would you rely on the expertise of a fire marshal or a medical doctor? If you were writing an essay on water pollution, would you consult scientific journals and EPA studies, or would you rely on the Web pages of chemical corporations? Readers are more likely to be moved by the soundness of your argument if your supporting evidence seems logical, objective, verifiable, and reasonable.

Having said that, it would be a mistake to dismiss arguments of pathos outright. In fact, we believe that many teachers and writers have too easily separated intellect and emotion when talking about arguments. Arguments of pathos can be unusually powerful and convincing because they appeal to our needs, desires, fears, values, and emotions. The statement, "You should get an iPod because they are just plain cooler than anything else out there" is an appeal to pathos. Notice how this claim ignores any information about warranties, durability, price, or functionality. Rather, the statement plays on our desire to be cool—a most powerful appeal. If you are truthful with yourself, you might be surprised just how often such arguments actually work.

Most television commercials and advertisements in popular magazines play on our sense of pathos. If you have found yourself moved by those Michelin tire commercials in which nothing much happens except a cute little baby plays around in an empty Michelin tire, then the good folks in the marketing department at Michelin have been successful. If you have fought back a tear at an image of an elderly couple holding hands, or believed (if even for an instant) that drinking a certain lite beer might get you more dates, then you have been moved by an appeal to your sense of pathos. Now, appeals to pathos are not necessarily bad or manipulative; on the contrary, they can be effective when statistics or logic feels cold and inhuman.

The authors believe that the most effective arguments are those that combine logos and pathos, and, as we discuss next, ethos. Emotional appeals without facts feel sleazy, and scientific data without human appeal feel cold. We still maintain that your essays should make appeals to logos over pathos, but we encourage you to build arguments in which emotion supports or enhances logic. Arguments that feature good combinations of logos and pathos make you and your essay appear both smart and human—a good mix.

Not only do you need to create an appropriate mix of logos and pathos for your intended audience, but you must also create an appropriate **ethos.** Greek for "character" or "disposition," a writer's ethos is his or her sense of credibility. For most conservative Republicans, Michael Moore has little credibility, so for them, he would have a low ethos. However, someone like Colin Powell enjoys the respect of many Republicans and Democrats. Most Americans trust him; they find him credible. Therefore, Powell's ethos is high. The ethos of public figures like Powell and Moore are easier to talk about than relatively unknown personalities, so as a beginning writer, you should be mindful of how you want to establish credibility and authority. If you are going to argue that the Vietnam

Veterans Memorial is the ideal example of public art, it might undermine your argument if your best friend is the architect (or if you conceal that your best friend is the architect). Alternatively, if you argue that the Washington Redskins should not change their mascot from the potentially offensive epithet "redskin" but fail to mention that you own stock in the Redskins, then your credibility might be in jeopardy, and people might not take your argument seriously. *Ethos, pathos,* and *logos* make up what we call the "rhetorical triangle," and most arguments are made up of some combination of the three. Based on your audience, you need to adjust your own rhetorical triangle so that your argument contains the right mixture of reason, emotion, and credibility.

A reading aside: It's also helpful in reading to understand whether or how a writer is effective by analyzing their argument on whether they are writing from *logos, pathos,* or *ethos.* For example, if Colin Powell writes about the need for international diplomacy in the Middle East, it would automatically carry more weight than one made by your local city councilwoman, even if she had her master's degree in international relations.

Making Claims

A **claim** is a kind of assertion that you make based on evidence, logical and emotional appeal, and solid reasoning. Other words for claims are "thesis" or "assertion."

It is important to distinguish between a claim and a fact, and a claim and an opinion. The sentence "Pearl Jam is a band from Seattle" is a fact. It is a true statement, and as such would not make a good thesis or a good topic sentence. The sentence "I think I prefer Pearl Jam to Soundgarden" is an opinion and, again, would not make a particularly good thesis or topic sentence, in part because this is not a disprovable statement. Maybe someone who knows you well could argue that in your heart of hearts you prefer Soundgarden to Pearl Jam, but the topic is so personal and so narrow, it holds little interest for other readers. However, the sentence "Although most critics prefer Nirvana, Pearl Jam has emerged as the most socially conscious Seattle grunge band" is a claim because it is something you could spend an essay supporting. It emerges from the small world of personal opinion ("I prefer") to the world of more universal interest.

Generally, there are three different types of claims—policy, value, and fact—and these claims are frequently linked to the kinds of appeals you make (ethos, pathos, logos). **Policy claims** are those claims that the writer thinks should happen. Often, one sees policy claims made in terms of ought, and they usually advocate action. These claims must be supported by a justification, and it is usually a good idea to address potential opposing ideas. Essays that argue for more funding for public art or that demand harsher penalties for graffiti are examples of policy claims. Ellen Staurowsky's (pp. 324–332) piece on getting rid of Native American sports mascots is an example of a policy claim essay.

The **value claim** is among the most popular of all claims; in fact, the Pearl Jam thesis is a value claim. These claims assert worth and value. If you were to argue that *The Simpsons* carries positive messages or that a certain building embodies anti-human architecture, you would be advancing a value claim. bell hooks makes such a claim in her essay on gender and *Waiting to Exhale* (pp. 374–379), and, similarly, in her piece in Chapter 2, Garance Franke-Ruta argues that *Heroes* has more to offer than *24* (pp. 131–133). Note that in both of these essays, the authors ground their arguments on standards and values. Although emotion can go a long way in these kinds of claims, it is never advisable to hinge value claims on pathos or emotion.

For many beginning writers, the most common claim is a **fact claim** (sometimes called a claim of truth). These types of assertions focus on classification or definition, and they assert that *X* is or is not *Y*. In fact claims, the thesis is incredibly important, because you do not want to argue something that is unprovable, nor do you want to argue for the obvious. For example, making the claim that *Talladega Nights* is a parody of NASCAR is pointless, because it is so clearly a parody of NASCAR. One of the most common mistakes writers make is confusing *truth* with *argument* (see our section on **thesis statements** for more help here). Fact claims attempt to clarify. They assert that a thing or idea should be seen in a certain way or considered from a particular perspective. For instance, in Chapter 7, concerning public space, William Hamilton makes a compelling argument, relying on reason and data, that suburban design is failing teenagers (pp. 516–519). In Chapter 3, E. G. Chrichton uses established criteria and expert opinion to assert and prove that the NAMES quilt *is* art (pp. 216–222).

The key to making supportable claims lies in framing your assertions with balance and reason. Students often feel as though their arguments must be extreme in their coverage. Those kinds of claims tend to be less convincing because so little in life is absolute. Instead of arguing that Pearl Jam is the "best" Seattle band (because concepts like "best" and "worst" are impossible to prove), make a claim that Pearl Jam is the most socially conscious band (citing their lyrics and political activism), or argue that they are the most influential Seattle band (citing other songs that mimic them, interviews with other bands that mention Pearl Jam, and the opinion of music critics). Also, make sure your claims are reasonable in scope. Don't be afraid to use qualifiers. Limiting the Pearl Jam argument to *Seattle* bands or *grunge* bands circumscribes your claim and makes it doable in a five- or six-page essay.

Finally, now that you have made a claim, you must support that claim. The most common types of support include

- *Expert Opinion:* Citing the opinion of top scholars in a field or established experts is one of the most persuasive forms of support.
- *Statistics:* We like numbers, facts, and percentages. Use credible statistics to lend objectivity and data to your claims.
- *Analysis:* Close readings of a text by an insightful person can be quite convincing. This is where being a savvy semiotician is useful.
- *Analogies and Comparisons:* One way of illustrating what something is, is to show what it is *not*. Comparing and contrasting can highlight the values you want to explore.

In the next section, we expand our discussion of support, claims, and evidence to discuss how one implements these strategies to build a comprehensive argument and actually *write* that essay.

Using claims and support to make arguments: some helpful tips.

Honesty and trust come into play when you actually make your arguments. You do not want to mislead your potential audiences, you do not want to alienate them, and you do not want to manipulate them in an unethical way. Making up facts, inventing sources, and leaving out important details are not merely bad argumentation—they are often unethical acts. More positively, writing is all about engagement. We write to make connections with others; we read to learn more about the world and our place in it. Next we provide some basic tips for making solid, convincing, ethical arguments.

Do not be afraid to acknowledge differing opinions.

Some students think that if they acknowledge any aspect of the other side of their argument that they poke a hole in their own. Actually, just the opposite is the case. Letting your readers know that you are well informed goes a long way toward establishing your credibility. What's more, if you are able not only to identify a differing opinion and then refute it or discount it, your argument could carry even more weight. For instance, if you want to argue that Mel Gibson's film *The Passion of the Christ* succeeds as a work of art, you would do well to acknowledge near the beginning of your essay that some critics have problems with the film. In fact, you may decide to use their complaints and their weaknesses to help you make your own assertions.

Use credible, detailed information and sources to help support your arguments.

This is perhaps the most important tip we can provide. Think about what kind of information convinces you to do anything. Are you persuaded by vagueness, or by specificity? If we wanted to convince you to meet us for dinner at a specific restaurant, which of the following would be the most persuasive?

- We heard from someone that the food is really good.
- A restaurant critic we respect said this is some of the best food in town.
- A restaurant critic, two chefs, and a group of our friends all recommend this place.
- We've been there a number of times, and the food is great, the service is fantastic, the scene is relaxed but cool, and the prices are reasonable.
- The restaurant's Web site claims it is the city's favorite restaurant.
- Your grandparents raved about it.

In general, we are persuaded by thorough, objective data. Although we trust people whose tastes are similar to our own, we tend not to trust people we do not know or who might have a stake in a certain argument. The best kinds of evidence are expert opinions, statistics from a reliable source (such as a scientific study), facts from an objective source (such as a newspaper or peer-reviewed journal), personal experience, and the testimony of others. However, if your grandparents previously recommended good restaurants, their ethos could match the so-called experts who recommended the place. But, then again, their tastes may be much different than yours. Understanding the criteria that one uses in judging restaurants, movies, and television shows is crucial. For example, Roger Ebert, the well-known critic, admits before some Adam Sandler movie reviews he writes that he is no fan of Adam Sandler, giving his readers a warning that his criteria may not match their own.

Establish your own credibility and authority, but try not to overdo it.

There are two different ways to establish authority—explicitly and implicitly. In the explicit method, you say up front that you are a specialist in a certain area. For instance, if you are going to write about the influence of Tejano music in South Texas, you might say in the opening paragraph that you are a Latina from Texas who grew up listening to your dad play in Tejano bands around San Antonio. The audience then knows your background and is likely to give your arguments more weight than if a white guy from Boston was making the same argument—unless, of course, the white guy in question was a scholar of Tejano music (which lends a different kind of credibility). Establishing authority implicitly may have less to do with you and more to do with the research you have done. Implicit authority is revealed to the reader slowly, in pieces, so that you carefully fill in gaps over the course of your essay.

There are, of course, many ways to establish authority—by being an expert, by quoting experts, and by building a knowledge base as a result of research—but however you establish authority, do so within reason (see "Supporting Claims"). If the essay becomes more about how much you know and less about your topic, you will alienate your reader. You want to keep your reader engaged.

Try to avoid fallacies.

Fallacies are, literally, falsities, gaps, and errors in judgment. Sometimes called **logical fallacies,** these missteps are mistakes of logic, and they have been around for centuries. We are all guilty of falling into the fallacy trap now and then, but avoid that trap if possible. Here are a few of the most common:

- *The Straw Man fallacy:* When the writer sets up a fake argument or a "straw man" (an argument that doesn't really exist), only to refute it later.
- *The* ad hominem *fallacy:* Latin for "to the man," this occurs when a writer attacks a person and not an argument. When a politician accuses his detractors of personal attacks in an attempt to avoid the real issues, he is claiming that his opponents are making *ad hominem* assertions.
- *The hasty generalization:* When a writer jumps to a quick and easy conclusion without thinking through the leap logically. A hasty generalization would occur if one made an argument that Parker Posey appeared in *every* independent movie in the 1990s.
- *The* post hoc ergo propter hoc *fallacy:* Latin for "after the fact therefore because of the fact," this fallacy is a favorite among beginning writers. Literally, it means that because *X* comes after *Y*, *Y* must have caused *X*. In other words, it is a faulty cause-and-effect relationship. Let's say someone observes that teen violence seems to be on the rise. This person also is beginning to notice more video games at the local video store. The *post hoc* fallacy would occur when this person concluded that the rise in teen violence was *because* of the increased video games.
- *The vague generality:* Also a favorite among college students, the fallacy of generalization takes place when a writer makes sweeping claims about a group but provides no specific detail or evidence to back up his claim. This can happen on a micro level with an overuse of the passive voice ("It is agreed that . . . " or "It is assumed that . . . ") that does not attribute responsibility. It happens on a macro level when a writer makes a broad generalization about a group of people, like immigrants, lesbians, Republicans, Jews, professors, or students. In some ways, this fallacy is the cause of racism, as it assumes that behavior (or imagined behavior) of one person is shared or mimicked by an entire group. This is a dangerous strategy.
- *The* non sequitur *fallacy:* This is not a particularly common fallacy, but it is still useful to know. Latin for "it does not follow," a non sequitur is a fallacy of conclusion, like a faulty assumption. An example would be, "No woman I know talks about wanting a baby, therefore, there can't be very many women in the world who want babies."

Use inductive and/or deductive reasoning when appropriate.

As you write your paper, as you make your arguments and present your evidence, your reader must think through your arguments. However, before that happens, you must also think through your arguments so that you can develop them in the most cogent way. The two types of argument organization are **inductive** and **deductive.** Deductive reasoning begins big and moves to small; or, in other terms, deductive reasoning starts with the macro and moves to the micro. In classic rhetoric, this is called a **syllogism.** A classic syllogism might go something like this: Most Hollywood movies have a happy ending. *Forrest Gump* is a Hollywood movie. Therefore, it is likely that *Forrest Gump* has a happy ending. A typical syllogism begins with two broad statements and arrives at a narrower proposition based on those statements.

Inductive reasoning resembles detective work. You start with many small observations or bits of evidence, and then based on that conglomeration, you make a generalization. For instance, let's say you noticed that Parker Posey starred in *Party Girl, Best in Show, The House of Yes, Short Cuts, Broken English,* and *A Mighty Wind.* You also then realize that all of these movies are independent films. Therefore, based on all of this information, you make an argument about Parker Posey's contribution to independent film. Both approaches are valid, but each has its own pitfalls. Be sure you do not make big leaps in logic (see **"hasty generalization"**) that you cannot support.

Papers that use deductive reasoning almost always begin with a thesis or main argument. Most professors prefer this type of reasoning because it indicates that the author has thought about his or her argument in advance. However, the inductive approach can also be effective in certain situations, particularly those where the writer has established credibility. Typically, essays that follow the inductive model build an argument over the course of the essay and position the thesis near the end. Although this strategy is valid, it can be more difficult for beginning writers to execute. Writing instructors tend to favor essays written in the deductive model because the formula is simpler—the writer places the thesis near the beginning of the essay and spends the rest of the paper unpacking, proving, and supporting that thesis.

Consider thinking like a lawyer when building an argument—make a case and prove it.

One of the best ways of making and proving an assertion with insight, clarity, and thoroughness is through what rhetoricians have come to call the **Toulmin system.** This term was derived from Stephen Toulmin, a British philosopher, who argued that the best way to win an argument is by making a strong case. This may sound like stating the obvious, but it really isn't. Rather than relying on airtight data to make an argument, Toulmin argued that in real-life situations, you can never be 100 percent certain of something. Someone always has a comeback or an opposing view to counter yours. So, for Toulmin (and many writing teachers), you make an argument by building a case, like a lawyer would in a trial. And, in essence, Toulmin's system resembles legal reasoning in that it makes a case and lays down evidence rather than pretending you have achieved complete certainty. Toulmin's system is useful because it does not insist on absolutes, which is important when writing about texts as subjective as those in popular culture. It is next to impossible to be "right" about what a movie like *Office Space* means, but it is possible to be convincing about your particular interpretation. You can't say with complete certainty why someone liked *Office Space,* but it is possible to make a strong case about why students like *Office Space.*

According to Toulmin, one makes a convincing case by first making a **claim** (see "Making Claims", p. 44) then by citing a "datum," or evidence, that would prompt someone to make a claim in the first place; then, one offers support for that datum via what he calls a "warrant." A **warrant** is a statement that underscores the logical connection between the claim and evidence. For instance, if you park your car outside a store, go inside, and return and it is gone, and say, "My car has been stolen," you are relying on the warrant that a car that is from a place one has left it must be stolen. Your claim: "My car has been stolen." Your datum: The car is missing. The warrant: Cars that are missing must have been stolen. But of course, another warrant could be argued—"A car that is missing might have been towed." The warrant is legitimized by what Toulmin calls "backing," or additional evidence.

How would this system work when arguing about popular culture? Let's use another film example. Say that you notice something about recent gangster movies. You observe that since *Reservoir Dogs* and *Pulp Fiction* were released, the gangster genre has become increasingly popular. Based on this observation, one could make an argument that Quentin Tarantino, the director for both movies, has had a rather significant impact on gangster films. In doing some research, we discovered that a number of recent directors cited either *Reservoir Dogs* or *Pulp Fiction* when asked about their films. In the car example, the backing might be that you have parked in a high-crime area or in a tow-away zone, depending on the warrant you use. According to Toulmin, we have here all the necessary information to make a convincing case:

Claim: Quentin Tarantino has had a significant impact on the gangster movie genre.

Datum: Two popular gangster movies, *Reservoir Dogs* and *Pulp Fiction,* were directed by Tarantino.

Warrant: Several directors cite either *Reservoir Dogs* or *Pulp Fiction* when talking about their own movies.

Backing: These comments appeared in respectable, reviewed publications.

Of course, if one were to build a paper out of this system, you would need one to two more pieces of data (what we called **points** or **reasons** earlier) and additional warrants; in this case, perhaps discussing how recent movies or television shows resemble specific scenes from the Tarantino movies.

The Toulmin system is not foolproof, but it does provide a model for argumentation, and it is particularly useful for making claims about popular-culture texts, or any text for which there is no clear "right" or "wrong" answer.

Synthesis: pulling it all together.

Writing is about synthesis—combining differing elements—so learning to synthesize makes you a much better writer (and a better thinker). In the world of composition, **synthesis** refers to a couple of different things. First, a writer must synthesize her ideas; that is, she must pull together the various half-baked premises, vague notions, and uncompleted thoughts into one cohesive, central concept. Usually, this concept becomes your thesis, and it is difficult in its own right. As stated previously, sometimes it may take a draft or two of writing and condensing and collapsing before you arrive at what you want to say.

Another form of synthesis involves combining all of the secondary sources you amass into the body of your essay. This is one of the hardest things to master—weaving other voices into the tapestry of your own. How much of another quote do you include? Should you paraphrase, or quote precisely? How does one lead into a quote succinctly and elegantly? We would love to provide some sure-fire tricks here, but, alas, that is impossible, as integrating secondary quotes, paraphrases, and ideas into your own work remains a kind of art that gets easier only with practice.

However, don't fear, because you engage in synthesis every day. Whenever you relate to your roommate what each person in your group thought about a concert or a movie, you synthesize. Take the process of deciding what movie to see. The entire process is one big act of synthesis—from seeing what's playing, to locating the best theater, to juggling the various reviews, to deciding whether you trust the opinion of your friends and family who have either seen the movie or talked to someone who has. You synthesize when you take all of the disparate material in your head, combine it, and from that whorl of data, arrive at a kind of personal claim: *I am going to see the new Harry Potter movie at the Balboa Theater at 9:15.*

Because synthesis is so important to becoming an inclusive, informed writer, increasingly more instructors require a synthesis essay. A **synthesis essay** is an essay that requires the writer to synthesize various kinds of information into one unified document. Typically, this means researching, paraphrasing, and presenting differing forms of data. That data could be opinions about a piece of art, quotations from experts on a new CD, or data from surveys on television use. How a writer delivers that information, however, is critical. A writer must either **paraphrase** (restate an idea in his or her own words) or **quote** (quote the phrase, sentence, graph, chart, or image using quotation marks) the material; in both cases, the writer must **cite** the material by indicating where the material comes from. *The writer cannot pass this information off as his or her own work.* Most instances of plagiarism occur in the synthesizing process—because students don't know how to cite or don't know how to paraphrase, or think they don't need to do either one.

To illustrate synthesis in action, we use synthesis itself as an example. To do this, we consulted the Drew University On-Line Guide for Writers and the Bellevue College Online Writing Lab. The Drew site offers a full definition of **synthesis writing:**

> Although at its most basic level a synthesis involves combining two or more summaries, synthesis writing is more difficult than it might at first appear because this combining must be done in a meaningful way and the final essay must generally be thesis-driven. In composition courses, "synthesis" commonly refers to writing about printed texts, drawing together particular themes or traits that you observe in those texts and organizing the material from each text according to those themes or traits. Sometimes you may be asked to synthesize your own ideas, theory, or research with those of the texts you have been assigned. In your other college classes you'll probably find yourself synthesizing information from graphs and tables, pieces of music, and art works as well. The key to any kind of synthesis is the same.

It also enumerates these three features of synthesis:

1. It accurately reports information from the sources using different phrases and sentences;
2. It is organized in such a way that readers can immediately see where the information from the sources overlap;
3. It makes sense of the sources and helps the reader understand them in greater depth.

Our decision to cut and paste the definition and the three features exactly as they appear on the Drew site is a form of quotation or citation. Acknowledging Drew lets the reader know that the features come from a reliable source and that they are not the products of Silverman and Rader.

However, the Bellevue site includes this explanation of synthesis:

WHAT IS A SYNTHESIS?

A synthesis paper is a certain kind of essay.

> According to the *Little, Brown Handbook* (Aaron & Fowler, 2001, p. 133), a synthesis is a way to "make connections among parts or among wholes. You can create a new whole by

drawing conclusions about relationships and implications." What this means is, in order to write a successful synthesis paper, you must conduct research on your chosen topic, contemplate what this unique collection of knowledge may mean to you and the world, and develop an argument about it. Specifically, this means discussing the implications of the knowledge you have gathered. You have amassed a collection of information on a certain topic, and now you must say something unique and interesting about it.

A synthesis is not: A summary

A synthesis is: An opportunity for you to create new knowledge out of already existing knowledge, i.e., other sources. You develop an argument, or perhaps a unique perspective on something in the world (a political issue, how something works, etc.), and use your sources as evidence, in order to make your claim (thesis statement) more believable.

Thus, at the risk of confusion, here is how one might synthesize two different takes on synthesis in college writing.

Though the Drew Online Writing Lab and the Bellevue Online Writing Lab approach the concept of synthesis differently, they ultimately have more similarities than differences. What connects the two sites is an emphasis on combining information from various sources in order to make connections. Drew tends to focus on synthesis as it applies to written texts and as a means of presenting and collating sources so that readers can better understand varying information. In addition to a generous definition of synthesis, the Drew site lists three key features of synthesis, all of which focus on accurate presentation of source material. Despite the fact that Bellevue distinguishes between summary and synthesis (something Drew does not), their site underscores Drew's argument that synthesis can perform important work by taking existing information and combining it in a way that makes it rounder, more comprehensive, and more fresh.

At its core, synthesis is about interpretation. In order to write this paragraph, we had to interpret what both sites had to say about synthesis. Notice how we did not just regurgitate the two sites. We made connections between the two (synthesized), and we unpacked the data from each so that we could 1) make it our own, and 2) distill it so that we could better explain it to you.

Synthesis takes work; one must be conscientious and careful while doing it. Do not take shortcuts and simply cut and paste—that's plagiarism. Consider each source separately, unpack each source, then present the theme of each source in your synthesis. This helps you avoid the traps of plagiarism and summary, and it enables you to connect with your audience.

Know your audience.

An outspoken advocate of the Internet's capacity to share vast amounts of information has been invited to speak at a gathering of music company executives, who are nervous about the thousands of people downloading free music. What kind of tone should she take when addressing this potentially hostile audience? Next, that person is going to speak to a gathering of college students, who are among the most avid downloaders of music. How would her presentation differ? Would she give the same presentation to both audiences? What strategies would she use with the hostile audience that she would not need for the sympathetic one? Keeping the assumptions, education, political leanings, and culture of your audience in mind helps you write a more appropriate essay than if you ignored these issues altogether.

As we write this section, Michael Moore's controversial movie *Sicko* has just been released nationwide. A scathing indictment of America's health-care industry, Moore's film polarized viewers and critics. There is no doubt that the film makes a powerful argument, but one might ask who the audience of the movie is. Is Moore making the movie for Republicans, Democrats, or those in the middle? Many believe that because the movie is so one-sided it will change few people's minds, whereas others contend that it could move people to actually do something about this nation's health-care shortcomings. We would argue that Moore's audience is mainstream America; people who are most affected by no or bad insurance. Moore knows that his movie will probably be seen by those on the Right as propaganda, but his persistent arguments in the movie seem aimed at those who defend the status quo. If Moore was interested in a broader audience, there are any number of ways he might have kept his message but changed his method of delivering it—including interviewing sympathetic and thoughtful defenders of HMOs, insurance companies, and the health-care lobby, toning down some of his own antics, and most importantly, editing the film differently.

These examples reflect the three types of audiences you should consider when writing your papers—a sympathetic audience, an undecided audience, and an antagonistic audience. You would likely not write the same paper for the three kinds of audiences, but tailor your arguments based on who would be reading your essay. We do this kind of tailoring all the time. For instance, when you tell the story of a fabulous date you had the previous night to your mother, your best friend, and your ex, you probably tell three radically different stories. The potentially hostile audience (the ex) gets one version, the undecided audience (mother) gets another, and the sympathetic audience (roommate) gets yet another. All your stories might be accurate, but shaded and delivered differently based on what you know about each listener.

When writing for a sympathetic audience, you already have them on your side, so you do not need to try to win them over. In this case, an argument grounded in pathos may be the most effective. Chances are, they already know the information that might make them think a certain way, so giving them facts, statistics, and details they are familiar with is ineffective, because it could come across as overstating the obvious or simply appearing repetitive. However, an emotionally powerful appeal supported by a strong ethos could be incredibly successful. Let's say you are going to write an essay on Kurt Cobain's contribution to American music for *Rolling Stone* or *Spin.* Most readers of these magazines are predisposed to agree with the facts you may present, so you do not need to list the number of records Nirvana sold or the awards they won. Instead, you may want to focus on how the music has affected you and your friends.

Alternatively, if you have been asked to write an article on Cobain for *Country Music Today,* the audience is less sympathetic to your topic. In this instance, you need to adjust your ethos and your approach. First, you could establish credibility by informing your readers that you are a fan of country music, perhaps even mention the important contributions of various artists you know these readers appreciate. When addressing a potentially antagonistic or skeptical audience, it is best to avoid an overly pathos-driven argument. You may come across as ill-informed and even irrational. Instead, you might want to point to specific songs or chords that resemble country songs. A good strategy might be to make connections thematically, arguing that even though the music is different, Cobain, Willie Nelson, Lyle Lovett, Merle Haggard, and Waylon Jennings all write smart, catchy songs about disaffected, blue-collar Americans. Look for instances of overlap. If you have time to research, you might find out that Cobain listened to country music or that the people in the area he grew up in have a strong affinity for country music. With these kinds of audiences, the best way to establish credibility is to let your audience know that you have done your homework, and that you know their world as well as you know your own.

In some ways, writing for an antagonistic audience is easier than writing for an uncertain one, because you know what you are getting into. Writing for the vast middle can be truly challenging. When writing for an undecided audience, the best strategy is to establish strong ethos and logos. How much you rely on ethos or logos depends on you and your topic. If you are arguing that advertisements featuring skinny, near-naked female models are empowering to women, you might need to adjust your argument based on your gender or age. If you want to argue that the NAMES quilt should be taken seriously as art, focus not simply on the formal or artistic qualities of the quilt, but mention how the quilt affected you, that it fostered an interest in folk art and a love for art that inspires social change. Your audience responds more favorably to your claims if they trust you and your evidence. Be honest. Do not try to manipulate. Write in your own voice.

Use common sense.

You know what arguments are likely to persuade you. You have examples of documents in this book and elsewhere of compelling, sound, reasonable arguments. Use them as your models. The best argument is one that comes from a position of reasonableness.

Overall, making an argument is a key element of writing successful papers, perhaps more important than any other. For one, knowing what you are arguing often leads to clearer writing; it allows you to separate to some degree the processes of thinking and actually putting those thoughts onto paper. In addition, while students sometimes focus on grammatical errors or sounding smart by using sophisticated vocabulary, making clear and nuanced arguments has the best chance of making the ultimate argument—that your paper is worth reading and deserves a grade that reflects such an effort.

PART V. HOW DO I GET INFO ON SONGS? RESEARCHING POPULAR CULTURE TEXTS

Thus far we have focused on the process of making arguments largely from processing and elaborating on one's observations. However, nontraditional texts can also be fruitful entering points for researching questions, both large and small, about culture.

For one, nontraditional texts often raise questions about the medium from which they come. When you watch a sitcom, it might make you think about other sitcoms. When you see a painting, it might make you think of other paintings. When you walk through another university's student union, you might think about how the two student unions are related—maybe a similar type of student goes to each university, or perhaps the student unions were built in different times. You might also notice that your student union has university-owned food and drink places, but your friend's union has chain restaurants. Researching the history of student unions would produce one type of paper, probably one more historical in nature, whereas researching the presence of corporations on campus would produce a paper that explored more explicitly political issues (the presence of corporations on campus is a highly sensitive issue for many associated with higher education). In either case, your walk through a public space might suggest to you some avenues for research.

Nontraditional texts can also raise issues about gender, race, and class, among other things. When observing stereotyped behavior on sitcoms, it can make you think about how other television shows present the same behavior, and perhaps how other creative genres do as well.

Nontraditional texts can also be places where one might explore how abstract concepts play out in practice, through portrayals of popular culture, as Katherine Gantz does with *Seinfeld* and the lens of queer theory. Gantz uses the concept of queerness (which is different than homosexuality) to demonstrate how *Seinfeld*'s characters have complicated relationships that test traditional definitions of masculinity. Queerness does not have to be the only lens— one could certainly use *Seinfeld* to explore issues of feminism, racism, and regionalism in current society. *Seinfeld* is ideal for this task because 1) it was for a number of years the most popular show in the country, and 2) it remains an active presence on television through syndication (reruns). That said, exploring such concepts in other, less popular media also has its value.

There are other ways of using nontraditional texts to engage research, but these methods are worth talking about further, because they offer relatively straightforward ways of using research to enhance understanding of both the texts at hand and the culture at large. In the first method of researching popular culture, the one used in student unions, the text is a window to further exploration of such issues as the corporatization of universities or the function of the environment in student lives.

In the second approach, examining the text and stereotypes in it, the text itself is the focus. In the third approach, the lens used to look at the nontraditional text is the focus; the nontraditional text is more a means to further discussion and elaboration of the concepts. In other words, queerness is the focus of Gantz's essay more than *Seinfeld*. All three approaches share the idea that these texts matter—that they reflect larger concerns in society.

There are other reasons why researching nontraditional texts might seem daunting. You may ask yourself who could have possibly written about Barbie dolls or *The Matrix*. Or you may not have written a paper that engages popular culture as a research topic. After all, isn't research about "serious" topics? Traditionally, you have probably written research papers about historical events or movements, or about the author of a literary work, or perhaps literary movements. Although research of nontraditional texts may seem more difficult, students writing research papers about popular culture have a lot of resources at their disposal. There is a large and ever-increasing amount of work written on popular culture, such as music, the movies, technology, art, found objects, and television. There's even more work done on the more political elements of this textbook, such as gender and the media.

Because researching popular culture topics seems daunting, you might be tempted to amass as much information as possible before beginning your writing. However, we believe that one of the best ways of researching a paper about popular culture is to make sure you have a take on whatever text you are analyzing before researching. That way, you have your ideas to use as a sounding board for others that might come your way. Finding out what you think about the text also allows you to research more effectively and probably more efficiently.

Generally, the trick to researching papers about popular culture is not only to find work that engages your specific topic, but something general or *contextual* about your topic. In the case of *The Matrix* (2000), a film popular with both viewers and critics, science fiction movies might be a good general subject to look up, but so might computers and culture. Broadly defined, *The Matrix* is a science fiction movie, but it's also a movie about the roles of computers in society. One of the movie's primary arguments is that our culture is quickly moving toward one that is run by computers with decreasing human control. That's the subject of more than a few movies, including *2001: A Space Odyssey* and *I, Robot*, but its message is even more crucial given the remarkable growth of the Internet since the mid-1990s. One could research the philosophical argument the movie is making, that humans and computers are somewhat at odds. One could research how other movies or books treat this subject, both within the science fiction genre and outside it. The movie also has a political bent, about the nature of not only computers but also about corporations, who seem to run Neo's life before he realizes what the Matrix is. It's also about the culture of computers, which Neo is immersed in before his transformation. In addition, it engages the idea of the future as well as the present, a temporal argument (about time). All these contexts—philosophical, genre-based, cultural, political, temporal—have strong research possibilities. You could write compelling papers on each of these topics, and each would be very different from the others. You can also see why understanding what you are arguing affects how you research a topic.

Another possibility for research is music CDs. Instead of thinking of particular contexts right away, you might begin by asking some questions of the text. For example, take as a text Johnny Cash's album *Solitary Man: American Recordings III*, which he released in 1999. Johnny Cash was a musician who recorded music for almost 50 years; he received his start about the same time and in the same place as Elvis Presley but had the same record producer as the Beastie Boys, a popular rap group. Such biographical constructions may shape your paper's direction, or they may not. In either case, in writing this paper, you might listen to the album and note some of the themes, symbols, and ideas. You might ask yourself: Was Johnny Cash writing about issues he had written about before? You could find this out by listening to other albums or seeking research materials about his recording career. You could also ask: What is it about the life of Cash that made him write songs like this? Material contained either in biographies of Cash himself or in general histories of country music could help this paper. Another question: Is Johnny Cash part of the recognizable genre of country music or a different genre altogether? Again, a general work about country music enables you to answer this question. Any of these questions can be the beginning of a good research paper. If you decided to focus only on the album, you could also read other reviews, and after you have staked out your own position, argue against other readings of this album.

Movies and music are good choices for research because they are texts that in some ways mirror traditional texts—movies have narratives like novels, and songs have lyrics that resemble poetry. But even found objects have strong possibilities for research. Objects like cars or dolls are not only easily described but have long traditions of scholarship, especially within cultural contexts. In the case of dolls, histories of dolls in American culture or the role of toys would provide historical contexts for your arguments; the same would be true for cars. As you get closer to the present, your methods of research may change. In the case of cars, current writers may not be writing about the context of a new model, but they certainly review them, and examining the criteria of car reviews may give you insight into the cultural context of a car. So might advertisements. Researching popular culture can include placing different primary sources (the source itself, like *Solitary Man* or *The Matrix* or advertisements for either of these texts) in context with one another, or using secondary sources—sources about the primary text, such as reviews, or scholarly articles, ones that are peer reviewed, reviewed by experts, and often have footnotes.

The most difficult thing about doing this research, somewhat ironically, is its flexibility; once you decide on researching popular culture, many different avenues, sometimes an overwhelming number, open to you. The authors have encountered students who enjoy this type of work but are overwhelmed by the possibilities in approaching popular culture texts as researchable topics. Most students eventually come away with not only a better understanding of their particular text but of researching generally.

Researching Nontraditional Texts: One Method

There are any number of ways to undertake the research process with nontraditional texts, given the complexities of the intersections among texts, issues, and culture. At Virginia Commonwealth University, where Dr. Silverman once taught, the department used the same approach in the university's required sophomore researched-writing class. Each student focused on what instructors called a "cultural text," which, for their purposes, meant nonliterary texts.

For the class, students were required in a four-step process to 1) identify and explore a particular cultural text and write about it; 2) choose research angles or avenues and write about the arguments between sources they encountered; 3) reread and write about the text through the research; and 4) merge the first three assignments (a kind of synthesis). The approach mimics to some extent the way many academics work, with a focus on text and context. This may involve doing a **close reading** of a text. A close reading examines the text details by paying attention to all of its inner workings, its colors, shapes, sounds, and symbols. When combined with research and larger cultural insight, a close reading can become a comprehensive paper. Peter Parisi's piece in Chapter 2 does this kind of work, for example. He uses for his text the "Black Bart" T-shirt, examines the concept of audience, and then looks at the phenomenon of the T-shirt using the terms and ideas laid out in his essay.

The advantages of this approach are many. For one, you get a sense of how to do in-depth research that's not done for its own end but to provide better understanding of a particular topic. It also makes you as a writer learn how to incorporate others' ideas into your essay—which is what you have to do in school and long after you leave, when you have to complete market research and prepare reports.

From a purely academic perspective, this approach also demonstrates the diversity and depth of research being done on nontraditional texts and the even deeper well of information for issues of cultural significance (such as race, gender, and class). When faced with the prospect of doing in-depth college research, not to mention research on popular culture topics, students often believe there is not enough information for their topic. Sometimes this is true, but most times the process requires some cleverness and ingenuity.

Nuts and Bolts Research

Clearly, your university library is the place to start. Books have a much more comprehensive perspective on any possible text than most Web sites. Think broadly when approaching what books you might look at; think about what category the books you are looking for might fall into. One of the best ways of doing this is through a keyword search involving "the perfect book." For a book about Johnny Cash, a simple keyword search on "Johnny Cash" might yield some useful sources. If not, a keyword search with "history," "country," and "music" might provide some results. If it does, write down a call number, the physical address of the book in the library, and head for the stacks; most libraries have separate floors or sections for their collection of books. When you get there, find the book number you have written down, but also be careful to look around on the shelves for other possibilities. Both authors have found that some of their best sources have come from browsing on the shelves of libraries.

Then it is on to periodicals. The *Reader's Guide to Periodicals* is a complete non-electronic guide to periodicals such as newspapers and major magazines. You may be tempted to skip anything not on line, but electronic sources generally go back only a decade, so for any type of historical research, you should probably hit the *Reader's Guide*.

If you do resort to the computer, try to use an electronic database your university subscribes to; search engines like Google or Yahoo! are limited in what they come up with and may lead users to sources that are not reliable. The authors both like electronic databases like Infotrac (or Academic Search Premier), JSTOR, and LexisNexis, which many universities subscribe to. The overall difference between Infotrac and LexisNexis and standard Internet searching is that Infotrac and LexisNexis, for the most part, have articles that appear in print form—generally, although not always—making them more reliable sources. Infotrac is an index to periodicals that tend to be scholarly, with footnotes, although some more-popular magazines are there as well. Some of the articles on Infotrac are full-text articles, which means the full version appears on the screen; some you have to head to the library to find. LexisNexis contains full-text articles from most large American and European newspapers as well as many magazines. It has a database geared toward general news and opinion and other databases geared toward sports, arts, science, and law. If you are working with popular culture sources, the arts index, which contains reviews, may be helpful. Speaking of computers, you may also find the Library of Congress Web site, http://www.loc.gov, or WorldCat, a database of the holdings in major libraries, helpful to find if there are any books on the subject; you can then use your library's interlibrary loan to request a needed book. Be aware, however, that some books may take some time to arrive from another library to yours. The Library of Congress site also has an excellent collection of images. Overall, in doing research, be creative and thorough.

Guerilla Research

Okay, if you've exhausted your library options and you *still* can't find what you need, try a bookstore like Borders or Barnes & Noble. Bring some index cards and a notebook, and take notes on the books you want. And if you want an alternative, look at Amazon.com, where you can research books, movies, and albums; sometimes you can see what you need, especially bibliographic information, in Amazon's "look inside the book" feature.

PART VI. HOW DO I KNOW WHAT A GOOD PAPER LOOKS LIKE? AN ANNOTATED STUDENT ESSAY

Sometimes, students have the ability to write good papers; they just can't visualize them. They simply don't know what a good paper looks like, what its components are.

An annotated student paper appears on the following pages. You see that we have highlighted the positive aspects of the essay and also some elements that need work. (Careful readers might notice additional stylistic and formatting inconsistencies.) One thing we like about this piece is a good move from general information to specific. The best papers are those with a clear, narrow focus. This student's thesis is also clear and well developed.

An unannotated version of this essay appears later in Chapter 10 if you want to consult it again. Sample student papers appear throughout *The World Is a Text*.

Matt Compton

Professor Silverman

English 101

9 December 2001

"Smells Like Teen Spirit"

In 1991 a song burst forth onto the music scene that articulated so perfectly the emotions of America's youth that the song's writer was later labeled the voice of a generation (Moon). That song was Nirvana's "Smells Like Teen Spirit," and the writer was Kurt Cobain; one of the most common complaints of the song's critics was that the lyrics were unintelligible (Rawlins). But while some considered the song to be unintelligible, to many youth in the early 90s, it was exactly what they needed to hear. Had the song been presented differently, then the raw emotions that it presented would have been tamed. If the lyrics had been perfectly articulated, then the feelings that the lyrics express would have been less articulate, because the feelings that he was getting across were not clear in themselves. One would know exactly what Kurt Cobain was saying, but not exactly what he was feeling. The perfect articulation of those raw emotions, shared by so many of America's youth, was conveyed with perfect inarticulation.

1991 was a year when the music scene had become a dilute, lukewarm concoction being spoon-fed to the masses by corporations (Cohen). The charts and the radio were being dominated by "hair bands" and pop ballads; popular music at the time was making a lot of noise without saying anything (Cohen). Behind the scenes "underground" music had been thriving since the early eighties. Much of this underground music was making a meaningful statement, but these musicians shied away from the public eye. The general public knew little about them, because they had adopted the ideology that going public was selling out (Dettmar). Nirvana was a part of this "underground" music scene.

In 1991 Nirvana broke the credo, signing with a major label, DGC, under which they released the chart-smashing *Nevermind*. "Smells Like

The title appears in quotes because it represents a song title.

Good beginning—the "burst forth" is passive, but here it seems to work.

Good clarification, although he almost moves too quickly into unintelligibility.

This is a strong explanation, although it probably could have been condensed a bit.

The thesis is great—it's argumentative and clever. We know here what the rest of the paper is about. However, the passive "was conveyed" could be turned into the active "Cobain conveyed."

The writer gives a good background of the atmosphere before the song. Those more familiar with the era might raise objections to the definitiveness of the conclusion, but he uses a source to back up his opinion. We may not agree, but have to respect this research.

The topic sentence is weak here—there's a lot going on in this paragraph, and the first sentence and even the second don't adequately prepare the reader for the information.

Teen Spirit" was the first single from the record, and it became a huge hit quickly (Cohen). Nirvana stepped up and spoke for the twenty something generation, which wasn't exactly sure what it wanted to say (Azerrad 223–233). A huge part of America's youth felt exactly what Cobain was able to convey through not just "Smells Like Teen Spirit" but all of his music. Nirvana shot into superstar status and paved the way for an entire "grunge" movement (Moon). No one complained that they could not hear Cobain, but many did complain that they could not understand what he was saying.

> The information itself is good—he's revisiting the ideas he talked about in his thesis, which in some ways makes up for the lack of organization in this paragraph.

Kurt Cobain did not want his music to just be heard and appreciated; he wanted it to be "felt" (Moon). His music often showed a contrast of emotions; it would change from a soft lull, to a screaming rage suddenly. And few could scream with rage as could Cobain (Cohen). There is a Gaelic word, "yarrrrragh," which "… refers to that rare quality that some voices have, an edge, an ability to say something about the human condition that goes far beyond merely singing the right lyrics and hitting the right notes." This word was once used to describe Cobain's voice by Ralph J. Gleason, *Rolling Stone* critic (Azerrad 231). It was that voice, that uncanny ability to show emotions that Cobain demonstrated in "Smells Like Teen Spirit."

> Good move to the songwriter, Kurt Cobain, although the transition might have been stronger. Good topic sentence.

> Cool Gaelic reference. Excellent research (although he could have cited a little more elegantly).

Cobain's raging performance spoke to young Americans in a way that no one had in a long while (Moon). Michael Azerrad wrote in his 1993 book, *Come as You Are: The Story of Nirvana,* "Ultimately it wasn't so much that Nirvana was saying anything new about growing up in America; it was the way they said it" (Azerrad 226). Cobain's music was conveying a feeling through the way that he performed. It was a feeling shared by many of America's youth, but it was also a feeling that could not have been articulated any other way than the way that Cobain did it (Cohen).

> Another good topic sentence.

> Again, a good use of research, although the repetition of *Azerrad* is unnecessary in parentheses.

> The strong final sentence supports not only the topic sentence of the paragraph, but also the thesis of the paper.

"Smells Like Teen Spirit" starts out with one of the most well-known guitar riffs of the 90s. The four chord progression was certainly nothing new, nothing uncommon. The chords are played with a single guitar with no distortion, and then suddenly the bass and drums come

> This topic sentence is a bit on the narrative side and does not connect well with the previous paragraph.

in. When the drums and bass come in the guitar is suddenly distorted, and the pace and sound of the song changes. The song's introduction, with its sudden change, forms a rhythmic "poppy" chord progression to a raging, thrashing of the band's instruments (Moon), sets the pace for the rest of the song.

The chaos from the introduction fades, and it leads in to the first verse, which gives the listener a confused feeling (Azerrad 213). In the first verse the tune of the song is carried by the drums and bass alone, and a seemingly lonely two-note guitar part that fades in and out of the song. The bass, drums and eerie guitar give the listener a "hazy" feeling. Here Cobain's lack of articulation aids in the confused feeling, because as he sings, one can catch articulate phrases here and there. The words that the listener can discern allow them to draw their own connections. Cobain's lyrics do in fact carry a confused message, "It's fun to lose, and to pretend" (Azerrad 213).

The pre-chorus offers up clear articulation of a single word, but this articulation is the perfect precursor to the coming chorus. As the first verse ends, the pre-chorus comes in; Cobain repeats the word "Hello" fifteen times. The repetition of the word Hello draws the confusion that he implicates in the first verse to a close, and in a way reflects on it. As the tone and inflection of his voice changes each time he quotes "Hello," one is not sure whether he is asking a question or making a statement, or both. It is like he is saying, "Hello? Is anybody at home?" while at the same time he exclaims, "Wake up and answer the door!"

The reflection that he implicates in the pre-chorus builds to the raw raging emotions that he expresses in the chorus, as the guitar suddenly becomes distorted, and he begins to scream (Azerrad 214, 226). In the chorus he screams, but somehow the words in the chorus are actually more articulate than those in the verse. As Cobain sings, "I feel stupid, and contagious," anyone who has ever felt like a social outcast understands exactly what Cobain is saying (Cohen), and they understand exactly why he must scream it.

I remember the first time that I heard that line and thinking about it; I was about thirteen, and I thought that there was no better word than

The description does an excellent job of describing how the song sounds. It's a very difficult task to do this well.

This is a very good topic sentence—it not only leads us from the last paragraph, but also sums up the current one.

Good quote from the song. (He might have cited the song itself, but wanted to include Azerrad's ideas.)

Another good topic sentence, and here the transition is much better implied than in those mentioned earlier.

An insightful analysis of what seems to be a pretty simple lyric. This is excellent work—complicating the simple is a staple of good work in reading culture. The writer also makes a good analogy here.

Omit unnecessary "actually." Again, good reading of the song. So far the writer has done a lot of strong work in (1) contextualizing the song, (2) studying its music, and (3) analyzing its lyrics. It's almost a formula for doing this type of work.

This personal aside adds to the paper, in our opinion—but you should check with your teacher before including it.

"contagious" to describe the way it feels being in a social situation and not being accepted. Because no one wants to be around that person, they will look at the person with disgust, as if they have some highly *contagious* disease. There is certainly a lot of anger and confusion surrounding those feelings. People needed to hear Cobain scream; they knew how he felt, because they knew how they felt.

People who were experiencing what Cobain was expressing understood what he was saying, because they understood how he felt. In much the same way when someone hits their hand with a hammer that person does not lay down the hammer and calmly say, "Ouch, man that really hurt." They throw the hammer down, and simultaneously yell an obscenity, or make an inarticulate roar, and one knows that they are going to lose a fingernail. Anyone who has smashed their finger with a hammer understands why that person is yelling; in the same way anyone who has felt "contagious" or confused about society knows why Cobain is screaming about feeling "stupid and contagious." Cobain is not examining society. He is experiencing the same things as his audience (Moon); he is "going to lose a fingernail." As the chorus draws to a close, the music still rages, but it changes tempo and rhythm slightly.

> Another analogy—comparison, done in reasonable doses, is an effective technique in doing analysis, particularly if one does it thoughtfully.

> The move back to narrative is jarring.

The chorus is the most moving part of the song; it is a display of pure emotion. In the chorus Cobain demonstrates what it was that connected with so many; his lyrics said what he meant (Moon). But what he said had been said before, and whether he was articulate or not, people felt what he meant. It was the articulation of that feeling that gained the song such high praise (Moon).

> Good topic sentence, although it could be condensed into one sentence.

The chorus ends with the phrase, "A mulatto, an albino, a mosquito, my libido"; this line is a reference to social conformity. Cobain is referring to things, or the ideas associated with them that are "outside" of social conformity, and then relating those things back to himself with the phrase "my libido" (Azerrad 210–215). This end to the chorus again goes back to reflect on the feelings expressed in the chorus, and ties them together with a return to the confusion expressed in the verses.

> See previous comment—the topic sentence is doing excellent work but not doing it as "writerly" as it could be done.

The articulation of the lyrics in the second verse gives the confusion more focus than in the first verse. He begins the second verse with the lyric, "I'm worse at what I do best, and for this gift I feel blessed." Although the lyrics are more articulate in the second verse, the feelings of confusion are still there, due to the tempo and rhythm of the music. After Cobain has sung the second verse he returns to the pre-chorus, the repetition of the word Hello. The cycle begins anew.

We like the way the writer connects ideas, music, and lyrics together again.

"Smells Like Teen Spirit" in its entirety gives the listener a complete feeling after listening to it, especially if that listener is feeling confused and frustrated. The song carries one through an entire cycle of emotions, from confusion, to reflection, to frustration. Tom Moon, a Knight-Ridder Newspaper writer, described Nirvana's music as having moments of "tension and release." Being carried through those emotions allows the listener to "vent" their own feelings of confusion and frustration, and at the same time know that someone else feels the same way (Azerrad 226–227). Despite the connection that Cobain made with many there were still many who did not "get" the song; these people often complained about the inarticulation of the lyrics (Azerrad 210).

Good summary of the song's meaning/content. The writer does a good job of making sure the reader is following his argument.

Weird Al Yankovic utilized the common criticism of the song in his parody "Smells Like Nirvana"; Yankovic parodied "Smells Like Teen Spirit," based entirely on Cobain's obscure articulation. Yankovic is known for parodying popular music, and with lines such as, "And I'm yellin' and I'm screamin', but I don't know what I'm saying," Yankovic stated exactly what so many of the song's critiques had, though he did it with a genuine respect for the song, and its impact (Rawlins).

Now, he switches to other voices. Because the choice is both surprising and apt, the use of Weird Al is a good choice for a source/comparison.

Weird Al Yankovic's version struck a note with many who liked Cobain's music but could not understand his lyrics (Rawlins). There were many people who did not understand the feelings of confusion, frustration, and apathy that Cobain was getting across. In 1991 when "Smells Like Teen Spirit" first came out I was only 9, and I did not like that kind of music at all. I remember my brother, who is nine years older than me, and who listened to a lot of "heavy metal," bought Yankovic's *Off the Deep End,* with his parody "Smells Like Nirvana" on it. He

Again, we like the personal reference. It's not as relevant as the other one, but it somehow gives the argument more weight if we know where the writer is "coming from."

thought it was funny because he did not like Nirvana. He never really connected with Cobain's message; even though he did not get what Cobain was saying, he could still enjoy the music. When I became older I did connect with Cobain's music, and Nirvana was one of my favorite bands. My brother never did understand, like many people who never did understand what it was that Cobain was saying (Azerrad 210).

Nirvana made the generation gap clear. It was Nirvana that spoke for a large part of that generation (Moon), where no one else had ever really addressed the confusion and frustration about growing up in America at that time, or at least no one had expressed it in the same way that Nirvana did. They were not the first to vocalize a problem with corporate America, but they were the first *popular* band to convey the feelings that many were feeling *because* of growing up in corporate America, in the way that they did. Cobain did not just show that he has experienced those feelings, but that he was still *experiencing* them, and many young people connected with that (Moon).

> The transition isn't strong here, but the topic sentence is good. It again summarizes—this time the band, not the song.

> The "corporate America" reference is not clear here. As readers, we know vaguely what he is talking about, but he doesn't use sources in the same way he has previously when making similar points.

In 1992 singer-songwriter Tori Amos illustrated why Cobain's "Smells Like Teen Spirit" had connected with so many by making a cover of the song that was a clear contrast to the original. She rendered the song with a piano, and a clear articulate voice. Her cover of the song became fairly popular, because it was different, and because many people could now understand the lyrics that Cobain had already popularized (Rawlins). The cover was interesting, to say the least; however, it would have been impossible for her version ever to have had the same impact as Cobain's (Rawlins). The lyrics to the song have meaning, and depth, but the emotions that the song conveyed were in and of themselves abstract.

> Again, the writer puts comparison to good use. Some writers make the mistake of doing multiple comparisons that all make the same point. Here, the writer uses Tori Amos, whose work is very different from that of both Nirvana and Weird Al, to useful effect—reinforcing his argument.

Amos's version of the song articulated each word clearly, her clear voice hit each note on key; her song was comparable to a ballad. Cobain's "Smells Like Teen Spirit" could be described as "sloppy," his guitar distorted through much of the song; he either screamed or mumbled most of the song (Azerrad 214). The two versions of the song illustrate a clear contrast: it is as if Cobain is "angry about being confused" (Azerrad 213), while Amos sings the song to lament Cobain's feelings.

Amos's version of the song became popular for the same reason that it could never have paved the way as Cobain's version did. It was like a ballad, and after everyone heard what Cobain was saying, about society, about America, about growing up, there is one clear emotion that follows the confusion and frustration: sadness. Her "ballad-like" cover of "Smells Like Teen Spirit" exemplified that sadness. But at the same time, people had written ballads about being confused or frustrated, and performed them as Amos performed "Smells Like Teen Spirit"; that was nothing new. However, no one had yet demonstrated such clear and yet abstract confused, frustrated emotions as Cobain did, and at that moment in time that was exactly what America needed to hear (Azerrad 224–225).

Cobain had written and performed a song about his own confusion, and in the process he had connected with young people all over the United States (Moon). He had helped those people to understand their own confusion better. The problem with "Smells Like Teen Spirit" was not that Cobain was not articulate; he could not have articulated his point more clearly than he did. The problem was that not everyone knew what he was talking about, just like not everyone knows what it is like to strike their finger with a hammer. And in the same way, if someone doesn't know what it is like they might say something foolish like, "That couldn't *hurt* that bad," or "What's *his* problem?" when someone else hits their finger with a hammer, and they make an inarticulate roar. That roar expresses exactly what that person is feeling, but only those who know that feeling, can really understand it. As Michael Azerrad, author of *Come as You Are: The Story of Nirvana*, put it, "you either get it, or you don't" (Azerrad 227). Thus was the case with Cobain's music. "Smells Like Teen Spirit" was his inarticulate roar; it was articulate in that it expressed exactly what he was trying to point out; however, not everyone could grasp what that was.

The writer does a good job of extending the comparison as a way of bringing his own argument to a close.

The conclusion approaches, with the writer putting the work into final context.
The conclusion could be a little stronger—the writer might have taken this argument beyond Nirvana, or put it in a little greater context. He chose instead to close the work by restating the thesis, which is an acceptable way to end the paper.
Overall, the work this paper does is outstanding—it approaches a "cultural text"—a famous song and brings the reader multiple perspectives on it, using comparison, literary and sound analysis, and analogy. It's a good model for doing this type of work.

Works Cited

Azerrad, Michael. *Come as You Are.* New York: Doubleday, 1993.

Cohen, Howard, and Leonard Pitts. "Kurt Cobain Made Rock for Everyone but Kurt Cobain." *Knight Ridder/Tribune* 8 Apr. 1994. Infotrac.

Dettmar, Kevin. "Uneasy Listening, Uneasy Commerce." *The Chronicle of Higher Education.* 14 Sept. 2001: 18. LexisNexis.

Moon, Tom. "Reluctant Spokesman for Generation Became the Rock Star He Abhorred." *Knight Ridder/Tribune* 9 Apr. 1994. Infotrac.

Nirvana. *Nevermind.* David Geffen Company, 1991.

Rawlins, Melissa. "From Bad to Verse." *Entertainment Weekly* 5 June 1992: 57. Infotrac.

PART VII. HOW DO I CITE THIS CAR? GUIDELINES FOR CITING POPULAR CULTURE TEXTS

As you probably know, you must cite or acknowledge any kind of text (written or otherwise) that you use in an academic or professional essay. Most students think that citing work has mostly to do with avoiding plagiarism—and that's certainly an important part of it—but there are other reasons why citing work is important.

As a researcher, your job is often to make sense of a particular phenomenon and in doing so, make sense of the work done before you on the same subject. When you do that, you perform a valuable service for your reader, who now not only has your perspective on this phenomenon, but also has an entry into the subject through the sources you cite. For this very reason, professional researchers and academics often find the works cited pages and footnotes as interesting as the text itself.

As writers in the humanities, you typically use MLA (Modern Language Association) formatting in your papers. There are two other major forms of citing—APA (American Psychological Association), often used in the social sciences and science, and "Chicago" (named for its association with the University of Chicago Press) or "Turabian," often used in history and political science.

All three ways of citing are part of a system of citation. How you *cite* (say where information comes from) is directly related to the bibliography or, in the case of MLA, the works cited page. You indicate in the text who wrote the article or book, and at the end of the paper, the sources are listed in alphabetical order, so the reader can see the whole work, but without the intrusion of listing that whole work within the text; seeing (Alvarez 99) is much easier than seeing (Alvarez, Julia. *How the Garcia Girls Lost Their Accents*, New York: Plume, 1992, p. 99.) in an essay.

Using Parenthetical References

In MLA, you cite using parenthetical references within the body of your essay. The format for the parenthetical reference is easy. If you know the author's name, you include the author's last name and the page number(s) in parentheses before the punctuation mark. For instance, if you are quoting from LeAnne Howe's novel *Shell Shaker,* your parenthetical reference would look like this:

> The novel *Shell Shaker* does a great job of conveying Choctaw pride: "I decide that as a final gesture I will show the people my true self. After all, I am a descendent of two powerful ancestors, Grandmother of Birds and Tuscalusa" (Howe 15).

If the author's name has already been used in the text in a particular reference (not earlier in the essay), then you simply provide the page number (15). If there are two or three authors, then list the authors' last names and the page number (Silverman and Rader 23). For more than three authors, use et al. (Baym et al. 234).

The same holds true for citing an article. Simply list the last name of the author of the article or story or poem, followed by the page number (Wright 7). You don't need to list the title of the book or magazine.

If you use works from the Internet, the system of citing is the same, except you sometimes do not have page numbers, and you often cannot find authors (although you should look hard—sometimes the authorship appears at the end of the text, rather than the beginning). In citing an article from the Internet, use if you can the page's title, rather than the home page. For example, if you are looking at admissions policies at Virginia Commonwealth University, you come to the page and it says "Admissions" at the top. You would then in the text, after your information, type: ("Admissions")—not "Virginia Commonwealth University" and definitely not the Web page address: http://www.vcu.edu/admissions. This form of citing also applies to non-Internet articles without authors. Some of your professors may ask you to tell them from which paragraph the information comes. If that is the case, your in-text citation might look like this: ("Admissions" par. 2).

Building the Works Cited Page

A works cited page consists of an alphabetized list of the texts that you cite in your paper. This list goes at the end of an essay in MLA format. This list tells your readers all of the pertinent publication information for each source. It is alphabetized by the last name of the author or, if there is no author, by the title or name of the text. Generally, works cited pages start on a new page and bear the heading "Works Cited." For books, you use the following format, not indenting the first line but indenting the remaining lines.

> Clements, Brian. *Essays against Ruin.* Huntsville: Texas Review Press, 1997.

Notice the crucial aspects in this citation—the author's name, the title of the work, the date it was published, and who was responsible for publishing it. The general rule of citing work is to find all four of these elements in order to help a fellow researcher (or your teacher) find the source and to give appropriate credit to both those who wrote the book and those who brought the book to the attention of the general public. Of course, citing a magazine requires a different format, but with the same idea, as does citing a Web page or a song or a movie. We provide examples of many different sources later.

Plagiarism

Citing your work is critical. If you quote from a text in your paper, or if you use information in any way but do not cite this source, the use of this material is plagiarism. At most institutions, plagiarism is grounds for failing the assignment and even the class. At many universities and colleges, students can be dismissed from the institution entirely if plagiarism can be proved.

A student can commit plagiarism in several different ways. One is the deliberate misrepresentation of someone else's work as your own—if you buy a paper off the Internet, get a friend's paper and turn it in as your own, or pay someone to write the paper, you are committing the most serious form of plagiarism.

Then there is the previous example of using someone's work in your text but without citing it, which is also a serious offense. Some students do this inadvertently—they forget where their ideas came from, or mean to find out where the information came from later, but do not. Still others want their teacher to think they are intelligent and think that using someone else's work may help. The irony of the last way of thinking is that teachers often are more impressed by the student who has taken the time to do research and incorporate those ideas thoughtfully into a paper—that's what real researchers do.

It is also possible to commit plagiarism without such intent. If you do not paraphrase a source's work completely—even if you cite the source—that is also plagiarism.

Besides the general ethical problem of using someone else's work as your own, the more practical issue with plagiarizing is that you are likely to get caught. As teachers, we become so familiar with the student voice in writing, and a particular student's voice, that it is often not very difficult to catch a cheating student.

Works Cited Examples

The examples shown here cover most citation contingencies; however, if you have trouble deciding how to cite a source, there are a number of options, the best of which is to consult the *MLA Handbook for Writers of Research Papers*, which your library owns, if you do not. Otherwise, you can find any number of web pages that provide examples of MLA documentation. We recommend the Purdue Writing Center site (http://owl.english.purdue.edu) and the award-winning "Guide for Writing Research Papers" site at Capitol Community College (http://webster.commnet.edu/mla.htm).

CITING BOOKS

Book entries include the following information:

Author's last name, Author's first name. *Title*. City of publication: Publisher, year of publication.

A Book by a Single Author

Clements, Brian. *Essays Against Ruin*. Huntsville: Texas Review Press, 1997.

A Book by Two or Three Authors

After the first author, list subsequent authors' names in published (*not* alphabetical) order.

Levitt, Steven D., and Stephen J. Dubner. *Freakonomics: A Rogue Economist Explores the Hidden Side of Everything*. New York: William Morrow, 2005.

Two or More Books by the Same Author

Arrange entries alphabetically by title. After the first entry, use three hyphens instead of the author's name.

Garber, Frederick. *Thoreau's Fable of Inscribing*. Princeton: Princeton UP, 1991.

---. *Thoreau's Redemptive Imagination*. New York: New York UP, 1977.

An Anthology or Compilation

Silverman, Jonathan, and Dean Rader, eds. *The World Is a Text: Writing, Reading, and Thinking about Culture and Its Contexts*. Upper Saddle River: Prentice Hall, 2003.

A Book by a Corporate Author

Bay Area AIDS Foundation. *Report on Diversity: 2001*. San Francisco: City Lights Books, 2001.

A Book with No Author

A History of Weatherford, Oklahoma. Hinton: Southwest Publishers, 1998.

A Government Publication

If no author is known, begin with the government's name, and then add the department or agency and any subdivision. For the U.S. government, the Government Printing Office (GPO) is usually the publisher.

United States. Forest Service. Alaska Region. *Skipping Cow Timber Sale, Tongass National Forest: Final EIS Environmental Impact Statement and Record of Decision*. Wrangell: USDA Forest Service, 2000.

The Published Proceedings of a Conference

Ward, Scott, Tom Robertson, and Ray Brown, eds. *Commercial Television and European Children: an International Research Digest. Proceedings of the Research Conference, "International Perspectives on Television Advertising and Children: The Role of Research for Policy Issues in Europe," Held in Provence, France, July 1–3 1984*. Brookfield: Gower, 1986.

An Edition Other Than the First

Gibaldi, Joseph. *MLA Handbook for Writers of Research Papers*. 5th ed. New York: Modern Language Association, 1999.

CITING ARTICLES

Articles use a similar format as books; however, you must include information for the article and the source of its publication. They follow the following format:

Author(s). "Title of Article." *Title of source* day month year: pages.

For newspapers and magazines, the month or the day and the month appear before the year, and no parentheses are used. When quoting from a scholarly journal, the year of publication is in parentheses. When citing articles from periodicals, the month (except May, June, and July) is abbreviated.

An Article from a Reference Book

Deignan, Hebert G. "Dodo." *Collier's Encyclopedia*. 1997 ed.
Voigt, David G. "America's Game: A Brief History of Baseball." *Encyclopedia of Baseball*. 9th ed. New York: Macmillan, 1993. 3–13.

An Article in a Scholarly Journal

Crawford, Rachel. "English Georgic and British Nationhood." *ELH* 65.1 (1998): 23–59.
Ingrassia, Catherine. "Writing the West: Iconic and Literal Truth in *Unforgiven*." *Literature/Film Quarterly* 26.1 (1998): 53–60.

A Work in an Anthology

Begin with the author of the poem, article, or story. That title goes in quotation marks. Then, cite the anthology, as before. Include the page numbers of the text you use at the end of the citation.
Haven, Chris. "Assisted Living." *The World Is a Text: Writing, Reading, and Thinking about Culture and Its Contexts*. Eds. Jonathan Silverman and Dean Rader. Upper Saddle River: Prentice Hall, 2003. 89–99.

An Article in a Monthly Magazine

Sweany, Brian D. "Mark Cuban Is Not Just a Rich Jerk." *Texas Monthly* Mar. 2002: 74–77.

An Article in a Weekly Magazine

If the article does not continue on consecutive pages, denote this with a plus sign (+).

Gladwell, Malcolm. "The Coolhunt." *The New Yorker* 17 Mar. 1997: 78+.

An Article in a Newspaper

Hax, Carolyn. "Tell Me about It." *The Washington Post* 29 Mar. 2002: C8.

An Article with No Author

"Yankees Net Bosox." *The Richmond Times–Dispatch* 1 Sept. 2001: D5.

A Letter to the Editor

McCrimmon, Miles. "Let Community Colleges Do Their Jobs." Letter. *The Richmond Times–Dispatch* 9 Mar. 1999: F7.

Silverman, Melvin J. "We Must Restore Higher Tax on Top Incomes." Letter. *The New York Times* 8 Mar. 1992: E14.

A Review

Smith, Mark C. Rev. of *America First! Its History, Culture, and Politics*, by Bill Kauffman. *Journal of Church and State* 39 (1997): 374–375.

A Cartoon

Jim. Cartoon. *I Went to College and It Was Okay*. Kansas City: Andrews and McNeel, 1991. N. pag.

ELECTRONIC SOURCES

A Book Published Online

If known, the author's name goes first, followed by the title of the document or page in quotation marks. If the document/page is part of a larger work, like a book or a journal, then that title is italicized. Include the date of publication, the date of access if known, and the address or URL (uniform resource locator) in angle brackets.

Savage, Elizabeth. "Art Comes on Laundry Day." *Housekeeping—A Chapbook. The Pittsburgh Quarterly Online*. Ed. Michael Simms. Dec. 1997. 20 Mar. 2002 <http://trfn.clpgh.org/tpq/hkeep.html>.

An Article from a Web site

Silverman, Jason. "*2001*: A Re-Release Odyssey." *Wired News* 13 Oct. 2001. 20 Mar. 2002 <http://www.wired.com/news/digiwood/0,1412,47432,00.html>.

A Review

Svalina, Mathias. Rev. of *I Won't Tell a Soul Except the World*, by Ran Away to Sea. *Lost at Sea* July 2001. 2 Mar. 2002 <http://lostatsea.net/LAS/archives/reviews/records/ranawaytosea.htm>.

A Mailing List, Newsgroup, or E-Mail Citation

If known, the author's name goes first, followed by the subject line in quotations, the date of the posting, the name of the forum, the date of access and, in angle brackets, the online address of the list's Internet site. If no Internet site is known, provide the e-mail address of the list's moderator or supervisor.

An E-Mail to You

Brennan, Brian. "GLTCs." E-mail to the author. 21 Mar. 2002.

An Electronic Encyclopedia

"Play." *Encyclopædia Britannica*. 2007. Encyclopædia Britannica Online. 27 July 2007 <http://www.britannica.com/eb/article-9060375>.

An Article from a Periodically Published Database on Infotrac

Gordon, Meryl. "Truly Deeply Maggie." *Marie Claire* 1 Sept. 2006. 31 July 2007. *LexisNexis Academic*.

(Some of your professors will ask for a more complete version of this, which includes the place you found it and the original page number.)

Gordon, Meryl. "Truly Deeply Maggie." *Marie Claire* 1 Sept. 2006: 208+. *LexisNexis Academic*. Henry Birnbaum Library, Pace University. 31 July 2007 <http://www.lexisnexis.com.rlib.pace.edu/universe>.

OTHER SOURCES

A Television or Radio Program

List the title of the episode or segment, followed by the title of the program italicized. Then identify the network, followed by the local station, city, and the broadcast date.

"Stirred." *The West Wing*. NBC. WWBT, Richmond, VA. 3 Apr. 2002.

A Published Interview

Morrison, Toni. Interview with Elissa Schnappell. *Women Writers at Work*: The Paris Review *Interviews*. Ed. George Plimpton. New York: Modern Library, 1998: 338–375.

A Personal Interview

Heinemann, Alan. Personal interview. 14 Feb. 2001.

A Film

Olympia. Dir. Bob Byington. King Pictures, 1998.
    Or (depending on emphasis in your paper)
Byington, Bob, dir. *Olympia*. Perf. Jason Andrews, Carmen Nogales, and Damien Young. King Pictures, 1998.

A Sound Recording from a Compact Disc, Tape, or Record

The Asylum Street Spankers. *Spanks for the Memories*. Spanks-a-Lot Records, 1996.

A Performance

R.E.M. Walnut Creek Auditorium, Raleigh, NC. 27 Aug. 1999.

A Work of Art in a Museum

Klee, Paul. *A Page from the Golden Book*. Kunstmuseum, Bern.

A Photograph by You

United States Post Office. Bedford, NY. Personal photograph by author. 15 Aug. 2001.

An Advertisement

Absolut. Advertisement. *Time* 17 Dec. 2002: 12.

Cars, Buildings, Outdoor Sculptures, and Other Odd Texts

Although many of your teachers would not require you to cite a primary text like a car or a building, if you have to do so (or want to), we suggest you follow the guidelines for a text like a movie, which has a flexible citing format, but always includes the title and the date, and hopefully an author of some kind. For example, if you were going to cite something like a Frank Lloyd Wright building, you might do something like this:

Wright, Lloyd Frank, arch. *Robert P. Parker House*. Oak Park, IL: 1892. ("arch." stands for *architect*, like "dir." stands for *director*.)

If, for some reason, you were to cite a car, you might do something like this:

Toyota Motor Company. *Camry*. 1992.

Or, if you knew where the car was built:

Toyota Motor Company. *Camry*. Georgetown, KY: 1992.

But if you knew the designer of the car, you could use that person as an author, similar to the way you can use a screenwriter or a director or an actor for the "author" of a movie.

PART VIII. HOW AM I A TEXT? ON WRITING PERSONAL ESSAYS

We think the best papers come from one's own viewpoint—after all, writing is thinking, and for the most part, the thinking you do is your own. The texts you have been writing about, however, were texts you read from a more general perspective.

But say your professor wants a personal essay, as many freshman composition instructors do. Is it possible to write one using the ideas and techniques of reading texts? Of course. You are a text, and so are your experiences, feelings, ideas, friends, and relatives. What's more, your experiences and emotions are not culture neutral—they have in some ways been influenced by the expectations living in our culture has generated. Take, for example, one of four ideas often used as personal essay topics in freshmen classes: the prom, the class trip to the beach, the loss of a loved one, or coming to college.

Just so you know, these are the topics we instructors often brace ourselves for, because students often have so little new to say about them. The essays are often laden with description of familiar landscapes, emotions, and events at the expense of any real reflection—they do not tell us anything new about the prom or grief.

Yet, in some way, even going to the beach should be a rich textual experience. Here's why: not only are you going to the beach, but going to the beach with ideas of the beach in mind, with cultural expectations of what beaches are like, what people do at beaches, and so on. For example, how do we know to wear bathing suits, wear sunscreen, and play volleyball at the beach? Not only because we have done it before, but because we have seen others do it before and have incorporated their ideas about beachgoing into our beachgoing.

So if you write about the prom or a loved one getting ill or dying, try to focus not only on the emotions attached to such an event, but your emotional expectations as well. Did you "not know how to feel"? Why? Was it because you had expected to feel a certain way? How did you know how to act? Were there cultural clues? Did you see a movie about a prom or about death? Proms are a particularly American phenomenon, and have been featured in any number of movies, usually teen romances. Use that knowledge about the prom (or any other subject) in your own writing.

Take another common example. Dying in America has any number of traditions attached to it, depending on what American subculture you belong to. Foreign cultures have very different ways of looking at death. How you view death or illness also may have to do with religious beliefs, the closeness of your family, and so on. But even these ideas about illness and death come from somewhere, and you owe your reader your best guess at how you came to them. So do ideas about what brothers, mothers, fathers, and grandmothers should be if you choose to write about them.

What we are talking about here is what personal essayists often call *reflection*—the idea that we are not only describing our lives but also contemplating them at the same time. Entering college is a particularly ripe time for contemplation; at a minimum, you have a new learning environment, but for most of you, there is a change in friendships and social environments as well. For some of you, it is time for even more upheaval—you may change your career path or your worldview. You probably won't know all this if you decide to write about entering college, but you have some ideas about what your expectations for college are and where you received them. The university setting is a rich cultural text; reading it may provide you additional insight into your own experiences there.

There are more subjects that are worthy of personal reflection than we can count here (the ones we already named are some of the hardest). The idea is to take an experience or event, put it in your own perspective, and reflect on how your perspective may fit in with others. Anything from a trip to the grocery store to a road trip to a phone call to a visit can be the subject of a reflective essay; so can relationships with other people. But what you have to do in these essays is to make sure they matter not only to you, but to others as well—that's why focusing on putting your experiences in a cultural perspective can make your writing worth reading (not just worth writing).

Some of you might object to this sort of self-analysis and wonder why you can't just simply describe your experiences in a paper. For some papers and some teachers, that might be acceptable. But if writing is thinking and writing about oneself is thinking and self-discovery, you owe your reader—and yourself—your best shot at unearthing cultural expectations.

One last note about personal essays: Students often misunderstand their purpose. Although the topic of the personal essay might be your experience, the personal essay is not written for you, but for your audience. The story that you tell about the beach or the prom or the death of a loved one is not as important as what you learned from the event. Simply recounting your trip to the beach is not nearly as interesting as what you saw, observed, and learned from your trip to the beach. Even more important is to consider what your audience can learn from what you learned. How can your experiences help the reader? The two great advantages you have as a personal essayist are recognition and discovery. In the best personal essay about a prom, the reader recognizes something familiar (an awkward moment, a romantic dance, the smell of hairspray), but also discovers something new about the text that is a prom because of your essay. So, as you sit down to draft a personal essay, think about how you might use this opportunity to help your reader learn something new about a topic they think they already know.

One last word on making the world your own text.

The authors are readers, which is why this book keeps changing. For every article that makes it in, we have often read anywhere from a half dozen to a dozen or more. We say this only to encourage you to read on your own. Some of our favorite periodicals include (many of which we drew from for this and previous editions): *Slate, Salon.com, The New York Times, Mental Floss, Good, Harper's, Wired, Vanity Fair, Mother Jones, Utne Reader, The Washington Post, The Village Voice, Rolling Stone,* and so on. We have placed a list of links on our Web site to many of these and other periodicals.

THE WORLD IS A TEXT READING THE WORLD

IS A TEXT READING THE WORLD IS A TEXT

READING THE WORLD IS A TEXT READING

THE WORLD IS A TEXT READING THE WORLD

reading

IS A TEXT READING THE WORLD IS A TEXT

READING THE WORLD IS A TEXT READING

THE WORLD IS A TEXT READING THE WORLD

IS A TEXT READING THE WORLD IS A TEXT

THE WORLD IS A TEXT THE WORLD IS A

This student's room is an array of intentional signs and signifiers designed to communicate ideas, values, and affiliations. What can you infer about her from her decor?

CHAPTER 1

"THERE WAS A TIME WHEN MEANINGS WERE FOCUSED AND REALITY COULD BE FIXED; WHEN THAT SORT OF BELIEF DISAPPEARED, THINGS BECAME UNCERTAIN AND OPEN TO INTERPRETATION." THIS OBSERVATION, FROM BRITISH PAINTER BRIDGET RILEY, SERVES AS A WAY INTO THE SECOND PART OF *THE WORLD IS A TEXT*, AND, IN PARTICULAR, TO THIS FIRST CHAPTER. HERE AND ELSEWHERE WE EMPHASIZE THE POSSIBILITY AND IMPORTANCE OF "READING" AND INTERPRETING THE WORLD AROUND YOU BY PAYING ATTENTION TO THE ARGUMENTS TEXTS MAKE.

In the Introduction, we gave you a theoretical basis for reading the world as a text; here we show you how writers might perform such a task. We asked colleagues and students to undertake analyses of topics of their choosing, using an approach that focused both on how to read such a text and that actually performed a reading of said text. In making their choices, they show us how diverse both the topics and the approaches might be.

The idea behind this chapter is to introduce you to the act of thinking about common texts as thought-out constructions designed to enable some kind of effect or reaction. Or, put in the language of rhetoric—we want you to learn to recognize how texts—even seemingly small texts—make arguments. For example, Elisabeth Piedmont-Marton unpacks numerous arguments various clothes can make by identifying our associations with jeans or shirts or sweaters. Dean Rader, one of the authors of this book, demonstrates how signs, plants, walls, and buildings that you pass every day on your college campus can make an argument about your institution. Of course,

paying attention to how other texts make arguments helps you when it comes time to make arguments of your own in your papers.

The essays in this chapter have two main purposes: to help model reading and writing about nontraditional texts. The writers walk readers through the interpretation of nontraditional texts in a sophisticated but accessible voice, putting the theory behind semiotics to work. Our hope is that these help you approach your own papers, and one way of making the transition to writing your own papers is by noticing how other writers are doing their work. As you read these essays, pay attention to the details the authors use to make their points. Do they have a thesis? Do they use specific examples? Do they back up their arguments with evidence? What processes do they use to "read" and "interpret" the various texts? If you recall the section on lenses from the Introduction, you might also ask yourself what lenses the authors use to interpret their texts. Our hope here is that you begin to notice the way other writers make connections, ground their observations in concrete examples, and take informal readings and make them formal. In other words, we want you to see how these writers decode the rhetoric of nontraditional texts and use this to make their own rhetorical constructions.

As we mention in the Introduction, this chapter is composed entirely of original, commissioned essays written especially for this issue of *The World Is a Text*. Dean Rader has published widely in the fields of American and Native American literature, rhetoric, and visual culture; he's also a published poet. He is a professor at the University of San Francisco and the curator of *The Weekly Rader,* an arts and culture blog that reads both as texts. Jonathan Silverman, the other author, has also published in a number of fields, including literary studies, American studies, and music. He is completing a book on Johnny Cash. Similar to Rader, Silverman looks at signs and signifiers along American highways. Elisabeth Piedmont-Marton is a professor at Southwestern University, where she directs the writing center. She, too, has published widely, including a number of essays on art, culture, and politics. Her essay decodes the visual signs of fashion. Jonathan Hunt, a professor in the highly regarded PWR program at Stanford, contributes a reading of the "fixie" bicycle—a phenomenon cropping up around San Francisco. Peter Hartlaub has one of the best jobs on the planet—he is the Pop Culture critic and the video game reviewer for the *San Francisco Chronicle*. His essay "reads" video games. Catherine Zimmer is an assistant professor of English and film studies at Pace University; her essay focuses on what YouTube really means. Lee Transue is a recent graduate of Pace University who is now working for a start-up publishing house in New York. His essay reads *Family Guy* through the lens of a stream-of-consciousness. Cristina DeLuca, the former editor-in-chief of *The Pace Press* and a recent graduate of Pace University, now works for the New York City Parks and Recreation Department. Her essay answers the question: What do those Facebook photographs really mean? Brandon Brown is a physicist and the associate dean for science at the University of San Francisco. Brown recently won first prize in *Seed Magazine's* science essay contest. His contribution examines a science lab as a complicated text. Finally, Rader and Silverman do a repeat performance—this time a collaborative how-to essay for reading an advertisement.

Reading and Writing About Your Campus

Dean Rader

INSTITUTIONS OF HIGHER LEARNING INVEST a great deal in their image. Like companies and corporations, colleges maintain a profound interest in branding and market recognition, although how a college develops and maintains that reputation is unique among large institutions. One of the most public sources of college image-building is its campus. It is rare to hear of a potential employee turning down a job at Yahoo! or GM because she found the building ugly, but how often do we hear students talk about the role a campus played in their decision about where to apply and attend college? Have you ever seen a college admissions brochure that did not feature its most attractive lawns and buildings?

This interest in campus aesthetic is not confined to current and prospective students. Administrators obsess about their physical plant because its main components like lawns, buildings, fountains, sculptures, statues, foliage (think: ivy), and signs all send messages about the institution. For example, why are so many buildings on campuses modeled on Greek and Roman structures? An initial response might be: Because Greek and Roman buildings look "important" or "imposing" or "learned" or "fancy" or "classical." But, then, the next step is to inquire into why a college might want to embody any of these ideals. What messages do columns, spires, fountains, gardens, gates, and walls send? How are these connected to the liberating power of education? Would a campus send a different message if its buildings resembled a Western mining town from the 1800s? Similarly, what purpose does green space serve on a campus? Why have lawns and fields? Why not construct as many buildings and classrooms as possible? Why plant flowers? Why not build more labs?

One answer might be that campuses want to feel inviting both to students and to the surrounding community. However, for better or worse, colleges in the United States have not always been the most welcoming places; in fact, for many years, many older, private institutions cultivated a reputation based on exclusion—how difficult it was to be admitted or how rigorous its classes were. With the rise of public universities and the community college system, college has become more accessible; accordingly, campus architecture and design have taken on a more welcoming posture. In fact, how a campus fronts the public—how it *welcomes*—can often say quite a bit about how a college wants to be seen. Consider campus signage. Signs on campus may seem utterly insignificant, but, in truth, they reveal a great deal—even among campuses just a few miles from each other. The University of San Francisco (USF), The City College of San Francisco (CCSF), and San Francisco State University (SFSU) are all first-rate institutions in the same city, yet their signs and points of campus entry differ dramatically. In the case of these colleges, region has less to do with their signage than institutional history, mission, and audience, all of which get encoded in their signage.

San Francisco State University is the only four-year public university in the city of San Francisco, and it enjoys a rich history of quality education, ethnic diversity, and open, progressive policies. The campus is located in the southwest part of the city, next door to one of the more popular shopping malls in the area. Although the neighborhood is largely residential and almost suburban, the campus fronts a major north–south artery in San Francisco and a major train route on the San Francisco Municipal Transportation line, situating the university at a crossroads of train, car, and foot traffic. The main access to the university (Fig. 1) is notable for its lack of pretense. The modern sign, a basic gray monolith, blends in well with the clean modern lines of the building behind it to the left. Both the sign and the building are free of flourish and are almost understated in their muted colors, rectangular shapes, and unobtrusive design. Notice how the sign refrains from boasting a date, a motto, or a mascot. To the right of the sign is an open sidewalk that runs along 19th Avenue, a busy street. You can see both cars and the train within a few feet of the campus entrance. At many institutions, one would expect a large wall or imposing shrubbery delineating the campus from the fray of the street, but at SFSU, no such barrier exists. In fact, Figure 2 reveals the openness of this part of campus. If you look closely to the right of the sign, you can make out the square umbrella-like tops of coffee and food kiosks. Here, the campus opens on to the sidewalk, the street, and the train stop, creating a sort of commons that is in concert with the university's image of an open, accessible, *public* university.

This sign seems consonant with SFSU's mission. Because San Francisco State enjoys a large enrollment of around 25,000 students of all ages and ethnicities, it's important that the institution send a message through its design that the campus is open, friendly, easily accessible, and familiar. The City College of San Francisco, one of the premiere community college systems in the country, makes similar arguments through its campus plan. Like San Francisco State, CCSF is a public institution, whose students are likely drawn to it not simply because

Fig. 2 The main access, San Francisco State University.

of its quality but also because of its affordability and convenience (in fact, CCSF has eleven different sites around San Francisco). Its main campus, also in the southern part of the city, features a number of elements that stand as metaphors for the college's mission. Like State, City College's signs (Figs. 3 and 4) at its main campus are functional and free of pompous gesture. The scrolling LED sign serves a practical purpose by disseminating valuable information to busy students, all of whom live off campus. This sign, like the ones in Figure 4, are helpful without being intimidating. In fact, that the second sign might resemble those found at many high schools may make students who are insecure about college feel like CCSF is a less scary transition. In addition, for the many commuting students at CCSF who also hold jobs and have families, easy parking is more important than stone walls or flower beds, so this aspect of the campus's physical plant sends the important message that the college meets student needs.

Fig. 1 Alternate view of SFSU along 19th Avenue and its coffee and food kiosks.

Fig. 3 Sign at the front entrance of the main campus of the City College of San Francisco.

Fig. 4 Signs fronting the main parking area at CCSF.

Fig. 5   Stairway and sculpture in front of the main building at CCSF.

Like those at San Francisco State, the signage and entry points encourage the public to the campus. As you can see in Figure 5, the campus features an easy ingress from the street to the stairs leading to the main building. Although it is not an official sign, the small sculpture of the woman with open arms, as if welcoming visitors, accentuates the campus's many inviting indicators. The main building at the University of San Francisco, a private university at the Northeast corner of Golden Gate Park, is also at the top of a hill, with stairs leading up to it, but, as you will see, USF's campus planners made different decisions about how the hill and the stairs should be adorned.

Students (or their parents) who are willing to pay more than $30,000 dollars per year for a private college education likely expect more in terms of campus design than students who opt to attend a state-funded institution. The University of San Francisco, my home institution, has won awards for urban campus design and beauty, and it is a stunning place, especially from atop Lone Mountain, but some aspects of USF's campus design may reveal more about its past ambitions than its present vision. Like SFSU and CCSF, USF has many points of entry, but the main sites of ingress run along Golden Gate Street, separating "lower campus" from the gate, walls, and stairs that lead to "upper campus" (Figs. 6 and 7). The upper campus, or Lone Mountain campus, used to be a Catholic women's college, which may explain the design choices here—gates, walls, and stairs constructed to keep nice girls in and bad boys out. But, these choices serve other purposes. Consider all the architectural elements at work in the grand entrance to Lone Mountain. There are the Italian- and Spanish-influenced stairs (which, perhaps not coincidentally, resemble a goblet). Then, one

Fig. 6 The University of San Francisco's entrance to its Lone Mountain Campus off of Golden Gate Street.

notices the sculpted archways and the fountain (difficult to see in the photograph, but just below the opening in the arch, a stream of water pours out of the mouth of a lion). Beyond all this, the stately palm trees seem to frame the arch, and behind them, the faint outline of a cross. Every detail here is intentional, from the finely wrought light on the column, to the decision to display the institution's founding date (1855), to the font of the lettering. The totality of these elements sends a clear message: This place is palatial, this place is imposing, this place is fancy, this is a place to be taken seriously. Interestingly, USF makes its sign part of the architecture of the space, advancing the argument that USF's education is as impressive as its design.

However, USF, a Jesuit university, also advances an overt mission of civic engagement and social justice, so one might argue that despite its beauty, the intimidating stairs, the walls, the columns, and the gates (that suggest separation) are at odds with key components of USF's identity as an institution of justice, engagement, and inclusion.

There is much more one could say about these signs. You can see here that even so humble an object as a sign can reveal a great deal about a university. It would be easy to devote an entire essay to decoding the semiotics of the USF stairway or the bustling, open point of entry at San Francisco State. Similar work could be done either comparatively or individually on many aspects of these campuses—and your campus too. To that end, you might ask big questions like, what are the connections between architecture, public space, and human need? Or, why doesn't my institution devote some of the money it spends on flowers, gardens, and trees to scholarships? If you don't know the answer to these questions, it may be

Fig. 7 USF's shrubbery sign on the Lone Mountain hill. Note the shrubbery wall on the far right of the photo.

best to start smaller. Begin with a semiotic reading of your campus and pay attention to the symbols, cues, and icons you see every day. Why do all of the buildings on my campus look alike (or different)? Does my campus combine architecture, plants, and signage to create a specific image? If so, what is it?

Without question, your campus is a rich text. Learning to look at that text through a semiotic lens enables you to see your campus and your education with a renewed interest and an informed clarity those admissions brochures can never replicate.

Reading and Writing About the Road

Jonathan Silverman

AMERICAN POPULAR CULTURE IS OBSESSED with the road, as witnessed by the enormous output of writers and movie-makers across time and place. Such works, ranging from the Jack Kerouac classic *On the Road* to Cormac McCarthy's Pulitzer-Prize winning novel *The Road* to movies like *Thelma and Louise* and *Easy Rider* and the Bob Hope–Bing Crosby road movies (e.g., *The Road to Rio, The Road to Morocco*), not to mention John Ford's adaptation of John Steinbeck's *The Grapes of Wrath*. Earlier works that focus on movement could also be classified as Road narratives; they include diaries by those crossing the Oregon Trail, letters by African American migrants from the South to North, and accounts by Native Americans regarding the Trail of Tears; even many narratives by the Puritans have elements of later conceptions of the Road in them. When reading these accounts, we often get a sense of both identity and continuity that mark movement in the United States.

As these examples illustrate, the Road in American culture is well traveled. Accordingly, in writing about such a familiar and mythic place, one might feel insecure about the ability to say anything new—such a feeling applies not only to the Road—but also other familiar topics as well. One way to approach such a subject is to simply discuss what we see; taking what we observe and analyzing it rather than worrying about trying to understand all of a subject is a way around this issue. It does not mean ignoring context, but it does mean relying on one's power of observation as the *primary* source of content. In other words, we can write our own Road stories.

With this in mind, I photographed a recent trip across the country. In the summer of 2007, I drove from Connecticut, where my parents live, to Santa Fe, New Mexico, making several stops along the way. I took photographs at every stop I made in an attempt to document what kinds of messages we encounter as we drive across the country. Following are some examples of photographs that make some statements about the Road, my encounter with it, and perhaps some larger truths associated with travel as well. I should note here that these photos are just a few of the hundred or so I took, and that my goal in writing about the Road was to combine my photography with analysis; such an approach requires *choosing*. Had I been required to write about all my photos and all my stops, there is no guarantee that I would have been able to come up with a coherent narrative. In writing about other nontraditional texts, you too will have to choose, in much the same way you might have to choose passages of a traditional text, like a poem or short story, to bolster an argument.

My approach also reflects a particular way of traveling across the country. Some like to move slowly, stopping at tourist destinations along the way, or pacing themselves by traveling only a short way each day. Some like to motor down the interstate in RVs, whereas others stick to the "Blue Highways," the national and state highways that preceded the Interstate, as termed by William Least Heat-Moon. And some like to travel like I did this time, in a hectic pace, marked by stops to visit friends, but with very little interaction with the culture beyond the road itself. Regardless of whether one stops to get to know a people or a place, signs, buildings, towns, people, and even the landscape seem to want to be looked at. Indeed, why would anything constructed near or along a road want to be *ignored*? Because traveling along a road presents a myriad of semiotic moments, traveling by road is always accompanied by a perpetual act of reading.

Consumption

Food is an essential part of travel. Westward travelers used to have to pack supplies in order to make the journey, though very quickly markets were created to cater to travelers. Now, we have convenience stores and travel stops (Fig. 1). For many travelers, the accessibility of food of both good nutrition or less so (Fig. 2) is an enjoyable part of venturing across the country. Consider the Moon Pie. It is not a national brand; you can find it mostly in the Midwest and the South, and so a hardy traveler venturing forth is buoyed by the find of this delectable mix of banana-flavor coating, cakelike filling, and marshmallow. (It's funny, too, that it bills itself as "The Only One On The Planet!" given the fact that one chooses one Moon Pie among a display of many.) I also like the

Fig. 1   This rest stop is just outside of Albuquerque, New Mexico, on I-40.

universality of the moon in the Moon Pie—the sky is one constant in traveling, and often a way of marking one's progress across the country is by the different views we have of the sky and the horizon.

Although it is often home to the delectable Moon Pie, the travel center itself (Fig. 1) goes beyond the convenience and corner store in that it is also a center of symbolic consumption. Until recently, most were associated with one gasoline brand and that's it. But here we see the trend of collaborating with other national brands, in this case, Dairy Queen. This particular center is devoted to nostalgia—note the Route 66 sign, which refers to the most romantic of former roads that was consonant with the first wave of pleasure road trips out West, as well as the path for migrants from Oklahoma to California during the Dust Bowl. Originally cutting a path from Chicago to Los Angeles, Route 66 has been replaced by I-40. You can't see it well, but Phillips 66 is behind the '50s inspired sign. This particular sign intentionally evokes the romanticized image of Route 66 that Lisa Mahar documents in her suite in Chapter 5, "Reading and Writing about Images." (Note, too, the faux space-age arrow seemingly straight out of the 1950s, an arrow that was supposed to signify progress. Now it points back to itself; it's a symbol of the future that harks back to the past.)

The travel stop is also a monument to American commercialism (Fig. 3). Here, more than 100 bottles of electrolyte drink are displayed in a scene that seems a form of deliberately constructed commercial beauty. My own view here is mediated by the photographs of Andres Gursky, particularly his *99 Cent*, a photograph of a convenience store in Los Angeles

Fig. 2   The Moon Pie (nestled on top of GoogleMaps). Purchased in a rest stop off I-70 in Ohio.

Fig. 3   America might be thirsty.

The bigger question is: can anyone be *that* thirsty? But the prominence of these drinks also might signal the transition to the Desert Southwest, where people worry about dehydration.

To me, the Moon Pie, Route 66, and Gatorade drinks form a triptych of road consumption, symbolizing the plenty one can find on the road, as well as the way images speak to us in unexpected—and sometimes unexpectedly beautiful—ways.

Landscape

Roads frame landscape by guiding travelers through a particular area; they then become part of what they frame, as the associated parts—guardrails, medians, exit signs, and others, not to mention the podlike businesses that surround the exits—become part of the landscape itself. In other words, the discussion about landscape actually began in the previous section. The road's landscape is also framed, however, by the response of its travelers. For some, highways are anonymous, empty routes that exist only as means of travel to one's destination. For others, seeing unfamiliar landscapes, even if they bracket a long, relatively unchanged road, is part of the exploration of travel.

A familiar landscape to one traveler might be exotic to another. Witness my own traveling through the mid-section of the country. For those who grow up on the coasts, the sheer flatness and vision of the land can be both breathtaking and in the case of weather, a little frightening. Shown are two shots taken from the road—the first (Fig. 4) driving North in Arkansas, and the second (Fig. 5) on I-70 in Kansas.

For me, someone who grew up in Connecticut, where the horizon is hidden by trees, the big sky and flat plains are fascinating and beautiful. They suggest the openness so commonly associated with the West and Westward expansion, a hypnosis-inducing means of crossing

Fig. 4 On I-55 in Arkansas.

Fig. 5 On I-70 in Kansas.

the country. But to others, they are just the background of daily living. When I was in graduate school in Texas, I took my first journey across West Texas on my way to Colorado to visit a friend. I was buoyed by the beauty of landscape throughout my travel, but I thought the cotton fields outside of Lubbock were particularly beautiful. I expressed this thought to a clerk at a convenience store, who demanded to know where I was from.

"Connecticut," I said.

She responded by saying something to the effect of "It's beautiful there. This is ugly."

Signs

Signs are literal markers on a highway, telling its travelers what to do (drive a speed limit, slow down, change lanes) or where to go (St. Louis, Exit 287, north). But signs are also signs of a different sort—they can be unpacked to show some of the idiosyncrasies of road travel. Figure 6, taken off I-70 in Utah, illustrates the many possibilities one might choose to view the landscape. Standing in the rest area, an arbitrary location carved out in this case to view the scenery, there is no possibility that one will go the wrong way. So when looking backward, I was struck by the repetition of a sign that seems superfluous in contrast to a "beautiful landscape."

For those who find direct religious expression difficult to process, landscape combined with religious signage sends several coded messages. Is the sign in Figure 7 referring to the afterlife, or this particular place? Is Hell an emotional state, or a destination? Maybe this sign is also about travel of a different sort.

And then we have signs that reveal much about the country we live in, such as the Homeland Security sign taken in a rest stop in Richfield, Utah (Fig. 8). Such a sign could reveal the political leanings of the owner—not necessarily a statement of risk.

Fig. 6 Utah rest stop.

Fig. 7 On I-71 in Ohio.

Fig. 8 Off I-70 in Utah.

The signs in Figure 9 suggest a great deal of options traveling across the country, a mix of various routes, subroutes, and in the case of Route 66, historic or even nostalgic routes. When approaching this intersection, knowing how (and not only where) one is going seems imperative.

And then we have these signs (Fig. 10) marking a bathroom in Utah, signaling the sort of universality of highway travel—bathrooms where distinction is both signified by inclusion of all three possible restroom symbols (and certainly a throwback—the symbol for the women does not reflect any sort of standard of female dress in the twenty-first century).

Although this is not actually a street sign (Fig. 11), the bear and the hedges do reveal through a close reading some of the concerns of this rest stop in Grand Junction, Colorado. The bear is native to the area, but also a symbol of wildness and, more important, of nature itself. In a way, so are the hedges next to the bear, on top of a constructed stone wall, in front of manicured grass. But taken together, they suggest a manicured nature, perhaps the nature that travelers prefer to encounter. Taken as a whole, this photograph also reminds the traveler of his or her own home as well as the pull of nature.

Another trip down another road might engender an entirely different semiotic experience and a different interpretation. The cultural and visual rhetoric of the road is always active, although because it is stationary, it may feel passive. However, we are the ones for whom the road and its many texts are designed. Paying attention to the various associations bears and signs and products carry may help us understand how the road tries to determine its own interpretation.

Fig. 9 In Flagstaff, Arizona.

Fig. 10 In a rest stop off I-70 in Utah.

Fig. 11   Off I-70 in Grand Junction, Colorado.

Reading and Writing About Fashion

Elisabeth Piedmont-Marton

MOST HIGH SCHOOL STUDENTS would be surprised to learn that they are highly skilled semioticians, or readers of signs. Able to recognize a complex array of signs and symbols at twenty paces or more, they can form remarkably reliable conclusions about the person heading toward them in the hall outside the cafeteria or dawdling in front of the kiosk in the mall. The guy with the oversized pants and the faux-hawk? Skate punk. A guy with short-sleeved white shirt and ill-fitting blue pleated chinos? Science teacher. Depending on geographic region, size, and the populations they serve, high schools have different categories into which fashion texts can be divided, but the reason most students are such skilled readers of these texts is that high school has a relatively fixed number of subject positions, or selves, that fashion can indicate. Even the girl with blue hair slumped against her locker signifies that she rejects the constraints of high school fashion by signifying that she belongs to the group of kids who wish to signal that They Don't Belong. Once free from the fixed taxonomy of high school, however, these skilled semioticians must broaden their symbolic lexicon and sharpen their skills at both reading and composing fashion texts.

Fashion, or more broadly, dress, is the outer text of the body, signifying basic information such as gender, class, age, and status and occupation. In high school, these categories are relatively stable: everyone is about the same age, and has neither a professional identity nor independent means. The terms that are variable communicate status, economic and otherwise; values, such as religion and politics; avocation, such as sports, art, computers, and other interests; and affiliation, such as what kind of music one listens to. Fashion can say a lot of things. It cannot, however, say nothing. In other words, if you want to dress in such a way to signify that you care nothing about fashion, then you must nevertheless use the language of fashion in order to construct that text. The dream of creating a meaning-neutral mode of dress is a powerful one: it's the rationale for both school uniforms and for the imaginary unisex jumpsuits of science fiction. If there is any doubt that the uniform cannot diffuse fashion's signifying charge, consider the rich variations schoolchildren and professional athletes display in their uniforms.

Even when we roll out of bed and pull on the first thing we can find, we are authoring a text. That text can say, "I just got out of bed and don't care what I look like at the moment." Or can also say, "I don't choose to participate in the textual exchange of fashion." What we cannot say with our haphazard and apparently artless dress is "Fashion is not a text," because we would have to use the language of fashion in order to send that message.

Although the text of fashion is incapable of refusing signification, it does not follow that what it signifies is narrowly determined. As many theorists have argued in recent decades, all sign systems are always indeterminate and unanchored, and fashion is no exception. From this perspective, the richness and the pleasure of the text is in the endless possibilities for play, for destabilizing fixed categories, subverting expectations, up-ending categories, and generally messing with people's heads. This play is perhaps most visible when women dress like men and vice versa, but also takes more subtle forms, such as when a young hipster wears pants that once apparently belonged to a professional golfer in 1970. The surprise and delight we experience when we read a text like that derives from the unexpected contrast between register of the wearer and the signifying charge of the plaid polyester pants. The same pleasure is not obtained if the hipster also dons a matching shirt and shoes. Then it's just a costume, which doesn't invite readers into the same level of engagement.

Like texts of all kinds, fashions won't yield immediately to our critical strategies. Encountering a fashion text that we don't quite "get" is one of the great pleasures of becoming attuned to the semiotics of dress. I'll close with a story of an encounter with an enigmatic fashion text that refused to yield to my exegetical powers. Several years ago, a young and quite successful fiction and screenwriter visited the campus where I work. He very much looked the part of the young literary star: long haired and rumpled clothing made from quality fabrics, punctuated with stylish and expensive shoes. At the dinner with invited faculty, however, he added a piece to his ensemble, as if to recognize the formality of the occasion where professors wear their once-a-year suits and dresses. He had added an ugly brown cardigan sweater made from acrylic fiber, a sweater only Mr. Rogers could have loved. At the end of the evening and after investigating at close range, I concluded that it was a hilarious ironic commentary on the mannered tweediness and trying-too-hard hipness of the professoriate. But then he also wore it the next night when he delivered his reading and lecture to a large audience. Far away on the stage the sweater just slumped there on his slight shoulders, not looking at all ironic. It may have been contemptuous ("I don't care enough about your little college to dress for the occasion, so I'm wearing this crappy sweater"), or reassuring ("I'm terribly insecure in these situations, and this sweater I got from my grandfather's closet after he died comforts me"), or hyper-cool ("What?! You don't know that brown polyester cardigans are featured in everyone's runway shows this season?").

Another important lesson from this experience is that there is often a potential gap between the *intention* of the wearer and the *reception* of the viewer. That is, this guy may have wanted to send one message by wearing the sweater, but, for whatever reason, I received a different message. Who knows what message other people received? Wearing Chuck Taylor sneakers with a suit could be interpreted a number of different ways—that the wearer is hip, that the wearer is homeless or out of pocket, or that the wearer has a long walk to public transportation. So, although we may obsess over the messages sent by the clothes our friends, boyfriends, girlfriends, teachers, parents, and idols wear, we must always keep in mind that fashion is a fluid text, contingent on interpretation. As any reader of a poem or short story knows, the key to accurate interpretation is context. So, what the guest writer may have been suggesting with the combination of hip clothes but ratty sweater is something like, "Even though I'm now a cool Hollywood writer, I'm also, really, at my core, a lot like you academic types." Of course, he also may have been mocking us academic types.

I could never decide what the sweater signified, but I'm sure it was trying to tell me something. If I ever run into the writer again, I'm going to ask him what the sweater meant, but who knows if he will tell the truth!

Reading and Writing About a Bicycle

Jonathan Hunt

NOT LONG AGO, and quite suddenly, it seemed, my neighborhood was overrun by bicyclists on a new kind of bike—a sort of *reduced* bike, with no brakes or gears. Or let me put it more precisely: *I* was nearly overrun. The culprit was a young person who sped through an intersection against the light and without slowing, leaving consternation and resentment behind her among the pedestrians and motorists who—naively, it now seemed—allowed their movements to be guided by illuminated signals. As she flew away down the street, I could see that she was on a track bike, a special kind of racing bicycle built

Fixie graffiti, downtown San Francisco (2007). © Jonathan Hunt. Some rights reserved.

Racers at Hellyer Park Velodrome (2007). © Steven Ryan. Some rights reserved.

Sylvester Stallone as Judge Dredd.

for indoor competition, characterized by a single fixed gear; hence its more popular name, the "fixie."

But the fixie subculture in my neighborhood had nothing to do with track racing, which shares most of the visual features of the professional road racing. If you have cable, you can watch it on *Versus* (the rodeo, kickboxing, deer-hunting, and cycling channel): brightly colored bicycles matching the tight Lycra outfits of their athletic riders, bicycles and cyclists alike splashed all over with the names and logos of corporate sponsors, all shaved legs and huge lungs topped with Judge Dredd helmets, chasing each other around and around according to complicated and opaque rules.

The skinny kids congregating in front of the coffee shop down the street or in certain corners of the local park didn't look like that. They had unruly hair and tattooed arms, and their astonishingly tight pants were scuffed black denim, not shiny Lycra. Their gleaming, matchy bicycles at first seemed a contrast to their scruffy appearance: I saw an orange bike with an orange seat, orange wheels, orange tires, orange pedals and orange handlebar tape, its few chrome bits polished to a gleam. Another bike, flawlessly powder blue, featured white handlebar tape with red hearts on it, and an ace of hearts playing card to match,

stuck jauntily in the spokes of the rear wheel. Among these pristine steeds, some bikes seemed to have the same careful carelessness as their owner's hairstyle: an old, chipped steel frame seemed to take pride in the worn decal with the name of a long-dead Italian frame-builder; a low-end ten-speed crusted with grease and dirt, converted to a fixie by removal of the brakes and replacement of the back wheel.

In fixie subculture, then, the bikes themselves vary widely, but two properties are invariably prized. The first of these is minimalism. None of the fixed-gear bikes I've spotted have racks, baskets, fenders, chain guards, cushy seats, bells, or other common bicycle accessories in the style of Pee-Wee Herman's beloved cruiser. The second property is a related lack of safety features: very few have reflectors or brakes (in fact, a T-shirt in circulation proclaims "If it's fixed, don't brake it")—in a related sartorial code, few fixie riders I've seen wear helmets, favoring faded cycling caps with Italian brand names: *Campagnolo, Cinelli, Bottecchia*.

In one sense, the values of a subculture are conveyed quite clearly in the choice of display objects (bikes, in this case, but hairstyles, handbags, or hot rods would do equally well). The fixie rider values sleek minimalism tinged with rebellious nostalgia, a reaction against the gadgetry-driven "newer-is-better" ethos that dominates the bicycle industry and American consumer culture more broadly. Against the ever-more-complicated gearing, braking, and suspension systems of mountain and road bikes, the fixie recalls a lost golden age of European cycling, an age before Lycra shorts, neon colors, and Styrofoam helmets (a sacred text is *The Impossible Hour*, Danish director Jørgen Leth's 1974 homage to cycling on the track). Against the square practicality of conventional bicycle advocates, the fixie rider values a stylish recklessness, an affiliation with outlaw bike messenger culture (which pioneered the fixed-gear trend decades ago). Steve Carell's character in *The 40-Year-Old Virgin* is the antithesis of fixie cool.

Trackstars (2007). © Randy Reddig. All rights reserved. Used by permission.

Still from *The Impossible Hour* (1974).

Yet the meaning of a display-oriented subculture goes beyond the conscious messages associated with choices of accessories, clothing, hairstyles, or music. The fixie cyclist (or fixist? fixster?) announces her or his difference or departure from the "parent" culture (and other bicycle subcultures), but in doing so, remains entwined in systems of sameness and difference that constitute all cultural affiliations. In short, fixie variation takes place within an overarching sameness: the fixie enthusiast seems free to choose colors (generally eschewing patterns) and certain limited accessories (the playing card in the spokes, the saddle), and in fact, the act of making these choices is strongly encouraged. The oohs and ahs down at the coffee shop are exclusively reserved for unique bikes, such as the one with mismatched wheels but perfect color coordination, a combination of components displaying the owner's creativity and design sense. Fixie cool has its boundaries, just as any kind of design or fashion statement: *cool* involves breaking certain sets of rules (and, in some cases, laws), but at the same time, it requires adherence to a strict new set of conventions.

The fixed-gear bike is thus not just a vehicle for transport (although it is that), but it is also a vehicle for communicating the values and characteristics of its owner. Many of these values and characteristics are transmitted intentionally, such as design sense, mechanical aptitude, and riding skills; the fixster values these traits in her- or himself and in fixie "colleagues." In selecting components, in assembling the bicycle, and in surviving urban traffic on a bicycle with no brakes, the fixist broadcasts these desirable traits—traits that, to those not attached to the subculture, seem annoying or irresponsible.

The fixie bicycle, then, is a marker of opposition to mainstream culture, with its sensible values and readily available consumer choices. Trapped in a world where people are defined

"Off-the-rack Masi" (2007). © Jonathan Hunt. Some rights reserved.

"Your Fixie Makes You Look Fat" (2006). © Franco Follini. Some rights reserved.

by the objects they buy at the mall, the fixist aspires to be different by assembling a unique machine—because of this aspiration, an off-the-rack Bianchi or Masi fixie from the bike shop is practically a badge of shame (note, however, that even corporate manufacture of fixies adheres to the style code: the dreaded Bianchi is all chrome, with minimalist decals). Like any consumers, fixsters seek to map out their individualities with a constellation of purchases, but as with purchasers of Levi's and Mini Coopers, their individuality is commodified by the very gesture (the purchase) that seeks to establish it.

The meaning of the fixed-gear bike—like the meaning of any object—depends on a play of sameness and difference: it is like other bikes, yet not like them; its rider is like other consumers, yet different. Like other texts, the fixie can be read in isolation or in relation to related systems of meaning (e.g., the fashion system, the gender system). Some of its meanings are explicit and intentional; others, less flattering to the rider, cannot be outrun no matter how fast they pedal.

Reading and Writing About Video Games

Peter Hartlaub

WE ARE AT THE BEGINNING, and there is only Pong.

Like a single-celled organism crawling out of the primordial ooze, it appears as an outhouse-size arcade game in a few bars and pizza parlors in 1972, before a much smaller take-home version starts selling at Sears. Both are as simple looking as a block of cheese.

Reading the game takes a split second, if you're slow. Two long rectangles moving on a vertical axis try to block a small square block traveling horizontally or diagonally, with numbers in the upper left and right corners of the screen that represent the score. Instructions aren't necessary—if you can operate a thermostat, you can play Pong. Two round dials control the paddles. A switch in the back turns the machine on and off.

The first mainstream video game says almost nothing about the people who enjoy it, or even its creator. What are his artistic influences? Is he an optimistic person, or filled with darkness and doubt? Does he have a humorous or whimsical side? You won't learn these things from playing Pong.

The Dragon's Lair arcade game is, in the words of a 10-year-old in 1983, "Totally rad." The front and sides have ornate and colorful drawings of knights and fire-spitting dragons, not unlike the ones that are appearing on the sides of conversion vans and the covers of heavy metal albums at this time in American popular culture.

The creator of the game, Don Bluth, has worked with Disney, but you knew that when you walk up to the monitor—which for the first time uses a laserdisc to simulate animation that is as good as anything you'll find in the theaters. The presentation is grand and musical and a bit funny, like a trip through the Pirates of the Caribbean ride at Disneyland.

Just a few years earlier, people in video games were basically stick figures. But your character Dirk the Daring looks and acts like a real person, whose body language alone tells the story of a man who is brave, foolish, and uncomfortable in his own skin. His lanky body and clumsy stride make you wonder how he got to be a knight in the first place. Did his father have connections in the royal guard?

There's a joystick and four buttons on the front of the game, with a few instructions written underneath the monitor in a medieval font. The only words on-screen are the "Credits = 0" text in the bottom right corner. Presumably, the creator of this game wanted nothing to clutter his artistic statement.

On-screen text in video games was like an arms race in the 1990s, and by the turn of the century there's enough readable information to tell a fairly complete story with a single image. The following is gathered from one screenshot, a pause in action from the 2001 Xbox video game *Halo:*

A ship hovers overhead, but the ornate writing on the side doesn't come from the world of Master Chief, the Earth-born commando whose movements you control from the first-person perspective. The ship's hostile intentions are confirmed from the frozen-in-time pink laser blasts in the space soldier's direction.

Master Chief is carrying a big gun, but it will soon be useless. The bulky blaster rifle carries sixty shots, but a counter on the gun that faces the player reveals that only four rounds are left—with no remaining clips.

Another counter at the top left part of the screen displays some more bad news: Master Chief's grenade reserve is down to three, and a gauge on the top right reveals that his shields have taken a hit.

In the lower left-hand corner of the screen a circular radar sensor shows that six heavily armed insect creatures are on foot, fifteen meters away, and closing ground fast. The space bugs are about to win.

The boxer trading punches with Muhammad Ali is you, assuming you chose to bother with the create-your-own-character mode in the 2007 video game *Fight Night Round 3.*

Read the Xbox 360 title like a text, and you can discover something about its creators, the real-life boxers whose likenesses are included in the game and the executives who make the marketing and business decisions for the company.

Unlike *Halo,* the game has no letters, numbers, or shaded meters to let players know the status of their fighter. (The boxer's heart rate can be felt on the controller, which rumbles heavily when he's about to fall.) But the background is filled with writing, including banners advertising an athletic clothing line that are visible at every angle, and background music that is carefully chosen to launch a hot new artist. Text displays the band's name and album information as each new song is played.

The game also says something about the person playing it. Do you attack your opponent, or lay back to parry blows? Is your boxer wearing simple clothing, or the sequined trunks of a modern-day Apollo Creed, with your name boldly emblazoned across the wasteline?

And if you chose to make the fighter on screen in your own image, does the character on-screen look like you, or the person you want to be? Do you give your video game doppelgänger love handles, a receding hairline and that bad tattoo you got in Mexico on Spring Break thirteen years ago, or will he be a new improved version of whatever really looks back at you in the mirror every morning?

Video games have evolved quickly since the early 1970s, beginning as toys and developing into an art form that is exceptionally participatory. With each new advance, the act of reading them becomes more dynamic.

Audiences influence many art forms, especially theater and music. Even a television show such as *American Idol* gives the viewer multiple chances to become part of the show. But with avatars, online cooperative play, and the *Grand Theft Auto* "digital sandbox" model of cities that players can freely explore, games are becoming less about the creators and more about the imaginations of whoever is playing.

As we move forward into an age of photorealism, accurate simulations, and controllers that are sensitive to the motions of the human body, is a walk down the street in a video game that much different than a walk down the street in your neighborhood?

During the Pong era, reading a video game wasn't much different than reading a hula hoop (or, perhaps more accurately, a game of catch between two robots). Years later, the process has become almost as complicated and nuanced as real life.

Reading and Writing About Social Networking Sites: Making Friends and Getting "Poked"

Cristina DeLuca

SO, HOW MANY FRIENDS DO YOU HAVE?

If this question immediately makes you think of the last time you logged on to your Facebook or MySpace page, then you already have the skills to "read" a social networking website (and all this time you thought you were procrastinating on the Internet). As you probably know firsthand, perfecting a Facebook or MySpace profile is an activity on which college students spend inordinate amounts of their time. This might be because between high school and college, students experience the freedom to shift away from their constraining high school identities toward something completely new. Once you arrive on campus, no one knows the "jock," "alpha girl," "nerd," or "drama queen" you may have been categorized as in high school, and for many students, this newfound anonymity can be quite liberating. In fact, the innumerable opportunities to remake identity are the main draws of these sites and the reason young people—the very demographic struggling toward identity—are turning to virtual sites instead of traditional social groups.

For many students, the transition from high school to college life is stressful because they are met with the arduous task of finding a new circle of friends. Because browsing their peers' Facebook or MySpace profiles online requires no personal contact, social networking sites allow students the liberty to look for potential friends without having to utter a single (potentially embarrassing) word or feel self-conscious about proper body language. Similar to how certain clothes or hairstyle make a first impression, social networking sites can provide flattering a first look into a student's personality. What type of music they listen to, books they've read, Internet video clips that make them laugh, and what their friends have to say about them all converge into a webpage that is their own unique cyber fingerprint. These pages are thoughtfully constructed and continuously managed—entirely not-random text. A profile page on a social networking site is the result of a series of careful choices based on information we want to reveal about ourselves.

The profile photo on the top of the page is the key component of all social networking websites and sets the tone for the entire profile. A site user's interests in books, movies, and music all seem secondary to this feature. Exploring this all-important feature semiotically can not only make you a savvier site user, but may also provide some insight into the presentation of your own profile page. Although there are minor exceptions, the profile photo exists in three varying forms: the photo of the user surrounded by friends or in a social situation, the artsy self-portrait, and the irreverent photo. All three types of images represent the first impression of the profile page, summing up the site user in one single frame.

For instance, a person would most likely want to be viewed as "social" if his profile photo displays him holding a plastic red cup with his arms around a bunch of equally happy guys and girls. This type of photo conforms to a popular category of users among friends, and it is a natural choice. Humans instinctively find comfort in groups of other people and showing to the world that we "fit in." This photo tells viewers, *I am well liked, and I am with other people who think I am friendly and fun too*. The red plastic cup probably contains beer, and that shows that the user isn't uptight and likes to have a good time. However, some users may see the photo and dismiss this person as a shallow frat brother. Users with social profile photos also risk looking insecure. If a person has to be surrounded by people to prove his self-worth, perhaps he doesn't know himself very well.

Attempting to present the opposite appearance that the social photograph does is the artsy self-portrait. A typical example of this picture includes a photo of a girl or guy in a dimly lit room, looking away from the camera very seriously. This common pose adds an element of mystery and intrigue to the profile. The darkness and stylized aspects of the photograph reveal characteristics that say, *I'm too deep for this website*. Perhaps the artsy self-portrait is the user's way of proclaiming his or her reluctance to join the social networking craze. Taking the picture themselves, and thereby controlling every aspect of the photograph, those who choose the self-portrait may be less interested in being perceived as well liked and more interested in creating a profile page that displays their unique perspective of the world. A viewer of this photo could be either intrigued by the user's resistance to prove his or her popularity, or possibly turned off by the user's potentially self-righteous (*It's all about me!*) attitude.

Of course, both of these photos can pigeonhole the user into a very specific category (such as "party animal" and "dramatic," respectively) before the viewer even reads the rest of the profile. That's where the irreverent, completely out of context, photo comes in. An irreverent photo is any one (animal, vegetable, or mineral) that is not actually a picture of the user himself. This may show that the user has a sense of humor, either about himself or the website. "Identifying" yourself as some physical person or object other than you goes against conventional wisdom.

For example, if someone has a photo of a panda bear on his profile page, you are forced to think, *This person is obviously not a panda bear*, and read further into it to devise some kind of meaning. Perhaps he is mocking the predictable structure of the site, or the mores we follow to express ourselves in the "correct" way. Or, he doesn't want to have his photo plastered on a website for millions to see. Or, of course, he just might really like panda bears. The viewer of this photo may laugh along at its absurdity or dismiss it as plain confusing. Viewers of the irreverent photo might also be disappointed that they cannot see what the individual actually looks like.

Whatever the photo, the site user's intended meaning will not always come across successfully to every viewer. As with face-to-face encounters, site users cannot completely control every aspect of how their profile pages will be received. These variables aside, social networking websites allow users to fashion an online identity that enables them to meet others that can appreciate their profile choices (and weed out those who don't). So I say, treat these next few years as an opportunity to remake yourself by logging on and discovering who is online. Not just another webpage in cyberspace, each profile on a social networking site is a cultural text brimming with meaning, and waiting to be examined.

PS: Facebook me, won't you?

Reading and Writing About *Family Guy:* The Semiotics of Stream of Consciousness

Lee Transue

IT IS THE CERTIFICATION OF TRUE TALENT when a storyteller can write that which he or she feels *can* be written, and not what *should* be written by typical literary standards, while the audience remains unaware of his or her slight of hand. There are many words and phrases to describe the technique, foremost amongst them *stream of consciousness;* however, such qualifications fail to embrace the varied and complex forms this type of writing takes for simple reasons: There are simply too many pieces of literature so vastly incomparable to the next that to call one piece a work written in stream of consciousness acts only to cyclically render other works of totally different execution, but also written in stream of consciousness, a different "style" of the form. Of course this creates a fundamental problem with stream of consciousness. The form becomes much like the color blue. Yes, the sky is often blue. Your parents may have once owned a blue Volkswagen Beetle. You may feel "blue" during the winter months, and you just might be reading this with Blue Öyster Cult's Donald Roeser singing "Ooooooh, Godzilla!" through your buds. So what is *blue*? And what is *stream of consciousness*? The easy answer is that they're both vague concepts with a great number of examples to define them. Typically, the form is written quickly, sometimes rabidly, by an author who is free-associating each word or concept with the next with no real concern for the immediate structure of the text. Rather, he or she is concerned with the work as a whole, representing the mass of competing ideas all masterfully packed into one story, somehow all coming together in the end through bits and pieces by way of the conscience splayed out in some poetic collage. And there is one example of a work of stream of consciousness that millions of both Americans and Europeans ingest happily and with ease on a weekly basis. That work being, of course, Seth MacFarlane's perennially successful animated television series, *Family Guy*.

Stream of consciousness is not an unfamiliar concept to sitcom viewers; however, *Family Guy's* brand of the form is alien to the free-association style of humor that, say, *Seinfeld* gained massive popularity with (often touted as "the show about nothing"). Unlike the famously loose plots of *Seinfeld*, the premise of *Family Guy* is the convention for most television sitcoms, live action or animated, present or past, in that it follows the Griffins, a standard nuclear American family (in its case a father, Peter; mother, Lois; two adolescent siblings, Chris and Meg; an infant, Stewie; and their dog, Brian) through their blue-collared existence in the fictional town of Quahog, Rhode Island. But unlike most typical sitcom families, there are certain exceptions that set the Griffins apart from the lot. Peter is an unapologetic drunk with the attention span and sense of humor of a seven-year-old; Lois is an articulate, strong woman from an exceedingly wealthy family; Meg is unpopular and unattractive (and is constantly reminded of both); Chris is simply dumb (but held a stint as a professional artist for one episode); Stewie, the infant (and a star of the series), continuously tries to kill Lois and obtain world domination (a bit more drastic than the occasional, "How rude!"); and Brian, the dog, can talk, drives a hybrid, and loves martinis. And Quahog beyond the Griffin household is just as colorful: The mayor is a delusional Adam West of *Batman* fame (voiced by Mr. West himself); Peter's neighbors and friends consist of a sexual deviant, a paraplegic police officer, and a gentle deli owner who is one of the few black characters on the show. Many other characters appear infrequently on the show, including a soft-voiced, elderly ephebophile, a giant chicken that battles Peter each time they come across one another, an evil monkey that lives in Chris's closet, and the Grim Reaper (who still lives with his mother and can't get dates). So, as Jerry Seinfeld and Co. all-too-perfectly present a stream-of-consciousness representation of life in New York City for the upper-middle class using loose, unpredictable plots, the Griffins take the audience through stories that are quite grounded in convention, but with unpredictable halts in the action that separate it from other styles of the form that television viewers are more familiar with. But what exactly are these halts in action that define it as a stream-of-consciousness text?

Despite its unique take on the sitcom formula, it isn't the absurd foundations on which *Family Guy* is built that makes it a stream-of-consciousness text. To understand that argument, one must look further than the barmy cast of characters because it's not the people (or animals) that define the form of a particular work; it's the way in which their story is told. And for those familiar with the show, and therefore with Seth MacFarlane's writing style, this argument comes easy. But for those who are outsiders in the *Family Guy* universe, its "stream of consciousness"-ness, and the many levels therein, might not become obvious until you familiarize yourself with the text, and with examples of the form.

An easy way to read *Family Guy* through the stream-of-consciousness filter is by examining the show's structure on a whole before getting down into the nitty-gritty of the characters' contribution to the form. The same can be said for nearly any work written in this way. Take, briefly, James Joyce's watershed novel *Ulysses* as an example. For their part, the characters in this stream-of-consciousness masterpiece are relatively identifiable and, I daresay, normal. Yes, Joyce's protagonist Leopold Bloom does have his quirks (the bar of soap he carries in his pocket, his enjoyment of flatulence, and the occasional bit of public masturbation), but on the whole he and the rest of the work's characters are *honest*, in that, like most characters in sitcoms, they are composed of both negative and positive characteristics that help the audience identify with them.

But just like *Family Guy*'s Peter Griffin, *Ulysses*' Leopold Bloom is not what defines the form of the novel (or in Peter's case, the show). That definition is all to do with the structure. With *Ulysses*, the story is presented in a way that was truly revolutionary at its time of full publication in 1922. Joyce's cast of strangely unique and believable characters simply existed inside of a story told like no other. Broken into eighteen "episodes," *Ulysses* ends with one of the most impenetrable examples of stream of consciousness ever printed. The eighteenth episode, "Penelope," is recited by Leopold's wife, Molly, in a roughly fifty-page soliloquy that consists of only eight sentences (each many pages long) with almost no punctuation to speak of for its entirety. Molly, like Leopold, is a character that could easily be found in most forms of literature. But it is how she and her words appear that define the work. It is why *Ulysses* stands apart, acting as a true archetype of the genre. And similarly, the manner in which episodes of *Family Guy* are built does the same for animated sitcoms. The structure of each very seldom changes. There is a distinct style MacFarlane relies on, and it is what makes the show unique and successful. Dispersed throughout each episode are brief, tangential jokes that are present for no purpose other than to entertain with their idiosyncratic deviations from the plot (which they never act to advance). The majority of these defining sight gags are introduced by Peter by way of what I'll call a trigger. For example, there is a scene in the episode "North by North Quahog" (original air date, May 1, 2005), during which Peter and Lois are involved in a car chase after stealing the film reel for a sequel to *The Passion of the Christ* from Mel Gibson's hotel room. During the chase, Peter states: "Oh man, this is even more intense than that time I forgot how to sit down." The scene immediately cuts to Peter at home walking up to an arm chair in the family's living room, staring at it blankly for a few moments, then leaping into it with a humorously violent result. In this case, the "Oh man . . ." statement is the trigger.

Nearly every one of *Family Guy*'s characteristic vignettes is introduced in a similar fashion. Although likely well thought out in advance by MacFarlane and his staff of writers, this joke and all of those like it are presented bundled within the main story; therefore, they appear to the viewer as full stops in the action for the sole purpose of inserting this sort of comical ADD into an otherwise linear plot. That, too, raises interesting implications about *Family Guy* being read as a stream-of-consciousness text. The development of the show's script is arguably not stream of consciousness, because one can assume that the show's writers spend many hours carefully constructing the jokes in the show. This is antithetical to the style itself; however, when the show is viewed at once by an audience, it then becomes stream of consciousness in a way that is unique to film and television. It is a visual representation of the form, not a literary one, and that is how it must be *read*. The human thought process is an erratic one. It jumps from idea to idea, and although these ideas may seem random, even unrelated, they all contribute to one cogent flow that somehow remains linear, or at least travels meanderingly to a clear end. It was an unprecedented achievement for authors like Joyce to translate that process into a work of literature, and so is it an achievement for *Family Guy* to do the same in the form of an animated television series. A text doesn't need to be written in the form to be perceived that way, and *Family Guy* pioneered that idea in its genre. And just as *Ulysses* should be read for its undeniable contribution to literature, so too should *Family Guy* for its similar invention.

In addition to the vignettes, most of the characters in the show have mannerisms that perpetuate the form. It should be remembered, however, that just because a character is quite strange indeed doesn't make for a stream-of-consciousness text; it is their actions that do so. I mentioned a few extraneous characters previously, including the evil monkey and the giant chicken. Yes, it's strange to have an evil monkey and a giant chicken as characters. But that's just silliness not stream of consciousness. The line there is crossed, however, when those characters act as triggers for the non-plot-advancing-full-stop sight gags. The evil monkey is the weaker of these two examples because he appears more frequently than the giant chicken. Although quite real, the evil monkey has been seen only by Chris (who is always met with ridicule when he suggests that the evil monkey, in fact, exists). Such mentions of the pernicious primate generally begin with a simple discourse between family members, but end with Chris making a comment such as, "I don't want to go to my room—there's an evil monkey that lives in my closet!" Predictably, the family laughs, but then it happens: Chris looks down a hallway, or to the top of the stairs, and there, accompanied by a jolt of ominous music, is a small monkey revealing a threatening set of fangs, his brow furrowed, an accusatory finger pointed in Chris's direction. Interestingly, but of little consequence to my argument, the episode "Ready, Willing, and Disable" (original air date, December 20, 2001) revealed that the evil monkey wasn't always evil, but was made that way when he returned from work one day to find his wife in bed with another monkey.

An even stronger example of stream of consciousness through character appearances is that of the giant chicken, who has been featured in just four episodes. In three of those four appearances, Peter and the giant chicken have randomly come across one another on the street, and on seeing one another, begin fighting incredibly violent battles that last for several minutes and take the two characters to dramatic locales across the city. These segments, which look a lot like modern action films, aren't properly explained in any way (aside from the chicken's first appearance, where he hands Peter an expired coupon on the street) until the fourth episode, in which a flashback shows Peter bumping into the chicken (whose name is revealed to be Ernie) at a country club while dancing with Lois. The chicken becomes enraged, but this friend calms him down, saying, "You'll probably never see him again" ("Meet the Quagmires," original air date, May 20, 2007). These epic battles always end with Peter as the victor. Bloodied and bruised, his clothing hanging in shreds, Peter walks off thinking that Ernie the giant chicken is finally dead, but at the last moment the camera pans to his lifeless body to show an eye dramatically cracking open, or the movement of a limb. To solidify these cut scenes as stream-of-consciousness meditations (or lack thereof), Peter always rejoins whatever conversation he was holding when he encountered Ernie, often in mid-sentence, acting as if the entire battle never happened. This, again, is a perfect example of how the form works by flowing naturally with the erratic patterns of the human thought process, and a perfect example of why reading *Family Guy* in this way is important. Yes, the fight with the giant chicken seems arbitrary. And it is. But arbitrariness is a staple of sitcoms, live action or animated. We typically don't realize the arbitrary nature of the sitcom until we are forced to see it (television is, after all, an escape for most of us). The giant chicken battles do just that. Once the battle is over and Peter returns to a scene mid-sentence, we must acknowledge that the story is unchanged by the absurd halt in action.

Perhaps it is the fact that *Family Guy* works so naturally with the human thought process that we find these vignettes to be so humorous. Critics might say that such comedy is forced, but, actually, the opposite is true. It is more difficult for our brains to follow the standard, unfalteringly linear structure of other sitcoms because they never allow our thought processes to occasionally derail, as they do naturally. *Family Guy* does allow that, and that makes it unique and very important. It, just like other sitcoms, follows a fairly linear path to a conclusion (and then the credits, of course). But for the benefit of our collective firing synapses, it meanders just like our brains do, and just like all great stream-of-consciousness works do.

These are but a few examples of how both *Family Guy*'s structure and its characters act to bring to life a text that can easily be read as stream of consciousness, even if it was originally written otherwise. And although unique to the medium, it is but one of the most recent works to use the ever-nebulous and in some ways ancient form of storytelling. Much like *Ulysses, Anna Karenina, The Garden of Cyrus, Metamorphosis,* and others that are quite different but tied with the stream-of-consciousness twine, *Family Guy* tells stories that are not obscure, but are rather quite grounded, or at least fundamentally and generally understood. It just does so in a way that breaks it from the traditional sitcom, animated or otherwise, much like M. C. Escher can take a flight of stairs and bend it on an impossible angle. It is still recognizable as a stair, but now it is quite obviously a stair through the eyes of the famous artist. In the case of *Family Guy,* the linear storylines are the stairs, and the artist—Seth MacFarlane— twists them with his wonderful vignettes.

The show remains a recognizable sitcom, but with a somewhat surreal and certainly eccentric study on stream of consciousness. It is almost like an experiment in which the audience is the object: Will the millions of viewers walk this broken stair? Fortunately for the series, they have, and have done so with much enthusiasm, making *Family Guy* one of the most successful animated television programs (and stream-of-consciousness texts) ever. And MacFarlane, like Faulkner or Woolf, continues to deliver a text that he has painstakingly crafted to an audience of millions to receive as a natural-flowing story with the occasional (although not unexpected) ninety-degree turn in the form of stream of consciousness. We, as the audience, make it what it is, and are therefore partially responsible for *Family Guy* being such an achievement artistically. And because the show adheres successfully to the "*can, not should*" ideal of storytelling while venturing into previously untapped territory with its audience interactivity, MacFarlane's *Family Guy* truly is one of the great modern texts.

Reading and Writing About a Laboratory

Brandon Brown

ENTER A SCIENTIFIC RESEARCH LABORATORY, and confront three levels of text: the linguistics, the success, and the humanity of specific science. All send coded messages to the studied reader.

Like any space inhabited by humans and technology, a science laboratory is a complicated place in which there are many levels of communication and grammar. By *scientific linguistics,* I simply mean the exact type of science conducted in that laboratory space. Organic or inorganic chemistry? Laser physics or condensed matter? Yeast genetics or mammalian cell cultures? These questions are akin to asking the language of a printed book. Italian or Spanish? Japanese or Korean? That's not a very interesting question—one could create a translation dictionary full of equipment types, fume-hood widths, pungent smells, and safety requirements. With a long enough compendium, any visitor could eventually learn to name the exact type of science at work. That kind of factual reading is useful, but is ultimately more limiting than looking beyond the superficial cues to interpret the interplay of work and accomplishment.

Reading success presents a subtler task. Is this research team bringing in grants? Are they publishing results at a good clip? Are they working intensely? On topics they believe to be important?

Key factors include activity, reading material, and the state of equipment. In a successful lab, people hustle more than lounge. Even if they crack wise with their lab mates, they do so while mixing solutions, labeling sample tubes, or recording numbers from recent measurements. The lab members sometimes ignore cell-phone rings. The laboratory hums—centrifuges, pumps, or agitators whir even when people are absent. When vacant, there is a tangible, "Oh, they just stepped out" feeling in the space. Several haphazard stacks of recent research articles should dot the horizontal surfaces, with notes and question marks scrawled in the margins. Equipment in the lab shines as if it was just removed from packaging. Stainless steel tubes gleam free of finger grease. Tiny red and green lights blink regularly.

Similarly, certain signs underline a stagnant lab culture, with scientists who are less than captivated by the questions they ask of nature. Although some ask the universe about its childhood or its sex life, others shrug, clear their throats and avoid eye contact with the divine. The room itself may smell strongly—mold from an untreated water leak, or a nose-twisting vapor from an organic solvent improperly contained. Lab notebooks lay open on a desk but look as though the pages haven't turned in months. People in the lab surf the web or play computer games. Other than the computers, chitchat, and perhaps music, there is little sound. On the walls and bulletin boards, data plots are rare in a sea of snowboarding or camping photos. Most of the equipment lies asleep, electronic eyes long closed, and a few cables snake unattached across the floor.

These readings are straightforward and should consume less than an hour. With more patience, a visitor can begin to read the humanity of a laboratory. Only an intensely curious and intrusive reader can hope to find this last text. The reader must be willing to linger and watch the inhabitants.

In approximately 400 years, the scientific enterprise has made little progress on recognizing the humanity of its practitioners. An unspoken veneer remains: the good scientist becomes a cold, objective robot when she conducts her experiments. Her facial expression and irrational thoughts disappear when she enters her laboratory. So forgive the space if only the most superficial elements of personal history and drama appear on your first inspection of a laboratory. You will always encounter a few photos of family and friends, an obligatory drawing from a child. In the less familial graduate students, workspaces include sub-pop-culture images and references—ironically bad television series or some such. But start poking around. Laboratories possess rich narratives of both competition and also awkward scientific adolescence.

The waters of intellectual ownership run murky and turbulent through a lab's culture. Not only does one lab member rush an experiment, hoping to complete and publish the work before rival scientists in other labs, but the boundaries of discovery can also smear within a single laboratory. Two geneticists start on separate problems but quickly find themselves examining the same gene—it happens to control two completely different things. Because an entire career rests on owning specific ideas and breakthroughs, emotions can flare far beyond the robotic scientific ideal. An observer may notice two people who intentionally turn away from one another, even in groups. One lab member may close her notebook quickly when the rival enters the lab. The process is entirely human. Identical situations could create a fast friendship and collaboration for one set of personalities, whereas other versions fester and swell until a new company and a university do legal battle over what once sat in a petri dish, between two sets of eyes.

Although tensions among equals can involve enormous stakes, the most poignant drama in a research lab replays parent–child separation. A graduate student moves steadily from admiration and respect for an advisor, through a realization that the advisor is imperfect, to eventually craving solo flight from the nest and an unfurling of her science wings. Each student–advisor relationship evolves uniquely, but for the students, their experience is more about their biological parents than their new intellectual parent. Was the student a wild child in high school? Watch to see if she deviates from her advisor's instructions for the next experiments. Or perhaps the student had a more obedient stance for his parents, oozing passive resentment. This young scientist complains openly in the lab when the advisor is absent, questioning the advisor's work habits, focus, or even wardrobe. Yet there are those who enjoyed famous friendships with mom and dad growing up. These students still call their parents regularly and enjoy a breezy open dialogue with their advisors in most cases.

In the end, a laboratory presents several major elements of a written text. Science sets the story in fluorescent lighting, with the humming of equipment, and inevitable clutter. Plastic wrap, notebooks, glass vials, cables, and computer disks coat the laboratory. An observer can quickly learn to recognize the language of the place. By turning a few pages in the first chapter, an experienced reader gets a sense of whether the narrative has quality, whether the writing is exceptional or amateur. And by carefully spending some time with the text, the reader enjoys character development. Dramatic scenes come to life, full of humor, remorse, and romance.

The omnipresent theme of obsession fills a lab. The obsession can spring from intense curiosity or desperation, appearing romantic or creepy. It can gaze serenely at a scientific problem with an adoration tempered by experience, or it can stare with foolish and feverish puppy love, destined for heartbreak. The obsession can be rewarded with discovery or rejected with inconclusive data and failed experiments. But it unifies the laboratories, drawing the characters from one chapter to the next.

Reading and Writing About YouTube: The You in YouTube

Catherine Zimmer

WHEN *TIME* MAGAZINE CHOSE TO DECLARE "You" their Person of the Year for 2006, their cover presented this choice with a square reflective material intended to offer the reader back to him- or herself at the same time that it indicated a computer screen.

Of course, the Person of the Year was not, in fact, *me* (or *you*, for that matter). What *Time* referred to was the rise of YouTube, the Internet video-sharing site that revolutionized the dispersal, and thus, in many ways production, of digital moving images. *Time* chose YouTube as not only representative of that particular website (and apparently, you), but also the larger arena of "peer production" or "consumer-generated content" characteristic of websites from YouTube to Wikipedia to MySpace.[1] Implicit in *Time*'s selection of You/YouTube/etc. as "person" of the year is the question of how much Internet users are themselves present in YouTube versus how much that site and the culture surrounding the Internet have already defined the persona of the "you" in YouTube (as well as other related sites). In other words, to what degree is our self-presentation via this website influenced or even determined by the technological, economic, and cultural milieux of YouTube? Arguably, despite the fact that a peer-produced website such as this provides a platform for "anybody" to share or view a diversity of video works, YouTube ultimately reflects the possibilities and limitations of the Internet market as much as, if not more than, it reflects "you."

The site's very name indicates the manner in which we must begin to consider the history and stakes of YouTube as a media environment. The "tube" seems to be a clear reference to one of the core televisual technologies: the cathode ray tube.[2] This tube was the primary element in the display, but not production, of both television and video images.[3] In other words, the cathode ray tube was the central technology literally behind the screen of your television monitor; "the tube" eventually became common slang for television. This did not, however, carry a particularly positive connotation. The added designation of "boob tube" to the term suggested a moronic dependence on television, an attitude that was in large part a result of the kinds of media critics that arose with the television era—most significantly, Marshall McLuhan. McLuhan's fa-

---

[1] Lev Grossman, "*Time*'s Person of the Year: You," *Time* December 13, 2006, http://www.time.com/time/magazine/article/0,9171,1569514,00.html (accessed July 2, 2007).

[2] Although if YouTube had not emerged the year before Congressman Ted Stevens infamously declared the Internet to be a "series of tubes," we might also read the site's name as an ironic commentary on the (mis)characterization of the Internet by legislative bodies.

[3] The distinction between television and video technologies is a vague one at best, because they are interrelated, but suffice it to say for now that the specificity of television has to do with the transmission of the television signal, whereas video seems to refer more to the magnetic tape technology on which video images were recorded in the era before they were immediately converted to digital information.

mous quote that "The medium is the message" has gained renewed attention in the digital era, when the content of our media seems increasingly informed by the manners in which that content can be produced and delivered technologically.[4] In other words, what we might find on the Internet is at times only marginally as important as the fact that we might be able to get that information on the new Apple iPhone.

Thus, YouTube, by virtue of its very name, as well as its base in a highly technologized media culture, seems to want to cast itself as both in the tradition of television entertainment, "the tube," and as a departure—this departure apparently constituted by the "you" in YouTube. So who, and what, is the "you"? If the tube is the form, is the "you" the content? Not exactly. Quite simply, the idea is that one

can find virtually anything on YouTube. Anything, everything, and conceivably, nothing people might want to see is available on YouTube—crucially, this content is entirely uploaded by users. YouTube thus markets itself as user-generated media, as truly democratic entertainment, information, and artistry. But, to what degree is this possible? Home videos are indeed a staple, particularly humorous videos, music, or stunts. In addition, you can find snippets of previously broadcast/published materials, such as clips of television shows that have become topics of conversation, or materials that are re-edited/digitally manipulated (these manipulations of existing material are a mainstay of digital audiovisual culture). Where else can one go to find a video of a housecat nursing an orphaned chipmunk, followed by a Duran Duran video from 1984, followed by a clandestine recording of Lindsay Lohan falling down drunk? It is also a simple matter to either "embed" the video stored on YouTube into an alternate website, or to link to YouTube from other sites. This is all to say that the premier site for video on the Internet *produces no content* itself—it is simply the platform for storage and dispersal.

It is this element that seems to suggest a you-ness to the system. In a television era in which, despite the proliferation of channels, media outlets are increasingly controlled by very few multinational media conglomerates, a democratizing resource such as YouTube and the other sites championed by *Time* in their cover story would seem to suggest that the peer-produced quality of the Internet is the most significant site of resistance to the kinds of entertainment and information control that have tended to characterize television, the original tube. Certainly, there is a

---

[4] McLuhan began to elaborate this concept in his book *Understanding Media: The Extensions of Man*, originally published in 1964 by McGraw-Hill, New York.

kind of "wild" element to both YouTube and the Internet at large—an "anything is possible" attitude that contrasts starkly with the sense of entrenchment, repetitiveness, and powerlessness that seems to reign broadly over other American media and political arenas. But despite the characterization of Internet media intervention as an uncontained organic force, I think we are still hard pressed to determine where the "you" is that has some sort of power in this environment.

A casual survey of the YouTube site reveals a mixture of self-produced video and material captured from already produced work. Any small video produced can catch hold of a wide Internet audience. Your video could gain international notoriety within a couple of days if your YouTube contribution gets taken up by any number of popular referring sites, such as Digg or BoingBoing. These videos are then forwarded between individuals ("Check out the video of this drummer I found on YouTube!"). Literally millions of people could see your video of your talented skateboarding dog. And despite the fact that I am using the more amusement-based, inconsequential examples of YouTube possibilities, there is the theoretical implication here that a talented filmmaker could gain a foothold in the popular imagination and eventually in the media industry without necessarily operating within the traditional power structures of the entertainment industry. Political interventions could be made on this site, as they have been on others, by providing alternative sources of news and a wider reach for activism and organizing. Thus, YouTube would seem, as a neutral web platform for video, to have endless possibilities for the democratization of media and the leveling of the information playing field.

A notable example of the kind of intervention possible via YouTube is the (in)famous video of former Senator George Allen from the 2006 election (dubbed "The YouTube Election" by *The New York Times*).[5] The video shows Allen during his reelection campaign, at a small speaking engagement, twice using the word *macaca*, a racial slur (http://youtube.com/watch?v=r90z0PmnKwI). The video was posted on YouTube, where it "rocketed to the top of the site's most viewed list."[6] It was then picked up by larger print and broadcast media; Allen eventually lost the election, despite having been favored to win. Obviously, the exposure of the Virginia senator's racism was a coup for the opponent's campaign, and it was, in fact, no accident: The video was recorded by a student working for Allen's opponent. Even more remarkable was the fact the racial slur was not just recorded by, but directed at the student recording the video. This student thus produced (through both his presence at and his recording of the event) and distributed an amateur video that constituted him as a very potent "you" on YouTube.

The form of the video itself suggests ways that we can understand the action and power of this "you." After a straightforward introductory title providing the senator's name, the name of the event, and the date and location, the video is simply an approximately one-minute recording of a moment from the event in which Allen points directly at the camera and refers to the man recording him as *macaca*, later repeating the word and saying, "Welcome to America." There is no commentary, editing, or anyone else visible within the frame of the video, seeming to allow the material to speak for itself and suggesting a lack of manipulation of the image and thus of the viewer. The camera is clearly handheld, shaking somewhat and zooming rather inexpertly. Positioned slightly below the eyeline of Allen, the video is presented to us as recorded by an "average person," a "you," a spectator at the Allen event. As viewers of the video, we are thus looking from the position of that student (through his "eyes" as it were), and when George Allen points at the young man holding the camera

---

[5] Ryan Lizza, "The YouTube Election," *The New York Times* (August 20, 2006).
[6] *Ibid.*

and demeans him racially, he is also pointing at *us*, putting us in a position to perhaps feel personally attacked by his comments, whatever our racial background might be. Thus, beyond simply providing a record of the senator's racism, we might see that the amateur structuring of the video itself encourages political action by creating a community of "yous."

And yet, it also seems reasonable to suggest at this point, despite this moment of apparent intervention, and despite *Time*'s cover story, that the democratization of media via the Internet, and the accompanying political possibilities, has not undermined the power of the larger media machine; despite the proliferation of "you" on the Internet, there does not seem to be any threat to the existing and overarching structures in place in both media and politics.[7] The Allen video, after all, only became what is considered "news" after it was picked up by newspapers and broadcast news shows—the established media outlets. Furthermore, it is not inconsequential that the student was working for the Democratic opponent of George Allen, and even if the video did influence the outcome of the election, that election was still defined by the *de facto* two-party system in place in the United States.

The fact is that we are living with what would seem to be a striking contradiction: the unparalleled democratizing power of information exchange on the Internet and the unprecedented centralization of media corporations. How can we explain why these two seemingly opposite situations co-exist fairly easily? One primary thing we must recognize is that YouTube and the Internet at large, although radical in their seeming existence as pure space that anyone might occupy with whatever they like, do not exist outside of an already present global economy. Despite the frequent characterization of the Internet as a free non-space of endless possibility for everyone, it is in fact a very real material space composed of technologies to which access is limited by social circumstances and a market economy. The Internet is *not* an alternate universe where all may play freely—it is part of the material world in which we live, and both the problems and the pleasures of that world find their place there. After all, when you go to YouTube you are as much surrounded by paid advertisements as you are by democratic content. And although the videos might be user-generated, everything from the software that makes them viewable to the established categories of video on the site are out of your hands. The idealism surrounding the Internet on the part of both the public and some media theorists thus comes up against a wall when we encounter the realities of the way technologies are deployed. Although it is certainly—and thankfully—true that the Internet has dispersed the control of information, and the possibility for creative distribution has thus greatly increased, to suggest that the Internet is entirely free of the economic and ideological constraints of the rest of media culture would be naive.

Beyond this general point that we cannot entirely separate the functioning of YouTube from other media outlets, it is instructive to return to some of the terminology with which we began in discussing the "tube" and the "you," and in that way to return to our initial investigation of what and who is presented/represented on YouTube. For instance, when a video (or, in fact, any item) takes hold and achieves a certain reach on the Internet, it is said to have "gone viral." Some websites even have a category for "viral videos." This is certainly not the first time

---

[7] Even the intensive restructuring of music distribution forced by Napster, Limewire, and other file-sharing sites has been relatively reabsorbed unclear into a corporate economy via Apple iTunes, Verizon VCAST, and others that take advantage of the new possibilities of digital music sales. This is not to deny that the digitally aided rebellion did, indeed, lower music prices and allow independent artists increased possibility for distribution; merely that although some of the players have changed and positions have shifted, the game remains the same in many significant ways.

that the idea of the "virus" has been used in relation to computer culture—obviously, it is the term most frequently used to describe computer code that makes its way into your computer system and breaks down certain elements of its functionality. The rhetoric of virus, infection, bugs, and so on, is prevalent here. What the notion of the viral video has done is reframe the thinking about infection in terms of the positive possibility of the Internet. Used to connote the infectious quality of certain Internet items that come and go like a brief hysteria, a viral video is generally very short, and usually has an immediate effect of great hilarity, amazement, or shock. In this way, viral videos, in both their short length and generally nonnarrative nature, can be broadly compared to the earliest forms of motion pictures, what Tom Gunning famously dubbed "the cinema of attractions."[8] In many ways, this is not a new form of entertainment, but a very old one, in which motion pictures were initially enjoyed in the same way as a brief circus attraction or magic trick, rather than immersed as one would be in a novel and later a narrative film (not that these need to be considered necessarily mutually exclusive). A recent example, "Dramatic Chipmunk" (http://youtube.com/watch?v=a1Y73sPHKxw), first picked up by Digg and then Gigglesugar, swept the Internet in days, and within a week had undergone at least five video incarnations as it made its rounds.[9]

But it is the characterization of the distribution of these works as "viral" that can be our best indicator of both their possibilities and limitations. As I note earlier, Internet media have the strength of an organic force, but what does it mean if that force is one characterized as microbial and infectious, rather than as that of a thinking, speaking, human subject? What I would like to suggest is that the organizing models of digital culture is both organic and dehumanizing at the same time. The "you" in YouTube begins as the human subject who places a video online, but only emerges as an Internet entity in the form of an infectious agent. Within traditional thinking, we might be asked to mourn this loss of the originary "human" subject in the rise of an Internet presence, but perhaps we should instead ask what we might gain by embracing both YouTube's and our own status as carriers of infection. If a virus is, arguably, the most powerful organism on Earth, we might look into what is to be gained by infecting certain systems (cultural, computer, political, and otherwise) with ourselves—and our creative productions—as viruses.

However, this characterization of the individual dispersal of media on the Internet as viral also carries with it a notion of a thoughtless, instinctive, parasitic, and thus wholly unethical existence. If we are again to ask why there has not been a media overhaul given the incredible possibility of YouTube and its like, I argue that it is partly because despite the great power inherent in the metaphor of the virus, the virus seems unable to have a political or social conscience. Its purpose is merely to reproduce itself—thus, the elements that "go viral" tend to be things that we consider relatively innocuous and without an agenda: kittens, songs, jokes. Indeed, one video, significantly to be found on an *alternate* video site, glumbert, parodizes the rise and fall of a viral Internet sensation: Mustard Face Dancing Guy (http://www.glumbert.com/media/internetsens).[10] As this video aptly points out, those things that go viral are often so completely arbitrary that they defy any reasonable explanation for their appeal beyond that very randomness. Thus, it seems reasonable to suggest that these are things that both we and the Internet are happy to serve as carriers because they seemingly propose no threat to the system at large. What seems clear is that if the ambiguous "you" in YouTube is to become the piv-

---

[8] I am indebted to my student, Tucker Dyer, at Pace University for initially pointing out the similarity between YouTube and the cinema of attractions to me.

[9] Accessed July 3, 2007.

[10] Accessed July 2, 2007.

otal player in Internet culture in a way that truly has effects on systems of media, one must consider the ways in which one's participation in that system is being offered and characterized, and how that characterization to a certain degree already positions your place in that system and your contributions to it. Viruses, after all, must mutate if they are going to progress.

Reading and Writing About Advertising: Two Case Studies

Dean Rader and Jonathan Silverman

YOU PROBABLY ENCOUNTER ADVERTISEMENTS on a daily basis. On television, on the radio, in magazines, on the Web, and now even at the movies, we confront advertisements in almost every aspect of our lives. Researchers suggest we see between 100 and 300 advertisements per day, whereas it would be unusual if you were to read 100 poems in an entire year. What's more, most experts agree that the American public believes or is open to at least one advertisement out of every eight that it sees. That may not sound like much, but if you see 100 ads per day for 365 days, that's 36,500 ads per year. If researchers are correct, then you probably believe or consider at least 4,562 commercials per year. Think that's a lot? Consider this: The average nineteen-year-old has probably been paying attention to advertisements for about thirteen years. So, if these estimates are correct, most nineteen-year-old Americans have taken into their consciousness and devoted some aspect of their reasoning ability to more than 59,000 ads over the course of their lifetime. If you are nineteen, then you have likely seen more than 450,000 ads. By the time you are thirty, it's probable that more than one million ads have made their way into your brain.

By now, it is a cliché to claim that ads sell an image, but . . . ads sell an image. They not only sell images of us and their products, but also of a culture. In advertiser's lingo, this is called the "promise." Ads make promises to people all the time, but they tend to be implied or suggested promises. When you read an advertisement, ask yourself what kind of promise the ad is making to you. In addition, ads also work to cultivate another image—their own. This is why so many companies are very protective of their names, trademarks, and product use. For instance, you may be familiar with the court case in which Mattel toys sued the rock band Aqua over a critical song about "Barbie." And, in an example closer to home, we were denied permission from Tommy Hilfiger to reprint the advertisement we describe later—even after personal letters from the authors. We suspect Tommy was worried about what our reading might do to their branding. So, keep in mind that although ads may be funny, informative, and persuasive, they also help promote the company's image.

Thus, reading the image that a company tries to cultivate is all part of the larger experience of reading an advertising text. It would appear that many advertisers worry about how we might *use* their ads. Understandably, they are concerned about how their ad, their product, their image might look out of context. So, because so much of advertising is about branding, where an ad appears is as important as the ad itself. Sadly, that means we must *describe* the ad, rather than provide it. At press time, the ad appeared as the first image on the following Web site: http://lime.mediacorppublishing.com/2000-07/win.htm.

We have chosen a widely published Tommy Hilfiger ad that features six young, handsome/ beautiful, smiley people (two white men, two black men, a white woman, and a black woman) lounging around in red, white, and blue Hilfiger clothes on the expansive front lawn of a country home. The large house stands in the right corner of the photo, and in the upper left corner of the photo, a big American flag waves just over the left shoulder of one of the models. Advertising Tommy cologne, the ad's tag line reads in large white letters along the bottom, "tommy: the real american fragrance."

When we began to read this ad so that we could write about it (the same process you will engage in), we asked ourselves, *What textual cues are in the ad?* Here is what we saw: In this ad for Tommy Hilfiger cologne, all the people in the photograph are young, well scrubbed, and attractive. And they are happy! Now, what about the setting of the photograph? Where does it take place? It appears to be a rural area, perhaps a country club or a farmhouse in New England. What other textual cues or signs do you see? In this ad, we see a large American flag waving in the upper left corner of the ad. The text, "tommy: the real american fragrance," runs along the bottom fourth of the image, while a picture of the featured cologne balances the flag in the bottom right corner. Smaller than the American flag but similar to it, the Tommy Hilfiger logo hovers above the writing, but seems to be affixed to the White woman's body.

Then we asked ourselves, *How do we describe the appearance of the people in the ad?* How are they dressed? Well, for one thing, they are all wearing Tommy Hilfiger clothes. This tells us a lot. What is the demographic for Tommy Hilfiger clothes? Who buys them? Who hangs out in large, well-kept farmhouses in New England? Who spends time at a country club? The answer to all of these questions seems to be middle-class or upper middle-class White Americans, although the ad suggests that Tommy Hilfiger clothes and cologne appeal to a plurality of people—perhaps even that Tommy clothes and cologne promise racial harmony, an upper middle-class lifestyle, *and* a good time.

But is this so? We decided to make a list of who or what is missing—what is *not* in this picture. Off the top of our heads, we came up with quite a list: people who look poor, anyone over 30, any sign of work (a briefcase, a shovel, a computer, a uniform), anyone who is even remotely overweight, a Mexican flag, a tenement building, any sign of anger, Native Americans, anything having to do with a city, any reference to a blue-collar or working-class situation, clothing other than Tommy Hilfiger, people who are unattractive, reading material such as books or a newspaper, and finally, any clue as to what these people are doing dressed in Tommy Hilfiger clothes out in the country. What message does the absence of these things send? Is this ad suggesting something about the role of these things in the "real America"? We don't know exactly, but by asking these questions we might come closer to understanding not only the ad, but also the culture from which it comes and the culture it tries to sell. Advertisers use various techniques to get us to respond to their ads, most of which involve making the viewer feel desired, accepted, important, or exclusive. What individual techniques does this ad use to make us feel these things? The flag? The pretty, happy people sitting close together? The sense of affluence suggested by the large house out in the country? The sense of racial harmony evoked by the people of various ethnicities laughing together? Now, when you combine all of these cues, what is the overall argument or promise of the ad? Take this one step further: What does this text suggest about how Tommy Hilfiger, the company, sees itself? And, what does this text suggest about how Tommy Hilfiger, the company, sees America? Does this version of America mesh with your own? Does this version of America reflect mainstream American values?

Although we ended up with more questions than answers here, finding what questions to ask helps us understand the text we're looking at. In more general terms, learning how to read advertisements not only makes you more aware about companies and how they market their products and themselves, but also how mainstream advertising and media outlets create a vision or even a myth of our culture. What's more (and perhaps at this moment, most important to you), learning how to read advertisements, poems, and public spaces helps you write better papers, as the reading process is fundamentally linked to the writing process.

While preparing the manuscript for this new edition, we were tempted to take out the previous reading of the Tommy ad, but we like the ad so much—we still don't know why we were denied permission—we thought we'd keep it and augment this section with a shorter semiotic reading of an ad that we could actually get permission to print. But we were denied permission here, too. The ad is part of the Soft-N-Dri "Strong and Beautiful" campaign.

Chances are, you would have noticed the same things we did. An attractive White woman (blonde), dressed in skimpy tight pink clothes, work gloves, and a pink gimme cap stands rather defiantly in front of a big, black (and rather menacing) semi-truck. Over the windshield, again in pink, are the words, "PRINCESS OF THE OPEN ROAD," and lower, in the middle of the page, where her legs would begin to show, her body is cut off by the black page. Over the line separating the text from the image are the words "STRONG & BEAUTIFUL," with the "strong" in white and the "beautiful" in pink.

Rather than walk you through this ad, we'll give you the questions we asked:

- Why did the ad folks put the model in pink? What does pink suggest?
- Why a semi-truck?
- Why a black semi-truck?
- Why is she wearing work gloves (leather) and a hat? Why aren't the gloves pink?
- Look closely at the model's body. What is different about her body from the body of a woman or girl you might see in a Calvin Klein or Victoria's Secret ad?
- Also, what do you notice about her features? Her facial expression?
- Given the fact that this deodorant features a "power stripe," why are her gloves and the truck important?
- Is it *clear* which is strong and which is beautiful—the truck or the model?
- How about the text copy at the bottom—what do you make of the use of the phrase "long haul"?
- This is a more delicate question, but how would the ad be different with an Asian model? An African-American model? A man dressed in pink?
- Do you think there is any relation between the whiteness of the model and the fact that the word "strong" is also in white? Why wouldn't it be the same color as the truck?
- Is this an effective ad? Is is sexist? What makes it effective or sexist? Could it be both?

Now it's time to read an ad yourself. Open any magazine and see how advertisers try to "sell" anything.

Based on our answers to these questions, we can then move on to the work of writing the essay. Remember that it is okay if you don't know what a text means right away, or if you don't know what you want to argue about that text. Persistent, careful, and insightful semiotic observations eventually lead you to the door of writing.

READING WRITING

This Text: Reading

1. What approach unifies these essays? In what ways are these pieces consistent, despite very different topics?

2. Pick three or four of the essays in this chapter and try to identify the "lens" each of the authors uses to read their particular text.
3. Each of these essays is relatively *persuasive*; that is, each is an argumentative essay that asserts a thesis. Look at the essays by Peter Hartlaub, Catherine Zimmer, and Cristina DeLuca—all three read video-based texts. How are their theses similar? Different?
4. Look at the first two essays by Silverman and Rader. Both incorporate semiotics to make sense of public space. What similarities do you see between their two approaches?
5. What is Elisabeth Piedmont-Marton's main argument in her essay on fashion?
6. Brandon Brown's essay on reading a science lab is not really like any other piece in this chapter. Traditionally, such spaces are not particularly concerned with décor, but Brown argues that such spaces are rich texts. Is his argument compelling? Why or why not?
7. Think of a few nontraditional texts. Now imagine these authors tackling the subjects. How would these various essays be different under these authors? How would they be different from the way you would want to approach these subjects?

Your Text: Writing
1. Find a readable text that is part of the world around you. Ask a series of questions about it the way Rader and Silverman do toward the end of their co-authored essay on advertising. Based on the questions and the answers to them, build a thesis and write a persuasive paper on your text.
2. Write a comparison paper on two of the essays in this chapter. Pick essays that differ either in style (Brown and Transue; Hartlaub and Zimmer) or in subject matter (Hartlaub and Brown; Piedmont-Marton and Silverman) and argue for a similar way of unpacking a text.
3. Write an essay in which you compare and contrast Rader's essay on campus signs and Frances Halsbland's essay on college campuses and public space in Chapter 7 concerning public and private spaces. How do the two authors approach campus space?
4. Gather photos you have taken in a day or on trip or even in a family scrapbook. Now try to write a paper that ties them together.
5. Find a text you want to explore. Instead of beginning writing right away, list at least five ways you might approach the text. Then, choose one approach to the text and begin drafting or freewriting!

READING BETWEEN THE LINES

Classroom Activities
1. Spend 10–15 minutes "reading" your classroom. Pay attention to details you might not normally notice—paint color, décor, windows, ceiling height, flooring, even the size and comfort of your desk or table. What visual cues about the classroom help the room "make an argument?"
2. A good homework assignment is for everyone to come to class having read someone else's dorm room. Why do we personalize our space? It's pretty easy to get an idea of someone's personality by intentional cues (Barack Obama posters, Dave Matthews Band cds, lots of philosophy books, posters of women in bikinis on Porches), but what about *unintentional* cues?
3. One of the author's favorite classroom activities is to take his class outside and have them read the semiotics of the Lone Mountain gate and stairway at the University of San

Francisco (see pages 76–82). Go outside and read various constructed spaces on your campus. What arguments do those spaces make?

4. Read the logo and team mascot of your college or university.

5. Do some research and see if your college has done any local or national advertising on radio, television or the Internet. Do a semiotic reading of the ads. Or, look at the college's recruiting materials and read those. What sorts of arguments is the college making about itself?

6. Next time you drive to campus or from campus, read the road. Look at normally ignored details—billboards, landscaping, guardrails, streetlights, fences, and signs. What feeling do you get? In what way are the areas along roads constructed texts? Is there disagreement in class about such spaces' "beauty" or "utility?"

7. Does your town or city have an official logo? Does it have official branding? If so, track it down and do a collaborative in-class reading of your city's visual branding? Does the message it sends mesh with your reading of the city?

8. Watch a YouTube video in class. Talk about the video as a constructed text. Does watching a video on YouTube differ from watching the same clip on TV? How? Why?

9. Locate and old map of your town/city and a new one. Read them side-by-side. What do you see? What information do the maps have? Or, find old and new postcards of your town. What has changed besides the obvious?

Essay Ideas

When reading the world around you, literally, the entire globe is your textbook, so feel free to look at things you never have before in ways that are totally new. Here are just a fraction of the options available to you.

1. Write an essay on any of the topics above. Do some research and be sure to use a lot of specific detail.

2. Write a comparison/contrast essay in which you read a science lab and an art studio. What are the similarities? Differences? How do the regular users of the spaces "brand" their rooms?

3. If you can, revisit one of your high school classrooms. Take some photos of it. Now, write an essay comparing your high school classroom with a typical college classroom. What stays the same? What changes? Are there semiotic texts that scream " high school" or "college?" If so, what and how?

4. Write a paper on the various forms of transportation in a college parking lot. Look at cars, SUVs, bikes, motorcycles, and scooters. What does the aggregate tell you about the demographic of your school? Do we tend to associate certain types of people with specific modes of transportation? If so, why? And what are the associations?

5. Write an essay on what you think are three new or interesting fashion trends: tattoos, a haircut, a kind of jean, a hip T-shirt, or the popularity of flip-flops. Give a semiotic reading of each fashion trend and explain what message the wearer intends to send by donning that accessory.

6. Write a comparison/contrast paper in which you read your university's dining hall and your favorite local restaurant. What is similar? What's different? Does your dining hall do anything to try to approximate a restaurant?

7. Give a semiotic reading of some space in your dorm/residence hall. Maybe you read all of the material on dorm room doors on your hall; maybe you read all of the notices and ads on a bulletin board; maybe you read the main entryway; or, maybe you give a semiotic reading of a bathroom on your floor.

Dude's gotta have his Teletubbies.

YOU MAY BE SURPRISED BY HOW MUCH YOU ALREADY KNOW ABOUT *READING* TELEVISION AS OPPOSED TO *WATCHING* TELEVISION. FOR EXAMPLE, YOU NO DOUBT KNOW THE STRUCTURE OF SITCOMS, TALK SHOWS, AND SPORTING EVENTS. YOU KNOW ABOUT THE PROBABLE AUDIENCES OF THESE PARTICULAR SHOWS, AND YOU PROBABLY KNOW SOMETHING ABOUT PLOT DEVICES AND LAUGH TRACKS, AND THE WAY TELEVISION NETWORKS SPREAD OUT AND TIME COMMERCIALS.

The fact that you are familiar with television shows is more help than hindrance when writing about them. But watching television is different than reading television. Watching is passive; reading is active. Take, for example, the act of reading a traditional text such as a poem or a short story. When reading these texts, they force us to confront and unlock their meanings. We read passages over and over and think about the way writers arrange words as well as more general concerns such as theme and plot. And we are taught to think about what short stories mean. Yet when we watch television, we rarely attend to these concerns. Most of us have been watching television since we were small children, with little guidance on how to watch; our parents, our friends, and newspapers and magazines may tell us what we can and should watch, but once we get in front of the television, we tend to let the show dictate our response without our interaction. To understand television, we must learn to question the structure and content of television shows as well as the presence and absence of ideas, people, and places. And so when watching television, consider a number of things.

The structure of television encourages passive viewing.

When we read a book or magazine or newspaper, the text is in our hands. We can start and stop reading whenever we want to; we can reread at our convenience. We can underline these texts and make notes on them. We can, of course, take this particular text with us on the bus, to the bathroom, or to the coffee shop. However, when we watch television, we are already physically disconnected from the text. Unless we have an iPhone or some small, portable television, we cannot pick it up, and worse, we cannot mark it up. Only recently have we been able to control its flow with a remote control. But even when we watch with the remote control, there is a laugh track telling us not only when but how to laugh, commercial interruptions telling us to wait, and familiar plot conventions telling us to respond in predictable ways.

Furthermore, various aspects of modern life contribute to a consumption of television that is not particularly critical. For instance, it's likely that your home lends itself to passive television watching. Most people arrange their dens so that the TV is the center of the room and focal point when they sit down. And, after a long day of work, there is often something comforting about settling down in front of the television for an episode of *The Family Guy*, a baseball game, or a movie. Our architecture, our work, and our home lives facilitate thinking of the act of watching television as an act of disengagement.

Are networks and television producers conspiring to have us watch this way? Some of television's harsher critics would say yes, but others might view television as a form of escape from the realities of modern life or even as educational. In either case, we can better understand television by watching a show with critical engagement, taking notes, and if possible, rewatching the show before sitting down to write about it.

Unlike works of literature, television shows have no recognizable author.

When we pick up a book, we know who has written it—the name of the author is usually displayed as prominently as the title. Once we know who has authored a book, we can use this information accordingly. Traditionally, when scholars study written texts, they often focus on the words on the page, the symbols, the themes, and the plot contained within, but many also use the life of the author and the author's other texts to gain a deeper understanding of a particular text. Although modern scholars have diminished the power of authorial reputation, the author, even if less important to scholars, still exists and may exist most profoundly for readers.

Who authors less traditional texts is not always clear. In movies, for example, we have two, and sometimes three people, to whom to attach authorship: the screenwriter, the director, and sometimes either the producer or cinematographer; in architecture, sometimes an entire firm serves as the author of a building.

In television, even more so than movies, there is no discernable author. We might consider the show's writers to be the authors, but as you well know, writing is only a small part of a visual text. There are the various settings, the clothing the actors wear, and the angles cameras use. In addition, we never know quite who has composed a particular show. There are writers listed, but we also hear stories about actors writing their own lines, as well as the presence of ad-libbed material. In addition, unlike authors of their own works who are responsible for virtually all of the production of the text (except, of course, for the book itself), the producers of a television show do not have the same direct connection to the texts they construct. They often play defining roles in shaping elements of the text that we can also make use of—the casting, the setting, the themes, even who technically writes the show—but do not do the writing, the set construction or the casting themselves.

So the question is, how do we (or can we) refer to a show's author? One way is to refer to the show's *authors,* and use as a possibility for discussion what the presence of group authorship means to a particular text as opposed to discussing a single author. In any case, the question of authorship is one large difference between television and more traditional texts.

Television shows are character driven, genre based, and plot oriented.

Television shows are much more genre driven than the traditional texts we read. Whereas literature contains a number of different types of forms, many of which do not fit into a particular genre, television shows operate almost exclusively within genres. A **genre** is a type of medium with established and expected formulas and devices. Romances and Westerns are prime examples of novel genres. Most works of fiction that critics consider to be literary do not fit into a particular category of novel such as romances, Westerns, and science fiction, and it's rare that a literature class discusses works from these categories. Literary critics often consider them to be formulaic, with easily predicted plots. In recent years, critics have begun to study these works more carefully, but their interest in such texts has probably not often made it into your classroom.

Television, however, is all about genre. Dramas, comedies, action shows, reality shows, or various hybrids like "dramedies," all have recognizable components. Traditional texts have these components as well, but in television shows, they are often omnipresent. We know what to expect from sitcoms, gritty police dramas, and shows about families. The fact that shows about hospitals, lawyers, and the police compose almost 80 percent of the hour-long dramas on prime-time network television speaks to the ubiquity of genre. One reason innovative programs like *The Days and Nights of Molly Dodd, Twin Peaks, Freaks and Geeks,* and *Wonderfalls* had short lives on television was because they could not be placed in any particular genre. Viewers didn't know how to watch them because they didn't know what to expect from them. One of the reasons television shows are neglected as a field of study in the college classroom is because they are genre oriented; if television shows were novels, we never would study them.

So in writing about television, we have to understand that in large part shows fall into a particular category. We may want to ask whether an individual show "transcends" the normal fare of that genre, as well as what conventions of that genre a particular show follows. Once we start thinking about genre, we might also think about how this might affect the audience's viewing experience.

The audience pays for its free television.

On its surface, network television appears to be free; however, on closer scrutiny, it turns out that we do pay for TV in a number of ways. First, we buy (and keep buying) more expensive television sets. Second, most Americans get their programming through monthly cable or satellite subscriptions that add up to between $300 and $800 per year. More people are subscribing to services like TIVO, which costs more money. Contrast the price of a TV set and cable with the fee of a library card, which is free, and TV may not seem like such a bargain.

These are direct costs that we remain aware of, for the most part. What we may not consider, however, are the indirect ways we pay for television. Instead of charging viewers to watch, television networks present commercials, paid for by advertisers. Advertisers, in turn, choose shows in which to advertise. Then, the price for those ads likely gets passed on to you in the purchase price of the items you buy.

But we pay for television in another way as well—with our time and attention. If you watch a commercial, then you are essentially paying for that program with your time.

Advertisers know this and plan accordingly. You can often tell what audience an advertiser thinks it is getting by watching its commercials. Because they in part are responsible for paying for a show, advertisers do play a role in what makes it to television, although the networks play a much larger role. If a show's content is considered controversial, advertisers may shy away, with the idea that it may lose potential customers who attach the advertisers to the show's content. If advertisers do not want to advertise with a show, the show may not survive.

The size of an audience may also play a factor in how we view the show. We might think about how a show geared toward appealing to millions differs from a novel, which often has (and can have) a more limited appeal. Television is entertainment for the masses, and its direct connection to commerce is another factor we have to look at when writing about it.

What is not there is often as important as what is.

What is not in a show is often as important as what is in it. For example, as Oprah Winfrey pointed out when the cast of *Friends* came on her show, there is no black "friend." Winfrey's observation raises another: What does the absence of minorities of any kind in a city of incredible diversity say about the creators of a show? (We can make the same comments about any number of sitcoms: see *Everyone Loves Raymond, Will and Grace, Frasier,* and *Seinfeld,* although *Seinfeld* is smart enough to talk about its relative whiteness.) The ethnicity of the casts may send a message about the target audience for the show, but also what kind of family, relationship, or group is considered "normal" or "cool." Unlike the 1970s, there are now a number of programs that feature people of color that are, in fact, written and perhaps even directed by people of color, which was rare even in the mid-1980s. Despite this notable improvement, many American groups get little or no representation on TV. For instance, as this book goes to press, there is no show that looks at Asian-American, Arab-American, or Native-American families, relationships, or culture on prime-time television. Whether it is people of a certain age, particular areas of the country or world, or specific jobs, many aspects of modern life do not appear on television.

When reading at sitcoms or other television shows, also note the presence or absence of traditional gender roles, realistic dialogue, and typical, real-time events. Looking for absence rather than presence is difficult, but rewarding; trying to understand what is missing often helps us understand the flaws of a show (or any text, for that matter).

Visual media have specific concerns.

Television is a decidedly more visual medium than more traditional texts, such as short stories and poems. Thus, we must take into account how a show looks as well as sounds. The visual presence comes most obviously in its setting. In some shows, the setting is crucial. In *Seinfeld,* for example, New York City drives a great deal of the plot. In *The Simpsons,* the midwestern averageness of Springfield often determines the issues the show addresses, sometimes explaining a character's actions. *Friends* is set in New York, but how much really is New York a "character" in the show (as opposed to in *Seinfeld,* for example)? We also might look at three other settings—the coffee shop, Rachel and Monica's apartment, and Joey and Chandler's apartment. Are they appropriate for people of their age and wealth? Are they particularly male or female? What does the coffee shop represent to these characters and the audience? And how come that sofa is never occupied by anyone else? *Grey's Anatomy* is the first television drama to have an African-American woman as the lead writer, and although there are black men and women in power positions in the show, Seattle's Seattle-ness feels more present than do issues of race.

You might also ask how the clothing of each cast member contributes to the audience member's idea of who and what the character is supposed to represent. On shows like *The King of Queens, The Bernie Mac Show, The Sopranos, Seinfeld, Friends, NYPD Blue,* and even *Oprah,* clothing plays a crucial role in what the audience is supposed to understand about the show's characters, or, in the case of *Oprah,* the host. Finally, you might ask how cameras are used and the colors that dominate the broadcast. Shows like *24* and *Alias* utilize hand-held cameras, ostensibly for a more realistic look. A soap opera uses close-ups held for a number of seconds before cutting away to another scene or commercial. The wonderful program *Arrested Development* incorporates fake flashbacks, home movies, and a voice-over narration by Ron Howard to create a homey yet disjunctive effect. What do these techniques say about the shows in which they appear? Overall, the visual elements are crucial to understanding some of the show's intended and unintended messages, and its distinction from more traditional texts.

Finding themes is easy, but finding meaningful ones is difficult.

Themes are the intended meanings that authors give their works. For example, a theme of Harper Lee's *To Kill a Mockingbird* would be that racism can interfere with justice, and this interference is highly destructive to a society's fabric. Every text has a theme, and whether we know it or not, we pick up on a text's thematics.

Of all the elements involved with watching television, theme is the most easily discerned and often the least interesting. Most often, television themes explore tolerance and patience and, above all, the problematic nature of jumping to conclusions. Although many critics sometimes justifiably complain about the violence of television shows, most shows favor right over wrong, happiness over sadness, lessons learned over lessons forgotten. Shows like *The Sopranos* and even *Seinfeld* play with these traditions, which is one reason critics tend to praise them. All in all, looking for a theme is often the easiest task a television reader has.

What's more difficult is trying to understand whether the television author(s) handled these lessons too simplistically or offensively, or at the expense of the quality of the show. In other words, does the theme take away from the show's other elements? In watching sitcoms, finding the theme is easy, but one must be careful. *The Simpsons,* for example, has a traditional television sitcom theme in many of its shows but often brutally satirizes American culture. So which message is more important? Clearly, what happens during the show matters more than what happens at its end, which the authors of *The Simpsons* often use to criticize the conventions of television itself.

Overall, the medium of television has a number of general concerns that play into our enjoyment as well as our critical stance. As a writer, you do not have to take all this into account, but thinking about them is a good way of breaking free of your traditional relationship to television. There are also more specific ways of analyzing a television show. Next, we give a list of questions you can ask of a television show.

THIS TEXT

1. How does the background of the authors influence their ideas about television?
2. Do the authors have different ideas about class, race, and gender, and their place in television? In what ways?
3. Although it is impossible for you to know this fully, try to figure out the writing situation of each author. Who is the audience? What does the author have at stake?
4. What is the writer's agenda? *Why* is she or he writing this piece?
5. What social, political, and cultural forces affect the author's text? What is going on in the world as he or she is writing?
6. What are the main points of the essay? Can you find a thesis statement anywhere?
7. How does the author support his or her argument? What evidence does he or she use to back up any claims he or she might make?
8. Is the author's argument valid and/or reasonable?
9. Do you find yourself in agreement with the author? Why or why not?
10. Does the author help you *read* television better (or differently) than you did before reading the essay? If so, why?
11. How is the reading process different if you are reading an essay as opposed to a short story or poem?
12. What is the author's agenda? Why does she or he want us to think a certain way?
13. Did you like this? Why or why not?
14. Do you think the author likes television?

BEYOND THIS TEXT: READING TELEVISION

Genre: What genre are we watching? How do the writers let us know this (visually, orally, etc.)?

Characters: Who are the characters? Do they represent something beyond actors in a plot? How do the writers want us to perceive them, and why? How would changing the characters change the show?

Setting: What are the settings? What do they say about the show? What do the writers want us to think about the setting? Could the show take place somewhere else and remain the same?

Plot: What happens? Is the plot important to understanding/enjoying the show?

Themes: What do the show's writers think about the issues/ideas/subjects they present? (*Themes* are what writers believe about issues, ideas, and subjects, *not* the ideas and issues themselves.)

Figurative language: What symbols, metaphors, and motifs present themselves in the show? What effect does their repetition have?

Visual/Audio constructions: How do the writers make us see (or hear) the show?

Absences: What is missing? What real-world notions are not represented in the show?

Conventional/nonconventional: In what ways is the show typical/atypical of its genre?

Race/ethnicity/gender/class: How do the writers talk (or not talk) about these issues? How do these issues show up in other categories we have mentioned, such as character, setting, plot, and theme?

Reality: In what way does what is depicted in a particular television show or on TV in general reflect the world as you normally experience it? What is different? Does this matter?

Life According to TV

Harry F. Waters

Harry Waters wrote this piece about television demographics for *Newsweek* in 1982. Although the article is mostly reportage, it does relay some of the assumptions about the world television viewers are exposed to. It also chronicles how many thought about television in the early 1980s—a time when most of you were not yet born. Have things changed in terms of how we read TV as we approach 2010? In what sense do you think Gerbner's observations remain true?

You people sit there, night after night. You're beginning to believe this illusion we're spinning here. You're beginning to think the tube is reality and your own lives are unreal. This is mass madness!

—Anchorman Howard Beale in the film *Network*

If you can write a nation's stories, you needn't worry about who makes its laws. Today television tells most of the stories to most of the people most of the time.

—George Gerbner, Ph.D.

THE LATE PADDY CHAYEFSKY, who created Howard Beale, would have loved George Gerbner. In *Network,* Chayefsky marshaled a scathing, fictional assault on the values and methods of the people who control the world's most potent communications instrument. In real life, Gerbner, perhaps the nation's foremost authority on the social impact of television, is quietly using the disciplines of behavioral research to construct an equally devastating indictment of the medium's images and messages. More than any spokesman for a pressure group, Gerbner has become the man that television watches. From his cramped, book-lined office at the University of Pennsylvania springs a steady flow of studies that are raising executive blood pressures at the networks' sleek Manhattan command posts. George Gerbner's work is uniquely important because it transports the scientific examination of television far beyond familiar children-and-violence arguments. Rather than simply studying the link between violence on the tube and crime in the streets, Gerbner is exploring wider and deeper terrain. He has turned his lens on TV's hidden victims—women, the elderly, blacks, blue-collar workers and other groups—to document the ways in which video-entertainment portrayals subliminally condition how we perceive ourselves and how we view those around us. Gerbner's subjects are not merely the impressionable young; they include all the rest of us. And it is his ominous conclusion that heavy watchers of the prime-time mirror are receiving a grossly distorted picture of the real world that they tend to accept more readily than reality itself.

The 63-year-old Gerbner, who is dean of Penn's Annenberg School of Communications, employs a methodology that meshes scholarly observation with mundane legwork. Over the past 15 years, he and a tireless trio of assistants (Larry Gross, Nancy Signorielli and Michael Morgan) videotaped and exhaustively analyzed 1600 prime-time programs involving more than 15,000 characters. They then drew up multiple-choice questionnaires that offered correct answers about the world at large along with answers that reflected what Gerbner perceived to be the misrepresentations and biases of the world according to TV. Finally, these questions were posed to large samples of citizens from all socio-economic strata. In every survey, the Annenberg team discovered that heavy viewers of television (those watching more than four hours a day), who account for more than 30 percent of the population, almost invariably chose the TV-influenced answers, while light viewers (less than two hours a day), selected the answers corresponding more closely to actual life. Some of the dimensions of television's reality warp:

- **Sex:** Male prime-time characters outnumber females by 3 to 1 and, with a few star-turn exceptions, women are portrayed as weak, passive satellites to powerful, effective men. TV's male population also plays a vast variety of roles, while females generally get typecast as either lovers or mothers. Less than 20 percent of TV's married women with children work outside the home—as compared with more than 50 percent in real life. The tube's distorted depictions of women, concludes Gerbner, reinforce stereotypical attitudes and increase sexism. In one Annenberg survey, heavy viewers were far more likely than light ones to agree with the proposition: "Women should take care of running their homes and leave running the country to men."

- **Age:** People over 65, too, are grossly underrepresented on television. Correspondingly, heavy-viewing Annenberg respondents believe that the elderly are a vanishing breed, that they make up a smaller proportion of the population today than they did 20 years ago. In fact, they form the nation's most rapidly expanding age group. Heavy viewers also believe that old people are less healthy today than they were two decades ago, when quite the opposite is true. As with women, the portrayals of old people transmit negative impressions. In general, they are cast as silly, stubborn, sexually inactive and eccentric. "They're often shown as feeble grandparents bearing cookies," says Gerbner. "You never see the power that real old people often have. The best and possibly only time to learn about growing old with decency and grace is in youth. And young people are the most susceptible to TV's messages."

- **Race:** The problem with the medium's treatment of blacks is more one of image than of visibility. Though a tiny percentage of black characters come across as "unrealistically romanticized," reports Gerbner, the overwhelming majority of them are employed in subservient, supporting roles—such as the white hero's comic sidekick. "When a black child looks at prime time," he says, "most of the people he sees doing interesting and important things are white." That imbalance, he goes on, tends to teach young blacks to accept minority status as naturally inevitable and even deserved. To assess the impact of such portrayals on the general audience, the Annenberg survey forms included questions like "Should white people have the right to keep blacks out of their neighborhoods?" and "Should there be laws against marriages between blacks and whites?" The more that viewers watched, the more they answered "Yes" to each question.

- **Work:** Heavy viewers greatly overestimated the proportion of Americans employed as physicians, lawyers, athletes and entertainers, all of whom inhabit prime-time in hordes. A mere 6 to 10 percent of television characters hold blue-collar or service jobs vs. about 60 percent in the real work force. Gerbner sees two dangers in TV's skewed division of labor. On the one hand, the tube so overrepresents and glamorizes the elite occupations that it sets up unrealistic expectations among those who must deal with them in actuality. At the same time, TV largely neglects portraying the occupations that most youngsters will have to enter. "You almost never see the farmer, the factory worker or the small businessman," he notes. "Thus not only do lawyers and other professionals find they cannot measure up to the image TV projects of them, but children's occupational aspirations are channeled in unrealistic directions." The

Gerbner team feels this emphasis on high-powered jobs poses problems for adolescent girls, who are also presented with views of women as homebodies. The two conflicting views, Gerbner says, add to the frustration over choices they have to make as adults.

- **Health:** Although video characters exist almost entirely on junk food and quaff alcohol 15 times more often than water, they manage to remain slim, healthy and beautiful. Frequent TV watchers, the Annenberg investigators found, eat more, drink more, exercise less and possess an almost mystical faith in the curative powers of medical science. Concludes Gerbner: "Television may well be the single most pervasive source of health information. And its overidealized images of medical people, coupled with its complacency about unhealthy life-styles, leaves both patients and doctors vulnerable to disappointment, frustration and even litigation."

- **Crime:** On the small screen, crime rages about 10 times more often than in real life. But while other researchers concentrate on the propensity of TV mayhem to incite aggression, the Annenberg team has studied the hidden side of its imprint: fear of victimization. On television, 55 percent of prime-time characters are involved in violent confrontations once a week; in reality, the figure is less than 1 percent. In all demographic groups in every class of neighborhood, heavy viewers overestimated the statistical chance of violence in their own lives and harbored an exaggerated mistrust of strangers—creating what Gerbner calls a "mean-world syndrome." Forty-six percent of heavy viewers who live in cities rated their fear of crime "very serious" as opposed to 26 percent for light viewers. Such paranoia is especially acute among TV entertainment's most common victims: women, the elderly, non-whites, foreigners and lower-class citizens.

  Video violence, proposes Gerbner, is primarily responsible for imparting lessons in social power: it demonstrates who can *do* what to whom and get away with it. "Television is saying that those at the bottom of the power scale cannot get away with the same things that a white, middle-class American male can," he says. "It potentially conditions people to think of themselves as victims."

At a quick glance, Gerbner's findings seem to contain a cause-and-effect, chicken-or-the-egg question. Does television make heavy viewers view the world the way they do or do heavy viewers come from the poorer, less experienced segment of the populace that regards the world that way to begin with? In other words, does the tube create or simply confirm the unenlightened attitudes of its most loyal audience? Gerbner, however, was savvy enough to construct a methodology largely immune to such criticism. His samples of heavy viewers cut across all ages, incomes, education levels and ethnic backgrounds—and every category displayed the same tube-induced misconceptions of the world outside.

Needless to say, the networks accept all this as enthusiastically as they would a list of news-coverage complaints from the Ayatollah Khomeini. Even so, their responses tend to be tinged with a singular respect for Gerbner's personal and professional credentials. The man is no ivory-tower recluse. During World War II, the Budapest-born Gerbner parachuted into the mountains of Yugoslavia to join the partisans fighting the Germans. After the war, he hunted down and personally arrested scores of high Nazi officials. Nor is Gerbner some videophobic vigilante. A Ph.D. in communications, he readily acknowledges TV's beneficial effects, noting that it has abolished parochialism, reduced isolation and loneliness and provided the poorest members of society with cheap, plug-in exposure to experiences they otherwise would not have. Funding for his research is supplied by such prestigious bodies as the National Institute of Mental Health, the surgeon general's office and the American Medical Association, and he is called to testify before congressional committees nearly as often as David Stockman.

Mass Entertainment

When challenging Gerbner, network officials focus less on his findings and methods than on what they regard as his own misconceptions of their industry's function. "He's looking at television from the perspective of a social scientist rather than considering what is mass entertainment," says Alfred Schneider, vice president of standards' and practices at ABC. "We strive to balance TV's social effects with what will capture an audience's interests. If you showed strong men being victimized as much as women or the elderly, what would comprise the dramatic conflict? If you did a show truly representative of society's total reality, and nobody watched because it wasn't interesting, what have you achieved?"

CBS senior vice president Gene Mater also believes that Gerbner is implicitly asking for the theoretically impossible. "TV is unique in its problems," says Mater. "Everyone wants a piece of the action. Everyone feels that their racial or ethnic group is underrepresented or should be portrayed as they would like the world to perceive them. No popular entertainment form, including this one, can or should be an accurate reflection of society." On that point, at least, Gerbner is first to agree; he hardly expects television entertainment to serve as a mirror image of absolute truth. But what fascinates him about this communications medium is its marked difference from all others. In other media, customers carefully choose what they want to hear or read: a movie, a magazine, a best seller. In television, notes Gerbner, viewers rarely tune in for a particular program. Instead, most just habitually turn on the set—and watch by the clock rather than for a specific show. "Television viewing fulfills the criteria of a ritual," he says. "It is the only medium that can bring to people things they otherwise would not select." With such unique power, believes Gerbner, comes unique responsibility: "No other medium reaches into every home or has a comparable, cradle-to-grave influence over what a society learns about itself."

Match

In Gerbner's view, virtually all of TV's distortions of reality can be attributed to its obsession with demographics. The viewers that prime-time sponsors most want to reach are white, middle-class, female and between 18 and 49—in short, the audience that purchases most of the consumer products advertised on the tube. Accordingly, notes Gerbner, the demographic portrait of TV's fictional characters largely matches that of its prime commercial targets and largely ignores everyone else. "Television," he concludes, "reproduces a world for its own best customers."

Among TV's more candid executives, that theory draws considerable support. Yet by pointing a finger at the power of demographics, Gerbner appears to contradict one of his major findings. If female viewers are so dear to the hearts of sponsors, why are female characters cast in such unflattering light? "In a basically male-oriented power structure," replies Gerbner, "you can't alienate the male viewer. But you can get away with offending women because most women are pretty well brainwashed to accept it." The Annenberg dean has an equally tidy explanation for another curious fact. Since the corporate world provides network television with all of its financial support, one would expect businessmen on TV to be portrayed primarily as good guys. Quite the contrary. As any fan of "Dallas," "Dynasty" or "Falcon Crest" well knows, the image of the company man is usually that of a mendacious, dirty-dealing rapscallion. Why would TV snap at the hand that feeds it? "Credibility is the way to ratings," proposes Gerbner. "This country has a populist tradition of bias against anything big, including big business. So to retain credibility, TV entertainment shows businessmen in relatively derogatory ways."

In the medium's Hollywood-based creative community, the gospel of Gerbner finds some passionate adherents. Rarely have TV's best and brightest talents viewed their industry with so much frustration and anger. The most sweeping indictment emanates from David Rintels, a two-time Emmy-winning writer and former president of the Writers Guild of America, West. "Gerbner is absolutely correct and it is the people who run the networks who are to blame," says Rintels. "The networks get bombarded with thoughtful, reality-oriented scripts. They simply won't do them. They slam the door on them. They believe that the only way to get ratings is to feed viewers what conforms to their biases or what has limited resemblance to reality. From 8 to 11 o'clock each night, television is one long lie."

Innovative thinkers such as Norman Lear, whose work has been practically driven off the tube, don't fault the networks so much as the climate in which they operate. Says Lear: "All of this country's institutions have become totally fixated on short-term bottom-line thinking. Everyone grabs for what might succeed today and the hell with tomorrow. Television just catches more of the heat because it's more visible." Perhaps the most perceptive assessment of Gerbner's conclusions is offered by one who has worked both sides of the industry street. Deanne Barkley, a former NBC vice president who now helps run an independent production house, reports that the negative depictions of women on TV have made it "nerve-racking" to function as a woman within TV. "No one takes responsibility for the social impact of their shows," says Barkley. "But then how do you decide where it all begins? Do the networks give viewers what they want? Or are the networks conditioning them to think that way?"

Gerbner himself has no simple answer to that conundrum. Neither a McLuhanesque shaman nor a Naderesque crusader, he hesitates to suggest solutions until pressed. Then out pops a pair of provocative notions. Commercial television will never democratize its treatments of daily life, he believes, until it finds a way to broaden its financial base. Coincidentally, Federal Communications Commission chairman Mark Fowler seems to have arrived at much the same conclusion. In exchange for lifting such government restrictions on TV as the fairness doctrine and the equal-time rule, Fowler would impose a modest levy on station owners called a spectrum-use fee. Funds from the fees would be set aside to finance programs aimed at specialized tastes rather than the mass appetite. Gerbner enthusiastically endorses that proposal: "Let the ratings system dominate most of prime time but not every hour of every day. Let some programs carry advisories that warn: 'This is not for all of you. This is for nonwhites, or for religious people or for the aged and the handicapped. Turn it off unless you'd like to eavesdrop.' That would be a very refreshing thing."

Role

In addition, Gerbner would like to see viewers given an active role in steering the overall direction of television instead of being obliged to passively accept whatever the networks offer. In Britain, he points out, political candidates debate the problems of TV as routinely as the issue of crime. In this country, proposes Gerbner, "every political campaign should put television on the public agenda. Candidates talk about schools, they talk about jobs, they talk about social welfare. They're going to have to start discussing this all-pervasive force."

There are no outright villains in this docudrama. Even Gerbner recognizes that network potentates don't set out to proselytize a point of view; they are simply businessmen selling a mass-market product. At the same time, their 90 million nightly customers deserve to know the side effects of the ingredients. By the time the typical American child reaches the age of reason, calculates Gerbner, he or she will have absorbed more than 30,000 electronic "stories." These stories, he suggests, have replaced the socializing role of the preindustrial church: they create a "cultural mythology" that establishes the norms of approved behavior and belief. And all Gerbner's research indicates that this new mythological world, with its warped picture of a sizable portion of society, may soon become the one most of us think we live in.

Who else is telling us that? Howard Beale and his eloquent alarms have faded into off-network reruns. At the very least, it is comforting to know that a real-life Beale is very much with us . . . and *really* watching.

READING WRITING

This Text: Reading

1. What is Waters's point in describing the world according to television? Do you agree or disagree? Why or why not?
2. What is Waters assuming about television's audience when describing this "world"? Do you think these assumptions are appropriate? Do they apply to you?
3. This piece is now more than twenty-five years old—what do you think has changed since he wrote it? Are the ideas Gerbner wrote still valid today?

Your Text: Writing

1. Pick a night of television and a network and do your own demographic study. Who makes up the casts of the shows? What values do the shows display? Imply?
2. One of the techniques the authors use for watching popular culture is to follow the implications of character action. For example, if a character is portrayed as strong or weak, smart or dumb, greedy or kind, what happens to them can be an indication of how the authors feel about that general type of character.
3. Imagine yourself in "television world"—what would it look like? How would people act in it? How would it sound? How would this world be different from the world you live in now? Write a short essay on your experiences in television world.

Beyond Fear: Heroes vs. *24*

Garance Franke-Ruta

Garance Franke-Ruta is a senior editor at *The American Prospect*, in which this essay was originally published in 2007. Although she grew up in Mexico, she has lived in New Mexico, New York City, and Washington, D.C. In this essay, Franke-Ruta argues that *Heroes* has surpassed *24* as the favorite action-adventure drama on American television. She links this shift to changing American values. Do you agree with the way she describes the connections between politics and television content? If not, what are some other theories about the relationship between politics and television?

WHEN PETITE, BLONDE DIXIE CHICKS lead singer Natalie Maines told a British audience ten days before the 2003 American invasion of Iraq: "Just so you know, we're on the good side with y'all. We do not want this war, this violence, and we're ashamed that the president of the United States is from Texas," the political climate was such that she rapidly found herself the subject of international controversy. War supporters burned the group's CDs, and the three-woman alternative country rock band lost half its audience, which at the time was more partial to Toby Keith's *Shock'n Y'all*-style bluster than to the Chicks' anti-war doubts, at concerts over the next year.

Go back to that moment in your mind. Imagine what would have happened if a television show had dared to suggest that the anniversary of September 11 was anything less than a sacred moment for national reflection and mourning, or that the president was a jingoistic impostor using the specter of terrorism for evil, selfish, and ultimately un-American ends. Most likely such a show would have sparked national outrage, advertisers would have fled, and the writers and actors would have been forced to grovel in apology on the national stage in order to keep working.

But, oh, how times have changed. The misguided invasion of Iraq has gone sour, and so, too, has the American public, among whom Bush supporters now number roughly 30 percent. In June, more than four years after the Chicks were bashed for opposing the president's war, Maines' husband, the actor Adrian Pasdar, portrayed on a prime-time network series a terrorism-era American president who is the living embodiment of evil—and won the best audience numbers in his time slot.

The hit show is NBC's *Heroes*, a meandering sci-fi epic about a band of normal looking men and women whose genetic anomalies grant them extraordinary powers and link them in a shared struggle to prevent a nuclear explosion in New York City. With the penultimate episode of its first season, which aired in May, the show moved from the realm of fantasy into biting political commentary, filled with ripped-from-the-headlines scenes unimaginable during the peak years of the Bush administration. In that episode, the show flashed forward to a post-attack future whose fifth-anniversary memorial service visually echoed the first September 11 commemoration, and was presided over by a platitudinous president who has used the terrorism attack to suspend laws and persecute those who disagree with him.

Middle East scholar Juan Cole has compared *Heroes* to FOX's anti-terrorism hit *24*; the affection of the lead character in that show, Jack Bauer, for "enhanced interrogation" techniques has become such a cultural touchstone that it cropped up during a Republican presidential primary debate. "I'm looking for Jack Bauer at that time, let me tell you," Colorado Rep. Tom Tancredo declared at the second GOP presidential debate, after being conveniently presented with a *24*-style ticking-nuclear-timebomb scenario by FOX's news division, which was hosting the debate.

24: Enhanced interrogation or torture?

"But while *24* skews to the right politically, *Heroes* seems like a left-wing response" to September 11 and the rise of international terrorism, Cole wrote. More than that, the show represents the passing of the moment in which fear of terrorists and fear of the president ruled, and both were used to justify actions that undermined America's values, legal traditions, and citizens' ability to freely criticize their leaders. While *24*, which airs Monday nights on FOX against *Heroes*, makes heroes of its torturing CIA agents, *Heroes'* heroes are everyday men and women called to greatness by the necessity of their times: a cheerleader, a Japanese salaryman, a bumbling cop who can never quite get that promotion. They are civilians hunted by the FBI—portrayed in the show's pre-attack moments as a feckless organization that fails to grasp what's truly going on, and that doesn't listen to whistle-blowers and warnings, to boot—and forced to fend off the storm troopers of the post-attack Department of Homeland Security with *Matrix*-like superpowers and samurai swords. To be sure, they sometimes go awry when using their powers, over which they have imperfect control, injuring inno-cents or endangering themselves. Trapped in a world they don't quite understand, with fresh betrayals and revelations in every episode, the heroes slowly recognize their destiny: to learn to control their powers, and through this self-restraint and self-mastery, to "save the world."

As such, they are descendents of an older tradition in American television, which pits heroic individuals against the corrupt political sphere or government forces. Where *24* makes heroes of its state agents, *Heroes* sharply questions their actions.

The plot of *Heroes* is complicated, going back and forth between time periods, with the narrative thread of past and future constantly evolving from episode to episode in response to the characters' interventions, and new mutants being revealed as old ones are captured or killed off. Even the characters rely on comic books that tell the future to help guide them through the plot twists and turns.

According to Franke-Ruta, *Heroes* is more about family and protection than *24*.

In the penultimate episode, the camera shows us one possible future in a Las Vegas club, where Niki, one of the ensemble show's many recurring characters, is working as a stripper in the wake of the heroes' inability to stop the nuclear bomb from exploding in New York, an attack that claimed her son and husband. In this episode, as the caption "America Remembers" flashes across a TV screen, overlaid on the image of fires licking the ruins of New York, Niki sighs, "Today's just another day." Her reaction to the anniversary of this fictional attack seems apposite given the real world, where the current mayor of New York, Michael Bloomberg, can tell reporters in the wake of a recent bomb scare: "There are lots of threats to you in the world. There's the threat of a heart attack for genetic reasons. You can't sit there and worry about everything. Get a life."

Later in the show, Niki sees President Nathan Petrelli (Adrian Pasdar)—a fellow mutant—on the TV screen at the fifth-anniversary memorial service, a huge American flag in the background, the stars of the presidential seal on his podium before him. Niki, earlier restrained in her grief, throws a glass at the screen as Petrelli launches into a speech filled with platitudes that should be recognizable to us all. He praises the "sacrifices" that the population has made and "the laws that we have had to pass to keep our citizens safe . . . We've all lost. We've all mourned. And we've all had to become soldiers, heroes. This is a battle that we've entered knowing that the enemy is ourselves," he intones, before declaring a false victory against the mutants in the form of a "cure" that is really a poison. "We've been vigilant. We have been uncompromising, and our efforts have paid off. The nightmare is finally over. The world is safe."

In fact, as the show continues, it is soon clear that the world has never been less safe, for that talking head is not Nathan Petrelli at all, but the evil Sylar, a man who kills the mutants to steal their powers. He's the show's vicious anti-hero, who, in the flash-forward, is believed to have caused the explosion, having stolen the powers of a radioactive man. At the time of his presidential impersonation, he has added shapeshifting to his repertoire of skills, and has dragooned the entire apparatus of the U.S. state into his quest for new mutants whose powers he can steal.

Sylar, in his own way, is a victim of the same lack of self-control as Nathan's brother Peter Petrelli, a former nurse who innocently absorbs other mutant's powers and who is revealed in an earlier episode to be the actual exploding man—a "human bomb"—who cannot control the radioactive powers he absorbed involuntarily from another character. Sylar, too, cannot control his urge to destroy. It's up to the others to stop him.

In the final episode of the first season, which jumps back to the main, pre-explosion plot five years earlier, Nathan, who can fly, saves Peter and the world by grabbing his brother and flying him up into space as his hands pulse orange, mere moments before he explodes (shades of Superman). Peter, who has absorbed the power of regeneration, will be back next season. But Nathan may well have made a real sacrifice, laying bare the ultimate lesson of this antidote to *24*. It is not in torture and the frantic tossing off of our legal standards that we find freedom and safety, but in learning to control our vast and growing power in response to the threats we know we face. And, should any individual fail to do so, we have a responsibility to rein that person in.

READING WRITING

This Text: Reading

1. The author opens her piece with a reference to the Dixie Chicks and September 11. In what way does this opening gambit influence how you read her arguments about *24* and *Heroes*?
2. The author argues that *24* feels like a right-wing show (conservative) and *Heroes* like a left-wing show (progressive). What is her rationale for this? Do you agree?
3. Franke-Ruta buries her thesis deep in the essay. Locate her main argument. Is it easy to see what her main points are? Does she support her assertions?

Your Text: Writing

1. Write a comparison/contrast essay about two television shows you think occupy opposite points of the spectrum. *Heroes* and *24* are vaguely located in the same genre—adventure/thriller—but are much different shows in a number of different ways. Make sure you pick shows of the same genre to support your case. Arguing that *That 70s Show* and *CSI* are radically different is not too compelling; however, a paper contrasting *Oz* and *Prison Break* might be interesting.
2. Take a different tack than Franke-Ruta—argue that *24* is a more appropriate response to 9/11. How will you support this assertion?
3. Many have compared *Lost* and *Heroes* to one another—the supernatural, ordinary people put in extraordinary circumstances, the interplay of past and present. Write a paper in which you explain the phenomenon of these two shows at *this* moment in history.

"Not That There's Anything Wrong with That": Reading the Queer in Seinfeld

Katherine Gantz

Katherine Gantz uses the lens of queer theory in her 2000 discussion of *Seinfeld*. Notice how Gantz strictly defines not only the term "queer" but the particular questions she intends to ask of her text using "queer."

THE WORLD OF MASS CULTURE, especially that which includes American television, remains overwhelmingly homophobic. Queer theory offers a useful perspective from which to examine the heterosexism at the core of contemporary television and also provides a powerful tool of subversion. The aim of this article is twofold: first, it will outline and explain the notion of a queer reading; second, it will apply a queer reading to the narrative texts that comprise the situation comedy *Seinfeld*. The concept of the queer reading, currently en vogue in literary analysis, has evolved from a handful of distinct but connected sources, beginning with the popularization of the term "queer." In

1989, the AIDS activist group ACT UP created Queer Nation, an offshoot organization comprised of lesbians and gays dedicated to the political reclaiming of gay identity under the positively recoded term "queer."[1] The group was initially formed as a New York City street patrol organized to help counteract escalating hate crimes against gays. As Queer Nation gained visibility in the public eye, the use of "queer," historically a derogatory slur for homosexuals, entered into standard parlance in the gay and lesbian press.[2] Eve Kosofsky Sedgwick's *Epistemology of the Closet*[3] appropriated the term with a broadened interpretation of "queer," suggesting not that literature be read with the author's possible homosexuality in mind but instead with an openness to the queer (homoerotic and/or homosexual) contexts, nuances, connections, and potential already available within the text. The concept of "queerness" was elaborated once more in 1991, with the publication of *Inside/Out: Lesbian Theories, Gay Theories;*[4] within this assemblage of political, pedagogical, and literary essays, the term was collectively applied to a larger category of sexual non-straightness, as will be further explained.

As the political construction of "queer" became increasingly disciplinized in academia, the emerging body of "queer theory" lost its specifically homosexual connotation and was replaced by a diffuse set of diverse sexual identities. Like the path of feminism, the concept of queerness had been largely stripped of its political roots and transformed into a methodological approach accessible to manipulation by the world of predominantly heterosexual, white, middle-class intellectuals. It is with this problematic universalization of queer theory in mind that I undertake an application of queer reading.

In what could be deemed a reinsertion of the subversive into a "straightened" discipline, Alexander Doty's book *Making Things Perfectly Queer: Reading Mass Culture*[5] has taken the queer reading out of the realm of the purely literary and applied it to analyses of film and television texts. From this ever-transforming history of the queer reading, the popular situation comedy *Seinfeld* lends itself well to a contemporary application.

In the summer of 1989, NBC debuted a tepidly received pilot entitled *The Seinfeld Chronicles,* a situation comedy revolving around the mundane, urbane Manhattan existence of stand-up comic Jerry Seinfeld. Despite its initially unimpressive ratings, the show evolved into the five-episode series *Seinfeld* and established its regular cast of Jerry's three fictional friends: George Costanza (Jason Alexander), ex-girlfriend Elaine Benes (Julia Louis-Dreyfus), and the enigmatic neighbor Kramer (Michael Richards). By its return in January 1991, *Seinfeld* had established a following among Wednesday-night television viewers; over the next two years, the show became a cultural phenomenon, claiming both a faithful viewership and a confident position in the Nielsen ratings' top ten. The premise was to write a show about the details, minor disturbances, and nonevents of Jerry's life as they occurred before becoming fodder for the stand-up monologues that bookend each episode. From the start, *Seinfeld*'s audience has been comprised of a devoted group of "TV-literate, demographically desirable urbanites, for the most part—who look forward to each weekly episode in the Life of Jerry with a baby-boomer generation's self-involved eagerness," notes Bruce Fretts, author of *The Entertainment Weekly "Seinfeld" Companion.*[6] Such obsessive identification and self-reflexive fascination seem to be thematic in both the inter- and extradiegetic worlds of *Seinfeld*. The show's characters are modeled on real-life acquaintances: George is based on Seinfeld's best friend (and series cocreator) Larry David; Elaine is an exaggeration of Seinfeld's ex-girlfriend, writer Carol Leifer; Kramer's prototype lived across the hall from one of David's first Manhattan apartments.[7] To further complicate this narcissistic mirroring, in the 1993 season premiere entitled "The Pilot" (see videography for episodic citations), Jerry and George finally launch their new NBC sitcom *Jerry* by casting four actors to portray themselves,

Kramer, and Elaine. This multilayered Möbius strip of person/actor/character relationships seems to be part of the show's complex appeal. Whereas situation comedies often dilute their cast, adding and removing characters in search of new plot possibilities, *Seinfeld* instead interiorizes; the narrative creates new configurations of the same limited cast to keep the viewer and the characters intimately linked. In fact, it is precisely this concentration on the nuclear set of four personalities that creates the *Seinfeld* community.

If it seems hyperbolic to suggest that the participants in the *Seinfeld* phenomenon (both spectators and characters included) have entered into a certain delineated "lifestyle," consider the significant lexicon of Seinfeldian code words and recurring phrases that go unnoticed and unappreciated by the infrequent or "unknowing" viewer. Catch phrases such as Snapple, the Bubble Boy, Cuban cigars, Master of My Domain, Junior Mints, Mulva, Crazy Joe Davola, Pez, and Vandelay Industries all serve as parts of the group-specific language that a family shares; these are the kinds of self-referential in-jokes that help one *Seinfeld* watcher identify another.[8] This sort of tightly conscribed universe of meaning is reflected not only by the decidedly small cast but also by the narrative's consistent efforts to maintain its intimacy. As this article will discuss, much of *Seinfeld*'s plot and humor (and, consequently, the viewer's pleasure) hinge on outside personalities threatening—and ultimately failing—to invade the foursome. Especially where Jerry and George are concerned, episodes are mostly resolved by expelling the intruder and restoring the exclusive nature of their relationship. The show's camera work, which at times takes awkward measures to ensure that Jerry and George remain grouped together within a scene, reinforces the privileged dynamic of their relationship within the narrative.

Superficially speaking, *Seinfeld* appears to be a testament to heterosexuality: in its nine-year run, Jerry sported a new girlfriend in almost every episode; his friendship with Elaine is predicated on their previous sexual relationship; and all four characters share in the discussion and navigation of the (straight) dating scene. However, with a viewership united by a common coded discourse and an interest in the cohesive (and indeed almost claustrophobic) exclusivity of its predominantly male cast, clearly *Seinfeld* is rife with possibilities for homoerotic interpretation. As will be demonstrated, the construction, the coding, and the framing of the show readily conform to a queer reading of the *Seinfeld* text.

Here I wish to develop and define my meanings of the word "queer" as a set of signifying practices and a category distinct from that of gay literature. Inspired by Doty's work, I will use "queer"—as its current literary usages suggest—as relating to a wide-ranging spectrum of "nonnormative" sexual notions, including not only constructions of gayness and lesbianism but also of transsexualism, transvestism, same-sex affinity, and other ambisexual behaviors and sensibilities. Queerness at times may act merely as a space in which heterosexual personalities interact, in the same ways that a queer personality may operate within an otherwise heterosexual sphere. In this system, "queer" does not stand in opposition to "heterosexual" but instead to "straight," a term that by contrast, suggests all that is restrictive about "normative" sexuality, a category that excludes what is deemed undesirable, deviant, dangerous, unnatural, unproductive. "Queer," then, should be understood not so much as an intrinsic property but more as the outcome of both productive and receptive behaviors—a pluralized, inclusive term that may be employed by and applied to both gay and nongay characters and spectators.[9]

The second point I wish to clarify about the use of the term "queer" as it relates to my own textual analysis of a mass culture text is the indirect, nonexplicit nature of the queer relationships represented in *Seinfeld*. Explicit references to homosexuality subvert the possibility of a queer reading; by identifying a character as "gay," such overt difference serves to mark the other characters as "not gay." Sexual perimeters become limited, fixed, rooted in traditional definitions and connotations that work contrary to the fluidity and subtle ambiguity of a queer interpretation. It is precisely the unspokenness ("the love that dare not speak its name") of homoeroticism between seemingly straight men that allows the insinuation of a queer reading. As Doty rightly notes, queer positionings are generated more often through the same-sex tensions evident in "straight films" than in gay ones:

> Traditional narrative films [such as *Gentlemen Prefer Blondes* and *Thelma and Louise*], which are ostensibly addressed to straight audiences, often have greater potential for encouraging a wider range of queer responses than [such] clearly lesbian- and gay-addressed films [as *Women I Love* and *Scorpio Rising*]. The intense tensions and pleasures generated by the woman–woman and man–man aspects within the narratives of the former group of films create a space of sexual instability that already queerly positioned viewers can connect in various ways, and within which straights might be likely to recognize and express their queer impulses. (8)

Of course, there is a multitude of possibilities for the perception and reception of queer pleasures, but, to generalize from Doty's argument, the implications in the case of the *Seinfeld* phenomenon suggest that while queer-identified viewers may recognize the domesticity between Jerry and George as that of a gay couple, straight viewers may simply take pleasure in the characters' intimate bond left unbroken by outside (heterosexual) romantic interruptions.

This is not to say that *Seinfeld* ignores the explicit category of homosexuality; on the contrary, the show is laden with references and plot twists involving gay characters and themes. In separate episodes, Elaine is selected as the "best man" in a lesbian wedding ("The Subway"); George accidentally causes the exposure of his girlfriend Susan's father's affair with novelist John Cheever ("The Cheever Letters"); and, after their breakup, George runs into Susan with her new lesbian lover ("The Smelly Car"). At its most playful, *Seinfeld* smugly calls attention to its own homosexual undercurrents in an episode in which Jerry and George are falsely identified as a gay couple by a female journalist ("The Outing").[10] Due to the direct nature of such references to homosexuality, these are episodes that slyly deflect queer reading, serving as a sort of lightning rod by displacing homoerotic undercurrents onto a more obvious target.

Such smoke-screen tactics seem to be in conflict with the multitude of queer-identified semiotics and gay icons and symbols at play within the *Seinfeld* text. Most notably, no "queer-receptive" viewer can look at the *Seinfeld* graphic logo (at the episode's beginning and before commercials) without noticing the inverted triangle—hot pink during the earliest seasons—dotting the "i" in "Seinfeld."[11] Although the symbol dates back to the Holocaust (used to mark homosexuals for persecution), the pink triangle has recently been recuperated by gay activists during ACT UP's widely publicized AIDS education campaign, "Silence Equals Death," and has consequently become a broadly recognized symbol of gayness.

Even if the pink triangle's proactive gay recoding remains obscure to the "unknowing" viewership (i.e., unfamiliar with or resistant to queerness), *Seinfeld* also offers a multitude of discursive referents chosen from a popular lexicon of more common gay signifiers that are often slurs in use by a homophobic public. In an episode revolving around Jerry and Kramer's discussion of where to find *fruit*—longstanding slang for a gay man—Jerry makes a very rare break from his standard wardrobe of well-froned button-up oxfords, instead sporting a T-shirt with the word "QUEENS" across it. Although outwardly in reference to Queens College, the word's semiotic juxtaposition with the theme of fruit evokes its slang connotation for effeminate gay men.

Like an old married couple, George and Jerry bicker about everything but always make up.

Narrative space is also queerly coded. Positioned as Jerry and George's "place" (or "male space"), the restaurant where they most often meet is "Monk's," a name that conjures up images of an exclusively male religious society, a "brotherhood" predicated on the maintenance of masculine presence/feminine absence, in both spiritual and physical terms.

Recurring plot twists also reveal a persistent interest in the theme of hidden or falsified identities. As early as *Seinfeld*'s second episode ("The Stakeout"), George insists on creating an imaginary biography for himself as a successful architect before meeting Jerry's new girlfriend. Throughout the *Seinfeld* texts, the foursome adopts a number of different names and careers in hopes of persuading outsiders (most often potential romantic interests) that they lead a more interesting, more superficially acceptable, or more immediately favorable existence than what their real lives have to offer: George has assumed the identity of neo-Nazi organizer Colin O'Brian ("The Limo"); Elaine has recruited both Jerry and Kramer as substitute boyfriends to dissuade unwanted suitors ("The Junior Mint" and "The Watch"); Kramer has posed as a policeman ("The Statue") and has even auditioned under a pseudonym to play himself in the pilot of *Jerry* ("The Pilot"). Pretense and fabrication often occur among the foursome as well. In "The Apartment," Jerry is troubled by Elaine's imminent move into the apartment above him. Worried that her presence will "cramp his style," he schemes to convince her that she will be financially unable to take the apartment. In private, Jerry warns George that he will be witness to some "heavy acting" to persuade Elaine that he is genuinely sympathetic. Unshaken, George answers: "Are you kidding? I lie every second of the day; my whole life is a sham." This deliberate "closeting" of one's lifestyle has obvious connections to the gay theme of "passing,"[12] the politically discouraged practice of hiding one's homosexuality behind a façade of straight respectability. One might argue that *Seinfeld* is simply a text about passing—socially as well as sexually—in a repressive and judgmental society. It must be noted, however, that George and Jerry are the only two characters who do not lie to each other; they are in fact engaged in maintaining each other's secrets and duplicities by "covering" for one another, thus distancing themselves somewhat from Kramer and Elaine from within an even more exclusive rapport.[13]

Another thematic site of queerness is the mystification of and resulting detachment from female culture and discourse. While Jerry glorifies such male-identified personalities as Superman, the Three Stooges, and Mickey Mantle, he prides himself in never having seen a single episode of *I Love Lucy* ("The Phone Message"). Even Elaine is often presented as incomprehensible to her familiar male counterparts. In "The Shoes," Jerry and George have no problem creating a story line for their situation comedy, *Jerry,* around male characters; however, when they try to "write in" Elaine's character, they find themselves stumped:

> JERRY: [In the process of writing the script.] "Elaine enters." . . . What does she say . . . ?
> GEORGE: [Pause.] What *do* they [women] say?
> JERRY: [Mystified.] I *don't know.*

After a brief deliberation, they opt to omit the female character completely. As Jerry explains with a queerly loaded rationale: "You, me, Kramer, the butler . . . Elaine is too much." Later, at Monk's, Elaine complains about her exclusion from the pilot. Jerry confesses: "We couldn't write for a woman." "You have *no idea?*" asks Elaine, disgusted. Jerry looks at George for substantiation and replies: "None." Clearly, the privileged bond between men excludes room for an understanding of and an interest in women; like Elaine in the pilot, the feminine presence is often simply deleted for the sake of maintaining a stronger, more coherent male narrative.

Jerry seems especially ill at ease with notions of female sexuality, perhaps suggesting that they impinge on his own. In "The Red Dot," Jerry convinces the resistant George that he should buy Elaine a thank-you gift after she procures him a job at her office. Despite George's tightfisted unwillingness to invest money in such social graces as gift giving, he acquiesces. The duo go to a department store in search of an appropriate gift for Elaine. Jerry confesses: "I never feel comfortable in the women's department; I feel like I'm just a *little* too close to trying on a dress." While browsing through the women's clothing, George describes his erotic attraction to the cleaning woman in his new office:

> GEORGE: . . . she was swaying back and forth, back and forth, her hips swiveling and her breasts—uh . . .
> JERRY: . . . convulsing?

George reacts with disdain at the odd word choice, recognizing that Jerry's depiction of female physicality and eroticism is both inappropriate and unappealing. (It should be noted that the ensuing sexual encounter between George and the cleaning woman ultimately results in the loss of both their jobs; true to the pattern, George's foray into heterosex creates chaos.)

Although sites of queerness occur extensively throughout the *Seinfeld* oeuvre, the most useful elucidation of its queer potential comes from a closer, more methodical textual analysis. To provide a contextualized view of the many overlapping sites of queerness—symbolic, discursive, thematic, and visual—the following is a critique of three episodes especially conducive to a queer reading of *Seinfeld*'s male homoerotic relationships.

"The Boyfriend" explores the ambiguous valences of male friendships. Celebrated baseball player Keith Hernandez stars as himself (as does Jerry Seinfeld among the cast of otherwise fictional characters), becoming the focal point of both Jerry's and, later, Elaine's attentions. Despite Elaine's brief romantic involvement with Keith, the central narrative concerns Jerry's interactions with the baseball player. Although never explicitly discussed, Jerry's attachment to Keith is represented as romantic in nature.

The episode begins in a men's locker room, prefiguring the homoerotic overtones of the coming plot. The locker room is clearly delineated as "male space"; its connection to the athletic field posits it as a locale of physicality, where men gather to prepare for or to disengage from the privileged (and predominantly homophobic) world of male sports. The locker room, as a site of potential heterosexual vulnerability as men expose their bodies to other men, is socially safe only when established as sexually neutral—or, better still, heterosexually charged with the machismo of athleticism. This "safe" coding occurs almost immediately in this setting, accomplished through a postgame comparison of Jerry's, George's, and Kramer's basketball prowess. As they finish dressing together after their game, it is the voracious, ambisexual Kramer who immediately upsets the precarious sexual neutrality, violating the unspoken code of locker-room decorum:

> KRAMER: Hey, you know this is the first time we've ever seen each other naked?
> JERRY: Believe me, *I* didn't see anything.
> KRAMER: [With disbelief.] Oh, you didn't sneak a peek?
> JERRY: No—did you?
> KRAMER: Yeah, I snuck a peek.
> JERRY: Why?
> KRAMER: Why not? What about you, George?
> GEORGE: [Hesitating] Yeah, I—snuck a peek. But it was so fast that I didn't see anything; it was just a blur.
> JERRY: I made a conscious effort *not* to look; there's certain information I just don't want to have.

Jerry displays his usual disdain for all things corporeal or carnal. Such unwillingness to participate in Kramer's curiosity about men's bodies also secures Jerry firmly on heterosexual ground, a necessary pretext to make his intense feelings for Keith "safe." The humor of these building circumstances depends on the assumption that Jerry is straight; although this episode showcases *Seinfeld*'s characteristic playfulness with queer subject matter, great pains are taken to prevent the viewer from ever believing (or realizing) that Jerry is gay.

After Kramer leaves, Jerry and George spot Hernandez stretching out in the locker room. With Kramer no longer threatening to introduce direct discussion of overtly homoerotic matters, the queer is permitted to enter into the narrative space between Jerry and George. Both baseball aficionados, they are bordering on giddy, immediately starstruck by Hernandez. Possessing prior knowledge of Keith's personal life, Jerry remarks that Hernandez is not only a talented athlete but intelligent as well, being an American Civil War buff. "I wish *I* were a Civil War buff," George replies longingly. Chronically socially inept, George is left to appropriate the interests of a man he admires without being able to relate to him more directly.[14]

Keith introduces himself to Jerry as a big fan of his comedy; Jerry is instantly flattered and returns the compliment. As the jealous and excluded George looks on (one of the rare times that Jerry and George break rank and appear distinctly physically separated within a scene), Keith and Jerry exchange phone numbers and plan to meet for coffee in the future. Thus, in the strictly homosocial, theoretically nonromantic masculine world of the locker room, two men have initiated an interaction that becomes transformed into a relationship, consistently mirroring traditional television representations of heterosexual dating rituals. The homoerotic stage is set.

Later, at Monk's, Jerry complains to Elaine that three days have passed without a call from Keith. When Elaine asks why Jerry doesn't initiate the first call, he responds that he doesn't want to seem overanxious: "If he wants to see me, he has my number; he should call. I can't stand these guys—you give your number to them, and then they don't call."

Here, in his attempts not to seem overly aggressive, Jerry identifies with the traditionally receptive and passive role posited as appropriate female behavior. By employing such categorization as "these guys," Jerry brackets himself off from the rest of the heterosexual, male dating population, reinforcing his identification with Elaine not as Same (i.e., straight male) but as Other (Elaine as Not Male, Jerry as Not Straight). Elaine responds sympathetically:

ELAINE: I'm sorry, honey.
JERRY: I mean, I thought he liked me, I really thought he liked me—we were getting along. He came over to *me,* I didn't go over to *him.*
ELAINE: [Commiserating.] I know.
JERRY: Here I meet this guy, this *great* guy, ballplayer, best guy I ever met in my life … well, that's it. I'm *never* giving my number out to another guy again.

Jerry is clearly expressing romantic disillusionment in reaction to Keith's withdrawal from their social economy. Elaine further links her identity—as sexually experienced with men—to Jerry's own situation:

ELAINE: Sometimes I give my number out to a guy, and it takes him a *month* to call me.
JERRY: [Outraged.] A *month?* Ha! Have him call *me* after a month—let's see if *he* has a prayer!

Thus, Jerry's construction of his relationship with Keith is one bound by the rules of heterosexual dating protocol and appropriate exchange; the intensity of his feelings and expectations for his relationship with Keith have long surpassed normative (that is, conventional, expected, tolerable), straight male friendship. By stating that Keith's violation of protocol will result in Jerry's withdrawal, it is clear that Jerry is only willing to consider any interactions with Keith in terms of a romantic model—one that, as suggested by Keith's relative indifference, is based in fantasy.

Elaine suggests that he simply put an end to the waiting and call Keith to arrange an evening out. Jerry ponders the possibility of dinner but then has doubts:

JERRY: But don't you think that dinner might be coming on too strong? Kind of a turnoff?
ELAINE: [Incredulous.] Jerry, it's a *guy.*
JERRY: [Covering his eyes.] It's all very confusing.

Throughout the episode, Jerry is content to succumb to the excitement of his newfound relationship, until the moment when someone inevitably refers to its homoerotic nature (terms such as "gay" and "homosexual" are certainly implied but never explicitly invoked). Elaine's reminder that Jerry's fears about a "turnoff" are addressed to a man quickly ends his swooning; he covers his eyes as if to suggest a groggy return from a dream-like state.

To interrupt and divert the narrative attention away from Jerry's increasingly queer leanings, the scene abruptly changes to George at the unemployment office, where he is hoping to maneuver a thirteen-week extension on his unemployment benefits.[15] There, George evades the questions of his no-nonsense interviewer Mrs. Sokol until she forces him to provide one name of a company with which he had recently sought employment.

Having in truth interviewed nowhere, he quickly concocts "Vandelay Industries," a company, he assures her, he had thoroughly pursued to no avail. Further pressed, he tells Mrs. Sokol that they are "makers of latex products." His blurting-out of the word "latex" must not be overlooked here as a queer signifier directly associated with the gay safe-sex campaigns throughout the last decade. Whereas "condoms" as a signifier would have perhaps been a more mainstream (straight) sexual symbol, latex evokes a larger category of products— condoms, gloves, dental dams—linked closely with the eroticization of gay safe-sex practices. When Mrs. Sokol insists on information to verify his claim, it is telling that George provides Jerry's address and phone number as the home of Vandelay latex. George's lie necessitates a race back to Jerry's to warn him of the impending phone call; once again, he will depend on Jerry's willingness to maintain a duplicity and to adopt a false identity as the head of Vandelay Industries.

As if to await the panicked arrival of George, the scene changes to Jerry's apartment, where he is himself anxiety ridden over his impending night out with Keith. In a noticeable departure from his usual range of conservative color and style, he steps out of his bedroom, modeling a bright orange and red shirt, colors so shocking that they might best be described as "flaming." Pivoting slightly with arms outstretched in a style suggesting a fashion model, he asks Elaine's opinion. Again, she reminds him: "Jerry, he's a guy." Agitated (but never denying her implication of homoerotic attraction), he drops his arms, attempting to hide his nervous discomfort.

Jerry's actual evening out with Keith remains unseen (closeted) until the end of the "date"; the men sit alone in the front seat of Keith's car outside of Jerry's apartment. In the setup that prefigures the close of Elaine's date with Keith later in the episode, Jerry sits in the passenger seat next to him; a familiar heterosexual power dynamic is at play. Keith, as both the car owner and driver, acts and reacts in his appropriate masculine role. Jerry, within the increasingly queer context of an intimate social interaction with another man, is left to identify with what we recognize as the woman's position in the car. As the passenger and not the driver, he has relinquished both the mechanical and social control that defines the dominance of the male role. In a symbolic interpretation of power relations, Jerry's jump into the feminized gender role is characterized by the absence of the steering wheel:

JERRY: [Aloud to Keith.] Well, thanks a lot, that was really fun. [Thinking to himself.] Should I shake his hand?

This anxiety and expectation over appropriate and mutually appealing physical contact expresses the same kind of desire—that is, sexual—that Keith will express with Elaine later on; whereas Keith will long for a kiss, Jerry's desires have been translated into a more acceptable form of physical contact between men. It would seem that part of Jerry's frustration in this situation comes from the multiplicity of gender roles that he plays. Whereas in his interactions with George, Jerry occupies the dominant role (controlling the discourse and the action), he is suddenly relegated to a more passive (feminine) position in his relationship with the hypermasculine Keith Hernandez. Part of the tension that comprises the handshake scene stems not only from Jerry's desire to interact physically *and* appropriately but also from wanting to initiate such an action from the disadvantaged, less powerful position of the (feminine) passenger's seat. I would suggest that the confusion arising out of his relationship with Keith is not strictly due to its potentially homosexual valences but is also the result of the unclear position (passive/dominant, feminine/masculine, nelly/butch) that Jerry holds within the homoerotic/homosexual coupling.

Once again, the humor of this scene is based on the presupposition that Jerry is straight and that this very familiar scene is not a homosexual recreation of heterosexual dating etiquette but simply a parody of it. Nonetheless, Jerry's discomfort over initiating a handshake betrays the nature of his desire for Keith. From behind the steering wheel (the seat of masculine power), Keith invites Jerry to a movie over the coming weekend. Jerry is elated, and they shake hands: a consummation of their successful social interaction. However, Keith follows up by telling Jerry that he would like to call Elaine for a date; the spell broken, Jerry responds with reluctance and thinly veiled disappointment.

Back in Jerry's apartment, George jealously asks for a recounting of Jerry's evening with Keith. Again, the handshake is reinforced as the symbol of a successful male-to-male social encounter:

GEORGE: Did you shake his hand?
JERRY: Yeah.
GEORGE: What kind of a handshake does he have?
JERRY: Good shake, perfect shake. Single pump, not too hard. He didn't have to prove anything, but firm enough to know he's there.

George and Jerry share a discourse, laden with masturbatory overtones, in which quantifying and qualifying the description of a handshake expresses information about the nature of men's relationships. This implicit connection between male intimacy and the presence and quality of physical contact clearly transcends the interpretation of the handshake in a heterosexual context. Upon hearing that Jerry had in fact shaken hands with Keith, George follows with the highly charged question: "You gonna see him again?" Here, the use of the verb "to see," implying organized social interaction between two people, is typically in reference to romantic situations; George has thus come to accept Jerry in a dating relationship with Keith.

Elaine enters and immediately teases Jerry: "So, how was your date?" Not only has she invaded Jerry and George's male habitat, but she has once again made explicit the romantic nature of Jerry's connection to Keith that he can only enjoy when unspoken. Jerry is forced to respond (with obvious agitation): "He's a guy." Elaine quickly reveals that she and Keith have made a date for the coming Friday, perhaps expressing an implicit understanding of a rivalry with Jerry. Realizing that such plans will interfere with his own "date" with Keith, Jerry protests with disappointment and resentment. Elaine mistakes his anger as being in response to some lingering romantic attachment to her:

ELAINE: I've never seen you jealous.
JERRY: You weren't even *at* Game Six—you're not even a fan!
ELAINE: Wait a second . . . are you jealous of *him* or are you jealous of *me*?

Flustered and confused, Jerry walks away without responding, allowing the insinuation of a queer interpretation to be implied by his silence.

Jerry steps outside of the apartment just as Kramer enters; he sits alone with Elaine as George disappears into the bathroom. Predictably, it is just as Kramer finds himself next to the phone that the call from the unemployment bureau arrives; Kramer, the only one uninformed about George's scheme, answers the phone and responds with confusion, assuring the caller that she has reached a residential number, not Vandelay Industries. Having overheard, George bursts from the bathroom in a panic, his pants around his ankles. Despite his frantic pleading with Kramer to pass him the phone, Kramer is already hanging up; the defeated

George collapses on the floor. Precisely at this moment, Jerry reenters the apartment. In a highly unusual aerial shot, the camera shows us Jerry's perspective of George, face down, boxer shorts exposed, and prone, lying before him on the floor in an obvious position of sexual receptivity. Jerry quips: "And you want to be my latex salesman." Once again, Jerry's reinvocation of latex has powerful queer connotations in response to seeing George seminude before him.

The next scenes juxtapose Elaine and Keith's date with Jerry's alternate Friday night activity, a visit to see his friends' new baby. Elaine, the focal point of a crowded sports bar discussing Game Six of the World Series with Keith, has occupied the very place (physically and romantically) that Jerry had longed for. In the accompanying parallel scene of Jerry, he seems both out of place and uncomfortable amid the domestic and overwhelmingly heterosexual atmosphere of the baby's nursery. The misery over losing his night on the town to Elaine is amplified by his obvious distaste for the nuclear family, the ultimate signifier of "straightness."

The scene again changes to Keith and Elaine alone in his car, this time with Elaine in the passenger seat that Jerry had previously occupied. Elaine, comfortable in her familiar and appropriate role as passive/feminine, waits patiently as Keith (in the privileged masculine driver's seat) silently wonders whether or not he should kiss her, mirroring Jerry's earlier internal debate over suitable intimate physical contact. Although they kiss, Elaine is unimpressed. Later, just as George had done, Jerry pumps Elaine for information about her date. When Elaine admits that she and Keith had kissed, Jerry pushes further: "What *kind* of kiss was it?" Incredulous at Jerry's tactlessness, Elaine does not respond. Jerry at last answers her standing question: "I'm jealous of everybody."

Keith calls, interrupting one of the few moments in the episode when Jerry and George share the scene alone. After hanging up, he explains with discomfort that he has agreed to help Keith in his move to a new apartment. George seems to recognize and identify with Jerry's apprehension over this sudden escalation in their rapport. "This is a big step in the male relationship," Jerry observes, "the biggest. That's like going all the way." Never has Jerry made such a direct reference to the potential for sexual contact with Keith. Of course, Keith has by no means propositioned Jerry, which makes the queer desire on Jerry's part all the more obvious in contrast with the seemingly asexual nature of Keith's request. However, Jerry has made clear his own willingness to homoeroticize his friendship with another man. By likening "going all the way" to moving furniture, Jerry is able to fantasize that Keith shares Jerry's homosexual desire. Ingeniously, he has crafted an imaginary set of circumstances that allow him to ignore Keith's preference for Elaine as a sexual object while tidily completing his fantasy: Keith has expressed desire for Jerry, but now Jerry has the luxury of refusing his advance on the moral ground that he will not rush sexual intimacy. Once Keith arrives, Jerry tells him that he cannot help him move, explaining that it is still too soon in their relationship. Again, by positing Keith in the masculine role of sexual aggressor, Jerry in turn occupies the stereotypically feminine role of sexual regulator/withholder.

Kramer and Newman arrive just as Jerry declines Keith's request; not surprisingly, Kramer jumps at the opportunity to take Jerry's place. As he and Newman disappear out the door to help Keith move his furniture, Jerry commiserates with Elaine over the phone: "You broke up with him? Me too!" Even as Jerry's homoerotic adventure has drawn to a close, Kramer's last-minute appearance lends an air of sexual unpredictability to end the episode on a resoundingly queer note.

In contrast to "The Boyfriend," in which the queer subtext is exploited as the source of the humor, "The Virgin" and its companion episode "The Contest" present an equally queer narrative expressed in subtler and more indirect ways. Within these interwoven episodes, the "knowing" spectator—one familiar with gay culture and receptive to potentially homo-erotic situations—is essentially bombarded by queer catchphrases and code words, gay themes, and gay male behavior, while the "unknowing" spectator would most likely only recognize a traditionally "straight" plot about heterosexual dating frustrations. "The Virgin" drops its first "hair-pins" almost immediately[16]; Jerry and George are drinking together in a bar when Jerry spots Marla, a beautiful woman whom he recognizes across the room. "She's in the closet business—reorganizes your closet and shows you how to maximize your closet space. She's looked into my closet." In the same instant that we are introduced to a potential female love object for Jerry, she is immediately identified with the closet, a widely recog-nized metaphor referring to a gay person's secret sexual identity. Queerly read, Marla could be interpreted as (and will in fact become) a nonthreatening, nonsexual female object. Having "looked into his closet," Marla functions as a woman who is aware of Jerry's homo-sexuality and will be willing to interact with him in ways that will permit him to pass while still maintaining the homoerotic connections to the men around him. By allowing him this duplicity, she will indeed maximize Jerry's "closet space."

While at the bar, George bemoans the fact that he is miserable in his relationship with television executive Susan, his first girlfriend in some time. He is instead more interested in the new partnership that he has developed with Jerry, writing his new situation comedy pilot for NBC. The ostensibly platonic nature of such privileged male–male relations becomes further queered by Jerry's insistence that George "maintain appearances" with Susan until she has persuaded the network to pick up their pilot. The Seinfeldian recurring theme of hidden identities and guarded appearances puts into place the knowing viewer's suspicions about the homosexual potential between George and Jerry.

In the following scene, the spectator is given a rare view of Jerry's bedroom, made even more rare by the presence of a woman with him. Although the scene employs the standard formula for a possible sexual encounter (a man and woman alone in his bed-room), the couple remains perpetually framed inside Jerry's open closet; Jerry's coded homo-sexuality, symbolically surrounding the couple as they speak, prevents the sex scene from occurring.

To further complicate Jerry's interaction with Marla, his friends start to invade the apart-ment, interrupting the potential for intimacy. First, Kramer intrudes, taking over the televi-sion in the living room. (He is desperate to see *The Bold and the Beautiful,* a show whose soap opera genre is largely identified with a female viewership.) Jerry kicks Kramer out only to have Elaine buzz over the intercom a moment later. In the few private moments left, Marla con-fesses that the reason for her breakup with her ex-boyfriend was his impatience with her virginity. Elaine arrives before they can discuss it.

Marla and Elaine, Jerry's current and past romantic interests, stand in stark contrast to one another. The timid, traditional, and virginal Marla is further desexualized in the pres-ence of the heterosexually active Elaine; this contrast is intensified by Elaine's crass descrip-tion of her embarrassment at a recent party when she accidentally let her diaphragm slip out of her purse. As she laughs knowingly, Jerry winces, sensing Marla's shock at Elaine's casual remark: "You never know when you might need it." This exaggerated reference to female sexuality makes Marla's virginity even more pronounced; she is unable to hide her discom-fort any longer and excuses herself in haste. It seems that Jerry, socially and romantically attached to a woman horrified by even the discussion of sex, could himself not be further from heterosexual activity.

Upon hearing that her indiscretion has lost Jerry a potential girlfriend, Elaine chases after Marla in hopes of repairing the damage. Over coffee at Monk's (clearly a female invasion of Jerry and George's male space), Elaine tries to dissuade Marla from her horror of sex with men. However, her lecture quickly dissolves into a listing of male failings: their thoughtlessness, manipulations, and fear of emotional attachment after sex. Despite Elaine's outward intentions to reunite Jerry and Marla, she has instead instilled an intensified mistrust of men. Once again, Jerry's friends have been the cause of his distancing from women; he remains insulated in the homoerotic network of his male friends and is ushered through acceptable straight society by his platonic female friend.

In a strange reversal of roles, George is still engaged in a romantic relationship with a woman (even if he is unwillingly "maintaining appearances" with Susan). At the crucial meeting with the NBC executives, George greets Susan with a kiss, an appropriate and public gesture of straightness. However, by exposing Susan as his girlfriend, George compromises her professional standing with the network. Not only is she fired, but she also breaks off her relationship with George (and consequently later "becomes" a lesbian).[17] Despite George's delight at having inadvertently rid himself of Susan, the overall message is clear: straying out of his queer context sparks destructive results in the straight world.

Juxtaposed with George's ultimately disastrous straight kiss is one of Jerry's own; he and Marla, back in his bedroom, are finally embracing passionately. The (hetero)sexual potential suggested in this scene is diffused, however, by the viewer's instant recognition that the couple is not only framed by Jerry's closet but in fact that they are embracing inside of it. Marla, as a nonsexualized female object with knowledge and access to Jerry's closet(edness), poses no threat of engaging in "real" sexual intimacy with Jerry. Their embrace is made comically awkward by the clutter of Jerry's hanging clothes around them; the encounter is again cut short as Marla recalls Elaine's unflattering depiction of typical male behavior after sex. Even in absentia, Jerry's friends precipitate the woman's departure and his own separation from the possibility of (hetero)sex.

"The Contest" follows up on this storyline; Jerry is still patiently dating the virginal Marla while, as usual, spending the bulk of his social time with George, Kramer, and Elaine. As George arrives to join them for lunch at Monk's, he announces sheepishly (yet voluntarily) that he had been "caught" by his mother. Although never explicitly mentioned, George is clearly making reference to masturbation. Believing himself to be alone in his mother's house, he was using her copy of *Glamour* magazine[18] as erotic material when his mother entered and discovered him masturbating. In her shock, Mrs. Costanza had fainted, hurt herself in the fall, and ultimately wound up in traction. It is essential to note the homosexual underpinnings of masturbation as a sexual act; the fetishization of one's (and in this case, George's) own genitalia is often closely linked in psychoanalytic theory to the narcissism and reflexive fixation associated with same-sex desire. Mrs. Costanza was not reacting so much to her recognition of her son as sexual but instead to his inappropriate sexual object choice, the (his) penis. George has paid dearly for being exposed to straight eyes while practicing queer pleasure.

Traumatized by his experience, George announces that he is swearing off such activity for good. Jerry and Kramer are skeptical of the claim, and the three men find themselves in a contest—regulated by the "honor system"—to see which of them can abstain the longest from masturbating. The wager is steeped in homoerotic potential; in fact, the three *Seinfeld* men have entered into a kind of sanitized "circle jerk" in which they monitor (and consequently augment) each other's sexual tension, voyeuristically waiting to see who will be the first to "relieve" himself. When Elaine, who has been listening to their conversation from the periphery of their queer circle, wants to enter the contest as well, the men protest that she would have an unfair advantage. As Kramer explains: "It's easier for women—it's part of *our lifestyle*." By creating a stiff binary opposition between women and "our lifestyle," he not only employs a phrase closely associated with the "alternative lifestyle" of homosexuality, but he also demonstrates an obvious ignorance and detachment from female sexuality, perpetuating myths about the limited appetite and imagination of the female sexual drive. Despite her protests, Elaine is forced to stake fifty dollars extra to even the odds before entering into the contest.

In the next scene, the foursome returns to Jerry's apartment, where Kramer immediately spots a naked woman in the window across the street.[19] The sexually ravenous Kramer is unable to control himself; he excuses himself immediately and returns to announce what we had been led to predict: "I'm out." Of the three male characters, Kramer takes on the most ambisexual valence, moving freely from the homoerotic circle shared with Jerry and George to the distinctly heterosexual desire he expressed for the naked woman. While highly sexualized, neither Kramer's intimate and often seductive relationship with Jerry and George nor his frequent erotic encounters with women serve to posit him in clear homo- or heterosexual territory. Functioning as a sort of sexual fulcrum depending on the social context, Kramer may well be acting as *Seinfeld*'s embodiment of queerness.

The three remaining contestants are left to their own frustrations. In her aerobics class, Elaine finds herself positioned behind John F. Kennedy Jr., the popular object of white, privileged heterosexual female desire. George is disturbed and aroused by his discovery that the privacy curtain separating his mother's hospital bed from her beautiful roommate's creates an erotic silhouette of the stranger's nightly sponge bath.[20] Locked in a passionate embrace in the front seat of Jerry's car, Marla pulls back and asks Jerry to "slow down"; he politely acquiesces, assuring Marla that her virginity is not hindering his enjoyment of their relationship.

On the surface, Marla's virginity is posited as an intensifying factor of her attractiveness; the withholding of not only sex but also of her sexuality seems to make the possibility of physical intimacy even more inaccessible—and thus desirable. In fact, Marla's virginity is a crucial element to balance (and perhaps camouflage) the more important discussions and representations of masturbation. Marla's introduction to the periphery of Jerry's bet with Kramer, George, and Elaine serves a twofold purpose. First, her virginity becomes both a presence and an obstacle between Jerry and Marla, impeding any progress toward a heterosexual encounter. Second, without Marla as Jerry's ostensible love object, the "masturbation episode" would take on a glaringly homosexual tone. Marla's presence serves to divert attention away from what is more or less a circle jerk among homosexualized men: a collective and voyeuristic study of each other's (auto)erotic activity, focusing—if we may momentarily exclude Elaine's participation—on the male orgasm brought on reflexively by the male participants. As a virgin, Marla serves to deflect the queerness of the contest away from Jerry while never threatening the homoerotic trinity of Jerry, George, and Kramer.

Elaine, by comparison, is indeed a heterosexually active female. Why is Elaine allowed to participate in the otherwise queerly coded masturbatory abstinence contest? In effect, she never truly is cast as an equal participant. Throughout the episode, she is consistently figured as the "odd man out"; at the restaurant table where the triangulated male bodies of Jerry, George, and Kramer construct the terms of the bet, Elaine is seated in the corner of the booth. Within the frames, she appears either alone or with her back partially turned to the camera, surrounded by the men who look toward her, clearly separated from the intimate boy talk of the others who share the booth with her. As mentioned before, the men's misconception that women are naturally predisposed to such masturbatory abstinence works to further distance female sexuality—and thus females—from their own collective experience of (same-sex) desire. Perhaps most importantly, Elaine's strongest connection to the trio is through her relationship with Jerry, a friendship that is predicated on their previous failure as (hetero)sexual partners. Her potentially menacing role as Straight Female is mitigated by her position as Not Love Object. Elaine may participate in the contest from the sidelines without truly interrupting its homosexual valence.

Despite the remaining contestants' boasts of being "queen of the castle" and "master of my domain," their sexual frustrations are evident in the four juxtaposed scenes of their private bedrooms: Jerry appears restless in his bed of white linens; George thrashes beneath his sheets printed with cartoon dinosaurs[21]; Elaine is sleepless in her darkened room; Kramer, however, long having satisfied his desire, snores peacefully.

Grumpy from his sleepless night, Jerry tells Kramer that he can no longer tolerate the view of the naked neighbor across the street. As he prepares to go over and ask the woman to draw her shades, the infuriated Kramer tries to stop him, doubting Jerry's sanity for wanting to block their view of a beautiful nude woman. Kramer has called into question Jerry's priorities, which seem to be clear: Jerry privileges his participation in the queerly coded contest over the visual pleasure Kramer experiences from the nude woman.

In the next series of juxtaposed bedroom shots, the viewer discovers from Elaine's restful sleep that she has given in. The next morning, as she sheepishly relinquishes her money, she explains that rumors of JFK Jr.'s interest in her had prompted her moment of weakness. Jerry marvels that "the queen is dead," thereby leaving only himself and George to compete for the pot.

In the following scene, two embracing figures are stretched out on the couch in Jerry's dark apartment. In the close-up shot, we see that Marla is on top of Jerry; not only does this physicality suggest a heightened potential for sexual intimacy between the ordinarily distant couple, but Jerry's positioning on the bottom of the embrace casts him in the stereotypically feminine, passive role of a woman in a straight couple (a role evocative of the one he occupied in his relationship with Keith Hernandez). In keeping with the episode's (and indeed the show's) pattern, such menacing circumstances should surely create chaotic results.

Taking her cue from Jerry's receptive position, the previously hesitant Marla becomes the aggressor, initiating a (masculine) invitation to have sex: "Let's go in the bedroom." From beneath her, Jerry's somewhat timid voice sounds unsure: "*Really?*" Now too close for comfort, Jerry must find a way to disengage from the heterosexual situation in which he is now entangled; Marla's virginity is no longer a sufficient buffer. When Marla asks why he looks so tense, he thoughtlessly (or so it would appear) recounts the details of the contest to explain his (ostensible) relief at the chance to have sex with her. Marla reacts with horror and disgust and quickly exits, leaving Jerry alone.

On the street, Marla bumps into Elaine, who is eagerly awaiting the arrival of JFK Jr. for their first arranged meeting. Marla pulls away from Elaine in revulsion: "I don't want to have anything to do with you or your perverted friends. Get away from me, you're horrible!" Having clearly identified Jerry, George, and Kramer as sexually deviant (i.e., not "straight"), Marla leaves, removing the safe, female heterosexual anchor that her presence provided to the otherwise transparently queer contest.

Believing that JFK Jr. stood her up, Elaine complains to Jerry only to hear from George that Kennedy had just driven away with Marla. As they look out the window, Jerry spots Kramer in the arms of the beautiful woman across the street.

In the final series of four bedroom shots, Jerry and George are at last also enjoying a restful sleep; Kramer snores next to his new lover, and Marla compliments "John" on his sexual prowess. Whereas the two latter scenes depict the postorgasmic satisfaction of the two heterosexual partners that share it, the two former scenes are ambiguous by contrast: no explanation is provided for how or why Jerry and George relieved their pent-up sexual energies at the same time. With no female love object available (no recent viewings of the erotic sponge bath for George, and Jerry's potential lover has left him) to dehomosexualize Jerry and George's two-member circle jerk, the viewer is left with the suggestion that they have satisfied their sexual frustrations together. Intensified by the "success" of the hypervirile JFK Jr. in the face of Jerry's sexual failure with Marla, the narrative closes with individual shots of George and Jerry—alone and yet paired off. Quite apart from the strong homoerotic sensibility of "The Contest"'s construction, the simple and familiar plot resolution—the duo's inability to sustain a romantic relationship with a woman leaves them again alone with each other—marks the episode as incontrovertibly queer.

Seinfeld's narrative design would, at first glance, seem to lack the depth necessary in character and plot to facilitate a discussion of the complexities of homoerotic male relationships. The sort of nonspecific, scattered quality of the *Seinfeld* text, however, makes it well suited to the fluid nature of a queer reading, whose project is more concerned with context than fixity, more with potential than evidence. Nonetheless, *Seinfeld* is full of both context and evidence that lead the text's critics toward a well-developed queer reading. *Seinfeld* enjoys a kind of subculture defined by a discursive code that unites its members in a common lexicon of meaning. The narrative restricts its focus to the foursome, containing and maintaining the intimate bonds between the show's three men and its one woman (the latter being clearly positioned as sexually incompatible and socially separate from the others). Directly related to this intense interconnection, the foursome often causes each member's inability to foster outside heterosexual romantic interests.

Jerry and George share the most intimate relationship of them all; they aid each other in perpetuating duplicities while remaining truthful only with one another. They are the two characters who most frequently share a frame and who create and occupy male-coded narrative spaces, whether in the domestic sphere of Jerry's apartment or in the public sphere at Monk's.

All of these relationships are in motion amid a steady stream of other discursive and iconic gay referents. Their visibility admits the "knowing" viewer into a queerly constructed *Seinfeld* universe while never being so explicit as to cause the "unknowing" viewer to suspect the outwardly "normal" appearance of the show.

Reading the queer in *Seinfeld* sheds a revealing light on the show's "not that there's anything wrong with that" approach to representations of male homoeroticism. While sustaining a steadfast denial of its gay under-currents, the text playfully takes advantage of provocative semiotic juxtapositions that not only allow but also encourage the "knowing" spectator to ignore the show's heterosexual exterior and instead to explore the queerness of *Seinfeld*.

Selected *Seinfeld* Videography
(*Seinfeld*. Created by Jerry Seinfeld and Larry David. NBC-TV, 1989–98.)

"The Apartment." Writ. Peter Mehlman. 4 Apr. 1991.
"The Boyfriend." Writ. Larry David and Larry Levin. 12 Feb. 1992.
"The Café." Writ. Tom Leopold. 6 Nov. 1991.
"The Cheever Letters." Writ. Larry David. 28 Oct. 1992.

"The Contest." Writ. Larry David. 13 Nov. 1992.
"The Dog." Writ. Larry David. 9 Oct. 1991.
"The Junior Mint." Writ. Andy Robin. 18 Mar. 1993.
"The Limo." Writ. Larry Charles. 26 Feb. 1992.
"The Outing." Writ. Larry Charles. 11 Feb. 1993.
"The Phone Message." Writ. Larry David and Jerry Seinfeld. 13 Feb. 1991.
"The Pilot." Writ. Larry David. 20 May 1993.
"The Red Dot." Writ. Larry David. 11 Dec. 1991.
"The Shoes." Writ. Larry David and Jerry Seinfeld. 4 Feb. 1993.
"The Smelly Car." Writ. Larry David and Peter Mehlman. 15 Apr. 1993.
"The Stakeout." Writ. Larry David and Jerry Seinfeld. 31 May 1990.
"The Statue." Writ. Larry Charles. 11 Apr. 1991.
"The Subway." Writ. Larry Charles. 8 Jan. 1992.
"The Virgin." Writ. Larry David. 11 Nov. 1992.
"The Watch." Writ. Larry David. 30 Sept. 1992.

Notes

All dialogue quoted in this essay, unless otherwise indicated, comes from my own transcriptions of the television programs in question.

1. Dave Walter, "Does Civil Disobedience Still Work?" *Advocate,* 20 Nov. 1990, 34–38.
2. For further discussion of the political and semiotic history of the word "queer," see Ernesto Laclau, *New Reflections on the Revolution of Our Time* (London: Verso, 1990); Teresa de Lauretis, "Queer Theory: Lesbian and Gay Sexualities," *differences* 3:2 (1991): iii–xviii; Michelangelo Signorile, "Absolutely Queer: Reading, Writing, and Rioting," *Advocate,* 6 Oct. 1992, 17.
3. Eve Kosofsky Sedgwick, *Epistemology of the Closet* (Berkeley: University of California Press, 1990).
4. Diana Fuss, ed. *Inside/Out: Lesbian Theories, Gay Theories* (New York: Routledge, 1991).
5. Alexander Doty, *Making Things Perfectly Queer: Reading Mass Culture* (Minnesota: University of Minnesota Press, 1993).
6. Bruce Fretts, *The Entertainment Weekly "Seinfeld" Companion* (New York: Warner Books, 1993), 12.
7. Bill Zehme, "Jerry and George and Kramer and Elaine: Exposing the Secrets of *Seinfeld*'s Success," *Rolling Stone* 660–61 (6–22 July 1993): 40–45, 130–31.
8. As evidence of this Seinfeldian shared vocabulary, I offer one of my primary resources for this paper, *The Entertainment Weekly "Seinfeld" Companion.* Author Bruce Fretts creates a partial glossary of these terms, situating them in their episodic contexts, cross-referencing them with the episodes in which the term recurs, and finally providing a chronological plot synopsis of episodes 1–61, ending with the 1993 season premiere, "The Pilot."
9. Doty outlines the political and semiotic complexities of the term "queer" in his insightful introduction to *Making Things Perfectly Queer.*
10. My essay takes its title from this episode; while combating the rumor of their homosexuality, the phrase "not that there's anything wrong with that" serves as Jerry and George's knee-jerk addendum to their denials. The catchphrase becomes a running joke through the episode, being echoed in turn by Jerry's and George's mothers and, later, by Kramer as well.
11. During the 1994 season, the *Seinfeld* triangle suddenly switched to blue. Might this suggest that the show's creators wished to distance themselves from an overly gay–identified icon, or does a queer interpretation suggest that Jerry is simply attempting to be more butch during that period? The 1995 season was marked with an ambiguous green triangle; the icon continued to change in each following season. One can only speculate that the shift away from the pink triangle is meant to mirror the shift away from the queerness of the early seasons—as evidenced by Susan's abrupt renunciation of lesbianism and subsequent return to George (my thanks to colleagues Melinda Kanner and Steve Bishop for their insightful ideas on this subject).

12. A particularly useful example of this theme occurs in "The Café," in which George, terrified of his girlfriend Monica's request that he take an IQ test, fears that he will not be able to pass. Out of desperation, he arranges for the more intelligent Elaine to take the test for him by passing it out to her through an open window. Jerry too has approved their secret plan to pass George off as an intelligent, appropriate partner for Monica: "Hey, I love a good caper!" Despite their best efforts to dupe Monica by presenting George in a false light, she discovers their duplicity and breaks up with him.

13. When questioned, Jerry makes no secret about the intensity of his "friendship" with George; in "The Dog," he confesses that they talk on the phone six times a day—coincidentally, the same number of times a day that he gargles.

14. A queer reading of the social differences between Jerry and George reveals a substratum of conflict: within the homoerotic dynamic that groups them together as a couple, George is constantly portrayed as crude, unrefined, and in need of direction. When George is paired with Jerry in the intimate, caretaking relationship they share, their connection suggests a domestic partnership in which Jerry, the more successful and refined of the duo, acts as their public voice, correcting George's social missteps allowing them to "pass" less noticeably through acceptable, urban, upper-middle-class society.

15. It should be noted that George's presentation as both unemployed and desperate accentuate the clear class differences between him and Jerry, the successful stand-up comic being courted by a celebrity athlete.

16. In *Gay Talk* (New York: Paragon Books, 1972), Bruce Rodgers defines the expression "drop hairpins" (also "drop beads" or "drop pearls") as "to let out broad hints of one's sexuality" (69). Historically rooted in gay male culture, this expression is useful here to express the texts' many links to gay icons and lexicon. It should be noted, however, that the intentionality suggested by the phrase "drop hairpins" is problematic in the context of this paper, as I am not entering into an analysis of whether or not the creators of *Seinfeld* have knowingly or inadvertently produced a heavily queer text.

17. In "The Smelly Car," George runs into Susan for the first time since their breakup and is shocked to see her with Mona, her new lover. Although Susan alludes to her longstanding attraction to women, George makes multiple references to how he "drove her" to lesbianism. After Mona is inexplicably seduced by Kramer's mystique, Susan makes a new romantic contact in Allison, another of George's ex-girlfriends. The implication is not only that George is a failure as a heterosexual but also that, even in his attempts to connect romantically with women, he is attracted to inappropriate (or equally conflicted) female object choices.

18. George's use of *Glamour,* a women's fashion magazine, is a notably odd choice for visual sexual stimulation in contrast to such heterosexual pornography as *Playboy,* in which nude women are presented in ways to elicit sexual responses from men. George has instead found sexual pleasure from a magazine whose focus is women's beauty culture—fashion, health, cosmetics—and not women themselves. It is essential to recognize that George's masturbatory activity was not in response to heterosexual desire for women's bodies but instead connected to something only indirectly related to their appearances.

19. In contrast to George's interest in *Glamour,* Kramer provides us with a more familiar example of an "appropriate" erotic stimulus for the heterosexual male; the sight of a nude woman directly and immediately enacts Kramer's sexual response.

20. This visual joke is revived in "The Outing": having been falsely identified in the newspaper as Jerry's lover, George attempts to set his shocked and still-hospitalized mother "straight." However, the tempting silhouette of the beautiful patient and her nurse has been replaced by the erotic shapes of a muscular male attendant sponge-bathing a brawny male patient.

21. Again, the spectator is privy to a subtle material reference to the class distinctions apparent within the coupling of Jerry and George; the contrast in their choices of bed linens—Jerry's tasteful white and George's childish, colorful pattern—provide a point of reference from which to understand the power dynamic between them as middle- to upper-middle-class (Jerry) and lower-middle- to working-class (George) gay men.

This Text: Reading

1. Gantz indicates to an extent her writing situation when she labels American television as homophobic. How does this play out in her essay?
2. Gantz focuses on "queer theory" in this essay, which she essentially uses as a lens to view her text. Are there other lenses we might use in discussing popular culture? Using another lens (such as gender, race, or class), examine *Seinfeld* or some other popular text.
3. What other works might yield the same type of results with examination by queer theory?
4. Why might *Seinfeld* be a particularly good show to examine? Does Gantz indicate this in her essay?
5. In what ways might queer theory apply in your daily experiences of reading?
6. What is the difference between "queer" and "homosexual"? Does Gantz make the distinction clear?

Your Text: Writing

1. Using the same lens of queer theory as Gantz, examine another popular television show.
2. Using another lens (such as race, gender, class), examine *Seinfeld* or another popular show. How does reading through a particular theory affect the writing process?
3. Write a short response paper to the essay itself. What did you like about it? What, if anything, disturbed you about it?

"Black Bart" Simpson: Appropriation and Revitalization in Commodity Culture[1]

Peter Parisi

As we work on the third edition of this book in the summer of 2007, the premiere of *The Simpsons Movie* is a little over a week away. Although programs like *South Park* and *Family Guy* have eclipsed *The Simpsons* in terms of popularity, the show remains the longest running animated show in the history of American TV, and the longest running program currently on American television. Of all contemporary comedies, only *Seinfeld* and *Friends* have had such an impact on culture. In this (1993) piece, Peter Parisi examines the phenomenon of the omnipresent cultural artifact: the T-shirt. Parisi uses the phenomenon as a window into the relationship artifacts audience.

DURING THE SUMMER OF 1990, the streets of cities across the country witnessed a striking and unusual gesture in popular culture: the appropriation and re-interpretation of a mass media figure by minority group members. That summer, *The Simpsons,* a crudely drawn television cartoon that itself portrayed the cultural impact of mass media upon ideals of family and small-town life, had completed a hit season. A merchandising blitz followed up on the success, flooding stores and streets with T-shirts depicting Matt Groening's highly publicized characters: the militant under-achiever Bart Simpson; his feckless and juvenile father Homer; patient, long-suffering mother Marge; and two sisters, bright, sensitive Lisa, and wide-eyed baby Maggie who perpetually and noisily sucks a pacifier.

The summer was not far advanced, however, before innumerable blacks, men and women, young and middle-aged, appeared in cities nationwide, wearing T-shirts adorned with the bootlegged image of Bart but now dark-skinned and posed in a variety of black identities.[2] Fusing Air Jordan and MC Hammer, "Air Bart" slam dunks a basketball and says, "you can't touch this." Home Boy Bart inquires pugnaciously, "Yo, homeboy, what the hell are you looking at?" "Rastabart, Master of Respect" sprouts dreadlocks, sports a red, green and gold headband and growls, "Watch it, Mon. 'Irie'," or, in a variation on the Rastafarian theme, becomes "Rasta-Dude Bart Marley" or "RastaBart." On other shirts, Black Bart and white Bart shake hands; Black Bart appears alongside Nelson Mandela, saying "Apartheid. No!" or "My Hero!" and Black Bart insists, "I didn't do it." "Asiatic Bart" wears the robes and skull cap of a Black Muslim and, borrowing the group's rhetoric, declares himself "Cream of the Planet Earth, Dude!" Bedecked with gold chain and snazzy sneakers, Black Bart glares from another shirt that reads, "You should understand," playing on another Afrocentric T-shirt motto: "It's a Black thing. You wouldn't understand." Still another shirt mixes a pacific message with a glaring Bart, joined by sister Lisa and a graphic of the African continent. The message read, "It's cool being black" and in a box beneath, "We are all brothers and sisters so live in unity, love and peace" (118).

One striking, scatological variant suggests how pungently these graphic figures could embody and play with social meanings. Across its top, the shirt carries the legend, "Crack Kills" and across the bottom "Black Power." Pictured between is a discomfited "white" Bart clenched between the buttocks of a sizable black woman with wavy hair and purple toenails. The shirt was striking in its irreverent treatment of phrases and terms—Crack Kills, Black Power— usually regarded as too solemn for parody.

Prices for the bootlegs in the summer of 1990 ranged from six to ten dollars, and dropped to five the following summer as the craze faded and authorities clamped down on copyright violations in the fashion industry. The total number of shirts sold is virtually impossible to determine. Obviously, no industry figures were kept. Nor would it be easy to enumerate all the designs. Unlicensed as they were, the bootleggers could freely crib, modify or invent ideas. At least two versions of the "Air Bart/'You Can't Touch This'" shirt circulated and another variant featured "BartHammer." There were apparent local variations. In Washington, Mills described shirts in which Bart utters lines from rap songs, a form that was uncommon in New York City.

Black Bart was not the first popular icon appropriated and modified to reflect African-American culture. *The New York Times* article about Black Bart noted that "there have been occasional blackened Betty Boops and a few attempts last year to recast Bat Man as 'Black Man' . . . " (Marriot C1). Also in 1988, New York street vendors sold sweatshirts depicting Mickey Mouse in a warm-up suit and gold chains, saying, "Yo Baby, Yo Baby, Yo! Let's get busy!" (i.e., let's make love). And a cartoonist and graphic artist, J. T. Liehr, who worked in a Philadelphia screen printing shop used by T-shirt designers, said his shop produced not only black versions of Bart Simpson, but also of Charlie Brown and Budweiser mascot Spuds Mackenzie, who was transmuted to a spliff-smoking Rastafarian, "Buds MacSensie" (a reference to high-grade, "sinsemilla" marijuana). "Whatever was popular at the time was modified to be black," Liehr said.

If not the first, the Black Bart T-shirt was yet the most popular Afrocentric appropriation of mass culture iconography. As illicit or anarchic as it may have been, the underground fashion industry that spawned the shirts managed to distribute them "coast to coast" ("When Life Imitates Bart" 61). The *Washington Post* (Mills), *New York Times* (Marriot) and *Newsweek* ("When Life Imitates Bart") found the phenomenon worthy of notice, with *The New York Times* calling Black Bart "one of the most enduring T-shirt images of the summer" (Marriot C1).

Wearing Black Bart Simpson shirt (Harlem), 125 St., NY, NY.

African Americans and the Active Audience

The consumption and display of Black Bart T-shirts represents a noteworthy case study within the growing scholarly interest in the creative activity of the mass audience, or, as Janice A. Radway puts it consumers' "power as individuals to resist or alter the ways in which... objects mean or can be used" (221). In *Reading the Popular,* John Fiske says popular culture "is always a culture of conflict, . . . involv[ing] the struggle to make social meanings that are in the interest of the subordinate and that are not those preferred by the dominant ideology" (2). "In the practices of consumption," he adds, "the commodity system is exposed to the power of the consumer, for the power of the system is not just top-down, or center-outward, but always two-way, always a flux of conflicting powers and resistances" (31).

Recent work on audience activity—see, for instance, David Eason and Fred Fogo's review (3–5)—has not much reflected on the contemporary culture-making activity of African-Americans. This is unfortunate not only because the influence of African-American culture on American popular culture is pervasive and under-estimated, but because "audience activity," in the sense of reaction to and upon dominant cultural products, has necessarily been essential to culture-making within the African diaspora. Both the frequently opposed views of E. Franklin Frazier—that African heritage was virtually erased during slavery—or of Melville Herskovits—that African-American culture takes shape around specific survivals of African civilization—imply vigorous interaction with Euro-American culture (see Holloway ix and Philips 225–226). Moreover, an essential feature of African-American culture is precisely the responsiveness of audience—consider the "call and response" pattern (Levine 218), the "second line" of musicians in jazz, or the dialectical interaction between improvising performer and inspired-and-inspiring audience that Charles Keil finds central to "the dialectics or mechanics of soul" (174–175).

Lawrence Levine in *Black Culture and Black Consciousness* and Charles Keil in *Urban Blues* have usefully studied both aspects of African-American popular culture. Keil describes a relationship of "appropriation and revitalization" (43) between African-American and Euro-American culture. This conception, developed in a discussion of LeRoi Jones' *Blues People,* envisions an essentially compensatory relationship in which dominant culture appropriates, largely through mass media "covers" of African-American work, and African-Americans respond by "reexpressing American Negro identity and attitudes in a new revitalized way" (45). However, if we focus too deeply on black culture as expropriated victim and reactor, we risk under-valuing its vitality and effectiveness. In culture-making it is often difficult to distinguish action from reaction, defense from offense. As Albert Murray has said:

> Much is forever being made of the deleterious effects of slavery on the generations of Black Americans that followed. But for some curious reason, nothing at all is ever made of the possibility that the legacy left by the enslaved ancestors of blues-oriented contemporary U.S. Negroes includes a disposition to confront the most unpromising circumstances and make the most of what little there is to go on, regardless of the odds—and not without finding delight in the process . . . (69–70)

Consequently, Levine's description of the appropriation–revitalization process proves somewhat more helpful in assessing the ongoing vitality of African-American popular culture. He describes the cultural interplay between African- and Euro-American culture as a "complex and multi-dimensional" relationship, "a pattern of *simultaneous* acculturation and revitalization" (*italics added,* 444). Cultural diffusion between whites and blacks was by no means a one-way street with blacks the invariable beneficiaries, he writes. Afro-American impact upon wide areas of American expressive culture has become increasingly obvious, though it has not yet been adequately assessed.

And in fact examples employed by Keil, Levine and others describe many instances in which black culture clearly acts upon dominant culture, not defensively or reactively, but actively, perspicaciously, and with satirical penetration. For instance, Keil acutely observes how a distinctively Negro style animates established white American entertainment forms, such as sports. He points to the nothing ball and sucker ball as pitched by Satchel Paige, the base as stolen by Maury Wills, the basket catches of Willie Mays, the antics of the Harlem Globetrotters, the beautiful ritualization of an ugly sport by Sonny Liston and Muhammed Ali (15). Similarly, George Nelson in *Elevating the Game* has described the growth in recent years of air-borne, slam-dunking basketball technique. These symbolic transformations, as Keil calls them, represent not a return to roots, but a genuine invigoration of the possibilities of popular cultural forms.

African-American culture by definition and necessity works in relation to dominant culture products. But the result is often distinct cultural invention. Speaking of black music, for instance, Schafer and Riedel note a basic force behind all genres and modes of black music in the ability to absorb, rework, and develop every musical material and influence, to be protean, taking on any shape yet remaining substantially the same in feeling or spirit (22). Maultsby describes how the black spiritual developed as slaves . . . frequently fashioned Protestant psalms, hymns, and spiritual songs into new compositions by altering the structure, text, melody, and rhythm. They thus created an essentially autonomous art form, a body of religious music created or adapted by slaves and performed in a distinctly African style (198).

Nor does African-American culture's ability to actively absorb, rework and develop operate solely in melodic spheres. As John W. Roberts says in *From Trickster to Badman,* the lyrics of the spiritual were not simple adoptions of Biblical texts but careful selections of figures and episodes significant to black historical and social experience. Roberts quotes Sterling Brown:

> Paul . . . is generally bound in jail with Silas, to the exclusion of the rest of his busy career. Favored heroes are Noah, chosen of God to ride down the flood; Joshua, who caused the wall of Jericho to fall . . .; Jonah, symbol of hard luck changed at last; and Job, the man of tribulation who still would not curse his God. (110)

Roberts continues, quoting Levine, in "the world of the spirituals, it was not the masters or the mistresses but God and Jesus and the entire pantheon of Old Testament figures who set the standards, established the precedents, and defined the values. . . ." It was a black world in which no reference was ever made to any white contemporary (110). A similar creative adaptation occurs in the Rastafarian re-interpretation of the Bible as a critique of dominant society ("Babylon") and manifesto of revolution and apocalypse, as Hebdige has described (33–35). A similar perspicacious and satiric adaptation is evident in dance: the cakewalk, John Storm Roberts notes in *Black Music of Two Worlds,* "began as a slaves' parody of white 'society' ways" (199).

The point of this survey is not simply and comfortably to assimilate the Black Bart T-shirt to this honorable tradition. But if, as Frederick Perls, Ralph Hefferline and Paul Goodman have pervasively argued (227–235), the process of creative adjustment is fundamental in all human conduct, we might expect it to persist even in the purchase and display of mass-produced commodities. The point is not that buying and wearing a T-shirt is as creative as singing the blues, or even dancing to them. But the deployment of such a commodity can constitute a cultural maneuver parallel to those we have just surveyed in the tradition of appropriation and revitalization as enacted in culture-making that employs the purchase of commodities. And the maneuver may engender group affirmations of some cultural significance.

Still, a variety of curiosities enter the picture when creative adjustment or appropriation and revitalization operate within the culture of mass media and commodities. As we shall see, the creators of Black Bart T-shirts may not be black, and some may question the cultural value of images of a self-declared dropout and mischief maker. Yet in the end, I will argue, the Black Bart T-shirt makes a significant comment upon the culture of mass media and enhances African-American identity. It also makes us aware of other instances of potential cultural power through the deployment of commodities.

Complications of Commodity Culture

T-shirts, however ephemeral or "commodified," are not entirely unlikely means of social communication. Since the mid-1970s when they emerged as outerwear embellished with product images and slogans, they have functioned as literal "fashion statements," a kind of personalized advertising. The commodities displayed on them are heavy with "lifestyle" connotations—not a jar of mayonnaise, say, but a brand of beer, a soft drink, a travel destination, a rock group—entities that presumably evoke occasions and emotions significant of the wearer's personality, taste and allegiances. Correspondingly, Behling's classification of T-shirt types for an empirical study (1988)—cynical, advertising, environmental, health and exercise, political, feminism, prestige, and off-color humor—suggests the association between the T-shirt and causes, issues and activities close to the wearer's central values. The affirmation involved can have tangible social significance. When stutterers, in a study by Silverman, wore a T-shirt saying, "I stutter. So what?" store clerks were found to perceive them more positively. The apparent personal transformations negotiated by the shirt occur on a more informal level too. A mother overhearing a discussion of Black Bart T-shirts, said, "Oh yes, my son wanted one of those, but I wouldn't get him one. He has enough attitude already." Merely to don the shirt is to be taken over by an "attitude."

The Black Bart T-shirt arguably furthers group identification and cohesion and makes as well a lively implicit commentary on contemporary media. The fact that the shirt appropriates figures from an ongoing television show carries a special impact. Although television, as separate studies by Richard Allen, Fred Bales, and Carolyn Stroman ("Mass Media Effects and Black Americans") have found, is a medium highly popular and credible with African-Americans, its origins and production are largely impervious to popular modification. To be sure, in the last 20 years African-Americans have been portrayed more frequently and more positively on television, as Stroman notes ("Twenty Years Later"). But other scholars have pointed out that this gain brings a reduction of significant dimensions of black culture. Sherry Bryant-Johnson remarks on the loss of significant expressive features of black ethnic background; Ilona Holland notes that the non-standard dialect employed by blacks on television is not true to black English as actually spoken, and Todd Gitlin and Martin Bayles contend that televised representations of African-Americans back away from the presentation of realistic characters in realistic backgrounds. Without overestimating the cultural impact of a mere T-shirt, we may yet suggest that sporting the blazonry of Black Bart "broadcasts" an unsanctioned commentary on *The Simpsons* show that reverses this tendency. As we will discuss in more detail below, the Black Bart T-shirt extends the social rules portrayed on the show to include raffish, urban personae—Rastafarians, "homeboys," rappers, and Black Muslims—all of whom may seem vaguely threatening and who find scant representation in the mass media.

But at the same time, an environment of commodities and post-modern "intertextuality" complicate this affirmative culture-making picture. Appropriation and revitalization in commodity culture turn and return upon each other. Matt Groening, creator of *The Simpsons,* has recognized both the economic expropriation and artistic creativity of the Black Bart phenomenon. "You have to have mixed feelings when you're getting ripped off," he said (qtd. in Mills). But his ambivalence did not prevent him from making the "rip-off" into material for further cartooning. In "Life in Hell," another of his strips, Groening depicts Akbar and Jeff, identical figures who inexplicably wear fezs and may be brothers or lovers, and who bootleg themselves. Working from "Akbar & Jeff's Bootleg Akbar & Jeff T-shirt Hut," they vend "Blakbar and Jeff" T-shirts, including "Air Akbar" and "Akbar and Jeff go funky reggae." Dreadlocks sprouting from under his fez, one says, "Irie, Mon." The other responds, "What?" Groening thus plays with the very cultural gaps that engender the Black Bart T-shirt. A warning label on the cartoon intones: "we will prosecute bootleggers of our bootlegs and don't you forget it."

Fox Television itself briefly adapted the possible connection between a white Bart and a black Bart to its own purposes. A black-oriented show, *True Colors,* was for a time programmed to follow *The Simpsons* presumably to compete more successfully with the top-10 *Bill Cosby Show.* Advertisements for the new pairing played upon the identity of Bart and the young black hero of *True Colors,* placing their images side by side, comparing the two dancing, and having Bart say of the young black star, "He's my idol!"

More fundamental matters arise when we ask, who are the creators of Black Bart Simpson T-shirts? It is not easy to offer a definitive answer. One might ask vendors and producers of the T-shirts, but given the illegality of their operations, they could easily suspect that a scholar's interest was but a clever ruse to hunt copyright violators. Nonetheless, in T-shirt screen printing shops some aspects of the production process comes into public view. And according to some testimony from this source, the designers and producers of Black Bart and other black-oriented T-shirts emerge from a group hardly associated with empathy for African-American culture—the "middleman minority" of immigrant Korean business people in the United States.

Korean merchants in general display a strong presence in "low-end retailing" of inexpensive items such as wigs, handbags, martial arts supplies, jewelry and casual apparel, including T-shirts, much of which makes an appeal to the cultural interests of low-income groups. J. T. Liehr, the graphic artist and cartoonist quoted earlier, said that about half a dozen Korean merchants regularly used his shop to order silk screens for black-oriented shirts that were vended in Center City and west Philadelphia. "Of all the shirts aimed at blacks, I rarely saw black people involved in making them," Liehr said. (White "progressives," he added, typically produced anti-apartheid and Nelson Mandela T-shirts.) Nor did the Korean producers of Afrocentric material with their shoestring budgets seem likely to employ much help of any sort, to say nothing of black artists or collaborators, Liehr said.

Origins exert a powerful conceptual spell. The cultural and economic conflicts between Koreans and African-Americans have received so much publicity that many observers are likely to aver that if Koreans designed Black Bart T-shirts, their cultural value cannot be high. Korean–black antipathies figure prominently in such recent African-American films as Spike Lee's *Do the Right Thing* and Frederick Singleton's *Boyz in the 'Hood*. Blacks cite such grievances as the failure of Korean merchants to live in the communities where they work, firing black workers, refusing credit to black customers, treating them as potential shoplifters, and failing to contribute to black charities.[3] The possible Korean production of Black Bart T-shirts can echo too closely the old story of the financial exploitation of black cultural interests and creations for the profit of other groups. Certainly too, the likely Korean origins of the Black Bart products sit oddly in the tradition of African-American cultural creativity sketched above. And in fact it might be suspected that the casual relation to value terms that we noted in the "Crack Kills/Black Power" T-shirt implies the detached and distant perspective of a culture alien to African-American concerns.[4]

Disapproval of the possible Korean production of the shirts links with a more general disapproval of the Bart figure, black or white, by authority figures of both races. A *People Weekly* article called "Eat My Shirts!" described how principals in California and Ohio banned Bart Simpson T-shirts bearing the label "Underachiever" or Bart's rude query, "Who the hell are you?" Bart's underachieving can be viewed as particularly dangerous when the school dropout rate among many young people, including African-Americans, stands at worrisome rates. T-shirt vendor Id-Deen said she had heard a Black Muslim imam criticize Bart's disrespect for his parents. In a *Jet* magazine article headlined "Black Bart T-shirt raises concern among blacks," a black man chastises wearers at a black fraternity picnic: "With all the Black heroes in the world—Mandela and Malcolm and Martin—and that's what you are showing our children?" (In fairness, Black Bart on one shirt himself declares Mandela his "hero.") But the very effort to dismiss the Black Bart T-shirt in the name of more "positive" African-American values can contradict itself. The *Jet* article approvingly quotes an African-American vendor from Baltimore who invokes the very negative stereotypes the article seems to protest: "We are the only people in the world that let somebody take a White cartoon character, paint it Black and then sell it to us for 10 bucks."

Condemning Black Bart on the basis of his possible origins may offer a comfortable sense of superiority to the buyers' presumed foolishness but it does nothing to explain his popularity. Thousands of urban blacks proudly donned and displayed the image of Black Bart Simpson. Many even sported the "Crack Kills" variant. They did not do it to make Koreans rich or increase school dropout rates. The financial economy of popular culture wherein Korean entrepreneurs produce Black Bart T-shirts and the cultural economy wherein African-Americans eagerly buy and display them are "parallel" and "semi-autonomous," as Fiske notes in *Understanding Popular Culture* (26). "Every act of consumption is an act of cultural production, for consumption is always the production of meaning," he says (35).

For its wearers, the Black Bart T-shirt must possess an active, affirmative meaning. And as we examine this popularity the idea reasserts itself that the phenomenon, for all the curiosities surrounding it, stands in discernible continuity with more traditional, creative acts of African-American adaptation of materials from dominant culture: Koreans and African-Americans do, after all, share minority status. Spike Lee acknowledges as much in *Do the Right Thing* when the film's hero Mookie, recognizing the bond, sees to it that a family of Korean greengrocers are spared the racial conflagration that closes the film. Furthermore, there is, as Simon Bronner has pointed out, ample procedent in American culture for a group apparently detached from the African-American community to nonetheless take a central role in circulating African-American culture more widely. Although these cultural brokers may be viewed with hostility by African-Americans (witness Spike Lee's treatment of Jewish nightclub owners in *Mo' Better Blues*), in many cases the broker evinces genuine aesthetic appreciation—consider Alan Freed's promotion of rock 'n' roll music or John Hammond's of jazz and blues. If an anonymous Korean entrepreneur understands how a black Betty Boop or Bart Simpson will appeal to African-American cultural interests, so be it. Cross-cultural understanding is not beyond the capacities of any ethnic or racial group.

Moreover, it is not as if the Black Bart figure is without its own positive vitality. Bart Simpson and Black Bart may hate school but they are at least "street smart." Black Bart's bold social assertiveness and multiplication of social roles is more imaginative than mindless. If Bart Simpson infuriates principals by calling himself an "underachiever—and proud of it," he must at least comprehend the schoolmaster's jargon. On the show Bart is certainly no scholar but is not without intellectual interest. He shows a near Jesuitical expertise with questions that torture his Sunday school teacher, like whether heaven will admit "a robot with a human brain." In other words, those concerned about the "model" set by the Bart figures might give more weight to the intelligence and penetration implicit in ironic play.

How Does a T-Shirt Mean?

What then is the social meaning of Black Bart and how is it engendered? Young wearers of Black Bart T-shirts formulate the pleasure and meaning of this imagery with full understanding of the cultural dissonance that circulates around the Bart figure. In interviews, 11 Black and Hispanic public school students at first vigorously condemned the show, charging that Bart uses bad language, even the "S-word" and "the F-word" (which of course are not heard on television). They acknowledged solemnly that Bart does not do his homework. A seven-year-old Hispanic boy showed best how the condemnation was "in the air." He could provide no specifics about the show, but nonetheless opined heatedly that it was unnecessarily obscene and violent. "You can't learn anything from that! You don't learn your A-B-C's!" he said. It is hardly likely that on their own children gather at recess to murmur this sort of disapproval of *The Simpsons*. This lad's opinions were adapted from the children's precocious presumptions about adult views of cartoons. A six-year-old boy described the essence of the process: "The parents, they don't like Bart Simpson because they don't want us to turn out cussing when we grow up because they don't want us turning out in jail."[5]

If they piously intoned the "dangers" of Bart, the children nonetheless all but universally could produce details about the show, and in many cases said they owned Simpsons T-shirts or other products. And their more active pleasure in its meanings soon surfaced. A nine-year-old girl, who solemnly called the show "a bad influence," also vividly described an incident in which Lisa comforted baby Maggie, her tone clearly indicating she found it touching. Two girls, aged 10 and 11, who were also best friends, spontaneously said of a "Bart Marley" T-shirt, "It's nice . . . It's colorful and stuff." With her friend's agreement, one stated explicitly that she recognized the show's "bad examples" to serve a larger function:

> I don't think Bart Simpson was made to offend anyone but to show how the kids act. And some kids . . . do act like that. But Bart Simpson, I don't think he was made to do bad things. Bart Simpson . . . is taking the children's offense and Homer and Maggie [Marge] are taking the parents' offense and it's showing how we all act together.

Allowing for a fourth-grader's vocabulary, this is the perceptive observation that the show portrays family dynamics rather than glorifying bad behavior. Of Black Bart, one of the pair said, "what's nice is that there is a black person in here, his name is Bart too and they have colorful colors too." Her friend seconded the political aspect:

> On the commercials they don't show that many black people and in the magazines they hardly show any black people. All you see is white. And I don't understand why white people are scared of us because there's nothing wrong with our color.

Youngsters construct the figure of Black Bart from an active, perceptive reinterpretation of materials on the show. They select particular features of Bart Simpson's style that resonate with African-American culture, particularly his hair and dress. Krebs quoted a 14-year-old boy holding that Bart Simpson himself seemed black: "You never see white people with spiked hair like that—that's the way blacks look." Another commented, "I think Bart acts more like a black kid than a white one, especially the way he wears clothing and styles his hair." Larger elements of Bart Simpson's character undergird Black Bart's appeal. Bart Simpson offends authority figures in part because he focuses on his own goals and pleasures, responding with singular detachment to the lures and values of adult society. One boy approved the way Bart "doesn't give a damn about anything" (qtd. in "When Life Imitates Bart"). Bart's "rowdiness" and "unvarnished chutzpah . . . speak particularly well to many black youngsters who are growing up in a society that often alienates them," said Russell Adams, chair of the Afro-American Studies Department at Howard University (qtd. in Marriott C3).

As noted earlier, the Black Bart T-shirts mobilize an implicit critique of the range of black roles on the show. The show's characterizations commendably include more than a token number of people of color. The show also plays with the sociology of racial and ethnic identity. For instance, the local convenience store is owned and operated by a regular character, Apu, who is Indian or Pakistani. African-Americans are numerous and presented in positive roles. Several of Bart's friends and schoolmates and Clarence, the mayor of Springfield City, along with the Simpson's family physician, are black. The physician, Dr. Hibbert, is an "intertextual" reference, the show's Bill Cosby. Hibbert relaxes at home in the multicolored sweaters favored by Cosby as Dr. Cliff Huxtable (*The Cosby Show* aired at the same time as *The Simpsons*). Bart knows plenty about alternative identities. He avidly collects "Radioactive Man" comics and pretends variously he is "Bart-Man," "The Caped Avenger," a ninja, and other characters. The Black Bart T-shirt builds on Bart's mischief and imagination along with the show's sociological realism to expand its spectrum of roles.

The T-shirts further domesticate these identities by steeping them in the show's acceptance and popularity. Correspondingly, many of the shirts feature a double gesture of pugnacious self-assertion and openness. "Rastabart" warns, "Watch it, Mon" but adds "Irie" ("everything's fine"). Black Bart glares and says, "It's cool being black," but a box on the T-shirt notes, "We are all brothers and sisters so live in unity, love and peace." Another changes the saying, "It's a black thing. You wouldn't understand" to "It's a black thing. You should understand"—a statement that at least opens the possibility that someone not black *could* potentially "understand." Even the "Crack Kills/Black Power" design considered from a wearer's perspective embodies a raw humor, assimilating "black power" to a carnivalesque, scatological tradition of "funky butt" humor.

Though he lives in and as a commodity, Black Bart's energetic transformations and evocations of multiple identities arguably connect with longer traditions from folk culture, recalling for instance the African-American trickster figure, whose transformations *From Trickster to Badman* Roberts has described. He also appears to draw upon the dynamic surrounding the figure of the entertainer in black culture. As Keil has described him, the African-American entertainer is not simply a charming personality skilled in some single area of public amusement. He is rather an "identity expert," whose mastery of stances and poses possesses ritual power to construct identity and social cohesion, in the process defining "a special domain of Negro culture wherein black men have proved and preserved their humanity" (15). Without effacing the difference between a T-shirt cartoon and actual, personal performance, it would nonetheless seem that Black Bart's tricky signifying evokes cultural identity and cohesion. Worn in the streets, the Black Bart figure makes a cultural assertion, a species of enacted rhetoric, commenting upon the arena of television and making it a forum for African-American values and images. As T-shirt vendor Deborah Id-Deen said, the Black Bart T-shirt "gives black people a sense that they're famous."

Conclusion

The possible political value of this sense of "fame" is easy to underestimate. As Levine points out,

> There has been an unfortunate if understandable tendency in our political age to conceive of protest in almost exclusively political and institutional terms. Thus group consciousness and a firm sense of the self have been confused with political consciousness and organization, "manhood" has been equated with armed rebellion, and resistance with the building of a revolutionary tradition.

Levine further explains how black song serves a constructive social function that may be extended even to the public display and deployment of commodities such as the Black Bart T-shirt:

> To state that black song constituted a form of black protest and resistance does not mean that it necessarily led to or even called for any tangible and specific actions, but rather that it served as a mechanism by which Negroes could be relatively candid in a society that rarely accorded them that privilege, could communicate this candor to others whom they would in no other way be able to reach, and, in the face of the sanctions of the white majority, could assert their own individuality, aspirations, and sense of being (240).

The Black Bart T-shirt too arguably mediates a communicative candor and assertion of self and group identification.

The Black Bart T-shirt is not alone as an expressive use of a commodity to support personal and social identity and convey resistant social messages. Consider, for instance, the insouciant rejection of school deportment expressed in the gracefully untied laces of urban high tops and super sneakers. The gesture rejects that fundamental school rule—"tie your shoelaces!"—yet the shoes stay on and in fact imply spirited, gymnastic agility. "Boom boxes" or "ghetto blasters" and cars fitted with elaborate sound systems blaring rap or salsa create mobile, auditory cultural environments that are expansive—and instantly collapsible. Dance party DJs, MCs and rappers enact an even more creative relation to the commodity. They treat the completed tape or record as itself artistic material. The DJs select, reorder, "sample" and "scratch" these existing commodities into a new composition or "mix," which "priest-like" they offer up for the dancing communion of "everybody in the house."

But as the appropriation–revitalization process works in the post-modernist era with pastiche and quotation of completed, existing texts, the cultural conflict Fiske describes also manifests itself in palpable cultural and legal controversy. The racial apocalypse that concludes

Spike Lee's *Do the Right Thing* begins over the use of a boom box. Sound control ordinances are passed to quell the sound-system cars (but allow exceptions for political sound trucks). Poaching on the territory of copyrighted mass media commodities, whether by T-shirt manufacturers or DJ samplers, meets prosecution for copyright violation.

But however contentiously or even illegally they go about it, these practices accomplish something significant for group life in commodity culture. They serve a social–psychological function akin to the "soul strategy" of the blues as Keil describes it: to "increase feelings of solidarity, boost morale, strengthen the consensus" (164–5). The Black Bart T-shirt and similar appropriated and revitalized commodities suggest the significant creative precisely, in the midst of commodity culture and post-modernism.

Notes

1. This paper was originally delivered at the 1991 annual meeting of the Popular Culture Association. For their helpful comments on versions of this essay, the author wishes to thank Simon Bronner, Gary Daily, Clemmie Gilpin, Charles Keil, Suren Lalvani and William Mahar. Craig Smith provided valuable information on T-shirt production.

2. This paper will not concern itself with the many other appropriations of the ubiquitous Bart Simpson. Suffice it to say that his mischievous image was used for a variety of causes and by no means did they all represent marginalized groups. Bart was swiftly enlisted in the Gulf War: Windbreakers in Tijuana cast him as Rambo, strangling Saddam Hussein and saying, "I am your worst nightmare." On a T-shirt he urinated on a map of Iraq. Editors of the conservative *Campus Review* at the University of Iowa put a slingshot in Bart's hands and had him threaten, "Back off Faggot!" sparking a lawsuit and complaints to local human rights organizations (see "Suits and debate follow display of cartoon poster"). In California, Republican campaign strategists used Bart's visage to accuse gubernatorial candidate Diane Feinstein of "cheating" in a debate ("The Rehabilitation of Bart Simpson"). A cartoon circulated within Xerox culture incorporated Bart as well. With obscene logic it fused two key traits in characters of the show—Bart's physicality and Baby Maggie's perpetual plying of her pacifier. The photocopied drawing, circulated in south central Pennsylvania and reported printed on a T-shirt in New Orleans, finds Bart, his pants about his knees, with baby Maggie, and Mother Marge screaming in the background. Bart says, "But Mom, she lost her pacifier!" We leave to the reader's imagination what means Bart found to replace it.

3. See Light and Bonacich 322. Kim in "The Big Apple Goes Bananas Over Korean Fruit Stands" and *New Urban Immigrants: The Korean Community in New York* and McKinley describe the relations of Blacks and Koreans in New York City. In general, as Light and Bonacich note, Korean merchants in low-end retailing gain valuable entry to the American market and in the process provide American corporate interests with a variety of indirect benefits. Koreans pioneer in and distribute corporate goods in low-productivity sectors of the market, help keep labor cheap and unorganized, and promote the idea that the United States is a land where hard work is rewarded (though most entrepreneurs in fact will spend generations working long hours for low pay) (354–400). The increased economic connections between Korea and the United States is also reflected in the fact that, as Basler reports, "The Simpsons" animation is produced at Akom Studio in Seoul.

4. In fact the shirt was more offensive than other Black Bart T-shirts. T-shirt vendor Deborah Id-Deen described it *sotto voce,* asserting solemnly that she may have sold Black Bart T-shirts but she would never sell the "Crack Kills" T-shirt. Yet it was also worn and distributed at least from New York City to Washington D.C., where Mills described it.

5. The students were members of a "student activities committee" representing grades from kindergarten through fifth at the Benjamin Franklin Academic Prep School, Harrisburg, PA. They spoke to me on the understanding they would not be identified. The author wishes to thank the children for their help, Norma Gotwalt, director of the Harrisburg Division of Elementary Education, and Joann Griffin, principal of the Benjamin Franklin Academic Prep School.

Works Cited

Allen, Richard L. "Communication Research on Black Americans." Paper presented at the Symposium on Minority Audiences and Programming Research. Lenox, MA, Oct. 1980. ERIC ED.

Bales, Fred. "Television Use and Confidence in Television by Blacks and Whites in Four Selected Years." *Journal of Black Studies* 16.3 (1986).

Basler, Barbara. "Peter Pan, Garfield and Bart—All Have Asian Roots." *The New York Times* 2 Dec. 1990.

Bayles, Martha. "Blacks on TV: Adjusting the Image." *New Perspectives* 17.3 (1985).

Behling, Dorothy U. "T-Shirts as Communicators of Attitudes." *Perceptual and Motor Skills* 66 (1988).

"Black Bart Simpson T-Shirt Raises Concern Among Blacks." *Jet* 27 Aug. 1990, 37.

Bronner, Simon. Personal Communication. 18 Sept. 1991.

Bryant–Johnson, Sherry. "Blacks on TV Soaps: Visible but Neutralized." *Perspectives: The Civil Rights Quarterly* 15.3 (1983).

de Certeau, Michel. *The Practice of Everyday Life.* Trans. Steven F. Rendall. Berkeley: U of California P, 1984.

Eason, David, and Fred Fogo. "The Cultural Turn in Media Studies." *Mass Comm Review* 15.1 (1988).

"Eat My Shirts! Pesky Bart Simpson Tees Off a California Principal—and Gets Kicked Out of School for Swearing." *People Weekly* 21 May 1990: 130.

Fiske, John. *Reading the Popular.* Boston: Unwin, 1989.

———. *Understanding Popular Culture.* Boston: Unwin, 1989.

Frazier, E. Franklin. *The Negro Church in America.* Boston, 1963.

Gitlin, Todd. "Prime-Time Whitewash." *American Film* 9.2 (Nov. 1983).

Groening, Matt. "Life in Hell." Cartoon. *Village Voice* 7 Aug. 1990: 8.

Hebdige, Dick. *Subculture: The Meaning of Style.* London: Methuen, 1979.

Herskovits, Melville J. *The Myth of the Negro Past,* 1941. Boston: Beacon, 1958.

Holland, Ilona E. "Nonstandard English on Television: A Content Analysis." Paper presented at the Annual Meeting of the International Communication Association. Chicago, 22–26 May 1986. ERIC ED.

Id-Deen, Deborah. Personal Interview. 10 Nov. 1990.

Keil, Charles. *Urban Blues.* Chicago: The U of Chicago P, 1966.

Kim, Illsoo. "The Big Apple Goes Bananas Over Korean Fruit Stands." Asia 4 (1981).

———. *New Urban Immigrants: The Korean Community in New York.* Princeton: Princeton UP, 1981.

Krebs, Jeanette. "Black Bart: T-Shirts Depict TV Kid with Dark Skin." *Patriot-News* [Harrisburg, PA] 29 July 1990.

Levine, Lawrence W. *Black Culture and Black Consciousness: Afro-American Folk Thought from Slavery to Freedom.* New York: Oxford UP, 1977.

Liehr, J. T. Telephone Interview. 20 Dec. 1990.

Light, Ivan, and Edna Bonacich. *Immigrant Entrepreneurs: Koreans in Los Angeles, 1965–1982.* Berkeley: U of California P. 1988.

Marriott, Michel. "I'm Bart, I'm Black and What About It?" *The New York Times* 19 Sept. 1990.

Maultsby, Portia K. "Africanisms in African-American Music." *Africanisms in American Culture.* Ed. Joseph E. Holloway. Bloomington: Indiana UP, 1990.

Mills, David. "Bootleg Black Bart Simpson, the Hip-Hop T-Shirt Star." *Washington Post.* 28 June 1990: D1.

Murray, Albert. *Stomping the Blues.* New York: McGraw-Hill, 1976.

Nelson, George. *Elevating the Game: Black Men and Basketball.* New York: Harper Collins, 1992.

Perls, Frederick, Ralph F. Hefferline, and Paul Goodman. *Gestalt Therapy: Excitement and Growth in the Human Personality.* New York: Dell, 1951.

Philips, John Edward. "The African Heritage of White America." Ed. Joseph E. Holloway, *Africanisms in American Culture.* Bloomington: Indiana UP, 1990.

Radway, Janice A. *Reading the Romance: Women, Patriarchy, and Popular Literature.* Chapel Hill: U of North Carolina P, 1984.

"The Rehabilitation of Bart Simpson." *Mother Jones* Jan.–Feb. 1991.

Roberts, John Storm. *Black Music of Two Worlds.* New York: Praeger, 1972.

Roberts, John W. *From Trickster to Badman: The Black Folk Hero in Slavery and Freedom.* Philadelphia: U of Pennsylvania P, 1989.

Schafer, William J., and Johannes Riedel. *The Art of Ragtime.* Baton Rouge: Louisiana State University, 1973.

Silverman, Franklin H., Michele Gazzolo, and Yvonne Peterson. "Impact of a T-shirt Message on Stutterer Stereotypes: A Systematic Replication." *Journal of Fluency Disorders* 15.1 (1990).

Stroman, Carolyn A. "Mass Media Effects and Black Americans." *Urban Research Review* 9.4 (1984).

——— et al. "Twenty Years Later: The Portrayal of Blacks on Prime-Time Television." Paper presented at the Annual Meeting of the Association for Education in Journalism and Mass Communication. Portland, OR, 2–5 July 1988.

"Suits and Debate Follow Display of Cartoon Poster." *The New York Times* 25 Nov. 1990.

"When Life Imitates Bart." *Newsweek* 23 July 1990.

Yoo, Woong Nyol. "Business Owners in New York's Harlem Struggle Against Anti-Korean Prejudice." *Koreatown* 19 Oct. 1981.

READING WRITING

This Text: Reading

1. What scholarly contexts does Parisi use in the article? How might these be useful for other phenomena?
2. Can you think of another phenomena that audiences have altered to make them reflect their interests?

Your Text: Writing

1. Find another T-shirt that's commonly worn and read it as a cultural text.
2. Go to a toystore and look at the toys related to TV shows or movies. What relationship between audience and show or movie does the related toy assume? In what ways does the toy reinterpret the show or movie?

Sex Sells: A Marxist Criticism of *Sex and the City*

Dave Rinehart

Student Essay

Dave Rinehart wrote this essay in 2006 while a student at the University of San Francisco. Rinehart's essay stands as a good example of reading a television text through a lens—in this case, the lens of Marxism. Rinehart recently graduated from USF and is teaching English in Japan.

Introduction

ARTHUR ASA BERGER, in his book *Media Analysis Techniques,* writes: "The bourgeoisie try to convince everyone that capitalism is natural and therefore eternal, but this idea, say the Marxists, is patently false, and it is the duty of Marxist analysts to demonstrate this" (51). It will be my duty over the course of this paper to expose and explicate the capitalist, consumerist,

Carrie Bradshaw: Feminist hero? Bourgeois hero? Or Capitalist hero?

and classist aspects of the TV show *Sex and the City* using Marxist criticism.

Sex and the City aired its final episode in spring 2004, concluding a massively successful six-season run on the HBO network. The series, created by Darren Star, is based on the sex advice columns of Candace Bushnell. The fictionalized TV version re-imagines Bushnell as Carrie Bradshaw (Sarah Jessica Parker), a young, single New York woman who narrates the show and serves as its primary focus. Each episode is based around her weekly column, with the topic typically regarding relationship dynamics between men and women. Over the course of an episode, Carrie will write on her laptop (with accompanying narrative voiceover), wine and dine with her group of closest friends Charlotte, Samantha, and Miranda, and carouse with her boyfriends, who come and go in and out of her life through various episode arcs. This essay will analyze, using Marxist techniques, Carrie's role as the "bourgeois hero," the show's capitalist and consumerist aspects, the ways in which its characters and viewers may engage in commodity fetishism, and the show's representation of classism.

Carrie Bradshaw as the "Bourgeois Hero"

Karl Marx wrote, "The ideas of the ruling class are, in every age, the ruling ideas; i.e., the class which is the dominant material force in society is at the same time its dominant intellectual force" (78). Throughout history, the ruling class has been responsible for the production of the most popular culture industry texts. It makes sense, then, that the ruling class would utilize the media to glorify and promote themselves, producing texts that celebrate the bourgeoisie lifestyle. The main characters that populate these texts, then, often function as "bourgeois heroes," who "maintain the status quo by 'peddling' capitalist ideology in disguised form and by helping keep consumer lust at a high pitch" (60). (To clarify, Berger separates "bourgeois heroes" and "bourgeois heroines," but I have made the term gender-neutral.)

As the show's main character and narrator, Carrie functions as *Sex and the City's* bourgeois hero. The series details her many travails through high society New York, mingling with wealthy socialites and dating powerful investment bankers and corporate executives — and then getting paid well to detail said interactions in her newspaper column. In a typical episode, Carrie will shop at upscale boutiques, dine in fancy restaurants, sip expensive wines, and/or receive dazzling gifts. While in the first two seasons she is seen wearing rather generic (though good-looking) clothing and flat-soled shoes, from season three on she seemingly only wears designer clothing and stilettos.

The show's producers, however, do attempt to portray Carrie as down-to-earth: she chain-smokes cigarettes, gets hangovers, cries, and ends up in many embarrassing situations. These situations make her relatable to the show's majority female viewership, while simultaneously placing her on a pedestal of bourgeois taste and lifestyle. While many female viewers might see themselves in Carrie's various character nuances, they will also be envious of her abundance of expensive possessions. To use an example from the opposite gender: male comic book readers see a little or a lot of themselves in gawky teen Peter Parker, but dream of rising beyond their real-life state and taking to the skyscrapers as Spider-Man.

Capitalism and Consumerism

In pretty much any episode, it is difficult to find scenes where characters are interacting without simultaneously consuming. Carrie is nearly always smoking a cigarette while writing, she talks to her friends over meals at nice restaurants, and she goes to bars and clubs with her beaus. Even while walking and talking, the friends will also be sipping lattes or have the obnoxious neon ads of Times Square as a backdrop.

One could argue that these types of scene setup are merely a reflection of the kind of interactions people have on a daily basis. I would argue, however, like Berger did in his quotation that introduced this paper, that this is just an example of the bourgeoisie trying "to convince everyone that capitalism is natural and therefore eternal" (51). *Sex and the City* is a celebration of capitalism, as its characters drift in and out of various capitalist outposts, finding new and exciting ways to consume. It is amazing, then, how rarely we see them actually in the act of spending money; but this is, again, Berger's argument of natural capitalism. Drinks are poured, food served, and pedicures administered as if this was the way of the world.

This style of episode structure fosters in its audience a false consciousness, "in leading people to believe that 'whatever is, is right' " (Berger 49). After being beaten over the head with images of the program's characters interacting and consuming, viewers may be led to believe that the one cannot happen without the other. In order to talk with friends about serious, thought-provoking matters, the characters must do it over drinks or dinner.

Commodity Fetishism

Operating at peak popularity with virtually no slowdown for the past several years, *Sex and the City* has, therefore, been a prominent trendsetter in the world of fashion. Many of the main characters' clothing, shoes, and various accessories have exploded in real-life as hot commodities among upper-class women. Specific examples include Carrie's "Carrie" necklace, which inspired women to get their own personalized necklace, and her distinctive Manolo Blahnik and Jimmy Choo stilettos. The show has functioned as a go-to source for fashion tips among the viewers who can afford to, both financially and physically, wear the same items.

But the commodity fetishism *Sex and the City* inspires in its audience would be nothing if not practiced by its own characters. Indeed, characters will often spend an entire episode wanting a particular commodity, and the majority of their dialogue will even focus around it. As a grand example of irony, one of the last episodes in season six had Charlotte, the naïve do-gooder of the group, indulging a salesman's shoe fetish in return for free high heels, so long as she let him fit her. She returns again and again, unwilling to let her personal shoe fetish go and simultaneously satiating his, far more sexual one.

Regarding Samantha, the group's vixen, it is important to bring in the concept of hegemony. The basest definition of the word is provided by Berger as "that which goes without saying," and in television it regards the different standards of conduct between the genders, races, ages, etc. that are taken for granted. John Fiske, in his essay "British Cultural Studies," writes: "women, so the hegemonic reading would go, are rewarded for their ability to use their beauty and talents to give pleasure to men" (303).

Sex and the City can easily be typified as antithetical to typical TV gender hegemony. While regular programming may portray men going through a series of female partners, *Sex* reverses this notion by portraying a group of independent, freethinking women who keep men at their mercy. But ultimately, the show's progressive feminism is canceled out by commodity fetishism, a condition which makes the women vulnerable and willing to lower their typically high standards.

For example, Samantha uses sex as a way to satisfy her expensive tastes. Until the final season, she exclusively dates exceedingly wealthy men who pay for her every indulgence. In season two, she even leads on a mid-70s executive-type man, remaining in bed with him so long as he whispers fantasies of dream vacations in her ear. Although Carrie chastises her for this decision, Samantha remains on, dreaming of happiness based on material wealth.

Classism

Class is an issue that is addressed on both latent and manifest levels in *Sex and the City*. Latently, differences can be shown with the four main women interacting with a dichotomy of workers: newspaper or hot dog vendors are usually always Hispanic males and beauty salon workers Asian females, while employees of the upscale restaurants and shops are usually always white men and women. Carrie, Samantha, Charlotte, and Miranda live life in a vacuum, staying on a narrow track that leads them from event to event with similar working, acting, and looking people.

Class differences are made manifest in episodes like one from season two where Miranda, a self-made millionaire, struggles with dating a blue-collar bartender, Steve, who in subsequent seasons becomes her husband and the father of her child. Unlike other TV programs, class is certainly not ignored or overlooked in *Sex and the City* but, as Berger states, it acts as an apologist "for the ruling class in an effort to avert class conflict and prevent changes in the political order" (51). *Sex and the City* portrays ethnic men and women doing the "dirty work" and white people enjoying the comforts of the bourgeois lifestyle as the natural, unbreakable order of the American class system.

Marxist Criticism

Marxist criticism seems to be the most heavily criticized of the five primary media analysis techniques. Berger has qualms with Marxists in that they are "prisoners of the categories of their thought, and the questions they ask of a work of popular art carried by the media are often rather limited" (66). Similarly, Theodor Adorno writes: "[T]he very intelligentsia that pretends to float freely is fundamentally rooted in the very being that must be changed and which it merely pretends to criticize" (Jay 116). Since the analysts are so firmly imbedded in the culture they are attempting to critique, their results cannot be trusted for objectivity and truth. I think that Mimi White says it best, however, in her essay "Ideological Analysis and Television." She writes:

> [T]he classical Marxist approach is limited by its inability to account for the fact that . . . most people watch television, most of the time, because they find it enjoyable. In this sense, classical Marxism does not provide sufficiently subtle critical and theoretical perspectives for dealing with the pleasures of contemporary culture, including watching TV. (166)

My Marxist criticism of *Sex and the City* is perhaps marred by my personal enjoyment of the show. It is difficult for me to abandon my appreciation of the show's sharp writing and clever scenarios to systematically tear down its capitalist overtones. Like White says, my critiques fail to take in the aforementioned ways in which fellow viewers could also enjoy the show, even ignoring its consumerist celebration and commodity fetishism. (For instance, fetishisms for expensive high heels and personalized necklaces are completely lost on me, a straight male viewer.)

Methods such as content analysis and semiotic analysis are more conducive to studying television. A content analysis of *Sex and the City* could count the frequency of scenes where characters are interacting and simultaneously consuming, and compare it to the amount of times they converse without the burden of consumerism. Semioticians could have a field day with the series, analyzing the signs and signifiers in its main title sequence, analyzing its characters' evolution over the six seasons using a diachronic perspective, and even applying Propp's dramatis personae to the main characters and revolving door of supporting characters. These are merely methods of analysis, however. In my opinion, Marxist criticism is best suited as a method for breaking down the series' most contemptible elements; those rooted in capitalism and consumerism.

Works Cited

Berger, Arthur Asa. *Media Analysis Techniques*. 3rd ed. Thousand Oaks: Sage, 2005.
Fiske, John. "British Cultural Studies." *Channels of Discourse, Reassembled*. 2nd ed. Ed. Robert C. Allen. Chapel Hill: Univ. of North Carolina Press, 1992.
Jay, Martin. *Adorno*. Cambridge: Harvard Univ. Press, 1984.
Marx, Karl. *Selected Writings in Sociology and Social Philosophy*. Ed. T. B. Bottomore, M. Rubel. New York: McGraw-Hill, 1964.
White, Mimi. "Ideological Analysis and Television." *Channels of Discourse, Reassembled*. 2nd ed. Ed. Robert C. Allen. Chapel Hill: Univ. of North Carolina Press, 1992.

READING WRITING

This Text: Reading

1. Rinehart does a nice job of using Marxism as a lens for reading *Sex and the City*. How does he explain how he will use the concepts of Marxism?
2. Does this essay make you see *Sex and the City* through a different light? Why or why not?
3. Although both authors like *Sex and the City,* it tends to be a show that appeals primarily to women. Do you think Rinehart's opinion of the show is affected by his gender? Is there evidence in his essay that he reads the show from a male perspective?

Your Text: Writing

1. Using a major concept as a lens for reading a text is a classic approach to an essay. Write an essay in which you read a television program through a particular ideological lens, like Democracy, Christianity, Capitalism, or Feminism.
2. Write an essay in which you compare the major themes of *Sex and the City* with *The L-Word*. How are they similar? Different? Or, write an essay comparing *Sex and the City* with *Entourage* (what some have called men's *Sex and the City*).

The *NEXT* Plague: MTV's Sexual Objectification of Girls and Why It Must Be Stopped

Maribeth Theroux

Student Essay

Maribeth Theroux wrote this essay for Dr. Patricia Pender's class at Pace University in 2007. For more information about the assignment, please see the "Third-Wave Feminism Suite" in Chapter 6, "Reading and Writing about Gender."

REALITY-BASED TELEVISION HAS become both a phenomenon and a plague in recent years. Each network broadcasts shows in this genre, one that can no longer be called simply a trend since it shows no signs of going away. MTV's reality shows are a huge part of their weekly schedule. The craze began with their *The Real World,* and today the network broadcasts such reality shows as *Road Rules, Date My Mom, Exposed, Room Raiders, Parental Control, True Life, Made, The Hills,* and *NEXT.* MTV is ranked the number one cable network for the 12- to 24-year-old demographic, with viewers in 342 million homes worldwide (Stern 1). In addition, girls between the ages of 12 and 19 comprise 30% of MTV's audience (Eads 5). On a network that broadcasts not only reality shows, but reality *dating* shows, it is crucial to analyze the messages that these shows send to viewers, especially girls. Eads explains, "Girls look to TV programming to decipher what it means to be a woman, to try out different roles, and to learn sexual expectations and behaviors" (14). It is my argument that in looking to these shows girls are taught to be sexual objects through seeing other girls forced into that role. In addition, the shows police female appearance and behavior in specific, harmful ways that rob girls not only of their control and power but also of their worth as individuals.

The third wave of the feminist movement and the reality television movement are both influencing American culture, but their messages are primarily in conflict with one another. In her article, "The Third Wave's Final Girl," Irene Karras writes, "Third wave feminists . . . are struggling to define their femaleness in a world where the naming is often done by the media and pop culture" (3). This is why cultural production is so important to third wave feminism. Positive female representations are necessary in movies, television, and music because otherwise stereotypes and societal expectations that restrict girls will be perpetuated. A 1998 *Time* article asks, "Is Feminism Dead?" If reality-based dating shows such as MTV's *NEXT* and the way they portray and treat girls continues, the answer to that question will ultimately be a resounding "yes." The article asks, "For the next generation, feminism is being sold as glitz and image. But what do the girls really want?" (60). Do girls want to be paraded off of a bus as a male contestant chooses between them based on their appearances, as *NEXT* does? Do they want to pose suggestively in front of a camera and make sexually explicit comments for the viewing pleasure of over 342 million homes worldwide? MTV turns girls into hypersexual objects for men and boys to look at and for other girls to emulate, and this needs to not only be analyzed and critiqued, but also put to an end.

NEXT and other television dating shows rely on the sexuality of contestants to attract viewers. In order to understand why this is so harmful to girl participants and viewers, the word "sexuality" itself must be understood. As feminist theorist Catharine MacKinnon writes, "What is sexual is what gives a man an erection" (480). By this definition, there is no possibility for empowerment that girls can gain through being made into sexual spectacles on shows like *NEXT.* This relates to the arguments of Laura Mulvey who has theorized that film intrinsically sets up females to be sexually objectified solely for male pleasure. She writes, "The way film reflects, reveals and even plays on the straight, socially established interpretation of sexual difference . . . controls images, erotic ways of looking and spectacle" (297). Mulvey is relating this idea to film during Hollywood's "Golden Age" in the 1930s and 40s, but unfortunately her theories lend themselves just as well to the television dating show genre of recent years. Mulvey explains that when sexual pleasure can only be gained from "watching, in an active controlling sense, an objectified other" this is an extreme perversion (298). There is no doubt that contestants on *NEXT* are in a controlled setting in which they are objectified. And if this is the case, is *NEXT* not trying to make all of its viewers throughout its 342 million homes worldwide into female objectifying perverts? MTV has a long tradition of producing reality-based shows such as *The Real World* in which "women partake in their own degradation, learning to make the male gaze their own" (Stern 3).

That being said, if females are given no other choice but to gain pleasure through watching other females being objectified, when will sexual objectification stop? Additionally, when a show like *NEXT* is as antifeminist and problematic as it is, how will girls even *know* that they are being sent dangerous messages that they should not accept, and more importantly, should not emulate?

The basis of *NEXT* is that there is one contestant who has the opportunity to go on five separate dates. To avoid confusion, I will call the person choosing between the five people the "contestant," and the people who she/he must choose between will be called the "dater/s." The majority of the episodes of *NEXT* feature dating under hetero-normative conditions in which the contestant is choosing between five dates of the opposite sex. There are also episodes featuring homosexual contestants and daters, but these are not aired regularly. The daters are concealed on a bus and leave the bus individually for their date with the contestant. This leaves the contestant in suspense of who else is on the bus throughout the episode. One of the most disturbing and revealing aspects of *NEXT* is the fact that daters receive $1 for each minute that they last before the contestant "nexts" them, sending them back to the bus. The title of the show comes from "nexting," in which the contestant tells their date "Next!," the date is forced to return to the bus with however much money they "earned," and the next date gets her/his turn with the contestant. In turn, if a contestant likes one of their dates enough to ask them on a *second* date, the dater must choose between however much money she/he has accumulated and a second date, forfeiting any money she/he has "earned" should she/he accept the second date. Shows like *NEXT* further normalize male objectification of females in a world where this kind of behavior is ever-present. MacKinnon writes, "Women cope with objectification through trying to meet the male standard, and measure their self-worth by the degree to which they succeed" (484). In terms of *NEXT*, the ultimate success for a female dater is being asked on a second date by the male contestant. Under these circumstances, the girl daters' only options are to decline the second date and receive their payment for each minute they were objectified, or to accept the second date. By forgoing all money they earned the male contestant can thus sexually objectify the girls free of charge, which is more realistic in regards to a world in which "all women live in sexual objectification like fish live in water" (MacKinnon 484). One female dater responds to being sent back to the bus with $1 by flashing the male contestant. Immediately after, she stands in front of the camera, waving her dollar, and says, "Usually on Spring Break I show my boobs for free." Girls have been so normalized to their sexual objectification that it has become not only something they are subjected to, but something they actively participate in. Shows like *NEXT* play a role is this normalization that cannot be ignored.

A spoof of *NEXT*, entitled *Jesus on NEXT*, makes light of the fact that female daters are nothing more than objects to the male contestant. The male contestant judges them solely on their appearances. The mere fact that a spoof of this kind exists is proof in itself of the impact and influence that MTV's reality dating programs have on young viewers. *Jesus on NEXT* features a male contestant, a representation of Jesus, who goes on dates with five females. At one point in the film that is featured on YouTube.com, Jesus "nexts" a girl who he has been getting along with very well for no other reason except, as he reasons, "I just have to see what else is on that bus" (*Jesus*). The use of the word "what" instead of "who" exemplifies the blatant objectification that occurs on actual episodes of *NEXT*. The people who produced this spoof realize the horrible messages that *NEXT* sends, but do all viewers? And more importantly, does realizing these messages do anything to prevent them from influencing viewers' perceptions?

The sad reality of actual episodes of *NEXT* is that they are in many cases more disgusting than any spoof. This is especially true of a special "Spring Break 2007" episode of *NEXT* in which a male contestant, Lorenzo, 25, goes on dates with five girls in the following order: Amaris, 19, Rachel, 21, Jenn, 25, Alysha, 18, and Catherine, 18. A particularly revealing moment on this episode is when one of the girls asks the others if they would ever consider appearing on a *Girls Gone Wild* video. Alysha, an 18-year-old aspiring go-go dancer who works at Hooters, replies, "Yeah, why not?" and the four other girls look at her, jaws dropped in disbelief. It is my argument, however, that *NEXT* objectifies girls in the same way that the *Girls Gone Wild* videos, which are notorious for showing girls flashing their breasts, kissing other girls, and dancing suggestively, do. While *Girls Gone Wild* is specifically marketed towards a male audience, *NEXT* has a wider and younger audience but provides the same basic, implied message that it is natural to sexually objectify girls, therefore proving *NEXT* more harmful.

When I first began researching *NEXT* I knew that it was far from anything even resembling third wave feminism, but I thought it might reflect some ideals of girlie feminism. Irene Karras states, "Girlie feminists claim their femininity as a source of power. . . . By embracing the feminine—make-up, clothing, and even Barbies—third wave feminists are sending the message to society that women are powerful on their own terms" (7). While the girls on *NEXT* embrace make-up and revealing clothing, they are in turn objectified and demeaned by boys. There is nothing empowering about girls dressing this way or wearing a lot of makeup because if they *do not* present themselves this way then they are most often "nexted" and sent back to the bus. This is an obvious form of policing female appearance and behavior.

Perhaps the most disturbing aspect of *NEXT* is that not only does the male contestant police female behavior, the female daters and a female narrator whose voice is heard throughout the episodes polices and demeans girls, as well. When Rachel exits the bus for her date with Lorenzo one of the four remaining girls on the bus asks the others if they think Rachel will "win." Jenn replies, "Maybe if she went on the salad diet like six months ago." Lorenzo instantly sends Rachel back to the bus. Their date would have consisted of them racing dune buggies on the beach, and as Rachel walks back to the bus the female narrator says, "When Rachel's clothes were a bit too snug, she didn't get to drive the dune bug." The input from this narrator is similar to a device used on the dating show, *Blind Date,* in which text pops up on the screen accompanying the action of the show. In the article, "Pop (Up) Goes the Blind Date: Supertextual Constraints on 'Reality' Television," the authors critique the show's "supertext," which they say "serves to maintain the social order and punish deviance from behavior traditionally regarded as normal" (185). The narrator on *NEXT* serves the same purpose, reinforcing insulting comments from contestants and daters. This further naturalizes the show's message to girls that there is an ideal image they must embody to "win" boys' approval and in turn their own self-worth.

Proponents of *NEXT* may claim that the show is empowering to girls because it allows one girl to choose between five male dates on some episodes. Although this gives the female contestant some agency, it does not reverse the objectified role that she is still forced into. Despite having the control to choose between five dates, these boys compensate for their lack of control by objectifying and bad-mouthing the girl even more when/if she decides to "next" them. This rejection in one episode led a boy to return back to the bus and declare to the other four boys, "The girl is flat. She's got stretch marks on her legs." In addition to these heteronormative episodes, on rare occasions MTV airs episodes of *NEXT* featuring homosexual contestants and daters. Rather than showing positive representations of gay girls and boys, however, *NEXT* makes spectacles of them by exaggerating gay stereotypes such as hypersexuality and flamboyancy. These episodes are even more laden with sexual innuendos and objectify homosexuality in the same way that female sexuality is on other episodes.

MTV is watched worldwide by millions of young viewers. The network therefore has a responsibility to send positive messages to this audience, instead of messages that perpetuate and further normalize the sexual objectification of females. Univision, as one of the only Spanish-speaking networks broadcast on American television, has its own responsibilities to its viewers. In February 2007 Univision was punished for filling up slots meant for children's educational programming with *telenovelas*, or soap operas. Univision agreed to pay the Federal Communications Commission (FCC) $24 million (Abrams). Univision failed to meet government rules for children's educational programming, instead showing racy, sexually explicit *telenovelas*. Univision failed its young viewers in the same way that MTV continues to fail its own. As Jennifer Eads states, "Girls look to TV programming to decipher what it means to be a woman, to try out different roles, and to learn sexual expectations and behaviors" (14). If MTV's programming is a source of education to girls and boys alike then they should be held just as responsible as the Univision network. Just because MTV may not be subject to government rules about children's educational programming does not mean that their programming is not used by children for educational purposes. The media is used for sexual and gender role education by young viewers and therefore must be held responsible for the messages it sends and the consequences of those messages. It is wrong for MTV to promote the sexual objectification of girls, and just as Univision was punished for its offences, as should MTV.

MTV promotes the expendability of people through its dating shows, turning daters into objects that can easily be thrown away. On its website, potential contestants are instructed, "The minute you get annoyed, angry, or just plain bored, simply kick 'em to the curb saying 'NEXT' and start over with someone new" (*NEXT* Summary). The way *NEXT* was designed works to rob daters of their dignity. A comment that dater, Jenn, makes to contestant, Lorenzo, exemplifies this point. She says, "Get me naked before you next me, idiot." Her words reveal that Jenn is basing her own worth solely on her physical appearance, and is offended that her looks were not enough to secure her a second date. The message that being "nexted" by a male contestant sends and that the narrated voice reinforces is that the girls are worthless. Girls' appearances and behaviors are thus policed when they realize how easily they can be replaced by a different girl whose appearance and behavior is more valued. Danielle Stern discusses the commodification of female sexuality in *The Real World,* and this commodification is even more clearly present in *NEXT* where girls are immediately given the money they "earned" after being "nexted." MTV, however, is earning far more for these girls' appearances on *NEXT*. Stern reports, "Advertisers are willing to spend anywhere from $10,000 to $20,000 for a 30-second slot to target MTV's young viewers" (2). Not only is MTV making money by sexually objectifying girls, the companies that advertise during *NEXT* are also capitalizing on the show's sexual displays, and it is girls who ultimately pay the very high price.

Shows like *NEXT* cannot be written off as simply innocent, silly television dating programs. Catharine MacKinnon writes, "only 7.8 percent of women in the United States are not sexually assaulted or harassed in their lifetimes" (476). Reality-based television cannot be disassociated from the role it plays in creating such alarming statistics. 92.2% of United States women have been sexually assaulted or harassed in their lifetimes, and the fact that 100% of women are sexually objectified on *NEXT* should be no less of an alarming statistic. The harsh realities of reality-based television dating shows must be realized before the harmful and dangerous roles that girls are forced into can or will ever change. MTV should not be allowed to define femaleness and it should not be allowed to turn girls into sexual, disposable objects. Sexual objectification is something that is even more prevalent than reality-based dating shows. Reality-based dating shows feed off of female sexual objectification, and this plague needs to be eradicated if girls will ever have the opportunity to base their worth on something other than male approval and subsequently gain the empowerment and agency they so deserve but are so rarely given the chance to claim.

Works Cited

Abrams, Jim. "Univision Agrees to Record $24M Fine From FCC Over Lack of Children's Programming." *Yahoo! Finance* 24 Feb. 2007. 27 Apr. 2007 <http://biz.yahoo.com/ap/070224/univision_fine.html?.v=4>.

Baumgardner, Jennifer and Amy Richards. "Third Wave Manifesta." *Feminist Theory: A Reader*. Comp. Wendy K. Kolmar and Frances Bartkowski. New York: McGraw-Hill, 2005. 568–569.

Derose, Justin, Elfriede Fursich, and Ekaterina Haskins. "Pop (Up) Goes the Blind Date: Supertextual Constraints on "Reality" Television." *Journal of Communication Inquiry* 27.2 (2003): 171–189. 20 Feb. 2007.

Eads, Jessica. *Construction of Adolescent Girls' Identity in the Age of Reality Television*. Diss. The Univ. of North Carolina at Greensboro, 2004.

Ferris, Amber. *Playing the Dating Game: the Relationship Between Viewing Reality Dating Programs on Television and College Students' Perceptions of Dating*. Diss. Michigan State Univ., 2004.

Jesus on NEXT. 7 Jan. 2007. *YouTube*. 23 Feb. 2007 <http://www.youtube.com/watch?v=f0ulGU19sP4>.

Labi, Nadya. "Is Feminism Dead?" 29 June 1998. *Time*.

Mulvey, Laura. "Visual Pleasure and Narrative Cinema." *Feminist Theory: A Reader*. Comp. Wendy K. Kolmar and Frances Bartkowski. New York: McGraw-Hill, 2005. 296–301.

"*NEXT* Summary." *MTV*. 18 Feb. 2007 <http://www.mtv.com/#/ontv/dyn/next/summary.jhtml>.

NEXT. MTV. 19 Mar. 2007.

Phillips, Lynn. "Sexuality." *The Girls Report*. New York: National Council for Research on Women, 1998. 33–43.

Stern, Danielle M. "MTV, Reality Television and the Commodification of Female Sexuality in the Real World." *Media Report to Women* 33 (2005): 13–22. 22 Feb. 2007.

Syvertsen, Trine. "Ordinary People in Extraordinary Circumstances: A Study of Paricipants in Television Dating Games." *Media, Culture & Society* 23 (2001): 319–337. 19 Apr. 2007.

READING WRITING

This Text: Reading

1. In what ways is Theroux effective in using her lens of third-wave feminism in analyzing *Next*?
2. Compare her work to the other essays in the Third-Wave Feminism Suite.
3. Are there other lenses that might be appropriate in examining this particular text?

Your Text: Writing

1. Using the lens of third-wave feminism, examine another dating reality show (like *The Bachelor*).
2. Using the lens of third-wave feminism, examine a different type of reality show, such as *The Real World*. In what ways do the producers use traditional stereotypes in both choosing their contestants and organizing the narratives?

Media Journal: *The Rosie O'Donnell Show*

Hillary West

Student Essay

Week of February 14, 1999

Rosie just might be a control freak. She controls her audience. She controls her guests and she controls her production.

The very young Olympic gold medalist, Tara Lapinski appeared as Rosie's first guest on Wednesday February 17. Rosie fired questions and comments at her left and right. Tara seemed to be ok with it. What else was she to do? She was trying to plug her special that was to air that night. Maybe Rosie knew ahead that Tara would need a lot of prodding. After the interview I noticed that I was standing in the middle of my kitchen staring at the television. There was nothing relaxing or restful about watching that bit. Now that I think about it I am always standing up when I watch the show. Rosie is quick witted and clever. It is part of her charm. But, maybe it is a little intense as well.

Rosie's next guest was fellow talk show host, Matt Lauer. Her demeanor was dramatically different. She immediately opens with the statement, "Matt, you threatened me." Evidently, earlier that morning Matt was hosting *The Today Show* and two young ladies appeared at his outside gate where the crowds gather for the show and on the air expressed their concern that they could not get on the Rosie show for that afternoon. Matt, on live TV, gave Rosie an ultimatum, put the girls on the show or he would not come on as a guest that afternoon. That afternoon Rosie accused Matt of threatening her. He agreed. Perhaps he realized he had stepped over a line. He had stepped over Rosie's line. It is Rosie's show and she is definitely in control. But, we should never underestimate the innate goodness of Rosie. Not only did the girls get into the Rosie show, they were invited on stage to sit with Matt Lauer during his interview. Rosie played it very cool. Was she kidding or was she genuinely irritated that she had been pushed into an awkward position? Throughout the interview with Matt, Rosie was very subdued, so unlike her encounter with Tara. But, by inviting the girls to come on stage, it certainly made Rosie look like the hero, even though she may not have appreciated having been manipulated. Or, the entire episode could have been a joke.

Rosie may feel a great need to control all that she can because she extends herself so much to others. We are always learning of how she is helping someone, family, friends, neighbors, or just fans who want to meet her or one of her guests. She is very friendly with her audience. It is as if they have all come over for a drink and she is the hostess. But, she has control over the audience. She is in the limelight and they are under the darker lights. She decides if members of the audience will be mentioned or not. It can be very spontaneous and at random. This Wednesday, while in the middle of a conversation with her band leader, John, she calls out, "Oh, I just realized it is Ash Wednesday!" Several people in the audience still had their ashes on their foreheads and she was trying to make out what it was that made them look so different from the others. She was friendly, amusing and made everyone feel at ease. But, Rosie was the one in charge. The cameras then shot to those in the audience to whom Rosie was referring.

Maybe this brief encounter with Matt Lauer has revealed a different Rosie. Or, it could be that she has a weakness: the need to control. She can control whether or not she wants to be overweight, funny, successful, or a good mom. It is interesting that there is no man in her life to share with the raising of her children. Maybe she doesn't want to share the opportunity because she will have to relinquish some of her control. To be as successful as Rosie has become, she must have some drive that pushes her along. If it is the need to control all that surrounds her, then fine. As long as she doesn't hurt anyone.

Week of March 15, 1999

It might be fake, but I don't think it is. Rosie is an honest, real life role model. She probably has some idea of the impact she makes, but maybe not. Everyone loves her and she seems to appear to be genuinely grateful when people are kind to her. As a role model she is generous, sincere, sensitive and moral.

Barbara Walters was a guest this week on Rosie. Rosie has mentioned many times that she would not and did not watch the Monica Lewinsky interview. Yet, Rosie is all too happy to have Barbara on her show and they are obviously very close. Rosie speaks her mind, though. She immediately reminds Barbara that she did not watch the interview and she doesn't want to talk about it because it upsets her so. Then Rosie launches into a two to three minute discourse about the fate of Hillary Clinton. Seldom does Rosie give a candid opinion about an issue. Perhaps it is because she is so adamant about things. Whatever the reason, the world listened and Rosie's opinion was duly noted. Tens of thousands of middle class moms heard her and have been influenced by what she had to say.

Rosie is believable because she is one of them. She cheats on her exercise and diet regime because she has had "a stressful week." What woman, what person could not relate to that? We crave her words, her thoughts, her opinions because she makes a difference and she is like us so maybe we could make a difference too even with all our faults. Rosie's stressful week began at an event, in her honor, whereby a celebrity friend was singing a song as a tribute to her and fell off the stage. The friend was alright but Rosie was not. She cried uncontrollably and all week she couldn't stop thinking about her friend. Each time she would mention the incident tears would well up in her eyes. Rosie was definitely not herself this week.

Her sensitivity makes her an emotional wreck and by some that may be perceived as a weakness. But her general audience relates to her sympathetic nature because they see themselves in the same light. For Rosie it means another session in therapy. For her viewers it probably means three more donuts and more exercise in the famous Rosie Chub Club.

What you don't want to do with Rosie is get on her list! Once the word is down, this stubborn Irish woman is not budging. If she doesn't like you, she doesn't like you. She has been very vocal about how she feels about Monica Lewinsky and consequently Bill Clinton. Although she loves the actors on *Party of Five,* her favorite TV show, she is very critical of their moral behavior. She is the last of the do gooders and does not allow R rated language on the show as she once again reminded Barbara Walters. Barbara, in mentioning the film *When Harry Met Sally* refrained, at Rosie's request from using the word orgasm. It's not even a swear word! Her strict Catholic upbringing must be the basis for her high moral fiber.

Every day members of the audience receive gifts. They are sponsor promotional pieces and the audience loves them. But Rosie's generosity stems far beyond that. She always pumps her celebrity guests for donations to E-bay to be auctioned off so that the proceeds will help needy children. And because she interacts so much with her audience, she learns quickly of a need. One visiting family lost their home and pets to a devasting fire. Rosie, sympathetic to the sorrow of the children, made arrangements for the family to receive a new cat and dog. Another elderly woman had not seen her sister in nine years and Rosie gifted her with a plane trip, car and driver and hotel room to visit her sister. Rosie confesses that giving things away makes her feel better and after all, she has had a "stressful week."

She isn't perfect, we all know that. But she is a positive role model for a sea of viewers who probably don't feel very good about themselves and spend too much time watching television and yelling at their kids. Rosie helps viewers see the good in themselves despite their faults because she is open about her own weaknesses. It is easy to look up to someone who is honest about who she is. I hope I don't discover one day that Rosie is a total hoax and I have been tricked into thinking she is a decent human being.

The Reality TV Suite

The authors of *The World Is a Text* live on opposite coasts, so they agreed to meet in the desert Southwest to work on the second and third editions of this book, and in particular, to write this new suite on reality TV. In a bizarre coincidence, as one of the authors was about to fly back to the West Coast, he found himself in an airport restaurant with the cast of *The Real World*. Cameras were everywhere; MTV handlers circled the restaurant and were staged at various places in the airport. Dozens of travelers peeked over into where the cast (and the author) were eating. It is entirely possible that one of the authors was in the background of an episode of *The Real World* long before you read this mini-introduction. The entire scene was profoundly unreal, and yet . . . not.

This suite explores the phenomenon of reality television. Reality TV first arrived in the United States in 1992, when MTV broadcast *The Real World*, a surprise hit. However, reality TV truly became a phenomenon in 2000, when *Survivor* appeared on CBS and completely entranced the American public. Since then, a plethora of reality shows have reached American viewers. Although the fact that so many shows are successful (and so many are given chances to be successful) indicates that the American public loves them, many are critical of a genre that promises "reality" but delivers something else.

Between the second edition of *The World Is a Text* and this one, scholarship on reality television has exploded. Trying to stay abreast of everything written, both here and in England, has been fascinating. Similarly, keeping up with new reality TV can prove both infuriating and engrossing. For example, while working on the third edition, we became transfixed by *The Biggest Loser*. Although we kept the reality TV suite in this edition, we changed all of the readings except the first one. This particular duet of short argumentative essays originally appeared in *Entertainment Weekly* in 2004. Ken Tucker, a television critic for the magazine, and Henry Goldblatt face off on the nature of reality television—Goldblatt is for, and Tucker is against. Although the piece is a bit dated, it provides a nice entrée into the reality TV debate. Laurie Ouellette and Susan Murray's piece comes from the introduction to their 2004 book, *Reality TV: Remaking Television Culture*. Here, Ouelette and Murray place reality TV in context and provide some useful terms for making sense of reality TV genres. In his essay—which is a chapter from his book, *Reality Television* (2006)—Richard M. Huff focuses on one of the most talked about aspects of this genre—the "reality" of reality TV. Finally, in one of our favorite essays, Stephanie Greco Larson reads *The Apprentice* through the lens of race. This piece, from the opening chapter of Larson's 2006 book *Media & Minorities: The Politics of Race in News and Entertainment*, links the popularity of *The Apprentice* with assumptions about "The American Dream" and racial stereotypes.

For the most part, media critics and conservative commentators lambaste reality TV as bad entertainment that has no basis in reality. Others contend that it is going to become the new soap opera and that it makes celebrities out of ordinary people. Television studios love reality TV because the shows are cheap to produce but bring in a great deal of money, suggesting the fad is not going away any time soon.

Consider, as you work your way through these essays, how reality TV has changed television, your own ideas about the world, and how we see the entire concept of "entertainment." Also, for those of you who have become hooked on *Survivor*, or like one of the authors, the first *Bachelor* series, think about where your overt interest in these shows comes from. Why is it we watch these shows? What do they give us that the everyday world does not?

Reality TV Bites— or Does It? The New Soap Opera or the End of Civilization: A Point-Counterpoint

Henry Goldblatt and Ken Tucker

Love It

Wasn't it jarring to hear that Jerri from *Survivor* stormed off the live reunion special last week? How could she do that? Rachel wouldn't be allowed to leave the last episode of *Friends* in a huff. Oh, wait a minute—Rachel's not real, but Jerri is: "She was a great 'character.' It's easy to forget she's a real person," said host Jeff Probst.

We need the reminder. It's easy to treat reality contestants as fiction because they're the types of characters we had been accustomed to seeing on TV before all those detectives without personal lives showed up. We're on a first-name basis with so many reality players—Rupert, Troy, Clay, and Shandi—because their emotions are so accessible. Apologies to *The O.C.,* but for fans of character-driven television, these series are the best prime-time soaps in years.

As Albert Camus said: "An intellectual is someone whose mind watches itself." Reality characters and the dramas encasing them are so compelling because they represent our dreams and lives. Look beyond the slick and (often) crass packaging of *American Idol*'s Kelly and Clay and reach into the deepest pit of your shame. Now admit it: They are your shower-singing, pop-star fantasies come true. Watching *The Apprentice*'s Omarosa, haven't you thought: *She's like that crazy #%!@ I work with?*

What puzzles me about the hate part of critics' love–hate relationship with reality is that no other genre of entertainment is maligned so harshly. In pop music, Usher is as commercial as any Idol and performs lightweight R&B (sample lyric: "yeah yeah yeah yeah yeah yeah")—but he's called infectious. (Before anyone writes letters, I'm a fan.) The film *Van Helsing* cost $148 million and bites, yet critics are barely fazed, since it'll be out of theaters soon enough. But when critics hear *Idol's* Jasmine hit a few wrong notes on Barry Manilow night? Quick, duck for cover—it's a sign of the apocalypse.

Speaking of the apocalypse, there's even redeeming value in the very worst of reality TV: (1) *The Swan* makes us feel good about ourselves in comparison (at least we have enough self-esteem not to enter a beauty pageant for former ugly people); and (2) *Are You Hot?* reminded us that under no circumstances does Lorenzo Lamas deserve a comeback.
—*Henry Goldblatt*

Hate It

As someone who originally got into this racket to explore what's vital, fun, and troublesome about popular culture. I'm glad I work at a magazine that doesn't accept or condemn any phenomenon at face value. Unlike a lot of my TV-critic colleagues, I don't go to bed hoping reality TV will vanish when I wake up in the morning simply because the decades-old sitcom/drama configuration was easier to deal with. There are reality shows—some editions of *Survivor, Big Brother, The Amazing Race,* and, delving into the netherworld of syndication for a moment, *Cheaters*—that are full of fascinating sociological details and, of course, laughs.

But ultimately, I find the majority of reality TV really depressing. For instance, I cannot muster enthusiasm for what's supposed to be the central conceit of *American Idol*—finding a first-rate young singer—when every piece of music the vocalists perform

The Reality TV Suite

is the kind of schlock I detested in my previous incarnation as a rock critic. (That's the reason I love Fantasia—like Aretha Franklin and Ray Charles, she bursts the flimsy bonds of cheap ballads with agile gospel and soul inflections.)

Nearly all of the young-folks-on-the-make shows, from *The Bachelor* to *Average Joe* to *The Real World,* strike me as a vast condemnation of the education system (no one on these shows speaks with any eloquence or wit, or makes cultural references beyond sports or pop music) and the failure of upbringing (these studs and babes hold their eating utensils like monkeys and get drunk at every opportunity). The fact that parents let their kids watch swill like *Fear Factor*—which celebrates swill, as long as a contestant can keep from barfing it up—fills me with dread for the future.

I'm not foolish enough to expect civilian non-performers to be profoundly self-analytical about their motives or to crack jokes as sharp-witted as a pro like, say, Larry David (though aren't his comments unscripted too? Gee, y'think it's because he has a frame of reference beyond just getting loaded or laid?). But is it asking too much for entertainment to be entertaining, and not a constant parade of people who, if I met them in real life, I'd dash across the room to avoid? —*Ken Tucker*

Americans seem to idolize *American Idol.*

Reality TV: Remaking Television Culture

Laurie Ouelette and Susan Murray

IN FALL 2002, THE CHARACTERS on *The Simpsons* appeared as contestants on a fictional reality TV program. Donning nineteenth-century clothing and giving up all modern conveniences, they agreed to be filmed around the clock by the Reality Channel while living in a nineteenth-century-style home complete with TV cameras and a video "confessional" room. When their show fails to generate high ratings, the producers move the house to a remote location in the Amazon, forcing the cartoon family to navigate the ravages of nature as well as the hardships of premodern life and the surreal process of living their lives in front of millions of TV viewers. When the Simpsons encounter a disillusioned "tribe" of North Americans assembled for another reality show, they join forces to overthrow the production team, escape the house, and return to the comforts of their suburban life, which—most important to the family—includes television viewing.

The episode pokes fun at the recombinant nature and ratings-driven sensationalism of much reality TV in scenes where producers copy the format of successful European shows and frenetically scan U.S. channels for ideas about attention-grabbing plot twists. Taking the conventions of programs like *Survivor, Big Brother,* and *1900 House* as a shared cultural reference point, it satirizes viewer fascination with the televisual display of "real" people, the agreed-on surveillance inherent to reality TV, and the commercial pressures that have coalesced to create simultaneously "authentic," dramatic, popular, and profitable nonfictional television programming. The parody suggests that reality TV is a pervasive and provocative phenomenon that is remaking television culture and our understandings of it.

Situating Reality TV

What is reality TV? The classification of generic labels is always contextual and historical, as several essays in this volume demonstrate. While there are certain characteristics (such as minimal writing and the use of nonactors) that cut across many reality programs, we are ultimately more concerned with the cultural and "branding" discourses that have coalesced to differentiate a particular moment in television culture. We define reality TV as an unabashedly commercial genre united less by aesthetic rules or certainties than by the fusion of popular entertainment with a self-conscious claim to the discourse of the real. This coupling, we contend, is what has made reality TV an important generic forum for a range of institutional and cultural developments that include the merger of marketing and "real-life" entertainment, the convergence of new technologies with programs and their promotion, and an acknowledgment of the manufactured artifice that coexists with truth claims.

We have seen the rapid proliferation of television programming that promises to provide nonscripted access to "real" people in ordinary and extraordinary situations. This access to the real is presented in the name of dramatic uncertainty, voyeurism, and popular pleasure, and it is for this reason that reality TV is unlike news, documentaries, and other sanctioned information formats whose truth claims are explicitly tied to the residual goals and understandings of the classic public service tradition. Although the current wave of reality TV circulates ideologies, myths, and templates for living that might be called educational in nature, it eschews the twin expectations of unpopularity and unprofitability that have historically differentiated "serious" factual formats from popular entertainment. If the reality programming that we examine here celebrates the real as a selling point, it also distances itself from the deliberation of veracity and the ethical concerns over human subjects that characterize documentary programming in its idealized modernist form.

While the convergence of commercialism, popularity, and nonscripted television has clearly accelerated, much of what we call popular reality TV can be traced to existing formats and prior moments in U.S. television history. The quiz formats of the late 1950s represent an early incarnation of highly profitable TV programming that hinged on the popular appeal of real people placed in dramatic situations with unpredictable outcomes. Other precursors include the staged pranks pioneered by *Candid Camera,* celebrations of ordinary people in unusual or unusually contrived situations (examples include *Queen for a Day, It Could Happen to You, That's Incredible,* and *Real People*), and the amateur talent contest first brought to television by *Star Search.* The landmark cinema verité series

An American Family, which is often cited as the first reality TV program, also provides an important reference point, as does low-budget, nonprofessionally produced television, from the activist and amateur programming shown on cable access stations to the everyday home video excerpted on *America's Funniest Home Videos*. Daytime talk shows, the favored reality format of the late 1980s and early 1990s, anticipated the confessional ethos and cultivation of everyday drama that permeate contemporary reality TV. Yet it wasn't until the premiere of *The Real World* on MTV in 1991 that we began to witness the emergence of many of the textual characteristics that would come to define the genre's current form. By casting young adults in a manner intended to ignite conflict and dramatic narrative development, placing the cast in a house filled with cameras and microphones, and employing rapid editing techniques in an overall serial structure, the producers created a text that would prefigure programs such as *Survivor* and *Big Brother*. It could also be argued that *The Real World* trained a generation of young viewers in the language of reality TV.

Today, reality TV encompasses a variety of specialized formats or subgenres, including most prominently the gamedoc (*Survivor, Big Brother, Fear Factor*), the dating program (*Joe Millionaire, Mr. Personality, Blind Date*), the makeover/lifestyle program (*What Not to Wear, A Wedding Story, Extreme Makeover*), and the docusoap (*The Real World, High School Reunion, Sorority Life*). Other examples include the talent contest (*American Idol*), popular court programs (*Judge Judy, Court TV*), reality sitcoms (*The Osbournes, My Life as a Sitcom*), and celebrity variations that tap into many of the conventions for presenting "ordinary" people on television (*Celebrity Boxing*). What ties together all the various formats of the reality TV genre is their professed abilities to more fully provide viewers an unmediated, voyeuristic, yet often playful look into what might be called the "entertaining real." This fixation with "authentic" personalities, situations, and narratives is considered to be reality TV's primary distinction from fictional television and also its primary selling point.

Beyond the textual characteristics and appearance of new subgenres, what differentiates today's cultural moment is a heightened promotion of the entertaining real that cuts across prime time and daytime, network and cable programming. For a variety of complex reasons that the authors explore, reality TV has moved from the fringes of television culture to its lucrative core as networks adopt reality formats to recapture audiences and cable channels formulate their own versions of reality formats geared to niche audiences. Consequently, not since the quiz show craze of the 1950s have nonfictional entertainment programs so dominated the network prime-time schedule. Talk shows and game shows have historically been relegated to daytime or late-night hours, while networks have relied on dramas and sitcoms to secure their evening audience base. While cable stations were the first to begin airing reality programs during prime time, the success of CBS's *Survivor* eventually led the networks to follow suit. By early 2003, the staying power of the genre, along with the success of new shows like *American Idol, The Bachelorette,* and *Joe Millionaire,* convinced networks to make long-term plans for reality TV and its accompanying business strategies. In a front-page story on the topic in the *New York Times*, Leslie Moonves, president of CBS Television, proclaimed that "the world as we knew it is over."[1] The networks plan to stagger the release of new reality programs throughout the year instead of debuting them en masse in September. They also plan to jettison repeats of the programs altogether. These additional scheduling shifts will help networks compete more aggressively with cable channels and, they hope, retain reality TV's young, upscale audience base. By January 2003, one-seventh of all programming on ABC was reality based. ABC executives, along with NBC, Fox, and CBS,

The Reality TV Suite

promised to bring even more reality to their schedule in the coming season and cut back on scripted fictional drama series and sitcoms.[2] A few months later, the first "reality movie," *The Real Cancun,* was released in theaters just as development plans for Reality Central, an all-reality cable channel scheduled to debut in 2004, were announced. While some industry insiders remain skeptical about the long-term viability of the reality craze, the spread and success of the genre has already exceeded expectations.

Is Reality TV Real?

Reality TV's staying power renders an investigation of its relationship to truth and authenticity even more urgent. Many reality formats maintain noticeable connections to the documentary tradition. In particular, the use of handheld cameras and lack of narration found in many reality programs is reminiscent of observational documentaries, and carries with it an implicit reference to the form's original promise to provide direct access to the experience of the observed subject. This has the effect of bolstering some of reality TV's claims to the real. Scholarly discussions of documentaries have tended to turn on issues of the ethics of representation and the responsibilities associated with truth telling and mediation. In *New Documentary: A Critical Introduction*, Stella Bruzzi points out that at the root of these discussions is a naive utopian belief in a future in which "documentaries will be able to collapse reality and fiction" by "bypass[ing] its own representational tools" with the help of particular techniques such as those commonly associated with cinema verité.[3] The reception of reality TV programming evokes similar questions and concerns as critics (but not necessarily audiences) wring their hands over the impact that editing, reconstruction, producer mediation, and prefab settings have on the audience's access to the real. Despite such similarities in claims and critical concerns, however, reality TV also establishes new relationships between "reality" and its representation.

Although reality TV whets our desire for the authentic, much of our engagement with such texts paradoxically hinges on our awareness that what we are watching is constructed and contains "fictional" elements. In a highly provocative and influential article in the *Television and New Media* special issue on *Big Brother*, John Corner claims that the commingling of performance with naturalism is a defining element of what he calls television's "postdocumentary context."[4] In this contradictory cultural environment, critics like Corner contend that viewers, participants, and producers are less invested in absolute truth and representational ethics and more interested in the space that exists between reality and fiction. Reality TV promises its audience revelatory insight into the lives of others as it withholds and subverts full access to it. What results is an unstable text that encourages viewers to test out their own notions of the real, the ordinary, and the intimate against the representation before them. Far from being the mind-numbing, deceitful, and simplistic genre that some critics claim it to be, reality TV supplies a multilayered viewing experience that hinges on culturally and politically complex notions of what is real, and what is not.

Central to what is "true" and "real" for reality TV is its connection to the increase in governmental and private surveillance of "ordinary" individuals. In an era in which a "total information awareness" of all U.S. citizens has been made a top governmental priority, the recording and watching of others—and ourselves—has become a naturalized component of our everyday lives. Surveillance cameras are everywhere in the United States. In fact, the American Civil Liberties Union found in 1998 that in New York City alone, 2,397 cameras (both privately and governmentally operated) were fixed on public places such as parks, sidewalks, and stores.[5] By 2001, a company providing security services, CCS International, reported that the average New Yorker was recorded seventy-three to seventy-five times a day.[6] Since the events of 11 September 2001, even more cameras have been installed. Reality TV mitigates our resistance to such surveillance tactics. More and more programs rely on the willingness of "ordinary" people to live their lives in front of television cameras. We, as audience members, witness this openness to surveillance, normalize it, and in turn, open ourselves up to such a possibility. We are also encouraged to participate in self-surveillance. Part of what reality TV teaches us in the early years of the new millennium is that in order to be good citizens, we must allow ourselves to be watched as we watch those around us. Our promised reward for our compliance within and support of such a panoptic vision of society is protection from both outer and inner social threats. Surveillance is just one of the promises of "public service" that reality TV makes. Reality TV is cheap, common, and entertaining—the antithesis of public service television and a threat to the well-informed citizenry that it promises to cultivate, according to conventional wisdom. And yet, a closer look at reality TV forces us to rethink the meaning and cultural politics of public service, democracy, and citizenship in the age of neoliberalism, deregulation, conglomeration, and technological convergence.

The Commercialization of the Real

If reality TV raises cultural and ethical questions, it also points to the medium's changing industrial context. In the late 1980s, a shifting regulatory climate, network financial troubles, and labor unrest forced the television industry to reconsider its programming strategies. Finding reality formats cheap to produce, easy to sell abroad, and not dependent on the hiring of unionized acting and writing talent, the industry began to develop more programs like *Unsolved Mysteries, Rescue 311*, and *America's Most Wanted*. In Europe, public television stations also embraced reality programming, mainly as a financial survival mechanism. Faced with deregulatory policies and heightened pressures to compete with commercial channels that aired popular (and often U.S.-produced) programs, public stations in the United Kingdom, the Netherlands, and other European locales developed the reality genre.

The explosion of reality programming in the 1990s was also the product of a changing industrial environment—both in the United States and abroad. Feeling threatened by new recording devices such as TiVo and ReplayTV (which contained commercial-skipping features) and an ever increasing number of cable stations, U.S. television networks were open to the possibility of new production and financing models, including the purchasing and selling of formats rather than completed programs, the expansion of merchandising techniques, an increased emphasis on audience interactivity, and the insertion of commercial messages within programs. (This last strategy isn't entirely new, of course, but is a variation on the indirect-sponsorship model used in the 1950s and revived within the deregulated policy milieu of the 1990s.)

If reality TV is at the center of major shifts within the television industry, its proliferation has also corresponded with the rapid development of new media technologies. Much of reality TV in the late 1980s and early 1990s, such as *Cops* and *America's Funniest Home Videos*, depended on the availability and portability of handheld video cameras. The most recent wave of reality programs has relied on small microphones and hidden cameras to capture private moments such as those that occur on *Big Brother* and *The Real World*. Yet the marketing and distribution of reality TV has also developed in particular ways in its use of the Internet, streaming video, cell phone technology, radio, and digital television. Viewers are no longer limited to just watching the completed text of a show, but can keep in touch through short message service (SMS) updates sent to their cell phones, by accessing live twenty-four-hour footage on websites, and by calling to cast their votes. New technologies have also facilitated new advertising strategies that enable sponsors to cut through the clutter of traditional television advertising.

One of the most compelling aspects of reality TV is the extent to which its use of real people or nonactors contributes to the diversification of television culture. *Survivor,* for example, has made it a point to use people from diverse age, racial, geographic, class, and sexual backgrounds. Reality TV opens up new possibilities and limitations for representational politics, as the authors in this volume demonstrate. The fifteen minutes of fame that is the principal material reward for participating on the programs limits the selection of "real people" to those who make good copy for newspaper and magazine articles as well as desirable guests on synergistic talk shows and news specials. Indeed, many of the participants on *Survivor* and other successful reality programs have gone on to star in Hollywood films, host television shows like MTV's *Spring Break,* and appear as contestants on new reality programs. While participation in reality TV doesn't seem to lead to an acting career, it does appear to provide a continuation of the observed life, as former participant/players' offscreen behaviors are tracked by the media even after their show airs. The celebrification of "average" folk further complicates the contours of television fame and the way that its star personas have been constructed as existing in a space between the ordinary and the extraordinary.

For some critics, reality TV's commercial orientation has co-opted its democratic potential. The dream of "the people" participating directly in television culture can be traced to the alternative video movements of the 1960s and 1970s, which sought to collapse the hierarchy between producers and receivers, and to empower everyone to participate in electronic image making. Influenced by the writings of Hans Magnus Enzensberger and Bertolt Brecht, video pioneers sought to "remake" television as a democratic endeavor, bypassing one-way transmission for a participatory model that allowed a full range of people to tell their stories and document their struggles, "unfiltered" by the demands of convention, stereotyping, and commercial sponsorship.[7] While this philosophy lives on in the alternative productions of Paper Tiger TV, Deep Dish TV, and Free Speech TV, it is now more commonly associated with the television industry itself, which emphasizes the democratic potential of reality TV by promising unscripted programs filled with (and sometimes made by) real people from all walks of life. Even advertisers have jumped on the trend, as the Gap uses real people to sell jeans and the Subway sandwich chain claims that a recent television commercial was "shot by real teenagers."

However opportunistic, the commercial embrace of popular reality programming does signal representational shifts, and with them, openings that warrant special consideration. The reality boom has spawned an opportunity to wrest control of television images and discourses away from the culture industries.

The theoretical assumptions and methodological principles on which we have come to depend are no longer sufficient tools to analyze an increasingly complex televisual environment. Television has become more sophisticated, not just in the presentation of reality programming that simultaneously claims authenticity yet rewards savvy viewers for recognizing constructed or fictional elements but in its reliance on interactive technologies, novel commercial strategies, and an intertextual environment in which real people slip in and out of the roles of celebrities, and vice versa. The global context in which reality programs are produced and shared is changing too: as media conglomerates become international entities, and as television formats are exchanged and revamped across national boundaries, we need to revise our political–economic frameworks and ways to understand how meaning can be both culturally specific and globally relevant.

Notes

1. Bill Carter, "Reality Shows Alters the Way TV Does Business," *New York Times*, 25 January 2003, A1.
2. Lynn Elber, "ABC Defends Increased Use of Reality TV," *Associated Press*, 15 January 2003.
3. Stella Bruzzi, *New Documentary: A Critical Introduction* (New York: Routledge, 2000), 255–59.
4. John Corner, "Performing the Real: Documentary Diversions," *Television and New Media* 3, no. 3 (August 2002): 255–60.
5. Dean E. Murphy, "As Security Cameras Sprout, Someone's Always Watching," *New York Times*, 29 September 2002, A1.
6. *Ibid.*
7. See Bertolt Brecht, *Brecht on Theatre*, ed./trans. John Willett (New York: Hill and Wang, 1964), and Hans Magnus Enzensberger, "Constituents of a Theory of the Media," in *Video Culture*, ed. John Hanhardt (New York: Visual Studies Workshop Press, 1986), 96–123. For an overview of the history and goals of alternative television, see Dee Dee Halleck, "Towards a Popular Electronic Sphere, or Options for Authentic Media Expression beyond *America's Funniest Home Videos*," in *A Tool, a Weapon, a Witness: The New Video News Crews*, ed. Mindy Faber (Chicago: Randolph Street Gallery, 1990), n.p.; Deirdre Boyle, "From Portapack to Camcorder: A Brief History of Guerilla Television," *Journal of Film and Video* 44, nos. 1–2 (1992): 67–79; William Boddy, "Alternative Television in the United States," *Screen* 31, no. 1 (1991): 91–101; and Laurie Ouellette, "Will the Revolution Be Television? Camcorders, Activism, and Alternative Television in the 1990s," in *Transmission: Toward a Post-Television Culture*, ed. Peter d'Agostino and David Tafler (Newbury Park, Calif.: Sage, 1995), 165–87.

⊔

"Reality" Television: American Myths and Racial Ideology

Stephanie Greco Larson

"No cultural representation can offer access to the 'truth' about what is being represented, but what such representations do provide is an indication about how power relations are organized in a society, at certain historical moments."[1]

"YOU'RE FIRED!" BECAME THE CATCHPHRASE in the spring of 2004 as the first season of *The Apprentice* captured public and media attention. The four-time Emmy-nominated NBC reality show brought sixteen ambitious business people together to compete for a position in Donald Trump's empire. Each week the participants were divided into two teams and given a sales, advertising, or negotiating task. At the end of each show, Trump eliminated one member from the less successful team.

NBC Universal's coordinated promotion contributed to the program's success and created a buzz that extended to other networks, print media, and the metaphorical watercooler.[2] The show received a popular time slot and aggressive advertising, and episodes aired more than once a week (on both NBC and CNBC). After being fired, contestants appeared on talk shows and soft news shows (like *Today* and *Larry King Live*). An entire *Dateline NBC* episode

The Apprentice is clearly about the Donald, but how is it also about race?

looked "Behind the Apprentice." The two-hour grand finale included a live reunion of the losing contestants and Trump's selection of the winner.

The advertising and network promotions may explain why viewers knew about the show and tuned into it initially but not why they kept watching. For it to become such a cultural phenomenon, *The Apprentice* had to appeal to large numbers of people. As with other popular reality television shows, audiences were invited to enjoy the blend of routine and drama, of unpredictability and familiarity, as well as the battle between appealing and annoying personalities. Viewers watched attractive young people compete, cooperate, emote, and reveal to the viewers their analysis of the game (and each other) as it unfolded. The casting made it easy to root for some competitors and against others. The editing made the weeks of work and cohabitation dramatic and thematic. The individual alliances and adversaries, the romantic possibilities, and the initial girls-versus-boys organization of teams became the show's story lines and guided media discussion. The talk centered on personalities and gender: Did Amy and Nick get together? Why did the women's team beat the men's so consistently? Did the women use their sexuality unfairly? Why did the women self-destruct on the mixed gender teams?

This attention to what the show might have told us about gender (particularly gender and the workplace) distracted us from what it said about race. Like most television programs and movies, *The Apprentice* was not explicitly about race. Yet, like other media, it contained (and reinforced) racial messages that are part of the dominant American ideology. Media (entertainment, news, and their hybrids) represent reality in a way that promotes certain meanings and interpretations of how the world works and why. These representations are selected and constructed in ways that consistently promote the status quo—the current beliefs, structures, and inequalities. This includes the racial hierarchy.

Media Discourse and the Racial Status Quo

The racial status quo is one of inequality with whites at the top of the hierarchy. Racial minorities are underrepresented in government, education, and corporations; they are overrepresented among the poor and in prison populations. The nation has a long history of legal and extralegal racial oppression; yet, this is inconsistent with American values of equality and fairness. Most Americans abhor the idea that political, social, and economic structures might be racists.[3] This is not the story they want to hear; it is not the one white people believe. So, mainstream media (the major television networks, newspapers, magazines, and motion pictures) do not tell it. Nevertheless, the stories told by the mass media help justify a system in which some groups (such as racial minorities) are subordinate to others by using narratives that reconcile the fact of racial inequality with belief in justice and equality. Ideologies that guide these stories make the status quo seem natural, inevitable, and right.[4] These discourses provide explanations for why things are the way they are. They deny the extent and the systemic causes of racial inequality.

American values and familiar narratives such as the "American Dream" make up one of the dominant discourses. This narrative holds that America is a "land of opportunity" where the circumstances of birth do not determine people's status in life, so anyone who works hard enough can go from "rags to riches."[5] Rather than being threatened by the existence of racial inequality, this narrative (which is so central to American identity) is used to understand racial inequality.[6] It focuses attention on the faults of individuals rather than the problems shared by groups and determined by social, economic, and political structures. The individualist perspective prevents people from seeing themselves as members of collective groups with different opportunities and access to power.[7]

The "assimilation narrative" says that once legal impediments to equality were lifted, racial minorities could "pull themselves up by their bootstraps" like other immigrants had.[8] Failure to do so was interpreted as the result of individuals' own inadequacies or attitudes. This simplistic explanation for failure reassures those who have succeeded and want to believe in the justness of the system. The media provide examples of racial-minority success stories in entertainment and news to show that minorities can enjoy the American Dream. If individuals from a minority group are shown overcoming adversity, the audience assumes that they all can, that is, as long as they are the "right kind" of individuals.[9]

Attention to the "wrong kind" of racial minorities also serves to justify the status quo. Due to continued racial segregation, the media are the primary forum through which whites come to "know" nonwhites; therefore, individual minorities in the media come to symbolize these groups for white audiences. Stereotypes use negative attributes of members of racial-minority groups to stigmatize the entire group.[10] These negative stereotypes help legitimate racism and the racial status quo by exacerbating white anxieties and fears.[11] In these ways, the popular media deny that racism exists and provide other explanations for the economic, criminal, and cultural problems racism creates.[12]

The Apprentice demonstrates many of the ways in which the media help maintain the racial status quo, including ignoring racial minorities and their problems, stereotyping racial minorities, and explaining and justifying racial inequality in a way that forestalls major reforms.

Ideology on *The Apprentice*

The Apprentice is a good example of how entertainment media convey the dominant ideology about race. Four of the sixteen competitors were racial minorities. Omarosa and Kwame were clearly identifiable as African Americans. Neither the show nor the official website made

The Reality TV Suite

clear that Katrina was a Cuban American.[13] Tammy's biography identified her as an Asian American from Seattle, but the show made no on-air references to this; nor was attention paid to her ethnicity in other ways. Although we can interpret Tammy's dismissal for disloyalty (when other women had been fired for being "too loyal") as reinforcing racial stereotypes of Asian Americans, the coverage of these two characters says more about invisibility and the denial of racial diversity than it does about stereotyping. Any influence race might have had on them or their experiences during the competition was overshadowed by their characterization as oversexualized and catty females.

Omarosa became the focus of most of the overt racial discussions. She talked about herself, her firing, and how the other contestants treated her in racial terms during and after the show. The most extended dialog about race and the show occurred in response to Omarosa's claim that Ereka used the "N word." This accusation was widely covered on the news, as was Trump's statement that a thorough review of the tapes found no evidence of this. Ereka denied the allegation and took a lie detector test on the *Howard Stern* radio show to prove it. This controversy helped solidify Omarosa's role as the antagonist on the show. Presented as embodying the "bad black" stereotype, she became the character the audience was invited to dislike (and most of them seemed to accept the invitation).

Consistent with this stereotype, Omarosa appeared to be a combative, lazy, self-pitying complainer who did not work well with others. Trump fired her because he thought she made too many excuses, was rude and abrasive, and had a chip on her shoulder. Yet, she remained on the show longer than her talents seen on screen seemed to justify. This served to extend the drama on the show, but it also invited criticism that she was getting "special treatment" because of her race.

Not only did these racial stereotypes seem to influence the casting of Omarosa and the way the show was edited and advertised, but their embodiment in a reality-show character helped to reinforce them. The "real" Omarosa can be seen as "evidence" of why racial inequality persists in America. This evidence is reassuring to white audiences because it says the problem is with "them" (blacks), not with "us" (whites) or the sociopolitical system.

Kwame fit the "good black" stereotype, which also supports the status quo. Soft-spoken, dignified, nonthreatening, and cooperative, he was shown as fitting comfortably in the "white world" with a Harvard MBA, his inability to communicate with hip-hop producer Russell Simmons (on episodic 6), and his deferential approach to Trump and the white players.

By focusing a lot of attention on Kwame's friendship with Troy (the only competitor with a drawl), the show fit him into the "white man's sidekick" stereotype. Their relationship illustrated that "race doesn't really matter" because on a personal level, "we can all get along." It also reinforced the racial hierarchy of whites as leaders and blacks as followers. Although Troy got fired before Kwame did, he was still shown as the leader of the pair. It was Troy's idea in episode 4 that Kwame sign basketballs to increase merchandise sales at Planet Hollywood (a strategy that used racial stereotypes to deceive consumers). Kwame eagerly went along with this and other suggestions from the guy he called his "main man." Even on tasks when Kwame was officially the leader, Troy seemed to call the shots. In episode 12, Tramp's decision came down to Troy and Kwame after Troy decided to go head-to-head with Kwame instead of Bill. In the boardroom, Troy said that Kwame was a "steady Eddie" but had never shone. Trump agreed that in three opportunities as project leader, Kwame never exhibited leadership. Yet, Trump fired Troy instead of Kwame, thereby inviting viewers to use a "reverse discrimination" explanation for the black man's success.

The fact that the competition came down to two men, one black and one white, conveyed another system-supportive message (messages that justify the status quo—its institutions, processes, and inequalities). It said that *The Apprentice* and all it represented (big business, competition, capitalism, American values) was fair and provided equal opportunity regardless of race. In fact, it did this explicitly when Kwame looked into the camera and said, "My grandfather signed his name with an 'X.' If this isn't the American dream, what is?"[14] The show makes this comforting and attractive idea more real. Kwame's example serves to refute the fact that there are a multitude of others for whom the dream does not come true. These people do not seem real: they are nameless and faceless; Kwame is not. Of course, viewers need only look at Omarosa to understand why some minorities fail to realize the American Dream.

Because of the all-or-nothing nature of the competition, Kwame's second-place finish put him in the same position as the fourteen other people who lost.[15] What did his loss to Bill in the final episode say about race? The simple answer might be that a "good black" is inferior to a "good white." But that sounds like old-fashioned racism and out of step with what a modern American audience wants to believe. A more convincing explanation needs to concern something within Kwame's control.

In episode 13, Kwame and Bill chose teams from the final six contestants, which they would lead in the final competition. Omarosa was not the last one selected; Kwame picked her before he selected Heidi (the Jewish New Yorker Omarosa said lacked class).[16] The final episode showed Omarosa bringing the same deficiencies shown earlier to this last task. She did not do her job, she blamed someone else for her mistakes, she was rude to an employee, she was late and irresponsible, and she lied to Kwame. Trump chastised Kwame for selecting Omarosa and for failing to fire her when she screwed up (something that Trump had failed to do in more than one boardroom). These decisions became the justification for Trump's choice of Bill as his apprentice.

Ultimately, the qualities that made Kwame the "good black'" and helped him stay in the game for so long ended up getting him fired. He was deferential when he needed to be a leader. He was calm and cool when he should have gotten angry. He stuck with the rules of the game when he should have thought outside of the box and fired Omarosa (an option he was unaware he had). His kindness was weakness. His loyalty was a character flaw. The lesson that the white audience got was that "good blacks" are brought down and held back by "bad blacks" because "they" stick together in a world that "we" know is color-blind. The implication is that "they" are at fault for any remaining racial inequality, not "us" or the system.

The Apprentice in its first season looked like the rest of America's mainstream popular culture. It presented race in America as white and black, overlooking the greater range of racial diversity. It created characters that fit dominant racial stereotypes through its contestant selection and video editing. In a variety of ways, it used dominant ideologies to defend and justify the race/sex/class status quo. It did this without most viewers even noticing because the ideologies are so familiar that they seem like common sense. The media help create this common sense through the continued use of racial discourses.

Notes

1. Lisa Taylor and Andrew Willis, *Media Studies: Texts, Institutions, and Audiences* (Oxford: Blackwell Publishers, 1999), 40.
2. NBC Universal is a corporation that includes a variety of news and entertainment vehicles. It was formed in May 2004. General Electric owns 80 percent of it, and Vivendi Universal controls 20 percent. See www.nbc.com.

3. Yet, many still hold antiblack attitudes and believe that blacks are too demanding. D. O. Sears, "Symbolic Racism," in *Eliminating Racism*, ed. P. A. Katz and D. A. Taylor, 53–84 (New York: Plenum, 1988).

4. Louis Althusser, *Lenin and Philosophy and Other Essays* (London: New Left Books, 1971).

5. Horatio Alger Jr., *Ragged Dick, Or Street Life in New York with the Boot-Blacks,* reissued ed. (New York: Signet Classics, 1990).

6. Stephanie Greco Larson and Martha Bailey, "ABC's 'Person of the Week': American Values on Television News," *Journalism and Mass Communication Quarterly* 75 (1988): 487–99.

7. Althusser, *Lenin and Philosophy*.

8. Gunnar Myrdal, *An American Dilemma*: *The Negro Problem and Modern Democracy* (New York: Harper and Row, 1962 [1944]).

9. Sut Jhally and Justin Lewis, *Enlightened Racism: The Cosby Show, Audiences, and the Myth of the American Dream* (Boulder, Colo.: Westview Press, 1992).

10. Oscar H. Gandy Jr., *Communication and Race: A Structural Perspective* (London: Arnold, 1998).

11. Teun A. Van Dijk, "New(s) Racism: A Discourse Analytical Approach," in *Ethnic Minorities and the Media*, ed. Simon Cottle, 33–49 (Buckingham, U.K.: Open University Press, 2000), 48; John Gabriel, "Dreaming of a White . . . ," in *Ethnic Minorities and the Media*, ed. Simon Cottle, 67–82 (Buckingham, U.K.: Open University Press, 2000), 80.

12. Christopher P. Campbell, *Race, Myth, and the News* (Thousand Oaks, Calif.: Sage Publications, 1995), 33.

13. See www.nbc.com/nbc/The_Apprentice (accessed August 15, 2004).

14. See www.hispeed.rogers.com/features/FeatureC.jsp?id = apprentice (accessed August 15, 2004).

15. It might have helped him parlay the show into more attention and opportunities.

16. In the boardroom during episode 6.

⊔

READING WRITING

This Text: Reading

1. What do you make of the *Entertainment Weekly* articles? Which one is the most convincing? Does one use better, more compelling arguments than the other?

2. Can you detect a bias in Ouelette and Murray's piece? Do they have a stance on the usefulness or importance of reality TV?

3. Huff's essay is a classic persuasive piece. He argues that reality TV is not *real*. That is not a unique argument, but his take is compelling. How successful is his argument?

4. We love Larson's essay on race and *The Apprentice*. Her reading is clearly done through a subjective lens. Do you find her observations sound and her assertions convincing?

5. When taken as a whole, what do these four pieces reveal about reality TV and American culture?

Your Text: Writing

1. Write a comparison/contrast essay in which you examine the pro/con arguments regarding reality TV.

2. Track down some of the old episodes of *TV Nation*. Is this show reality TV? How about Sunday morning political talk shows? *Queer Eye? What Not to Wear?* All of those home-makeover shows? Are these reality TV? Write a paper in which you define reality TV and give examples of what is and is not reality TV.

3. Write an essay in which you read American culture and tastes through the popularity (and unpopularity) of certain reality TV programs.
4. Take a cue from Huff. Write an essay in which you explain exactly why and how reality TV programs are *not* "real."
5. Write an essay in which you explain why reality TV is so popular in the United States and Europe. Why has it caught on *now*? If it does die, what will be the cause of its death?

READING BETWEEN THE LINES

Classroom Activities

Realistic?

Watch a show in class taking notes on what is realistic about the show. Do you find its setting realistic? Its dialogue? The characters—both in the way they act and their gender, ethnic, and class make-up? In what ways do the show's creators try to be realistic? In what ways are they admitting that television shows are not realistic? Do you think whether a show is realistic an important consideration in whether you watch it? What are the differences between television shows and "real life"?

Advertising

Watch the commercials in a particular television show. Can you tell from them who its target audience is? Do you think advertisers are reaching their intended audience?

Is This a Good Show?

What are your criteria for saying a show is "good"? Are they similar or different than the ones you might use for literature and/or movies?

Casting

Who would play you in a sitcom about your life? Why would you make this choice?

Genre

What is your favorite type of television show? Why? Do you feel you have something in common with others who like these types of shows?

Show Loss

Talk about a show that went off the air that you miss. What emotions did you feel when this show ended its run? Do you think the run ended too early? What do you think makes a successful television show?

Essay Ideas

The General Television Assignment

In this paper, read an episode of a television show and write a paper analyzing some aspect of it. What do we mean by "read" and "analyze"? You might start by describing the text at hand, performing an inventory of sorts. Then think about what these elements say about the text. What conclusions can you draw about the work from the observations you have made? A television show has traditional elements of texts such as a narrative and symbolic language of one sort or another, as well as visual elements that contribute to the show's meaning.

Look at the Fashion

For this paper, notice the way the characters dress on a particular television show. From what you know about fashion, what are the creators of the show trying to convey with their choices of fashion for their characters? Are they hoping to tie into prevailing opinions about the way certain groups (e.g., those of color, class, gender, and age) dress in providing clues on how we're supposed to understand these characters? Taken together, what conclusions can we draw from the fashion choices of the creators?

Analyze the Theme

In most sitcoms and many dramas, there is an explicit "moral of the story" that those who script the episode attach to the ending. Taking one such show, a night of shows on a particular network, or an accumulation of the same shows, what sorts of morals are presented to the audience? Do you think the creators think these morals are important? If so, do they present an honest attempt to educate the audience, or are they a vehicle for laughs? Do you know any shows that do not have "a moral of the story"? How would you compare them to the shows that do have morals?

The Unintended vs. the Intended

Sometimes television shows are explicit about what they are trying to convey. Sometimes, however, what is not present in a show says as much about the show as what is there. For example: Oprah Winfrey made a comment to the cast of *Friends* on her show: "Why isn't there a black 'friend' on your show?" Look at a popular sitcom and try to determine what may or may not be missing on a show. You might focus on the racial make-up of the characters or their gender, class, or age.

Real vs. Unreal

Many people may say that they watch television "to escape reality." In what ways do the producers of shows try to be "real"? In what ways do they ignore reality? You may already have noticed that we tend to watch characters in action with other characters, and that basic human functions like bathing, eating, sleeping, and going to the bathroom are ignored. On a more philosophical level, you may also notice that the problems these characters face are resolved relatively quickly, and the communication between characters is highly evolved. For this paper, you might discuss what overall effect the inclusion of "reality" might have on the audience.

Understand the Audience

Creators of television shows often target their shows to particular audiences—or their advertisers do, in order to see a greater return on their investment. Watch a television show, or several, and see if you can determine what demographic they are appealing to or what show their advertisers feel they are. Are the two audiences different? Is one more broad than the next? What do you think are some of the problems inherent in targeting a particular demographic?

Race and Ethnicity

For a long time, race and ethnicity has been an issue on television. Watch a show and see what they say and do not say about questions of race and ethnicity. Do members of a particular race play a particular role on the show? Do these roles embrace or reject previous stereotypes?

Honor the Show

Write an essay on why you feel a show is "good." Your first step, of course, is defining what you mean by "good". Does "good" mean writing that is funny, realistic, philosophical, or a combination of these factors or others? Is good defined by the quality of the actors? Can you define what a good television show is without constructing the criteria from the show you like? What other shows fit into the definition you constructed?

Disparage the Show

Write an essay on why you feel a show is "bad," going through the same process as you did when you defined what "good" meant. A useful exercise is to write both positive and negative reviews.

Follow the Character

What single character on a television show do you most identify with? Why? Does this identification make you at all uncomfortable? What does this identification say about you and the television character?

Media Journal

Using the worksheet at the front of the book as a guide, we want you to follow a phenomenon for the length of the course. It could be a television show, a continuing story in the newspaper (make sure you choose one that will continue), or a continuing event (such as a sport). Each journal entry should provide some sort of commentary on the phenomenon, moving beyond general plot concerns. A brief (two- or three-sentence) summary is fine but should not dominate the entry. See "Media Journal, *The Rosie O'Donnell Show*," by Hillary West, for an example.

Even though Marnie Spencer's *Between the Devil and the Deep Blue Sea* appears to be a collage, it is entirely painted. However, Spencer does create a collage of icons, memorabilia, and visual fragments that feel both classical and postmodern.

Source: Courtesy of the artist and Julie Baker, Fine Art, Grass Valley, California.

ART AND VISUAL CULTURE OFTEN INTIMIDATE US. WHEN CONFRONTED WITH A PIECE OF ARTWORK, PARTICULARLY IF IT IS ABSTRACT (MADE MORE FROM SHAPES RATHER THAN RECOGNIZABLE FIGURES), WE DO NOT OFTEN KNOW HOW WE SHOULD LOOK AT IT. WE WANT TO APPRECIATE ART BECAUSE WE KNOW "PEOPLE" THINK IT'S IMPORTANT, BUT HOW TO DO SO CAN BE A MYSTERY. THAT'S WHERE THIS CHAPTER COMES IN—WE HOPE TO MAKE IT EASIER FOR YOU TO APPROACH WHAT CAN BE A REWARDING AND EVEN ENJOYABLE PROCESS. IN FACT, IT COULD TURN OUT TO BE ONE OF THE MOST REWARDING SKILLS IN YOUR REPERTOIRE AS A HUMAN BEING.

Let's begin with a quick overview of what we mean by visual art. Although visual art has undergone transformations with technological innovations, we generally mean paintings, sculpture, and photographs, though items like artistic installations (large works of art often taking up entire rooms) or collages are often considered visual art. In addition, there is public or "street art," which merges traditional art with atraditional exhibition. Examples of this type of art include murals and graffiti. Traditionally, these texts make meaning through visual signs— colors, shapes, shadings, and lines—as opposed to texts that make meaning with words or music, though modern art has sought to bring both of these into its world. Like everything else we talk about in this book, works of visual art are complex texts that you are encouraged and invited not simply to look at but to *read*.

In helping you make sense of art as a medium, one of the most important aspects to recognize about art is its uni-versality and longevity. Long before there were written languages, there were visual ones. Since human beings could hold sticks and daub them in mud, there has been art. In caves in France, on cliffs in Utah, on tablets in the Middle East, on paper in the Orient, and on tombs in Egypt, men and women have been drawing pictures. If you have visited any of these places and seen these texts, you get a sense of the artist's overwhelming urge to represent the world—that is to represent or remake the world. That is really all art of any kind is—an individual's way of presenting the world in a new way. Van Gogh's sunflowers, Monet's water lilies, Picasso's musicians, Georgia O'Keeffe's flowers, El Greco's Jesus, even Jackson Pollock's splatterings are attempts to make us experience some aspect of the world in a way we had not before.

For a variety of reasons, art resonates with us in ways other media don't and perhaps can't. For one, we are visual creatures. We see millions of things every day, and in so doing rely heavily on our sight. Visual artists take our enormous practice of seeing the world and use it to make us see something new. So, in some regard, there is very little to learn. Artists use what you already use. All you have to do is get an idea of the very few tools they use to make their art do what they want it to.

Now, on to some hints for reading and writing about art:

Test your first reactions, both emotionally and intellectually.

Painting and photography often have definite advantages over poetry and fiction in that when you look at a painting, you don't immediately ask yourself what a certain tree symbolizes or what the rain is a metaphor for, although in abstract art, some of the same questions come up. Accordingly, you can approach reading them in different ways. Instead of trying to figure out what the painting "means," try to pay attention to what the painting or photo "evokes." What sort of reaction or response does the piece elicit? Is there a mood or tone? Does the painting or its colors create any particular emotion? You might also ask yourself how the artist works with notions of beauty. Is the picture or sculpture conventional in its use of beauty, or does he or she challenge typical ideas of beauty? If Hieronymus Bosch's *Garden of Earthly Delights* makes you uncomfortable, then the painting has succeeded as a rhetorical and semiotic text. If Monet's paintings of waterlillies give you a sense of calmed, pastoral elegance, then Monet has probably achieved his goal. If you find Georgia O'Keeffe's paintings of flowers, pistils, and stamens strangely erotic, then you are probably experiencing the kind of reaction that she intended. Works like Picasso's *Guernica* might affect you emotionally first, then begin to move you on an intellectual level—or vice versa. Either way, artists use shapes, colors, scale, and tone to make you feel a certain way. Thus, you may be reading the text of the painting on a subconscious level and not even know it.

In many ways, poetry resembles painting more than prose; so, like poetry, paintings may take a while to work on you. But that's okay; be patient. Let yourself be drawn into the text.

Pay attention to the grammar or syntax of visual art.

Like written language, visual art enjoys its own set of rules and structures. You don't have to know many of these terms or ideas to enjoy or understand art, but knowing some does help to decode individual artistic texts. For instance, let's look at the notion of **composition**. Chances are that you are in a composition course right now, and while artistic composition is slightly different, there are similarities. To compose means to "put together" or "assemble." It comes from two Latin words: *com*, which means "together," and *poser*, which means to "place or to put down." Accordingly, "composition" means to place together. In this way, the composition of a painting resembles the composition of your essays: both are texts that have been assembled from various "components" (a word with the same origin). So then the composition of a work of art is the plan or placement of the various elements of the piece. Most of the time, a painting's composition is related to the principles of design, such as balance, color, rhythm, texture, emphasis, and proportion.

Let's say you are looking at Leonardo da Vinci's masterpiece, *The Last Supper*. You might notice the symmetry or balance of the painting, how the table and the men are perfectly framed by the walls of the building, and how Jesus is framed in the very center of the piece by the open doorway. Placing Jesus in this position, lighting him from the back, gives him a certain emphasis the disciples lack. His red robe and his blue sash add to his stature, as does his posture. He looks as though he is offering a blessing, a gesture that underscores da Vinci's interpretation of Christ as a giver and a healer. Thus, how the artist places his subject (at the center) and how he depicts him (as offering both thanks and blessing) and how his subject is contrasted against the rest of the painting (in red and almost radiating light, power, and glory) is a kind of argument or thesis to the painting, just as you will create an argument or thesis for your own composition.

Taken all together, then, the various components of a painting or a photograph contribute to the piece's effect.

How we see, evaluate, and interpret "art" is influenced by a number of forces.

The visual arts extend beyond paintings we find in museums—they include digital images, installations, LED texts, performances, collages, comics, and a host of other media. For a long time, there has been a rift between "high" and "low" art. People then believe artists like Picasso, Monet, Manet, van Gogh, da Vinci, Michelangelo, Goya, Degas, and the like produce high art, where say, Nagel prints, photos of cars, most outdoor murals, much folk or "primitive" art, digital images, cartoons, Hummel figurines, Precious Moments statuettes, and any mass-produced

Fig. 1 C. M. Coolidge, *A Friend in Need.*
Source: Getty Images, Inc.

design is seen by many as "low" or "populist" art. For instance, we love the Dogs Playing Poker series (Fig. 1), but you are unlikely to see any of these paintings (despite how funny they are) in the Louvre, the Metropolitan Museum of Modern Art, or the Chicago Art Institute because they are considered "blue collar" or "pedestrian" or "unsophisticated." That said, William Wegman's photos of dogs (Fig. 2) *are* considered art. You can find calendars and postcards in the gift shops of most museums and the photos themselves on the walls.

It's unclear from the content why one is "art" and one is "tacky." Both are color images of dogs at tables. What makes the Wegman piece art? (One reason might be that the Wegman dogs in a way are mocking the dogs playing poker. Of course, the dogs playing poker might be themselves mocking something.) These kinds of questions are at the heart of the art world and continue to serve as cultural markers of education, sophistication, social class, and good taste. There are many, many people who would judge your sense of taste depending on which

Fig. 2 William Wegman, *Jack Sprat.*

of these two images you think is the best "art." Now, if you "like" the poker dogs better than the eating dogs, that's one thing; but if you argue that the poker dogs are better *art*, that is another matter altogether.

Art reflects not only the artists themselves, but also their culture.

Like music, literature, and film, the visual arts are products not only of artists but also of the culture in which the artist lives and works. It should come as no surprise that during the Middle Ages and the Renaissance, when the Catholic Church dominated the religious and political landscape of Europe, that most of the paintings reflected Biblical themes. Similarly, during the Romantic period, large, dark, brooding, tumultuous paintings tended to mimic "romantic" characteristics that worked their way into both architecture and fiction. Even the earliest cave paintings and rock art focuses on themes important to the artists of the time—hunting, fishing, keeping warm, and invoking the gods. The belief that art reflects the world in which it exists is called **mimesis.** Some people may argue that artistic movements such as Surrealism and Cubism were movements away from mimetic art because people like Marcel Duchamp, Georges Braque, Picasso, and Man Ray distorted reality in their work. However, if we consider that, at this time, most artists, writers, and thinkers found the early twentieth century to be a time of chaos, disorder, violence, alienation, and fragmentation, then one can make a compelling argument that Picasso's and Braque's fissured pictoral landscapes reflected a fissured cultural and political landscape.

Currently, as our culture becomes more politically conscious, so too does our art. Andres Serrano has become famous for his photographs of guns, murdered corpses, and Ku Klux Klan members; Native American artist Jaune Quick-to-See Smith assembles journalism articles about violence toward American Indians, sports mascots from teams whose mascots are Indians, and stereotypes of "natives" such as toy tomahawks and moccasins to make comments on contemporary American Indian life; photographer Cindy Sherman did a series of disturbing photographs of mutilated female mannequins as a commentary on the violence toward and objectification of women; and Michael Ray Charles, an African-American painter, has made a career out of augmenting representations of "Sambo," a disturbing stereotype used to mock African Americans. In each of these situations, art crosses over from the aesthetic world and into the world of ethics, becoming not just artistic statements but political statements.

Often, there is a gap between the artist and the public.

It's somewhat of a cliché by now, but what an artist finds appealing is not always what the public finds appealing. The furor over the *Sensation* exhibition in 1999 is one of the most recent in a long line of controversial artistic moments. In 1989, three men—Jesse Helms (a Republican senator from North Carolina), the conservative politician and commentator Patrick Buchanan, and art critic Hilton Kramer—launched an all-out attack on *The Perfect Moment*, a traveling exhibit of photographs by Robert Mapplethorpe that was funded by the National Endowment for the Arts (which gets some of its money from tax dollars).

Some of Mapplethorpe's photographs crossed the line of decency, according to those critics and others, because of their explicit homoerotic themes and because two photographs were of naked children. What resulted was a long legal and cultural battle over pornography, public funding for the arts, morality, and artistic freedom. Similarly, Andres Serrano's wildly controversial photograph *Piss Christ* nearly got the NEA shut down for good. This 1987 photograph of a crucifix dropped in urine angered so many people that it brought about the most thorough scrutiny of public financial support for the arts in American history. But America is not the only battleground for art and culture. To this day, if you visit Picasso's famous painting *Guernica* in Madrid, you will likely be accosted by locals who will want to give you a revisionist reading of the painting, which still remains behind glass to protect it from vandalism.

Photography tends to draw more fire than other art forms because people do not always see photographs as texts but as a reflection of the actual world. Along these same lines, think about how public art can be. Paintings and photos hang on walls of hotels and libraries, and the grace the walls of museums. We encourage our children to go to museums to get "enlightened." If what parents find at the museum disturbs them, then the public role of art often gets called into question. As readers of the world, be aware of the various forces that determine how we see art and how we see art's role in forging a vision of contemporary culture.

As we note above, art is not just social and economical, it is also political. Some of the images in the Censorship Suite have caused a lot of people a lot of grief. Because, for centuries, specific values and ideals have been associated with the term "art," when certain texts that challenge those ideas are marketed or displayed as "art," some aspects of American society get pretty worked up. In other words, for some, "art" is more than aesthetics, more than how something looks. Content also comes into play.

Works of modern and contemporary art deserve your attention because they are often important texts about the contemporary world.

Chances are, if you are like most people, you are totally confused by modern art, which often seems like an endless series of nonsensical images: people with square heads, splatters of paint, chaos. What's important to recognize about modern art is the audience's role in constructing the text. While modern artists do create work that may reflect their perspective and their culture, they also rely on the viewer to bring to their work an idea about what art is and how art functions. Frequently, viewers of modern art complain that they could have done the work themselves; they focus on the craftsmanship of modern art. But the artist might argue that the conception of art and the discussion of what art is and what it means is what makes modern art so compelling, and being a good reader of modern and contemporary art can give you valuable insights into recent social, political, and artistic moments.

Modern art saw the rise of the most recognizable schools: cubism, expressionism, fauvism, futurism, abstract expressionism, pop art, and collage. Figures like Pablo Picasso, Paul Klee, Wassily Kandinsky, Joan Miro, Gustav Klimt, Georges Braque, Edvard Munch, Henri Rousseau, Henri Matisse, Jackson Pollock, Robert Motherwell, Andy Warhol, and a host of others ushered in an entirely new way of looking at art. Most modern art is abstract or **nonrepresentational,** which means that the subjects of the paintings may not be nature or people but ideas, politics, or art itself (but they might just look like shapes). It's no coincidence that art took such a radical turn in the twentieth century: The innovations in technology, literature, film, psychology, and communication found commensurate innovations in the art world; those innovations, like art itself, tend to focus on destabilizing traditional forms and narratives. Modern artists believe that if you change the way you see the world, you change the world. So you have artists playing with reality: Paul Klee said he wanted to make the nonvisible, visible; Kandinsky claimed that form was the outer expression of inner content; Picasso once wrote that if he wanted to express the roundness of a glass, he might have to make it square. Thus the changes in the world, the growths in perspective and innovation, get reflected and chronicled in our art.

Reproduction and technology have changed how we see and value art.

One of our favorite books is *Ways of Seeing* by British writer John Berger. Based on a BBC television series, *Ways of Seeing* walks the reader through various "ways" we see the world. Berger's analysis ranges from looking at landscape to art to advertisements to fashion. For example, Berger makes a compelling argument about how women are posed and presented in modern ads. According to Berger, these seductive images are a reproduction of the way male artists would position the "ideal" woman in Renaissance and Enlightenment paintings. Notice, for example, how many early nude paintings feature women in unnatural and uncomfortable poses and how, quite often, they look directly at the viewer (assumed, at the time, to be male). Contemporary artist Cindy Sherman plays with this tradition in many of her photographs.

Another of Berger's more enduring observations involves what happens to a work of art when it is reproduced over and over and over again. For Berger, the ability to reproduce art—to put the *Mona Lisa* on T-shirts, to place Van Gogh paintings on coffee mugs, to make huge blow up dolls of Edvard Munch's *The Scream*, to be able to hang a poster of Gustav Klimt's *The Kiss* in every residence hall in the United States—translates into the ability to change the meaning of that art based on how it is used. For example, one of the most famous American paintings—perhaps *the* most famous American painting—is Grant Wood's *American Gothic.*

You have likely seen an image of the painting hundreds of times, though you probably have never stood before the *actual* work of art. Indeed, even though the original hangs in the Chicago Art Institute, you don't have to travel to the Windy City to see *American Gothic*—you can just search the web.

But is double-clicking on a photo of *American Gothic* on Google really "seeing" *American Gothic?* For instance, what is the painting made of? What are its dimensions? Thousands of people visit Chicago to see it every year; however, by the time they get there, they have probably been exposed to reproductions and alterations of the painting hundreds of times over the course of their lives. These issues make some wonder about the specialness or uniqueness of a work of art in the age of reproduction.

The famous German thinker Walter Benjamin first posed these questions in a remarkably influential essay called "The Work of Art in the Age of Mechanical Reproduction" (1936).

Grant Wood, *American Gothic,* 1930. Oil on Beaver Board. 29 7/8″ x 24 7/8″. Friends of American Art. Photograph © 2005 The Art Institute of Chicago. All Rights Reserved.

According to Benjamin, even the best, most perfect reproduction lacks the original work's "presence in time and space, its unique existence at the place where it happens to be." For Benjamin, this raises important questions about authenticity (which we talk about later in the Authenticity Suite in Chapter 10), particularly in regard to photography's ability to print images over and over again. Can a photograph be a unique, original work of "art" if you can print hundreds of them?

One of Benjamin's most enduring arguments is that the mass reproduction of art changes how the masses respond to art. Or, put another way, the ability to reproduce famous paintings can turn high culture into popular culture. For instance, people who wear *American Gothic* ties might be honoring the painting, or they might see it as an ironic gesture. Twenty years ago, Gustav Klimt was a sort of fringe artist, but the proliferation of *The Kiss* has transformed him into another Monet or Degas or Picasso—not because thousands were wowed by the painting while visiting the Österreichische Galerie Belvedere in Vienna—but because folks have been wowed by the reproduction of the painting they have seen on cards and posters around the world. In fact, the great irony is that most who love the *image* have never seen the original *painting*.

On one hand, this is great for art, artists, and museums. On the other hand, however, Berger and Benjamin argue that these instances of reproduction strip the original of its power (what Benjamin calls **aura**). For example, how does it change your regard for the "authentic" *American Gothic* when you see this?

Neither Berger nor Benjamin could have predicted the proliferation and alteration of artistic images in the digital age. What's more, computer programs like Photoshop make it easy to take Wood's painting in all sorts of directions:

AMERICAN GOTH

What makes these images funny is that they not only play on the original painting, they also play on the overuse of the original painting—proving Berger's and Benjamin's points. The repetitive use and overexposure of *American Gothic* has altered the meaning of the original painting, transforming it into a kind of icon to be parodied.

Even the images you see in this chapter are reproductions; in fact, they are reproductions of reproductions. And yet, the ability for Prentice Hall to print these images relatively cheaply means you get to see the works of Marnie Spencer, Chris Ofili, Warhol, and, of course, dogs playing poker from the comfort of your dorm room, library, or favorite coffee shop. The question is, now that you have seen reproductions of an Andres Serrano photograph or an Andy Warhol piece, will you be more likely or less likely to seek out the original? Does it even matter? Is art more or less than the original work? What is important to remember is that the ubiquity of an image affects how we see and think about that image—for better or worse.

Reading art helps you see the world in new ways.

Again, look at the perspective of the picture or the sculpture. Has the artist made you see the world or nature or a person or an object differently? If so, how? Ask yourself how the artist has represented the world, that is, how has he or she re-presented the world? Why might an artist be interested in altering your perception of something? Perhaps because if you learn to see the world in a new way fairly often, then looking at the world will be a way of creating your own art.

A chapter of suites.

Rather than present a menu of various essays, we decided to cluster the readings in this chapter and offer, in essense, a chapter of three different suites. We found we kept coming back to the same questions in regard to the visual arts—censorship, photography and reliability, and the biggest question of all, what makes art? We hope you like these suites. We think they make for some of the most interesting reading in the book.

THIS TEXT

1. While it will be impossible for you to know this fully, try to figure out the writing situation of each author. Who is the audience? What does the author have at stake? What is his or her agenda? Why is she or he writing this piece?
2. What are the main points of the essay? Can you find a thesis statement? Remember, it doesn't have to be one sentence—it can be several sentences or a whole paragraph.
3. What textual cues does the author use to help get his or her point across?
4. How does the author support his or her argument? What evidence does the author use to back up any claims he or she might make?
5. Is the author's argument valid? Is it reasonable?
6. Do you find yourself in agreement with the author? Why or why not?
7. Does the author help you read the visual arts better than you did before reading the essay? If so, why?
8. What issues about race, ethnicity, class, and gender does the writer raise? Do you think the writer has an agenda of sorts?
9. Did you like the piece? Why or why not?

WORKSHEET

BEYOND THIS TEXT

1. What are the major themes of the work? What is the artist trying to suggest?
2. What techniques does the artist use to get his or her message across? Why *these* techniques?
3. What are we to make of the characters in the painting or photograph? What is their function? What is their race? Their social class? Are they like you? How?
4. Where does the text take place? When is it set?
5. What are the main conflicts of the text? What issues are at stake?
6. What kinds of issues of identity is the artist working on in the text?
7. Is there tension between the self and society in the text? How? Why?
8. What is the agenda of the artist? Why does she or he want me to think a certain way?
9. How is the text put together? What is its composition? How does it make meaning?
10. What techniques is the author using? How does it adhere to issues of artistic design?
11. Did you like this artwork? Why or why not?

The "Is It Art?" Suite

As we discussed earlier, art often frustrates us. Given a piece of modern art or even folk art, we might exclaim, "That isn't art!" This is true especially if the work seems to rely on idea rather than craftsmanship. But what we're really saying is, "That isn't *good* art." It's not hard to argue that someone who intends to create art is indeed creating art of one kind or another. This suite—our largest—looks at the provocative question, "Is it art?" and encourages you to come up with an answer.

What makes something *art*? Is it technique, theme, the support of famous people, or the adherence to specific criteria? Can "popular" art be "good" art? Can texts not intended as art objects be art? What is at stake if something is or is not art? The following essays discuss these questions and others as they explore the nature of art and criteria for judging it.

There is a lot at stake with this question, both for the artist and for the culture at large. Artists hold special places in our culture, so being an "artist" can mean more money, more commissions, a higher profile, museum collections, and eventually, maybe even postcards, neckties, magnets, and totebags with reproductions of one's work. If a text gets elevated to the level of "art," it is often assumed to have some sort of relevance to or comment on our culture. If a text becomes art, then the values embodied by that text are often seen as sanctioned, even valuable. For example, if the NAMES quilt is, officially, art, according to American cultural and artistic values, that signals for some that America approves of gay culture—even aestheticizes it. In other words, if we decide that something is art, we place it in an important place in our culture.

These issues and many others are the topic of E. G. Chrichton's essay (1988) on the NAMES quilt, which discusses folk and community in the context of high art in trying to answer whether the quilt qualifies as art. His is a good example of a definitional essay; note how Chrichton defines what he thinks art is, then demonstrates how the NAMES quilt meets those criteria. Similarly, Diana Mack (1999) argues that questions surrounding "good" art have resonances beyond the art world. In writing about the *Sensation* exhibition, she wonders who can and should define the standards for good or even acceptable public art. In classic definitional manner, Mack lays out three principles for evaluating art. The next two essays deal with street art. Steve Grody is a martial arts specialist and a choreographer who has also become a specialist on Los Angeles graffiti. In this 2006 piece, he offers a close semiotic reading of two works of graffiti art, and he introduces this art with an original piece written especially for this edition of *The World Is a Text*. Similarly, Theresa George argues for reading graffiti through an inclusive lens in her essay for Professor Devon Holmes's Rhetoric and Composition 210 class at the University of San Francisco in 2007. In an attempt to argue for Andy Warhol's effectiveness as an artist, Alan Pratt gives a semiotic and cultural reading of Warhol's art and critical reception (2000). Pratt suggests that because Warhol divided critics and audience alike, he is perhaps the most controversial artist of the century. What makes Pratt's approach intriguing is that he explores the major hot button issues surrounding art and artists—their persona as artists and their "originality." Among the most well known of Cindy Sherman's works is her *Untitled Film Stills* in which, using herself as a model, she creates staged scenes that could have been derived from black and white movies from the 1950s. None of these photographs were based on any specific film; they were meant to portray stereotypical female roles as created by or perpetuated by these movies in particular. Virginia Commonwealth University student Anne Darby reads a particular Sherman photograph not through the lens of art but through the lens of gender.

Finally, comic artist and theoretician Scott McCloud integrates the themes advanced in the previous essays in two related comics about the nature of art and our participation in making it. These "essays" come from Scott McCloud's *Understanding Comics* (1994), a comic about the importance— and semiotics—of comics and comic books.

Is the NAMES Quilt Art?

E. G. Chrichton

IT IS BEAUTIFUL, POWERFUL, and inspirational. But is it art? The NAMES Project Quilt started in San Francisco with one cloth panel to commemorate one AIDS victim. In a little more than a year it has grown to over 5000 panels from every region in the country. For each person who has taken up needle and thread, paint, and mixed media to create a piece of the Quilt, there are many more who have walked among its connected grids, often in tears. No one with this experience would deny its force and magic as a national symbol of the AIDS tragedy. But from where does this power derive? Why has the NAMES Project Quilt captured our hearts and minds like no other project to come out of the gay community? One answer lies in the Quilt's power as art: art that lives and grows outside established art channels.

The NAMES Project organizers promote the Quilt as the "largest community arts project in the nation." They are aided by a national media that is surprisingly willing to report on events surrounding its display. The art world, however—that ivory tower that is reported to us via a handful of glossy national art magazines—has overlooked the Quilt. The art critics who write in these magazines are not rushing to interpret the Quilt's significance in the history of art.

Art is important, most people agree, but the reasons why are sometimes elusive. There is nothing elusive, though, about the NAMES Project Quilt; it is extremely concrete as visual communication. This accessibility is exactly what throws the Quilt's status as "real art" into question. Unlike much of what we find in galleries and museums, the Quilt has a connection to our daily lives that seems unrelated to the remote world of "high art," or "fine art"— art that is promoted by critics, museum curators, and art historians. To understand the source of discrepancies about how our culture defines art, it helps to look at some of the assumptions made about art and who makes them.

Art, in Western culture, is first and foremost made by the artist—that individual genius whose work and life we come to recognize through a network of museums, media, dealers, and historians. Despite the fact that a myriad of people make art, a very select few are promoted in a way that grabs our attention. This process works like any good marketing strategy: we are told which art is hot, and why, by those who seem to know best. As a result, our taste is inevitably influenced by what appears to be an objective window on aesthetics. It is very hard to regard art found outside these institutional channels as serious. We don't go to the local craft fair to find serious art. It is not the needlepoint your grandmother did, nor the sketches you do in your spare time. And it's not a project like the NAMES Quilt that thrives entirely outside the art world. "Real art" is a luxury item for sale in an elite marketplace that takes it away from the artist's hands, and any community connection we might relate to.

Critics argue a bit about art, trying to maintain the illusion of democratic options, but they essentially define "good art" around a fairly narrow set of assumptions. It is virtually impossible to understand most modern mainstream art without the translation of these intermediaries. They generally promote obscurity as a desirable feature, and cast accessibility in an untrustworthy light; art we can too easily understand is more like entertainment. And, if you want to include a social message, make it vague at best.

Given this milieu, it is no wonder that potential art fans often feel suspicious of famous artists, seeing them as con-artists instead who try to fool us into thinking their enigmatic puzzles are great art. In contrast, the Quilt seems trustworthy partly because we are the artists. Although not for sale on the art market, it generates important funding for local AIDS services networks. It is not the offspring of a famous artist, yet its scale is monumental and attention grabbing. And it isn't found where most important art is found; the "museums" where we view the Quilt are convention centers, pavilions, gymnasiums, and the Capitol Mall—hardly the retreats of high art. Yet one thing is clear: the Quilt has succeeded in creating a visual metaphor for the tragedy of AIDS that transcends individual grieving to communicate beauty and hope. What more could be expected of a great work of art?

If the establishment art world places the NAMES Quilt outside the holy realm of high art, other art traditions do not. In the early seventies, feminist artists working within the art world successfully revived an interest in the folk art of quilting and sewing bees—"low art" historically associated with women. New materials explored during this period gained acceptance as legitimate fine art ingredients: cloth, clay, and rope, for example. Many artists, both male and female, started to inject more personal and autobiographical content into their work. In general, the division between high and low art melted a little.

Several large-scale projects were also organized that introduced the idea of bringing together many people's labor into one artistic vision. Judy Chicago attracted hundreds of craftspeople to her "Dinner Party" project. The end result was a huge and complex installation illustrating the lives of specific women throughout history with china place settings around a huge table. In a very different project, the artist Christo engaged the help of hundreds of people to set up a "Running Fence" of fabric that wound for miles through northern California countryside, focusing attention on the land and its natural contours. In both cases, people skeptical about the initial vision were drawn in and became enthusiastic through participation. Chicago and Christo are the rare mainstream artists whose work and vision have crossed out of the exclusive art world to be accessible. The Vietnam War Memorial, designed by an architectural student named Maya Ying Lin, set a precedent for the simple naming of victims of a tragic war instead of merely immortalizing the warmonger leaders.

Tribal art from all ages has influenced Western artists interested in introducing ritual to their work. The holistic integration of art with the spiritual and survival needs of a community, characteristic of tribal art, appeals to many of us brought up on the doctrine of "art for art sake." Many artists have also been influenced by ancient art like the prehistoric Stonehenge. Monuments like this reveal a very different set of assumptions about art and the artist. No one knows exactly who created them—their massive scale obviously required the labor and creativity of many people, over many life spans. It seems as though the individual artistic ego was not important here, and that art had a function in society beyond visual aesthetics.

The contemporary art that is perhaps most similar to the NAMES Project Quilt are the *arpilleras* created by anonymous Chilean women resisting the fascist junta ruling their country. Pieced together from scavenged factory remnants, these patchwork pictures use decorative imagery to protest specific government policies or to commemorate "disappeared" political prisoners, often relatives of the artists. They are smuggled out of the country to communicate the conditions in Chile to the rest of the world. The *arpilleras* are also the only surviving indigenous Chilean visual art, now that murals have been destroyed and artists of all kinds murdered and imprisoned.

What the NAMES Project Quilt has in common with feminist, environmental, ancient, tribal, and Chilean art is a tradition of collaboration, a mixing of media, and an emphasis on process that makes the reason for the art just as important as the finished product. In art like this, the individual artist's identity is less important than the purpose of the art in the life of a community or people. This purpose might be the need to remember a part of history in a visual way, a means of marking time, or a tribute to the dead created not by a government, but by those who mourn. The NAMES Project Quilt started as one panel, one person's need to commemorate a dead friend. It soon expanded to a collaborative vision with a plan for how the Quilt could grow: panels approximately the size of a human body or a casket; panels to remember people who are most often cremated and leave no grave plot to visit; panels sewn together into grids—individual lost lives stitched together, woven into an enormous picture of the effect of AIDS.

This vision is dependent on the contributions of a growing number of individual artists who work alone or with others to stitch and paint a memory of someone they loved. They do this in the best tradition of quilting, using pieces from the person's life, articles of clothing, teddy bears, photographs, messages to the dead from the living who mourn them. People who have never before felt confident about making art testify about the healing nature of this participation in a larger artwork—one that also allows them to "come out" around AIDS. Instead of mourning alone, they link their grief to others both visually and organizationally. Finally, in keeping with the unifying principle of the whole Quilt, they stitch or paint the person's name who died, committing that name to an historical document that physically shows real people, not mere statistics.

Art needs an audience. The NAMES Project Quilt has an unusually large one: hundreds of thousands of us across the nation who have walked amidst the panels, stood in the sea of colorful memories, cried, found panels of people we've known, hugged strangers—in general been awed, moved, and inspired by the power of the total vision. We, the audience, have received much of the healing communicated by the artists through the ritual reading of names and physical beauty of the Quilt. It is a rare work of art that can transcend its material components to communicate this kind of collective power. A political demonstration could not have done the same. Neither could a single memorial service nor a walk through a graveyard.

■ ■ ■

There are other reasons the Quilt is effective art. The quilt form itself feels very American. It is almost apple pie in its connotations, and when used to communicate thoughts and feelings about AIDS with all the stigma, a powerful dialectic occurs. Tangible evidence of individuals who lie outside of society's favored status gets woven into a domestic metaphor. The Quilt reveals that these people had domestic lives of one kind or another—family, friends, lovers who banded together to make the panels. The quilt form historically is a feminist metaphor for integration, inclusiveness, the breaking down of barriers, the pieces of someone's life sewn together. It is not surprising that women and gay men would pick up on this traditional women's art. Sewing and weaving have been metaphors for life, death, creation, and transformation in many cultures. Just as the spider weaves from material that is pulled from inside, women have woven their ideas and emotions into cloth decorated with the symbols of their culture. The NAMES Quilt picks up on all these traditions.

The grid pattern is another important part of the Quilt's effect as art. Formed by a huge (and growing) number of individually made panels, the pattern signifies inclusiveness and equality. Unlike a cemetery where class differences are obvious, this grid unites the dead regardless of who they were. It is as though the dead are woven together, visually mirroring the networks the living form to create the quilt. Within this grid pattern there is an amazing and unplanned repetition of imagery. Items of clothing dominate—remnants of someone's wardrobe, T-shirts, jeans, jewelry, glittery gowns, and sashes. Teddy bears are common, too, a kind of cuddly accompaniment to the dead, a lively symbol of rest and sleep. The dates that show up so often are shocking because of the abbreviated life spans they illustrate. Some of the most powerful panels contain messages written directly to the dead, stitched or painted: "Sweet dreams," "I miss you every day."

The NAMES Quilt bridges the gap between art and social consciousness. Art is too often peripheral to our society, seen as superfluous fluff. Political activism, on the other hand, is often perceived as uncreative and separate from culture. The Quilt is a rare successful integration of these two worlds so separate in Western culture. We should be proud of an art form that originated in the gay community and that is able to communicate beyond to other communities. What is communicated is as complex as any art would strive for, something that will have historical significance beyond all of our lives. Developed outside established art channels, shown mostly in non-art environments, the Quilt could nevertheless teach the art world a great deal about organization, collaboration on a grand scale, and the communication of an aesthetic that crosses many boundaries. Very few artists or art projects are able to reach so many people in such a way.

Parts of the art world have started to hear about the Quilt. At least two or three well-known artists have created panels. In Baltimore, the Quilt will not be hung in one of the pavilions, gymnasiums, and civic centers that house the Quilt elsewhere on its national tour—it will be hung on the walls of the Baltimore Art Museum. Organizers are excited by

The *NAMES Project AIDS Memorial Quilt*, October 1989.

Volunteers and others walk on the 21,000 panel *NAMES Project AIDS Memorial Quilt* in Washington.

these developments, viewing them as evidence of the far-reaching effects of the Quilt. But what will happen to the present spirit of the Quilt? Will focus turn to "famous" panels more than others? Will museums become a more targeted locale for the Quilt, changing the vantage point from ground to wall? These are important questions because so much of the Quilt's power lies in its existence outside the official art world. It would be unfortunate if the category of "non-artist" became accentuated by more of a focus on "real" artists, and intimidated wider participation. I would hate to see the Quilt swallowed up in the land of institutional art and co-opted from its community roots.

We should be proud of the Quilt, but we should also stand back and reflect on its process as often as necessary. The NAMES Project is growing at an overwhelming pace, one that demands a look at how centralized the vision can remain. The power of the Quilt is fully communicated when people walk among the squares, physically becoming part of the vast grid, feeling tiny in scale compared to the whole. Its power also lies in its capacity to educate about AIDS in the universal language of quilting. I am concerned that continuing centralization will make the Quilt unwieldy, both in organization and in size. Will continuous expansion make it impossible to display in one location? Will people have to see it only in pictures, or only in its home resting place of San Francisco?

What about communities deeply affected by AIDS but not yet familiar with the NAMES Project Quilt? In New York City, for instance, women of color and their children form a growing percentage of victims, yet I wonder how many panels reflect this. A continued centralization of the Quilt could stand in the way of the outreach that makes the Quilt's vision so powerful. One possible solution would be regional quilts that are more accessible to

AIDS Quilt—overhead shot.

people. Smaller cities have already created their own quilts and displayed them locally before sending them to join the larger work. This link to something larger is an important part of the Quilt process, and it could easily continue with local areas concentrating on new outreach before joining together regionally. Stores in areas where there are many AIDS deaths could be organized to hang quilt grids in their windows. People could get involved who would never travel to Phoenix, or Baltimore, or other places on the tour, people who would never hear about the Quilt through existing channels.

It must be hard to think about giving up control of a project that has been so successful so quickly—especially in an age of media co-optation of art and social movements. But one of the most important roles the Quilt has played is as a tool for organization: individuals networking to make panels, groups networking to form local quilt tour organizations. A central vision has been important and may be for some time to come. But AIDS is unfortunately with us for longer than that, and the vision could become stronger by branching out. The ritual unfolding of the panels and reading of names might change from region to region. New cultural influences would add new dimensions. The Northeast's Quilt might take on a very different character from the Southwest's. These differences would be exciting and would expand the Quilt's dimensions as art. It would reach more people. And the inevitable difficulties of large organizations would be strengthened by more autonomy at the local level. People could still feel part of a larger-than-life whole, yet not be subsumed by an abstraction out of reach. If four football fields of panels are overwhelming, are ten necessarily better?

These are questions and reactions I have amidst my own emotions about the power of the Quilt and its significance as art in an age when the institutions of art can be so devoid of spirit. Art and artists survive regardless of art market trends, and most art will never be seen in a museum or gallery. It is the art made by your neighbor or your lover, the art that someone is compelled to make for reasons other than money. I hope the Quilt will never be a commodity on the art market, never owned by an individual or corporation, never laid to rest in one museum. The NAMES Project Quilt is a living, breathing, changing work of art, one that was inspired by grief and grew to communicate hope. Let it continue to live in good health.

It Isn't Pretty ... But Is It Art?

Diana Mack

Diana Mack

FEW AMERICANS WAKE UP MORNINGS contemplating the question of what makes a good work of art. But surprisingly enough, three belligerent public disputes have recently centered on this very question.

New York Mayor Rudolph Giuliani made headlines last month when he vowed to withhold municipal funding if the Brooklyn Museum of Art went through with its controversial British art exhibition, *Sensation.* The major object of contention: an image of the Virgin Mary, her breast rendered in elephant dung (see page 268).

Then, a few weeks later, parents in South Carolina, Georgia, and Minnesota protested the presence in public school classrooms of J. K. Rowling's bestselling Harry Potter series, one mother claiming this fantasy literature carried "a serious tone of death, hate . . . and . . . evil."

Finally, there was the public uproar in Seattle over the heavily bosomed and pregnant *Picardo Venus*, a community garden statue many find too suggestive.

In each case, those objecting to the disbursement of public funds for the display of art they find offensive insist they are not for censorship. They claim they merely want publicly funded and publicly presented artwork to reflect community standards of taste, decency, and respect for religious faith. All well and good; but who is to define those standards? Chris Ofili, painter of the *Sensation* exhibition's much maligned *Holy Virgin Mary*, claims that Mr. Giuliani falsely assigned deprecatory motives to his work. He is not out to desecrate the image of the Virgin Mary, he says.

Rather, he's a Roman Catholic earnestly coming to terms with his faith, his African heritage, and a long Western tradition of representing the Madonna.

Similarly, J. K. Rowling might claim that the Harry Potter books also stand in a long "pre-apologetic" literary tradition: Yes, they deal with magic and witchcraft. Their tone is dark. But no less a devout Christian than C. S. Lewis understood the power of pagan imagery in preparing the young imagination for the moral rigors and spiritual comforts of biblical religion. Indeed, if there is something wrong with a "tone of death" in children's literature, then we might as well jettison all our volumes of fairy tales. For these distilled popular narratives exert their charm and power precisely, as Bruno Bettelheim pointed out, because they allow children a reality-removed way to confront the "existential predicament."

And what of the *Picardo Venus*? Must she be rejected, as one citizen–critic contended, because she "glorifies fertility a little too much for kids," or because, as another said, "no normal woman looks like that"?

Do "normal" women look like Picasso painted them? Or Rubens? Did not Botticelli's immortal *The Birth of Venus* also glorify fertility? The point is that almost all the arguments we bring against public support of controversial new works are at best specious, at worst manifestly wrongheaded. Informed aesthetic judgments seem to elude us.

Faced with creative works that seem to us alien and unappealing, we are forced to fall back on that proverbial disclaimer, "I don't know much about it . . . I only know what I like."

Just because an artwork doesn't make us feel warm and fuzzy doesn't mean it's worthless. The Seattle man who protests against the *Picardo Venus* on the basis that "art is supposed to evoke all these good feelings" is wrong. Good art is not necessarily pleasing. It is, however, disciplined. It is about mastery of medium, form, and style. And good art must communicate something comprehensibly worthwhile, something worthy of contemplation. And here we get closer to the aesthetic problem facing the American public today. More and more so-called artists today call attention to themselves by shocking and agitating rather than by promoting reflection. In reaction to these salvos, the public has come to anticipate offense.

How do we move past the disturbing impasse of public contention over art and toward a healthier, more vital cultural life? One answer is to be guided in our aesthetic judgments by three important principles:

1. Art doesn't do. It says. Art is not action; it is speculation. It is looking, listening, digesting, speaking. Art can make a controversial statement; but it cannot do controversial things. If the primary effect of a so-called artwork is physical repulsion or titillation, if it acts on us rather than speaks to us, it is simply not up to the standards of art. If it makes us think, however, we should take up the challenge.

2. Art is about content, not context. Art is the schematic arrangement of forms and symbols through specific, culturally recognized mediums. If we exhibit, say, a cow's embryo in an art museum, it does not suddenly become a work of visual art simply by virtue of its surroundings.

3. Similarly, if we hung a print of Titian's *Woman on a Couch* in a biology lab, it would scarcely transform that painting into a science display. We need to be open to the possibilities of the creative process; yet, we must recognize that not everything offered up in the artistic arena is art.

The greater the knowledge, the sounder the judgment. When we venture onto the battlefield of the culture wars, we owe it to our artists and ourselves to come armed with knowledge. In a multicultural society such as America's, that means making the attempt to familiarize ourselves with the major artistic traditions of Europe, Asia, and Africa. Before we criticize, we need first to understand. Indeed, there is nothing more inspiring to good artists than a public that can be communicated with on the highest and most subtle levels of creativity and skill.

Graffiti: The Anatomy of a Piece

Steve Grody

BEFORE LOOKING AT THE DIAGRAM ON PAGE 217, it is useful to acknowledge the human tendency towards snobbery and how that can put on blinders. The development of aesthetic sensitivity tends to be specific to an individual's focus. While a modern jazz fan would immediately recognize an Eric Dolphy solo as distinct from John Coltrane, those with no appreciation of jazz might not hear any difference, even if they had a sensitivity to orchestral or pop music. Bringing the issue closer to home, even artists familiar with modernist abstract artists such as Robert Motherwell or Franz Kline tend to regard modern graffiti pieces (such as those in the diagram on p. 217) with condescension, even while grudgingly acknowledging their craft as contemporary urban folk practice.

Because graffiti is vernacular, it is rarely seen by outsiders as something expressing "transcendent poetics"—which means a kind of overreaching sense of the beautiful and often, a dividing line between "high" and "low" art. The difference between snobbery and simply having individual preference for one aesthetic mode or another is the moral presumption carried. That is, those doing gallery-career oriented art often (albeit unconsciously) presume that a high-art or gallery-based endeavor is intrinsically more worthy, of greater moral value, than graffiti (and here we are referring to the technically sophisticated high-end spray can work). It is that moral stance that keeps one from engaging less familiar modes of expression. Interestingly, most veteran graffiti writers speak of the emotional impact that they felt, and felt was expressed by the work seen, when they first viewed a powerful graffiti piece. Snobbery, of course, cuts in any direction: most graffiti writers have blinders on preventing them from appreciating or deeply understanding much of the art done throughout history. While some might recognize a Matisse, for example, it would be rare for any to understand how radical his art is in its treading the line between representation and abstraction, as well as his exquisite color formalism. (Of course most art history Ph.Ds know Matisse's formalism as well.)

Critic Christopher Knight makes a strong argument that the prominent art critic from the 50s and 60s, Clement Greenberg, did a great disservice to following generations of artists and critics by proposing a cultural dividing line between High Art and popular art: since we can easily see examples of supposedly High art that are empty and sterile in effect and can also see examples of Pop forms of art that are emotionally moving, should we not, Knight argues, throw out those categories with and simply look at a given piece of art and judge it for how it works on its own terms? This is not the same as a nihilistic view that argues against High/Low categories, stemming from a belief that work made from a moral basis (read: life affirming) is empty cultural pretense— that is, morality is merely a concept relative to a particular dominant culture.

In terms of reading the context of graffiti, it's useful to think of three continuums. The first is the continuum from legal to illegal; legal being those spaces where there is permission to paint, and illegal where arrest is possible. Within the "illegal" part of that continuum is a second continuum of vandalistic to non-vandalistic intention. That is, there is graffiti (for example, on storefronts) where the intention is clearly vandalism, and then there is a great deal of illegal work that is on a back alley wall, industrial rooftop or abandoned sites where it would be hard to classify the work as defacing anything. In this regard, the terms "damage" or "destruction" which are often used in relation to graffiti are entirely inappropriate: a construction barrier or formerly bare freeway wall has never been "destroyed" by graffiti. The wall fully maintains its function. This is not to say that people should like graffiti, just a clarification of a fact. The third continuum is simply that of legibility, from easy to read block fonts, to letters only the writer of the piece would be able to decipher.

There is no doubt that the two pieces on p. 217 contain some of the same compositional techniques of high art. One could draw comparisons between these works and large-scale paintings by Juan Gris and Willem de Kooning. Ultimately, if these works and those of so-called high art are both thoughtful, technically astute, aesthetically constructed texts, why ask if one is intrinsically superior than another?

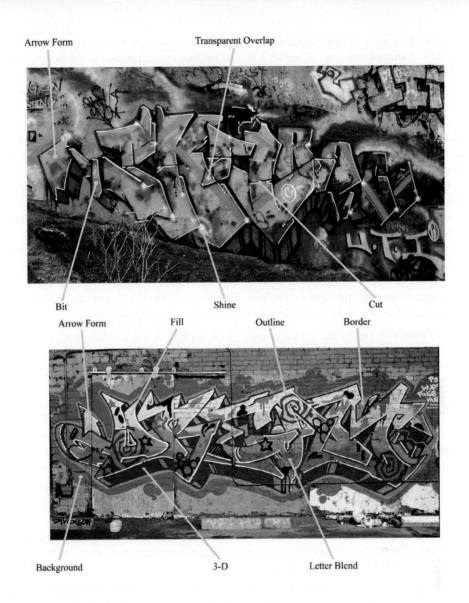

Arrow Form   Transparent Overlap

Bit   Shine   Cut

Arrow Form   Fill   Outline   Border

Background   3-D   Letter Blend

The Multifaceted Nature of Street Art

Theresa George

Student Essay

"THESE MYSTERIOUS HEROES of wild communication, these spontaneous artists whose signs were volatile and abrupt, tough and angry, vehement and vital, created a great fresco . . . irreverent and complicit, committed and contrary, implicated and distant, sentimental and caustic." Here, Lea Vergine, author of *Art on the Cutting Edge: A Guide to Contemporary Movements,* speaks of graffiti, a passionate form of art and expression that is rarely regarded as such. This unique art form provides a feeling of social belonging, literacy practice, and political and educational outreach for many of its creators. Unfortunately, a great number of city planners and

The "Is It Art?" Suite

criminologists have worked together in efforts to try to eliminate street art and in effect the stigmas that allegedly go along with it. The problem we must face is not how to control these spontaneous, and many times planned, events of artistic ability but how to approach each of these works as authentic and meaningful as they relate to their creators and their environments.

Just like many other socially accepted phenomena, street art can and does take many different forms, from innocent public displays of individuality to upscale alternative art. It takes on names of "tagging," graffiti," and even "writing," all of which will be used synonymously in this paper to refer to street art for the sake of discussion. As Lea Virgine describes, graffiti includes "graphic-isms, graphemes, scratches, clashes, grazes, twistings and lacerations of the world or the surface on which they are applied" (215). She passionately declares that they are the "grapho-spasms of love" (215). Regrettably, the majority of graffiti's onlookers do not regard it with the same respect and admiration. What Virgine believes is "the painting of desire or wild communication" (215) is seen as "symbolic of the collapse of the [societal] system" (qtd. in Gladwell 183) by New York City subway director David Gunn. His remark surfaced amidst a citywide effort to eliminate graffiti from the subway stations and cars. Graffiti was believed to be a significant contributor to the high crime rate in New York City at the time. On behalf of criminologists James Q. Wilson and George Kelling, the "Broken Windows theory" explains,

> If a window is broken and left unrepaired, people walking by will conclude that no one cares and no one is in charge. Soon, more windows will be broken, and the sense of anarchy will spread . . . relatively minor problems like graffiti . . . are . . . the equivalent of broken windows (Gladwell 182).

And with the birth of this sociological theory came swift yet diligent action to rid New York City of street art. Subway cars with graffiti were labeled "dirty cars" while those lacking any signs of life were clean cars (Gladwell 183). In effect, indication of any creativity or interpersonal memos from city dwellers was associated with filth and the undesirable. This is not, however, the correct representation street artists would like their art to be identified with. In photographing and assessing the street art in New York City, David Robinson states in the introduction of his book, *SoHo Walls: Beyond Graffiti:*

> Whereas the city establishment sponsored or at least tolerated community murals, it viewed graffiti as defacement and vandalism. For the writers themselves . . . the graffiti created points of beauty and something positive amid the pervasive decay, desolation and brutal ugliness of their neighborhoods (6).

It is crucial for onlookers to understand that street art does not serve just one purpose or create only one reaction. It does more than merely exist on a wall for visual pleasure or disgust. Not only does graffiti create beauty for those living in hostile environments, it can be a source of educational outreach for those same inhabitants. Laurie MacGillivray, author of "Tagging as a Social Literacy Practice," explains,

> In vilifying the practice of tagging, society too easily overlooks its evolving symbol system and the complexities of the phenomenon. The public's misunderstanding is particularly relevant for . . . teens from working-class backgrounds because of their historical academic underachievement . . . (354).

The inaccessibility to canvases for artistic expression and other activities that middle and upper class adolescents usually have leads lower class adolescents to the streets to utilize "public canvases" of walls and sidewalks. In this sense, graffiti holds special significance for thek creators and their creators' communities. Many associate graffiti with gang communities since many violent gangs mark their territory with types of graffiti. But MacGillivray clarifies that there is a well-defined difference between gangs who tag to inform other gangs of their territory and those who tag because of the innocent desire to tag: "Taggers are not gang members . . . tagging is a social practice. Tagging has its own rules and codes, it is a literacy practice imbued with intent and meaning" (354). This statement may be a shock to those who generally see street art as random, undisciplined, and meaningless. However random acts of graffiti may be, they are surely not undisciplined, as MacGillivray discovers when researching and interviewing taggers.

Just as subway directors and criminologists see graffiti as undesirable, street artists see poor and meaningless art or tags as extremely unwanted as well. It is of great significance to the street art community that every piece of writing on walls, sidewalks, or subways possesses meaning and signs of talent. In interviewing taggers educated on the subject, MacGillivray finds, "While anyone can participate in tagging, it is only those who display talent that are valued in the tagging culture" (363). She cites that one tagger even stated, "if individuals are not talented, they should not engage in tagging" (363). MacGillivray continues on with this idea: "Most of our participants talked with disdain of those who tag poorly and explained that it hurts the reputation of taggers as artists" (363). This attitude towards their way of life illustrates the "social responsibility and non-elitism advocated by most graffiti artists" that Robinson experienced while photographing their work (Robinson 8). In assessing the artists' system of tagging MacGillivray expands on this idea of responsibility within their community: "In choosing the nature of their message and deciding on placement, taggers displayed sophisticated decision making which parallels the values of conventional writers" (367). This recognition of street artists as comparable to "conventional writers" qualifies them for a place in society far beyond what the average onlooker would imagine. Perhaps if more people were aware and understanding of the codes of conduct that exist within the graffiti community, as does exist with mural communities, then street art might be more welcomed and perhaps respected.

There are many similarities between murals—communal art completed on public spaces by a group of people with permission—and graffiti. Malcolm Miles, author of *Art, Space and the City: Public Art and Urban Futures,* even categorized graffiti as "unofficial street murals" (206). Of his observations, Robinson adds, "The motives of graffiti writers seem to have been similar to those of the community muralists: self-assertion, pride and self-expression" (6). These comments are quite foreign to the paradigm of public art that Jane Golden, author of *Philadelphia Murals and the Stories They Tell* and an active member of the Philadelphia Anti-Graffiti Network, accepts. Her value of murals stands high above her regard for graffiti and tagging. She has the following admirable remarks to say about murals in the preface of her book: "Murals work on a symbolic level, providing opportunities for communities to express important concerns, values, and aspirations . . ." (2). In the foreword of Golden's book, Timothy W. Drescher states, "murals express community, but they also help create it . . . sometimes designing and producing a local mural begins a process of social connections and political activism that previously did not exist" (8–9). However distinct Golden and Drescher may find their observations of murals to be from that of graffiti, let's recall and compare comments made by Laurie MacGillivray in assessing the purposes and consequences of tagging:

> Tagging . . . can be conceived of as a local literacy practice and as an avenue into the construction of youth identity and group affiliation . . . [it is able] to sustain social relationships; it is a form of dialogue and conversation . . . Another purpose of tagging can be to provide commentary on larger social issues (355, 360, 362).

The word use of Golden and Drescher ("community," "values," "concerns," and "social connections") to describe murals closely identifies with that of MacGillivray's in regards to graffiti ("identity," "group affiliation," "social issues," and "social relationships"). Most appropriately in this sense and for the respect of varying ways of expression in our culture, the two should be regarded with similar, if not the same, value. It appears here that street art provides just as much community building and strengthening as does mural creation. Onlookers, sociologists, and criminologists must not forget the crucial value that street art holds for those who have little if nothing else in their lives.

As stated above, graffiti can be a means of expressing views on larger social issues when no other means is available, especially to young adults with low-income and undereducated backgrounds. Graffiti is the result of "an individual event [that] takes place in response to the social relationships with the expectations and norms of others" (MacGillivray 367). This unique style of communication between people of limiting backgrounds developed from "a need to express shared urban experiences" (MacGillivray 357) as well as to educate each other on social and world events. Images that MacGillivray came across in her observations included genuine reactions to political occurrences such as the recent bombings in Iraq and the "negative effects of corporate-sponsored deforestation on the environment" (362). It is an amazing ability of young urban dwellers to communicate such information to each other and to the public when the common means of obtaining it are generally inaccessible to them. Joe Austin, author of *Taking the Train: How Graffiti Art Became an Urban Crisis in New York City,* believes graffiti's

> development follows one of several pathways by which young people's political education
> became transformed . . . demonstrating some of the ways that youth cultures have con-
> tinued to create and appropriate cultural and physical spaces of relative autonomy (270).

Rather than seeing graffiti as "dirty" and representative of a lack of education and discipline it should be viewed as the collective experiences, desires, and desperation for communication between city dwellers and their peers. Whether or not these progressive feelings towards graffiti infiltrate the mainstream way of thought graffiti will remain active: "In all likelihood the . . . effort will continue, undertaken by individual artists outside the mainstream who want to express themselves, make a point and provoke others while claiming their own freedom" (Robinson 15). The freedom to express oneself or one's experiences in an artistic way is a highly respected manner in the United States; it is only just that this freedom be granted to persons of all ages, education level, and socioeconomic backgrounds.

Among the profound purposes of street art such as political and education outreach lies an aesthetic purpose—the expression of the organic nature of art. While David Robinson photographed the art-covered walls of SoHo, New York City, he discovered an intense nature possessed by graffiti that he had not expected:

> Art was in the SoHo air, its energy palpable, spilling out of the lofts onto the streets—and onto
> the walls . . . I found the "public galleries," out on the streets, just as compelling as the art dis-
> played indoors . . . the art . . . was organic, not restricted to white walls and neutral space (8, 5).

His experiences with the art in New York City were so powerful that he compared the essence of the art on the walls to that of Abstract Expressionism. There are even many art critics who see graffiti as a form of modem art, hence its presence in numerous galleries around the world, including the famous Museum of Modern Art in New York City.

If the great importance of graffiti art to the art community can be recognized by the prestigious taste of famous galleries, then the public too can recognize its societal, educational, and political importance to the communities that create it. From literacy practice to social belonging, street art serves multiple essential purposes to its creators and their surrounding environments. Whether the public chooses to accept the messages that artists display on walls and subway cars or continue to refute their art as legitimate, street art will not relinquish its existence. And as David Robinson so vehemently declares, "Their voices cannot be silenced, their creativity cannot be erased" (15).

Works Cited

Austin, Joe. *Taking the Train: How Graffiti Art Became an Urban Crisis in New York City*. New York: Columbia University Press, 2001.

Gladwell, Malcolm. "The Power of Context." *The Tipping Point: How Little Things Can Make a Big Difference*. N.p.: n.p., 2000. Rpt. in *The New Humanities Reader*. Ed. Richard E. Miller and Kurt Spellmeyer. 2nd ed. Boston: Houghton Mifflin Company, 2006. 178–195.

Golden, Jane, Robin Rice, and Monica Yant Kinney. *Philadelphia Murals and the Stories They Tell*. Philadelphia: Temple University Press, 2002.

MacGillivray, Laurie, and Margaret Sauceda Curwen. "Tagging as a Social Literacy Practice."*Journal of Adolescent and Adult Literacy* 50.5 (Feb. 2007): 354–369.

Miles, Malcolm. *Art. Space and the City: Public Art and Urban Futures*. New York: Routledge, 1997.

Robinson, David. *Soho Walls: Beyond Graffiti*. New York: Thames and Hudson Inc., 1990. 5–15.

Vergine, Lea. *Art on the Cutting Edge: A Guide to Contemporary Movements*. Milan: Skira, 1996.

Andy Warhol: The Most Controversial Artist of the Twentieth Century?

Alan Pratt

WHEN ANDY WARHOL HIT HIS STRIDE in the early sixties by appropriating images from advertising design and serializing them with a hands-off austerity, he became a lightning rod for criticism.

Studying the public perception of the artist in 1966, critic Lucy Lippard noticed that "Warhol's films and his art mean either nothing or a great deal. The choice is the viewer's...." In retrospect, Lippard's early, tentative appraisal is revealing. While the images Warhol stumbled across have a deep resonance with the public, the problem of interpreting them is, depending on one's point of view, simple or complex.

In the current polemic, Warhol's reputation still depends on the reviewer's ideological or art-historical preoccupations. If, as has been suggested, Warhol succeeded in redefining the art experience, then the critical response required redefinition as well. In retrospect, it appears that one problem that confronted critics and journalists was that established critical approaches simply didn't lend themselves to an art which they perceived as "artless, styleless, and anonymous."

While the debate still hasn't resolved itself, three interconnected issues figure prominently in the disagreements about Warhol's reputation: his persona, his originality, and his antecedents.

Warhol's Persona

The problematic nature of Warhol's critical reputation is attributable, in part, to the evasive, equivocal persona he cultivated—the calculated indifference, the monosyllabic rejoinder, the flat, vacuous affect of the I-think-everybody-should-be-a-machine Warhol. And while it's true that he suffered from a debilitating shyness, he nevertheless delighted in baffling his critics.

The "Is It Art?" Suite

In reviewing Warhol's life it's often impossible to distinguish the authentic Warhol from the act. As a result, a significant portion of the critical response, if only anecdotally, is to Warhol's personality. And with little that's reliable to go on, critics have wide latitude in extrapolating or inventing motives for him. Currently, psychological interpretations of Warhol's work are the fashion.

Warhol's Originality

Like the problems of personality which have intrigued critics for years, the issue of Warhol's artistic legitimacy has also been the basis of ongoing debate. The subjects of some of his most famous works—the soup cans, Coke bottles, dollar bills, flowers, and cows—were apparently recommendations.

That Warhol borrowed his images from others, from photographs, advertisements, and food labels and developed a technique by which they were serially mass-produced by anonymous factory hands remains one of the most contentious issues in the criticism.

By erasing himself from his creations, minimizing the artist's responsibility, the significance of talent, and the value of originality, Warhol challenged presumptions about what art is supposed to be and how one is to experience it. This abnegation of responsibility was deemed unethical, if not subversive, by the critical audience, further fueling the controversy about whether or not his work should even be regarded as art.

Warhol's Antecedents

From the beginning, critics have addressed the connections between what Warhol was doing and what Marcel Duchamp had done. It was Duchamp who in 1914 broke the rules and outraged the art world when he began exhibiting his objets trouvés, the coat-stands, bottle racks, and bicycle wheels. Duchamp, critics suggested, had shown Warhol that appropriating common consumer items could be art.

Warhol was a particularly culpable pioneer of cultural nihilism because the silkscreened readymades—soup cans, bottles, and such—were perceived to be the apotheoses of the objets trouvés.

So why is Warhol the most controversial artist of the century? Read on:

Warhol's Place in Modernism

As a study of the criticism makes clear, Warhol appalled the art establishment because he represented a complete transvaluation of the aesthetic principles that had dominated for several generations. What for years modernists had deliberately ignored or contemptuously spurned, Warhol embraced. As appropriated mass-culture images—such as his *Turquoise Marilyn* (1962)—his "art" was indistinguishable from advertising—meaning it was crass and pedestrian—and thus lampooned the modern emphasis on noble sentiment and good taste. No doubt Warhol's comments about art, that it should be effortless, that it's a business having nothing to do with transcendence, truth, or sentiment, also infuriated detractors.

Both Warhol's subject matter and his flippant attitudes toward the conventions of the art world were the antithesis of the high-seriousness of modernism. And the rub of it was that his celebrations of the inconsequential were being taken seriously. It was a nasty slap in the face for those steeped in the myths of modernism.

Source: Marilyn Monroe, Andy Warhol, 1962. Oil on canvas. 81" × 66¾".™ 2002 Marilyn Monroe LLC by CMG Worldwide Inc. www.MarilynMonroe.com. © 2003 Andy Warhol Foundation for the Visual Arts/ARS, New York.

Warhol's aesthetic contributed to the breakdown of the hierarchial conventions of modernism, dissolving distinctions between commercial design and serious art and the boundaries between popular taste and high culture—or, as some would have it, between trash and excellence.

Warhol and Postmodernism

As many observers now agree, the early 1960s mark the beginnings of a postmodern sensibility, where the modernist desire for closure and aesthetic autonomy has been rapidly replaced with indeterminacy and eclecticism.

If that's true, Warhol's art forecast and then highlighted the changes that were occurring. And it has been argued that his art anticipated many ploys of this aesthetic new world, including the emphasis on irony, appropriation, and commonism, as well as promoting intellectual engagement through negation.

So What's Warhol's Place in the Criticism?

> *"Criticism is so old fashioned. Why don't you just put in a lot of gossip?"*
>
> —Warhol to Bob Colacello, longtime editor of Warhol's magazine *Interview*

In reviewing the critical record, one can conclude that Warhol's role in art history is as a transitional figure. Stylistically his work is a bellwether, and the critical issues raised about him often

The "Is It Art?" Suite

Source: Andy Warhol (1928–1987), *One Hundred Cans,* 1962, synthetic polymer paint on canvas, 72 × 52 in. © 2003. The Andy Warhol Foundation for the Visual Arts/ARS, New York. Albright Knox Art Gallery, Buffalo, New York. The Andy Warhol Foundation, Inc.

converge with those at the center of the modern/postmodern debate. As a "mirror of the times," Warhol criticism reflects the trepidation and enthusiasm in response to shifting paradigms. Lucy Lippard's proposition is still valid—Warhol's images are ambiguous. It's this ambiguity that gives his work its edge. His images function as a sort of cultural Rorschach blot allowing for the projection of personalities, theoretical orientations, and ideological biases.

Why put fifty Cambell's soup cans on canvas? So far, there are scores of explanations. And the debate rages on . . .

#27: Reading Cindy Sherman and Gender

Anne Darby

Student Essay

THE WOMAN IS SEATED, and the photograph is cropped from the middle of her forehead to the table on which her hands are resting. In her right hand she holds a half-smoked cigarette, and her left hand is curled distractedly around some indistinguishable object. In front of her right hand are a glass of champagne and a decorative ashtray. Before her left hand lies a pack of wooden matches, and on the ring finger of that hand there is a ring with a dark stone. It is impossible to discern whether it is merely a piece of jewelry or an indication of engagement, but either way it is enough to make the viewer speculate about her future marital status and, by association, her future in general.

The table is strewn with cigarette ash, which alludes to her preoccupation. She is wearing a low cut dress with a faux leopard fur collar that spans almost the width of her shoulders. The most noticeable aspect of the photograph is the emotion displayed on her face. Her heavy eye makeup is smeared by the tears which have run down her face in dark lines. Tears have caught on her eyelashes, held there by the heavy mascara. Light glints off of the excessive liquid, distorting and accentuating her eyes. Her mouth is partially open and her collarbones protrude, which indicate that she is in mid-gasp.

We are all familiar with that moment, near the end of a heavy cry, when we begin to try to compose ourselves and regain the oxygen we have lost. It is my assumption that the moment portrayed will be more poignant and powerful to female viewers, though it is possible male viewers would be able to relate on some level. The photograph stands for me as a symbol of the struggle between a person's façade and their soul. The symbols shown can be divided into those that stand as signifiers of façade and those that portray the true self coming through.

The dress, specifically the low neckline, suggests that this woman has dressed for someone other than herself. The idea that a woman, seen as a sexual object, lets (whether passively or actively, consciously or not) other parts of her character and psyche suffer is a predominant theme in Sherman's early work. For example, her *Centerfolds* series acts as commentary on pornographic images of women, and many of those images depict women in what could be sensual poses, were it not for the emotion or in some cases fear or sickness, that pervades the scene.

It has been my experience that the great majority of women to some extent project an image of who they think they are expected to be. (I know that this is also an issue with men, but that is a whole different topic, about which I am not qualified to write.) We *want* to be all of these things: beautiful, collected, intelligent, happy, witty (yet demure!) and successful. Furthermore the presence of the alcohol and the cigarette, as well as the subject's outfit, lead me to believe that she is involved in a certain lifestyle in which a woman plays a slightly different role than she does in the home or the workplace.

In a bar, at a party, or at any sort of gathering which is meant on the surface to be celebratory, most of us switch gears, and attempt to maintain a pleasant front. At a party one drinks, smokes, and talks about nothing. One is attractive and easy to get along with, never tired or moody, never undergoing stressful situations or tragedy. For a little while, that is amusing, even positive, but any length of time spent in that world causes detriment to the body and the soul. Again, this is more applicable to women than to men, and especially in the movies on which this photograph was based, but certainly not specific to those.

Alcohol and cigarettes are crutches on which one may rely to numb pain, pass time, or ignore real issues. Drinking makes one dull, and in the long term, stunts emotional growth. It causes one to lose touch with one's self. The juxtaposition of the tears with the traditional meanings associated with champagne is what makes the photograph so real. In fact, the champagne works more effectively to make this comparison than any other form of alcohol would.

The theme of a woman's misery threatening her façade has found its way many times into art and literature. I am automatically reminded of Justine, a character in Lawrence Durell's *Alexandria Quartet*. Succinctly, Justine is a beautiful woman, married to a wealthy banker, who is haunted by events of her past, most of which she is not at liberty to talk about. She had a child that was stolen from her, and she was constantly reminded of the presence of a man who had taken advantage of her in her youth, to name just a few of her woes. On the surface, she was highly visible socially, and in a position to be envied; she was untouchably beautiful, was the wealthiest woman in the city, had a husband who loved her, but inside she was ravaged by her regrets and neuroses. In a similar vein, Neil Jordan wrote a short story about a woman making idle conversation at a party while in the back of her mind wondering where it was that her soul had gone. Granted, all of the stories here have very different elements, but that particular theme ties them all together.

For me, and possibly for many other women, the smeared makeup is the most powerful single signifier of this woman's self breaking through her projected persona. When a woman prepares herself to face the world, she puts on a mask. It is a defense mechanism, as well as a beauty aid. Some women rely on this more than others, some are more conscious of it than others, but the effect is essentially the same. The activities that smear eye makeup are the activities that threaten our façade of coolness. Sleeping, crying, or a mistake in application all reveal our real human qualities. If the photograph were to be narrowed down to just the eyes and the streaks of stained tears, it would still be a loaded visual text; the rest of the photograph only elaborates on what the eyes have already said.

This photo is of Sherman herself, but because she uses herself in every image she creates, through repetition she herself is phased out of significance, giving the spotlight to each specific persona. Sherman becomes a non-element in each photograph. The significance is placed on the aspects that are different from picture to picture, which create the person, or the stereotype. Of course, if the viewer sees only one of Sherman's photographs, this is not an issue. The image is so strikingly genuine that it is difficult, even with knowledge of the subject, to imagine its staging. Also, the woman's failure to acknowledge the camera makes us believe that we really are glimpsing straight into the scene, uninvited and unnoticed.

Through staged photographs Sherman is able to solidify this nebulous concept. The success of the photograph is in the fact that it has pinpointed the perfect image to display such a moment, and such an emotion. Its delivery relies on the viewer to make it anything other than thoughtless voyeurism, but it is unlikely that an image this powerful will miss its mark.

Works Cited

Durrell, Lawrence. *The Alexandria Quartet*. 4 vols. New York: Dutton, 1957.
Jordan, Neil. *The Collected Fiction of Neil Jordan*. London: Vintage, 1997.
Krauss, Rosalind. *Cindy Sherman, 1975–1993*. New York: Rizzoli Internation, 1993.
Photography Exhibitions: Videocassette #No. 11. Writ. Mark Miller. Art/New York, 1982.
Sherman, Cindy. *Centerfolds*. New York: Skarstedt Fine Art, 2003.
———. *Untitled Film Stills*. New York: Rizzoli, 1990.

Sequential Art: "Closure" and "Art"

Scott McCloud

These "essays" come from Scott McCloud's *Understanding Comics* (1994), a comic about the importance—and semiotics—of comics and comic books. McCloud forces us to think about what art is and how we see it. He also raises interesting questions about the intersection of comics and art.

THIS PHENOMENON OF *OBSERVING THE PARTS* BUT *PERCEIVING THE WHOLE* HAS A *NAME*.

IT'S CALLED *CLOSURE*.

IN OUR DAILY LIVES, WE OFTEN COMMIT CLOSURE, MENTALLY COMPLETING THAT WHICH IS *INCOMPLETE* BASED ON *PAST EXPERIENCE*.

SOME FORMS OF CLOSURE ARE *DELIBERATE INVENTIONS* OF *STORYTELLERS* TO PRODUCE *SUSPENSE* OR TO *CHALLENGE AUDIENCES*.

OTHERS HAPPEN *AUTOMATICALLY*, WITHOUT MUCH *EFFORT*... PART OF *BUSINESS AS USUAL*.

IN *RECOGNIZING* AND *RELATING TO OTHER PEOPLE*, WE *ALL* DEPEND *HEAVILY* ON OUR LEARNED ABILITY OF CLOSURE,

IN AN *INCOMPLETE WORLD*, WE MUST *DEPEND* ON CLOSURE FOR OUR VERY *SURVIVAL*.

CLOSURE CAN TAKE *MANY FORMS*. SOME *SIMPLE*, SOME *COMPLEX*.

SOMETIMES, A MERE *SHAPE* OR *OUTLINE* IS ENOUGH TO TRIGGER CLOSURE.

THE MENTAL PROCESS DESCRIBED IN *CHAPTER TWO* WHEREBY THESE LINES BECOME A *FACE* COULD BE CONSIDERED CLOSURE.

EVERY TIME WE SEE A *PHOTOGRAPH* REPRODUCED IN A *NEWSPAPER* OR *MAGAZINE*, WE COMMIT CLOSURE.

OUR *EYES* TAKE IN THE *FRAGMENTED, BLACK-AND-WHITE* IMAGE OF THE *"HALF-TONE"* PATTERNS--

--AND OUR MINDS TRANSFORM IT INTO THE *"REALITY"*--

--OF THE *PHOTOGRAPH!*

IN *ELECTRONIC MEDIA,* CLOSURE IS *CONSTANT,* EVEN *OVER-POWERING!*

IN *FILM,* CLOSURE TAKES PLACE *CONTINUOUSLY--* TWENTY-FOUR TIMES PER *SECOND,* IN FACT-- AS OUR MINDS, AIDED BY THE *PERSISTENCE OF VISION,* TRANSFORM A SERIES OF *STILL PICTURES* INTO A STORY OF *CONTINUOUS MOTION.*

A MEDIUM REQUIRING EVEN *MORE* CLOSURE IS *TELEVISION,* WHICH, IN REALITY, IS JUST A *SINGLE POINT OF LIGHT,* *RACING ACROSS* THE SCREEN SO *FAST* THAT IT'S DESCRIBED MY FACE *HUNDREDS OF TIMES* BEFORE *YOU* CAN EVEN SWALLOW THAT *CORN CHIP!!**

BETWEEN SUCH *AUTOMATIC ELECTRONIC* CLOSURE AND THE SIMPLER CLOSURE OF *EVERYDAY LIFE--*

--THERE LIES A MEDIUM OF COMMUNICATION AND EXPRESSION WHICH USES CLOSURE LIKE *NO OTHER...*

...A MEDIUM WHERE THE AUDIENCE IS A WILLING AND CONSCIOUS *COLLABORATOR* AND CLOSURE IS THE AGENT OF *CHANGE,* *TIME* AND *MOTION.*

* MEDIA GURU TONY SCHWARTZ DESCRIBES THIS AT LENGTH IN HIS BOOK *MEDIA, THE SECOND GOD,* ANCHOR BOOKS, 1983.

The "Is It Art?" Suite

COMICS PANELS *FRACTURE* BOTH *TIME* AND *SPACE,* OFFERING A *JAGGED, STACCATO RHYTHM* OF *UNCONNECTED MOMENTS.*

BUT CLOSURE ALLOWS US TO *CONNECT* THESE MOMENTS AND *MENTALLY CONSTRUCT* A *CONTINUOUS, UNIFIED REALITY.*

The "Is It Art?" Suite

TO KILL A MAN BETWEEN PANELS IS TO CONDEMN HIM TO A THOUSAND DEATHS.

PARTICIPATION IS A *POWERFUL FORCE* IN *ANY* MEDIUM. FILMMAKERS *LONG AGO* REALIZED THE IMPORTANCE OF ALLOWING VIEWERS TO USE THEIR *IMAGINATIONS.*

BUT WHILE *FILM* MAKES USE OF AUDIENCES' IMAGINATIONS FOR *OCCASIONAL EFFECTS,* *COMICS* MUST USE IT FAR MORE *OFTEN!*

FROM THE *TOSSING* OF A *BASEBALL* TO THE *DEATH OF A PLANET,* THE READER'S *DELIBERATE, VOLUNTARY CLOSURE* IS COMICS' *PRIMARY* MEANS OF SIMULATING *TIME AND MOTION.*

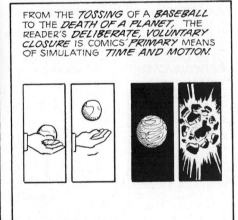

CLOSURE IN COMICS FOSTERS AN INTIMACY SURPASSED ONLY BY THE *WRITTEN WORD,* A SILENT, SECRET CONTRACT BETWEEN *CREATOR* AND *AUDIENCE.*

HOW THE CREATOR *HONORS* THAT CONTRACT IS A MATTER OF BOTH *ART* AND *CRAFT.*

LET'S TAKE A LOOK AT THE *CRAFT.*

The "Is It Art?" Suite

TRAPPED ON THE EDGE OF A *CLIFF*, HIS MIND CAN ONLY CONCEIVE OF *ONE PATH* TO *SURVIVAL!*

HE TAKES IT!

AND *SURVIVES.*

ROOOAARR

HIS *NEXT* MOVE MIGHT BE TO LOOK FOR FOOD (*SURVIVAL*) OR PERHAPS ANOTHER *FEMALE* (*REPRODUCTION*).

BUT *INSTEAD...*

THPLPLP!!

ART.

IT'S A *HAPPY FACT OF HUMAN EXISTENCE* THAT WE SIMPLY *CAN'T* SPEND OUR *EVERY* WAKING HOUR *EATING* AND *HAVING SEX!* NO MATTER HOW FRANTICALLY WE PURSUE OUR GOALS, THERE WILL *INEVITABLY* BE TIMES WHEN WE *JUST DON'T HAVE A THING TO DO!*

UGH.

UGH.

HRMMM...

The "Is It Art?" Suite

FIRST, THEY PROVIDE EXERCISE FOR MINDS AND BODIES NOT RECEIVING *OUTSIDE STIMULUS.*

SECOND, THEY PROVIDE AN *OUTLET* FOR *EMOTIONAL IMBALANCES,* AIDING IN THE RACE'S *MENTAL* SURVIVAL.

THIRD AND PERHAPS MOST *IMPORTANTLY* TO OUR SURVIVAL AS A RACE, SUCH RANDOM ACTIVITIES OFTEN LEAD--

--TO *USEFUL DISCOVERIES!*

AAH!!

FUMF!

THIS FUNCTION WOULD ALSO BE PERFORMED IN *LATER* CENTURIES BY *SPORTS* AND *GAMES.*

ART AS *SELF EXPRESSION,* THE ARTIST AS *HERO;* FOR MANY, ITS *HIGHEST PURPOSE.*

ART AS *DISCOVERY,* AS THE PURSUIT OF *TRUTH,* AS *EXPLORATION;* THE SOUL OF MUCH *MODERN* ART AND THE FOUNDATIONS OF *LANGUAGE, SCIENCE* AND *PHILOSOPHY.*

A LOT HAS *CHANGED* IN HALF A MILLION YEARS, BUT SOME THINGS *NEVER* CHANGE.

OH NO! I'M GONNA BE LATE FOR THAT *JOB INTERVIEW!*

THE PROCESSES ARE MORE *COMPLEX* NOW, BUT THE INSTINCTS *REMAIN THE *SAME. SURVIVAL AND REPRODUCTION* STILL HOLD THE *UPPER HAND.*

YET IN ALMOST EVERYTHING WE DO THERE IS AT LEAST AN *ELEMENT* OF ART.

PERHAPS A LITTLE *UNNECESSARY CHOREOGRAPHY* ON THE *ASSEMBLY LINE.*

OOOH, BEHBEE!

OR THE *PERSONAL STYLE* OF A *BICYCLE MESSENGER.*

HONK! HONK!

OR JUST THE WAY WE *SIGN OUR NAMES!*

IN *SOME* OCCUPATIONS, THE LATITUDE FOR SELF-EXPRESSION IS *GREATER.* *SURVIVAL*--MAKING A LIVING--GOES HAND IN HAND WITH *CREATIVE DESIRE.*

I THINK IT'S FAIR TO SAY THAT SOME ACTIVITIES HAVE MORE ART *IN* THEM THAN OTHERS.

LIFE IS A SERIES OF *MINUTE DECISIONS,* SOME MOTIVATED BY *SURVIVAL,* SOME *NOT,* AND PROPORTIONS DO *VARY.*

BUT TO PROCLAIM, AS SO MANY SO OFTEN *DO,* THAT--

THAT'S NOT ART!

--PRESUMES THAT ART IS AN *EITHER/OR* PROPOSITION. I DON'T THINK IT IS.

RARE IS THE PERSON IN *ANY* OCCUPATION WHO EXPRESSES *NOTHING...*

...AND RARE IS THE *ARTIST* WHO CARES NOTHING FOR *SUCCESS,* I.E., *SURVIVAL!*

The "Is It Art?" Suite

BUT THE **IDEAL** OF THE LATTER IS ALIVE IN THE HEARTS OF MANY ARTISTS WHO MAY **HOPE** FOR SUCCESS, BUT WON'T ALTER THEIR WORK TO **OBTAIN** IT.

THE "FINE ARTIST"--THE **PURE ARTIST**-- SAYS TO THE WORLD: "I DIDN'T DO THIS FOR **MONEY!** I DIDN'T DO THIS TO MATCH THE COLOR OF YOUR **COUCHES!**

"I DIDN'T DO THIS TO GET **LAID!** I DIDN'T DO THIS FOR **FAME** OR **POWER** OR **GREED** OR **ANYTHING ELSE!** I DID THIS FOR **ART!**"

IN **OTHER** WORDS: "MY ART HAS NO PRACTICAL VALUE WHATSOEVER!"

"BUT IT'S **IMPORTANT!**"

AND SOMETIMES IT **IS**, THOUGH IT MIGHT TAKE A **CENTURY** OR TWO FOR THE **REST** OF THE WORLD TO FIND OUT!

"PURE" ART IS ESSENTIALLY TIED TO THE QUESTION OF **PURPOSE**-- OF DECIDING WHAT YOU **WANT** OUT OF ART.

THIS IS AS TRUE IN **COMICS** AS IT IS IN **PAINTING, WRITING, THEATRE, FILM, SCULPTURE,** OR **ANY OTHER FORM**...

...BECAUSE THE CREATION OF **ANY** WORK IN **ANY** MEDIUM WILL ALWAYS FOLLOW A CERTAIN **PATH.**

The "Is It Art?" Suite

READING WRITING

This Text: Reading

1. According to Chrichton, is the *NAMES Quilt* art?
2. How does Chrichton distinguish between "real" or "high" art and the *NAMES Quilt*? Do you agree with this distinction?
3. Do you agree with Mack's three principles for evaluating art?
4. What is Mack's thesis statement? Does she rely on ethos, pathos, or logos for her argument?
5. How are Grody's and George's arguments similar? Different?
6. Darby does not really make an argument about Cindy Sherman's photograph as "art," rather as a document of gender. Does this affect its artistry? What about the fact that it is a staged photograph?
7. What are the three areas that Pratt cites as being important to Warhol's success and controversy? Are these important areas?
8. How does presenting McCloud's ideas in comic form change the way you view the information? Is it appropriate to present "serious" information in comic form? What might prevent us from receiving this information in the way the author might have intended it?
9. Do you agree with McCloud's idea about the role of the audience in determining meaning? Do you feel you have such a role in what you watch? When do you perform such a role?

Your Text: Writing

1. Write an essay in which you define art. Then look at two or three different texts and explain why they either are or are not art, according to your definition.
2. If you can see the *NAMES Quilt,* do so. If not, try to watch a video about it or find pictures of it. Write an essay on the experience of seeing the *NAMES Quilt.* What kind of text is it?
3. Write your own essay on art. Give 2–3 criteria for what makes good art. Be sure to explain and support your assertions.
4. Write an essay on a piece of public art in your city. Find a sculpture or a mural and talk about its relationship to its environs. What makes good *public* art?
5. Look at some of Warhol's art. Is he an important artist? Is his art important? Is there a distinction between being an important artist and making important art?
6. Using the criteria of Mack and Chrichton, write an essay on Warhol's work as effective art.
7. Write your own definition of art based on your own experience as a reader.
8. Write about your own experience as a reader in participating in making meaning.

The Reading a Photograph Suite

When photography entered the world of the visual arts, it was denigrated for being imitative, derivative, and not original—after all, it was merely reflecting what was already there. Later, however, critics praised it for some of the same reasons they had dismissed it before—photographs could truly capture reality in a way "artist-driven" work could not. Like writing, photography can be both commonplace and artistic. It can grace our scrapbooks, splash the front pages of a newspaper, and be displayed in a gallery or museum. But the question of whether photography captures reality is one that many critics struggle with.

As several recent examples have shown, photography—especially in the age of Photoshop—may be more open to manipulation than painting. With the ability to crop, erase, and superimpose, we wonder how reliable photographs are any more. In one prominent case, *Time* magazine was criticized for altering O. J. Simpson's face on its cover, making him look more menacing than in the original photograph. Indeed, in some court cases, photographs are inadmissible evidence because they can be so easily tampered with.

Reading a photograph also presents its own challenges. When one encounters a painting or a sculpture, one assumes the piece was intentionally designed a certain way, with artistic traces that indicate a signature style and help the viewer with a possible interpretation. Additionally, we are prepared to read sculpture and painting as fiction—imaginative renderings of the world. Photographs carry more overt connotations of reality, even if they have been altered in a studio. On the other hand, photographs can be candid in a way painting and sculpture cannot. Renoir, for all of his talents, would have problems busting out a quick and secret sculpture of someone exiting a limo, but photographers can snap several speedy photos without anyone noticing.

This issue of candor and intention is at the heart of this suite on photographs. We begin with two photographs (and essays) of seemingly shocking photos of young people appearing to be unmoved by disaster. On September 10, 2006, *The New York Times* columnist Frank Rich used Thomas Hoepker's now famous (infamous?) photograph of five New Yorkers lounging on the Brooklyn waterfront during 9/11 as a kind of window into the state of America (see our section windows and lenses in the introduction). Three days later, David Plotz, the deputy editor of *Slate*, offered an entirely different reading of the same photograph. Here, we print Hoepker's photo and the columns by both Rich and Plotz. Notice how both writers rely on semiotic cues in the photo to arrive at their (differing) interpretations of the photo and America.

When American photographer Spencer Platt won the coveted World Press Photo of the Year Award in 2006 for his photograph, controversy erupted—not only because of the behavior of the well-groomed people in the car ("disaster tourism") but also because of the aesthetic quality of the photograph. Reading Platt's photo through the lens of semiotics raises a series of questions, but so, too, does reading the photo through the lenses of class, gender, war, and race. Testing your reaction toward the subjects between photograph one and photograph two speaks to how visual (and cultural) rhetoric affects our emotions and our ideas.

Errol Morris is, perhaps, the most important documentary filmmaker in the United States. Much of his work, such as the film *The Thin Blue Line,* focuses on the difficulty of certainty when interpreting what appears to be objective evidence. In his piece that appeared in *The New York Times* in the summer of 2007, Morris asks how "true" photographs and images can really be.

One Photo, Two Lenses: Frank Rich and David Plotz on One of the Most Controversial Photos of 9/11

"THE MOST FAMOUS PICTURE NOBODY'S EVER SEEN" is how the Associated Press photographer Richard Drew has referred to his photo of an unidentified World Trade Center victim hurtling to his death on 9/11. It appeared in some newspapers, including this one, on 9/12 but was soon shelved. "In the most photographed and videotaped day in the history of the world," Tom Junod later wrote in *Esquire*, "the images of people jumping were the only images that became, by consensus, taboo."

Five years later, Mr. Drew's "falling man" remains a horrific artifact of the day that was supposed to change everything and did not. But there's another taboo 9/11 photo, about life rather than death, that is equally shocking in its way, so much so that Thomas Hoepker of Magnum Photos kept it under wraps for four years. Mr. Hoepker's picture can now be found in David Friend's compelling new 9/11 book, "Watching the World Change," or on the book's Web site, watchingtheworldchange.com. It shows five young friends on the waterfront in Brooklyn, taking what seems to be a lunch or bike-riding break, enjoying the radiant late-summer sun and chatting away as cascades of smoke engulf Lower Manhattan in the background.

Lounging or mourning? Thomas Hoepker's photo can be read many ways.

Mr. Hoepker found his subjects troubling. "They were totally relaxed like any normal afternoon," he told Mr. Friend. "It's possible they lost people and cared, but they were not stirred by it." The photographer withheld the picture from publication because "we didn't need to see that, then." He feared "it would stir the wrong emotions." But "over time, with perspective," he discovered, "it grew in importance."

Seen from the perspective of 9/11's fifth anniversary, Mr. Hoepker's photo is prescient as well as important—a snapshot of history soon to come. What he caught was this: Traumatic as the attack on America was, 9/11 would recede quickly for many. This is a country that likes to move on, and fast. The young people in Mr. Hoepker's photo aren't necessarily callous. They're just American. In the five years since the attacks, the ability of Americans to dust themselves off and keep going explains both what's gone right and what's gone wrong on our path to the divided and dispirited state the nation finds itself in today.

What's gone right: the terrorists failed to break America's back. The "new" normal lasted about 10 minutes, except at airport check-ins. The economy, for all its dips and inequities and runaway debt, was not destroyed. The culture, for better and worse, survived intact. It took only four days for television networks to restore commercials to grim news programming. Some two weeks after that Rudy Giuliani ritualistically welcomed laughter back to American living rooms by giving his on-camera imprimatur to *Saturday Night Live*. Before 9/11, Americans feasted on reality programs, nonstop coverage of child abductions and sex scandals. Five years later, they still do. The day that changed everything didn't make Americans change the channel, unless it was from "Fear Factor" to "American Idol" or from Pamela Anderson to Paris Hilton.

For those directly affected by the terrorists' attacks, this resilience can be hard to accept. In New York, far more than elsewhere, a political correctness about 9/11 is still strictly enforced. We bridle when the mayor of New Orleans calls ground zero "a hole in the ground" (even though, sadly, he spoke the truth). We complain that Hollywood movies about 9/11 are "too soon," even as *United 93* and *World Trade Center* came and went with no controversy at multiplexes in middle America. The Freedom Tower and (now kaput) International Freedom Center generated so much political rancor that in New York freedom has become just another word for a lofty architectural project soon to be scrapped.

The price of all New York's 9/11 P.C. is obvious: the 16 acres of ground zero are about the only ones that have missed out on the city's roaring post-attack comeback. But the rest of the country is less invested. For tourists — and maybe for natives, too—the hole in the ground is a more pungent memorial than any grandiose official edifice. You can still see the naked wound where it has not healed and remember (sort of) what the savage attack was about.

But even as we celebrate this resilience, it too comes at a price. The companion American trait to resilience is forgetfulness. What we've forgotten too quickly is the outpouring of affection and unity that swelled against all odds in the wake of Al Qaeda's act of mass murder. If you were in New York then, you saw it in the streets, and not just at ground zero, where countless thousands of good Samaritans joined the official responders and caregivers to help, at the cost of their own health. You saw it as New Yorkers of every kind gathered around the spontaneous shrines to the fallen and the missing at police and fire stations, at churches and in parks, to lend solace or a hand. This good feeling quickly spread to Capitol Hill, to red states where New York had once been Sodom incarnate and to the world, the third world included, where America was a nearly uniform object of sympathy and grief.

At the National Cathedral prayer service on Sept. 14, 2001, President Bush found just the apt phrase to describe this phenomenon: "Today we feel what Franklin Roosevelt called 'the warm courage of national unity.' This is the unity of every faith and every background. It has joined together political parties in both houses of Congress." What's more, he added, "this unity against terror is now extending across the world."

The destruction of that unity, both in this nation and in the world, is as much a cause for mourning on the fifth anniversary as the attack itself. As we can't forget the dead of 9/11, we can't forget how the only good thing that came out of that horror, that unity, was smothered in its cradle.

When F.D.R. used the phrase "the warm courage of national unity," it was at his first inaugural, in 1933, as the country reeled from the Great Depression. It is deeply moving to read that speech today. In its most famous line, Roosevelt asserted his "firm belief that the only thing we have to fear is fear itself—nameless, unreasoning, unjustified terror which paralyzes needed efforts to convert retreat into advance." Another passage is worth recalling, too: "We now realize as we have never realized before our interdependence on each other; that we cannot merely take but we must give as well; that if we are to go forward, we must move as a trained and loyal army willing to sacrifice for the good of a common discipline, because without such discipline no progress is made, no leadership becomes effective."

What followed under Roosevelt's leadership is one of history's most salutary stories. Americans responded to his twin entreaties — to renounce fear and to sacrifice for the common good — with a force that turned back economic calamity and ultimately an axis of brutal enemies abroad. What followed Mr. Bush's speech at the National Cathedral, we know all too well, is another story.

On the very next day after that convocation, Mr. Bush was asked at a press conference "how much of a sacrifice" ordinary Americans would "be expected to make in their daily lives, in their daily routines." His answer: "Our hope, of course, is that they make no sacrifice whatsoever." He, too, wanted to move on — to "see life return to normal in America," as he put it — but toward partisan goals stealthily tailored to his political allies rather than the nearly 90 percent of the country that, according to polls, was rallying around him.

This selfish agenda was there from the very start. As we now know from many firsthand accounts, a cadre from Mr. Bush's war cabinet was already busily hyping nonexistent links between Iraq and the Al Qaeda attacks. The presidential press secretary, Ari Fleischer, condemned Bill Maher's irreverent comic response to 9/11 by reminding "all Americans that they need to watch what they say, watch what they do." Fear itself—the fear that "paralyzes needed efforts to convert retreat into advance," as F.D.R. had it—was already being wielded as a weapon against Americans by their own government.

Less than a month after 9/11, the president was making good on his promise of "no sacrifice whatsoever." Speaking in Washington about how it was "the time to be wise" and "the time to act," he declared, "We need for there to be more tax cuts." Before long the G.O.P. would be selling 9/11 photos of the president on Air Force One to campaign donors and the White House would be featuring flag-draped remains of the 9/11 dead in political ads.

And so here we are five years later. Fearmongering remains unceasing. So do tax cuts. So does the war against a country that did not attack us on 9/11. We have moved on, but no one can argue that we have moved ahead.

Frank Rich Is Wrong About That 9/11 Photograph: Those New Yorkers Weren't Relaxing!

David Plotz

SOON AFTER THIS ARTICLE WAS POSTED, one of the people in the photograph e-mailed Slate *to respond. A day later, photographer Thomas Hoepker joined the debate.*

In his Sept. 10 column, Frank Rich of the *New York Times* describes a "taboo 9/11 photo," one so "shocking" that photographer Thomas Hoepker didn't publish it for four years. The photo, which the *Times* did not run but which is reproduced here (and which *Slate* also wrote about here), shows five people on the Brooklyn waterfront, engaged in conversation while the smoke from the fallen towers billows over Manhattan behind them.

In an interview with David Friend—who published the photo in a new book, *Watching the World Change: The Stories Behind the Images of 9/11*—Hoepker said his subjects "were totally relaxed like any normal afternoon" and that he didn't publish the picture in 2001 because "we didn't need to see that, then." Rich, who quotes the Hoepker interview, evidently agrees with the photographer's characterization of the image, writing, "What he caught was this: Traumatic as the attack on America was, 9/11 would recede quickly for many. This is a country that likes to move on, and fast. The young people in Mr. Hoepker's photo aren't necessarily callous. They're just American. In the five years since the attacks, the ability of Americans to dust themselves off and keep going explains both what's gone right and what's gone wrong on our path to the divided and dispirited state the nation finds itself in today."

But wait! Look at the photograph. Do you agree with Rich's account of it? Do these look like five New Yorkers who are "enjoying the radiant late-summer sun and chatting away"? Who have "move[d] on"? Who—in Rich's malicious, backhanded swipe—"aren't necessarily callous"? They don't to me. I wasn't there, and Hoepker was, so it may well be that they were just swapping stories about the Yankees. But I doubt it. The subjects are obviously engaged with each other, and they're almost certainly discussing the horrific event unfolding behind them. They have looked away from the towers for a moment not because they're bored with 9/11, but because they're citizens participating in the most important act in a democracy—civic debate.

Ask yourself: What are these five people doing out on the waterfront, anyway? Do you really think, as Rich suggests, that they are out for "a lunch or bike-riding break"? Of course not. They came to this spot to watch their country's history unfold and to be with each other at a time of national emergency. Short of rushing to Ground Zero and digging for bodies, how much more patriotic and concerned could they have been?

So they turned their backs on Manhattan for a second. A nice metaphor for Rich to exploit, but a cheap shot. I was in Washington on 9/11. I spent much of the day glued to my TV set, but I also spent it racing home to be with my infant daughter, calling my parents and New York relatives, and talking, talking, talking with colleagues and friends. Those discussions were exactly the kind of communal engagement I see in this photo. There is nothing "shocking" in this picture. These New Yorkers have not turned away from Manhattan because they have turned away from 9/11. They have turned away from Manhattan because they have turned toward each other for solace and for debate.

Rich and Hoepker and I have all characterized what these five people were doing and how they were feeling, but none of us really know. Wouldn't you like to hear from the five themselves? I would. If they're out there and they'd like to respond to Rich or me, they can e-mail me at plotzd@slate.com.

Editors' note: After Plotz's column ran in *Slate,* one of the men from the photo e-mailed the magazine. You can read his letter here: http://www.slate.com/id/2149578/

Award-Winning Photo Puts Subjects On Defensive

Gert Van Langendonck

Editor's Note: Spencer Platt's image of Lebanese residents driving through South Beirut on Aug. 15, 2006, won the World Press Photo of the Year award. A reporter later identified the subjects in the photo as Noor Nasser, 21 (hidden behind Lihane Nacouzi), Lihane Nacouzi, 22 (with face mask), Bissan Maroun, 29 (with cellphone), Jad Maroun, 22 (driving), and Tamara Maroun, 26 (in the front passenger seat).

Some saw the image as a symbol of how war affects rich and poor, while others saw the subjects as callously indifferent to the mayhem around them; PDNOnline referred to them as "cavalier." Platt himself never spoke to the subjects.

But in an interview with freelance journalist Gert Van Langendonck, the people in the car tell their side of the story. Van Langendonck, on assignment for the Belgian newspaper *De Morgen, says* he showed Platt's photo to everyone he met, and eventually someone recognized one of the women in the car, Bissan Maroun, who works as a bank teller.

A former foreign editor and U.S. correspondent for *De Morgen,* van Langendonck also has written for *NRC Handelsblad* in the Netherlands, *Die Zeit and Die Welt* in Germany, and other papers in Europe, as well as GNN.TV, a left-wing blog based in the U.S. A translation of Van Langendonck's story follows.

It was around 1 p.m. on August 15th, the second day of the ceasefire that ended the 33-day war between Israel and the armed Shia resistance group Hezbollah, and all of Lebanon was in upheaval. While tens of thousands of refugees from the South were

© Spencer Platt, USA, Getty Images

The Reading a Photograph Suite

clogging the roads on the way back to their homes, many others headed for the Dahiye, the Hezbollah-controlled southern suburbs of Beirut. Some wanted to check if their houses had survived the massive bombing campaign by the Israeli air force; others were simply curious.

It was at that moment that a red car caught photographer Spencer Platt's eye. He shot four or five frames, he says, but this was the only one he sent to his agency.

"I liked it because it showed another, fabulous side to Beirut," Platt says from his home in New York City. "It is important to show the cliches, the refugees, because that was the reality of what was happening. But this is Beirut too. It is this dichotomy that makes Lebanon such a fascinating place. But I never thought it was the picture."

Jad Maroun, 22, and his sisters Bissan, 29, and Tamara, 26, were not feeling all that fabulous on that sunny day in August. Despite the fact that they are Christian, they all lived in the Dahiye, which was once a Christian neighborhood. At the start of the war they had fled the bombing and settled in the Plaza Hotel in Hamra, a Sunni part of Beirut. It was there that they had met Noor Nasser, 21, a Muslim, and Liliane Nacouzi, 22, a Christian, who were working as waitresses in a sandwich shop in the hotel. They too were refugees from Beirut's Southern suburbs.

It was also where they ran into Lana El Khalil, 25, the owner of the Mini Cooper in Platt's picture. El Khalil, who calls herself an atheist, had given up her apartment in Hamra to make room for Shia refugees from the South and moved back to her parents' house. But she was hardly ever at home. When the war began, she was part of a sit-in in downtown Beirut to call attention to the Palestinian cause. As soon as the bombing started, she threw herself into relief work. She joined an NGO called Samidoun that was set up specifically to help the displaced people from the South. During the first days of the war, El Khalil helped evacuate people who were trapped in the Dahiye. Later on she would ferry food and medical supplies to the neighborhood. The little convertible came in handy.

But on August 15, two days into the ceasefire, it had served its purpose. When Jad and the others asked if they could borrow the Mini Cooper to go check on their houses in the Dahiye, El Khalil was happy to oblige them.

Six months later, they are all gathered in the apartment of Bissan's fiance in the Christian neighborhood of Achrafieh. Only Tamara, the blonde girl in the picture, is missing; she is getting ready for her engagement the next day. Jad, who was driving the car that day, admits that he had second thoughts about opening up the convertible. "I was worried that it would give people the wrong idea. But it was a hot day. There were five of us in a tiny car and we all wanted to get a good look at what had happened to the neighborhood."

They never saw Spencer Platt. The first they heard about his picture was when it was published in *Paris Match* in September. It is not so much the picture that bothered them; it was the caption that often went with it in publications around the world: rich Lebanese Christians doing war tourism in the ravaged suburbs of Beirut.

"Take a good look at the picture," says Bissan Maroun, a bank employee, "I can assure you that we were not having fun. The looks on our faces show consternation at what was done to our neighborhood. And I can tell you that not one person in this photo belongs to the Christian bourgeoisie."

There is the obvious question. What were they thinking dressing up in tight t-shirts and designer sunglasses on a day like this, and in a conservative part of town? "Hey, we're Lebanese," says Noor. "It's not like we dressed up like this to go visit the Dahiye. We dress like

© Karim Ben Khelifa/Oeil Public

Reporter Gert Van Langendonck located the subjects of Spencer Platt's prize-winning photo from the Lebanon war. From left to right: Bissan Maroun, 29, Noor Nasser, 21, Jad Maroun, 22, Lana El Khalil, 25 (the owner of the car, not seen in Platt's photograph), and Lihane Nacouzi, 22. Not shown here is Tamara Maroun, 26, who was in the front seat of the car.

this every day. On any other day, nobody would have given us a second glance. It was the contrast with the destruction in the background that made the difference." There is something the world needs to understand about Lebanon, adds El Khalil. "Glamour is a very important part of life here. It transcends class. Even if you're poor, you want to look glamorous."

A lot has been read into Platt's picture based on what viewers thought it conveyed. But such are the intricacies of life in Lebanon that they don't entirely disagree with its message, either. "It is a very interesting picture," says El Khalil. "And, yes, there was war tourism going on in Lebanon at the time; just not in this case."

It can be difficult for people in the West to grasp what life in a war zone is like. During the last war with Israel, many Lebanese who could afford it went up to places like Faraya, a ski resort in winter time. They settled in five-star hotels there and spent the day shopping or lounging around the swimming pool while the Southern suburbs were being bombed. Many of Beirut's designer boutiques and even some of its trendy night clubs followed their clientele to the mountain resorts. "I went to Faraya myself one weekend during the war", says El Khalil, "and I too was shocked by some of the things I saw there." But she doesn't judge. "Everybody reacts to war in their own way. Me, I chose to help people. Others went to la-la-land and partied. There is a survival instinct that kicks in. It's another form of resistance, to try and keep living your life the way you want to despite the war."

The choice of Platt's picture for the World Press Photo has stirred up quite a debate in the photojournalism community. Some critics applauded the break from more traditional war photography. In interviews with Le Monde in France and Hebdo magazine in Lebanon, Lebanese photographer Samer Mohdad described the jury's choice as "an insult to all news photographers who have risked their lives to cover this horrible war."

The young Lebanese in the picture are not quite that angry. But they ask themselves why Platt's picture was chosen, "and not, for instance, the picture of a dead young boy being taken from the rubble after an Israeli bombing in Qana." Could it be, asks El Khalil, "that the photo of the dead boy shows the reality of a war, and that this makes people in the West uncomfortable?" This is why she feels Platt's photo is dangerous. "It distracts attention from the harsh reality of war. It confirms what many people in the West think already, that war only happens to people who don't look like them."

Bissan Maroun's boyfriend Wissam Awad, 32, takes the argument one step further. "Giving the award to the picture of the dead boy would have harmed the reputation of Israel in the world. Platt's picture doesn't do that. On the contrary, it suggests that the Christians had nothing to do with the war, that they were all against Hezbollah and on the side of Israel. And that's just not true."

Spencer Platt never knew who the people in his picture were. He wants it known that he never meant to judge them. "I never talked to them. For all I knew, they might have lost members of their family. No one was immune to hardship in that conflict. And I certainly didn't mean to make a political statement, as some have said. My fixer, Wafa, was of a very similar type to the people in the car, and her life had been turned upside down by the war." In the end, he says, "What I think this image partly asks us, the viewer, is to challenge our stereotypes of victims of war."

Liar, Liar Pants on Fire

Errol Morris

PICTURES ARE SUPPOSED TO BE WORTH a thousand words. But a picture unaccompanied by words may not mean anything at all. Do pictures provide evidence? And if so, evidence of what? And, of course, the underlying question: do they tell the truth?

I have beliefs about the photographs I see. Often—when they appear in books or newspapers—there are captions below them, or they are embedded in explanatory text. And even where there are no explicit captions on the page, there are captions in my mind. What I think I'm looking at. What I think the photograph is about.

I have often wondered: would it be possible to look at a photograph shorn of all its context, caption-less, unconnected to current thought and ideas? It would be like stumbling on a collection of photographs in a curiosity shop—pictures of people and places that we do not recognize and know nothing about. I might imagine things about the people and places in the photographs but know nothing about them. Nothing.

This collection could even involve my own past. I recently was handed a collection of photographs taken by my father—dead now for over fifty years. I looked at it, somewhat confused. I suppose saddened by the passage of time. Even though I am in the photographs, the people in them are mysterious, inherently foreign. Maybe because photographs tamper with the glue that holds life and memory together.

Who are these people? Do they have anything to do with me? Do I really know them?

As disconnected from the present as these photographs might be, they do not seem devoid of context. I know too much about them—even if I know very little. They are pictures of

my own family. It's too easy for me to concoct some story about them. To find a picture shorn of context, it would be important to pick a photograph that's sufficiently removed for me in time and context—a photograph preternaturally unfamiliar. Perhaps a war photograph, but a war photograph from an unfamiliar war. It should be a war six or seven wars ago. Passions, presumably, have been diminished. No one in the photographs will still be alive.

I want to ask a relatively simple question. Are these photographs true or false? Do they tell the truth?

Look at the photograph on the next page. Is it true or false?

I find the question ridiculous: "True or false in regard to what?"

Without a caption, without a context, without some idea about what the picture is a picture of, I can't answer. I simply cannot talk about the photograph as being true or false independently of beliefs about the picture. A captionless photograph, stripped of all context, is virtually meaningless. I need to know more.

And yet, this idea that photographs can be true or false independent of context is so ingrained in our thinking that we are reluctant to part with it.

Let's add a caption to the photograph.

Only now can we ask questions that have true or false answers. The caption asserts that this is a photograph of the *Lusitania*, a British ship launched in 1907. I found the photograph on a website entitled "Maritime Quest." I made no effort to check it; I simply took their word for it. That could be a mistake on my part. With no malice intended, the wrong caption could have inadvertently been placed under the photograph. The photograph could actually be a photograph of the *Titanic*. Or malice could have been involved. Someone could have maliciously switched the captions of pictures of the *Lusitania* and the *Titanic*.

But one thing is clear. When I look at these pictures—whether it is a picture of the *Lusitania* or the *Titanic*—I imagine that someone stood on a dry dock, or some vantage point, looked through the viewfinder of the camera, and took a photograph of something that was floating out there in the water. If it was the *Lusitania*, then he took a photograph of the *Lusitania*. If it was the *Titanic*, then he took a picture of the *Titanic*. This may seem hopelessly obvious, but I have this saying—and I believe there's something to it—that there is nothing so obvious that it's obvious.

The Lusitania

But we need language, and we need context, in order to know which ship it is, and a host of other sundry facts.

In discussing truth and photography, we are asking whether a caption or a belief—whether a statement about a photograph—is true or false about (the things depicted in) the photograph. A caption is like a statement. It trumpets the claim, "This is the *Lusitania*." And when we wonder "Is this a photograph of the *Lusitania*?" we are wondering whether the claim is true or false. The issue of the truth or falsity of a photograph is only meaningful with respect to statements about the photograph. Truth or falsity "adheres" not to the photograph itself but to the statements we make about a photograph. Depending on the statements, our answers change. All alone—shorn of context, without captions—a photograph is neither true nor false.

But why this photograph? It's so terribly bland. I wanted to begin this series of essays on photography with an image chosen particularly for its blandness. Removed in time, far from our core knowledge, it is unfamiliar. We know little about it. We most likely do not recognize it as the *Lusitania*. We might think it's an early-20th-century ocean liner, and perhaps even imagine it may be the *Titanic*—at which point we have placed a kind of mental caption under the photograph, and we begin to see the photograph in terms of our associations and beliefs, about what it seems to say about reality.

It is also interesting how a photograph quickly changes when we learn more about what it depicts, when we provide a context, when we become familiar with an underlying story. And when we make claims about the photograph using language. For truth, properly considered, is about the relationship between language and the world, not about photographs and the world.

So here's a story.

The Reading a Photograph Suite

On the evening of May 7th, 1915, the RMS *Lusitania* was off the coast of Ireland en route to Liverpool from New York when it was torpedoed by a German U-Boat and sank. Nearly 2,000 passengers and crew drowned, including 128 Americans. The loss of life provoked America out of a hereunto neutrality on the ongoing war in Europe. With cries of "Remember the *Lusitania*" the U.S. entered into WWI within two years.

To modern viewers, this image of the Lusitania is emotionally uncharged, if not devoid of interest. But to a viewer in the summer of 1915, it was charged with meaning. It was surrounded by many, many other photographs, images and accounts of the sinking of the *Lusitania,* a cause célèbre.

Let's look at some of these other images.

"ENLIST" was a WWI Recruitment poster designed by Fred Spears. Spears' design was inspired by a news report from Cork, Ireland, that described, among the recovered bodies from the *Lusitania*, "a mother with a three-month-old child clasped tightly in her arms. Her face wears a half smile. Her baby's head rests against her breast. No one has tried to separate them."

And here is a photograph from the same period with the following caption.

"SOME OF THE SIXTY-SIX COFFINS BURIED IN ONE OF THE HUGE GRAVES IN THE QUEENSTOWN CHURCHYARD."

The caption is from a two-page pictorial spread in the May 30, 1915, *New York Times*: "BURYING THE LUSITANIA'S DEAD AND SUCCORING HER SURVIVORS."

One more photograph and an accompanying article from the *Toronto Star*.

The photograph is of a pocket watch. We learn from the accompanying article that the watch belonged to Percy Rogers and that the watch stopped at exactly 2:30 after "ticking off 30 of the most terrible minutes in history." Mr. Rogers was in a stateroom when the torpedo struck the *Lusitania*. He spent his last minutes on board helping women and children climb into lifeboats. Then he climbed into a lifeboat as well. And then the ship sank. The last paragraph of the article is memorable. It quotes "the official German statement" following the sinking of the *Lusitania*: "Every German heart is filled with joy, pride and gratification."

Now look at the photograph of the ship one more time.

The image remains the same, but clearly we look at it in a different way.

Watch's Fixed Hands Record Lusitania's Last 30 Minutes

At 2.30 p.m. today it will be exactly 27 years since a small pocket watch owned by Percy Rogers, Toronto, was stopped by the action of a German submarine.

It was 2 o'clock on the afternoon of May 7, 1915. The giant Cunard liner, Lusitania, with 1,906 aboard, was eight miles off the south coast of Ireland, and New York bound. In the domed dining saloon, Percy Rogers, then secretary of the C.N.E., had just finished lunch.

Mr. Rogers got up from the table, glanced at his watch and walked to his stateroom. At the very moment he was reaching to pick up a letter, he heard a "tremendous thud." He rushed on deck.

"People were running around like a flock of sheep with no one to direct them," he recalls. "Some of them clambered into lifeboats. The ship took a heavy list," His watch ticked off the fateful minutes. It was 2.15.

"I helped women and children near me into a boat. Then, as there were no more there, I got in. We had barely pulled a little way off before the ship turned on its side and sank." Five minutes had ticked by. It was 2.20.

"There was very little suction from the ship's sinking. But our boat upset, I struck out. Women and children were floating, mothers seeking to hold babies up. . . ." The watch ticked on, minute after minute. More than 1,000 lives were being snuffed out, and as the cold salt water seeped through Percy Rogers' clothes and finally into the delicate mechanism, his watch stopped. The minute hand, which had ticked off 30 of the most terrible minutes in history, was turned downward in defeat. It was exactly 2.30.

Mr. Rogers floated with the help of a cupboard for an hour and a half. He was then picked up by a trawler and taken to Queenstown. When he looks at his watch today, one thing sticks in his mind. It is the official German statement at the time of the torpedoing: "Every German heart is filled with joy, pride and gratification." Mr. Rogers has never had the watch repaired. The hands have remained where they stopped as a reminder of the Lusitania.

Is that really a photograph of the *Lusitania*? When was it taken? Could it have been taken on May 7, 1915? If it was, what was the exact time that it was taken? Two o'clock? Two fifteen? Just seconds before the German torpedo hit? Ah, can we see the torpedo in the water? Is that the mother and her child (depicted in the poster) standing on the deck looking out over the water? Is that Percy Rogers with his pocket watch, helping that same woman and child climb into a lifeboat?

The idea that photographs hand us an objective piece of reality, that they by themselves provide us with the truth, is an idea that has been with us since the beginnings of photography. But photographs are neither true nor false in and of themselves. They are only true or false with respect to statements that we make about them or the questions that we might ask of them.

The photograph doesn't give me answers. A lot of additional investigation could provide those answers, but who has time for that?

Pictures may be worth a thousand words, but there are two words that you can never apply to them: "true" and "false."

This Text: Reading

1. How is it possible that two smart people like Rich and Plotz can have such different reactions to the same photograph? To what degree is the Hoepker photo misleading?

2. Whose opinion to you agree with—Rich or Plotz? Who makes the most compelling argument?

3. Plotz relies on classic semiotic techniques—paying close attention to the details of the photo—in order to arrive at his interpretation. Does he give an accurate reading of Hoepker's photo?

4. Why do you think Platt's photo—of all of the photographs taken in 2006—won this award?

5. Does this photograph say something about war that traditional "war photography" does not? If so, what does it say?

6. To what degree does Platt's photograph make an argument? Does it invite you to "read into" the photo? Is the photo value free?

7. Find two or three family photos or some of you and your friends and give a reading of these texts. What do the photos say about the people in them if you read the texts through the lens of race? Culture? If you give a semiotic reading of them, what does that suggest? Do the photos make an argument?

8. Look at some of the photographs in this book. Now imagine them without captions. How does this change how you *see* the photos?

Your Text: Writing

1. Write an essay in which you evaluate Rich's and Plotz's reading of the photograph. Identify each writer's main thesis. What sort of argument is each making?

2. Give your own reading of Hoepker's photograph. Based on the semiotic cues in the photo, what do *you* think the photo suggests? How would you interpret either the behavior of the people or the motives of Hoepker?

3. Write an essay in which you compare Hoepker's photo with Seymour Platt's controversial photo of several young people cruising through war-torn Lebanon in a convertible. Why did these photos create such controversy? What do they tell us about the expectations of people after and during disaster?

4. Write a comparison/contrast essay in which you read the two photographs alongside each other. Each is a kind of portrait, but each uses context to send a different message. Describe your emotional reactions to each.

5. Write an essay in which you read Platt's photo and Hoepker's photo of the young people lounging during the 9/11 attacks.

6. Write an essay using old family photos as a point of departure. How hard is it to read texts from the past through the lens of the present?

The Censorship Suite

"Every work of art is an uncommitted crime," according to the German philosopher Theodore Adorno. Similarly, Pablo Picasso, a painter whose name probably rings a bell, said in 1935 that for him, "a picture is a sum of destructions." Those of you who think of art as primarily "pretty" or "uplifting," might find both of these statements rather shocking. We tend not to think of art as either dangerous or criminal, yet for many, that is what it has become.

Since the late 1980s, a number of artists, museums, and granting agencies have lost funding, incurred fines, been shut down, and in some cases arrested for supporting, producing, and exhibiting art that some have found indecent. Indeed, one of the great clashes of American democracy occurs when freedom of expression bumps up against laws and civil codes prohibiting pornography and hate speech. Fundamental American values clash with questions about morality, standards, and public funding. For example, who decides what is pornography and what is art? Is art that employs racist images and ideas itself racist? Who gets to censor art? What are the criteria for art censorship? Should art that is funded by tax dollars be subject to public approval?

These questions came to the fore in 1987 with the appearance of two separate art events. The first was a photograph by Andres Serrano, who was awarded a $15,000 grant by the Southeastern Center for Contemporary Art in Winston–Salem, North Carolina, a program funded by the National Endowment for the Arts (NEA). The photograph in question featured a crucifix in a golden, bubbly haze. According to *The New York Times,* Serrano's photo "appears reverential, and it is only after reading the provocative and explicit label that one realizes the object has been immersed in urine." Of course, the artwork in question is the now infamous *Piss Christ.* That same year, the Philadelphia Institute of Contemporary Art (ICA) received an NEA grant to host a retrospective of Robert Mapplethorpe's photographs, entitled "The Perfect Moment." The show included some homoerotic photographs and a couple of portraits of naked children (commissioned by their parents). The exhibit ran in Philadelphia and Chicago without incident. However, enraged by federal funding for *Piss Christ,* some conservative congressmen such as Jesse Helms (R–N.C.), Alphonse D'Amato (R–N.Y.), and Dick Armey (R–Tex.) got wind of the NEA-funded Mapplethorpe exhibit, slated to arrive at the Corcoran Gallery in Washington, D.C. In June 1989, 108 congressmen filed a formal complaint against the NEA, charging it supported indecent art with public funds. Two days previously, the director of the Corcoran had cancelled the Mapplethorpe exhibit out of fear of negative publicity, but it did no good. The war over art, decency, and public monies was ratcheted to a new level, and public art and the public funding for visual art has never been the same in the United States.

Not only does this debate raise questions about funding for art, but it also brings the role of visual art into the spotlight as a particularly vulnerable and powerful text. Why is it that visual texts remain a lightning rod for censorship over written ones? Granted, on occasion novels like *Catcher in the Rye* or *The Adventures of Huckleberry Finn* find themselves in a touchy case with a local schoolboard, but we rarely hear of people banning essays or poetry. On the contrary, paintings, sculptures, movies, and especially photographs worry watchdog groups a great deal and are the examples most commonly used to decry the immorality of American art. On the other hand, artists, professors, and critics hailed this debate as proof that art *matters,* that it is powerful, and that people must take it seriously.

All of the images in this suite have incurred some kind of censorship or controversy. We reprint them here not to add to that controversy but to foreground the symbolic importance of visual texts. This entire book makes the argument that texts, signs, and symbols carry enormous social and cultural weight—that these images engender such strong reactions is proof that the world is a text full of complicated texts. We also believe that it is important to engage any text that elicits powerful responses; in fact, almost nothing makes for better writing. Forcing yourself to articulate why a painting moves you (either positively or negatively) is one of the most effective strategies for vigorous writing and compelling argument.

As a side note, we got the idea for this suite from two sources—a free public information pamphlet from the National Coalition against Censorship (NCAC) and a photo–timeline based on this pamphlet that appeared in a wonderful book by the National Arts Journalism Program (NAJP) titled *The New Gatekeepers: Emerging Challenges to Free Expression in the Arts*. We wish to thank Svetlana Mintcheva, Director of the Arts Advocacy Project at the NCAC, for her help with this suite.

Andres Serrano, *Piss Christ*. © A. Serrano. Courtesy of the artist and the Paula Cooper Gallery, New York.

Dread Scott, *What Is the Proper Way to Display a US Flag?*

Avalus, Hock, and Sisco, *Welcome to America's Finest Tourist Plantation*

Andres Serrano, *Klanswoman*. © A. Serrano. Courtesy of the artist and the Paula Cooper Gallery, New York.

Gran Fury, *Kissing Doesn't Kill*

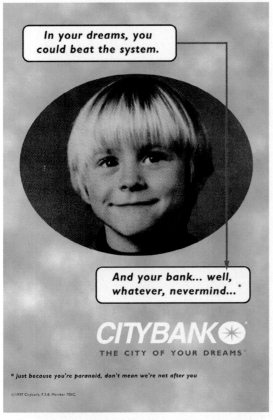
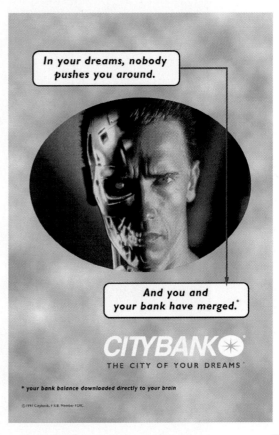

Andres Andy Cox, *CityBank Posters*

Chris Ofili, *The Holy Virgin Mary*

Alma Lopez, *Our Lady*

Renee Cox, *Yo Mama's Last Supper*. Courtesy Robert Miller Gallery

READING WRITING

This Text: Reading

1. Some might argue that some of these images are not, in fact, "art." Would you agree? Which ones are "art" and which ones are not? How do you make your determination?
2. Does the artistry or aesthetics of a visual text affect how you perceive it? That is, if its form is beautiful but its content is disturbing, can it still be art? Does its content diminish (or enhance) its artistry?
3. Which of the images is the most disturbing? Why?
4. If you could own any of these pieces, which would you want? Why?
5. If *Piss Christ* had a different title would it have caused such an uproar? What if it had been titled *Golden Christ* or *What the Modern World Has Done to Religion?* How does the title affect how we see the photograph?
6. In 1997, author Anthony Julius wrote a paper called "Art Crimes," in which he argues for "the creative complicity of art with crime—what he calls "crimes of art that are also crimes *against* art." He favors these kinds of art crimes because they challenge the boundaries of what is art and what is law. Are any of these texts crimes against art?
7. Do you think these works of art mirror American values and culture or ignore them?
8. In his engaging book *Arresting Images: Impolitic Art and Uncivil Actions,* Steven C. Dubin argues that "a combination of two critical elements is required for art controversies to erupt: there must be a sense that values have been threatened, and power must be mobilized in response to do something about it." In what ways do these art works *threaten* American values? In what ways do they uphold American values?

Your Text: Writing

1. Write an argumentative paper in which you claim that these works should or should not be censored. Be sure to supply reasonable information to support your assertions.
2. Write a definitional paper on art and show why and how these pieces are (or are not) art.
3. Write an essay comparing one of the works here with a classic work of art. For instance, you might compare *Piss Christ* with a more revered painting of a crucifixion from the middle ages or even more recently, such as Eugene Carriere's 1897 *Crucifixion.* Or, perhaps *Yo Mama's Last Supper* with da Vinci's; Mapplethorpe's photographs of nude men with Michaelangelo's *David.*
4. Write a personal essay about looking at these images in your classroom. Is it odd to be confronted with disturbing images in a college classroom? Is it appropriate?

The Censorship Suite

5. Write an argumentative essay in which you take a stance on public funding for art. Should taxpayer dollars go to fund controversial exhibits? What is the difference between funding art and funding wars? Paintings vs. missiles? Sculptures over monuments?

6. Write an essay on the placement of this suite in this book. Do the authors make an argument about censorship and art with this suite? Are they objective?

7. Do a semiotic analysis of one of the works in this suite. Talk about the various signs, symbols, and codes the artist uses to achieve an effect.

READING BETWEEN THE LINES

Classroom Activities

1. Bring in a slide or a photograph of a famous work of art. As a class, read the artistic text. How does reading it as a group change how you see it?
2. As a class, select an image from the book. Then, spend 15 minutes trying to redraw or reproduce the image. How does that change the image? How does it change how you see the image?
3. Bring a reproduction of a painting by Elsworth Kelley or Barnett Newman or Morris Louis to class. Or, look at a sculpture by Claes Oldenburg or Jeff Koonz. Have a discussion on whether these pieces are art. Why? Why not?
4. Look at a particularly incendiary artistic text in class, like Andres Serrano's *Piss Christ* or a Robert Mapplethorpe photograph or the Chris Ofili painting from the *Sensation* exhibit. What is the role of art, decency, and public opinion? Where and how do aesthetics and ethics meet? What cultural forces might prompt this kind of art?
5. Look at some Warhol prints in class. Are his pieces art? Why or why not?
6. Talk about the differences between painting and photography. What can one do that the other cannot?
7. Take a field trip to look at some pieces of sculpture near or on your campus. How does sculpture adhere to the principles of artistic design?
8. Talk about the role of art in American culture. Compare how you think about art to how you think about television, film, and literature.

Essay Ideas

1. Write a paper in which you define art, then show why three paintings, photographs, or sculptures meet your definition of art.
2. Write a poem about one of the images in this chapter, and then write an essay about the process of writing a poem about the image.
3. What is the relationship between gender and art? Many of the most famous paintings, photographs, and sculptures are of nude women. How has art altered how men and women see the female body?
4. In what way is how we see the world affected by what we believe or what we know? How does our background, our beliefs, our interests, and our personality affect how we see art? How does the political climate of our society affect how we see art?
5. Compare a Diane Arbus photograph with a classic painting. Are both art? Compare what della Francesca or da Vinci or Vermeer tries to do in his art with what Arbus tries to accomplish in hers. How might their respective cultures influence their ideas of what art should do?
6. Write an essay comparing Chrichton's questions about art and the NAMES quilt with Mack's questions about art and the *Sensation* exhibit. How do both pieces rise out of social or political unrest?
7. Look at some of the advertisements in this book. Using Acton's notion of composition, argue how advertisements adhere to notions of artistic design.

8. Write an essay in which you demonstrate and explain how a work of art makes a political statement.

9. Do you believe that public funding for the arts should be cut if the public finds the art objectionable? Can the public, if it supports an exhibit with its tax dollars, censor a work of art?

10. Write an essay on the artistic situation for one of the texts. What cultural or societal forces may influence what or how an artist creates?

READING AND WRITING ABOUT
race and ethnicity

Tommie Smith and John Carlos raise their fists at the 1968 Olympics.

OF ALL THE INTRODUCTIONS WE HAVE WRITTEN, THIS ONE MADE US FEEL THE MOST UNCOMFORTABLE. WRITING ABOUT PEOPLE, SKIN COLOR, AND THE RELATIONSHIP BETWEEN APPEARANCE AND ATTRIBUTED BEHAVIOR IS A MINEFIELD FOR ANY PROSPECTIVE AUTHOR. WE WANTED TO PUT OUR ANXIETY ON THE TABLE RIGHT AWAY BECAUSE WE BELIEVE THAT THIS ANXIETY MIRRORS THE WAY YOU MIGHT FEEL WHEN YOU ARE TALKING ABOUT RACE AND ETHNICITY WHETHER YOU ARE HISPANIC, AFRICAN AMERICAN, ASIAN AMERICAN, AMERICAN INDIAN, WHITE, OR, MOST LIKELY, SOME COMBINATION OF ETHNICITIES.

As you will notice in reading this introduction, we are constantly hedging—saying "to a degree" or "to some extent." And there is a reason for this hesitation. When it comes to race or ethnicity, there are few if any absolutes; yet, unfortunately, the world of racism seems to operate within a system of ignorant absolutes. Assumptions about individuals because of skin color and perceptions about ethnicities based on unexamined stereotypes lump individuals into groups where it is easy to make sweeping generalizations that never take into account individual nuances, abilities, and personalities. When these experiences occur because of perceived common characteristics, an individual experience becomes a group one. Prejudice, then, projects perceived or assumed group characteristics on a single person or groups of people. Again, saying a group of people is not qualified to do particular work because of how they look or the ethnicity they belong to is a clear example of prejudice.

To an overwhelming degree, these experiences are socially constructed. Indeed, most scientists believe that race is a social, not a biological, construction. In other words, race as it was commonly perceived in the past—as a means of attributing characteristics to individuals of a common group—is not scientifically or biologically defensible. Scientists believe that perceived traits of races are a product of social experiences, despite the way we often visually identify someone of a particular race. To put it a different way, one's skin color does *not* determine race; factors contributing to one's race are far more complex.

We are *not* saying that biology does not determine the color of one's skin; clearly, biology determines skin pigmentation, as it does the color of our eyes, our hair, and our acne. What we are saying (and what most scientists also argue) is that the idea that biological traits are associated with a particular skin color is false. As humans of different shades of color, we are much more alike biologically than we are different. Even if some groups do have higher incidents of disease (African Americans with sickle-cell anemia, Jews with Tay-Sachs disease), environmental factors largely shape their existence. For example, Americans are much more likely to have heart conditions compared to the French. The characteristics of Americans are more alike than characteristics of people from Tibet, which is to say that our biology and our cultural community connect us in more ways than our perceptions of race might suggest.

Self-perception is even more of a factor in racial or ethnic identity, as people often "switch" ethnicities or at least change their affiliation with a certain group. For instance, a recent study shows that more than one-third of respondents in a census identified themselves as a different ethnicity than when they responded to the same census only two years later. This is not to say that race is not important—it is. Race and ethnicity, even if socially constructed, guide much of our public life. By putting the burden on social constructions of race, we have to think about the way we construct race more completely rather than accept that things like skin color and racial traits are simply the way things are.

In the past, people from various groups had a tendency to impose a set of values onto certain groups based simply on skin color, a tendency that has certainly diminished in the last 50 years (though we would be the last people to claim that this type of behavior is gone, and the first to acknowledge that prejudice is still very much a part of too many people's lives). Our goal in this chapter is to help you become more sensitive readers of race and ethnicity by becoming more aware of the social forces that construct the volatile texts of race and racism.

The determination that race, ethnicity, and class are socially constructed has led to new ways of thinking about our identity that carry political and social implications.

Not too long ago, and for most of the history of the Western world, people made assumptions about other people based on their appearance, most notably their skin color. White people wrongly, and often tragically, assumed blacks were inferior or that American Indians were "savages." For centuries, groups have enslaved other groups based on that group's race or ethnicity. In the last few decades, we have gone from the biological construction of race—one based on parentage—to one based more on social groups and associations. "Hispanic" means something different than it did twenty years ago, as does "Native American." For example, there has been a persuasive shift in identification. We tend to view Native Americans by tribe or nation, and those from Central and South America, the Caribbean, and Mexico by country of origin and nationality, rather than the catchall of ethnicity. We talk of Choctaw, Zuni, and Osage rather than "Indian." We identify folks as Cuban, Columbian, or Mexican, rather than "Hispanic." At the University of San Francisco, there is a resistance to Pan–Asianism among students. There are, for example, a number of different Filipino student organizations, each more or less political than the others. Precise linguistic markers more accurately articulate identity, as anyone familiar with racial and cultural history can tell you.

To a degree, race and ethnicity are visually constructed, but those visual constructions are hardly without controversy.

We tend to categorize people by their appearance, not by their biological background, for the most obvious reason: we have no other way of reading people. We do construct race, ethnicity, and gender, and its multiplicity of meanings and ideas visually, not only through a person's skin but also through what they wear, how they walk, how tall or short they are. We are not trying to demonize this process as much as we are trying to draw attention to it. Like other visual constructions, it must be slowed down and digested more actively. Thus, every time we see someone and register that person's skin color, we are doing a reading of his or her ethnicity. We pick up on external codes that we think cue us into that person's racial background, but what, really, do those cues tell us? For one, even if we can determine if someone is Chinese or Russian or Kenyan or Navajo, that tells us very little about who she is as a person, what he likes to eat, what she is good at, how smart he is, what sports she plays, or what his values are.

As we indicate earlier, for centuries people in power (mostly white but not always) used skin color as a means of identifying both ethnicity and character. One of the worst and most tragic fallacies one can commit is to conflate external and internal in regard to race; to see "Asian" or "African American" and think _____. There is a funny scene in the movie *Carbon Copy*, when George Segal (anglo) assumes his black son (Denzel Washington), a grown man who he has just met, is good at basketball. In an attempt to make money, Segal challenges a father and son who are shooting hoops to a pickup basketball game for cash. Segal's expectations, those of the other father and son, and those of the viewers, are undermined when the Denzel Washington character is terrible at basketball. Here Segal engages in a classic misreading of race. In this instance, he only lost money; however, in the case of slavery, Japanese internment, and Native removal, the consequences of misreading were much more significant.

To some extent, reading the "otherness" in someone's appearance makes us uncomfortable because of reasons both political and personal.

We want to be—and are explicitly trained to be—democratic in the way we view others, by the way they act toward us, not the way they look. "Don't judge a book by its cover," we say, but we are always judging books by their covers and people by their appearance, and this makes many of us *very* uncomfortable. This discomfort is magnified when it comes to race, ethnicity, gender, and class because we know our constructions have political, cultural, social, and personal consequences for us and for the people we are trying to read. Our democratic nature wants us to read neutrally, but our less controllable side does not, because we have been conditioned through decades and even centuries of reading values into otherness. Perhaps you have noticed or even commented on someone's ethnicity, then felt strange about it. In one classic episode of *Seinfeld*, George and Elaine muse over the ethnicity of Elaine's new boyfriend, an endeavor that makes George extremely uncomfortable. Throughout the episode, he keeps saying, "I don't think we're supposed to be talking about this." This is because we want things that seem to be mutually exclusive—to acknowledge someone's difference but not be affected by it. Yet, how can we *not* be affected by something we notice and then think about?

The simple act of noticing that someone's ethnicity is different from your own creates an immediate otherness for both of you. Moreover, with this perception of otherness comes, perhaps, assumptions about that person and about yourself—that you are scarier or smarter or wealthier or poorer. In fact, in the history of America, the fact that we can and do see otherness in our fellow Americans has caused more hardship, violence, and death than we can even imagine.

Definitions of race are always changing.

In the late nineteenth and early twentieth centuries and to some extent afterwards, race and ethnicity were often conflated. For instance, at the turn of the century, Jews and Italians were considered racial groups (not ethnic groups). Similarly, fewer than fifty years ago, many places in the South considered anyone to be African American if they had an African American ancestor; this was called the "one-drop" rule. Because the vast majority of Americans do not think this way now, it may seem difficult to believe that this past existed, but understanding it is crucial in understanding contemporary notions of race and race theory.

As casinos bring more money, power, and prestige to American Indian reservations and communities, Indian identity has become an increasingly sensitive issue. For some tribes, one must have a certain "blood quantum" level and/or be an enrolled member of a tribe. A hundred years ago, someone with any amount of Indian blood could be imprisoned or killed, but now the same level of "Indianness" that could have gotten you killed in the 1800s might not be enough to enable you to become a member of a tribe.

Race, like gender and class, are fluid texts, so it is important *not* to assume too much about individuals or groups based on what they appear to be.

Although we claim to be nondiscriminatory now, discriminatory practices in the past have influenced the present social, political, economic, and cultural structure of our country.

This may seem like a highly political statement, and it is. However, the authors believe that discrimination in the past gave the white male majority a head start in this generation; race theorists call this phenomenon "white privilege." As you know, blacks, Asians, Hispanics, and Native Americans were frequently, if not regularly, denied admission to colleges, job interviews, loans, and access to restaurants and hotels and even basic medical service. Affirmative action, the idea that employers and schools should actively seek historically underrepresented individuals to fill their slots, is a response to this phenomenon by ensuring that minorities get fair consideration by employers and admission offices (for the most part, affirmative action does *not* involve a quota system, despite misconceptions popularly articulated). But the theory behind affirmative action, looking for ways to engage the past while living in the future in making decisions about schools and employment, is not only a government program but also a factor in admitting legacies to colleges, incorporating one's progeny into a family business, and so on. While preferential treatment may be decried as un-American in some quarters—after all, the Bill of Rights says all men are created equal—the fact is the past has always shaped how people are treated in the present.

What's more, generations of broken promises, abuses of power, and institutional discrimination and oppression have left some members of minority communities bitter toward institutions of power and law. People are smart. They know that history repeats itself; they know that the past is always present in some form or another. Thus, the reality of slavery, the history of American Indian genocide and removal, and the memory of Asian internment constitute a legacy that still affects how members of these groups see America and its institutions, and it is a legacy that contemporary America must take seriously.

Race, ethnicity, and gender are political constructions as well as social ones.

We now think of members of so-called races as political groups as well as social ones. If you read about politics, you will notice commentators talking about how a candidate was trying to "appeal to African Americans" or "appeal to women" (or more specific groupings like "soccer moms" or "the Catholic Latino vote"). The recognition that these groups have political power in one sense has empowered members of these groups and given them political power in ways they may not have had. However, of course, some people within these groups do not want to be identified as group members; it too easily reminds them of the way society constructs their identity negatively. For example, Toni Morrison, the Nobel Prize-winning author, has said that she does not want to be thought of as an African American writer but merely as a writer. The tendency, the need, in America to preface any such statement with the racial descriptor, goes to show how completely we see race and, perhaps, how often we cannot see past it.

Even more important, the goals of an ethnicity as a whole may not be those of the individual. In fact, it may be impossible to state, with any certainty, what the goals of any one ethnicity may be, as all people are complex and in the process of change. Supreme Court Judge Clarence Thomas will have very different ideas about what African Americans need than will the Reverend Jesse Jackson or Minister Louis Farrakhan, even though all are intelligent, upper class African American men. Which of the three best represents black Americans? That may depend on what group of black Americans you poll.

Stereotyping occurs as a result of our perceived view of racial or ethnic characteristics.

Unless you are the rare completely neutral human being, someone the authors feel does not exist, you attach stereotypes to groups—even if they seem like stereotypes that are positive, such as all professors are smart, nuns are nice, textbook authors are cool, and so on. You may also, without knowing it, hold negative stereotypes. The problem, of course, with all stereotypes is their propensity to attribute group characteristics to individuals. Believing all Jews are smart or all African Americans are athletic can have subsequent negative effects that balance out any positives.

How do we acquire our stereotypes? Some believe stereotypes are based on a grain of truth. That sort of thought makes the authors and others nervous, because the next logical step is thinking that traits or behaviors are inherent or natural. Researchers believe we pick up stereotypes in a variety of ways, including through popular culture and our upbringing. That is why we have stressed throughout this book the importance of looking for treatments of race and ethnicity as they appear—or do not appear—in texts.

There is also disturbing evidence that people mirror stereotyped expectations. As we discuss in the chapter on gender, mainstream American society has a tendency to punish those individuals who operate outside of the perceived norms of a certain group. Thus, stereotypes keep getting reinforced generation after generation, despite efforts from all groups to eradicate them. As the suite in this chapter suggests, many American Indian groups are frustrated by their inability to do much about the sanctioned stereotyping of Native Americans through sports mascots and nicknames. One wonders and worries about what messages these stereotypes send to both Native and non-Native communities—especially children. Similarly since 9/11 Arab Americans have had to face unfair suspicion and discrimination based on the radical behavior of a *very, very,* small number of extremists.

Your view of these issues probably depends on your personal relationships as well as political affiliation.

When surveying the landscape of these issues, we are likely to take our personal experiences and make them universal. If we are white and have African American friends or relatives, not only are we more likely to be more sympathetic to black causes, we are probably going to take the part of the whole for better or worse. If we have no friends of color, and our only exposure is through popular culture and our political affiliations, that too will shape the way we look at race and ethnicity. It is an overgeneralization to be sure, but the authors believe that proximity brings understanding in ways that reading about race and ethnicity can never bring. So does, we believe, actively thinking about the ways we construct race and ethnicity.

Sadly, in the United States, views on race are often influenced by financial concerns. We wonder about the number of people who are critical of immigrants from Latin American countries but whose standard of living relies on illegal immigrant labor. Similarly, in the 1800s, Asians suffered horrible forms of racism, but investors were eager to have them build railroads for almost no money.

Every bit of evidence suggests that racism is a learned behavior, which means that we are taught to *read* ethnicity. There is a famous scene on an episode of the television show *Montel*, when the children of black guests and white extremists are shown playing together in the Green Room. Despite such harmful lessons, personal relationships can often overcome flawed teaching and empty stereotyping.

Class is a more crucial element in American life than many people think.

Class also has similar connections to both self-identity and outside reality. Studies show most Americans believe they are middle class. And because there is no set way of determining what someone's class is, a person making $200,000 a year can call himself middle class; so can someone earning $20,000 a year. Are their lives different? Absolutely. However, they may not see that. Of course, class issues run through issues of race and ethnicity, in ways both simple and complex. Some researchers believe that race and ethnicity are mostly a class problem, with the members of ethnic groups disproportionately represented among the nation's poor. There probably is some validity to this claim. However, because the nation has had a long bloody history of clashes between ethnicities of the same class, it is hard to see class as the primary issue in racial or ethnic discrimination.

On the other hand, perceptions of reality can be as strong or stronger than reality itself, and in a capitalist country that tends to link economic prosperity with personal worth, the prevailing perceptions of what groups have more can shape how we see certain people. Thus, although class may not be the primary factor in racial discrimination, it is difficult when talking about race to separate it from issues of class. As this book goes to press, the website *Stuff White People Like* is turning into a cultural phenomenon. But, as many argue (including one of the authors of this book), the site is about what left-leaning yuppies like than, say, what blue collar whites from the deep south like. In other words, the site pretends to be about race, but it's really about class, and the assumptions Americans make about how class and race manifest.

The complicated nature of race and ethnicity is reflected here in the selections, which include a variety of perspectives and methodologies to consider.

THIS TEXT

1. While it will be impossible for you to know this fully, try to figure out the writing situation of each author. Who is the audience? What does the author have at stake? What is his or her agenda? *Why* is she or he writing this piece?

2. What social, political, and cultural forces affect the author's text? What is going on in the world as he or she is writing?

3. How does the author define race and ethnicity? Is the definition stated or unstated?

4. When taken as a whole, what do these texts tell you about how we construct race and ethnicity?

5. How do stories and essays differ in their arguments about race and ethnicity?

6. Is the author's argument valid and reasonable?

7. Ideas and beliefs about race and ethnicity tend to be very sensitive, deeply held convictions. Do you find yourself in agreement with the author? Why or why not? Do you agree with the editors' introduction?

8. Does the author help you *read* race and ethnicity better than you did before reading the essay? If so, why? How do we learn to read race and ethnicity?

9. Did you like this? Why or why not?

10. What role does science play in the essay?

BEYOND THIS TEXT: READING RACE AND ETHNICITY

Media: How are different ethnicities portrayed in the news or magazine articles? Is the author taking the "part for the whole" (talking to one member of a group as representative of all members of the group)?

Advertising: How are different ethnicities portrayed in the print or broadcast ad? Is there anything that "signals" their ethnicity—is clothing used as a "sign" of their color or identity? Is the advertiser using a "rainbow effect" in the ad, appearing to be inclusive by including multiple ethnicities? Does this effect seem forced or genuine?

Television: How are different ethnicities portrayed in a particular television show? Do they conform to predictable stereotypes? Are the people of color more than merely representative? Is there a lone African American or Hispanic American on a mostly white show? One white person on an African American dominated show? Are the members of different races allowed to date? Does their dating engage the idea of intergroup dating or ignore it?

Movies: How are different ethnicities portrayed in the movie? Do they conform to predictable stereotypes? Are the people of color the first to be targeted for death (if it's an action movie)? Are the people of color more than merely representative? Is there a lone African American or Hispanic American in a mostly white movie? One white person in an African American dominated movie? Are the members of different races allowed to date? Does their dating engage the idea of intergroup dating or ignore it?

In Living Color: Race and American Culture

Michael Omi

Michael Omi is a scholar who often writes about race and ethnicity. In this argumentative essay (1989), he takes on the stereotypes television "speaks" in when it talks about race and ethnicity.

IN FEBRUARY 1987, Assistant Attorney General William Bradford Reynolds, the nation's chief civil rights enforcer, declared that the recent death of a black man in Howard Beach, New York and the Ku Klux Klan attack on civil rights marchers in Forsyth County, Georgia were "isolated" racial incidences. He emphasized that the places where racial conflict could potentially flare up were "far fewer now than ever before in our history," and concluded that such a diminishment of racism stood as "a powerful testament to how far we have come in the civil rights struggle."[1]

Events in the months following his remarks raise the question as to whether we have come quite so far. They suggest that dramatic instances of racial tension and violence merely constitute the surface manifestations of a deeper racial organization of American society— a system of inequality which has shaped, and in turn been shaped by, our popular culture.

In March, the NAACP released a report on blacks in the record industry entitled "The Discordant Sound of Music." It found that despite the revenues generated by black performers, blacks remain "grossly underrepresented" in the business, marketing, and A&R (Artists and Repertoire) departments of major record labels. In addition, few blacks are employed as managers, agents, concert promoters, distributors, and retailers. The report concluded that:

> The record industry is overwhelmingly segregated and discrimination is rampant. No other industry in America so openly classifies its operations on a racial basis. At every level of the industry, beginning with the separation of black artists into a special category, barriers exist that severely limit opportunities for blacks.[2]

Decades after the passage of civil rights legislation and the affirmation of the principle of "equal opportunity," patterns of racial segregation and exclusion, it seems, continue to characterize the production of popular music.

The enduring logic of Jim Crow is also present in professional sports. In April, Al Campanis, vice president of player personnel for the Los Angeles Dodgers, explained to Ted Koppel on ABC's *Nightline* about the paucity of blacks in baseball front offices and as managers. "I truly believe," Campanis said, "that [blacks] may not have some of the necessities to be, let's say, a field manager or perhaps a general manager." When pressed for a reason, Campanis offered an explanation which had little to do with the structure of opportunity of institutional discrimination within professional sports:

> [W]hy are black men or black people not good swimmers? Because they don't have the buoyancy.... They are gifted with great musculature and various other things. They're fleet of foot. And this is why there are a lot of black major league ballplayers. Now as far as having the background to become club presidents, or presidents of a bank, I don't know.[3]

Black exclusion from the front office, therefore, was justified on the basis of biological "difference."

The issue of race, of course, is not confined to the institutional arrangements of popular culture production. Since popular culture deals with the symbolic realm of social life, the images which it creates, represents, and disseminates contribute to the overall racial climate. They become the subject of analysis and political scrutiny. In August, the National Ethnic Coalition of Organizations bestowed the "Golden Pit Awards" on television programs,

---

[1] Reynolds' remarks were made at a conference on equal opportunity held by the bar association in Orlando, Florida. *The San Francisco Chronicle* (February 7, 1987).

[2] Economic Development Department of the NAACP, "The Discordant Sound of Music (A Report on the Record Industry)," (Baltimore, Maryland: The NAACP, 1987), pp. 16–17.

[3] Campanis's remarks on *Nightline* were reprinted in *The San Francisco Chronicle* (April 9, 1987).

commercials, and movies that were deemed offensive to racial and ethnic groups: *Saturday Night Live*, regarded by many media critics as a politically "progressive" show, was singled out for the "Platinum Pit Award" for its comedy skit "Ching Chang" which depicted a Chinese storeowner and his family in a derogatory manner.[4]

These examples highlight the *overt* manifestations of racism in popular culture—institutional forms of discrimination which keep racial minorities out of the production and organization of popular culture, and the crude racial caricatures by which these groups are portrayed. Yet racism in popular culture is often conveyed in a variety of implicit, and at times invisible, ways. Political theorist Stuart Hall makes an important distinction between *overt* racism, the elaboration of an explicitly racist argument, policy, or view, and *inferential* racism which refers to "those apparently naturalized representations of events and situations relating to race, whether 'factual' or 'fictional,' which have racist premises and propositions inscribed in them as a set of *unquestioned assumptions*." He argues that inferential racism is more widespread, common, and indeed insidious since "it is largely *invisible* even to those who formulate the world in its terms."[5]

Race itself is a slippery social concept which is paradoxically both "obvious" and "invisible." In our society, one of the first things we notice about people when we encounter them (along with their sex/gender) is their *race*. We utilize race to provide clues about *who* a person is and *how* we should relate to her/him. Our perception of race determines our "presentation of *self*," distinctions in status, and appropriate modes of conduct in daily and institutional life. This process is often unconscious; we tend to operate off of an unexamined set of *racial beliefs*.

Racial beliefs account for and explain variations in "human nature." Differences in skin color and other obvious physical characteristics supposedly provide visible clues to more substantive differences lurking underneath. Among other qualities, temperament, sexuality, intelligence, and artistic and athletic ability are presumed to be fixed and discernible from the palpable mark of race. Such diverse questions as our confidence and trust in others (as salespeople, neighbors, media figures); our sexual preferences and romantic images; our tastes in music, film, dance, or sports; indeed our very ways of walking and talking are ineluctably shaped by notions of race.

Ideas about race, therefore, have become "common sense"—a way of comprehending, explaining, and acting in the world. This is made painfully obvious when someone disrupts our common sense understandings. An encounter with someone who is, for example, racially "mixed" or of a racial/ethnic group we are unfamiliar with becomes a source of discomfort for us, and momentarily creates a crisis of racial meaning. We also become disoriented when people do not act "black," "Latino," or indeed "white." The content of such stereotypes reveals a series of unsubstantiated beliefs about who these groups are, what they are like, and how they behave.

The existence of such racial consciousness should hardly be surprising. Even prior to the inception of the republic, the United States was a society shaped by racial conflict. The establishment of the Southern plantation economy, Western expansion, and the emergence of the labor movement, among other significant historical developments, have all involved conflicts over the definition and nature of the *color line*. The historical results have been distinct and different groups have encountered unique forms of racial oppression—Native

---

[4] Ellen Wulfhorst, "TV Sterotyping: It's the 'Pits,'" *The San Francisco Chronicle* (August 24, 1987).
[5] Stuart Hall, "The Whites of Their Eyes: Racist Ideologies and the Media," in George Bridges and Rosalind Brunt, eds., *Silver Linings* (London: Lawrence and Wishart, 1981), pp. 36–37.

Americans faced genocide, blacks were subjected to slavery, Mexicans were invaded and colonized, and Asians faced exclusion. What is common to the experiences of these groups is that their particular "fate" was linked to historically specific ideas about the significance and meaning of race.[6] Whites defined them as separate "species," ones inferior to Northern European cultural stocks, and thereby rationalized the conditions of their subordination in the economy, in political life, and in the realm of culture.

A crucial dimension of racial oppression in the United States is the elaboration of an ideology of difference or "otherness." This involves defining "us" (i.e., white Americans) in opposition to "them," an important task when distinct racial groups are first encountered, or in historically specific periods where preexisting racial boundaries are threatened or crumbling.

Political struggles over the very definition of who an "American" is illustrates this process. The Naturalization Law of 1790 declared that only free *white* immigrants could qualify, reflecting the initial desire among Congress to create and maintain a racially homogeneous society. The extension of eligibility to all racial groups has been a long and protracted process. Japanese, for example, were finally eligible to become naturalized citizens after the passage of the Walter–McCarran Act of 1952. The ideological residue of these restrictions in naturalization and citizenship laws is the equation within popular parlance of the term "American" with "white," while other "Americans" are described as black, Mexican, "Oriental," etc.

Popular culture has been an important realm within which racial ideologies have been created, reproduced, and sustained. Such ideologies provide a framework of symbols, concepts, and images through which we understand, interpret, and represent aspects of our "racial" existence.

Race has often formed the central themes of American popular culture. Historian W. L. Rose notes that it is "curious coincidence" that four of the "most popular reading-viewing events in all American history" have in some manner dealt with race, specifically black/white relations in the south.[7] Harriet Beecher Stowe's *Uncle Tom's Cabin*, Thomas Ryan Dixon's *The Clansman* (the inspiration for D. W. Griffith's *The Birth of a Nation*), Margaret Mitchell's *Gone with the Wind* (as a book and film), and Alex Haley's *Roots* (as a book and television miniseries), each appeared at a critical juncture in American race relations and helped to shape new understandings of race.

Emerging social definitions of race and the "real American" were reflected in American popular culture of the nineteenth century. Racial and ethnic stereotypes were shaped and reinforced in the newspapers, magazines, and pulp fiction of the period. But the evolution and ever-increasing sophistication of visual mass communications throughout the twentieth century provided, and continue to provide, the most dramatic means by which racial images are generated and reproduced.

Film and television have been notorious in disseminating images of racial minorities which establish for audiences what these groups look like, how they behave, and, in essence, "who they are." The power of the media lies not only in their ability to reflect the dominant racial ideology, but in their capacity to shape that ideology in the first place. D. W. Griffith's aforementioned epic *Birth of a Nation*, a sympathetic treatment of the rise of the Ku Klux Klan during Reconstruction, helped to generate, consolidate, and "nationalize" images of

---

[6] For an excellent survey of racial beliefs see Thomas F. Gossett, *Race: The History of an Idea in America* (New York: Shocken Books, 1965).

[7] W. L. Rose, Race and *Region in American Historical Fiction: Four Episodes in Popular Culture* (Oxford: Clarendon Press, 1979).

blacks which had been more disparate (more regionally specific, for example) prior to the film's appearance.[8]

In television and film, the necessity to define characters in the briefest and most condensed manner has led to the perpetuation of racial caricatures, as racial stereotypes serve as shorthand for scriptwriters, directors, and actors. Television's tendency to address the "lowest common denominator" in order to render programs "familiar" to an enormous and diverse audience leads it regularly to assign and reassign racial characteristics to particular groups, both minority and majority.

Many of the earliest American films deal with racial and ethnic "difference." The large influx of "new immigrants" at the turn of the century led to a proliferation of negative images of Jews, Italians, and Irish which were assimilated and adapted by such films as Thomas Edison's *Cohen's Advertising Scheme* (1904). Based on an old vaudeville routine, the film featured a scheming Jewish merchant, aggressively hawking his wares. Though stereotypes of these groups persist to this day,[9] by the 1940s many of the earlier ethnic stereotypes had disappeared from Hollywood. But, as historian Michael Winston observes, the outsiders of the 1890s remained: the ever-popular Indian of the Westerns; the inscrutable or sinister Oriental; the sly, but colorful Mexican; and the clowning or submissive Negro.[10]

In many respects the Western as a genre has been paradigmatic in establishing images of racial minorities in film and television. The classic scenario involves the encircled wagon train or surrounded fort from which whites bravely fight off fierce bands of Native American Indians. The point of reference and viewer identification lies with those huddled within the circle the representatives of civilization who valiantly attempt to ward off the forces of barbarism. In the classic Western, as writer Tom Engelhardt observes, the viewer is forced behind the barrel of a repeating rifle and it is from that position, through its gun sights, that he receives a picture history of Western colonialism and imperialism.[11]

Westerns have indeed become the prototype for European and American excursions throughout the Third World. The cast of characters may change, but the story remains the same. The humanity of whites is contrasted with the brutality and treachery of nonwhites; brave (i.e., white) souls are pitted against the merciless hordes in conflicts ranging from Indians against the British Lancers to Zulus against the Boers. What Stuart Hall refers to as the imperializing white eye provides the framework for these films, lurking outside the frame and yet seeing and positioning everything within; it is the unmarked position from which observations are made and from which, alone, they make sense.[12]

Our common sense assumptions about race and racial minorities in the United States are both generated and reflected in the stereotypes presented by the visual media. In the crudest sense, it could be said that such stereotypes underscore white superiority by reinforcing the traits, habits, and predispositions of nonwhites which demonstrate their

---

[8]Melanie Martindale-Sikes, "Nationalizing 'Nigger' Imagery Through *Birth of a Nation*," paper prepared for the 73rd Annual Meeting of the American Sociological Association (September 4–8, 1978) in San Francisco.

[9]For a discussion of Italian, Irish, Jewish, Slavic, and German stereotypes in film, see Randall M. Miller, ed., *The Kaleidoscopic Lens: How Hollywood Views Ethnic Groups* (Englewood, N.J.: Jerome S. Ozer, 1980).

[10]Michael R. Winston, "Racial Consciousness and the Evolution of Mass Communications in the United States," *Daedalus*, Vol. III, No. 4 (Fall 1982).

[11]Tom Engelhardt, "Ambush at Kamikaze Pass," in Emma Gee, ed., *Counterpoint: Perspectives on Asian America* (Los Angeles: Asian American Studies Center, UCLA, 1976), p. 270.

[12]Hall, "Whites of Their Eyes," p. 38.

inferiority. Yet a more careful assessment of racial stereotypes reveals intriguing trends and seemingly contradictory themes.

While all racial minorities have been portrayed as less than human, there are significant differences in the images of different groups. Specific racial minority groups, in spite of their often interchangeable presence in films steeped in the Western paradigm, have distinct and often unique qualities assigned to them. Latinos are portrayed as being prone toward violent outbursts of anger; blacks as physically strong, but dim-witted; while Asians are seen as sneaky and cunningly evil. Such differences are crucial to observe and analyze. Race in the United States is not reducible to black/white relations. These differences are significant for a broader understanding of the patterns of race in America, and the unique experience of specific racial minority groups.

It is somewhat ironic that *real* differences which exist within a racially defined minority group are minimized, distorted, or obliterated by the media. All Asians look alike, the saying goes, and indeed there has been little or no attention given to the vast differences which exist between, say, the Chinese and Japanese with respect to food, dress, language, and culture. This blurring within popular culture has given us supposedly Chinese characters who wear kimonos; it is also the reason why the fast-food restaurant McDonald's can offer Shanghai McNuggets with teriyaki sauce. Other groups suffer a similar fate. Professor Gretchen Bataille and Charles Silet find the cinematic Native American of the Northeast wearing the clothing of the Plains Indians, while living in the dwellings of Southwestern tribes:

The movie men did what thousands of years of social evolution could not do, even what the threat of the encroaching white man could not do; Hollywood produced the homogenized Native American, devoid of tribal characteristics or regional differences.[13]

The need to paint in broad racial strokes has thus rendered "internal" differences invisible. This has been exacerbated by the tendency for screenwriters to "invent" mythical Asian, Latin American, and African countries. Ostensibly done to avoid offending particular nations and peoples, such a subterfuge reinforces the notion that all the countries and cultures of a specific region are the same. European countries retain their distinctiveness, while the Third World is presented as one homogeneous mass riddled with poverty and governed by ruthless and corrupt regimes.

While rendering specific groups in a monolithic fashion, the popular cultural imagination simultaneously reveals a compelling need to distinguish and articulate "bad" and "good" variants of particular racial groups and individuals. Thus each stereotypic image is filled with contradictions: The bloodthirsty Indian is tempered with the image of the noble savage; the *bandido* exists along with the loyal sidekick; and Fu Manchu is offset by Charlie Chan. The existence of such contradictions, however, does not negate the one-dimensionality of these images, nor does it challenge the explicit subservient role of racial minorities. Even the "good" person of color usually exists as a foil in novels and films to underscore the intelligence, courage, and virility of the white male hero.

Another important, perhaps central, dimension of racial minority stereotypes is sex/gender differentiation. The connection between race and sex has traditionally been an explosive and controversial one. For most of American history, sexual and marital relations between whites and nonwhites were forbidden by social custom and by legal restrictions. It was not until 1967, for example, that the U.S. Supreme Court ruled that antimiscegenation laws were unconstitu-

---

[13]Gretchen Bataille and Charles Silet, "The Entertaining Anachronism: Indians in American Film," in Randall M. Miller, ed., *Kaleidoscopic Lens*, p. 40.

tional. Beginning in the 1920s, the notorious Hays Office, Hollywood's attempt at self-censorship, prohibited scenes and subjects which dealt with miscegenation. The prohibition, however, was not evenly applied in practice. White men could seduce racial minority women, but white women were not to be romantically or sexually linked to racial minority men.

Women of color were sometimes treated as exotic sex objects. The sultry Latin temptress—such as Dolores Del Rio and Lupe Velez—invariably had boyfriends who were white North Americans; their Latino suitors were portrayed as being unable to keep up with the Anglo-American competition. From Mary Pickford as Cho-Cho San in *Madame Butterfly* (1915) to Nancy Kwan in *The World of Suzie Wong* (1961), Asian women have often been seen as the gracious "geisha girl" or the prostitute with a "heart of gold," willing to do anything to please her man.

By contrast, Asian men, whether cast in the role of villain, servant, sidekick, or kung fu master, are seen as asexual or, at least, romantically undesirable. As Asian American studies professor Elaine Kim notes, even a hero such as Bruce Lee played characters whose "single-minded focus on perfecting his fighting skills precludes all other interests, including an interest in women, friendship, or a social life."[14]

The shifting trajectory of black images over time reveals an interesting dynamic with respect to sex and gender. The black male characters in *The Birth of a Nation* were clearly presented as sexual threats to "white womanhood." For decades afterwards, however, Hollywood consciously avoided portraying black men as assertive or sexually aggressive in order to minimize controversy. Black men were instead cast as comic, harmless, and nonthreatening figures exemplified by such stars as Bill "Bojangles" Robinson, Stepin Fetchit, and Eddie "Rochester" Anderson. Black women, by contrast, were divided into two broad character types based on color categories. Dark black women such as Hattie McDaniel and Louise Beavers were cast as "dowdy, frumpy, dumpy, overweight mammy figures"; while those "close to the white ideal," such as Lena Horne and Dorothy Dandridge, became "Hollywood's treasured mulattoes" in roles emphasizing the tragedy of being of mixed blood.[15]

It was not until the early 1970s that tough, aggressive, sexually assertive black characters, both male and female, appeared. The "blaxploitation" films of the period provided new heroes (e.g., *Shaft, Superfly, Coffy,* and *Cleopatra Jones*) in sharp contrast to the submissive and subservient images of the past. Unfortunately, most of these films were shoddy productions which did little to create more enduring "positive" images of blacks, either male or female.

In contemporary television and film, there is a tendency to present and equate racial minority groups and individuals with specific social problems. Blacks are associated with drugs and urban crime, Latinos with "illegal" immigration, while Native Americans cope with alcoholism and tribal conflicts. Rarely do we see racial minorities "out of character," in situations removed from the stereotypic arenas in which scriptwriters have traditionally embedded them. Nearly the only time we see young Asians and Latinos of either sex, for example, is when they are members of youth gangs, as *Boulevard Nights* (1979), *Year of the Dragon* (1985), and countless TV cop shows can attest to.

Racial minority actors have continually bemoaned the fact that the roles assigned them on stage and screen are often one-dimensional and imbued with stereotypic assumptions. In theater, the movement toward "blind casting" (i.e., casting actors for roles without regard

---

[14] Elaine Kim, "Asian Americans and American Popular Culture" in Hyung-Chan Kim, ed., *Dictionary of Asian American History* (New York: Greenwood Press, 1986), p. 107.
[15] Donald Bogle, "A Familiar Plot (A Look at the History of Blacks in American Movies)," *The Crisis*, Vol. 90, No. 1 (January 1983), p. 15.

to race) is a progressive step, but it remains to be seen whether large numbers of audiences can suspend their "beliefs" and deal with a Latino King Lear or an Asian Stanley Kowalski. By contrast, white actors are allowed to play anybody. Though the use of white actors to play blacks in "black face" is clearly unacceptable in the contemporary period, white actors continue to portray Asian, Latino, and Native American characters on stage and screen.

Scores of Charlie Chan films, for example, have been made with white leads (the last one was the 1981 *Charlie Chan and the Curse of the Dragon Queen*). Roland Winters, who played Chan in six features, was once asked to explain the logic of casting a white man in the role of Charlie Chan: "The only thing I can think of is, if you want to cast a homosexual in a show, and you get a homosexual, it'll be awful. It won't be funny ... and maybe there's something there."[16]

Such a comment reveals an interesting aspect about myth and reality in popular culture. Michael Winston argues that stereotypic images in the visual media were not originally conceived as representations of reality, nor were they initially understood to be "real" by audiences. They were, he suggests, ways of "coding and rationalizing" the racial hierarchy and interracial behavior. Over time, however, "a complex interactive relationship between myth and reality developed, so that images originally understood to be unreal, through constant repetition began to *seem* real."[17]

Such a process consolidated, among other things, our "common sense" understandings of what we think various groups should look like. Such presumptions have led to tragicomical results. Latinos auditioning for a role in a television soap opera, for example, did not fit the Hollywood image of "real Mexicans" and had their faces bronzed with powder before filming because they looked too white. Model Aurora Garza said, "I'm a real Mexican and very dark anyway. I'm even darker right now because I have a tan. But they kept wanting to make my face darker and darker."[18]

Historically in Hollywood, the fact of having "dark skin" made an actor or actress potentially adaptable for numerous "racial" roles. Actress Lupe Velez once commented that she had portrayed "Chinese, Eskimos, Japs, squaws, Hindus, Swedes, Malays, and Japanese."[19] Dorothy Dandridge, who was the first black woman teamed romantically with white actors, presented a quandary for studio executives who weren't sure what race and nationality to make her. They debated whether she should be a "foreigner," an island girl, or a West Indian.[20] Ironically, what they refused to entertain as a possibility was to present her as what she really was, a black American woman.

The importance of race in popular culture is not restricted to the visual media. In popular music, race and race consciousness has defined, and continues to define, formats, musical communities, and tastes. In the mid-1950s, the secretary of the North Alabama White Citizens Council declared that "Rock and roll is a means of pulling the white man down to the level of the Negro."[21] While rock may no longer be popularly regarded as a racially subversive musical form, the very genres of contemporary popular music remain, in essence, thinly veiled racial categories. "R & B" (Rhythm and Blues) and "soul" music are clearly references to *black* music, while

---

[16] Frank Chin, "Confessions of the Chinatown Cowboy," *Bulletin of Concerned Asian Scholars*, Vol. 4, No. 3 (Fall 1972).

[17] Winston, "Racial Consciousness," p. 176.

[18] *The San Francisco Chronicle*, September 21, 1984.

[19] Quoted in Allen L. Woll, "Bandits and Lovers: Hispanic Images in American Film," in Miller, ed., *Kaleidoscopic Lens*, p. 60.

[20] Bogle, "Familiar Plot," p. 17.

[21] Dave Marsh and Kevin Stein, *The Book of Rock Lists* (New York: Dell Publishing Co., 1981), p. 8.

Country & Western or heavy metal music are viewed, in the popular imagination, as *white* music. Black performers who want to break out of this artistic ghettoization must "cross over," a contemporary form of "passing" in which their music is seen as acceptable to white audiences.

The airwaves themselves are segregated. The designation "urban contemporary" is merely radio lingo for a "black" musical format. Such categorization affects playlists, advertising accounts, and shares of the listening market. On cable television, black music videos rarely receive airplay on MTV, but are confined instead to the more marginal BET (Black Entertainment Television) network.

In spite of such segregation, many performing artists have been able to garner a racially diverse group of fans. And yet, racially integrated concert audiences are extremely rare. Curiously, this "perverse phenomenon" of racially homogeneous crowds takes place despite the color of the performer. Lionel Richie's concert audiences, for example, are virtually all-white, while Teena Marie's are all-black.[22]

Racial symbols and images are omnipresent in popular culture. Commonplace household objects such as cookie jars, salt and pepper shakers, and ashtrays have frequently been designed and fashioned in the form of racial caricatures. Sociologist Steve Dublin in an analysis of these objects found that former tasks of domestic service were symbolically transferred onto these commodities.[23] An Aunt Jemima-type character, for example, is used to hold a roll of paper towels, her outstretched hands supporting the item to be dispensed. "Sprinkle Plenty," a sprinkle bottle in the shape of an Asian man, was used to wet clothes in preparation for ironing. Simple commodities, the household implements which help us perform everyday tasks, may reveal, therefore, a deep structure of racial meaning.

A crucial dimension for discerning the meaning of particular stereotypes and images is the *situation context* for the creation and consumption of popular culture. For example, the setting in which "racist" jokes are told determines the function of humor. Jokes about blacks where the teller and audience are black constitute a form of self-awareness; they allow blacks to cope and "take the edge off" of oppressive aspects of the social order which they commonly confront. The meaning of these same jokes, however, is dramatically transformed when told across the "color line." If a white, or even black, person tells these jokes to a white audience, it will, despite its "purely" humorous intent, serve to reinforce stereotypes and rationalize the existing relations of racial inequality.

Concepts of race and racial images are both overt and implicit within popular culture—the organization of cultural production, the products themselves, and the manner in which they are consumed are deeply structured by race. Particular racial meanings, stereotypes, and myths can change, but the presence of a system of racial meanings and stereotypes, of racial ideology, seems to be an enduring aspect of American popular culture.

The era of Reaganism and the overall rightward drift of American politics and culture has added a new twist to the question of racial images and meanings. Increasingly, the problem for racial minorities is not that of misportrayal, but of "invisibility." Instead of celebrating racial and cultural diversity, we are witnessing an attempt by the right to define, once again, who the "real" American is, and what "correct" American values, mores, and political beliefs are. In such a context, racial minorities are no longer the focus of sustained media attention; when they do appear, they are cast as colored versions of essentially "white" characters.

---

[22] Rock & Roll Confidential, No. 44 (February 1987), p. 2.
[23] Steven C. Dublin, "Symbolic Slavery: Black Representations in Popular Culture," *Social Problems*, Vol. 34, No. 2 (April 1987).

The possibilities for change—for transforming racial stereotypes and challenging institutional inequities—nonetheless exist. Historically, strategies have involved the mobilization of political pressure against an offending institution(s). In the late 1950s, for instance, "Nigger Hair" tobacco changed its name to "Bigger Hare" due to concerted NAACP pressure on the manufacturer. In the early 1970s, Asian American community groups successfully fought NBC's attempt to resurrect Charlie Chan as a television series with white actor Ross Martin. Amidst the furor generated by Al Campanis's remarks cited at the beginning of this essay, Jesse Jackson suggested that a boycott of major league games be initiated in order to push for a restructuring of hiring and promotion practices.

Partially in response to such action, Baseball Commissioner Peter Ueberroth announced plans in June 1987 to help put more racial minorities in management roles. "The challenge we have," Ueberroth said, "is to manage change without losing tradition."[24] The problem with respect to the issue of race and popular culture, however, is that the *tradition* itself may need to be thoroughly examined, its "common sense" assumptions unearthed and challenged, and its racial images contested and transformed.

READING WRITING

This Text: Reading

1. Omi's work engages popular culture actively and takes it seriously. Why do you think Omi thinks television is important to write about?
2. From what perspective is Omi writing? Do you think the problems he identifies in 1987 are still around today?
3. Who do you think is Omi's intended audience? Do you think they watch television?

Your Text: Writing

1. Watch an evening of television and note the presence of race and ethnicity. Do the same issues come up? Do you think things have changed since 1987? Why or why not? Write a paper assessing the status of race and ethnicity in American television, focusing either on a particular show or evening of television.
2. What stereotypes generally remain present in American television? Are the same stereotypes present in American movies? If stereotypes in movies and television are different, what differences between the two media do you think account for the difference in portrayals?
3. Take a television show you like and note how it treats those of different ethnicities. Do these portrayals show an understanding of members of these groups or rely on previously held ideas about them?

Mother Tongue

Amy Tan

Amy Tan is the well-known author of *The Joy Luck Club* and other novels. In this 1991 piece, she writes about her experiences with her mother and her mother's use of language.

I AM NOT A SCHOLAR OF ENGLISH OR LITERATURE. I cannot give you much more than personal opinions on the English language and its variations in this country or others.

---

[24] *The San Francisco Chronicle* (June 13, 1987).

I am a writer. And by that definition, I am someone who has always loved language. I am fascinated by language in daily life. I spend a great deal of my time thinking about the power of language—the way it can evoke an emotion, a visual image, a complex idea, or a simple truth. Language is the tool of my trade. And I use them all—all the Englishes I grew up with.

Recently, I was made keenly aware of the different Englishes I do use. I was giving a talk to a large group of people, the same talk I had already given to half a dozen other groups. The nature of the talk was about my writing, my life, and my book, *The Joy Luck Club*. The talk was going along well enough, until I remembered one major difference that made the whole talk sound wrong. My mother was in the room. And it was perhaps the first time she had heard me give a lengthy speech, using the kind of English I have never used with her. I was saying things like, "The intersection of memory upon imagination" and "There is an aspect of my fiction that relates to thus-and-thus"—a speech filled with carefully wrought grammatical phrases, burdened, it suddenly seemed to me, with nominalized forms, past perfect tenses, conditional phrases, all the forms of standard English that I had learned in school and through books, the forms of English I did not use at home with my mother.

Just last week, I was walking down the street with my mother, and I again found myself conscious of the English I was using, the English I do use with her. We were talking about the price of new and used furniture and I heard myself saying this: "Not waste money that way." My husband was with us as well, and he didn't notice any switch in my English. And then I realized why. It's because over the twenty years we've been together I've often used that same kind of English with him, and sometimes he even uses it with me. It has become our language of intimacy, a different sort of English that relates to family talk, the language I grew up with.

So you'll have some idea of what this family talk I heard sounds like, I'll quote what my mother said during a recent conversation which I videotaped and then transcribed. During this conversation, my mother was talking about a political gangster in Shanghai who had the same last name as her family's, Du, and how the gangster in his early years wanted to be adopted by her family, which was rich by comparison. Later, the gangster became more powerful, far richer than my mother's family, and one day showed up at my mother's wedding to pay his respects. Here's what she said in part: "Du Yusong having business like fruit stand. Like off the street kind. He is Du like Du Zong—but not Tsung-ming Island people. The local people call putong, the river east side, he belong to that side local people. That man want to ask Du Zong father take him in like become own family. Du Zong father wasn't look down on him, but didn't take seriously, until that man big like become a mafia. Now important person, very hard to inviting him. Chinese way, came only to show respect, don't stay for dinner. Respect for making big celebration, he shows up. Mean gives lots of respect. Chinese custom. Chinese social life that way. If too important won't have to stay too long. He come to my wedding. I didn't see, I heard it. I gone to boy's side, they have YMCA dinner. Chinese age I was nineteen."

You should know that my mother's expressive command of English belies how much she actually understands. She reads the *Forbes* report, listens to *Wall Street Week*, converses daily with her stockbroker, reads all of Shirley MacLaine's books with ease—all kinds of things I can't begin to understand. Yet some of my friends tell me they understand 50 percent of what my mother says. Some say they understand 80 to 90 percent. Some say they understand none of it, as if she were speaking pure Chinese. But to me, my mother's English is perfectly clear, perfectly natural. It's my mother tongue. Her language, as I hear it, is vivid, direct, full of observation and imagery. That was the language that helped shape the way I saw things, expressed things, made sense of the world.

Lately, I've been giving more thought to the kind of English my mother speaks. Like others, I have described it to people as "broken" or "fractured" English. But I wince when I say that. It has always bothered me that I can think of no way to describe it other than "broken," as if it were damaged and needed to be fixed, as if it lacked a certain wholeness and soundness. I've heard other terms used, "limited English," for example. But they seem just as bad, as if everything is limited, including people's perceptions of the limited English speaker.

I know this for a fact, because when I was growing up, my mother's "limited" English limited my perception of her. I was ashamed of her English. I believed that her English reflected the quality of what she had to say. That is, because she expressed them imperfectly her thoughts were imperfect. And I had plenty of empirical evidence to support me: the fact that people in department stores, at banks, and at restaurants did not take her seriously, did not give her good service, pretended not to understand her, or even acted as if they did not hear her.

My mother has long realized the limitations of her English as well. When I was fifteen, she used to have me call people on the phone to pretend I was she. In this guise, I was forced to ask for information or even to complain and yell at people who had been rude to her. One time it was a call to her stockbroker in New York. She had cashed out her small portfolio and it just so happened we were going to go to New York the next week, our very first trip outside California. I had to get on the phone and say in an adolescent voice that was not very convincing, "This is Mrs. Tan."

And my mother was standing in the back whispering loudly, "Why he don't send me check, already two weeks late. So mad he lie to me, losing me money."

And then I said in perfect English, "Yes, I'm getting rather concerned. You had agreed to send the check two weeks ago, but it hasn't arrived."

Then she began to talk more loudly. "What he want, I come to New York tell him front of his boss, you cheating me?" And I was trying to calm her down, make her be quiet, while telling the stockbroker, "I can't tolerate any more excuses. If I don't receive the check immediately, I am going to have to speak to your manager when I'm in New York next week." And sure enough, the following week there we were in front of this astonished stockbroker, and I was sitting there red-faced and quiet, and my mother, the real Mrs. Tan, was shouting at his boss in her impeccable broken English.

We used a similar routine just five days ago, for a situation that was far less humorous. My mother had gone to the hospital for an appointment, to find out about a benign brain tumor a CAT scan had revealed a month ago. She said she had spoken very good English, her best English, no mistakes. Still, she said, the hospital did not apologize when they said they had lost the CAT scan and she had come for nothing. She said they did not seem to have any sympathy when she told them she was anxious to know the exact diagnosis, since her husband and son had both died of brain tumors. She said they would not give her any more information until the next time and she would have to make another appointment for that. So she said she would not leave until the doctor called her daughter. She wouldn't budge. And when the doctor finally called her daughter, me, who spoke in perfect English—lo and behold—we had assurances the CAT scan would be found, promises that a conference call on Monday would be held, and apologies for any suffering my mother had gone through for a most regrettable mistake.

I think my mother's English almost had an effect on limiting my possibilities in life as well. Sociologists and linguists probably will tell you that a person's developing language skills are more influenced by peers. But I do think that the language spoken in the family, especially in immigrant families which are more insular, plays a large role in shaping the language of the child. And I believe that it affected my results on achievement tests, IQ tests, and the SAT. While my English skills were never judged as poor, compared to math, English could not be considered my strong suit. In grade school I did moderately well, getting perhaps B's, sometimes B-pluses, in English and scoring perhaps in the sixtieth or seventieth percentile on achievement tests. But those scores were not good enough to override the opinion that my true abilities lay in math and science, because in those areas I achieved A's and scored in the ninetieth percentile or higher.

This was understandable. Math is precise; there is only one correct answer. Whereas, for me at least, the answers on English tests were always a judgment call, a matter of opinion and personal experience. Those tests were constructed around items like fill-in-the-blank sentence completion, such as, "Even though Tom was _____, Mary thought he was _____." And the correct answer always seemed to be the most bland combinations of thoughts, for example, "Even though Tom was shy, Mary thought he was charming," with the grammatical structure "even though" limiting the correct answer to some sort of semantic opposites, so you wouldn't get answers like, "Even though Tom was foolish, Mary thought he was ridiculous." Well, according to my mother, there were very few limitations as to what Tom could have been and what Mary might have thought of him. So I never did well on tests like that.

The same was true with word analogies, pairs of words in which you were supposed to find some sort of logical, semantic relationship—for example, "Sunset is to nightfall as _____ is to _____ ." And here you would be presented with a list of four possible pairs, one of which showed the same kind of relationship: red is to stoplight, bus is to arrival, chills is to fever, yawn is to boring. Well, I could never think that way. I knew what the tests were asking, but I could not block out of my mind the images already created by the first pair, "sunset is to nightfall"—and I would see a burst of colors against a darkening sky, the moon rising, the lowering of a curtain of stars. And all the other pairs of words—red, bus, stoplight, boring—just threw up a mass of confusing images, making it impossible for me to sort out something as logical as saying: "A sunset precedes nightfall" is the same as "a chill precedes a fever." The only way I would have gotten that answer right would have been to imagine an associative situation, for example, my being disobedient and staying out past sunset, catching a chill at night, which turns into feverish pneumonia as punishment, which indeed did happen to me.

I have been thinking about all this lately, about my mother's English, about achievement tests. Because lately I've been asked, as a writer, why there are not more Asian Americans represented in American literature. Why are there few Asian Americans enrolled in creative writing programs? Why do so many Chinese students go into engineering? Well, these are broad sociological questions I can't begin to answer. But I have noticed in surveys—in fact, just last week—that Asian students, as a whole, always do significantly better on math achievement tests than in English. And this makes me think that there are other Asian-American students whose English spoken in the home might also be described as "broken" or "limited." And perhaps they also have teachers who are steering them away from writing and into math and science, which is what happened to me.

Fortunately, I happen to be rebellious in nature and enjoy the challenge of disproving assumptions made about me. I became an English major my first year in college, after being enrolled as pre-med. I started writing nonfiction as a freelancer the week after I was told by my former boss that writing was my worst skill and I should hone my talents toward account management.

But it wasn't until 1985 that I finally began to write fiction. And at first I wrote using what I thought to be wittily crafted sentences, sentences that would finally prove I had mastery over the English language. Here's an example from the first draft of a story that later made its way into *The Joy Luck Club*, but without this line: "That was my mental quandary in its nascent state." A terrible line, which I can barely pronounce.

Fortunately, for reasons I won't get into today, I later decided I should envision a reader for the stories I would write. And the reader I decided upon was my mother, because these were stories about mothers. So with this reader in mind—and in fact she did read my early drafts—I began to write stories using all the Englishes I grew up with: the English I spoke to my mother, which for lack of a better term might be described as "simple"; the English she used with me, which for lack of a better term might be described as "broken"; my translation of her Chinese, which could certainly be described as "watered down"; and what I imagined to be her translation of her Chinese if she could speak in perfect English, her internal language, and for that I sought to preserve the essence, but neither an English nor a Chinese structure. I wanted to capture what language ability tests can never reveal: her intent, her passion, her imagery, the rhythms of her speech and the nature of her thoughts.

Apart from what any critic had to say about my writing, I knew I had succeeded where it counted when my mother finished reading my book and gave me her verdict: "So easy to read."

READING WRITING

This Text: Reading

1. Tan points out that language is a sign for others trying to read her mother. What other nonvisual elements might be signs? How do we normally read them?
2. Talk about the way we discuss or react to people with accents. Why do accents mark, or set off as different, people? Is there any established non-marked way of speaking? Who speaks this way?
3. How do you think Tan feels about the situation in which she is placed by having to serve as her mother's "agent"? Is there a way around it?

Your Text: Writing

1. Write an essay talking about ways we mark people as different through non-visual means through popular culture. What forms of popular culture are especially guilty of this?
2. One of the things that Tan's essay brings up is the idea of Americanness. How should we define such a concept? Are there degrees of Americanness? Research and see what others say about this.
3. In what way is this piece an argument? What is Tan arguing? In your own work, use a story to argue a particular point.

True Tales of Amerikkkan History Part II: The True Thanksgiving

Jim Mahfood

Jim Mahfood is a comic artist who often takes on stereotypes and race in his work. Here is his 1998 response to popular ideas about Thanksgiving.

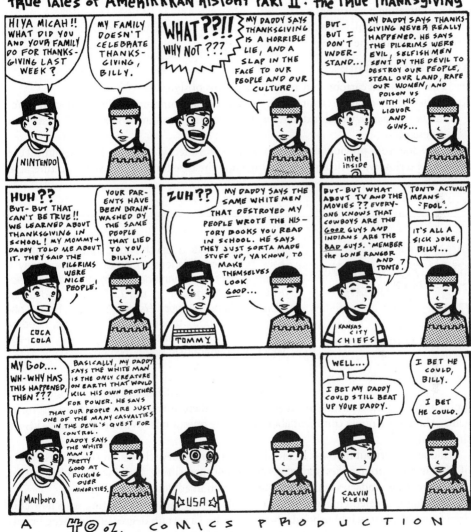

Source: *Stupid Comics* © 1998 by Jim Mahfood

READING WRITING

This Text: Reading

1. If you have read Scott McCloud's piece, what do you think he would say about this cartoon? In what ways does the reader participate in making meaning here?
2. Compare Mahfood's approach to those taken in this chapter's suite.
3. What other subtext does Mahfood address with the boy's T-shirt? With the girl's Native American garb? Are these relevant to the main storyline? Why or why not?
4. What perspective do you think Mahfood is writing/drawing from? What do you think is motivating his writing?
5. Who do you think is Mahfood's audience? Does your answer depend on consideration of the medium he's using?

Your Text: Writing

1. Find a political cartoon and analyze it in terms of signs.
2. Write a short essay discussing why visual texts can communicate ideas effectively. You might compare a visual text and written text that have similar ideas but present them differently.
3. How does your previous experience with comics affect your ability to take political cartoons seriously? Write a short essay making the case for teaching visual culture at an early age.

Why Are All the Black Kids Sitting Together in the Cafeteria?

Beverly Daniel Tatum

Beverly Tatum is a psychologist who writes about race and race relations in America. This essay is taken in part from her book, *Why Are All the Black Kids Sitting Together in the Cafeteria? And Other Conversations About Race* (1999). Here she argues that both teachers and students need to talk actively about race, especially in the teen-age years when identity is being formed.

WALK INTO ANY RACIALLY MIXED high school cafeteria at lunch time and you will instantly notice an identifiable group of black students sitting together. Conversely, there are many white students sitting together, though we rarely comment about that. The question is "Why are the black kids sitting together?"

It doesn't start out that way. In racially mixed elementary schools, you often see children of diverse racial boundaries playing with one another, sitting at the snack table together, crossing racial boundaries with an ease uncommon in adolescence.

Moving from elementary school to middle school means interacting with new children from different neighborhoods than before, and a certain degree of clustering by race might therefore be expected, presuming that children who are familiar with one another would form groups. But even in schools where the same children stay together from kindergarten through eighth grade, racial grouping begins by the sixth or seventh grade. What happens?

One thing that happens is puberty. As children enter adolescence, they begin to explore the question of identity, asking "Who am I? Who can I be?" in ways they have not done before. For black youths, asking "Who am I?" includes thinking about "Who am I ethnically? What does it mean to be black?"

Why do black youths, in particular, think about themselves in terms of race? Because that is how the rest of the world thinks of them. Our self-perceptions are shaped by the messages we receive from those around us, and when young black men and women reach adolescence, the racial content of those messages intensifies.

Here is a case in point. If you were to ask my 10-year-old son, David, to describe himself, he would tell you many things: that he is smart, that he likes to play computer games, that he has an older brother. Near the top of his list, he would likely mention that he is tall for his age. He would probably not mention that he is black, though he certainly knows that he is. Why would he mention his height and not his racial group membership?

When David meets new adults, one of the first questions they ask is "How old are you?" When David states his age, the inevitable reply is, "Gee, you're tall for your age!"

It happens so frequently that I once overheard David say to someone, "Don't say it, I know. I'm tall for my age." Height is salient for David because it's salient for others.

When David meets new adults, they don't say, "Gee, you're black for your age!" Or do they?

Imagine David at 15, six-foot-two, wearing the adolescent attire of the day, passing adults he doesn't know on the sidewalk. Do the women hold their purses a little tighter, maybe even cross the street to avoid him? Does he hear the sound of automatic door locks on cars as he passes by? Is he being followed around by the security guards at the local mall? Do strangers assume he plays basketball? Each of these experiences conveys a racial message.

At 10, race is not yet salient for David, because it's not yet salient for society. But it will be.

Understanding Racial Identity Development

Psychologist William Cross, author of *Shades of Black: Diversity in African American Identity*, has offered a theory of racial identity development that I have found to be a very useful framework for understanding what is happening with those black students in the cafeteria. In the first stage of Cross's five-stage model, the black child absorbs many of the beliefs and values of the dominant white culture, including the idea that it's better to be white.

Simply as a function of being socialized in a Eurocentric culture, some black children may begin to value the role models, lifestyles and images of beauty represented by the dominant group more highly than those of their own cultural group. But the personal and social significance of one's racial group membership has not yet been realized, and racial identity is not yet under examination.

The Encounter Stage

Transition to the next stage, the encounter stage, is typically precipitated by an event—or series of events—that forces the young person to acknowledge the personal impact of racism.

For example, in racially mixed schools, black children are much more likely to be in a lower track than in an honors track. Such apparent sorting along racial lines sends a message about what it means to be black. One young honors student said, "It was really a very paradoxical existence, here I am in a school that's 35 percent black, you know, and I'm the only black in my class. That always struck me as odd. I guess I felt that I was different from the other blacks because of that."

There are also changes in the social dynamics outside the school. In racially mixed communities, you begin to see what I call the "birthday party effect." The parties of elementary school children may be segregated by gender, but not by race. At puberty, when the parties become sleepovers or boy–girl events, they become less and less racially diverse.

Black girls who live in predominantly white neighborhoods see their white friends start to date before they do. One young woman from a Philadelphia suburb described herself as "pursuing white guys throughout high school" to no avail. Because there were no black boys in her class, she had little choice. She would feel "really pissed off" that those same white boys would date her white friends.

Another young black woman attending a desegregated school to which she was bussed was encouraged by a teacher to attend the upcoming school dance. Most of the black students did not live in the neighborhood and seldom attended the extracurricular activities. The young woman indicated that she wasn't planning to come. Finally the well-intentioned teacher said, "Oh come on, I know you people love to dance." This young woman got the message.

Coping with Encounter

What do these encounters have to do with the cafeteria? Do experiences with racism inevitably result in so-called self-segregation?

While a desire to protect oneself from further offense is understandable, it's not the only factor at work. Imagine the young eighth-grade girl who experienced the teacher's use of "you people" and the dancing stereotype as a racial affront. Upset and struggling with adolescent embarrassment, she bumps into a white friend who can see that something is wrong. She explains. Her white friend responds—perhaps in an effort to make her feel better—and says, "Oh, Mr. Smith is such a nice guy, I'm sure he didn't mean it like that. Don't be so sensitive."

Perhaps the white friend is right, but imagine your own response when you are upset, and your partner brushes off your complaint, attributing it to your being oversensitive. What happens to your emotional thermostat? It escalates. When feelings, rational or irrational, are invalidated, most people disengage. They not only choose to discontinue the conversation but are more likely to turn to someone who will understand their perspective.

In much the same way that the eighth-grade girl's white friend doesn't get it, the girls at the "black table" do. Not only are black adolescents encountering racism and reflecting on their identity, but their white peers—even if not racist—are unprepared to respond in supportive ways.

The black students turn to each other for the much needed support they are not likely to find anywhere else.

We need to understand that in racially mixed settings, racial grouping is a developmental process in response to an environmental stressor, racism. Joining with one's peers for support in the face of stress is a positive coping strategy. The problem is that our young people are operating with a very limited definition of what it means to be black, based largely on cultural stereotypes.

This Text: Reading

1. Do you find yourself personally involved (or implicated) in Tatum's analysis? How do you think she would respond to your response?
2. In what ways is Tatum performing a semiotic analysis of the idea of race? In what ways have race and ethnicity contributed to "semiotic situations" in your own life?
3. Where does her analysis fit into what we traditionally think of as the American Dream?
4. Why is the cafeteria such an important location for a discussion like this? What happens in a cafeteria that might not happen in a classroom?

Your Text: Writing

1. Using your own experiences, write an essay about the role race and ethnicity have played—or didn't play—in your experiences growing up.
2. Tatum's essay balances personal experience with research; do you think this method of writing is effective? Why or why not? Do you think this is important for this type of topic? Why or why not?
3. Can you think of a personal topic that would benefit from a combined research/personal approach?

The Sports Taboo

Malcolm Gladwell

Malcolm Gladwell is a writer for *The New Yorker* who often writes about social issues. In this essay (1997) he uses an analogy to describe the relationship between perceived race and sports achievement.

1.

THE EDUCATION OF ANY ATHLETE BEGINS, in part, with an education in the racial taxonomy of his chosen sport—in the subtle, unwritten rules about what whites are supposed to be good at and what blacks are supposed to be good at. In football, whites play quarterback and blacks play running back; in baseball whites pitch and blacks play the outfield. I grew up in Canada, where my brother Geoffrey and I ran high-school track, and in Canada the rule of running was that anything under the quarter-mile belonged to the West Indians. This didn't mean that white people didn't run the sprints. But the expectation was that they would never win, and, sure enough, they rarely did. There was just a handful of West Indian immigrants in Ontario at that point—clustered in and around Toronto—but they owned Canadian sprinting, setting up under the stands at every major championship, cranking up the reggae on their boom boxes, and then humiliating everyone else on the track. My brother and I weren't from Toronto, so we weren't part of that scene. But our West Indian heritage meant that we got to share in the swagger. Geoffrey was a magnificent runner, with powerful legs and a barrel chest, and when he was warming up he used to do that exaggerated, slow-motion jog that the white guys would try to do and never quite pull off. I was a miler, which was a little outside the West Indian range. But, the way I figured it, the rules meant that no one should ever outkick me over the final two hundred metres of any race. And in the golden summer of my fourteenth year, when my running career prematurely peaked, no one ever did.

When I started running, there was a quarter-miler just a few years older than I was by the name of Arnold Stotz. He was a bulldog of a runner, hugely talented, and each year that he moved through the sprinting ranks he invariably broke the existing four-hundred-meter record in his age class. Stotz was white, though, and every time I saw the results of a big track meet I'd keep an eye out for his name, because I was convinced that he could not keep winning. It was as if I saw his whiteness as a degenerative disease, which would eventually claim and cripple him. I never asked him whether he felt the same anxiety, but I can't imagine that he didn't. There was only so long that anyone could defy the rules. One day, at the provincial championships, I looked up at the results board and Stotz was gone.

Talking openly about the racial dimension of sports in this way, of course, is considered unseemly. It's all right to say that blacks dominate sports because they lack opportunities elsewhere. That's the "Hoop Dreams" line, which says whites are allowed to acknowledge black athletic success as long as they feel guilty about it. What you're not supposed to say is what we were saying in my track days—that we were better because we were black, because of something intrinsic to being black. Nobody said anything like that publicly last month when Tiger Woods won the Masters or when, a week later, African men claimed thirteen out of the top twenty places in the Boston Marathon. Nor is it likely to come up this month, when African-Americans will make up eighty per cent of the players on the floor for the N.B.A. playoffs. When the popular television sports commentator Jimmy (the Greek) Snyder did break this taboo, in 1988—infamously ruminating on the size and significance of black thighs—one prominent N.A.A.C.P. official said that his remarks "could set race relations back a hundred years." The assumption is that the whole project of trying to get us to treat each other the same will be undermined if we don't all agree that under the skin we actually are the same.

The point of this, presumably, is to put our discussion of sports on a par with legal notions of racial equality, which would be a fine idea except that civil-rights law governs matters like housing and employment and the sports taboo covers matters like what can be said about someone's jump shot. In his much heralded book *Darwin's Athletes*, the University of Texas scholar John Hoberman tries to argue that these two things are the same, that it's impossible to speak of black physical superiority without implying intellectual inferiority. But it isn't long before the argument starts to get ridiculous. "The spectacle of black athleticism," he writes, inevitably turns into "a highly public image of black retardation." Oh, really? What, exactly, about Tiger Woods's victory in the Masters resembled "a highly public image of black retardation"? Today's black athletes are multimillion-dollar corporate pitchmen, with talk shows and sneaker deals and publicity machines and almost daily media opportunities to share their thoughts with the world, and it's very hard to see how all this contrives to make them look stupid. Hoberman spends a lot of time trying to inflate the significance of sports, arguing that how we talk about events on the baseball diamond or the track has grave consequences for how we talk about race in general. Here he is, for example, on Jackie Robinson:

> The sheer volume of sentimental and intellectual energy that has been invested in the mythic saga of Jackie Robinson has discouraged further thinking about what his career did and did not accomplish.... Black America has paid a high and largely unacknowledged price for the extraordinary prominence given the black athlete rather than other black men of action (such as military pilots and astronauts), who represent modern aptitudes in ways that athletes cannot.

Please. Black America has paid a high and largely unacknowledged price for a long list of things, and having great athletes is far from the top of the list. Sometimes a baseball player is just a baseball player, and sometimes an observation about racial difference is just an observation about racial difference. Few object when medical scientists talk about the significant epidemiological differences between blacks and whites—the fact that blacks have a higher incidence of hypertension than whites and twice as many black males die of diabetes and prostate cancer as white males, that breast tumors appear to grow faster in black women than in white women, that black girls show signs of puberty sooner than white girls. So why aren't we allowed to say that there might be athletically significant differences between blacks and whites?

According to the medical evidence, African-Americans seem to have, on the average, greater bone mass than do white Americans—a difference that suggests greater muscle mass. Black men have slightly higher circulating levels of testosterone and human-growth hormone than their white counterparts, and blacks overall tend to have proportionally slimmer hips, wider shoulders, and longer legs. In one study, the Swedish physiologist Bengt Saltin compared a group of Kenyan distance runners with a group of Swedish distance runners and found interesting differences in muscle composition: Saltin reported that the Africans appeared to have more blood-carrying capillaries and more mitochondria (the body's cellular power plant) in the fibres of their quadriceps. Another study found that, while black South African distance runners ran at the same speed as white South African runners, they were able to use more oxygen—eighty-nine per cent versus eighty-one per cent—over extended periods: somehow, they were able to exert themselves more. Such evidence suggested that there were physical differences in black athletes which have a bearing on activities like running and jumping, which should hardly come as a surprise to anyone who follows competitive sports.

To use track as an example—since track is probably the purest measure of athletic ability—Africans recorded fifteen out of the twenty fastest times last year in the men's ten thousand-metre event. In the five thousand metres, eighteen out of the twenty fastest times were recorded by Africans. In the fifteen hundred metres, thirteen out of the twenty fastest times were African, and in the sprints, in the men's hundred metres, you have to go all the way down to the twenty-third place in the world rankings—to Geir Moen, of Norway— before you find a white face. There is a point at which it becomes foolish to deny the fact of black athletic prowess, and even more foolish to banish speculation on the topic. Clearly, something is going on. The question is what.

2.

If we are to decide what to make of the differences between blacks and whites, we first have to decide what to make of the word "difference," which can mean any number of things. A useful case study is to compare the ability of men and women in math. If you give a large, representative sample of male and female students a standardized math test, their mean scores will come out pretty much the same. But if you look at the margins, at the very best and the very worst students, sharp differences emerge. In the math portion of an achievement test conducted by Project Talent—a nationwide survey of fifteen-year-olds—there were 1.3 boys for every girl in the top ten per cent, 1.5 boys for every girl in the top five per cent, and seven boys for every girl in the top one per cent. In the fifty-six-year history of the Putnam Mathematical Competition, which has been described as the Olympics of college math, all but one of the winners have been male. Conversely, if you look at people with the very lowest math ability, you'll find more boys than girls there, too. In other words, although the average math ability of boys and girls is the same, the distribution isn't: there are more males than females at the bottom of the pile, more males than females at the top of the pile, and fewer males than females in the middle. Statisticians refer to this as a difference in variability.

This pattern, as it turns out, is repeated in almost every conceivable area of gender difference. Boys are more variable than girls on the College Board entrance exam and in routine elementary-school spelling tests. Male mortality patterns are more variable than female patterns; that is, many more men die in early and middle age than women, who tend to die in more of a concentrated clump toward the end of life. The problem is that variability differences are regularly confused with average differences. If men had higher average math scores than women, you could say they were better at the subject. But because they are only more variable the word "better" seems inappropriate.

The same holds true for differences between the races. A racist stereotype is the assertion of average difference—it's the claim that the typical white is superior to the typical black. It allows a white man to assume that the black man he passes on the street is stupider than he is. By contrast, if what racists believed was that black intelligence was simply more variable than white intelligence, then it would be impossible for them to construct a stereotype about black intelligence at all. They wouldn't be able to generalize. If they wanted to believe that there were a lot of blacks dumber than whites, they would also have to believe that there were a lot of blacks smarter than they were. This distinction is critical to understanding the relation between race and athletic performance. What are we seeing when we remark black domination of elite sporting events—an average difference between the races or merely a difference in variability?

This question has been explored by geneticists and physical anthropologists, and some of the most notable work has been conducted over the past few years by Kenneth Kidd, at Yale. Kidd and his colleagues have been taking DNA samples from two African Pygmy tribes in Zaire and the Central African Republic and comparing them with DNA samples taken from populations all over the world. What they have been looking for is variants—subtle differences between the DNA of one person and another—and what they have found is fascinating. "I would say, without a doubt, that in almost any single African population—a tribe or however you want to define it—there is more genetic variation than in all the rest of the world put together," Kidd told me. In a sample of fifty Pygmies, for example, you might find nine variants in one stretch of DNA. In a sample of hundreds of people from around the rest of the world, you might find only a total of six variants in that same stretch of DNA—and probably every one of those six variants would also be found in the Pygmies. If everyone in the world was wiped out except Africans, in other words, almost all the human genetic diversity would be preserved.

The likelihood is that these results reflect Africa's status as the homeland of Homo sapiens: since every human population outside Africa is essentially a subset of the original African population, it makes sense that everyone in such a population would be a genetic subset of Africans, too. So you can expect groups of Africans to be more variable in respect to almost anything that has a genetic component. If, for example, your genes control how you react to aspirin, you'd expect to see more Africans than whites for whom one aspirin stops a bad headache, more for whom no amount of aspirin works, more who are allergic to aspirin, and more who need to take, say, four aspirin at a time to get any benefit—but far fewer Africans for whom the standard two-aspirin dose would work well. And to the extent that running is influenced by genetic factors you would expect to see more really fast blacks—and more really slow blacks—than whites but far fewer Africans of merely average speed. Blacks are like boys. Whites are like girls.

There is nothing particularly scary about this fact, and certainly nothing to warrant the kind of gag order on talk of racial differences which is now in place. What it means is that comparing elite athletes of different races tells you very little about the races themselves. A few years ago, for example, a prominent scientist argued for black athletic supremacy by pointing out that there had never been a white Michael Jordan. True. But, as the Yale anthropologist Jonathan Marks has noted, until recently there was no black Michael Jordan, either. Michael Jordan, like Tiger Woods or Wayne Gretzky or Cal Ripken, is one of the best players in his sport not because he's like the other members of his own ethnic group but precisely because he's not like them—or like anyone else, for that matter. Elite athletes are elite athletes because, in some sense, they are on the fringes of genetic variability. As it happens, African populations seem to create more of these genetic outliers than white populations do, and this is what underpins the claim that blacks are better athletes than whites. But that's all the claim amounts to. It doesn't say anything at all about the rest of us, of all races, muddling around in the genetic middle.

3.

There is a second consideration to keep in mind when we compare blacks and whites. Take the men's hundred-metre final at the Atlanta Olympics. Every runner in that race was of either Western African or Southern African descent, as you would expect if Africans had some genetic affinity for sprinting. But suppose we forget about skin color and look just at country of origin. The eight-man final was made up of two African-Americans, two Africans (one from Namibia and one from Nigeria), a Trinidadian, a Canadian of Jamaican descent, an Englishman of Jamaican descent, and a Jamaican. The race was won by the Jamaican-Canadian, in world-record time, with the Namibian coming in second and the Trinidadian third. The sprint relay—the 4 3 100—was won by a team from Canada, consisting of the Jamaican-Canadian from the final, a Haitian-Canadian, a Trinidadian-Canadian, and another Jamaican-Canadian. Now it appears that African heritage is important as an initial determinant of sprinting ability, but also that the most important advantage of all is some kind of cultural or environmental factor associated with the Caribbean.

Or consider, in a completely different realm, the problem of hypertension. Black Americans have a higher incidence of hypertension than white Americans, even after you control for every conceivable variable, including income, diet, and weight, so it's tempting to conclude that there is something about being of African descent that makes blacks prone to hypertension. But it turns out that although some Caribbean countries have a problem with hypertension, others—Jamaica, St. Kitts, and the Bahamas—don't. It also turns out that people in Liberia and Nigeria—two countries where many New World slaves came from—have similar and perhaps even lower blood-pressure rates than white North Americans, while studies of Zulus, Indians, and whites in Durban, South Africa, showed that urban white males had the highest hypertension rates and urban white females had the lowest. So it's likely that the disease has nothing at all to do with Africanness.

The same is true for the distinctive muscle characteristic observed when Kenyans were compared with Swedes. Saltin, the Swedish physiologist, subsequently found many of the same characteristics in Nordic skiers who train at high altitudes and Nordic runners who train in very hilly regions—conditions, in other words, that resemble the mountainous regions of Kenya's Rift Valley, where so many of the country's distance runners come from. The key factor seems to be Kenya, not genes.

Lots of things that seem to be genetic in origin, then, actually aren't. Similarly, lots of things that we wouldn't normally think might affect athletic ability actually do. Once again, the social-science literature on male and female math achievement is instructive. Psychologists argue that when it comes to subjects like math, boys tend to engage in what's known as ability attribution. A boy who is doing well will attribute his success to the fact that he's good at math, and if he's doing badly he'll blame his teacher or his own lack of motivation—anything but his ability. That makes it easy for him to bounce back from failure or disappointment, and gives him a lot of confidence in the face of a tough new challenge. After all, if you think you do well in math because you're good at math, what's stopping you from being good at, say, algebra, or advanced calculus? On the other hand, if you ask a girl why she is doing well in math she will say, more often than not, that she succeeds because she works hard. If she's doing poorly, she'll say she isn't smart enough. This, as should be obvious, is a self-defeating attitude. Psychologists call it "learned helplessness"—the state in which failure is perceived as insurmountable. Girls who engage in effort attribution learn helplessness because in the face of a more difficult task like algebra or advanced calculus they can conceive of no solution. They're convinced that they can't work harder, because they think they're working as hard as they can, and that they can't rely on their intelligence, because they never thought they were that smart to begin with. In fact, one of the fascinating findings of attribution research is that the smarter girls are, the more likely they are to fall into this trap. High achievers are sometimes the most helpless. Here, surely, is part of the explanation for greater math variability among males. The female math whizzes, the ones who should be competing in the top one and two per cent with their male counterparts, are the ones most often paralyzed by a lack of confidence in their own aptitude. They think they belong only in the intellectual middle.

The striking thing about these descriptions of male and female stereotyping in math, though, is how similar they are to black and white stereotyping in athletics—to the unwritten rules holding that blacks achieve through natural ability and whites through effort. Here's how *Sports Illustrated* described, in a recent article, the white basketball player Steve Kerr, who plays alongside Michael Jordan for the Chicago Bulls. According to the magazine, Kerr is a "hard-working overachiever," distinguished by his "work ethic and heady play" and by a shooting style "born of a million practice shots." Bear in mind that Kerr is one of the best shooters in basketball today, and a key player on what is arguably one of the finest basketball teams in history. Bear in mind, too, that there is no evidence that Kerr works any harder than his teammates, least of all Jordan himself, whose work habits are legendary. But you'd never guess that from the article. It concludes, "All over America, whenever quicker, stronger gym rats see Kerr in action, they must wonder, How can that guy be out there instead of me?"

There are real consequences to this stereotyping. As the psychologists Carol Dweck and Barbara Licht write of high-achieving schoolgirls, "[They] may view themselves as so motivated and well disciplined that they cannot entertain the possibility that they did poorly on an academic task because of insufficient effort. Since blaming the teacher would also be out of character, blaming their abilities when they confront difficulty may seem like the most reasonable option." If you substitute the words "white athletes" for "girls" and "coach" for "teacher," I think you have part of the reason that so many white athletes are underrepresented at the highest levels of professional sports. Whites have been saddled with the athletic equivalent of learned helplessness—the idea that it is all but fruitless to try and compete at the highest levels, because they have only effort on their side. The causes of athletic and gender discrimination may be diverse, but its effects are not. Once again, blacks are like boys, and whites are like girls.

4.

When I was in college, I once met an old acquaintance from my high-school running days. Both of us had long since quit track, and we talked about a recurrent fantasy we found we'd both had for getting back into shape. It was that we would go away somewhere remote for a year and do nothing but train, so that when the year was up we might finally know how good we were. Neither of us had any intention of doing this, though, which is why it was a fantasy. In adolescence, athletic excess has a certain appeal—during high school, I happily spent Sunday afternoons running up and down snow-covered sandhills—but with most of us that obsessiveness soon begins to fade. Athletic success depends on having the right genes and on a self-reinforcing belief in one's own ability. But it also depends on a rare form of tunnel vision. To be a great athlete, you have to care, and what was obvious to us both was that neither of us cared anymore. This is the last piece of the puzzle about what we mean when we say one group is better at something than another: sometimes different groups care about different things. Of the seven hundred men who play major-league baseball, for example, eighty-six come from either the Dominican Republic or Puerto Rico, even though those two islands have a combined population of only eleven million. But then baseball is something that Dominicans and Puerto Ricans care about—and you can say the same thing about African-Americans and basketball, West Indians and sprinting, Canadians and hockey, and Russians and chess. Desire is the great intangible in performance, and unlike genes or psychological affect we can't measure it and trace its implications. This is the problem, in the end, with the question of whether blacks are better at sports than whites. It's not that it's offensive, or that it leads to discrimination. It's that, in some sense, it's not a terribly interesting question; "better" promises a tidier explanation than can ever be provided.

I quit competitive running when I was sixteen—just after the summer I had qualified for the Ontario track team in my age class. Late that August, we had travelled to St. John's, Newfoundland, for the Canadian championships. In those days, I was whippet-thin, as milers often are, five feet six and not much more than a hundred pounds, and I could skim along the ground so lightly that I barely needed to catch my breath. I had two white friends on that team, both distance runners, too, and both, improbably, even smaller and lighter than I was. Every morning, the three of us would run through the streets of St. John's, charging up the hills and flying down the other side. One of these friends went on to have a distinguished college running career, the other became a world-class miler; that summer, I myself was the Canadian record holder in the fifteen hundred metres for my age class. We were almost terrifyingly competitive, without a shred of doubt in our ability, and as we raced along we never stopped talking and joking, just to prove how absurdly easy we found running to be. I thought of us all as equals. Then, on the last day of our stay in St. John's, we ran to the bottom of Signal Hill, which is the town's principal geographical landmark—an abrupt outcrop as steep as anything in San Francisco. We stopped at the base, and the two of them turned to me and announced that we were all going to run straight up Signal Hill backward.

I don't know whether I had more running ability than those two or whether my Africanness gave me any genetic advantage over their whiteness. What I do know is that such questions were irrelevant, because, as I realized, they were willing to go to far greater lengths to develop their talent. They ran up the hill backward. I ran home.

READING WRITING

This Text: Reading

1. What do you think of the analogy that Gladwell raises? What are some objections you have or do you think others have had? How would Gladwell answer those?
2. Why is the sports question in regard to race such an important and generally sensitive one?
3. What role does Gladwell attribute to sociology in achieving sports success?
4. What are some of the signs of sports—some elements of sports that can be read as signs, items to interpret? Are there semiotic situations you can think of?
5. Who is Gladwell's audience? Why do you think he's writing about this topic?

Your Text: Writing

1. Gladwell uses the personal voice in the essay, but the essay's content is mostly about what research has been done on this topic. What do you think of this approach? Is this one you can imitate? Think of a social issue that you have a stake in and try your hand at this approach, using this article as a model.
2. What are some other issues that are "taboo"? Write an essay exploring another subject that is generally off limits for discussion.

Qallunaat 101: Inuits Study White Folks in This New Academic Field

Zebedee Nungak

A long-time Inuit activist, Zebedee Nungak is also the co-author with Eugene Arima of *InuitStories: Povungnauk-Légendes inuic Povungnituk* (1988). In this wry piece, Nungak turns the traditional anthropologist subject-observer relationship on its head.

LIKE MANY INUIT BOYS OF MY GENERATION, I had a fascination with Qallunaat that bordered on awe. The few we encountered lived in warm wooden houses, while we grew up in igloos. They seemed to lack no material thing. Their food was what the word *delicious* was invented for, all their women were beautiful, and even their garbage was impressive! As a boy, I had an innocent ambition to be like them. The measure of my success would be when my garbage equaled theirs.

I lived among the Qallunaat for seven years. In my time in their land, my discoveries of their peculiarities sparked my interest in what could be called Qallunology.

Many of us who have been exposed to Qallunaat-dom through deep immersion in their world could write some credible discourses on the subject. Their social mores and standards of etiquette could fill several volumes. Their language contains all sorts of weirdness. Their sameness and distinctness can be utterly baffling. An Irishman from Northern Ireland looks exactly the same as one from the Irish Republic. A close look at Albanians and Serbs has them all looking like bona fide Qallunaat. Why such savage conflict among such same-looking civilized people?

Look, Look! See Sally Run! Oh Dick, Oh Jane! Why do your parents have no name? Are all dogs in Qallunaat-dom Spot, all cats Puff? There was absolutely no Fun with Dick and Jane as we Inuit children crashed head-on into the English language. The cultural shocks and tremors have never completely worn off those of us who were zapped with such literature.

The Qallunaat custom of abbreviating first names does not seem to follow a standard formula. Robert can be Rob, Robbie, Bob, Bobby or Bert. Joseph is Joe, James/Jim, Sidney/Sid, Arthur/Art, and Peter/Pete. Charles is Charlie but can be Chuck. What sleight of hand makes a Henry a Hank? And how does Richard become a Dick, if not a Rich or a Rick? Do you see a B in William on its way to be a Bill? Don't ever say *Seen* for Sean (sh-AWN) or *John* for Jean, if the person is a francophone male.

Qallunaat women can have very masculine names clicked feminine by ending them with an A: Roberta, Edwina, Phillippa. Shortened names are mostly chopped versions— Katherine/Kate, Deborah/Debbie—except for some ready-made like Wendy and Kay. Liz is drawn from the midsection of Elizabeth, unlike in Inuit use, where these names are entirely separate as Elisapi and Lisi. Many names can fit both sexes: Pat, Jan, Leslie, Kit.

One of the most distinctive features of life among Qallunaat, the one most markedly different from Inuit life, can be summed up in this expression of theirs: keeping up with the Joneses. Not much is communal and few essentials are shared. Life is based on competition, going to great lengths to "get ahead," and amassing what you gain for yourself. People around you may be in want, but that is their problem.

We know Qallunaat, of course, by the way they eat: with a fork and a dull knife known by Inuit as *nuvuittuq* (without point). There is a whole etiquette to eating too cumbersome to describe in detail. But, if one has the misfortune to burp, belch, or fart during the meal, one has to be civil and say "Excuse me!" in a sincere enough demeanor. Never forget to say "please" in asking for the salt or potatoes to be passed. Don't ever just up and walk away from the table.

Having visitors over (company) is mostly attached to some ritual or activity, such as a bridge game. If alcohol is served to guests, it is amazingly incidental, and not the main item of attention. Nobody gets drunk, but there is a lot of talking! Then there seems to be an obligation to talk even more at the door before leaving. Guests and hosts lingering forever at the entrance to talk about nothing in particular is one of the surest trademarks of being in Qallunaat-dom.

There is a ritual called dating, which is hard to describe in Inuit terms. It can't really be described as husband- or wife-hunting. Maturing people of opposite sexes mutually agree to "go out" to some form of enjoyable activity. Sometimes it is to test their compatibility as a possible couple, sometimes simply to genuinely enjoy each other's company. It seems to be a permanent occupation of some, whom Inuit might call *uinitsuituq* or *nulianitsuituq*, meaning "un-attachable to a husband or wife."

I don't proclaim to be an expert on Qallunaat and what makes them tick. But my commentaries on Qallunology are based on having eaten, slept, and breathed their life for some years, learning their language, and tumbling along in their tidy-square thought processes. The resulting recollections are no more superficial than those of the first Qallunaat to encounter the Inuit, who unwittingly illustrated their educated ignorance when they tried to describe us. That has changed. Today, even Qallunaat with strings of academic degrees attached to their names are more often seeking guidance from the reservoir of traditional Inuit knowledge.

Eskimology has long been a serious field of study by Qallunaat. Scores of museums and universities all over the world have great departments and sections devoted solely to the subject. Serious Qallunologists, on the other hand, are likely to sweat and toil in unrewarding anonymity until the academic currency of their field of study attains the respectability of being labeled officially with an "-ology."

Eskimologists have carted off traditional clothing, artifacts, hunting implements, tools, ancient stories and legends, and human remains for display in museums, bartering these for very little. Qallunologists will find nothing worth carting away for display. All Qallunaat stuff is for immediate use, much of it disposable, easily replaceable, and now available in mass quantities to Inuit as well. It all costs quite a lot, and one will be prosecuted for stealing any of it.

Eskimology was triggered by others' curiosity about who we are and how we live. It has flourished to the point that we Inuit have in some ways benefited from it by reclaiming some essences of our identity from various collections in others' possession. Qallunaat, meanwhile, are not in any danger of having to go to museums to pick up remnants of who they once were.

READING WRITING

This Text: Reading

1. Do you think this piece is funny? Why or why not?
2. What points is Nungak making about the relationships between Inuits and whites? Have you heard these issues before? Is Nungak treating these ideas differently?
3. Does anyone study white people as an anthropological study? If not, should they? If so, who does?

This Text: Writing

1. Do your own anthropological study of a group or phenomenon that seems familiar but can still be studied (cafeteria, gym, supermarket, etc.).
2. Find a traditional anthropological study and write a compare and contrast piece.

Race Is a Four-Letter Word

Teja Arboleda

In this piece, taken from his 1998 book, *In the Shadow of Race,* Arboleda explores what it means to be multiracial. A producer and peformer, Arboleda wrote and directed *Got Race,* his first feature-length movie, which premiered in October 2003.

I'VE BEEN CALLED *nigger* and a neighbor set the dogs on us in Queens, New York.

I've been called *spic* and was frisked in a plush neighborhood of Los Angeles.
I've been called *Jap* and was blamed for America's weaknesses.
I've been called *Nazi* and the neighborhood G.I. Joes had me every time.
I've been called *Turk* and was sneered at in Germany.
I've been called *Stupid Yankee* and was threatened in Japan.
I've been called *Afghanistani* and was spit on by a Boston cab driver.
I've been called *Iraqi* and Desert Storm was America's pride.

I've been called *mulatto, criollo, mestizo, simarron, Hapahaoli, masala, exotic, alternative, mixed-up, messed-up, half-breed,* and *in between.* I've been mistaken for Moroccan, Algerian, Egyptian, Lebanese, Iranian, Turkish, Brazilian, Argentinean, Puerto Rican, Cuban, Mexican, Indonesian, Nepalese, Greek, Italian, Pakistani, Indian, Black, White, Hispanic, Asian, and being a Brooklynite. I've been mistaken for Michael Jackson and Billy Crystal on the same day.

I've been ordered to get glasses of water for neighboring restaurant patrons. I've been told to be careful mopping the floors at the television station where I was directing a show. Even with my U.S. passport, I've been escorted to the "aliens only" line at Kennedy International Airport. I've been told I'm not dark enough. I've been told I'm not White enough. I've been told I talk American real good. I've been told, "Take your hummus and your pita bread and go back to Mexico!" I've been ordered to "Go back to where you belong, we don't like *your* kind here!"

I spent too much time and energy as a budding adult abbreviating my identity and rehearsing its explanation. I would practice quietly by myself, reciting what my father always told me: "Filipino-German." He never smiled when he said this.

My father's dark skin told many stories that his stern face and anger-filled tension couldn't translate. My mother's light skin could never spell empathy—even suntanning only made her turn bright red. My brother Miguel and I became curiosity factors when we appeared in public with her. During the past 34 years, my skin has lightened, somewhat, but then in the summers (even in New England where summers happen suddenly, and disappear just as quickly), I can darken several degrees in a matter of hours. This phenomenon seems a peculiar paradigm to which people's perceptions of my culture or race alter with the waning and waxing of my skin tone. I can almost design others' perceptions by counting my minutes in the sun. My years in Japan, the United States, Germany, and the numerous countries, cities, and towns through which I've traveled, have proven that my flesh is irrelevant to the language I speak, to the way I walk and talk, or the way I jog or mow my lawn or to the fact that I often use chopsticks to eat. It is irrelevant to *who* or *what* I married, my political viewpoints, my career, my hopes, desires and fears.

I don't remember being taught by my parents never to *question* skin color, yet when I compare the back of my hand to these pages, I cannot help myself—I must know. Like a sickness coursing through my veins with the very blood that makes me who I am, I ask: What color am I? And, what color was I yesterday? Tomorrow? There is also that pesky, familiar feeling I get when, in the corner of my eye, I catch passing strangers with judgments written on their brows. Maybe paranoia, maybe vanity, but the experiences and memories of too often being "different" or "undefinable" have left me with a weary sense of instant verdict on my part. And sometimes I study their thousands of faces, hoping somehow to connect. I know that they ask themselves the same questions, as they are plagued by the same epidemic, asking and reasking themselves, ourselves, "Who and what are we?"

Overadapting to new environments has become second nature to me, as my father and my mother eagerly fed me culture. As a child I felt like I was being dragged to different corners of the planet with my parents, filling their need for exploration and contact, and teaching us the value and beauty of difference. Between packing suitcases and wandering through unfamiliar territory, all I had ever wanted was to be "the same."

They were successful in some respects—I do believe I am liberal in my thinking—but inevitably there was a price to pay. With each step, each move, each landing through the thick and tenuous atmosphere of a new culture, my feet searched for solid ground, for something familiar. The concept of home, identity, and place become ethereal, like a swirl of gases circling in orbit, waiting for gravity to define their position.

In a sense, I have been relegated to ethnic benchwarmer, on a hunt for simplicity in a world of confusing words that deeply divide us all. In response, I learned to overcompensate. New places and new faces have rarely threatened me, but I have a desperate need to belong to whatever group I'm with at any particular moment. I soak in the surrounding elements to cope with what my instincts oblige, and deliver a new temporary self. I am out of bounds, transcending people and places. I carry within my blood the memories of my heritage connected in the web of my mind, the marriage of history and biology. I breathe the air of my ancestors as if it were fresh from the sunrises of their past. I am illogical, providing argument to traditional categories of race, culture, and ethnicity. I am a cultural chameleon, adapting out of necessity only to discover, yet again, a new Darwinism at the frontiers of identity.

"What are you, anyway?" sometimes demandingly curious Americans like to ask. "I'm Filipino-German," I used to say. I have never been satisfied with abbreviating my identity to the exclusion of all the other puzzle pieces that would then be lost forever in shadowy corners where no one ever looks.

Do I throw a nod at a Black brother who passes me on the street? And if I did so, would he understand why I did? Do I even call him "brother?" Does *he* call *me* "brother?" If not, should he call me a "half-brother," or throw me a half nod? In the United States do I nod or bow to Japanese nationals in a Japanese restaurant? Would they know to bow with me? In Jamaica Plain, Massachusetts, if a Hispanic male gestures hello to me, is it a simple greeting, or a gesture of camaraderie because I might be Hispanic? Do I dress up to go to a country club because, in the eyes of its rich White men, I would otherwise live up to their idea of the stereotypical minority? Should I dance well, shaking and driving my body like Papa's family afforded me, or should I remain appropriately conservative to preserve the integrity of a long-gone Puritan New England? Do I shave for the silver hallways of white-collar highrises so as not to look too "ethnic?" Do I agree to an audition for a commercial when I know the reason I'm there is just to fill in with some skin color for an industry quota?

"I know you're *something*," someone once said. "You have some Black in you," another offered. "He must be ethnic or something," I've overheard. "I've got such a boring family compared to yours," another confided. "You're messed-up," an elementary school girl decided. "Do you love your race?" her classmate wondered. "*What* did you marry?" I've been asked. "*Who* did you marry?" I've been asked. "Is she just like you?" I've been asked. "You are the quintessential American," someone decided.

■ ■ ■

America continues to struggle through its identity crisis, and the simple, lazy, bureaucratic checklist we use only serves to satisfy an outdated four-letter word—*race.* Like the basic food groups, it is overconsumed and digested, forming a hemorrhoid in the backside of the same old power struggle. I am only one of many millions of Americans, from this "League of Outsiders," demanding a change in the way we are designated, routed, cattle-called, herded, and shackled into these simplified classifications.

The United States is going through growing pains. The immigrants coming to the United States and becoming citizens are no longer primarily of European origin. But let's not fool ourselves into thinking that America is only now becoming multicultural.

In 1992, *Time* magazine produced a special issue entitled, "The New Face of America" with the subtitle, "How immigrants are shaping the world's first multicultural society." The cover featured a picture of a woman's face. Next to the face was a paragraph that suggested her image was the result of a computerized average of faces of people of several different races.

The operative words on the cover are "races," "culture," and "first." Race and culture are very different words. Race in America is predominantly determined by skin color. Culture is determined by our experiences and our interactions within a society, large or small.

Then there is this idea of being "first." Are we to say that this continent was never populated by a mix of people? Are we to say that the Lacota and Iroquois were of exactly the same culture? What about the different Europeans who settled here later on? Of course, African slaves were not all from the same tribe, and they certainly were not of the same culture as the slave traders.

In the middle of the magazine, there was a compilation, more like a chart of photographs of people from all over the world. The editor and computer artist scanned all the pictures into a computer. Then, by having the computer average the faces together, they produced a variety of facial combinations. Remember, however, they said on the cover, "People from different *races* . . . to form the world's first *multicultural* society." But in the body of the article and its accompanying pictures, many people were not identified by their *race*, but rather by their *nationalities*—such as Italian and Chinese—in other words *citizenship*, a very different word.

Through it all, *Time* was trying to educate us, but at the same time, we're miseducated. The world—not just this country—has always been and always will be a multicultural environment. So what is it about the words *multicultural* or *diversity* that is confusing or overwhelming?

In the next 20 years, the average American will no longer be technically White. This will have to be reflected in the media, in the workplace, and in the schools, not out of charitable interest, but out of necessity. More people are designating themselves as multiracial or multicultural. People continue to marry across religious, cultural, and ethnic barriers. A definition for "mainstream society" is harder to find.

■ ■ ■

My mother's father, Opa, died a year after Oma passed away. The day after the funeral in Germany, my mother's relatives told her, for the first time, that her father was not really her father (i.e., biologically). All the people who knew the true identity of her father have long since passed away. So, if my mother's biological father was, let's say, Italian or Russian, does that make her German-Italian or German-Russian? She says no. German, only German, because that's how she was raised.

My brother, Miguel, married a Brazilian. (*Pause.*) Do you have an image in your head of what she looks like? I did when he first told me about her over the phone. Well, she is Brazilian by culture and citizenship, but her parents are Japanese nationals who moved to Brazil in their early 20s to escape poverty in Japan after World War II. So she *looks stereotypically* Japanese. But she speaks Portuguese and doesn't interact socially like most Japanese do.

■ ■ ■

I offer myself as a case study in transcending the complex maze of barriers, pedestals, doors, and traps that form the boundaries that confine human beings to dominant and minority groups.

I am tired. I am exhausted. I am always looking for new and improved definitions for my identity. My very-mixed heritage, culture, and international experiences seem like a blur sometimes, and I long for a resting place. A place where I can breathe like I did in my mother's womb: without having to open my mouth.

READING WRITING

This Text: Reading

1. In what ways does Aborleda present himself as a text? In what ways do people "mis-read" him?

2. The author writes in a vivid first person style; in what ways would this story be different if it were in the third person?

3. How does Aborleda describe his identity? How is his idea of identity different from the identity he finds in others' reactions to him?

Your Text: Writing

1. Write about a time when you were mistaken for another group, whether enthnicity, gender, class, or age. What assumptions did the people mistaking you for someone else make?

2. Do research on multiracial identity and determine what issues are "in the air." *Hint:* Both the recent census and Tiger Woods's statements about his identity have made this issue more prominent. Then re-read this text or another one that involves this issue, such as the movie *The Human Stain.* In what ways do the text and research speak to one another?

Censoring Myself

Betty Shamieh

Betty Shamieh, an Arab American, is a highly regarded writer and performer. Her play *Chocolate in the Heat—Growing Up Arab in America* was staged in 2001 in New York. A graduate of Harvard and the Yale School of Drama, Shamieh's essay (2003) is about being read as a certain kind of text—an Arab American—in the wake of 9/11.

I AM A PALESTINIAN-AMERICAN PLAYWRIGHT—and I'm Christian. Significant numbers of Arabs are Christian, which is something many Americans do not know; Arab society is not by any means homogeneous.

I was born in San Francisco, so I'm a citizen of this country. I went to Harvard and Yale and what attending institutions like that provides is access to people in positions of power.

Yet, part of me is terrified to be writing these words singling myself out as an Arab-American at this stage in American history, because I don't know what the ramifications of that are or will be. Part of me wants to heed President Bush when he lets it be known on national television that he thinks citizens better "watch what they say," but part of me is extremely cognizant of the fact that over a thousand Arab- and Muslim-Americans were picked up and held for months without trials and without our government releasing their names following the attacks of Sept. 11; that it was 18 months after Pearl Harbor that Japanese Americans were sent to internment camps; and that this country does not have a history of showing tolerance toward any racial minority whose members are easy to pick out of a crowd.

There are certainly acts of intolerance short of internment of which governments are capable. I have been censored in many ways. But I think the most overt example of censorship I have yet faced is my experience with a project called the Brave New World Festival.

The Brave New World Festival at New York City's Town Hall was—as its Web site declared—designed for artists to explore "the alternate roots of terrorism." For the most part, only very well-established playwrights were asked to participate, but I—who had just finished Yale School of Drama a year before—was invited partly because of my work at the "Imagine: Iraq" reading, which drew 900 people to Cooper Union in New York City in November 2001, to hear plays about the Middle East. I am an actress as well as a playwright, and, at the "Imagine: Iraq" reading, I performed a monologue I wrote about the sister of a suicide bomber who mourns not knowing what her brother planned to do and not being able to stop him. The piece is very clearly a plea for non-violence.

When the organizers of the Brave New World Festival asked me to perform the same monologue for them, my first thought was that I did not want to be in Town Hall on the first anniversary of Sept. 11 presenting a play that deals with such potent subject matter. Then I realized that it was especially important at that time and in that place to present precisely such work. So, despite all my fears and concerns, I agreed to their request—but asked the organizers to get Marisa Tomei (who was already involved in the project) or an actress of that caliber to play the role. I felt that if there was going to be a backlash, I didn't want to be dealing with it alone.

I got a call from an organizer a few weeks later. She told me she loved the piece and that—at my request—she had given it to Marisa Tomei. But she also said that some of her colleagues had objected to the content of my piece. She informed me that I was welcome to write something different but that they were rescinding their offer to present my monologue.

At this time, I did not know that they were also censoring people like Eduardo Machado, who is the head of the playwriting MFA program at Columbia and one of the best-known playwrights of his generation.

So, in an Uncle Tom–like manner, instead of holding my ground, I wrote another piece. I did so because I was the only Arab-American playwright in the lineup. Arab-American artists are largely faceless in this country and I felt that, by dropping out, I would be helping those who are trying to keep it that way.

The new piece I wrote for them was a very mild and humorous short play. The narrator, an Arab-American girl, tells the audience of a fantasy she has about ending up on a hijacked plane and talking the hijackers out of their plans. The people on the plane listen to the hijackers' grievances and actually refuse to get off the flight until all people have a right to live in safety and freedom. Then, in her fantasy, the narrator ends up on "Oprah," and has a movie made about her starring Julia Roberts.

Harmless, right? Especially for a forum designed to present theater that asked real questions.

But when I got into rehearsal on the day of the performance with the director, Billy Hopkins, and actresses including Rosie Perez, I realized someone had censored the text, deleting chunks of my work that deal with the main character talking to the hijackers and making them see the error of their ways.

Of course, I had my own original copy with me. I had just begun to distribute it when the stage manager stepped into the rehearsal. She announced that because the performance schedule had grown overlong, my piece, the token Arab-American playwright's play, had been cut, along with a number of others.

What made the experience particularly disturbing was that the organizers had touted this event as a venue for alternative ideas and voices. To censor voices that present exactly those perspectives made it seem as though those voices don't exist.

Many people ask me if I—as a Palestinian-American playwright living in New York in a post–Sept. 11 world—have been facing more censorship in the wake of that horrific event that changed all of our lives. The answer—which might surprise many—is no.

The reason is that there was such as astounding level of censorship in American theater when it comes to the Palestinian perspective before Sept. 11, that I really haven't felt a difference in the past two years.

Indeed, the last time there was a serious attempt to bring a play written by a Palestinian to a major New York stage was in 1989. Joe Papp, artistic director of the Joseph Papp Public Theatre, asked a Palestinian theater troupe that had toured throughout Europe to bring its highly acclaimed show, "The Story of Kufur Shamma," to his theater.

Joe Papp was a theatrical visionary. In other words, he wasn't going to stick a piece of mindless propaganda on his theater's stage. But his board objected to his decision to bring the show to New York.

Papp, arguably the most powerful man in the history of American theater, did not feel he could stand up to his board members. He rescinded his offer because, as the *Philadelphia Inquirer* reported, "he had come under a great deal of pressure and that he could not jeopardize his theater."

I'm telling this story only because I think its relationship with my work is intriguing. For the three years I was a graduate student at the Yale School of Drama, I, in effect, censored myself. I did not produce a single play about the Palestinian experience, which is an enormous part of who I am as a person and an artist.

I wanted to avoid confronting the kind of censorship anybody faces when portraying the Palestinians as human beings. I wanted to avoid that kind of controversy until I had a bit of a name for myself, a bit of a following.

Unfortunately, what happened as a result of my self-censorship was my work was eviscerated. Now, I write about the Palestinian experience not only just because it deserves—as all stories deserve—to be heard, but also because if I hope to make vital theater I can only write about what I care deeply about. And vital theater is the only kind of theater I'm interested in making.

It came down to a very clear choice for me. I either had to give up writing for the stage or decide to write about what I knew and cared about and, therefore, face what it meant to be a Palestinian-American playwright working in New York at this time. I, either wisely or unwisely, have chosen the latter.

When you think of all the ethnic minorities in this country who have had their story told multiple times in the theater, you wonder—would it do such harm to add to that mosaic one story about the Palestinian perspective?

Are the people involved in the incidents I mentioned being rational when they try so hard to keep a Palestinian perspective out of the public eye, which they unfortunately and—in my opinion—unnecessarily see as contrary to their own?

Aren't they overreacting a little bit? I mean, really. Is theater that powerful?

The answer is yes. A good play, a play that makes you feel, allows you to see its characters as fully human, if only for two hours.

If more people actually saw Palestinians as human beings, our foreign policy could not and would not be the same.

This Text: Reading

1. What are some of the problems Shamieh has had to face as an Arab American?
2. Shamieh refers to a decision as being Uncle Tom-esque. What does she mean by this?
3. How is this essay about identity? Does Shamieh have a thesis? If so, what is it?

Your Text: Writing

1. Write a first-person essay, like Shamieh's, in which you talk about your own identity as a text. How have people read and misread you?
2. Write an essay in which you respond to Shamieh's. What did you learn from her piece?
3. Write a comparison/contrast paper on Shamieh's essay and Amy Tan's "Mother Tongue." How are they similar? How does gender figure in to issues of race?

Gender Expectations and Familial Roles Within Asian American Culture

Amy Truong

Student Essay

Amy Truong wrote this essay for Professor Brian Komei Dempster's Asian American Literature survey course at the University of San Francisco. Here, she reads the texts of gender, race, and family alongside Lan Samantha Chang's novella *The Unforgetting*. Dempster says of Truong's essay, "I admire the synthesis of literary analysis and family history." To achieve this effect, Truong shifts back and forth between readings of Chang and Truong.

> In Mercy Lake he started his new job as a photocopy machine repairman . . . He maintained the new Chevrolet sedan—changed the oil, followed the tune-up dates, and kept good records of all repairs . . . He labored on the yard. (Chang, 135–136, 140)

> She laundered Ming's new work clothes: permanent-press shirts with plastic tabs inserted in the stiff, pointed collars; bright, wide ties . . . In the kitchen, Sansan learned to cook with canned and frozen foods. She made cream of tomato soup for lunch, and stored envelopes of onion soup mix for meat loaf or quick onion dip. More often . . . Sansan consulted the Betty Crocker cookbook. (138–139)

Are these from an episode of *Leave It to Beaver*? No. These are excerpts from Lan Samantha Chang's, "The Unforgetting." Ask yourself what these excerpts mean to you. They may just simply remind some of you of an episode of *Leave It to Beaver* because these were the characteristic roles of men and women some decades ago when television sets only came in black and white—men were the breadwinners while women were the caretakers. For others, including myself, they are reminders of the life that still exists; a life that is representative of many Asian American families today.

In many Asian cultures, gender plays a role in dictating what you do. Certain members of the family are designated specific responsibilities that compliment their respective gender roles much like the characters in *Leave It to Beaver*. The males support the family financially and control the household, and the women take care of the family and household chores. Lan Samantha Chang's novella, "Hunger," parallels the events in my life and shows how gender roles are still very apparent in today's Asian American families. This essay seeks to capture that parallel experience of interpreting Chang's text and the texts of my own experiences.

Within Asian culture, women are raised and taught to be silent and obedient. I am a first generation Vietnamese American and growing up, I was told, "Do not comment or speak up," whenever I wanted to voice my opinion. My opinion was considered unimportant. And for many years of my life I believed that this was true. I never spoke a word unless I was asked to speak or spoken to; until I finally became tired of being mute. As a young teenager, my parents were going through difficult times with their marriage. One night, my mother, father, grandmother, brother and I sat down to have a family meeting about the issues between my parents. My dad did all the talking while my mom sat in silence like she always did. "Your mother has committed terrible sins and has destroyed our family," he said to us sternly in our native language. Not once during the entire family meeting did anyone in the family speak other than my father. Before the meeting ended, I finally worked up the nerve to defend my mother since she refused to defend herself. "Daddy, you shouldn't speak about Mommy like that in front of us," I declared. As soon as I said it, my father slapped me hard on the back of my head and told me, "Do not ever speak unless you have been instructed to." I immediately received a scolding from my mother and grandmother as well. Ironically, it was my mind that they thought was poisoned, and they blamed America for my "rebellious" breaking of silence.

The characters in Lan Samantha Chang's "Hunger" also suffer from silence. Min, the wife, very rarely speaks a word when she does not agree with her husband. Instead, she lets him do as he pleases and remains quiet as a good Asian wife. For instance, her husband treats their youngest daughter in ways that she does not particularly agree with. Her husband places a lot of pressure on their daughter and that is not how she wants their children to grow up. Yet she remains silent, because she believes that it is her place to let her husband control their family and their daughter in the way that he wants. For example, the mother's silence is demonstrated on one occasion when her daughter and husband are screaming:

> Baba, let me stop! You go ahead and cry! . . . You cry all you want! . . . You cry! But—play! . . . As I ironed I watched Anna fiddle with the frayed towels that had once been pink but now were faded to a creamy white . . . I opened my mouth but my throat was dry. (59)

She wishes to protect her daughter and attempts to speak, but chooses to refrain from doing so due to her respective roles as a woman and wife. Ironically, it is only after her death that she is able to voice her thoughts. In essence, the novella's point-of-view is symbolic and emphasizes how a woman's voice can be silenced due to her gender role.

Ruth, the youngest daughter, is also silenced and lets her father live vicariously through her. Though she hates it, she does not speak against his wishes. For example, her father makes her play the violin and has her practice for hours on end. She practices so much everyday that it brings her to tears and causes her to resent her father, because she cannot do or say anything that will prevent him from forcing her to play. For instance, when she and her father are locked in the practice room, he tells her,

> Do you understand? From now on, you work. You practice everyday . . . No no no no—Her voice rose to a shriek. There was a slam as he closed the door, and they were trapped inside the room together. . . . He clapped and counted. She played and cried. (60)

Though she cries and screams, she continues to play because this is her father's desire. Irony once again occurs. Just as Tian leaves his family to pursue his passion for music, Ruth's passionate hate for that same music drives her to leave her family as well. As a woman, she is put in an impossible position: her breaking of silence and fighting back is a form of defiance and shows a lack of respect towards the male figure, causing the destruction of this family.

In Vietnamese culture, the oldest daughter is also expected to play a major role in the house—she is expected to handle household chores and responsibilities in the absence of a mother. My mother is the oldest daughter and was only fourteen when she arrived in the United States after the Vietnam War. My mother came to this country with her older brother, Nihn (age 18), her two younger brothers, Can (10) and Toan (4), and her younger sister, Ngoc (5). "Life was very hard and unbearable sometimes," she said. My mother had to take on the difficult responsibility of taking care of all her siblings. At the tender age of fourteen, she assisted her siblings with their schoolwork, put food on the table and clothes on their backs, attended school, worked a part-time job, and attempted to learn the English language. My grandparents finally arrived in the United States (along with two more children) when my mother was 22 years old. "I thought it was over," she told me. But this was not the case. My grandparents expected more from my mother because after eight years in the United States she spoke the English language, understood how the system worked, and already seemed to have things under control. My grandparents soon developed a bad gambling habit and left my mother to take on the burden of caring for her six siblings. I ask my mother why she continued to put up with it. She responded only by saying, "I am obligated, Amy." Till this day my mother is the one who holds her family together, and one day she expects me (the oldest and only daughter) to do the same for my siblings and our family.

In "Hunger," Anna is the oldest daughter who, like my mother, has the responsibility of taking care of the home in the absence of her mother. She hires men to work on the home, decorates it so that it will be more presentable, and even gives tours to interested buyers. Strangely, she denies bids on the house and does not move out into a beautiful loft, a comfy townhouse or spacious condominium. As much as Anna longs to sell the house in order to rid of all their unhappy memories, a part of her feels obligated to stay there. For instance, Anna's mother watches her as she lays in bed and notices, "through all this, Anna sleeps; but on some nights, as the melodies fade away, she shudders and sits up in bed . . . Perhaps she has been dreaming of her greatest hope and fear—that the house is gone, that it is destroyed, and nothing more remains of it" (114). Anna's personal desire to forget her family's past conflicts with her duty to her family to keep their home. Anna stays loyal to her gender and familial role by remaining in that home, resulting in restless nights due to her split conscience.

On the other hand, men play a very different role in an Asian family. They are the primary (and often only) breadwinner in the family. My father came to the United States when he was 23. Because of his limited knowledge of English, he found it difficult to obtain good work or even go back to school. "No one would hire me because my English was very hard to understand," he explains. This affected him ten years later when he and my mother married. Because my father did not know the language well, my mother was the breadwinner in their relationship. This made my father "lose face." Not being able to contribute to the household as much as your wife was a shameful thing and made him lose a lot of his pride. "I was very embarrassed that your mother made more than me. I was too ashamed to even go out because I worried that others would see me and speak badly of me," my father states, no longer embarrassed. Not being able to provide for the family financially, my father expressed his "manliness" in other ways. Though my mother made most of the money, he decided where that money would go and how it would be distributed. He was also very strict, held strongly to Vietnamese traditions, and made sure we knew that he still wore the pants. He made sure that I was never out late, because traditionally it was not appropriate for a young lady to be out past dark. Even to this day, I am expected to be home and in bed at 10 p.m. He made sure that we never spoke English in the house so that we would remember where we came from and so that others would know that we were still very Vietnamese even though we were born American. When we spoke English, he either ignored what we said or scorned us for doing so. "You must remember your origins. This house is not a white man's house," he droned in our native language. He also made sure of this by having my mother cook traditional Vietnamese meals every day and restricted us from having things such as burgers, fries and sodas. He told us, "Vietnamese food is healthier than American food . . . tastes better too. All Americans know how to do is fry their food. The Vietnamese, on the other hand, are real chefs." My father is now trying to regain his respect and honor by taking night courses and practicing his English with my mother and his children. He hopes that by doing this he will earn a better job with better money so that he can fulfill his duty as a man and father.

Tian, the father in "Hunger," is the breadwinner and the head of his household, much like my father. He provides the only source of income and does so by first working as a music professor, then in a restaurant. He also calls all the shots and makes all the decisions for each member of his family. For example, he decides that Ruth is going to play the violin and that she is going to play it well by forcing her to practice whenever she has free time. According to the novella, "All morning during summer vacations, plus two evenings a week, he sat in the tiny room for hours and helped her practice" (62). Though the text indicates that he is helping Ruth, no normal teenager wants to be locked in a room practicing a craft that he/she has no interest in. Therefore, force is used on Tian's part to get her to do so. He also decides that she is not going to attend the university where he once taught even after they offer her a scholarship. They have an argument and he demands,

> You're staying here.
> Let go of my arm! You're hurting me!
> You are not leaving this house as long as you are still a child. Do you hear me? I'm not a child!
> You're my daughter and I'm your father! (72)

It is not traditional among Asian families for a child to leave the home to attend school. His refusal to succumb to this American tradition represents his need to control the family.

Tian also tells his wife Min what to do. One such incident occurs after his recital. Tian's colleagues want him to stay and have some drinks. He tells them that Min is tired, but it is she who insists that they stay. He hushes her quickly and tells her that they are going to go home. Min urges him,

> It is okay. My [Min's] voice cracked against the words . . . Come on, said Tian. He took my arm and pulled me around the corner, to the coatrack. I'm not that tired; I could have gone out with them . . . Why did you want to leave so much?
> . . . I want to go home. (22)

Though Min is persistent that her husband mingle with his American friends, his desire is apparently more important than hers, displaying both his power and her silence. Tian, like many other Asian men, including my father, is the money-earner and controller of the family. They both support the family financially and make all the decisions pertaining to each member of the family whether or not protest occurs.

Male sons also have a respected role in the Asian family. They are expected to bring in income and help with the household expenses as well. My younger brother, Tim (19), lives with my parents and has paid rent every month since he was seventeen and received his first job. My parents do not like to call it rent. They prefer to term it "duty" or "obligation." Tim is still young and would prefer to spend his money to go out and have fun with his friends. He and my parents constantly argue about this topic but my parents do not budge. "Tim, it is your responsibility to contribute to the needs of the family. This is only preparing you so that one day you can handle the responsibility of being a father, the man of the house, when it is your time," they continually insist to him in Vietnamese. Likewise, they tell Tim that American traditions have made him ungrateful and lazy. In due time, they will be lecturing the same thing to my other younger brother, Will (5), as well.

In "Hunger," all of the characters, like my brother, struggle between achieving their individual desires and observing their respective gender and familial roles. Min wishes to speak her thoughts, but her role as a wife prevents her from doing so. Min has other desires and yet after "Twenty-one years . . . I had never admitted my disappointment with him. I had not complained about a lack of money or time together. I had taken what he brought home and made it into our daily lives" (94). Min is very unhappy and though she yearns to express her disappointment and opinion, she can not because she has to maintain her role as dutiful wife.

Tian decides to pursue his love for music but at the cost of abandoning his family and his responsibilities to them. According to Tian,

> Everyone . . . has things they want to do in their lives. But sometimes there is only one thing— one thing that a person must do. More than what he is told to do, more than what he is trained to do. Even more than what his family wants him to do. It is what he hungers for. (28)

Unlike some members of his family, Tian chooses his own personal longing over his obligation to his respective gender and familial role, claiming that it is something that he must do, as though he has no choice.

Ruth challenges her prescribed role as a daughter so that she can live the life that she always wanted to, also at the cost of her family. She searches for freedom from her duties, saying, " 'I'm quitting! I'm never going to pick up a violin again for as long as I live.' And without a pause, he cried, 'Then I don't want you! You are not my daughter! You are nothing!' " (88). After this heated exchange, Ruth "walked to the door, opened it, and stepped outside" (90). Ruth and Tian have their differences, but they are very much alike. As stated earlier, they both leave their families to pursue their dreams, disregarding their responsibilities to their family.

Anna wishes to forget all her memories by selling their home. Instead, she is true to her respected role and remains in that home even against her own wishes. For example, "One day she opened the door to a brisk young couple full of plans, the woman's belly swollen with hope like freshly risen dough . . . They bid, and Anna refused to sell" (107). Anna has invested much money into fixing the house so that she can begin to forget the past it holds, but her obligation to stay in that house so that her family's story can be saved keeps her from doing so.

Like my brother, the characters of "Hunger" make sacrifices in order to fulfill their roles. Likewise, those who follow their desires make huge sacrifices as well. Their personal longings and respected gender and familial roles create internal conflicts that are a part of their everyday lives just as is so with members of today's Asian American families.

It has been thirty years since my parents first arrived in the United States. Most people would expect them to assimilate to the American culture by now but they are deep-rooted in their Asian traditions and way of thinking, just as Min and Tian from "Hunger" are. They raised my brothers and me by attempting to pass on their way of thinking, hoping that we honor our roots. We are Vietnamese and were raised to understand and adhere to Vietnamese values, meaning that we are to accept our gender and familial roles as many of Chang's characters do. What my parents fail to understand is that we are also American and have been greatly immersed in and influenced by the American culture as well. My siblings and I believe that gender roles are a thing of the past . . . a thing that belongs to the generation, time, and country in which my parents grew up.

In essence, my siblings and I are Anna and Ruth in "Hunger" while my parents are Min and Tian. We are a great representation of an Asian American family torn apart by our prescribed gender and familial roles. Reminiscent of the family in "Hunger," my family is one of many Asian American families conflicted with such issues. These issues tear apart the family in Chang's story, but many Asian American families are learning to cope with these problems by finding a balance between familial responsibilities and personal desires instead of letting one or the other dictate their lives completely. For us, these issues have become an everyday part of our lives and our struggles seem to be far from over. There is much that my siblings and I need to understand about the immigrant generation and vice versa. Whether or not these conflicts will ever disappear is still a mystery and has yet to stand the test of time.

Works Cited

Chang, Lan Samantha. *Hunger: A Novella and Stories.* New York: Penguin Books, 1998.

The Native American Mascot Suite

The very day we sat down to write the introduction to this suite for the second edition, we read in the papers that Southeast Missouri State University had decided to drop their Native American mascots. The board of regents voted unanimously to cease using "Indians" for its men's athletic teams and "Otahkians" for the women's teams and instead use "Redhawks." This time around, the mascot issue making the news is Chief Illiniwek and the University of Illinois, where a close friend of one of the authors has taken over as director of the Native American House. Unrest over Chief Illiniwek has been percolating for some time, but a 2005 policy by the National Collegiate Athletic Association (NCAA) that prohibits institutions with Indian mascots and imagery from displaying either at NCAA events, thrust the Chief and the University into an uncomfortable spotlight. The issue polarized the campus, and some Native scholars at the university have had property vandalized and even received death

threats. However, in February 2007, the University officially announced that it would cease using Native imagery and that Chief Illiniwek would dance no more.

The move by Illinois is one of more than 300 mascot changes that have occurred since the early 1980s. Activists first began raising questions about the ethics of Native American mascots in 1968, when the National Congress of American Indians began a campaign to address issues of stereotypes in the media. The following year, students, faculty, and other interested parties protested Dartmouth College's "Indian" nickname. It was on April 17, 1970, however, that the dam burst. The University of Oklahoma, a sports powerhouse with a visible Native mascot, retired "Little Red," its disturbing mascot that it had used since the 1940s. Over the next few years, Marquette, Stanford, Dickinson State, Syracuse, St. Bonaventure, and Southern Oregon all got rid of their Indian mascots. Since then, a number of groups such as the United Methodist Church, the state of Minnesota, the American Jewish Committee, the State of Wisconsin Department of Public Instruction, the U.S. Patent and Trademark Office, the United States Commission on Civil Rights, and even the NCAA have taken official public stances against the use of American Indian stereotyping.

That said, there remains a strong enclave of support for Native American mascots. Fans of the Washington Redskins, Cleveland Indians, Chicago Blackhawks, Kansas City Chiefs, Illinois Illini, and Florida State Seminoles have repeatedly fought movements to do away with Indian mascots. The issue at the University of Illinois is among the most public and the

most hotly contested. Alumni, students, and administrators remain divided over the use of an Indian in full headdress as the university's mascot and in particular the "chiefing" (an invented ritualistic dance) of Chief Illiniwek. Supporters of the mascot and the chief claim that both honor the dignity, nobility, and bravery of Native peoples, whereas opponents claim the mascots and the dance engender and perpetuate stereotypes, racism, and bigotry.

The following texts explore the cultural, racial, aesthetic, historical, emotional, and political issues surrounding the Native American mascot issue. Scholar Ellen J. Staurowsky is a professor and chair in the Department of Sport Management at Ithaca College. In this recent essay (2007), Staurowsky uses the NCAA's 2005 policy as a springboard for an analysis of the ethics and politics of Native mascots. C. Richard King and Charles Fruehling Springwood's piece, "Imagined Indians, Social Identities, and Activism," comes from the introduction to their book *Team Spirits: Native Mascots* (2001). King and Springwood do not simply trace the history of Native mascots and resistance to them; they also make connections between the pervasive acceptance of mascots and the history of the United States' treatment of American Indians. King and Springwood also advocate social activism on this front. S. L. Price's article, "The Indian Wars," appeared in a 2002 issue of *Sports Illustrated* and stands as perhaps the most widely accessible piece on the mascot issue, even though it has been decried by some American Indian scholars and activists for allegedly inaccurate statistics regarding the stance of reservation Indians on mascots. An excellent rhetorical assignment would be to read the article closely to determine whether you find the arguments balanced. Finally, we included some fun pieces— a series of hilarious political cartoons and a cycle of funny prose poems by the Choctaw writer LeAnne Howe (known for her award-winning novel *Shell Shaker*). Howe's pieces come from her book of poems, *Evidence of Red*, which won the Oklahoma State Book award in 2006.

The mascot issue remains a critical topic of public debate because it hones in on the conflicts between freedom of expression and civil rights. It also marks an interesting overlap among politics, sports, and visual culture. Do images carry weight? To what degree are caricatures racist? Do these comical, infantilizing, and hostile images contribute—even subconsciously—to the way in which most Americans view American Indians? Finally, how do these images affect Native American identity?

"You Know, We Are All Indian": Exploring White Power and Privilege in Reactions to the NCAA Native American Mascot Policy

Ellen J. Staurowsky

IN THE 1920S AND 1930S, ENGLISHMAN ARCHIE BELANEY became one of the most famous "Red Indians" in the world when, under the guise of the assumed identity of "Grey Owl," he published books about the Canadian wilderness and advocated for nature conservation on the lecture circuit in North America and Europe (Canadian Broadcasting Company [CBC], 1972; Root, 1998). An impostor whose public image was shaped in significant part by White audiences who expected to see a man in buckskins and headdress, his carefully constructed and maintained fraudulent "Indian" identity would not come to light until just after his death (CBC, 1972; Root, 1998). Although Belaney's duplicity was viewed as a betrayal by some of his followers, his misappropriation of Indian identity could not have been accomplished if not for the expectations of the very people who were fascinated with him and/or enamored of his message precisely because he "looked like" an Indian. In 1972, Belaney's Iroquois wife Gertrude Bernard spoke about this in a CBC documentary. She commented, "I was aghast when he said that he was going as an Indian chief to lecture in England. And I said, 'why not as the woodsman you are?'" In response to his wife's query, Belaney replied, "They expect me to be an Indian." From the perspective of Lovat Dickson, the British publisher who arranged the lecture tour, "[Belaney] looked just like what I would have expected or hoped he would look like—an Indian. He was wearing the right clothes, everything I had hoped to unveil to the English public" (CBC, 1972).

Scholar Deborah Root (1998) points out that individual acts of cultural appropriation such as the one perpetrated by Belaney "do not float in space but are underlain by very precise systems of authority" (p. 103). In effect, Grey Owl did not become one of the most famous "Red Indians" in the world by accident. Rather, the existence of Grey Owl speaks to a sociopolitical power structure that renders Indianness tolerable to Whites as long as it is represented on terms acceptable to them. When seen within the larger context of White colonial control over indigenous populations, "how Indians look through the other man's eyes" (Baca, 2000b) is laden with multiple meanings. As a consequence, "In a society where land theft is legitimized by law, and where communities and individuals are repressed to facilitate the colonization of territory, the taking up and popularizing of the culture under siege are not neutral acts" (Root, 1998, p. 105).

For more than a century, U.S. colleges and universities have participated in laying siege to American Indian culture. Through a mass process of misappropriation in the form of American Indian mascots, fight songs, and other forms of imagery, legions of students, graduates, sports fans, and citizens have been encouraged to enact their own versions of the Grey Owl scenario, selectively becoming American Indian impostors themselves and accepting American Indian impersonation as a normative and expected part of school and team identity.

Contrary to the case of Grey Owl, whose masquerade was not known at a conscious level by most of his followers, supporters of "Chief Osceola" at Florida State University (FSU), "Chief Illiniwek" at the University of Illinois, and the "Fighting Sioux" of the University of North Dakota (UND) express few qualms about images manufactured for White consumption designed to achieve an agenda that serves a White power structure. Thus, these images and personalities are celebrated because of their attendant qualities of fighting prowess and bravery but not because they represent peoples, whether they be Sioux or Seminole, who were, and are at times now regarded, in quite literal terms, as enemies of the United States. Within the context of a college sport spectacle, the scripted form of White people "becoming" American Indian renders invisible the ignominious history of American Indian genocide by the U.S. government, replacing it with a culturally comfortable and comforting myth of the "American Indian warrior." It further obscures the White supremacist center of the debate that remains ever present but rarely in full view, unless revealed in the form of someone like Ralph Englestad, a collector of Nazi memorabilia with a penchant for hosting parties on Hitler's birthday, whose $35 million gift to the UND athletic department was linked to the retention of their Fighting Sioux imagery (Dorhmann, 2001).

Inasmuch as the cultural appropriation of American Indians is not neutral, neither are attempts to interrupt the use of this imagery. Nowhere in recent years has this been more forcefully demonstrated than in the negative reaction to the National Collegiate Athletic Association's (NCAA) decision in August of 2005 to bar institutions with hostile or abusive Native American imagery from displaying those images while participating in NCAA-sponsored championships or from hosting championships on campuses where Native American imagery was used (Lederman, 2005; Williams, 2005).

Notably, in the grand scheme of issues that the NCAA has dealt with during its 100-year span of history—persistent academic fraud issues, overcommercialization, allegations of exploiting athletes, and gender equity—none have produced the sustained level of rancor as the Native American mascot issue from the time the policy was announced through the present. Acknowledging the widespread criticism of the NCAA as a result of the policy, noted Cheyenne and Hodolugee Muscogee author Suzan Shown Harjo (2005) wrote in *Indian Country Today*, "The NCAA is learning what it's like to be mocked, cartooned, lampooned and vilified—in short, what it's like to be Indian" (p. A3).

The question of who controls the representation of Native Americans in the college sport context is very much at issue in the reactions to the NCAA Native American mascot policy. Although the presenting focal point for the dialogue surrounding the mascot controversy is a conception of Native Americans, in point of fact, the master narrative running through this discourse is about White supremacy. How else can we explain why images initially invented by White people without the permission of Native Americans have become contested "Indian" terrain, defended by state boards of education, college and university presidents, and state legislatures that are predominantly White? (For detailed histories of these images as White inventions, see Deloria, 1999; King & Springwood, 2001; Spindel, 2000; Staurowsky, 2000; Tovares, 2002.)[1] Even for institutions such as FSU, which has the qualified support of what has come to be called its namesake tribe, it is notable that in none of these cases did American Indian tribes lobby for this recognition. The engagement of American Indian tribes in these discussions is only after the fact, and well after the fact at that.

The Native American Mascot Suite

Whatever umbrage some take to the NCAA policy being achieved by what they call administrative fiat (Kupchella, 2005), the very existence of these images was a matter of White groups or individuals in power acting by fiat.[2]

The remainder of this article addresses the ways in which White power and privilege have played out in the debate that has ensued in the aftermath of the announcement of the NCAA Native American mascot policy, with a focus primarily on the case of the UND Fighting Sioux.

Advised by recent efforts of sport scholars to map Whiteness in sport (King, 2005; McDonald, 2005), the discussion to follow adheres to what McDonald (2005) describes as a reversal that "moves the analytic gaze away from an exclusive preoccupation with the effects of racism on people of color toward inquiry that targets the knowledge and subjects perpetuating racism" (p. 246). In an effort to pursue the question of what the NCAA Native American mascot controversy reveals about White people, power, and privilege, consideration will be given to the complications associated with who gets to claim being "Indian" and the racial trappings contained within the continuum of sustainable racism emerging in the scheme of NCAA policy exemptions. The article ends with a reflection on the role racialized Native American mascots play in perpetuating a culture whose high level of tolerance for offenses directed toward Native Americans cannot be reconciled with the central mission of higher education to treat students fairly and with respect.

"We Are All Indian. At Least, Those of Us Who Went to McMurry."

Reacting to the placement of McMurry University on the NCAA list because of its nickname, the "Indians," Grant Teaff, executive director of the American Football Coaches Association and former McMurry coach, commented, "You know, we are all Indian. At least those of us from McMurry anyway. We all are McMurry Indians, and we always will be" (Griffin, 2006, p. 1C). The sentiment expressed by Mr. Teaff is a familiar one among those affiliated with schools that have Native American sport imagery, perpetuated by the practices of the institutions themselves. Florida State regularly corresponds with their athletic boosters using the standard address, "Dear Seminole" (Black, 2002). Student supporters of the UND call themselves the Sioux Crew, the largest student organization on the campus ("Sioux Crew," 2006). On the surface, this seems like a harmless enough claim embedded as it is in a feeling of solidarity, a desire to belong to groups for whom one has affection and affinity. It is the ease with which the claim is made, however, that is significant. Most assuredly, the desire on the part of non-American Indians who wish to assume the affectations and appearance of being American Indian cannot actually mean that they are Indians or they have authority to speak as Indians. They cannot mean that they would volitionally set themselves on a path to be subjected to the ongoing forces of assimilation designed to "kill the Indian and save the man" (Churchill, 2004). And yet, they perceive themselves to be Indians with a legitimate voice of authority regarding control of "their" imagery.

This assumption of Indianness, this presumption of Indianness on the part of non-American Indians, relies on an understanding that the status conferred by mascots is imbued with the "benefits" of being American Indian without ever suffering the price exacted by the U.S. government and American society at large. As psychologist Stephanie Fryberg (2001) found in studying the effects of Native American imagery on the self-esteem of White and Native American youth, both may support the imagery, but it is Whites, not Native Americans, who experience a boost in self-esteem from being exposed to it. In effect, mascots represent a quintessential consumerist form of no fuss, no muss Indianness made easy. Thus, as Philip Deloria (2004) so eloquently describes, Indians are everywhere in symbolic form throughout American material culture.

This problematic of a freewheeling entitlement to being Indian is explained by Jason Black (2002), a non–American Indian scholar who graduated from Florida State and became, courtesy of the athletic boosters, a Seminole. In interpreting the phenomenon of the "mascotting" of Native America, Black theorized that it served to further White hegemony. About the essential falsity at the core of the "mascotting" process, Black wrote:

> On the one hand, I carry with me a so-called misrepresented identity, a Seminole persona I do not understand but apparently assume through attending football games and hanging framed parchment on my wall. On the other hand, without a lived experience—replete with cultural understanding, prejudicial suffering, and a sense of heritage—how can Florida State University actually refer to me in good faith as "Dear Seminole"? (p. 605).

American Indian identity within this construction is a matter of choice that denies the implications of what it is to be an American Indian.

When viewed through the expanse of history, the taking up and taking on of American Indian identity by Whites has paralleled the taking of land and the taking over of the land mass now commonly referred to as the North American continent. From the time of the Boston Tea Party to the present, Whites have masqueraded as Indians (Deloria, 1999). Strong (2004) points out that assuming the guise of American Indian within the context of a university sport team, however, "is a form of playing Indian in which there is an unusual degree of economic and emotional investment" (p. 79). "As a Foucaltian process of 'self making and being made' within 'hierarchical schemes of racial and cultural difference,'" mascots are a form of cultural citizenship that "defines who does and does not belong within the nation-state and civil society" (p. 83). As normalized activities, the use of Indian sports mascots, logos, and rituals serves to "exclude contemporary Native Americans from full citizenship by treating them as signs rather than as speakers, as caricatures rather than as players and consumers, as commodities rather than citizens" (p. 83).

Beyond the subtle ways in which mascots block paths to what Strong (2004) refers to as full participatory citizenship for American Indians, the cultural shorthand of mascots avoids the very real problem of Whites pretending to be American Indian for their own social and economic gain. As a case in point, in 2000, then president of the National Native American Bar Association Lawrence Baca challenged the integrity of statistics reported by the American Bar Association that suggested American Indians were represented in law schools at higher rates than within the American Indian population overall, a figure that suggested something had gone awry in the reporting given that 40% of American Indian students drop out of high school. He went on to attribute the flawed numbers to "certain students who check the Native American box when they apply to law school even though they are not American Indian" (Baca, 2000a, p. 18).

As Springwood (2004) points out, "The selective (mis)use and inflation of American Indian identity is hardly a new practice" (p. 56). However, disingenuous claims to Indianness affect the entire dialogue surrounding the Native American mascot debate. The obsession with polling American Indians and others on the mascot issue (King, Staurowsky, Baca, Davis, & Pewewardy, 2002) reflects the degree to which the public relies on a belief that "Native voices embody a genuine authenticity that renders them more authoritative" (Springwood, 2004, p. 56). Locating that authentic Native voice, however, or even recognizing it when it is asserted, is problematic because of the "ways in which people who are not 'ethnically Indian' have strategically claimed Indianness in favor of Native American mascots" (Springwood, 2004, p. 56).

TABLE 1   How the NCAA's Mascot Ruling Has Affected 19 Colleges

College	Nickname	Postseason Eligibility
Alcorn State University	Braves	Ineligible unless it changes its nickname.
Arkansas State University	Indians	Ineligible unless it changes its nickname.
Bradley University	Braves	Eligible after dropping its American Indian mascot and logos more than a decade ago (it uses its moniker generically), but placed on a watch list for 5 years.
Carthage College	Red Men	Eligible after changing name from Red Men.
Catawba College	Indians	Ineligible while appeal is pending to keep its nickname.
Central Michigan University	Chippewas	Eligible after receiving support from eponymous tribe.
Chowan University	Braves	Changing its nickname to become eligible.
College of William and Mary	The Tribe	Ineligible while appeal is pending to keep its nickname.
Florida State University	Seminoles	Eligible after receiving support from eponymous tribe.
Indiana University of Pennsylvania	Indians	Ineligible after losing appeal to keep its nickname.
McMurry University	Indians	Ineligible while appeal is pending to keep its nickname.
Midwestern State University	Mustangs	Eligible after changing its nickname from Indians.
Mississippi College	Choctaws	Eligible after receiving support from eponymous tribe.
Newberry College	Indians	Ineligible while appeal is pending to keep its nickname.
Southeastern Oklahoma State University	Savage Storm	Eligible after changing name from Savages.
University of Illinois at Urbana-Champaign	Illini	Won appeal to keep using Illini and Fighting Illini nicknames but lost appeal to bring Chief Illiniwek mascot to tournament games. Ineligible unless it does not bring its mascot. Considering lawsuit against NCAA to keep mascot.
University of Louisiana at Monroe	Warhawks	Eligible after changing its nickname from Indians.
University of North Dakota	Fighting Sioux	Ineligible after losing appeal. Suing association to keep its nickname and logo.
University of Utah	Utes	Eligible after receiving support from eponymous tribe.

Note: In August, 2005, the NCAA ruled that 19 colleges would be ineligible to participate in or play host to NCAA postseason events unless the colleges dropped their American Indian mascots and town nicknames. This table provides an update on the status of those colleges.

When considered in this light, one of the harms of Native American sport team imagery is the day-to-day, easily accessible instruction it provides in how to inappropriately claim symbolic American Indian identity without thought to the individual and collective consequences of doing so. As a tool of social control, non-American Indians become adept at misappropriating without conscience or consideration while creating mass confusion as to who is an Indian.

In this sense, Native American mascots serve as primers of White privilege, where taking without asking or regard is not socially impolite, morally corrupt, educationally harmful, or legally criminal but an acceptable mode of behavior for masses of Americans educated in schools believed to possess, according to Hoftstadter (1963), the moral conscience of the society. As a result, the facially shallow imagery of American Indians that resides in the recesses of the American subconscience exempts the populace from accountability for genocide and makes possible the naive belief that a meaningful answer as to whether these images are objectionable can be ascertained from forced choice opinion polls alone. When examined objectively, the problematic of the "we are all Indians" mascot mentality as incorporated into college and university identity and transmitted through athletic departments violates the fundamental core of the academy and the right of American Indian students to access an education free from the limitations and pressures imposed by the racialized stereotypes that far outnumber them in the higher education landscape.

Notes

1. According to the Institute on Money in State Politics (Moore, 2006),

   Although non-white populations across the country continue to grow, the minority presence in many state legislatures is not representative of the diversity of state populations. . . . Fifty Native American legislators were elected in 12 of the 48 states that held elections in the 2004 election cycle. (p. 8)

   More generally, 13% of those who won election belonged to a minority group. In consulting the list of Native Americans in state legislators, there are none in the state of Florida (http://www.ncal.org/programs/statetribe/2006tcibig.htm).

2. Kupchella mentions this information in several exchanges with the NCAA and in his interview with U.S. College Hockey Online.

3. The incident that occurred in the 1990s, homecoming, when a group of Native Americans riding on a float in the parade were decided by fraternity and sorority members, reportedly subjected to verbal abuse, such as "go back to the reservation," "dirty Indians," "tell your parents to get off welfare," accompanied by war whoops (Tovares, 2002).

4. The university has expressed concern that views of the racial climate at the University of North Dakota (UND) have been based on hearsay (see Braine, 2004).

5. Kupchella (2005) reports that American Indian programs on campus have been funded by $12 million in support, all but $400,000 of it coming from federal sources and tribes. Although Kupchella uses this information to suggest that funders would not entrust the university with the funding if there was a racially hostile environment, one could question whether the university could get more funding if it dropped the Fighting Sioux Name.

6. According to reports in the *Las Vegas Weekly* and *Sports Illustrated*, Englstad hosted parties on two occasions in the 1990s displaying his collection of Adolf Hitler memorabilia. Although Englstad being a supporter of Hitler's, his Imperial Casino was the source of publishing bumper stickers that read "Hitler was right." The Nevada Gaming Control Board fined Englstad $1.5 million and placed restrictions on his gaming license (Dorhmann, 2001; Hodge, 2003; for reference to the $35 million figure, see B.R.I.D.G.E.S., n.d).

7. Three events occurred around the same window of time on the UND campus in June 2006. The lawsuit against the NCAA was arroundced, the decision to move to Division I was arrounced, and a new Sioux Scholarship Endowment was arrounced. The convergence of these three things created an impression on the part of some that the new scholarship program was intended as a bribe to quiet dissent. As Jesse Taken Alive, A Standing Rock Council member said, "It sounds like extortion when dealing with communities that are impoverished," ("Kupchella: Scholarship," 2006). The university denied that this was the motive.

8.. In September 2005, the Standing Rock Sioux passed another resolution opposing the use of the Fighting Sioux nickname. See letter from Ron His Horse is Thunder, Chairman, Standing Rock Sioux Tribe to Bemard Franklin, National Collegiate Athletic Association. This was Resolution No. 438-05.

References

Baca, L. R. (2000a). American Indians overrepresented in law schools? How can that be? *Student Lawyer, 29*(1), 17–18.

Baca, L. R. (2000b). *Being Indian 101* [Lecture]. Ithaca, NY: Ithaca College.

Baca, L. R. (2005). American Indians, the racial surprise in the 1964 Civil Rights Act: They may, more correctly, parhaps, be denominated as a political group. *Howard Law Journal, 48*, 971–991.

Bergland, B. (2006, June 16). UND v. NCAA: State board says no public funds can be used to pay for lawsuit. *Grand Forks Herald*. Retrieved July 7, 2006, from http://www.grandforksherald.com

Black, J. E. (2002, Fall). The "mascotting" of Native America. *American Indian Quarterly, 26*, 605–622.

Braine, M. (Producer). (2004). *If the name has to go …* [Motion picture]. Washington, DC: Quiet Coyote Productions.

B.R.I.D.G.E.S. (n.d.). *Letter from Ralph Englestad to President Kupchella*. Retrieved July 7, 2006, from http://www.und.edu/org/bridges/index2.html

Canadian Broadcasting Company. (1972, December 11). *Grey Owl: Trapper, conservationist, anthor, fraud*. Retrieved August 23, 2006, from http://archives.cbc.ca/IDC-1-69-1931-12551/life_society/saskatchewan_100/clip5

Christianson, E. (2005, August 19). *NCAA executive committee approves Native American mascot review process* [Press release]. Retrieved July 17, 2006, from http://www.ncaa.org

Churchill, W. (2004). *Kill the Indian, and save the man: The genocidal impact of American Indian residential schools*. San Francisco: City Lights.

Copeland, J. (2006, May 22). Mutual of Omaha selected for basic accident program. *The NCAA News*. Retrieved July 7, 2006, from http://www.ncaa.org

Crowley, J. N. (2006). *In the arena: The NCAA's first century*. Indianapolis, IN: NCAA Publishing.

Deloria, P. (1999). *Playing Indian*. New Haven, CT: Yale University Press.

Deloria, D. (2004). *Indians in unexpected places*. Lawrence: University Press of Kansas.

Dodds, D. (2006, January 13). UND: Senate calls for name change. *Keep Media*. Retrieved July 7, 2006, from http://www.keepmedia.com

Dorhmann, G. (2001, October 8). Face-off. *Sports Illustrated*, pp. 44–48.

Falla, J. (1981). *NCAA: The voice of college sports*. Mission, KS: NCAA Publishing.

Fryberg, S. (2001). *Really! You don't look like an American Indian*. Unpublished doctoral dissertation, Stanford University, Palo Alto, CA.

Griffin, T. (2006, June 29). Tradition dies hard. *San Antonio Express-News*, p. 1C.

Harjo, S. S. (2005, August 15). The NCAA is learning what it is like to be Indian. *Indian Country Today, 25*(10), A3.

Hodge, D. (2003). Finer things: What does a casino have to do to be fined? We have A list. *Las Vegas Weekly*. Retrieved July 7, 2006, from http://www.lasvegasweekly.com/2003/05_08/news_upfront3.htm

Hoftstadter, R. (1963). *Anti-intellectualism in American life*. New York: Vintage.

Johnson, P. (2006, June 21). *UND to move all athletic programs to Division I*. Retrieved July 7, 2006, from http://www.fighting.sioux.com/sports/news/release.asp?RELEASE_ID=4957

King, C. R. (2005). Cautionary notes on Whiteness and sport studies. *Sociology of Sport Journal, 22*, 397–408.

King, C. R., & Springwood, C. F. (Eds.). (2001). *Team spirits: The Native American mascot controversy.* Lincoln: University of Nebraska Press.

King, C. R., Staurowsky, E. J., Baca, L., Davis, L., & Pewewardy, C. (2002, November). Of polls and race prejudice: *Sports Illustrated*'s errant "Indian wars." *Journal of Sport and Social Issues, 26,* 381–402.

Kupchella, C. (2005, August 30). *Letter to Myles Brand and Bernard Franklin, National Collegiate Athletic Association.* Retrieved July 1, 2006, from http://www.universityrelations.und.edu/logoappeal/news.html

Kupchella, C. (2006, June 7). *Why the "Sioux" may have to "Sioux."* Retrieved July 1, 2006, from http://www.universityrelations.und.edu/logoappeal/openletter_6-07-06.html

Kupchella, C. (2006, June 19). Scholarship not a bribe for support. *In Forum.* Retrieved July 7, 2006, from http://www.in-forum.com/

Lederman, D. (2005, September 29). Shunning the "Fighting Sioux." *Inside Higher Education.* Retrieved July 7, 2006, from http://www.insidehighered.com/news/2005/09/29/mascot

McDonald, M. (2005). Mapping Whiteness and sport: An introduction. *Sociology of Sport Journal, 22,* 245–255.

Miller, P. C. (2006, June 21). *Interview: UND president continues search for nickname solution.* Retrieved July 7, 2006, from http://www.uscho.com

Minority report from the American Indian Student Services and the Campus Committee for Human Rights. (2005, May). Retrieved July 7, 2006, from http://www.und.nodal.edu/org/bridges/minority_report.html

Moore, M. (2006, March). *Money and diversity: 2004 state legislative elections. A report published by the Institute of Money in State Politics.* Retrieved July 17, 2006, from http://www.followthemoney.org

Native American Rights Fund. (2006). *Individual Indian Money (IIM) accounts: Fact sheet.* Retrieved July 7, 2006, from http://www.narf.org/cases/iimgeninfo/htm

Reynolds, J. (2006, April 19). Cobell trust case enters critical phase. *Indian Country Today, 25*(45), A1-A2.

Root, D. (1998). *Cannabal culture: Art, appropriation, & the commodification of difference.* Boulder, CO: Westview.

Sack, A. L., & Staurowsky, E. J. (1998). *College athletes for hire: The evolution and legacy of the NCAA amateur myth.* Westport, CT: Greenwood.

Sioux Crew. (2006). *Welcome.* Retrieved July 7, 2006, from http://www.und.edu/org/siouxcrew/

Spindel, C. (2000). *Dancing at halftime: Sports and the controversy over American Indian mascots.* New York: New York University Press.

Springwood, C. F. (2004, February). "I'm Indian too!" Claiming Native American identity, crafting authority in mascot debates. *Journal of Sport & Social Issues, 28*(1), 56–70.

Staurowsky, E. J. (2000, November/December). The Cleveland "Indians": A case study in American Indian cultural dispossession. *Sociology of Sport Journal, 17,* 307–330.

Strong, P. T. (2004, February). The mascot slot: Cultural citizenship, political correctness, and pseudo-Indian sports symbols. *Journal of Sport and Social Issues, 28*(1), 79–87.

Tovares, R. (2002, January). Mascot matters: Race, history, and the University of North Dakota's "Fighting Sioux" logo. *Journal of Communication, 26*(1), 76–94.

UND Alumni Association. (2006). *UND litigation fund.* Retrieved August 23, 2006, from http://www.undalumni.org/NCAALitigationFund.htm

UND Indian Related Programs. (2000). *A statement to President Charles Kupchella from 21 separate Indian-related programs at UND.* Retrieved July 7, 2006, from http://www.und.nodak.edu/org/bridges/indianprograms.html

UND Fighting Sioux Club. (2006). *Membership: Levels & benefits.* Retrieved July 7, 2006, at http://www.undalumni.org/FSC-letterwinners/fsc-benefits.htm

United States Commission on Civil Rights. (2000). *Statement of the U.S. Commission on Civil Rights on the use of Native American images and nicknames as sport symbols.* Retrieved August 23, 2006, from http://aistm.org/fr.education.htm

University Relations. (2006a). *American Indian viewbook*. Retrieved July 7, 2006, from http://www.universityrelations.und.edu/logoappeal/vbook.html

University Relations. (2006b). *History of the Fighting Sioux name*. Retrieved July 8, 2006, from http://www.universityrelations.und.edu/logoappeal/history.html

Williams, B. (2005, August 5). *NCAA executive committee issues guidelines for use of Native American mascots at championship event*s [Press release]. Retrieved July 7, 2006, from http://www.ncaa.org/

Imagined Indians, Social Identities, and Activism

C. Richard King and Charles Fruehling Springwood

NATIVE AMERICAN MASCOTS are a pervasive, ubiquitous feature of American culture. Dozens of professional and semi-professional sports teams have (or have had) such monikers. A quarter of a century after Stanford University, the University of Oklahoma, and Dartmouth College retired "their" Indians, according to the National Coalition on Racism in Sports and Media, more than eighty colleges and universities still use Native American mascots (Rodriguez 1998). Innumerable high schools continue to refer to themselves and their sports teams as the Indians, the Redskins, the Braves, the Warriors, or the Red Raiders.

Euro-American individuals and institutions initially imagined themselves as Indians for a myriad of reasons. Whereas some institutions, such as Dartmouth College, had historically defined themselves through a specific relationship with Native Americans, more commonly, especially at public universities, regional histories and the traces of the Native nations that formerly occupied the state inspired students, coaches, and administrators to adopt Indian mascots, as in the University of Utah Running Utes or the University of Illinois Fighting Illini. Elsewhere, elaborations of a historical accident, coincidence, or circumstance seem to account for the beginnings of playing Indian. The students at Simpson College, in Indianola, Iowa, became the Redmen, later adopting a victory cheer known as the "Scalp Song" and using idioms of Indianness in their annual rituals such as homecoming, following remarks that they played like a bunch of red men. Similarly, St. John's University teams were known as the Redmen initially because their uniforms were all red; only later did fans and alumni transform this quirk into a tradition of playing Indian. Whatever the specific origins of these individual icons, Euro-Americans were able to fabricate Native Americans as mascots precisely because of prevailing sociohistorical conditions. That is, a set of social relations and cultural categories made it possible, pleasurable, and powerful for Euro-Americans to incorporate images of Indians in athletic contexts. First, Euro-Americans have always fashioned individual and collective identities for themselves by playing Indian. Native American mascots were an extension of this long tradition. Second, the conquest of Native America simultaneously empowered Euro-Americans to appropriate, invent, and otherwise represent Native Americans and to long for aspects of their cultures that had been destroyed by conquest. Third, with the rise of public culture, the production of Indianness in spectacles, exhibitions, and other sundry entertainments proliferated, offering templates for elaborations in sporting contexts.

Importantly, Native American mascots increasingly have become questionable, contentious, and problematic (Banks 1993; Churchill 1994; Davis 1993; Frazier 1997; Jackson and Lyons 1997; King 1998; King and Springwood forthcoming; Pewewardy 1991; Slowikowski 1993; Springwood and King forthcoming; Vanderford 1996; Wenner 1993). Across the United States and Canada, individuals and organizations, from high school students and teachers to the American Indian

Movement and the National Congress of American Indians, passionately and aggressively have contested Native American mascots, forcing public debates and policy changes.

At the professional level, in April 1999, the federal Trademark Trial and Appeal Board voided the trademark rights of the Washington Redskins of the National Football League, finding that the name and logo used by the team were disparaging and hence violated the law (Kelber 1994; Likourezos 1996; Pace 1994; see also Sigelman 1998). The seven prominent Native Americans who brought the case in 1992, including contributors Vine Deloria Jr. and Susan Shown Harjo, hoped that the cancellation of trademark protection would encourage the franchise to drop its derogatory moniker. In an effort to fend off similar claims and defuse criticism, the Cleveland Indians have offered an origin myth of sorts that suggests the name and logo memorialize a past player and thus honor Native Americans more generally (Staurowsky 1998).

Arguably, collegiate mascots have evoked more debate than their professional counterparts. In the past decade, several colleges and universities have taken great strides in response to public concern. Whereas a handful of institutions, including the University of Utah and Bradley University, have *revised* their use of imagery, many others, including St. John's University, the University of Miami (Ohio), Simpson College, the University of Tennessee at Chattanooga, and Adams State College (Colorado) have *retired* their mascots. Some schools without Native American mascots, such as the University of Wisconsin and the University of Minnesota, have instituted policies prohibiting their athletic departments from scheduling games against institutions with racist icons. At the same time, countless communities and boards of education have confronted the issue. Many have deemed Native American mascots to be discriminatory, opting as the Minnesota State Board of Education and the Los Angeles and Dallas School Districts did, to require that schools change them. Of course, many other schools have retained them, often becoming the site of intense protest and controversy, such as the highly visible struggle continuing to unfold at the University of Illinois at Urbana-Champaign (see King 1998; King and Springwood forthcoming; Prochaska, this volume; Spindel 1997; Springwood and King forthcoming). Not surprisingly, media attention has increased markedly. On the one hand, the media have detailed numerous local and national struggles, while on the other hand, they have taken a leading role in modifying public perceptions of mascots, such as when the *Portland Oregonian* changed its editorial policy and refused to print derogatory team names. In both capacities, they have opened a crucial space of public debate about mascots. . . .

For all of this, Native American mascots remain understudied, too often taken for granted, and rarely questioned by scholars and citizens alike. *Team Spirits* challenges these tendencies, reinterpreting the forgotten histories of many of these "invented" Indians, unraveling their significance for players, coaches, spectators, students, and Native Americans more generally, and, finally, revealing their complicated relevance for an array of postcolonial American social relations and identities.

■ ■ ■

Native American mascots perpetuate inappropriate, inaccurate, and harmful understandings of living people, their cultures, and their histories (Banks 1993; Churchill 1994; Davis 1993; Frazier 1997; Gone 1999; Jackson and Lyons 1997; King 1998; King and Springwood forthcoming; Pewewardy 1994; Slowikowski 1993; Springwood and King forthcoming; Vanderford 1996; Wenner 1993). Through fragments thought to be Indian—a headdress, tomahawk, war paint, or buckskin—Native American mascots reduce them to a series of wellworn clichés, sideshow props, and racist stereotypes, masking, if not erasing, the complexities of Native American experiences and identities. Halftime performance, fan antics, and mass merchandizing transform somber and reverent artifacts and activities into trivial, shallow, and lifeless forms. Indeed, Native American mascots misappropriate sacred ideas and objects, such as the headdress war bonnet, relocating them in sacrilegious contexts. They misuse and misunderstand the elements of Native American cultures and their symbolic meanings. Importantly, since many Euro-Americans encounter Native Americans *only* as mascots and moving images, these unreal Indians materialize the most base images of Native Americans, presenting them as warriors battling settlers and soldiers, noble savages in touch with nature, uncivilized barbarians opposing the civilized and ultimately triumphant advance of Euro-America.

The many invented Indians used in sporting contexts reveal a nuanced system of signs comprising a broad performative space. This space, largely designed by and for a white America, has broad historical dimensions that turn on imaginary images of Native Americans (see Berkhofer 1979; Bird 1996; Dilworth 1996; Drinnon 1980; Mihesuah 1996; Pearce 1988; Steedman 1982). These embodied "Indian" caricatures have been *tropically* produced as, variously, the warring body (Berkhofer 1979; King 1998; Springwood and King forthcoming), the drunken Native (Duran 1996), the dancing Native (Drinnon 1980; Bloom 1996; King and Springwood forthcoming), the sexual Native (van Lent 1996), the magical Native (Colin 1987; Duran 1996), and the maiden Native (Albers and James 1987; Green 1975; Sparks 1995). These Indian mascots conceptually *freeze* Native Americans, reducing them to rigid, flat renderings of their diverse cultures and histories. Moreover, these invented mascots indicate moments of writing and rewriting a Euro-American identity in terms of conquest, hierarchy, and domination. From center courts to athletic turfs, Indian mascots typically stage the historical relations between Native Americans and Euro-Americans as unmarked by violence. Indian mascots are often situated as warlike and bellicose, while others—commonly barefooted and bare-chested—imply a constellation of savagery and sexualized wildness. We suggest that these kinds of images dehumanize and demonize Native Americans, constraining the ability of the non-Indian community to relate to Indians as contemporary, significant, and real human actors. The narratives inscribed by these mascot exhibitions are punctuated by an ambivalence that includes contact, friendship, and subsequent submission. It is a sensual narrative that turns on wildness, sexuality, and savagery, and it is a nostalgic narrative mourning the loss of these once great warriors and their glorious society. To be sure the performance seeks on some level to "honor" the Indian, but it does so through unconscious forms, by allowing white America to simultaneously enact its grief for and consecrate the memory of the Indian. It is a celebration of the Indian sacrifice in the name of imperial progress according to the divine plan of Manifest Destiny. It is a celebration of imperial power then that ritually incorporates the tragic figure of the Indian into the "Imagined community," in Benedict Anderson's (1983) words, of the United States of America. It allows white America to primitively reimagine itself as a partial embodiment of Indianness and, in the process, attempts to psychically and sympathetically join with the Indian in the formation of a "shared" American consciousness. But, as the contributors to the volume demonstrate, it is not a liberating ritual, for it remains comfortably informed by oblique relations of power.

Significantly, then, Native American mascots do not merely craft disparaging images of others but facilitate the dynamic stagings of self. They permit Euro-Americans to construct an individual identity—as fans, athletes, students, citizens, and the like—while solidifying a transcendent sense of community, a unifying communitas. In essence, Native American mascots are masks, which when worn enable Euro-Americans to do and say things they cannot in everyday life, *as though by playing Indian they enter a transformative space of inversion wherein new possibilities of experience reside* (Deloria 1998; Green 1988; Huhndorf 1997; Mechling 1980). For example, on numerous occasions all-male, fraternal clubs have chosen to name and ritually adorn themselves after particular Native American tribes in ways that

The Native American Mascot Suite

3 2 6

CHAPTER 4 • READING AND WRITING ABOUT RACE AND ETHNICITY perhaps allow them to bond at spiritual and emotional levels that—to their non-Indian selves—may seem otherwise unattainable.

Thus, Native American mascots are one instance within a much broader complex of practices of playing Indian. We would argue that in the present moment, such mascots represent the most conspicuous, hotly contested, and broadly consumed form of playing Indian. To fully appreciate the significance of such mascots, the ideological and political economy grounding them must be examined. Playing Indian has always opened a space in which to articulate American identities, as illustrated here by a handful of examples. At the (much celebrated and so-called) Boston Tea Party of December 16, 1773, for instance, a group of locals who fashioned themselves as "Indians" by smearing their faces and shouting "war calls" relieved the British ship *Dartmouth* of its East India Company's tea (see Deloria 1998). Later, as the new republic and its citizens searched for symbols and stories through which to create themselves, they invariably poached Native American communities or at least idealized notions of their Indianness. Perhaps most important, as early as the late eighteenth century, was a proliferation across the young nation of fraternal orders—often secret "clubs" joining learned, masculine patriots—(in)vested in invented Indianness (Deloria 1998:46). The importance of these homosocial organizations intensified precisely as industrial modernity reshaped the racial and gender contour of everyday life. If sport promotes contexts in which to negotiate these crises, sporting clubs often enhanced the productivity of play by playing Indian (Davis 1993). Moreover, throughout the nineteenth century, Euro-Americans played at being Indian on stage and in literature, while encouraging Native Americans to enact notions of Indianness at fairs, in museums, and for other public performances. These stagings peaked in their popularity and sophistication in the late nineteenth and early twentieth centuries at world's fairs (Rydell 1984) and in Wild West shows (Moses 1996). Importantly, the increased use of Native American culture to (re)create self and society for fun and profit corresponded with the final stages of the Euro-American subjugation of Native America in which reformers and politicians endeavored through increasingly ambitious programs and policies to assimilate Native Americans and in the process sought to restrict their traditional practices and precepts, particularly dance, ritual, and spirituality. It was in this context of well-worn and accepted patterns of playing Indian, imperial nostalgia, and the imperial momentum to control Indian expression that Euro-Americans began to fashion Native American mascots.

Scholars and Native American activists have invested great energy in constructing a critique of Indian mascots by foregrounding their colonial legacies and deconstructing the stereotypes they embody. Efforts to challenge mascots emerged from a broader movement to reclaim sovereignty, redress historical inequities, and assert a sociopolitical identity in American public culture (Cornell 1988; Johnson, Nagel, and Champagne 1997; Nagel 1996; Smith and Warrior 1996). Fueled by the civil rights movement, anti-colonial struggles, including opposition to the Vietnam War, and using demands for self-determination in Native American communities, activists and allies demanded a voice in the representation of Native American cultures throughout popular culture. Importantly, struggles over images, although lacking the violence and spectacle of many earlier interventions, have been among the most visible and arguably the most successful examples of American Indian activism and socio-cultural resurgence. Importantly, efforts to challenge and retire Native American mascots have largely been left out of this history. . . .

■ ■ ■

Students and their allies called for the retirement of Native American mascots, rightly highlighting the hurtful images, hateful practices, and hostile learning environments associated

The Native American Mascot Suite

with them. Initially, as detailed above, their struggles resulted in a measure of success, forcing the retirement of mascots at Stanford University and Dartmouth College and the alteration of practices at Oklahoma University and Marquette University. Over the next thirty years, activists and organizations have continued to struggle against mascots, using litigation, petitions, and protests. Indeed, during this period, combining sociopolitical intervention with sociohistorical education, they have raised formerly unspeakable and unremarkable issues to the forefront of current debates about public culture. Moreover, as discussed in greater detail above, they have encouraged many colleges, universities, and communities to rethink their uses and understandings of Indianness. The results of these reconsiderations have been quite impressive, as prominent schools have retired or modified "their" Indians.

For all of their success, activism against mascots has met vigorous reactionary responses. Indeed, many Euro-Americans, even well-intentioned ones, and some Native Americans do not understand such criticisms or grasp the significance of implementing such changes. The 1995 World Series clarifies some of the difficulties associated with this counter-hegemonic, anti-imperial sociopolitical movement. When members of the American Indian Movement as well as representatives from other Native American organizations demonstrated with placards and bull horns outside Atlanta's Fulton County Stadium during baseball's 1995 World Series—pitting the Atlanta Braves against the Minnesota Twins—they voiced objections to the Braves' spectators, many of whom carried large, colorful Styrofoam tomahawks to wave during the now famous "chop." These demonstrations apparently caught the attention of Jane Fonda, the one-time activist and movie star, who met with the leaders of some of these groups. After listening to Clyde and Vernon Bellecourt of AIM (American Indian Movement), she promised that she would no longer do the "tomahawk chop." Braves' fans tend to collectively stand and perform this syncopated chop to stadium organ music—a rhythmic "Indian" beat. The promise of Jane Fonda, married to the team owner, millionaire Ted Turner, was significant. And yet, a few games further into the series, with the Braves "rallying," Fonda stood, along with her husband and some 60,000 other spectators, to do the tomahawk chop. Clearly, Native American activism, for all of its success, continues to struggle against racist ideologies.

References

Albers, Patricia C., and William R. James. 1987. "Illusion and Illumination: Visual Images of American Indian Women in the West." In *The Women's West,* ed. Susan Armitage and Elizabeth Jameson, pp. 35–50. Norman: University of Oklahoma Press.

Anderson, Benedict. 1983. *Imagined Communities.* New York: Verso.

Banks, Dennis J. 1993. "Tribal Names and Mascots in Sports." *Journal of Sport and Social Issues* 17: 5–8.

Berkhoffer, Robert F., Jr. 1979. *The White Man's Indian.* New York: Vintage Press.

Bird, S. Elizabeth, ed. 1996. *Dressing in Feathers: The Construction of the Indian in American Popular Culture.* Boulder, CO: Westview Press.

Bloom, John. 1996. "There Is Madness in the Air: The 1926 Haskell Homecoming and Popular Representations of Sports in Federal Indian Boarding Schools." In *Dressing in Feathers: The Construction of the Indian in American Popular Culture,* ed. S. Elizabeth Bird. Boulder, CO: Westview Press.

Brown, Bill. 1991. "The Meaning of Baseball in 1992 (with Notes on the Post-American)." *Public Culture* 4(1): 43–69.

Churchill, Ward. 1994. "Let's Spread the 'Fun' Around." In *Indians Are Us? Culture and Genocide in Native North America,* pp. 65–72. Monroe, ME: Common Courage Press.

Colin, Susi. 1987. "The Wild Man and the Indian in Early 16th Century Book Illustration." In *Indians and Europe,* ed. C. F. Freest. Herodot, Netherlands: Rader Verlag.

Comoroff, John, and Jean Comoroff. 1991. *From Revolution to Revelation.* Chicago: University of Chicago Press.

Cornell, Stephen. 1988. *The Return of the Native: American Indian Political Resurgence.* Oxford: Oxford University Press.

Davis, Laurel. 1993. "Protest against the Use of Native American Mascots: A Challenge to Traditional, American Identity." *Journal of Sport and Social Issues* 17(1): 9–22.

Deloria, Philip. 1998. *Playing Indian.* New Haven: Yale University Press.

Dilworth, Leah. 1996. *Imagining Indians in the Southwest: Persistent Visions of a Primitive Past.* Washington DC: Smithsonian Institution Press.

Drinnon, Richard. 1980. *Facing West: The Metaphysics of Indian-Hating and Empire-Building.* Minneapolis: University of Minnesota Press.

Duran, Bonnie. 1996. "Indigenous versus Colonial Discourse: Alcohol and American Indian Identity." In *Dressing in Feathers: The Construction of the Indian in American Popular Culture,* ed. S. Elizabeth Bird, pp. 111–28. Boulder, CO: Westview Press.

Frazier, Jane. 1997. "Tomahawkin' the Redskins: 'Indian' Images in Sports and Commerce." In *American Indian Studies: An Interdisciplinary Approach to Contemporary Issues,* ed. Dane Morrison, pp. 337–46. New York: Peter Lang.

Gone, Joseph P. 1999. "Not Enough Indians, Too Many Chiefs: Authority and Performance in the Movement to End Chief Illiniwek." Unpublished manuscript.

Green, Rayna. 1975. "The Pocahontas Perplex: The Image of Indian Women in American Culture." *Massachusetts Review* 16: 698–714.

———. 1988. "The Tribe Called Wannabee: Playing Indian in America and Europe." *Folklore* 99: 30–55.

Hall, Stuart, ed. 1997. *Representation: Cultural Representations and Signifying Practices.* Thousand Oaks, CA: Sage.

Harvey, David. 1990. *The Condition of Postmodernity.* Cambridge, MA: Blackwell.

Huhndorf, Shari. 1997. "Playing Indian, Past and Present." In *As We Are Now: Mixblood Essays on Race and Identity,* ed. William S. Penn, pp. 181–98. Berkeley: University of California Press.

Jackson, E. N., and Robert Lyons. 1997. "Perpetuating the Wrong Image of Native Americans." *Journal of Physical Education, Recreation, and Dance* 68(4): 4–5.

Jameson, Fredric. 1991. *Postmodernism, or, the Cultural Logic of Late Capitalism.* Durham, NC: Duke University Press.

Johnson, Troy, Joane Nagel, and Duane Champagne, eds. 1997. *American Indian Activism: Alcatraz to the Longest Walk.* Urbana: University of Illinois Press.

Jordan, Glenn, and Chris Weedon. 1995. *Cultural Politics: Class, Gender, Race and the Postmodern World.* Oxford: Blackwell.

Kaplan, Amy, and Donald E. Pease, eds. 1993. *Cultures of United States Imperialism.* Durham, NC: Duke University Press.

Kelber, B. C. 1994. "Scalping the Redskins": Can Trademark Law Start Athletic Teams Bearing Native American Nicknames and Images on the Road to Reform? *Hamline Law Review* 17: 533–88.

King, C. Richard. 1998. "Spectacles, Sports, and Stereotypes: Dis/Playing Chief Illiniwek." In *Colonial Discourse, Collective Memories, and the Exhibition of Native American Cultures and Histories in the Contemporary United States,* ed. C. Richard King, pp. 41–58. New York: Garland.

King, C. Richard, ed. 2000. *Postcolonial America.* Urbana: University of Illinois Press.

King, C. Richard, and Charles Fruehling Springwood. Forthcoming. "Choreographing Colonialism: Athletic Mascots, (Dis)Embodied Indians, and EuroAmerican Subjectivities." In *Cultural Studies: A Research Volume,* vol. 5, ed. Norman Denzin. Stamford, CT: JAI Press.

Likourezos, G. 1996. "A Case of First Impression: American Indians Seek Cancellation of the Trademarked Term 'Redskins.' " *Journal of the Patent and Trademark Office Society* 78: 275–90.

Mechling, Jay. 1980. " 'Playing Indian' and the Search for Authenticity in Modern White America." *Prospects* 5: 17–33.

Mihesuah, Devon A. 1996. *American Indians: Stereotypes and Realities.* Atlanta: Clarity Press.

Moses, L. G. 1996. *Wild West Shows and the Images of American Indians, 1883–1933.* Albuquerque: University of New Mexico Press.

Nagel, Joane. 1996. *American Indian Ethnic Renewal: Red Power and the Resurgence of Identity and Culture.* Oxford: Oxford University Press.

Pace, K. A. 1994. "The Washington Redskins and the Doctrine of Disparagement." *Pepperdine Law Review* 22: 7–57.

Pearce, Roy Harvey. 1988. *Savagism and Civilization: A Study of the Indian and the American Mind.* Rev. ed. Berkeley: University of California Press.

Pease, Donald E., ed. 1994. *National Identities and Post-Americanist Narratives.* Durham, NC: Duke University Press.

Pewewardy, Cornel D. 1991. "Native American Mascots and Imagery: The Struggle of Unlearning Indian Stereotypes." *Journal of Navaho Education* 9(1): 19–23.

Rodriguez, Roberto. 1998. "Plotting the Assassination of Little Red Sambo." *Black Issues in Higher Education* 15(8): 20–24.

Rydell, Robert W. 1984. *All the World's a Fair: Visions of Empire at American International Expositions, 1876–1916.* Chicago: University of Chicago Press.

Sigelman, Lee. 1998. "Hail to the Redskins? Public Reactions to a Racially Insensitive Team Name." *Sociology of Sport Journal* 15: 317–25.

Slowikowski, Synthia Sydnor. 1993. "Cultural Performances and Sports Mascots." *Journal of Sport and Social Issues* 17(1): 23–33.

Smith, Paul Chaat, and Robert Allen Warrior. 1996. *Like a Hurricane: The Indian Movement from Alcatraz to Wounded Knee.* New York: New Press.

Sparks, Carol Douglas. 1995. "The Land Incarnate: Navajo Women and the Dialogue of Colonialism, 1821–1870." In *Negotiators of Change: Historical Perspectives on Native American Women,* ed. Nancy Shoemaker, pp. 135–56. New York: Routledge.

Spindel, Carol. 1997. "We Honor Your Memory: Chief Illiniwek of the Halftime Illini." *Crab Orchard Review* 3(1): 217–38.

Springwood, Charles Fruehling, and C. Richard King. Forthcoming. "Race, Ritual, and Remembrance Embodied: Manifest Destiny and the Symbolic Sacrifice of 'Chief Illiniwek.'" In *Exercising Power: The Making and Remaking of the Body,* ed. Cheryl Cole, John Loy, and Michael Messner. Albany: SUNY Press.

Staurowsky, Ellen J. 1998. "An Act of Honor or Exploitation? The Cleveland Indians' Use of the Louis Francis Sockalexis Story." *Sociology of Sport Journal* 15(4): 299–316.

Steedman, Raymond William. 1982. *Shadows of the Indian: Stereotypes in American Culture.* Norman: University of Oklahoma Press.

Vanderford, Heather. 1996. "What's in a Name? Heritage or Hatred: The School Mascot Controversy." *Journal of Law and Education* 25: 381–88.

van Lent, Peter. 1996. "'Her Beautiful Savage': The Current Sexual Image of the Native American Male." In *Dressing in Feathers: The Construction of the Indian in American Popular Culture,* ed. S. Elizabeth Bird, pp. 211–27. Boulder, CO: Westview Press.

Wenner, L. 1993. "The Real Red Face of Sports." *Journal of Sport and Social Issues* 17: 1–4.

A Suite of Mascot Poems

Leanne Howe

Noble Savage Confronts Indian Mascot

NOBLE SAVAGE: What are you doing in my closet?
INDIAN MASCOT: Sugar, can I wear your loin cloth to the big game tonight?
NOBLE SAVAGE: No, and don't call me sugar.
INDIAN MASCOT: C'mon. Besides, you've outgrown it.
NOBLE SAVAGE: No I haven't. Take off those feathers.
INDIAN MASCOT: You said you liked my ostrich boa.
NOBLE SAVAGE: Only that one time. I wish you'd forget it.
INDIAN MASCOT: I will never forget it.
NOBLE SAVAGE: I don't feel the same about you.
INDIAN MASCOT: Don't pull that colonizer shit with me, baby.

> First you say you love me, then you say you don't. I'm not
> your toy baby. Listen, I'm the better half of you six days of
> the week, and twice on Sunday. (He screams and goes a
> little crazy.) And don't you forget it!

(Long Pause)
NOBLE SAVAGE: (shrugs) Sorry.

Noble Savage Contemplates His Fate

Dear Diary;
I can't fall in love with anyone.
I'm here to make all men believe
They're just like me.

Indian Mascot Joins The Village People

At last,
I'm in step with Hollywood,
No longer a transitory subaltern
On center stage
I surpass Fred Astaire,
Michael Jackson,
his sister,
and,
(You can't touch this)
Beatboxer Alien Dee.

I'm masculine prowess
a male dancer in beads and skins,
See the stadium crowd
how they jump to their feet in a

Reverent,
Religious,
Fervent,
Fit.
"YMCA, YMCA, YMCA, YMCA"
an old chant—
Young Men's Christian Association
Young Men's Christian Association
Young Men's Christian Association
Young Men's Christian Association.

Yeah, some decades are more ironic than others.

Indian Mascot Encounters Prejudice (from real Indians)

My own people hate me.
When the Red woman and her child see me,
They weep.
And I weep, too.
"He's white," the Indians, cry. "He's a bestial impersonator."
1 try to humor them with my beautiful smile,
My half-time fancy footwork,
but they throw rotten apples.
At moi.
"You're a fiction." They shout.
"A character, that much is certain." I reply.
"An invention?" They chant.
"No more than you!"
"A failure?" They charge.
"Not a chance. I have fans."
And the show must go on.

American Indians Attempt to Assassinate Indian Mascot

Now,
only the whites protect me.
Indians scream, "Monster."
"He inspires disgust," they cry.
Their words sting like bullets.
Where is my Noble Savage when I need him?
He always defends the weak.

In defiance, I mock my detractors,
"Not butch enough for you, *eh*?"
I pull out all the stops.
Listen,
"I fought beside Red Shoes against the British in 1720."

"I fought with Little Turtle at the 1794 Battle of Fallen Timbers."
"I fought at Horseshoe Bend in the 1814 Red Stick War."
"And, I *KILLED* Custer at the Battle of Little Big Horn."

An Indian boy will not stand for my blasphemy.
He draws his revolver from a backpack,
Aims,
Fires,
Dead on,
Straight.
At the last possible moment my beloved
rides to the rescue on a white horse,
and
we take the bullet simultaneously.
Mortally wounded,
We sigh together.

Ah, my love.

What happened to Indian Mascot and Noble Savage—After the shooting?

Nothing.
They were never real.
This is Hollywood.

A Suite of Cartoons
Three Comics on the
Mascot Issue

5/10

Source: © 2002 Lalo Alcaraz/Universal Press Syndicate.

READING WRITING

This Text: Reading

1. Which of the previous text do you find the most compelling? What evidence does the author use to help make his point? Why are *these* bits of evidence the most convincing?
2. It is easy to discern the position of Staurowsky and King and Freuling, but Price's stance is more difficult. Is he writing from a particular perspective? Elements of the essay make it feel more balanced than the others, but is it?
3. What techniques does Price use to make his essay feel more balanced? What objective data does he use to help make his argument sound convincing?
4. Based on this chapter, do you think the authors of this book take a position regarding the mascot issue? What evidence is there that we make a particular argument here?
5. How do the comics and Howe's poems add to the arguments that Staurowsky makes?

Your Text: Writing

1. Write an essay in which you take a stand on the Native American mascot issue. What evidence will you use to help support your assertions?
2. Write an essay in which you analyze the rhetorical strategies of Staurowsky and Price. Look closely at the "evidence" each uses to help make their points.
3. Write an essay in which you explore why there are still dozens of Native American mascots in the United States. Why is there resistance to changing them? Why do non-Indians have so much invested in holding on to Native American mascots?
4. Write an essay in which you look at the mascot issue through the lens of freedom of expression.
5. Write an essay on the mascot issue through the lens of hate speech and civil rights.
6. Are there other arguments for or against the mascot issue that these writers and artists have not provided? What are they?
7. Write a comparison and contrast essay in which you read the comics alongside the LeAnne Howe piece. How do the authors use humor to defuse the mascot tension?

READING BETWEEN THE LINES

Classroom Activities

1. Although most scientists believe that race is socially constructed, that still leaves open the question of how we construct our ideas of race. In class, discuss some of the ways you see this process working in culture attributed to particular ethnic groups, and in white America as well.
2. In his essay, "In Living Color: Race and American Culture," Michael Omi discusses the way race and ethnicity are portrayed on television. Using your own observations, discuss how popular culture treats race and ethnicity.

3. Discuss clothing and what pieces of clothing signify in general. Do you tend to characterize different groups by what clothes they wear?

4. After reading Beverly Tatum's piece, talk about the presence of race and ethnicity on campus. Do you notice patterns that can be inferred? Do you feel your campus is enlightened about race and ethnicity?

5. Some people still believe races and ethnicities have particular cultures, or cultures that are generated from groups from particular ethnicities. Discuss the phenomenon of people from different cultures participating in each other's culture.

6. Watch *Do the Right Thing* in class. What ideas about race does Spike Lee explore? What about his narrative makes you uncomfortable? What do you think his ideas about race are?

7. Watch *Mississippi Burning* with *Rosewood*. Compare how the two treat the idea of African American participation in remedying racism. What problems do you see in the narratives? What have the filmmakers emphasized in their narratives? Is it at the expense of more "real" or important issues?

8. Watch two television shows, one with an all white or largely white cast, and one with an all African American or largely African American cast. How does each treat the idea of race and ethnicity?

9. Using the same shows, notice the commercials playing—how do these construct a view of race and/or ethnicity?

10. Rent the movies *Smoke Signals*, and, if you can find it, *Naturally Native*—two of the more common films about Native American realities. How do the movies address the issue of Native American representation?

11. On the Web, look at paintings by Jaune Quick-To-See Smith, Michael Ray Charles, and Freddy Rodriguez. Give a semiotic reading of the work by these authors. How do they deal with the visual politics of race?

Essay Ideas

1. Trace the evolution of the portrayal of race and/or ethnicity in a particular medium—television, movies, art, public space. Has it changed in your lifetime? Why or why not?

2. Go to the library or the computer and do a keyword search on a particular ethnicity and a politician's name (example: "Cheney" and "African American"). What comes up when you do this? Is there a trend worth writing about?

3. Do some research on the nature of prejudice. What do researchers say about its nature?

4. Get stories or novels from 75 years ago; look and see how different authors, African/American, white, Italian, Jewish, and so on, portrayed people of different skin color and ethnicity. How would you characterize the treatment as a whole?

5. What are the signs that are encoded in race and ethnicity? How are they portrayed in popular culture and the media? Do a sign analysis of a particular show or media phenomenon.

6. Watch two television shows, one with a largely white cast, one with a largely African-American cast. Compare how each deals with the idea of race or ethnicity.

7. Using the same shows, notice the commercials playing—how do these construct a view of race and/or ethnicity?

8. Look at a film or films made by African American, Hispanic, or other ethnic directors. How do these directors deal with the idea of race and ethnicity, compared to white directors dealing with similar ideas?

9. Write an essay on racially questionable comments uttered by celebrities (e.g., Michael Richards, Fuzzy Zoeller, Joseph Biden, Frederic Rouzaud, Mel Gibson, and George Allen) and what these transgressions say about race, our culture, and the people who made them.

The set of *X-Men* is a carefully constructed text.

CHAPTER 5

THE CONTEMPORARY AMERICAN POET LOUIS SIMPSON WRITES IN ONE OF HIS POEMS: "EVERY AMERICAN IS A FILM CRITIC." HE IS PROBABLY RIGHT. JUST ABOUT EVERYONE WE KNOW LOVES MOVIES, AND AS MUCH AS WE LOVE MOVIES, WE LOVE TALKING ABOUT THEM. WHAT'S MORE, WHEN WE WATCH MOVIES, WE OFTEN FEEL QUALIFIED AS CRITICS; WE FREELY DISAGREE WITH MOVIE REVIEWERS AND EACH OTHER. ANDRE MAUROIS ONCE QUIPPED THAT IN LITERATURE AS IN LOVE, WE ARE ASTONISHED BY WHAT OTHERS CHOOSE. THAT MAY BE DOUBLY SO FOR MOVIES.

Despite our familiarity with movies and our apparent willingness to serve as movie critics, we sometimes resist taking a more analytical approach to them. For many of us, movies are an escape from school or critical thinking. After a long day at school or at work, most of us want to sit in front of a big screen and veg out with *Talladega Nights* or *Terminator 2* for a couple of hours. Your authors confess that we have been known to veg out too, so we aren't knocking the idea of losing oneself in front of a seemingly mindless action flick. However, we do want you to be aware of the fact that movies are never *just* mindless action flicks. They are always some kind of cultural text, loaded with ideas about a particular culture, either consciously or unintentionally expressed.

For instance, some film and cultural critics have argued that despite the futuristic special effects, the *Star Wars* movies create a sense of nostalgia for the value systems of the 1950s, values that by today's standards may seem racist, sexist, and blindly patriotic. In fact, one of our students has written an essay along these lines, which we have included here. For others, the 90s favorite *Fatal Attraction* is more than a suspenseful movie about a crazed psycho-killer boiling

a bunny. Some see the film as an allegory on AIDS, claiming the film reinforces the central fear of AIDS: if you sleep around, you risk death. Still others see the film as a document that confirms the backlash against women during the conservatism of the Reagan years. In a much different vein, cultural critics and film historians have argued that genre movies like comedies, family melodramas, and gangster flicks tell stories about and support mainstream American values— the centrality of parenting, traditional heterosexual marriage, the necessity of law enforcement, and the security of suburbia. In fact, some film and cultural critics like Thomas Shatz and Andre Bazin have argued that Westerns like *The Searchers, Red River,* and *Broken Arrow* reflect an era's views on race, justice, and "American values." You may disagree with these particular readings, but they show how movies can be a rich source for cultural exploration and debate.

However, there are obstacles when reading movies through a purely cultural lens. In some ways, our familiarity with movies becomes a liability when trying to analyze them. Because you have seen so many movies, you may believe that you already know how to read them. In some ways, you do. As informal movie critics, you are geared toward analyzing the plot of a movie or determining whether a film text is realistic or funny or appropriately sad. And if asked about music, fashion, setting, and dialogue, you would likely be able to talk about these aspects of filmmaking. But, when reading literature, you probably prepare your brain for a more intense act of *analysis* than you do when you watch *Legally Blonde 2.* You probably have not been taught to look *through* the plot and dialogue of movies to see the film as a cultural text. Though at times difficult, the process is often rewarding.

For instance, pay attention to how many Asian or American Indians you see in contemporary movies. Watch for roles for strong, confident women. Look for movies in which poor or blue-collar people are treated not as a culture but as interesting individuals. See how many films are directed by women or minorities. Pay attention to product placements (that is, brand products such as soda cans, cereal, kinds of cars, or computers) in movies. Work on seeing cinematic texts as products, documents, and pieces of evidence from a culture. Rather than diminishing your enjoyment of movies, this added component of movie watching should enhance not only the actual film experience but also your understanding and appreciation of movies as produced, constructed texts.

Like literature and music, movies are comprised of genres.

Movies, perhaps even more than literature and music, are comprised of genres, such as Westerns, science fiction, comedy, drama, adventure, horror, documentaries, and romance. You may not think about film genres that often, but you probably prepare yourself for certain movies depending on the genre of that particular film. You come to comedies prepared to laugh; you arrive at horror movies prepared to be scared; you go to "chick flicks" expecting romance, passion, and a happy ending. If you don't get these things in your movie experience, you will likely feel disappointed, as though the film didn't hold up its end of the bargain. Notice, in reading the selections here and movie reviews generally, how critics do or do not pay attention to genre. Though they should be familiar with genre, many critics insist on reviewing all movies as if they are supposed to be as earnest and dramatic as *Casablanca* or *Titanic,* when movies like *Borat* or *Knocked Up* clearly try to do different things.

The idea of genre in movies is as old as film itself. In the early days of Hollywood, the studio system thrived on genre movies, and in fact, genre films were pretty much all that came out of Hollywood for several decades. Even today, blockbuster movies are most often genre pieces that adhere to the criteria of a particular genre. *I, Robot* is not *The 40-Year Old Virgin.* Different genres evoke different emotions, and they comment on (and reinforce) different values.

Being aware of genres and their conventions will help you when it comes time to write a paper on movies. When you "read" a film, think about how it fits into a particular genre. Taking into account formal, thematic, and cultural forces (the Cold War, civil rights, Vietnam, feminism, the Great Depression, the economic pressure to turn a profit) will allow you to see movie production as a dynamic process of exchange between the movie industry and its audience. You should be mindful of why we like certain genres and what these genres tell us about our culture and ourselves. The fact that some writers and critics distinguish between "movies" (cinema for popular consumption) and "films" (cinema that tries to transcend or explode popular genre formulations) suggests the degree to which genres influence how we read movie texts.

Movies are a powerful cultural tool.

A hundred years ago, people satisfied their cravings for action, suspense, and character development by reading books and serials; today, we go to the movies, or, more and more frequently, avoid the communal experience of the theater for the private experience of renting DVDs. Innovations like TiVo and Netflix have made staying at home even easier. Still, we are living in a visual age. In America, video and visual cultures have become the dominant modes of expression and communication, and learning to "read" these media with the same care, creativity, and critical acumen with which we read written texts is crucial. To better understand the phenomenon of movies, we need to contextualize the movie experience within American culture, asking in particular how thoroughly American movies affect (and reflect) American culture.

In addition, movies are not just indicators for American culture—they determine culture itself. Fashion, songs, modes of behavior, social and political views and gender and racial values are all underscored by movies. For instance, *Wayne's World* made certain songs and phrases part of everyday American life. On a more complex level, many critics claim the movie *Guess Who's Coming to Dinner,* in which a wealthy white woman brings home her black fiancé, went a long way toward softening racial tensions in the 1960s. We even define eras, movements, and emotions by movies—the 1960s is often symbolized by *Easy Rider;* the 1970s by *Saturday Night Fever* and *Star Wars;* the 1980s by movies like *Fast Times at Ridgemont High* and *Do the Right Thing;* and the 1990s by *Titanic* and *You've Got Mail.* Because more people see movies than read books, one could argue that the best documents of American popular culture are movies. Thus, we tend to link the values and trends of certain eras with movies from those eras. Movies help us understand culture because they embody culture.

Movies also guide our behavior. In contemporary society, we often learn how to dress, how to talk, and even how to court and kiss someone, from the cinema. In fact, for many young people, their model for a date, a spouse, and a romantic moment all come from what they have seen in movies. In other words, influential models of behavior, aspects of their hopes and dreams, come not from life but from movies. So, as you read the following pieces and as you watch movies, ask yourself if the things you desire, you desire because movies have planted those seeds in your heads.

The advertising and marketing of a movie affect how we view the movie and how the studio views itself and us.

Next time you watch previews in a theatre or on a video or DVD you have rented, pay attention to how the film being advertised is presented to you. Be aware of how movies are packaged, how they are marketed, how actors talk about them in interviews. Whether you know it or not, you are being prepped for viewing the movie by all of these texts. Even independent films have become mainstream by marketing themselves as similar to other (popular) independent movies. Marketing is selling, and studios fund, market, and release movies not so much to make the world a better place but primarily to make money (though directors and actors may have different motivations). Also, unlike a book publisher, a studio has likely paid tens of millions of dollars to make a movie, so it needs a lot of us to go see it. We might ask ourselves how these considerations affect not only the advertising but also the movie itself.

In addition, Hollywood studios rarely have your best interest at heart. This is not to say that studios want to make you an evil person, but moviemakers have only rarely seen themselves as educators. For instance, few studios fund documentaries—and the controversy over Disney/Miramax refusing to distribute Michael Moore's incendiary documentary *Fahrenheit 9/11* is a testament to this fact. Few studios seem eager to make movies about poets, painters, composers, or philosophers because they know that not many people will go to see them. Movie studios began as a financial enterprise; studios and the film industry grew as America and American capitalist ideals grew. Nowadays, the topics and subjects of movies have been largely market tested just like any other consumer product such as toys, soft drinks, and shoes.

Movies use various techniques to manipulate audiences.

Manipulation is not necessarily a negative term when we talk about the manipulation of everyday objects; but when we move into the realm of emotions, manipulative texts become problematic. Film is such a wonderful medium because directors have so many tools at their disposal; however, it is relatively easy to use those tools to manipulate audiences. Directors employ music, lighting, special effects, and clever editing to help make their movies more powerful. Music reinforces feelings of excitement (*Lord of the Rings*), fear (*Jaws*), romance (*Titanic*), or anger (*Do the Right Thing*). Lighting and filters can make people, especially women, appear more delicate or fragile. The famous film star from the 1930s and 1940s, Marlene Dietrich, would only be shot from one side and insisted on being illuminated with overhead lights. The first several minutes of *Citizen Kane,* widely considered the best American film ever made, are shot largely in the dark to help drive home the sense that the reporters are "in the dark" about media mogul Charles Foster Kane. In movies like *I, Robot, The Matrix* trilogy, and *Lord of the Rings,* special effects make the story we are watching seem less like light and shadow and more like reality. Even how a filmmaker places a camera affects how we view the film. The close-up, spookily lit shots of Anthony Hopkins's face in *Silence of the Lambs* make us feel like Hannibal Lecter might eat *our* liver with some fava beans and a nice Chianti. Similarly, in many Westerns, the camera is placed at knee level, so that we are always looking up at the cowboy, reinforcing his stature as a hero. Director Orson Welles uses similar techniques in *Citizen Kane.* Alfred Hitchcock was a master of placing the camera in manipulative places. From *Psycho* to *Rear Window* to *Rope,* we see exactly what he wants us to see and how he wants us to see it. We see nothing more than what the camera shows us.

There are other forms of manipulation as well. Many people feel Steven Spielberg's movies end with overly manipulative scenes that pluck at the heartstrings of the audience, forcing overdetermined emotions and over-the-top melodrama. Such accusations are often leveled at teen romance flicks and so-called bio-pics because they make a person's life seem more maudlin, more heart wrenching than it could possibly be.

Costumes, colors, sounds and sound effects, editing, and set design all contribute to how the movie comes to us. Sound and music are particularly effective. In *Star Wars,* for instance, each character has a specific musical profile—a kind of theme song—whose tone mirrors how you are supposed to feel about that character. You probably all remember the dark, deep foreboding music that always accompanies Darth Vader. Like music, the clothes a character wears tell us how to feel about that person. The costumes worn by Ben Affleck and Will Smith in various movies probably reinforce gender expectations, as do the clothes of Julia Roberts or Jennifer Lopez. How a spaceship or a dark, scary warehouse looks puts us in the mood so that the plot and action can move us. Savvy viewers of movies will be aware of the ways in which films try to manipulate them because in so doing, they will be better able to read other forms of manipulation in their lives.

Movies are not just about ideas and action; they are also about values.

Next time you see a Hollywood movie, consider the value system the movie supports. By value system, we mean the values, priorities, and principles a movie advocates. For instance, although we liked the first *Legally Blonde* movie, we were shocked by how traditional the movie's ending was. While the entire movie demonstrates the ways in which the underappreciated female character gets the best of boys, law school colleagues, and professors—even her enemies in the courtroom—all of these very important successes take a back seat to the fact that, ultimately, she lands the hunky guy. It is as though all of her accomplishments were important *so* that she could win the cute boy in the end. The ultimate message, then, is that what women accomplish on their own is fine, if that is of interest, but the real victory, the real triumph, is snagging the man.

Similarly, many Hollywood movies advocate the importance of social class, as Michael Parenti points out in his now famous essay "Class and Virtue." Movies like *Maid in Manhattan* and *Jerry Maguire* and classic romantic comedies such as *Pretty Woman, Trading Places,* and *My Fair Lady* spend most of their energy figuring out ways for their characters to make a jump in social class. It is worth asking how many truly popular Hollywood movies are at the same time truly radical and how many reinforce traditional, mainstream middle-class values. We are not suggesting traditional middle-class values are *bad;* rather, we urge you to consider the value system advocated by the most powerful cultural machinery in the country. Our contention here is that this value system directly affects the movies you see, the stars acting in the movie, the plot structures, and the ultimate messages these movies send. They also affect how you see your own life, as you may find yourself, without knowing it, comparing your own life to that of Elle Woods. Again, paying attention to these issues will make you a smarter watcher of movies and a better writer about them as well.

THIS TEXT

1. While it will be impossible for you to know this fully, try to figure out the writing situation of each author. Who is the audience? What does the author have at stake? What is his or her agenda? Why is she or he writing this piece? For instance, would David Denby, a white male, give the same reading of *Waiting to Exhale* as bell hooks?

2. What are the main points of the essay? Can you find a thesis statement?

3. Do you think the authors "read into" movies too much? If so, why do you say this?

4. As you read the essays, pay attention to the language the critics use to read movies.

5. If you have not seen the movies the authors mention, rent and watch them—preferably with a group of people from your class.

6. Try to distinguish between a review and an argumentative or persuasive essay. You should also be aware of a distinction between a short capsule review, which is more of a summary, and a longer analytical review (like the ones printed here).

BEYOND THIS TEXT: FILM TECHNIQUE

Camera angles and positioning: How is the camera placed? Is it high, low, to the side? And how does it move? Is it a hand-held camera, or is it stationary? How does it determine how you *see* the movie?

Lighting: Light and shading are very important to movies. Are there shadows? Is the film shot during the day or mostly at night? How do shadows and light affect the movie and your experience of it?

Color and framing: Often, directors try to give certain scenes an artistic feel. Is the shot framed similar to a painting or photograph? Does the movie use color to elicit emotions? How does the movie frame or represent nature?

CONTENT

Theme: What are the themes of the movie? What point is the director or writer trying to get across?

Ideology: What ideas or political leanings does the movie convey? Are there particular philosophies or concepts that influence the message the movie sends?

THE WHOLE PACKAGE

Celebrities: What movie stars appear (or don't appear) in the movie? How do certain stars determine what kind of movie a film is? Do the actors ever look ugly or dirty or tired or sloppy?

Technology: What kind of technology is at work in the film? How do special effects or stunts or pyrotechnics affect the film viewing experience?

Genre: What genre does a particular movie fit into? Why? What are the expectations of that genre?

Culture: As a cultural document, a cultural text, what does this movie say about its culture? How does it transmit values? What kinds of ideas and values does it hold up or condemn?

Effectiveness: Does the movie "work" as a movie? Why or why not? What cultural forces might be influencing your criteria of effectiveness?

Great Movies and Being a Great Moviegoer

Roger Ebert

Roger Ebert is probably the most famous movie reviewer in the country. A Pulitzer-prize winning columnist for the *Chicago Sun-Times,* he became a household name through his participation in *Siskel and Ebert at the Movies,* a popular television show in which he and the late Gene Siskel argued (sometimes bitterly) about current movies. Ebert wrote this piece in 2000 to celebrate reaching the milestone of 100 "great movies" in his ongoing series. We like it because Ebert talks about why he likes certain movies and what it takes to be a good watcher of them. As you read, think about how movies are both public and private texts. Why do we love them, and what roles do they play in our lives? The entire Great Movies project can be found at http://rogerebert. suntimes.com/apps/pbcs.dll/section?category-greatmovies_first100.

EVERY OTHER WEEK I VISIT a film classic from the past and write about it. My "Great Movies" series began in the autumn of 1996 and now reaches a landmark of 100 titles with today's review of Federico Fellini's *8½,* which is, appropriately, a film about a film director. I love my job, and this is the part I love the most.

We have completed the first century of film. Too many moviegoers are stuck in the present and recent past. When people tell me that *Ferris Bueller's Day Off* or *Total Recall* are their favorite films, I wonder: Have they tasted the joys of Welles, Bunuel, Ford, Murnau, Keaton, Hitchcock, Wilder or Kurosawa? If they like Ferris Bueller, what would they think of Jacques Tati's *Mr. Hulot's Holiday,* also about a strange day of misadventures? If they like "Total Recall," have they seen Fritz Lang's *Metropolis,* also about an artificial city ruled by fear?

I ask not because I am a film snob. I like to sit in the dark and enjoy movies. I think of old films as a resource of treasures. Movies have been made for 100 years, in color and black and white, in sound and silence, in wide-screen and the classic frame, in English and every other language. To limit yourself to popular hits and recent years is like being Ferris Bueller but staying home all day.

I believe we are born with our minds open to wonderful experiences, and only slowly learn to limit ourselves to narrow tastes. We are taught to lose our curiosity by the bludgeon-blows of mass marketing, which brainwash us to see "hits," and discourage exploration.

I know that many people dislike subtitled films, and that few people reading this article will have ever seen a film from Iran, for example. And yet a few weeks ago at my Overlooked Film Festival at the University of Illinois, the free kiddie matinee was *Children of Heaven,* from Iran. It was a story about a boy who loses his sister's sneakers through no fault of his own, and is afraid to tell his parents. So he and his sister secretly share the same pair of shoes. Then he learns of a footrace where third prize is . . . a pair of sneakers.

"Anyone who can read at the third-grade level can read these subtitles," I told the audience of 1,000 kids and some parents. "If you can't, it's OK for your parents or older kids to read them aloud—just not too loudly."

The lights went down and the movie began. I expected a lot of reading aloud. There was none. Not all of the kids were old enough to read, but apparently they were picking up the story just by watching and using their intelligence. The audience was spellbound. No noise, restlessness, punching, kicking, running down the aisles. Just eyes lifted up to a fascinating story. Afterward, we asked kids up on the stage to ask questions or talk about the film. What they said indicated how involved they had become.

Kids. And yet most adults will not go to a movie from Iran, Japan, France or Brazil. They will, however, go to any movie that has been plugged with a $30 million ad campaign and sanctified as a "box-office winner." Yes, some of these big hits are good, and a few of them are great. But what happens between the time we are 8 and the time we are 20 that robs us of our curiosity? What turns movie lovers into consumers? What does it say about you if you only want to see what everybody else is seeing?

I don't know. What I do know is that if you love horror movies, your life as a film-goer is not complete until you see *Nosferatu.* I know that once you see Orson Welles appear in the doorway in *The Third Man,* you will never forget his curious little smile. And that the life and death of the old man in *Ikiru* will be an inspiration every time you remember it.

I have not written any of the 100 Great Movies reviews from memory. Every film has been seen fresh, right before writing. When I'm at home, I often watch them on Sunday mornings. It's a form of prayer: The greatest films are meditations on why we are here. When I'm on the road, there's no telling where I'll see them. I saw *Written on the Wind* on a cold January night at the Everyman Cinema in Hampstead, north of London. I saw *Last Year at Marienbad* on a DVD on my PowerBook while at the Cannes Film Festival. I saw *2001: A Space Odyssey* in 70mm at Cyberfest, the celebration of HAL 9000's birthday, at the University of Illinois. I saw *Battleship Potemkin* projected on a sheet on the outside wall of the Vickers Theater in Three Oaks, Mich., while three young musicians played the score they had written for it. And Ozu's *Floating Weeds* at the Hawaii Film Festival, as part of a shot-by-shot seminar that took four days.

When people asked me where they should begin in looking at classic films, I never knew what to say. Now I can say, "Plunge into these Great Movies, and go where they lead you."

There's a next step. If you're really serious about the movies, get together with two or three friends who care as much as you do. Watch the film all the way through on video. Then start again at the top. Whenever anyone sees anything they want to comment on, freeze the frame. Talk about what you're looking at. The story, the performances, the sets, the locations. The camera movement, the lighting, the composition, the special effects. The color, the shadows, the sound, the music. The themes, the tone, the mood, the style.

There are no right answers. The questions are the point. They make you an active movie watcher, not a passive one. You should not be a witness at a movie, but a collaborator. Directors cannot make the film without you. Together, you can accomplish amazing things. The more you learn, the quicker you'll know when the director is not doing his share of the job. That's the whole key to being a great moviegoer. There's nothing else to it.

READING WRITING

This Text: Reading

1. What makes a "great movie" for you? Do you think it would differ from Ebert's criteria? Based on his essay, what does it take for a movie to be "great" in Ebert's eyes?
2. What does Ebert mean when, in the final paragraph, he asks you to be a "collaborator?" How is this similar to being an active reader of texts?
3. What is Ebert's thesis in this essay? Does he have a clear argument, and if so, what is it? How would you describe his tone?

Your Text: Writing

1. Write an essay in which you argue that a certain movie is "great." This is a wonderful opportunity to write a definitional essay. Define what a great movie must be, then show how your movie is, in fact, great.
2. Take an oppositional stance to Ebert regarding one of the movies on the list. Make a compelling argument why a certain movie is *not* great. Be sure that your argument is more logos-based than pathos-based.
3. Write a paper about the entire process of labeling "great" movies. Why do we care if a movie is great or not? What is at stake in movie hierarchies like this?

The New Hollywood Racelessness: Only the Fast, Furious, (and Multiracial) Will Survive

Mary C. Beltrán

Mary C. Beltrán is an assistant professor at the University of Wisconsin-Madison, where she teaches communication studies and Chicano/a studies. In this exceedingly well-researched and well-documented essay from 2005, she reads two popular action movies through the lens of race. Fans of *Romeo Must Die* and *The Fast and the Furious* who assumed the movies were value-free adrenaline flicks will be astonished at how much information about race and racelessness the films carry. Beltrán's essay is a fine model of using a lens and research to make serious points about popular texts.

RECENT HOLLYWOOD FILMS SUCH AS *Romeo Must Die* (Andrzej Bartkowiak, 2000) and *The Fast and the Furious* (Rob Cohen, 2001) are notable for their multiethnic casts and stylized urban settings. Correspondingly, the key to the survival of the protagonists in these "multiculti" action narratives is their ability to thrive in environments defined by cultural border crossings and pastiche. Perhaps not coincidentally, the heroes who command these environments increasingly are played by biracial and multiethnic actors, such as Vin Diesel in *The Fast and the Furious* and *XXX* (Rob Cohen, 2002) and Russell Wong, who plays a pivotal role in *Romeo Must Die*.[1]

This trend reflects contemporary shifts in U.S. ethnic demographics and ethnic identity, while subtly reinforcing notions of white centrism that are the legacy of the urban action movie. In particular, as I shall argue, the new, ethnically ambiguous protagonist embodies contemporary concerns regarding ethnicity and race relations with respect to the nation's burgeoning cultural creolization and multiethnic population. The analysis presented here shall be situated in the history of Hollywood representations of the multiethnic inner city, as well as in relation to shifts in the country's ethnic demographics, cultural interests, and popular culture.

Romeo Must Die and *The Fast and the Furious* present two visions of the millennial city and its multiethnic inhabitants that at first glance appear radically different. *Romeo Must Die* tells the story of a struggle between African American and Chinese crime syndicates in the San Francisco Bay Area, a cityscape marked by extreme cultural divisions. In this millennial urban environment, ethnic groups are at war, "getting along" is just a dream used to sell ethnic-oriented clothes and music, and treading on another's territory can have deadly consequences. Two nonwhite and "bicultural" stars (with respect to crossing over from other cultural worlds of the mass media), Hong Kong film star Jet Li and the late R&B and hip-hop artist Aaliyah, rise within the narrative to end a bloody battle between the two factions.

In contrast, *The Fast and the Furious* depicts Los Angeles as racially harmonious. The story of a young white cop who goes undercover in the world of illegal street racing, *The Fast and the Furious* presents the inner city as a place where ethnic groups, although they know their own turf, compete amicably. Biracial actor Vin Diesel portrays the ethnically ambiguous leader of this culturally diverse, utopic subculture. This essay explores how the distinct settings, narratives, characters, and actors in these two films reflect and comment on contemporary American race relations, particularly its increasing multiracial/multiethnic dimension.

The Multiculti Millennial Audience

The evolution of urban action films and their respective heroes have, to a large degree, mirrored national sociopolitical changes. Developments that have had an impact, both on U.S.

cities and on national race relations, include the shift to postindustrialism and the rise of the suburbs in the 1950s, the subsequent economic decay of many cities, the inner-city protests and riots of the 1960s, and, in more recent decades, the redevelopment of some urban centers. Civil rights efforts over the last half-century, as well as changes in the attitudes of Hollywood film producers, have also influenced racial attitudes and perceptions about American cities. Particularly influential in this regard have been the ethnic demographic shifts of the last two decades, which have entailed a "complete shakeup of the country's ethnic and racial composition."[2] As a result of these developments, many younger Americans have a more open approach to matters of race and ethnicity than do their older counterparts.

With respect to ethnic demographics, notions of a white majority also no longer fit the country neatly. Speaking of today's teens, who have been referred to variously as Generation Y, the Echo Boomers, and the Millennial Generation, Neil Howe and William Strauss assert that "demographically, this is America's most racially and ethnically diverse, and least Caucasian generation."[3] As tallied by the U.S. Census, almost 36 percent of Americans eighteen and younger fell under the racial classification of nonwhite in 1999, while nonwhites made up only 14 percent of the GI Generation, born between 1901 and 1924. In addition, as Howe and Strauss state, "One millennial in five has at least one immigrant parent, and one in ten has at least one noncitizen parent."[4] Thus, we could expect to see a broad, multicultural perspective in many millennials—a cohort large enough to displace the baby boomers with respect to dictating popular culture.[5] The proportion of nonwhites rises exponentially when California—home to the film industry and other producers of global entertainment—is considered. In 2000, California became the second mainland state where whites are a minority; Latinos have outnumbered whites in California by one million since 1998.[6] Undoubtedly, nonwhites have reached an important critical mass through which their presence is beginning to be felt, even in the formerly white-dominated story worlds of Hollywood.

Meanwhile, the percentage of multiethnic or, as they are more popularly described, mixed-race families and individuals in the United States is also rising. In a revolutionary shift, in the 2000 census, respondents were given the option for the first time to describe themselves as biracial or multiracial; 6.8 million or 2.4 percent of the respondents indicated that they belonged to two or more races.[7] Given that many multiracial individuals also choose to identify themselves by only one ethnic or racial signifier, we can assume that the multiracial population in the United States is even higher. The number of mixed-race youth in particular has boomed and is expected to continue to increase with the decriminalization of mixed-race marriages and increasing social acceptance of marriages to those outside one's ethnic group. The impact of this growing mixed-race population is just beginning to be realized.

Moreover, as cultural critics such as Marilyn Halter and Leon Wynter assert, a "postmodern ethnic revival" has taken hold in the United States with respect to individuals of both European and non-European heritage expressing a greater interest in their ethnic origins than Americans in previous decades.[8] This renaissance in ethnic exploration and related consumer practices has been prompted by several factors, including increasing ethnic diversity and cultural pride since the peak of the civil rights and counterculture movements of the 1960s and 1970s. Related to these developments, a paradigm shift has taken place. In marked contrast to the racial attitudes that motivated the tragic mulatto discourses in the early part of the twentieth century, as described by film historian Donald Bogle and others, nonwhite ancestry now has cachet. According to Wynter, "Blackness (or nonwhiteness) now suffers less and less of a discount in the marketplace, while whiteness commands less and less of a premium."[9] Nonwhite ancestry also has, I argue here, a particular cachet when combined with whiteness.

Young people of all ethnic backgrounds also are demonstrating in their media habits an interest in performers of diverse backgrounds. For example, one BBDO study of television viewing in the 1990s found that people aged seventeen to twenty-four are more likely than older viewers to watch television programs starring actors of ethnicities different from their own.[10] Many American entertainment producers, manufacturers, and advertisers are capitalizing on this evolution, as reflected in the commodification of ethnic-inflected fashion, products, and popular culture texts.

Alongside, and probably because of these demographic shifts, ethnically ambiguous media figures are gaining greater cultural visibility.[11] This trend can be seen in the ascendance of ethnically ambiguous models and actors, including mixed-race and light-skinned performers of color. In addition, "white" actors and models increasingly are modifying their appearance to promote an ethnic look, whether by increasing the size of their lips, making their eyes more almond-shaped, or adding curves by inserting implants.

The political potential of this new ethnic visibility has been the subject of continuing debate. Wynter, for one, says that mixed-race actors and models represent the ultimate challenge to traditional attitudes about race in the United States. The performers are "high-status billboards for the natural and perhaps inevitable positive resolution of the tension imposed on the freedom to enjoy an individual identity in a multiracial society."[12] How audiences "read" mixed-race actors with respect to notions of race and ethnicity is unclear, however, particularly when these actors portray white characters in films. Are we witnessing the beginning of a more racially egalitarian perspective or merely a bronzing of whiteness, repackaged to emphasize the aesthetic trappings of cultural creolization? As an analysis of *The Fast and the Furious* and *Romeo Must Die* illustrates, despite the apparent shifts in attitudes, a white ethos is still a potent frame of reference.

This brings us to scholarship on biracial and multiethnic representations in film and other forms of popular culture. While many of the earliest film images of biracial characters portray them as tragic mulattos, as described by Bogle, Jane Gaines, and Freda Scott Giles, later images are markedly more positive.[13] In her "Genealogy of Black Film Criticism," Anna Everett argues that Peola, in *Imitation of Life* (John Stahl, 1934), was the first biracial film character to break with previous negative characterizations.[14] Fredi Washington, a light-skinned African American, "imbues the character with an authenticating aura unavailable to a Caucasian actress attempting to pass for a black attempting to pass for white."[15] Washington also refused to pass in real life, despite her ability to do so, increasing her appeal with African Americans.[16] Teresa Kay Williams underscores the resonance for contemporary audiences of mixed-race individuals like Washington. According to Williams, the unique physical appearance of multiethnic public figures can have distinct appeal because of the "ambiguity and multiple otherness" associated in the popular imagination with miscegenation.[17] From this perspective, mixed-race individuals serve as resonant ethnic enigmas in U.S. society.

Many scholars now argue that the fluid identities that some feel characterize mixed-race individuals are the new wave in American racial identity. Gloria Anzaldúa was one of the first scholars to posit the unique strengths of the "new mestiza," and the potential for the mestiza to overcome traditional racial categories through the combining, rather than the denial, of diverse cultural attributes.[18] Naomi Zack describes this dynamic as embracing "racelessness," which she says is the basis of a future-leaning "identity founded on freedom and resistance to oppression rather than immanence and acceptance of tradition."[19] Such an identity, according to Zack, is constantly recreated in a dynamic process rather than based on origins or affiliation. There is a danger, however, as Carol Roh Spaulding points out, of this utopic ideal becoming merely "another version of biological homogeneity,"[20] in which mestizaje swallows racial divisions and material histories whole. The two films that are analyzed here present distinct Hollywood perspectives on these concerns.

"Racelessness" in *Romeo Must Die*

Of the two films, *Romeo Must Die* is more rooted in Hollywood racial paradigms, despite the relatively little screen time devoted to white characters. As a "hip-hop martial arts film" (producer Joel Silver's description) in the tradition of the white-centric urban gang movie,[21] *Romeo Must Die* presents the San Francisco Bay Area and particularly the city of Oakland as culturally divided. Only its multicultural protagonists and, arguably, those afforded symbolic whiteness have what it takes to survive. Set amid a struggle between black and Chinese organized crime families—and behind the scenes, a wealthy, white developer—over Oakland waterfront property, *Romeo Must Die* echoes actual political and racial struggles that have plagued the area for decades.

Jet Li stars as Han Sing, the son of the Chinese crime family and thus the Romeo who his enemies feel must die. Juliet to his Romeo is the late singer Aaliyah, who plays Trish, the daughter of the African American crime family. As performers with proven appeal to both

Jet Li and Aaliyah in *Romeo Must Die*.

whites and nonwhites, Li and Aaliyah are particularly suited to portray characters who easily navigate an ethnically divided and dangerous cityscape. Moreover, the narrative situates them as simultaneously able to embrace and transcend race.

Through abundant aesthetic display, the culturally diverse cityscape of the Bay Area is paired with vitality and energy, in contrast to Hong Kong, which is presented as repressed and monocultural through drab tones and gray skies. Boundaries between ethnic communities in the Bay Area are also emphasized through aesthetics and musical cues. Warm, multicolored hues in clothing and décor and hip-hop and R&B music are used to represent the African American community, while more austere design and Oriental motifs stand in for the Chinese culture of the Sing family. Even more austere, or "cultureless," is the white developer's work environment. A paean to impersonal, pricy minimalism, it is decorated in gleaming chrome and glass that offer no hint at cultural heritage, community, or family connection. Ultimately, the visual and aural signifiers associated in the film's early scenes with African American and Asian culture are blended when Han and Trish are shown together, contributing to an underlying narrative message that harmony can be achieved through sharing and consuming multiple cultures.

While the presence of Jet Li as the chief protagonist marks a shift in traditional Hollywood casting, also pertinent is the casting of Russell Wong as Kai, the right-hand man to Han's father, the powerful Mafia boss Ch'u Sing (Henry O.). As portrayed by Wong, Kai serves as a symbol of multiracial America, despite the fact that the character's ethnicity as monoracial Chinese goes unquestioned. Given Wong's distinct Eurasian facial features, he literally and figuratively embodies national fears and fantasies of miscegenation, albeit at a submerged level. Wong's mixed ethnicity, Chinese and Dutch American, arguably lends credence to Kai's ability to know and respect the cultural codes in various ethnic communities, to cross cultural borders when necessary, and to serve as the Asian Mafia's chief liaison in negotiations with the African American gang. Given that Kai ultimately betrays his Chinese family, he also serves as the ideological "trouble in the text" with whom the main character must battle. His role thus coincides with previous representations of film protagonists that did not fit easy racial or ethnic categories.

Kai's introduction into the narrative highlights his bicultural mastery. In the first scene in which he appears, Kai adeptly saves Ch'u Sing's youngest son, Po (Jonkit Lee), from certain danger in an Oakland nightclub that is part of the African American syndicate's territory. Kai thereby establishes his cultural ease and competence, even on enemy turf. In contrast, Po is young and foolish; he does not know he has set himself up for a hostile confrontation that could cost him his life. When a fight ensues with several African Americans in streetwise garb, Kai easily and competently defends himself and Po. (In Hollywood action films, cultural mastery often translates into the ability to better one's opponent and maintain one's dignity, even in another's territory.)

Ultimately, however, Kai is revealed to be a villain. In one of the final plot twists, Han realizes that Kai, not the African American crime syndicate, killed Po, his brother. In his greed for power, Kai has chosen to betray his employer and sacrifice his ethnic allegiances. In the process, he also ignores the delicate boundaries between ethnic factions in the underground economy. If read as a mixed-race character because of Wong's ethnic heritage and appearance, Kai thus could be viewed as yet another cinematic illustration of the dangers of miscegenation. From this perspective, Kai is like other Hollywood mixed-race characters who are deceitful and dangerous in their drive to achieve the privileges of whiteness, a pattern that D. W. Griffith's *Birth of a Nation* established in 1915.

The character of Han is less ambiguous in this regard. Despite his recent arrival in the United States (at the beginning of the film, he is languishing in a Hong Kong prison for a crime his father committed), Han gradually asserts his cultural mastery in the Oakland milieu. As the hero, Han is a naturally superior fighter; his opponents, the African American men who work for Trish's father, ultimately are made to look foolish. In one scene, for instance, these men invite Han to play football, but the game is in fact a cover for their plan to rough him up. But after being battered a bit, Han quickly turns the tables on the men by using martial arts moves and assaulting each one in turn. Through such display, Han is elevated racially in relation to his African American opponents, thus gaining symbolic whiteness.

Ultimately, both Han and Trish rise above their conflicts by turning their backs on their families and friends and, in effect, on their ethnic identities. Trish owns a popular shop that specializes in African American and other ethnic-oriented clothes and music, a multihued example of the postmodern ethnic revival in American patterns of consumption. Her young, hip staff, in fact, is a virtual United Colors of Benneton; the shop clerks appear to hail from a rainbow spectrum of ethnicities. But despite being the owner of a store that encourages its customers to embrace cultural diversity, Trish is socially and culturally isolated. She will not consort with the African Americans in her life because of their connections with organized crime. This is evident in her cool response when two men who work for her father flirt with her and in her strained relations with her father and brother.

Similarly, Han experiences only disappointment with respect to his dealings with his mob boss father and knows no one in the United States except for Trish. His climactic fight scene with Kai and subsequent face-off with his father mark the conclusion of Han's figurative struggle with his Chinese origins. In the face of these racialized dilemmas, a more fluid, idealized ethnic identity is posed as an alternative (and narrative solution) for both Trish and Han. Ultimately, the duo survives by embracing "racelessness," ethnic identities that are achieved through the consumption and sharing of music, fashion, and cultural forms such as martial arts, rather than by accepting their former ethnic community allegiances and in-group prejudices.

Utopic Multiculturalism in *The Fast and the Furious:* Only the Multiethnic Will Survive

In sharp contrast to *Romeo Must Die, The Fast and the Furious* presents a more optimistic vision of race relations in the millennial city. As director Rob Cohen has explained, the film was inspired by an article by journalist Ken Li on illegal drag racing on the East and West Coasts. Young Asian American men have been at the forefront of the craze since it was started in Southern California in the early 1990s.[40] Cohen chose to set the narrative in Los Angeles, the city described by Edward Soja and many others as the paradigmatic American city at the turn of the century. Many scholars consider it a continuing repository of American dreams and urban nightmares, particularly regarding human relations.[23] As such, the narrative in large part centers on the vibrancy of racial and ethnic diversity in the millennial city.

In Cohen's cinematic version of the world of street racing, *The Fast and the Furious* retains the subculture's primary tenet that speed rules, rather than the color of one's skin or even the amount of money in one's wallet. The racers, racing teams, and fans are extremely diverse. The extras in fact were actual street racers, and Asian Americans, Latinos, and African Americans far outnumber whites. Cohen also recruited Asian American street racer R. J. DeVera to be a technical consultant and to play a small speaking role.[24]

Part of the multicultural cast of *The Fast and Furious*

While the extras lend an air of authenticity to the diegesis, the lead characters reflect the legacy of Hollywood whiteness that strongly influences *The Fast and the Furious*.[25] All but one of the lead teams in the racing scenes are nonwhite, but these characters are not well developed. They serve mainly as one-dimensional opponents with whom the main characters compete, as in the case of Asian American Johnny Tran (Rick Yune), or as comic relief, in the case of African American racer Edwin (played by hip-hop performer Ja Rule). Moreover, the one team that is ostensibly white rules the road and is the one with which audiences identify. I say ostensibly white because this team is led by Dominic Torretto (Dom), played by Diesel, a biracial actor of African American and Italian descent. Jordana Brewster, who plays his sister, is part Brazilian, while Michelle Rodriguez, cast as his girlfriend, is Latina as well. Again, while the multiethnicity of these actors is not made concrete in the narrative, related visual referents serve as submerged or not so submerged elements in the development of their characters. This makes for an ensemble with significant box-office appeal because of its multicultural roots and experience.

The ethnic ambiguity of Diesel as Torretto, the undisputed king of the street-racing world, in particular cannot be fully submerged. While it is established early on that Dom is Italian (white), Diesel's ambiguous looks and acknowledgment of his mixed ethnic origins in extra-textual publicity raise questions about the hero's ethnic identity. This ambiguity, in turn, lends credence to Dom's strength of character, mobility, and mastery in the diverse subculture of the film, or what can be termed "new ways of knowing" on the part of his character. Dom's Latina girlfriend also provides evidence of his ability to cross cultural borders and easily navigate and dominate in the diverse street scene. The director no doubt was aware that Diesel's biraciality would lend something unique to his performance: In Cohen's commentary accompanying the DVD of the film, he describes Diesel as a "new kind of leading man."

The addition of team members who are unambiguously white contributes to Dom's group ultimately being associated with whiteness, arguably easing their appeal for viewers weaned on traditional Hollywood racial paradigms. Even so, the "white" team members sport ethnic-oriented apparel, including a heavy sprinkling of cholo-style tattoos and woven caps. These visual signifiers symbolize the nonwhite "ethnicity by consent" of these individuals, all of whom are described as having grown up in multicultural LA.[26] Through such narrative construction, Dom's team is shown to possess both the prized skills and knowledge associated with whiteness as well as those qualities presumably acquired by nonwhites in urban environments.

In contrast, Brian Spillner (Paul Walker), a mysterious stranger fresh on the scene, is described as a golden white boy from Arizona. While Brian is a competent and professional undercover police officer (unbeknownst to the racers), as well as a daring driver, his distinctly Anglo-Saxon whiteness offers little to no cachet in this culturally colorful landscape. His expensively renovated "rice rocket" (the racing term for a mega-amped Japanese street racer) afford him no quick respect either. When Brian appears on the scene, Mexican American racer Hector (Noel Gugliemi) jokingly points him out to his friends as the "snowboy" standing by his car. Edwin also tells Brian that "it's not how you stand by your car, it's how you race your car" that is important. In this manner, the "raceless" credo of street racing is communicated: racing ability and cultural savvy determine status and leadership, not whiteness or money. Only by proving himself as a competitive racer and gaining the affiliation of the leading team does Brian gain respect and acceptance.

The valence of whiteness within this world is complicated and at times contradictory. Most notably, the power of whiteness is diminished. Status is set dynamically through performance; speed literally rules. Like the 'hood films of the 1990s, *The Fast and the Furious* also is unusual in turning the camera on a slice of Los Angeles life that has rarely been seen on film. Much of the racing, as in real life, takes place at night, on streets that are normally packed with drivers. The film also reveals the rich culture that exists in neighborhoods like the primarily Latino Echo Park that seldom serve as backdrops for films. In addition, Cohen's focus on the consumer habits of the racers and their fans, who pour their money into expensive car accessories, street-savvy fashion, and other pop-culture items, highlights the social and economic vibrancy and vitality of the subculture.

Despite these progressive, color-blind elements, *The Fast and the Furious* privileges a white-centrist perspective and notions of natural white superiority. Perhaps most notably, white characters are posited as dominant within a subculture in which they are often absent or marginal. For instance, Asian American R. J. DeVera, who is acknowledged in real life to be one of the top street racers in Southern California, plays Danny, a small-time wannabe destined to be beaten by the white leads in the film. Conversely, Brian's ability to be accepted by the lead racing team, while nonwhite racers are not afforded similar respect, goes unquestioned.

The privilege afforded whites is painted in broad strokes during Brian's first chance to prove himself, in a drag race against Dominic, Edwin, and Danny. Hector is not allowed to compete; he is told, jokingly, he is too slow. Brian easily beats Edwin and Danny and ultimately competes head to head with Dom. The inability of the Asian American and African American racers to truly compete with these two "white" racers is not highlighted as remarkable in any way, although Asian Americans, Latinos, and African Americans dominate the actual subculture. The false hierarchy constructed in the narrative goes unnoticed, reinforcing traditional racial expectations.

The casting of Vin Diesel problematizes Hollywood tradition in this regard, however. Diesel's ambiguous ethnic identity, conjoined with his character's natural leadership in this environment, has new and unique implications for the action film. Despite Brian's positioning as central to the narrative, it is Dom, possessing what might be termed a bronzer whiteness, who demonstrates the inherent traits necessary to master this cultural landscape. Brian's ultimate sacrifice of his career to save Dom from a prison sentence also demonstrates Dom's narrative purpose: to be a leader in this new, culturally pluralistic society.

The production design and casting of *The Fast and the Furious* also contain ambiguous and contradictory elements. The camera often lingers on the young fans of the racers, particularly young women of color and smartly dressed interethnic couples. In addition, the soundtrack underscores Cohen's urban-oriented aesthetic. However, even in this carefully constructed multicultural narrative, Hollywood norms of white beauty have primacy. In particular, while the young women featured as extras are mostly Asian American and Latina, many are tall and very thin, approximating an Anglo-centric standard of beauty. This is true even of the Mexican American racing team's crowd on what is presumably its own turf. This is a far cry from the actual physical diversity within the subculture. Arguably, it also includes young women who are short and curvaceous, a body type celebrated in the low-rider subculture, from which the racing scene borrows heavily. Ultimately, the aesthetics of the constructed setting reflect Hollywood standards, to the extent that "diversity" is limited to particular body types.

The New Raceless Aesthetic

Given demographic developments, it is not surprising that cinematic action narratives are becoming increasingly multicultural in their focus and aesthetics. Examples of these trends, both *Romeo Must Die* and *The Fast and the Furious,* posit through their casting and narratives that the embracing of an idealized "raceless" ethnic identity is key to mastery in the urban environment. Contradictions abound, however, when such narratives are rooted in Hollywood tradition and aim to appeal to white as well as nonwhite audiences. As Guerrero states, even in recent decades, Hollywood has "continued to stock its productions with themes and formulas dealing with black issues and characters that are reassuring to the sensibilities and expectations of an uneasy white audience."[27] In this respect, multiculti film narratives soothe white sensibilities even while attempting simultaneously to appeal to young viewers with "urban," media-savvy tastes.

A number of points can be made regarding the representation of race and race relations in multicultural action movies. For one, ideologies of white superiority and nonwhite subordination continue to have a powerful influence, even while the casting, production design, and other manifest components of the films promote a multicultural aesthetic. In *Romeo Must Die,* whites are seldom seen but nevertheless dominate the narrative environment by "pulling the strings" of both the African American and Chinese crime syndicates. Jet Li also is elevated to symbolic whiteness through the continual devaluing of African American characters, particularly in the fight sequences. In *The Fast and the Furious,* by contrast, white characters ostensibly rule the drag-racing subculture but in real life generally play marginal roles. However, Vin Diesel's presence as a chief protagonist complicates racialized expectations in this regard.

There are multiple ways to interpret the cultural implications of the boom in casting mixed-race actors. An emphasis on actors with an "is she or isn't she?" off-white look can be said to erase ethnic difference and, by extension, to deny the nation's and film industry's history of racial discrimination. When multiracial actors replace monocultural actors of color, perhaps for easier consumption by audiences, they erase darker ethnic bodies in the process. In addition, when multiethnic identity plays even a submerged role in film narratives, as in the case of the characters played by Vin Diesel and Russell Wong, it tends to raise tensions that must be resolved within the narrative. The conflicts between Han and Kai in *Romeo Must Die* and Brian and Dom in *The Fast and the Furious* bear this out. On the one hand, multiethnic actors and characters often provide the "trouble in the text" of contemporary films, as they have throughout Hollywood cinema history. On the other hand, the rise in and popularity of mixed-race and multiethnic performers can be interpreted as a reflection and celebration of the increasing cultural diversity in the nation.

Audience reception to narratives involving "passing" is a matter for future research. Action heroes portrayed by biracial actors are still likely to be read as white. While scholars such as Williams and Antonia Grace Glenn have begun to explore the marketing of and audience reception to mixed-race actors, questions remain unanswered.[28] A number of successful actors have chosen not to foreground their mixed ethnicity in their star publicity; their ranks include Keanu Reeves, Jennifer Beals, and Meg Tilly.[29] These actors generally "pass" without question despite their nonwhite ancestry. Similarly, biracial actors such as Halle Berry and Vanessa Williams have been coded consistently as African American without discussion of the complexity of their dual heritage. There is much to be learned from critical scholarship on these questions. Regardless of audience interpretation, biraciality is increasingly less submerged in Hollywood narratives, which is a powerful trend of contemporary concern.

Notes

1. As Michael Omi, Howard Winant, and other scholars have argued, while racial categories are social constructions, race has a material impact on individuals, families, and communities. Continuing, although decreasingly strong, taboos about miscegenation, for example, serve as indicators of the valence of racial boundaries in the United States. Nevertheless, growing numbers of U.S. citizens are of mixed racial or ethnic descent. For the purposes of this essay, "biracial" will be used to refer to individuals who can claim two racial backgrounds as defined by the U.S. Bureau of the Census, while "multiracial" will refer to individuals with more than two racial backgrounds. The racial groups identified by the Bureau of the Census in 2000 included white; black, African American, or Negro; Asian/Pacific Islander; and American Indian or Alaskan native. Multiethnic and the more popularly used term "mixed race" will be used here more generally to identify individuals who belong to two or more ethnic or racial groups or who are of indeterminate but mixed racial or ethnic status.
2. Marilyn Halter, *Shopping for Identity: The Marketing of Ethnicity* (New York: Schocken Books, 2000), 3.
3. Neil Howe and William Strauss, *Millennials Rising: The Next Great Generation* (New York: Vintage, 2000), 15.
4. Cited in *ibid*.
5. Quoted in Leon E. Wynter, *American Skin: Pop Culture, Big Business, and the End of White America* (New York: Crown, 2002), 180.
6. Rudolfo Acuña, *Anything but Mexican: Chicanos in Contemporary Los Angeles* (London: Verso, 1996), 3.
7. U.S. Census Bureau, "The Two or More Races Population: 2000," Census Bureau brief, November 2001, www.census.gov/prod/2001pubs/c2kbr01-6.pdf.
8. Halter, *Shopping for Identity*, 83. Wynter describes the same development in *American Skin*, 136.
9. Wynter, *American Skin*, 136.

10. "TV Viewing Habits Differ in Black Households: While Black vs. White TV Viewing Habits Continue to Polarize, There Is Growing Mutuality of Preferences among Black and White Viewers 12–17," *Minority Markets Alert* 7, no. 5 (May 1995): 2.

11. Halter, *Shopping for Identity,* 171, and Wynter, *American Skin,* 170.

12. Wynter, *American Skin,* 170.

13. Bogle, Toms, Coons, Mulattoes, Mammies, and Bucks, 9. See also Jane M. Gaines, *Fire and Desire: Mixed-Race Movies in the Silent Era* (Chicago: University of Chicago Press, 2001), and Freda Scott Giles, "From Melodrama to the Movies: The Tragic Mulatto as a Type Character," in Naomi Zack, ed., *American Mixed Race: The Culture of Microdiversity* (Landham, Mass.: Rowman & Littlefield, 1995), 64.

14. Everett, *Returning the Gaze,* 221.

15. *Ibid.*

16. Everett and Bogle both point to a number of indicators of Washington's intense popularity among black moviegoers. Everett, *Returning the Gaze,* 220–23, and Bogle, *Brown Sugar: Eighty Years of Black Female Superstars* (New York: Da Capo Press, 1980), 76–82.

17. Teresa Kay Williams, "The Theater of Identity: (Multi-) Race and Representation of Eurasians and Afroasians," in Zack, *American Mixed Race,* 91.

18. Gloria Anzaldúa, *Borderlands/La Frontera: The New Mestiza* (San Francisco: Aunt Lute Books, 1987), 79.

19. Naomi Zack, *Race and Mixed Race* (Philadelphia: Temple University Press, 1993), 164.

20. Carol Roh Spaulding, "The Go-Between People," in Zack, *American Mixed Race,* 110.

21. Joel Silver, producer's commentary, *Romeo Must Die* DVD, Warner Bros., 2000.

22. Rob Cohen, director's commentary, *The Fast and the Furious* DVD, Universal, 2001.

23. See, for example, Edward Soja, Postmodern Geographies: The Reassertion of Space in Critical Social Theory (New York: Verso, 1993), 223, and Mike Davis, City of Quartz: Excavating the Future in Los Angeles (London: Verso, 1990).

24. *The Fast and the Furious* DVD.

25. For further scholarship on the legacy of whiteness in Hollywood film, see Richard Dyer, *White* (London: Routledge, 1997), and Ella Shohat and Robert Stam, *Unthinking Eurocentrism: Multiculturalism and the Media* (London: Routledge, 1994). A number of seminal essays on this subject can be found in Daniel Bernardi, *The Birth of Whiteness* (New Brunswick, NJ: Rutgers University Press, 1996).

26. Werner Sollers, *Beyond Ethnicity: Consent and Descent in American Culture* (New York: Oxford University Press, 1986).

27. Guerrero, *Framing Blackness,* 162.

28. Antonia Grace Glenn, "Hapa Passing (and Non-passing) in Contemporary Film and Television," paper presented at the conference of the Northeast Modern Language Association, Toronto, April 12, 2002; Williams, "The Theater of Identity," 86.

29. According to numerous publicity sources, Keanu Reeves is of Hawaiian and other mixed descent, while Jennifer Beals is of African American and Irish heritage. Meg Tilly is purportedly of Chinese and Canadian descent.

READING WRITING

This Text: Reading

1. Find Beltrán's thesis. What does she argue about the two films?

2. How does Beltrán make her case here? How does she use scholarship about race to make her points?

3. You are the multiculti millennial generation Beltrán writes about and that the films are aimed at. Do your own values merge with those presented in the essay and in the film?

Your Text: Writing

1. Find two movies that seem *not* to be about race and read them through the lens of race. Use scholarship on race and ethnicity to undergird your assertions.
2. Compare Beltrán's essay on film and race to the following essay by bell hooks. How are the essays similar? Different? Are they shaped by their eras? Write an essay in which you compare/contrast Beltrán's and hooks' manner of film criticism.
3. Write an essay on some other kind of text—an ad, a TV show, music—in which you explore this notion of racelessness.

Deciphering *I, Robot:* Random Thoughts from an Evolving Film Reviewer

Jason Silverman

Below are two different pieces by Jason Silverman, both written in 2004. The first is an original essay on the process of watching movies from the perspective of a movie reviewer, with specific examples from the recent movie *I, Robot.* Following the essay is Silverman's actual review of *I, Robot* that he wrote for wired.com. Silverman has been working in the film industry for over a decade. A former artistic director for the Taos Moving Pictures Festival, Silverman is active in all facets of the independent movie scene. Currently, he is a film reviewer for wired.com and other publications.

I'VE SPENT A GOOD CHUNK of the last 12 years watching and thinking about movies, and I still don't know what I'm doing. I'm not sure how to prepare or how to "watch" the movie once it starts. A kind of schizophrenia sets in when I'm in the theater, with voices in my head competing for attention: the (pseudo)-intellectual forcing me to take notes on sociopolitical– aesthetic issues; the eager-to-please freelance writer testing out witty phrases to use; and the little kid yanking on my sleeve, saying, "Loosen up! It's just a movie!"

It's not surprising that I'm conflicted while watching a movie. Movies are *complicated.* They rely on highly technical processes, and their mechanics remain a mystery to most viewers. Though the movies are mostly a form of amusement—a colossally expensive one—some film lovers insist that cinema is the ultimate form of art—a medium that incorporates all other media. Then there are the watchdogs, who are concerned that the movies have a variety of negative effects on our culture. They are right to worry; movies, after all, are persuasive transmitters of information, the favored medium of both propagandists and advertising firms.

For these and other reasons, cinema is a tricky medium to write about. The more I learn, the more I realize I don't know. But I have seized upon a few concepts to help me tackle the film reviews, articles, and essays I write. Here's how these concepts helped shape a review I wrote of *I, Robot* (reprinted below) for the online magazine *Wired News* (wired.com).

There are lots of pieces in this puzzle.   Every second of a movie is packed with information, far too much to take in. But I try and get a sense of how the various elements—the writing, music, lighting, camera angles, performances, film stock, effects, editing—work together. Doing that helps me understand why the filmmakers made the choices they did.

- In Hollywood films, clumsy elements can jump out at me—an awkward edit, dialogue that feels staged, an especially bogus special effect. Studio films are generally supposed to be seamless. *I, Robot*'s team built a smooth-running film, and the cinematography, sets and performative, and editing style well suited to the subject matter. From a technical standpoint, at least, *I, Robot* is highly proficient.

The most impressive element of *I, Robot* was the convincing interaction between the computer-generated (CG) characters (the CG imaging work is done long after the human actors have left the set). And, while I didn't think much of the screenplay as a whole (more on that below), the writers created a good part for the star, Will Smith. Like most Hollywood scores, the *I, Robot* music was overwrought and intrusive.

Story rules.   Filmmakers say it again and again: good movies come from telling good stories. It's a cliché, maybe, but it's also true, especially if you expand your notion of what a story can be. Most feature films rely on conventional narratives—boy meets girl, alien attacks planet, detective hunts murderer, king grows paranoid, etc.—and unfold in specific three-act structure. Occasionally, artistic-minded filmmakers will experiment with more adventurous narrative forms. Experimental, non-narrative films (some have no characters, dialogue or plot) seek to tell stories of some kind. The form of the story is less important than its relevance—does it matter to me?—and the level of passion and ingenuity the film-makers use in transmitting it.

- The many loose ends and nonsensical scenes in *I, Robot* left me wondering how much the filmmakers cared about the integrity of the story. Give the plot a few lingering thoughts and it begins to disintegrate. More importantly, the filmmakers chose to take a highly relevant subject—our relationship to technology—and turn it into a relative caricature (robots bad, humans good).

It's more than entertainment.   I think movies can influence behavior. Not that there is a one-to-one correlation—watching some dumb violent movie won't make every teen in the audience start knocking over convenience stores. But every movie, intentionally or not, can serve as a political and sociological text, transmitting information that can challenge or reinforce what we believe about ourselves and the world.

- I was initially excited at the prospect of an *I, Robot* movie—it's based on a 1950 Isaac Asimov book that explores the tension between humans and their increasingly sophisticated machines. The book feels a bit dated, but there's plenty of meaty, brainy stuff for an ambitious film to delve into. Unfortunately, this *I, Robot* movie sends simplistic, technophobic messages: Smart machines are to be feared, but human ingenuity will save the day.

On the surface *I, Robot* takes an anti-corporate stance (the villain is a big robotics company). Look a bit deeper, though: the film was made by 20th Century Fox—owned by the same multinational corporation that runs the business-friendly Fox News and scores of conservative newspapers—and it's filled with product placements (those mini-commercials for things like sneakers and soft drinks that Hollywood studios sneak onto the screen).

There are also interesting gender and race issues in the movie. Smith, playing the African-American policeman Del Spooner, is accused of being an anti-robot bigot, while oldfashioned, anti-black racism never becomes an issue. Nancy Calvin, the female protagonist, is the latest in a long Hollywood line of lonely, frigid female professionals who have problems connecting with men. What does that stereotype tell us? That women who are successful in the workplace lead miserable personal lives.

Movies are magic.   I try not to get *too* caught up in the politics of every single movie—a good one can be a mind-altering substance, transporting me to new, weird and/or wonderful places. I'm at my best when I can tune in intellectually to a film *and* experience it on a gut level.

- With special effects becoming more spectacular every month, it's easy to take for granted how great the new breed of sci-fi/fantasy films look. Five years ago, the visuals in *I, Robot* would have been groundbreaking, but the computerized, futuristic landscapes somehow don't seem quite as startling in this age of digital wizardry, when any visual is possible. I found the robots to be remarkable, and genuinely frightening in a plastic, banal way. The lead robot, Sonny, was especially convincing. Unfortunately, the magical moments weren't sustained for very long—*I, Robot*'s narrative gaps shook me out of any brief reverie.

Business rules.   Entrepreneurs built the American film industry and, 100 years later, money still drives the movies. The average Hollywood film costs nearly $100 million to produce and market, so there's lots at stake with every release. Filmmakers are not immune to the profit motive—even Martin Scorsese and Woody Allen juggle financial considerations with artistic concerns.

- It's difficult to balance philosophical discourse and blockbuster action. When in doubt, Hollywood generally slugs it out—disposing of the brainy stuff and emphasizing fight and chase scenes. That's certainly true in *I, Robot*, which radically diverges from Asimov's edgy book. Did the producers worry that an idea-driven movie would scare off audiences? Perhaps. There are other signs of financial pressures here, including the movie's implausible happy ending, the casting of a beautiful young actress as Susan Calvin (she's something of an old bat in the book); and the inclusion of liberal amounts of product placements.

Beware the tricks.   The so-called "moving image" is actually a physiological fluke: flash a series of images past the human eye and the human brain will read them as seamless motion. The idea that cinema exists thanks to a trick of the eye represents one level of movie manipulation. I'm also wary of the other tricks filmmakers have developed: the schmaltzy music to try and make me cry, the shrouding of a villain in sinister shadow, an explosion so fiery that I fear for my eyebrows. I admire a good cinematic trick as much as anyone, but also am aware that these tricks too often cover up inept storytelling.

- *I, Robot*, a film about the future, enjoyed showing off futuristic machinery. That's the advantage of sci-fi and other tech-oriented stories. I liked the filmmakers' relationship with gadgetry. It wasn't fetishistic; instead, they showed enough of the robots to give me an understanding of how they worked. The CG imagery was also used to good effect. Other standard-issue tricks—the button-pushing music, the sappy ending, the film noir–inspired lighting—were restrained, at least in terms of Hollywood blockbusters.

Don't be seduced by style. What passed for great filmmaking 50 years ago can today look stilted and clumsy. I've seen films made on laptops that have better effects than the original *Star Wars.* Styles that seem innovative and timeless right now will pass into obsolescence sometime soon (yes, that includes *The Matrix* and *The Lord of the Rings*). Style in itself does not qualify a film as a work of art. The stylistic choices in any good film reflect and deepen that film's intent. That's not to say I don't *ooh* and *aah* over eye-bending effects or stunning cinematography. I just try to avoid confusing them with artful filmmaking.

- *I, Robot* made some smart stylistic choices. The cinematographer shot the film, probably using filters, striving for a sci-fi/pulp fiction look, with shades of blue replacing the shades of gray familiar to fans of classic film noir. The result was relatively subtle and unified, and not especially memorable or innovative. But it was appropriate and served the story well.

Watch old stuff, too. The movies are only a century old—an infant compared to other forms of expression—and they continue to evolve at a fast pace. I don't claim a comprehensive knowledge of film history (there's just too many movies out there) but the more old movies I watch, the better I understand cinema's evolutionary path. That gives me more confidence when I critique a new film.

- What makes great science fiction, and why did *I, Robot* fall short? To me, the best sci-fi films do at least one of two things: they build a complete world and live within the rules that govern that world; or they use the future as prism through which to investigate issues that affect our culture today. I love the first two *Terminator* films, both of which fulfil the first rule. You could think about them over and over and they still seemed to make sense. I remain one of the few defenders of *A.I: Artificial Intelligence,* which was as moving and troubling an examination of human–machine relationships as I've seen. Other sci-fi movies I've been impressed with: *A Clockwork Orange, Alphaville, Metropolis, Close Encounters, The Truman Show.* It's not a long list, partly because good sci-fi is hard to create. Special effects make these films expensive, and expensive movies usually don't have the luxury of exploring deep, philosophical issues. To me, that's *I, Robot's* central problem: Despite its potentially rich subject matter, it dedicated most of its resources to more conventional action sequences.

Read some books, too. My favorite film writers are able to put movies into the context of art, history, sociology, literature, theory, philosophy, geography, geology, theology . . . anything and everything. Good film writers do more than just compare one film to another. They offer a context in which to understand the movies as an artistic and cultural form, and as a window into the world.

- I re-read *I, Robot,* which I last picked up as a teenager, to prepare for this film. It's amazing how sharp and relevant Asimov's thoughts on artificial intelligence remain, given that the book predates the computer age. Reading the book, far more than seeing the movie, reinforced the urgency of considering our relationship to technology. Movies like *I, Robot* may not do all of the intellectual and philosophical work I want them to, but they do help push important issues into the pop-cultural slipstream.

■ ■ ■

I, Robot, No Deep Thinker

Near the beginning of his classic 1950 novel *I, Robot,* Isaac Asimov laid out the three commandments governing robot behavior: Thou shalt not allow harm to come to a human, thou shalt obey humans, thou shalt protect thyself.

Hollywood blockbusters have their own set of rules, too: Drop in little commercials for products whenever you can, replace meaningful dialogue with witty repartee, build lots of fight scenes, end happily (by saving the world, if budget permits) and dilute any brainy stuff.

In the movie version of *I, Robot,* Hollywood's rules rule. Asimov fans and others who like their sci-fi on the chewy side will probably revolt—the essence of the book is gone. But the average popcorn muncher will appreciate *I, Robot*—it's a good example of why the blockbuster formula works. It's funny, has a chilly, blue visual style (the robots look like the clamshell iBooks) and moves fast.

This *I, Robot* began life as a screenplay called *Hardwired,* about a robot alleged to have killed a human. The film's producers then acquired the rights to the Asimov book and decided to combine the two stories.

It's not clear how the novel influenced the finished film (the credits describe *I, Robot* as "suggested by," rather than "adapted from," Asimov). But this movie definitely has made the book's most sensational bit—the idea that robots could follow the three laws and take over the world—central to the plot.

I. Robot. You, lame film?

Of course, if any alien group is plotting a hostile global takeover, best to cast Will Smith to stop them—he's a one-man Department of Homeland Security. In *I, Robot*, Smith plays Officer Del Spooner, a guy with a grudge against robots—he's even been accused of being an anti-tech bigot. Spooner also hates United States Robotics, the world's largest "mecha" manufacturer.

USR is preparing to roll out its new Automated Domestic Assistant, the almost-human NS-5, when one of the company's founders, Alfred Lanning, jumps to his death, leaving Spooner a cryptic message.

Convinced that Lanning's death is part of a bigger plot, Spooner sets out to investigate with help from USR scientist Susan Calvin (played by Bridget Moynahan as a distant relation, at best, to the Calvin of the book) and a robot named Sonny. His opponents include some pesky mecha assassins and Lawrence Robertson, USR's hard-edged CEO. *I, Robot* displays plenty of high-tech wizardry—cars rolling on balls instead of wheels; a slow-mo, airborne robot fight and, best of all, Sonny, who is one of the best movie robots yet. The film is set in 2035, and the NS-5s are still a few generations behind the Terminators and Steven Spielberg's A.I. mechas. Sonny is much more robot than human, a plastic, nearly affectless, truly creepy creature.

I've yet to see a convincing CG replication of human movement. Sonny, however, is supposed to move like a machine—like CG itself, Sonny is mechanical but aspires to be more lifelike.

Through Sonny, director Alex Proyas (*The Crow, Dark City*) takes a few stabs at exploring deeper man–machine questions. How will artificial intelligence parallel human thought processes? How can robots reconcile a complex world with their rigid rules of behavior? What happens when machines grow conflicted about the wisdom of their creators?

But Proyas' film never settles down long enough to dig deep. He's nodding in Asimov's general direction, not exploring his ideas.

Worse, Proyas' *I, Robot* stops making sense once you think about it. There are too many loose ends, too many plot-convenient moments and far from enough rigorous thought. To enjoy this *I, Robot,* you'll have to turn off your brain.

That may be what moviegoers expect to do over the summer, but it's the last thing Asimov, a master of clear, sharp logic, would have wanted.

READING WRITING

This Text: Reading

1. What connections do you see between Silverman's observations in the first essay and his actual review?
2. In what ways does Silverman read movies as "texts"?
3. What is the most interesting (or unexpected) aspect of the way in which Silverman looks at movies? How is his system similar or different than your own?
4. Find Silverman's thesis (it's pretty clear). How does he try to "prove" his thesis throughout the essay?

Your Text: Writing

1. Write a rebuttal to Silverman's review of *I, Robot*. What don't you like about his review?
2. Find a more positive review of *I, Robot* and write a comparison/contrast paper on the two reviews. Which review is the more convincing? Why?

Mock Feminism:
Waiting to Exhale

bell hooks

Taken from her provocative book *Reel to Reel: Race, Sex, and Class at the Movies,* bell hooks' essay (1996) offers a reading of the popular movie *Waiting to Exhale.* Unlike most reviews that praised the film for its depiction of black women, hooks' review charges the film merely masks harmful stereotypes. Though the essay is now more than ten years old, it still feels current and relevant and is a nice example of both lens and window.

IN THE PAST A BLACK FILM was usually seen as a film by a black filmmaker focusing on some aspect of black life. More recently the "idea" of a "black film" has been appropriated as a way to market films that are basically written and produced by white people as though they in fact represent and offer us—"authentic" blackness. It does not matter that progressive black filmmakers and critics challenge essentialist notions of black authenticity, even going so far as to rethink and interrogate the notion of black film. These groups do not have access to the levels of marketing and publicity that can repackage authentic blackness commodified and sell it as the "real" thing. This was certainly the case with the marketing and publicity for the film *Waiting to Exhale.*

When Kevin Costner produced and starred in the film *The Bodyguard* with Whitney Houston as co-star, the film focused on a black family. No one ever thought to market it as a black film. Indeed, many black people refused to see the film because they were so disgusted by this portrayal of interracial love. No one showed much curiosity about the racial identity of the screenwriters or for that matter, anybody behind the scenes of this film. It was not seen as having any importance for black women by the white-dominated mass media. Yet *Waiting to Exhale*'s claim to blackness, and black authenticity, is almost as dubious as any such claim being made about *The Bodyguard.* However, that claim could be easily made because a black woman writer wrote the book on which the movie was based. The hiring of a fledgling black director received no critical comment. Everyone behaved as though it was just normal Hollywood practice to offer the directorship of a major big-budget Hollywood film to someone who might not know what they are doing.

The screenplay was written by a white man, but if we are to believe everything we read in newspapers and popular magazines, Terry McMillan assisted with the writing. Of course, having her name tacked onto the writing process was a great way to protect the film from the critique that its "authentic blackness" was somehow undermined by white-male interpretation. Alice Walker had no such luck when her book *The Color Purple* was made into a movie by Steven Spielberg. No one thought this was a black film. And very few viewers were surprised that what we saw on the screen had little relationship to Alice Walker's novel.

Careful publicity and marketing ensured that *Waiting to Exhale* would not be subjected to these critiques; all acts of appropriation were carefully hidden behind the labeling of this film as authentically a black woman's story. Before anyone could become upset that a black woman was not hired to direct the film, McMillan told the world in *Movieland* magazine that those experienced black women directors in Hollywood just were not capable of doing the job. She made the same critique of the black woman writer who was initially hired to write the screenplay. From all accounts (most of them given by the diva herself) it appears that Terry McMillan is the only competent black woman on the Hollywood scene and she just recently arrived.

It's difficult to know what is more disturbing: McMillan's complicity with the various acts of white supremacist capitalist patriarchal cultural appropriation that resulted in a film as lightweight and basically bad as *Waiting to Exhale,* or the public's passive celebratory consumption of this trash as giving the real scoop about black women's lives. Some bad films are at least entertaining. This was just an utterly boring show. That masses of black women could be cajoled by mass media coverage and successful seductive marketing (the primary ploy being that this is the first film ever that four black women have been the major stars of a Hollywood film) to embrace this cultural product was a primary indication that this is not a society where moviegoers are encouraged to think critically about what they see on the screen.

When a film that's basically about the trials and tribulations of four professional heterosexual black women who are willing to do anything to get and keep a man is offered as a "feminist" narrative, it's truly a testament to the power of the mainstream to co-opt progressive social movements and strip them of all political meaning through a series of contemptuous ridiculous representations. Terry McMillan's novel *Waiting to Exhale* was not a feminist book and it was not transformed into a feminist film. It did not even become a film that made use of any of the progressive politics around race and gender that was evoked however casually in the novel itself.

Loretta Devine, Lela Rochon, Angela Bassett, and Whitney Houston in *Waiting to Exhale* (1995).
Source: 20th Century Fox/The Kobal Collection.

The film *Waiting to Exhale* took the novelistic images of professional black women concerned with issues of racial uplift and gender equality and turned them into a progression of racist, sexist stereotypes that features happy darkies who are all singing, dancing, fucking, and having a merry old time even in the midst of sad times and tragic moments. What we saw on the screen was not black women talking about love or the meaning of partnership and marriage in their lives. We saw four incredibly glamorous women obsessed with getting a man, with status, material success and petty competition with other women (especially white women). In the book one of the women, Gloria, owns a beauty parlor; she is always, always working, which is what happens when you run a small business. In the movie, girlfriend hardly ever works because she is too busy cooking tantalizing meals for the neighbor next door. In this movie food is on her mind and she forgets all about work, except for an occasional phone call to see how everything is going. Let's not forget the truly fictive utopian moment in this film that occurs when Bernie goes to court divorcing her husband and wins tons of money. This is so in the book as well. Funny though, the novel ends with her giving the money away, highlighting her generosity and her politics. McMillan writes: "She also wouldn't have to worry about selling the house now. But Bernadine wasn't taking that fucker off the market. She'd drop the price. And she'd send a nice check to the United Negro College Fund, something she'd always wanted to do. She'd help feed some of those kids in Africa she'd seen on TV at night.... Maybe she'd send some change to the Urban League and the NAACP and she'd definitely help out some of those programs that BWOTM [Black Women on the Move] had been trying to get off the ground for the last hundred years. At the rate she was going, Bernadine had already given away over a million dollars." Definitely not a "material girl." It would have taken only one less scene of pleasure fucking for audiences to have witnessed Bernie writing these checks with a nice voiceover. But, alas, such an image might have ruined the racist, sexist stereotype of black women being hard, angry, and just plain greedy. No doubt the writers of the screenplay felt these "familiar" stereotypes would guarantee the movie its crossover appeal.

Concurrently, no doubt it helps that crossover appeal to set up stereotypically racist, sexist conflicts between white women and black women (where if we are to believe the logic of the film, the white woman gets "her" black man in the end). Let's remember. In the novel the movie is based on, only one black man declares his love for a white woman. The man Bernie meets, the lawyer James, is thinking of divorcing his white wife, who is dying of cancer, but he loyally stays with her until her death, even though he makes it very clear that the love has long since left their marriage. Declaring his undying love for Bernie, James moves across the country to join her, sets up a law practice, and gets involved with "a coalition to stop the liquor board from allowing so many liquor stores in the black community." Well, not in this movie! The screen character James declares undying love for his sick white wife. Check out the difference between the letter he writes in the novel. Here is an excerpt: "I know you probably thought that night was just something frivolous but like I told you before I left, it meant more to me than that. Much more. I buried my wife back in August, and for her sake, I'm glad she's not suffering anymore... I want to see you again, Bernadine, and not for another one-nighter, either. If there's any truth to what's known as a 'soul mate,' then you're as close to it as I've ever come... I'm not in-terested in playing games, or starting something I can't finish. I play for keeps, and I'm not some dude just out to have a good time... I knew I was in love with you long before we ever turned the key to that hotel room." The image of black masculinity that comes through in this letter is that of a man of integrity who is compassionate, in touch with his feelings, and able to take responsibility for his actions.

In the movie version of *Waiting to Exhale,* no black man involved with a black woman possesses these qualities. In contrast to what happens in the book, in the film, James does not have a one-nighter with Bernie, because he is depicted as utterly devoted to his white wife. Here are relevant passages from the letter he writes to Bernie that audiences hear at the movie: "What I feel for you has never undercut the love I have for my wife. How is that possible? I watch her everyday. So beautiful and brave. I just want to give her everything I've got in me. Every moment. She's hanging on, fighting to be here for me. And when she sleeps, I cry. Over how amazing she is, and how lucky I've been to have her in my life." There may not have been any white women as central characters in this film, but this letter certainly places the dying white wife at the center of things. Completely rewriting the letter that appears in the novel, which only concerns James's love and devotion to Bernie, so that the white wife (dead in the book but brought back to life on-screen) is the recipient of James's love was no doubt another ploy to reach the crossover audience: the masses of white women consumers that might not have been interested in this film if it had really been about black women.

Ultimately, only white women have committed relationships with black men in the film. Not only do these screen images reinforce stereotypes, the screenplay was written in such a way as to actively perpetuate them. Catfights between women, both real and symbolic, were clearly seen by the screenwriters as likely to be more entertaining to moviegoing audiences than the portrayal of a divorced black woman unexpectedly meeting her true love—an honest, caring, responsible, mature, tender, and loving black man who delivers the goods. Black women are portrayed as so shrewish in this film that Lionel's betrayal of Bernie appears to be no more than an act of self-defense. The film suggests that Lionel is merely trying to get away from the black bitch who barges in on him at work and physically attacks his meek and loving white wife. To think that Terry McMillan was one of the screenwriters makes it all the more disheartening. Did she forget that she had written a far more emotionally complex and progressive vision of black female–male relationships in her novel?

While we may all know some over-thirty black women who are desperate to get a man by any means necessary and plenty of young black females who fear that they may never find a man and are willing to be downright foolish in their pursuit of one, the film was so simplistic and denigrating in its characterization of black womanhood that everyone should be outraged to be told that it is "for us." Or worse yet, as a reporter wrote in *Newsweek,* "This is our million man march." Whether you supported the march or not (and I did not, for many of the same reasons I find this film appalling), let's get this straight: We are being told, and are telling ourselves that black men need a political march and black women need a movie. Mind you—not a political film but one where the black female "stars" spend most of their time chainsmoking themselves to death (let's not forget that Gloria did not have enough breath to blow out her birthday candle) and drowning their sorrows in alcohol. No doubt McMillan's knowledge of how many black people die from lung cancer and alcoholism influenced her decision to write useful, unpreachy critiques of these addictions in her novel. In the novel the characters who smoke are trying to stop and Black Women on the Move are fighting to close down liquor stores. None of these actions fulfill racist fantasies. It's no accident that just the opposite images appear on the screen. Smoking is so omnipresent in every scene that many of us were waiting to see a promotional credit for the tobacco industry.

Perhaps the most twisted and perverse aspect of this film is the way it was marketed as being about girlfriend bonding. How about that scene where Robin shares her real-life trauma with Savannah, who is busy looking the other way and simply does not respond? Meaningful girlfriend bonding is not about the codependency that is imaged in this film. At its best *Waiting to Exhale* is a film about black women helping each other to stay stuck. Do we really believe that moment when Savannah rudely disses Kenneth (even though the film has in no way constructed him as a lying, cheating dog) to be a moment of profound "feminist" awakening? Suddenly audiences are encouraged to believe that she realizes the dilemmas of being involved with a married man, even one who has filed for a divorce. Why not depict a little mature communication between a black man and a black woman? No doubt that too would not have been entertaining to crossover audiences. Better to give them what they are used to, stereotypical representations of black males as always and only lying, cheating dogs (that is, when they are involved with black women) and professional black women as wild, irrational, castrating bitch goddesses.

Nothing was more depressing than hearing individual black women offering personal testimony that these shallow screen images are "realistic portrayals" of their experience. If this is the world of black gender relations as they know it, no wonder black men and women are in serious crisis. Obviously, it is difficult for many straight black women to find black male partners and/or husbands. Though it is hard to believe that black women as conventionally feminine, beautiful, glamorous, and just plain dumb as the girlfriends in this film can't get men (Bernie has an MBA, helped start the business, but is clueless about everything that concerns money; Robin is willing to have unsafe sex and celebrate an unplanned pregnancy with a partner who may be a drug addict; Gloria, who would rather cook food for her man any day than go to work; Savannah has sex at the drop of a hat, even when she does not want to get involved). In the real world these are the women who have men standing in line.

However, if they and other black women internalize the messages in *Waiting to Exhale* they will come to their senses and see that, according to the film, black men are really undesirable mates for black women. Actually, lots of younger black women, and their over-thirty counterparts, go to see *Waiting to Exhale* to have their worst fears affirmed: that black men are irresponsible and uncaring; that black women, no matter how attractive, will still be hurt and abandoned, and that ultimately they will probably be alone and unloved. Perhaps it feels less like cultural genocide to have these messages of self-loathing and disempowerment brought to them by four beautiful black female "stars."

Black women seeking to learn anything about gender relationships from this film will be more empowered if we identify with the one black female character who rarely speaks. She is the graceful, attractive, brown-skinned lawyer with naturally braided hair who is a professional who knows her job and is also able to bond emotionally with her clients. Not only does she stand for gender justice (the one glimpse of empowering feminist womanhood we see in this film), she achieves that end without ever putting men down or competing with any woman. While we never see her with a male partner, she acts with confident self-esteem and shows fulfillment in a job well done.

The monetary success of a trashy film like *Waiting to Exhale,* with its heavy sentimentality and predictable melodrama shows that Hollywood recognizes that blackness as a commodity can be exploited to bring in the bucks. Dangerously, it also shows that the same old racist/sexist stereotypes can be appropriated and served up to the public in a new and more fashionable disguise. While it serves the financial interests of Hollywood and McMillan's own bank account for her to deflect away from critiques that examine the politics underlying these representations and their behind-the-scenes modes of production by ways of witty assertions that the novel and the film are "forms of entertainment, not anthropological studies," in actuality the creators of this film are as accountable for their work as their predecessors. Significantly, contemporary critiques of racial essentialism completely disrupt the notion that anything a black artist creates is inherently radical, progressive, or more likely to reflect a break with white supremacist representations. It has become most evident that as black artists seek a "crossover" success, the representations they create usually mirror dominant stereotypes. After a barrage of publicity and marketing that encouraged black people, and black women in particular, to see *Waiting to Exhale* as fictive ethnography, McMillan is being more than a bit disingenuous when she suggests that the film should not be seen this way. In her essay, "Who's Doin' the Twist: Notes Toward a Politics of Appropriation," cultural critic Coco Fusco reminds us that we must continually critique this genre in both its pure and impure forms. "Ethnographic cinema, in light of its historical connection to colonialist adventurism, and decades of debate about the ethics of representing documentary subjects, is a genre that demands a special degree of scrutiny." Just because writers and directors are black does not exempt them from scrutiny. The black female who wrote a letter to the *New York Times* calling attention to the way this film impedes the struggle to create new images of blackness on the screen was surely right when she insisted that had everyone involved in the production of this film been white and male, its blatantly racist and sexist standpoints would not have gone unchallenged.

READING WRITING

This Text: Reading

1. At first, you might find hooks overly critical of *Waiting to Exhale*. But are her contentions reasonable? Why? Why not? What standards is she holding the film to?
2. What political and cultural forces are influencing her review of the film? Or, what can you glean about her political leanings from her review? What is hooks's writing situation?
3. Do you agree with hooks that a seemingly harmless film like *Waiting to Exhale* is culturally dangerous?

Your Text: Writing

1. Write your own review of *Waiting to Exhale*. Will you focus on the representations of gender, or are you more interested in plot and character development?
2. Compare *Waiting to Exhale* with *How Stella Got Her Groove Back*. Both movies are adaptations of Terry McMillan novels. How are the films similar? How are they different? How does the film version depart from the novel?
3. Write a personal essay in which you analyze Hollywood representations of *your* gender and ethnicity. For instance, if you are a Hispanic male, write an essay in which you analyze how Hispanic males are represented in movies. What do you notice?
4. Write a comparative paper analyzing what hooks has to say about women in *Waiting to Exhale* with the suite in Chapter 6. How do women define representations of women?

Indians and Cowboys: Two Poems That Re-Cast Hollywood Indians

Of the many disturbing legacies of Hollywood, perhaps the most disturbing is its history of Native American representation. Although Hollywood films have not always been friendly to women, African Americans, and the poor, no group has likely gotten as much negative and potentially harmful screen time as American Indians. In fact, for some Americans their only information about Indian culture, behavior, and values comes from Western movies. The two poems that follow take a critical look at Westerns and their impact on the Native American community. "Dear John Wayne" (1984), by Ojibwe writer Louise Erdrich "reads" the Western icon John Wayne through a Native lens, noting the violent overtones of Western films. In "My Heroes Have Never Been Cowboys" (1993), Spokane/Coeur d'Alene writer Sherman Alexie also notes the overwhelming cultural presence of Wayne, but like Erdrich, deconstructs the iconography of Wayne and Westerns in general. Alexie even has a short story entitled "Dear John Wayne," influenced by Erdrich's poem. As you read, think about what it might be like to watch a Western from a Native American perspective.

Dear John Wayne

Louise Erdrich

August and the drive-in picture is packed.
We lounge on the hood of the Pontiac
surrounded by the slow-burning spirals they sell
at the window, to vanquish the hordes of mosquitoes.
Nothing works. They break through the smoke screen
for blood.

Always the lookout spots the Indians first,
spread north to south, barring progress.
The Sioux or some other Plains bunch
in spectacular columns, ICBM missiles,
feathers bristling in the meaningful sunset.

The drum breaks. There will be no parlance.
Only the arrows whining, a death-cloud of nerves
swarming down on the settlers
who die beautifully, tumbling like dust weeds

into the history that brought us all here
together: this wide screen beneath the sign of the
bear.

The sky fills, acres of blue squint and eye
that the crowd cheers. His face moves over us,
a thick cloud of vengeance, pitted
like the land that was once flesh. Each rut,

each scar makes a promise: *It is*
not over, this fight, not as long as you resist.

Everything we see belongs to us.

A few laughing Indians fall over the hood
slipping in the hot spilled butter.
The eye sees a lot, John, but the heart is so blind.
Death makes us owners of nothing.
He smiles, a horizon of teeth
the credits reel over, and then the white fields

again blowing in the true-to-life dark
The dark films over everything.
We get into the car
scratching our mosquito bites, speechless and small
as people are when the movie is done.
We are back in our skins.

How can we help but keep hearing his voice,
the flip side of the sound track, still playing:
Come on boys, we got them
where we want them, drunk, running.
They'll give us what we want, what we need.
Even his disease was the idea of taking everything.
Those cells, burning, doubling, splitting out
of their skins.

My Heroes Have Never Been Cowboys

Sherman Alexie

1.

In the reservation textbooks, we learned Indians were invented in 1492 by a crazy mixed-blood named Columbus. Immediately after class dismissal, the Indian children traded in those American stories and songs for a pair of tribal shoes. *These boots are made for walking, babe, and that's just what they'll do. One of these days these boots are gonna walk all over you.*

2.

Did you know that in 1492 every Indian instantly became an extra in the Great American Western? But wait, I never wondered what happened to Randolph Scott or Tom Mix. The Lone Ranger was never in my vocabulary. On the reservation, when we played Indians and cowboys, all of us little Skins fought on the same side against the cowboys in our minds. We never lost.

3.

Indians never lost their West, so how come I walk into the supermarket and find a dozen cowboy books telling me *How The West Was Won?* Curious, I travel to the world's largest shopping mall, find the Lost and Found Department. "Excuse me," I say. "I seem to have lost the West. Has anybody turned it in?" The clerk tells me I can find it in the Sears Home Entertainment Department, blasting away on fifty televisions.

4.

On Saturday morning television, the cowboy has fifty bullets in his six-shooter; he never needs to reload. It's just one more miracle for this country's heroes.

5.

My heroes have never been cowboys; my heroes carry guns in their minds.

6.

Win their hearts and minds and we win the war. Can you hear that song echo across history? If you give the Indian a cup of coffee with six cubes of sugar, he'll be your servant. If you give the Indian a cigarette and a book of matches, he'll be your friend. If you give the Indian a can of commodities, he'll be your lover. He'll hold you tight in his arms, cowboy, and two-step you outside.

7.

Outside it's cold and a confused snow falls in May. I'm watching some western on TBS, colorized, but the story remains the same. Three cowboys string telegraph wire across the plains until they are confronted by the entire Sioux nation. The cowboys, 19th century geniuses, talk the Indians into touching the wire, holding it in their hands and mouths. After a dozen or so have hold of the wire, the cowboys crank the portable generator and electrocute some of the Indians with a European flame and chase the rest of them away, bareback and burned. All these years later, the message tapped across my skin remains the same.

8.

It's the same old story whispered on the television in every HUD house on the reservation. It's 500 years of that same screaming song, translated from the American.

9.

Lester FallsApart found the American dream in a game of Russian Roulette: one bullet and five empty chambers. "It's Manifest Destiny," Lester said just before he pulled the trigger five times quick. "I missed," Lester said just before he reloaded the pistol: one empty chamber and five bullets. "Maybe we should call this Reservation Roulette," Lester said just before he pulled the trigger once at his temple and five more times as he pointed the pistol toward the sky.

10.

Looking up into the night sky, I asked my brother what he thought God looked like and he said "God probably looks like John Wayne."

11.

We've all killed John Wayne more than once. When we burned the ant pile in our backyard, my brother and I imagined those ants were some cavalry or another. When Brian, that insane Indian boy from across the street, suffocated neighborhood dogs and stuffed their bodies into the reservation high school basement, he must have imagined those dogs were cowboys, come back to break another treaty.

12.

Every frame of the black and white western is a treaty; every scene in this elaborate serial is a promise. But what about the reservation home movies? What about the reservation heroes? I remember this: Down near Bull's Pasture, Eugene stood on the pavement with a gallon of tequila under his arm. I watched in the rearview mirror as he raised his arm to wave good-bye and dropped the bottle, glass and dreams of the weekend shattered. After all these years, that moment is still the saddest of my whole life.

13.

Your whole life can be changed by the smallest pain.

14.

Pain is never added to pain. It multiplies. Arthur, here we are again, you and I, fancydancing through the geometric progression of our dreams. Twenty years ago, we never believed we'd lose. Twenty years ago, television was our way of finding heroes and spirit animals. Twenty years ago, we never knew we'd spend the rest of our lives in the reservation of our minds, never knew we'd stand outside the gates of the Spokane Indian Reservation without a key to let ourselves back inside. From a distance, that familiar song. Is it country and western? Is it the sound of hearts breaking? Every song remains the same here in America, this country of the Big Sky and Manifest Destiny, this country of John Wayne and broken treaties. Arthur, I have no words which can save our lives, no words approaching forgiveness, no words flashed across the screen at the reservation drive-in, no words promising either of us top billing. Extras, Arthur, we're all extras.

READING WRITING

This Text: Reading

1. What arguments do these two poems make about Indians, Westerns, America, and Hollywood?
2. Consider the "form" of each poem. How does the poem's formal qualities (its typography, how it looks on the page, its language) contribute to its overall meaning? Which poem is more "poetic"?
3. bell hooks argues that a seemingly harmless movie like *Waiting to Exhale* is dangerous to African Americans. How dangerous, then, are movies like Westerns to American Indians? Is there a difference in the dangers they pose?

Your Text: Writing

1. Write a comparison/contrast paper on these two poems. Pay close attention to language, form, symbolism, and metaphor. Be sure you make an argument in your essay.
2. Watch a famous movie starring John Wayne, like *The Searchers* or *Rio Bravo*. Write a paper in which you compare your own reading of Wayne with Erdrich's and Alexie's.
3. Talk to your parents or professor about John Wayne. Ask them how important he was during the 1950s and 1960s. Write a paper in which you analyze the power certain Hollywood stars have over American culture—even American politics.

Star Wars and America

Whitney Black

Student Essay

Whitney Black wrote this essay while a student at the University of San Francisco in 2003. In her short persuasive essay, she takes what is perhaps to most readers an unpopular stance. Black reads *Star Wars* through the lens of a classic American Western, arguing that the film essentially replicates the standard formula of Hollywood Westerns—even the good guys wear white and the bad guys, black. As you work through her essay, you might ask if Black reads too much into the film. Or, does she pick up on deep-seeded American values that many people are reluctant to question? Finally, is it possible to identify problematic aspects of a movie but still love it?

THOUGH *STAR WARS* TAKES PLACE in the far off frontier of space, and is less concerned with recreating America's past than it is with imagining the future, the film is still a classic American

Western, right down to the requisite good versus evil, us against them dualities. Like all formulaic Westerns, *Star Wars* is about opposition and the promotion of good old-fashioned American values. The environment is the unfamiliar galaxy, but the underlying message is pure Americana; *Star Wars* subverts patriotism within the rebel forces and religious "force," and establishes the rebellion's struggle against the tyrannical Empire as a pro-American ideological battle. The rebel forces, with their pared down attire and allegiance to the old "force" religiosity, are the antithesis to the techno-driven, machine heavy homogeneity of the Evil Empire; similar to how the American identity, with its commitment to traditional democratic values, differed from the oppressive threat of communism. Communism, during both the Red Scare and the Vietnam War, served as both a threat to American ideals as and a way to glorify those ideals by contrast. The un-American construct of the Empire, like the un-American Communist mentality, function as the perfect counterparts; both are outsider systems, whose differences illuminate America's "greatness," and generate a need to preserve that "greatness." The Rebellion is obligated to defend *a way of life,* a sense of individual freedom, from the Empire.

Like the Western's struggle between Cowboy and Indian, civilization and savagery, *Star Wars* simply modernizes the conflict, replacing cowboys with Jedi and Indians with evil empire affiliates. Though the characters have changed, the implicit Western message of expelling a threatening "other" remains. Both *Star Wars* and the classic Western are filmic homage to an American ideal; while the classic Western re-writes the past to stabilize and reassure the present, *Star Wars* acts as a cautionary tale against what an absence of those ideals means for the future. The "us against them" duality is less about racial differences than it is about America's ideological system. It is glorious democracy against a "bad" countergovernment. Though *Star Wars* does not directly ally itself with America's geography, location is inconsequential; the rebels are as American as Indians killing cowboys, symbols of a filmic tradition advocating American values by setting them against an external threat.[1]

Star Wars succeeds at its "Western-ness" because of its dependence on opposition. Nothing solidifies the righteousness of "good" as much as the presence of a contrasting evil. The Evil Empire justifies the Rebellion (obviously a *force* is necessary to confront the manifestation of evil) while divulging the danger of sacrificing the rebel cause to the empire. The Empire is the ominous threat and represents everything opposing the rebel value system, persona, and way of life. The result is audience approval of the rebel cause; audiences, whether aware of it or not, identify with the rebels as individual heroes fighting against a different, and thus threatening, authority. While the rebellion, and its association to the Imperial Senate, most certainly symbolizes the people's voice, the Empire is ignorant of the wants of the common people, and is a realization of abused power, and a warning against forces opposed to American democracy. While America, with its own structured Senate, associates its ideals with a "power to the people" mentality, the Empire is in obvious contrast, determined to exploit technology (the Death Star) and become an ultimate power and oppressive regime.

Not only does *Star Wars* link technology to tyranny and oppression, but it also creates another opposition of technology versus nature, with nature encompassing the rural American identity of honor, duty, and goodness while technology embodies the age-old fear of change. Clearly, the death star is both an example of misused power, and a warning against change. The machine, because of its relation to the Evil Empire, is a digression away from humanity; technology threatens the existence of individual power and becomes an instrument for proliferating evil. The protagonist Luke Skywalker succeeds against the Empire by

relying on the power of his subconscious, turning off his computerized tracking system to respond on instinct. He uses his faith in the force, a religion of nature, and old fashioned and unquestioned belief; the outcome of his success, his ability to defeat the Empire, perpetuates yet another American notion. Believe in its value systems and justice will be restored.

The film's message is clear: Hold fast to our present way of life and the future will be saved. Like any Western, *Star Wars* is a cinematic love letter to Americana, and the country's perpetual fear of confrontation. Westerns deal in oppositions, because the rebel in space or in the west is always sacrificing their own safety to salvage a community. Community salvation mirrors American salvation, and the protagonist's determination and commitment to deep-rooted American rightness serves as the best possible form of American patriotism and duty. The Western always needs a hero willing to die for the cause, ready to save America from the threat of change. Westerns contend that America is the "best and only way," oppositions are the worst imagined evil; both feared and destroyed and ultimately never tolerated.

Note

1. For more information on *Star Wars* and American values, see Peter Lev's *American Films of the 70s: Conflicting Visions*.

Works Cited

Lev, Peter. *American Films of the 70s: Conflicting Visions*. Austin: University of Texas Press, 2000.

The *Sicko* Suite

The documentary has become an important and controversial text in American culture. Because most documentaries combine techniques from feature films and journalism, they can often blur the boundaries between fact and reality. Traditionally, documentaries have been assumed to be "objective," nonpartisan presentations of an actual story or topic, a sort of extended piece of reporting delivered visually instead of printed in a magazine or book. Over the past few decades, however, filmmakers have turned to the documentary not simply to "document" an issue but to make an argument about an issue. Most filmmakers have a point of view before undertaking their projects, and that point of view has to make it into the film. The difference now is that the point of view is more often explicit. In his important book *Theorizing Documentary,* Michael Renov claims that documentary films have four possible motives: to record, reveal, or preserve; to persuade or promote; to analyze or interrogate; and to express.

Michael Moore's films arguably do all four, which rankle some who carry the belief that documentaries should be objective—or at least appear so. Like him or hate him, Moore's movies are groundbreaking. They include *Roger and Me* (1989), *Bowling for Columbine* (2002), *Fahrenheit 9/11* (2004), and now *Sicko* (2007). Moore is arguably the most divisive filmmaker in the United States—enemies decry him as a propagandist, a phony, and a liar; fans hold him up as a much-needed voice of reason, reality, and righteousness. Moore won an Academy Award for *Bowling for Columbine,* but that only solidified for his detractors that he is a mouthpiece for the "liberal left."

His most recent project, *Sicko,* takes on America's health-care system and is the subject of this suite of reviews. Like most of Moore's movies, the reception of *Sicko* has been mixed. However, one difference with *Sicko* is that reviews of the movie have not necessarily fallen along political lines. Conservative media outlets like Fox News gave *Sicko* a glowing review,

Michael Moore and a doctor from *Sicko.*

calling it "brilliant and uplifting," whereas traditionally progressive publications like *The New Yorker* and *The Washington Post* were critical of the film.

The reviews here read the movie through four different lenses. Mick LaSalle of *The San Francisco Chronicle* and Kyle Smith of *The New York Post* write about the film from their perspective as movie reviewers, but, clearly, their political and aesthetic biases influence how successful they find Moore's project. Maggie Mahar has worked as a financial journalist, writing for *Money, Institutional Investor,* and *Barron's* before specializing in health care. Her review reads *Sicko* through the lens of America's health-care bureaucracy. As the director of the Center for Bioethics at the University of Pennsylvania, Arthur Caplan offers yet another take on *Sicko*—in his case, from the perspective of human and medical ethics.

As it happens, ethical questions remain at the fore in any discussion of documentaries. Documentary films can be a powerful form of visual rhetoric, and learning to recognize how and why such texts persuade is an important step to reading all kinds of documentary texts, such as reports, photographs, essays, and even novels. Even seemingly objective documentaries like *Nanook of the North* or *March of the Penguins* have a point of view, even if the film's political overtones are difficult to parse. For example, one could argue that if the directors of *March of the Penguins* had no agenda, they would not have included a voice-over narration, but they did. Plus, they hired Morgan Freeman, who is impossible to dislike, to tell us the ways in which penguins resemble humans. Although the film (or Freeman) never comes out and says anything like, "We must save the penguins!" or "Understanding these penguins may give us insight into animal and human behavior and relations," we get the sense that the film makes both arguments. Under the larger rubric of persuasion and documentary is **propaganda**—a term that comes up in a couple of the reviews of *Sicko*—which carries both positive and negative connotations. Because they can alter beliefs, shape behavior, and manipulate factual detail to make a more persuasive text, documentaries are often also propaganda. Does that make them less "true"? Not necessarily, but it does make them less objective. Although Moore may claim his film is "nonpartisan," he would never claim it is "objective."

Before writing about *Sicko*, you should, of course, see the movie. *Reading* a documentary is slightly different from reading a typical feature film. You should pay attention to the various techniques the director uses to make an argument—music, editing, real versus created footage, comedy, and the sense of "reality" that the film creates. Remember, even a supposedly real text like a documentary is a constructed text—shot, edited, and assembled so that it has a specific impact on the viewer. As you read these reviews, note how each one picks up and comments on *Sicko*'s main arguments and the way Moore makes them.

Need a Doctor? That's Too Bad

Mick LaSalle

MICHAEL MOORE DOES SOMETHING very shrewd in *Sicko*, his new documentary about the health care crisis in America. He doesn't address his film to the 50 million Americans who don't have health care, but to the 250 million who do. And he makes the case that things need to

change not by appealing to sympathy or to common decency but to self-interest. He tells people who have health insurance that, even if they think they're safe, they're not—and he shows them why. *Sicko* will scare people, and it probably should.

Moore makes two arguments in this documentary, one that's entirely persuasive and another that's at least intriguing. The first is that health care in America is in a state of escalating crisis—that people are getting swindled and people are dying. Moore documents a corrupt and scandalous situation in which doctors and health care gatekeepers get rewarded for denying coverage and the HMOs rack up profits in the billions—which they then use to buy off politicians. If what Moore is saying is true, if health care companies really are making billions by deliberately defrauding customers and letting them die, then we're witnessing the moral equivalent of war profiteering, or perhaps war crimes.

Having made the case that our system isn't working, Moore launches his second argument, that what we need in this country is what France, England and Canada already have: a single-payer system. He then proceeds to present the national health systems in these countries as nothing short of idyllic, with short waits in emergency rooms, house calls (in France), happy doctors and expert care. It's here that I wish Moore would have striven for more balance, not because he's obligated to be fair, but because a balanced approach might have been more informative and persuasive. For example, in his French, English and Canadian interviews he never asks the one key question: What are you paying in taxes? Yet there's no mistaking the pride these people have in their system, not just because of what it does for them but for what it says about them and their culture.

Indeed, even if Moore is guilty of propagandizing, he shows enough for us to realize that we've been on the receiving end of propaganda for years without knowing it—that "socialized medicine" is a nightmare, that doctors are so poorly paid that there's no incentive to enter the profession, that people don't get to choose their own doctor and that governments, to save money, let serious illness go untreated.

Moore does a good job of knocking down those arguments and demonstrates how, if anything, that state of affairs actually exists more and more under our system. A woman relives the nightmare of having her daughter turned away for emergency treatment at a hospital because her plan covered only treatment at another hospital. The child died on the way. He interviews a young woman denied treatment for cervical cancer because her plan considered her too young to get cervical cancer. Promising treatments are denied desperately ill patients on the basis of being "experimental." One of the patients Moore interviewed has since died, and another woman, who appears to be in her mid-20s, has seen her cancer metastasize.

But these are just isolated incidents, aren't they? Apparently not. A health care company screener breaks down in tears, talking about the system by which she is forced to refuse care, and a former investigator for an HMO discusses the ways in which his department looked for excuses not to pay legitimate claims. "You're not slipping through the cracks," he says. "Someone made that crack and is sweeping you toward it."

Moore may be an imp, a manipulator and a provocateur, but he keeps his vaudevillian antics to a minimum, and to the extent they're there, they're welcome: They provide enough diversion, grim laughter and gallows humor to make this dispiriting topic bearable. *Sicko* is enraging, alarming and terribly sad, but Moore takes care that it's never anything less than fascinating, a series of compulsively watchable stories and incidents, interspersed with masterfully edited sequences. Some might prefer other Moore films for

The *Sicko* Suite

their subject matter. But in terms of pure storytelling and filmmaking, this is his most accomplished work.

In a jaw-dropping prank, Moore takes Sept. 11 rescue workers—denied coverage for respiratory ailments contracted while pulling bodies from the rubble—and brings them to Cuba for medical treatment. He captains a small flotilla of ships to Guantanamo Bay, so that these Americans can get the health care that the terrorists and alleged terrorists are getting, and when that doesn't work, he just takes them to a Cuban hospital. It's Moore at his best. He contrives situations, but then real things happen.

In the process, Moore rescues 9/11 from its heinous use as a stealth weapon for the teardown of American values and uses it in the interest of restoring true American values, like "looking out for the other guy," as James Stewart once said in an old Capra film. No one should consider *Sicko* the last word on the health care issue, but it just might spark the demand for a genuine, honest discussion.

Botched Operation

Kyle Smith

MICHAEL MOORE'S LATEST DOCUMENTARY, *Sicko,* is an urgent bipartisan plea. Liberals and conservatives, Democrats and Republicans, Yankees and Red Sox can surely all agree, says Moore, that our health-care system ought to be run by Fidel Castro.

The silliness of Moore's oeuvre is so self-evident that being able to spot it is not liberal or conservative, either; it's a basic intelligence test, like the ability to match square peg with square hole. His documentaries are political slapstick that could have been made by a third Farrelly brother or a fourth Stooge. I will pay him the honor of treating him with his own meds. (How else to deal with a film that calls Hillary Clinton "sexy"?)

The film doesn't open until June 29, but already has been leaked on the Internet, free, with Moore's blessing. The central pleasure offered by Marxism is observing the way it is programmed to destroy itself.

The bulk of *Sicko* is given over to the stories of Americans who got the run-around from health insurers, being told they didn't qualify for benefits because the requested procedures were too experimental or because of pre-existing conditions. Perhaps the most absurd example is that of the woman who says that after she received benefits, the check was stopped because she had previously suffered an undisclosed yeast infection.

No one doubts that lots of insured and uninsured Americans face health-care crises. So far, Moore is master of the obvious. Where do we go from here? To France, Britain and Canada, says Moore.

But lots of people in those countries have health-care nightmares of their own. Checking out France's free, universal health system, Moore gets blissed out by French happiness. But this phrase is as close to an oxymoron as French rock. In a poll, 85 percent of the French recently said their country is heading in the wrong direction. Right direction? Nine percent. In France in 2003, 15,000 mostly elderly hospital patients died in an August heat wave—because hospitals lack air conditioning and doctors (who, like everyone in France, sometimes go on strike) were on vacation.

Moore also marvels at the free health care in Britain, but he knows the Brits have a two-tier health system: The smart set carries private insurance, which Moore wants to

The *Sicko* Suite

outlaw in the United States. The cliché in London is that the well-shod go to the same doctor as the suckers on the National Health Service. The difference is that private clients get treated right away, while the NHS losers wait two years to get their strep throat looked at.

Moore hopes his audience is too stupid to know about wait times. He asks a handful of Canadian patients how long they had to wait to see the doctor. Oh, 20 minutes, 45 minutes, everyone says. So if Moore finds five people who didn't have to wait, there's no waiting for anybody! Check out the Canadian movie *The Barbarian Invasions* (which is, like *Sicko*, a fiction film) for a view of how Canadians view their system: agonizing waits, trips across the border to Vermont to get access to modern technology and fetid facilities modeled, seemingly, on an American one—the Confederate field hospital in *Gone with the Wind*.

What about stats? Moore emphasizes life-expectancy figures in which the U.S. slightly lags some other countries. But life expectancy involves many factors; two that Moore is especially knowledgeable about, obesity and firearms homicide, are special American plagues. Here's a stat: The percentage of patients having to wait more than four months for non-emergency surgery is about five times higher in Canada and seven times higher in Britain than it is here.

In *Entertainment Weekly*, Moore tacitly admitted that *Sicko* lies about wait times, saying, "Well, OK, let's set up a system where we don't have the Canadian wait." Er, what Canadian wait? *Sicko* says there isn't one. "Let's set up a system," Moore says, "where we take what they do right and don't do the things that we do wrong." And let's make it so every girl is the prettiest one in town. Deciding who gets what and when involves rationing, either by price or by waiting or some combination of both. The law of supply and demand can no more be repealed than the law that all documentary films must be left-wing.

Moore is outwardly a genial buffoon, but inwardly he is an authoritarian buffoon, as he shows in two long episodes: a straight-faced interview with the United Kingdom's house Commie, Tony Benn, and the famous-before-anyone-saw-it sequence, first reported in *The Post*, in which Moore takes some 9/11 rescue workers with lingering health problems to Cuba.

Moore, at a Havana hospital, says he requested that his group receive exactly the same care as any Cuban–"and that's exactly what they got." As comedy, this statement is on a par with the sex scene in *Knocked Up*, the chest waxing in *The 40-Year-Old Virgin* and the moment in *An Inconvenient Truth* when Al Gore tells us that the ecology's No. 1 threat, China, is in fact "on the cutting edge" of environmentalism.

In the Cuba section of *Sicko*, so many guys in white coats scurry around Moore's patients listening to symptoms, peering at X-rays and firing up high-tech medical equipment that the scene might have been co-written by Groucho and Karl Marx. If Fidel himself gets this level of care, it's no wonder the guy has outlasted nine presidents.

I expected Moore to protect himself with a thin coat of disclaimer, just a line to say, "Look, I know Cuba is actually a Caribbean Alcatraz where nobody's gotten a new car since Fredo betrayed Michael, but I'm just using this as an extreme example for ironic purposes." Instead, his irony runs the other way: He plays scare music over an image of Castro and expects you to giggle along. Cuban health care, Moore declares, is among the best in the world. Actually, Cuba is short on everything from clean drinking water to aspirin and on up.

Despite Moore's apparent belief that he can seem moderate by narrating in a sing-song, I'm-talking-to-a-child-or-moron tone, the man can no more hide his Marxism than his belly. He presents not only Tony Benn but Che Guevara's daughter as voices of sanity. Through a French doctor, Moore sneaks in the Marxist slogan "from each according to his ability, to each according to his needs." Moore also runs lots of old Soviet propaganda footage with comical music on the soundtrack as if to suggest that Stalin was just another campy, overhyped entertainment figure—Martin Short with a mustache.

Let's not give too much credit to Moore for his gift to the guy running an anti-Moore Web site who was going to be forced to shut it down—because of a health crisis he couldn't afford. When Moore found out, he anonymously sent a $12,000 check, or .0005 percent of the money he was paid to make this movie. An anonymous check is not actually anonymous if you announce it in a movie; then, it becomes simply a bargain method for buying press accounts of you as a nice guy.

Moore, of course, has a Castro-ish history of suppressing dissent. But he is free to disprove me by anecdote. He can send my check care of *The Post.*

Sicko and Healthcare Reform

Maggie Mahar

MICHAEL MOORE'S *SICKO* DOES TWO THINGS VERY WELL.

First, the film makes it clear that in the U.S., even if you have health insurance, this does not mean that you are "covered." Everyone knows that many Americans are uninsured. But now, millions of middle-class Americans are beginning to realize that they are *under*insured, and Moore drives that point home.

For-profit insurers spend a great deal of time designing policies that will limit their "losses"—i.e., limit the amount that they have to pay out. These "Swiss cheese" policies are filled with holes: for example, a policy may pay for surgery, but not rehabilitation after surgery. And this omission is deliberate. As a former claims adjuster tells Moore, when an insurer denies payment, "You're not slipping through the cracks. They made the crack and are sweeping you toward it."

Secondly, *Sicko* underlines the signal difference between healthcare in the U.S. and healthcare in other countries: the citizens of other countries take a collective view of the problem. Or as Moore puts it, they realize that when it comes to sickness and dying, all of us are vulnerable. "In the end, we truly are all in the same boat . . . they live in a world of 'we' not 'me.'"

Of course people in the U.K., Canada and France know that healthcare is not free. (And contrary to what some of Moore's critics say, he does not pretend that it is.) But since they think of healthcare as a right—something we all deserve simply because we are human—it seems to them fair that, "You pay according to your means [through taxes] and receive according to your needs." In this, national health programs that are funded by taxes resemble Medicare: the higher your salary, the more you pay into Medicare. The sicker you are, the more you will take out in benefits. If you're lucky, you put in more than you take out.

What *Sicko* doesn't do is focus on the waste in our system. We can't afford to pay for everything that someone might possibly want. We need to be sure that we are getting value for our healthcare dollars. In one case, Moore tells the story of a man dying of kidney cancer. Desperate to save him, his wife valiantly tries to persuade insurers to pay for new treatments— including a bone-marrow transplant that the insurance company calls "experimental." But the insurer refuses, and a few weeks later her husband dies. This is one of the saddest moments in the film—both husband and wife are very appealing.

Yet it is not clear that the insurer was wrong to refuse to cover the bone-marrow transplant. It is very difficult to tell from the few details given in the film whether it might have helped—but advanced kidney cancer is not curable. Even the newest drugs give the patient, at most, a few more weeks of life. At the same time, it is understandable that both the husband and the wife (and apparently Moore) assume that the insurer was merely trying to save money.

After all, when it comes to making coverage decisions based on medical evidence, for-profit insurers have a pretty spotty record. In the 1990s, when insurers said they were trying to "manage care," many were simply "managing costs." For example, some decided which drugs to include in their formularies based simply on whether the manufacturer would give them a deep discount. In return for the discount, the insurance company would assure the drug-maker that it would not cover a competing product.. This had nothing to do with which drug was more effective.

The public will always be suspicious of decisions made by for-profit insurers—even when their decisions are based on sound medical evidence. For-profit insurers just don't have the political or moral standing to make these judgments. (By contrast, most patients are much more comfortable with Medicare's coverage decisions—which is why we need a federal agency testing and comparing the effectiveness of new treatments.)

But if Moore skips over the problems of overt treatment it may be because he knows that at this point more Americans are worried about undertreatment. And to be fair, no one could examine all of the problems in our dysfunctional healthcare system in a single film. What is important is that Moore says what he says loudly and clearly. He tells a vivid, memorable story—and in the process, he has managed to spur the national conversation about healthcare reform.

This is what scares people like Peter Chowka. If people begin talking about healthcare, they may begin to think about it. It may even occur to them that perhaps it wouldn't be so terrible to borrow a few ideas from other countries. As Moore points out, "If another country builds a better car, we buy it. If they make a better wine, we drink it. If they have better healthcare . . . what's our problem?"

It's conceivable, Moore suggests, that we might even learn something from Cuba, a country that spends 1/27 of what we do on care. Of course the film's Cuban adventure is controversial—and purposefully so. I've written about it on *TPM Café* where I recount a very funny story Moore tells about his experience with Standards and Practices at NBC— a tale which shows that he knew exactly what he was doing when he took part of *Sicko*'s "cast" to Cuba. Looking back on *Sicko* Moore says, "I could have played it safe, I know. I could have gone to Ireland. . . . Everyone loves the Irish. . . . But you know you have to get people's attention."

And, as usual, Michael Moore has succeeded in doing just that.

The *Sicko* Suite

Nothing Funny About *Sicko*: Gitmo Prisoners Get Better Medical Treatment than September 11 Rescue Workers

Arthur Caplan

A NUMBER OF REVIEWERS HAVE described *Sicko*, Michael Moore's new documentary film about health care in the United States, as funny. It isn't.

Sure there is a chuckle or two to be had. You have to smile when Moore uses '50s-style anti-communist film clips to mock the fear-mongering American politicians engage in whenever the subject turns to "socialized" medicine, or when he is bellowing through a bullhorn while bobbing in a boat in Guantanamo Bay, Cuba, begging for the same level of health care for workers injured in Sept. 11 rescue efforts as we afford the evildoers locked up in maximum security at Gitmo.

But *Sicko*, which opens nationwide Friday, is not funny. It is tragic. You should not come out of the movie theater smiling. You should leave angry. *Sicko* is right on target about the mess that is American health care.

Moore's critics would like you to believe *Sicko* is slicko. Those with vested interests in preserving the current status quo in health care have already activated their lobbyists, media flacks, think-tank mouthpieces and trade organizations to go after Moore and his movie. There are nearly $2 trillion worth of vested interests out there in insurance, managed care, hospitals, doctors, advertisers and salespeople looking to keep their share of the health care pot of gold.

But there's no disputing the key flaws in our system that *Sicko* makes abundantly clear: Nearly one in five Americans doesn't have health insurance. And even those with insurance often face incredible and sometimes lethal hurdles to adequate health care— from crushing out-of-pocket expenses and co-payments to snail-like bureaucracies unresponsive to the needs of their clients (usually by design in the hope that they simply go away).

As if that's not trouble enough, your doctor may be motivated to deny medical care as he climbs the corporate ladder. Your employer could go bankrupt and leave retirees high and dry. Insurance companies may deny your claim and drop coverage for pre-existing conditions.

And when insurance payments dry up, hospitals have literally tossed patients onto the street. *Sicko* tells these stories irrefutably and grimly.

Paying More for Less

Worse, if that is possible, Americans pay more for this mess than anyone else in the world for health care—and we get less for our money. Despite our love of the free market, the rest of the industrialized world delivers care to more of its populations with much more economic efficiency than we do. The only parts of the U.S. health system that approximate the efficiencies of Canada, Germany, Singapore, Australia, France, the Netherlands and Sweden are Medicare and the Veterans Affairs hospital system. Moore goes so far as to visit Cuba to show that even those under Fidel's dictatorial thumb have easier access to health care than many Americans.

Why do we put up with a broken, bloated, bureaucratic and increasingly barbaric health system? Because your politicians are in the thrall of the people who profit from it. And just enough of us have access to a fairly decent level of care that the misery of the uninsured, underinsured and tapped out does not move us to care.

And Moore doesn't get into this, but even if you have great health insurance, don't get comfortable. You, too, could be getting the runaround or finding yourself on the outside looking in unless reform comes to American health care.

Will Boomers Bankrupt the System?

Baby boomers are getting older. And while it is chic to babble on about 50 being the new 40 and for 60-year-old women to grab the headlines by having babies, the fact remains that this group is entering into old age, a time of heavy reliance on health care.

A system that barely can get by dealing with chronic illnesses and the demand for long-term care will soon be tipped over by an entire cohort of geezers who, no matter how religiously they jog and or how much pomegranate juice they drink, will use health care to a degree never seen anywhere in the world at a price that, if nothing is done, will bankrupt the country.

The boomers are partly to blame. They built a health care system to suit their medical needs when they were middle-aged. We have some of the finest acute care hospitals in the world for treating heart attacks and transplanting organs. But we are not prepared to deal with long-term care, home care or hospice, a lack of health care personnel willing to work in these settings and the complete absence of insurance to pay for most of what you need when you are old, disabled or both.

Not only will the ranks of the elderly be exploding but we'll also soon see a rise in genetic testing. More and more of us will find out that we are at risk of various ailments. This means your insurance company and HMO will have even more tools to use to figure out how to chop the risky off their rolls.

Moore has it right in *Sicko*. American health care is in serious need of rehaul and repair. Ignore the bleatings of those out to discredit Moore by saying he is too flip with his depiction of health care in Canada or France, who chafe at his cheekiness in noting that we guarantee imprisoned terrorists better health care than we do our own sick neighbors, or that he never says that many have to wait 18 months in England to get a hip replacement.

No one in Canada or France would even contemplate exchanging their systems for our health care mess. Prisoners do enjoy a more meaningful right to health care than many Americans. And while you may wait a long time for a new hip in England, a fair number of people in the U.S. will never get that hip replacement because they cannot pay for it.

If you think Moore is exaggerating the woes of the health care system and if you think—as his often bought and paid-for critics charge—that he is just a sloppy, overfed left-wing ideologue, then go down to your local hospital emergency room or nursing home and tell it to those waiting there for care and compassion. Except for luck and a few ticks of the clock, they might be you. If Moore's call to action is not heeded, such a visit tells you all you need to know about what awaits you in terms of health care in America. Nothing funny at all about that.

ARTHUR CAPLAN • NOTHING FUNNY ABOUT *SICKO*: GITMO PRISONERS **3 8 7**
GET BETTER MEDICAL TREATMENT THAN SEPTEMBER 11 RESCUE WORKERS

The *Sicko* Suite

READING WRITING

This Text: Reading

1. If you have not already seen it, track down a copy of *Sicko* and watch it for yourself. Which of the four reviews seem the most on target to you? Why do you advocate one over another?
2. Would it be possible for a review of *Sicko* to change your mind about the movie or about your own views of the American health-care situation? How persuasive can rhetorical texts be? In what ways do the rhetorics of visual texts differ from the rhetorics of written texts?
3. LaSalle and Smith disagree on the value of Moore's film rather dramatically. Clearly, they were viewing the film through two different political lenses. Which review is the more convincing? Why?
4. Health-care issues cut across boundaries of politics, gender, race, and class. Democrats and Republicans want good, reliable, affordable health care, as do men and women. Can you identify the lenses of Mahar and Caplan? What do they have at stake in *Sicko*'s success or failure?
5. Look up some definitions of **propaganda.** In what ways is *Sicko* propaganda? Is that a bad thing?

Your Text: Writing

1. Write your own essay on *Sicko,* but pick a lens through which to read it. How does the movie's form of persuasion alter depending on the lens you adopt?
2. Write a comparison/contrast paper on *Sicko* and one of Moore's other films. What makes *Sicko* different? Even though Moore (and others) claim the film is nonpartisan, is it really? *Can* it be?
3. Compare *Sicko* to another well-known documentary designed to right injustice—*The Thin Blue Line, Harlan County U.S.A.,* or *Paradise Lost*—demonstrating and analyzing how these texts try to persuade.

READING BETWEEN THE LINES

Classroom Activities

1. As a class, watch one of the movies under review in this section. Write your own review of the movie without talking to anyone else in class about the movie. Then, after a class discussion, write yet another review of the movie. How does your own reading of the movie change after class discussion?
2. Watch a movie in class and write a group review. What are the major points of disagreement? On what was it easy to agree?
3. View any of the movies that you have read about in the previous texts. Do you agree with the writers? Why or why not?
4. Is watching a movie in class different than watching one at home or in a theater? Why? Have a class discussion on the space of watching movies.
5. Write a poem about the *experience* of watching a particular film (like Erdrich's "Dear John Wayne"). How does writing a poem about a movie differ from writing a journal entry or a formal paper? Is there a relationship between poems and film?

6. Bring advertisements or commercials about particular movies to class. Discuss the demographic the studio is targeting. Do the commercials and ads *tell* you how to read the movie?
7. As you watch a movie in class, write down every form of manipulation you notice (such as music, close-ups, special effects, camera angles, unusual editing, intense colors).
8. Watch a recent movie that was praised by critics but was seemingly ignored by the general public (these might include *The Lives of Others, Tully, The Fast Runner, Three Kings, Red, Simple Men, Vanya on 42nd Street, The Straight Story, Rushmore, Secrets and Lies, You Can Count on Me, Boys Don't Cry, American Movie, The Winslow Boy, Ghost World*). Why do you think not many people saw these films? Why do you think critics loved these particular movies? Is there tension between critical and popular taste?
9. Talk about the criteria and expectations of different genres in class. What characteristics must a romantic comedy have? What is the purpose of a Western? What does an action–adventure movie need to do? What makes a good scary movie?
10. Find a copy of the American Film Institute's top 100 American movies. Talk about the list in class. Why did these movies make the list? What movies are missing? Why?

Essay Ideas

1. What is the "greatest" movie you've seen? Write an essay in which you argue why your choice is the greatest.
2. Chances are, you have seen *Sicko* or *The Fast and the Furious*. Write your own analytical review of one of these films. Feel free to reference one of the reviews you have read. Perhaps you will agree or disagree with one (or many) of the reviewers. Be sure to analyze the film; don't simply write a plot summary.
3. bell hooks's review of *Waiting to Exhale* is a provocative text. Track down a positive review of the film and write a comparison/contrast paper in which you not only identify but also explore the variant readings of the film.
4. Write an essay on a director's body of work. People like Steven Spielberg, Woody Allen, Quentin Tarantino, Penny Marshall, Stanley Kubrick, John Sayles, Spike Lee, Michael Bay, Paul Verhoven, or Howard Hawkes, who have directed a number of different movies, will make your essay more interesting. Is there an overarching theme to their movies? How have they contributed to film history? To American culture?
5. Write an essay in which you explore issues of gender in one or two recent movies. Perhaps you can pick a movie directed by a woman and one directed by a man. How are women represented? How are women's bodies presented or framed? Male bodies? Do the women have strong roles, or are they limited, stereotypical roles? Do the women date or love men their own age, or are the men much older? Do the women have good jobs and healthy lifestyles?
6. Write an essay in which you explore issues of race. As in gender, how are issues of race and power represented in the film? What kind of music runs through the film? Are minority characters filmed or framed differently than Anglo characters? There is an old joke that the one black character in a horror film is one of the first to die. Is this still the case? While there are a number of wonderful movies by people of color (*Do the Right Thing, Smoke Signals, The Joy Luck Club, Mississippi Masala, El Mariachi*), you might also consider how minorities are represented in movies made by Anglos.
7. Explore notions of class in American cinema. How often are poor people in movies? While there may be women and people of color in Hollywood and in the studio system,

how well does Hollywood understand low-income America? Are there realistic film portrayals of working-class or low-income families? Some would say that America is more classist than racist: Is this theory proved or refuted by Hollywood?

8. Write an essay in which you offer a reading of a film based solely on the film techniques: sound, lighting, camera angles, music, framing, and editing. How can technique determine meaning?

9. *Star Wars* is beloved by millions. Do you agree with Whitney Black's critical reading of the film?

READING AND WRITING ABOUT
images

WITH THE PROLIFERATION OF TELEVISION, MOVIES, VIDEO GAMES, COMPUTERS, AND ADVERTISING, WE HAVE BECOME A CULTURE THAT TENDS TO DEFINE ITSELF THROUGH VISUAL IMAGES. EVEN THE ACT OF READING THESE WORDS ON THIS PAGE REMAINS A VISUAL ACTIVITY. AS WE EXPLAIN IN THE INTRODUCTION, READING IS NOTHING MORE THAN VISUAL DECODING OF IMAGES SO FAMILIAR THAT WE DO NOT EVEN THINK OF THEM AS IMAGES. WE DON'T IMAGINE TEXT ON THE PAGE AS PICTURES, BUT EACH WORD IS A SMALL PICTURE OF CURVED, SLANTED, AND DOTTED MARKS THAT WE CALL "LETTERS." WHEN WE PUT CERTAIN COMBINATIONS OF THESE LETTERS TOGETHER, THEY CONJURE UP A PARTICULAR IDEA OR

image in our heads. While words are images themselves and reflect other images, we're more concerned here with the way we constantly decode, (often with little conscious effort) the multiple images that we encounter each day—from people's faces to television shows to book covers to signs to architecture. One of this book's main ideas, in fact, is slowing down the reading process of visual images. As you may have noticed, almost all of the chapters in this book involve visual decoding of some sort.

Our book's insistence on this type of reading stands behind our idea to present some images as a way of focusing our attention on the visual. The kinds of images we offer need little introduction, but we will provide a brief entrée into our thinking behind this chapter. First, we present pairs of

images. We remain interested in how images speak (both directly and indirectly) to each other and how details of specific images become highlighted or accentuated when placed in context with another picture. For instance, a small, older wooden house in a working-class neighborhood may appear quite different depending on its context. Next to the White House, it may seem tiny and almost shabby, but next to a grass hut from a poor country, it could appear downright spacious and luxurious. In this chapter, you are given several combinations of images. Our hope is that you will engage in a semiotic reading of the individual images and that you will do a semiotic analysis of the pair as well.

To this end, we've identified and reiterated a few points about reading visual images:

Images are texts that can and should be read.

Again, as we point out in our discussion of semiotics in the Introduction, we ask that you apply the vocabulary and attention you devote to reading written texts to reading visual texts. When we open a book or look at directions or scan a newspaper, we are conscious of the act of reading. We know that our eyes move across a page and process information, and most important, we are conscious of the information that this process of looking produces. That is, we know we are reading for information, for content—we know that there is a message to most written texts.

However, the title and the thesis of this book is that the world is a text; that means that all images are texts, and as such demand to be read as thoroughly as a poem or textbook. In fact, we would argue that visual images such as advertisements, television and movies, photographs, album covers, movie posters, and T-shirts should be read with particular care because images transmit many values and assumptions but do so quietly and subconsciously. Because images do not come in the language of analysis (words), we tend not to analyze them as closely, if at all. We urge you to analyze all images.

Reading images is usually an informal rather than a formal process.

As we noted earlier, reading images tends to be an informal process—that is, we are not always aware of the process of reading images. We take them in and move on, giving very little thought to the thousands of visual cues we see every few seconds. To formalize the process, all we need to do is become conscious readers of images as constructed texts. For instance, this morning if you combed your hair, washed, shaved, put on makeup—if you thought about what to wear at all—then you did some work in constructing yourself as a text. You knew that today, like every other day, you were going to be read, on some level, and you wanted to send certain cues. Perhaps you wanted to suggest that you are alternative, conservative, athletic, bookish, or sophisticated. Depending on the image you wanted to project, you would don the appropriate signifiers.

When the other students look at you as you walk into class or when patrons in the coffee shop regard you as you order a latte, they do an informal reading of you—even if it is very brief and even if they don't know they are doing it at all. They might notice something has changed about you, but they would likely acquire even this information informally—virtually no one would actively ask the question, "How has *X* changed her appearance today? Let me take a thorough inventory of hairstyle, clothing, grooming." The same kind of quick informal reading usually goes into our appraisal of images. How often do we really stop to consider everything, all the details, that contribute to the overall message of the image? Here is where reading images mirrors reading visual arts—we must be aware of issues of composition, how the image is put together. As soon as you begin asking questions about what message a certain image is supposed to send, as soon as you read the image on your own terms—that is, when you begin to read the image not as the image wants to be read but as something to analyze—then you will formalize the reading process and begin to see the world in a more complex way.

The reader/viewer always participates in the construction and significance of the image.

The Confederate flag, the "Stars and Bars," has become one of the most controversial American images in the past 50 years. Perhaps more than any other American icon, the Stars and Bars reveals how deeply our own backgrounds, culture, and political beliefs determine how we "read" images. For some white Southerners, the flag stands as a symbol of rebellion and independence. For white Northerners or those not from the South, the Stars and Bars may reinforce negative stereotypes about Southern culture. For yet another population, African Americans, the Stars and Bars stand as a salient and prominent symbol of slavery and racism. Why do each of these groups have such different interpretations of a simple red rectangle, crossed by two blue bars and some white stripes? The answer is simple. We cannot "see" the flag (or any image) outside of our own ideas.

Whether the image under debate is a photo of Osama bin Laden, Bill Clinton talking with Monica Lewinsky, a topless supermodel, a multiracial couple, an electric chair, a fetus, a church, or a chemistry textbook, we each bring to the image our own set of assumptions and prejudices. This realization is important because it underscores the gap between intention and reception. By intention or intent, we mean the motivation behind producing or displaying the text, whereas reception is the reaction to the text—how the text is received. In many instances, intention and reception have nothing to do with each other. Not long ago, the chief justice of the Alabama Supreme Court, Roy Moore, was removed from office for placing a monument of the Ten Commandments in the rotunda of the courtroom. A number of people were outraged, claiming that hanging up the Ten Commandments was publicly stating that the judge would rule from a position that is sympathetic to an Old Testament Judeo–Christian perspective, thereby admitting *de facto* discrimination against non-Christians. Was the judge intending to send this message? Maybe, maybe not. Is this message a valid reception of the text? Probably.

In addition, the American flag means something different in Afghanistan than it does in Ireland. The logo for the Atlanta Braves sends one message to folks in Georgia and another to folks on the Rosebud Indian Reservation in South Dakota. The photograph of incoming First Lady Hillary Rodham Clinton holding hands with outgoing First Lady Barbara Bush incites very different reactions depending on your political leanings. Our point is that no reading of an image is ever value-free. We are active participants in the construction and reception of an image, and by extension, the world.

What follows is a series of images, without captions or explanations, that we feel make rich visual texts.

Two Images of Gender

Source: Leonardo da Vinci (1452–1519), *Mona Lisa,* oil on canvas, 77 × 53 cm. Inv. 779. Photo: R.G. Ojeda. Louvre, Paris. Reunion des Musees Nationaux/Art Resource, NY.

Two Images of Gender

The Semiotics of Architecture

Flags

Laundry

Laundry

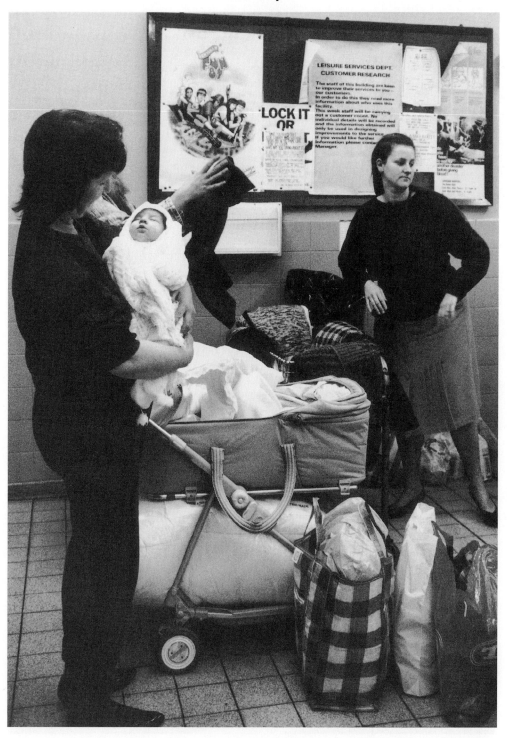

Neighborhoods

Cars

Signs

Signs

Private Symbol/Public Space: The Virgin of Guadalupe

Two Murals by Rigo

Diners

Postcards from Texas

READING WRITING

This Text: Reading

1. The photograph of John Wayne contains a number of signifiers. How many icons or symbols do you see in the photograph?
2. Does the photo of Jackie Chan seem out of place next to John Wayne? Why? If the shot of Chan included all of the icons in the photo of Wayne, would it seem even more odd?
3. What are the similarities between the *Mona Lisa* and Britney Spears?
4. How do a photograph and painting differ in terms of their signifiers? Does one allow more input from the viewer?
5. Greek revival houses in the United States often have unsavory connotations, namely as fraternity houses and plantations. Why do you think this is the case?
6. How do the two "laundry" photographs represent different notions of what laundry does and is?
7. Can you gauge your physical reaction when looking at the American flag versus the Mexican flag? Do the colors symbolize different things for you in each flag?
8. Which flag do you find more aesthetically pleasing?
9. What do you make of the Diane Arbus photographs? Both are about families/friends, yet both are a bit discomfiting. Why?
10. What is your immediate reaction to the neighborhood photos?
11. Are you surprised the two bizarre postcards are from Texas? Why? Why not? What symbols (racist or otherwise) are at work in the El Jardin hotel postcard?
12. Which of the two cars would you like? What would you assume about the owner of each based on the "text" of each car?

Your Text: Writing

1. Write a comparison/contrast essay on the cowboy images. How does race figure into the myth of the American West?
2. Give a semiotic reading of the images of the *Mona Lisa* and Britney Spears. Identify at least three signifiers in each image.
3. Why do you think the White House and many other official buildings are modeled on the Parthenon and Greek architecture in general? What kind of message does such a structure send?
4. Write a descriptive paper on the place where you do your laundry. How is the act of doing or hanging laundry in a public place an intimate act?
5. Compare or contrast the laundry photos. How are they similar? What is missing from each?
6. Write down the first five things that pop into your head when you see the Mexican flag. Do the same for the American flag. Write an essay in which you explore the different values you assign to each.
7. Write a paper in which you unpack the two Diane Arbus photographs. What is going on in them? Are they exploitive?
8. Write a comparison/contrast paper looking at the murals by Rigo and the murals of the Virgin de Guadalupe. All four are public art and versions of public "texts." How are they similar? Different?

9. Do a semiotic reading of the neighborhoods. What assumptions do you make about each neighborhood based on the photographs?
10. Write a paper in which you give a semiotic reading of the two cars. What messages does each send?
11. Give a semiotic reading of the diners. What does each evoke?

The American Signs
on Route 66 Suite

In reading through dozens and dozens of books for the 2nd edition of this book, we came across what both of the authors think is one of the coolest books we have seen in years— *American Signs: Form and Meaning on Route 66,* by Lisa Mahar. One of the authors grew up in a small town in which Route 66 was the town's main street, and he is familiar with many of the signs featured, but even without that personal connection, the book is simply amazing.

Mahar begins with the premise that the roadside sign is not simply a symbol of the open road but a marker of economic, social, and cultural trends. Signs are larger-than-life clues to the values, images, icons, and traditions of the areas in which they exist. Examining motel signs on both a micro and macro level, Mahar traces their influences, shows their arguments, unpacks their conceptual framework, and explains their appeal.

We have reprinted here (with the gracious help of Mahar herself) the opening pages of Chapter 3. What we like about these images is not simply how Mahar notes the influences of popular signs, but the care and detail with which she reads them. The book is also a model of document design—it is itself a text as rich and provocative as the motel signs it features.

PLASTIC: USED AS A UNIFORM LIGHT
SOURCE TO ACCURATELY PORTRAY
ILLUSTRATIONS AND TRADEMARKS

BULBS: USED FOR VARIETY AND
DYNAMIC FLASHING EFFECTS

NEON: USED FOR ILLUMINATING AND
OUTLINING LETTERS AND FOR ANIMATION

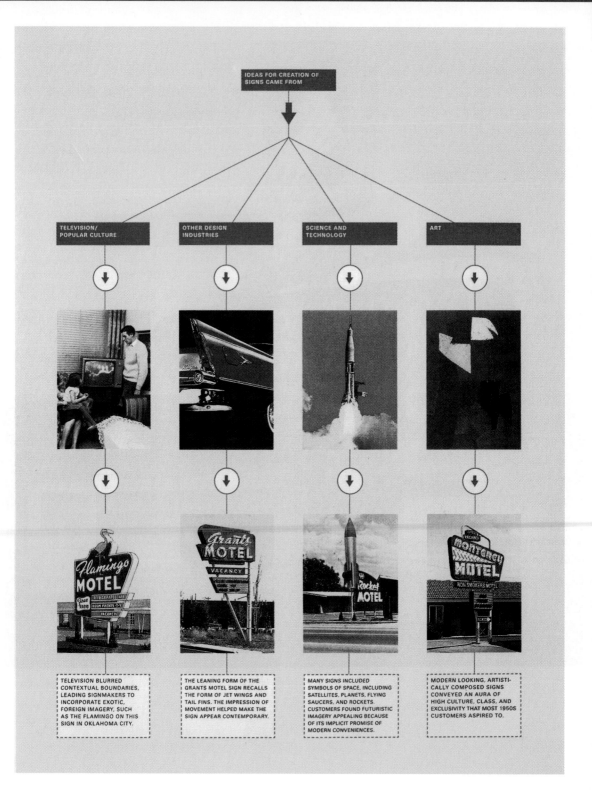

IDEAS FOR CREATION OF SIGNS CAME FROM

TELEVISION/ POPULAR CULTURE

OTHER DESIGN INDUSTRIES

SCIENCE AND TECHNOLOGY

ART

TELEVISION BLURRED CONTEXTUAL BOUNDARIES, LEADING SIGNMAKERS TO INCORPORATE EXOTIC, FOREIGN IMAGERY, SUCH AS THE FLAMINGO ON THIS SIGN IN OKLAHOMA CITY.

THE LEANING FORM OF THE GRANTS MOTEL SIGN RECALLS THE FORM OF JET WINGS AND TAIL FINS. THE IMPRESSION OF MOVEMENT HELPED MAKE THE SIGN APPEAR CONTEMPORARY.

MANY SIGNS INCLUDED SYMBOLS OF SPACE, INCLUDING SATELLITES, PLANETS, FLYING SAUCERS, AND ROCKETS. CUSTOMERS FOUND FUTURISTIC IMAGERY APPEALING BECAUSE OF ITS IMPLICIT PROMISE OF MODERN CONVENIENCES.

MODERN LOOKING, ARTISTI- CALLY COMPOSED SIGNS CONVEYED AN AURA OF HIGH CULTURE, CLASS, AND EXCLUSIVITY THAT MOST 1950S CUSTOMERS ASPIRED TO.

3

3.2 > FORMAL ETYMOLOGY

The Hacienda Holiday Motel sign in Oklahoma City is an example of how far signmakers went to create original compositions for their clients. Fearing that they might lose control over the design process to an emerging class of professional designers, signmakers looked for inspiration in other disciplines, especially art and science.

The use of abstract symbols common in art of the period, such as this detail from Joan Miro's *Woman in Front of the Sun* (1950), made signs appear up-to-date.

Script lettering was used to convey uniqueness and add visual drama to the sign.

Forms and structures were often angled to create more dynamic, and therefore noticeable, compositions, as seen in this late 1950s building.

Bold, stylized arrows were common additions to signs during this period. Artists such as Paul Klee also found them enticing.

Abstracted figurative elements were also found in the design world, as seen in this mid-1950s engraved bowl designed by Ingeborg Lundin.

Irregular shapes were non-traditional and therefore appropriate forms for signmakers looking to create original signs. Artists also made use of them, as in this 1959 mobile, "Big Red," by Alexander Calder.

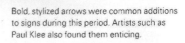

Asymmetrical compositions, as in this plate design by Florence Wainwright, conveyed individuality and uniqueness.

Nowhere was the break from tradition seen more dramatically than in a sign's form. Signmakers chose irregular, asymmetrical shapes over traditional ones, whether or not the business the sign identified was new. By the mid-1950s, many signmakers had begun creating their signs as fragmented compositions, a final abandonment of traditional form.

In the mid-1950s, the Wishing Well Motel in Springfield, Missouri, replaced its traditional sign, which was based on a 1:2 rectangular sign box, with an L-shaped composition of four elements. Though the L shape recalls earlier Main Street signs, the shape of the Wishing Well's sign box is irregular, more dramatic, and includes decorative elements. The words "Wishing Well" and "motel" are treated as separate elements through the use of different colors and type styles.

The asymmetrical form, large wrapping arrow, script type, and advertising panels of the Rest Haven Court's mid-1950s sign are characteristic features of motel signs from the period.

The only elements that remained the same on these two signs from the mid-1940s and the early 1950s were the name (although depersonalized with the removal of "Clark's") and the square, sans serif letters. The newer sign has no formal relationship to its context. The angled structure, palette-shaped sign box, and bright red paint all help to separate it from nearby buildings and natural elements.

The updated Tower Motel sign in Santa Rosa, New Mexico, formally distances itself from the traditional inverted T form of the mid-1940s sign. Each element on the new sign is perceived as a distinct component: the name "Tower" is spatially segregated from "motel," and the letters are treated as individually articulated elements.

The simple, symmetrical sign for the Skyline Motel in Flagstaff, Arizona, was replaced with a larger and bolder asymmetrical arrangement.

Early signs, like the one for the Conway Motel in El Reno, Oklahoma, were often composed of geometrically pure shapes. In this example, the form also reflected the circular motel office. The late-1950s replacement was designed with only contemporary stylistic trends in mind—it was no longer important to maintain a formal connection to the motel's architecture.

Although motel chains did not gain widespread popularity until the late 1950s, Holiday Inn had begun to expand nationwide much earlier. The most visible aspect of the first major chain's growth was the "great sign," as it was referred to. And like the older signs it took its aesthetic cues from, the Holiday Inn sign garnered recognition that attested to the skill with which independent motel owners and signmakers were able to define their businesses' identity. A sign functioned as the motel's logo; it appeared on stationery, ads, and other materials. While independent motel signs influenced the first Holiday Inn sign, as the chain expanded it was the Holiday Inn sign that began to influence the vernacular.

BEFORE 1952

STAR

The star, a traditional symbol used in vernacular signs, denoted quality of service.

WRAPPING ARROW

Early arrows were generally thin and functioned more as a border than as a primary visual element.

LEANING FORM

By the late 1940s, a "slant" form was used to add visual interest and to attract the attention of passing motorists.

COLOR

NAME

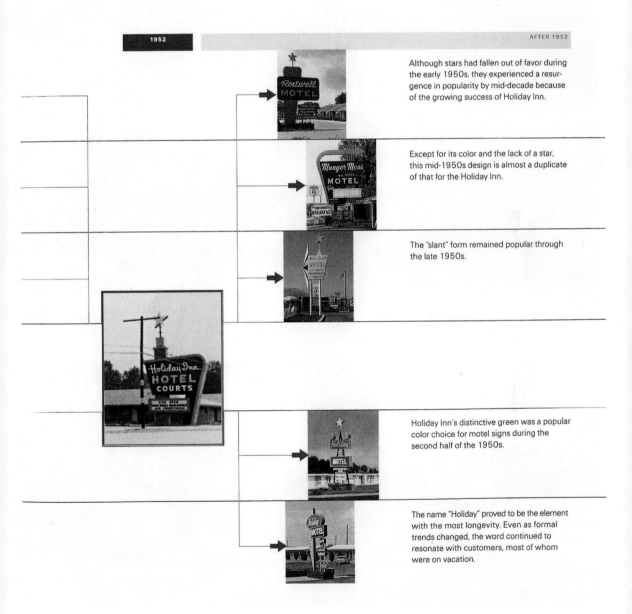

Although stars had fallen out of favor during the early 1950s, they experienced a resurgence in popularity by mid-decade because of the growing success of Holiday Inn.

Except for its color and the lack of a star, this mid-1950s design is almost a duplicate of that for the Holiday Inn.

The "slant" form remained popular through the late 1950s.

Holiday Inn's distinctive green was a popular color choice for motel signs during the second half of the 1950s.

The name "Holiday" proved to be the element with the most longevity. Even as formal trends changed, the word continued to resonate with customers, most of whom were on vacation.

As compositions became more complex, structure became an increasingly important element of the sign. Structure was used either as an abstract framework for organizing the sign's varied elements or as a conceptual and visual connection to a motel's architecture. Only rarely was it used as an overtly thematic component of the sign, as it had been during the late 1940s and early 1950s.

Early attempts to make structure an important aesthetic component were focused on creating a solid, relatively permanent visual barrier that contrasted with the natural context and related to the man-made one. This early-1950s structure for the Pine Tree Lodge in Gallup, New Mexico, was massive and therefore more noticeable. It was built from the same materials as the motel building, thus creating a visual connection between the sign and the architecture.

The sign box for the Tower Motel sign in Oklahoma City conveyed the visual weight of earlier, architectural structures like the Pine Tree Lodge's, but the structure consisted of easy-to-install metal poles. Unlike traditional pole structures, however, their placement was determined as much by aesthetic reasons as by functional ones. The gradual return to pole-based structures also made it possible to build taller signs—those constructed from architectural building materials had to remain relatively small.

Poles made it easy to arrange separate, irregular components such as those on the Flamingo Motel sign in Elk City, Oklahoma. They were readily available and did not require specialized labor, as did architectural materials like brick.

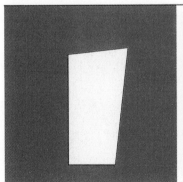 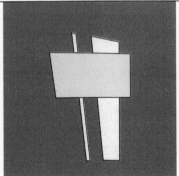 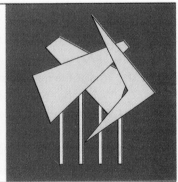

READING WRITING

This Text: Reading

1. What do you make of Mahar's connection between motel signs and rockets, cars, Miro paintings, and fish? Are her arguments solid?
2. Mahar argues that in the 1950s signs entered a kind of revolution, becoming irregular, asymmetrical, and original. What cultural and artistic forces might account for this shift in signs and sign making?
3. Look at the various arguments about art (e.g., Chricton's and Diana Mack's) in Chapter 3: Reading and Writing About Art. Based on their criteria, are these signs art? Why or why not?
4. Why do you think Mahar chose motel signs? Why motel and not restaurant signs?

Your Text: Writing

1. Find some classic motel or restaurant signs in your town. Write a paper in which you read them in the same way as Mahar.
2. Write a paper in which you break down the logo of your college. What kind of symbolism is at work?
3. Many of these signs appear in Oklahoma, New Mexico, and Arizona. Is there something about the Southwest that lends itself to these kinds of irregular images? Write a paper in which you examine the cultural influences on these signs.
4. Write a comparison/contrast paper in which you read the sign of a popular local chain hotel (Wyndham, Hyatt, Marriott, Hampton Inn, La Quinta) against one of the classic signs in the book. What "work" does each sign do? How does it do that work?

WORKSHEET

THIS TEXT

1. What is the semiotic situation of the image? What are its signifiers?
2. What social, political, and cultural forces affect the image?
3. What visual cues appear in the text?
4. What kinds of details, symbols, and codes send messages in the image?
5. What is the composition of the image?
6. Do you think there might be any tension between the image's intention and reception?
7. What kind of story does the image tell? How does it tell that story?
8. Does the image rely on patriotic or sentimental associations to manipulate the viewer?
9. Can you sum up the theme of the image?

BEYOND THIS TEXT

Media: How do news programs, magazines, and newspapers use images to tell stories or convey ideas?

Advertising: Advertising is perhaps the most notorious user of loaded images. How do magazine ads and billboards use images to help sell products? What values do we tend to see in ads? What kind of associations, people, and cultures tend to reappear over and over?

Television: To what degree does television rely on images? Would you sit in front of a TV if there were only words and no picture? How are characters in shows carefully constructed texts? And, what about commercials? How do commercials use images to manipulate viewers?

Movies: Do movies use images differently than television? If so, how?

Icons: The swastika. The peace symbol. The bald eagle. A cactus. A white cowboy hat. The McDonald golden arches. The American flag. The Mexican flag. High heels. All of these are icons. How do icons rely on strong values associated with visual images? How are icons constructed texts?

Public space: How do public and private areas rely on images to get us to feel a certain way? More specifically, what roles do billboards and murals play in public life? What about things like posters or framed art in a dorm room, bedroom, or house?

Music: How does what a band looks like, or what an album looks like, influence the way we look at a band?

READING AND WRITING ABOUT
gender

Various gender signifiers transform RuPaul Andre Charles into "RuPaul!"
Source: © Mitchell Gerber/Corbis/Getty Images Entertainment, Inc.

"**H**OW IN THE WORLD DOES SOMEONE *READ* GENDER? ISN'T GENDER OBVIOUS?" IF YOU ARE LOOKING AT THIS INTRODUCTION FOR THE FIRST TIME, WE SUSPECT THIS IS WHAT A LOT OF YOU ARE THINKING RIGHT NOW. FOR MANY OF YOU, DETAILS OF GENDER ARE CUT AND DRIED, BLACK AND WHITE, MALE AND FEMALE. THIS BOOK DEALS WITH GENDER AS A TEXT, AND, AS YOU WILL SOON SEE, THERE ARE MANY OTHER REASONS WHY ONE MIGHT BE INTERESTED IN READING GENDER IN A SOPHISTICATED WAY.

Without question, gender has become one of the most hotly contested subjects in recent American culture, but this issue is not new. On the contrary, it's been at the forefront of public debate for centuries. Ancient poets like Sappho and Greek plays like Aristophanes' *Lysistrata* explored issues of inequality between the genders long before Gloria Steinem (perhaps the most public feminist of the past four decades). More recently than Sappho or Aristophanes, an amazing Mexican nun named Sor Juana de la Cruz wrote poems and letters extolling the virtues of education for women, citing Biblical passages as examples for equality. And more than 200 years before Susan Faludi's *Backlash* (a controversial book appearing in 1992 that posited a backlash against American women), Mary Wollstonecraft wrote an important and influential essay entitled "A Vindication of the Rights of Women" in which she called for a recognition of women as "rational creatures" capable of the same intellectual and emotional proficiency as men. So while certain aspects of this chapter may feel new to you, in truth, people have been reading (and writing about) gender for centuries.

Still, perhaps it would be beneficial to talk about what we mean by the term "gender." When we use "gender" we refer to socially constructed behaviors and identity tags, such as "feminine" and "masculine." Gender should not be confused with "sex," which speaks only to biological differences between males and females. "Sex," then, refers to biology, whereas "gender" refers to culture and society.

If you've read the chapters on movies or television, then you know that having experience reading a certain text is not the same as reading it well. Similarly, many of you have significant experience reading genders, but you may not be very *probing* readers of gender. This chapter in particular (and college in general) is designed to remedy that. On one hand, reading gender implies a kind of superficial determination of another person's sex. In some cultures, that used to be easier than it is now; in fact, it can be somewhat difficult to tell if a person is a man, a woman, or neither. Those of you with a soft spot for classic rock may remember a similar line from the long-haired Bob Seeger, who, in his song "On the Road Again," adopts the persona of someone making a critical remark about his long hair: "Same old cliché / Is it a woman or a man?" This statement and the simple fact that we assume that we can tell if a person is male or female suggests that there are traits or cues that might tip us off about gender. Using or reading these codes or behaviors is called "doing gender," and we all do gender at some point. "Doing gender" means participating in any behavior associated with a certain gender such as painting your nails, growing a beard, and wearing high heels, earrings, makeup, neckties, and sports jerseys. In each of the previous examples, every one of you associated a certain trait with a certain gender. Did you link painting nails with men or wearing neckties with women? Probably not, but it is likely that most of you have seen a man sport painted nails or a woman wear a necktie. These people are playing with typical expectations of gender, and to some degree, we all do that a little bit. In fact, if, like us, you've lived in New York or San Francisco, where gender diversity is more common and more accepted, then you've likely encountered women sporting facial hair and men donning heels.

If there are external traits in a culture, then it's probable that there are assumed internal gender traits in a culture as well. Although these external indicators may seem minor, ultimately, as you have probably noticed by now, doing gender often translates into men doing dominance and women doing submission. For instance, in America, most people tend to associate nurturing behavior with women and aggressive behavior with men. Similarly, women are "dainty" while men are "rough;" women are "refined," whereas men are "brutish." But is this always the case? As you read this, you are probably thinking of some dainty guys you know and some brutish women. What's more, you should be able to identify specific moments in your own lives and in the lives of your parents, siblings, and close friends when they have, even for an instant, done something that reminded you of another gender. The point is that we carry so many assumptions—many of them dangerous—about genders that we may discover that we have already *interpreted* gender before we have read and thought deeply about gender and genders.

Our goal in this chapter is to encourage you to rethink any preconceptions about and expectations of gender. Why do we expect women to be "emotional"? Why do we expect men to be "responsible"? Why is there societal pressure on women to be thin? Why aren't men expected to wear makeup and shave their legs? Why is there no male equivalent for "slut"? Why aren't women taught to see marriage as the end of a certain kind of independence the same way men are? Why don't boys get dressed up and play groom? Why are all of our presidents men? Why are most kindergarten teachers women? These are puzzling phenomena that raise more questions than answers; however, what we do know is that learning to read gender as a text will help you make sense of the world as roles become less black and white, less right and wrong, less male and female.

Social scientists remind us that gender is socially constructed, and therefore, in a way, we are recruited to gender. Consequently, society tends to punish those who don't conform to its gender roles. The goal of this chapter is to help you read the various means of recruitment; we want you to become savvy readers of the texts that encourage you to *do* gender.

While one's sex may be determined by biology, gender is constructed.

What we mean by "constructed" is that gender is built, invented, created. Of course, while some gender traits might seem to be related to one's biological make-up, gender can still be constructed or "performed." We can think of these traits in both external and internal terms. For instance, our culture assigns certain behaviors or characteristics to maleness. These may include strength, rationality, virility, affluence, and stability. To send out cues that he possesses all these things, a man may bulk up, he may wear designer clothes and drive a sports car, he may watch and play a lot of sports, he may date a lot of women or men. However, what if the values our culture assigned to maleness were grace, daintiness, refinement, monogamy, and nurturing? What if *these* traits were the most male traits? Would men still bulk up, watch football, go hunting, watch *Rambo* movies, and drive pickups? Some might, but most would not. Why? Because they would be ostracized and stigmatized, not seen as "real" men, according to society's expectations of masculine behavior. Men who adhere to socially constructed codes of gender behavior have read the texts of maleness and America well—they know how to fit in.

Just as external elements connote gender, so do internal elements. For instance, what if mainstream heterosexual female behavior were characterized by aggression, dominance, sexual assertiveness, and independence? Would women still wait for men to make the first move? Would women still link their sense of identity with men? Would women think of marriage in the same way? Would women feel differently about their bodies? Would women be afraid to beat their dates in bowling, or fear appearing smarter than their male partners? So, without even knowing it, you are probably performing or doing gender in various aspects of your lives. There is not necessarily anything wrong with this; however, you should be aware that there can be negative implications, and we would encourage you to read your own gender and the genders of others with increased care and sensitivity.

Though we've talked mostly about gender in heterosexual terms, doing gender is not reserved for straight folks. Chances are, you are familiar with terms like "butch," "femme," and "queen." That these terms exist suggests how important gender constructs are to our identities, and they reveal how, even in same-sex relationships, we do gender. What's more, as many gay and lesbians will confirm, gender has nothing to do with biology. Most gays and lesbians would argue that genders are, in fact, fluid. For many, having a penis does not prohibit someone from being or living as a woman, just as having breasts and a vagina does not prohibit many people from living or passing as a man. Here, the distinction between "sex" and "gender" is critical. You may have your own assumptions about how gay men and women do gender, just as you have expectations about how straight men and women do gender.

Our perceptions of gender can be influenced by a number of factors, including stereotypes, tradition, popular culture, and family.

We are all aware of stereotypes surrounding gender: Women are better communicators, men are stronger; men like power tools, women like chick flicks. Without realizing it, you may make gendered assumptions about traits of women all the time. For instance, if you are in a grocery store, and you want to know the ingredients for a cake, who are you most likely to ask: a woman or a man? If someone tells you they have a wonderful new doctor, are you more likely to assume its a man or a woman? If you hear that someone went on a shooting spree in a school, are you most likely to assume that person was male or female? Stereotypes are amazingly powerful, and we may not realize the degree to which our thoughts, beliefs, and actions are shaped by them.

Similarly, cultural and family traditions continue to affect how we see ourselves and other genders. We have a number of female and male friends who complain about how, after every holiday dinner, the men adjourn to the living room to watch sports, while the women clear the tables and do the dishes. At that same dinner, it is likely that the father or grandfather carves the turkey or ham and even says the prayer. One might say that these are roles that both genders silently agree to, yet others might say that these behaviors reflect and inscribe a pattern suggesting that the important duties are reserved for men, while the menial tasks remain women's work. Thus, we grow up not merely ascribing values to genders but linking the importance of specific genders to the importance our society places on the kind of duties we think of as female and male.

Equally persuasive is popular culture. How many of our preconceptions about gender come from billboards, television shows, advertisements, movies, and commercials? Research indicates quite a bit. For instance, psychologists and advertisers suggest that the average viewer believes about one in eight commercials she or he watches. That may not seem like a great deal, but over the course of eighteen or nineteen years, you have seen (and probably internalized) a number of commercials, many of which have, no doubt, influenced your own views of gender. From rock and country music lyrics to commercials for cleaning products to NFL pregame shows to advertisements for jeans and tequila to television sitcoms to the infamous beer commercials, images of men and women doing gender flood us from all sides. Because of this, pop culture can fuse into stereotype, and tradition can meld into popular culture; at times, we may not know which comes from which. So many people conform to the expectations of gender roles, that gender roles appear natural or innate. We urge you to stop and think for a moment before assuming anything about gender.

Oddly, perhaps the most influential source for our gender roles comes from our own families. Before we are even aware of it, we see our mothers *be* women, and we see our fathers enact maleness. In fact, most agree that our early caretakers—whether it is our mothers, grandmothers, nannies, fathers, uncles, or siblings—provide for us the foundations of gender roles. What we see our fathers do, we think is what most men do, and more importantly, what men are supposed to do. As you get older, you will be shocked at how easily you slip into the same gender roles and gendered duties you observed your family engaging in for eighteen years. What's more, over time, these behaviors get coded, recoded, and coded again. Every time you see your father turn on the TV and not help clear the table, it sends messages about what men and women do and don't do. Similarly, every time you do see your father change a diaper or your mom fix a car, it sends other messages about what men and women can do. Most importantly, these behaviors can send subtle but powerful messages about what *you* can do. So, as you think about gender roles in your own life, consider how gender in your family is a complex but powerful text.

Feminism (or feminisms) can and should be supported by both men and women.

Often we ask our students if they believe that women should be paid the same as men. They say yes. We ask them if they think men are inherently smarter than women. They say no—usually an emphatic no. We ask them if they believe that women should be afforded the same opportunities for employment as men. They all say yes. We ask them if they think that there should be equality between men and women. All claim there should. Yet, when we ask how many are feminists, virtually none raise their hands. This reality continues to be perplexing and frustrating. The authors of this book are straight men, and both identify as feminists—so why the resistance among students?

One reason may be the text "feminism." There are any number of definitions of feminism, ranging from very open definitions (if you think men and women should be treated equally, then you are a feminist) to more forceful definitions, such as Barbara Smith's ("Feminism is the political theory and practice that struggles to free *all* women: women of color, working-class women, poor women, Jewish women, disabled women, lesbians, old women—as well as white, economically privileged, heterosexual women"). Some people think that a definition of feminism must be religiously conceived, since much discrimination has ties to religious conservatism (a feminist is a person who supports the theory that God the Mother is equal to God the Father). Though neither of the authors are women, both lean toward a definition of feminism that is broad enough to take in all interested parties. For us, feminism is the understanding that there has been an imbalance between how men and women have been treated, and that balance between genders must be restored. We also tend to believe that feminism implies more than a passing interest in bringing about this change; feminists must, on some level, act in a way that helps facilitate a more equitable balance. These actions might be as small as refraining from using sexist language or as large as protesting in front of the Capitol. Thus, we prefer the term "feminisms" because it acknowledges the fact that feminism is as individual as each individual.

For some reason, many students associate feminism with hating men, refusing to shave legs, being bitchy, being militant, being strident, and, in general, being unlikable. None of these traits has ever been part of the mission of feminism. Rather, feminism as an idea, as an ideology, has always been about equality. In fact, there remains no single feminism but, as we've suggested, inclusive and intriguing "feminisms." Instead of thinking of feminisms as exclusionary, it is more helpful and more accurate to think of feminisms as inclusive. And, like any text, feminism is always open to revision.

There is a double standard in America regarding men and women.

You really don't need a textbook to tell you this—most of you already know it. Many women would acknowledge that they feel a palpable pressure to be thin, virginal, and refined, whereas American culture not only allows but also encourages males to be physically comfortable, sexually adventurous, and crass. Similarly, women who work in the corporate world have argued for decades that female behavior characterized as bitchy, cold, and calculating when enacted by women, is praised and considered commanding, rational, and strategic when carried out by men. On the other hand, both men and women have suggested recently that cultural pressure on men to be in control, in charge, and emotionally cool leaves little room for personal growth and fulfillment.

Even though America has grown immensely in terms of gender equity, there remain dozens of unwritten or even unspoken codes that both men and women feel compelled to adhere to. Thus, how people of different genders act in the world has everything to do with cultural expectations placed on their genders. Moreover, when men and women do gender properly—that is, as society dictates they should—they make gender seem invariable and inevitable, which then seems to justify structural inequalities such as the pay gap, the lack of elected female politicians, or even good roles for women in theater, film, and television.

In short, issues of gender involve more than leaving the toilet seat up; they arise out of personal, public, private, and cultural worlds. We hope that this chapter will make you a more engaged reader of how gender gets enacted in each of these worlds.

THIS TEXT

1. While it will be impossible for you to know this fully, try to figure out the writing situation of each author. Who is the audience? What does the author have at stake? What is his or her agenda? Why is she or he writing this piece?

2. What social, political, and cultural forces affect the author's text? What is going on in the world as he or she is writing?

3. This is a chapter about gender, so, obviously, you should be aware of the gender of the author.

4. How does the author define "gender"? Does she or he confuse "gender" and "sex"?

5. When taken as a whole, what do these texts tell you about how we construct gender?

6. How do stories and essays differ in their arguments about gender?

7. Is the author's argument valid? Is it reasonable?

8. Ideas and beliefs about gender tend to be very sensitive, deeply held convictions. Do you find yourself in agreement with the author? Why or why not? Do you agree with the editors' introduction?

9. Does the author help you read gender better than you did before reading the essay? If so, why? How do we learn to read gender?

10. If you are reading a short story or poem, then where does the text take place? When is it set?

11. What are the main conflicts in the text? What issues are at stake?

12. What kinds of issues of identity is the author working with in the text?

13. Is there tension between the self and society in the text? How? Why?

14. How do gender codes and expectations differ among cultures?

15. Did you like this? Why or why not?

BEYOND THIS TEXT

Media: How are men and women portrayed in television shows, movies, video games, and music videos? Do the media try to set the criteria for what is "male" and what is "female"? How do they do this?

Advertising: How are women and men portrayed in magazine ads? Do advertisers tend to associate certain products or tasks with a specific gender? How do ads influence how we read gender roles?

Television: Is there much variance in how men are portrayed on television? What kinds of shows are geared toward men? What about women? What kinds of activities do we see women engage in on television? Are gender roles related to stereotypes about race, class, and geography?

Movies: Many actors and actresses bemoan the lack of good movie roles for women. Why is this the case? Can you think of many movies in which a younger man falls for an older woman? How often do women rescue men in movies? Why is male nudity so rare and female nudity so coveted?

Public space: How do we know that a place is geared toward men or women? What visual clues do we see?

Marked Women, Unmarked Men

Deborah Tannen

Linguist Deborah Tannen uses a conference as a semiotic setting to read three other women. Based on textual cues (or signs) of the women's hair, clothes, and mannerisms, this 1993 essay gives a reading of each of these "texts," suggesting that women, more than men, are marked by cultural expectations.

SOME YEARS AGO I was at a small working conference of four women and eight men. Instead of concentrating on the discussion I found myself looking at the three other women at the table, thinking how each had a different style and how each style was coherent.

One woman had dark brown hair in a classic style, a cross between Cleopatra and Plain Jane. The severity of her straight hair was softened by wavy bangs and ends that turned under. Because she was beautiful, the effect was more Cleopatra than plain.

The second woman was older, full of dignity and composure. Her hair was cut in a fashionable style that left her with only one eye, thanks to a side part that let a curtain of hair fall across half her face. As she looked down to read her prepared paper, the hair robbed her of bifocal vision and created a barrier between her and the listeners.

The third woman's hair was wild, a frosted blond avalanche falling over and beyond her shoulders. When she spoke she frequently tossed her head, calling attention to her hair and away from her lecture.

Then there was makeup. The first woman wore facial cover that made her skin smooth and pale, a black line under each eye and mascara that darkened already dark lashes. The second wore only a light gloss on her lips and a hint of shadow on her eyes. The third had blue bands under her eyes, dark blue shadow, mascara, bright red lipstick and rouge; her fingernails flashed red.

I considered the clothes each woman had worn during the three days of the conference: In the first case, man-tailored suits in primary colors with solid-color blouses. In the second, casual but stylish black T-shirts, a floppy collarless jacket and baggy slacks or a skirt in neutral colors. The third wore a sexy jump suit; tight sleeveless jersey and tight yellow slacks; a dress with gaping armholes and an indulged tendency to fall off one shoulder.

Shoes? No. 1 wore string sandals with medium heels; No. 2, sensible, comfortable walking shoes; No. 3, pumps with spike heels. You can fill in the jewelry, scarves, shawls, sweaters—or lack of them.

As I amused myself finding coherence in these styles, I suddenly wondered why I was scrutinizing only the women. I scanned the eight men at the table. And then I knew why I wasn't studying them. The men's styles were unmarked.

The term "marked" is a staple of linguistic theory. It refers to the way language alters the base meaning of a word by adding a linguistic particle that has no meaning on its own. The unmarked form of a word carries the meaning that goes without saying—what you think of when you're not thinking anything special.

The unmarked tense of verbs in English is the present—for example, visit. To indicate past, you mark the verb by adding ed to yield visited. For future, you add a word: will visit. Nouns are presumed to be singular until marked for plural, typically by adding s or es, so visit becomes visits and dish becomes dishes.

The unmarked forms of most English words also convey "male." Being male is the unmarked case. Endings like ess and ette mark words as "female." Unfortunately, they also tend to mark them for frivolousness. Would you feel safe entrusting your life to a doctorette? Alfre Woodard, who was an Oscar nominee for best supporting actress, says she identifies herself as an actor because "actresses worry about eyelashes and cellulite, and women who are actors worry about the characters we are playing." Gender markers pick up extra meanings that reflect common associations with the female gender: not quite serious, often sexual.

Each of the women at the conference had to make decisions about hair, clothing, makeup and accessories, and each decision carried meaning. Every style available to us was marked. The men in our group had made decisions, too, but the range from which they chose was incomparably narrower. Men can choose styles that are marked, but they don't have to, and in this group none did. Unlike the women, they had the option of being unmarked.

Take the men's hair styles. There was no marine crew cut or oily longish hair falling into eyes, no asymmetrical, two-tiered construction to swirl over a bald top. One man was unabashedly bald; the others had hair of standard length, parted on one side, in natural shades of brown or gray or graying. Their hair obstructed no views, left little to toss or push back or run fingers through and, consequently, needed and attracted no attention. A few men had beards. In a business setting, beards might be marked. In this academic gathering, they weren't.

There could have been a cowboy shirt with string tie or a three-piece suit or a necklaced hippie in jeans. But there wasn't. All eight men wore brown or blue slacks and nondescript shirts of light colors. No man wore sandals or boots; their shoes were dark, closed, comfortable and flat. In short, unmarked.

Although no man wore makeup, you couldn't say the men didn't wear makeup in the sense that you could say a woman didn't wear makeup. For men, no makeup is unmarked.

I asked myself what style we women could have adopted that would have been unmarked, like the men's. The answer was none. There is no unmarked woman.

There is no woman's hair style that can be called standard, that says nothing about her. The range of women's hair styles is staggering, but a woman whose hair has no particular style is perceived as not caring about how she looks, which can disqualify her for many positions, and will subtly diminish her as a person in the eyes of some.

Women must choose between attractive shoes and comfortable shoes. When our group made an unexpected trek, the woman who wore flat, laced shoes arrived first. Last to arrive was the woman in spike heels, shoes in hand and a handful of men around her.

If a woman's clothing is tight or revealing (in other words, sexy), it sends a message—an intended one of wanting to be attractive, but also a possibly unintended one of availability. If her clothes are not sexy, that too sends a message, lent meaning by the knowledge that they could have been. There are thousands of cosmetic products from which women can choose and myriad ways of applying them. Yet no makeup at all is anything but unmarked. Some men see it as a hostile refusal to please them.

Women can't even fill out a form without telling stories about themselves. Most forms give four titles to choose from. "Mr." carries no meaning other than that the respondent is male. But a woman who checks "Mrs." or "Miss" communicates not only whether she has been married but also whether she has conservative tastes in forms of address—and probably other conservative values as well. Checking "Ms." declines to let on about marriage (checking "Mr." declines nothing since nothing was asked), but it also marks her as either liberated or rebellious, depending on the observer's attitudes and assumptions.

I sometimes try to duck these variously marked choices by giving my title as "Dr."—and in so doing risk marking myself as either uppity (hence sarcastic responses like "Excuse me!") or an overachiever (hence reactions of congratulatory surprise like "Good for you!").

All married women's surnames are marked. If a woman takes her husband's name, she announces to the world that she is married and has traditional values. To some it will indicate that she is less herself, more identified by her husband's identity. If she does not take her husband's name, this too is marked, seen as worthy of comment: she has done something; she has "kept her own name." A man is never said to have "kept his own name" because it never occurs to anyone that he might have given it up. For him using his own name is unmarked.

A married woman who wants to have her cake and eat it too may use her surname plus his, with or without a hyphen. But this too announces her marital status and often results in a tongue-tying string. In a list (Harvey O'Donovan, Jonathan Feldman, Stephanie Woodbury McGillicutty), the woman's multiple name stands out. It is marked.

I have never been inclined toward biological explanations of gender differences in language, but I was intrigued to see Ralph Fasold bring biological phenomena to bear on the question of linguistic marking in his book *The Sociolinguistics of Language.* Fasold stresses that language and culture are particularly unfair in treating women as the marked case because biologically it is the male that is marked. While two X chromosomes make a female, two Y chromosomes make nothing. Like the linguistic markers s, es or ess, the Y chromosome doesn't "mean" anything unless it is attached to a root form—an X chromosome.

Developing this idea elsewhere, Fasold points out that girls are born with fully female bodies, while boys are born with modified female bodies. He invites men who doubt this to lift up their shirts and contemplate why they have nipples.

In his book, Fasold notes "a wide range of facts which demonstrates that female is the unmarked sex." For example, he observes that there are a few species that produce only females, like the whiptail lizard. Thanks to parthenogenesis, they have no trouble having as many daughters as they like. There are no species, however, that produce only males. This is no surprise, since any such species would become extinct in its first generation.

Fasold is also intrigued by species that produce individuals not involved in reproduction, like honeybees and leaf-cutter ants. Reproduction is handled by the queen and a relatively few males; the workers are sterile females. "Since they do not reproduce," Fasold says, "there is no reason for them to be one sex or the other, so they default, so to speak, to female."

Fasold ends his discussion of these matters by pointing out that if language reflected biology, grammar books would direct us to use "she" to include males and females and "he" only for specifically male referents. But they don't. They tell us that "he" means "he or she," and that "she" is used only if the referent is specifically female. This use of "he" as the sex-indefinite pronoun is an innovation introduced into English by grammarians in the 18th and 19th centuries, according to Peter Muhlhausler and Rom Harre in "Pronouns and People." From at least about 1500, the correct sex-indefinite pronoun was "they," as it still is in casual spoken English. In other words, the female was declared by grammarians to be the marked case.

Writing this article may mark me not as a writer, not as a linguist, not as an analyst of human behavior, but as a feminist—which will have positive or negative, but in any case powerful, connotations for readers. Yet I doubt that anyone reading Ralph Fasold's book would put that label on him.

I discovered the markedness inherent in the very topic of gender after writing a book on differences in conversational style based on geographical region, ethnicity, class, age and gender. When I was interviewed, the vast majority of journalists wanted to talk about the differences between women and men. While I thought I was simply describing what I observed—something I had learned to do as a researcher—merely mentioning women and men marked me as a feminist for some.

When I wrote a book devoted to gender differences in ways of speaking, I sent the manuscript to five male colleagues, asking them to alert me to any interpretation, phrasing or wording that might seem unfairly negative toward men. Even so, when the book came out, I encountered responses like that of the television talk show host who, after interviewing me, turned to the audience and asked if they thought I was male-bashing.

Leaping upon a poor fellow who affably nodded in agreement, she made him stand and asked, "Did what she said accurately describe you?" "Oh, yes," he answered. "That's me exactly." "And what she said about women—does that sound like your wife?" "Oh yes," he responded. "That's her exactly." "Then why do you think she's male-bashing?" He answered, with disarming honesty, "Because she's a woman and she's saying things about men."

To say anything about women and men without marking oneself as either feminist or anti-feminist, male-basher or apologist for men seems as impossible for a woman as trying to get dressed in the morning without inviting interpretations of her character. Sitting at the conference table musing on these matters, I felt sad to think that we women didn't have the freedom to be unmarked that the men sitting next to us had. Some days you just want to get dressed and go about your business. But if you're a woman, you can't, because there is no unmarked woman.

READING WRITING

This Text: Reading

1. What do you make of Tannen's claim that women are "marked"? Is that an appropriate word?
2. Would you agree with her that men are not marked?
3. What is Tannen's evidence for her claims? Is it solid evidence? Do Tannen's arguments follow a logical progression?

Your Text: Writing

1. Go to a coffee shop or a restaurant and read a group of women sitting together. Are they marked? How? Then write an essay, similar to Tannen's, on your reading of the women. How do contemporary cultural expectations of women influence how you read other women?
2. Write an essay on how men are marked.
3. Are there other female markings that Tannen does not mention? Write an essay in which you give a reading of other kinds of female markings.
4. Read Maxine Hong Kingston's "No Name Woman," and write an essay in which you demonstrate how the aunt was marked.

Out of Style Thinking: Female Politicians and Fashion

Annette Fuentes

Hillary Clinton was one of the leading Democratic candidates for president for the 2008 presidential elections—the first time a woman has been in this position. Annette Fuentes, a journalist who covers health and policy issues for a number of American publications, is a contributing editor at *In These Times* magazine. In her short 2007 piece for *USA Today,* Fuentes argues that many

Americans—even journalists—look at female politicians through a lens of gender or a lens of fashion rather than seeing them first and foremost as politicians. Note Fuentes' thesis, and note how she backs up her thesis with specific examples and quotes.

IF SOME THINGS HAVE CHANGED, the news media's take on female politicians has a tendency to recycle the same old clichés about them. Coverage of first female House Speaker Nancy Pelosi's fashion sensibility in the media is Exhibit A.

First there was a *Washington Post* article published shortly after the elections on the presumptive new House speaker, "Muted Tones of Quiet Authority: A Look Suited to the Speaker." It offered the information that "Pelosi's suit was by Giorgio Armani—the Italian master of neutral tones and modern power dressing—and she wore it well." The article at least appeared in the newspaper's Style section, but was chock-full of psychoanalytic forays into Pelosi's wardrobe choices, asserting that "an Armani suit, for a woman, is a tool for playing with the boys without pretending to be one." I would wager that Pelosi is one woman who doesn't play around with anyone.

A "Fashion Leader"

Then there was a *New York Times* article in January in its Thursday Styles section titled "Speaking Chic to Power." While noting that Pelosi, barely in her new job a month, had brought the House to votes on a minimum wage increase, stem cell research, and Medicare drug prices, the article said "she did it looking preternaturally fresh, with a wardrobe that, while still subdued and overreliant on suits, has seldom spruced the halls of Congress."

Similar articles appeared in the *Baltimore Sun* and *Chicago Tribune*. Mentioned were other women politicians and their fashion choices, such as Sen. Hillary Clinton's hair style and preference for black pantsuits or Florida Rep. Debbie Wasserman Schultz's haircut. The question is whether focusing on the clothing choices of serious female political players risks rendering them less than serious. Another question is whether such reports warrant precious space. After all, with rare exceptions, male politicians are seldom scrutinized for their choice of suits.

Some reporters and editors haven't figured out a way to cover female politicians that doesn't rely on the old stereotypes, says Gail Dines, sociology and women's studies professor at Wheelock College in Boston. "To be a woman politician, you have to strategize and work hard, and yet what matters is what designer you're wearing. It's a way to make women in power less scary." Dines notes, "it's putting women into a comfort zone for those who are still baffled by how to treat strong women."

Trivializing Women

The articles seem a throwback to a time when women were only spouses, not players, says Ruth Mandel, director of the Eagleton Institute of politics at Rutgers University. "To focus on their attire, the cut of their clothes . . . is to be in danger of trivializing who they are, the important role they play and the meaning behind women's advancement to positions of power: That is, we're moving to a true democracy of shared leadership."

The problem is the media haven't quite caught up. "A woman who rises to a leadership position at any level is going to dress appropriately," says Kathleen Hall Jamieson, professor at the Annenberg School of Communications at the University of Pennsylvania. "It underscores her competence and is not a distraction. You take for granted that it would not be worthy of comment any more."

Jamieson thinks the underlying motivation for reporting on female politicians' style is "the natural news interest in talking about what changes, and men don't look different. There is a uniform for men in power and we all know what it looks like. The only thing to change is the color of the shirt or tie."

Because women have greater fashion options, changes they make are more obvious and invite analysis. Now that Pelosi's "uniform" has been established, that should be the end of it. Ditto for Clinton. "Clinton now has a range of what she wears," Jamieson says. "She hasn't been changing hairstyles or her pantsuits. That is our definition of what she wears, and that should end it."

Tom Rosenstiel, director of the Project for Excellence in Journalism, thinks reporting that describes women politicians' appearance is justified in profiles of them. "Beyond that, there comes a point where it reflects badly on the press," he says. "The only way the appearance of a politician is really politically relevant is if they are so dazzlingly charismatic or strange looking that people can't look at them. Whether it's Condoleezza Rice, Madeleine Albright or Nancy Pelosi, they all fall into the same zone as their male counterparts. They all look like regular people, none is a runway model or the elephant man."

Female politicians will certainly survive such silly coverage, and, some argue the stories are harmless. But these women are role models for young women and offer an alternative to the fashion model and celebrity in setting the standard for female beauty and worth.

Dines worries that when the media emphasize the appearance of women, it perpetuates attitudes in the larger world that devalue and limit women. "These are fortunate, privileged women," Dines notes of politicians, "but for young women trying to make it in the world, how they look can affect their opportunities."

READING WRITING

This Text: Reading
1. What is Fuentes' thesis here? Can you locate it?
2. Do you agree that the articles she cites "trivialize" women? Why or why not?
3. What do you make of the argument that there is a "uniform" for men in power?

Your Text: Writing
1. Write a comparison/contrast essay in which you look at the pieces by Fuentes and the previous essay by Tannen. How do they make similar arguments?
2. Most of us watched Hillary Clinton run for president. Be honest with youself—did you expect specific "female" behavior from her? If so, what was it? Write an essay on Hillary Clinton's run for president. How did you, men, the media *read* her?

Being a Man

Paul Theroux

In this 1985 essay, Theroux offers a reading of masculinity from the perspective of someone who "always disliked being a man." Theroux is troubled by the expectations of masculine behavior and finds writing at variance with many of them.

THERE IS A PATHETIC SENTENCE in the chapter "Fetishism" in Dr. Norman Cameron's book *Personality Development and Psychopathology.* It goes, "Fetishists are nearly always men; and their commonest fetish is a woman's shoe." I cannot read that sentence without thinking that it is just one more awful thing about being a man—and perhaps it is an important thing to know about us.

I have always disliked being a man. The whole idea of manhood in America is pitiful, in my opinion. This version of masculinity is a little like having to wear an ill-fitting coat for one's entire life (by contrast, I imagine femininity to be an oppressive sense of nakedness). Even the expression "Be a man!" strikes me as insulting and abusive. It means: Be stupid, be unfeeling, obedient, soldierly, and stop thinking. Man means "manly"—how can one think about men without considering the terrible ambition of manliness? And yet it is part of every man's life. It is a hideous and crippling lie; it not only insists on difference and connives at superiority, it is also by its very nature destructive—emotionally damaging and socially harmful.

The youth who is subverted, as most are, into believing in the masculine ideal is effectively separated from women and he spends the rest of his life finding women a riddle and a nuisance. Of course, there is a female version of this male affliction. It begins with mothers encouraging little girls to say (to other adults) "Do you like my new dress?" In a sense, little girls are traditionally urged to please adults with a kind of coquettishness, while boys are enjoined to behave like monkeys towards each other. The nine-year-old coquette proceeds to become womanish in a subtle power game in which she learns to be sexually indispensable, socially decorative, and always alert to a man's sense of inadequacy.

Femininity—being ladylike—implies needing a man as witness and seducer; but masculinity celebrates the exclusive company of men. That is why it is so grotesque; and that is also why there is no manliness without inadequacy—because it denies men the natural friendship of women.

It is very hard to imagine any concept of manliness that does not belittle women, and it begins very early. At an age when I wanted to meet girls—let's say the treacherous years of thirteen to sixteen—I was told to take up a sport, get more fresh air, join the Boy Scouts, and I was urged not to read so much. It was the 1950s and if you asked too many questions about sex you were sent to camp—boy's camp, of course: the nightmare. Nothing is more unnatural or prisonlike than a boy's camp, but if it were not for them we would have no Elks' Lodges, no pool rooms, no boxing matches, no Marines.

And perhaps no sports as we know them. Everyone is aware of how few in number are the athletes who behave like gentlemen. Just as high school basketball teaches you how to be a poor loser, the manly attitude towards sports seems to be little more than a recipe for creating bad marriages, social misfits, moral degenerates, sadists, latent rapists, and just plain louts. I regard high school sports as a drug far worse than marijuana, and it is the reason that the average tennis champion, say, is a pathetic oaf.

Any objective study would find the quest for manliness essentially right-wing, puritanical, cowardly, neurotic, and fueled largely by a fear of women. It is also certainly philistine. There is no book-hater like a Little League coach. But indeed all the creative arts are obnoxious to the manly ideal, because at their best the arts are pursued by uncompetitive and essentially solitary people. It makes it very hard for a creative youngster, for any boy who expresses the desire to be alone seems to be saying that there is something wrong with him.

It ought to be clear by now that I have something of an objection to the way we turn boys into men. It does not surprise me that when the President of the United States has his customary weekend off he dresses like a cowboy—it is both a measure of his insecurity and his willingness to please. In many ways, American culture does little more for a man than prepare him for modeling clothes in the L.L. Bean catalogue. I take this as a personal insult because for many years I found it impossible to admit to myself that I wanted to be a writer. It was my guilty secret, because being a writer was incompatible with being a man.

There are people who might deny this, but that is because the American writer, typically, has been so at pains to prove his manliness that we have come to see literariness and manliness as mingled qualities. But first there was a fear that writing was not a manly profession—indeed, not a profession at all. (The paradox in American letters is that it has always been easier for a woman to write and for a man to be published.) Growing up, I had thought of sports as wasteful and humiliating and the idea of manliness was a bore. My wanting to become a writer was not a flight from that oppressive role-playing but I quickly saw that it was at odds with it. Everything in stereotyped manliness goes against the life of the mind. The Hemingway personality is too tedious to go into here, and in any case his exertions are well known, but certainly it was not until this aberrant behavior was examined by feminists in the 1960s that any male writer dared question the pugnacity in Hemingway's fiction. All the bullfighting and arm wrestling and elephant shooting diminished Hemingway as a writer, but it is consistent with a prevailing attitude in American writing one cannot be a male writer without first proving that one is a man.

It is normal in America for a man to be dismissive or even somewhat apologetic about being a writer. Various factors make it easier. There is a heartiness about journalism that makes it acceptable—journalism is the manliest form of American writing and, therefore, the profession the most independent-minded women seek (yes, it is an illusion, but that is my point). Fiction-writing is equated with a kind of dispirited failure and is only manly when it produces wealth—money is masculinity. So is drinking. Being a drunkard is another assertion, if misplaced, of manliness. The American male writer is traditionally proud of his heavy drinking. But we are also a very literal-minded people. A man proves his manhood in America in old-fashioned ways. He kills lions, like Hemingway; or he hunts ducks, like Nathanael West, or he makes pronouncements like, "A man should carry enough knife to defend himself with," as James Jones once said to a *Life* interviewer. Or he says he can drink you under the table. But even tiny drunken William Faulkner loved to mount a horse and go fox hunting, and Jack Kerouac roistered up and down Manhattan in a lumberjack shirt (and spent every night of *The Subterraneans* with his mother in Queens). And we are familiar with the lengths to which Norman Mailer is prepared, in his endearing way, to prove that he is just as much a monster as the next man.

When the novelist John Irving was revealed as a wrestler, people took him to be a very serious writer, and even a bubble reputation like Eric (*Love Story*) Segal's was enhanced by the news that he ran the marathon in a respectable time. How surprised we would be if Joyce Carol Oates were revealed as a sumo wrestler or Joan Didion active in pumping iron. "Lives in New York City with her three children" is the typical woman writer's biographical note, for just as the male writer must prove he has achieved a sort of muscular manhood, the woman writer—or rather her publicists—must prove her motherhood.

There would be no point in saying any of this if it were not generally accepted that to be a man is somehow—even now in feminist-influenced America—a privilege. It is on the contrary an unmerciful and punishing burden. Being a man is bad enough; being manly is appalling (in this sense, women's lib has done much more for men than for women). It is the sinister silliness of men's fashions and a clubby attitude in the arts. It is the subversion of good students. It is the so-called Dress Code of the Ritz-Carlton Hotel in Boston, and it is the institutionalized cheating in college sports. It is the most primitive insecurity.

And this is also why men often object to feminism, but are afraid to explain why: of course women have a justified grievance, but most men believe—and with reason—that their lives are just as bad.

This Text: Reading

1. Why does Theroux not like being a man? Are his reasons valid? Is his argument and progression well reasoned?
2. Can you think of "any concept of manliness that does not belittle women"? What do you make of the way Theroux claims we turn boys into men? Do you agree with him? Do you share his distaste?
3. Do Theroux's claims about manliness and writing still hold true? Why? Why not? His piece seems a bit dated—how can you tell it was written in a previous era?

Your Text: Writing

1. Write an essay entitled "On Being a Woman." How will yours differ from Theroux's?
2. Write an essay about being the opposite gender. What would be good about being the other gender? What would not be so good?
3. This is the only text in this section written by a man. Write an essay on the fact that there is only one piece by a man in a chapter about gender. Should it be evenly balanced? Is the rest of *The World Is a Text* balanced in terms of gender? Should there be a female co-author?

You Would Have Me White

Alfonsina Storni

One of South America's most important poets, Alfonsina Storni spent most of her life in Argentina until her death in 1938. "Tú me quieres blanca" was published in 1918 and remains her most famous poem and a significant text for North and South American women. Edgy and poetic, angry and beautiful, her poem is a strong statement on the universal stereotyping of women. As a side note, you should know that in Spanish, "white" is *blanca*. However, *blanca* also means "empty" and "blank."

Tú me quieres alba,	You want me white,
me quieres de espumas,	you want me foam,
me quieres de nácar.	you want me pearl.
Que sea azucena	That I would be white lily,
sobre todas, casta.	above all the others, chaste.
De perfume tenue.	Of tenuous perfume.
Corola cerrada.	Closed corolla.
Ni un rayo de luna	That not even a ray of filtered
filtrado me haya.	moonlight have me.
Ni una margarita	Nor a daisy
se diga mi hermana.	call itself my sister.
Tú me quieres nívea,	You want me snowy,
tú me quieres blanca,	you want me white,
tú me quieres alba.	you want me dawn.

Tú que hubiste todas	You who had all
las copas a mano,	the cups in hand,
de frutos y mieles	Your lips purple
los labios morados.	with fruits and honey.
Tú que en el banquete	You who at the banquet
cubierto de pámpanos	covered with ferns
dejaste las carnes	relinquished your flesh
festejando a Baco.	celebrating Bacchus.
Tú que en los jardines	You who in black
negros del engaño	gardens of deceit
vestido de rojo	dressed in red
corriste al estrago.	ran yourself to ruin.
Tú que el esqueleto	You whose skeleton
conservas intacto	is still intact
no sé todavía	by what miracles
por cuáles milagros,	I'll never know,
me pretendes blanca	you want me to be white
(Dios te lo perdone),	(God forgive you),
me pretendes casta	you want me to be chaste
(Dios te lo perdone),	(God forgive you),
¡me pretendes alba!	you want me to be dawn!
Huye hacia los bosques;	Go to the woods;
vete a la montaña;	go to the mountains;
límpiate la boca;	wash out your mouth;
vive en las cabañas;	live in a hut;
toca con las manos	touch the damp earth
la tierra mojada;	with your hands;
alimenta el cuerpo	nourish your body
con raíz amarga;	with bitter roots;
bebe de las rocas;	drink from stones;
duerme sobre escarcha;	sleep on frost;
renueva tejidos	restore your body
con salitre y agua;	with saltpeter and water;
Habla con los pájaros	Speak with birds
y lévate al alba.	and get up at dawn.
Y cuando las carnes	And when your flesh
te sean tornadas,	is restored to you,
y cuando hayas puesto	and when you've put
en ellas el alma	back into the flesh
que por las alcobas	which was entrapped
se quedó enredada,	in bedrooms,
entonces, buen hombre,	then, good man,
preténdeme blanca,	pretend I'm white,
preténdeme nívea,	pretend I'm snowy,
preténdeme casta.	pretend I'm chaste.

This Text: Reading

1. How do the connotations of *blanca* in Spanish alter your reading of the poem?
2. Why does Storni want her man to "go to the mountains," "wash out his mouth," and "live in a hut"? Why must he restore his flesh? Why will returning to nature accomplish this?
3. How is Storni using the various symbolisms surrounding "white"?
4. Why does Storni think the man in question needs God's forgiveness?

Your Text: Writing

1. Who is Storni addressing here? Write an essay in which you explore issues of male and female gender in the poem.
2. Give a feminist reading of the poem. What kind of statement is Storni making about how men see women?
3. Write an essay in which you explore the various connotations of whiteness in Storni's poem and *Snow White*.

Playing Doctor: The Pro-Life Movement's New Plan for Family Planning

Siobhan O'Connor

We like this essay not simply because it tackles a difficult issue facing young women, but also because it offers a semiotic reading of family planning pamphlets. In this 2007 piece, Siobhan O'Connor, a features editor for *Good* (a new magazine focused on the various "good" things to be aware of), unpacks the rhetorical strategies of Crisis Pregnancy Centers and their public relations literature.

IT'S 7:47 ON A SATURDAY MORNING in the Bronx, and a 32-foot-long RV, plush considering the surroundings, is taking up almost three full parking spots near the corner of Southern Boulevard on East 149th Street. Inside, the floors are carpeted, there's a comfortable couch, a microwave, a dishwasher, a mini-stove. There's a box of half-eaten Entenmann's danish on the counter, and a flat screen computer monitor on the table. It would almost look like a tour bus, were it not for the ultrasound machine in the back.

A few yards up the street is an abortion clinic— though you'd likely miss it if you didn't know to look. There is a man in a security vest by the clinic's front door; next to him stands a woman who later identifies herself as Mary, with a half-dozen plastic rosaries dangling from her wrist and a fistful of pink pamphlets. With wild eyes, she watches oncoming foot traffic, approaching every young woman and couple she sees, bar none.

A tough-looking girl with a bold gait—hair wrapped in a do-rag and legs poured into low-cut jeans—veers when Mary jumps into step with her. Nearby, a small group has convened in what appears to be a prayer for the unborn. Mary hands the young woman a few of her brochures; without stopping, the young woman sashays right past her—not inside the clinic, but down the block. It's impossible not to wonder if she rounded the corner and went in through the facility's back door. One can only guess.

Consider this a very literal iteration of a battle that's going on in state legislatures across the country; in Congress and the Supreme Court; in medical clinics and the nearby pro-life centers that look just like them. This roving RV, one of roughly 3,400 pro-life counseling outposts nationwide known as crisis pregnancy centers, is evidence of a tactical shift in the anti-abortion movement—the idea being: Take the "choose life" message, dress it up to look medical (ideally with an ultrasound machine), and, in this case, take it on the road. Many of the centers offer free pregnancy tests, baby clothes and diapers, adoption referral, and parenting classes. What they don't offer is pregnancy prevention other than abstinence, abortion referral, or—in most cases—access to medical professionals. Since half the pregnancies in the country are unintended, critics say it's dangerous to be funding centers that don't offer complete family-planning options in addition to counseling.

As it stands, CPCs have a PR problem. They have a well-documented reputation of persuading young women to continue pregnancies they say they don't want, showing them gruesome videos about abortion, and providing medical misinformation. One center even went so far as to pretend to offer a woman an abortion only to then delay the procedure until it was no longer a legal option.

In response, less radical CPCs have been working hard to change that tainted reputation— one pro-life umbrella group has even gotten behind proposed legislation to regulate CPCs in Oregon. " They have really changed their tactics and techniques," says Sarah Wheat of Planned Parenthood Austin. "I think they are being a little more strategic about how they present themselves in an effort to increase their funding." Of course, the more organized and well-funded CPCs become, the more eyes are on them—and for CPCs that isn't always good news. A recent report by Representative Henry Waxman, Democrat of California, shook the abortion debate, confirming what reproductive-rights advocates have been saying for decades: that 87 percent of the centers investigated provided false and misleading medical information about abortion and contraception. This runs the gamut from claims that birth control leads to breast cancer to citing "evidence" that abortion causes women to later commit suicide.

The Waxman report also tallied up the amount of federal funding these centers have received under the Bush administration. Since 2001, CPCs have received more than $30 million in federal dollars, and many states have also been generous (Texas has earmarked $5 million for counseling that steers women to abortion alternatives). In the last few years, these centers' funding strategies have changed dramatically. In the past, they relied heavily on private, often tax-deductible donations, as well as creative indirect money-gathering strategies, such as federal abstinence-only education contracts and state "Choose Life" license plates—for an extra $20 to $50, people can customize their plates with a pro-life message; the extra cash goes straight to CPCs. "There's a new trend with governors and state legislatures being much more bold in their willingness to secure direct funding for CPCs," Planned Parenthood's director of government relations, Jackie Payne, confirms.

Currently, in the United States, there are two CPCs for every abortion clinic, a ratio that will only grow more lopsided as abortion becomes more regulated, bans are upheld, and national and state family-planning dollars are redirected to CPCs. "Only 13 percent of counties in the U.S. have abortion providers," says Payne. "Soon everyone will have to look at ultrasounds of a fetus they don't want because they won't be able to find a family-planning clinic."

New York State has the dubious distinction of being the abortion capital of America— it performs 10 percent of the country's abortions, making it a focal point for some pro-lifers. "This is the front line for abortion in America," says Chris Slattery, from the passenger seat of the RV in the Bronx. Slattery runs the RV and 15 other pregnancy centers in the city, many of which are strategically positioned across the street from (or in the same buildings as) Planned Parenthood centers. After about an hour and a half of sidewalk counseling, Slattery's coworkers, joined by Mary from the Helpers of God's Precious Infants, have stopped dozens of passersby, handing out as many leaflets. A knock on the van's door animates the sonographer, who has shimmied into a nurse-blue vest, ready to get to work. The visitor is a 20-year-old, light-skinned black woman, dressed Saturday casual in a gray sweat suit and Nikes, hair yanked into a high ponytail. She is a mother of two—she had her first child at 18, her second at 19, both unplanned— and she came here unsure, she says. The counselor asks her if she believes in God (she does); if she has heard about the "medical risks associated with abortion" (she has); and if she wants to watch a video about fetal development (sure). Finally, it's sonogram time. The sonographer slides the accordion door shut, and the young women can be heard giggling, as echoes and white noise fill the bus. "That's the baby's heartbeat," Slattery tells me matter-of-factly. We later find out that the pregnancy was six weeks along. After the woman leaves, it's smiles all round. "Another save!" he says.

Herein lies the crux of the controversy surrounding CPCs: their increasing use of the sonogram as a persuasive tool and their dispersal of health information refuted by every major medical association in the country, as well as the government. This is the heart of the debate—both sides fundamentally disagreeing on the science behind the information they provide. Do pro-lifers actually believe the National Cancer Institute is so entangled with the pro-choice movement that it is obscuring a causal relationship between abortion and breast cancer, or is this assertion merely an effective tool for coercion they don't want to give up? Depends on whom you ask.

"What concerns me is that if a woman goes to a CPC and has an ultrasound," says Jessica Farrar of the Texas State House of Representatives, "she thinks she's receiving medical care. But there might be a birth defect or some other issue related to her health that would fail to be diagnosed because there are not the right medical staff there. CPCs are often the first line of observation, but a woman could walk out that door thinking everything is fine with her, when it's not." Some reproductive-rights advocates are asking that CPCs be required by law to post a sign that says "This is not a medical facility" in the entranceway.

Meanwhile, 550 pregnancy centers are already equipped with ultrasound, with another 100 in the works this year, says Beth Chase, the executive director of the medical advancement division of the pro-life umbrella group National Institute of Family and Life Advocates. According to an article by NIFLA's president, Thomas Glessner, CPCs are reporting fewer and fewer clients seeking abortions, so a "major challenge . . . will be to find new methods to attract abortion-minded women." The strategy? A nationwide effort to convert CPCs into what they call full-blown medical facilities. "Full-blown," of course, is a relative term.

Chase is a thoughtful, soft-spoken woman—the kind of person who uses your first name when she talks to you, whom you can hear smiling as she describes the positive impact CPCs have had on her clients. The new centers she calls "pregnancy help medical clinics" are equipped with ultrasound machines and many are offering free early prenatal care, Sexually Transmitted Infection testing, and standard medical services associated with that appointment. What they don't offer is abortion referral, contraception or, in most cases, visits with a licensed OB-GYN. "Under the supervision of a licensed physician, an ultrasound exam is performed by a medical professional to confirm a viable intrauterine pregnancy," she says. "And during that time a woman can also be introduced to her baby for the first time."

A woman named Bethany, with 13 years of experience at a Dallas abortion clinic, finds this particularly troubling. "It isn't the sonogram itself that is objectionable, but the highly unethical purpose for which it is used," she says. "A sonogram picture from a medical facility has information printed on it, such as measurements in millimeters for purposes of determining the stage of pregnancy. I have had pictures from CPCs handed to me by 16-year-old [clients of mine], with the words 'Hi, Mommy!' where the medical data should be."

As crisis pregnancy centers become more like medical clinics, other problems emerge. Right now there are no sweeping regulations for these centers, though Oregon and Texas have proposed Senate bills attempting to change that. On the other hand, some people are concerned that the more medical CPCs become, the more powerful they will actually be. And as it stands, women have often reported confusion about the difference between a CPC and a medical clinic. Amanda Hill, for example, was 19 and living in a trailer home in Huntsville, Texas, when her period was a week late. She looked in the phone book and found a large ad boasting "free, anonymous pregnancy tests and pregnancy options counseling." She headed over that afternoon.

After her test, she says, she was left alone in a pamphlet-filled room for half an hour. "Finally, a counselor wearing a white lab coat and carrying a clipboard came into the room pulling a TV on a rolling cart behind her," she says. She suspected that the clipboard had her results, but before she could get them, she'd have to watch a video about prenatal development. "It started with a quote about how at the moment of conception you are given a road map to be complete as a woman," Amanda recalls. "It was really powerful, heart-wrenching stuff, and the pictures of the fetuses looked like full babies."

The counselor then asked Amanda what she would do were she pregnant. "When I told her, she asked me how my parents would feel about me killing their grandkid," she says. She was told she was on a destructive life path, and was encouraged to pray with the counselor (Amanda is not Christian). About an hour later, the counselor sent her on her way with a bunch of pamphlets. She wasn't even pregnant.

The RV has been parked by the clinic's front door almost every morning for two months now. Its presence has been without major incident, though it's impossible to know the impact it's had on the young women passing by, preparing to make one of the most personal decisions of their lives. Planned Parenthood has called it a trap. The clinic staff declined to comment.

Slattery, for his part, feels his work has been an unqualified success. In his 20-odd years of pro-life work, he says he's counseled 70,000 women. "We could fill Madison Square Garden with our saves," he says. "They come in here more afraid of their child, and they leave more afraid of abortion."

The morning sun is getting brighter, and around 10 a.m. another sidewalk counselor turns up with his two young daughters, the youngest monkeyed around his waist, the other by his side. His glasses are thick and it's hard to see his eyes, but he has the demeanor of the deeply spiritual—stoic, squinty, gentle. Soon, the three of them will join the growing vigil set up by the clinic's front door.

Inside, the clinic's waiting room looks like any-medical triage center—tidy rows of chairs, every seat taken, a few people slumped against the taupe walls, mouths open, fast asleep. Couples sit with their fingers clenched so tightly that the blood appears to be draining from their knuckles. Some girls giggle and whisper, other girls sit alone.

Just outside the back door, by the waiting room, a man of about 25 is smoking a Newport, shifting his weight from one foot to the other. "They tried to stop us on our way in," he says, cocking his chin without looking up. Across the parking lot, a lone man holds a stack of blue and green pamphlets. "They were persistent, too." He shakes his head and with a swift exhale says, "We're going to be okay. We'll come out the back door."

This Text: Reading

1. What is O'Connor's thesis in this piece? What is her main argument?
2. Is O'Connor fair to CPCs? What kind of lens is she reading CPC literature through?
3. Do you get a sense of O'Connor's political leanings through her piece? It would be difficult to call her essay "objective," but is it fair? Based on the information she provides, does she give a reasonable reading of the CPC project?

Your Text: Writing

1. Find some public relations literature or recruiting brochures from some organization—particularly one with a political or social leaning—and give a rhetorical reading of their publications. How do they make their arguments? What sorts of appeals to they make?
2. Track down some obviously biased pamphlets or literature—political campaign brochures, military recruitment materials, religious tracts, university admissions packets, or travel packages—and analyze the rhetorical strategies of these publications. How do they attempt persuasion? What techniques are most effective?
3. Write a comparison/contrast paper in which you look at CPC brochures and Planned Parenthood materials. How are they similar? How are they different? What kinds of appeals does each organization make?

The Third Wave Feminism Suite

Although there is no official definition or starting point of "Third Wave Feminism," most scholars place its inception in the early 1990s when a number of different writers, journalists, and critics simultaneously called into question some of the approaches of the so-called "second wave" of feminism of the 1960s and 70s. These new voices called for new notions of feminism at the end of the twentieth century. Most credit Rebecca Walker's 1992 essay about the Anita Hill/Clarence Thomas scandal in which she distances herself from previous forms of feminism by declaring, "I am the third wave" as the jumping off point for third wave feminism. Third wavers are, generally, women born in the 60s and 70s who have grown up in a world in which feminism was already part of American culture. In their 2000 book *Manifesta: Young Women, Feminism, and the Future,* Jennifer Baumgardner and Amy Richards advance a defense of contemporary "girl culture," arguing that characters like Xena, Ally McBeal, and Madonna embody the best female values—strength, determination, autonomy, liberation, and sexual freedom. Like Richards and Baumgardner, other writers and performers have argued for a more inclusive definition of feminism that allows for all kinds of femininity. For example, rap and hip-hop are often decried as sexist and demeaning, but both bell hooks and Eisa Davis claim those sites as locales of strong, black womanhood. Essentially, Third Wave Feminism embraces popular culture in ways previous *feminism* would have resisted; this enables new feminists to forge an individual feminism that, to them, is inclusive rather than exclusive. But there is never an uncontroversial definition of feminism, and what the term is or should be remains the topic of much and often heated discussion.

In this suite on Third Wave Feminism, we have done something unusual—we pair a professor's work with that of her students. Professor Patricia Pender has written extensively on *Buffy the Vampire Slayer*. Here, we print an essay by Dr. Pender on Buffy as a Third Wave Feminist icon. Dr. Pender also teaches a class called "Girls on Film," in which students engage films about and by women through various theoretical lenses. We include three student responses to an assignment that asks the students to look at a piece of popular culture through the lens of Third Wave Feminism.

We thought we would present some of Dr. Pender's materials for her class and paper in order for you to see the context in which these papers were prepared.

Here is a section from Dr. Pender's syllabus that explains the class's focus:

> This class explores the phenomenon of "girl culture" as it has been represented in recent mainstream cinema in the United States. It examines the unlikely feminist heroines of twentieth and twenty-first century popular film; Alicia Silverstone's Cher in the classic "chick flick" *Clueless,* Reese Witherspoon's rampaging Vanessa in the explosive *Freeway,* and Michelle Rodriguez's feisty Diana in Karyn Kusama's *Girl Fight.* Paying particular attention to issues of race, class, ethnicity, education, sexuality, psychology, and geography, the class will attempt to interrogate and destabilize mainstream media representations of female adolescence as predominantly white, heterosexual, and upper-middle class. We will examine recent cinematic representations of African-American (*Just Another Girl on the IRT*), Latina (*Girlfight*), queer (*All Over Me*), and transgender (*Boys Don't Cry*) adolescents, and employ a variety of methodologies: anthropological, cinematic, psychological, and economic.

As part of the course, Dr. Pender requires a significant research component that culminates in a research paper that also involves an active reading of a text associated with the class.

Here were the more specific requirements:

- Focus on representations of GIRLS (not women) on FILM (including TV).
- Make sure your film is MADE and SET sometime between 1980 and now (unless you have talked it over with me already)
- Make explicit connections to Third Wave Feminism—either in terms of your film's representation of girls, its subject matter (the issues it addresses), its narrative, its aims, its intended audience, its reception in popular media, or a combination of the above.

Following are examples of completed assignments (also look at Maribeth Theroux's paper on *NeXT* in the television chapter). In the first paper, Catherine Kirfrides looks at *Marie Antoinette*. In the second, Lara Hayhurst writes about *Grey's Anatomy;* and in the third, Gwendolyn Limbach looks at *Veronica Mars*. All three papers take different approaches to the assignment, although the commonality of the subject matter remains strong.

'Kicking Ass Is Comfort Food': Buffy as Third Wave Feminist Icon

Patricia Pender

BUFFY: *I love my friends. I'm very grateful for them. But that's the price of being a Slayer . . . I mean, I guess everyone's alone, but being a Slayer—that's a burden we can't share.*

FAITH: *And no one else can feel it. Thank god we're hot chicks with superpowers!*

BUFFY: *Takes the edge off.*

FAITH: *Comforting! (Buffy the Vampire Slayer, 'End of Days')*

I definitely think a woman kicking ass is extraordinarily sexy, always ... If I wasn't compelled on a very base level by that archetype I wouldn't have created that character. I mean, yes, I have a feminist agenda, but it's not like I made a chart. (Joss Whedon qtd. in Udovitch, Rolling Stone)

WHAT ACCOUNTS FOR THE EXTRAORDINARY FEMINIST APPEAL of the hit television series *Buffy the Vampire Slayer,* and how has its ex-cheerleading, demon-hunting heroine become the new poster girl for third wave feminist popular culture?[1] In this article I examine *Buffy* through the problematic of third wave feminism, situating the series as part of a larger cultural project that seeks to reconcile the political agenda of second wave feminism with the critique of white racial privilege articulated by women of colour and the theoretical insights afforded by poststructural analysis. I suggest that if one of the primary goals of third wave feminism is to question our inherited models of feminist agency and political efficacy, without acceding to the defeatism implicit in the notion of 'postfeminism,' then *Buffy* provides us with modes of oppositional praxis, of resistant femininity and, in its final season, of collective feminist activism that are unparalleled in mainstream television. At the same time, the series' emphasis on individual empowerment, its celebration of the exceptional woman, and its problematic politics of racial representation remain important concerns for feminist analysis. Focusing primarily on the final season of the series, I argue that season seven of *Buffy* offers a more straightforward and decisive feminist message than the show has previously attempted, and that in doing so it paints a compelling picture of the promises and predicaments that attend third wave feminism as it negotiates both its second wave antecedents and its traditional patriarchal nemeses.

'Third wave feminism' functions in the following analysis as a political ideology currently under construction. Buffy makes a similar claim about her own self-development when (invoking one of the more bizarre forms of American comfort food) she refers to herself as unformed 'cookie dough' ('Chosen' 7022). Ednie Kaeh Garrison proposes that the name 'third wave feminism' may be 'more about desire than an already existing thing' (165), and Stephanie Gilmore has suggested that, ironically, the defining feature of third wave feminism 'may well be its inability to be categorized' (218). Transforming such indeterminacy into a political principle, Rory Dicker and Alison Piepmeier state that one of the aims of their recent anthology, *Catching a Wave: Reclaiming Feminism for the 21st Century,* is to 'render problematic any easy understanding of what the third wave is' (5). While there are arguably as many variants of third wave feminism as there are feminists to claim or reject that label, the characteristics I have chosen to focus on here are those that provide the most striking parallels to *Buffy*'s season seven: its continuation of the second wave fight against misogynist violence; its negotiation of the demands for individual and collective empowerment; its belated recognition and representation of cultural diversity; and its embrace of contradiction and paradox.

Combining elements of action, drama, comedy, romance, horror, and occasionally musical, *Buffy* sits uneasily within the taxonomies of television genre. Darker than *Dawson,* and infinitely funnier than *Felicity, Buffy* was explicitly conceived as a feminist reworking of horror films in which 'bubbleheaded blondes wandered into dark alleys and got murdered by some creature' (Whedon qtd. in Fudge par. 2). From its mid-season US premiere in 1997 to its primetime series finale in 2003, the chronicles of the Chosen One have generated, in the affectionate words of its creator and director Joss Whedon, a 'rabid, almost insane fan base' (Longworth 211). Subverting the conventional gender dynamics of horror, action, and sci-fi serials, as well as the best expectations of its producers, the series has followed the fortunes of the Slayer as she has struggled through the 'hell' that is high school, a freshman year at U.C. Sunnydale, and the ongoing challenge of balancing the demands of family, friends, and relationships, and work with her inescapable duty to fight all manner of evil. As the voiceover to the show's opening credits relates: 'In every generation there is a Chosen One. She and she alone will fight the demons, the vampires and the forces of darkness. She is the Slayer.'

Television critics and feminist scholars alike have been quick to appreciate the implicit feminist message of the series as a whole. Buffy has been celebrated as a 'radical reimagining of what a girl (and a woman) can do and be' (Byers 173); as a 'prototypical girly feminist activist' (Karras par. 15); and as a 'Hard Candy-coated feminist heroine for the girl-power era' (Fudge par. 17). Her ongoing battle with the forces of evil is seen as symbolic of several second wave feminist struggles: the challenge to balance personal and professional life (Bellafante, 'Bewitching' 83), the fight against sexual violence (Marinucci 69), and the 'justified feminist anger' young women experience in the face of patriarchal prohibitions and constraints (Helford 24). More metacritically, the series has been analysed in terms of its 'wayward' reconfiguration of the mind/body dualism (Playden 143), and its refusal of the 'inexorable logic' of binary oppositions (Pender 43). Despite the fact that the series itself has ended, the furor of attention it continues to generate both within and outside the academy assures *Buffy* an active afterlife. The last two years alone have seen an online journal, three one-day conferences, and four anthologies devoted to the burgeoning field of 'Buffy Studies' with at least another six publications, and three further conferences in the academic pipeline.[2]

But what propels such feminist fandom? What inspires this excess of affect? Rachel Fudge addresses this question directly when she writes that the impulse that propels Buffy out on patrols, 'night after night, forgoing any semblance of "normal" teenage life,' is identical to the one

The very feminine Buffy with a traditionally masculine weapon.

'that compels us third-wavers to spend endless hours discussing the feminist potentials and pitfalls of primetime television' (par. 8). Fudge claims that Buffy 'has the sort of conscience that appeals to the daughters of feminism's second wave,' women for whom 'a certain awareness of gender and power is ingrained and inextricably linked to our sense of identity and self-esteem (par. 8). In her examination of Buffy as the third wave's 'final girl,' Irene Karras argues that Buffy's appeal lies in her intentional 'slaying [of] stereotypes about what women can and cannot do' (par. 15). Karras applauds the show's combination of sexuality and what she calls 'real efforts to make the world a better and safer place for both men and women' (par. 15). Blending an exhilarating athleticism with a compulsion to activism, Buffy's spectacular agency—her (literally) fantastic facility for kicking ass—has come to function as feminist comfort food.

When fellow Slayer Faith consoles Buffy with the thought '[t]hank god we're hot chicks with superpowers' (first epigraph), the gesture is offered as sympathy and support; it helps to 'take the edge off' the burden they 'can't share.' In this exchange, the Slayer's burden is assuaged in part by what Whedon refers to as her 'sexiness' (second epigraph); in part by the very exceptional qualities or superpowers that isolate her to begin with; and perhaps ultimately by the sharing of confidences and, by extension, of responsibilities. The 'comfort' offered here is a complex conglomerate, and one that rewards further scrutiny. The title of this chapter, 'kicking ass is comfort food,' comes from the episode 'The Prom' (3020), which occurs immediately prior to season three's apocalyptic Ascension. Buffy has just been told by her lover, Angel, that—in the event that they survive the imminent end-of-the-world—he will be abandoning their relationship and leaving town. To complicate matters, a jilted senior denied a prom date has secretly been training hellhounds to attack partygoers wearing formal attire. Buffy's mentor Giles attempts to console his devastated charge with the conventional cure for a broken heart:

> GILES: Buffy, I'm sorry. I understand that this sort of thing requires ice cream of some sort.
> BUFFY: Ice cream will come. First I want to take out psycho-boy.
> GILES: Are you sure?
> BUFFY: Great thing about being a Slayer—kicking ass is comfort food. ('The Prom')

Kicking ass becomes comfort food for Buffy when her supernatural abilities provide her with an extraordinary outlet for more conventional frustrations. Action—in this case a cathartically violent form of action—serves up a supernatural solace for a range of quotidian, human afflictions.

Kicking ass offers Buffy psychological and physical relief: it allows her to simultaneously redress straightforward social evils and to palliate more personal sorts of demons. For the feminist viewer, the spectacle of Buffy kicking ass is similarly comforting; equally, exhilarating and empowering, Buffy provides the compound pleasures of both the hot chick and her superpowers. Recent feminist critiques of the heteronormative assumptions and moral policing that underlie second wave theories of visual pleasure ensure that as feminist viewers, we too can find the spectacle of 'a woman kicking ass . . . extraordinarily sexy' (second epigraph).[3] At the same time, as Elyce Rae Helford has argued, Buffy can stand metaphorically for young women everywhere who are angered by having 'their lives directed by circumstances or individuals beyond their control' (24). In an era which can sometimes seem saturated with condemnations of feminism's increasing frivolity, Buffy's indomitable militancy—her unrelenting vigilance—can be consumed by the feminist spectator as primetime panacea. Buffy's predilection towards, and consummate abilities in, the art of kicking ass thus simultaneously soothe and sustain, and inspire and incite the compulsion to feminist activism.

While over the last seven years the series has addressed a staggering range of contemporary concerns— from the perils of low-paid, part-time employment to the erotic dynamics of addiction and recovery—it is significant that the final season of *Buffy* makes a decisive shift back to feminist basics. Season seven eschews to a certain extent the metaphorical slipperiness and pop-cultural play that is typical of its evocation of postmodern demons and instead presents a monster that is, quite literally, an enemy of women. The principal story arc pits an amorphous antagonist, The First Evil, against the Slayer and her 'army,' a group that has swelled to include in its ranks 'Potential' Slayers from around the globe. Staging the series' final showdown with a demon that is overtly misogynist and creating an original evil with a clearly patriarchal platform, *Buffy*'s season seven raises the explicit feminist stakes of the series considerably.

Unable to take material form, The First Evil employs as its vessel and deputy a former preacher turned agent-of-evil called Caleb. Spouting hellfire and damnation with fundamentalist zeal Caleb is, of all of the show's myriad manifestations of evil, the most recognisable misogynist: 'There once was a woman. And she was foul, like all women are foul' (Dirty Girls' 7018). Dubbed 'the Reverend-I-Hate-Women' by Xander ('Touched' 7020), Caleb is a monstrous but familiar representative of patriarchal oppression, propounding a dangerous form of sexism under the cover of pastoral care. 'I wouldn't do that if I were you sweet pea,' Caleb at one point warns Buffy; 'Mind your manners. I do believe I warned you once' ('Empty Places' 7019). At other times he calls her 'girly girl' ('End of Days' 7021), a 'little lady' ('Empty Places'), and, once (but only once), 'whore' ('Touched'). Buffy's response (after kicking him across the room) is to redirect the condescension and hypocrisy couched in his discourse of paternal concern: 'You know, you really should watch your language. Someone didn't know you, they might take you for a woman-hating jerk' ('Touched'). In comparison with the supernatural demons of previous episodes, Caleb's evil might seem unusually old-fashioned or even ridiculous, but successive encounters with the Slayer underscore the fact that his power is all the more insidious and virulent for that. Mobilising outmoded archetypes of women's weakness and susceptibility—'Curiosity: woman's first sin. I offer her an apple. What can she do but take it?' ('Dirty Girls')—Caleb effectively sets a trap that threatens to wipe out the Slayer line. Within the context of the narrative, Caleb's sexist convictions— 'Following is what girls do best' ('Dirty Girls')—and, more importantly, their unconscious internalisation by the Slayer and her circle pose the principal threat to their sustained, organised, collective resistance.

In its exploration of the dynamics of collective activism, *Buffy*'s final season examines the charges of solipsism and individualism that have frequently been directed at contemporary popular feminism. 'Want to know what today's chic young feminist thinkers care about?' wrote Ginia Bellafante in her notorious 1998 article for *Time* magazine: 'Their bodies! Themselves!' ('Feminism' 54). One of the greatest challenges Buffy faces in season seven is negotiating conflicting demands of individual and collective empowerment. Trapped by the mythology, propounded by the Watcher's Council, that bestows the powers of the Slayer on 'one girl in all the world,' Buffy is faced with the formidable task of training Potential Slayers-in-waiting who will only be called into their own power in the event of her death. In the episode 'Potential' (7012) Buffy attempts to rally her troops for the battle ahead:

> The odds are against us. Time is against us. And some of us will die in this battle. Decide now that it's not going to be you ... Most people in this world have no idea why they're here or what they want to do. But you do. You have a mission. A reason for being here. You're not here by chance. You're here because you are the Chosen Ones.

The Third Wave Feminism Suite

This sense of vocation resonates strongly with feminist viewers who feel bound to the struggle for social justice. However, such heroism can still be a solitary rather than collective endeavour. On the eve of their final battle, after decimating her advance attack, Caleb makes fun of what he calls Buffy's 'One-Slayer-Brigade' and taunts her with the prospect of what we might think of as wasted Potential:

> None of those girlies will ever know real power unless you're dead. Now, you know the drill . . . 'Into every generation a Slayer is born. One girl in all the world. She alone has the strength and skill . . .' There's that word again. What you are, how you'll die: alone. ('Chosen' 7022)

Such references make it clear that loneliness and isolation are part of the Slayer's legacy.

Balancing the pleasures and price of her singular status, Buffy bears the burden of the exceptional woman. But the exceptional woman, as Margaret Thatcher and Condoleezza Rice have amply demonstrated, is not necessarily a sister to the cause; a certain style of ambitious woman fashions herself precisely as the exception that proves the rule of women's general incompetence. In one of the more dramatic and disturbing character developments in the series as a whole, season seven presents Buffy's leadership becoming arrogant and autocratic, and her attitude isolationist and increasingly alienated. Following in the individualist footsteps of prominent 'power feminists,' Buffy forgoes her collaborative community and instead adopts what fans in the United States and elsewhere perceived as a sort of 'You're-Either-With-Me-Or-Against-Me' moral absolutism ominously reminiscent of the Bush administration (Wilcox)—an incipient despotism exemplified by what Anya calls Buffy's 'Everyone-Sucks-But-Me' speech ('Get It Done' 7015).

The trial of Buffy's leadership is sustained up to the last possible moment, and its resolution repudiates recurring laments about the third wave's purported political apathy. 'According to the most widely publicized construction of the third wave,' describe Leslie Heywood and Jennifer Drake, '"we" hate our bodies, ourselves, our boring little lives, yet we incessantly focus on our bodies, and our boring little lives. . . . "We" believe that the glamorization of nihilism is hip and think that any hope for change is naive and embarrassing' ('We Learn America' 47). Jennifer Baumgardner and Amy Richards respond to such allegations directly when they write 'imagine how annoying it is to hear from anyone (including the media and especially Second Wave feminists) that young women aren't continuing the work of the Second Wave, that young women are apathetic, or "just don't get it"' (85). Baumgardner and Richards state that they have reacted 'by scrambling to be better feminists and frantically letting these women know how much we look up to them.' Ultimately, however, they have 'refused to accept this myth' (85).

Drawing attention to the Slayer's increasing isolation, Caleb highlights the political crisis afflicting her community, but in doing so he inadvertently alerts Buffy to the latent source of its strength, forcing her to claim a connection she admits 'never really occurred to me before' ('Chosen'). In a tactical reversal Giles claims 'flies in the face of everything . . . that every generation has ever done in the fight against evil,' Buffy plans to transfer the power of the Chosen One, the singular, exceptional woman, to the hands of the Potentials—to empower the collective not at the expense of, but by force of, the exception. In the series finale, Buffy addresses her assembled army in the following terms:

> Here's the part where you make a choice. What if you could have that power *now?* In every generation one Slayer is born, because a bunch of men who died thousands of years ago made up that rule. They were powerful men. This woman [pointing to Willow] is more powerful than all of them combined. So I say we change the rules. I say *my* power should be *our*

power. Tomorrow, Willow will use the essence of the scythe to change our destiny. From now on, every girl in the world who might be a Slayer, *will* be a slayer. Every girl who could have the power, *will* have the power. Can stand up, will stand up. Slayers—every one of us. Make your choice: are you ready to be strong? ('Chosen'; emphasis in original)

At that moment—as the archaic matriarchal power of the scythe is wrested from the patriarchal dictates of the Watcher's Council—we see a series of vignettes from around the world, as young women of different ages, races, cultures, and backgrounds sense their strength, take charge, and rise up against their oppressors. This is a 'Feel the Force, Luke' moment for girls on a global scale. It is a revolution that has been televised.

In transferring power from a privileged, white Californian teenager to a heterogeneous group of women from different national, racial, and socioeconomic backgrounds *Buffy*'s final season addresses, almost as an afterthought, the issue of cultural diversity that has been at the forefront of third wave feminist theorising. Garrison has drawn attention to the connections between Chela Sandoval's articulation of 'US Third World Feminism' and US third wave feminism, representing the latter as a movement fundamentally indebted to the feminist critique articulated by women of colour. Garrison claims that, 'unlike many white feminists in the early years of the Second Wave who sought to create the resistant subject "women," in the Third Wave, the figure "women" is rarely a unitary subject' (149). This understanding of third wave feminism is borne out by Baumgardner and Richards, who argue that 'the third wave was born into the diversity realized by the latter part of the second wave,' a diversity represented by the works of African American and Chicana feminists, Third World feminists of colour, and US Third World feminists (77). Heywood and Drake make the third wave's debts to Third World feminism explicit when they state that the arguments that women of colour scholars introduced into the dominant feminist paradigms in the 1980s 'have become the most powerful forms of feminist discourse in the 1990s' ('We Learn America' 49). They claim that while third wave feminism owes 'an enormous debt to the critique of sexism and the struggles for gender equity that were white feminism's strongest provinces, it was U.S. Third World feminism that modeled a language and a politics of hybridity that can account for our lives at the century's turn' (Introduction 13).

From some of its earliest incarnations academic third wave feminism has presented itself as a movement that places questions of diversity and difference at the centre of its theoretical and political agenda. However, as Stacy Gillis and Rebecca Munford have pointed out, the 'extent to which third wave feminism has learned how to incorporate, rather than to exclude' (5) remains an issue for ongoing concern. Examining what she sees as the serious limitations of predominantly Western third wave feminism, Winifred Woodhull warns that the third wave risks repeating the exclusionary errors of earlier feminist practices. 'Given the global arena in which third wave feminism emerges,' she writes, 'it is disappointing that new feminist debates arising in first-world contexts address issues that pertain only to women *in* those contexts' (6; emphasis in original). Woodhull claims that the significance and potential of third wave feminism 'can be grasped only by adopting a global interpretive frame, that is, by relinquishing the old frameworks of the west and developing new ones that take seriously the struggles of women the world over' (6). In its most rigorous and responsible guise, then, third wave feminism's call for cultural diversity is the political response to the critique of white racial privilege articulated by second wave feminists of colour, and the theoretical consequence of incorporating the discourse of difference elaborated by poststructural theory more broadly. In its less careful incarnations, as *Buffy* demonstrates admirably, it can perform the very strategies of occlusion and erasure that its more critical proponents are at pains to redress.

Buffy's racial politics are inarguably more conservative than its gender or sexual politics, a situation pithily summarised by one of the few recurring black characters of the show's first three seasons, Mr. Trick: 'Sunnydale' . . . admittedly not a haven for the brothers—strictly the Caucasian persuasion in the Dale' ('Faith, Hope, and Trick' 3003). While the final season of the show has seen an expansion of *Buffy*'s exclusively white, middle-class cast with the introduction of character Principal Robin Wood and the international expansion of the Slayer line, such changes can easily be dismissed as mere tokenism. Season seven makes repeated recourse to racial stereotypes—most notably in its primitivist portrayal of the 'First Slayer' and the 'Shadow Men' as ignoble savages, and its use of formulaic markers of cultural difference to distinguish the international Slayers. As Gayle Wald has warned in a slightly different context, feminist scholarship must be wary of uncritically reproducing simplistically celebratory readings of popular culture that focus on gender performance 'as a privileged site and source of political oppositionality,' in which 'critical questions of national, cultural, and racial appropriation can be made to disappear' (590). A critical analysis *of Buffy*'s racial representations need not be considered a critique of the palpable pleasures provided by the show but rather, as Wald suggests, 'a critique of the production of pleasure through gendered and racialized narratives that signify as new, transgressive, or otherwise exemplary' (595).

In extending the Slayer's powers to young girls across the globe, *Buffy*'s season seven can be seen to begin to redress—albeit belatedly and incompletely—the national, cultural and racial privilege the show has assumed through its seven-year cycle. Bringing ethnic diversity and racial difference to the Slayer story, a generous reading of *Buffy*'s finale might see it as an exemplary narrative of transnational feminist activism. A more critical reading might see it as yet another chapter in a long, repetitive story of US imperialism. I would suggest that these readings are not as inimical as they might initially seem; season seven's narrative implies that both of these readings are admissible, perhaps even mutually implicated. In her analysis of what she calls 'the globalization of Buffy's power,' for instance, Rhonda Wilcox has argued that '*Buffy* be seen as both a metaphor for and an enactment of globalization,' one that contemplates both its negative and positive aspects. Wilcox claims that the series celebrates capitalist institutions such as the mall at the same time that it recognises and critiques the 'cultural presumption' inherent in the idea of 'all-American domination of the world . . . through the spread of technological goods and through governmental aggression.' Similarly, I would suggest that the idealised vision of universal sisterhood with which *Buffy* concludes needs to be read against the immediate political context in which its final season is screened; a context that illuminates some of the same gestures of cultural imperialism that the series elsewhere successfully critiques. *Buffy*'s celebration of what is effectively an international military alliance under ostensibly altruistic American leadership demands special scrutiny in our current political climate. In the context of the indefensible arrogance of Bush's 'War on Terror' and the spurious universalism of his 'Coalition of the Willing,' *Buffy*'s final gesture of international inclusivity is imbued with unwittingly inauspicious overtones.

It would be a mistake, I think, to underestimate or to collapse too quickly the contradictions embedded in *Buffy*'s cultural politics, contradictions that are in turn indicative of the crosscurrents that distinguish the third wave of feminism. The refusal of misogynist violence, the battle against institutionalised patriarchy, and the potential of transnational feminist activism are issues that remain at the forefront of the third wave agenda, and themes that *Buffy*'s final season explores with characteristically challenging and satisfying complexity. The fact that its success in critiquing its own cultural privilege is equivocal should be read less as a straightforward sign of failure than as a reflection of the redoubtable contradictions that characterise third wave feminism itself. Fudge has suggested that *Buffy* 'constantly treads the fine line between girl-power schlock and feminist wish-fulfillment, never giving satisfaction to either one' (par. 17). Adopting one of the signature rhetorical and political strategies of feminism's third wave, *Buffy* has consistently welcomed such apparent contradiction with open arms. I suggest that in its examination of individual and collective empowerment, in its ambiguous politics of racial representation, and its willing embrace of contradiction, *Buffy* is a quintessentially third wave cultural production. Providing a fantastic resolution—in both senses of the word—to some of the many dilemmas confronting third wave feminists today, *Buffy* is comfort food for girls who like to have their cake and eat it too.

Notes

1. I would like to thank the students in my Stanford class, *Girls on Film: Cultural Studies in Third Wave Feminism,* for their creative and critical engagement with this material. Thanks also to Caitlin Delohery and Falu Bakrania who provided invaluable comments on earlier versions of this essay.
2. See the *Academic Buffy Bibliography,* the *Encyclopaedia of Buffy Studies* and David Lavery's '"I Wrote My Thesis on You": *Buffy* Studies as an Academic Cult.'
3. For more on this see Debbie Stoller.

Works Cited

Academic Buffy Bibliography. Ed. Derik A. Badman. 20 Apr. 2003. 22 Sept. 2003. <http://madinkbeard.com/buffy/index.html>.

Baumgardner, Jennifer, and Amy Richards. *Manifesta: Young Women, Feminism, and the Future.* New York: Farrar, Straus and Giroux, 2000.

Bellafante, Ginia. 'Bewitching Teen Heroines.' *Time* 5 May 1997. 82–85.

———. 'Feminism: It's All About Me.' *Time* 29 June 1998. 54–62.

Buffy the Vampire Slayer. By Joss Whedon. Perf. Sarah Michelle Gellar, Alyson Hannigan, and Nicholas Brandon. Twentieth Century Fox, 1997–2003.

Byers, Michelle. 'Buffy the Vampire Slayer: The Next Generation of Television.' *Catching a Wave: Reclaiming Feminism* for *the 21st Century.* Ed. Rory Dicker and Alison Piepmeier. Boston: Northeastern UP, 2003. 171–187.

Dicker, Rory, and Alison Piepmeier. Introduction. *Catching a* Wave: *Reclaiming Feminism for the 21st Century.* Ed. Rory Dicker and Alison Piepmeier. Boston: Northeastern UP, 2003. 3–28.

Encyclopaedia of Buffy Studies. Ed. David Lavery and Rhonda V. Wilcox, I May 2003.

Slayage: The Online Journal of Buffy Studies. 22 Sept. 2003. <http://www.slayage.tv/EBS>.

Fudge, Rachel. 'The Buffy Effect: Or, A Tale of Cleavage and Marketing.' *Bitch: Feminist Responses to Popular Culture* 10 (1999). 20 June 2000. <http://www.bitchmagazine.com/archives/08_01/buffy/buffy.htm>.

Garrison, Ednie Kaeh. 'U.S. Feminism–Girl Style! Youth (Sub)Cultures and the Technologics of the Third Wave.' *Feminist Studies* 26.1 (2000): 141–170.

Gillis, Stacy, and Rebecca Munford. 'Harvesting Our Strengths: Third Wave Feminism and Women's Studies.' *Third Wave Feminism and Women's Studies.* Ed. Stacy Gillis and Rebecca Munford. Spec, issue of *Journal of International Women's Studies* 4.2 (2003). <http://www.bridgew.edu/SoAS/jiws/April03/>.

Gilmore, Stephanie. 'Looking Back, Thinking Ahead: Third Wave Feminism in the United States.' *Journal of Women's History* 12.4 (2001): 215–221.

Helford, Elyce Rae. '"My Emotions Give Me Power": The Containment of Girls' Anger in *Buffy*.' *Fighting the Forces: What's at Stake in* Buffy the Vampire Slayer. Ed. Rhonda Wilcox and David Lavery. Lanham: Rowman and Littlefield, 2002. 18–34.

Heywood, Leslie, and Jennifer Drake. Introduction. *Third Wave Agenda: Being Feminist, Doing Feminism.* Ed. Leslie Heywood and Jennifer Drake. Minneapolis: Minnesota UP, 1997. 1–20.

_____. 'We Learn America Like a Script: Activism in the Third Wave; Or, Enough Phantoms of Nothing.' *Third Wave Agenda: Being Feminist, Doing Feminism.* Ed. Leslie Heywood and Jennifer Drake. Minneapolis: Minnesota UP, 1997. 40–54.

Karras, Irene. 'The Third Wave's Final Girl: *Buffy the Vampire Slayer.' Thirdspace* 1.2 (2002). <http://www.thirdspace.ca/articles/karras.htm>.

Lavery, David. '"I Wrote My Thesis on You": *Buffy* Studies as an Academic Cult.' Sonic Synergies/Creative Cultures Conf. University of South Australia, Adelaide. 21 July 2003.

Longworth Jr, James L. 'Joss Whedon: Feminist.' *TV Creators: Conversations with America's Top Producers of Television Drama.* Ed. James L. Longworth Jr. Syracuse: Syracuse UP, 2000.197–220.

Marinucci, Mimi. 'Feminism and the Ethics of Violence: Why Buffy Kicks Ass.' Buffy the Vampire Slayer *and Philosophy: Fear and Trembling in Sunnydale.* Ed. James B. South. Chicago: Open Court, 2003. 61–75.

Pender, Patricia. '"I'm Buffy and You're . . . History": The Postmodern Politics of *Buffy the Vampire Slayer.' Fighting the Forces: What's at Stake in* Buffy the Vampire Slayer. Ed. Rhonda Wilcox and David Lavery. Lanham: Rowman and Littlefield, 2002. 35–44.

Playden, Zoe-Jane. '"What You Are, What's to Come": Feminisms, Citizenship and the Divine.' *Reading the Vampire Slayer: An Unofficial Critical Companion to Buffy and Angel.* Ed. Roz Kaveney. London: Tauris Parke, 2002. 120–147.

Stoller, Debbie. 'Introduction: Feminists Fatale: BUST-ing the Beauty Myth.' *The BUST Guide to the New Girl Order.* Ed. Marcelle Karp and Debbie Stoller. New York: Penguin,1999. 42–47.

Udovitch, Mim. 'What Makes Buffy Slay? *Rolling Stone* July 2000. 40–41, 110.

Wald, Gayle. 'Just a Girl? Rock Music, Feminism, and the Cultural Construction of Female Youth.' *Signs: Journal of Women in Culture and Society* 23.3 (1998): 585–610.

Wilcox, Rhonda. '"Show Me Your World": Exiting the Text and the Globalization of *Buffy.*' Staking a Claim: Global Buffy, Local Identities Conf. University of South Australia, Adelaide. 22 July 2003.

Woodhull, Winifred. 'Global Feminisms, Transnational Political Economies, Third World Cultural Production.' *Third Wave Feminism and Women's Studies.* Ed. Stacy Gillis and Rebecca Munford. Spec. issue of *Journal of International Women's Studies* 4.2 (2003). <http://www.bridgew.edu/SoAS/jiws/April03/>.

Classically Different: Sofia Coppola's *Marie Antoinette* Takes a New Look at What It Means to Be a Girl

Catherine Kirifides

Student Essay

CROWDS GATHER, TOMATOES ARE THROWN and angry expletives are yelled in French at one young girl. Surprisingly enough this is not 1793, but 2006 and the anger is directed at Sofia Coppola whose new film *Marie Antoinette* has just been unveiled at the Cannes Film Festival. The reaction of the French people to this revisionist take on the famed teen queen binds Coppola to her main character due to the perception of Coppola as a foreign girl with status.

Like the general French public, critics pulverized Coppola's newest film for being historically inaccurate, cheesy, and mere pop fluff. "A case of never mind the history books," many have wondered, "why Coppola is bothering with reality if she's going to be so cursory about it" (Gilbey 1). These accusations came as a shock considering the young Coppola's track record of feature films, which include *The Virgin Suicides* and *Lost in Translation*. Both films dealt with heavy issues of adolescence and were heralded for their seriousness and complexity. The impression, on the other hand, of *Antoinette* as "silly fizz makes it simpler and less creepy than her [Coppola's] earlier projects" claimed *The New Yorker,* though the opening sequence was "codified to death" (Lane 3, 1). How is it that Sofia Coppola, the golden child of Hollywood greatness, could possibly have made such a shallow film? Considering Coppola's past films and the subject matter she most likes to explore— adolescent girls— one must come to the conclusion that there is a rhyme and reason as to why *Marie Antoinette* was made the way it was. Coppola doesn't seem like a girl who makes mistakes.

Though the film does take on a more teen pop feel than her earlier works, from the cinematography to the costuming and editing, form still follows function. The pop feel of the production is used to magnify Antoinette's parallel to contemporary girlhood. These artistic decisions reflect Coppola's portrayal of Antoinette as a young vibrant girl who is discovering a new world, and growing up in it, throughout the course of the film. Focusing on Antoinette's youth, Coppola highlights the generational differences between the young Queen and her mother and other ladies at court. By being thrust into an adult life at an early age, Coppola's Antoinette tries to recapture her childhood through her more radical behavior. Coppola asks if the negative connotation of the name Marie Antoinette is justified. Based on Antonia Fraser's biography *Marie Antoinette: The Journey*, Coppola has written and directed a tale that looks at the iconic queen for what she truly was: merely a girl.

Barbara Amiel writes that Marie Antoinette's life "took place at a punctuation mark in history" (2). Coppola's film shows us a girl who did not only just happen to be at the wrong place at the wrong time, but one who challenged the norm and the institutions of the time. Though she ended up on the chopping block, Coppola's Antoinette is depicted as a rebel and a revolutionary; just not in the patriotic sense. By highlighting the generational differences between Antoinette and her mother, Empress Maria Teresa of Austria, we see how this young girl was, in a way, bucking the system. Maria Teresa said, the year Marie Antoinette was born, "They are born to obey and must learn to do so in good time" (Fraser 21). The film is narrated some of the time by the voice of Maria Teresa, as she reads pieces from the constant correspondence she kept with her youngest daughter. Like the ominous voice from above, Maria Teresa's words truly affect young Antoinette. Whether we see her try and brush off her mother's advice by diving into the French ways of doing things (for which she is being reprimanded), or slowly sink to the ground because of them, we have to take into account the fact that her mother's word and opinion has great influence over her. After one such letter from her mother Antoinette states, "Letting everyone down would be my greatest unhappiness." This need to seek approval from the women around her, and the depression the lack of this approval leads to, is very similar to the dynamic girls today have with the 2nd wave feminists many of their mothers were.

Unable to totally conform to all the rules of etiquette that Versailles required, Antoinette is depicted as someone who is constantly fighting against the older regime of royalty and prestige. The film begins with Antoinette's passage from Austria to France, showing the young girl's open compassion for her ladies in waiting, dog, and mother. She is met with an intrigued coldness by the French for this display of affection when she hugs goodbye and hello to the people around her. After arriving at Versailles she is watched by everyone and we see her engaging in easy conversation with the children around her. This fondness and ease with children foreshadows her future woes in motherhood as well as the fact that there were not many people remotely close to her age at court. Coppola also made the artistic decision to have Antoinette's close circle of friends and admirers of the young and beautiful persuasion (which is not historically correct) in order to further highlight this generational difference. Antoinette's relationship with her husband's (the dauphin, Louis Auguste) aunts is another

The Third Wave Feminism Suite

Coppola's Marie Antoinette: Fashionista or feminist? Both?

of woman/girl strain. Unable to understand Antoinette's disinclination for intrigue and pompous etiquette, they first mock her and then try to make her the elitist queen they wish her to be. They eventually gain influence over the young girl by coaxing her to snub the king's mistress, Du Barry, who also flouts the rules of etiquette at court. Once the aunts' influence causes Antoinette trouble, she is reprimanded by her mother, she resorts to her own ways of handling people and situations. This helps in winning over the king and her husband, but hurts her in terms of friends she later makes and promotes. Antoinette is seen as a girl who is being pulled between the older generation's ways of how to gain power as a woman and how she wants to enjoy her own life. As her mother states, "Everything depends on the wife, if she is willing and sweet [. . .] never ill humor," showcasing the mentality of the older generation of women about a woman's duty, place, and influence.

Since Coppola's film generally focuses on the issue of girlhood and what it means to grow up in a specific time period, it is very telling that she chose this girl and this time. "I didn't set out on a campaign to correct the misperceptions about her; I just wanted to tell the story from her point of view," said Coppola in an interview. "I was struck by the fact that Louis and Marie were teenagers—in charge of France at the most vulnerable time in its history" (Covington 2). Highlighting Antoinette's rebellion of serious adulthood, we see her life as the flash of intoxicating glamour and fun that whirls about and that "her royal privilege is to get lost in the superficial pleasure of the moment" (Johnson 2). Coppola condenses many years of Antoinette's life, mixing up the order of events, to give us the feeling that everything was happening to the young girl all at once. This consolidation of facts allows us to see the essence of her life and some of the more interesting events in it, rather than the hum drum of day to day court life. This long and tedious existence is seen by the pacing and cinematography Coppola employs in the first thirty minutes of the film. Gradually speeding up the very monotonous start to the film, the days fly by until Antoinette takes her life, or at least amusement, into her own hands. When you are sent away to be married at 14, don't consummate that marriage until age 21 and become queen of France at 18 you inevitably skip the most important time of female adolescence. This teen adolescence age is when most girls are just discovering who they are and are coping with low self-esteem, personality changes, and responsibility. Antoinette was forced to act like an adult, with no questions or wavering allowed. This stifled childhood leads to a rebellion expressed in all things girly and childish. Most girls are deemed women once they are married, have sex and children, and have a job (i.e. being queen). Antoinette refuses all of those factors and ferociously throws herself into fashion, the arts, and game playing. Always acting for her own amusement, Antoinette has no other knowledge of what life is like outside of her bubble. The extravagance associated with Antoinette is excused by the fact that "her actions would have been excessive or greedy only if she had had no sense of entitlement and believed herself to be getting away with something [...] She did her best at what she was supposed to do, being the leader of French style" (Amiel 5). These elements of Antoinette's influence and role in society, as well as her extravagance, are all addressed in Coppola's film.

Coppola drives home (through editing) the idea that Antoinette's fling into fashion and other stereotypical simple female pleasures are a result of her unhappiness in her pseudo-adult life. By juxtaposing scenes of domestic inadequacy and frustration with those of pleasure, we see the extremes that dominated Antoinette's life. The contrasting looks and forms of each type of scene help to highlight this difference. The dark and naturally lit scene where Antoinette is rebuffed in bed by Louis' "I'm exhausted" is directly followed by the sequence showing the fast paced life of riding, parties, and unfixed movement. Similarly, after Antoinette's sister-in-law gives birth, we see Antoinette's masked unhappiness and despair as she cries curled up in a ball of the floor of her apartment's back room. There isn't a more telling action to show a child who feels she's failed. This muted painful image directly cuts to the montage showing extravagant shoes, drink, food, and gambling to the music of "I Want Candy." With the heightened coloring and pace, Coppola's implication is, "Can't have a baby? Buy some shoes and get drunk." This escapist behavior is one way to look at Antoinette's excessive spending and flagrant personality.

How Coppola deals with Marie Antoinette's iconic image is very telling of her own experiences. All of Coppola's films have been said to have some autobiographical thread to them. Antoinette's wealth, family privilege, and youthful age while she makes a name for herself produce a compelling parallel with Coppola's life. Coppola has practically worked on films since she came out of the womb (she first appeared on film as the baby boy in the christening scene in her father's film *The Godfather*), been given chances to try many different aspects of her field (she has a clothing label, done camerawork and costume design, writes, directs, and acts), and has been heralded as a young genius. "It is, perhaps, this combination of celebrity status, privilege and talent that causes some to regard Sofia Coppola's achievements with ambivalence," writes Pam Cook (36). Born into "her own bubble of Hollywood royalty" (Johnson 2), in the extravagant 1980s, we can see her cloistered childhood as paralleling Antoinette's, which stylistically evokes the pastel frippery, obscene spending, and punk music of the 1980s. Besides this personal comparison, there is much to be said for the Paris Hilton like quality Coppola gives to Antoinette. She is portrayed as a socialite who doesn't know any better (in terms of how much she is spending and how ridiculously opulent her lifestyle is). Antoinette breaks the norm of what is expected of a proper queen of her role and stature, is dragged through the dirt by the paparazzi and tabloids, has a tight clique of other socialite friends, and even carries her dog around as if it's the latest fashion accessory. The cute blondeness and pouty look of Kirsten Dunst (who plays Antoinette, and is a Hollywood child star herself) only helps to highlight the similarities between Hilton and Antoinette, socialite sisters 200+ years apart. The stereotypical connection between Antoinette and twenty-first century socialites is an unfavorable one. Amiel addresses this connection by saying, "In modern usage, the name Marie Antoinette has become the negative sobriquet of the female consumer gone mad" (2). The negative reputation today's socialites have hits a familiar chord with audiences (mainly adolescent girls) as they watch *Antoinette*. Coppola doesn't seem to be disregarding the possible validity of some of these tabloid accusations. With the "unembarrassed devotion to the superficial" (Lane 2) elitist clique Antoinette kept around her and the flagrant disregard for politics, Coppola gives us material to decide for ourselves about Antoinette's personality. Contrarily, Coppola justifies many of the queen's extravagant actions by showing Antoinette's unhappy life and naiveté, claiming she kept her characters, "in this bubble, because none of them realized what was going on outside their world" (Johnson 2). Overall the statement that these girls are being judged extremely harshly due to their presence in the spotlight, which they were born into, is being made. The film forces the viewer to re-examine the situation and decide for themselves how much of Antoinette's bad PR was of her own doing, and how much was unfairly attributed to her. Seen as a purposefully sympathetic image of the queen by some, Amiel claims that the film's main point is to show us, "Whether it is the 18th century or the 21st, the same pitfalls await anyone who achieves any sort of social prominence" (5).

The way in which we view the socially prominent is an important factor in the film. Image, the creation and destruction of it, is commented on continually. The portrait of Antoinette and her children in the garden by Adolf Ulrik von Wertmüller is recreated in the film. This portrait was considered "unflattering and insufficiently formal," showcasing the royal family in plainer clothing and less reserved positioning (Fraser 296–297 insert). Also shown in the film is the more austere and famous portraits of the royal family and Antoinette by Louise-Elisabeth Vigée-Lebrun. The portraits are utilized as a device to illustrate the passage of time, events, and the changing sentiments towards the queen. We see the image of Antoinette as the solitary object in the film frame. Only the banners with slogans "Beware of Deficit," "Queen of Debt," and "Spending France into Ruin" change throughout the shot, marking how the image of the queen is perceived by onlookers. The personal life of the queen is also determined through images of her. The painting out of Antoinette's fourth child (third in the film version) in the Lebrun family portrait is shown to convey the passage of time and familial events as the public would have seen them. Through using the iconic portraits of the queen, we catch a glimpse of how the *image* of Marie Antoinette plays into this story.

The image, and the use of it, is very important since we are first and foremost discussing a visual representation of a historical figure, and not fact. As her mother warns in the film, "all eyes will be on you." Much of Antoinette's life was just that, watched. Antoinette described this life as a voyeur's subject in a 1770 letter when she stated, "I put my rouge on and wash my hands in front of the whole world." She was watched as she got dressed, went to church, ate, walked around her home and even gave birth. In the film, we see the famed incident where Antoinette is left standing naked for several minutes because new and more prestigious, courtiers kept entering her chambers and the etiquette of who got the privilege to dress her had to be upheld. To this, Antoinette states, "This is ridiculous," and the Comtesse des Noailles retorts, "This is Versailles." The dinner ceremonies where courtiers and guests were allowed to walk by and watch the royal family eat is also depicted several times in the film. As time progresses we get the sense that Antoinette is starting to get used to this constant attention, but never as much as her husband who can furiously eat despite the confines of strict etiquette while Antoinette merely picks at her food.

Antoinette inevitably flouts this, and other standards of etiquette at Versailles, by hosting private gatherings and "handing out meats to a hunting party." Most representative of these rule-breaking behaviors is Antoinette's use of the Petit Trianon at Versailles. Although the actual time and reason she made this her second home is muddled in the film, what this place represented to Antoinette and to the public is much more important. The root of Antoinette's desire for the Petit Trianon is due to the simple fact that "She wanted a domain reserved for her intimate circle of friends" (Covington 4). In the film, we see Antoinette's love for the retreat as related to a longing for a more casual setting which she has dominion over. She plays with her daughter there, picking flowers and strawberries. The facade of this being a casual place is illustrated in the film by a scene which shows servants cleaning the chicken eggs before Antoinette takes her daughter to find them. The Petit Trianon was also the setting for many of the tabloid exploits of Antoinette. By cloistering herself off even more from the world, she had free reign to do and act as she pleased. This access to freedom is seen as a chance for wrongdoing by much of the eighteenth century press who imagined orgies, seduction, and extravagant parties at the Petit Trianon. This portion of the film is also representative of a shift in Antoinette's personality. The Petit Trianon sequence starts after she becomes a mother and we see Antoinette take pleasure in the seemingly more simple way of life. She is seen reading Rousseau to her friends asking, "What is the natural state?" as they sit in the garden in their new romantic frock dresses which, "suited Marie Antoinette's romantic idea of a simplified life" (Fraser 176). This is a contrast from her earlier character who asked, "Which sleeve do you like; with ruffles or without?" during a political briefing.

Another way Coppola uses Antoinette's disregard for etiquette is as an indictor of the public opinion of her. A scene in which Antoinette claps at the opera (which Princess de Lamballe tells her "is not usually permitted at court appearances") and everyone in the crowd happily follows her example is later juxtaposed by her acting in the same manner, though she is met with cold silence the second time. Her ability to pioneer trends, fashion, or behavior is diminishing as her rule-breaking is seen as menacing rather than refreshing.

For all of its controversy and extravagance, what exactly is Sofia Coppola trying to say with her rendition of *Marie Antoinette*? She seems not merely to be painting a more sympathetic picture of the famed queen, but to be looking closely at the girl, and what it means to be one. Exploring the allure of close female friends and safe home spaces, signified by the Petit Trianon and the de Polignac crowd, Coppola maintains an ambivalent attitude about the relationships between Antoinette and her closest friends, the Princess de Lamballe and Comtesse de Polignac. History and gossip has called them evil, lovers, and meddlesome females but Coppola looks at them like a high school clique. The claiming and owning one's sexuality, which we see Antoinette do once she meets Count Fersen, is also a rite of passage for girls that most of society today still ignores. Coppola comments on the many ways women employ their time and resources by showing the extravagance of the shopping and beauty industries, but also shows the joy it can bring as well. Power for girls is gained in this film through strong and pleasing personalities, malicious gossip and truthful exchanges, learning to play by the rules and by breaking them. Ironically, it is Coppola's refusal of the gravitas that historical dramas usually command that makes her revisionist version of Marie Antoinette as subversive and revolutionary as the girl she's portraying. This fluffier way of looking at history entices market audiences (i.e. teenage girls) and gives them something to relate to. Whether she gets the critics on her side or not, Coppola has succeeded in looking at a historical figure from a new perspective—that of the girl. Echoed by Antoinette to her newborn daughter, Coppola's *Marie Antoinette* tells us, "Poor little girl. You were not what was desired, but you are no less dear to me."

Works Cited

Amiel, Barbara. "Misunderstood Marie Antoinette." *Maclean's* 119 (2006): 48–50. Academic Search Premier. Pace U Lib., New York, NY. 24 Jan. 2007 <http://web.ebscohost.com/>.

Cook, Pam. "Portrait of a Lady: Sofia Coppola." *Sight & Sound* 16 (2006): 36–40. Academic Search Premier. Pace U Lib., New York, NY. 24 Jan. 2007 <http://ebscohost.com/>.

Covington, Richard. "Marie Antoinette." *Smithsonian* 37 (2006): 56–65. Academic Search Premier. Pace U Lib., New York, NY. 24 Jan. 2007 <http://ebscohost.com/>.

Doane, Mary Anne. *Femmes Fatales: Feminism, Film Theory, Psychoanalysis.* New York, London: Routledge, 1991.

Drake, Jennifer, and Leslie Heywood. "Introduction." *Third Wave Agenda.* Minneapolis: U of Minnesota P, 1997. 1–20.

_____. "We Learn America Like a Script: Activism in the Third Wave; or, Enough Phantoms of Nothing." *Third Wave Agenda.* Minneapolis: University of Minnesota Press, 1997. 40–54.

Fraser, Antonia. *Marie Antoinette: The Journey.* New York, London: Random House, 2001.

Gilbey, Ryan. "Never Mind the Bastille, Here's a Sexy Picture." *New Statesman* 23 Oct. 2006: 43.

Grossberger, Lewis. "Film Rouge." *Media Week* 16 (2006): 13–13. Communication & Mass Media Complete. Pace U Lib. New York, NY. 24 Jan. 2007 <http://ebscohost.com/>.

Gussow, Mel. "A Resolute Biographer and a Kinder, Gentler Antoinette." *The New York Times* 4 Sept. 2001: E1.

Harris, Anita. "Introduction." *All About the Girl: Culture, Power, and Identity.* Taylor & Francis, Routledge, 2004. xvii–xxv.

Heyman, Marshall. "Kirsten." *W* Apr. 2007: 256–267.

Johnson, Brian D. "Sex and the City in Versailles." *Maclean's* 119 (2006): 72–72. Academic Search Premier. Pace U Lib., New York, NY. 24 Jan. 2007 <http://ebscohost.com/>.

Lane, Anthony. "Lost in the Revolution." *New Yorker* 82 (2006): 93–95. Academic Search Premier. Pace U Lib., New York, NY. 24 Jan. 2007 <http://ebscohost.com/>.

Mantel, Hilary. "The Perils of Antoinette." *New York Review of Books* 54 (2007): 59–63. Academic Search Premier. Pace U Lib., New York, NY. 24 Jan. 2007 <http://ebscohost.com/>.

Marie Antoinette. Dir. Sofia Coppola. Perf. Kirsten Dunst, Jason Schwartzman. DVD, 2006. Columbia Pictures, Sony Pictures, 2007.

Pastor, Jennifer et al. "Makin' Homes: An Urban Girl Thing." *Urban Girls: Resisting Stereotypes, Creating Identities.* Ed. Leadbeater, B.J.R., and N. Way. New York: New York UP, New York, 1996. 15–34.

Phillips, Lynn. *The Girls Report: What We Know & Need to Know About Growing Up Female.* New York: National Council for Research on Women, 1998.

Vigée-Lebrun, Louise-Elisabeth. *Marie Antoinette, aged twenty-eight.* 1783. Bridgeman Art Library, Versailles. *Marie Antoinette: The Journey.* By Antonia Fraser. New York: Doubleday. 296–297, second picture.

_____. *The Queen with Three of Her Children.* 1787. Giraudon/Bridgeman Art Library, Versailles. *Marie Antoinette: The Journey.* By Antonia Fraser. New York: Doubleday. 360–361, second picture.

von Wertmüller, Adolf Ulrik. *The Queen with Her Children in the Park of the Trianon.* 1784. National Museum, Stockholm/Bridgeman Art Gallery, Versailles. *Marie Antoinette: The Journey.* By Antonia Fraser. New York: Doubleday. 296–297, ninth picture.

Putting the "Me" Back in Medical Drama: *Grey's Anatomy's* Adventures in McFeminism

Lara Hayhurst

Student Essay

FEMINISM'S THIRD WAVE longs to use popular culture and the media as a weapon of empowerment for women rather than an obstacle hindering their progression. The Third Wave propagates itself as not just a compromise between strident Second Wave ideals and the gutted superficiality of the Girlie Feminism movement, but as its own, progressive breed of feminism that is integrated, inclusive, open-minded, and tangible to all females. With this in mind, analyzing specific cultural productions that should ideally be serving as Weapons of Female Empowerment is an important exercise. Television holds an important place in our contemporary media, and by analyzing a television show with a large female viewership, such as *Grey's Anatomy*, that also quietly promotes itself as a progressive and feminist piece of pop culture, we can determine if this part of contemporary media and television is beneficial or detrimental to the ideals of the Third Wave.

When perusing critical responses to *Grey's Anatomy*, one encounters conflicting critiques that alternately brush the series off as daytime drama or consider it a dynamic, culturally progressive piece of television. This leads me to believe that while *Grey's Anatomy* has certainly taken the female fantasy narrative made so popular by *Sex and the City* much further on the feminist radar by including a multiracial cast and professional, yet flawed, women, the series also misrepresents itself as a progressive piece of VIT, or Very Important Television. It seems that *Grey's Anatomy* merely satisfies the appetite of cultural norms with a suggestive gloss of progressive feminism and color-blind casting. It cannot be denied, however, that this formula, and *Grey's Anatomy's* operation within it, certainly appeals to the sensibilities of today's average female viewer, which *Grey's Anatomy* identifies as its primary fan base: young women between the ages of 18–49 with generally upper levels of income (Lisotta 1). These women, whose ideas and writing can be read in a number of online *Grey's Anatomy* blogs and fansites, also seem to be self-identifying feminists interested in the series' portrayal of "strong, successful women" ("Feminism Friday").

Although *Grey's Anatomy* is now in its third season of prime time television on the ABC network, the program was initially a mid-season replacement that occupied a strategic time placement after the network's fantastical juggernaut, *Desperate Housewives*. However, *Grey's* soon developed enough of a fan base and high enough ratings to move into a night of its own (Gilbert 1). Set in the fantasy world of Seattle Grace Hospital, the series features a gaggle of surgical interns just beginning their residencies, and we experience their lives and loves as narrated by Meredith Grey, our protagonist. Though sometimes denigrated and brushed off as "nighttime soap opera with scalpels and condoms" (Gilbert 1), it cannot be denied that the series has momentum, significance, and a fiercely loyal and far-reaching fan base.

Ellen Pompeo, who portrays lead intern Meredith Grey on the series, claims that the girls of *Grey's* are more evolved and different from the "flawed bimbo" female stereotype that consistently appears on television (Freydkin and Keck 1), which is exactly what creator Sondra Rhimes had in mind when she began writing *Grey's Anatomy*. Rhimes, who must be credited as the first African American woman to create and produce a top-10 network series (McDowell 2), found TV drama's leading ladies existing "purely in relation to the men in their

The Third Wave Feminism Suite

Doctors talking in *Grey's Anatomy*.

lives," and then decided that she wanted to see more women on TV like those she knew—women who were "competitive and a little snarky . . . complex, ambitious, clever, confused women" (McDowell 2). The inaccurate representation of women on TV is nothing new; "although popular TV dramas . . . appear to present characters and plotlines that defy gender stereotypes, [Susan] Douglas still finds telltale signs of cultural bias against women in such programs" (Maasik and Solomon 270). Susan Douglas, in her essay "Signs of Intelligent Life on TV," reiterates the point that modern television strives "to suck in those women [middle and upper-income folks between the ages of 18–49] whose lives have been transformed by the women's movement while keeping guys from grabbing the remote" (272). This is exactly what *Grey's Anatomy* is striving to do; it appeases and appeals to first-world feminists, but hidden contradictions abound in their devotion to both the series and Third Wave Feminism.

One extensive feminist blog on the series, *The Thinking Girl*, praises the number of female characters on *Grey's Anatomy*, and how they are portrayed as "dedicated and deserving"(2), but it later admits that the men continually have the upper hand of the girls within the show. Dr. McDreamy (a.k.a. Derek Shepard), an attending surgeon involved in a complicated relationship with Meredith, is obviously superior to her because, as the site writes:

> He holds all the cards in his *marriage* because his wife cheated on him, and he feels that gives him a moral superiority that allows him to be an asshole to her. And [Meredith] has to deal with accusations of sleeping her way to the best surgeries, and claims of favoritism, while [McDreamy's] morality is never questioned in any way. But, he's just so darn dreamy! With that floppy hair and dimples, he is oh-so-hard to resist! (2)

Although many find McDreamy hard to resist, viewers also cheered Meredith during Season Two of the series when she issues a verbal diatribe to her boss, and former lover, after he decided to return to his aforementioned wife. Meredith begins dating and pursuing one-night stands after the break-up, and McDreamy, now devoid of the "moral superiority" that *The Thinking Girl* awarded him earlier, becomes jealous that he no longer holds Meredith and Addison in the palm of his hand. Now known colloquially among fans as the "Whore Speech" (Freydkin and Keck 6), Meredith rants:

> You don't get to call me a whore. When I met you, I thought I had found the person I was going to spend the rest of my life with. I was done. So all the boys, and all the bars, and all the obvious Daddy issues—who cared? Because I was done. *You* left me. *You* chose Addison. I'm all glued back together now. I make no apologies for how I chose to repair what *you* broke (Greysanatomyinsider.com 1).

This seems like a feminist message; girl talks back to man who did her wrong and unapologetically pursues her own sexual interests in his absence. It's smatterings of occurrences like this that provides *Grey's* with a feminist vibe. But what becomes of this exchange? McDreamy storms off, later recants and dumps the wife, and we are left with a simpering Meredith pleading to His Floppy-Hairedness; "Pick me . . . choose me . . . love me" (Greysanatomyinsider.com 1).

More examples of feminist contradiction occur when one fan/blogger later complements the "smart dialogue" and "good friendships" (Greysanatomyinsider.com 1) within the series, and then a few pages later rants, "wouldn't it be incredible if some writer out there could damn well come up with some real compelling female conversation?" (Greysanatomyinsider.com 7), because she feels that the girls, although important and professional, limit their conversations amongst themselves to that suitable to a gaggle of high school girls. But my thought is: would *Grey's Anatomy* be as successful as it is if they didn't? When fans are saying things like, "The setting, the medical emergencies—that's all secondary—in the end, I'm tuning in every week to watch [the girls] find love . . . and hope they get loved in return" (Freydkin and Keck 5), and, "My favorite is Callie. She's real. She rocks a size-12 body and she's Hispanic, which is awesome . . . and she's got the best lip gloss" (8), it appears that "feminist" women may long for a more stereotypical, culturally cookie-cutter life and romance then they may let on, and they may not be interested in the altruistic somberness of *Grey's Anatomy*'s older siblings such as *ER* and even *House, MD.*

Because *Grey's* fan base is over 68% women, and it is ranked number two in female viewership (second to *Desperate Housewives*), it is clear that women are buying what *Grey's Anatomy* is selling to them; a brand of McFeminism that makes them feel like progressive peers of the ladies of Seattle Grace. In reality, however, this McFeminism is merely a dressed up version of the same old thing; girls that need the leveling weakness of a messy love life, existential angst, and unflattering blue scrubs in order to make them culturally tolerable (Stanley 1). The men of *Grey's Anatomy*, who consistently have the upper hand in their female intern's lives, also happen to be a giant McSelling Point for the female viewers. Creator Wilson herself has said of *Grey's* men; "They were my fantasy men . . . they got to say and do things I wish men would say and do" (McDowell 2). So, these "fantasy men" are doing what their creator wished all men would say and do: punishing their respective intern's sexual/romantic mistakes by assigning them inferior duties at the hospital. Countless times in the series, if Meredith or Christina are acting inappropriately to their lovers, Drs. McDreamy and Burke, they will be denied access to surgeries by their respective attending, so the doctors' control over the interns extends past the romantic and into the educational as well.

To the credit of *Grey's Anatomy*, however, it does present us with a more utopian view of humanity that varies from TV dramas of the past where, as Susan Douglas puts it:

> . . . female friendships are nonexistent or venomous . . . Asian and Latina women are rarely seen, and African American women are generally absent except as prostitutes, bad welfare moms, and unidentified nurses. In the ER emergency room, the black women who are the conscience and much-needed drill sergeants of the show don't get top billing, and are rarely addressed by name (273).

Rhimes explains the racial diversity of her cast by saying, "If you have a show in which there's only one character of color— which is what most shows do— then you have a weird obligation to make that person slightly saintly because they are representing all the people of color . . . But if you have all different races, people get to be good or bad, flawed, selfish, and competitive" (Ogunnaike 3). These advances help make *Grey's Anatomy* more progressive than some of its earlier counterparts, and the series is also sometimes credited for the defibrillation of medical dramas like *ER* and the success of medical comedies like *Scrubs*, although fans of both shows have sometimes looked down upon *Grey's* for being short on altruism and long on "Hospital High School" drama (Gilbert 2), like when Addison Shepard (McDreamy's wife) finds Meredith's panties in her husband's operating room and posts them on the hospital callboard under a sign that says "Lost and Found." Instances like these humanize the serious world of the hospital, which viewers find appealing, but some critics think that it creates mere cartoons of characters that would be better served in a more austere medical drama (Gilbert 2).

What all of this information and critique boils down to, however, is that *Grey's Anatomy*, much like its fan base, is complicated and contradictory (an interesting thought, as the show's original working title was *Complications*). These are girls and women that want professional careers, personal control, and success; all the things that the femmes of *Grey's Anatomy* seem to have, but deep down inside they, and the surgeons, may just really want dysfunctional romance and some great lip gloss. With this brand of Diet Third Wave Feminism, we have upper-middle class females that don't identify with the commercial "girls-can-do" attitude of Girlie Feminism per say, but neither do they relate to the rigidness of the Second Wave. Are these women who can become active enough to actually do something and join the ranks of what Third Wave Feminism is all about? Or do they just want to put on the glossy veneer of a Very Important Feminist, much like *Grey's Anatomy* is Very Important Television?

Grey's Anatomy may actually be fostering a generation of young females who aren't, and don't want to be, blind to the issues of race, gender, class, and socioeconomic hardship, but nor do they want to mess up their aforementioned lip gloss. This is a generation that isn't quite as self-centered or issue-blind as the Ally McBeals of yesteryear, but neither are they the great, altruistic humanitarians of today . . . and *Grey's Anatomy* seems to be catering to those McFeminists just fine.

Works Cited

Albiniak, Paige. "Why 'Grey' Seems So Bright." *Broadcasting & Cable* 30 May 2005. *Business Source Premier Database.*

Douglas, Susan. *Where the Girls Are: Growing Up Female With the Mass Media.* New York: Three Rivers Press, 2005.

"Feminism Friday; *Grey's Anatomy.*" *The Thinking Girl.* 10 Nov. 2006. <http://www.thinkinggirl.wordpress.com/2006/11/10/feminism-friday-greys-anatomy.htm>.

Freydkin, Donna, and William Keck. "*Grey's* Ladies: Hospital Show's Appeal Lies with its Strong, but Flawed, Women." *USA Today* 21 Sept. 2006.

Gilbert, Matthew. "*Anatomy* of a Hit: It Doesn't Want to Save the World. And That's Why We Love It." *The Boston Globe* 7 May 2006.

Grey's Anatomy Insider Fansite. 26 Feb. 2007. <http://www.greysanatomyinsider.com>.

Grey's Anatomy. Internet Movie Database 26 Feb. 2007. <http://www.imdb.com/title/tt0413573>.

"*Grey's Anatomy*." *Wikipedia*. 26 Feb. 2007. <http://www.en.wikipedia.org/wiki/Grey's_Anatomy>.

Lisotta, Christopher. "Upscale Young Viewers Go For *Anatomy*." *Television Week*. 2 Oct. 2006 *Business Source Premier Database*.

Maasik, Sonia, and Jack Solomon. *Signs of Life in the USA: Readings on Popular Culture for Writers*. New York: Bedford/St. Martins, 2006.

McDowell, Jeanne. "A Woman and Her *Anatomy*." *Time* 22 May 2006.

Ogunnaike, Lola. "*Grey's Anatomy* Creator Finds Success in Surgery." *The New York Times* 28 Sept. 2006.

Stanley, Alessandra. "Television Review: Male Misery Just Loves Female Company." *The New York Times* 3 Jan. 2007.

"*La Femme Veronica*": Intelligence as Power in *Veronica Mars*

Gwendolyn Limbach

Student Essay

A CRITIC FAVORITE AND CULT HIT, *Veronica Mars* is hailed simultaneously as "so not the new Nancy Drew" and younger sister of *Buffy the Vampire Slayer* (Bianco). Yet this neo-noir, teen crime drama heroine goes beyond both female predecessors in not only her investigative prowess but also her agency on screen. Whereas Buffy finds her power in super-human physical strength to vanquish demons, Veronica locates her own agency in her intelligence, which enables her to solve her life and her town's many mysteries. Veronica's world is a complex puzzle unto itself: throughout the television series' first season Veronica must solve the murder of her best friend, Lilly Kane, whose suspects include the girl's father, brother, boyfriend, and lover; find the person who drugged and raped her at a party; and discover her true paternity. As Joss Whedon, creator of *Buffy*, writes, "Welcome to the funniest and most romantic show on television." Because of its complex plot and intricate characters, *Veronica Mars* goes beyond the usual teen genre fodder of other shows to explore classic noir themes as well as class and race conflict, sexuality, and familial relationships. Through Veronica's intelligence as a detective, she is able to exploit a traditionally male genre and role and expectations of girlhood, allowing her to survive not only high school but also the precarious culture of teen girls in the media market.

From the beginning of the first episode it is obvious that Veronica Mars is not an average high school student. Only when the camera rests momentarily on her textbook and she reveals that she has a Calculus test in four hours does the viewer realize this private investigator is a teenage girl. Veronica excels in school, as is apparent when she wakes from a daydream in her Advanced Placement English class to quote Pope's "Essay on Man." Her sassy attitude also reveals itself in this scene when she sums up Pope's meaning succinctly: "Life's a bitch, and then you die" ("Pilot"). But to define Veronica's intelligence solely in terms of school-learned knowledge and good study habits would only contain her in the "smart girl" stereotype of girlhood. Instead, she shows that her intelligence encompasses the world outside of school; she does not sit in the library pouring over books for answers, but instead uses intricate ploys, advanced technology, loyal friends, and skills gleaned from her professional P.I. father to solve her cases. For example, in the episode "The Wrath of Con," Veronica exposes college-aged computer

The Third Wave Feminism Suite

Veronica Mars looks at crime and culture in innovative ways.

scam artists through a myriad of tricks: disguising herself at once as a Japanime-looking gamer to steal an ID and then as a nerdy freshman to break into the suspects' dorm room; bugging the suspects' room; learning the code to the students' security system by recognizing keypad tones; luring the boys out of the room to see a game demo with another (imposter) prospective student; breaking into the dorm room again and dismantling the students' hard drive and backup drive. Here, and in many other cases, Veronica employs her knowledge of technology and of other people's psyches as well as the help of trusted allies to figure out not just the whodunit but also how to catch them. Many times, as one reviewer put it, "Veronica out-savvies people" through her use of "wit, spunk, and smarts" (Armstrong).

By the end of every episode Veronica possesses the necessary knowledge to solve the mystery of the day and says so rather than retreating into silence, which many young girls are forced into. In most instances she declares "I know who did it" or "I know what happened" when she has solved the mystery. Throughout the 22-episode first season, she makes these statements 19 times; unlike non-nerd smart girls who "simply [sublimate] their intellect into achieving recognition" in the social sphere, Veronica proudly announces her knowledge regardless of how others will judge her (Shary 244). Social acceptance is clearly not Veronica's goal as she reveals that she was once a part of the popular group because of her social connections, dating rich Duncan Kane and befriending his sister Lilly, but quickly fell out of favor with the others after Lilly's murder and the ensuing investigation. As Timothy Shary notes, most films today suggest that the "more valuable assets that grant girls success (popularity and respect) are fashion sense, physical beauty, agreeable attitude, and the attainment of a boyfriend" (236). However, Veronica Mars tends to contradict, and many times manipulate, some of these preferred assets to expand her investigations. When Veronica is commissioned by the vice principal to investigate the kidnapping of the school mascot, she

CHAPTER 6 • READING AND WRITING ABOUT GENDER

infiltrates the competing high school and quickly ingratiates herself with the jock in-crowd, noting, "Whoever said it's a man's world had no idea how easy it is sometimes to be a girl" ("Betty and Veronica"). By dressing like the in-crowd and acting the part of a ditzy ingenue, she quickly earns a seat at the popular table and asks questions of her suspects without suspicion. Veronica exploits cultural expectations of petite, blonde girls to get information from those that underestimate her.

In other instances Veronica utilizes her father's personal expectations of her intelligence to get away with rule-breaking in the name of investigating a mystery, at the same time living up to a rebuking patriarchal standards of gendered intelligence. Shary notes that non-nerdly smart girls are expected to be studious but not appear too smart. Veronica never shies away from appearing "too" smart, and she knows that appealing to her father's wish for her academic success allows her to accomplish more than simply telling him the truth. Four times in the season Veronica claims that she's doing a "school project" to either hide her investigations from her dad or get information from him. In one episode Veronica claims that she is trying to take a blood sample for a health class assignment on HIV. By playing on her girlish fear to prick her finger and her desire for good grades, Veronica tricks her father into giving his blood sample for what turns out to be a paternity test. Keith Mars jokes that his "bad-ass, action-figure daughter is scared to take a little tiny drop of blood" but in fact the joke is on him ("Drinking the Kool-Aid").

Whereas with her father Veronica plays on the "girly" stereotype of girlhood, once she is among her peers Veronica refuses to rely on any stereotypes to survive. Part of *Buffy*'s premise, and its major appeal to teens, is that "high school is hell, literally"; a similar concept can be applied to *Veronica Mars*. As Roz Kaveney notes, high school life is not easy for Veronica because she is "stigmatized as a slut because of her behavior under the date-rape drug [actually, GHB, not Rohypnol] and because she no longer has social power as Lilly's friend, consort of Lilly's brother Duncan, and the daughter of the sheriff" (178). Until she meets Wallace, a new student who is the victim of bullying by the town biker gang, Veronica has no friends or allies at Neptune High School. She endures snide quips from the school's "obligatory psychotic jackass," Logan Echols, and even a guest-starring Paris Hilton who remarks that "no one cares what you think Veronica Mars, not anymore" ("Pilot," "Credit Where Credit's Due"). Yet rather than retreating into silence, Veronica stands up to these in-crowd kids and creates a space for herself in which she is feared by some if not respected by all. When her reputation is once again tarnished along with that of a remaining popular friend, Meg, Veronica's advice is to "get tough . . . get even"; once she asserts herself, Meg tells her "people are afraid of you" ("Like a Virgin"). Here it is apparent that Veronica refuses to be relegated to the smart-girl trope where "either the smart girl is made to minimize her intellectual qualities or those qualities negatively affect her" (Shary 244). The friendship of her popular former friends is never a goal for this heroine; she has learned all too well that the rich, white, and powerful group is the most destructive one.

According to Anita Harris's introduction to *All About the Girl*, many researchers in girls' studies have noted the "now popular idea that girls lose their resistant and authentic voices when they engage with cultural requirements to shape their identities in line with dominant femininities" (xviii). In the case of *Veronica Mars*, viewers see through flashbacks that this popular idea was true of Veronica's life before Lilly's death and her own rape. Veronica caves to Lilly's peer-pressure over skipping the homecoming dance and isolates a potential friend after a misunderstanding at a party. When Veronica interacts with popular friends during these flashbacks her customary sarcasm and "green-apple personality" are conspicuously absent (Flynn, "Life on *Mars*"). It is only after Veronica encounters a peril too common among girls, rape, that she rebukes the dominant femininities she once tried to uphold, stating, "I'm no longer that girl" ("Pilot"). The new Veronica takes an active role in her life and relationships. Later in the season Veronica investigates the night of her rape and finally receives some answers. By having the conclusion to this plot thread delayed until the penultimate episode, Thomas does not place Veronica in a victim subject position throughout the season. Unlike some rape survivors, Veronica does not lose her voice like so many other girls but rather finds a stronger voice through her experience.

Veronica's voice, its authenticity, snarkiness, and the self-assured quality it gives Veronica, is one of the protagonist's most distinctive characteristics. Her voice is also key to the show itself through her voice-over narration and flashbacks, which reveal the teen's complex world and her reactions to it, making "Veronica sound like a hurt child one minute and Philip Marlowe the next" (Kelleher). This is Veronica's show, and we see it from her point of view; her authentic voice resists societal expectations of docility from teenage girls and instead makes itself heard in a patriarchal world. In her essay on Feminist Television Criticism, Ann Kaplan contends that "radical feminists emphasize that the silencing of the female voice results from male domination (252). Though this emphasis does not seem to be a specifically "radical" type of feminism, the author's point, especially in connection to *Veronica Mars*, holds true. Neptune, and the world at large, is dominated by men who exercise their agency over women. Until her rape, Veronica seems to be unaware of the patriarchal authority she is under, unaware that she is being silenced. After this experience, she realizes the extent to which her agency has been withheld from her and therefore reclaims it through raising her voice. Rather than launching into bra-burning protests to be heard, Veronica remarks on the state of her world through pop-culture awareness and references. *Entertainment Weekly* writer Gillian Flynn describes Veronica as "blithely brushing off adversity, launching bubble-gum-flavored retorts at everyone from disappointing beaus to bullying FBI agents . . . Veronica Mars is like a cute female Fletch" ("*Mars* Attracts"). Veronica mocks the expectations of quiet, studious girls repeatedly through the series. For instance, when Keith leaves town to chase a bail-jumper he suggests that Veronica stays with a friend and she replies, "And miss the opportunity to have the apartment to myself so I can raid the liquor cabinet and watch Skinemax? No, wait, I'm a girl. I'm gonna do all my homework, secure the locks, brush, floss, and crawl into bed with an overly protective pit bull. You don't have to worry about me" ("A Trip to the Dentist"). Though it looks like she places herself in this quiet, "girly" position, statements like this one mock the silence that society tries to force upon her. Frequently we see Veronica use her pop culture sensibility and language to confront the hegemonic white upper-class group and gain agency.

The theme of this hegemonic group as corrupt appears pervasively in the series. Veronica explains in the first episode that Neptune is "a town without a middle class . . . where your parents are either millionaires or work for millionaires" ("Pilot"). Though Veronica's character and her other lower-class friends look like and are usually coded as middle class, "her poverty status [exists] in comparison with the Kanes and Echols of her world" (Kaveney 181). One *Entertainment Weekly* writer notes that "the wealthy Southern California town of Neptune has a heightened-reality vibe" (Flynn). Veronica's class status is repeatedly the target of derision, especially by her antagonist Logan, the son of movie stars, but viewers identify with Veronica, Wallace, and computer wiz Mac rather than with the rich kids. Throughout the series, the sons and daughters of millionaires commit offenses more often than their low class counterparts that include drug trafficking, steroid use, student government election corruption, stealing money from each other, binge drinking that results in a coma, raucous parties, faking a kidnapping, extortion, and slipping GHB into drinks at parties. As Tom Gilatto notes in a review in *People*, "the show has definitely been flavored . . . by the nasty cultural down-trickle of real-life crimes of pampered West Coasters" ("Veronica Mars"). These infractions are much more visible than the crimes committed by the PCH (Pacific Coast Highway) biker gang, a group of tattooed, working class Latinos who frequently fail to graduate, yet the former group seems to evade any type of punishment. That is, of course, until Veronica Mars is on the case.

When it is up to Veronica is solve the crime, her first suspects are usually those at the top of the high school hierarchy; however, viewers see in the first two episodes that Veronica's first investigations take her to first suspect the same person, Weevil. He is the leader of the biker gang and is seen as a threat to Wallace and Veronica after he tapes the former to the school flagpole naked and taunts the latter about her reputation repeatedly. Keeping in line with the dominant cultural conceptions of the white power structure of Neptune, Veronica singles Weevil out as the "obvious" suspect after his grandmother is arrested for opening credit accounts in her employer's name. Both the grandmother's lawyer and the sheriff, and even Keith, believe that Weevil is the real culprit, so Veronica begins her investigation on this premise. Veronica has seen Weevil's criminal behavior previously, but when evidence shows that he could not have used the credit card she quickly reconsiders her position. Unlike the men around her, Veronica can shed class prejudices and expand her inquiries to other avenues. Instead of investigating someone who fits the criminal description in terms of Neptune's white upper-class standards, Veronica turns her attention to Logan Echols, noting that "80% of credit fraud is committed by a close relative" ("Credit Where Credit's Due"). Unfortunately the show fails to pursue the idea of the wayward upper-class delinquent by revealing that Weevil's cousin is guilty of fraud. However, creator Thomas does not swiftly send him to jail like so many other shows might do; instead, his crime is shown to be about betrayal of friends, family, and race (partly because the cousin used the stolen credit card to take out a rich white girl) rather than a transgression against the system. Veronica's attitudes towards race and class become more distant from those of Neptune's hegemony as the show progresses, revealing Veronica as one of the most socio-economically aware characters on teen-targeted television.

Veronica is also very aware of the existence, and dominance, of the patriarchy in Neptune and this knowledge allows her to resist containment within it. Within Veronica's world there are two main representations of patriarchal agency that she must confront: her father Keith and the school vice principal, Mr. Clemmons. Veronica's relationship with her father Keith is quite a rare one on television today and is, as magazine writer Jaime Weinman notes, "a bright spot in the world of television fatherhood." At the same time that the show is not one "in which father knows best," creator Thomas says that " '[a]s clever as we play Veronica, we always try to play Keith one step more clever' " (Weinman). This tension of who can outsmart whom sets up a struggle between not just parent and child but also dominant and dominated societal forces. Veronica as the lower-class teenage girl must work harder to gain knowledge and prove her intelligence than her already established P.I. dad, whose wealthy clients provide access to upper-class means of detecting through their ability to pay for any on-the-job expenses such as bugging equipment, etc. Even though Keith appears to know more than his daughter at times, Veronica is still a formidable force against him. She uses some of the contacts her father made as sheriff to get information and, as discussed above, can pursue investigations under Keith's nose by claiming to do mere school projects. And although Thomas wishes to play Keith as cleverer than his daughter, Veronica shows a keen detective prowess than amazes both her father and the viewer. For example, after stealing a crime scene photo of Lilly's room from her father's safe and comparing it to a video of a police press conference, Veronica proves that the evidence linking Lilly's convicted killer to the victim was planted in the killer's home. In the end, it is Veronica and not Keith who finds her friend's real murderer and turns him over to the police.

The scene in which she does this has met with criticism by some, including Kaveney. She contends that "the episode's culmination places Veronica in serious physical danger from which she does not escape by her usual intelligence—she has to be rescued by her father . . . in the season finale, it is a worrying drift away from message" (184). Though Kaveney makes a fair point that Keith must save Veronica, she fails to note that Veronica immediately then saves her father from being horribly burned. Not only this, she then takes his gun and finds Lilly's killer, Aaron Echols (Logan's father), and orders a bystander to call the authorities. In this instance Veronica possesses agency by solving Lilly's murder and controlling the resultant situation by wielding a gun. Although the series shows Keith as the main patriarchal representation in Veronica's life, it also reveals that Veronica has legitimate and successful tools to confront and defy this form of domination.

Her main device to do so, of course, is her intelligence and her use of it when others attempt to contain her, as is the case with the vice principal. Though Clemmons tries to be the authority in school, Veronica reveals in the first episode that she possesses more knowledge of Neptune High: "The [locker] searches aren't really random. I know when they're going to happen before Vice Principal Clemmons does" ("Pilot"). We realize that even though Veronica is an outcast among her peers and considered a problem student among her teachers, she still has agency in her school environment. Throughout the season we see Veronica reading students' permanent files, bugging an administrator's office, and even impersonating the school board president to get information. By the sixteenth episode Clemmons explicitly recognizes Veronica's intelligence when he hires her to investigate the disappearance of the school mascot. Though the two are positioned in traditional places of school administrator and student, with Clemmons standing behind his desk and Veronica sitting in front of him expecting to be punished for a crime she did not commit, the places of power are actually reversed. The vice principal lacks knowledge and must defer to Veronica as the most capable seeker of knowledge. Their positioning is ironic in that when a client appeals to a detective for help, the P.I. is behind the desk and the client in front. This reversal questions the physical and metaphorical positions of power within a school setting that tends to disenfranchise the working-class students.[1]

With "a girl scout's face and Philip Marlowe's jadedness" *Veronica Mars* is a singular representation of young female agency on television today (Poniewozik). With the influences of both third wave feminism and pop culture, this complex show confronts issues of class and race conflict, rape, murder, and personal identity. Through Veronica's possession and use of her intelligence, along with her continuous search for further knowledge, she is able to find an agency that would otherwise be denied to her. Her awareness of the hegemonic and patriarchal systems that attempt to control her world better equips Veronica to challenge these institutions. Although the series was canceled after its third season, fans and cultural critics alike must hope that Veronica Mars's influence can extend to female viewers as well as fellow teen girls on television.

---

[1] See episode 1.6 "Return of the Kane." School activities such as sports and student government, which require lengthy after-school commitments that many students with jobs cannot do, are awarded "Pirate Points." These accumulated points allow students special privileges, like ordering outside food for lunch among others.

Works Cited

Armstrong, Jennifer. "Bell of the Fall." *Entertainment Weekly* no. 796 (Dec. 2004): 36–7. OmniFile Full Text Select. H.W. Wilson. 23 Feb. 2007 <http://vnweb.hwwilsonweb.com>.

Bianco, Robert. "*Veronica Mars*: Intelligent Life." *USA Today* (Sept. 2004). Academic Search Premier. 23 Feb. 2007 <http://search.ebscohost.com>.

Flynn, Gillian. "Life on Mars." *Entertainment Weekly* no. 790 (Oct. 2004): 59–60. OmniFile Full Text Select. H.W. Wilson. 23 Feb. 2007 <http://vnweb.hwwilsonweb.com>.

———. "*Mars* Attracts." *Entertainment Weekly* no. 865 (Feb. 2006): 53. OmniFile Full Text Select. H.W. Wilson. 23 Feb. 2007 <http://vnweb.hwwilsonweb.com>.

Gilatto, Tom. "Veronica Mars." *People* 64.19 (Nov. 2005): 41. Academic Search Premier. 16 Feb. 2007 <http://search.ebscohost.com>.

Harris, Anita. "Introduction." *All About the Girl: Culture, Power, and Identity*. Ed. Anita Harris. London: Routledge, 2004. xvii–xxv.

Kaplan, Ann. "Feminist Criticism and Television." *Channels of Discourse, Reassembled*. Chapel Hill: UP of North Carolina, 1992.

Kaveney, Roz. "Watching the Teen Detective: *Veronica Mars*." *Teen Dreams: Reading Teen Films from Heathers to Veronica Mars*. London: I.B. Tauris & Co., 2006. 177–185.

Kelleher, Terry. "*Veronica Mars*." *People* 62.13 (Sept. 2004): 42. Academic Search Premier. 23 Feb. 2007 <http://search.ebscohost.com>.

Poniewozik, James. "6 Best Dramas on TV Now." *Time* 165.14 (Apr. 2005): 70. Academic Search Premier. 16 Feb. 2007 <http://search.ebscohost.com>.

Shary, Timothy. "The Nerdly Girl and Her Beautiful Sister." *Sugar, Spice, and Everything Nice: Cinemas of Girlhood*. Frances Gateward and Murray Pomerance, ed. Detroit: Wayne State UP, 2002. 235–250.

Weinman, Jaime J. "Wow! A Show with a Smart Father!" *Maclean's* 119.39 (Oct. 2006): 60. Academic Search Premier. 23 Feb. 2007 <http://search.ebscohost.com>.

Whedon, Joss. "Ace of Case." *Entertainment Weekly* no. 844 (Oct. 2005): 131. OmniFile Full Text Select. H.W. Wilson. 23 Feb. 2007 <http://vnweb.hwwilsonweb.com>.

READING WRITING

This Text: Reading

1. What is Third Wave Feminism? Which student paper most directly engages Dr. Pender's definition?
2. In what way is Third Wave Feminism related to the original ideas of feminism? In what ways is it a departure?
3. For what other television shows or movies would it be useful to use Third Wave Feminism as a lens?
4. What do you think a "Fourth Wave Feminism" might look like? What might popular culture in a fourth wave look like? Do you see any precursors now?
5. What might you find if you ventured outside the period defined by Dr. Pender and used the lens of Third Wave Feminism and examined a show like *I Love Lucy* or *The Mary Tyler Moore Show*?

Your Text: Writing

1. Do a close reading of a current television show through the lens of Third Wave Feminism.
2. Do a close reading combined with a research angle (similar to Dr. Pender's assignment).

The Third Wave Feminism Suite

3. Write an annotated bibliography on Third Wave Feminism or feminism in general. What trends do you note in both scholarship generally and the subject matter specifically?

4. After undertaking number 3, use this information to approach a text, and write this as a paper.

READING BETWEEN THE LINES

Classroom Activities

1. Send all of the males to another room to discuss a specific text. Now that all the guys are absent, hold a discussion for 20 minutes on one or two texts in this section. How is your classroom experience different without males around? Why is it different?

2. In class, watch a television show from the '50s or '60s like *Leave It to Beaver* or *Father Knows Best* or *Bonanza*. Compare the gender roles to those in a show like *Will & Grace*, *Frasier*, or *Ally McBeal*. What has changed? What hasn't? How do cultural norms and mores affect how gender gets represented?

3. Go around the room, and ask students to identify how they are themselves "marked," or ask them to provide one example of how they "do gender."

4. As a class, identify five famous women. How do they "do gender"?

5. Do the same with five famous men.

6. As a class, discuss why words like slut, whore, bitch, easy, loose, cold, frigid, and manipulative are generally reserved for females. Why are similar words used to describe males, like stud, player, gigolo, pimp, shrewd, and rational, so different from those used to describe women?

7. As a class, write a companion poem to Storni's "You Would Have Me White," but from a male perspective. What would the male's claim be? "You Would Have Me _____"

8. Is America more racist or sexist? Do you think we will have a African Amerian male or a white woman president first? What's your reasoning here?

9. Have everyone in the class bring in a magazine ad that has to do with gender or gender roles. When taken together, what emerges?

10. Break up into groups and discuss the contradictions of gender we see in television, movies, music, and magazines. Compare your answers.

11. Listen to some rap, country, pop, and folk songs in class. How are issues of gender reinforced by song lyrics, album covers, and videos?

Essay Ideas

1. Write a paper in which you examine and debunk three stereotypes about gender.

2. Most of the essays here have dealt with gender issues and women. Write an essay in which you examine how music, sports, business, movies, and even pornography determine what admirable "masculine" traits are.

3. Write a personal essay in which you examine three ways in which you "do gender." What do your means of doing gender say about you?

4. Write an argumentative essay about certain texts that you think are harmful in terms of how they perpetuate gender stereotypes.

5. Read a magazine that is aimed at another gender. If you are a woman, read *Maxim*, *Sports Illustrated*, *GQ*, *Details*, *Men's Health*, or *Field and Stream;* if you are a man, read

Cosmopolitan, Shape, Redbook, Ladies Home Journal, Martha Stewart Living, Ms., or *Working Woman*. Write a paper in which you give a semiotic analysis of the magazine.

6. Write a paper on daytime television. What messages do the commercials and the programming send to women (and men) about women (and men)?

7. As this book goes to press, there is a proliferation of pro-anorexia sites on the World Wide Web. Write a paper that is a reading of anorexia and/or bulimia. Why does this disease affect mostly middle-class white women? Why don't men suffer from these ailments?

8. Give a semiotic reading of male/female dating. What roles are men and women supposed to play early in the dating process? What behavior is okay? What is forbidden? How do we know these rules?

9. Go to the room or the apartment of a friend of yours of a different gender. Give a semiotic reading of that person's room. How is it different from yours? How does your friend's room reflect his or her gender?

10. Give a reading of the gender dynamics in your household. What gender roles do your parents or stepparents fall into? Your siblings?

READING AND WRITING ABOUT
public and
private space

REAL OR FAKE?: New York, New York Casino, Las Vegas.

WHETHER WE ARE IN OUR BEDROOMS, BATHROOMS, COFFEEHOUSES, CLASSROOMS, STADIUMS, OR RECORD STORES, WE ARE ALWAYS SOMEPLACE, AND UNDERSTANDING OUR RELATIONSHIP TO THESE PLACES AND SPACES GIVES US A BETTER UNDERSTANDING OF THE WORLD. HOW? BY PROVIDING US TOOLS TO UNDERSTAND THE WAY THE PHYSICAL WORLD INFLUENCES OUR INNER WORLD, THE WAY THOSE CONSTRUCTING SPACES INFLUENCE US—OR ATTEMPT TO.

In this introduction, we will talk about public and private space, architecture, and design as constructed texts. What we mean by **space** is the environment created by human-made activities, including built areas, such as classrooms, stadiums, shopping malls, and dorm rooms. Architecture and design are forces that help construct these places and spaces and give them their particular personality.

In a sense, architects and designers are the authors of buildings and public spaces; they construct these texts through a series of decisions. And if you look around you, not only will you see patterns of decisions made by architects and designers but you will also see the influence of those who pay the designers and the people who use or live in that particular space.

For example, architects may have had some leeway in designing your classroom, but their decisions about certain aspects of design or comfort might have been affected by their cost. The kind of institution you attend, whether it's a private or public university or college, probably had some impact on these decisions. The designers and architects were limited by function— putting a fireplace or a wet bar in a classroom would be inappropriate. And the designers were undoubtedly influenced by the period in which they lived; if you think about it, you can pinpoint the date within twenty years of construction based on colors, materials, and lighting. For instance, rectangular buildings built with brick or cinder blocks reflect the architectural style of the '60s and '70s, whereas a wooden Victorian house was probably built as much as 100 years earlier.

Such decisions also exist in corporate and retail venues. If you walk into a Starbucks, for example, you will see the results of a series of carefully made judgments: the color scheme, the décor and the lighting, the font type of the signs that describe coffee products, and where all of this is placed. It's not hard to gather from these aspects of design that Starbucks is going for both "cool" and familiar in its space. They want customers to feel they are not only purchasing coffee but that they are having some unexpressed secondary experience as well.

Is it one element that gives us this idea? No—it's a series of details taken together. Drawing conclusions from architectural decisions and public space is not much different than making these conclusions from reading literature; each has its own "grammar," symbols, and themes that we interpret to get a picture of the work as a whole. Here are some other things to think about when considering public space and architecture.

Colors and shapes often have symbolic value.

Part of the grammar we wrote about in the last paragraph (color and shape) helps architects and designers speak to the public in a language they understand, either consciously or subconsciously. Psychologists have shown that particular shapes and colors have psychological effects on their viewers. Designers and architects also draw on traditional uses of color and shape, again, as a sort of grammar of construction. Of course, homeowners may think they choose certain shapes or shades because they look "pretty," or "nice," but what they mean by pretty is of course arbitrary as well. Still, it is very unlikely that the walls in your classrooms are red or black. They are probably also not adobe, wood, or steel. We venture that they are not painted in a checkerboard style or with stripes. Rather, they are probably white or off-white, neutral in some way so as not to distract you from the process of listening and learning.

Combinations of these colors and shapes often form recognizable designs that are imitated repeatedly, especially in regard to public structures that want to suggest something beyond mere functionality. For example, arches, columns, and white picket fences often symbolize ideas that transcend their simple presence—arches and columns have often stood for power and tradition, and the white picket fence stands for tradition as well, but perhaps a different kind of tradition. The Washington Monument, for instance, on the National Mall in Washington, D.C., is, from a functional perspective, a poor use of space. You can't do anything in there. Its significance is symbolic; accordingly, a great deal of thought went in to selecting a design that would signify the values the government wanted. As important as the structures themselves are the spaces surrounding the structures. A house with a white picket fence around it is a much different text than a house with a high metal security gate enclosing it.

We associate certain kinds of structures with economic and social class—brick versus mobile homes, skyscrapers versus corrugated tin buildings, strip malls versus warehouses. Buildings and spaces are rarely *just* buildings and spaces. When it comes to public space, almost nothing is random.

Cost and community preferences often contribute to the design of a public or private space.

Although most designers seek to make buildings and spaces both beautiful and useful, there are other factors that often interfere with stated goals. Cost is always an issue—people can only build what they can afford, and some materials are prohibitively expensive for a given function. Design help can also cost money, as does land, construction and so on.

The surrounding community also plays a role in design. Community standards, often in the form of zoning laws, will have an effect on what something looks like. Zoning regulations determine the use of a particular piece of property and, depending on the locale, can also determine the size and function of what's built on that property. Even politics can help determine how something is designed. For example, at the University of Texas at Austin in the 1970s, a prominent student meeting-place was significantly altered when the administration built large planters to restrict student gatherings protesting administration policies. Similarly, at the State University of New York at Binghamton, a beloved and locally famous open space in the center of campus called the "Peace Quad," where students gathered to read, protest, talk, eat, and listen to music, was paved over so that a large new building could be erected in its place. Issues of class and race can also affect public and private spaces. For example, there are very few upper class communities near industrial plants, nor does one often find a poor neighborhood that has easy access to the attractive elements of a city.

In some cases entire communities determine how a city can look. Santa Fe, New Mexico, has a city ordinance that requires new buildings to have an adobe look. Hilton Head, South Carolina, prohibits certain kinds of signs. San Francisco, California, has some prohibitions on large chains and franchises. These communities are particularly aware that how a space looks can affect how we feel in that space.

Space can be manipulative, comforting, or both.

Designers have conscious ideas about the world they construct, and they often think about how and where they want people involved with their work. If you have ever found yourself frustrated in a poorly designed building, you may have wondered what idiots designed the place. The design of casinos, for instance, is most interesting. Casinos have no windows, usually only one or two exits, and you almost always have to walk through the slot machines to get to either of them. Why might this be the case?

In your life, how do elements of design work? Think about sidewalks. Do they always take you where you want to go? What about doorways? Are they always at the most convenient place? In your own room, think about where you put your desk, your chairs, and your bed: What is your main concern in placing them—your convenience or someone else's? All of those decisions influence those who enter your room. Think too about most classrooms at your institution. What do they resemble? Do they create a certain mood? For example, is talking about a movie or a story different in a large classroom than in a café? Why or why not? Sometimes places are friendly to their visitors or inhabitants; others are less so, either through oversight by designers, or more deliberately, as in the case of the Peace Quad or student protest space at the universities mentioned before.

What is important to know is that your emotional reaction to certain spaces is *intended*. If you have been to a court, then you know that the heightened judicial bench inspires a bit of trepidation; if you have walked in a particularly beautiful cathedral, the sense of awe you feel is not arbitrary; if you enter the library of an old or prestigious university, you probably experienced a hushed sense of tradition that was designed to be elicited in you when it was still in blueprints.

Users have ways of altering landscapes that can have personal and political implications.

One of these ways is through decoration. Humans love to personalize their spaces, whether it's a cubicle, an office, a dorm room, their computer desktop, or their cars. How we inhabit space is a means of establishing identity; space is a text we are always making and re-making. Think about your own spaces. Posters lining a room, particularly in the dorm rooms and bedrooms of your contemporaries, are usually there to send a message—that the inhabitant is a man or a woman, or someone concerned with music, art, beer, and/or cars. Some rooms scream that the inhabitants are trying to be cool, while others ooze sophistication.

When one gets older, it is usually time to say goodbye to the rock posters, M.C. Escher prints, and the beer ads, but what to replace them with becomes a question all of us grapple with for the rest of our lives. Some people decide they have a style they feel comfortable with and make their decisions based on that; others feel their way through the process; still others delegate their design choices to someone else. However, there are effects from these decisions, whether they are intended or unintended. The space you live in—how you decorate it, your traces within it—is a kind of text that people can (and do) read to understand something about you.

Entities as large as cities can try to influence the way its inhabitants and visitors feel. If you have visited Santa Fe, for example, you know that art is everywhere—in front of the state capitol, in parks, outside buildings, in restaurants, in courtyards, in and outside of private homes. The message this sends is not simply that Santa Fe and its residents like to decorate their landscape but that it is a place that values art, how things look, and how art makes you feel. The abundance of art sends a message of sophistication, worldliness, and a progressiveness that is welcoming. You may not always be conscious of it, but spaces that pay close attention to design and beauty probably make you feel quite good.

Of course, there can also be a gap between what the occupant of the space wants to suggest and what is actually suggested—in this way, spaces can be revealing texts. Knowing about space will help you not only be better readers of someone else's space, but may also help you avoid pitfalls of constructing unwelcoming space yourself. You may think that posters of near-naked women reclining on cars are cool, or you may think black mammy figurines are quaint, but there will be a sizeable audience out there who might wonder about you and your values based on how you arrange and decorate your space.

Other elements can change the landscape in ways not imagined by designers.

Graffiti alters the public landscape, and so does public art. Neglect can change public space, as well as new construction surrounding a previous design. How we use and design space gives some indication of our personality, among other things. Walking into someone's dorm room, office, or living room gives us a clue of who they are (and who they think they are). When you walk into a business, you also receive some indication of how they view themselves. For example, compare the interior at McDonalds to a fancy restaurant, or to a TGI Fridays, Applebee's, or Chili's; the interiors and exteriors are littered with clues about what these places think they are about. Similarly, how do Mexican restaurants tell us that they serve Mexican food? How do Chinese restaurants create an "Asian" setting? Think too about the way movies and television shows set scenes; often the settings of movies give us an indication of how we're supposed to view the characters. In *Frasier* or *Friends,* for example, we see the presence of couches, bright lighting, the expensive, clean apartments (in the case of *Friends,* far too expensive for New Yorkers their age) as clues to how we are supposed to relate to them.

Public spaces are especially curious in this way. Dams completely alter natural environments, flooding entire valleys. Roads paved through forests bring cars and tourists and pollution. In urban areas, for example, some public parks have become centers for both drug use and needle exchange programs—no doubt a *very* different use of public space than was intended. The authors live in New York City and San Francisco, and the two great parks in both cities—Golden Gate Park and Central Park—get used in ways the designers never could have imagined. We leave our imprint everywhere. And, just as we make our rooms or cubicles our own, so, too, do we make public space our own—for better or worse.

Ultimately, the space that surrounds us says a number of things about that particular location—who inhabits that space, what the space is used for, and how we are to read that space. Additionally, we can discern a great deal about what kinds of spaces or buildings are important given the amount and kind of space devoted to them. As you read this chapter, think about how certain spaces force you to interpret the world in a certain way.

THIS TEXT

1. How does the background of the authors influence their ideas about public space?
2. Do they define public space differently? In what ways?
3. Do the authors have different ideas about class, race, and gender? In what ways?
4. Try to figure out the writing situation of each author. Who is the audience? What does the author have at stake? What is the agenda of the author? Why does she or he want me to think a certain way?
5. What is his or her agenda? Why is she or he writing this piece?
6. What social, political, and cultural forces affect the author's text? What is going on in the world as he or she is writing?
7. What are the main points of the essay? Is there a specific thesis statement? Remember that it doesn't have to be one sentence—it could be several sentences or a whole paragraph.
8. What type of evidence does the author use to back up any claims he or she might make?
9. Is the author's argument reasonable?
10. Do you find yourself in agreement with the author? Why or why not?
11. Does the author help you *read* public space better than you did before reading the essay? If so, how?
12. How is the reading process different if you are reading an essay as opposed to a short story or poem?
13. Did you like this? Why or why not?

BEYOND THIS TEXT

Shapes: What are some of the dominant shapes you see in a public space or building? Do they symbolize anything to you? Are they supposed to? Do they remind you of other shapes in other spaces? How do the shapes relate to the space's use?

Colors: What are the dominant colors? What emotions do they evoke? Why? How would the space or architecture change if the color changed? How does the color relate to the space's use?

Size: How big is this place? How does this affect the way you view it, and the feelings it inspires? Is there a way to change the size to evoke different feelings? In what ways do the space's or architecture's size relate to its use?

Use: What is the use of this particular space or architecture? How do we know from the elements you see? Do you see unintended uses that might result from this construction? Do you see an emphasis on practicality or ornament in this space?

Interaction between architecture and space: How do the two work together? What elements in the architecture affect the way the space is constructed? Are there ways of changing this interaction?

Overall beauty: What is your general view of the place's beauty? What standards or criteria do you find yourself relying on?

Emotional response: What is your overall emotional response to this place? Why? What elements contribute to this response? What elements could you change that might provoke a different response?

Overall statement: What do you think this space or architecture says? What is it trying to say? How might this gap between what it says and is trying to say be changed?

Campuses in Place

Frances Halsband

Frances Halsband has worked on and in campuses for many years—as part of the New York architectural firm R. M. Kliment & Frances Halsband, as a professor at various universities, and as a former dean at Pratt Institute. Her firm has designed or renovated buildings as well as completed master plans on a number of campuses including Arcadia University, Brown University, Columbia University, Dartmouth College, New York University, Princeton University, Smith College, and Yale University. Here, Halsband examines the increasingly complex text that is the modern college campus. As you read, think about your own campus—how does it compare to Halsband's notion of what a campus should do and be?

Websites, View Books, and finally, campus visits.
Lost downtown.
No place to park.
"Mom, Dad, this is The Place. This is where I want to be."

THE BEST UNIVERSITY CAMPUSES are places that have been carefully designed over decades, even centuries. They are places that speak to us of continuing care, thoughtful decision-making, reverence for tradition and ritual, and a harmony of nature, landscape, and architectural design. They are places that invite us to participate in the thoughtful creation of our communal environment. They are familiar, inviting, alluring, mysterious. Richard Brodhead has defined the university as home: "a defensive structure," and a "world of belongingness thrown up against a larger world of exposure and strangeness"—but also, essentially and fundamentally, a "terra incognita," a place of "disorientation, defamiliarization."[1] Walking through the gates, we walk into the world of our future.

These qualities raise important questions for designers of new campus buildings and open spaces. Many American university campuses began on open land outside developed areas, but our cities have now grown to envelop them, complicating the distinction between "town" and "gown." Today, many American universities are called upon to be simultaneously inward-focused learning communities and outward-oriented providers of service and amenity. Embedded in urban settings, their greens may be, in some sense, public parks; their libraries, theaters and athletic facilities invite outsiders; and students and nonstudents mingle in adjacent residential neighborhoods and commercial streets—spaces whose rhythms are defined by the campus calendar, but which are fully open to the outside world.

Many of the most difficult issues faced by universities are apparent at their perceived edges. It is here that the characteristic tension between the university's desire to be both included and separated from the larger *polis* becomes most apparent. On campus, pressure to increase the density and scale of buildings often threatens the very qualities of space and social interaction which make campuses memorable. But when universities try to push outward, surrounding neighborhoods are likely to push back—and often with good reason, since these neighborhoods themselves have evolved into historic districts, with their own memorable and distinctive qualities of space and architecture. As a result, campus edges are frequently flashpoints of bitter controversy.

Faced with such strong opposition to external growth, university planners have recently begun to look for new ways to coexist. One consequence is that the original design paradigm of academic life around a campus green, so carefully considered and nurtured through the last century, is everywhere giving way to new informal places which hide their academic roots. Starbucks is now at the center—and at the edge. Off-campus housing is the new solution to on-campus life. Remotely located biotechnology laboratories are the new norm.

Are these new university spaces "campuses"? Or are they something else entirely? Have we lost the clarity of the original idea of "collegial" life to a blurring of domains; or are dynamic new typologies of mixed-use places for research and learning emerging? Will the next generation of children get out of the car in the middle of this new melange of university and city and announce *"Mom, Dad, this is The Place. This is where I want to be!"*

An American Ideal

In the United States, the early twentieth century was a period of intense focus on campus design. The Olmsted Brothers, Warren Powers Laird, Paul Cret, Ralph Adams Cram, Frank Day, Charles Klauder, and others provided campus plans for numerous universities. These places continue to serve as cultural paradigms. Early Olmsted plans showed individual buildings gathered around green lawns with curving boundaries and paths. Typical were the oval lawns of Smith College, shaded with (now) enormous trees, ringed with energetically Victorian buildings, and affording tantalizing glimpses of Paradise Pond. Later designs by Laird, Cret and Klauder kept the sanctity of campus greens, but interpreted them as formal rectangles, bounded by connected ranges of buildings, "where one building serve[d] to enhance, because of proximity, the value of another."[2]

The shape and style of these places was not merely scenographic. Woodrow Wilson, president of Princeton from 1902 to 1910, envisioned a collegiate system of educating the whole man, in and out of the classroom. To him, the college experience required "a certain seclusion of mind preceding the struggle of life, a certain period of withdrawal and abstraction." He described Princeton as "this little world, this little state, this little commonwealth of our own."[3]

Wilson himself sketched a physical reconstruction of the Princeton campus which joined the buildings into quadrangles, or separate colleges, such as he had seen at Oxford and Cambridge. Wilson's Quad Plan was realized in Klauder's romantic design for dormitories that recalled Gothic precedents. The success of such plans at Princeton later influenced Cret, Day, and James Gamble Rogers to make drawings of the Gothic quads which would become the signature elements of Yale in the 1920s.

But the idea of designing a series of quads to define an inner campus space was also not limited to Oxbridge styles. Klauder designed infill buildings at Brown University based on its colonial precedents. He also invented a Tuscan Country style to frame the quads of the rapidly growing Boulder campus of the University of Colorado. These campuses have since been admired, copied, and identified as special places.

Qualities of Space and Building

As Barbara Stanton explains in this issue, the essential ingredients of campus are greensward and trees, in a ratio favoring green over buildings. But a campus is also a place that expresses a complex mix of privacy and public purpose. The territories of many older campuses are today defined by iron fences and gates—though the gates are always open and the spaces inside welcome outside participation and use.

Campus landscapes are also furnished with signs, maps and information kiosks; artwork and commemorative plaques (free of commercial advertising) reward visitors' attention; and amenities such as benches, night lighting, and bicycle racks make them safe, convenient, and pleasant to use. Some of the great university campuses also include broad flights of steps which still invite us to sit and watch the passing scene.

In addition, the elimination of much vehicle traffic on campuses creates an oasis of safety and quiet. With fewer cars, there is no need for wide road beds, harsh street lights, or clearly defined sidewalks. A simple lane, wide enough for a fire truck, edged with granite, speaks of a great freedom of pedestrian activities—walking, meandering, contemplating, even sitting down. It is no wonder that rituals such as "chalking the walk" have become much loved traditions in such settings.

Memorable university campuses may also be distinguished by a prevailing architectural style. However, uniformity is less an end in itself than a means to provide the sense of continuity, background and identity against which distinctive individual buildings may stand out. In design terms it is a question of establishing a "ground" against which a "figure" may become visible. An identifiable building style may also inspire a sense of belonging. Thus one may think of Princeton and Duke as Gothic, Harvard as Georgian, and University of Virginia as Classical—even when closer inspection reveals far more diversity among individual buildings.

The sense of a planned building ensemble is clearly important to the sense of a campus. Even on campuses where relatively little effort is made to arrive at a uniformity of style, a sense of appropriate scale still emerges. Often in such cases the landscape is made to do the principal work of tying the whole together. Thus, the intense green leafy canopy of Amherst College unites two hundred years of building design; the University of Oregon is distinguished by a finely woven tapestry of tiny inhabited spaces; and, the bold new master plan for the University of Cincinnati creates a unified setting for a variety of contemporary buildings.

Still other campuses, such at that of Brown University, find their identity as places with deliberately contrasting styles. Brown's buildings are diverse, quirky, often brilliant, always individualistic—all qualities that embody the character of the place. At Brown one has to ask which came first, the diversity of thought characteristic of its intellectual atmosphere, or the diversity of its buildings?

While campuses are distinctive as ensembles, their best individual buildings also proclaim a certain public orientation. Signs tell you their names and what you may expect to find inside. Grand front doors welcome entry. Public buildings are located in many other places in our cities, but rarely do we find the same quality of invitation.

Qualities of Campus Life

In the city, informal interaction is rare, sometimes dangerous, and requires extraordinary circumstances. But on a campus a sense of containment and common purpose, the coordination of schedules, and the existence of shared spaces for dining and living increase everyone's changes of encountering others with common interests, goals and desires. Add to this the social vitality of young adults, and one can see how a high level of informal interaction is typical of campus environments. On campuses there are people moving about at all times of the day and night: outdoor furnishings will be used.

Creativity blossoms in such free-flowing nonhierarchical environments, and college leaders have long defined their mission as going beyond mere classroom learning. The founders of Pembroke College sought to create "a new academic atmosphere with that inner quietness which only spacious and dignified surroundings permit."[4] Likewise, the trustees of Brown in 1925 recognized that even dormitory rooms were integral to the college experience: "A student's room is not only an effect, but a cause of his character, and a worthy and dignified environment is felt at once in the student's intellectual and moral life."[5]

Well-designed outdoor spaces, and plenty of them; in-door spaces like libraries and student centers; numerous and diverse places where people feel welcome: these are all ultimately essential settings for the nurture of informed citizens.

Campuses Today

Many of the qualities described above have characterized American campuses for more than two hundred years. But the campus of the twenty-first century is also a very different place than it was fifty, or even fifteen, years ago.

As noted earlier, the most obvious change has to do with physical growth. Maps of Brown clearly illustrate this exponential increase of size. Such growth reflects the reality of increasing numbers of students, faculty and staff. Students need classrooms and places to live; professors need offices and laboratories; and library collections will continue to expand and require more space.

Along with growth in the number of buildings has come an increasing differentiation and specialization of building types. Yesterday's multipurpose gym has given way to today's indoor track, basketball and hockey arena, fitness center, swim center, and squash courts. Laboratory space has become similarly specialized. And to support the growing number of employees and students living off campus, parking garages are now needed, despite the best efforts at demand management.

The size and scale of individual buildings also continues to increase. The footprint of a research laboratory is now about 60,000 sq. ft., and a width of 130 ft. is deemed desirable. Such a behemoth will not fit easily on a carefully crafted historic campus. If located in an existing neighborhood, its associated impacts, including increased traffic congestion, will often be fiercely resisted by nearby residents.

As the old campus becomes a revered historic artifact—a "garden of delights" in which to enact historic rituals—it also becomes, ironically, less amenable to changes that might keep it vital in everyday use. Campus design guidelines, historic designations, tradition, nostalgia, and the force of alumni sentiment all combine to limit needed flexibility and change. Yet simultaneously, the desire to constantly reinvent and regenerate the institution requires expression in new forms, new styles, creating a parallel demand for associated places where new things are welcome.

Of course, there are very few, if any, old campuses which are so perfect that they cannot tolerate positive change. Architecture magazines and Websites show infill projects of subtlety and charm: new buildings, additions, and renovations which transform worthy old containers into exciting spaces for new programs. Indeed, the opportunity to work in a context rich with association, with a client group willing to take intellectual risks, makes campus commissions among the most highly desired by architects. Similarly, the best current campus plans manage to identify new building sites and craft design guidelines for them that reflect awareness of both contemporary and historical values.

A Question of Boundaries

Even so, the reality is that as universities face pressures for growth they have been trying to expand beyond their traditional edges. Examined collectively, such efforts seem to indicate that different types of campuses exhibit different potentials for development. In particular, some edges seem to invite incremental expansion, while others seem to demand a more radical leapfrogging to distant sites.

Campuses with clearly defined edges are more likely to expand by taking the form of the adjacent city. These extensions are likely to be commercial in character and made up of large-scale buildings which hug the street line. In such buildings, public uses are allowed to occupy the ground floor, and little attempt is made to continue patterns of associated open space or landscaping that might tie them to older campus traditions. Their style may express an overt rejection of historical campus precedents (even if the real choice was dictated by the necessity of making peace with the neighbors).

Designing new campus buildings to look like a part of the adjacent city, and including services, commercial and office space in them, are clearly strategies of camouflage and disguise. To appeal further to residents of surrounding communities, such "stealth" expansion may even involve inviting private developers to construct the buildings. Thus commercial housing developers are increasingly being called on to build and operate university housing, and Barnes & Noble may now be the university bookstore of choice.

Following this paradigm, Columbia's new student dormitory on Broadway includes a public library and a video store on the ground floor. Access to these spaces is from Broadway, while the students must enter their residence from a side street. In this case, the local community board indicated that its approval of the project was contingent on it being clad in Upper West Side yellow brick, not Columbia red brick.

The story of Ohio State's High Street development, described in this issue by David Dixon, shows the lengths to which campus planners have gone to address community concerns.

> Here is the key to the whole matter: The object of the college, as we have known and used and loved it in America, is not scholarship (except for the few, and for them only by way of introduction and first orientation), but the intellectual and spiritual life. What we should seek to impart in our college, therefore, is not so much learning itself as the spirit of learning. This spirit, however, they cannot get from the classroom unless the spirit of the class-room is the spirit of the place as well, and of its life, and that will never be until the teacher comes out of the class-room and makes himself a part of that life. Contact, companionship, familiar intercourse, is the law of life for the mind. The comradeships of undergraduates will never breed the spirit of learning. The circle must be widened. It must include the older men, the teachers, the men for whom life has grown more serious and to whom it has revealed more its meanings. So long as what the undergraduates do and what they are taught occupy two separate, air tight compartments in their consciousness, so long will the college be ineffectual.

—Woodrow Wilson
1905 Phi Beta Kappa oration at Harvard University[9]

Fuzzy vs. Hard Boundaries

Criteria for expansion are not as clear-cut at campuses whose edges are less well defined. Here opportunities may exist for expansion following a more gentle continuum, easing the tensions of the visible and fixed boundary, and paving the way for closer interconnection and interaction between town and gown.

Brown is one such place with fuzzier boundaries. Shared streets have provided an opportunity for limited expansion of its campus within the surrounding College Hill neighborhood. Such conditions have recently made it possible to plan for an extension of the campus walkway system to link the cores of the old Pembroke and Brown campuses across two city streets. The centerpiece of this plan is a new Walk, whose furnished green spaces are bounded by new academic buildings that open both internally to the greens and externally to neighboring streets. Among other things, the plan envisions retaining and reconfiguring significant historic buildings for new uses, while it also proposes moving one old house whose location conflicts with the new open areas to fill a gap elsewhere in the historic district.[6]

Another less obvious example of a university with fuzzy boundaries is New York University. Indeed, its edges are nearly impossible to identify. Over the years NYU has managed to expand largely by buying and renovating commercial loft buildings, transforming them into offices, classrooms, laboratories and housing, while maintaining commercial tenancies on the ground floor. While it has faced major battles in constructing new space, such gradual inhabitation of existing buildings continues without comment. In technical terms, New York zoning limits classroom uses to the area west of Broadway, but this boundary is visible only to university planners. On the street, the principal visual clue to the presence of NYU are the purple flags flown on all its buildings.

Moving Off Campus

In some cases, the edges of a university may ultimately prove immovable, and it may be essential to start anew in a distant place. This has long been the policy of the University of California, which has developed new campuses around the state rather than centralize its operations in a few locations. Today this process continues with the design and construction of a tenth UC campus in the town of Merced in the fast-urbanizing Central Valley. However, even in such situations, they point out, important questions surround the location and design of campus spaces, especially as they may be used to create new poles of growth or stabilize older patterns of development.

Smaller institutions can also employ a leapfrog strategy, especially when it comes to siting large new buildings. Brown is choosing to locate several large departments in buildings away from its existing campus on historic College Hill in areas of Providence dominated by abandoned manufacturing buildings and underutilized commercial properties. Eventually, it hopes to join the city in a broader redevelopment of one of these areas.

To maintain an identification with Brown, a new campus will need to have a physical connection through a clearly defined circulation infrastructure involving such elements as bicycle lanes, shuttle routes, and signage. The new satellite campus will also need many essential elements of the old campus: inviting furnished open spaces separated from traffic and surrounding commercial life, recognizable and permeable boundaries relevant to campus functions and the life of nearby communities, and buildings of public character and related scale.

Columbia University, long confined to an extremely hard-edged campus, is also planning a major expansion. Its new ensemble of buildings at Manhattanville will leapfrog geographic barriers and nearby neighborhoods and provide a link to their medical school campus further north. The redevelopment of Manhattanville is planned as a simultaneously urban and academic environment.

Literally and figuratively, this mixed-use precinct is being conceived as a "sandwich." It will be built on a "factory" of below-grade infrastructure and services provided by Columbia. But the three floors closest to street level will be devoted to public use. Above that, spaces will be occupied by university laboratories and other academic spaces. Renzo Piano has described this new effort as follows:

> The idea is not to make a citadel. One century ago, the only way to design a campus was monumental architecture, giving a sense of security. Today the university is in communication with life, so the story to tell today is completely different. It's more about permeability, more about participation. The model of the university today is more related to reality.[7]

Such a stratification of public urban space with academic space may well provide a new prototype for accommodating the variety of desires at the edges of the most urban university campuses. It allows local communities to maintain their identity, local governments to maintain the social fabric of the city, and deeply embedded urban universities to expand their facilities to compete with their peers.

The Future

There are some who would question the need for a "bricks and mortar" campus in our time. Stuart Strother recently described his experience teaching in a strip mall. Such "satellite campuses" offer the possibility for classes taught almost anywhere, books delivered by mail, and unlimited free parking. But he points out that students miss campus life, "the sidewalk culture of protest, music, art, free-love groups, and even hate groups that encourages students to think about life in new ways . . . the expansive common areas and green space of traditional universities [that] nurture expansive thinking and lively debate."[8]

The models for the future, then, include campuses disguised as extensions of the adjacent city, pieces of campuses constructed by commercial builders, satellite campuses of rented space, and Starbucks everywhere. Amidst such a collision of new ideas, however, it is important to continue to ask about the obligation, and the opportunity, that only an academic institution can bring to the city.

Is this not to continue to construct and maintain those very qualities of open space, architecture, and social structure that invite free participation and dialogue, the informal mixing places that nurture creativity, and the public spaces that offer a forum for learning in a free society?

Notes

1. Richard H. Brodhead. *The Good of This Place: Values and Challenges in College Education* (New Haven. CT: Yale University Press, 2004), pp. 3–4, 53–54.
2. Charles Z. Klauder and Herbert C. Wise. *College Architecture in America* (New York: Charles Scribner's Sons, 1920), p 40.
3. August Heckscher. *Woodrow Wilson: A Biography* (New York: Charles Scribner's Sons, 1991), pp. 145–53.
4. From *Bulletin of Brown University. Report of the President to the Corporation.* Vol. IV, No. 4 (October 1907), p. 31.

5. From *Bulletin of Brown University. Report of the President to the Corporation*. Vol. 1, No. 4 (October 1904), p. 9.
6. R. M. Kliment & Frances Halsband Architects/Todd Rader & Amy Crews Landscape Architecture LLC. "The Walk: A Proposed Design for the Extension of the Brown University Campus Joining Lincoln Field and Pembroke Green," May 27, 2004.
7. As cited in Robin Pogrebin. "A Man About Town, In Glass and Steel." *The New York Times*, Jan. 5, 2005, p. E1.
8. Stuart C. Strother. "The Stripped-Down College Experience." *The Chronicle of Higher Education*, February 4, 2005, p. B5.
9. As reported by President Faunce of Brown in the *Bulletin of Brown University. Report of the President to the Corporation*. Vol. II, No. 4 (October 1905), pp. 21–23.

This Text: Reading

1. What is Halsband's thesis? How does she support it?
2. Through what kind of lens does Halsband read college campuses? If this is a difficult question, think about what kinds of universities she mentions and how that colors her analysis. Are there community colleges here? Small state colleges? Would her reading of campus space work for your institution?
3. Toward the end of the piece, Halsband brings up the need for brick and mortar campuses. What function do actual campuses serve? How might be taking a class on a traditional college campus different than taking one online or in a strip mall?

Your Text: Writing

1. Give a semiotic reading of your campus. You can either read the campus as a whole—making an argument that it sends a specific kind of message—or, you can read a specific part as a microscope (a small thing that functions as a symbol of something larger). You might consult Dean Rader's essay in Chapter 1 on reading a campus for some help.
2. Write an essay on how the commercial and the educational merge at your institution. Does your campus have commercial enterprises run by outside vendors? Are there advertisements in rooms, in dorms or on campus elsewhere? In what ways does that affect the campus atmosphere, if at all? Does it detract from the stated mission of your university?
3. Find some aspect of your campus that seems nontraditional in its construction or use and give a reading of that space. You might consider off-campus housing, a virtual classroom, a space that merges with the community, or even a new dorm. What makes this place nontraditional?
4. Write about the college campus as a public place. What makes a campus public? Should a private university be a public place?

Spatial Segregation and Gender Stratification in the Workplace

Daphne Spain

Daphne Spain wrote this essay as part of a larger work, *Gendered Spaces* (1992). In this work, she writes about the way a specific type of public space—the workplace—and gender interact, an argument that you might find has implications beyond the workplace.

TO WHAT EXTENT DO WOMEN AND MEN who work in different occupations also work in different spaces? Baran and Teegarden (1987, 206) propose that occupational segregation in the insurance industry is "tantamount to spatial segregation by gender" since managers are overwhelmingly male and clerical staff are predominantly female. This essay examines the spatial conditions of women's work and men's work and proposes that working women and men come into daily contact with one another very infrequently. Further, women's jobs can be classified as "open floor," but men's jobs are more likely to be "closed door." That is, women work in a more public environment with less control of their space than men. This lack of spatial control both reflects and contributes to women's lower occupational status by limiting opportunities for the transfer of knowledge from men to women.

It bears repeating that my argument concerning space and status deals with structural workplace arrangements of women as a group and men as a group, *not* with occupational mobility for individual men and women. Extraordinary people always escape the statistical norm and experience upward mobility under a variety of circumstances. The emphasis here is on the ways in which workplaces are structured to provide different spatial arrangements for the typical working woman and the typical working man and how those arrangements contribute to gender stratification....

Typical Women's Work: "Open-Floor Jobs"

A significant proportion of women are employed in just three occupations: teaching, nursing, and secretarial work. In 1990 these three categories alone accounted for 16.5 million women, or 31 percent of all women in the labor force (U.S. Department of Labor 1991, 163, 183). Aside from being concentrated in occupations that bring them primarily into contact with other women, women are also concentrated spatially in jobs that limit their access to knowledge. The work of elementary schoolteachers, for example, brings them into daily contact with children, but with few other adults. When not dealing with patients, nurses spend their time in a lounge separate from the doctors' lounge. Nursing and teaching share common spatial characteristics with the third major "women's job"—that of secretary.

Secretarial/clerical work is the single largest job category for American women. In 1990, 14.9 million women, or more than one of every four employed women, were classified as "administrative support, including clerical"; 98 percent of all secretaries are female (U.S. Department of Labor 1991, 163, 183). Secretarial and clerical occupations account for over three-quarters of this category and epitomize the typical "woman's job." It is similar to teaching and nursing in terms of the spatial context in which it occurs.

Two spatial aspects of secretarial work operate to reduce women's status. One is the concentration of many women together in one place (the secretarial "pool") that removes them from observation of and/or input into the decision-making processes of the organization. Those decisions occur behind the "closed doors" of the managers' offices. Second, paradoxically, is the very public nature of the space in which secretaries work. The lack of privacy, repeated interruptions, and potential for surveillance contribute to an inability to turn valuable knowledge into human capital that might advance careers or improve women's salaries relative to men's.

Like teachers and nurses, secretaries process knowledge, but seldom in a way beneficial to their own status. In fact, secretaries may wield considerable informal power in an organization, because they control the information flow. Management, however, has very clear expectations about how secretaries are to handle office information. Drawing from their successful experience with grid theory, business consultants Robert Blake, Jane Mouton, and

Artie Stockton have outlined the ideal boss–secretary relationship for effective office teamwork. In the first chapter of *The Secretary Grid,* an American Management Association publication, the following advice is offered:

> The secretary's position at the center of the information network raises the issue of privileged communications and how best to handle it. Privileged communication is information the secretary is not free to divulge, no matter how helpful it might be to others. And the key to handling it is the answer to the question. "Who owns the information?" The answer is, "The boss does." . . . The secretary's position with regard to this information is that of the hotel desk clerk to the contents of the safety deposit box that stores the guest's valuables. She doesn't own it, but she knows what it is and what is in it. The root of the word *secretary* is, after all, *secret:* something kept from the knowledge of others. (Blake, Mouton, and Stockton 1983, 4–5; emphasis in original)

In other words, secretaries are paid *not* to use their knowledge for personal gain, but only for their employers' gain. The workplace arrangements that separate secretaries from managers within the same office reinforce status differences by exposing the secretary mainly to other secretaries bound by the same rules of confidentiality. Lack of access to and interaction with managers inherently limits the status women can achieve within the organization.

The executive secretary is an exception to the rule of gendered spatial segregation in the workplace. The executive secretary may have her own office, and she has access to more aspects of the managerial process than other secretaries. According to another American Management Association publication titled *The Successful Secretary:* "Probably no person gets to observe and see management principles in operation on a more practical basis than an executive secretary. She is privy to nearly every decision the executive makes. She has the opportunity to witness the gathering of information and the elements that are considered before major decisions are made and implemented" (Belker 1981, 191).

Yet instructions to the successful executive secretary suggest that those with the closest access to power are subject to the strictest guidelines regarding confidentiality. When physical barriers are breached and secretaries spend a great deal of time with the managers, rules governing the secretary's use of information become more important. The executive secretary is cautioned to hide shorthand notes, remove partially typed letters from the typewriter, lock files, and personally deliver interoffice memos to prevent unauthorized persons from gaining confidential information from the boss's office (Belker 1981, 66).

The executive secretary has access to substantial information about the company, but the highest compliment that can be paid her is that she does not divulge it to anyone or use it for personal gain. Comparing the importance of confidentiality to the seal of the confessional, Belker counsels secretaries that "the importance of confidentiality can't be overemphasized. Your company can be involved in some delicate business matters or negotiations, and the wrong thing leaked to the wrong person could have an adverse effect on the result. . . . Years ago, executive secretaries were sometimes referred to as confidential secretaries. It's a shame that title fell out of popular usage, because it's an accurate description of the job" (Belker 1981, 73–74).

Typical Men's Work: "Closed-Door Jobs"

The largest occupational category for men is that of manager. In 1990, 8.9 million men were classified as "executive, administrative, and managerial." This group constituted 14 percent of all employed men (U.S. Department of Labor 1991, 163, 183). Thus, more than one in ten men works in a supervisory position.

Spatial arrangements in the workplace reinforce these status distinctions, partially by providing more "closed door" potential to managers than to those they supervise. Although sales and production supervisors may circulate among their employees, their higher status within the organization is reflected by the private offices to which they can withdraw. The expectation is that privacy is required for making decisions that affect the organization. Rather than sharing this privacy, the secretary is often in charge of "gate-keeping"—protecting the boss from interruptions.

Just as there are professional manuals for the successful secretary, there are also numerous guidelines for the aspiring manager. Harry Levinson's widely read *Executive* (1981) (a revision of his 1968 *The Exceptional Executive*) stresses the importance of managerial knowledge of the entire organization. A survey of large American companies asking presidents about suitable qualities in their successors revealed the following profile: "A desirable successor is a person with a general knowledge and an understanding of the whole organization, capable of fitting specialized contributions into profitable patterns. . . . The person needs a wide range of liberal arts knowledge together with a fundamental knowledge of business. . . . A leader will be able to view the business in global historical and technical perspective. Such a perspective is itself the basis for the most important requisite, what one might call 'feel'—a certain intuitive sensitivity for the right action and for handling relationships with people" (Levinson 1981, 136).

The importance of knowledge is stressed repeatedly in this description. The successful manager needs knowledge of the organization, of liberal arts, and of business in general. But equally important is the intuitive ability to carry out actions. This "feel" is not truly intuitive, of course, but is developed through observation and emulation of successful executives. Levinson identifies managerial leadership as "an art to be cultivated and developed," which is why it cannot be learned by the book; rather, "it must be learned in a relationship, through identification with a teacher" (Levinson 1981, 145).

Because the transfer of knowledge and the ability to use it are so crucial to leadership, Levinson devotes a chapter to "The Executive as Teacher." He advises that there is no prescription an executive can follow in acting as a teacher. The best strategy is the "shine and show them" approach—the manager carries out the duties of office as effectively as possible and thereby demonstrates to subordinates how decisions are made. There are no formal conditions under which teaching takes place; it is incorporated as part of the routine of the business day. In Levinson's words, "The process of example-setting goes on all the time. Executives behave in certain ways, sizing up problems, considering the resources . . . that can be utilized to meet them, and making decisions about procedure. Subordinates, likewise, watch what they are doing and how they do it" (Levinson 1981, 154).

Just as in the ceremonial men's huts of nonindustrial societies, constant contact between elders and initiates is necessary for the transmission of knowledge. Levinson implies that it should be frequent contact to transfer most effectively formal and informal knowledge. Such frequent and significant contact is missing from the interaction between managers and secretaries. Given the spatial distance between the closed doors of managers and the open floors of secretaries, it is highly unlikely that sufficient contact between the two groups could occur for secretaries to alter their positions within the organization.

In addition to giving subordinates an opportunity to learn from the boss, spatial proximity provides opportunities for subordinates to be seen by the boss. This opportunity has been labeled "visiposure" by the author of *Routes to the Executive Suite* (Jennings 1971, 113). A combination of "visibility" and "exposure," visiposure refers to the opportunity to "see and be seen by the right people" (Jennings 1971, 113). Jennings counsels the rising executive that "the abilities to see and copy those who can influence his career and to keep himself in view of those who might promote him are all-important to success." The ultimate form of visiposure is for the subordinate's manager to be seen by the right managers as well. Such "serial visiposure" is the "sine qua non of fast upward mobility" and is facilitated by face-to-face interaction among several levels of managers and subordinates (Jennings 1971, 113–14).

Both Levinson and Jennings acknowledge the importance of physical proximity to achieving power within an organization, yet neither pursues the assumptions underlying the transactions they discuss—that is, the spatial context within which such interactions occur. To the extent women are segregated from men, the transfer of knowledge—with the potential for improving women's status—is limited.

Office Design and Gender Stratification

Contemporary office design clearly reflects the spatial segregation separating women and men. Secretaries (almost all of whom are women) and managers (nearly two-thirds of whom are men) have designated areas assigned within the organization. . . .

Privacy can be a scarce resource in the modern office. Empirical studies have shown that privacy in the office involves "the ability to control access to one's self or group, particularly the ability to *limit others' access to one's workspace*" (Sundstrom 1986, 178; emphasis added). Business executives commonly define privacy as the ability to control information and space. In other words, privacy is connected in people's minds with the spatial reinforcement of secrecy. Studies of executives, managers, technicians, and clerical employees have found a high correlation between enclosure of the work space (walls and doors) and perceptions of privacy; the greater the privacy, the greater the satisfaction with work. Employees perceive spatial control as a resource in the workplace that affects their job satisfaction and performance (Sundstrom, Burt, and Kemp 1980; Sundstrom 1986).

Not surprisingly, higher status within an organization is accompanied by greater control of space. In the Sundstrom study, most secretaries (75 percent) reported sharing an office; about one-half (55 percent) of book-keepers and accountants shared an office; and only 18 percent of managers and administrators shared space. Secretaries had the least physical separation from other workers, while executives had the most (Sundstrom 1986, 184).

Two aspects of the work environment are striking when the spatial features of the workplaces for secretaries and executives are compared: the low number of walls or partitions surrounding secretaries (an average of 2.1), compared with executives (an average of 3.5), and the greater surveillance that accompanies the public space of secretaries. Three-quarters of all secretaries were visible to their supervisors, compared with only one-tenth of executives. As one would expect given the physical description of their respective offices, executives report the greatest sense of privacy and secretaries the least (Sundstrom 1986, 185). Doors do not necessarily have to be closed or locked in order to convey the message of differential power; they merely have to be available for closing and be seen as controlled at the executive's discretion (Steele 1986, 46).

The spatial distribution of employees in an office highlights the complex ways in which spatial segregation contributes to gender stratification. Workers obviously are not assigned space on the basis of sex, but on the basis of their positions within the organization. Theoretically, managers have the most complex jobs and secretaries have the least complex, yet research on secretaries and managers with equal degrees of office enclosure suggests that women's space is still considered more public than men's space. Sundstrom found that "in the workspaces with equivalent enclosure—private offices—[respondents] showed differential ratings of privacy, with lowest ratings by secretaries. This could reflect social norms. Secretaries have low ranks, and co-workers or visitors may feel free to walk unannounced into their workspaces. However, they may knock respectfully at the entrance of the workspaces of managers. . . . *Perhaps a private office is more private when occupied by a manager than when occupied by a secretary*" (Sundstrom 1986, 191; emphasis added). This passage suggests that even walls and a door do not insure privacy for the typical working woman in the same way they do for the typical working man. Features that should allow control of workspace do not operate for secretaries as they do for managers.

Works Cited

Baran, Barbara, and Suzanne Teegarden. 1987. "Women's Labor in the Office of the Future: A Case Study of the Insurance Industry." In *Women, Households, and the Economy*, edited by Lourdes Beneria and Catharine R. Stimpson, pp. 201–24. New Brunswick, N.J.: Rutgers University Press.

Belker, Loren. 1981. *The Successful Secretary*. New York: American Management Association.

Blake, Robert, Jane S. Mouton, and Artie Stockton. 1983. *The Secretary Grid*. New York: American Management Association.

Jennings, Eugene Emerson. 1971. *Routes to the Executive Suite*. New York: McGraw-Hill.

Levinson, Harry. 1981. *Executive*. Cambridge: Harvard University Press.

Steele, Fritz. 1986. "The Dynamics of Power and Influence in Workplace Design and Management." In *Behavioral Issues in Office Design*, edited by Jean D. Wineman, pp. 43–64. New York: Van Nostrand Reinhold.

Sundstrom, Eric. 1986. "Privacy in the Office." In *Behavioral Issues in Office Design*, edited by Jean Wineman, pp. 177–202. New York: Van Nostrand Reinhold.

Sundstrom, Eric, Robert Burt, and Douglas Kemp. 1980. "Privacy at Work: Architectural Correlates of Job Satisfaction and Job Performance." *Academy of Management Journal* 23 (March): 101–17.

U.S. Department of Labor. 1991. *Employment and Earnings* 38 (January). Washington, D.C.: Bureau of Labor Statistics.

READING WRITING

This Text: Reading

1. Do you think such constructions of public space matter? Are symbolic values of space crucial in our world?
2. Do you think genders have different ways of looking at public space? If so, where does this difference come from? Why does it persist?
3. What do you think Spain's "writing situation" is? Is she writing from experience or observation? Can you tell by reading her essay? Why does this distinction matter?

Your Text: Writing

1. Find another environment where gender and space interact. What about the space you describe makes it connect to the particular gender?
2. Think about other public spaces or buildings where separation of people into genders, races, or classes is built into the design. (*Hint:* Think of places where people spend more or less money to sit in different places.) Are those spaces considered

problematic in the same way Spain thinks about the workplace? Write a paper that addresses this question.

3. Look at several dorm rooms or apartments of friends both male and female. Write a short paper that discusses which elements in particular define these spaces as particularly male or female.

4. Look at other things that are "gendered," such as advertisements, clothing, and cars. How do these gendered texts compare to the gendered spaces you described earlier? What elements do designers of any text use to designate gender? Write a paper that ties gendered space to another gendered text.

Making Space on the Side of the Road: Towards a Cultural Study of Roadside Car Crash Memorials

Bob Bednar

Bob Bednar has long been fascinated with the way we interact with public space. Here he writes about roadside shrines and the complex relationship that he has with documenting them. He is a professor of communication studies at Southwestern University in Georgetown, Texas. He previously wrote about tourist spaces for this collection's first and second volumes.

Road/Work

It's my first day of intense fieldwork while I am based in Santa Fe. I'm at the second of many stops on US-84/285, a four-lane divided highway north of Santa Fe that is under heavy construction. I'm running a fever, and the pace of my work is making it worse.

I have just finished photographing a set of three separate crosses near a busy intersection just north of Tesuque. The three crosses are all lined up in a row just on the outside of the guardrail on the east side of the road facing northbound drivers. The first displays a Harley insignia and the name Jerry Gurule (Fig. 1). About 30 feet ahead of that one is a five-foot-tall cross that says, "MOM." Fifteen feet farther up is a cross with a bear but no name.

Fig. 1

Standing there taking the pictures with cars buzzing by and nothing but a guardrail between them and me, I can begin to visualize why there are so many crosses here.

After filling up with gas, I take a U-turn to photograph a white cross I had seen a few hundred yards from the other three and on the other side of the road. Like the other three across the road, this memorial is just on the edge of the right of way. Unlike them, this cross is engulfed by road construction and blends into the collection of construction signs, surveyor's stakes, and recently-cleared brush. I miss it and have to circle back.

After I locate the cross again, I park in the only partially safe place I find: a wide shoulder where a group of trucks and cars belonging to the road crew are parked. I pop on the hazards and grab my cameras, hop out of the car, and run across the field of freshly graded dirt and gravel, dodging a water truck, a grader, and two front-end loaders in the process.

The cross is old, dedicated to Herman Padilla, Age 18, October 59 to February 78 (Fig. 2). The road crew seems to have left it undisturbed, but its space is entirely circumscribed.

The dash back to the car is even more daunting than the way there. "What the hell am I doing?" I'm telling myself as I approach the car. Out of the corner of my eye, I notice a white highway department truck driving up behind me on the shoulder. Its flashing lights are on. "Maybe he is going somewhere else?" I think.

I have enough time to make it back to my car and drop off my cameras before he is out of the truck and walking towards me. I meet him at the back of my car. He is wearing a hardhat and inscrutable wrap-around sunglasses. His face is sunburned. The traffic is buzzing by. His face is more than sunburned: it is angry.

"You having some kind of car trouble here?"

"No. Just taking some pictures."

"Well, buddy, this is no place to take pictures. There's a nice spot up there at Camel Rock where there's a parking lot and an overlook. Try that. But we can't have you out here like this. You're gonna get yourself killed."

The rest of the day, the rest of the trip, I feel more personally involved in a research project than I ever have before. I'm beginning to see that the connection is thematic. Early on in the project, I had wondered what was at stake in the practice of roadside memorials. Now I knew what was at stake for me, at least in the field. Roadside memorials speak in different voices simultaneously, functioning as testaments to lives lived and violently lost, but also as cautionary tales.

At each stop, I'm there on the side of the road taking pictures, thinking about the memorials, thinking about the horrible scene that must have taken place, thinking about the terrible but also often beautifully indifferent scene that now sits before me, trying to read between the spaces of silence and exuberance. And at each stop—especially the ones with narrow shoulders or blind curves, or the ones buzzing with traffic—I begin to think: Someone died right here. Right here! And here I am taking a picture of it. What if I die taking a picture of the place where someone else died?

Overlooking Violence

> In looking there is always something that is not seen, not because it is perceived as missing—as in the case of fetishism—but because it does not belong to the visible.
>
> Victor Burgin, In/Different Spaces: Place and Memory in Visual Culture (1996)

When I am driving doing mobile fieldwork, my eyes are peeled—on the lookout for anything resembling a cross. Some scream out to be noticed even at highway speeds.

Others blend into their surroundings, easily overlooked among other, more institutional road signs (Figs. 3 and 4).

Fig. 2

Fig. 3

Fig. 4

Fig. 5

Fig. 6

Fig. 7

I find a lot, but I know from recursive traveling that I miss a lot as well (and see ones once that I cannot find later). I also get a little jumpy about it: often mistaking fire hydrants for crosses, for instance. When you are looking for something, you find it—and you find other things that you can't recognize at all because your head is spinning with one command: "find the shrine."

It's an odd space to inhabit. Part of you hopes that you will see no sites at all, that no one else has died, that everything is going to be OK for just a moment or a mile longer. Part of you hopes there are more—for "research purposes." And unfortunately, on the roads of Northern New Mexico, there are lots of opportunities to feel the conflict in your gut.

■ ■ ■

The first few times I stopped at memorials, I felt horribly self-conscious, almost shameful. If you have ever stopped at a stranger's memorial, you know what I mean. If you haven't, I hope some day you will. You feel as though you have been suddenly transported into a stranger's bedroom, and there are people watching you look through other people's stuff (Fig. 5).

There I am on the side of the road looking at, photographing, and sometimes touching the intimately symbolic objects of a person's life, and I don't know who they are or how they lived or how they died (Fig. 6).

And yet, these are not bedrooms—or even living rooms—but spaces on the side of the road visible to all who drive by (Fig. 7).

Whatever else we might see communicated by the memorials, one thing rings through clearly: that the people who attach crosses and flowers to fences and trees and guardrails and build grottoes and shrines along the right of way think that they have the right to do so—think that there is room for them (or at least should be room for them) in public space (Figs. 8 and 9).

The memorials say, "I want to carve out a space in the landscape, and thus the culture." As folklorist Alberto Barrera says, "roadside crosses are a way of saying to the departed loved one, 'I will remember you always, but I also want for the community to remember you as they come face-to-face with the cross on the roadside.'"

This is particularly the case in New Mexico. In some states—Texas, for instance—it is illegal to construct and maintain a roadside memorial, but in New Mexico the state has embraced the practice, using it in billboards and other official public media DWI messages. There is even a descanso at the edge of the parking lot at the State Police headquarters in Taos (Fig. 10).

Even here, though, the state has followed other states in offering an official DOT roadsign to memorialize drunk driving victims (Fig. 11).

The personal sites mark space in a different way, creating a space for private grief to be memorialized in an already circumscribed public landscape, but what do they "say" to those who drive by? What actually is there at the site and what/how does it communicate and to whom? There are so many things there at some of the sites that it is overwhelming. Are the sites themselves so "multiplicitous" that they are rendered mute? Or is it that they are so personal that they are illegible to those of us "outside the code"? You know the objects are meaningful to someone, but what do they mean to you the visitor? These are texts open to public consumption, but not necessarily constructed for it. The content of the message—especially the story of how the person died—is an absent presence, sometimes simply an absence (Fig. 12).

On the other hand, when you find yourself face-to-face with a cross emblazoned with silk flowers spelling the word "MOM," you can't help but notice the subjectivity of it: it pulls you in and pushes you away at the same time, saying, "This looks familiar and intimate, but it really isn't (Fig. 13)." This is no objective statement about a person with a name you and I could say and be talking about the same person. This is no historical marker put up by the

Fig. 8

Fig. 9

Fig. 10

Fig. 11

Fig. 12

Fig. 13

Fig. 14

state to tell public history. This is constructed by someone who is radically situated and located—a person who defines themselves in relation to the person who has died. This is the place where someone's Mom died.

And yet, the flower arrangements themselves are standardized. Any person with a mom can go into the store and see the exact same Mom arrangement and think it will provide a fitting tribute to their own Mom.

And that is exactly where my mind is now on the side of the road, where I see the distinction between the two main functions of the memorials—to remember and to caution—

Fig. 15

Fig. 16

collapse. As much as I know my own mom is alive and well, I see the Mom cross and see it as my own mom. Or I see it as a memorial my daughter Anika and I might put up for Danielle if she were to die on the road.

And this last association is not at all random. You see, I am not alone on this fieldwork trip. Except for a day and a half while we are based in Santa Fe—when I am out working and they are playing in town—Danielle and Anika are right there with me the whole time, a barely absent presence always at least metaphorically and sometimes literally at the edge of the frame of my photographs (Fig. 14).

Mobile fieldwork is always intense and surreal, but it is particularly surreal while you are also doing a family vacation with a two-year-old: Each site we see generates an instant cost-benefit analysis based on a quick glance at the memorial: what impact would stopping have on everyone else? Is it too soon for another stop? Is everyone maxed out on memorials for a while? Is this site really worth a stop?

Fig. 17

When we are moving, we trade off driving and playing with Anika in the backseat. When Danielle is driving, I am in the backseat playing with Anika. I hate to admit that it takes me a while to learn to trust Danielle to see memorials and tell me about them.

When we stop, we say something like, "Anika, Daddy is going to stop to take some pictures." And Anika responds, "CHEESE!"

When I am driving and Anika is napping, Danielle is usually reading, creating a space for herself within the car, enjoying the moment of silence between bursts of toddler energy. I am doing something similar. I try to make mental notes of milemarkers in case we reach critical mass and the conditions are right for turning around at the end of the nap. Mostly I just talk to myself about letting go, or about what I've gained instead.

The car looks a little like our back room at home, and so do our activities: Living out of our car, dwelling in motion, we have taken our home on the road and made a home on the road. Distinctions between what we are researching and what we are playing and what we are thinking and what we are saying and what we are dreaming–they all bleed together.

Danielle and I have begun to call the trip "Winnie the Pooh and Descansos Too."

■ ■ ■

Anika is awake after a rare long nap.

"I thought you had him."
"I did, until Anika fell asleep."
"Oh, shit."

Winnie the Pooh is missing.

We finally figure out that we left him at a place fifty miles on the other side of Taos from where we are now. Driving the route again, I notice a memorial I missed the other two times I drove by that day. When I see it, I forget about my frustration with Pooh and am yet again happy that Anika is with me. It is about fifty yards up the road from a massive three-cross site I had stopped to photograph (Figs. 15 and 16).

The site I missed is unique, though: instead of crosses, this one features a Star of David. The wood on the Star is weathered and gray, which makes it blend into its surroundings. But this is only one reason I missed it. I was so busy looking for roadside crosses that I looked right past it—not just once but twice. What else have I not seen? What else do I not understand?

■ ■ ■

"In the Blink of an Eye"

> Performance, for me, functions as an episteme, a way of knowing, not simply an object of analysis.
>
> Diana Taylor, The Archive and the Repertoire:
> Performing Cultural Memory in the Americas (2003)

Back at home, I continually watch the paper for new deathsites to contemplate and photograph. In October, as I am finishing my paper for ASA, two separate groups of high school students in small towns south of Austin are involved in car crashes seven days apart. In the first, five kids die near Lockhart as the driver of the car overcorrects while steering around an Igloo Cooler sitting in the middle of the highway. In the second, a car plows into a high school cross-country team kneeling and praying on the roadside before their regular Saturday morning run. One runner is killed. Both stories run on the front page of the Austin paper. The second runs just above a story about how a disproportionate number of troops dying in Iraq are from small towns.

As with the space of fieldwork, here also I feel torn between the pain of imagining the actual losses for the families pictured in the paper and the excitement that I will have another site to explore. It's getting ghoulish, really.

The paper quotes Dale Guzman, one of the cross-country team members who was injured:

Guzman said he feels lucky to be alive, though sad that one of his teammates didn't survive. "He was one of our better runners and he was a good friend. I remember yesterday being in class with him . . . and the next day, in the blink of an eye, he's gone," he said.

In the blink of an eye. It seems an apt metaphor: Car crashes are so sudden that the victims and those who grieve the victims don't have time to process them. My guess is that no one who dies accidentally—not even a drunk driver—thinks it is going to happen to them until it is too late. Maybe that's why people construct roadside memorials: for those left to live and live with the story to have a place to physically embody their grief over time. But why on the roadside, and not in the home, or at the cemetery? Such a site could be (and often is) constructed in the homes of the survivors and at cemeteries, but the existence of ostensibly private memorials in public space shows that the people who made it want to remember publicly. A roadside memorial not only says "I remember you, and I will remember you," but also "I want the community to remember you."

■ ■ ■

A final moment . . .

I'm in New Mexico. I'm photographing another MOM site. This one is just a few miles from where we were camping for a couple of days, taking a break from the road. Part of the memorial is attached to the guardrail, and part is set just outside it (Fig. 17).

The cross carries the name, "Martha Martinez." The guardrail has a nasty dent in it. Is that from the crash?

Fig. 18

I'm moving around the site when something catches my eye: a child's handprint in the concrete holding up the memorial. The handprint is surrounded by several names. I assume that they are her children, the people for whom "Mom" means "My Mom." I move closer, feeling compelled to place my hand near it—for scale and for connection (Fig. 18).

I glance back at the car, which is idling on the shoulder up the road at the next safest pullout spot. Anika is napping and Danielle is sitting in the backseat next to her. I had to slip out of the window of the driver's side door to avoid waking Anika up with a beeping door.

I frame a photograph with the cross and the car together. Would I want Danielle and Anika to put up a memorial if I died taking this picture? What would I hope it "said" about me? What would it look like? How would their site be related to the existing one in the same exact place? What if they were hit in our parked car and died while I was out of the car taking pictures? Would I create a memorial? How would I mark the space? What would it look like? Would I answer these questions differently if it happened closer to home, where I could visit more often? What if we all died?

Standing there on the side of the road, witnessing yet another deathsite, I see that these are not idle questions . . .

READING WRITING

This Text: Reading

1. How much of this is storytelling and how much of it is analysis? Does it work?
2. Why do you think Bednar tells the reader how he feels when doing his work?
3. What other type of documentation might bring on the same mixed feelings that Bednar shares?

Your Text: Writing

1. Take some photographs, but as you are doing so, document what you are thinking about while you take them. Write about this experience.
2. Write a paper comparing this essay to one of the essays in the first chapter.
3. Write a paper researching the public displays of mourning. Where does Bednar's essay fit in this tradition?

How Suburban Design Is Failing Teen-Agers

William L. Hamilton

In this 1999 piece written in the wake of the Columbine shootings, William L. Hamilton, a reporter for *The New York Times*, writes about the inherent failings of suburban design and the way they affect teenagers in particular.

AS QUICKLY AS THE WORD "alienation" can be attached to the idea of youth, the image of isolation can be attached to a picture of the suburbs. Is there an unexplored relationship between them? It is a question parents and urban planners alike are raising in the aftermath of the Columbine High School shootings in Littleton, Colo.

At a time when the renegade sprawl of suburbs themselves is being intensely scrutinized, the troubling vision of a nation re-pioneered in vast tracts of disconnected communities has produced uneasy discussion about the psychological disorientation they might house. Created as safe havens from the sociological ills of cities, suburbs now stand accused of creating their own environmental diseases: lack of character and the grounding principles of identity, lack of diversity or the tolerance it engenders, lack of attachment to shared, civic ideals. Increasingly, the newest, largest suburbs are being criticized as landscapes scorched by unthoughtful, repetitive building, where, it has been suggested, the isolations of larger lots and a car-based culture may lead to disassociation from the reality of contact with other people.

Designers of the newest American suburbs say they have largely ignored or avoided one volatile segment of the population—teen-agers. In recent conversations, three dozen urban planners, architects, environmental psychologists and sociologists, and experts on adolescent development agreed that specific community planning and places for teen-agers to make their own are missing.

"They're basically an unseen population until they pierce their noses," said William Morrish, a professor of architecture and the director of the Design Center for American Urban Landscape at the University of Minnesota. "They have access to computers and weaponry. The sense of alienation that might come from isolation or neglect will have a much larger impact than it might have before. And there are no questions coming from the design community about what we can be doing about this. We don't invite them in."

Virtually every other special interest has been addressed by enlightened suburban designers—the elderly, the disabled, families with young children. But, said Andres Duany, a planner who is a leading proponent of the "new urbanism," a model of suburban design based on principles of traditional towns, "it's the teen-agers I always bring up as a question mark." Mr. Duany said that he had only once or twice included teen-agers in the public process of planning a suburban development.

"It's a good point," he said, as though it were an unlikely idea. "I should talk to the kids."

Though teen-agers tend to resist advice and choose their own turf as a territorial issue of establishing self-identity, most experts interviewed say that design could constructively anticipate and accommodate anxieties of adolescence. They agreed that teen-agers need a place to congregate in and to call their own; it is a critical aspect of relieving the awkward loneliness of adolescence. Between home and school—spheres compromised by the presence of parents or the pressure of performance—places for teen-agers in the suburbs are as uncommon as sidewalks.

"It's a paradoxical situation," said Ray Suarez, host of "Talk of the Nation" on National Public Radio and author of *The Old Neighborhood* (The Free Press, 1999), a study of suburban migration. "Parents move there for their children; their children are dying to get out." Like much of the Western United States, Denver is experiencing vertiginous suburban growth. From 1990 to 1996, the metropolitan area expanded by two-thirds, to its current size of 535 square miles.

"Typical of the Denver metro area are the new suburbs, where 'downtown' is a four-way intersection with three shopping centers and a condo development," said Charles Blosten, community services director for Littleton's city planning division. Highlands Ranch, Denver's largest suburban development, has its own ZIP code, "nothing but rooftops and miles and miles of nothing," he said of the numbing vista of houses. "It's got to affect people."

The idea that place has an impact on adolescent development and socialization is accepted by most experts on the suburbs but is only now beginning to be studied. "A culture of impersonality has developed in the suburbs by the way they're laid out," said Jonathan Barnett, a professor of regional planning at the University of Pennsylvania and author of *The Fractured Metropolis* (HarperCollins, 1996). In the newer suburbs, "the standard of houses is high, but the standard of community isn't," he continued, adding, "It's most people's impression of modern life."

And the people it stands to impress the most are children. "They are the most vulnerable people growing up there," said Dr. Jose Szapocznik, a professor of psychiatry and behavioral sciences and director of the Center for Family Studies at the University of Miami. "As a child you're disabled by not being able to walk anywhere. Nothing is nearby."

Mr. Morrish said he thought that public transportation to metropolitan downtowns was crucial for high school students. He said that the ability to access "the system"—the world adults create—was a vital form of empowerment.

"What to do after school, how to get to the city, to see other people and how to negotiate this without parents," he said, posing the issues. "Teen-agers have to have better access to the public realm and public activity." He recalled a conversation with a group of high school students who met with the Design Center, which invites teen-agers to group meetings when it is commissioned to study neighborhoods.

"One girl said, 'All I've got is the Pizza Hut,'" Mr. Morrish said. "'You go there a lot or you go to somebody's house—we're tired of both.'"

Between home and school, in a landscape drawn by cars and the adults who drive them, is there even a particular place that teen-agers can call their own? Peter Lang, a professor of architecture at the New Jersey Institute of Technology and an editor of *Suburban Discipline* (Princeton Architectural Press, 1997), a collection of essays, said: "In most suburbs, there's not even a decent park, because everyone has a backyard. But older kids never play in the backyard. They'll find even the crummiest piece of park."

Typically, the students at Columbine High School went to Southwest Plaza, a two-level mall that has video arcades, food courts and stores, supervised by security guards and closed by 9 P.M. "Like any suburban community, there's not a lot of places to go and hang out," Mr. Blosten said of Littleton. "I tell you this because that's where my daughter goes—the mall."

Mr. Lang said he thought that places like malls were not adequate gathering spaces for teen-agers, calling them, like many public suburban venues, commercially and environmentally "controlled space." He added, "They are not places for free expression or hanging out."

Disagreeing that suburbs create greater alienation is Dr. Laurence Steinberg, a professor of psychology at Temple University and director of the MacArthur Foundation Research Network on Adolescent Development and Juvenile Justice. But he said that he thought recent tragedies like the incident in Littleton do "wake people up to the notion that there is parental disengagement in affluent suburbs." He added: "We did a study on latchkey kids. The kids most likely to be left unattended for long periods were middle class, in sprawling professional suburbs. Isolated for long periods of time, there's no counterbalancing force to fantasy."

The desire for more and cheaper land that has pushed suburbs to rural exurbia may result in teen-agers who are alone for large parts of the day. Mr. Morrish pointed out that in communities like Modesto, in the San Joaquin Valley in central California, people commute to jobs in the San Francisco area, where they enroll their children in schools.

"Some people in California are taking their kids with them," he said, "making the kids commute."

The planners who have been most vocally and visibly at work on restructuring the suburban model have been "new urbanists" like Mr. Duany. Their solutions to the wheeling nebulae of tract development are based on tighter concentrations of houses, businesses and public spaces connected by townlike elements—porches, sidewalks and parks—that have largely disappeared from the new residential landscape.

If teen-agers find their place there, in new towns like Columbia and Kentlands in Maryland or Celebration, the Disney-built town in Florida, it is not because of any bravery on the planners' part. They often foster nostalgic views of families with young children. But like conventional suburbs, they overlook the inevitability of teen-agers in their design.

Peter Katz, who with Vincent Scully wrote *The New Urbanism: Toward an Architecture of Community* (McGraw-Hill, 1993), spoke of the importance to teen-agers of a place that existed only for them, neither hidden and ignored nor exposed and supervised—in effect, a secret place in full view.

On a visit, Mr. Katz discovered that for Celebration's teen-agers, it was a narrow bridge, "with low railings, that goes from downtown to the health club." He continued: "They find each other. They sit on the railing. It's on the route to daily life—not a back alley, but not the town square." Mr. Katz suggested that such a structure could become a conscious part of a community design for teen-agers.

For Diane Dorney, a mother with two teen-age children who lives in Kentlands, Md., a 10-year-old "new urban" suburb of some 1,800 people, the hallmarks of town life work well for both parents and children. Ms. Dorney and her husband, Mark, moved their family from a typical town-house development.

"We wanted to raise our kids in a place that provided more than just a house," she said. "It's a diverse community, of age and income," with older people, young couples, families. Ms. Dorney said that she thought the gaze of the town created a sense of extended family and moral weight that were its most important success.

"Someone sneaking down the street to have a cigarette—they don't get away with it," she said. "I don't think teen-agers should be left on their own until they're caught at the small things." She continued, "When they go into the big things, they know how big they are." She added: "And we have another way of knowing these kids, other than the bad things. They're your neighbors, too. You're always seeing them. You give them another chance."

READING WRITING

This Text: Reading

1. Although this is a work of journalism, does the author emphasize one side over another?
2. What do you think are the strongest arguments for or against teenagers' lives in suburbia made in the article?
3. In what ways did you find Hamilton's article addressed your own experiences? How much of teenage alienation has to do with public space?

Your Text: Writing

1. Write a short piece about your experience in the suburbs.
2. What would you say the philosophy of suburban life is? Write a paper articulating what you think this philosophy is.
3. What are the defining architectural ideas behind living in the suburbs? How do these ideas affect the way people live?
4. Drive through some suburban communities—both old and new. What do you notice about the public spaces and the way houses look? What do those aspects of the suburbs suggest about life there?
5. Write a short piece about the positive nature of the suburbs. Are there any cultural texts that would aid in your examination?
6. If you have grown up in the suburbs, think about your relationship to the suburbs at different times in your life. Is there a point at which you remember changing your ideas about where you live?
7. If you do not live in the suburbs, think about when you realized that there were places different from where you lived. Think about what you thought about these places growing up and what you think about them now.

Media and the City

Hugh Hardy

Hugh Hardy is an architect at H³ Hardy Collaboration Architecture in New York City. Among his most celebrated projects are: the new New York Botanical Garden Leon Levy Visitor Center (Bronx, N.Y.); reconstruction and addition of the Baseball Hall of Fame and Museum (Cooperstown, N.Y.); restoration of the Brooklyn Academy of Music's façade (Brooklyn, N.Y.); and the Packer Collegiate Institute's new school in a nineteenth-century James Renwick church (Brooklyn, N.Y.). In this short piece, Hardy argues that contemporary media "animates" a city. What are Hardy's arguments about media and the streets of New York? Is he convincing?

WHAT DEFINES A CITY? Cities are all about people, about their interaction, finding different ways to reach them with new forms of communication. Tall buildings, yes, and complex transportation systems, yes, and busy streets, yes; but what animates these urban places is the reciprocal actions of people. The media now make it possible for this interchange to take place in the streets at an unprecedented scale. The physical fact of New York's street grid roots everything in place as much as any of its individual buildings. The permanence of the streets continues to define a sense of place more strongly than any single piece of architecture or any electronic display.

The public realm is changing under the onslaught of new reproduction techniques. Whether these employ electronics or injection-molded plastic, they create "synthetic cities" like those found on late-night television talk shows. In TV studios the experience of performance is electronic *and* actual. It takes place in enclosed spaces where audiences can view both images of performance on monitors *and* the actual performance in front of them. Both are "real" in that they take place at the same point in time with the same people and settings, but what appears on the monitors can be more intense because they are viewed through the cross-cut images of different cameras at different focal lengths. By comparison the "real" actors and settings have less power and become the means to create a packaged product whose ultimate reality is electronic.

New forms of media have made communication in the public realm possible in ways that both define and embellish the urban environment. No place represents this more than Times Square, New York's L.E.D playground. This place of animated commercial messages assaults the senses in a glowing expanse of popular entertainment. It is where the diagonal of Broadway cuts through Manhattan's rectangular street grid to create the distinctive street plan of a "bow tie."

Shakespearean Theater Proposals

Joe Papp believed theater could be an effective way to reach the general public. He began in 1954 by using the streets as performance spaces and staging productions of Shakespeare with American actors, proving these four-hundred-year-old-plays could still come alive, revealing the human condition. He entertained the public for free, in the same way advertisers now delight the public with their colorful, digital displays in Times Square.

To honor Joel Papp, new performance spaces designed by H³ Hardy Collaboration Architecture form part of an exhibition on the subject of a Shakespearean theater for the twenty-first century, at the National Building Museum in Washington, D.C. H³'s design proposes two sites, one in Times Square and the other in waterfront parks around the city. Conceived as a way for major corporations to link their advertising programs to the cultural ambitions of this hypothetical theater, and to simultaneously present events to a larger public, we imagine a building that rises over the intersection of Broadway and Seventh Avenue. Here the auditorium and public spaces would be visually linked to the surrounding displays, programmed to enhance performance. The experience of attending plays would thus take place in an enhanced dimension that uses commerce to subsidize art.

To further pursue Joe Papp's idea of free, public theater brought to audiences where they live, a second building, designed to float, would offer possibilities for mooring in neighborhood parks in all five boroughs. When this mysterious non-nautical form is spotted gliding toward shore, it will excite curiosity and anticipation for the theatrical wonders it might bring. These productions would be visibly sponsored by the same corporations as those that inhabit Times Square.

Corporate sponsorship of cultural events is a long-standing part of the American scene, but in this project it offers a direct link between public advertising and the experience of performance in the city. In Times Square, instead of installing a simple billboard representing Shakespeare, we propose integrating images of the playwright and his history with simulcast presentations from the theater onto surrounding jumbotrons. Unlike simulcast presentations from the Metropolitan Opera House, which now take place in movie theaters across the nation, these productions would not be broadcast from hermetic, enclosed rooms. Rather, they would form part of an interactive environment, where both the production *and* the urban environment are visible at the same time.

This exploitation of the "synthetic city," of an electronic realm whose appearance is ephemeral and constantly changing, becomes possible at street scale. Instead of being represented by the permanent buildings of an enclosed architecture, where the public is separated from its surroundings, this project accepts an expanded realm of multistory digital displays. Even with these new frontiers of community definition, the permanence of the New York streets continues to convey both the historic and "synthetic" cities. These live side by side. Traditional theater performances will retain their importance—as will the traditional city, which survives as the measure of change that, by itself, can offer no orientation to time or place.

READING WRITING

This Text: Reading

1. How does Hardy define a city? Do you agree with his definition?
2. Why does Hardy think "the public realm is changing"? What evidence does he give to support his assertions?
3. How does Hardy connect media, the city, and theater? Do you agree with his assertions about these relationships?

Your Text: Writing

1. Give a semiotic reading of your hometown—city, town, village, whatever it may be—paying attention to how it defines itself in terms of public space. What argument does

your town make about the importance of public space, community, or even democracy?

2. Locate a specific example of media in a town or city—Times Square in New York, television sets in store fronts, music over loudspeakers, ads in subways, billboards along highways, and loops—and give a semiotic reading of that media. What does it say about the city? How does it affect human interaction? In what ways does it define the public space that contains it?

3. Hardy argues that media animates the city. Write an opposing essay in which you argue that increased media creates a static, distancing effect.

Reading the Nautical Star

Matthew King

Student Essay

Matthew King was a student in English 101 at Virginia Commonwealth University when he wrote this piece.

HUMAN BEINGS ARE EXTREMELY SUSCEPTIBLE to becoming creatures of habit. We go about our day without taking much notice of the people around us. We follow the beaten path on a kind of autopilot. One of the most traveled pathways near us is Schafer Court, and especially the newly installed Nautical Star (I have determined this title, for that is what it appears to be). Sitting and watching how people use the Star is a study in human behavior and habit. After a few hours of unintentionally voyeuristic "people-watching" I have found that the populace has turned an intended pathway into a place of congregation.

The Nautical Star is located directly in front of Virginia Commonwealth University's Branch-Cabell Library, a hub of student activity. Constructed out of tan and slate grey brick and bronze metal, it is inlaid into the burnt orange brick of the surrounding pathways. Four points around the Star illustrate the directions orientating the star, with North being slightly to the right of the library. The Star is surrounded also by the Hibbs Building, Schafer Court, and a pathway to VCU's Life Sciences Building. Given the immense traffic these respective locations draw, the Nautical Star becomes a hub for students and faculty who pass through it on the way to classes or meetings.

The first trend I noticed while studying the diurnal flux of VCU's student body was that the Nautical Star, seemingly intended as a centerpiece for Schafer Court, had succeeded in that regard. The heaviest flow of traffic was always on or around the Star, given that it has four main entrances and exits leading to some of VCU's busiest buildings. Viewing the people milling about the circular brick decoration reminded me of looking down at the flow of people going through New York's Grand Central Station. The determined, tight-lipped looks seen in New York were the same I saw at the Star, as well. These looks were evidence to me that most people used the Star as a pathway, focused only on their respective destinations and not on the newly built brickwork that they were treading upon.

Despite the mass amounts of people going their various ways, there is a sense of calm amidst the chaos. There are no collisions between human and bike, no traffic flow issues, and no heated run-ins. There seems to be a pervasive flow or path that all participants in the journey seem to subconsciously follow. In fact, it appears as if this circular star fed by four outlets of traffic maintains a strange, unexplainable sense of efficiency, upholding the Star's intent as a way to move people through a complex courtyard to the buildings and class-rooms where they need to be.

And yet, despite the seeming success of the Star's purpose (moving people and providing direction), I noticed that the people have quietly, perhaps unintentionally, changed the use of the Star. While the majority of the people follow the motion flow and move through the Star to their destination, a small faction have decided to buck the trend and instead use the Star as a meeting place, a destination as opposed to a gateway to a destination.

Given this fact, it is ironic that the designers of the Star saw no need to install seating anywhere near the Star. They did not think to allow a structure in which to facilitate people's lollygagging. The Star remains a directional guide, pushing the people through it, around it, anywhere but onto it. That said, the desire for people to congregate there and remain there seems at once unnatural and yet completely logical, despite the obvious irony of a directional device being used as a destination in itself.

Perhaps the explanation for the student body's decision to remain on the Star can be found in the layout and flow of the rest of the university. Being an extremely far-flung university, there are few main areas where mass amounts of the students congregate. In addition to the Schafer Court area, only the Student Commons (located approximately 3/4 of a block away) serves as a communal "meet market" and congregational area. That being said, however, the various designers that have toiled away at the university over the years have usually included ample seating around the veins of transportation. Benches, tables, unusually wide stairs and the like have been included to make student R&R an easily afforded benefit of campus life. Even walls near walkways have historically been constructed so as to facilitate easy seating and gathering, as evidenced by the Schafer Court/Cabell Library shared spaces. So it seems odd that VCU's latest addition to its conduit system would lack simple elements such as seating and gathering space. And yet, the students have created these things in a non-material way, simply seating when the mood strikes and consistently meeting with friends at the Star's center or edges.

In a way, the whole system is reminiscent of Fiske's comment in "Shopping for Pleasure" of the weak unseating the powerful. The intent of the designers was for the Star to be a place for mobility and information-giving, not a place to meet fellow students or friends. So why has the Star turned into something seemingly not intended when it was built? Perhaps the designers were too successful in constructing an attractive yet functional centerpiece for Schafer Court.

One main purpose of the Star, besides the ones mentioned above, was for it to be an attractive centerpiece for the university. Perhaps it was just that—an attractive centerpiece that people found so magnetic that they congregated there, drawn by the uniqueness and symmetry. Numerous groups of people gather on all points of the Star, engaging in conversation and gossip, scanning the hordes of passing students for friends and acquaintances. Meanwhile, solitary students dot points on the outside perimeter of the Star, waiting to meet friends and significant others for shared classes or a quick bite to eat at Hibbs. Some talk on cell phones, giving directions to the Star or encouraging the other party to hurry up. Whatever reason has drawn these people here, their behavior has turned the Nautical Star on its ear, so to speak. They have made a decision, though not necessarily a conscious one, to mold the Star to fit their needs and to make its seeming unfaithfulness to previous university constructs a seemingly meaningless issue in regards to seating and gathering.

Surprisingly, what I learned from this experiment was that taking a small slice of a person's day (their passage through Schafer Court and the Star) can actually tell one a tremendous amount about human behavior in general. People are often so set in their routine (or so tired or hung over) that they seem to blur out everything but their destination. In fact the zombie-like look of some members of the student body are almost frightening in their one-dimensionality. People seem bound to a sense of flow, almost unable to break free of a predetermined path. However unconscious these movements may be, a few of them tend to shatter the paradigm with outright force, neglecting the intent or focus of architects and work-a-day construction workers in favor of simple convenience. All of these observations prove that habit is a powerful force in our lives, and even if we don't realize it, we can subconsciously shift the intent of the powerful.

The Mall Suite

In his essay "The 'Magic of the Mall,'" cultural geographer Jon Goos claims "Shopping is the most important contemporary social activity, and, for the most part, takes place in the shopping center." If Goos is correct, then the most important social space in contemporary American culture is the mall. Much has been written about malls—from their appeal to consumerism, their constant persuasive techniques, and their connection to the American dream. In regard to this last point, Güliz Ger argues that malls accrue power precisely because they create and fuel personal and societal fantasies:

> Fantasies can be played out in a mall as a shopper walks in the mall, sits in a mall atrium, or is "waited on" by a responsive retail sales associate. Shopping malls provide semiotic messages, fuel consumer emotions and fantasy, and provide a stage for acting. The mall is a theatre where consumers can create their own world and fantasize their parts in a play.

The questions many observers have about these fantasies is how healthy they are, what they say about American life, and what is their future given the rise of a cyberspace that is already draining sales from a phenomenon that was thought to be invulnerable. This suite explores the mall as an almost monolithic text that plays on private emotions, desires, and fears.

Malls offer consumers a number of choices that on the surface are appealing to many visitors—shopping, movies, food, and even entertainment in the form of amusement park rides. But malls are also places where some refuse to shop if they can, because they find the space forbidding and deadening. Malls have addressed these concerns over the years, as potential clients have increasingly taken their chain stores to urban areas, which in themselves have caused critics to bemoan the urban mall in the making.

Although mall designers have become increasingly conscious of their design and function over the years, many city planners, social critics, architects, and cultural geographers have blamed malls for encouraging suburban sprawl, the rise of the strip mall, the deterioration of downtowns, the increased emphasis on cars, and even "white flight," which means white migration from cities to the suburbs, a trend of the 1960s and 1970s that mirrored the growth of mall development. How malls contribute to how lived and built spaces interact with each other (and the landscape) remains a sensitive issue. Just as the internal spaces of malls are complex texts, so, too, are the external designs and locations of malls.

The following essays read malls through various lenses. Nancy Backes views the mall through a semiotic lens, paying attention to the visual cues malls rely on. In her 1997 essay, she makes a connection between the mall and the city, arguing that malls try to convince us that they, like cities, can be lived in. James Farrell takes an entirely different approach in his analysis of the seemingly politics-free aura of malls. This piece comes from his 2003 book, *One Nation under Goods: Malls and the Seductions of American Shopping*. In the last essay, William Severini Kowinski traces the history of what he claims is the first black mall through a close examination of an important shopping center in Washington, D.C. His essay is also a chapter from a book, his 2002 collection, *The Malling of America*. We recommend all of these books for further reading on the semiotic, aesthetic, cultural, and architectural significance of malls.

The Politics of No Politics

James Farrell

THE GRAND OPENING of a shopping center is a festive occasion. Shopping centers help put communities on the map, because good shopping is understood as an essential element of the good life; towns without a mall are the backwaters of a consumer society. So as a sign of civic boosterism, the mayor of Mall City comes to cut the ribbon. Other officials put in an appearance, too, giving public approval to the new venture. But when the mayor goes back to the office and the cleaning crew begins sweeping up the confetti, the mall reverts to a private enterprise. The mall is the town square of American suburban culture; some malls are even called Town Square. But this doesn't mean that the mall is public space. According to mall management, the shopping center is a center for shopping, not for politics.[1]

Yet even if there's no politics *in* the mall, there is a politics *of* the mall. Shopping centers are inevitably political places; in fact, shopping center executives exercise a lot of political power to maintain their malls' apolitical policy. Malls are intimately involved in a politics of free speech, a local politics of zoning and financing, a state politics of taxes and growth management, and a national politics of regulation and environmental issues. Finally, along with the cultural politics of race and gender and class and desire, malls reflect and affect America's politics of consumption and citizenship. As historian Lizabeth Cohen says, "The commercializing, privatizing, and segmenting of the physical gathering places that has accompanied mass consumption has made more precarious the shared public sphere upon which our democracy depends." This chapter traces the basic contours of the politics of no politics in American malls.[2]

The Politics of Public Places

As Americans started going to malls in the 1950s and 1960s, and malls celebrated themselves as community centers, they began to look like public spaces—a combination of park and village square. With their large common areas, they simply felt more public than a store on the street. People in malls acted as if they were in public. They took pleasure in visiting stores and shops, in people watching and pedestrianism. Like the seaside promenade or the city park, the mall provided a space to go public with friends.

As it happened, the crowds of shoppers were also crowds of citizens. If you wanted to reach the public in person, therefore, the mall was a good place to do it. Community organizations like the Red Cross held blood drives, and charities sponsored book and bake sales. In the early 1970s, some shopping center managers felt that shoppers "bring both their money and their civil rights. They expect to be accepted with both and to be treated fairly and equally. They also naturally think of the center as a forum and maybe it should be, for constructive social and political activism." But the complications of politics on the premises were problematic, because the exercise of activists' civil rights caused customers to complain about "infractions of their human rights (Consumerism)."[3]

Since the 1970s, shopping centers have fought legally to keep politics outside the shopping center. Like broadcasters who depend on the advertising dollars of the mall's retail chains, shopping centers have tried to avoid activities that might offend customers—and, in a relentlessly privatist era, politics can be offensive. It turned out that some ideas were more "malleable" than others. When unions tried to picket at the mall, when political activists tried to leaflet, when groups tried to assemble to hear a speaker, they discovered that mall managers considered the shopping center private property and prohibited such exercises of free speech. Court battles ensued. Over the last fifty years, as Lizabeth Cohen suggests, "American courts all the way up to the Supreme Court struggled with the political consequences of having moved public life off the street and into the privately owned shopping center."[4]

Legally, the malls argued that shopping centers were a private business and could be harmed by the practice of free speech. Mall managers opposed demonstrations not because they didn't care about politics but because they cared about the sensibilities of their customers. Mall managers often marketed shopping as an escape from everyday life, and they expected people to be left alone (at least politically) in the shopping center. Many shopping centers, therefore, banned what has come to be called "non-commercial expressive activity." In essence, mall managers contended that you could have any kind of community life you wanted, as long as it didn't interfere with sales.[5]

At first, the courts contended that free speech rights didn't end at the property line of the shopping center. But a series of Nixon appointees to the Supreme Court modified that rule, suggesting, for example, that antiwar leafleting was an unwarranted infringement of property rights, because leaflets could be distributed in other places without distracting mall customers from the distractions of shopping. A 1980 decision, *Prune Yard Shopping Center v. Robbins,* affirmed both rights of free speech and private property, and essentially left the matter up to the states, where it remains. California and New Jersey have upheld the most liberal guidelines for free speech: according to attorney Suzanne Schiller, they decided that "a regional shopping center is the functional equivalent of a city street, and the free speech rights that people enjoy in a downtown area—to leaflet, for example—apply to shopping centers." But even states upholding the rights of free speech have given shopping centers a lot of discretion about where and when and how people may speak in the center. Mall management, for example, can determine where tables will be placed, how many people may be there, how they must be dressed, and what times are permissible.[6]

When we park our cars at the shopping center, therefore, we also park most of our rights to free speech, to assembly, and to privacy. We trade political rights for commercial opportunities. At one Colorado mall, a sign welcomes customers at the entrance by establishing the rules of dress and conduct. It requires "appropriate non-offensive attire" and requests that patrons "use trash receptacles located throughout the mall." It prohibits disorderly and disruptive conduct, including running, skateboarding, roller blading, and, less strenuously, loitering. It bans radios, pets (except seeing-eye dogs), and "dress that is commonly recognized as gang-related." And it asserts that "picketing, distributing handbills, soliciting and petitioning require the prior written consent of mall management." In some cases, when we enter the mall, we even give up our right to ask questions or take photographs. Basically, the rule is that we enter the mall to do what mall managers want us to do, and not much else.[7]

The result is that the primary political expression allowed at the mall is the politics of consumption, which is politically more powerful than any other politics. In fact, one of the latent functions of a shopping center is to create a space in which politics is seemingly suspended. In this way, shopping centers have been a part of the relentless privatization of American life, the *republican* agenda of the late twentieth century. Mall designs may evoke a feeling of public space, but it's primarily a simulation, meant to call up good feelings more than good citizenship.[8]

The Mall Suite

Local Politics

The pretense of no politics is itself political, but it's not the only political involvement of the shopping center. The politics of no politics often begins at the local level with zoning and tax-increment financing. Usually shopping centers locate on sites that have already been zoned for commercial development. But sometimes the mall displaces homeowners and other businesses, so the politics of zoning is part and parcel of developing shopping center parcels. In the search for a site, too, commercial developers can play one political jurisdiction against another, trying to get the best deal possible. And a good deal often comes from tax-increment financing.

You might think that people who believe in the privacy of shopping malls would insist on private capital markets for financing their projects, but you would be wrong. Tax-increment financing is a process that basically allows developers to build shopping centers now with the property taxes the malls will generate in the future. It's like a credit card for development costs, especially the costs of capital. A city or government agency sells bonds to provide money for infrastructure costs like land acquisition and clearance, and construction of roads and sewers. The bonds are secured by the promise of profits in the future, when the increased value of the land parcel generates increased property taxes for the city. The increased revenue is the "increment," and it constitutes the payoff to taxpayers.

Tax-increment financing is often used in special districts that need redevelopment, but it may also be used for new projects that seem to have a substantial future payoff. And malls often possess those payoffs. They generate jobs first in construction, and then in sales, and each of those jobs supports other jobs. They eventually generate tax revenues through real estate taxes and sales taxes. They often catalyze new construction and additional sales near the mall site, as restaurants and other retailers try to capitalize on the traffic flow to the mall. Shopping centers have important multiplier effects in the local economy.

But tax-increment financing isn't without its costs. Since the taxes generated by the new development go to paying off the bonds, they don't go to other projects, at least until the bonding is paid off. For the term of the bonds, the tax increment doesn't help school boards or counties or other governmental agencies that normally benefit from property taxes. Nor can the tax increment be used for the normal expenses of a city: police and fire protection, park and road construction, municipal programming or historic preservation. Those expenses are still paid by other businesses and taxpayers, some of whom could also use the sort of assistance the mall gets. And if the municipality overextends itself, its bond rating (which affects its borrowing costs) could be downgraded.

In general, tax increment financing favors the national chains of the shopping center over the independent mom-and-pop stores of the community. Independent merchants find it difficult to pay the increased rents in the vicinity of the mall, and they have a hard time, too, matching the advertising of the national chains. So the tax-increment financing of shopping centers can sacrifice the local character of retailing for the predictably larger incomes produced by national merchants. It can drive some shops off the tax rolls even as it adds others.[9]

Tax-increment financing often depends on unexamined assumptions about government responsibility for economic growth and ecological destruction. When City Hall considers whether to offer tax-increment financing for a development project, it seldom questions the assumption that more is better. It tends to focus on the financial benefits for the specific community, not on costs to other communities. It focuses more on economic considerations and less on social and cultural and familial consequences, and it focuses on the construction of a mall, not on the ecological consequences of consumption. It's politics in the service of private enterprise—and their privatized consumers.

State Politics and Sales Taxes

Shopping centers are not just a drain on public finances. Indeed, to the contrary, they are one of the primary sources of public finances, especially at the state and local level. Both sales taxes and real estate taxes are ways that shopping centers provide for the public treasury. The sales tax is a way of converting individual consumption to collective purposes. It's a way of making sure that a percentage of our private desire ends up in public projects. So even as we go to the private space of the mall, we're engaged in a public activity because in many states the sales clerk is also a tax collector. In 2000, shopping centers collected $46.6 billion in sales taxes.[10]

The sales tax is one of America's most regressive taxes. Poor people pay proportionately more in sales taxes than rich people do. With a 5 percent sales tax, a person who makes $300,000 a year pays ten times less (as a percentage of income) for the sales tax on a $30 pair of Levi's than a person in the same community making $30,000 a year. The tax, $1.50 on the jeans, is the same for both people, but the tax bite is very different. This doesn't sound like much for a single purchase, but since people with moderate incomes spend twice as much on clothes (as a percentage of income) as rich people do, the costs mount up quickly. The regressiveness of sales taxes is the main reason that progressive states exempt food and clothing from the sales tax. Localities that tax these items, and governments that depend on sales taxes, have made a political decision to let poor people pay proportionately more taxes than rich people.

The real estate tax is a levy on the assessed valuation of property. It's a way that people who have property, at least property of a certain sort, support the governments that protect their property and enhance its value with public improvements and services. Shopping centers aren't cheap, so they pay a lot in real estate taxes. They also tend to raise the value of land adjacent to the center, thus indirectly contributing more money to the public purse. Few types of retail development generate more money for communities than shopping centers.[11]

These contributions help our state and local governments, but they also amount to another example of government cooperation with commercialism and consumerism. With sales taxes, state and city income depends to some extent on consumer spending. As Ken Jones and Jim Simmons suggest, "State governments that depend on sales tax revenues have as large a stake in consumer spending as the K Mart Corporation." And it's not wise, presumably, to bite the hand that feeds you.[12]

The issue of suburban sprawl shows how the International Council of Shopping Centers gets involved in state and local politics. During the late 1990s, for example, the sprawl issue seemed to pose a threat to the shopping center industry. Vice President Al Gore proposed a "livability agenda" that included the regulation of suburban sprawl, and growth control referenda appeared on more than two hundred state and local election ballots in 1998. In an article "Antisprawl Raises PR Issues for Industry," Edmund Mander summarized the early responses. The ICSC responded with public relations releases reminding legislators that "people still want to live in a single-family home in the suburbs where there are new schools and there are new shopping centers, and they have a little more open space and they have a nice backyard." The organization also joined with the National Association of Homebuilders to publish a joint paper opposed to growth restrictions, and they worked with the American

Legislative Exchange Council, a group of three thousand state legislators dedicated to free-market principles and limited government, to draft legislation to require economic impact studies before enacting limits to growth.[13]

National Politics

At the national level, there's not much direct support for malls. The Federal Interstate Highway Act indirectly supports suburbs and suburban institutions like shopping centers. Federal transportation policy helped create the infrastructure for malls, because highways attract the business of Americans who mainly get about in cars. There are not massive national subsidies for shopping centers, but the federal government still sets important parameters for America's malls.

Consequently, the ICSC also engages in Washington politics. "Politics is serious business," the council says. "The passage of one bill in the U.S. Congress alone can make a greater impact on the future of our industry than many decisions made by your own management." The ICSC web page thus includes a "Government" section that begins, "On behalf of our members, ICSC works with legislative offices and agencies on timely regulatory issues pertaining to the shopping center industry. ICSC operates a grassroots mobilization program, the Shopping Center Action Network, SCAN, an annual Congressional Contacts Meeting, and a Political Action Committee, ICSC PAC. Our Government Relations staff works closely with ICSC members who voluntarily serve on Committees and Subcommittees pertaining to their areas of interest."[14]

The ICSC Government Relations people monitor issues at both state and federal levels. At the national level, their primary issues are economic and environmental. Economically, the organization is interested in taxation of Internet sales, capital gains, the Americans with Disabilities Act, bankruptcy reform, and cost recovery of leasehold improvements. Environmentally, the shopping center industry worries about regulations that put undue restrictions on private property rights. So they support reforms of the Endangered Species Act and of wetlands regulations in the Clean Water Act. They also support regulatory relief in brownfields redevelopment, and promote restraint of "smart growth" initiatives that try to contain suburban sprawl.[15]

In addition, a "fast action" page on the organization's web site makes it easy for members to register their opinions with their legislators. In June 2000, the site instructed members to "Tell Congress You Want a Fair and Level Playing Field." Concerned that "the competitive tax advantage that Internet-based retailers currently enjoy could result in the loss of billions of dollars in future revenues to shopping centers, traditional merchants, and local communities," the ICSC advised its members to lobby for a sales tax on both Internet and catalogue sales.[16]

In addition to getting members involved in politics, the ICSC takes a part in electing and lobbying federal officials. Its political action committee, ICSC PAC, was established in 1988 "to help elect federal office candidates who favor the shopping center industry and its goals and initiatives." In the 1996 elections, the shopping center industry funded 120 campaigns, and "seventy percent of Senate candidates and 84 percent of House candidates supported by ICSC PAC won their respective elections." Consequently, "visiting with ICSC staff and members has now become a routine stop for most federal candidates."[17]

The ICSC is assisted in the politics of shopping malls by organizations like the National Retail Federation (NRF) and the International Mass Retail Association (IMRA). The National

Retail Federation asserts that "when NRF speaks, government listens. It listens because NRF is the world's largest retail trade association, a true federation made up of major nationally known retailers and independent stores, 50 state retail associations, and more than 30 national retail organizations." Recently, the NRF has lobbied for the elimination of the estate tax, for bankruptcy reform, for free trade with China, against new ergonomics standards for the workplace, and against increases in the minimum wage. Like the ICSC and NRF, the IMRA also supports "reasonable" regulation, defined generally as regulation with fewer restrictions on commercial enterprises. It also opposes increases in the minimum wage, supports free trade, and calls for civil justice reforms restricting class action and product liability lawsuits. There's a lot of politics in American commerce, and vice versa.[18]

Trade industry organizations set a political agenda that provides for the health of the industry, but other issues could also prove helpful to shopping centers. An end to poverty, for example, would be good business for America's malls. The ICSC's own statistics show that poor people make up almost 20 percent of the American population but only about 7 percent of mall shoppers. Still, poverty tends not to be a priority in ICSC political discussions. People who sell status apparently can't afford to mess too much with the status quo.[19]

The Politics of Consumption

Even though they prohibit politics on the premises, shopping centers are deeply involved in American politics at every level. They regularly use America's political institutions to support the politics of no politics at the mall, lobbying for legislation that makes selling stuff easier. But they also have a deeper influence on American politics because malls perform cultural work that helps to shape American political culture. Shopping and consumption shape our assumptions about the place of politics in our lives, so that consumption itself becomes a political statement. We can see this in the creation of what Lizabeth Cohen calls "a consumer's republic" in the 1950s.[20]

During the 1950s, consumption was a political act. Jane Pavitt notes that "in the postwar West, against the backdrop of the Cold War, to be an active participant in a consumer society became increasingly regarded as a basic human right. The idea of citizenship [was] framed around the idea of consumership." Politicians in both parties heralded "the American way of life," and the material goods that symbolized American freedoms. At the Brussels World's Fair of 1958, the American pavilion included a fully stocked supermarket. At the Moscow trade show of 1959, the American exhibit featured even more consumer goods, including a fully furnished suburban home. Such exhibits praised Americans' freedom of choice in the supermarket and the shopping center, and implied (not inaccurately) that they were somehow related to American democracy. In the famous Kitchen Debate at the Moscow show, Vice President Nixon expressed this popular idea, making materialism a primary measurement of American cultural superiority. "The good life" was good political propaganda.[21]

Lizabeth Cohen notes that citizenship and consumption have always been essential elements of American political culture, but that the balance between them has shifted over time. During the early twentieth century, Progressives and New Dealers shaped a political system based on what Cohen calls "citizen consumers"—people who saw consumer issues as a catalyst for political reform. Citizen consumers believed that democracy offered a way to make capitalism work for the public good, and so they supported ideals like a living wage, the eight-hour day, minimum wages, workmen's compensation, pure food and drug acts, antitrust legislation, and, during World War II, price controls, rent regulations, and rationing restrictions. Both the Depression and World War II convinced Americans that they could act effectively as citizens to assure that they could act freely as consumers.[22]

After World War II, however, businesses attacked the restrictive regulations of the New Deal state and began to promote a new conception of citizenship and consumption: Cohen's "consumer's republic." In this "new and improved" political culture, "customer consumers" replaced "citizen consumers." The government would be responsible for promoting economic growth and assuring elementary fairness in the marketplace, but decisions about the character of consumption would be shifted from democratic politics to the market. The consumer's republic promoted "a new post-war ideal of the *customer as citizen* who simultaneously fulfilled personal desire and civic obligation by consuming." In this social construction of reality, Americans hardly had to think about the public good, because it would be the inevitable result of private consumption. Indeed, consumption became one of the highest forms of citizenship. Immigrants had always come to America for both political and personal freedom. The consumer's republic continued to celebrate this combination. It still promoted American ideals of freedom, democracy, and equality, but it adapted these ideas to an increasingly commercial culture. In the consumer's republic, Americans voted for the pleasures of private life.[23]

During this period, Americans increasingly subscribed to what sociologist Richard Flacks calls "the postwar charter." This new social contract specified that Americans wouldn't bother the government as long as the government provided both security and economic growth. This "motivated disengagement" wasn't apathy: Americans freely chose not to participate in politics. Instead of fighting for the Four Freedoms, as they had in World War II, they chose to fight for the freedoms of private consumption. Experiencing freedom and choice in institutions like shopping centers and the home, they trusted the government to preserve their other freedoms. Instead of engaging in politics, they engaged in what Flacks calls "the politics of everyday commitment." Following that tradition, shoppers today don't want to be bothered by politics in malls, in part because Americans don't want to be bothered by politics, period.[24]

The "people's capitalism" of the postwar period seemingly solved the problem of the distribution of wealth; while it privileged present inequities (many the result of prior political decisions), its promise of growth assured increased abundance for everybody. Proponents of the consumer's republic contended that American capitalism distributed goods better than Soviet socialism, and they conflated capitalism with democracy. Consequently, in the cold war world, when the United States attempted to "make the world safe for democracy," it usually made it safe for capitalism.[25]

Consumption was also a good answer to the crisis of democratic theory. As historian Edward Purcell has shown, American intellectuals increasingly doubted the capacity of the American people for deliberative politics. But the consumer's republic didn't require much deliberation about the public good. If people were smart enough to understand their own pleasure principle and self-interest, they would be choosing wisely for the political community. The politics of shopping fit perfectly with an "end of ideology" ideology, which counterpoised American pragmatism and practicality against Soviet ideological rigidity. Like abstract expressionism, which was celebrated as an expression of American freedom, the shopping center stood as a symbol of the promise of American politics.[26]

But even as Americans correctly contrasted the freedom of the American way of life with the coercive constraints of life in the Communist bloc, they often forgot the seductive constraints of their own seemingly apolitical system. Ideology hadn't really ended; it just took new forms in a culture of seduction (see Table 1).

TABLE 1 Coercive Versus Seductive Cultures

	Coercive Culture	Seductive Culture
Center of Power	Military/party	Commerce
Expansive ambition	Global empire	Global market
Order of leadership	Centralized	Decentralized
	Highly visible and fixed	Invisible and mobile
	Dictator/general	Corporate board
Philosophical presumptions	RATIONAL Materialism	Rational MATERIALISM
	Commerce serving state	State serving commerce
	Science serving party line	Science serving bottom line
	Religion as enemy	Religion as commodity
Ultimate value	Power	Money
Social status	Proximity to power (Soviet May Day picture)	Conspicuous consumption Lifestyles of the rich and famous
Cultural character	Repressive	Expressive
	Masculine	Feminine
	Patriotic	Self-centered
	Puritanical	Sexual
	Earnest	Sentimental
Cultural mythos	Ideology	Fantasy
	Party line	Pop culture
	State "hero"	Pop "star"
Modes of control	Command and conquer	Tempt and co-opt
	Conscription	Addiction
	Physical threat	Financial debt
	Party loyalty	Brand loyalty
	Fiat	Fashion
	Censorship	Saturation
	The Big Lie	The Big Top
Representative art form	Collage	Montage
Communication	Three-hour speech	Thirty-second ad
Structure	Berlin Wall	Mall of America
Profession	Apparatchik	Salesman/adman
Psychosis	Paranoia	Narcissism
Model world	Skinner box	Circe's Isle

Source: Bosworth, "Endangered Species," 224–45.

Under cover of this ideology of no ideology, American postwar consumption exploded. The pent-up demand of twenty years, coupled with the government's promotion of consumption with programs like the CI Bill and federal housing programs, led to unprecedented economic expansion. To people in the 1950s, of course, this abundance didn't seem extravagant. It seemed like a return to normalcy, a fulfillment of the promise of American life. In the process, though, the American standard of living came to substitute for the American way of life, with its social, political, and religious activities.

Shopping centers grew up in this materialistic milieu, and served, along with supermarkets, as symbols of American affluence. Although the first shopping centers were built during the 1920s and 1930s, the Depression and World War II delayed further development. Starting in the 1950s, however, malls mushroomed throughout the United States. In 1957, International Council of Shopping Centers was created to coordinate and promote the growth of the burgeoning industry. Although some shopping center pioneers expected malls to serve as centers of civic life, their plans fell victim to the cultural priorities of privatism and profit. The long-term decline in American political participation hasn't been caused by shopping centers, but America's malls have reinforced the politics of "customer consumers" in the postwar era.[27]

During the 1960s, radicals preached that "the personal is political," and celebrated the virtues of participatory democracy. Affirming the importance of consumption, they used economic tools like boycotts to pressure businesses to live up to the ideals of the consumer's republic. In 1960, for example, four civil rights activists sat down at the lunch counter at Woolworth's in Greensboro, North Carolina, and demanded the same service that white customers received. Their action inspired sit-ins and boycotts, both North and South, directed at retail stores that supported southern racial segregation, and at the laws that countenanced such discrimination. This political counterculture hoped to revolutionize the counter cultures of American retail establishments. "With their demands for more access to the stores, more respect inside them, and more African American employees working for them," historian Ted Ownby suggests, "protesters wanted full access to two central aspects of consumer culture. They saw shopping as a potentially democratic experience and hoped to find pleasure and dignity in the experience. Even if they did not emphasize the idea, they were defining the right to shop as a basic element in American freedom." African Americans demanded not just equal citizenship but also the equality of consumers. Shopping was part of their American Dream.[28]

American consumers supported other boycotts, too—like the boycott of grapes by Cesar Chavez and the United Farmworkers—to reform the market system. And antiwar activists asked Americans to boycott consumer goods produced by companies, like Dow Chemical, that also manufactured munitions for the Vietnam War. The market responded in two ways. In many cases, as in southern retail stores, companies acted to remedy wrongdoing, or at least to explain it with public relations. In the South, for example, the segregation of retail markets soon gave way to the segmentation of markets, as stores began to cater to the African American market.[29]

In other cases, the market responded by marketing the social revolution, turning a serious critique of profligate consumerism into a new style of consumerism. American commercial culture co-opted the counterculture of communes and simple living, commodifying dissent, and selling it back to the dissenters. Capitalists found that antimaterialism sold very well to selected customers. The more the counterculture could be construed as a life-style apart from politics, the more capitalists could sell the style without the substance. By marketing the outward signs of hippie life—music, psychedelic posters, clothes, beads, and drug paraphernalia—merchandisers found that they could make a profit on the ephemera of prophecy.[30]

Malls and their assumptions have increasingly defined other aspects of American life, including politics. "Liberal democracy still defines America," notes political scientist Alan Wolfe, "but liberty is coming more and more to mean that everything is, and ought to be, for sale, and democracy is being turned into the notion that whatever people want the most must be the best for them." Ironically, our "ideology of liberty" reinforces our liberty from politics. If we're really free, we should be free of politics too. So we still generally fulfill our duties to the polity by fulfilling ourselves.[31]

During the 1980s, the Reagan revolution reinforced the privatism of American political culture. When the government failed to uphold its side of the postwar charter, when real incomes failed to rise in the 1970s, American citizens got political to preserve their private American dreams. They fueled the tax revolt, which was designed to give consumers the money they needed to fulfill their part of the postwar charter: self-fulfillment. Republicans used private consumption as a counter against public provision, and the Reagan administration guided this sentiment into an attack on Big Government and on politics itself. As the president spun fanciful stories about the shopping habits of welfare queens, he cut taxes so that Americans could go on a spending spree. And we did.[32]

Because conservatives like Ronald Reagan decided to conserve the free market more than anything else, they succeeded in conserving little else. As Alan Wolfe suggests, "By the time Reaganism finished working its way through American society, such quaint notions as uninterrupted family meals, commerce-free Sundays, unspoiled places, and unindebted self-reliance had almost completely disappeared." And given the marketeers' penchant for putting a price tag on everything, market culture undermines "the ties of solidarity associated with friendship and family—ties that, if they are to endure through thick and thin, must be non-economic in nature." Conservatives believe that liberals have undermined American institutions and values, but the market is much more powerful than mere liberals.[33]

Unfortunately, as it happens, a consumer's republic is almost a contradiction in terms. The word "republic" derives from the Latin "res publica," the public things. In early America, republicanism worked because the culture itself encouraged restraint and self-government. Frugality was both an economic benefit and a political virtue, because it demonstrated the self-government that could restrain the desires of mass democracy. These days, however, the institutions that teach frugality and moderation are often overwhelmed by the market's emphasis on self-indulgent freedom.

During the last twenty-five years, conservatives have succeeded in convincing Americans about the evils of Big Government and high taxes. They have promoted and passed big tax cuts on the unproven theory that the American people can spend their money more wisely than our government can. They have repeatedly argued that you can't solve problems by throwing money at them. Such policies promote private enterprises like shopping centers, where, in fact, we go to throw money at our own problems.[34]

Shopping centers use politics to keep politics out of the mall and to keep the mall profitable. In the process, they also perform cultural work for Americans. The private consumption encouraged by shopping centers, for example, affects our taste for public goods. The more we can buy at the mall, the less we want to contribute to public projects. Why pay for good police protection when you can buy a private security system for your house and "the Club" for your car? Why pay for public playgrounds when you can buy one for your own backyard?

Indeed, shopping centers help to keep public issues out of sight and out of mind. They're just one institution that reinforces our penchant for political compartmentalization. It might affect the business of the food court if there were signs about hunger in the United States. It might be harder to buy toys for our children at KayBee if we were reminded about the scope of child poverty. We might think twice about a computer game if we were thinking about our school district's bond levy. Indeed, the shopping center is meant to center our attention on private spending, not public spending of any sort. We learn to satisfy our desires by buying individual "solutions" from private enterprise, instead of buying social solutions in the public sphere.[35]

Despite the claims of shopping center management, however, there's no such thing as "not political," there's just consciously or unconsciously political, intentionally and unintentionally political, and formally and informally political. Even the so-called free market is neither private nor free but the consequence of many prior public decisions. Shopping centers and retailers, for example, depend on currency, public roads, postal service, and police and fire departments. They depend on a legal system that defines and protects private property, enforces contracts, and prosecutes fraud and shoplifting. Corporations depend on the limited legal liability of investors and on the legal fiction that corporations are persons, able to sue and be sued. Corporations and credit card companies tend to do business in states that have structured their politics with loose regulations on taxes and interest rates. Lenders and developers depend on interest rates and tax incentives to motivate investments. As real estate investment trusts (REITs), shopping center companies can avoid paying corporate income taxes and still distribute quarterly dividends to stockholders. Manufactures depend on tariff and trade laws, and they tend to do business in countries with minimal wages and environmental regulations. Once their product is made, they depend on the protections of patent and trademark law. Advertisers depend on the public airwaves, the post office, and minimal governmental oversight. Market researchers depend on the Census Bureau and the Commerce Department. We all depend on the confidence generated by specific pieces of protective legislation, especially involving consumer safety. And these companies also benefit from campaign finance laws that make it easy for businesses to assure that, as Calvin Coolidge once said, "the business of America is business." So despite the apparent politics of no politics, our shopping both affects and reflects American democracy and political culture.[36]

Notes

1. Ironically, there's even a virtual Town Square at www.townsquareshops.com/index.htm.
2. Cohen, "From Town Center to Shopping Center," 1080–81.
3. Kowinski, *Malling of America,* 354–59.
4. *Ibid.,* 1068.
5. Satterthwaite, *Going Shopping,* 114–17.
6. Cohen, "From Town Center to Shopping Center," 1068–69; Michael Fickes, "Freedom of Speech in the Mall," *Shopping Center World,* 1 September 2000, 150–53. See also ICSC, "Scorecard of Pruneyard Litigation," at www.icsc.org/law/prune.pdf.
7. Kowinski, *Malling of America,* 355.
8. Coady, "Concrete Dream," 618.
9. *Ibid.,* 568–69.
10. ICSC, "Scope USA."
11. Beyard et al, *Shopping Center Development Handbook,* 66.
12. Ken Jones and Jim Simmons, *The Retail Environment* (New York: Routledge, 1990), 1.
13. Edmund Mander, "Antisprawl Raises PR Issues for Industry," *Shopping Centers Today* (May 1999), at www.icsc.org/srch/sct/current/sct9905/48.htm.
14. ICSC, "ICSC PAC," at www.icsc.org/government/pac.html, and ICSC, "Government," at www.icsc. org/government.
15. ICSC, "Government Relations Issues," at www.icsc.org/cgi/dispgri.
16. ICSC Fast Action Center, at www.capitoloconnect.com/icsc.
17. ICSC, "ICSC PAC."
18. "Government Affairs," at www.imra.org/govaff-fed_agenda.asp.

19. Gentleman, "1997 Mall Customer Shopping Patterns Report," 17.

20. Lizabeth Cohen, *A Consumer's Republic: The Politics of Mass Consumption in Postwar America* (New York: Knopf, 2003).

21. Jane Pavitt, "In Goods We Trust?" in *Brand.new*, ed. Jane Pavitt (Princeton: Princeton University Press, 2000), 32. For an excellent discussion of the Kitchen Debate, see Karal Ann Marling, "Nixon in Moscow," in her *As Seen on TV*, 243–83.

22. Lizabeth Cohen, "Citizens and Consumers in the United States in the Century of Mass Consumption," in *The Politics of Consumption: Material Culture and Citizenship in Europe and America* (Oxford: Berg, 2001), 204–5.

23. *Ibid.*, 213–20.

24. Richard Flacks, "Making Life, Not History," in *Making History: The American Left and the American Mind* (New York: Columbia University Press, 1988), 32–37, 51–57.

25. Godfrey Hodgson, *America in Our Time* (Garden City, N.Y.: Doubleday, 1976), 51.

26. Edward Purcell, *The Crisis of Democratic Theory: Scientific Naturalism and the Problem of Value* (Lexington: University of Kentucky Press, 1973), David and Cecile Shapiro, "Abstract Expressionism: The Politics of Apolitical Painting" in *Prospects* 3 (1977): 175–214.

27. "Cheers to 100 Years . . . 20th Century Timeline," *Shopping Center World* (1 December 1999), at www.industryclick.com/magazinearticle.asp?releaseid=4532&magazinearticleid=52314&siteid=23 &magazineid=109.

28. Ownby, *American Dreams in Mississippi*, 149–58.

29. *Ibid.*

30. Lipsitz, "Who'll Stop the Rain? Youth Culture, Rock 'n' Roll, and Social Crises," in *The Sixties: From Memory to History*, ed. David Farber (Chapel Hill: University of North Carolina Press, 1994), 224. For a brilliant analysis of this story, see especially Thomas Frank, *The Conquest of Cool* (Chicago: University of Chicago Press, 1997).

31. Alan Wolfe, "Undialectical Materialism," *New Republic*, 23 October 2000, 29. According to Dan Cook, this ideology of liberty applies even to children: "The children's market works because it lives off of deeply-held beliefs about self-expression and freedom of choice—originally applied to the political sphere, and now almost inseparable from the culture of consumption." Cook, "Lunchbox Hegemony?"

32. Gary Cross, *An All-Consuming Century: Why Commercialism Won in Modern America* (New York: Columbia University Press, 2000), 193–213.

33. Wolfe, "Undialectical Materialism," 30–31.

34. Holsworth and Wray, *American Politics and Everyday Life*, 40.

35. *Ibid.*, 43.

36. *Ibid.*, 213–14.

D.C. Panoply— and the First Black Mall

William Severini Kowinski

MOST OF THE BOOMTOWN PUBLICITY of recent years has gone to places like Houston and Phoenix, while New York City and Boston still retain their images as the nation's centers of wealth and culture. Even the suburbs of Chicago have been studied more than those of Washington. But the facts show that Greater Washington is the richest metropolitan area in the country, that it has been growing in wealth and population through thick and thin, especially since the 1960s, and that much of this growth has occurred in a wide swath of suburbia.

Washington also has the highest education level in the nation, the highest percentage of heads of household between the ages of twenty-five and thirty-four, and of women in the work force, and the lowest percentage of the population over age sixty-five. Most of the money is out in the suburbs, which, except for Prince George's County, are virtually all white. (The city of Washington has a majority black population.) Five of the twenty most affluent suburbs in the nation are in the Washington metro area.

So it should hardly be surprising that in the late 1960s and early 1970s, suburban Washington experienced a boom of major shopping-mall construction. Developers fought one another for potentially lucrative properties, and the sheer number of malls and their greater and greater opulence as the years have passed made mall-to-mall competition probably the fiercest in America. This is another kind of mall war, pitting developer against developer for the rights to mall empires.

Jean Callahan, another friend from *Newsworks* days, took me out to the first truly major mall in the area, Tysons Corner Center. It opened in 1968, just as that part of suburbia in Fairfax County Virginia, was beginning to boom. Before the mall, there was nothing at Tysons Corner except what you would expect had you happened on its name on a map of the South—a gas station, a general store, and a fruit and vegetable stand. But it was exactly the kind of corner for a shopping mall: the intersection of three major highways, including the Capital Beltway.

In fact, two developers wanted to build on this site: the Lerner Corporation, a local outfit, and the Rouse Company, from not far away in Maryland. Both developers submitted proposals to the Fairfax County Planning Commission, which recommended the Rouse plan. But then there was a tumultuous ten-hour meeting of the County Board of Supervisors, featuring expert witnesses for both sides armed with drawings and plans, charts and studies. Whether the actual meeting was where the decisive action took place or not, by the end of it the supervisors had voted, 4–2, to go against the Planning Commission and award the mall rights to Lerner.

It was a fateful decision. These were the early days of the mall boom, and the meeting influenced more malls than this one. With this foothold, Lerner became the master mall builder of metro Washington, and the Rouse Company looked elsewhere for its spheres of influence.

According to contemporary accounts, Tysons Corner mall was a revelation to suburban Washington. Overnight it created a mall sensibility—an appreciation, if not a hunger, for comfort-controlled, plushly appointed and richly stored, bejeweled and begardened enclosures. It was immediately perceived as the perfect expression of suburban affluence and the appropriate symbol of suburban prestige. If your suburb was going to be anywhere, you had to have a major mall. Otherwise, nowheresville. Without a mall you were a *rube*.

By the time I visited Tysons Corner, however, there were many newer malls, and in areas of high competition, newness counts. All the same, Tysons looked to be a community center still; perhaps less of a spectacle than before but nonetheless the place for a significant population to shop and eat and hang out, and to call its own. In fact, one of its problems had become urban-sized traffic jams around the parking lot.

Nothing much interesting happened to us as Jean and I walked around Tysons, except that during lunch in the Magic Pan Crêperie our waitress flubbed one of her programmed lines ("I'll take your check when you're ready," she said as she handed me my change) and realizing her error she almost fell apart, like those movie computers that start to spew smoke and nonsense when they make a mistake.

I learned more about the place from an excellent piece in the *Washingtonian* magazine, written by Lynn Darling. Darling interviewed old people at the mall (some of them purposely sitting where they could watch children's pictures being taken with the Easter Bunny) and teenagers ("Why would I go to another shopping center? I wouldn't know anybody there.

Here, if I wait around long enough, I can see just about everybody I know") and mall store employees (one of whom repeated the line I was to hear often: "You work here long enough, you find out this center is a regular Peyton Place," but when the teller is pressed for details, the stories turn out to be pretty tame, quite familiar, and of decidedly local interest).

Darling also got a middle-aged shopper to come close to admitting what is otherwise implied: "We come here because it has everything we want and nothing we don't want. There aren't any problems with parking, or crowds, or crime, or . . . well, we don't have to say what the other problems are."

The other problems that white suburbia perceives are black people, and Washington's racial situation was going to figure in the future of the next mall Jean and I went to, Landover Mall.

At the time we visited it. Landover intrigued me for another reason—its head-to-head competition, via very pointed media advertising, with another mall. In the short time I'd been back in Washington, I'd noticed television ads for Springfield Mall, accompanied by the slogan, "Springfield Mall—it's something else!" spoken in a bubbly voice. Television ads for malls outside the holiday seasons were rare then, but not really strange. What did catch my eye—and ear—was a television spot for Landover Mall. It featured an innocuous video montage of mall scenes but with a sizzling sound track: a woman's voice proclaiming in the semi-hysterical tones of a rabid game-show contestant, "I used to have the Springfield habit, but now I go to Landover Mall—it's *more fun!*" Her voice then collapsed into deep throaty giggles, accompanied by the clinking of glasses and assenting male laughter.

Aside from the fact that nobody said anything about shopping in these ads, or prices, or even stores; aside from referring to regular mall-going in the language of drug addiction; aside from the idea that malls were selling themselves as being "something else" and "more fun," there was the startling tactic of naming the competitor, at the time pretty daring in advertising.

That, and the sexual implications of the ad piqued my interest, so I got Jean to drive out to Landover Mall to see what might attract bored suburban housewives and men of leisure for afternoons of wild abandon.

What we found was a slightly down-at-heel mall, dark and severe, with a polluted pond as a centerpiece, its picturesque wishing well pennies lying among cigarette butts, plastic forks, and foam under an oily slick. Apart from the Tropica plant store and two beauty salons, I couldn't imagine what would entice a suburban woman. The ads, it seemed, were all competitive hype.

By then it was Happy Hour at the Porch on the Mall, and our tour was therefore over for the day. As we got into our half-price drinks, we chanced to overhear a man and woman at the next table arranging an extramarital tryst. So maybe there was something to this sexy image-making after all. "Maybe their spouses are at Springfield Mall," I suggested to Jean.

Then Jean told me about a story she had just done on single women in Washington. It turned out that the women she interviewed were meeting men not so much at bars and parties, as she expected. Most of them were meeting men at shopping malls.

There was an even more interesting twist to the Landover Mall story which developed after my visit. It seems that I had seen Landover when it was coming close to its all-time low point. The mall had opened in 1972 with high hopes of joining the other big malls as a citadel of affluence, with its own market sphere, catering to the ever-expanding and ever wealthier white middle class. Market projections showed that Prince George's County would grow to a million mostly monied inhabitants. But as the 1970s went on, that's not what happened.

Fewer people moved to the county than expected, and many of those who did were black. Instead of the unbroken march of single-family houses on neat white streets, there were apartments and low-income housing as well. The upper-middle-class whites headed for other suburbs, and those who lived in the Landover area soon began shopping at the newer malls elsewhere.

So Landover, a huge mall with four major department stores and, at its height, more shops than Tysons Corner, was that rarity in malldom, a suburban mall on the skids. Predictably, mall management and mall stores were at each other's throats, as nighttime vandalism in the parking lot spread and beer cans were strewn along the mall courts. Landover sank into a Muzak-glazed depression.

Then, gradually, Landover's merchants began to accept the fact that black people made up 70 percent of their customers instead of 35 percent when the mall opened. They began to treat them as a clientele by adding merchandise that appealed to them, and soon found that there was enough of a market to revive the mall's business. One store reported that 80 percent of its sales were from the "high fashion young black trade." Mall management was inspired to clean things up and restore the fountain and pond with sparkling fresh water. Another ad campaign was started, this one more realistic. Landover Mall experienced a rebirth, as possibly the first successful black shopping mall in suburbia.

Later on this trip, I visited two of the newest shopping-mall expressions of Washington's recent affluence. I'd already seen White Flint, the grandest so far, but there were others, closer to the city of Washington itself. They were also "specialty malls," which began coming into vogue in the late seventies. Technically a specialty mall has mostly high-fashion shops and a greater variety of eating places, anchored either by the most fashionable department stores or by no department store at all. But essentially what a specialty mall specializes in is rich people, or people who spend money as if they were rich. In the retail euphemisms of the day, these are the "upscale" customers or, even more obnoxiously, the "high end" market.

Washington was a prime place for these centers, for no matter what community functions malls fulfill (Tysons Corner hosts the Vienna Society of Artists show each year; Lakeforest Mall in Gaithersburg had its own Shakespearian festival, complete with "sonnet readings and Shakespearian proclamation in the Penney's court area"), the major function of a Washington mall is usually to express the affluence of its customers.

Affluent Washington is pretty much a nouveau riche city, having grown very fast in the last generation, and it is still looking for legitimacy among the urban centers of America. One of its bids for both prestige and urban efficiency was the Metro subway system. The major Metro stations are strange and wondrous: spacious enclosures out of which shoot long escalators, climbing at some stations so steeply that, going up, you seem to be riding directly into the sky. The stations themselves, resembling the bare shells of Victorian-era terminals brought underground, add a sci-fi ambience with electronic fare-card machines and circles of light inlaid along the tracks that silently blink when a train approaches.

Especially when the system was new and pristine, when the blink of the lights in the eerie quiet of the station was followed by the efficient hum of the train, one felt a quality of a clean but quaintly adventurous future already under way. Somewhat in this spirit, down the tracks (which were already down the rabbit hole) lay a brand-new mall, a kind of logical extension of the Metro.

Out past the Pentagon and Pentagon City stops was Crystal City and, attached to its station, the specialty mall called Crystal City Underground. The same brick floor that covered the station led gently into the mall, where the decor dropped the Metro's austere efficiency and assumed a more fanciful air, with gingerbread-house motifs and cute shops like Larimer's wine and cheese store, which proclaimed, "Established, though not on this spot, 1894." Welcome to Wonderland.

Crystal City Underground was something of a theme mall, designed by a Santa Monica, California, architect to resemble the turn-of-the-century streets of (for some reason) New York City. But the basic themes of the mall were money and newness. For just as it bore no resemblance to the chaos of shops and kiosks in New York or Boston subway stations, the mall did not serve subway patrons only. Even though it was underground, it had other entrances connecting to the fifty thousand people living in high-priced condominiums just above it, and in a series of eight hotels stretching to the nearby National Airport. Altogether, this is the lucrative market it was designed to serve.

As I walked through Crystal City Underground for the first time, I came upon a wine and cheese party celebrating the opening of a new shop, the Bed 'n Bath. Though this was perfectly appropriate for a contemporary Wonderland, it was a good deal fancier than the Mad Hatter's tea party.

I chatted with a laconically polite woman in an expensive pants suit who said she was a friend of the owner. (The Underground began with many locally owned shops, but eventually shifted to specialty chain outlets, like Casual Corner and Crabtree & Evelyn.) At one point I mentioned Tysons Corner Mall. "It's all right, I suppose," she said, "but it smells like hot dogs." So much for the erstwhile capital of suburban splendor in Washington. The king is dead; long live the Underground.

The last new specialty mall on my tour was the Mazza Gallerie, developed by the Neiman-Marcus department store, which was also its anchor. Although in a business sense Neiman's may have overextended itself here, psychologically the Texas-Washington connection makes perfect sense. The unquestioning clear-eyed worship of wealth I found most prominently displayed in two places in my travels: Washington and Houston. But that may have been because I didn't get to Dallas, where Neiman-Marcus is headquartered.

So perhaps the most expressive of Washington's mix of mall fantasies is this Mazza Gallerie, a severe structure of white Italian marble, not unlike what a Washington presidential monument might look like if it, too, were anchored by a Neiman-Marcus store.

The Gallerie opened with a typical Washington social event, the black-tie celebrity gala, with charity as the usual pretext for Washingtonians to dress up and mingle with power. In this instance they had the additional thrill of having the huge Neiman-Marcus store all to themselves for an evening's worth of private pawing of pavéed-diamond watches, cabochon rubies, mulberry silk dinner dresses, nylon storm coats, brown velvet evening suits, silk crepe de chine tunics, and lambskin patch-pocket blazers.

The Gallerie eventually got forty-five posh stores, including Ted Lapidus and other designer outlets based on Rodeo Drive in Beverly Hills, but as this opening gala was being prepared, only Neiman-Marcus was opening. The store's management office was awhirl. "Get me Pearl Bailey again," someone shouted to a secretary. A copy of *The Social List of Washington* sat on one desk amid sandwich remains and ad proofs. Press kits were being prepared, complete with photographs of Richard Marcus and the manager of the Washington store, plus fact sheets on them that included the first names of their wives.

Meanwhile, in the store itself, salesgirls were sorting out shoe boxes on a woven beige rug that looked like an enormous sweater. A black fashion model was being photographed while a high-powered young woman was giving her sales staff a pep talk, emphasizing the goal of getting the *very best* clientele in Washington. Since then, that goal has had to be broadened somewhat and the Gallerie changed, but ambience still matches these aspirations.

Before I left, I peeked into the still embryonic mall, the shops mere outlines drawn in slightly surreal, Thurber-esque wobbles on plasterboard walls. But soon it would be a mall, and for all its glitter and all the high-fashion charge Washington would get from it, there were things that would always be part of it—inescapable, intrinsic to the mall environment—no matter how far above the hot dogs of an aging suburbia Washington and its new malls might aspire. One of them was represented by a panel truck parked outside. It was from Muzak.

A few days later, just before I left Washington, I had lunch with Marcia and Larry, and reported to them my final mall activities. I'd finally made it out to the Beltway Plaza Mall on Greenbelt Road at Exit 28 of the Beltway. There was something primal about all those names—here was a mall that was on the highway and bragged about it, offered obeisance to it with its own name. It was enclosed and air-conditioned; it had more than eighty stores and room for five thousand cars to park. There was no pretense.

Next I would be turning my attention west, to the newest parts of America. There, migration had occurred not only in past centuries but again and in great numbers after World War II, both in the West and in areas of the South—which together have become known as the Sun Belt. This last great migratory wave had splashed back new cultural ideas and fashions upon the whole country. The centers of the Sun Belt, in particular, had taken the shopping mall to their literal hearts. No story of the mall would be complete without the West and South, just as no account of the Sun Belt can neglect the mall, its social and cultural role, and its style.

As I talked to Marcia and Larry about my western plans, I remembered a moment in White Flint Mall when the three of us were standing together. While my eyes were scanning the mall, Marcia's were darting to the various products on display, and Larry had looked at both of us and laughed. "If you're not a consumer here," he said to me, "you must feel like an agnostic touring the cathedrals of Europe. Most people here are worshipers."

It was true. What I was doing was counter to the mall's nature and purpose, and certainly different from what everyone else was doing in the mall. I did shop in malls, I roamed around them thinking of nothing, I ate and drank there, I watched people, and I enjoyed myself, pretty much like everybody else. But the main business of my mall odyssey was to be empathetic and objective, observant and receptive, a listener and an analyzer, alien and human.

Now I would be leaving the more familiar East and Midwest, where I had friends and guides to help me and accompany me, and going off to places I had never been, and where I would be largely on my own. As we concluded lunch in Washington, I mentioned some of these thoughts. I must have been pretty poignant about it, because suddenly Marcia looked a little concerned.

I laughed. "Aw, shucks, Marcia, don't worry," I said. "It's a lonely job, but somebody's got to do it."

READING WRITING

This Text: Reading

1. Where do the authors agree about malls? Where do they disagree?
2. Which writer best reflects your own experience with malls?
3. Why do you think the authors chose their subjects? What importance do malls have in American culture?

4. What other, less scholarly commentary have you seen about malls? Where does it disagree or agree with these observations?
5. Do these authors think of the mall as a public or private space—or both? In what ways does this characterization matter?

Your Text: Writing

1. Using the lens of class, read your local mall.
2. Using the lens of race and ethnicity, read your local mall.
3. Using the lens of gender, read your local mall.
4. If you can, do a comparison of two local malls or a mall and a local downtown. What differences do you see? Similarities? What does your comparison say about some of the issues these authors raise about class, race, and gender? What about consumption?
5. What are some of the symbols malls use to indicate class? How do malls use decoration to create an atmosphere? What assumptions do they rely on in using these symbols?
6. Find someone who disagrees with your like or dislike of malls, and take a trip to a mall. Write a paper that outlines some of the observations and interpretations you both make.

READING BETWEEN THE LINES

Classroom Activities

1. Look around your classroom. How do you know it's a classroom? Of course, there are the chalkboard and the desks, but what other qualities does this room have that makes it a classroom? How is it designed? Does it facilitate learning, alertness, and discussion?
2. Walk outside the classroom. What elements identify the walk as a college campus? What emotions does the walk evoke? Could it be improved?
3. What does the public space outside the classroom building say? Does it identify the campus as any particular type of school—private, public, urban, rural, suburban? What would a potential student read into this particular space? Would they be inclined to come to school or not because of this reading? Why or why not?
4. What particular place makes you feel the most comfortable? Least? Frightened? What is it about the spaces themselves that evoke these emotions? Are they human driven or architecturally or design driven? Can you think of a space that has bad or good memories driven mostly by the space itself?
5. Design the perfect classroom. What would it look like? What would it have in it? Where would everyone sit? What tools would everyone have? How would being in this classroom change your learning experience?
6. Design the perfect building at college. What would it look like? What would it have in it?

Essay Ideas

Building as analogy

Find a building you want to write about. Does it remind you of something besides a building in 1) its physical construction; 2) the emotional response it encourages; 3) its purpose; or 4) its structure? In what way are these disparate elements alike? Different? What does the analogy in general say about commonalties of texts generally?

Emotional response

Walk around a building or a public area such as a mall or your school's common area. What do you "feel"? What about the place makes you feel such an emotion? Are these effects intended or unintended?

Commercial versus artistic

What dominates this particular building or space—its artistic aspects or commercial ones? Or do the two work together?

My favorite place

If possible, analyze a place you feel close to and figure out why you feel that way. Is there a theme attached to this place? How would you describe the décor? The architecture? Do you feel your attachment to this place—or places like it—is unique?

Does this building or space "work"?

Find a place—do you think it succeeds on its own terms? What are its "terms"—what criteria is it trying to fulfill? Does is succeed? Why or why not?

The person from the space

Go to an office or a dorm room or car, or some place that "belongs" to someone. What can you tell about this person from the space? How did you arrive at your judgments? Are there other ways to interpret the information?

The common element

Compare similar spaces. What makes them similar? What are their differences? What do their differences or similarities say about this type of space?

READING AND WRITING ABOUT
advertising,
journalism,
and the media

The Colbert Report: journalism, entertainment, or both?

Anything from books to magazines to news programs to radio shows to films is technically a medium (media is the plural of medium). For the purposes of this chapter, we will define the media as organizations or companies that seek to cover any kind of news in whatever form. Probably the most technically correct way to refer to news organizations would be just that—news organizations—but because "media" has itself become a hot text, we want to engage it here. We include advertising in this chapter as well, because although it does not cover anything, often it helps pay for the coverage we see. "The media" has become a symbol of a world whose happenings are broadcast 24 hours a day, where no subject seems too trivial to be covered. Everyone seems to think the media are too intrusive. And yet . . . we watch, and we watch, and we read, and we watch. If we did not watch or read, the media would change because the media are not one entity but many, which are always changing. For instance, there was no cable television when the authors of this book were born, and thus no CNN. Moreover, when many of you were born, the Internet was only a military communications system, hardly the consuming force it is today. So, whatever we write and think about the media now is destined to change for better or worse as our world changes.

You might also be wondering why we have decided to combine advertising, journalism, and the media in one chapter, when, clearly, each could be its own chapter or its own book. For better or worse, the distinctions between media, advertising, and journalism are fuzzy at best. Is an infomercial news, an advertisement, or a form of television media? On the CNN.com Web site, one finds a news story about America's favorite cities to visit within eyeshot of an ad for Orbitz—is this coincidence? In 2004, CBS ran a segment on *60 Minutes* in which Dan Rather interviewed Bill Clinton about his forthcoming memoir; however, the network came under fire when some blogs explained that CBS would receive a cut from the sales of the book if it was purchased through an Amazon.com link on the CBS.com Web site. But, even beyond these instances, the texts of media and advertising and the media are so interdependent, that it seems both prudent and responsible to link them semiotically.

Even though the media are diverse in nature, they share a number of concerns that connect them. Almost all forms of media struggle to balance various concerns: public interest versus profit, fairness and objectivity versus bias, national coverage versus local, depth of coverage versus breadth of coverage, as well as some other more temporal concerns, though more partisan blogs, in their role in both advocating positions and criticizing more traditional media, are deliberately biased, and certainly part of the media landscape today. The first conflict, balancing the public interest and the need to have the public watch, read, or listen, is often the one that gets the media into the most trouble; it leads to the charge that the media are shallow, intent on sensationalizing news. Nevertheless, all the conflicts lead to our sense that there is something "wrong" with the media, that something is not quite working right in the system. Yet, while the media are far from perfect (what is, after all?), they do perform a crucial role in American life and American culture. This introduction will begin to explain some of the difficulties and misconceptions attached to the media before going into articles that explore the media in more depth.

Separate but related elements of the media are advertisers and marketers who have a crucial financial relationship with newspapers, magazines, Web pages, television news, and television shows. In essence, advertising pays for our free television and subsidizes our purchase of magazines and newspapers—without ads, we would pay for broadcast television (it's why cable television generally and premium channels like HBO cost money) and pay a lot more for newspapers and magazines. What do advertisers get in return for their ads? The simple answer is public exposure for their products or services. The more complicated (and perhaps unintended) one is an influence in public life. Although some critics object to the very existence of advertising in public life, most everyone acknowledges that advertising is the price we pay for living in a capitalist society. What is most criticized about advertising is the way advertising seeks to sell us products through manipulation and base appeals—its use of implicit and often inflated promises of various forms of happiness (sexual gratification, satiation of hunger, thinness, coolness) with the purchase of advertised items. When we consider these issues plus the sheer proximity of where and how ads and other media appear, it makes sense to think of these two entities as two sides of the same coin. While advertisers are not what people automatically think of as the media, their influence and importance in American society and their impact on various media outlets cannot be denied.

This introduction may seem one of our more political ones, but there is a reason for that: everyone, from liberals to conservatives, from the rich to the poor, from young to old, seems to criticize what the media do. Our purpose in asking you to "read" media and advertising in a complex way is to help you broaden and complicate your view of them. Following are some things to consider about the media.

The media are businesses, not a public service.

Although they cover the news, the media are in the business of selling newspapers or garnering ratings points. But as accepted protectors of the public interest, they also have obligations to the public—their connection to public interest is part of their business credibility. Some argue that because of the advantages given to television and radio networks by the government—exclusive use of broadcast frequencies for radio stations and various broadcast advantages to the big three television networks (NBC, CBS, and ABC)—that media outlets have further obligations to the public interest.

And yet, at the heart, the media are business organizations. As a way of trying to maintain some distance between the business side and the editorial (news) side, media organizations often try to separate the two divisions: the editorial side covers the news; the business side gets advertising and does accounting work. But these two elements often meet anyway. Special sections in magazines and in newspapers in which coverage is devoted to a particular event or phenomenon are the most obvious examples, but when we watch television some decisions seem motivated by the business component; local coverage of a business opening or prominently mentioning sponsorship of local events is an example of this interchange.

Nevertheless, in a media outlet with split organizations, keeping the business and editorial sides completely separate is impossible. Even the editorial side of large newspapers like *The New York Times* and *The Washington Post* may have unconscious motivations toward the business end; a newspaper is generally designed toward highlighting the most important stories, a tactic that "sells" the newspaper to the patron. However, the editorial side does not solicit ads directly and makes few of those types of decisions. On the other hand, small-town papers may make even less of a distinction between the editorial and business side. In smaller communities, the publisher, who either represents the owner or is the owner, *does* often influence editorial decisions, especially in the editorials of a paper.

So, what are we to do with such information? Again, given the fact that the basic structures of media organizations are unlikely to change, the most important thing to do is to watch or read news with an active, sometimes skeptical eye, looking for links between business interests and media outlets. Even more importantly, read news widely. Look at "alternative" papers or read media criticism. Taking such steps will help you become a better reader of the media.

The media are made up of a variety of people.

Do you think Katie Couric and the local weekly's columnist have similar roles in the media? Of course not—but the latter is as much a media member as the former. The large differences between members of the media (some of whom claim not to be) demonstrate what the media mean and do is complicated rather than simple. When columnists, politicians, or sports figures refer to the media, whom, specifically, do they mean? Miss Manners? National Public Radio? The folks at the History Channel? The obituary writer of your hometown newspaper? Probably they are thinking of the very few, very public media outlets like the major television networks, the overly aggressive talk radio personalities, and perhaps some writers for national newspapers and magazines. However, most members of "the media" are regular, virtually anonymous people who try to bring you interesting, important stories.

Although many members of the media have similar aims, their format and their audience shape their content. Radio news can only read a few paragraphs of a traditional newspaper story in its allotted time and has to rely on taped interviews to enhance it. A television news report has to focus on visual material, and national newspapers have different expectations attached to them than does the local weekly. To an extent, the format and mission of a news organization will dictate how it covers an event and sometimes even whether it will cover that event.

Additionally, different media do different things well, and the variety is what gives our media wonderful breadth and scope. Newspapers analyze long-term events better than television does, and magazines do it even better. But in covering house fires and the weather, and showing sports highlights, television is significantly better. Overall, the media have different elements that make various organizations better suited to do one job rather than another. There are very few absolutes when it comes to the media. Some newspapers and television stations are civic-minded organizations dedicated to upholding the public trust. Sometimes newspapers seem motivated more by financial concerns. Some ads are very entertaining. Some are offensive. Some media outlets try to present the news in the most balanced, most objective way they can. Other sources make no bones about being biased. The crucial thing is to be able to view the media generally, and advertising and the news specifically, with a critical eye.

Despite what your favorite conservative radio or television talk show host says, the media are not particularly liberal.

You may not be familiar with the ongoing controversy of the supposed "liberal bias" of the media, but if you spend any time watching or reading columnists—both from the left (liberal) and right (conservative)—you will encounter claims of a liberal media. Actually, the fact that someone points out that there is a liberal bias itself undermines the idea of one. If there is such a liberal bias, then how have we heard about it? Through the conservative media.

You may think we exhibit a so-called liberal bias in taking this stance, but the business element that often shapes editorial content, especially in small communities and perhaps the networks as well, tends to be more sympathetic to conservative political ideals. In addition, the fact that most media outlets recognize many conservative commentators probably shows how baseless this idea of a liberal media really is. Most publications also do not foreground information that is of concern to liberals or liberal organizations. For instance, do you know of any major news publication with a "Labor" section? How about a section entitled "Feminism"? Or, for that matter, "Racial Equality"? Does your local radio station give an environmental awareness update? Probably not (though with the rise of awareness in global warming, perhaps that may change). However, every major paper devotes a great deal of time to its business section, and just about every radio station gives some kind of market news or stock report. Sports never get the short shrift, yet many sportswriters, owners of sports franchises, and many athletes themselves tend to be both politically and socially conservative. Finally, simple coverage of events can reflect bias. In the September 2002 issue of *Harper's Magazine,* for example, the *Harper's* index lists the number of appearances made by corporate representatives on U.S. nightly newscasts in 2001 at 995, while the number of appearances of labor representatives was 31.

On the other hand, it may be unfair to accuse the media of leaning too far to the right. Most actors, filmmakers, and singers find affinity with left-leaning causes and, as you know, entertainment always makes the news. Both liberal and conservative groups assail the media for bias, which probably indicates that the media's bias falls somewhere in the middle. The media's political bias may or may not be of concern to you now, but it is one aspect of the media you will continually hear about as they play a larger and larger role in public discourse.

The media are not objective, but its members try to be fair.

Reporters and editors are human beings with political, social, and cultural preferences that they hope to acknowledge and put away when reporting. Reporters quickly learn they have to ask both (or many) sides of questions when it comes to an issue. News stories often have this "she said, he said" quality. Does that mean the media always do a good job of being objective or fair? Definitely not, but they generally aim to do so. Those outlets with a specific political agenda are usually responsible enough to make that orientation clear in their editorial page or early in the publication or program. It is also worth noting that editorial writers and columnists are absolutely under no obligation to be fair or objective; their object is to deliver their opinion for better or worse. Calls for their objectivity miss the point of what an editorial is supposed to do—deliver opinions.

Questions of objectivity and fairness are not only important when talking about the media but in your own work. As writers and researchers, we hope we are being objective when we undertake a subject, but we naturally come to any subject with a viewpoint that is shaped by our experiences and the ideas that come from them. That is why we may disagree with each other over whether we liked a movie or a book, or over which candidate we support in an election (or even who we find attractive or not).

Though reporters come to the news with biases, they generally do understand their obligations to report fairly and generally serve the public interest, just as editorial writers and columnists understand their *mission* to seek to influence public opinion. The bigger point here is that critics who claim a lack of objectivity from the media are uninformed about the reality of the media (sometimes deliberately so). The media often deserve the criticism they get from both liberals and conservatives, but an imperfect media is destined in any system— in particular, one whose primary focus is business. Understanding these concerns will help you understand the media in a more inclusive and a more informed way.

Advertisers reflect consumers' desires as well as business's desire to sell to them.

There is a long-standing belief that advertising is manipulative and somehow unsavory. While we won't argue fully with those ideas, we believe it is important to think about what exactly advertising does. For one, we do think that advertising generally tries to sell us things we want (even if we "shouldn't" want them). Advertising items that consumers do not want is not a particularly effective use of advertiser's dollars. If you look at the majority of what advertisers sell, they consist of consumer items such as food, cars, clothing, electronics, and services—things that people want, though again the issue of how many of these things we should have or want is another question. Advertising can only influence a consumer so much—if a new snack food tastes like soap or broccoli, endorsements by every celebrity will still fail to sell it. Accordingly, some advertising experts believe that the greatest influence happens in choosing a brand at the point of sale, not in actually choosing to buy the product itself. Most of the marketing research that businesses do is not geared toward learning how to manipulate but learning what consumers will buy.

Yet the question of how far advertisers go in changing our attitudes about our world and what we should want is an open question that researchers continue to try to answer. We think that blaming advertisers for the perceived shallowness of human desire oversimplifies the role advertisers and consumers play in deciding what they want.

In addition, both authors have been confronted in the classroom with the idea that the public is not very smart compared to the students themselves. This kind of thinking on the part of students probably underestimates the intelligence of the public. If you assume the public is as savvy as you are, you will avoid many pitfalls both now and in the future.

Advertising and graphic design can be considered artistic.

Artistic components abound in advertising. Advertisers and directors of commercials compose their ads so that they are both aesthetically pleasing and effective at getting us to buy. Advertisers often use the same principles as artists by seeking tension, drama, comedy, and beauty in their work. And sometimes directors and artists do both commercial and more "artistic" work. For instance, film directors such as David Lynch and the Coen brothers have all done television commercials, and many artists do graphic design (including those involved in the Absolut Vodka campaign). What complicates graphic design and television commercials as art is their associations with commercial interests. Americans like to separate art from commerce; we would rather have our artists make their money from selling their art to the community, not to companies. However, increasingly, the two worlds are merging.

What do we do when we see a funny or clever commercial or a piece of advertising that is particularly striking? Perhaps we feel at war with ourselves in trying to place within a context what is clearly artistic expression and yet is trying to sell us something. Can we enjoy the art of advertising while decrying its influence? It is a difficult question. There are a lot of clever advertisements and interesting graphic design out there; to make a false distinction between high art and commercialism is to ignore how the texts of advertising and the texts of art actually work.

Advertisers appeal to us through common images whose meaning we have already learned.

Advertisers appeal to us through images that are iconic—standing directly in for something—or symbolic. Diamond manufacturers do not have to tell us that diamonds serve as an icon for sophistication and wealth—we already know that. Thus, the diamond ring has become an icon for luxury, as has a spacious car with a leather interior and adjustable seats. We have learned what manicured lawns, Bermuda shorts, and gold jewelry mean by association. We know what it means to see a beach, golf clubs, a city, or any number of things or settings in a commercial. Because advertisers communicate through images as much as they do words, and these images seem to convey what they want without too much effort, looking at the visual language they use can tell us more about the role these images play in American culture.

Researchers disagree about advertising's effects on consumers.

Many researchers, including some of the writers included here, believe there is a connection between advertisements and harmful behavior. Jean Kilbourne (not included here), for example, suggests that ads influence our children in harmful ways, particularly young women. William Lutz argues that the way in which advertisers alter the meaning of words can have a harmful effect on language and how we use it. Others are not so sure.

The authors are not convinced in one particular way, with this caveat. We believe the relationship between humans and any form of culture is complicated. We are not denying that there is a relationship between advertising and behavior—we are just not convinced about how direct it is. Similarly, we are not making any specific claims about the relationship between the media and advertising except to say that the two are increasingly intimately related and that we urge you to continue to be literate readers of both.

NEWS MEDIA

Medium: What form of media are you watching or reading? How does form contribute to coverage?

Bias: What point of view does the story seem to have? Are there some key words that indicate this? Do all the same stories seem to have the same viewpoint? If there is a bias, is the story still "fair"—does the reporter seek multiple perspectives?

Signs: When watching a newscast, how does the program communicate in image (video, photograph, graphic)? What symbols does it use? Are there any unintended meanings? How does the clothing of the reporters and anchors contribute to what we take from the newscast?

Audience: To what audience does the news article or news report appeal? How can you tell? Will others outside the target audience feel alienated by the report or article? What are news organizations assuming about their audience in a particular piece or the newscast, magazine, Web site, or newspaper as a whole?

Reality: Do the images and ideas match your idea of reality? Are they supposed to? Do they (the people reporting and presenting the news) see the world the way you do?

Race, ethnicity, gender, class: How are images of any or all of these groups presented? Can you tell the bias of the reporter or news organization from their presentation?

ADVERTISING

Signs: How does the advertisement speak to you through images? What do the images symbolize? Are there unintended meanings attached to the symbols? Can you classify the symbols into types? What do advertisers assume about the connections you will make between the signs presented and what researchers call "the point of purchase"?

Audience: What is the target audience of this advertisement? How do you know? What assumptions are advertisers making about their audience?

Race, ethnicity, gender, class: How are images of any or all of these groups presented? Can you tell what advertisers think of these groups through their portrayal? Or their absence?

Before Jon Stewart: The Growth of Fake News. Believe It.

Robert Love

The Daily Show with Jon Stewart has altered how an entire demographic approach television news. The satirical news program has won dozens of awards, including an Emmy and a Peabody, and has spurred interest in "fake news." Robert Love's article on the history and rise of fake news originally appeared in the *Columbia Journalism Review* (2007). He is the executive editor of *Best Life* and an adjunct professor at Columbia University's Graduate School of Journalism.

JUST BEFORE HIS FAMOUS CONFRONTATION with Tucker Carlson on CNN 's *Crossfire* two years ago, Jon Stewart was introduced as "the most trusted name in fake news." No argument there. Stewart, as everyone knows, is the host of *The Daily Show*, a satirical news program that has been running since 1996 and has spun off the equally funny and successful *Colbert Report*. Together these shows are broadcast (back to back) more than twenty-three times a week, "from Comedy Central's World News Headquarters in New York," thus transforming a modest side-street studio on Manhattan's West Side into the undisputed locus of fake news.

The trope itself sounds so modern, so hip, so *Gawkerish* when attached to the likes of Stewart or Stephen Colbert, or dropped from the lips of the ex-*Saturday Night Live* "Weekend Update" anchor Tina Fey, who declared as she departed SNL, "I'm out of the fake news business." For the rest of us, we're knee deep in the fake stuff and sinking fast. It comes at us from every quarter of the media—old and new—not just as satire but disguised as the real thing, secretly paid for by folks who want to remain in the shadows. And though much of it is clever, it's not all funny.

Fake news arrives on doorsteps around the world every day, paid for by You, *Time* magazine Person of the Year, a.k.a. Joe and Jane Citizen, in one way or another. Take for instance, the U.S. government's 2005 initiative to plant "positive news" in Iraqi newspapers, part of a $300 million U.S. effort to sway public opinion about the war. And remember Armstrong Williams, the conservative columnist who was hired on the down low to act as a $240,000 sock puppet for the president's No Child Left Behind program? Williams's readers had no idea he was a paid propagandist until the Justice Department started looking into allegations of fraud in his billing practices.

Fake news has had its lush innings. The Bush administration has worked hand-in-glove with big business to make sure of it. Together, they've credentialed fringe scientists and fake experts and sent them in to muddy scientific debates on global warming, stem cell research, evolution, and other matters. And as if that weren't enough, the Department of Health and Human Services got caught producing a series of deceptive video news releases—VNRs in p.r.-industry parlance—touting the administration's Medicare plan. The segments, paid political announcements really, ended with a fake journalist signing off like a real one—"In Washington, I'm Karen Ryan reporting," and they ran on local news shows all over the country without disclosure. All of this fakery taken together, it may be fair to say that the nation's capital has been giving Comedy Central a run for its money as the real home of fake news.

But let's dispense with the satire, whose intentions are as plain as Colbert's arched eyebrow. And let's step around the notion of fake news as *wrong* news: The 1948 presidential election blunder DEWEY DEFEATS TRUMAN, for instance, or even the *New York Post*'s howler from the 2004 campaign, DEM PICKS GEPHARDT AS VP CANDIDATE. Those are honest mistakes, set loose by overweening editors perhaps, but never with the intention to deceive. That wasn't always the case, as we shall see. In the early days of American journalism, newspapers trafficked in intentional, entertaining hoaxes, a somewhat puzzling period in our history. In modern times, hoaxes have migrated from the mainstream papers to the tabloid outriders like the old *National Enquirer*, the new *Globe*, and the hoaxiest of them all, *The Weekly World News*, purveyor of the "Bat Boy" cover stories.

The mainstream press covers itself with the mantle of authority now. Six of ten Americans polled in 2005 trusted "the media" to report the news "fully, fairly and accurately," a slight decline from the high-water mark of seven-in-ten during the Woodward-and-Bernstein seventies. What's more, in a veracity dogfight between the press and the government, Americans say they trust the media by a margin of nearly two to one.

But here's a question: Can we continue to trust ourselves? Are we prepared for the global, 24-7 fake news cage match that will dominate journalism in the twenty-first century? Let's call it *Factual Fantasy: Attack of the Ax-Grinding Insiders*. The boundaries have vanished, the gloves are off, our opponents are legion and fueled with espresso. Both CNN and *The New York Times* were used by the U.S. military as unwitting co-conspirators in spreading false information, a tactic known as *psychological operations*, part of an effort to convince Americans the invasion of Iraq was a necessary piece of the war on terror.

But let's not leave out the technology. Leaks may be the time-tested tactic for manipulating the press, but the new digital toolbox has given third-party players—government, industry, politicians, you name 'em—sleeker weapons and greater power to turn the authority of the press to their own ends: to disseminate propaganda, disinformation, advertising, politically strategic misinformation—to in effect use the media to distort reality. Besides a vast and sophisticated degree of diligence, the rising generation of journalists would be wise to observe two rules for working in this new environment: Beware of profiteers and hyperpatriots, and check out a little history—lest it repeat itself.

Fake news has been with us for a long time. Documented cases predate the modern media, reaching as far into the past as a bogus eighth century edict said to be the pope-friendly words of the Roman emperor Constantine. There are plenty of reports of forgeries and trickeries in British newspapers in the eighteenth century. But the actual term "fake news"—two delicious little darts of malice (and a headline-ready sneer if ever there was one)—seems to have arisen in late nineteenth century America, when a rush of emerging technologies intersected with newsgathering practices during a boom time for newspapers.

The impact of new technology is hard to overestimate. The telegraph was followed by transAtlantic and transcontinental cables, linotype, high-speed electric presses and halftone photo printing—wireless gave way to the telephone. The nation, doubled in population and literacy from Civil War days, demanded a constant supply of fresh news, so the media grew additional limbs as fast as it could. Newly minted news bureaus and press associations recruited boy and girl reporters from classified ads—"Reporting And Journalism Taught Free Of Charge"—and sent their cubs off to dig up hot stories, truth be damned, to sell to the dailies.

By the turn of the century, the preponderance of fakery was reaching disturbing proportions, according to the critic and journalist J.B. Montgomery-M'Govern. "Fake journalism," he wrote in *Arena*, an influential monthly of the period, "is resorted to chiefly by news bureaus, press associations and organizations of that sort, which supply nearly all the metropolitan Sunday papers and many of the dailies with their most sensational 'stories.'"

Montgomery-M'Govern delivers a taxonomy of fakers' techniques, including the use of the "stand-for," in which a reputable person agrees to an outrageous lie for the attendant free publicity; the "combine," in which a group of reporters concoct and then verify a false story; the "fake libel" plant, in which editors are duped by conspirators into running false and litigious articles; the "alleged cable news" story, in which so-called "foreign reports," dashed off in the newsroom or a downtown press association, are topped with a foreign dateline and published as truth. The editors of huge Sunday editions, with their big appetites for the juiciest stuff (what M-M calls "Sunday stories") naturally set the bar lower for veracity than they did for hot-blooded emotional impact.

Have I mentioned that news was suddenly big money? By the century's turn, the tallest buildings in New York and San Francisco were both owned by newspapers. And the business became so hypercompetitive that some reporters not only made things up but stole those fake scoops and "specials" from one another with impunity. The Chicago Associated-Press fell into a trap set by a suspicious client, who set loose a rumor at two in the morning that President Grover Cleveland had been assassinated! True to its reputation, Chicago AP ran with it—no fact-checking here—and put it up on the wires. The assassination story ran in newspapers all over the country the next day, amid much chuckling and finger pointing.

The further away the newsworthy event, the more likely it was to involve fakery. BOGUS FOREIGN NEWS ran the headline in *The Washington Post* of February 22, 1903, but the subheads that followed it are so illustrative as to deserve full reproduction below.

POPE HAS DIED TWENTY-TWO TIMES IN FIVE YEARS
YELLOWNESS ACROSS THE SEA
AMERICANS OUTSTRIPPED IN THIS SORT OF THING BY ENGLISH AND
GERMAN MANUFACTURERS-EDITORS VICTIMS
BECAUSE REPORTS ARE SOMETIMES TRUE-RIVALRY FOR NEWS AMONG
ORIENTAL ENGLISH DAILIES

It was a global problem. Even twenty true words cabled from London about an Indian Ocean hurricane could grow to a story ten times that length, padded out with imaginary details and encyclopedia facts. Mo' words, mo' money.

The loudest whoops at the fake news fiesta were shouted at William Randolph Hearst's *New York Journal*. Hearst, the legendary publisher and proud leading light of the "yellow press," propounded two combustible ideas at the height of his influence in the late 1890s. First, he believed in the "journalism of action," an activist press solving crimes, supporting charities, investigating corruption—taking charge in the arenas of national and international affairs. Second, he held unvarnished truth to be a somewhat negotiable commodity, especially when its subversion could lead to profit or power.

By 1897, the stage was set for a little international combustion. Cuba, ruled as a Spanish colony since 1511, had grown an insurgency, which was put down with terrific cruelty by its European overlords. In the U.S. there was a growing sentiment for a free and independent Cuba, along with the feeling that we should be mobilized for war to help out. Teddy Roosevelt, Joseph Pulitzer, and Hearst, among many others, felt that aggression was the proper response, but President McKinley was slow to act. And so began the first privately funded propaganda push to war in modern media history.

It kicked off in earnest on February 15, 1898, when the warship *USS* Maine, docked in Havana Harbor, exploded, killing 266 crewmen. Hearst first placed an ad offering $50,000 REWARD! FOR THE DETECTION OF THE PERPETRATOR OF THE MAINE OUTRAGE! He then threw all of his paper's resources at covering the explosion and its investigation, sending boatloads of reporters and illustrators to Cuba and Key West. Hearst's *Journal*—along with Pulitzer's *World*—not only produced the bulk of the news coming out of Cuba, but within days began spinning it to blame Spain for the explosion.

Competing papers cried foul! "Nothing so disgraceful as the behavior of these two newspapers has ever been known in the history of journalism," wrote E.L. Godkin in the *New York Evening Post*. He alleged "gross misrepresentation of the facts, deliberate intervention of tales calculated to excite the public and wanton recklessness in construction of headlines."

Nevertheless it was headlines that propelled the United States to war with Spain, headlines that swayed the populace with somewhat dubious evidence. War was declared and in two weeks it was over; we had freed Cuba, gained three new territories, and ended Spain's influence in the Western Hemisphere.

Okay, headlines can lie, but can you better determine the truth in a photo or the voice of a trusted colleague? With the advent of faster and easier halftone reproduction in the 1920s came the photo-driven tabloid newspapers like the *New York Illustrated Daily News*. In 1924 the most tabloidy of all tabloids arrived, the *New York Evening Graphic* (nicknamed the Porno-graphic), which launched the gossip careers of Ed Sullivan and Walter Winchell and the vaunted Composograph photo. The Composograph was actually a technique that combined real and staged pictures to depict events where no cameras had ventured. *The Graphic's* editors had a blast with the pop star Rudolph Valentino, documenting the singer's unsuccessful surgery, funeral, and his meeting in heaven with the departed Enrico Caruso—the headline: RUDY MEETS CARUSO! TENOR'S SPIRIT SPEAKS!

Telephones meant faster, more accurate newsgathering at a time when speed was prized and "extra" editions meant extra profits. The telephone necessitated the creation of two-man urban reporting teams—leg men and rewrite men—which irritated H.L. Mencken to no end. "Journalism," he wrote in 1927, "is in a low state, mainly due to the decay of the old-time reporter, the heart and soul of the American newspapers of the last generation. The current rush to get upon the streets with hot news, even at the cost of printing only half of it, has pretty well destroyed all his old qualities. He no longer writes what he has seen and heard; he telephones it to a remote and impersonal rewrite man. . . . But it must be manifest that, hanging on his telephone, maybe miles away from the event he is describing, he is completely unable to get into his description any of the vividness of a thing actually seen. He does the best he can, but that best is to the reporting of a fairer era as a mummy is to a man."

Of course Mencken's selective memory harks back to the glory days of yellow journalism, when the worst (or best) fakery in history took place, but never mind that. He seems to have completely forgotten his own role ten years earlier in a great classic newspaper hoax, "A Neglected Anniversary," a fake history of the bathtub, which ran in the *New York Evening Mail* on December 28, 1917.

"Not a plumber fired a salute or hung out a flag," Mencken lamented. "Not a governor proclaimed a day of prayer. Not a newspaper called attention to the day," the purported seventy-fifth birthday of the bathtub. Mencken's piece provided a vivid and full history of the introduction of the tub to American life. It singled out for praise Millard Fillmore for his role in bringing one of the first tubs to the White House, giving it "recognition and respectability in the United States."

"A Neglected Anniversary" was so finely rendered that it literally sprang back to life—like a reanimated mummy—and found its way into print dozens of times, criticized, analyzed, and repeated as a real chapter in American history.

Hoaxes like this seem so *Colbert* now, like mutant cousins to his notion of "truthiness." But hoaxers are historically not comedians; they are, like Mencken, journalists who write entertaining stuff that sounds vaguely true, even though it's not, for editors who are usually in on the joke. The hoaxing instinct infected newsrooms throughout the early days of modern newspapers to a degree that most of us find puzzling today. Newspapers contained hundreds, if not thousands of hoaxes in the late nineteenth and early twentieth centuries, most of them undocumented fakes in obscure Western weeklies. The subjects were oddball pets and wild weather, giants, mermaids, men on the moon, petrified people (quite a few of those), and (my favorite) the Swiss Navy. As a novice editor at the Virginia City, Nevada, *Territorial Enterprise*, a young Mark Twain put his talent to the test with a hoax of hoaxes. "I chose to kill the petrification mania with a delicate, a very delicate satire," he wrote. He called it "A Petrified Man."

Who knew? The twinning of news and entertainment that plagues us today grew not from some corporate greedhead instinct of the go-go eighties, but from our own weird history. The reasons for hoaxing were mostly mercenary: for the publisher, it was to fill column inches and bring in eyeballs. For the journalist, it was sport, a freelance fee or a ploy to keep his job. Strange to say, readers didn't seem to mind too much.

The first major fake news event of the modern media age was the Great Moon Hoax of 1835. A series of articles began appearing in the *New York Sun* on August 25, the late-summer brainchild of its ambitious publisher, Benjamin Day. Day wanted to move papers, like every publisher, and came up with a novel method. He began publishing a series of articles, allegedly reprinted from a nonexistent scientific journal, about Sir John Herschel, an eminent British astronomer on his way to the Cape of Good Hope to test a powerful new telescope.

What Herschel saw on the moon was . . . Life! Not just flora and fauna but living men—hairy, yellow-faced guys, four feet tall with enormous wings that "possessed great expansion and were similar in structure of those of the bat." It was all too much, but New Yorkers had to see for themselves and the *Sun*'s circ hit a new high of 15,000. Even after its men-in-the-moon story was revealed to be a hoax, the paper retained its popularity with readers.

Edgar Allan Poe, famous but destitute in 1844, wrote another well-known hoax for the *Sun*. THE ATLANTIC CROSSED IN THREE DAYS! Poe's story began, and it went on to describe a lighter-than-air balloon trip that wouldn't actually take place for another sixty years. Thirty years later, at the behest of its publisher, James Gordon Bennett Jr., the *New York Herald* ran what's often been called the Central Park Zoo Hoax. ESCAPED ANIMALS ROAM STREETS OF MANHATTAN the headline warned. The article maintained that twenty-seven people were dead and 200 injured in terrible scenes of mutilation. State militiamen were called in to control the situation, and sensible New Yorkers barricaded themselves in their homes.

In 1910, *The Washington Post* waxed nostalgic over the old men-on-the moon hoax, with a short item under a no-nonsense headline: THIS WAS A FAMOUS HOAX. In fact, that kind of warm retrospective began to appear as an occasional column or feature, illustrating a growing trend among newspapers to look back with a smile on the bad old days of great hoaxes. In the intervening years, the newspaper business had grown up into the Fourth Estate; hoaxes, for better or worse, were a part of its wild-child adolescence. By 1937, it was pretty much over, at least according to Marvin H. Creager, the president of the American Society of Newspaper Editors who addressed the group's fifteenth annual convention. "The day of the fake and the hoax . . . seems to have passed," he said, "and with it the reporters and editors who delighted in perpetrating them."

Creager, speaking to his confident colleagues at a time of rising circulation, added, "The reporter with a box of tricks is out of place in the newspaper world today."

Times change and so do the tricksters. The newspaper, the first mass-marketed medium to enter American living rooms, was a jack of all trades, a witty parlor guest with a deck of cards. Over time, mass distribution of movies, radio, TV, and the Internet arrived to entertain Americans and eventually to eat the lunch of the great newspaper dynasties. From the days of the Yellow Press onward, publishers began to see themselves as public servants and guardians of truth; editors learned the wisdom of marking off news columns from opinion pages and imparting a higher level of veracity even to soft features. Hoaxes? The Fourth Estate has no use for hoaxers, even of the pathetic dysfunctional variety; our tribal councils cast out fabulists like Jayson Blair or Stephen Glass with great harrumphing fanfare.

Today, people expect the news media to give them relevant, accurate information. Serious journalists have for decades thought of themselves as the descendants of muckrakers, reformers, and watchdogs.

But hold the applause for a moment. This presumption of good faith makes us the perfect marks for the new agenda-based fakers. Just last year, the Center for Media and Democracy identified sixty-nine news stations that ran clearly marked government- or industry-produced VNRs as unbiased news during a ten-month period. Many station managers, it was reported, even disguised those advertisements to look like their reporters' own work and offered no public disclosure.

Doctored pictures from war zones? The *Los Angeles Times* ran one in 2003, and Reuters ran one last year. Grassroots organizations with Orwellian names like Project Protect, funded not by conservation-minded voters, but the timber industry? The investigative reporter Paul Thacker brought that one to light, along the way revealing that a Fox News science reporter named Steven Milloy had undisclosed ties to the oil and tobacco industries. Milloy discredited reports of the danger of secondhand smoke as "junk science" on foxnews.com, never letting on he was on the payroll of Phillip Morris.

Welcome to journalism's latest transitional phase, where another rush of technology is changing the business in ways not imaginable ten years ago. Picture, cell, and satellite phones, wireless Internet, cheap digital cameras, Photoshop, and blogger software make it easier to deliver the news and also easier to fake it. If you're the kind of person who thinks there ought to be a law, there is one, at least for the conduct of our elected officials. Federal statutes prohibit the use of funding for "publicity or propaganda purposes" not authorized by Congress. The ban seems to have been observed as closely as speeding laws in recent years. For the rest of us, however, it's what they call a self-policing situation.

Late last year, Armstrong Williams, the conservative commentator who took undisclosed payments to promote President Bush's education agenda, settled his case with the Justice Department. The feds had pursued him not for propaganda violations, though they might have, but under the False Claims Act, for false or fraudulent billing. A weary Armstrong agreed to repay $34,000 to the government and said he was happy to be done with it. He admits no wrongdoing and has committed no crime.

In the exposure, however, he lost his syndicated column and suffered an eighteen-month investigation. The notoriety of his case jump-started a government-wide inquiry into the use of fake news as propaganda, which may actually have done some good. According to *USA Today*, "the Government Accountability Office, Congress's nonpartisan watchdog, in 2005 found that the deal violated a ban on 'covert propaganda.'"

But make no mistake; it's a small, isolated victory. In a time of falling circulation, diminishing news budgets, and dismantled staffs, the fakers are out there, waiting for their opportunities to exploit the authority that modern journalism conveys. Some of us, I fear, aren't doing all we can to help readers and viewers know the difference between the fake and the honest take. In early January, *The Huffington Post* reported that *The Washington Post*'s Web site was talking to Comedy Central about enlisting *The Daily Show* staff to cover the 2008 presidential campaign. Jon Stewart, the elder statesman of fake news, working for *The Washington Post*? There was no confirmation of a deal at press time.

So, here's my totally mock serious signoff: If General Pervez Musharraf, the president of Pakistan, who has already appeared once on *The Daily Show*, returned to announce that he had captured Osama bin Laden, would that be fake news? And what would we call it when it ran in *The Washington Post*?

Just asking.

READING WRITING

This Text: Reading
1. What does Love think of "fake news"? Do you agree with him?
2. Do you think he fairly characterizes Jon Stewart and Comedy Central? In what ways do those entities differ from mainstream media organizations?

Your Text: Writing

1. Watch *The Daily Show* one night and critique the presentation of news.
2. Compare *The Onion* to *The Daily Show*. What functions do each perform?
3. Watch *The Daily Show* and a network news evening broadcast. In what ways do they differ in their presentation? Where does *The Daily Show* borrow from network news? Which show informs you better?

Advertising and People of Color

Clint C. Wilson and Felix Gutierrez

By giving semiotic readings of some disturbing advertisements, Wilson and Gutierrez demonstrate how people of color and stereotypes about ethnicities have been exploited to sell various items (1995). As you read, pay attention to how the authors blend research and their own interpretation of visual texts.

Also, as we mention in "Reading an Advertisement" in Chapter One, it is often difficult to obtain permission to reprint advertisements. As it turns out, we were denied permission to print all three ads that appear in the original version of this essay—most likely because companies have become more sensitive to the personal and legal ramifications of racial stereotyping. In one ad for Cream of Wheat, Rastus, a black servant in a chef's cap, holds a blackboard containing information about Cream of Wheat written in African-American dialect. The other, an ad for Crown Royal aimed at Hispanic audiences, shows five clearly wealthy, well-dressed Latinos and Latinas drinking Crown Royal at what appears to be a fancy birthday party. The text for the ad, "Comparta sus riquezas" ("Share the Wealth") is in Spanish. Finally, though AT&T did deny us permission to print the original ad, they did agree to let us run an updated one. The original shows a young Chinese girl holding a phone. Appearing in Chinese newspapers in the United States, the ad ran only in Chinese.

GIVEN THE SOCIAL AND LEGAL RESTRICTIONS on the participation of racial minorities in the society of the United States during much of this country's history, it is not hard to see how the desire to cater to the perceived views of the mass audience desired by advertisers resulted in entertainment and news content that largely ignored people of color, treated them stereotypically when they were recognized, and largely avoided grappling with such issues as segregation, discriminatory immigration laws, land rights, and other controversial issues that affected certain minority groups more than they did the White majority. Although the entertainment and editorial portrayal of non-Whites is amply analyzed in other chapters of this book, it is important to recognize that those portrayals were, to a large extent, supported by a system of advertising that required the media to cater to the perceived attitudes and prejudices of the White majority and that also reinforced such images in its own commercial messages. For years advertisers in the United States reflected the place of non-Whites in the social fabric of the nation either by ignoring them or, when they were included in advertisements for the mass audience, processing and presenting them in a way that would make them palatable salespersons for the products being advertised. These processed portrayals largely mirrored the stereotypic images of minorities in the entertainment media that, in turn, were designed to reflect the perceived values and norms of the White majority. In this way, non-White portrayals in advertising paralleled and reinforced their entertainment and journalistic images in the media.

The history of advertising in the United States is replete with characterizations that, like the Frito Bandito, responded to and reinforced the preconceived image that many White Americans apparently had of Blacks, Latinos, Asians, and Native Americans. Over the years advertisers have employed Latin spitfires like Chiquita Banana, Black mammies like Aunt Jemima, and noble savages like the Santa Fe Railroad's Super Chief to pitch their products to a predominately White mass audience of consumers. In 1984 the Balch Institute for Ethnic Studies in Philadelphia sponsored an exhibit of more than 300 examples of racial and ethnic images used by corporations in magazines, posters, trade cards, and storyboards. In an interview with the advertising trade magazine *Advertising Age,* institute director Mark Stolarik quoted the catalog for the exhibit, which capsulized the evolution of images of people of color and how they have changed.

"Some of these advertisements were based on stereotypes of various ethnic groups. In the early years, they were usually crude and condescending images that appealed to largely Anglo-American audiences who found it difficult to reconcile their own visions of beauty, order and behavior with that of non-Anglo-Americans," said Stolarik. "Later, these images were softened because of complaints from the ethnic groups involved and the growing sophistication of the advertising industry."[1]

The advertising examples in the exhibit include positive White ethnic stereotypes, such as the wholesome and pure image of Quakers in an early Quaker Oats advertisement and the cleanliness of the Dutch in a turn-of-the century advertisement for Colgate soaps. But they also featured a late 19th century advertisement showing an Irish matron threatening to hit her husband over the head with a rolling pin because he didn't smoke the right brand of tobacco. Like Quaker Oats, some products even incorporated a stereotypical image on the package or product line being advertised.

"Lawsee! Folks sho' whoops with joy over AUNT JEMIMA PANCAKES," shouted a bandanna-wearing Black mammy in a magazine advertisement for Aunt Jemima pancake mix, which featured a plump Aunt Jemima on the box. Over the years, Aunt Jemima has lost some weight, but the stereotyped face of the Black servant continues to be featured on the box. Earlier advertisements for Cream of Wheat featured Rastus, the Black servant on the box, in a series of magazine cartoons with a group of cute but ill-dressed Black children. Some of the advertisements played on stereotypes ridiculing Blacks, such as an advertisement in which a Black school teacher standing behind a makeshift lectern made out of a boldly lettered Cream of Wheat box, asks the class "How do you spell Cream of Wheat?" Others appeared to promote racial integration, such as a magazine advertisement captioned "Putting it down in Black and White," which showed Rastus serving bowls of the breakfast cereal to Black and White youngsters sitting at the same table.

Racial imagery was also integrated into the naming of trains by the Santa Fe railroad, which named one of its passenger lines the Super Chief and featured highly detailed portraits of the noble Indian in promoting its service through the Southwestern United States. In another series of advertisements, the railroad used cartoons of Native American children to show the service and sights passengers could expect when they traveled the Santa Fe line.

These and other portrayals catered to the mass audience mentality by either neutralizing or making humor of the negative perceptions that many Whites may have had of racial minorities. The advertising images, rather than showing people of color as they really were, portrayed them as filtered through Anglo eyes. This presented an out-of-focus image of racial minorities, but one that was palatable, and even persuasive, to the White majority to which it was directed. In the mid-1960s Black civil rights groups targeted the advertising industry for special attention, protesting both the lack of integrated advertisements including Blacks and the stereotyped images that the advertisers continued to use. The effort, accompanied by support from federal officials, resulted in the overnight inclusion of Blacks as models in television advertising in 1967 and a downplaying of the images that many Blacks found objectionable.

"Black America is becoming visible in America's biggest national advertising medium," reported the *New York Times* in 1968. "Not in a big way yet, but it is a beginning and men in high places give assurances that there will be a lot more visibility."[2]

But the advertising industry did not generalize the concerns of Blacks, or the concessions made in response to them, to other groups. At the same time that some Black concerns were being addressed with integrated advertising, other groups were being ignored or singled out for continued stereotyped treatment in such commercials as those featuring the Frito Bandito.

Among the Latino advertising stereotypes cited in a 1969 article[3] by sociologist Tomás Martínez were commercials for Granny Goose chips featuring fat gun-toting Mexicans, an advertisement for Arrid underarm deodorant showing a dusty Mexican bandito spraying his underarms after a hard ride as the announcer intones, "If it works for him it will work for you," and a magazine advertisement featuring a stereotypical Mexican sleeping under his sombrero as he leans against a Philco television set. Especially offensive to Martínez was a Liggett & Meyers commercial for L&M cigarettes that featured Paco, a lazy Latino who never "feenishes" anything, not even the revolution he is supposed to be fighting. In response to a letter complaining about the commercial, the director of public relations for the tobacco firm defended the commercial's use of Latino stereotypes.

"'Paco' is a warm, sympathetic and lovable character with whom most of us can identify because he has a little of all of us in him, that is, our tendency to procrastinate at times," wrote the Liggett & Meyers executive. "He seeks to escape the violence of war and to enjoy the pleasure of the moment, in this case, the good flavor of an L&M cigarette."[4] Although the company spokesman claimed that the character had been tested without negative reactions from Latinos (a similar claim was made by Frito-Lay regarding the Frito Bandito), Martínez roundly criticized the advertising images and contrasted them to what he saw as the gains Blacks were then making in the advertising field.

"Today, no major advertiser would attempt to display a black man or woman over the media in a prejudiced, stereotyped fashion," Martínez wrote.

> Complaints would be forthcoming from black associations and perhaps the FCC. Yet, these same advertisers, who dare not show "step'n fetch it" characters, uninhibitedly depict a Mexican counterpart, with additional traits of stinking and stealing. Perhaps the white hatred for blacks, which cannot find adequate expression in today's ads, is being transferred upon their brown brothers.[5]

In 1970 a Brown Position Paper prepared by Latino media activists Armando Rendón and Domingo Nick Reyes charged that the media had transferred the negative stereotypes it once reserved for Blacks to Latinos, who had become "the media's new nigger."[6] The protests of Latinos soon made the nation's advertisers more conscious of the portrayals that Latinos found offensive. But, as in the case of the Blacks, the advertising industry failed to apply the lessons learned from one group to other racial minorities.

Although national advertisers withdrew much of the advertising that negatively stereotyped Blacks and Latinos, sometimes replacing them with affluent, successful images that were as far removed from reality as the negative portrayals of the past, the advances made by those groups were not shared with Native Americans and Asians. Native Americans' names and images, no longer depicted either as the noble savage or as cute cartoon characters, have all but disappeared from broadcast commercials and print advertising. The major exceptions are advertising for automobiles and trucks that bear names such as Pontiac, Dakota, and Navajo and sports teams with racial nicknames such as the Kansas City Chiefs, Washington Redskins, Florida State University Seminoles, Atlanta Braves, and Cleveland Indians. Native Americans and others have protested these racial team names and images, as well as the pseudo-Native American pageantry and souvenirs that accompany many of them but with no success in getting them changed.

Asians, particularly Japanese, continue to be dealt more than their share of commercials depicting them in stereotypes that cater to the fears and stereotypes of White America. As was the case with Blacks and Latinos, it took organized protests from Asian American groups to get the message across to the corporations and their advertising agencies. In the mid-1970s, a Southern California supermarket chain agreed to remove a television campaign in which a young Asian karate-chopped his way down the store's aisles cutting prices. Nationally, several firms whose industries have been hard-hit by Japanese imports fought back through commercials, if not in the quality or prices of their products. One automobile company featured an Asian family carefully looking over a new car and commenting on its attributes in heavily accented English. Only after they bought it did they learn it was made in the United States, not Japan. Another automobile company that markets cars manufactured in Japan under an English-language name showed a parking lot attendant opening the doors of the car, only to find the car speaking to him in Japanese. For several years Sylvania television ran a commercial boasting that its television picture had repeatedly been selected over competing brands as an off-screen voice with a Japanese accent repeatedly asked, "What about Sony?" When the announcer responded that the Sylvania picture had also been selected over Sony's, the off-screen voice ran off shouting what sounded like a string of Japanese expletives. A 1982 *Newsweek* article observed that "attacking Japan has become something of a fashion in corporate ads" because of resentment over Japanese trade policies and sales of Japanese products in the United States, but quoted Motorola's advertising manager as saying, "We've been as careful as we can be" not to be racially offensive.[7]

But many of the television and print advertisements featuring Asians featured images that were racially insensitive, if not offensive. A commercial for a laundry product featured a Chinese family that used an "ancient Chinese laundry secret" to get their customer's clothes clean. Naturally, the Chinese secret turned out to be the packaged product paying for the advertisement. Companies pitching everything from pantyhose to airlines featured Asian women coiffed and costumed as seductive China dolls or exotic Polynesian natives to pitch and promote their products, some of them cast in Asian settings and others attentively caring for the needs of the Anglo men in the advertisement. One airline boasted that those who flew with it would be under the care of the Singapore Girl.

Asian women appearing in commercials were often featured as China dolls with the small, darkened eyes, straight hair with bangs, and a narrow, slit skirt. Another common portrayal featured the exotic, tropical Pacific Islands look, complete with flowers in the hair, a sarong or grass skirt, and shell ornament. Asian women hoping to become models sometimes found that they must conform to these stereotypes or lose assignments. Leslie Kawai, the 1981 Tournament of Roses Queen, was told to cut her hair with bangs by hairstylists when she auditioned for a beer advertisement. When she refused, the beer company decided to hire another model with shorter hair cut in bangs.[8]

The lack of a sizable Asian community, or market, in the United States was earlier cited as the reason that Asians are still stereotyped in advertising and, except for children's advertising, are rarely presented in integrated settings. The growth rate and income of Asians living in the United States in the 1980s and 1990s, however, reinforced the economic potential of Asian

Americans to overcome the stereotyping and lack of visibility that Blacks and Latinos challenged with some success. By the mid-1980s there were a few signs that advertising was beginning to integrate Asian Americans into crossover advertisements that, like the Tostitos campaign, were designed to have a broad appeal. In one commercial, television actor Robert Ito was featured telling how he loves to call his relatives in Japan because the calls make them think that he is rich, as well as successful, in the United States. Of course, he adds, it is only because the rates of his long distance carrier were so low that he was able to call Japan so often.

In the 1970s mass audience advertising in the United States became more racially integrated than at any time in the nation's history. Blacks, and to a much lesser extent Latinos and Asians, could be seen in television commercials spread across the broadcast week and in major magazines. In fact, the advertisements on network television often appeared to be more fully integrated than the television programs they supported. Like television, general circulation magazines also experienced an increase in the use of Blacks, although studies of both media showed that most of the percentage increase had come by the early 1970s. By the early 1970s the percentage of prime-time television commercials featuring Blacks had apparently leveled off at about 10%. Blacks were featured in between only 2% and 3% of magazine advertisements as late as 1978. That percentage, however small, was a sharp increase from the 0.06% of news magazine advertisements reported in 1960.[9]

The gains were also socially significant, because they demonstrated that Blacks could be integrated into advertisements without triggering a White backlash among potential customers in the White majority. Both sales figures and research conducted since the late 1960s have shown that the integration of Black models into television and print advertising does not adversely affect sales or the image of the product. Instead, a study by the American Newspaper Publishers Association showed, the most important influences on sales were the merchandise and the advertisement itself. In fact, while triggering no adverse effect among the majority of Whites, integrated advertisements were found to be useful in swaying Black consumers, who responded favorably to positive Black role models in print advertisements.[10] Studies conducted in the early 1970s also showed that White consumers did not respond negatively to advertising featuring Black models, although their response was more often neutral than positive.[11] One 1972 study examining White backlash, however, did show that an advertisement prominently featuring darker-skinned Blacks was less acceptable to Whites than those featuring lighter-skinned Blacks as background models.[12] Perhaps such findings help explain why research conducted later in the 1970s revealed that, for the most part, Blacks appearing in magazine and television advertisements were often featured as part of an integrated group.[13]

Although research findings have shown that integrated advertisements do not adversely affect sales, the percentage of Blacks and other minorities in general audience advertising did not increase significantly after the numerical gains made through the mid-1970s. Those minorities who did appear in advertisements were often depicted in upscale or integrated settings, an image that the Balch Institute's Stolarik criticized as taking advertising "too far in the other direction and created stereotypes of 'successful' ethnic group members that are as unrealistic as those of the past."[14] Equally unwise, from a business sense, was the low numbers of Blacks appearing in advertisements.

> "Advertisers and their ad agencies must evaluate the direct economic consequences of alternative strategies on the firm. If it is believed that the presence of Black models in advertisements decreases the effectiveness of advertising messages, only token numbers of Black models will be used,"

wrote marketing professor Lawrence Soley at the conclusion of a 1983 study.

"Previous studies have found that advertisements portraying Black models do not elicit negative affective or conative responses from consumers. . . . Given the consistency of the research findings, more Blacks should be portrayed in advertisements. If Blacks continue to be under-represented in advertising portrayals, it can be said that this is an indication of prejudice on the part of the advertising industry, not consumers."[15]

Notes

1. "Using Ethnic Images," p. 9.
2. Cited in Philip H. Dougherty, "Frequency of Blacks in TV Ads," *New York Times,* May 27, 1982, p. D19.
3. Martínez, "How Advertisers Promote," p. 10.
4. Martínez, "How Advertisers Promote," p. 11.
5. Martínez, "How Advertisers Promote," pp. 9–10.
6. Domingo Nick Reyes and Armando Rendón, *Chicanos and the Mass Media* (Washington, DC: The National Mexican American Anti-Defamation Committee, 1971).
7. Joseph Treen, "Madison Ave. vs. Japan, Inc.," *Newsweek* (April 12, 1982), p. 69.
8. Ada Kan, *Asian Models in the Media,* Unpublished term paper, Journalism 466: Minority and the Media, University of Southern California, December 14, 1983, p. 5.
9. Studies on increase of Blacks in magazine and television commercials cited in James D. Culley and Rex Bennett, "Selling Blacks, Selling Women," *Journal of Communication* (Autumn 1976, Vol. 26, No. 4), pp. 160–174; Lawrence Soley, "The Effect of Black Models on Magazine Ad Readership," *Journalism Quarterly* (Winter 1983, Vol. 60, No. 4), p. 686; and Leonard N. Reid and Bruce G. Vanden Bergh, "Blacks in Introductory Ads," *Journalism Quarterly* (Autumn 1980, Vol. 57, No. 3), pp. 485–486.
10. Cited in D. Parke Gibson, *$70 Billion in the Black* (New York: Macmillan, 1979), pp. 83–84.
11. Laboratory studies on White reactions to Blacks in advertising cited in Soley, "The Effect of Black Models," pp. 585–587.
12. Carl E. Block, "White Backlash to Negro Ads: Fact or Fantasy?" *Journalism Quarterly* (Autumn 1980, Vol. 49, No. 2), pp. 258–262.
13. James D. Culley and Rex Bennett, "Selling Blacks, Selling Women."
14. "Using Ethnic Images," p. 9.
15. Soley, *The Effect of Black Models,* p. 690.

READING WRITING

This Text: Reading

1. It's likely that you found the descriptions of some of these ads shocking. What do these advertisements tell you about how America and Americans used to see people of color?
2. This is one of the few essays that examine how all people of color have been represented. Were you surprised to read about images of Hispanics and American Indians? If so, why?
3. What is the argument of the essay?

Your Text: Writing

1. With some research, you should be able to track down some images of a similarly disturbing nature. What is the semiotic setting of these ads? Write a paper in which you analyze the ads from today's perspective but are mindful of the ad as being a cultural document.

2. Write an essay on advertising and white people. Based on ads, what assumptions can we make about Anglos?

3. Write a comparative paper examining what Wilson and Gutierrez say about race with a similar essay from the Race chapter.

Hanes Her Way

Brittany Gray

Student Essay

Brittany Gray was a freshman at Virginia Commonwealth University in Richmond when she wrote this analysis of a "Hanes Her Way" ad in 2001. In her analysis of an ad piece, Gray reads her ad through the lens of the familiar vs. fantasy.

IT KNOWS WHO YOU ARE. It knows what you want. It gets into your psyche, and then—onto your television, your computer screen, your newspapers and your magazines. It is an advertisement, folks, and it's studying every little move you make, be it in the grocery store or the outlet mall. These advertisement executives know just what the consumer needs to hear to convince him or her to buy the product. Grocery stores even consult such advertisement firms on matters such as just how to set up the store in order to maximize consumer purchase. It has been watching, and it knows just what mood to set to get into the head of the consumer, and just how to set the scene.

This particular scene is a mild, relaxed morning. The sun streams in through the windows. The lighting is a tranquil yellow, and the background music is "Fade Into You" by Mazzy Star, a soft and haunting ballad which perfectly complements the temperate setting. Through a doorway a man watches a woman who is wearing a white t-shirt and white cotton underwear as she makes a bed, snapping a sheet into the air and watching it drift back down onto the bed in slow motion. Then a voiceover begins. The man talks over the music about how when they were dating, his girlfriend used to wear such tiny, sexy underwear. Then he says that now that they are married she just wears old worn cotton underwear by Hanes. He goes on to say that there is something comforting about the cotton underwear. He says he loves when he opens the laundry hamper and sees the worn out underwear in there waiting to go into the wash, because it reminds him of his mother and his childhood. The commercial then fades out on the Hanes trademark.

The ethical appeal in this commercial is particularly strong. For starters, the brand name of Hanes goes back a long way and has been trusted for years. There is nothing more comforting about buying a product than knowing that millions of people aside from oneself also trust the product. Also, the people in the ad seem to trust the product. It seems that trust and stability are the qualities that Hanes wants the customer to attribute to their underwear.

The pathos in this commercial was the strongest of all the appeals. The fact that, first of all, the couple is married, and also that the man seems to love and accept his wife so openly plays a part in the emotional appeal. It is not often that couples on television are married anymore, and when they are, their lives and marital stress are often the topic of comedy. This couple is not only happily married, but obviously has been married for a while as well, given the fact that the wife has had time to change her style of underwear *and* the fact that her Hanes Her Way cotton briefs are well worn.

Another aspect of the pathos is the setting of the scene. The tranquility of the lighting, the airy atmosphere consisting of so much white cotton and linen, and the relaxing background music all play a role in the manipulation of emotion. The way the man stands there with such a nostalgic look on his face, watching his wife and speaking about her so wistfully is meant to really touch something inside—and it does. Not only that, but the man still finds his wife beautiful, even after so many years, and even after the underwear that he initially found so attractive is gone. The entire ad evokes a sense of tranquility and comfort, seeming to say, "our product will fulfill you just the way these people are fulfilled."

The appeal to logic in this ad was for the most part absent, aside from one thing. After all, there is no real logic to a man liking his wife's underwear, nor is there any rhyme or reason behind the comfort that seeing the underwear lying in the hamper brings him, reminding him of his childhood and his mother. Hanes underwear does not make the sun come out in the morning, and it certainly won't find someone a spouse. The logic of the commercial, as well as the fact of the matter, is that Hanes underwear is comfortable—especially Hanes Her Way white cotton briefs.

The audience targeted in this commercial was without question middle-class women, probably aged 12 and up. Most men do not get misty-eyed hearing pretty music, and they are not particularly struck watching a man speak so fondly of his wife. However, women thrive on such things. Every woman loves to see a man talk about his wife as though she were the only woman on the earth, because it is such a rare occurrence.

That is not the only aspect of the ad directed at women, however. The lighting in the commercial, paired with the beautiful sunny morning, as well as the crisp white linens shown throughout the commercial, are all aimed at women in middle-class families. Women love to see that level of comfort and cleanliness within a home, as it all touches on a woman's romantic, idealistic side. Also, the fact that the couple and their home is so completely average shows that Hanes is for average, normal people. Everyone wants to feel that what they do is normal and accepted, especially women trying to run a home. It is one less thing to worry about, one less thing that can be criticized when it comes to a woman's running of her home. It also shows that the happiness of the couple is not out of reach—they are just like every other working class American couple.

These audience clinchers are not entirely in opposition to the ones used in men's underwear commercials. Many men's underwear commercials portray scenes containing rumpled beds in the morning, and fresh white linen. Underwear commercials in general seem to abound in their portrayal of morning sunrises and beautiful people making beds. In men's commercials, though, it seems that there is always that bittersweet touch of masculinity. There is constantly some muscular role model, doing the types of things that strong, ideal men should do. The man in the commercial always seems to do the same stereotyped things. He gives the dog a bath, he plays with the kids. He does the dishes with a smile, pausing to toss a handful of bubbles at his adoring wife. He goes jogging in the morning before his coffee. He shows his son how to throw a baseball just right, and of course he doesn't neglect his daughter—he tosses her into the air, and playfully dodges her blows during a pillow fight. And of course, he feels perfectly comfortable sitting around in nothing but his white cotton briefs.

Women on the other hand don't need examples of femininity. They know how to be women, and showing what the typical woman does in a day would be cheesy and clichéd. Just show a woman a good old fashioned love scene and most likely she's sold.

This commercial probably shouldn't appeal to me so strongly. It is exactly like most other commercials for women's underwear I have seen. They all have the same basic elements: white linen, sunny mornings, happy families, and beautiful, smiling people. I'm not sure if I can place my finger on exactly what made this commercial stand out for me. I think it was the combination of the music and the couple. I've never heard music like that in an underwear commercial. The music used is normally that sunny, get-up-and-go type of music, but this commercial utilized the softer sound of Mazzy Star. The voiceover and the utilization of romance really struck me too. Though the ad was not particularly original, I still felt that it was a beautifully done commercial.

The ethos of this commercial was definitely strong. The name of Hanes is one of the most trusted in underwear, and the advertisers used the stability of the marital relationship to illustrate this. However, the pathos was the most outstanding of the appeals in this ad. The fact that the underwear was made by Hanes was made known, as well as the reasons why Hanes should be trusted. However, the vivid sensory imagery in this commercial which made it so pleasing to the eye and such a joy to watch rules over the ethical appeal. A sunny morning means much more to me personally than the comfort of knowing that I'm wearing sturdy underwear, which is a comfort that is forgotten soon after putting the underwear on. A morning as beautiful as the one on TV is not commonly seen, nor is a couple more obviously in love. It is simple joys such as these that the commercial strikes at, and the joys seem to overpower the main ethical and logical appeal—that Hanes makes good underwear.

READING WRITING

This Text: Reading

1. What qualities of the advertising does Gray identify as worthy of discussion? If you have seen the ad, do you agree with her emphasis?
2. Have you purchased underwear based on commercials? Where do you think your influences to purchase come from?
3. In what ways do the home generally and bedroom specifically serve as a sign? What products are most appropriate for this approach? Can you think of other places that serve similar purposes?

Your Text: Writing

1. Perform a similar sign analysis using an advertisement that uses another familiar place (a front lawn, an office, sports field, etc.). What about the place's familiarity is part of the appeal?
2. Write a paper discussing the presence of fantasy and familiarity in a typical advertisement. What types of ads rely more on fantasy? Which on familiarity?
3. Examine the types of intimate relationships portrayed in advertisements. Write a paper examining how advertisers use those relationships to appeal to their target audience.

Weasel Words

William Lutz

In his classic essay on words in advertising, taken from his book *Doublespeak* (1989), William Lutz, a professor of English at Rutgers University, points out code words that advertisers use to make false claims about their products.

ONE PROBLEM ADVERTISERS HAVE when they try to convince you that the product they are pushing is really different from other, similar products is that their claims are subject to some laws. Not a lot of laws, but there are some designed to prevent fraudulent or untruthful claims in advertising. Even during the happy years of nonregulation under President Ronald Reagan, the FTC did crack down on the more blatant abuses in advertising claims. Generally speaking, advertisers have to be careful in what they say in their ads, in the claims they make for the products they advertise. Parity claims are safe because they are legal and supported by a number of court decisions. But beyond parity claims there are weasel words.

Advertisers use weasel words to appear to be making a claim for a product when in fact they are making no claim at all. Weasel words get their name from the way weasels eat the eggs they find in the nests of other animals. A weasel will make a small hole in the egg, suck out the insides, then place the egg back in the nest. Only when the egg is examined closely is it found to be hollow. That's the way it is with weasel words in advertising: Examine weasel words closely and you'll find that they're as hollow as any egg sucked by a weasel. Weasel words appear to say one thing when in fact they say the opposite, or nothing at all.

"Help"—The Number One Weasel Word

The biggest weasel word used in advertising doublespeak is "help." Now "help" only means to aid or assist, nothing more. It does not mean to conquer, stop, eliminate, solve, heal, cure, or anything else. But once the ad says "help," it can say just about anything after that because "help" qualifies everything coming after it. The trick is that the claim that comes after the weasel word is usually so strong and so dramatic that you forget the word "help" and concentrate only on the dramatic claim. You read into the ad a message that the ad does not contain. More importantly, the advertiser is not responsible for the claim that you read into the ad, even though the advertiser wrote the ad so you would read that claim into it.

The next time you see an ad for a cold medicine that promises that it "helps relieve cold symptoms fast," don't rush out to buy it. Ask yourself what this claim is really saying. Remember, "helps" means only that the medicine will aid or assist. What will it aid or assist in doing? Why, "relieve" your cold "symptoms." "Relieve" only means to ease, alleviate, or mitigate, not to stop, end, or cure. Nor does the claim say how much relieving this medicine will do. Nowhere does this ad claim it will cure anything. In fact, the ad doesn't even claim it will *do* anything at all. The ad only claims that it will aid in relieving (not curing) your cold symptoms, which are probably a runny nose, watery eyes, and a headache. In other words, this medicine probably contains a standard decongestant and some aspirin. By the way, what does "fast" mean? Ten minutes, one hour, one day? What is fast to one person can be very slow to another. Fast is another weasel word.

Ad claims using "help" are among the most popular ads. One says, "Helps keep you young looking," but then a lot of things will help keep you young looking, including exercise, rest, good nutrition, and a facelift. More importantly, this ad doesn't say the product will keep you young, only "young *looking*." Someone may look young to one person and old to another.

A toothpaste ad says, "Helps prevent cavities," but it doesn't say it will actually prevent cavities. Brushing your teeth regularly, avoiding sugars in foods, and flossing daily will also help prevent cavities. A liquid cleaner ad says, "Helps keep your home germ free," but it doesn't say it actually kills germs, nor does it even specify which germs it might kill.

"Help" is such a useful weasel word that it is often combined with other action-verb weasel words such as "fight" and "control." Consider the claim, "Helps control dandruff symptoms with regular use." What does it really say? It will assist in controlling (not eliminating, stopping, ending, or curing) the *symptoms* of dandruff, not the cause of dandruff nor the dandruff itself. What are the symptoms of dandruff? The ad deliberately leaves that undefined, but assume that the symptoms referred to in the ad are the flaking and itching commonly associated with dandruff. But just shampooing with *any* shampoo will temporarily eliminate these symptoms, so this shampoo isn't any different from any other. Finally, in order to benefit from this product, you must use it regularly. What is "regular use"—daily, weekly, hourly? Using another shampoo "regularly" will have the same effect. Nowhere does this advertising claim say this particular shampoo stops, eliminates, or cures dandruff. In fact, this claim says nothing at all, thanks to all the weasel words.

Look at ads in magazines and newspapers, listen to ads on radio and television, and you'll find the word "help" in ads for all kinds of products. How often do you read or hear such phrases as "helps stop . . . ," "helps overcome . . . ," "helps eliminate . . . ," "helps you feel . . . ," or "helps you look . . ."? If you start looking for this weasel word in advertising, you'll be amazed at how often it occurs. Analyze the claims in the ads using "help," and you will discover that these ads are really saying nothing.

There are plenty of other weasel words used in advertising. In fact, there are so many that to list them all would fill the rest of this book. But, in order to identify the doublespeak of advertising and understand the real meaning of an ad, you have to be aware of the most popular weasel words in advertising today.

Virtually Spotless

One of the most powerful weasel words is "virtually," a word so innocent that most people don't pay any attention to it when it is used in an advertising claim. But watch out. "Virtually" is used in advertising claims that appear to make specific, definite promises when there is no promise. After all, what does "virtually" mean? It means "in essence of effect, although not in fact." Look at that definition again. "Virtually" means *not in fact*. It does *not* mean "almost" or "just about the same as," or anything else. And before you dismiss all this concern over such a small word, remember that small words can have big consequences.

In 1971 a federal court rendered its decision on a case brought by a woman who became pregnant while taking birth control pills. She sued the manufacturer, Eli Lilly and Company, for breach of warranty. The woman lost her case. Basing its ruling on a statement in the pamphlet accompanying the pills, which stated that, "When taken as directed, the tablets offer virtually 100 percent protection," the court ruled that there was no warranty, expressed or implied, that the pills were absolutely effective. In its ruling, the court pointed out that, according to the *Webster's Third New International Dictionary,* "virtually" means "almost entirely" and clearly does not mean "absolute" (*Whittington* v. *Eli Lilly and Company,* 333 F. Supp. 98). In other words, the Eli Lilly company was really saying that its birth control pill, even when taken as directed, *did not in fact* provide 100 percent protection against pregnancy. But Eli Lilly didn't want to put it that way because then many women might not have bought Lilly's birth control pills.

The next time you see the ad that says that this dishwasher detergent "leaves dishes virtually spotless," just remember how advertisers twist the meaning of the weasel word "virtually." You can have lots of spots on your dishes after using this detergent and the ad claim will still be true, because what this claim really means is that this detergent does not *in fact* leave your dishes spotless. Whenever you see or hear an ad claim that uses the word "virtually," just translate that claim into its real meaning. So the television set that is "virtually trouble free" becomes the television set that is not in fact trouble free, the "virtually foolproof operation" of any appliance becomes an operation that is in fact not foolproof, and the product that "virtually never needs service" becomes the product that is not in fact service free.

New and Improved

If "new" is the most frequently used word on a product package, "improved" is the second most frequent. In fact, the two words are almost always used together. It seems just about everything sold these days is "new and improved." The next time you're in the supermarket, try counting the number of times you see these words on products. But you'd better do it while you're walking down just one aisle, otherwise you'll need a calculator to keep track of your counting.

Just what do these words mean? The use of the word "new" is restricted by regulations, so an advertiser can't just use the word on a product or in an ad without meeting certain requirements. For example, a product is considered new for about six months during a national advertising campaign. If the product is being advertised only in a limited test market area, the word can be used longer, and in some instances has been used for as long as two years.

What makes a product "new"? Some products have been around for a long time, yet every once in a while you discover that they are being advertised as "new." Well, an advertiser can call a product new if there has been "a material functional change" in the product. What is "a material functional change," you ask? Good question. In fact it's such a good question it's being asked all the time. It's up to the manufacturer to prove that the product has undergone such a change. And if the manufacturer isn't challenged on the claim, then there's no one to stop it. Moreover, the change does not have to be an improvement in the product. One manufacturer added an artificial lemon scent to a cleaning product and called it "new and improved," even though the product did not clean any better than without the lemon scent. The manufacturer defended the use of the word "new" on the grounds that the artificial scent changed the chemical formula of the product and therefore constituted "a material functional change."

Which brings up the word "improved." When used in advertising, "improved" does not mean "made better." It only means "changed" or "different from before." So, if the detergent maker puts a plastic pour spout on the box of detergent, the product has been "improved," and away we go with a whole new advertising campaign. Or, if the cereal maker adds more fruit or a different kind of fruit to the cereal, there's an improved product. Now you know why manufacturers are constantly making little changes in their products. Whole new advertising campaigns, designed to convince you that the product has been changed for the better, are based on small changes in superficial aspects of a product. The next time you see an ad for an "improved" product, ask yourself what was wrong with the old one. Ask yourself just how "improved" the product is. Finally, you might check to see whether the "improved" version costs more than the unimproved one. After all, someone has to pay for the millions of dollars spent advertising the improved product.

Of course, advertisers really like to run ads that claim a product is "new and improved." While what constitutes a "new" product may be subject to some regulation, "improved" is a subjective judgment. A manufacturer changes the shape of its stick deodorant, but the shape doesn't improve the function of the deodorant. That is, changing the shape doesn't affect the deodorizing ability of the deodorant, so the manufacturer calls it "improved." Another manufacturer adds ammonia to its liquid cleaner and calls it "new and improved." Since adding ammonia does affect the cleaning ability of the product, there has been a "material functional change" in the product, and the manufacturer can now call its cleaner "new," and "improved" as well. Now the weasel words "new and improved" are plastered all over the package and are the basis for a multimillion-dollar ad campaign. But after six months the word "new" will have to go, until someone can dream up another change in the product. Perhaps it will be adding color to the liquid, or changing the shape of the package, or maybe adding a new dripless pour spout, or perhaps a _____. The "improvements" are endless, and so are the new advertising claims and campaigns.

"New" is just too useful and powerful a word in advertising for advertisers to pass it up easily. So they use weasel words that say "new" without really saying it. One of their favorites is "introducing," as in, "Introducing improved Tide," or "Introducing the stain remover." The first is simply saying, here's our improved soap; the second, here's our new advertising campaign for our detergent. Another favorite is "now," as in, "Now there's Sinex," which simply means that Sinex is available. Then there are phrases like "Today's Chevrolet," "Presenting Dristan," and "A fresh way to start the day." The list is really endless because advertisers are always finding new ways to say "new" without really saying it. If there is a second edition of this book, I'll just call it the "new and improved" edition. Wouldn't you really rather have a "new and improved" edition of this book rather than a "second" edition?

Acts Fast

"Acts" and "works" are two popular weasel words in advertising because they bring action to the product and to the advertising claim. When you see the ad for the cough syrup that "Acts on the cough control center," ask yourself what this cough syrup is claiming to do. Well, it's just claiming to "act," to do something, to perform an action. What is it that the cough syrup does? The ad doesn't say. It only claims to perform an action or do something on your "cough control center." By the way, what and where is your "cough control center"? I don't remember learning about that part of the body in human biology class.

Ads that use such phrases as "acts fast," "acts against," "acts to prevent," and the like are saying essentially nothing, because "act" is a word empty of any specific meaning. The ads are always careful not to specify exactly what "act" the product performs. Just because a brand of aspirin claims to "act fast" for headache relief doesn't mean this aspirin is any better than any other aspirin. What is the "act" that this aspirin performs? You're never told. Maybe it just dissolves quickly. Since aspirin is a parity product, all aspirin is the same and therefore functions the same.

Works Like Anything Else

If you don't find the word "acts" in an ad, you will probably find the weasel word "works." In fact, the two words are almost interchangeable in advertising. Watch out for ads that say a product "works against," "works like," "works for," or "works longer." As with "acts," "works" is the same meaningless verb used to make you think that this product really does something, and maybe even something special or unique. But "works," like "acts," is basically a word empty of any specific meaning.

Like Magic

Whenever advertisers want you to stop thinking about the product and to start thinking about something bigger, better, or more attractive than the product, they use that very popular weasel word, "like." The word "like" is the advertiser's equivalent of a magician's use of misdirection. "Like" gets you to ignore the product and concentrate on the claim the advertiser is making about it. "For skin like peaches and cream" claims the ad for a skin cream. What is this ad really claiming? It doesn't say this cream will give you peaches-and-cream skin. There is no verb in this claim, so it doesn't even mention using the product. How is skin ever like "peaches and cream"? Remember, ads must be read literally and exactly, according to the dictionary definition of words. (Remember "virtually" in the Eli Lilly case.) The ad is making absolutely no promise or claim whatsoever for this skin cream. If you think this cream will give you soft, smooth, youthful-looking skin, you are the one who has read that meaning into the ad.

The wine that claims "It's like taking a trip to France" wants you to think about a romantic evening in Paris as you walk along the boulevard after a wonderful meal in an intimate little bistro. Of course, you don't really believe that a wine can take you to France, but the goal of the ad is to get you to think pleasant, romantic thoughts about France and not about how the wine tastes or how expensive it may be. That little word "like" has taken you away from crushed grapes into a world of your own imaginative making. Who knows, maybe the next time you buy wine, you'll think those pleasant thoughts when you see this brand of wine, and you'll buy it. Or, maybe you weren't even thinking about buying wine at all, but now you just might pick up a bottle the next time you're shopping. Ah, the power of "like" in advertising.

How about the most famous "like" claim of all, "Winston tastes good like a cigarette should"? Ignoring the grammatical error here, you might want to know what this claim is saying. Whether a cigarette tastes good or bad is a subjective judgment because what tastes good to one person may well taste horrible to another. Not everyone likes fried snails, even if they are called escargot. (*De gustibus non est disputandum,* which was probably the Roman rule for advertising as well as for defending the games in the Colosseum.) There are many people who say all cigarettes taste terrible, other people who say only some cigarettes taste all right, and still others who say all cigarettes taste good. Who's right? Everyone, because taste is a matter of personal judgment.

Moreover, note the use of the conditional, "should." The complete claim is, "Winston tastes good like a cigarette should taste." But should cigarettes taste good? Again, this is a matter of personal judgment and probably depends most on one's experiences with smoking. So, the Winston ad is simply saying that Winston cigarettes are just like any other cigarette: Some people like them and some people don't. On that statement, R. J. Reynolds conducted a very successful multimillion-dollar advertising campaign that helped keep Winston the number-two-selling cigarette in the United States, close behind number one, Marlboro.

Can't It Be Up to the Claim?

Analyzing ads for doublespeak requires that you pay attention to every word in the ad and determine what each word really means. Advertisers try to wrap their claims in language that sounds concrete, specific, and objective, when in fact the language of advertising is anything but. Your job is to read carefully and listen critically so that when the announcer says that "Crest can be of significant value . . . ," you know immediately that this claim says absolutely nothing. Where is the doublespeak in this ad? Start with the second word.

Once again, you have to look at what words really mean, not what you think they mean or what the advertiser wants you to think they mean. The ad for Crest only says that using Crest "can be" of "significant value." What really throws you off in this ad is the brilliant use of "significant." It draws your attention to the word "value" and makes you forget that the ad only claims that Crest "can be." The ad doesn't say that Crest *is* of value, only that it is "able" or "possible" to be of value, because that's all that "can" means.

It's so easy to miss the importance of those little words, "can be." Almost as easy as missing the importance of the words "up to" in an ad. These words are very popular in sales ads. You know, the ones that say, "Up to 50 percent Off!" Now, what does that claim mean? Not much, because the store or manufacturer has to reduce the price of only a few items by 50 percent. Everything else can be reduced a lot less, or not even reduced. Moreover, don't you want to know 50 percent off of what? Is it 50 percent off the "manufacturer's suggested list price," which is the highest possible price? Was the price artificially inflated and then reduced? In other ads, "up to" expresses an ideal situation. The medicine that works "up to ten times faster," the battery that lasts "up to twice as long," and the soap that gets you "up to twice as clean" all are based on ideal situations for using those products, situations in which you can be sure you will never find yourself.

Unfinished Words

Unfinished words are a kind of "up to" claim in advertising. The claim that a battery lasts "up to twice as long" usually doesn't finish the comparison—twice as long as what? A birthday candle? A tank of gas? A cheap battery made in a country not noted for its technological achievements? The implication is that the battery lasts twice as long as batteries made by other battery makers, or twice as long as earlier model batteries made by the advertiser, but the ad doesn't really make these claims. You read these claims into the ad, aided by the visual images the advertiser so carefully provides.

Unfinished words depend on you to finish them, to provide the words the advertisers so thoughtfully left out of the ad. Pall Mall cigarettes were once advertised as "A longer finer and milder smoke." The question is, longer, finer, and milder than what? The aspirin that claims it contains "Twice as much of the pain reliever doctors recommend most" doesn't tell you what pain reliever it contains twice as much of. (By the way, it's aspirin. That's right; it just contains twice the amount of aspirin. And how much is twice the amount? Twice of what amount?) Panadol boasts that "nobody reduces fever faster," but, since Panadol is a parity product, this claim simply means that Panadol isn't any better than any other product in its parity class. "You can be sure if it's Westinghouse," you're told, but just exactly what it is you can be sure of is never mentioned. "Magnavox gives you more" doesn't tell you what you get more of. More value? More television? More than they gave you before? It sounds nice, but it means nothing, until you fill in the claim with your own words, the words the advertisers didn't use. Since each of us fills in the claim differently, the ad and the product can become all things to all people, and not promise a single thing.

Unfinished words abound in advertising because they appear to promise so much. More importantly, they can be joined with powerful visual images on television to appear to be making significant promises about a product's effectiveness without really making any promises. In a television ad, the aspirin product that claims fast relief can show a person with a headache taking the product and then, in what appears to be a matter of minutes, claiming complete relief. This visual image is far more powerful than any claim made in unfinished words. Indeed, the visual image completes the unfinished words for you, filling in with pictures what the words leave out. And you thought that ads didn't affect you. What brand of aspirin do you use?

Some years ago, Ford's advertisements proclaimed "Ford LTD—700 percent quieter." Now, what do you think Ford was claiming with these unfinished words? What was the Ford LTD quieter than? A Cadillac? A Mercedes Benz? A BMW? Well, when the FTC asked Ford to substantiate this unfinished claim, Ford replied that it meant that the inside of the LTD was 700 percent quieter than the outside. How did you finish those unfinished words when you first read them? Did you even come close to Ford's meaning?

Combining Weasel Words

A lot of ads don't fall neatly into one category or another because they use a variety of different devices and words. Different weasel words are often combined to make an ad claim.

The claim, "Coffee-Mate gives coffee more body, more flavor," uses Unfinished Words ("more" than what?) and also uses words that have no specific meaning ("body" and "flavor"). Along with "taste" (remember the Winston ad and its claim to taste good), "body" and "flavor" mean nothing because their meaning is entirely subjective. To you, "body" in coffee might mean thick, black, almost bitter coffee, while I might take it to mean a light brown, delicate coffee. Now, if you think you understood that last sentence, read it again, because it said nothing of objective value; it was filled with weasel words of no specific meaning: "thick," "black," "bitter," "light brown," and "delicate." Each of those words has no specific, objective meaning, because each of us can interpret them differently.

Try this slogan: "Looks, smells, tastes like ground-roast coffee." So, are you now going to buy Taster's Choice instant coffee because of this ad? "Looks," "smells," and "tastes" are all words with no specific meaning and depend on your interpretation of them for any meaning. Then there's that great weasel word "like," which simply suggests a comparison but does not make the actual connection between the product and the quality. Besides, do you know what "ground-roast" coffee is? I don't, but it sure sounds good. So, out of seven words in this ad, four are definite weasel words, two are quite meaningless, and only one has any clear meaning.

Remember the Anacin ad—"Twice as much of the pain reliever doctors recommend most"? There's a whole lot of weaseling going on in this ad. First, what's the pain reliever they're talking about in this ad? Aspirin, of course. In fact, any time you see or hear an ad using those words "pain reliever," you can automatically substitute the word "aspirin" for them. (Makers of acetaminophen and ibuprofen pain relievers are careful in their advertising to identify their products as nonaspirin products.) So, now we know that Anacin has aspirin in it. Moreover, we know that Anacin has twice as much aspirin in it, but we don't know twice as much as what. Does it have twice as much aspirin as an ordinary aspirin tablet? If so, what is an ordinary aspirin tablet, and how much aspirin does it contain? Twice as much as Excedrin or Bufferin? Twice as much as a chocolate chip cookie? Remember those Unfinished Words and how they lead you on without saying anything.

Finally, what about those doctors who are doing all that recommending? Who are they? How many of them are there? What kind of doctors are they? What are their qualifications? Who asked them about recommending pain relievers? What other pain relievers did they recommend? And there are a whole lot more questions about this "poll" of doctors to which I'd like to know the answers, but you get the point. Sometimes, when I call my doctor, she tells me to take two aspirin and call her office in the morning. Is that where Anacin got this ad?

Read the Label, or the Brochure

Weasel words aren't just found on television, on the radio, or in newspaper and magazine ads. Just about any language associated with a product will contain the doublespeak of advertising. Remember the Eli Lilly case and the doublespeak on the information sheet that came with the birth control pills. Here's another example.

In 1983, the Estée Lauder cosmetics company announced a new product called "Night Repair." A small brochure distributed with the product stated that "Night Repair was scientifically formulated in Estée Lauder's U.S. laboratories as part of the Swiss Age-Controlling Skincare Program. Although only nature controls the aging process, this program helps control the signs of aging and encourages skin to look and feel younger." You might want to read these two sentences again, because they sound great but say nothing.

First, note that the product was "scientifically formulated" in the company's laboratories. What does that mean? What constitutes a scientific formulation? You wouldn't expect the company to say that the product was casually, mechanically, or carelessly formulated, or just thrown together one day when the people in the white coats didn't have anything better to do. But the word "scientifically" lends an air of precision and promise that just isn't there.

It is the second sentence, however, that's really weasely, both syntactically and semantically. The only factual part of this sentence is the introductory dependent clause—"only nature controls the aging process." Thus, the only fact in the ad is relegated to a dependent clause, a clause dependent on the main clause, which contains no factual or definite information at all and indeed purports to contradict the independent clause. The new "skincare program" (notice it's not a skin cream but a "program") does not claim to stop or even retard the aging process. What, then, does Night Repair, at a price of over $35 (in 1983 dollars) for a .87-ounce bottle do? According to this brochure, nothing. It only "helps," and the brochure does not say how much it helps. Moreover, it only "helps control," and then it only helps control the "*signs* of aging," not the aging itself. Also, it "encourages" skin not to *be* younger but only to "look and feel" younger. The brochure does not say younger than what. Of the sixteen words in the main clause of this second sentence, nine are weasel words. So, before you spend all that money for Night Repair, or any other cosmetic product, read the words carefully, and then decide if you're getting what you think you're paying for.

Other Tricks of the Trade

Advertisers' use of doublespeak is endless. The best way advertisers can make something out of nothing is through words. Although there are a lot of visual images used on television and in magazines and newspapers, every advertiser wants to create that memorable line that will stick in the public consciousness. I am sure pure joy reigned in one advertising agency when a study found that children who were asked to spell the word "relief" promptly and proudly responded "r-o-l-a-i-d-s."

The variations, combinations, and permutations of doublespeak used in advertising go on and on, running from the use of rhetorical questions ("Wouldn't you really rather have a Buick?" "If you can't trust Prestone, who can you trust?") to flattering you with compliments ("The lady has taste." "We think a cigar smoker is someone special." "You've come a long way baby."). You know, of course, how you're *supposed* to answer those questions, and you know that those compliments are just leading up to the sales pitches for the products. Before you dismiss such tricks of the trade as obvious, however, just remember that all of these statements and questions were part of very successful advertising campaigns.

A more subtle approach is the ad that proclaims a supposedly unique quality for a product, a quality that really isn't unique. "If it doesn't say Goodyear, it can't be polyglas." Sounds good, doesn't it? Polyglas is available only from Goodyear because Goodyear copyrighted that trade name. Any other tire manufacturer could make exactly the same tire but could not call it "polyglas," because that would be copyright infringement. "Polyglas" is simply Goodyear's name for its fiberglass-reinforced tire.

Since we like to think of ourselves as living in a technologically advanced country, science and technology have a great appeal in selling products. Advertisers are quick to use scientific doublespeak to push their products. There are all kinds of elixirs, additives, scientific potions, and mysterious mixtures added to all kinds of products. Gasoline contains "HTA," "F-130,"

"Platformate," and other chemical-sounding additives, but nowhere does an advertisement give any real information about the additive.

Shampoo, deodorant, mouthwash, cold medicine, sleeping pills, and any number of other products all seem to contain some special chemical ingredient that allows them to work wonders. "Certs contains a sparkling drop of Retsyn." So what? What's "Retsyn"? What's it do? What's so special about it? When they don't have a secret ingredient in their product, advertisers still find a way to claim scientific validity. There's "Sinarest. Created by a research scientist who actually gets sinus headaches." Sounds nice, but what kind of research does this scientist do? How do you know if she is any kind of expert on sinus medicine? Besides, this ad doesn't tell you a thing about the medicine itself and what it does.

Advertising Doublespeak Quick Quiz

Now it's time to test your awareness of advertising doublespeak. (You didn't think I would just let you read this and forget it, did you?) The following is a list of statements from some recent ads. Your job is to figure out what each of these ads really says.

Domino's Pizza: "Because nobody delivers better."
Sinutab: "It can stop the pain."
Tums: "The stronger acid neutralizer."
Maximum Strength Dristan: "Strong medicine for tough sinus colds."
Listermint: "Making your mouth a cleaner place."
Cascade: "For virtually spotless dishes nothing beats Cascade."
Nuprin: "Little. Yellow. Different. Better."
Anacin: "Better relief."
Sudafed: "Fast sinus relief that won't put you fast asleep."
Advil: "Better relief."
Ponds Cold Cream: "Ponds cleans like no soap can."
Miller Lite Beer: "Tastes great. Less filling."
Philips Milk of Magnesia: "Nobody treats you better than MOM (Philips Milk of Magnesia)."
Bayer: "The wonder drug that works wonders."
Cracker Barrel: "Judged to be the best."
Knorr: "Where taste is everything."
Anusol: "Anusol is the word to remember for relief."
Dimetapp: "It relieves kids as well as colds."
Liquid Drano: "The liquid strong enough to be called Drano."
Johnson & Johnson Baby Powder: "Like magic for your skin."
Puritan: "Make it your oil for life."
Pam: "Pam, because how you cook is as important as what you cook."
Ivory Shampoo and Conditioner: "Leave your hair feeling Ivory clean."
Tylenol Gel-Caps: "It's not a capsule. It's better."
Alka-Seltzer Plus: "Fast, effective relief for winter colds."

The World of Advertising

In the world of advertising, people wear "dentures," not false teeth; they suffer from "occasional irregularity," not constipation; they need deodorants for their "nervous wetness," not for sweat; they use "bathroom tissue," not toilet paper; and they don't dye their hair, they "tint" or "rinse" it. Advertisements offer "real counterfeit diamonds" without the slightest hint of embarrassment, or boast of goods made out of "genuine imitation leather" or "virgin vinyl."

In the world of advertising, the girdle becomes a "body shaper," "form persuader," "control garment," "controller," "outerwear enhancer," "body garment," or "anti-gravity panties," and is sold with such trade names as "The Instead," "The Free Spirit," and "The Body Briefer."

A study some years ago found the following words to be among the most popular used in U.S. television advertisements: "new," "improved," "better," "extra," "fresh," "clean," "beautiful," "free," "good," "great," and "light." At the same time, the following words were found to be among the most frequent on British television: "new," "good-better-best," "free," "fresh," "delicious," "full," "sure," "clean," "wonderful," and "special." While these words may occur most frequently in ads, and while ads may be filled with weasel words, you have to watch out for all the words used in advertising, not just the words mentioned here.

Every word in an ad is there for a reason; no word is wasted. Your job is to figure out exactly what each word is doing in an ad—what each word really means, not what the advertiser wants you to think it means. Remember, the ad is trying to get you to buy a product, so it will put the product in the best possible light, using any device, trick, or means legally allowed. Your own defense against advertising (besides taking up permanent residence on the moon) is to develop and use a strong critical reading, listening, and looking ability. Always ask yourself what the ad is *really* saying. When you see ads on television, don't be misled by the pictures, the visual images. What does the ad say about the product? What does the ad *not* say? What information is missing from the ad? Only by becoming an active, critical consumer of the doublespeak of advertising will you ever be able to cut through the doublespeak and discover what the ad is really saying.

Professor Del Kehl of Arizona State University has updated the Twenty-third Psalm to reflect the power of advertising to meet our needs and solve our problems. It seems fitting that this chapter close with this new Psalm.

The Adman's 23rd

The Adman is my shepherd;
I shall ever want.
He maketh me to walk a mile for a Camel;
He leadeth me beside Crystal Waters In the High Country of Coors;
He restoreth my soul with Perrier.

READING WRITING

This Text: Reading

1. Lutz's essay is now almost 20 years old, yet it still feels relevant. What about his essay rings the most true?
2. Does Lutz have a clear thesis here? If so, can you locate it? How would you summarize his main argument?
3. Has advertising changed in the last 20 years? Are ads now savvier?

Your Text: Writing

1. Write an essay in which you read a series of ads through a Lutzian lens. Use his terminology to offer a semiotic and rhetorical reading.
2. Write a comparison/contrast essay in which you analyze an ad you find particularly manipulative with one you find reasonable and straightforward. Give specific analytic examples of how the two ads differ from each other.

Sister Act (sís-ter ákt) *N*. 1. A Destructive Form of Writing

Arianne F. Galino

Student Essay

In this essay, written for Rhetoric and Composition 220 (a class similar to Composition II) at the University of San Francisco, Arianne Galino responds to Evan Wright's now well-known essay, "Sister Act," a scathing indictment of the Greek system at Ohio State that appeared in *Rolling Stone* in 1999. Galino deftly analyzes the way in which Wright makes his arguments, poking holes in his seemingly objective account of Greek life.

THROUGH THE CONSTITUTION, upon which our great nation is solemnly grounded, and the Emancipation Proclamation of 1863 that released thousands from the two hundred year shackles of slavery, one can gain an understanding of the power of the written word. As a writer, one is often bound to certain ethical responsibilities. Such limitations ensure the protection of the reader and keep the writer up to par in conveying information that is truthful and ethically sound. Alice Walker, award-winning author of *The Color Purple*, claims, "Deliver me from writers who say the way they live doesn't matter. I'm not sure a bad person can write a good book. If art doesn't make us better, then what on earth is it for," "Authors". On the contrary, certain literary works may be lacking in this principle. Such works include Evan Wright's "Sister Act," which is a destructive form of writing since it aims to entertain rather than provide solutions and uses stereotypical reasoning.

In October 1999, Evan Wright's "Sister Act" appeared in the pages of *Rolling Stone* magazine. The article takes an insider's view of the Greek system in one of the nation's largest universities, Ohio State. It takes on an interesting form as the individuals interviewed come to life and engage in a series of college activities. Through Wright's vivid descriptions, the reader is able to grasp the raw reality of the Greek system, its members, non-members, and the surrounding college atmosphere.

The technique used in "Sister Act" is most similar to that initiated by today's "reality TV" shows, such as MTV's *The Real World* and the CBS hit *Survivor*. According to Vida Zorah Gabe, the "unscripted coverage of ordinary people being themselves" gives this form of entertainment its "edge." Gabe further claims that these shows are edited to ensure that it is "real—but still entertaining" (bit 1–2). In the case of "Sister Act," the notion that "alcohol and sex sells" is used to its advantage in that it is entertaining.

The thematic and literal use of alcohol is extensive in the article. For instance, one of the first activities described in "Sister Act" is Alcohol Awareness Day, where a sorority member "throws up" between her two "wobbly-legged" sisters after the event (473). The article then closes with Jeff, a Kappa Sig member, in dire need of medical attention as a result of his drinking. Furthermore, throughout Wright's writing, the word "alcohol," along with alcohol-related terms like "beer" and "drunk," appears more than thirty times. One passage states, "Fraternities . . . are allowed to serve *beer* . . . to get *drunk*" (473, my emphasis). Such usage of the word "alcohol" in the context of the Greek system, induces the reader to create a correlation between the two. This, in turn, leads to a stereotype that all Greek members are drunks.

A similar technique of repetition is used with the term "sex" and other sex-related notions. According to an ABC News article by Joanne Ramos, "American culture is permeated with sex . . . That sex sells is nothing new" (par. 1–2). In "Sister Act," the words "clit," "whore," "fuck," "porno," "ass," and "jerking off" are used time and again. Not only does this also create a correlation between sex and the Greek system, but it clearly shows Evan Wright's devious method of drawing attention to his article. Where his negligence begins, his writing goes awry. He uses such strong explicit words with no concern for how it may affect his readers and without any real guidance as to the ethics of such principles. It almost seems as though Evan Wright's primary goal is to entertain rather than find solutions.

Although Wright's guidance is generally and apparently absent in his article, he manages to speak amid the mayhem and clutter of people in "Sister Act." His description of specific people and events surrounding the Greek system serves as a passage to his condemnation of the institution. In this way, he draws on the editing technique used by reality TV shows once again. But the manner in which he presents his views through stereotypes is further evidence of his recklessness.

A rift between social classes is clearly depicted in "Sister Act." Wright begins by saying, "Some people say that the Greek system is a sort of apartheid, enabling children from predominately white, upper-middle-class enclaves to safely attend a messily diverse university . . . without having to mix with those who are different" (475). His "theory seems . . . to be affirmed" through the example of Andrea, a former cheerleader and sorority member. At first, she points to a black area and warns that it is a "total ghetto a few blocks from here" (475). Wright seems to ridicule Andrea, who points out, to her own surprise, that five of her sorority sisters were dating black guys. She now has a black boyfriend, who used to chase her around because she was "scared of the fact that he was black" (476). Thus, Andrea seems to be solely motivated by her fellow sisters to date a black guy. However, her stereotypical views remain, as she warns Wright about the ghettos and recounts her first impression of her boyfriend. In this case, the author is able to use Andrea to prove the statement he made earlier.

In the passage above, Wright emphasizes the social class requirements for Greek members. Furthermore, he describes a person who did not meet the qualifications in the system. Wright begins by describing an individual named Mary. He states, "Mary is Hispanic and on full financial aid." Mary then says, "I could never get in. A sorority is a class thing. It's a breeding ground for the next conservative America" (qtd. in Wright 476). The author, therefore, employs his description of one "on full financial aid" as a stereotype for people who cannot be a part of a sorority or fraternity.

Evan Wright continues to reveal similar stereotypes on the basis of physical appearance. Wright depicts two young women in the main pedestrian crossroads. He writes, "One has hair dyed flashbulb yellow; the other has dark purple hair braided in strands around alphabet beads. They are both first-year students, and neither would dream of joining a sorority . . . Yellow hair leads the way to a residential tower on north campus" (474). Wright then switches his criticism to the Greek novice, Heather. He states, "Heather says her own sorority is cruelty-free. Even if it weren't, she has little to worry about since her teeth are straight, her body is slim and her skin is as pure as a cold glass of pure milk . . . Heather is soon to be a resident of Chi Omega's sandstone-and-brick mansion" (474). Through Wright's unique method of characterization, he is able to depict the qualities that separate a Greek member from a non-Greek. He also points out that fitting into the Greek member model certainly has its benefits. The "mansion," after all, is more appealing than the "residential tower on north campus" (474). Once again, such reasoning cannot help but lead many readers to stereotypes, according to which these superficial qualities become universal truths that apply to all people.

Lastly, the author introduces a partition of gender roles as expressed in various passages. Wright claims that fraternities "offer the only Greek parties that sorority girls can go to in order to get drunk" (473). He ends his essay with Jeff, a fraternity member, who upholds his fellow members' ideals by saying, "we learn how to treat girls like ladies" (479). After surveying the dismal turnout of the party, he declares, "Let's go fuck some sorority girls. It can be arranged. Anyone you want" (479). The fraternity men are apparently the authoritative figures in the system. First, they determine when the sorority girls can party and "get drunk." And they are very much in control of their sex lives. In this way, the author seems to uphold a clear generalization of a woman and a man's place in the Greek system with the latter dictating and the former adhering to her superior's orders.

One may argue that Evan Wright is merely revealing the stereotypes that are already present in the Greek system. In other words, he had no hand in creating them. However, by recalling Vida Zorah Gabe's essay "How Real is Real?" one can grasp Wright's usage of the same method in reality TV shows throughout his essay. Gabe writes, "Never mind that unscripted doesn't necessarily mean unedited. Never mind that *ordinary people* generally refers to a . . . diverse group of . . . men and women with strong personalities that make for much more interesting conflict or that these people themselves have sometimes been charged with . . . playing up to the camera by deliberately being provocative or stereotypical . . . Never mind, in other words, that the *reality* in *reality TV* isn't very real, after all." In "Sister Act," we seldom see a Greek member or non-member cross the other's definitive territory. A fusion between the two groups is revealed only in the character of Rachel Glass—a sorority member and feminist. But even Rachel claims the rarity of such an emergence. She states, "I'm probably one of the only . . . feminists in my sorority" (477). Notice the individuals that Wright uses in his essay. He describes them vividly and categorizes these descriptions as Greek or non-Greek. The emphasis on alcohol and sex in Wright's essay is almost absurd. It may have sparked the interest of more readers, but it also raises questions. For example, what ever happened to going to school, doing homework, being sober, and abstaining from sex? Wright's generalizations, usage of certain individuals, and overemphasis of certain issues are evidence enough of his role in not only generating stereotypes but also distorting the truth.

There is an old saying that goes, "the truth shall set you free." In this case, however, "Sister Act" constrains the reader's perspective on all aspects of the Greek system. The impact of the essay on my thinking, which may or may not be shared by other readers, is immense. Never again can I look at a Greek system member without associating him or her with being a white upper-middle class, sex-driven alcoholic. Perhaps it is immature for me to think in this manner, but with such an effect on thinking, Wright cannot "wash his hands clean" of generating such ideas in the minds of his readers.

Moreover, Evan Wright falls short of conveying his message on a higher level of communication. As mentioned earlier, writers have an ethical responsibility toward their readers. Yet, Wright's representation of alcohol, sex, social classes, physical appearances, and gender roles in the context of the Greek system are overtly stereotypical. His form of writing presents a series of stereotypes without a differentiation between right and wrong or the guidance of his personal opinions. He fails to unveil the destructive consequences of such thinking. Thus, he makes readers, such as myself, highly susceptible to stereotypical reasoning. The readers are not the only victims of such writing. It is also unfair to the misrepresented members and non-members of the Greek system. They should not be made to feel that by falling under one of these groups, one is predisposed to a particular manifestation. Such close-mindedness can make the world a more difficult place to live.

The destruction ensues when we are unable to live in a world in which we cannot be recognized and appreciated for who we are, and in which our daily lives are clouded by unethical, close-minded thinking. Until we can all learn to approach all aspects of life—from the words we speak to the books we read—with prudence, we will continue to be victims of and contributors to a destructive world.

Works Cited

"Authors: Alice Walker." *Brainy Quote*. 2002. 8 Sep. 2002. <http://www.brainyquote.com/quotes/authors/a/a125270.html>.

Gabe, Vida Zorah. "How Real Is Real?" *M/C Reviews Features* 4 May 2001. 10 Sep. 2002. <http://moby.curtin.edu.au/~ausstud/mc/reviews/features/realitytv/realitytv.html>.

Ramos, Joanne. "For Adults Only?" *ABCNews.com Original Report* 12 June. 2002. 10 Sep. 2002. <http://abcnews.go.com/sections/business/DailyNews/Ramos_adultproducts_020612.html>.

Wright, Evan. "Sister Act." *Good Reasons with Contemporary Arguments*. Ed. Lester Faigley and Jack Selzer. Boston: Allyn and Bacon, 2000. 472–80.

READING WRITING

This Text: Reading

1. Can you identify Galino's thesis? What is she arguing here? Is she persuasive?
2. What do you make of Galino's introductory paragraph? What effect does it have on the reader? On her overall argument?
3. Note how Galino's final paragraph moves the essay from the specific back to the general. Why is this effective?

Your Text: Writing

1. Track down Evan Wright's essay and write a response to it. Is it good journalism?
2. Write a comparison/contrast piece on Wright's and Galino's essays. How does each make their respective argument? Does one rely more on ethos or logos than the other?
3. Write an exposé of the Greek system at your own college. How can one be objective in this situation? Is objectivity something a writer of essays should strive for?

The Future of Journalism Suite

If you are like most people in America, you get your news through outlets other than newspapers. Some of you probably watch news on television, but increasingly, you likely get a lot of information via the Internet, through blogs, on-line only news sources (like *Slate* and *Salon*), from collaborations between on-line sites and other media outlets (like CNN and MSNBC), and newspapers' Web sites. The question of how or in what form newspapers will survive is hotly debated by those in the journalism field. Since newspapers have always been the bedrock of journalism, the discussion about the state of newspapers and journalism's future points to important issues facing contemporary news outlets and the people who look to them for information:

- **Amateur vs. professional.** Professional journalists have been slow to acknowledge the role that bloggers play in breaking news but more crucially in becoming voices of media criticism. Bloggers sometimes are slow to acknowledge how dependent they are on mainstream outlets.
- **Objectivity.** Even within the journalism profession, the idea of objectivity is coming under fire; critics such as Tom Rosenstiel and Bill Kovach argue that truth is a more important goal for journalists than the presenting of all sides in hopes the reader can make sense of the material presented. Bloggers would agree.
- **Business model.** Internet organizations like Craigslist and Monster.com have chipped away at a huge source of money for journalistic organizations—classified ads. Decreasing readership has also cut ad rates and money from subscriptions. Arguably, more people are actually reading the content produced by newspapers, but newspapers have not found a way to make Internet users pay for content.
- **Focus.** Some newspapers, including the Lawrence, Kansas, *Journal-World* and *The Rocky Mountain News,* have gone "hyper-local," rededicating their focus on their communities rather than news pages dedicated to international and national news, for which they do not have reporters—traditionally that space is filled with material from wire services like the Associated Press.
- **The environment.** Even with the advent of recycled newsprint, one could argue that printing of newspapers is environmentally unfriendly.
- **Timeliness.** Online media outlets, including newspaper, websites, and blogs can post photos and a story within seconds, whereas traditional newspapers may not be able to run a story until the following day. In a culture of speed and immediacy, viewers and readers may trade quickness for depth.

Those of us in the United States tend to take a free press for granted, but newspapers are folding at an alarming rate, large outlets are buying up all the papers in a city (making journalistic competition impossible), and media outlets are cutting back on overseas bureaus and writers (*The San Francisco Chronicle* just laid off 25% of its staff). In an increasingly complicated world in which there are coups, wars, impeachments, ethnic cleansing, terrorism, and record-setting corporate fraud, journalism helps keep citizens informed. How it will change to meet the needs of a new culture is the topic of this particular suite.

Mark Glaser, a columnist for Mediashift, a PBS blog about journalism, writes about why journalists should be optimistic about the future. Paul Fahri, a reporter with *The Washington Post* as well as a media critic, writes about one reaction to the changing newspaper landscape—the decision to go "hyper-local" in coverage. And Michael Kinsley, a well-known journalist and founder of *Slate* (an electronic journal from which we have drawn a few articles), writes about the seemingly antiquated (and environmentally unfriendly) way newspapers are produced.

⊔

Techno-Optimism: 10 Reasons There's a Bright Future for Journalism

Mark Glaser

There's been a lot of debate lately about the future of newspapers, the future of TV, the future of radio—the future of journalism itself—in the face of drastic change brought by technology and the Internet. I've asked MediaShift readers whether they thought journalism's metaphorical cup was half empty or half full and most people saw a pretty bright future.

As you might imagine, I share their enthusiasm for the future, and wouldn't be writing this blog if I didn't believe we will end up in a better place. But I'm also a hardened realist and natural skeptic, and I know there are painful months and years ahead for the (dwindling number of) people working in traditional media. Not everything new and shiny will be good for us, and there are plenty of ethical and technological pitfalls ahead.

But rather than dwell on the negative, rail against change, or damn the upstarts at Google and Craigslist, I'd like to take a walk on the sunny side of life in new media, consider the positive aspects of all that is happening, and how we could end up in a renaissance era for journalism. While I do believe large media companies will have the most difficult time adapting to the changes, they can learn a lot from the successful business models of smaller sites such as TMZ or The Smoking Gun (both owned by media companies).

10 Reasons There's a Bright Future for Journalism

1. More access to more journalism worldwide. One of the undersung advantages of the Internet is that it gives us access to content from newspapers, TV channels, blogs and podcasts from around the world. No longer are we limited to our local media for news of the world. Now we can go directly to that corner of the world to get a local angle from far away. No one has figured out how to sell advertising that would be relevant to all those international readers, but that doesn't mean they won't figure it out eventually.

2. Aggregation and personalization satisfies readers. Tired of being programmed to, we now have the tools online to program our own media experience. Whether that's through Google News or personalizing My Yahoo or an RSS newsfeed reader, we can get quick access to the media outlets and journalism we want on one web page. Some newspaper executives have railed against Google News, but the vast majority are working on their own ways of aggregating content from other sources or offering up personalized versions of their sites (see mywashingtonpost.com). It's a more open way of doing journalism than saying "we have all the answers here."

3. Digital delivery offers more ways to reach people. Before the web became popular, traditional media offered up just one way to get their content—in a print publication, by watching TV or listening to the radio. Now you can get their content online, in email newsletters, on your mobile phone and in any way that digital bits and bytes can be delivered. That's journalism unbound from traditional format constraints.

4. There are more fact-checkers than ever in the history of journalism. Maybe it's true that professional fact-checking has taken a big hit in the layoffs at mainstream media outlets, but it's also true that bloggers and free-thinkers online have provided an important check and balance to reporting. They might have an axe to grind or a political bias, but if they uncover shoddy reporting, plagiarism or false sourcing, it's a good thing for journalists and the public.

5. Collaborative investigations between pro and amateur journalists. The Internet allows ad-hoc investigations to take place between professional reporters and amateur sleuths. The Sunlight Foundation gave tools to citizen journalists so they could help find out which members of U.S. Congress were employing their spouses . The *Los Angeles Times* and various amateur investigators worked together to unmask the LonelyGirl15 video actress as Jessica Rose. Many more of these collaborative investigations are possible thanks to easy communication online and experiments such as NewAssignment.net.

6. More voices are part of the news conversation. In the past, if you wanted to voice your opinion, correct a fact or do your own reporting, you had to work at a mainstream news organization. Now, thanks to the rising influence of independent bloggers and online journalists, there are more outsiders and experts exerting influence over the news agenda. Not only does that mean we have a more diverse constellation of views, but it also takes the concentrated agenda-setting power out of a few hallowed editorial boardrooms.

7. Greater transparency and a more personal tone. Thanks to blogs and the great wide pastures of the web, reporters can go onto media websites and explain their conflicts of interest in greater detail, leading to more transparency. Plus, online writing tends to be more personal, giving reporters, editors and news anchors the chance to be more human and connect with their audience in deeper ways.

8. Growing advertising revenues online. While old-line media people complain that online ads aren't bringing in enough revenues to replace what's lost in the transition from the old advertising formats, that doesn't mean all is lost. Almost every forecast for online advertising shows double-digit percentage increases in revenues over the next five years, and it's hard to believe none of that will trickle down to media companies. What might well happen is that media concentration will lessen, and more of the revenues will be spread out to smaller independent sites than just the big conglomerates.

9. An online shift from print could improve our environmental impact. Very few people consider just how much our love for print newspapers and magazines harms the environment. It's true that publishers are trying to use more recycled paper, but use of online media has a much less drastic ecological impact. Choosing online over print actually saves trees, which in turn means that media companies that transition wisely could be helping to reduce global warming. Many people expect that some type of reusable, flexible e-ink readers will eventually replace ink-on-dead-tree publications.

10. Stories never end. Perhaps one of the weakest points about traditional journalism is that there's rarely any follow-ups on big stories. It usually takes a professional reporter having to go back and report what's happened since the big story. But online, stories can live on for much longer in flexible formats, allowing people to update them in comments or add more facts as they happen. Wikinews is one example of user-generated news stories that can be updated and edited by anyone.

What do you think? What other reasons do you think journalism has a bright future ahead? Or are you a techno-pessimist who thinks none of this will presage better days for journalism?

Rolling the Dice

Paul Farhi

Media companies have high hopes that hyperlocal news online will bolster their newspapers' futures. But early returns suggest the financial outlook for such ventures is not bright.

IT SEEMED LIKE A GOOD IDEA AT THE TIME. With blogging flourishing and citizen journalism just budding, Mark Potts and Susan DeFife thought they had a winning formula for a new kind of journalistic enterprise. One evening in the summer of 2004, they sketched out their common vision: A series of hyperlocal, news-oriented Web sites whose tone and content—news, commentary, blogs, photos, calendar listings—would be supplied primarily by the people who knew each community best, its residents. By May of 2005, the venture, dubbed Backfence.com, was up and running, with sites serving two affluent Virginia towns in Washington D.C.'s suburbs, McLean and Reston.

The idea of virtual town squares seemed so promising that within months Potts (a veteran reporter and editor at the *Washington Post* and cofounder of its digital division) and DeFife (founder and chief executive of Womenconnect.com for women in business) had attracted $3 million from two venture capital firms, including one headed by eBay founder Pierre Omidyar. The money funded an expansion program that would have made Starbucks proud (see "Dotcom Bloom," June/July 2005). By early 2007, Backfence had grown to 13 sites serving towns around Washington, Chicago and the San Francisco Bay area. The partners began talking about creating as many as 160 sites in 16 markets.

And then? And then the bottom dropped out. Backfence's rapid expansion burned up its $3 million war chest. The partners have split; Backfence's staff, which once numbered as many as 25, was laid off. The company's online communities are largely ghost towns now. "We ran out of money," says a somewhat chastened Potts today. "And we ran out of runway."

The failure of Backfence may offer no greater lesson than the old one about pioneers being the ones with arrows in their backs. New ventures fail all the time. But it could also sound a cautionary note about the present—and immediate future—of hyperlocal news sites. As big-media companies and entrepreneurs alike rush into the hyperlocal arena (see "Really Local," April/May), it's worth pausing and asking: Is there a real business in this kind of business?

So far—and admittedly it's still very early—the answer is no. A few of the estimated 500 or so "local–local" news sites claim to show a profit, but the overwhelming majority lose money, according to the first comprehensive survey of the field. The survey, conducted by J-Lab: The Institute for Interactive Journalism (affiliated with the University of Maryland's Philip Merrill College of Journalism, as is AJR), documents a journalism movement that is simultaneously thriving and highly tenuous. While independent sites such as WestportNow.com (Connecticut), iBrattleboro.com (Vermont) and VillageSoup.com (Maine) have sparked useful civic debates and prodded established media outlets to compete more vigorously, the field as a whole is so far financially marginal. As the report puts it, "their business models remain deeply uncertain."

In fact, many operators don't really have a business model. The first wave of hyperlocal sites has featured seat-of-the-pants operations, staffed part-time by dedicated volunteers, community activists and impassioned gadflies. About half of the 141 respondents to the J-Lab survey said they didn't need to earn revenue to stay afloat, thanks to self-funding and volunteer labor. A full 80 percent said their sites either weren't covering their operating costs—or that they just weren't sure. Only 10 of the 141 said they were breaking even or earning a profit.

This is why industry observers such as Peter Krasilovsky remain skeptical: "I don't really see a model right now that allows [hyperlocal sites] to build up a sales staff and an editor beyond a very limited point," says Krasilovsky, a consultant and blogger (Localonliner. com).

Then again, money isn't necessarily the issue, says Jan Schaffer, J-Lab's executive director and the author of a report accompanying the survey. "When they talk about success, they're not talking about revenue," she says. "They're talking about the impact they've had on their communities." She adds, "I'm not sure in this iteration, these [operators] see themselves as making big salaries and having big offices. I'm not saying it won't happen somewhere down the road, but in this iteration it isn't there yet."

These days, the category's shining star—the anti-Backfence—is Baristanet.com, a scrappy, snarky local-news-and-commentary site that covers the tony New York City suburbs of Montclair and Bloomfield in New Jersey. Co-owned by a novelist (Debbie Galant) and a journalist (Liz George), Baristanet is by all appearances thriving just three years after its founding. Its mix of news stories big (the arrest of a local murder suspect) and small (a debate over artificial turf at a local playing field) as well as reader-supplied commentary and photos attracts about 80,000 unique visitors a month, according to co-owner George. It's also selling ads—to local supermarkets, real-estate agents and restaurants. Baristanet has gotten so much buzz that Galant and George have recently branched out as consultants to other hyperlocal entrepreneurs.

But Baristanet (the name was picked to conjure news "baristas" serving up daily scoops) isn't exactly a big business. In fact, it's just barely a small one. The site generated about $60,000 in revenue last year. That's enough for Galant and George to hire a full-time freelance editor and a few part-time employees. Although George projects revenue of $100,000 this year, Baristanet isn't close to generating enough profit to support its owners, who aren't quitting their regular jobs. "As soon as the money's there, I'll commit to it" full-time, says George, a special sections editor at New York's *Daily News*. "We're growing, but we're not there yet."

Despite such modest returns, mainstream news organizations seem determined to enter the field. Sparked by such early hyperlocal innovators as the *Journal-World* (www2. ljworld.com) in Lawrence, Kansas, and the *Rocky Mountain News* in Denver (YourHub.com), established media companies see hyperlocalism as a way to win back lost readers and to target mom-and-pop advertisers who can't afford to, or simply don't want to, reach every household in a region. New entrants include Gannett, the nation's largest newspaper chain, and the *Chicago Tribune,* which in April launched Triblocal.com, aimed at nine towns in the southern and western suburbs.

The *Tribune's* foray into the burbs is "a way to make the [paper] more relevant to people who are farther and farther away from the central city," says Ted Biedron, who heads Chicagoland Publishing Co., the *Tribune* subsidiary overseeing the project. "Every major metro paper," he adds, "has this issue." True, but the *Tribune* isn't making any bold pronouncements about Triblocal, including revenue projections. The project seems modest so far: Triblocal has hired only four journalists to collect and organize material for the eight towns it is initially targeting online.

But Biedron notes that the project may prove more successful as an offline venture than an online one. This summer, the company will "reverse publish" its hyperlocal content, creating tabloid papers that will be inserted into copies of the *Tribune* bound for the distant towns.

A more ambitious hyperlocal effort is unfolding in my backyard, via my employer, the *Washington Post*. A 10-member team at Washingtonpost.Newsweek Interactive, the company's online division, has been working since October on the first of what it hopes will be a series of "microsites" covering the *Post's* home circulation area. The first such site, scheduled to go up in June, will target Loudoun County, Virginia (population: 255,518), a sprawling, exurban locale about 40 miles from downtown Washington. This is, in many ways, uncharted territory for the *Post,* which has tended to train its journalistic resources on Washington's government institutions, war zones and exotic foreign capitals.

WPNI picked Loudoun for its first hyperlocal effort because of the county's growth rate and affluence—its median household income of $98,483 is among the highest in the nation—and because Loudoun has just one moderately large municipality, Leesburg. This means that Loudoun's many subdivisions receive services from the county government, giving an otherwise disconnected place a common identity. Or so the folks at WPNI hope.

"What we're struggling with, and every major paper is struggling with, is how to reach our audience on a granular level, in a way we've never reached them before," says Jonathan Krim, WPNI's assistant managing editor for local and a co-leader on the Loudoun project. "People in the community want to know when that danged Dunkin' Donuts is finally going to move in. Or why there isn't a stoplight at the intersection where there have been a lot of accidents. There's a whole range of stories that, let's face it, a lot of newspapers and Web sites aren't engaged in, but that we know are really important to readers."

The *Post* already prints two Loudoun Extra sections a week with a staff of four reporters. But LoudounExtra.com, as the new microsite will be called, will also rely on its own "citizen army," as Krim puts it—a network of bloggers and amateur contributors who live in the county.

The site will also have several new features that the printed paper can't match. Rob Curley, WPNI's vice president of product development, takes on a nearly evangelical fervor as he talks up what he's got in store. Whipping out his ever-present Apple laptop and clicking frantically, he shows off a database that includes panoramic photos of every high school football field in the county; click on sections of the grandstands and you can see the sight lines to the field. There will be podcasts of some local church sermons, real-time accounts of high-school games and highly detailed restaurant guides, too. "You want to know which [county] restaurants are open after 11 p.m. on a Thursday? Boom! There you go!" he says, triumphantly displaying such a list.

Curley, a much-heralded veteran of similar projects at the *Journal-World* and at Florida's *Naples Daily News,* says newspapers can't afford not to add such bells and whistles.

"As my publisher in Lawrence used to say, 'Newspapers have to start driving with their brights on,'" he says. "My gut feeling is that a lot of newspapers aren't doing that right now. I don't know what it is about the newspaper industry, but it has a way of taking great ideas and making them into OK ideas."

But let's get back to the bottom line again and ask a simple question: Will initiatives like LoudounExtra.com have much of an impact on a newspaper that generated about $675 million last year from print and online ads? Will such efforts add up to much for an industry that seems to be grasping daily for the lifeboats?

Krim is hesitant. "We don't really know yet," he answers.

Still, he adds, "It's important to do this, even if it isn't a panacea. No one thing is going to change [the newspaper industry's] future. But a lot of things might. That's why we have to do this, even if we can't say for certain what kind of business success we might have. It's part of our mission. It has to be part of our mission in serving our readers and our communities. Do we hope, at the very least, that people looking at LoudounExtra.com will give the *Washington Post* a second look? Sure we do."

There are, of course, some good reasons for modesty. The *Post,* after all, isn't the first media company to discover Loudoun County. In addition to a local radio station, *Yellow*

Pages publishers and coupon mailers, LoudounExtra.com will have to compete for local advertising with no fewer than 11 weekly newspapers, says Paul Smith, the executive editor of the county's biggest weekly, the *Loudoun Times-Mirror*.

Smith points out that most of the weeklies have larger editorial and sales staffs than the *Post* in Loudoun (the *Times-Mirror* has 15 full- and part-time newsroom employees). What's more, the weeklies have an unquantifiable advantage over the big-city paper: local brand names and strong ties to the community. The *Times-Mirror,* for one, can trace its founding to 1798.

"The *Washington Post* is a great paper," says Smith. "I love to read it every morning. But sometimes when you're a little bigger, you think bigger is better. It's not necessarily so." Online restaurant guides are nice, but Smith says bread-and-butter news still sells: "Can they cover the school board meetings?" he asks. "Can they go to local sporting events? Because people still want to read about those things."

Mark Potts, late of Backfence.com, can tell you all about the pitfalls of hyperlocal journalism. Although Backfence had its internal stresses, with the partners clashing over strategy (DeFife eventually resigned because of them), the company had two basic structural problems: getting the word out and getting the money in.

Raising awareness among residents of a community was a constant challenge, he says, particularly since Backfence's competitors were reluctant to sell advertising to a would-be rival. So, Potts and DeFife tried grassroots promotion, such as handing out flyers at civic events and speaking to community groups. But such efforts are difficult to sustain. "Where we fell down was getting the initial traffic in," he says. "When it works, it's mind-blowing. But it takes time to build, and it's difficult if you don't have a big media organization behind you."

Attracting local advertisers wasn't really an issue; Backfence had more than 400 of them on its many sites. "We were happy with the advertising we got, but it didn't grow as quickly as we thought it would," Potts says. Some ads sold for as little as $50. Laments Potts, "Small businesspeople just don't have a lot of money to spend" on advertising. (Indeed, Krasilovsky, the industry consultant, estimates that two-thirds of small businesses don't even advertise in traditional *Yellow Pages* books, let alone online.)

But Potts remains optimistic. "I believe there's huge pent-up demand for this," he says. "It's still a good idea. And it's going to happen. It's just a question of where and who and how all the pieces come together."

He thinks hyperlocal news sites will succeed if they can keep operating costs to a rock-bottom minimum, and if the sites are clustered–that is, strung together over a wide territory. That way, he says, a publisher won't be dependent on ads from just the local pizza parlor or the neighborhood dry cleaner. With enough "mass," a hyperlocal publisher might even attract regional and national advertisers, too.

It's a paradoxical notion, one that seems to strike at the whole notion of "hyperlocal" journalism: To stay very small, you may have to get very big.

Extra! Extra! The Future of Newspapers

Michael Kinsley

SOMEWHERE IN THE FOREST, a tree is cut down. It is loaded onto a giant truck and hauled a vast distance to a factory, where the trees are turned into huge rolls of paper. These rolls are loaded onto another truck and hauled another vast distance to another factory, where the rolls of paper are covered in ink, chopped up, folded, stacked, tied, and loaded onto a third set of trucks, which fan out across cities and regions dropping bundles here and there.

Printing plants no longer have the clickety-clack of linotype machines and bubbling vats of molten lead. The letterpress machines that stamped the ink on the paper have been supplanted by offset presses that transfer it gently. There is computer-controlled this and that. Nevertheless, the process remains highly physical, mechanical, complicated, and noisy. As we live through the second industrial revolution, your daily newspaper remains a tribute to the wonders of the first one.

Meanwhile, back to those bundles. Some of them are opened and the newspapers are put, one-by-one, into plastic bags. Bagged or unbagged, they are loaded onto a fourth set of vehicles—bicycles by legend, usually these days a car or small truck—and flung individually into your bushes or at your cat. Other bundles go to retail establishments. Still other newspapers are locked into attractive metal boxes bolted into the sidewalk. Anyone who is feeling lucky and happens to possess the exact change has a decent shot at obtaining a paper or, for the same price, carting away a dozen.

What happens next is aided by a flat surface, especially on a Sunday near Christmas. The proud owner of up to four or five pounds of paper and ink begins searching for the parts he or she wants. The paper has multiple sections, each of which is either folded into others or wrapped around others according to an ancient formula known only to newspaper publishers and designed to guarantee that no one section can either be found on the first go-through or removed without putting half a dozen other sections into play. Newspaper-industry regulations do not require any particular labeling system for sections, but they do require that if letters are used, the sections cannot be in alphabetical order.

And so, at last, there are two piles of paper: a short one of stuff to read, and a tall one of stuff to throw away. Unfortunately, many people are taking the logic of this process one step further. Instead of buying a paper in order to throw most of it away, they are not buying it in the first place.

Bill Gates says that in technology things that are supposed to happen in less than five years usually take longer than expected, while things that are supposed to happen in more than 10 years usually come sooner than expected. Ten years ago, when I went to work for Microsoft, the newspaper industry was in a panic over something called Sidewalk—a now-forgotten Microsoft project to create Web site entertainment guides for a couple dozen big cities. Newspapers were convinced that Microsoft could and would put them out of business by stealing their ad base. It didn't happen. The collapse of the Internet bubble did happen. And, until very recently, the newspapers got complacent. Some developed good Web sites, some didn't, but most stopped thinking of the Web as an imminent danger.

Ten years later, newspapers are starting to panic again. But merely slobbering after bloggers may not be enough. In 1996, the oldest Americans who grew up with computers and don't even understand my tiresome anecdotes about how people used to resist them ("What's a typewriter, Mike?") were just entering adulthood. Now they are most of the working population, or close to it.

The trouble even an established customer will take to obtain a newspaper continues to shrink, as well. Once, I would drive across town if necessary. Today, I open the front door and if the paper isn't within about 10 feet I retreat to my computer and read it online. Only six months ago, that figure was 20 feet. Extrapolating, they will have to bring it to me in bed by the end of the year and read it to me out loud by the second quarter of 2007.

No one knows how all this will play out. But it is hard to believe that there will be room in the economy for delivering news by the Rube Goldberg process described above. That doesn't mean newspapers are toast. After all, they've got the brand names. You gotta trust something called the "Post-Intelligencer" more than something called "Yahoo!" or "Google," don't you? No, seriously, don't you? OK, how old did you say you are?

And newspapers have got the content. The first time I heard myself called a "content provider," I felt like a guy who'd been hired by the company that makes Tupperware to make sure there was plenty of Jell-O salad. As a rule, anyone who uses the term "content provider" without a smirk needs to consider getting content from someone else.

There is even hope for newspapers in the very absurdity of their current methods of production and distribution. What customers pay for a newspaper doesn't cover the cost of the paper, let alone the attendant folderol. Without these costs, even zero revenue from customers would be a good deal for newspapers, if advertisers go along. Which they might. Maybe. Don't you think? Please?

READING WRITING

This Text: Reading

1. Where do the writers agree about the future of newspaper? Disagree?
2. Notice how the writers use the word technology. Is it seen as a good or bad thing?
3. Notice too how the word bloggers is used.
4. Why do you think the writers, whatever their stance, are concerned with newspapers and journalism? Do you share their interest or concern?
5. What advantages do newspapers have over the Internet? Disadvantages?

This Text: Writing

1. Write a short paper comparing the front pages of an electronic version of the front page of a newspaper.
2. Spend an afternoon taking notes on a newspaper site that updates. In what ways is the newspaper taking advantage of new technology? Is it undermining or enchancing the newspaper?
3. Read a few bloggers linked on the newspaper page and some other bloggers. Write about the differences and similarities in tone.
4. Take one of the above assignments and re-think it as if it were electronic. What things could you link to? Does this detract or enhance your paper?

The Iraq War Suite

Since 2003, this country has been at war in Iraq. The war has been covered from a variety of angles that illustrate both the changing nature of journalism, and the tension—some would say inherent—between the government and media trying to cover an increasingly unpopular war. Blogs, such as *Daily Kos*, a self-described Democratic blog, have offered commentary as well as a way for people to comment on the Bush administration's decisions about the conflict in Iraq.

These questions matter because journalism is the source of information for Americans about their government generally and war specifically. One can even determine the nature of dissent between the government and its people by its journalism. During World War II, newspaper reports were often aimed at keeping morale high, both at home and abroad. However, during the Vietnam War, investigative reporting by people like David Halberstam were responsible not only for exposing the shocking realities of war but also for uncovering shameful transgressions on the part of the U.S. military.

Accordingly, when America is at war, journalists are often faced with seemingly contradictory tasks—reporting the truth and supporting the troops. And, even the most independent-minded newspapers find themselves caught in these crosshairs—especially if the issue involves National Security. For example, *The New York Times* held off reporting a story about President Bush authorizing the National Security Agency to conduct domestic eavesdropping for an entire year because they feared they might tip off terrorists.

The role of the reporter, then, is often confusing. In the Iraq war, these roles became even more confusing as many journalists became "embedded" with U.S. military forces; meaning the reporters actually lived, ate, traveled with, and were protected by American soldiers on patrol. Many have asked how objective (or critical) such reporters could possibly be on the troops that were ensuring their safety. This suite of articles about journalism and the Iraq war explores all of these issues and more.

John Hockenberry, writing in *Wired*, discusses how Army bloggers were telling the story. Writing in *Slate*, Jack Shafer discusses the pros and cons on the embedding experiment undertaken by the U.S. military; Matt Sanchez, an embedded journalist and a Marine, claims most journalistic accounts of the horrors of war are inaccurate. We also have a blog from *Daily Kos* that details soldiers' deaths and their impact on local communities.

Note: With all the commentary offered on Iraq, this suite only is a small portion of the relevant material. We encourage you to go to our Web site, where we have additional links.

Live from Baghdad: The Press's War

Matt Sanchez

In Baghdad, at an informal meeting of the incoming U.S. ambassador to Iraq and members of the media, the ambassador got an earful about how difficult it was to cover this war. Despite the dainty hors d'oeuvre and wine (in the first real glasses I have seen since my arrival in Iraq), the press brought out a laundry list of issues preventing them from doing their job: checkpoints, transportation, the bureaucracy of blood tests at the border, and the need for more personal security. For what was supposed to be a meet and greet, the greet did not last long. Ambassador Ryan Crocker was gracious, and some thanked him for inviting us to his home, which was rumored to be the former residence of

Saddam's sister. But like so many things here in country it's not always possible to separate the rumored from the real. Discerning facts from fiction is an obstacle the media trips over daily.

As the current center of national government, the Green Zone is a high-security, exclusive neighborhood, where checkpoints are more common than monuments. On the way back from the ambassador's residence, we were asked to get out of the car and submit to a search. Several members of the press and State Department were livid; they insisted there was no need for them to break the usual protocol of VIP express entry. The Peruvian guard, whose English was not up to the task of explaining his urgency, tersely insisted everyone leave the vehicle.

While waiting in line for the x-ray machine, I asked the Peruvian if this was normal. He assured me that it was not, and nervously explained they had received very specific information about a bomb threat. The following day, a suicide bomber attacked a hotel just a stone's throw away. But at the inconvenient checkpoint, a *New York Times* reporter raised even more of a fit for the guard than he did for the ambassador. With the Iraq War being one of the most dangerous to cover, you'd think some journalists would appreciate the extra security measures, but you'd be wrong about a lot of assumptions concerning the wartime press.

After spending some time with the mainstream media, it's not hard to understand why the coverage coming from Iraq is, as Staff Sergeant Rodriguez from the 4-9 cavalry out of Texas put it, "Completely wrong . . . in my opinion."

The media has a conflict of values. A successful insurgent will always get more recognition than a successful infantryman—no matter how many successful infantrymen there are. In an arm-wrestling match between progress and propaganda, the reward of media coverage for bad behavior has a Pavlovian effect on attention-seeking terrorists.

On my trip north, our convoy was hit by an IED. An explosion is a split-second flash, something you could miss if you blink. Like attempting to photograph a lightning bolt when the sky is clear, explosions are tricky to catch on film. You have to point at the right place in the right moment, and even then you'd need luck. Unless, of course, you know when, where, and how the bomb is about to go off.

Unlike any other player on the board, the press has no oversight, no mandate, few penalties, and even fewer consequences. In Fallujah, a suicide bomber kills one victim, but an "unidentified police officer" reports 20 dead and just as many casualties. Because there are not enough reporters on the ground, too many bureaus have outsourced both their reporting and standards to third-party "stringers" whose spectacular videos of explosions and inflated body counts have shown up on both jihadist recruiting sites and American television screens, simultaneously. These hacks-for-hire literally get more bucks for each bang.

Nothing happens? No cash from an image-driven 24-hour news cycle. Have the media made mistakes in coverage? No doubt. But in an industry where some claim to be "keeping them honest," there's no penalty for false or misleading reports. With accountability about as valid as last week's newspaper, reporters still maintain carte blanche in their work. For a group that habitually decries abuse of power and unilateralism, who watches the watchmen?

In 2004, the Iraqi prime minister banned Al Jazeerah from the country for "presenting a negative image of Iraq." The Al Jazeerah spokesman, whose first name is Jihad (no joke), called the ousting "unjustifiable" and "contrary to the promises of freedom of speech." Presenting a negative image of the United States is hardly grounds for dismissal and it may even earn an ambitious journalist a Pulitzer Prize, but the men and women fighting in this war have consistently protested against biased coverage that "never shows all the good things that happen."

Everywhere I have traveled throughout Iraq, I've heard troop horror stories of seemingly friendly reporters "burning" them, but reporters defend themselves. An *LA Times* correspondent insisted she was meticulous about getting quotes right, another journalist from the *Army Times* said soldiers sometimes regret saying things that look dumb in print. Misled or misspoken? The truth probably lies somewhere in between, but there should be no doubt about the friction between those on post and those in the press. Reporting as if the war were some type of game show, media coverage has been reduced to a running tally of dead servicemen and "expert commentary" from the faraway, air-conditioned offices of a midtown Manhattan newsroom.

Setting a Guinness record for distance to commute to work, *Time* magazine's Iraq "expert" Joe Klein has managed to get his opinion and analysis to audiences worldwide since 2003. With no military experience (which seems to be a prerequisite for reporting from Iraq), perched above his keyboard in Westchester, N.Y., Klein has been a persistent back-seat driver in the "rush to war". Finally, after four years of his articles have influenced millions of readers and news outlets throughout the world, Joe Klein has made it into Iraq just in time to declare the effort hopeless.

As I read much of the Western press I wonder, whose side are these guys on? Of course, the answer is that they're supposed to remain neutral, but this neutrality is a luxury afforded the media by a standard that only one side will meet. When *Time* magazine interviewed a bombmaker claiming to be responsible for "rising American casualties," they forgot to ask the "sophisticated and tenacious enemy" the tough questions like, "What's your exit strategy?" or "How broken is the insurgency?" "Could you define victory?" or even the most basic, "Why are you doing this?" The fact that the press demands accountability from one side and offers servility to the other is a very cunning strategy to win an asymmetrical war. That is, it's as if the press were conducting a war of its own.

The Press Dun Good in Iraq. But They Could Have Dun Better

Jack Shafer

The "embed" program, in which the Pentagon attached some 600 print, radio, and TV reporters with coalition forces for the Iraq invasion, gave reporters unprecedented access to the battlefield, allowing them to file uncensored views of the action in real time. In return, embeds vowed not to reveal anything that would endanger "operational security"—troop strength, location, strategy, etc.

Compared to the media freeze-outs of the Afghanistan campaign, the Panama invasion, and the taking of Grenada, the embed program is a huge improvement. Never in the history of war have more reporters been able to cover the conflict from the front as it happened. And just because the military ended up liking the embed program—Gen. Tommy Franks told Fox News that he was "a fan"—doesn't mean the program was bad.

Assessing the "embed war" in any complete way is beyond the scope of any single writer, even one who read voluminously while it raged and watched television into the wee a.m. But what can be ascertained in talking to individual reporters who covered the war as embeds and so-called "unilaterals" (unattached to any military unit) is—perhaps predictably—that the program was good but not perfect. Not every commander fully honored the terms of the Pentagon's program. One reporter who covered the war estimates that only 50 to 70 of the 600 embeds saw any interesting combat during the conflict. Others found themselves embedded with units that saw little action or were never deployed.

One troubling side effect of the program was that it created a credentialing system among reporters: The embedded were considered official journalists, to whom the military would generally talk, and the unilaterals were often treated as pests with no right to the battlefield. In many instances, the military prevented unilaterals from covering the war, especially in the southern cities left in the invasion's wake: Basra, Umm Qasr, Nasiriyah, and Safwan.

And while embedded TV journalists beamed back to the studio compelling footage of battlefield bang-bang, the networks failed to place the action in proper context. Exchanges of small-arms fire were inflated into major shootouts by television, and minor (though deadly) skirmishes became full-bore battles. Also, the journalistic tendency to put a human face on every story hyperbolized coalition setbacks, such as the ambush of Pfc. Jessica Lynch and her comrades.

Who's to blame? How can journalists work to make future war coverage better? Several reporters and editors who shaped coverage of the Iraq war speak their minds.

When Peter Copeland covered Gulf War I's ground war for Scripps Howard News Service, commanders made him privy to every aspect of the battle plan and allowed him to accompany troops into battle. But all this access was for naught. The technology was inadequate—there were no tiny, mobile satellite phones and no Internet.

"My technology was a battery-operated printer that I would try to have faxed. Or give guys to take back to the rear," Copeland says.

"There were reporters out in the front who were getting good stories. But we depended on the military to distribute our stories, which was a mistake, he says. "I didn't know if my stories were getting back or not. After the ground war was over I called my office. 'Where the hell have you been?' 'Iraq.' 'Why the hell didn't you file?!' "

Currently Scripps Howard's editor and general manager, Copeland and other experienced war reporters and editors worked with the Pentagon to create a program that would allow reporters to tell the war's story while it was happening.

Copeland applauds the embed program 1) for creating so many embedded slots that not all the offered slots were taken; 2) for educating the military on the fact that the press wouldn't endanger the troops or the battle plan; and 3) because it would protect reporters: "I didn't want my reporters driving around the battlefield during a high intensity conflict looking for stories, because they'll get killed."

But the embed program also taught Copeland that the press should do a better job of training people for the next conflict and reduce its dependency on the military.

Copeland resists reducing the discussion about Iraq war reporting to embeds versus unilaterals: "I am in favor of embedded reporters, but also reporters working on their own. You need to have both kinds and as many eyes as possible," he says.

No single vantage point gave an adequate view of the war, but one of the best seats went to *U.S. News & World Report* reporter Mark Mazzetti. Mazzetti (see his November *Slate* "Diary" about "embed school") covered the brass inside the 1st Marine Expeditionary Force's mobile command, which packed up and moved twice during the Baghdad blitz.

"Before the war started, they briefed us on the whole battle plan for the Marines. We got to see where they scrapped the plan," Mazzetti says. He heard everything from the calling of the first "audible" to invade, which resulted in the Marines securing the oil fields, to the end of the war. Mazzetti observed up close the planning of missions and the ever-changing positions of the blue (coalition) and red (Iraqi) icons on the laptops and monitors as the battles unfolded.

The Iraq War Suite

Although his viewpoint was limited, in some sense it was a clearer perspective than the TV networks were able to convey: From the mobile-command vantage point, the war was going exceedingly well—even during the weekend of March 29, when Army generals, TV generals, and the press worried that a quagmire had swallowed U.S. forces. The Marines told the journos they were smashing Iraqi forces and gaining excellent yardage on Baghdad—which conflicted with the TV images of selected units broadcast that weekend.

Cloistered inside the Marine tent, Mazzetti had trouble determining whether the Marines were spinning him and his three fellow embeds or whether the war really was going well.

"There were times during that bad week when the four of us were thinking that we were drinking the Kool-Aid and not getting the whole picture," Mazzetti says.

The Marines' optimistic message clashed with what U.S. News was hearing stateside. Ultimately, Mazzetti conveyed the Marines' message to his editors, who used it as one of many data points in shaping the story.

"We were able to present a picture to our editors: 'Hey, don't fall off a ledge,'" says Mazzetti.

It takes a lifetime of study to discern a defeat from a setback or to see a campaign's complete context. The military calls this skill "situational awareness," and many of the people who think they have it don't. The press corps' poor performance in reading the Iraq battlefield indicates that you can be embedded all the way up to the four-star generals and still not understand the meaning behind the action. Press organizations might want to think about teaching the TV generals more about journalism or, better still, schooling their correspondents and anchors in remedial situational awareness programs.

The embed program proved to be only as good as the commanders overseeing it. Embeds on the carrier USS Abraham Lincoln had to mutiny against the military to report the war. When they boarded the ship, Rear Adm. John M. Kelly forced them to agree to ground rules that were more restrictive than the Pentagon-imposed rules. The *Washington Post's* Lyndsey Layton, who covered the Navy's air war from the carrier, says the rear admiral assigned a Navy "minder" to sit in on every interview and note every question asked and every reply made. He banned reporters from the general mess deck, essentially preventing them from interacting with sailors. After five days of this treatment, Layton and her colleagues took their complaint to Navy brass in Bahrain. Only then were the ad hoc restrictions on reporters' movements lifted; eventually the escorts, who had previously shadowed the reporters' every step, vanished.

"I wasn't breaking any news on that ship," Layton says. "I was there in case a plane went down." But when a carrier-based Navy F/A-18 Hornet was lost over Iraq, Centcom released the information to the press swarm in Qatar, not via the carrier group.

Aside from Rear Adm. Kelly's overreaching—"He didn't want us there"—Layton thinks the embed program works but only as long as the senior people sign on. She does reflect, however, on the limitations of covering a war from the claustrophobic confines of a carrier. All of her dispatches were sent through the Navy's e-mail system, making them easy to hack if the Navy wanted to.

"When you're on the ground, you can always find your way to other sources," Layton says. "But on a ship, you can't place a phone call or send an e-mail to a source."

Washington Post military affairs reporter Thomas E. Ricks gives "two thumbs up" to the embed program. Working in Washington, Ricks fielded a flood of information each day—

anywhere from 60 to 70 pages of memos and dispatches from the front—that he and his fellow *Posties* melded into a daily overview of the campaign.

Ricks, who covered the Somalia intervention as an embed, says the program will have a lasting effect on the reporting of military affairs.

"Out of the 500 embeds, a goodly portion will continue to cover the military. There are a lot of Ernie Pyles out there who will know fielded military operations. I think too many reporters focus on the Pentagon. And calling yourself a military reporter and covering the Pentagon is like going to Yankee Stadium to report on baseball and covering George Steinbrenner," Ricks says. To adequately report war, Ricks insists, you must have witnessed it firsthand.

Some independent-minded journalists chaffed at embed restrictions, which required embeds to stay with assigned units. Or they feared, quite rationally, that their natural affinity for the troops who were protecting their lives might impede their objectivity. For these and other reasons, some journalists covered the war unilaterally by choice.

Many of them complain about the second-class role they were relegated to. They speak of broken promises made by the military to helicopter them into southern Iraq—perhaps broken because the desired visual of Iraqis celebrating the liberation of Basra never materialized. Instead of helicopters, buses ferried unilats to conventional photo ops of the rescued oil fields or of relief ships docking in Umm Qasr. It's rumored that some unilats, frustrated by the lack of access, ignored the Geneva Conventions by dressing their vehicles in Red Cross disguise to sneak across the Kuwait-Iraq border after the invasion.

As far as the "coalition military press machine" was concerned, writes Jamie Wilson in the *Guardian,* unilaterals were one level lower than Republican Guardsmen.

Richard Leiby of the *Washington Post's* "Style" section went to war as a unilateral with just one order from his editor, Gene Robinson: Don't get killed.

Leiby argues that while the war "at the tip of the spear" got extraordinary coverage, the conflict left in its wake, in the rear, was grossly under-covered. What was the collateral damage wrought by the war? While Leiby played it safe, he says his *Post* colleagues, David Finkel, Keith Richburg, Susan Glasser, and Lucian Perkins risked their lives to report the war in the south without the benefit of the military guardians most embeds were assigned. Just getting inside Iraq from the press tent in Kuwait took journalistic ingenuity, he says. You'd have to beg your way onto a convoy or attempt to join one at a berm crossing or even bootleg your way into Iraq by finding a gap in the border and sprinting in.

Los Angeles Times unilateral Sam Howe Verhovek dittos Leiby.

"If this had been a war that had only been covered by embedded reporters, as great a job as they've done, they would have only gotten a part of the story," says Verhovek, who documented the sufferings of Iraqi villagers in the south with fellow *Times*man Mark Magnier.

"There's an inherent conflict built into embedding. From the military's point of view, when you embed somebody in your unit, they become family," says Verhovek. "For the reporter, that's very tricky. You want to keep objective distance from your source."

The *New Yorker's* Jeffrey Goldberg declined an embed slot for the freedom of a unilateral approach because he wasn't sure the unit the military offered him would see combat. (It didn't.)

"The risk of embedding is that you won't be able to see anything," says Goldberg. He estimates that 50 to 70 reporters had "really interesting experiences."

"The real danger is not being killed but being seriously out of position," says Goldberg.

Reporting the war in the north, Goldberg's experience was a mixed bag. Some GIs wouldn't talk to him because he was a unilateral but would speak to the embed standing nearby.

Gradually he gained access to U.S. forces at the front and the hospitality of the U.S. Air Force on the way out. Goldberg cracked a few ribs when the Kurdish guerrilla driving the SUV he was riding in swerved to avoid mortar rounds and rolled onto its side. When the war looked all but won, he asked for a ride out on an Air Force C-130 departing from a northern airstrip.

"I assumed I wouldn't get it because I was a unilateral," says Goldberg, who thought of himself as an outsider. "This captain said, 'No problem, we're all on the same team.'"

Still, what sticks in Goldberg's craw about the embed program is the way it turns one group of reporters into "official reporters" and another group into "the unapproved," not unlike the official credentialing that reporters in nearly every Middle East country must endure.

"Somebody should be able to stand outside and find fault other than the people inside," Goldberg says.

But who? And how?

Scripps Howard's Copeland holds the press, not the Pentagon, accountable for the journalistic shortcomings in Iraq.

"You don't want to get the Army in the position of acting as assignment editor," Copeland says, shuttling embeds and others around to battlefield hot spots. "That was one of the problems in the first Gulf War, they'd decide where we wanted to go."

"Critics who don't like the coverage should put some of the burden on the media and stop trying to blame everything on 'censorship.' I don't think we should expect the Pentagon to do our jobs for us. It's our responsibility—not the military's—to figure out how to cover the story," Copeland writes in e-mail.

A more diligent press would have covered the Iraq war by hiring experienced, Arabic-speaking reporters and translators in greater numbers and assigning more experienced war reporters to follow behind advancing U.S. forces as unilats.

"I'd be willing to talk with other news organizations about sending in our own team of people together but independent of U.S. forces," says Copeland.

The Blogs of War

John Hockenberry

The snapshots of Iraqi prisoners being abused at Abu Ghraib were taken by soldiers and shared in the digital military netherworld of Iraq. Their release to the world in May last year detonated a media explosion that rocked a presidential campaign, cratered America's moral high ground, and demonstrated how even a superpower could be blitzkrieged by some homemade downloadable porn. In the middle of it all, a lone reservist sergeant stationed on the Iraqi border posed a simple question:

I cannot help but wonder upon reflection of the circumstances, how much longer we, like other bloggers, will be able to carry with us our digital cameras, or take photographs and document the experiences we have had.

The writer was 24-year-old Chris Missick, a soldier with the Army's 319th Signal Battalion and author of the blog *A Line in the Sand*. While balloon-faced cable pundits shrieked about the scandal, Missick was posting late at night in his Army-issue "blacks," with a mug of coffee and a small French press beside him, his laptop blasting Elliot Smith's "Cupid's

Trick" into his headphones. He quickly seized on perhaps the most profound and crucial implication of Abu Ghraib:

> Never before has a war been so immediately documented, never before have sentiments from the front scurried their way to the home front with such ease and precision. Here I sit, in the desert, staring daily at the electric fence, the deep trenches and the concertina wire that separates the border of Iraq and Kuwait, and write home and upload my daily reflections and opinions on the war and my circumstances here, as well as some of the pictures I have taken along the way. It is amazing, and empowering, and yet the question remains, should I as a lower enlisted soldier have such power to express my opinion and broadcast to the world a singular soldier's point of view? To those outside the uniform who have never lived the military life, the question may seem absurd, and yet, as an example of what exists even in the small following of readers I have here, the implications of thought expressed by soldiers daily could be explosive.

His sober assessments of the potential of free speech in a war zone began attracting a wider following, eventually logging somewhere north of 100,000 pageviews. No blogging record, but rivaling the wonkish audience for the Pentagon's daily briefing on C-Span or DOD press releases. Missick is just one voice—and a very pro-Pentagon one at that—in an oddball online Greek chorus narrating the conflict in Iraq. It includes a core group of about 100 regulars and hundreds more loosely organized activists, angry contrarians, jolly testosterone fuckups, self-appointed pundits, and would-be poets who call themselves milbloggers, as in military bloggers. Whether posting from inside Iraq on active duty, from noncombat bases around the world, or even from their neighborhoods back home after being discharged—where they can still follow events closely and deliver their often blunt opinions—milbloggers offer an unprecedented real-time real-life window on war and the people who wage it. Their collective voice competes with and occasionally undermines the DOD's elaborate message machine and the much-loathed mainstream media, usually dismissed as MSM.

Milbloggers constitute a rich subculture with a refreshing candor about the war, expressing views ranging from far right to far left. They also offer helpful tips about tearing down an M16, recipes for beef stew (hint: lots of red wine), reviews of the latest episode of 24, extremely technical discussions of Humvee armor configurations, and exceptionally raw accounts of field hospital chaos, gore, and heroism. For now, the Pentagon officially tolerates this free-form online journalism and in-house peanut gallery, even as the brass takes cautious steps to control it. A new policy instituted this spring requires all military bloggers inside Iraq to register with their units. It directs commanders to conduct quarterly reviews to make sure bloggers aren't giving out casualty information or violating operational security or privacy rules. Commanding officers shut down a blog that reported on the medical response to a suicide bombing late last year in Mosul. The Army has also created the Army Web Risk Assessment Cell to monitor compliance. And Wired has learned that a Pentagon review is under way to better understand the overall implications of blogging and other Internet communications in combat zones.

"It's a new world out there," says Christopher Conway, a lieutenant colonel and DOD spokesperson. "Before, you would have to shake down your soldiers for matches that might light up and betray a position. Today, every soldier has a cell phone, beeper, game device, or laptop, any one of which could pop off without warning. Blogging is just one piece of the puzzle."

Strong opinions throughout the military ranks in and out of wartime are nothing new. But online technology in the combat zone has suddenly given those opinions a mass audience

The Iraq War Suite

and an instantaneous forum for the first time in the history of warfare. On the 21st-century battlefield, the campfire glow comes from a laptop computer, and it's visible around the world.

"In World War II, letters basically didn't arrive for months," says Michael Bautista, an Idaho National Guard corporal based in Kirkuk whose grandfather served in World War II and who blogs as Ma Deuce Gunner (named for the trusty M2 machine gun he calls Mama). "What I'm doing and what my fellow bloggers are doing is groundbreaking."

If you're stuck in southern Baghdad in the dusty gray fortress called Camp Falcon and find yourself in need of 50-caliber machine-gun ammo, chopper fuel, toilet paper, or M&M's, you call Danjel Bout, a 32-year-old captain and logistics officer from the California National Guard who blogs as Thunder 6. He's been stationed here with the Army's 3rd Infantry Division for most of 2005. When he's not chasing down requisitions of supplies or out on patrol hunting insurgents, Bout is posting about the details of Army life in language evocative of literary warbloggers of yore like Thucydides, Homer, Thomas Paine, and John Donne.

> Sleep, blessed, blissful, wonderful sleep. Mother's milk. A full harvest in a time of famine. The storm that breaks the drought. It is the drug of choice here—assiduously avoided because of the never-ending chain of missions, but always craved. If rarity is the measure of a substance's worth, then here in Iraq, sleep carries a price beyond words. There is no more precious moment in my day than the sublime instant where my mind flickers between consciousness and the dreamworld. In that sliver of time the day seems to shimmer and melt like one of Dali's paintings—leaving only honey sweet dreams of my other life far from Arabia.

Bout's blog, *365 and a Wakeup*, is unlikely to put you to sleep. It's one of the most genuine accounts anywhere of what life is like for a soldier in Iraq. The captain can be spotted composing and editing his posts on his laptop from the roof of one of Camp Falcon's dusty buildings in the dark early-morning hours, or in a scarce patch of shade during a rare moment of daylight downtime. His posts are sharply rendered parables and small, often powerful scenes built on details of the violent world around him.

"I just kind of bookmark the things I see during the day so I can reflect on them later. There's almost nothing about life here that isn't interesting in some way." Thunder 6 is the oldest of eight siblings in a devout Catholic family. His dad is a computer technician, his mom a horticulture therapist. This former altar boy and longtime reservist left the touchy-feely psychology PhD program at UC Davis after September 11, grabbed an M16 rifle and a Beretta 9-mm sidearm and went all-infantry. Trained as an Army Ranger, he saw action in Kuwait and Bosnia and claims to have no yearning for his former scholarly life.

"I was coasting through college," he says, "and the Army spoke to honor and camaraderie and things I really believed in." While Bout's blog is all about his emotional connection to the Army and very little about the daily bang-bang of Iraq, there are lots of milbloggers who will take you straight to the front lines, posting first-person accounts of the fighting and beating some newspaper reports of the same battle filed by embedded journalists. By the crude light of a small bulb and the backlit screen of his Dell laptop, Neil Prakash, a first lieutenant, posted some of the best descriptions of the fighting in Fallujah and Baquba last fall:

> Terrorists in headwraps stood anywhere from 30 to 400 meters in front of my tank. They stopped, squared their shoulders at us just like in an old-fashioned duel, and fired RPGs at our tanks. So far there hadn't been a single civilian in Task Force 2-2 sector. We had been free to light up the insurgents as we saw them. And because of that freedom, we were able to use the main gun with less restriction.

The Iraq War Suite

Prakash was awarded the Silver Star this year for saving his entire tank task force during an assault on insurgents in Iraq's harrowing Sunni Triangle. He goes by the handle Red 6 and is author of *Armor Geddon*. For him, the poetry of warfare is in the sounds of exploding weapons and the chaos of battle. "It's mind-blowing what this stuff can do," Prakash tells me by phone from Germany, where his unit moved after rotating out of Iraq earlier this year. One of his favorite sounds is that of an F16 fighter on a strafing run.

"It's like a cat in a blender ripping the sky open—if the sky was made out of a phone book." He is from India, the land of Gandhi, but he loves to talk about blowing things up. "It's just sick how badass a tank looks when it's killing."

Prakash is the son of two upstate New York dentists and has a degree in neuroscience from Johns Hopkins. He's a naturalized American citizen, born near Bangalore, and he describes growing up in the U.S. and his decision to join the military as something like *Bend It Like Beckham* meets *The Terminator*. He says he admired the Army's discipline and loved the idea of driving a tank. He knew that if he didn't join the Army, he might end up in medical school or some windowless office in a high tech company.

With a bit of bluster, Prakash claims that for him, the latter would be more of a nightmare scenario than ending up in the line of fire of insurgents. "It was a choice between commanding the best bunch of guys in the world and being in a cubicle at Dell Computer in Bangalore right now helping people from Bum-fuck USA format their hard drives."

It's taken some adjustment, but Prakash says his parents basically support his Army career, although his father can't conceal his anxiety about having a son in Iraq. Prakash says he blogs to assure the folks back home that he's safe, to let his friends all over the world know what's going on, and to juice up the morale in his unit.

"The guys get really excited when I mention them." By the time Prakash left Iraq early this year, the readers of *Armor Geddon* extended far beyond family and friends. He still posts from his base in Germany and is slowly trying to complete a blog memoir of his and his fellow soldiers' experiences in the battle for Fallujah.

The most widely read milbloggers engage in the 21st-century contact sport called punditry, and like their civilian counterparts, follow few rules of engagement. They mobilize sympathizers to ship body armor to reserve units in combat, raise funds for families of wounded soldiers, deliver shoes to barefoot Afghani kids, and even take aim at media big shots.

It was milblogger pundits who helped bring down Eason Jordan, a senior executive at CNN who resigned earlier this year over remarks he made that U.S. troops were targeting reporters in Iraq. One important milblogger who weighed in on the Jordan affair is a secretive 20-year-career Army GI who goes by the handle Greyhawk. His blog, the *Mudville Gazette*, investigated the incident and concluded that Iraq-based reporters disputed Jordan's claim. He's unhappy that a more thorough news investigation wasn't conducted. Other bloggers call Greyhawk "the father of us all" and credit him with coining the term milblogger shortly after he started *Mudville* in March 2003.

In an email interview—Greyhawk wouldn't agree to "voice-com" or a "face-to face"— he writes proudly of his lifetime pageviews, which recently exceeded 1.7 million (700,000 of those have come in 2005): "*Mudville* is far and away the largest, oldest, widest-read active-duty MilBlog in the World. It's all in how you make the words line up and dance."

Then there's Blackfive: "I'm just a guy with a blog and I know how to use it," says this modest former Army intelligence officer and paratrooper who gives his real name only as

Matt. He prefers the nom de guerre of his popular site. His peers voted *Blackfive* the best military blog in the 2004 Weblog Awards, beating out such contenders as *Froggy Ruminations,* the *Mudville Gazette, 2Slick,* and *My War.*

Blackfive is a popular forum for analysis of the war and strident, argumentative warnings about media bias. It's nearly as cluttered with ads as the *Drudge Report,* and the sales pitches mostly hawk "liberal-baiting merchandise." There are pictures of attractive women holding high-powered weapons, dozens of links to conservative books and films, and even the occasional big spender like Amazon.com. Blackfive also sells his own T-shirts to benefit military charities. He says that milblogging is the result of an explosion of communications technology throughout the military and an increase in brainpower among the lower ranks.

"The educational level of sergeants and below is out of control." Blackfive himself has degrees in archaeology and computer science and avidly follows the postings of fellow bloggers. He describes Neil Prakash as "borderline Einstein" and Danjel Bout as "a real rock star." In his last deployment, Blackfive's unit had two such brainiacs, a sergeant with an MBA and another with a master's in economics from the University of Chicago.

Blackfive is retired now, honorably discharged and working as an IT executive for a big civilian company. He blogs from Chicago and confidently claims he can mobilize thousands of people and their wallets, all from a wireless hot spot at his local Starbucks. He stays in the shadows because he believes that his company would not approve of his blog or of his unabashed support for the U.S. war. The site has become a destination for thousands of information junkies and influential opinion makers.

According to TruthLaidBear, which tracks blog traffic for advertisers, *Blackfive* is regularly in the top 100 blogs and averages 5,000 unique visits a day. During the height of the war, traffic to *Blackfive* spiked when some high-profile conservatives linked to the site.

"My brother followed a link from *National Review* to me, and somebody, I think it was Jonah Goldberg"—a somebody who is only the editor of *National Review*—"told him that four or five of the biggest think tanks read my blog every day."

Goldberg confirms that at times he turns to military blogs to supplement and sometimes contradict information coming out of traditional media sources. "*Blackfive* was good, and in the blog world if you offer something unique, you make eyeballs sticky."

Since World War I, the military has opened the letters soldiers sent back home from the battlefield and sometimes censored the dispatches of war correspondents. Now mail leaves the battlefield already open to the world. Anyone can publicly post a dispatch, and if the Pentagon reads these accounts at all, it's at the same time as the rest of us. The new policy requiring milbloggers to register their sites does not apply to soldiers outside Iraq, but nearly all of the bloggers contacted for this article say that the current system of few restrictions can't possibly last.

Blackfive and Greyhawk wonder what the landscape will look like after the Pentagon finishes its review of global digital security. So far, the DOD is giving no hints. Michael Cohen, a major and doctor with the 67th Combat Support Hospital based in Mosul, touched a nerve at the Pentagon late last year with his blog, 67cshdocs. Before he began posting, Cohen turned himself into a local private broadband provider in order to set up his own network outside the one provided to the field hospital.

"Some of the docs suggested that life would be really good if we could get Internet into our nice trailers." Cohen bought his network setup online and had it shipped directly to him in Mosul. For the oversize satellite dish, he had to get creative. He ordered it from Bentley Walker, a satellite broadband service provider, and they sent it to his wife's house in Germany. On a medical escort flight to Germany for a wounded soldier, Cohen persuaded the Air Force to let him hand-carry the dish onto a transport for the return trip. After about six weeks of agonized troubleshooting on a hot rooftop, the network was up and running.

"We had pretty decent bandwidth," he says, "2 meg downlink and 1 meg up. It was better than the hospital." Cohen says the system supported webcams linking people back home, its own instant messaging system, live gaming, and, he theorizes, a robust trade in porn.

"If you were to make the series *M*A*S*H* about today's Army, Radar would be an IT guy and he'd be more popular than Hawkeye." Then Cohen started to blog on his homegrown network. Originally it was an attempt to stay in touch with family and friends, but when a suicide bomber killed 22 people last December in a mess tent, Cohen began detailing how doctors dealt with the carnage.

His moving account drew attention from worldwide press as well as parents desperate to know the fate of their loved ones:

> The lab was running tests and doing a blood drive to collect more blood. The pharmacy was preparing intravenous medications and drips like crazy. Radiology was shooting plain films and CT scans like nobody's business. We were washing out wounds, removing shrapnel, and casting fractures. We put in a bunch of chest tubes. Because of all the patients on suction machines and mechanical ventilators, the noise in the ICU was so loud everyone was screaming at each other just to communicate. Here are some of our statistics. They are really quite amazing: 91 total patients arrived. 18 were dead on arrival. 4 patients died of wounds shortly after arrival—all of these patients had non-survivable wounds. Of the 69 remaining patients, 20 were transferred to military hospitals in other locations in Iraq. This left 49 patients for us to treat and disposition.

Cohen posted mesmerizing details about the medical hardware and surgical procedures used to save lives on that bloody day. And then, without warning, it was over. "My doctor boss came to me and said, hey, we need to talk. There are some people in the chain of command who believe there are things in your blog that violate Army regulations."

Cohen was shocked. He hadn't used names or talked about military operations. But his impression was that the information he provided about medical capability in the field worried senior officers at Central Command. At first the Army asked Cohen to shut down his entire satellite network, which at its peak was serving 42 families, but ultimately decided against it.

"I think they didn't want a hornet's nest," Cohen says. Instead, Cohen stopped blogging. Back in Germany now, where he says he spends more time delivering the latest R&R babies than treating battlefield casualties, Cohen says that he was tempted to challenge the shutdown, but since he was close to going home anyway, he went along with the decision.

The Pentagon will not comment specifically on Cohen's situation except to reiterate its policy that blogs should not reveal any casualty information that could upset next of kin or any details that might jeopardize operational security. Army reservist Jason Hartley's popular and notoriously irreverent blog, *Just Another Soldier,* also provoked the higher-ups; last

The Iraq War Suite

summer, his commanding officer ordered him to shut it down. Hartley wrote with a fuck-you swagger that may partly explain why he's not blogging anymore:

> Being a soldier is to live in a world of shit. From the pogues who cook my food and do my laundry to the Apache pilots and the Green Berets who do all the Hollywood stuff, our lives are in a constant state of suck.

Hartley got a lot of mileage out of a post about a soldier who was assembling a rifle blindfolded. Another soldier in his unit, as a joke, handed the assembler a certain piece of his anatomy instead of the tool he asked for.

"I told the story and asked the question, Who is more gay, the guy who touches a dick, or someone who allows a soldier to touch his dick?" This pressing infantry-level controversy hit a chord with über-blogger and noted pundit-of-all-things-queer Andrew Sullivan.

"Sullivan was kind and wrote that he liked my site," Hartley recalls. The Pentagon won't say why, but it ordered Hartley to shut down his blog. He did for a while. Then he resumed blogging a few months later, without asking permission, and was busted for defying a direct order and demoted from sergeant to specialist. He chose not to file an appeal and has returned to civilian life, though he's still in the reserves. His memoir about his time in Iraq will be published next month by HarperCollins.

If you read *A Line in the Sand,* it's hard to imagine Chris Missick offending Pentagon brass. He is careful not to criticize his superiors and will tell you he has aspirations to run for Congress. While waiting for an early-morning plane to take him back home to southern California, Missick confesses that his biggest blog-related scandal is a romantic one. His stateside girlfriend when he left for Iraq was displaced by another woman, someone Missick says fell in love with him by reading his blog.

"When I get home I kinda need to sort that out." (He kinda did and now has yet another girlfriend. Let's hope she likes Elliot Smith music.) Prakash remains in Germany, awaiting orders to jump back into his beloved tank, which he calls Ol' Blinky. He says he has no plans to resume his study of neuroscience, although it wasn't completely useless in Iraq.

"Neuroscience actually came in handy when I had to explain to my guys exactly why doing ecstasy in a tank when it's 140 degrees out on a road that's blowing up every day is a really bad idea." Danjel Bout, a.k.a. Thunder 6, is looking to get home safely, keeping his head down on the streets of southern Baghdad and in his blog. He says the real value of milblogging may be that it brings to the U.S. the reality of what is becoming a long war.

"I don't purposely leave out the moments when our bodies hit the adrenal dump switch, I just don't focus exclusively on them." More typical are his vignettes of Iraqi civilians interacting with U.S. soldiers, or the sad tale of the death of a guardsman who had the chance to go home and instead requested another tour of duty, only to be killed by an improvised explosive device.

"Americans are raised on a steady diet of action films and sound bites that slip from one supercharged scene to another," he says, "leaving out all the confusing decisions and subtle details where most people actually spend their lives. While that makes for a great story, it doesn't reveal anything of lasting value. For people to really understand our day-to-day experience here, they need more than the highlights reel. They need to see the world through our eyes for a few minutes." Which suggests, at the very least, that this UC Davis psych-major dropout turned milblogger was perhaps paying more attention in class than he lets on.

Red State, Blue State: Hometown News

Meteor Blades

In between my unfettered rage at the ideologues who lied us into the Iraq war and my cautious elation that we may elect someone who brings an end to that nightmare, I sometimes catch myself going numb. The statistics are numbing. Perhaps 25,000 people dead, most of them civilians. Perhaps 100,000 wounded, many of them maimed forever. Who knows how many tens of thousands of insurgents recruited, not only in Iraq but also around the planet.

And all because of the machinations of some war criminals—sorry, no other description will do—who hijacked our patriotism, grief and anger in the service of a foul crusade that they mask with "liberty" and "democracy." In their mouths, these are simultaneously trigger words, soporific words, numbing words.

Yet every day, sometimes twice or three times a day, for the past 19 months, somewhere in America, a dead soldier or Marine is memorialized by her or his family. Whatever appears on the surface of the bereaved at these rituals, beneath they are anything except numb.

In the national media, we occasionally hear one of these stories, but mostly what we get—if anything at all—are the statistics. If only the personal stories in the local media—even the merged, oligopolistic chains that now pass for most local media—if only one of these stories made front-page news in the *New York Times* or the lead item on ABC—and if it were combined with an equivalent story about an Iraqi family at the burying grounds—numb would never describe us.

Here, in brief, are 14 of those stories from Winkelman, Ariz.; Bismarck, N.D.; North Lauderdale and Hollywood, Fla.; Bremerton, Wash.; New Florence, Pa.; Muscoda, Wisc.; Sandhills, N.C.; Santa Cruz, Calif.; Honolulu, Hawai'i; Normal, Ill.; Maynard, Ohio; Warwick, R.I.; Little Rock, Ark.

Winkelman, Arizona. *Arizona Republic*
Rural Arizona gives up another son

When a car bomb struck Army Pvt. Carson J. Ramsey's convoy Sunday near a market east of Baghdad, another Arizona country boy gave his life.

Ramsey was the state's 34th death since the war in Iraq began, and nearly half of the 34 hailed from small towns and rural backroads even though those residents make up just 12 percent of the Grand Canyon State's population.

Ramsey, a 22-year-old raised near the confluence of the San Pedro and Gila rivers between the mining towns of Winkelman and Mammoth, was typical of those enlistees who turn to America's military for opportunity, escape and an embrace of patriotism.

"His big thing was being in the service," recalls Christalee Jurado, 21, who graduated with Ramsey in 2001 from Ray High School's Junior ROTC program in Kearny. "We all enlisted in different branches. . . . It's the best opportunity for us to get anywhere, a military career."

Jurado, who wound up having a baby instead of going through with an Air Force enlistment, said high school seniors in copper country have three choices: work at the mines, go to school or enlist.

With the number of mining jobs declining and the cost of college going up, Uncle Sam's call is hard to resist. It's not just a chance for travel and adventure but an opportunity to get job training, veterans benefits and a government-paid college education afterward.

Bismarck, North Dakota. KXMA Channel 2
Friends and family talk about fallen soldier

Friends and family of an Army soldier killed in Iraq say Anthony Monroe loved North Dakota and joined the military to travel and get an education.

The 20-year-old Bismarck man was killed Sunday while serving in Iraq.

Private First Class Monroe was serving with the First Cavalry Division, based in Fort Hood, Texas. He had been in the Army since the fall of 2002 and had been in Iraq for the past couple of months. He was a mechanic.

Jeff Monroe says his grandson was "a laid back kid" who volunteered for the Army. He says his grandson was supposed to return to Bismarck next March.

Judi Mackie was Monroe's friend and boss at a pretzel store in Bismarck. She says she tried to talk Monroe out of joining the military. But she says he wanted to see the world and get an education. . . .

Monroe is the ninth U.S. service member from North Dakota or serving with North Dakota military units to be killed while on duty in Iraq.

North Lauderdale, Fla. *Florida Sun Sentinel*
Broward Marine, Army sergeant killed in Iraq attacks

A Marine from North Lauderdale and an Army sergeant from Hollywood were both killed in Iraq this week, officials said.

Marine Pfc. Oscar A. Martinez, 19, died Tuesday when a mortar fired by insurgents exploded at a U.S. base where he was eating with his unit, said his sister, Morena Martinez. He was a member of the I Marine Expeditionary Force stationed in Camp Pendleton, Calif.

"Ever since he was little he dreamt of being a Marine," said Morena Martinez, who flew back to the family's North Lauderdale home Wednesday from the University of Central Florida in Orlando. "It hasn't really sunk in yet."

Martinez joined the Marines last year, shortly before graduating from North Lauderdale High School. He played center for the school's football team. . . .

Two days earlier, Army Supply Sgt. Pamela G. Osbourne, 38, was killed when two rockets hit the camp where she was stationed with the Army's Division Artillery, First Cavalry Division.

A native of Jamaica, the slain soldier came to the United States when she was 14, said Rohan Osbourne, her husband. He learned of his wife's death Monday.

Pamela Osbourne lived in Miami, then in Hollywood, where she worked as a certified nurse's assistant at the Washington Manor nursing home. She had three children, ages 19, 14 and 9. And she had two dreams—to become a U.S. citizen and to serve in the military. "That was her life," her husband said. "She loved what she did."

Bremerton, Washington. KITSAP.COM
Local man killed in Iraq

A 1988 Bremerton High School graduate with a stellar Army career who was due to arrive home from Iraq in two weeks died in combat Monday in Mosul, Iraq.

Staff Sgt. Michael Lee Burbank was killed when insurgents steered a bomb-filled pickup truck, disguised as a produce truck, toward the Stryker convoy he was riding in.

Standing in the open hatch of his Stryker vehicle, Burbank was exposed to the blast and killed. He was 34.

Burbank lived in Bremerton for about 12 years until he enlisted in the Army in 1997. He is survived by his wife Shawna, 29, a 1994 South Kitsap High School graduate.

"I'm missing him a lot," Shawna said late Tuesday night, "and I'm incredibly proud."

The Iraq War Suite

Burbank's unit, the 1st Squadron, 14th Cavalry Regiment, is set to arrive home at Fort Lewis in about two weeks after a year in the Middle East.

"His unit will probably be here either before or at the same time his body gets here," said Burbank's father-in-law, Brant Culley, a Federal Way resident who grew up in Port Orchard and lived in South Kitsap for more than 40 years. . . .

Burbank is the second Bremerton resident to have died during the Iraq war and the sixth with ties to Kitsap. . . .

"He was a nice kid," retired Bremerton High history teacher Al Smith said. "He was a friendly kind of one-on-one kid, but in class getting him to talk was like pulling teeth.

"He was the kind of kid who you'd expect to get a job in the Navy yard, do a little fishing, have a wife and a kid and just be a rock of the community."

New Florence, Pa. *Tribune Democrat*
Area soldier killed in Iraq

A former New Florence man and Central Cambria graduate was killed in Iraq on Sunday morning—less than a month after he arrived.

Army Spc. Aaron Rusin, 19, was killed by sniper fire while patrolling in a Humvee, family members confirmed yesterday.

Rusin is the son of Tim Rusin of Youngstown, Westmoreland County, and Sandi Rusin of Mundys Corner.

The family was notified early yesterday that young Rusin had died.

"He was an outstanding young man and a kid that everyone loved," said his uncle, Jerry Rusin of Seward. "He was a 2003 graduate of Central Cambria High School. We learned of his death at about 10 a.m. Monday.

"Aaron joined the service for the opportunities to get an education later on the GI Bill."

Muscoda, Wisconsin. *Wisconsin State Journal*
Wisconsin Marine killed in Iraq was active student

The death of Andrew Halverson, 19, killed Saturday in Al Anbar Province in Iraq, has left the southwestern Wisconsin community of Muscoda grieving.

Halverson was more than just a Riverdale High School football player. He was a well-rounded student who was a senior class officer and a member of the Future Farmers of America and the forensics team. He was voted class clown during his senior year, his friends said.

Shortly after he graduated from the Muscoda high school last year, Halverson enlisted in the Marine Corps and was assigned to the 2nd Battalion of the 5th Marine Regiment.

Pfc. Halverson was killed in enemy action, according to the U.S. Department of Defense. He was the 22nd Wisconsin soldier to die in combat in Iraq.

"He wanted to fight for our community and country," former classmate Rebecca Broadbent said Sunday. Broadbent remembered Halverson as a "character" who got along with anybody.

Sandhills, North Carolina. *The Pilot*
Roadside bomb kills Moore guardsman

The flags at Sandhills Community College fly at half-staff this week.

Staff Sgt. Michael S. Voss, 35, an honor student from Carthage, lost his life last Friday fighting in Iraq. He leaves behind a wife and two small children. He was in the National Guard.

Emily Voss had taken their daughters, 5-year-old Lauren and 4-year-old Madelyn, on a weekend trip when two Army chaplains arrived at the Voss home to bring sad news. . . .

Voss died when a roadside bomb blew up near his Humvee. Voss was in the lead vehicle of a convoy heading north to a base near Kirkut.

The Iraq War Suite

He had deployed to Iraq early this year with his unit, the Army National Guard's 1st Battalion, 120th Infantry Regiment, headquartered in Wilmington. The unit is scheduled to come home in February, according to Maj. Robert Carver, a spokesman for the North Carolina National Guard.

Carver said no other soldiers were hurt in the blast. He called Voss a real Army hero.

"He was a very dedicated and decorated soldier," Carver said. "He had a lot of medals. I will hit the highlights: Purple Heart in Panama, 1989, three commendation medals, four Army achievement medals. He had his Airborne wings, and of course the CIB (Combat Infantry Badge). He was a squad leader, assigned to headquarters company."

Voss was a regular Army soldier before entering the National Guard. He served with the 82nd Airborne Division. He joined the Army in 1988 and was wounded during the Panama operation the next year.

Santa Cruz, California. *Santa Cruz Sentinel*
Soquel soldier killed in Iraq leaves legacy of friendship

Ask about Morgen Jacobs, and you'll probably hear about all his friends.

Morgen was the one who brought people together, his buddies said. Whether it was skimboarding with friends in Santa Cruz or organizing barbecues for his battalion in Iraq, the handsome 20-year-old with blond hair and a bright smile always knew who to invite.

His circle of friends was an eclectic mix; it included a mad scientist, a punk, an engineer, students and soldiers, said his dad, Todd Jacobs, from a chair on the patio of Santa Cruz Memorial Park Funeral Home on Tuesday.

Those buddies stopping by make it just a little easier to cope with his son's death, he said. Spc. Jacobs was assigned to the 1st Infantry Division, 1/18th Infantry Battalion, Company B, 7th Army. He died Oct. 6 after a roadside bomb exploded next to the Humvee on which he was riding near Bayji, Iraq, about 90 miles north of Baghdad. The blast wounded him severely, his father said.

"It was his decision. He didn't have to go," said Ryan Parola, 19, who finished school a year behind the 2002 graduate of Soquel High School.

In fact, Morgen's parents and friends tried to talk him out of joining the Army two years ago.

But Morgen wouldn't have it, and signed up for eight years.

Honolulu, Hawai'i. *Honolulu Advertiser*
Soldier told wife little of real danger

Pvt. 2 Jeungjin "Nikky" Kim went to Iraq thinking no one he knew would get hurt.

But that changed on the dangerous streets of Ar Ramadi, 70 miles west of Baghdad, an insurgent stronghold and frequent scene of clashes with the soldiers and Marines who patrol the region.

Kim, 23, a South Korean national who loved Hawai'i and considered it his home, didn't talk much with his wife about the dangers he faced with the 2nd Battalion, 17th Field Artillery.

Those dangers caught up with him last Wednesday, when he was killed in a roadside bomb and small-arms attack while on patrol.

Kim had deployed with the 2nd Infantry Division out of Camp Hovey, South Korea, in August, spending a month in Kuwait and arriving in the Sunni Triangle of Iraq just before his first child was born on Sept. 7.

A Young-Kim, who followed her husband into the Army, knew he was an artilleryman. She was surprised to learn he was out on patrols.

The Iraq War Suite

"I said, 'What kind of patroling?'" said Young-Kim, who grew up in Hawai'i and graduated from Hawaiian Mission Academy in 1999. "He didn't tell me he was patroling in a vehicle. He always tried to sound cheerful for me on the phone because I just had a baby." . . .

Young-Kim, 23, a private first class stationed in South Carolina, is still on maternity leave and staying at her mother's apartment in Makiki. She's trying to stay positive and celebrate her husband's life, rather than dwell on his death.

Normal, Illinois. *Bloomington Pantagraph*
Normal resident killed in Iraq

A soldier from Normal was killed and two others seriously injured Wednesday in an explosion as their convoy traveled a main supply route in Iraq, the Illinois Army National Guard announced Friday.

Spc. Jessica L. Cawvey, 21, was remembered Friday as a dedicated young mother, good college student and an independent-minded woman.

"I just feel so sorry for her family."

Cawvey lived in Normal and was part of a detachment based in Decatur.

She was a 2001 graduate of Mahomet-Seymour High School, where her younger brother, Josh, is now a senior, said school principal Del Ryan. He said she had graduated in three and a half years with a B-plus average.

"She was a great young lady," Ryan said. "A very intelligent girl, very responsible, hard-working."

She later completed an associate's degree in business administration at Parkland College in 2003 and was on the dean's list, college spokeswoman Margot Williams told The (Champaign) News-Gazette.

Maynard, Ohio. *Times-Leader*
Morgan returning home as a hero

Staff Sgt. Richard Lynn Morgan, Jr., 38, of Maynard was killed in Iraq on Oct. 5 when he drove a Humvee over a land mine, family members said Wednesday.

Morgan served in the 660th Transportation Company based in Iraq. He had been stationed in Iraq since December 2003.

Morgan joined the Army right after he graduated from St. Clairsville High School in 1984. He served in the Gulf War and was in his second tour of Iraq when he was killed.

"He just loved what he did," said his sister, Bonita Girty. "He wanted to go back and he said if no one wanted to volunteer he would go back."

Morgan met and married his wife Diana while stationed in Germany, Girty said. He returned from Iraq in August for two weeks to celebrate his 16th wedding anniversary and Diana's birthday.

At the time of his death, Morgan was an active duty staff sergeant. He was also involved in Operation Just Cause in Panama in 1989–1990.

According to his family, was a 1984 graduate of St. Clairsville High School where he was an original member of the St. C. Singers and was a member of the St. C. Red Devil football team. He was an employee of Conway Central Express at Uhrichsville, Ohio.

Warwick, Rhode Island. *Providence Journal*
A fallen soldier comes home

Sgt. Christopher Potts arrived home from Iraq yesterday, passing through a blue airport cargo door, which rose like a theater curtain to reveal a grim tableau of war.

The colors of the American flag that draped his silver coffin appeared to glow as the door rose ever higher and sunlight poured into the darkened airline warehouse.

Six stoic members of the National Guard casket team flanked his coffin as it rode a hydraulic lift down to the pavement. The throaty engines of 14 escorting police motorcycles rumbled. In the limousine, parked behind the hearse, Potts' widow, Terri, dabbed a tissue into the corner of her eye.

The man who tried saving Chris Potts a week ago this afternoon arrived home almost a full day ahead of him.

It was dark by the time the plane carrying Sgt. Russell Collier's body touched down in Little Rock, Ark., late Friday.

Carolyn Pfaus, Collier's only sibling, greeted him there, along with a National Guard representative.

"He was all I had left," Pfaus said yesterday afternoon by telephone, while 1,400 miles away the U.S. Air flight carrying Potts' remains descended to T. F. Green Airport.

They were strangers, these two men, Potts and Collier, when they met 10 months ago.

Potts, 38, of Tiverton, served with A Battery, 1st Battalion, 103rd Field Artillery of the Rhode Island National Guard. . . .

When his unit was called up in January, Potts confided to friends how much he would miss his wife and his two children. But he was resolute in the mission, telling his commanding officer in Texas, as their unit waited for a medic to be assigned to them, that he served hoping his sons Christopher Jr., 16, and Jackson, 2, would not have to later.

Collier, 49, had done stints in both the Army and the Navy before he joined the Arkansas Army National Guard in 1999. He worked in a chicken-processing factory before earning his emergency medical technician license last year.

Like Potts, Collier loved to read, his sister said. And cook. And he dreamed about one day owning a Harley-Davidson, the way Potts had carried on about owning his bright red Ford pickup truck.

They were both husbands and fathers, and when their two artillery units—the 103rd and the 206th—joined, each shared a similar duty: to look out for the others.

Collier "was in his element" in Iraq, his sister said. "We come from a military family and he was excited about going to serve his country, and to help people."

Potts was one of eight squad leaders in the 103rd and "the best of the eight," Maj. Christian Neary, of Cumberland, his commanding officer, said in a telephone interview from Taji, 18 miles north of Baghdad.

"Just his attention to details," Neary explained, "taking care of his guys, never settling for an easy answer, double-checking everything."

I wish I could say Rest in Peace to these men and women. But that will be hard for me to do in good conscience until those who concocted this war pay for their actions. Unfortunately, like most war criminals, they aren't likely to see justice done.

READING WRITING

This Text: Reading

1. What are some of the differences between writers and the way they view the war?
2. Do you think the excerpting of material is fair—does it capture fairly the intention of the speaker or writer?
3. What power do the writers place on information?
4. In what ways do each of the pieces indicate who is liberal or conservative?
5. Which is the most effective piece? Why?

Your Text: Writing

1. What symbols and metaphors do the writers use to make their points? Write a literary analysis of the war coverage.
2. Using your electronic databases at your library, write a paper about the change in coverage of the war.
3. Write a persuasive essay about which form of media—broadcast, print, or Internet—has done the best coverage.

READING BETWEEN THE LINES

Classroom Activities

1. Find an event or occurrence—a Supreme Court decision, a major decision or action made by the President, a law passed or not passed by Congress—and find an article from a conservative newspaper or magazine, a liberal one, and one that seems to be moderate. Compare how they evaluate the decision or action. What are their criteria? Can you tell what they value based on how they argue their point?
2. Watch and tape an episode of the local news. Do some sign-reading first. What impressions do you get from the set itself? How do you know it's a news set? What are the anchors wearing? Why is that important? What about the symbols—both in the "field" and the graphics section? How might this differ from a newspaper's coverage?
3. Share your experiences with dealing with a reporter, either from a school newspaper, a television station, or local newspapers. What are some common elements of these perceptions? Do you find yourself wishing the reporters handled themselves differently? In what way?
4. As a class, come up with a code of ethics, a set of ideas that all media should live by. Now critique it. What practical restrictions would this place on media outlets? How would it change the interpretation of the first amendment (freedom of speech)? How would it affect the way you receive news?
5. If you were a reporter, what type of reporter would you want to be? Why? What do you think the rewards of being a member of the media are?
6. Looking at some advertisements, either print or broadcast, what trends do you notice? Have these trends changed over time? What human characteristics do you think advertising appeals to? Do you think advertisers know you well enough to appeal to you? To the general public?
7. Notice the signs of advertisements. What elements do you see again and again?
8. Write a code of ethics for advertisers, advising them of the tactics they should or should not use when selling products to the public. If put into place, how would this change advertising as we know it?

Essay Ideas

1. Read a week of editorial pages from a local newspaper. What are some things you notice? How do columnists use particular words? What do they stand for?
2. See the attached handout on a rhetorical analysis.
3. Examine some of the signs of an advertisement.

4. Put yourself in the shoes of an advertiser for a particular product. Write an ad campaign for that product taking into account target audience, signs, and the medium you would use to advertise it.
5. What issues on campus could be covered better (or at all) by the local media? Why do you think they are not covered now?

ASSIGNMENT: THE RHETORICAL ANALYSIS

One of the easiest ways of analyzing an advertisement is by using Aristotle's three appeals; the appeals provide a natural organization of the paper.

Aristotle's Three Appeals: Ethos, Pathos, Logos

Ethos—The Ethical Appeal

An advertisement or other visual text uses the trustworthiness and credibility of the author to make its appeal. The ethos many times is the brand name itself—a brand we are familiar with may bring credibility. Or the advertiser may use someone famous or with expertise to present the advertisement. Politicians often use endorsements to provide credibility. Many times the ethical appeal is the weakest in an advertisement, however.

Pathos—Appeal to Emotions

This appeal tries to get the reader to feel a particular emotion through the use of images or words, or both. An advertisement typically wants us to be motivated to purchase the particular item. The copywriters may do this by presenting images, colors, people, letters, or a combination of the above to evoke feelings of intrigue, happiness, or pleasure in some form. The images are often aimed at reminding us of other ideas or images. The appeal to emotions is often the strongest in an advertisement.

Logos—Appeal to Reason or Logic

Advertisements often try to present a logical appeal, using facts of one sort or another. For example, an advertisement might use claims that it is the most popular brand or has won the most awards. It might claim the time to purchase the item is sooner rather than later because of the discounts its manufacturer is providing.

The Target Audience

When talking about visual texts, you might also talk about who its target audience is—how old or young, how rich or poor, where they are from, and so on.

A Typical Paper

1. An introduction talking about advertising.
2. A thesis statement describing the argument you are making about the ad.
3. A paragraph providing an organized general description of the ad.
4. Three or more paragraphs about the strengths and weaknesses of the three appeals.
5. A paragraph that talks about the target audience.
6. A concluding paragraph that explains why one appeal is stronger than the other.

How many different relationships are in this scene? Can our relationship to technology and shopping intercede on the human ones?

But of course, we are always reading relationships, trying to make sense of why people we know, love, or observe behave the way they do. Think about it—how much time have you spent going over a conversation you had with someone, trying to interpret the actual words as well as the sentiment behind them? Your conversation, in this case, is the text; you are doing similar work that you might do with a poem or a passage in a novel (not to mention the other texts we have talked about here). Any time you try to make sense of a relationship, you are attempting to de-code that relationship, interpret the signs that signify one thing or another.

And though we do much of this work in romantic or close family relationships, we also do this kind of interpretation with those who may be less close, such as professors, acquaintances, sorority sisters, distant relatives, clerks in stores, and even physical objects. *Seinfeld* is essentially about the difficulty of interpretation, as the characters go through each day reading (and re-reading) their interactions with each other, strangers, potential romantic partners, and employers. Both of the authors are professors, and we are constantly trying to read you guys. Do you

get the material? Are you paying attention? Do you like how class is going? Is that guy sleeping or just hung over? There is no question that relationships are constructed texts—built by our expectations of them, our behavior in them and the power differentials behind them.

While reading the small details of a relationship is something we all do, reading the larger issues in relationships is something that intrigues the authors as well. For example, we may think about the proper roles of professors and students both inside and outside the classroom, what constitutes a committed relationship (and when to pursue one), what the rules are for interacting with family members, and the relationship we have to our country. While each of these can be an extremely powerful relationship, each one is marked by its own demands and its own unique contexts. When we take a close look at these relationships, we see that we are the authors (at least co-authors) of such texts and that we imbue them with shades, themes, tones and rhythms, like a writer, composer, or painter.

When reading relationships on a detail level or a structural level, here are some things to consider:

Our readings of specific relationships are influenced by a number of factors.

Personal experiences and societal expectations influence the way we think about and behave in relationships. If we have good relationships with family members, we might think of the family as a positive aspect of our lives; if we have terrible relationships with our teachers, we might think negatively about the whole idea of higher education. The difficult part is separating personal experiences from what we see and read in popular culture. Whether you argue that television reflects or influences society (or both), you may unconsciously compare your own experience with those portrayed on screen. The family relationship we see in *The Brady Bunch*, for example, is a text that we might compare to the text that is our own family relationship. How we view and read relationships is based on a number of complicating factors, such as income, geography, gender, race, age, sexual orientation, and education, just to name a few. Understanding the aspects of a relationship can help us understand what it does for us and how we can be better in it.

Sometimes we feel trapped by relationships; we are bored, confused, and even angry. If we feel this way while watching a movie, we can walk out of the theater or turn off the television. It's harder to "turn off" a relationship, but we can change the terms of those relationships. We can, in effect, revise and rewrite the texts that are our relationships.

Relationships are fluid texts.

One of the most difficult things about reading relationships is how often they vary from day to day and even hour to hour. One reason for this is that when you talk about human relationships you are talking about complexities that often the two parties in the relationship do not understand completely. Some of the work psychologists do, in fact, is try to understand why people act the way they do, often with mixed results.

But such work is not easy because people are not fixed in their personalities over time; indeed, our personalities vary in our interactions with different people. Think about how much you have changed over the years, most notably how you have changed from junior high or high school to the person you are now, in college. Now think about all of the relationships in your life—your relationship with your parents, your boyfriend or girlfriend, your hometown, your favorite songs, your group of friends, your faith, your educators— and consider how these relationships have (or have not) changed along with you. Now imagine all of the people in your life and all of the changes *they* have gone through. It's not surprising that we move in and out of relationships so frequently.

College is a particularly volatile time for relationships. There may be no other time in your life when so many of your relationships change so drastically as they do when you begin college. Suddenly, your relationship with your parents is different, as it is with your friends from home. Most people experience their first mature romantic relationships in college, and they also have to deal with this new and somewhat bizarre phenomenon—the roommate. The nurturing, friendly presence of high school teachers and coaches gives way to a much different relationship with professors. In fact, almost every significant relationship undergoes some kind of transformation when you enter the world of the college student. So many new texts, all with their own subtexts, can make *reading* them unusually complicated.

You cannot be objective about relationships.

No matter how hard you try to take yourself out of a discussion about relationships, it seems impossible to see a relationship from an unbiased perspective. For one, you often have a stake in the reading you do—it matters to you, and not only on an academic basis, that you do a good job of interpreting. You also have a rooting interest that your discussion puts you in a better light than someone else.

Just as you cannot be objective about your favorite movie or song, so, too, can you not read the text of a relationship objectively. William Butler Yeats once wrote that you cannot tell the dancer from the dance, and this is particularly the case for relationships. *Sicko* exists in the world whether you do or not, but *your* relationship with your grandparents does *not* exist if you don't. Every relationship you have relies on your being part of that text. It should be no surprise, then, that reading certain relationships with a critical eye is difficult (and uncomfortable).

The Tracy Seeley essay printed here is a wholly subjective reading of her relationship with her mother. She can *try* to get outside of that relationship, and she may succeed to some degree but never completely. We may also find that we do not want to read our relationships objectively. If you've ever had someone criticize your brother or sister, you can relate to the sense of subjective loyalty. Of course, *you* can criticize your sibling, but no one else can.

What constitutes "good relationships" varies over time, place, and culture.

What we think of as good relationships here and now may not have been the case for our parents, or for people who live in other cultures or other parts of the country. For example, the authors have noticed their friends treat their children differently than they themselves were treated. Other observers have noted that the generation gap between this generation of college students and their parents is not as pronounced as in previous eras. Studying the differences between the way we look at relationships now, and how people in other times and places view them, can result in insights about gender, race, class, and cultural difference. Power also affects relationships. We often hear our students make comments about how they think other professors *see* them: "Professor X *hates* me. I can tell by the way she looks at me—like I'm stupid—when I make a comment that isn't what she's looking for." The professor–student dynamic is one of power inequity, and often students are searching for cues from their professor on their performance, their intelligence, and their grade. Students often scrutinize professors and their reactions to them because students have something at stake in the relationship, and professors retain a measure of power over something important—the grade. So, that imbalance can skew how we read each other.

In addition, problems sometimes arise when we have expectations of how a relationship *should* be and find that in reality it is much different. Thus, we can experience a disturbing gap between the text we have constructed in our heads and the text that is our actual relationship. For instance, you may have found that your "good" friendships in college bear little resemblance to those from high school. Or, there is no doubt that you each had an idea of what "college" should be and were probably shocked and unsettled when your own college experience was a text for which you felt unprepared.

For instance, one of the authors has worked as a professor in Europe and India. While the role of a professor and the relationship a professor has with his or her students varies dramatically from Europe to India, both are vastly different than typical professor-student interactions in the United States. Also, both authors have taught at universities in different parts of the country, including the South, the Southwest, and the Northeast. We have also been graduate students at large, competitive universities. Though all are American colleges, each place and each dynamic was unique—as were our relationships with each place.

As you grow older, your relationships will also change. You'll author new texts and with each one, revise your sense of who you are and what you *mean* to yourself and others.

Texts of all sorts spend much of their energy trying to explain relationships.

Of all the chapters we have put together, this one cries out most for inter-chapter connection. Many (if not all) texts either explore what relationships mean and how they work or narrate them. In fact, all of the readings in this book reveal a relationship with a certain text. That text might be race, gender, music, or film, and those relationships are themselves complicated texts that the authors try to "interpret" by writing about them. And, as you may have gathered by now, this book is about the texts we all construct. Understanding the texts that are our relationships can help us understand a world that is both familiar and confusing.

THIS TEXT

1. How does the background of the authors influence their ideas about relationships?
2. Do the authors have different ideas about relationships?
3. While it will be impossible for you to know this fully, try to figure out the writing situation of each author. Who is the audience? What does the author have at stake?
4. What is his or her agenda? *Why* is she or he writing this piece?
5. What social, political, and cultural forces affect the author's text? What is going on in the world as he or she is writing?
6. What are the main points of the essay? Can you find a thesis statement anywhere?
7. How does the author support the argument? What evidence does he or she use to back up any claims made?
8. Is the author's argument valid and/or reasonable?
9. Do you find yourself in agreement with the author? Why or why not?
10. Does the author help you *read* relationships better (or differently) than you did before reading the essay? If so, why?
11. How is the reading process different if you are reading an essay as opposed to a short story or poem?
12. What is the agenda of the author? Why does she or he want us to think a certain way?
13. Did you like this? Why or why not?

BEYOND THIS TEXT: READING RELATIONSHIPS

1. What are the traditional structures and roles of the relationships you are analyzing? How does the relationship coincide or disagree with these roles and structures?
2. What role do you play in the relationship you are describing? What determined your role?
3. How has the relationship you are describing changed over time? What has made it change?
4. In what ways does the "setting" of your relationship change the relationship? Have you experienced a relationship that was altered because of the place and/or time in which it was located?
5. How have your relationships been different or not because of differences in backgrounds— races, gender, sexual orientation, class, and age?
6. Think about how you came to your ideas about relationships. As an exercise, write down the "unwritten rules" about relationships you carry around with you.

Happy Endings

Margaret Atwood

Margaret Atwood is one of the world's most well-known writers having published more than twenty books, including *The Handmaid's Tale* (1985), *The Blind Assassin* (2000) (which won the Booker Prize for literature), and *Oryx and Crake* (2003). So it's perhaps a little surprising that she wrote the following piece, which both describes and analyzes the nature of romantic relationships. One question to ask of this piece is whether she means to critique fiction or fact; in other words, whether it's life that is so predictable or writing about life.

John and Mary meet.
What happens next?
If you want a happy ending, try A.

A. John and Mary fall in love and get married. They both have worthwhile and remunerative jobs which they find stimulating and challenging. They buy a charming house. Real estate values go up. Eventually, when they can afford live-in help, they have two children, to whom they are devoted. The children turn out well. John and Mary have a stimulating and challenging sex life and worthwhile friends. They go on fun vacations together. They retire. They both have hobbies which they find stimulating and challenging. Eventually they die. This is the end of the story.

B. Mary falls in love with John but John doesn't fall in love with Mary. He merely uses her body for selfish pleasure and ego gratification of a tepid kind. He comes to her apartment twice a week and she cooks him dinner, you'll notice that he doesn't even consider her worth the price of a dinner out, and after he's eaten the dinner he fucks her and after that he falls asleep, while she does the dishes so he won't think she's untidy, having all those dirty dishes lying around, and puts on fresh lipstick so she'll look good when he wakes up, but when he wakes up he doesn't even notice, he puts on his socks and his shorts and his pants and his shirt and his tie and his shoes, the reverse order from the one in which he took them off. He doesn't take off Mary's clothes, she takes them off herself, she acts as if she's dying for it every time, not because she likes sex exactly, she doesn't, but she wants John to think she does because if they do it often enough surely he'll get used to her, he'll come to depend on her and they will get married, but John goes out the door with hardly so much as a goodnight and three days later he turns up at six o'clock and they do the whole thing over again.

Mary gets run down. Crying is bad for your face, everyone knows that and so does Mary but she can't stop. People at work notice. Her friends tell her John is a rat, a pig, a dog, he isn't good enough for her, but she can't believe it. Inside John, she thinks, is another John, who is much nicer. This other John will emerge like a butterfly from a cocoon, a Jack from a box, a pit from a prune, if the first John is only squeezed enough.

One evening John complains about the food. He has never complained about the food before. Mary is hurt.

Her friends tell her they've seen him in a restaurant with another woman, whose name is Madge. It's not even Madge that finally gets to Mary; it's the restaurant. John has never taken Mary to a restaurant. Mary collects all the sleeping pills and aspirins she can find, and takes them and half a bottle of sherry. You can see what kind of a woman she is by the fact that it's not even whiskey. She leaves a note for John. She hopes he'll discover her and get her to the hospital in time and repent and then they can get married, but this fails to happen and she dies.

John marries Madge and everything continues as in A.

C. John, who is an older man, falls in love with Mary, and Mary, who is only twenty-two, feels sorry for him because he's worried about his hair falling out. She sleeps with him even though she's not in love with him. She met him at work. She's in love with someone called James, who is twenty-two also and not yet ready to settle down.

John on the contrary settled down long ago: this is what is bothering him. John has a steady respectable job and is getting ahead in his field, but Mary isn't impressed by him, she's impressed by James, who has a motorcycle and a fabulous record collection. But James is often away on his motorcycle, being free. Freedom isn't the same for girls, so in the meantime Mary spends Thursday evenings with John. Thursdays are the only days John can get away.

John is married to a woman called Madge and they have two children, a charming house which they bought just before the real estate values went up, and hobbies which they find stimulating and challenging, when they have the time. John tells Mary how important she is to him, but of course he can't leave his wife because a commitment is a commitment. He goes on about this more than is necessary and Mary finds it boring, but older men can keep it up longer so on the whole she has a fairly good time.

One day James breezes in on his motorcycle with some top-grade California hybrid and James and Mary get higher than you'd believe possible and they climb into bed. Everything becomes very underwater, but along comes John, who has a key to Mary's apartment. He finds them stoned and entwined. He's hardly in any position to be jealous, considering Madge, but nevertheless he's overcome with despair. Finally he's middle-aged, in two years he'll be bald as an egg, and he can't stand it. He purchases a handgun, saying he needs it for target practice—this is the thin part of the plot, but it can be dealt with later—and shoots the two of them and himself.

Madge, after a suitable period of mourning, marries an understanding man called Fred and everything continues as in A, but under different names.

D. Fred and Madge have no problems. They get along exceptionally well and are good at working out any little difficulties that may arise. But their charming house is by the seashore and one day a giant tidal wave approaches. Real estate values go down. The rest of the story is about what caused the tidal wave and how they escape from it. They do, though thousands drown. Some of the story is about how the thousands drown, but Fred and Madge are virtuous and lucky. Finally on high ground they clasp each other, wet and dripping and grateful, and continue as in A.

E. Yes, but Fred has a bad heart. The rest of the story is about how kind and understanding they both are until Fred dies. Then Madge devotes herself to charity work until the end of A. If you like, it can be "Madge," "cancer," "guilty and confused," and "bird watching."

F. If you think this is all too bourgeois, make John a revolutionary and Mary a counterespionage agent and see how far that gets you. Remember, this is Canada. You'll still end up with A, though in between you may get a lustful brawling saga of passionate involvement, a chronicle of our times, sort of.

You'll have to face it, the endings are the same however you slice it. Don't be deluded by any other endings, they're all fake, either deliberately fake, with malicious intent to deceive, or just motivated by excessive optimism if not by downright sentimentality.

The only authentic ending is the one provided here:

John and Mary die. John and Mary die. John and Mary die.

So much for endings. Beginnings are always more fun. True connoisseurs, however, are known to favor the stretch in between, since it's the hardest to do anything with.

That's about all that can be said for plots, which anyway are just one thing after another, a what and a what and a what.

Now try How and Why.

READING WRITING

This Text: Reading

1. Would you say Atwood is referring more to real life or fairy tales here? What is the difference?
2. What aspects of relationships is Atwood leaving out? Why does she do this?
3. What is a happy ending? Is there any such thing? What would Atwood say?

This Text: Writing

1. Watch a romantic comedy such as *You've Got Mail* or any teen movie. What "relationship texts" do these movies construct? What do they leave out?
2. Read Jane Yolen's piece on Cinderella in the gender section. In what ways does her essay comment on this one? Is this piece about gender? Write a paper analyzing this piece through the lens of gender.

To Make a Friend, Be a Friend

David Sedaris

Over the past decade, David Sedaris has become one of America's most popular essayists. Along with Anthony Lane, Sarah Vowell, and George Saunders, he is also one of America's funniest writers. This essay was originally broadcast on *This American Life* on National Public Radio and appeared in 2001 in Esquire. It was also published in *The Best American Nonrequired Reading 2002* under this title. This piece looks primarily at friendships but also at other kinds of relationships, both from the perspective of a teenager and an adult.

EVERY NIGHT BEFORE GOING TO BED, my boyfriend, Hugh, steps outside to consider the stars. His interest is not scientific—he doesn't pinpoint the constellations or make casual references to Canopus. Rather, he just regards the mass of them, occasionally pausing to sigh. When asked if there's life on other planets, he says, "Yes, of course. Consider the odds."

It hardly seems fair we'd get the universe all to ourselves, but on a personal level I'm highly disturbed by the thought of extraterrestrial life. If there are, in fact, billions of other civilizations, where does that leave our celebrities? If worth is measured on a sliding scale of notoriety, what would it mean if we were all suddenly obscure? How would we know our place?

In trying to make sense of this, I think back to a 1968 Labor Day celebration at the Raleigh Country Club. I was at the snack bar, listening to a group of sixth graders who lived in another part of town and sat discussing significant changes in their upcoming school year. According to the girl named Janet, neither Pam Dobbins nor J. J. Jackson had been invited to the Fourth of July party hosted by the Pyle twins, who later told Kath Matthews that both Pam and J. J. were out of the picture as far as the seventh grade was concerned. "Totally, completely out," Janet said. "Poof."

I didn't know any Pam Dobbins or J. J. Jackson, but the reverential tone of Jane's voice sent me into a state of mild shock. Call me naive, but it had simply never occurred to me that other schools might have their own celebrity circles. At the age of twelve I thought the group at E. C. Brooks was, if not nationally known, then at least its own private phenomenon. Why else would our lives revolve around it so completely? I myself was not a member of my school's popular crowd, but I recall thinking that, whoever they were, Janet's popular crowd couldn't begin to compete with ours. But what if I was wrong? What if I'd wasted my entire life comparing myself with people who didn't really matter? Try as I might, I still can't wrap my mind around it.

They banded together in the third grade. Ann Carlsworth, Christie Kaymore, Deb Bevins, Mike Holliwell, Doug Middleton, Thad Pope: this was the core of the popular crowd, and for the next six years my classmates and I studied their lives the way we were supposed to study math and English. What confused us most was the absence of any specific formula. Were they funny? No. Interesting? Yawn. None owned pools or horses. They had no special talents, and their grades were unremarkable. It was their dearth of excellence that gave the rest of us hope and kept us on our toes. Every now and then they'd select a new member, and the general attitude among the student body was *Oh, pick me!* It didn't matter what you were like on your own. The group would make you special. That was its magic.

So complete was their power that I actually felt honored when one of them hit me in the mouth with a rock. He'd gotten me after school, and upon returning home I ran into my sister's bedroom, hugging my bloody Kleenex and crying, "It was Thad!!!"

Lisa was a year older, but still she understood the significance. "Did he *say* anything?" she asked. "Did you save the rock?"

My father demanded I retaliate, saying I ought to knock the guy on his ass.

"Oh, Dad."

"Aww, baloney. Clock him on the snot locker and he'll go down like a ton of bricks."

"Are you talking to *me?*" I asked. The archaic slang aside, who did my father think I was? Boys who spent their weekends making banana-nut muffins did not, as a rule, excel in the art of hand-to-hand combat.

"I mean, come on, Dad," Lisa said. "Wake *up.*"

The following afternoon I was taken to Dr. Povlitch for x-rays. The rock had damaged a tooth, and there was some question over who would pay for the subsequent root canal. I figured that since my parents had conceived me, given birth to me, and raised me as a permanent guest in their home, they should foot the bill, but my father thought differently. He decided the Popes should pay, and I screamed as he picked up the phone book.

"But you can't just . . . call Thad's house."

"Oh, yeah?" he said. "Just watch me."

There were two Thad Popes in the Raleigh phone book, a Junior and a Senior. The one in my class was what came after a Junior. He was a Third. My father called both the Junior and the Senior, beginning each conversation with the line, "Lou Sedaris here. Listen, pal, we've got a problem with your son."

He always said the name as if it meant something, as if we were known and respected. This made it all the more painful when he was asked to repeat it. Then to spell it.

A meeting was arranged for the following evening, and before leaving the house, I begged my father to change his clothes. He'd been building an addition to the carport and was wearing a pair of khaki shorts smeared with paint and spotted here and there with bits of dried concrete. Through a hole in his tattered T-shirt, it was possible to see his nipple.

"What the hell is wrong with this?" he asked. "We're not staying for dinner, so what does it matter?"

I yelled for my mother, and in the end he compromised by changing his shirt.

From the outside, Thad's house didn't look much different from anyone else's—just a standard split-level with what my father described as a totally inadequate carport. Mr. Pope answered the door in a pair of sherbet-colored golf pants and led us downstairs to what he called the "rumpus room."

"Oh," I said. "This is nice!"

The room was damp and windowless and lit with hanging Tiffany lampshades, the shards of colorful glass arranged to spell the words *Busch* and *Budweiser*. Walls were paneled in imitation walnut, and the furniture looked as though it had been hand-hewn by settlers who'd reconfigured parts of their beloved Conestoga wagon to fashion such things as easy chairs and coffee tables. Noticing the fraternity paddle hanging on the wall above the television, my father launched into his broken Greek, saying, "*Kalispera sas adelphos!*"

When Mr. Pope looked at him blankly, my father laughed and offered a translation. "I said, 'Good evening, brother.'"

"Oh . . . right," Mr. Pope said. "Fraternities are Greek."

He directed us toward a sofa and asked if we wanted something to drink. Coke? A beer? I didn't want to deplete Thad's precious cola supply, but before I could refuse, my father said sure, we'd have one of each. The orders were called up the stairs, and a few minutes later Mrs. Pope came down carrying cans and plastic tumblers.

"Well, *hello* there," my father said. This was his standard greeting to a beautiful woman, but I could tell he was just saying it as a joke. Mrs. Pope wasn't *un*attractive, just ordinary, and as she set the drinks before us I noticed that her son had inherited her blunt, slightly upturned nose, which looked good on him but caused her to appear overly suspicious and judgmental.

"So," she said. "I hear you've been to the dentist." She was trying to make small talk, but due to her nose, it came off sounding like an insult, as if I'd just had a tooth filled and was now looking for someone to pay the bill.

"*I'll* say he's been to the dentist," my father said. "Someone hits you in the mouth with a rock, and I'd say the dentist's office is pretty much the first place a reasonable person would go."

Mr. Pope held up his hands. "Whoa, now," he said. "Let's just calm things down a little." He yelled upstairs for his son, and when there was no answer he picked up the phone, telling Thad to stop running his mouth and get his butt down to the rumpus room ASAP.

A rush of footsteps on the carpeted staircase, and then Thad sprinted in, all smiles and apologies. The minister had called. The game had been rescheduled. "Hello, sir, and you are . . . ?"

He looked my father in the eye and firmly shook his hand, holding it in his own for just the right amount of time. While most handshakes mumbled, his clearly spoke, saying both *We'll get through this* and *I'm looking forward to your vote this coming November.*

I'd thought that seeing him without his group might be unsettling, like finding a single arm on the sidewalk, but Thad was fully capable of operating independently. Watching him in action, I understood that his popularity was not an accident. Unlike a normal human, he possessed an uncanny ability to please people. There was no sucking up or awkward maneuvering to fit the will of others. Rather, much like a Whitman's Sampler, he seemed to offer a little bit of everything. Pass on his athletic ability and you might partake of his excellent manners, his confidence, his coltish enthusiasm. Even his parents seemed invigorated by his presence, uncrossing their legs and sitting up just a little bit straighter as he took a seat beside them. Had the circumstances been different, my father would have been all over him, probably going so far as to call him son—but money was involved, so he steeled himself.

"All right, then," Mr. Pope said. "Now that everyone's accounted for, I'm hoping we can clear this up. Sticks and stones aside, I suspect this all comes down to a little misunderstanding between friends."

I lowered my eyes, waiting for Thad to set his father straight. "*Friends?* With *him?*" I expected laughter or the famous Thad snort, but instead he said nothing. And with his silence, he won me completely. A little misunderstanding—that's *exactly* what it was. How had I not seen it earlier?

The immediate goal was to save my friend, so I claimed to have essentially thrown myself in the path of Thad's rock.

"What the hell was he throwing rocks for?" my father asked. "What the hell was he throwing them at?"

Mrs. Pope frowned, implying that such language was not welcome in the rumpus room.

"I mean, Jesus Christ, the guy's got to be a complete idiot."

Thad swore he hadn't been aiming at anything, and I backed him up, saying it was just one of those things we all did. "Like in Vietnam or whatever. It was just friendly fire."

My father asked what the hell I knew about Vietnam, and again Thad's mother winced, saying that boys picked up a lot of this talk by watching the news.

"Aww, you don't know what you're talking about," my father said.

"What my wife meant —"

"Aww, baloney."

The trio of Popes exchanged meaningful glances, holding what amounted to a brief, telepathic powwow. "This man crazy," the smoke signals read. "Make heap big trouble for others."

I looked at my father, a man in dirty shorts who drank his beer from the can rather than pouring it into his tumbler, and I thought, You don't belong here. More precisely, I decided that he was the reason *I* didn't belong. The hokey Greek phrases, the how-to lectures on mixing your own concrete, the squabble over who would pay the stupid dentist bill—little by little, it had all seeped into my bloodstream, robbing me of my natural ability to please others. For as long as I could remember, he'd been telling us that it didn't matter what other people thought: their judgment was crap, a waste of time, baloney. But it did matter, especially when those people were *these* people.

"Well," Mr. Pope said, "I can see that this is going nowhere."

My father laughed, saying, "Yeah, you got that right." It sounded like a parting sentence, but rather than standing to leave, he leaned back in the sofa and rested his beer can upon his stomach. "We're all going nowhere."

At this point, I'm fairly sure that Thad and I were envisioning the same grim scenario. While the rest of the world moved on, in a year's time my filthy, bearded father would still be occupying the rumpus room sofa. Christmas would come, friends would visit, and the Popes would bitterly direct them toward the easy chairs. "Just ignore him," they'd say. "He'll go home sooner or later."

In the end, they agreed to pay for half the root canal, not because they thought it was fair, but because they wanted us out of their house.

Some friendships are formed by a commonality of interests and ideas: you both love judo or camping or making your own sausage. Other friendships are forged by mutual hatred of a common enemy. On leaving Thad's house, I decided that ours would probably be the latter. We'd start off grousing about my father, and then, little by little, we'd move on to the hundreds of other things and people that got on our nerves. "You hate olives?" I imagined him saying. "I hate them, *too!*"

As it turned out, the one thing we both hated was me. Rather, I hated me. Thad couldn't even work up the enthusiasm. The day after the meeting, I approached him in the lunchroom, where he sat at his regular table, surrounded by his regular friends. "Listen," I said. "I'm really sorry about that stuff with my dad." I'd worked up a whole long speech, complete with imitations, but by the time I finished my mission statement, he'd turned to resume his conversation with Doug Middleton. Our perjured testimony, my father's behavior, even the rock throwing: I was so far beneath him that it hadn't even registered.

Poof.

The socialites of E. C. Brooks shone even brighter in junior high, but come tenth grade, things began to change. Desegregation drove a lot of the popular people into private schools, and those who remained seemed silly and archaic, deposed royalty from a country the average citizen had ceased to care about.

Early in our junior year, Thad was jumped by a group of the new black kids, who yanked off his shoes and threw them in the toilet. I knew I was supposed to be happy, but part of me felt personally assaulted. True, he'd been a negligent prince, yet still I believed in the monarchy. When his name was called at graduation, it was I who clapped the longest, outlasting even his parents, who politely stopped once he'd left the stage.

I thought about Thad a lot over the years, wondering where he went to college and if he joined a fraternity. The era of the Big Man on Campus had ended, but the rowdy houses with their pool tables and fake moms continued to serve as reunion points for the once popular, who were now viewed as date rapists and budding alcoholics. While his brothers drifted toward a confused and bitter adulthood, I tell myself he stumbled into the class that changed his life. He's the poet laureate of Liechtenstein, the surgeon who cures cancer with love, the ninth-grade teacher who insists that the world is big enough for everyone. When moving to another city, I'm always hoping to find him living in the apartment next door. We'll meet in the hallway and he'll stick out his hand, saying, "Excuse me, but don't I—*shouldn't I*—know you?" It doesn't have to happen today, but it does have to happen. I've kept a space waiting for him, and if he doesn't show up, I'm going to have to forgive my father.

The root canal that was supposed to last ten years has now lasted more than thirty, though it's nothing to be proud of. Having progressively dulled and weakened, the tooth is now the brownish gray color the Conran's catalog refers to as "kabuki." While Dr. Povlitch worked out of a converted brick house beside the Colony Shopping Center, my current dentist, Docteur Guige, has an office near the Madeleine, in Paris. The receptionist calls my name and it often takes a while to realize she's referring to me.

On a recent visit, Dr. Guige gripped my dead tooth between his fingertips and gently jiggled it back and forth. I hate to exhaust his patience unnecessarily, so when he asked me what had happened, it took me a moment to think of the clearest possible answer. The past was far too complicated to put into French, so instead I envisioned a perfect future, and attributed the root canal to a misunderstanding between friends.

READING WRITING

This Text: Reading

1. The essay begins by invoking celebrities. What is our relationship with celebrities? What roles do they play in our lives?
2. How are relationships when we are teenagers different when we move into college? How do high school relationships differ from those in college?
3. See if you can identify a thesis in Sedaris's essay. What is his argument?

Your Text: Writing

1. Write a personal essay in which you *read* a particularly bizarre or unusual relationship from your past. Now that you have distance, what does this relationship tell you about yourself?
2. Write an essay in which you define friendship. What do you *want* from a friendship? Do you have different types of friendships? Why?
3. Write an essay in which you explain what celebrity you would most like to be friends with. Explain why *this* celebrity.

My Mother's Hands

Tracy Seeley

Tracy Seeley's piece (2004) is part of a longer memoir project that looks at the intersections of geographic place and the human body. In this short essay, Seeley *reads* her mother via her mother's hands, making them a kind of semiotic text that reveals a great deal about her mother's character, her duties, the setting, the era, and Seeley's own family. As you read, you might pay attention not only to the essay's content but also to its form.

THE DAY BEFORE SHE WENT TO HOSPICE, she polished her nails. We found, on her dressing table, 18 shades of pink.

Afterwards, we divided the photos, the one box she kept.

Standing against the Rockies, looking into the sun, she is wearing her Aran Isle sweater, cabled to catch the light. She almost smiles in that cool way that says, no big deal. No big deal to be living in Aspen, leaving Balsam Lake, Wisconsin, behind, teaching kindergarten in the morning, schussing through powder every afternoon, and tutoring Gary Cooper's child. Her left hand drapes the wooden fence post, an unblemished row of fingers, all smooth skin and manicured nails. In her right hand, the two thin strips of her skis stand upright, their curved tips sprouting above her light fingers touch. She wears a ring, three colors of gold in a braided wreath around a dark red stone. It is 1948. She is 20.

They merge into one dark figure against the flowered drapes, his black suit and her black dress like ebony against the marble of their skin. Her face, in profile, yearns upward to kiss his mouth, the fingers of her right hand spreading gently across his back. Her other hand cups his neck, her thumb a feather against his hair line, while his hand around her waist pulls her close. The air is electric, their flesh luminous. Behind them, the wedding candles burn. Later, her exquisite fingers hold a bite of frosted cake, her wrist wrapped in pearls. It is 1953.

Leaning against the Studebaker, cream over bronze, she poses in her fitted blue print sundress. It falls just below her knees, well above her crossed ankles and high-heeled pumps. This car is headed into the future, its chrome bubble front like the prow of a ship, like a wide-open mouth, like, wow! a brand new car for this brand new marriage in a neighborhood too new for grass or trees! The sun glints off the windshield, off the chrome, off the paint. Her left hand must be burning; it lies atop the blazing hood, her thumb and pinky lifted into arcs above the metal—but she holds the pose.

Glenn Miller glamour, big bands and ballrooms, she clung to those rhythms all of her life. Her real father played a big band clarinet, licorice-stick swing, and she intoned the names Ginger and Fred as though they'd been friends in school. Once, when she went out dancing with my father, draped in black taffeta and rhinestones, she bent over our beds to kiss our foreheads goodnight. Her halo cloud of Chanel Number Five lingered after she'd quietly closed the door and gone. But mostly, she danced at home. When they began the beguine on the record player, she would sway and dip and whirl across the carpet in her white Keds and Capri pants, her sun-speckled shins shining, one hand at her invisible swain's waist, the other resting lightly in his uplifted palm.

At other times, in the midst of dusting or carrying in the mail, she'd break out a few little dance steps, wagging her finger, Charleston style, in the suburban air.

That's when I knew she had once been a person, before she became a mother, like when she taught us to whistle with a blade of grass. Pluck a fat reed, stretch it tight between your pressed-together thumbs, put your lips right there and blow. Like a high wailing clarinet when the joint was really jumpin. She knew how to play.

Sometimes my mother sat still. But not her pointer finger. It wrote secret, invisible words and runes on the surface of the glass-topped table. Little circles, lines, messages, the sign of something moving through her that was not worry or work. The moving finger was always dancing. No matter what, there was joy in her hand.

She has Carol Merrill hands at Christmas and birthdays, the hands of the game show hostess. Carol, will you show our contestant what she has won? Holding up the red boots, the Play-Doh, the red dress with petticoats. Showing the presents to the camera, to the birthday girl. Delivering the Christmas boxes to our pajamaed laps, our legs stuck straight out in front on the floor.

We found an 8-mm reel in the dusty bottom of the cardboard box.

Take One. 1965. Her hands are on TV. We are all on TV! Faking excitement, my sisters and I jump up and down, throwing tinsel on a Christmas tree, also imitation. Cut to close-up. Her blue-veined right hand and perfect pink nails glide atop the cabinet of a brand new RCA. Carol Merrill again. See the lovely hand caress the RCA, the pale, pointed fingers reflected in the sheen of polished wood. Cut to the star on the Christmas tree, glinting in the studio lights. Cut to the RCA Logo. The Most Trusted Name in Electronics.

Take Two. Sitting close together on tall stools, she and Dad smile and confer over the scrolling Christmas list that unfurls in her delicate hands. I can't hear what they're saying. For some reason, the sound has disappeared. The camera glides past their shoulders to reveal the RCA's behind them. Move to close-up and pan across five new models, each one bigger than the last. Then Mom and Dad stroll into the showroom, and Mom lays a big red bow on the biggest TV.

Wearing a bonnet and looking doubtful, I sit in her lap, and she sits behind me with an unconvincing smile. It's 1959. We both look off to the left. Her hand holds me close, pressing into the small, white buttons of my coat. Her smooth girl's hands now have bones and blue veins. Her thumb and finger make a little oval, like a puppet mouth, like a long, flat *o*.

Four years later, she said that Daddy would be living somewhere else. On Saturdays, she said, she would pack us a little lunch and we would spend the day with him. She cried and I cried, and she asked if we wanted to go for a walk, but I was the only one who did, so she took my hand and we walked outside, where we stood on the burnt summer grass and my mother talked to Annie, our neighbor, in a quiet, grown-up voice. I stared at the trickle of sprinkler water creeping through the powdery dirt in the gutter, and at the sailboats on my tennis shoes. I wasn't wearing any socks. Three days later or was it a week?—my father came home and they hugged, then holding the back of his neck with her hands, she studied his face up close and cried. I didn't know what was happening. When Saturday came, Daddy wasn't living somewhere else and we didn't get little lunches. I decided that my mother was lying.

Sometime in the 60's, she started painting her nails and never stopped. Frosted Melon; Paint the Town Pink; Love Me Red.

1961. Was this the year she dragged the Christmas tree home, her hands cracked and bleeding?

In 1964, my father bought her three slim gold bands, one for each daughter, to wear next to her wedding ring. I loved to see myself wrapped around her finger.

Up and down the back of her hand, I traced the blue veins that stood up like mine, her long, thin fingers. Bony knuckles, perfect nails, Frosted Rose. She was sitting on the couch with her hand on the armrest, talking to company. It was 1967. I camped at her feet and softly pinched the translucent skin on her hand, making a little ridge. She let me. When I let go, it stayed there. And she let it.

By 1957, since the wedding in Juneau, they've moved to Colorado, Los Angeles, Des Moines, Los Angeles again, then back to Colorado, Montrose this time. Her hands have kept busy wrapping, unwrapping, boxing, unboxing, lining shelves in new closets, cleaning new windows, waxing another new house full of floors, diapering two babies, 14 months apart; the new one, me, born in April. In 55 in California, she had buried a baby, born too soon. Before she let it go, did she stroke its quiet head?

Pumping the peddles on her tricycle fast, my older sister Tara tore up the block, one neighbor kid perching on her handlebars and two riding shotgun on the platform behind. My mother was pushing the mower across the new green Colorado lawn, the motor roaring and green grass smell all around. The circus act careened around the corner and spilled on to the sidewalk, my sister's arm broke and all four kids started screaming. Shutting off the mower, my mother lifted up the wailing wounded. Two weeks later, my sister Shannon was born. That year, 1960, we moved three times. My mother had her hands full.

My grandmother sent dresses to my sister and me in our third Kansas house: skirts out to here with crisp crinolines; sailor dresses with red ties; polished yellow cotton; stripes and lavender plaid; red with bows and white collars. We wore white anklets and a different dress to school every day. My mother, who in 1962, had seen the handwriting on yet another wall, was finishing her teaching degree, even as she washed and ironed ten dresses a week then hung them up in the closet. But before she washed them, she took out the hems. And before she ironed them, she put the hems back up. Ten hems a week, down, up. So that when we grew and she lowered the hems, the old line wouldn't show.

She didn't know how to sew on a button. She said she wasn't handy.

The day she posed in Aspen with her skis and nonchalance, back in 48, that very afternoon, a man, a friend, held her hand as they talked their way home from the slopes, held her hand as they walked through town, held her hand as he pulled her into an abandoned house. Did she struggle, strike his chest, gouge his face, as the Aran Isle sweater was wrenched and torn, as the ski pants were ripped, as she bled, a virgin? She never told. Not for fifty years.

Box, unbox, box, unbox. By 1970, she had moved eighteen times since she married, one for every year. She wasn't moving again. She put her wedding band in her jewelry box and adorned her bare fingers with red stones and green, party rings and everyday. One, at least, for her pinky. Hands off marriage, she said. She wasn't going to pick up someone else's socks. Ever. Again. She never did. And she didn't move again either, not for eighteen years.

When the child support didn't come, she took a second job. Until three o'clock, she taught first grade and after school, she went to Lewin's, where she helped women with money and husbands try on every season's latest. She hauled sizes smaller, larger, longer, shorter and colors brighter, darker, more muted, more fun and options what do you think of this, have you considered something like that—to the dressing room and back. Carol Merrill again, this time a little depressed. After seven, she cooked dinner, graded papers, wrote lesson plans, folded laundry, and wrote checks, pulling the shoebox of bills down from the closet shelf, licking envelopes and stamps. On weekends, at home, she polished the windows then got down on her knees, dunking a scrub brush into the Pine-Sol suds.

In 1973, her fingers crawled up the wall like a spider, a little bit higher each day. Up the wall and down. Up the wall and down. The mastectomy excised muscle, damaged nerves, tightened tendons. Every day, her fingers moved up the wall. Stretch.

The grandchildren begin to arrive in 1978. In the photos, she holds babies in her arms, her hands holding theirs. Then toddlers in her lap, her hands around their tummies, or holding a storybook, a puzzle, a Raggedy Ann. The grandchildren multiply and begin to grow up. First communion pictures, her hands in theirs. Her arm around a teenager's waist. Fingers laying down a Scrabble tile, slapping down a queen of hearts for War or Go Fish. Rings on her fingers, polish on her toes, she plays with children wherever she goes.

Eyes smile at the camera and her hand gladly grasps my sister's arm. A few tawny spots sprinkle wrinkling flesh. Every fall, she taught 25 fidgety six-year-olds how to fold their hands quietly in their laps. Now at her retirement party, in 1989, her pinky ring shines.

When she was six, her father the clarinetist had knelt in front of her, kissed her goodbye and wept. She never saw him again, never heard him play. At 62 in Arizona, she became Ginger Rogers, finally learning to tap dance to her long-dead father's tunes. A vision in feathers and satin and bows, she glided and shuffle-ball-changed, her six-year-old heart swinging with Benny, her hands held aloft like birds.

When her retirement funds dried up in 1991, she became a Wal-Mart greeter, waving hello and shaking hands, patting the babies arms. Not exactly Carol Merrill. But she liked the babies.

She wanted to play Scrabble with her grandchildren. Besides, Arizona was getting crowded. So she retired from sunshine and tap dancing and moved to Indiana in 1997. Her finger danced above the tiles as she carefully chose her words. She didn't care if she won. While she waited her turn, her pointer finger wrote its secrets.

1999. An Indiana January. Cancer has moved in. Fresh snow, opalescent and quiet, spreads itself across the dark fields. As she dozes in her recliner, her hands folded as if in prayer, I stare at her closed eyes and parted lips, her stilled hands.

2000. June. Her grandchildren and her daughters, and our husbands and partners, carry a box of ashes into the mountains of Glacier National Park, up Avalanche Gorge, along the streambed, under the shade of summer trees. One at a time, we dip into the box, hold her powdery bones in our hands, and let them go, cinders like sand through our fingers. The ashes dance, held aloft in a watery cloud, then begin to separate and, easing toward the center of the stream, pause for a moment, suspended. Then the current catches hold and she surges away in the turbulent rush of early summer snow melt, merging with the splash and play of flashing water, racing over boulders, over ledges, over stones, down toward the valley to become soil, streambed, life. We wash our hands in the icy water.

In the grainy, jittery frames of the 8-mm print, her hands hold mine, steering my lumbering steps toward the chocolate frosting on the two-layer cake and the single burning candle.

Naked, squat, glistening with bath water, I stand in the tub and grip the edge, grinning at the camera with two sharp teeth, doing the jerky bouncy dance of the proud, standing baby. It's a Loony Tunes home movie. Two slender hands reach into the frame, lifting me just enough to plop my bottom down in the water. The hands disappear, and I stare unsmiling, saucer eyes wide. I scowl at the water around my waist. I shoot the camera a dirty look, lean forward onto one hand, grip the tub edge with the other, plant one stolid leg then the other, and haul myself, wobbling, up. With two chubby hands clutching the tub, I look into the camera, straight-faced and innocent, then break out the two-tooth grin and begin the jerky bouncy dance again. The silent, honky-tonk jug band plays for eight more beats, then the hands reappear, reach under my arms, and my bent, shining legs fly through the air.

READING WRITING

This Text: Reading

1. What is Seeley's argument in this essay? Does she have a thesis statement? If so, where is it?
2. Make a list of the various things Seeley's mother's hands represent. What sorts of signs does Seeley pay attention to regarding her mother's hands?
3. How is this essay not simply about Seeley's mother's hands but about Seeley herself? What do we learn about the author by learning about the author's mother's hands?

Your Text: Writing

1. Write an essay in which you *read* someone close to you by focusing on a specific physical attribute of that person. It could be that person's nose, or dialect, or height, or hair color. What does this attribute reveal about this person?

2. Write an essay in which you read someone based not on a physical attribute but on a chosen obsession or hobby, such as a musical interest, a devotion to a sport, the participation in a club or activity, a beloved car or bicycle, a certain way of dressing. How is identification by object different than identification by physical attribute?
3. Write an essay in which you read your relationship with your guardian (parent, stepparent, grandparent) through something specific. How does this specific item speak for this person?
4. Write a comparison/contrast essay on "My Mother's Hands" and Amy Tan's "Mother Tongue."

Say Everything

Emily Nussbaum

Emily Nussbaum is a writer for *The New York Times* where she contributes the "Rerun" column in the Arts & Leisure section. Recently, she has been featured in various media outlets—including a stint on *The Today Show*—as a kind of expert on teen blogging. This essay appeared in 2007 in *New York Magazine*, although Nussbaum was writing about blogs as far back as 2004, when her piece "My So-Called Blog" ran in the *Times*. As Nussbaum notes, more and more young people look for, cultivate, and maintain relationships through social networking sites, chat rooms, and blogs. Without question, the Internet has changed our notion of what a good and "real" relationship is.

"YEAH, I AM NAKED ON THE INTERNET," says Kitty Ostapowicz, laughing. "But I've always said I wouldn't ever put up anything I wouldn't want my mother to see."

She hands me a Bud Lite. Kitty, 26, is a bartender at Kabin in the East Village, and she is frankly adorable, with bright-red hair, a button nose, and pretty features. She knows it, too: Kitty tells me that she used to participate in "ratings communities," like "nonuglies," where people would post photos to be judged by strangers. She has a MySpace page and a Livejournal. And she tells me that the Internet brought her to New York, when a friend she met in a chat room introduced her to his Website, which linked to his friends, one of whom was a photographer. Kitty posed for that photographer in Buffalo, where she grew up, then followed him to New York. "Pretty much just wanted a change," she says. "A drastic, drastic change."

Her Livejournal has gotten less personal over time, she tells me. At first it was "just a lot of day-to-day bullshit, quizzes and stuff," but now she tries to "keep it concise to important events." When I ask her how she thinks she'll feel at 35, when her postings are a Google search away, she's okay with that. "I'll be proud!" she says. "It's a documentation of my youth, in a way. Even if it's just me, going back and Googling myself in 25 or 30 years. It's my self—what I used to be, what I used to do."

We settle up and I go home to search for Kitty's profile. I'm expecting tame stuff: updates to friends, plus those blurry nudes. But, as it turns out, the photos we talked about (artistic shots of Kitty in bed or, in one picture, in a snowdrift, wearing stilettos) are the least revelatory thing I find. In posts tracing back to college, her story scrolls down my screen in raw and affecting detail: the death of her parents, her breakups, her insecurities, her ambitions. There are photos, but they are candid and unstylized, like a close-up of a tattoo of a butterfly, adjacent (explains the caption) to a bruise she got by bumping into the cash register. A recent entry encourages posters to share stories of sexual assault anonymously.

Some posts read like diary entries: "My period is way late, and I haven't been laid in months, so I don't know what the fuck is up." There are bar anecdotes: "I had a weird guy last night come into work and tell me all about how if I were in the South Bronx, I'd be raped if I were lucky. It was totally unprovoked, and he told me all about my stupid generation and how he fought in Vietnam, and how today's Navy and Marines are a bunch of pussies." But the roughest material comes in her early posts, where she struggles with losing her parents. "I lost her four years ago today. A few hours ago to be precise," she writes. "What may well be the worst day of my life."

Talking to her the night before, I had liked Kitty: She was warm and funny and humble, despite the "nonuglies" business. But reading her Livejournal, I feel thrown off. Some of it makes me wince. Much of it is witty and insightful. Mainly, I feel bizarrely protective of her, someone I've met once—she seems so exposed. And that feeling makes me feel very, very old.

Because the truth is, at 26, Kitty is herself an old lady, in Internet terms. She left her teens several years before the revolution began in earnest: the forest of arms waving cell-phone cameras at concerts, the MySpace pages blinking pink neon revelations, Xanga and Sconex and YouTube and Lastnightsparty.com and Flickr and Facebook and del.icio.us and Wikipedia and especially, the ordinary, endless stream of daily documentation that is built into the life of anyone growing up today. You can see the evidence everywhere, from the rural 15-year-old who records videos for thousands of subscribers to the NYU students texting come-ons from beneath the bar. Even 9-year-olds have their own site, Club Penguin, to play games and plan parties. The change has rippled through pretty much every act of growing up. Go through your first big breakup and you may need to change your status on Facebook from "In a relationship" to "Single." Everyone will see it on your "feed," including your ex, and that's part of the point.

Hey Nineteen

It's been a long time since there was a true generation gap, perhaps 50 years—you have to go back to the early years of rock and roll, when old people still talked about "jungle rhythms." Everything associated with that music and its greasy, shaggy culture felt baffling and divisive, from the crude slang to the dirty thoughts it was rumored to trigger in little girls. That musical divide has all but disappeared. But in the past ten years, a new set of values has sneaked in to take its place, erecting another barrier between young and old. And as it did in the fifties, the older generation has responded with a disgusted, dismissive squawk. It goes something like this:

> Kids today. They have no sense of shame. They have no sense of privacy. They are show-offs, fame whores, pornographic little loons who post their diaries, their phone numbers, their stupid poetry—for God's sake, their dirty photos!—online. They have virtual friends instead of real ones. They talk in illiterate instant messages. They are interested only in attention—and yet they have zero attention span, flitting like hummingbirds from one virtual stage to another.

"When it is more important to be seen than to be talented, it is hardly surprising that the less gifted among us are willing to fart our way into the spotlight," sneers Lakshmi Chaudhry in the current issue of *The Nation*. "Without any meaningful standard by which to measure our worth, we turn to the public eye for affirmation."

Clay Shirky, a 42-year-old professor of new media at NYU's Interactive Telecommunications Program, who has studied these phenomena since 1993, has a theory about that response. "Whenever young people are allowed to indulge in something old people are not allowed to, it makes us bitter. What did we have? The mall and the parking lot of the 7-Eleven? It sucked to grow up when we did! And we're mad about it now." People are always eager to believe that their behavior is a matter of morality, not chronology, Shirky argues. "You didn't behave like that because nobody gave you the option."

None of this is to suggest that older people aren't online, of course; they are, in huge numbers. It's just that it doesn't come naturally to them. "It is a constant surprise to those of us over a certain age, let's say 30, that large parts of our life can end up online," says Shirky. "But that's not a behavior anyone

under 30 has had to unlearn." Despite his expertise, Shirky himself can feel the gulf growing between himself and his students, even in the past five years. "It used to be that we were all in this together. But now my job is not to demystify, but to get the students to see that it's strange or unusual at all. Because they're soaking in it."

One night at Two Boots pizza, I meet some tourists visiting from Kansas City: Kent Gasaway, his daughter Hannah, and two of her friends. The girls are 15. They have identical shiny hair and Ugg boots, and they answer my questions in a tangle of upspeak. Everyone has a Facebook, they tell me. Everyone used to have a Xanga ("So seventh grade!"). They got computers in third grade. Yes, they post party pictures. Yes, they use "away messages." When I ask them why they'd like to appear on a reality show, they explain, "It's the fame and the— well, not the fame, just the whole, 'Oh, my God, weren't you on TV?'"

After a few minutes of this, I turn to Gasaway and ask if he has a Web page. He seems baffled by the question. "I don't know why I would," he says, speaking slowly. "I like my privacy." He's never seen Hannah's Facebook profile. "I haven't gone on it. I don't know how to get into it!" I ask him if he takes pictures when he attends parties, and he looks at me like I have three heads. "There are a lot of weirdos out there," he emphasizes. "There are a lot of strangers out there."

There is plenty of variation among this younger cohort, including a set of Luddite dissenters: "If I want to contact someone, I'll write them a letter!" grouses Katherine Gillespie, a student at Hunter College. (Although when I look her up online, I find that she too has a profile.) But these variations blur when you widen your view. One 2006 government study— framed, as such studies are, around the stranger-danger issue—showed that 61 percent of 13-to-17-year-olds have a profile online, half with photos. A recent Pew Internet Project study put it at 55 percent of 12-to-17-year-olds. These numbers are rising rapidly.

It's hard to pinpoint when the change began. Was it 1992, the first season of *The Real World*? (Or maybe the third season, when cast members began to play to the cameras? Or the seventh, at which point the seven strangers were so media-savvy there was little difference between their being totally self-conscious and utterly unself-conscious?) Or you could peg the true beginning as that primal national drama of the Paris Hilton sex tape, those strange weeks in 2004 when what initially struck me as a genuine and indelible humiliation—the kind of thing that lost former Miss America Vanessa Williams her crown twenty years earlier—transformed, in a matter of days, from a shocker into no big deal, and then into just another piece of publicity, and then into a kind of power.

But maybe it's a cheap shot to talk about reality television and Paris Hilton. Because what we're discussing is something more radical if only because it is more ordinary: the fact that we are in the sticky center of a vast psychological experiment, one that's only just begun to show results. More young people are putting more personal information out in public than any older person ever would—and yet they seem mysteriously healthy and normal, save for an entirely different definition of privacy. From their perspective, it's the extreme caution of the earlier generation that's the narcissistic thing. Or, as Kitty put it to me, "Why not? What's the worst that's going to happen? Twenty years down the road, someone's gonna find your picture? Just make sure it's a great picture."

And after all, there is another way to look at this shift. Younger people, one could point out, are the only ones for whom it seems to have sunk in that the idea of a truly private life is already an illusion. Every street in New York has a surveillance camera. Each time you swipe your debit card at Duane Reade or use your MetroCard, that transaction is tracked. Your employer owns your e-mails. The NSA owns your phone calls. Your life is being lived in public whether you choose to acknowledge it or not.

So it may be time to consider the possibility that young people who behave as if privacy doesn't exist are actually the sane people, not the insane ones. For someone like me, who grew up sealing my diary with a literal lock, this may be tough to accept. But under current circumstances, a defiant belief in holding things close to your chest might not be high-minded. It might be an artifact—quaint and naïve, like a determined faith that virginity keeps ladies pure. Or at least that might be true for someone who has grown up "putting themselves out there" and found that the benefits of being transparent make the risks worth it.

Shirky describes this generational shift in terms of pidgin versus Creole. "Do you know that distinction? Pidgin is what gets spoken when people patch things together from different languages, so it serves well enough to communicate. But Creole is what the children speak, the children of pidgin speakers. They impose rules and structure, which makes the Creole language completely coherent and expressive, on par with any language. What we are witnessing is the Creolization of media."

That's a cool metaphor, I respond. "I actually don't think it's a metaphor," he says. "I think there may actually be real neurological changes involved."

Change 1: They Think of Themselves as Having an Audience

I'm crouched awkwardly on the floor of Xiyin Tang's Columbia dorm room, peering up at her laptop as she shows me her first blog entries, a 13-year-old Xiyin's musings on Good Charlotte and the perfidy of her friends. A Warhol Marilyn print gazes over our shoulders. "I always find myself more motivated to write things," Xiyin, now 19, explains, "when I know that somebody, somewhere, might be reading it."

From the age of 8, Xiyin, who grew up in Maryland, kept a private journal on her computer. But in fifth grade, she decided to go public and created two online periodicals: a fashion 'zine and a newsletter for "stories and novellas and whatnot." In sixth grade, she began distributing her journal to 200 readers. Even so, she still thought of this writing as personal.

"When I first started out with my Livejournal, I was very honest," she remembers. "I basically wrote as if there was no one reading it. And if people wanted to read it, then great." But as more people linked to her, she became correspondingly self-aware. By tenth grade, she was part of a group of about 100 mostly older kids who knew one another through "this web of MySpacing or Livejournal or music shows." They called themselves "The Family" and centered their attentions around a local band called Spoont. When a Family member commented on Xiyin's entries, it was a compliment; when someone "Friended" her, it was a bigger compliment. "So I would try to write things that would not put them off," she remembers. "Things that were not silly. I tried to make my posts highly stylized and short, about things I would imagine people would want to read or comment on."

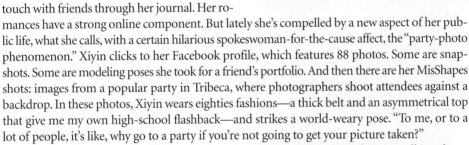

Since she's gone to college, she's kept in touch with friends through her journal. Her romances have a strong online component. But lately she's compelled by a new aspect of her public life, what she calls, with a certain hilarious spokeswoman-for-the-cause affect, the "party-photo phenomenon." Xiyin clicks to her Facebook profile, which features 88 photos. Some are snapshots. Some are modeling poses she took for a friend's portfolio. And then there are her MisShapes shots: images from a popular party in Tribeca, where photographers shoot attendees against a backdrop. In these photos, Xiyin wears eighties fashions—a thick belt and an asymmetrical top that give me my own high-school flashback—and strikes a world-weary pose. "To me, or to a lot of people, it's like, why go to a party if you're not going to get your picture taken?"

Among this gallery, one photo stands out: a window-view shot of Xiyin walking down below in the street, as if she'd been snapped by a spy camera. It's part of a series of "stalker photos" a friend has been taking, she informs me: He snaps surreptitious, paparazzi-like photos of his friends and then uploads them and "tags" the images with their names, so they'll come across them later. "Here's one where he caught his friend Hannah talking on the phone."

Xiyin knows there's a scare factor in having such a big online viewership—you could get stalked for real, or your employer could bust you for partying. But her actual experience has been that if someone is watching, it's probably a good thing. If you see a hot guy at a party, you can look up his photo and get in touch. When she worked at American Apparel, management posted encouraging remarks on employee MySpace pages. A friend was offered an internship by a magazine's editor-in-chief after he read her profile. All sorts of opportunities—romantic, professional, creative—seem to Xiyin to be directly linked to her willingness to reveal herself a little.

When I was in high school, you'd have to be a megalomaniac or the most popular kid around to think of yourself as having a fan base. But people 25 and under are just being realistic when they think of themselves that way, says media researcher Danah Boyd, who calls the phenomenon "invisible audiences." Since their early adolescence, they've learned to modulate their voice to address a set of listeners that may shrink or expand at any time: talking to one friend via instant message (who could cut-and-paste the transcript), addressing an e-mail distribution list (archived and accessible years later), arguing with someone on a posting board (anonymous, semi-anonymous, then linked to by a snarky blog). It's a form of communication that requires a person to be constantly aware that anything you say can and will be used against you, but somehow not to mind.

This is an entirely new set of negotiations for an adolescent. But it does also have strong psychological similarities to two particular demographics: celebrities and politicians, people who have always had to learn to parse each sentence they form, unsure whether it will be ignored or redound into sudden notoriety (Macaca!). In essence, every young person in America has become, in the literal sense, a public figure. And so they have adopted the skills that celebrities learn in order not to go crazy: enjoying the attention instead of fighting it— and doing their own publicity before somebody does it for them.

Change 2: They Have Archived Their Adolescence

I remember very little from junior-high school and high school, and I've always believed that was probably a good thing. Caitlin, 17, has spent her adolescence making sure this doesn't happen to her. At 12, she was blogging; at 14, she was snapping digital

FEATURES

Text Size: A | **A** | A

Say Everything

caitlin.

caitlin
email/text/IM.

caitlin
News Hour borefest

caitlin
AP Eng. vocab test. AP Gov. test, getti...

INSTANT MESSAGE
She talks to her friends online. Even when she's offline, her "Away" message often lets a viewer know where she is.

WEBSITE
Caitlin designed her own Website

|**contact**|
aim: caitlin
caitlin@yahoo.com

|**languages**|
english (native)
french (proficient)
chinese (novice)

 **myspace.com**
a place for friends

Caitlin's Blurbs

I want to be a celebrated graphic designer.

Books	The Three Musketeers, Angels & Demons, The Da Vinci Code, Harry Potter series, The Lord of the Flies, Night, The Scarlet Letter, Gossip Girl, Assassination Vacation, Me Talk Pretty One Day
Heroes	Tina Fey, Amy Poeler, Maja Ivarsson
Television	Project Runway, Absolutely Fabulou... Word, Sex and the City, Grey's Ana... F.R.I.E.N.D.S., The Real World: Par... Desperate Housewives, Boston Lega... Apprentice, Blow Out, Sex & The C...

Caitlin's Interests

General

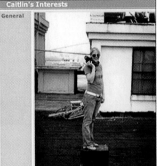

MYSPACE
Caitlin is not a fan of MySpace, but she joined so that she could look at other people's photos.

VISIT MY SITE

VIMEO
Her videos include scenes of her hula-hooping in Washington Square Park and a clip in which she asks for feedback on her new haircut.

VISIT MY SITE

vimeo

Clip Total	Appears in	Likes	Contacts
70	41	783	92

Emails are my favorite thing. Go for it!
caitlin(at)yahoo.com

IM me: caitlin

Activity on Your Clips   Newer / Older

Today	Mon	Sun	Sat	Fri	Thu	Wed

Your Clips   Newer / Older

LIKES	16	11	14	21	6
COMMENTS	26	12	12	8	19
VIEWS	227	250	291	350	549

VISIT MY
SITE

flickr GAMMA™

---

facebook
Caitlin's Profile

Sex:	Female
Relationship Status:	Single
Birthday:	
Political Views:	Very Liberal

Contact Info

Email: caitlin@yahoo.com
Mobile: **123-456-7890**

▼ **Courses**

▼ Mini-Feed
Displaying 10 stories.   See All

Yesterday

💬 Caitlin commented on John's note a mortgage on your dorm room? 6:09pm

January 29

👤 Caitlin is ecstatic...because she got into MICA. 6:15pm

January 25

👥 Caitlin joined the g... 11:23pm

January 24

📅 Caitlin plans to attend Julia's Sweet 16. 4:52pm

ON Stuco, NHS, Faraday Society, dancing, Check
The Pockets 2006, traveling, designing,
socializing, tennis, hooping!, talking, taking
photos & videos, scribbling, ON Tennis

- 1. AB/H Calculus AB (Obenhaus)
- 2. English (Greiner)
- 3. ge Chem (Reist)
- overnment (Cotsworth)
- 4. Drawing 3 (Trapp)
- 5. Distinguished Scholars Visual Arts (Trapp)
- 6. Chinese II (Lin)
- 7. AP Portfolio (Trapp)

↗
FACEBOOK
Caitlin's page
links to 91
friends at her
high school.
Her "feed"
displays the
latest news as
she edits her
profile.

VISIT MY
SITE

photos; at 15, she edited a documentary about her school marching band. But right now the high-school senior is most excited about her first "serious project," caitlin.com. On it, she lists her e-mail and AIM accounts, complains about the school's Web censors, and links to photos and videos. There's nothing racy, but it's the type of information overload that tends to terrify parents. Caitlin's are supportive: "They know me and they know I'm not careless with the power I have on the Internet."

As we talk, I peer into her bedroom. I'm at a café in the West Village, and she is in the Midwest—just like those Ugg girls, who might, for all I know, be linked to her somehow. And as we talk via iChat, her face floats in the corner of my screen, blonde and deadpan. By swiveling her Webcam, she gives me a tour: her walls, each painted a different color of pink; storage lockers; a subway map from last summer, when she came to Manhattan for a Parsons design fellowship. On one wall, I recognize a peace banner I've seen in one of her videos.

I ask her about that Xanga, the blog she kept when she was 12. Did she delete it?

"It's still out there!" she says. "Xanga, a Blogger, a Facebook, my Flickr account, my Vimeo account. Basically, what I do is sign up for everything. I kind of weed out what I like." I ask if she has a MySpace page, and she laughs and gives me an amused, pixellated grimace. "Unfortunately I do! I was so against MySpace, but I wanted to look at people's pictures. I just really don't like MySpace. 'Cause I think it's just so . . . I don't know if *superficial* is the right word. But plastic. These profiles of people just parading themselves. I kind of have it in for them."

Caitlin prefers sites like Noah K Everyday, where a sad-eyed, 26-year-old Brooklyn man has posted a single photo of himself each day since he was 19, a low-tech piece of art that is oddly moving—capturing the way each day brings some small change. Her favorite site is Vimeo, a kind of hipster YouTube. (She's become friends with the site's creator, Jakob Lodwick, and when she visited New York, they went to the Williamsburg short-film festival.) The videos she's posted there are mostly charming slices of life: a "typical day at a school," hula-hooping in Washington Square Park, conversations set to music. Like Caitlin herself, they seem revelatory without being revealing, operating in a space midway between behavior and performance.

At 17, Caitlin is conversant with the conventional wisdom about the online world—that it's a sketchy bus station packed with pedophiles. (In fact, that's pretty much the standard response I've gotten when I've spoken about this piece with anyone over 39: "But what about the perverts?" For teenagers, who have grown up laughing at porn pop-ups and the occasional instant message from a skeezy stranger, this is about as logical as the question "How can you move to New York? You'll get mugged!") She argues that when it comes to online relationships, "you're getting what you're being." All last summer, as she bopped around downtown Manhattan, she met dozens of people she already knew, or who knew her, from online. All of which means that her memories of her time in New York are stored both in her memory, where they will decay, and on her site, where they will not, giving her (and me) an unsettlingly crystalline record of her seventeenth summer.

Caitlin is not the only one squirreling away an archive of her adolescence, accidentally or on purpose. "I have a logger program that can show me drafts of a paper I wrote three years ago," explains Melissa Mooneyham, a graduate of Hunter College. "And if someone says something in instant message, then later on, if you have an argument, you can say, 'No, wait: You said *this* on *this* day at *this* time.'"

As for that defunct Xanga, Caitlin read it not long ago. "It was interesting. I just look at my junior-high self, kind of ignorant of what the future holds. And I thought, *You know, I don't think I gave myself enough credit: I'm really witty!*" She pauses and considers. "If I don't delete it, I'm still gonna be there. My generation is going to have all this history; we can document anything so easily. I'm a very sentimental person; I'm sure that has something to do with it."

Change 3: Their Skin Is Thicker than Yours

The biggest issue of living in public, of course, is simply that when people see you, they judge you. It's no wonder Paris Hilton has become a peculiarly contemporary role model, blurring as she does the distinction between exposing oneself and being exposed, mortifying details spilling from her at regular intervals like hard candy from a piñata. She may not be likable, but she offers a perverse blueprint for surviving scandal: Just keep walking through those flames until you find a way to take them as a compliment.

This does not mean, as many an apocalyptic op-ed has suggested, that young people have no sense of shame. There's a difference between being able to absorb embarrassment and not feeling it. But we live in a time in which humiliation and fame are not such easily distinguished quantities. And this generation seems to have a high tolerance for what used to be personal information splashed in the public square.

Consider Casey Serin. On Iamfacingforeclosure.com, the 24-year-old émigré from Uzbekistan has blogged a truly disastrous financial saga: He purchased eight houses in eight months, looking to "fix 'n' flip," only to end up in massive debt. The details, which include scans of his financial documents, are raw enough that people have accused him of being a hoax, à la YouTube's Lonelygirl15. ("ForeclosureBoy24," he jokes.) He's real, he insists. Serin simply decided that airing his bad investments could win him helpful feedback—someone might even buy his properties. "A lot of people wonder, 'Aren't you embarrassed?' Maybe it's naïve, but I'm not going to run from responsibility." Flaming commenters don't bug him. And ironically, the impetus for the site came when Serin was denied a loan after a lender discovered an earlier, friends-only site. Rather than delete it, he swung the doors open. "Once you put something online, you really cannot take it back," he points out. "You've got to be careful what you say—but once you say it, you've got to stand by it. And the only way to repair it is to continue to talk, to explain myself, to see it through. If I shut down, I'm at the mercy of what other people say."

Any new technology has its victims, of course: the people who get caught during that ugly interregnum when a technology is new but no one knows how to use it yet. Take "Susie," a girl whose real name I won't use because I don't want to make her any more Googleable. Back in 2000, Susie filmed some videos for her then-boyfriend: she stripped, masturbated, blew kisses at the Webcam—surely just one of many to use her new computer this way. Then someone (it's not clear who, but probably her boyfriend's roommate) uploaded the videos. This was years before YouTube, when Kaazaa and Morpheus ruled. Susie's films became the earliest viral videos and turned her into an accidental online porn star, with her own Wikipedia entry.

When I reached her at work, she politely took my information down and called back from her cell. And she told me that she'd made a choice that she knew set her outside her own generation. "I never do MySpace or Facebook," she told me. "I'm deathly afraid to Google myself." Instead, she's become stoic, walling herself off from the exposure. "I've had to choose not to be upset about it because then I'd be upset all the time. They want a really strong reaction. I don't want to be that person."

She had another option, she knows: She could have embraced her notoriety. "I had everyone calling my mom: Dr. Phil, Jerry Springer, *Playboy*. I could have been like Paris Hilton, but that's not me. That thing is so unlike my personality; it's not the person I am. I guess I didn't think it was real." As these experiences become commonplace, she tells me, "it's not going to be such a big deal for people. Because now it's happened to a million people."

And it's true that in the years since Susie's tapes went public, the leaked sex tape has become a perverse, established social convention; it happens at every high school and to every B-list celebrity. At Hunter College last year, a student named Elvin Chaung allegedly used Facebook accounts to blackmail female students into sending him nude photos. In movies like *Road Trip*, "oops porn" has become a comic convention, and the online stuff regularly includes a moment when the participant turns to the camera and says, "You're not going to put this online, are you?"

But Susie is right: For better or worse, people's responses have already begun to change. Just two years after her tapes were leaked, another girl had a tape released on the Internet. The poster was her ex, whom we'll call Jim Bastard. It was a parody of the MasterCard commercial: listing funds spent on the relationship, then his "priceless" revenge for getting dumped—a clip of the two having sex. (To the casual viewer, the source of the embarrassment is somewhat unclear: The girl is gorgeous and the sex is not all that revealing, while the boy in question is wearing socks.) Then, after the credits, the money shot: her name, her e-mail addresses, and her AIM screen names.

Like Susie, the subject tried, unsuccessfully, to pull the video offline; she filed suit and transferred out of school. For legal reasons, she wouldn't talk to me. But although she's only two years younger than Susie, she hasn't followed in her footsteps. She has a MySpace account. She has a Facebook account. She's planned parties online. And shortly after one such party last October, a new site appeared on MySpace: seemingly a little revenge of her own. The community is titled "The Society to Chemically Castrate Jim Bastard," and it features a picture of her tormentor with the large red letters loser written on his forehead—not the most high-minded solution, perhaps, but one alternative to retreating for good.

Like anyone who lives online, Xiyin Tang has been stung a few times by criticism, like the night she was reading BoredatButler.com, an anonymous Website posted on by Columbia students, and saw that someone had called her "pathetic and a whore." She stared at her name for a while, she says. "At first, I got incredibly upset, thinking, *Well now, all these people can just go Facebook me and point and form judgments.*" Then she did what she knew she had to do: She brushed it off. "I thought, *Well, I guess you have to be sort of honored that someone takes the time to write about you, good or bad.*"

I tell Xiyin about Susie and her sex tape. She's sympathetic with Susie's emotional response, she says, but she's most shocked by her decision to log off entirely. "My philosophy about putting things online is that I don't have any secrets," says Xiyin. "And whatever you do, you should be able to do it so that you're not ashamed of it. And in that sense, I put myself out there online because I don't care—I'm proud of what I do and I'm not ashamed of any aspect of that. And if someone forms a judgment about me, that's their opinion."

"If that girl's video got published, if she did it in the first place, she should be thick-skinned enough to just brush it off," Xiyin muses. "I understand that it's really humiliating and everything. But if something like that happened to me, I hope I'd just say, well, that was a terrible thing for a guy to do, to put it online. But I did it and that's me. So I am a sexual person and I shouldn't have to hide my sexuality. I did this for my boyfriend just like you probably do this for your boyfriend, just that yours is not published. But to me, it's all the same. It's either documented online for other people to see or it's not, but either way you're still doing it. So my philosophy is, why hide it?"

Future Shock

For anyone over 30, this may be pretty hard to take. Perhaps you smell brimstone in the air, the sense of a devil's bargain: Is this what happens when we are all, eternally, onstage? It's not as if those fifties squares griping about Elvis were wrong, after all. As Clay Shirky points out, "All that stuff the elders said about rock and roll? They pretty much nailed it. Miscegenation, teenagers running wild, the end of marriage!"

Because the truth is, we're living in frontier country right now. We can take guesses at the future, but it's hard to gauge the effects of a drug while you're still taking it. What happens when a person who has archived her teens grows up? Will she regret her earlier decisions, or will she love the sturdy bridge she's built to her younger self—not to mention the access to the past lives of friends, enemies, romantic partners? On a more pragmatic level, what does this do when you apply for a job or meet the person you're going to marry? Will employers simply accept that everyone has a few videos of themselves trying to read the Bible while stoned? Will your kids watch those stoner Bible videos when they're 16? Is there a point in the aging process when a person will want to pull back that curtain—or will the MySpace crowd maintain these flexible, cheerfully thick-skinned personae all the way into the nursing home?

And when you talk to the true believers, it's hard not to be swayed. Jakob Lodwick seems like he shouldn't be that kind of idealist. He's Caitlin Oppermann's friend, the co-founder of Vimeo and a co-creator of the raunchy CollegeHumor.com. Lodwick originated a popular feature in which college girls post topless photos; one of his first online memories was finding Susie's videos and thinking she seemed like the ideal girlfriend. But at 25, Lodwick has become rather sweetly enamored of the uses of video for things other than sex. His first viral breakthrough was a special-effects clip in which he runs into the street and appears to lie down in front of a moving bus—a convincing enough stunt that MSNBC, with classic older-generation cluelessness, used it to illustrate a segment about kids doing dangerous things on the Internet.

But that was just an ordinary film, he says: no different from a TV segment. What he's really compelled by these days is the potential for self-documentation to deepen the intimacy of daily life. Back in college, Lodwick experimented with a Website on which he planned to post a profile of every person he knew. Suddenly he had fans, not just of his work, but of him. "There was a clear return on investment when I put myself out there: I get attention in return. And it felt good." He began making "vidblogs," aiming his camera at himself, then turning it around to capture "what I'd see. I'd try to edit as little as possible so I could catch, say, a one-second glimpse of conversation. And that was what resonated with people. It was like they were having a dream that only I could have had, by watching this four or five minutes. Like they were remembering my memories. It didn't tell them what it was like to hang out with me. It showed them what it was like to be me."

This is Jakob's vision: a place where topless photos are no big deal—but also where everyone can be known, simply by making him-or herself a bit vulnerable. Still, even for someone like me who is struggling to embrace the online world, Lodwick's vision can seem so utopian it tilts into the impossible. "I think we're gradually moving away from the age of investing in something negative," he muses about the crueler side of online culture. "For me, a fundamental principle is that if you like something, you should show your love for it; if you don't like it, ignore it, don't waste your time." Before that great transition, some Susies will get crushed in the gears of change. But soon, he predicts, online worlds will become more like real life: Reputation will be the rule of law. People will be ashamed if they act badly, because they'll be doing so in front of all 3,000 of their friends. "If it works in real life, why wouldn't it work online?"

If this seems too good to be true, it's comforting to remember that technology always has aftershocks. Surely, when telephones took off, there was a mourning period for that lost, glorious golden age of eye contact.

Right now the big question for anyone of my generation seems to be, endlessly, "Why would anyone do that?" This is not a meaningful question for a 16-year-old. The benefits are obvious: The public life is fun. It's creative. It's where their friends are. It's theater, but it's also community: In this linked, logged world, you have a place to think out loud and be listened to, to meet strangers and go deeper with friends. And, yes, there are all sorts of crappy side effects: the passive-aggressive drama ("you know who you are!"), the shaming outbursts, the chill a person can feel in cyberspace on a particularly bad day. There are lousy side effects of most social changes (see feminism, democracy, the creation of the interstate highway system). But the real question is, as with any revolution, which side are you on?

READING WRITING

This Text: Reading

1. Note how Nussbaum begins her essay. Literally, look at the very first sentence. Why is this an effective opening?
2. Nussbaum buries her thesis. Can you locate on the page her actual argument—the main point of her essay?
3. Many professors, linguists, and critics have decried e-mail and blogs, claiming the casual, shorthand approach to language, grammar, and syntax has eroded writing skills and an awareness of complex language. How would you describe Nussbaum's language? Does it change to fit the tone and style of online writing?

Your Text: Writing

1. If you keep a blog, write a first-person essay about the experience of keeping a blog. Be sure and quote yourself (your entries) in your paper. Is it difficult making an argument about your own text?
2. Write an essay on an intriguing Facebook, Nerve.com, YouTube, or Match.com site. What kind of argument(s) does the page make?
3. Dig up some written personal ads from newspapers from the '70s and '80s. You can find them in the back of *The New York Review of Books, The New Yorker*, and many major weekly newspapers in large cities. Write a comparison/contrast essay in which you examine pre-Internet personal ads and the ads on sites like Match.com or Eharmony.com. What is similar? What has changed?

The College Relationship Suite

For some, college is the first significant choice one makes; for many it marks the beginning of independence as students leave home and go to a place they have chosen to live for the first time. While society has conventionally described college as the best four years of one's life, it can also be a confusing time, as old ties may weaken and new ties forged. Students, faculty, and parents often have conflicting ideas about what college should represent; faculty expect students to devote their time to studies—students may seek this too, but also want to experience a social life for their first time away from home; parents hope that college will lead to some sort of employment.

As we note in the introduction to this chapter, college marks the beginning not simply of new relationships but of new *kinds* of relationships. In fact, almost every relationship dynamic in college is new—you likely never had roommates before, dating is likely different in college, professors are not the same as high school teachers, you have never been in a sorority/fraternity before—even your friends are likely different. Negotiating these new contexts can be difficult. This suite looks specifically at college relationships and their unique demands and expectations.

Relationships between students can be complicated, as some want different things from one another, as Emily Littlewood (2000) describes in her essay on the types of college dating. Littlewood, a student at Virginia Commonwealth University, identifies three kinds of romantic relationships in college and reads each of them as specific texts with their own codes, rules, and expectations. Libby Copeland (2004) also looks at romantic relationships, most notably the pain of the unrequited crush, which exists in high school, but seems to intensify in college, perhaps because of the ubiquitous opportunities for dating.

The other three readings in this suite take a look at another new relationship in college—the professor/student relationship. While regulations at colleges and universities govern some of the behavior of faculty and students, there exists a great deal of ambiguity, not only in the popular topic of student–teacher romantic relationships (they make it into every movie and television show about college), but how students and teachers should act with one another on a daily basis.

Both authors are professors and both value collegial, friendly relationships with students. Both also feel very strongly that professor–student dating is not a good idea. Yet, more and more colleges and universities are encouraging faculty to spend educational time with students outside of class, fostering seamless learning environments, research and publication opportunities, and service learning experience. But what kind of student–professor relationship is "proper"? Laura Kipnis (2004), author of *Against Love: A Polemic,* argues that we should alter how we think about relationships between students and professors rather than banning them altogether. Kathleen Dean More and Lani Roberts, professors of philosophy at Oregon State, take two differing stances on whether professors should hug students. In this article and the next, you might find it interesting to see how professors feel about their relationships with students—they are often as anxious as you are. Deni Elliott and Paul Martin Lester are life partners as well as professors. In their essay, published in the *Chronicle of Higher Education* in 2001, they provide questions that professors should ask before initiating non-classroom meetings with students. Are these the same questions students should ask?

The authors have had professors whose classes, writings, and ideas have changed their worlds. And we have also had students in our classes whose commitment, humor, and liveliness have enriched our lives tremendously. We hope that this suite (and your college days) lead to similar experiences for you.

⊔

Can You Handle the Commitment?: Three Types of College Relationships

Emily Littlewood

Student Essay

EVERYONE PARTICIPATES in some type of romantic relationship at some point in his or her life. On campus there are, unsurprisingly, many different types of these relationships, few with specific boundaries or limits. There is a lot of "gray area" when dealing with relationships between people who are just "coming of age," such as college students. Though there are just about as many different types of these relationships as there are people participating in them, there are three main categories in which they fall. These groupings are simply split by level of commitment, which boils down to true underlying emotions. Of these groupings, the random hook up category has the least amount of commitment, followed by the dating/friends with benefits group, with the going out grouping being the "ultimate" commitment level. The fact that there are so many different levels of commitment and intimacy just goes to show that while in this period of selfconfusion, students have varied views upon how much effort and emotion should be placed into a romantic relationship.

The relationships that fall into the random hook up group contain the least amount of attachment and emotional involvement. This category is most likely the broadest because there are so many different definitions of what a hook up is, which makes explaining the exact boundaries of the category difficult. The one thing which all hook ups must have in common is their singularity. Anything from a kiss to sex can be a hook up, as long as there is no intent of forming any emotional bond with the person. A hook up is a singular occasion with that specific person, and no type of stronger relationship forms because of it. The people who are most likely to participate in these hook ups are either those who fear commitment or those who simply enjoy being single (or both).

Most hook ups occur for the sake of instant gratification, the claimed motto of our generation, the apparent reincarnate of the '60's. Hooking up is a non-committal way of satisfying sexual needs but very rarely has an impact upon an emotional level. This type of relationship seems to be most popular with college-aged students, because many do not feel comfortable with a serious commitment. Hooking up also provides the most convenient way of making physical contact with other people. Being in a situation where one meets huge amounts of new people, and in a state of change in general, a person seems to be most at ease with an interaction that needs no effort put into it.

The next level of commitment consists of the "dating" or "friends with benefits" category. This entails a semi-relationship, still without full emotional involvement. Dating requires the *repetition* of hook ups with the same person, taking hooking up to a more serious level. This type of relationship lacks any type of exclusiveness, though a slight concept of loyalty does exist. This loyalty leads to the repetitiveness. By dating the same person again and again, one is staking a claim that, yes, the sense of caring and desire to be with that other person subsists. This desire, however, lacks the amount of strength needed to invoke fidelity. Dating includes slight emotional involvement other than loyalty, requiring the two people involved to at least like each other enough to be around the other on more than one occasion. Friends with benefits requires a bit more caring on the part of the two people. Friends take their relationship that began as a platonic one and has, over time incorporated the physicality of a sexual relationship. Most people who are in this type of situation have the mindset that they are in a relaxed form of "going out," not having to deal with the issue of fidelity but being able to have everything else, mainly sexual and some emotional support.

The plus side of these types of relationships is that the people involved get most of the perks of an exclusive relationship, without having to actually make a commitment. There is an emotional connection between the partners, a sense of caring and *liking*. These relationships are much more laid back than their exclusive counterparts, not requiring the selfcontrol needed to be completely committed. There are a few downsides to these relationships, however. There may be underlying jealousy because either of the partners can date other people, and this jealousy cannot truly be addressed, because the relationship is not exclusive. In general, one of the people involved cares more than the other, which creates a problem because that person usually asks to "upgrade" the relationship to exclusiveness, while their partner protests their happiness with the freedom of dating many people.

The third type of relationship is the "going out" category. These relationships are mutually exclusive and are meant to satisfy all emotional needs. If one of the partners were to "hook up" with someone other than their relationship partner, he or she would be cheating. When a couple has decided to go out, it often shows that their emotional bond has become much stronger, and they want to become even closer. This type of relationship exhibits a much more powerful sense of caring than the other two types, as well as a sense of devotion. By agreeing to see only each other, the two people involved are agreeing to be devoted to one another. In a *good* relationship, the two people care deeply about each other's happiness, as well as maintaining a sense of respect for the other person.

When talking about this type of relationship, the pros and cons seem to be to the extreme. One gains a safety net, in a sense, not needing to look for random hook ups anymore. There should be a sense of extreme like, or even love, between the two people, which generally adds to one's well being. There is always someone to connect to, and trust. On the other hand, to be in a relationship like this one must make themselves vulnerable, and completely opening one's self to another is a very hard and dangerous thing to do. To be devoted to the other person, one needs to be willing to trust them, and just by doing that a world of pain can be brought about. At the college age, many people are just finding the ability to be devoted and reliable, which makes it hard to expect those qualities in another person. Many people at this age feel stifled by the exclusive nature of these relationships, because they are under the impression that college is the time to have fun, which, to them, means dating many different people.

Different people choose to be in particular types of relationships for different reasons. That decision usually includes consideration of how much physical attraction there is between the people as well as how strong of an emotional connection is present. When choosing what level of intensity to make the relationship, a person must decide how much emotional support and attachment, as well as how strong of a physical relationship, he or she wants. There must be a weighing of how devoted and committed a person can be to someone else against how much of a desire for the freedom to be with as many people as they choose. Making this choice shows character. People who are afraid to commit, or prefer to "play the field" generally stick to random hook ups, avoiding any need to becoming emotionally attached or devote themselves to another person. Those who choose to either date or begin a sexual relationship with a friend are usually craving some type of emotional support but without the desire of relying too heavily on anyone else. The people that choose to commit themselves to the status of "going out" seem to have the most maturity and will power. They exude self-control and confidence, able to, on most occasions, remain faithful to their partner and remaining emotionally steadfast. Just by choosing what type of relationship to participate in, people are telling others their secret fears of being hurt, or the stability of their being, by having someone rely upon them. By knowing this information, the world can look at teenage relationships in a new light. The choices that teenagers make regarding levels of commitment or physicality are not always careless. Changes affect teenagers as an age group in almost every aspect of life, and do play a role in what type of relationships a college aged student may want to involve themselves in. So maybe we have *reason* to not commit ourselves completely to one person, instead of the general view that we simply lack the capability to do it.

Boy Friend: Between Those Two Words, a Guy Can Get Crushed

Libby Copeland

THE WORST KIND OF TEMPTATION, as Tantalus found out, is the sort that's closest, the fruit that's barely out of reach. This holds true for infatuation, which is why the cruelest crush is one between friends.

We call this the friend-crush, and it happens when one member of a platonic relationship secretly harbors a desire for something more. The friend-crush survives through crying jags and significant others and drunken walks home. And when it ends, it often goes out with a humiliating fizzle, accompanied by something like, "I can't date you, Jason/Bobby/Steven/Mike. I value our friendship too much."

Apparently, no one talks about the friend-crush, about the fact that it's quite common, that it usually seems to be the guy doing the crushing, and that it is endemic to high schools and college campuses. Last autumn a college kid named Matt Brochu wrote about it in his school newspaper, and it was as if he'd just translated the Rosetta Stone of adolescent longing.

When Brochu's column ran in the University of Massachusetts paper in November, a cry of recognition arose from the young people of this nation. At last, someone had given voice to their silent suffering. Through instant messaging, the column spread from Amherst, Mass., to Boston to Austin to Muncie to Berkeley. It spread to England and Belgium and to a Navy enlistee in the middle of the Pacific Ocean and to a woman in eastern Canada who "almost cried" when she read it.

The Web site for the Massachusetts *Daily Collegian*, where Brochu's column was posted, was flooded. A typical column gets at most 1,000 readers in one month. Brochu's got 570,000 hits from November to March.

The column was an anatomy of Brochu's real-life crush, embellished by past experiences and by a sprinkling of imagination. Brochu, now a 21-year-old senior, fell into infatuation last summer, after he became friends with a girl from his home town of East Longmeadow, Mass. She was three years younger, an incoming freshman at UMass and—the way Brochu tells it—burdened by a boyfriend who wasn't good enough for her. (They never are.)

She was flirtatious and beautiful and had an air of innocence. She and Matt wound up in psychology class together, where they chatted through each seminar and Brochu's roommate took notes for both of them. Then she broke up with her boyfriend.

Brochu started writing. When he finished, the column was effusive and tragic the way love paeans usually are. It was called "What she doesn't know will kill you," and it was written in the second person and filled with references specific to his slice of generation.

> You met her a few months ago, and somehow she managed to seep into your subconscious like that "Suga how you get so fly" song. . . . She's gorgeous, but gorgeous is an understatement. More like you're startled every time you see her because you notice something new in a "Where's Waldo" sort of way.

It described how a crush works on memory, causing the desirer to remember everything ever told to him by the object of his desire. It talked about the guy's everyday indecisions, such as what to get the girl for her birthday and whether to instant-message her at any given moment. It talked of "that cute little scar on her shoulder," and her love for calzones, and her utter obliviousness to his ardor. It talked of her boyfriend, the "tool," who didn't appreciate her.

Collegian Web site readers are allowed to write responses to articles. Most columns get three or four. Brochu's column got over 500, nearly all in gratitude and praise. Eventually, the exhausted editor running the feedback section told readers they couldn't write in any more. But the old messages are still up there, steeped in the drama of young love.

> "Thank you for showing me that I'm not alone on this in this crazy world," wrote someone under the name "Hobbes."
> "By the time I finished it, I was speechless and light-headed from the truthfulness of it all," wrote "Abel."
> "i laughed when i saw resemblances of myself, yet inside i was really crying," wrote "Krunk."

Readers were inspired by the end of Brochu's column, a romantic call to arms that included a blank space where each reader could write the name of his beloved. The last lines are these:

> Now cut this out, fill in her name, and give it to her, coward. Just let me know how it works out.
> "Damn, I wish I could be so eloquent," wrote "P. Che." "Maybe it really is worth a shot no?"

Brochu thought so. He'd made up his mind to tell the girl.

Unlike the infatuation from afar, the friend-crush is especially powerful because the romance seems so almost possible. By its very nature, the friend-crush encourages Talmudic dissections of the beloved's psyche, hashing and rehashing of missed opportunities, optimistic interpretations of neutral behavior.

There's Brad Clark, 17, of Glen Burnie, who years ago became friends with a girl he had a crush on and tried to ask her out via a passed note. She wrote back, "I think you're really cool so we can be friends but I have a boyfriend."

For a week, Clark listened to moody Dashboard Confessional songs and analyzed the note over and over. He considered the phrase, But I have a boyfriend.

> "Have. That's not a very strong word there," he thought.

There's Carl M. Schwarzenbach, a 17-year-old high school junior in Southwick, Mass., who had a crush on a certain girl since the first moment he saw her, 2½ years ago, on the first day of school. It was the beginning of fifth period, choir class, at 12:03 p.m., as he recalls. He was a freshman. She was a senior. She was blond and beautiful and wearing a black tank top and jeans. They became close. Schwarzenbach says they kissed a few times, but they stayed just friends.

"She always had this mind-set that she was afraid of commitment and she didn't want to commit to anything 'cause she was afraid she would hurt me," Schwarzenbach says.

When Brochu's column came out, Schwarzenbach e-mailed it to the girl, with her name filled out in the blank. She's in college now, and they haven't seen each other much. She e-mailed him back, in pink, as always.

"She just said, uh, that it was really, really sweet and it made her smile," Schwarzenbach says. "I think it might have brought us a little closer."

The friend-crush is largely a phenomenon of adolescence, when hope is more persuasive then experience. Though it happens in high school, it blossoms in college, when a new culture shakes everything up. College is when you consider important questions like: Is there such a thing as a platonic back rub? Is there such a thing as a long-distance boyfriend?

It might have to do with the coed dorm setting, where near-strangers are thrust into an intimacy previously reserved for family. (Suitemates pass by in towels.) It might be the fluidity of college dating, in which nothing is defined, and in any case, no one knows what the definitions mean. Are you friends? Are you taking it slow? One person's "seeing each other" is another person's "dating each other," which is another person's "hanging out," which is another person's "friends with benefits."

Consider the experience that countless college guys have had. At a party, a certain girl—one you thought was taken—seems to be flirting with you. She takes your arm when you walk her home. The next day, when you instant-message her with the vaguely suggestive "I had a nice time last night," she says, "Me, too," and then mentions her boyfriend. What could it possibly mean?

Brian Murphy, a freshman at Robert Morris University in Pittsburgh, met a girl from his dorm on move-in day, and they became best friends. They walked to class together, ate lunch and dinner together, went to parties together. After parties, they had a ritual where they would go back to her room and cuddle. Murphy fell for her, hard. He says it was the kind of situation where—forced to choose between going out with guy friends and staying in with her to watch a chick flick—he'd watch the chick flick.

But she had a boyfriend of three years.

Murphy and the girl shared one guilty kiss, then they went home for Christmas break. During the break, Murphy read Brochu's column, and inspired by it, resolved to tell the girl how he felt. He made a scrapbook filled with pictures of the two of them. When they came back to school, he gave her the scrapbook and confessed his feelings.

"Get over me," she said. She said she had realized how much she loved her boyfriend. Murphy was crushed.
"It's definitely the first time that I ever fell in love," he says.

Love is like wealth, or the world food supply. Some people hog it; others get nothing at all. To scroll down the feedback column below Matt Brochu's article is to realize how much love goes unrevealed, unrecognized and unrequited. If only there were some mechanism for spreading love around, everybody could get enough.

Instead, the postings sit static in cyberspace, declarations of love to people who may never read them.

"I've seen the sun rise over the mountains of Vermont and seen it set over the Caribbean. I've swam with tropical fish and seen the view from the top of Katahdin. But none of that even begins to compare to how beautiful she is."

"Katie Norris—if you ever read this, you know how I felt about you during that first month when I was in Mexico . . . look me up sometime. . . . I'd still like to try again."

"Shandie although i only just met you it seems like u are the one . . . dang girl ur perfect"

Some female readers, impressed by Brochu's way with words, try to woo the author himself.

"As a woman that constantly prays for a man with those sensitive values and beautiful words, you definitely took the right approach with this lucky lady. And as a little side note . . . if she didn't think she was as lucky as everyone thought she was; I would love to hear back from you."

A reader incensed by the number of girls praising Brochu writes:

"Girls, stop saying you hope to find someone like the guy who wrote this . . . you already have but you call them your best friend and what you don't know is that they are In Love with you."

The feedback column is a strange sort of conversation, taking place among 500 strangers over the course of months. Readers post responses that reference other posts and debate the efficacy of Brochu's just-tell-her approach. All the theories on love present themselves. There are the cynics. They write that if romance hasn't happened yet, it isn't meant to. They suggest that women want jerks more than "nice guys," and they question whether it's even possible to move from friendship to love. They offer cautionary tales.

"I guess all good stories aren't supposed to have a happy ending and all heroes are not supposed to win," writes a fellow named "Ryan," who posts a harrowing account of running two miles in the rain to a woman's house to declare his love. The woman listened, then told him they were better off as friends. "It was a long walk home that day, the rain. . . . laughing at me in a steady and harsh flow."

But there are more romantics than cynics. A girl writes in to reconsider the "dateability" of guys who are "right under my nose." Another writes in to say she knows a guy has a crush on her and she thinks she feels the same way, but she needs to take it slow. Some confess their love to the people they like, and contacted later, two guys say it actually worked out.
Someone named "Kate" writes:

"As heard one thousand times before . . . amazing article. But, answer us all one question, because we're all dying to know . . . did you get the girl?!"

The answer is: After the story ran, Brochu sent the link over instant messaging to his crush. She wrote back, asking who the column was about. He sent her a cautious, rambling set-up, which he saved, along with her responses, so that he could analyze them later. His set-up started like this:

"First off, I'm not really obsessed with this girl, I'm just interested, and I have been since the day I met her, and she doesn't have to worry about letting me down easy, b/c I'm not the type of person to let things get awkward and let it ruin the friendship we already have, b/c she's gotta realize. . . ."

It went on like this for a while. Then: "So yeah, it's you, sorry I had to make things all weird."

She called it the "sweetest thing" she'd ever read and the "nicest thing" that had ever happened to her, and they agreed to sleep on it and talk the next day.

She called him.

"You never know whether to believe it or not, whether she was letting me down nicely," Brochu says. She talked about her long relationship with her ex-boyfriend, and how she didn't want to get into something serious, and how she felt she'd get too serious with Brochu.

"She said that she could only hang out with people in that way that she couldn't see herself getting to like," Brochu says.

It hurt, but the strange thing is, it hurt only for two days and then Brochu was over it. He says it was as if a light switch inside of him was turned off. He wonders now how much of the crush was just him enjoying the chase, the thrill of the unattainable.

"I think it goes to show that my crush was just building upon itself from me not knowing," he says. "It was completely constructed."

They're still friends, and Brochu says he's totally over her.

Anyway, he's dating someone now. Or, seeing someone. He doesn't quite know what to call it. At the very least, they're hanging out.

Off Limits: Should Students Be Allowed to Hook Up with Professors?

Laura Kipnis

The burning academic question of the day: Should we professors be permitted to "hook up with" our students, as the kids put it? Or they with us? In the olden days when I was a student (back in the last century) hooking up with professors was more or less part of the curriculum. (OK, I went to art school.) But that was a different era, back when sex—even when not so great or someone got their feelings hurt—fell under the category of experience, rather than injury and trauma. It didn't automatically impede your education; sometimes it even facilitated it.

But such things can't be guaranteed to turn out well—what percentage of romances do?—so colleges around the country are formulating policies to regulate such interactions, to protect against the possibility of romantic adversity. In 2003, the University of California's nine campuses ruled to ban consensual relationships between professors and any students they may "reasonably expect" to have future academic responsibility for; this includes any student known to have an interest in any area within the faculty member's expertise. But while engineering students may still pair-bond with professors of Restoration drama in California, many campuses are moving to prohibit all romance between any professor and any student.

Feminism has taught us to recognize the power dynamics in these kinds of relationships, and this has evolved into a dominant paradigm, the new propriety. But where once the issue was coercion or quid pro quo sex, in institutional neo-feminism the issue is any whiff of sexuality itself—or any situation that causes a student to "experience his or her vulnerability." (Pretty much the definition of sentience, I always thought.) "The unequal institutional power inherent in this relationship heightens the vulnerability of the student and the potential for coercion," the California code warns, as if any relationship is ever absent vulnerability and coercion. But the problem in redressing romantic inequalities with institutional blunt instruments is that it just confers more power on the institutions them-selves, vastly increasing their reach into people's lives.

Ironically, the vulnerability of students has hardly decreased under the new paradigm; it's increased. As opportunities for venting injury have expanded, the variety of opportunities to feel injured have correspondingly multiplied. Under the "offensive environment" guidelines, stu-dents are encouraged to regard themselves as such exquisitely sensitive creatures that an errant classroom remark impedes their education, such hothouse flowers that an unfunny joke creates a lasting trauma—and will land you, the unfunny prof, on the carpet or in the national news.

My own university is thankfully less prohibitive about student–professor couplings: You may still hook up with students, you just can't harass them into it. (How long before hiring committees at these few remaining enclaves of romantic license begin using this as a recruiting tool? "Yes the winters are bad, but the students are friendly.") But don't think of telling them jokes! Our harassment guidelines warn in two separate places that inappropriate humor violates uni-versity policy. (Inappropriateness—pretty much the definition of humor, I always thought.)

Seeking guidance, realizing I was clinging to gainful employment by my fingernails, I signed up for a university sexual-harassment workshop. (Also two e-mail communiqués from the dean advised that nonattendance would be noted.) And what an education I received—though probably not the intended one.

Things kicked off with a "Sexual Harassment Pretest," administered by David, an earnest mid-50ish psychologist, and Beth, an earnest young woman with a masters in social work. It con-sisted of unanswerable true–false questions like: "If I make sexual comments to someone and that person doesn't ask me to stop, then I guess that my behavior is probably welcome." Every-one seemed grimly determined to play along—probably hoping to get out by cocktail hour—until we were handed a printed list of "guidelines." No. 1: "Do not make unwanted sexual advances."

Someone demanded querulously from the back, "But how do you know they're unwanted until you try?" (OK, it was me.) David seemed oddly flummoxed by the question, and began anx-iously jangling the change in his pants pocket. "Do you really want me to answer that?" he asked.

Another person said helpfully, "What about smoldering glances?" Everyone laughed. A theater professor guiltily admitted to complimenting a student on her hairstyle that very afternoon (one of the "Do Nots" on the pretest)—but wondered whether as a gay male, not to have complimented her would be grounds for offense. He started mimicking the female student, tossing her mane around in a "notice my hair" manner. People shouted suggestions for other pretest scenarios for him to perform. Rebellion was in the air. Someone who stud-ies street gangs whispered to me, "They've lost control of the room." David was jangling his change so frantically you had to strain to hear what anyone was saying.

My attention glued to David's pocket, I recalled a long-forgotten pop psychology guide to body language that identified change-jangling as an unconscious masturbation substi-tute. (And isn't Captain Queeg's habit of toying with a set of steel marbles in his pants pocket diagnosed by the principal mutineer in Herman Wouk's Caine Mutiny as closet masturba-tion?) If the very leader of our sexual harassment workshop was engaging in potentially of-fensive public masturbatory-like behavior, what hope for the rest of us!

Let's face it: Other people's sexuality is often just weird and creepy. Sex is leaky and anxiety-ridden; intelligent people can be oblivious about it. Of course the gulf between desire and knowledge has long been a tragicomic staple; these campus codes do seem awfully optimistic about rectifying the condition. For a more pessimistic account, peruse some recent treatments of the student-professor hook-up theme—Coetzee's *Disgrace;* Francine Prose's *Blue Angel;* Mamet's *Oleanna*—in which learning has an inverse relation to self-knowledge, in which professors are emblems of sexual stupidity, and such disasters ensue that it's hard not to read these as cautionary tales, even as they send up the new sexual correctness.

Of course, societies are always reformulating the stories they tell about intergenerational desire and the catastrophes that result, from Oedipus to faculty handbooks. The details vary, also the kinds of catastrophes prophesized—once it was plagues and crop failure, these days it's trauma and injury. Even over the last half-century the narrative has drastically changed. Consider the Freudian account, yesterday's contender as big explanatory story: Children desire their parents, this desire meets up with prohibitions—namely the incest taboo—and is subject to repression. But the desire persists nevertheless, occasionally burbling to the surface in the form of symptoms: that mysterious rash, that obsessional ritual.

Today, intergenerational desire remains the dilemma; what's shifted is the direction of arrows. In the updated version, parents (and parent surrogates) do all the desiring, children are innocent victims. What's excised from the new story is the most controversial part of the previous one: childhood sexuality. Children are returned to innocence, a far less disturbing (if less complex) account of childhood.

Excising student sexuality from campus romance codes just extends the same presumption. But students aren't children. Whether or not it's smart, plenty of professors I know, male and female, have hooked up with students, for shorter and longer durations. (Female professors do it less, and rarely with undergrads.) Some act well, some are assholes, and it would definitely behoove our students to learn the identifying marks of the latter breed early on, because post-collegiate life is full of them too. (Along with all the wellestablished marriages that started as student-teacher things, of course—another social reality excised from the story.)

Let's imagine that knowledge rather than protectionism (or institutional powerenhancement) was the goal of higher education. Then how about workshops for the students too? Here's an idea: "10 Signs That Your Professor Is Sleeping With You To Assuage Mid-Life Depression and Will Dump You Shortly Afterward." Or, "Will Hooking Up With a Prof Really Make You Feel Smarter: Pros and Cons." No doubt we'd all benefit from more self-knowledge about sex, but until the miracle drug arrives that cures the abyss between desire and intelligence, universities might try being educational instead of regulatory on the subject.

Case Study: Harmful Hug?

Kathleen Dean More and Lani Roberts

[Editors' note: This case study is one of several posted on the Web site for the Program for Ethics, Science and the Environment within the Department of Philosophy at Oregon State University. The Web site provides the following disclaimer/introduction:

The case studies (all of which are constructed and modified from actual situations) and commentaries that constitute this issue of Reflections explore perennial issues, such as academic freedom, deception and cheating, and cooperation with perceived moral wrong. We begin, however, with two situations that pointedly raise issues of relationship and responsibility between student and professor. As academia readies itself for a new millennium, we hope that these scenarios contribute to a discussion about the ethical integrity and meaning of a university.]

AT THE BEGINNING OF A COURSE on death and dying, a philosophy professor is delighted to see a student who has taken a prior course from him enrolled in the class. As the term progresses, the

The College Relationship Suite

student seems to be having difficulty in the course, which she attributes on one occasion to the fact that her grandmother is dying. However, upon reading her class journal, the professor realizes that the student is experiencing a lot of other things that are difficult and contributing to stress.

On the day an important assignment is due, the student misses class. She drops by the professor's office the next day to turn in the assignment. It is apparent to the professor from the student's sad countenance and tear-stained cheeks that the student is experiencing great distress, and he asks, "do you want to talk about things?" The student hesitates for a moment, then says "yes," and the professor invites her into his office. The student talks about her life situation for close to an hour and a half, often breaking into tears as she relates her story, and as she and the professor think about different courses of action. As the conversation comes to an end, and the student rises to leave, the professor is inclined to give the student a shoulder hug of reassurance. Should he?

Commentary: Kathleen Dean More

Call me cold. Call me cautious. I just don't think any professor should hug any student. Part of my response is simply self-protective. The meaning of a hug is not only in the mind of the person giving a hug, but in the mind of the recipient as well. It follows that no matter what the professor intends, no matter what feelings of compassion or paternalism move him to embrace his troubled student, the student's response to the hug will be an important part of its meaning. She may welcome it as an offer of comfort, but she may just as well see it as a sign of aggression, or paternalism, or presumption. Again, she may welcome the embrace in the warmth of the moment, but then reconsider later. In any event, no matter what his intent, a professor who hugs a student is open to justifiable charges of making unwelcome, uninvited physical contact. And that is a very unpleasant position to be in.

But, someone might object, doesn't a professor have a moral duty to risk being unfairly accused, in order to offer comfort to a person in need? Isn't the spontaneous offer of loving beyond criticism? No, and no again. A hug is comforting, when it is comforting, just because it is an act of intimacy. It crosses the barriers between people, closes the distance. But when a hug is not comforting, it is an invasion—of personal space, surely, of privacy, perhaps—as anyone who knows who has been held in an uninvited, unwelcome embrace. So a professor who hugs his student is either inappropriately intimate or inappropriately presumptuous—an unfortunate choice.

Far better to keep a conversation from getting to the point where it would end with a hug. Professors aren't pastors. We aren't professional counselors. We aren't parents to our students. We are human beings who happen to know a lot about some sorts of things—higher mathematics, or the endocrinology of chimpanzees, or the history of the Roman Empire. The professor should have helped the student find a person who could help her.

Commentary: Lani Roberts

Are there any conditions under which it is permissible for a professor to hug a student? Although the situation that gives rise to this question involves a male professor and a female student, it could just as easily apply to a female professor and male student, or a same sex professor and student. In this broader context of professor-student relationships, the question at issue can be answered in two distinct ways: morally, and prudentially. It is entirely possible for a professor to hug a student without committing an immoral act, yet, he or she may still be well advised not to do so for very practical reasons. It would be foolish to overlook or minimize considerations and dangers of gender, sexual orientation, and race that complicate the inherent power differences between students and professors. The unfortunate facts of actual, potential, and perceived abuse involved in physical touching challenge any presuppositions that every hug is an act of consolation, empathy, and concern. Given these prudential considerations, and acknowledging that there may be opposing arguments, I nonetheless argue that we are embodied selves, needing affirmation and assurance, and therefore advocate a middle ground: proceed with caution.

Before proceeding, a caveat is in order. I am deeply concerned that my position can be misused in the service of the evil of professorial exploitation of vulnerable students. I am not providing any justification for use and abuse of power between teacher and student.

There is nothing inherently immoral in a professor hugging a student; indeed, within an area of great care, there are good reasons that professors may hug specific students and have it be the right thing to do. Students are not disembodied minds; they are persons, intelligent and embodied beings, rational and also emotional and spiritual. I conceive of myself as teaching and learning from whole dynamic beings. As such, I read body language and facial expressions in the classroom to gauge whether the students and I are communicating. I am also fully aware that students' lives are as complex and multifaceted as my own. They simply are not compartmentalized into their "student selves," somehow distinct from the whole persons they are.

Some will argue that the professor-student relationship is a professional one in which expressions of intimacy, such as a hug, are entirely out of place. However, when a student is confiding pain and confusion, as illustrated by this case, it can be argued that this crosses a boundary precluding inappropriate intimacy. Sharing personal information and concerns is often more intimate than physical expressions. Although some professors are unapproachable, most are not going to refuse to be a sounding board for a struggling, even desperate, student seeking guidance. The appropriate institutional action for the professor is, of course, to refer the student to counseling resources on campus. This, though, does not negate the value of a hug as a gesture of personal concern in such a situation.

If a hug is a gift, offered to an upset student solely for the benefit of the student, to console, affirm or encourage her or him, then I do not see it as immoral. On the rare occasions when I have hugged a student, the following common conditions were in play:

The student was tearful and confiding, seeking an anchor in a storm;

I listen and gain commitment from the student to seek counseling, sometimes calling myself to set up the appointment;

I offer a hug to the student, prefaced with a question, "Could you use a hug?", or "Would you like a hug?"

Only if the student says, "yes," only if there is no question of coercion or expectations on my part, will I then hug the student. If a hug is offered with expectations that it will be accepted, there is subtle coercion and what is offered as a gift is a gift no longer.

Some students decline; others accept. The very thought of a young person, away from home, experiencing her or his life as overwhelming and tenuous moves me to reach out to the person across an abyss created by power and professionalism, and offer a hug, subject to the conditions described above. With great care and caution, if the professor in the case offers a hug to the distraught student, with no expectations of an affirmative response, and she accepts, he may hug her without committing a moral wrong.

When Is It OK to Invite a Student to Dinner?

Deni Elliott and Paul Martin Lester

DON'T HAVE SEX WITH YOUR STUDENTS.

It would be hard to find faculty members who do not know that sex with their own students is taboo. But, if reciting that rule is the extent to which professors examine the boundaries of their student-teacher relationships, they ignore a whole set of norms and conventions. They may cross the line without even knowing it. Or they may avoid contact with students, out of fear of crossing the line, and deny both themselves and their students some rich educational experiences.

Boundaries are the moral and sometimes legal protective limits that help define any relationship. Some are set by explicit negotiation of those involved, but most are governed by ritual and custom. Without much effort, most people can describe the boundaries that define a marital relationship, a lawyer-client relationship, or a parent–child relationship.

The two of us think and talk constantly about boundaries, both in our lives and in our work. We are life partners as well as professional colleagues. We write a monthly column together for a national magazine, but are also deeply engrossed in separate projects and research.

One of us directs a University of Montana program, which offers a master's degree on how to teach practical ethics, and the other serves as an informal mentor in the program from time to time. The program attracts a diverse group of students who range in age from 23 to 63. Academic norms are unfamiliar to many of them and often a mystery. Because the program is intensive—with the possibility of earning the master's in a calendar year—students and professors are thrown together quite often in both academic and social settings. From our interactions with students in the program, we've learned a few things about the boundaries of the teacher-student relationship.

Taking that relationship to a more personal level is morally acceptable when it enhances the educational experience of the student. A friend of ours who is a kindergarten teacher, Leslie Black, inspired our favorite example of that. For most of her 30-plus years of teaching, Mrs. Black has invited her students—one 5-year-old at a time—to have dinner with her and her family. Decades later, former students recall how valued they felt by that attention and how receptive it made them to her teaching in the classroom.

Our variation is to invite graduate students in the program and their partners—two couples at a time—to our house for dinner. These dinners, planned for the first months of study, help set a tone of informality and clearly state our honest interest in each student. In return the students report that they have an easier time taking intellectual risks and trusting in the support and criticism that is offered.

Even in the most common of campus settings, professors can find ways to break from the conventional teacher-student relationship in an acceptable way. Most instructors, at one time or another, run into trouble attempting to coach a student one-on-one about a problem or a paper. The student is frustrated and uncomprehending. She seems to be creating obstacles to keep her from using what the instructor offers. Both teacher and student feel the tension in their guts.

Rather than abandoning the student to her own devices with phrases like, "Why don't you think about this on your own for a while," or "We don't seem to be getting anywhere on this," we look for an approach that keeps professor and student connected. "Let's go get coffee," "How about a walk around the block," or even, "Let's both stand up and stretch for a minute" are examples of how we cut the tension. The change in venue or even just the unexpected distraction opens up alternative ways for mentor and student to examine the challenge at hand.

We also begin our initial student appointments with a firm handshake and good eye contact. Few young adults are practiced in such social interchange, but the ability to greet an interviewer with poise and confidence can make the difference in a job or internship decision. As time goes on and a comfortable relationship is established, the appointments may end with a hug or a hand on a student's shoulder.

Sometimes professors face less-than-ideal situations in which they are called upon to step outside the norm of the teacher-student relationship. Our Montana community of Missoula, like many university towns, is small enough that students and professors trip over one another in a variety of settings. It is rare that a faculty member can enjoy an afternoon soak at a hot springs, take a morning yoga class, listen to music at a local bar, shop at the Saturday morning farmer's market, or attend a church service without running into students who are doing the same.

How a professor handles these unintentional, but largely unavoidable, meetings is critical. It is up to the professor to set the tone. Ignoring students in these settings can be perceived as rejection or arrogance, but neither is it necessary to invite students into the faculty member's circle of friends. As long as the student is unlikely to be harmed or made more vulnerable, a range of social interactions is acceptable. What is inappropriate is for professors to allow external settings to turn into annex offices. Physicians do not provide clinical judgments outside of their professional settings. Neither should professors.

Professors have gone too far when students are made to feel more vulnerable than the power imbalance in the faculty-student relationship already implies. That's one of the problems of sexual intimacy between instructors and students, but sex is not the only example.

The most commonplace violations occur when professors put their own agenda or egos above the educational experience of their students. It is wonderful when the lab director's research project and the student's thesis topic are naturally interwoven, but that kind of symbiosis is rarely a product of coincidence. More often, students adjust their learning goals and expectations to fit the lab that supports them. Even more often, students are expected to put aside their own studies in favor of the director's research agenda. That conflict is not confined to graduate students in labs. It is common for research and teaching assistants across campus to be pressured to put the professor's needs ahead of their own studies.

Even more depressingly common is the professor who uses the office or the lectern to demonstrate his or her brilliance and the corresponding students' ignorance. This run-of-the-mill abuse of faculty power interferes with students' education, and professors should be called on it.

Here are some questions that we ask ourselves, and that may guide you, as we examine our own relationships with students:

- If a professor extends a social invitation, is it easy for the student to decline? When we send out our e-mail messages at the beginning of the year alerting graduate students to a forthcoming dinner invitation, we include the information that some students have chosen not to come. We make it safe for them to say no.
- When students and professors gather socially, is it a model for how students can better interact with one another? Departmental parties for professors and graduate students, or faculty suggestions that a seminar group gather afterward for dinner or dessert, are accomplishing their teaching goals if those opportunities spark student study groups and independent socializing among peers.

- Are students taking inappropriate advantage of the relationship? When students start asking for special favors, it is time to re-examine what we are willing to do. We talk directly with students who make such requests about why granting the favor would be unfair.
- What about students who are left out of the social loop? Some students require more clear and formal boundaries than others do. Some may want to be included, but are shy in expressing themselves. Occasionally, we have students with whom we are nervous about extending boundaries. The trick is to be flexible enough to meet the needs of each student and still be consistent. If a student requires more formal interaction, so be it. Likewise, if a student needs repeated invitations from her peers and instructor to join the group meeting outside the formal classroom, those invitations should be forthcoming. However, we keep aware of our own comfort zone and refrain from extending invitations that make us uncomfortable.
- How willing are we to talk openly about this with colleagues and students? As with most acts that go against convention, publicity is a good test for moral permissibility. If we are willing to be direct and open about our relationships with students, it is more likely than not that these relationships are in the students' interest.

Ultimately, academics must examine their views about the ideal teaching role. Few faculty members emulate Charles W. Kingsfield Jr., the irritable and intimidating professor made famous by John Houseman in *The Paper Chase* or Harry Bailey, the dope-smoking, counter-culture radical graduate student played by Elliott Gould in *Getting Straight*. But, when we were students, most faculty members encountered both types along with teachers somewhere in the middle. We all were taught by professors who we called by their first names and by those, who even today, we would be uncomfortable addressing with such familiarity. To some extent, how most of us teach best reflects how we best learned. Considering the unique learning needs of each student, and noticing opportunities for interaction both within and outside of classrooms and offices, enhances the learning experience for all.

READING BETWEEN THE LINES

Classroom Activities

Compare and Contrast

Watch a sitcom and/or drama and see how television producers use traditional ideas of relationships in their shows. Which use relationships more traditionally—sit-coms or dramas? Why do you think that is?

Advertising

Watch the commercials in a particular television show. How do they use traditional ideas of relationships as a point of selling?

The "Perfect" Relationship

Talk about what the perfect relationship with your significant other, friend, parent, and/or professor would be. Where did you get your ideas for this? Now think about how the opposing person would feel about this relationship—would they find it perfect?

Relationships

On the board, make a list of different kinds of relationships. How many do you come up with? Which make the best material for writing?

Objects

Talk about our complicated relationships with objects—cars, stuffed animals, jewelry, old T-shirts, pictures, books, records. How are these relationships formed? What makes them strong?

Places

Spend class time talking about how we have special relationships with places. How are these relationships different than those we have with objects?

Essay Ideas

1. Write a short essay examining your favorite relationship and what made it so.
2. Write an essay comparing the reality of relationships with their mythic counterparts, as often displayed in popular culture.
3. Watch a reality television show. How would you describe their relationships? What does the television camera do to change their relationships? As part of this essay, try to imagine the presence of the camera in every filmed scene. How would you act in this scenario?
4. Write an essay in which you articulate what you *expected* your relationship to be like with your college professor versus what it is *really* like. What are some unexpected benefits and drawbacks?
5. Write a personal essay chronicling the first month with your new roommate(s). What is your room like as a text? How would you describe the text that is this new relationship?
6. Write an essay in which you *read* your college as a text. How would you describe your relationship with your college?
7. *Read* your relationship with your parent(s). How has that relationship changed since you went off to college?

Johnny Cash flips the "bird" while playing at San Quentin prison in 1969.

E CAN'T ESCAPE MUSIC. ALMOST ANY PLACE WE GO MUSIC IS PLAYING—IN THE SUPERMARKET, AT STARBUCKS, IN THE CAR, AND ON TELEVISION. IN FACT, AS WE WRITE THIS, WE'RE LISTENING TO SUFJAN STEVENS' *ILLINOIS*. ACCORDINGLY, MUSIC OFTEN SERVES AS THE SOUNDTRACK FOR OUR LIVES; WE ATTACH MEMORIES TO PARTICULAR SONGS, AND THOSE SONG—MEMORY ATTACHMENTS TEND TO BE LONG LASTING.

Music too is one medium we are at once reading actively and passively as we emotionally connect to the sounds and tones—we don't think so much about the mood a song evokes as much as how it makes us feel. Accordingly, we actively read music, if we read it at all, by focusing on its lyrics—after all, the content of what's sung in a song is the easiest element to interpret. In addition, we have the tools for interpreting words already: We know how to read and make sense of language or literature. And such tools can be useful in understanding music.

Still, interpreting music has its difficulties. Of all the texts in this book, music may be the most emotionally powerful. We can argue about books and movies and television shows, but discussions about music—favorite artists, what albums you would take to a desert island, who is better, the Beatles or the Stones—elicit the most passionate responses. And we often put that passion to good use. We turn to music to put us in a romantic mood, to celebrate events, to announce the arrival of the bride, to begin graduation ceremonies, to initiate all sporting events. Our lives are framed by music—it may be the text we are the most unable to live without, which is why it is particularly important to be a good reader of it.

But we have any number of other considerations to decipher a song's intentional meanings, as well as some of its unintentional ones. Here are some to keep in mind when listening to and writing about music.

Music is made up of genres.

Both professional and amateur listeners often classify a music's type in trying to understand or enjoy it. There are many genres of music—classical, rhythm and blues, rock and roll, rap, country, jazz, and "pop," as well as numerous subgenres within these groups (alternative, emo, trip-hop, fusion, etc.). Bands often combine genres, transcend genres, or even comment on them as they play within them. Sometimes, for example in the case of rap music, the commentary is part of the music itself. Some people place an enormous amount of importance on genres when deciding to listen to particular music—they want ways to understand what experience is ahead of them, and whether, based on past experience, they will like a particular song or band.

Of the genres we've listed, the one hardest to qualify is "pop music" (which is why we place it in quotes). For many, the term has negative connotations—it stands for "popular," which in some circles means unsophisticated or that it panders to a popular sensibility instead of artistic integrity. For the authors, pop music is an umbrella that often covers parts or wholes of entire genres at one time or another—classical music was the pop music of its day, as was early jazz or swing. Even much "classic rock" was once popular. Having said that, what is popular oftentimes is worth studying for the light it may shed on our contemporary world.

Yet, musical genres are not value free. We tend to associate certain traits with particular genres. If we see a number of country and western CDs in someone's car, we may (often incorrectly) assume something about them or their socioeconomic class. Genres are themselves complex texts whose significations change over time as culture, tastes, and people change.

Music is (or isn't) a reflection of the culture that surrounds it.

Music is often of a time and place and can offer clues to the society in which it's written. For example, much of Bob Dylan's work in the turbulent 1960s directly reflects the world around it; his songs frequently engage the protest movements of the time. Gangsta rap also seemingly helps tell stories from disadvantaged areas with its focus on the dilemmas of living in such areas. These forms of music can bring a broader understanding of various social ailments to the "average" listener. By a bizarre and unfortunate coincidence, Ryan Adams's catchy tribute to New York City, "New York, New York," was just gaining popularity when the events of September 11, 2001, occurred. The song became an unintended anthem and tribute that has, for many, come to symbolize the hope and sacrifice that New Yorkers felt after the attacks.

But making automatic leaps from music to culture and vice versa can be problematic. Songwriters sometimes have social aims that go along with their music, and sometimes they don't. Even if they do, there can be unintended messages that flow from their music; music may unintentionally reflect society as well. For example, some people believe that disco music with its programmed beats and the sexual innuendo in many of its lyrics reflected the so-called shallow values of the 1970s, though those writing the music probably did not intend their music to have this effect. Similarly, since Kurt Cobain's suicide, some critics have associated the entire grunge sound with nihilism—something Cobain never would have wanted.

On a purely musical level, we can also listen to a song and place it in a particular era because of certain musical conventions of the period—identifiable instruments or sounds in general often give this away. Can you think of some conventions used today? Some we associate with a previous era? Think not only of songs but also of commercials. Do you remember when rap beats became a big part of commercials? It wasn't always so. . . .

Finally, sometimes musicians write songs that seem not to be of a time and place. Gillian Welch's popular album *Revival* sounds as though it is a relic from early twentieth-century Appalachia, yet Welch, a Californian with classical music training, recorded the record in 1995. Smash Mouth could fool some into believing they were around in the early '60s. What qualities do these artists convey in their songs? What do they avoid?

The packaging of music reflects the aims of the bands, or the record companies, or both, and it has an effect on the way we view the music.

The packaging of music involves a variety of things. Consumers are presented bands not only with their music, but their record cover, their band name, the album or song name—components that sit outside of the actual music itself. As you know, how musicians present themselves can be crucial to how we perceive them and probably how we perceive their music. For example, how would we view the music of Britney Spears coming from Tupac Shukar, and vice versa? Would Justin Timberlake be as popular if he looked like Dick Cheney? The persona of each of these artists contributes to the way we perceive them and their work.

Often we read performers not only from the packaging of an album but also visually through photographs in rock magazines, reports on entertainment shows, live concerts, and videos. In particular, the handlers of the musician or the musician himself or herself use the music video to provide another way of determining how potential consumers see the artist. Web sites do similar work but may offer different portrayals of the performer if the artist, a fanatical listener, or the record company sponsors the site.

Sometimes the packaging of an artist helps us understand what musicians think they are doing; other times the package is a wall that interferes with our experiencing music honestly or directly. Accordingly, we have to recognize that packaging comes as a part of listening to the music, and we can do with that information as we will. For example, many fans of musicians assume that these musicians "sell out" when they sign a record deal with a large corporation, often looking for evidence of such behavior in the music, as did the fans of the band R.E.M. in the 1990s when they moved from the independent label I.R.S. to the mega-label Warner Brothers. Others just listen to the music with little regard to packaging, marketing, or in some instances, lyrics.

Packaging also can reflect the times—if we see an image of a band from a different decade we may understand a more complex relationship between the band and its era. But in reading packaging of bands from past eras we have to take into account the same factors we do in evaluating packaging from our own era.

While the music we like may reflect personal taste, it may also reflect cultural tastes.

How many of you have heard of Toni Price? The Derailers? The Gourds? The Damnations? Dale Watson? Texan students may recognize these names, as all of these performers are hugely popular in the Austin, Texas, area, selling out concerts and receiving considerable air time on local radio stations. Yet, few people outside of Austin and even fewer outside of Texas know this music, despite the fact that Austin enjoys a reputation as a progressive musical city. Similarly, if you have grown up in a small town outside of Austin, rap, grunge, and trip-hop may never make it to local radio stations or to the record collections of your friends, and, therefore, by extension, it may never make its way into your life (although MTV's presence now makes that less likely). Even worse, if you are from the United States, you may never get exposure to British punk bands, fado music from Portugal, or Bulgarian *a cappella* choruses. Record stores and video music channels have gotten much better at featuring international music in the past few years, and the Internet provides much more opportunity for fans to find this music, but there remain vast quantities of music we will never hear, simply because those forms of music belong to other cultures and places.

In addition, for many people, what they encounter on television, the Internet, and in print determines their musical tastes. If bands do not make videos or are not featured in popular magazines, we may never know they exist. Many forms of alternative music never make it onto the airwaves; accordingly, potential listeners never find music outside of the mainstream. American trends toward playing and replaying market-tested music like pop, rock, country, and rap tends to reinforce listening tastes and habits. In short, you may like the music you do simply because that's all you've been exposed to. Thus, our tastes may depend less on comparison shopping or eclectic listening than the demands of the marketplace.

The music itself contains readable elements that contribute to the listener's experience.

Music creates moods as well as meaning. It's often hard to isolate the aspects of songs that make us feel a particular way. Often, performers intend the pace of a song, its intensity, or the sounds of the notes to affect listeners in specific ways. Hard-driving punk, smooth jazz, rap with samples and scratches, and string concertos with a lot of violins spark conscious and subconscious reactions. Sometimes, these reactions are strong and mysterious; other times, we know all too well why we feel what we do. Music functions much like poetry in that it evokes as much as it overtly states.

We can often tell by the pace of a song what the mood is—a fast song means something different than a slow song. The instruments in a song indicate/signify something (for example, the presence of trumpets or violins tells the listener something about the intentions of the artist). They are there to make the song sound better, but the way they sound better is often indicative of something else as well. Similarly, how the lyrics are sung may indicate how we are to read the song. For instance, Kurt Cobain's voice demands a kind of response that Celine Dion's does not; how we read Johnny Cash's voice will differ from how we read Aretha Franklin's.

The recent popularity of MP3 players such as the iPod have completely altered our relationship to music and public space. On the bus, the subway, while walking down the street or across campus, we see people bobbing their heads in giddy oblivion, and until we see the headphones protruding from their ears, we may think they are suffering some kind of seizure from an unknown malady. But these compact players have increased our ability to add sound-tracks to our days. In fact, in the past few months, psychologists have argued that listening to music this way actually makes people happier—and if you listen in the morning, it can dramatically affect your mood for the entire day.

The listeners create the music.

What we as listeners make of this sound, the packaging, and lyrics is largely up to us. We can choose to ignore the packaging, the lyrics, or the music, or a combination of the above, and arrive at one kind of interpretation. We can read biographies of musicians, watch their videos, or read the lyric sheets in a CD to get at a more complete reading of a musician or band. We can choose to listen to music on an expensive system that enhances the effects of a CD, listen to them on a car stereo, or a Walkman, and have that transform our understanding of the song. Or we can put our car radios on scan and find the first song that we like. . . .

THIS TEXT

1. Notice how each writer approaches the music generally, or a song or artist differently. Why do you think that's the case?

2. Do you think all the writers are music critics? What distinguishes a critic from a writer?

3. Do you think the writers are fans of the music they are writing about? What about their writing makes you draw that conclusion? Do you think writers should be fans of the music they write about?

4. Notice whether you can get the criteria for each writer's idea of what a good song or album would be.

5. How much do these writers think about the social impact of the music they write about? Do you think they think about it enough, or too much?

6. How are elements such as race and gender a part of the analysis here?

7. How does the background of the authors influence their ideas about music?

8. While it will be impossible for you to know this fully, try to figure out the writing situation of each author. Who is the audience? What does the author have at stake?

9. What social, political, economic, and cultural forces affect the author's text? What is going on in the world as she is writing?

10. What are the main points of the essay? Can you find a thesis statement anywhere?

11. How does the author support his argument? What evidence does he use to back up any claims he might make?

12. Is the author's argument valid and/or reasonable?

13. Do you find yourself in agreement with the author? Why or why not?

14. Does the author help you read music better than you did before reading the essay? If so, why?

15. How is the reading process different if you are reading an essay, as opposed to a short story or poem?

16. What is the agenda of the author? Why does she or he want me to think a certain way?

17. Did you like this? Why or why not?

BEYOND THIS TEXT

LYRICS

Theme: What are some of the themes of the song (themes are generally what the author thinks of the subject)? Are there both intentional and unintentional themes?

Plot: Is there a plot to the song? Does the song tell a story or convey a narrative?

Literary devices: Do you notice any such devices such as the use of figurative language (metaphor, simile) or repetition or rhyme? Are there notable symbols? Are these devices effective? Do they add to your enjoyment?

"Literariness": Do you think the lyrics have literary quality? Would the lyrics stand alone as a poem? Why or why not?

MUSIC

The instruments: What instruments does the band use? Does it use them effectively? Does their use symbolize anything outside of normal use?

Mood: What is the mood of the song? How does the music reflect this—through the makeup of its instruments, its speed, its tone (minor or major), or a combination of factors?

Technology: Are there technological aspects in the song? What are they? What effects do they have on the song?

THE WHOLE PACKAGE

Genre: How would you classify this song by genre? Would you do so by the lyrics or music? Why? Are there ways that songs resist classification? If so, in what ways?

Effectiveness: Does this song "work"? Why or why not? Is there an element of the song that's stronger than the others?

How and where it's played: Unlike a poem, you can hear songs in the car, in a dance club, in the elevator, on a date, in the doctor's office, and at church. How does setting influence how you hear a song?

Musical Cheese: The Appropriation of Seventies Music in Nineties Movies

Kevin J.H. Dettmar and William Richey

In this piece (1999), Kevin Dettmar and William Richey use the term **cheese** to examine the idea of music in movies. In doing so, they acknowledge the power that directors have in shaping not only audience responses to the music but to the movies in which music appears.

RECENTLY, WROQ, A GREENVILLE, SOUTH CAROLINA, radio station with a "classic rock" format, had a seventies weekend, featuring all the music from the 1970s that the station's moguls are trying to smuggle in under the classic rock umbrella (primarily dreck like Boston, Kansas, Aerosmith, et al.). At one point late on Saturday afternoon, the DJ came on the air at the close of a song and pleaded, with a note of some real desperation in his voice, not to have to field any more requests for the Bee Gees or Barry Manilow.

In our local battle of the FM airwaves, the other new player is a station, called "The New Q," that fashions itself as a homey, corporate alternative-rock venue (playing bands such as Pearl Jam, R.E.M., Soundgarden, Collective Soul, and Nirvana). Every Friday morning, however, they have an all-request show that features extended dance-mix versions of disco songs you haven't heard or thought about in years (but remember instantly—with a groan— when they come on). Listeners sat by helplessly the other morning as the full, unedited, and unexpurgated "Disco Duck" came on, followed in short order by Donna Summer's witty and sublime "MacArthur Park." In the few months since its inception, this retrodisco show has been successful enough that a local nightclub has installed a lighted, shamrock-shaped dance floor on which eighteen and ups can shake their boo-tays all night long: they can boogie-oogie-oogie till they just can't boogie no more. As we write this, we've now learned that they've instituted a platform-shoe night on Tuesdays. Lawsuits just waiting to happen.

So what's going on here? Just when you thought it was safe to turn the radio back on, seventies' schlock is back, in spades (and in bell-bottoms). And remember, this is South Carolina we're talking about, not L.A. or New York or Chicago. We're not a remarkably avantgarde group; this state has been sending Strom Thurmond to the U.S. Senate since before we were born.

What we would argue is that this new fondness for the disco decade is simply the South Carolina manifestation (or, to use a more regionally appropriate metaphor, infestation) of the national phenomenon that some commentators have called "cheese." Like "camp"—which Susan Sontag in the 1960s saw as so uniquely characteristic of the modern sensibility—cheese is a highly rhetorical embrace of those things that many would consider to be in bad taste. But, as a postmodern version of this mentality, cheese—we believe—differs from camp in two primary ways. First, it is somewhat more exclusive than camp, in that cheese is derived solely from the detritus of consumer culture. Thus, while Sontag can list both "The Brown Derby restaurant on Sunset Boulevard in LA" and "Bellini's operas" in her "canon of Camp," cheese is almost entirely a celebration of canceled TV shows, artless pop songs, and useless cultural artifacts like the lava lamp and the Chia Pet.[1] Second, we would argue that the attitudes encoded in cheese are even more indecipherable than those of camp. Despite camp's apparent delight in things usually considered excessive or overwrought, it never really loses sight of what good taste is. With cheese, however, the distinction between good and bad taste threatens to break down altogether, to the point that it becomes nearly impossible to tell when something is being celebrated and when it is being parodied.[2]

To explore the rather twisted metaphysics of cheese, we wish to examine how this current taste for third-rate music, to which WROQ's request line and The New Q's disco-on-demand program bear witness, has begun to assert itself in recent films, specifically how, over the past few years, movie soundtracks have started recycling some of the very worst of seventies' and eighties' pop/rock.[3] Our first example is Ben Stiller's *Reality Bites* (Universal Pictures, 1994), a film that at first glance appears to exemplify the concept of cheese perfectly. For the film's central quartet, the flotsam and jetsam of seventies' and eighties' popular culture assume an almost cultic status; they adorn their apartments with posters of Shawn Cassidy and disco-era Travolta, they pass their days watching reruns of seventies' sitcoms such as *Good Times* and *One Day at a Time,* and, of course, they delight in listening to the most mindless music from this thoroughly forgettable period in rock 'n' roll history. The most glaring instance of this adoration of cheese occurs when the Knack's "My Sharona" comes on the radio as the main characters are purchasing Pringles and diet Pepsis at an AM/PM mini-mart. After persuading the clerk to pump up the volume, the two women (Lalaina and Vicki) begin a manic but clearly choreographed dance routine to the song, much to the amazement of the forty-something clerk and the apparent distaste of their friend, Troy, the group's resident grunge philosopher.

Though the film's trailer would emphasize Lalaina and Vicki's giddy gyrations, the scene in its original context indicates that Troy's disdain is the appropriate response. Once the women have abandoned themselves to their dance, the camera cuts to a long shot in which we see them boogalooing wildly through the window of the convenience store. Seemingly, then, this moment of ironized fun soon gives way to some rather dour social commentary in which Stiller equates the music of the Knack with the disposable consumerism of contemporary society. This is junk music for a junk food culture, the film none too subtly says—or, to put it in Jamesonian terms, "post-modernism is the consumption of sheer commodification as a process."[4] The Knack, of course, provides perfect fodder for such a reading as they never pretended that they were anything more than a hit-making machine. In fact, as the *Meet the Beatles*-inspired cover of their first album suggests, the Knack's primary model was the Fab Four of the early sixties, the producers of catchy, easy-to-dance-to hits, not the Beatles' later incarnation as the prophets of universal peace and love. And "My Sharona" is essentially "I Want to Hold Your Hand" repackaged to cash in on the relaxed sexual mores of the seventies ("When you gonna give it to me, give it to me/It's just a matter of time, Sharona").[5]

A similarly ironic use of seventies' music immediately follows this scene. The film cuts directly from the convenience store back to Lalaina's apartment as she is getting ready for a date with Michael, a rising executive for a new music video network (it's "like MTV, but with an edge") whom Troy instantly deems a "yuppyhead cheeseball." Though somewhat sympathetically portrayed by Stiller himself, we soon realize that Michael is bad news, and again it is the soundtrack that provides the principal clue. As Michael and Lalaina sit in his BMW convertible drinking Big Gulps, Peter Frampton's "Baby I Love Your Way" plays in the background. When Lalaina naively asks, "Who's this again?" Michael replies incredulously, "I can't believe you don't remember *Frampton Comes Alive.* That album like totally changed my life." Frampton's music—though wildly popular in the late seventies—is no less gimmicky or vapid than the Knack's (e.g., "Ooh baby I love your way/Wanna tell you I love your way"); and so the film clearly indicates that the only fitting response to a man who claims his life was changed by such music is, "Get a life."[6] When Frampton serves as the accompaniment to Michael's seduction of Lalaina, it forcefully demonstrates how morally and aesthetically tainted she is becoming in this relationship: it's as if she's sleeping with her father's record collection. But, if Lalaina has temporarily lost her ironic distance from this seventies' dreck, Troy has not. Happening along just as Lalaina and Michael begin making love, he seems as disgusted by the Frampton as by Lalaina's taste in men. Once again, music acts as a kind of diacritical marker alerting us to the presence of irony. And the filmmakers assume that we can read the clues. While otherwise there might be some ambiguity to Michael's character, the music serves as a surefire sign that Michael is as slickly shallow as an Abba single.

Despite the film's gestures toward cheese, then, its irony ultimately takes a rather stable and traditional form: it enacts, in effect, a kind of a musical morality play. As her documentary about Gen Xer's "trying to find [their] own identity without having any real role models or heroes or anything" suggests, the character of Lalaina represents her generation's potential for optimism, and so her relationship with Michael poses the danger that her idealism might become corrupted. By contrast, Troy's problem is a deep-seated, almost crippling cynicism. During a club appearance with his band, Hey That's My Bike, he performs "I'm Nuthin'," a song that neatly sums up his sense of aimlessness and resentment. Here, he not only characterizes the nineties as a time of diminishing expectations ("I'm sick of people talkin'/About American dreams"), but he explicitly blames the previous generation, the baby boomers, for causing this situation.[7] By abandoning their youthful sixties' ideals for the greedy consumerism of the seventies and eighties, the boomers have at once destroyed their own moral credibility and sold the next generation down the river ("Before I was born/It was all gone"). In short, they pawned the future in exchange for big TVs, flashy garages, and designer drugs. The song's most potent irony, however, comes from its sly appropriation of the opening riff to the Stones' "Street Fighting Man." Whereas this sixties' rock anthem exhibits a similar sense of alienation ("'Cause in sleepy London town/There's no place for a Street Fighting Man"), the speaker's outrage seems on the verge of erupting into decisive action ("the time is right for a palace revolution").[8] For the despairing speaker of "I'm Nuthin'," this kind of action—thanks to the failed example of the boomers—has ceased to be a viable option. Sixties-style rebellion has become just another discredited cliché, a cultural myth that is no more believable than the American dream; the Beatles' "Revolution" is now just a Nike commercial. Thus, unlike the "street fighting man," who can define himself through his opposition to the status quo, this speaker has lost all sense of identity. He's "nuthin,'" as alienated by the left as by the right, by the counterculture as much as by the establishment.

Ultimately, though, Troy's jaded perspective is no more valorized than Lalaina's naïveté because something like sixties' idealism consistently threatens to rear its long-haired head from beneath the film's ironic surface. Lalaina—as we have seen—hopes that her documentary will have some impact on her g-g-g-generation and makes a promise to herself not to "unintentionally commercialize it." And even Troy says that he would like his band to "travel the country like Woody Guthrie," harking back to a time before music had become a multimillion dollar industry. As a result, much of the soundtrack has a distinctly sixties' flavor. While several selections sound like warmed-over psychedelic rock (e.g., Dinosaur Jr.'s "Turnip Farm"), others have a retro-folk (Lisa Loeb's "Stay") or sixties-revival quality (the Posies' "Going, Going, Gone") that contrasts with the slickly produced hits of contemporary Top 40. But, predictably, the film's touchstone for sincerity and commitment comes from those poster boys of socially conscious rock, U2, whose ballad "All I Want Is You" accompanies the "Dover Beach"–like efforts of Lalaina and Troy to find love and security amid the chaos of nineties' America, to blend their respective idealism and skepticism into a harmonious and productive union. Clearly, then, the film's sensibility is a long way from the irony Jameson sees as characteristic of our postmodern moment, an attitude characterized by "a new kind of flatness or depthlessness, a new kind of superficiality."[9] This is not to say that Jameson misunderstands postmodernism but rather that *Reality Bites*—for all its hipper-than-thou attitude—is just faux po-mo. Troy talks bravely about "riding his own melt," and most of the characters, for most of the film, seem happy enough with Bono's injunction to "slide down the surface of things";[10] but when the going gets really tough—when Troy's dad dies, and Troy and Lalaina's relationship seems on the verge of breaking up—the film shows its true colors. It comes through with a big, orchestrally reinforced ballad to reassure us that everything'll be all right.

By now, we hope it's clear how much the value system that *Reality Bites* promotes grows out of, or is disseminated through, its soundtrack. The Knack and Frampton, we are led to believe, are "bad" because their vacuousness is symptomatic of the commercialism of the seventies and eighties; U2 and the other usually acoustic, sixties-tinged music on the soundtrack is "good" because it symbolizes the social commitment of that decade. Still, despite the simplicity of this allegory, the film's use of music is actually more sophisticated than that of most rock soundtracks. Rather than using a sixties' song simply to evoke the decade of the sixties as *The Big Chill* or *Forrest Gump* do, *Reality Bites* uses the music and musical styles of the sixties, seventies, and eighties to frame and comment on its Generation X narrative. Moreover, unlike most soundtracks, it is not simply our response to this music that is important but that of the characters as well. Throughout *Reality Bites*, we regularly see the central characters listening to, reacting to, and talking about the songs on the soundtrack, and it is principally these reactions that enable us to assess their states of mind and values. In Bret Easton Ellis's *American Psycho*,[11] we know not to trust Patrick Bateman in part because he can narrate entire chapters about Huey Lewis and the News and (post-Peter Gabriel) Genesis; in *Reality Bites*, we know that Troy and Lalaina are OK because Bono sings at their reunion.

A purer, less processed form of cheese appears in *Wayne's World*, the 1992 Mike Myers film that we would argue began this trend toward ironically recontextualizing baby boomer music in Gen X movies. Of course, *Wayne's World* takes nothing from the previous generation seriously. The movie opens with some poor middle-aged schmuck named Ron Paxton showcasing his new invention, the Suck Kut, on Wayne and Garth's public-access cable show. Bad idea, Ron. Wayne's first comment is that Ron's brain-child "certainly does suck," and while Ron's doing a demo trim on Garth's melon, Wayne surreptitiously calls in the "Get-A-Load-Of-This-Guy Cam." Poor Paxton's sent packing as the show ends, with Wayne remarking that the Suck Kut is "a totally amazing, excellent discovery. Not!" Later in the film, of course, the hapless, terminally unhip video arcade tycoon Noah Van Der Hoff gets much the same treatment when Wayne uses his idiot cards as message boards with which to make an idiot of the founder of Noah's Arcades during his live interview on "Wayne's World," calling Van Der Hoff a "sphincter boy," suggesting that "this man has no penis," and insisting that "he blows goats. I have proof."

But like *Reality Bites, Wayne's World*'s most sublime irony, for our money, comes when Myers gets his hands on the boomers' music. The obvious place to start is with the film's use and abuse of Queen's "Bohemian Rhapsody." Wayne, cruising down the street in the passenger's seat of his buddy Garth's vintage AMC Pacer (a.k.a. the Mirthmobile), queries the passengers about car tunes: "I think we'll go with a little 'Bohemian Rhapsody,' gentlemen?" His pilot, Garth, answers in the affirmative ("Good call"), and Wayne pops his cassette into the tape deck (though we almost expect an 8-track player), while the whole carful—including a drunk guy in the back seat named Phil who's upright only because he's wedged between two others—sing along and begin to thrash their stringy hair (in fact, obviously cheap hairpieces, like Wayne's and Garth's) in synch with the music and one another. In the process, seventies' superstars Queen—and particularly one of their signature songs, "Bohemian Rhapsody"—get "spun" in *Wayne's World*. It seems clear to us that Myers is sending the band up; the overproduced and deadly self-important music of Queen and the torch singer role so eagerly adopted by Freddie Mercury make a great source of cheese, and Myers uses Wayne and Garth's devotion to them as a way to flesh out their characterization. But it's finally a judgment call, for there's no firm textual or contextual evidence that the boys in the Mirthmobile think the song is anything but "Excellent": Wayne maintains a steady accompaniment of air guitar and air drums throughout and has a beatific grin on his face (as does Garth) as the song fades out that looks strangely like afterglow. Indeed, the sing-along participation in the song in the tight space of Garth's Pacer represents, among other things, a socially sanctioned moment of male bonding in a youth culture that provides few such opportunities. How bad can a song be, finally, if it allows adolescent males to connect in the midst of a homophobic atmosphere that forbids absolutely any such engagement?

This is the kind of unstable, postmodern irony that Linda Hutcheon describes: suspicious of "transcendental certitudes of any kind, including the subject" (and, we might add, taste), "postmodern irony . . . denies the form of dialectic and refuses resolution of any kind in order to retain the doubleness that is its identity."[12] Try as you might, you'll find no way to establish an ironic reading of this scene. To judge it an ironic treatment of "Bohemian Rhapsody," as we are, one must assert a distance between Mike Myers as writer and Wayne Campbell as narrator. This is doubly difficult because part of the dynamic in *Wayne's World* is that Myers is himself a late boomer rather than a Generation Xer: his character, Wayne, however, is an Xer, a slacker, all dressed up in black T-shirt and blue jeans—as well as "an extensive collection of name tags and hair nets"—but no place to go. It thus seems to us that the irony of "Bohemian Rhapsody" in the Mirthmobile—Schlock Opera lip-synched in the 1970's version of the Edsel—cuts two ways. The music of Queen is shown up as cheesy through the comic stylings of Wayne, Garth, and crew; thus Myers points a condemning finger at the excesses and narcissism of the progressive seventies' art rock with which he must have grown up that contrasts so sharply with the self-consciously disposable pop of "My Sharona." At the same time, however, Wayne and Garth are indicted, for they've pulled

"Bohemian Rhapsody" from the trash heap of contemporary history, dusted it off, and popped it into the tape deck; no saturation airplay has forced them to listen to, and hum along with, Queen against their will. They've brought this on themselves.

But wait: there's more. It gets weirder. After *Wayne's World*'s theatrical release, and the MTV video of the boys popping their heads to "Bohemian Rhapsody" in their Pacer got a lot of airplay, Queen actually enjoyed something of a renaissance, akin to the brief *Reality Bites*–inspired rebirth of the Knack—including a retrospective (and, in Freddie Mercury's case, posthumous) live album and live videos released and put in heavy rotation on MTV—which leads us to suspect that the irony that we think we see was missed by much of the audience. Freddie Mercury's death from AIDS in November 1991, only months before the film's release, doubtless had something to do with the revival of Queen's fortunes, and we don't wish to downplay this aspect. But an entire generation of music consumers was introduced to Queen, and "Bohemian Rhapsody," by *Wayne's World,* and they didn't see anything wrong with it: indeed, they thought it was "Excellent."

There are any number of other examples of this unstably ironic use of boomer tunes in the film. One thematic that we'd like to note briefly is the way that this avowedly cheesy music determines the structure of romantic and sexual desire in the Dynamic Duo. Garth's pure, chaste love of the Dreamwoman who works behind the counter at Stan Mikita's donut shop is figured in the soundtrack by Tchaikovsky's "Fantasy Overture" from *Romeo and Juliet,* surely a musical cliché of romantic love if ever there was one. But tellingly, when spurred on by Cassandra actually to break his silence and speak to her, Garth soundtracks his daydream/fantasy with Jimi Hendrix's "Foxy Lady." The choreography of this number is absolutely masterful; at one point in his waltz toward the counter, it appears as though Garth is being pulled toward his Dreamwoman by an invisible fishhook in the zipper of his trousers; as he gyrates toward her, he looks down in amazement at his seemingly possessed crotch. And as for the lyrics: well, most of us who listened to Hendrix before he was retro didn't listen for the lyrics, and when Garth makes little feral ears with his fingers while calling his Lady "Foxy," we're painfully reminded of *why* we ignored the lyrics. Ouch. As for Wayne and his lady, Cassandra, his theme song is—gulp—Gary Wright's eminently forgettable "Dream Weaver."

Aerosmith is the moral/aesthetic equivalent of Queen in *Wayne's World 2.* How many folks turned out to see *Wayne's World 2* simply because it contains live footage of Aerosmith? This makes for very complicated irony, of course, because Aerosmith, we think, takes itself pretty seriously even if Mike Myers doesn't. As with all interesting, postmodern irony, the use of Queen and Aerosmith in the *Wayne's World* films poses one particularly tricky question: *you* know that Mike Myers doesn't take Steve Tyler as seriously as Tyler takes himself, and *we* know it, but *how* do we know it? This irony is unstable because one can never prove with any certainty that it is even irony. Watching Aerosmith at Waynestock, the spectator is at some loss to discover precisely how s/he's to read Aerosmith's concert performance and Steve Tyler's adolescent mike humping. It's as if Wayne and Garth put Aerosmith up on the Waynestock stage and announce, "Hey, these guys are great! Not!!" But that "not" teasingly remains unvoiced.

In fact, the closest we get to a theory of irony in the *Wayne's World* films is at the end of the first movie, after the credits have been rolling for a time. Wayne and Garth are suddenly back up on the screen, to bid us adieu, and Wayne says into the camera: "Well, that's all the time we have for our movie. We hope you found it entertaining, whimsical, and yet relevant, with an underlying revisionist conceit that belied the film's emotional attachments to the subject matter." Wow! This is Wayne Campbell talking? Suddenly Wayne's become a native philosopher of postmodernism, positing in one economical sentence a theory of postmodern irony as compelling as anything written by Jameson or Hutcheon. But Wayne and Garth are a team; Wayne's brief disquisition is only half the story without Garth's rejoinder: "I just hope you didn't think it sucked." For postmodern irony can allow nothing to stand un-scathed, not even Wayne's definition of postmodern irony itself.

In the soundtracks to the films of Quentin Tarantino, we also find something approaching an aesthetics of pure cheese. The director's fondness for bad pop music is unmistakable, for rather than simply mixing in an occasional rock song for period color, he constructs entire soundtracks out of successions of not-quite-forgotten pop singles. *Reservoir Dogs,* for example, uses nothing but K-Billy's "Super Sounds of the Seventies" for the film's musical score, a strategy that, according to Tarantino himself, provides "somewhat of an ironic counterpoint to what you are seeing on the screen."[13] This is, for the most part, an accurate assessment: these unrelentingly superficial songs generally do help to distance us from the blood and often gut-wrenching violence of the film. Plus the cheesiness of the soundtrack constantly reminds us of the fact that this is a story about cheap hoods. Unlike its precursors in the heist movie genre—*The Asphalt Jungle, Riffifi, The Killing*—*Reservoir Dogs* does not ask us to empathize with the characters or to find tragic dignity in their plight, something that would be far more likely to happen if it had used a more conventional Miklos Rozsa/Jerry Goldsmith score. At the same time, though, we have to take the "somewhat" in Tarantino's statement seriously. Often, his specific musical choices have an unexpected aptness as in the most famous and memorable scene from the film: the torture sequence performed to Stealers Wheel's "Stuck in the Middle with You."[14] At first, the bouncy, hand-clap-accented beat of this "Dylanesque, pop, bubble-gum favorite" seems thoroughly out of keeping with the uncom-promising violence of the scene. But without this accompaniment, we would miss the glee that the torturer, Mr. Blonde, takes in his task, especially when he breaks into an impromptu dance in between his assaults on the young cop tied to the chair. Moreover, as the scene continues, the nasal drone of Gerry Rafferty's vocal becomes increasingly irritating, thereby intensifying the agony of this already agonizing scene. And, finally, if we can bring ourselves to concen-trate on the lyrics to the song, we notice that Tarantino himself seems to be taking an almost sadistic glee in the grim ironies of the scene. While the opening line, "I'm so scared I guess I'll fall off my chair," clearly contrasts with the condition of this thoroughly bound and gagged cop, the words of the song's title become cruelly literalized. The cop is stuck in the middle of this warehouse where his torturer is sticking him in the gut with a razor.

In *Pulp Fiction,* Tarantino's use of music is even more creative and unorthodox. With its eclectic mix of various music genres from the sixties, seventies, eighties, and nineties, the soundtrack exhibits the kind of "depthlessness" that Frederic Jameson decries in his jeremi-ads against postmodern art, and so—in sharp contrast to most rock soundtracks—it provides no reliable contextual clues to ground the narrative or situate the viewer. The opening cred-its sequence exemplifies how this kind of aesthetic and temporal destabilization works. First, we hear Dick Dale's sixties' surf guitar instrumental, "Misirlou," and then, in what may be an ironic nod at the soundtrack of *Reservoir Dogs,* the channel is changed to a new station on which Kool and the Gang's R&B hit "Jungle Boogie" is playing. Tarantino's rationale for these choices is instructive. "Misirlou" he describes as sounding like "the beginning of *The Good, the Bad, and the Ugly* with those trumpets, that almost Spanish sound. Having 'Misir-lou' as your opening credits, it just says, 'You're watching an epic, you're watching this big old movie, just sit back.'" The sudden switch to Kool and the Gang, however, works both to star-tle the viewer and to signal the film's "other personality": its appropriation of "this black ex-ploitation thing."[15]

In this way, Tarantino provides his viewer with quite a bit of information. There is no whiter music on the planet than surf music, while "Jungle Boogie" is obviously very black and urban. The only common denominator is their mutual cheesiness. With the coming of the British Invasion, psychedelia, and the Summer of Love, surf music was—until its recent Dick Dale–led renaissance—rendered terminally uncool, its clean-cut, All-American image being totally out of step with the increasingly radicalized atmosphere of the sixties. Similarly, Kool and the Gang are never going to be confused with Stevie Wonder or Marvin Gaye, and this song in particular seems designed to create as insulting a stereotype of African-American culture as possible. Nonetheless, Tarantino claims to be genuinely fond of both songs. He says that he "always really dug surf music," and while he admits "if I had to choose between Al Green or 'Jungle Boogie' I would probably choose Al Green," he maintains that "the early Kool and the Gang records were great." Here, then, the irony seems to be at least as unreadable as anything in *Wayne's World*. While in that film the distinction between Wayne and Mike Myers occasionally blurs, in *Pulp Fiction* such a distinction is impossible to find because Tarantino seemingly recognizes the ironic effect that such musical choices have but refuses to pass judgment on them or to acknowledge them as bad. This is a man who truly likes surf music and who can distinguish between the early, golden age of Kool and the Gang and their later decadence—who can distinguish for us among the good, the bad, and the ugly.

This suspension of judgment—this mixture of emotional involvement and ironic detachment—is, we believe, the principle on which Tarantino's brand of postmodernism depends. To construct his narrative, he creates a pastiche of B-movie allusions (*Kiss Me Deadly, The Killers, The Set-Up*) as well as several references to more mainstream fare (*Rocky, Deliverance*), but he puts them to unfamiliar, unexpected ends; he carefully creates atmosphere and attitude but divorces them from any clearly identifiable content or message. His use of pop music works similarly. These familiar or seemingly familiar songs set our toes tapping and heads bobbing involuntarily, even as our minds ask, "What *is* this shit?" They both draw us in and draw attention to themselves. During the episode in which the hit man, Vincent Vega, takes Mia Wallace, his boss's young wife, out on a date, we see two more examples of this strategy in action. When Vincent first comes to pick her up, she is playing Dusty Springfield's "Son of a Preacher Man" on the stereo. According to Tarantino, he wrote the scene with this song in mind: "That whole sequence, I've had in my head for six or seven years. And it was always scored to 'Son of a Preacher Man.' That was the key to the sequence. I can't even imagine it without 'Son of a Preacher Man'." But to most viewers—ourselves included—the immediate reaction would be simply, "Why?" What is it about this song that is so central to this scene? First of all, that Mia would be playing this song seems highly unlikely given the fact that it was released before she would have been born. Plus, when we consider the lyrics to the song, they seem to contradict the situation in the film flatly: this heroin-shooting hit man is unlikely to be taken for the son of a preacher man. And yet—as in Tarantino's earlier use of "Stuck in the Middle with You"—there is indeed something right about the way the song works in this scene. Much of the tension in the episode results from the fact that Mia, like the preacher's son, is off limits; it's not just that she's the wife of Vincent's boss but that her husband reportedly ordered another employee to be thrown out of a four-story building for giving Mia a foot massage. She's forbidden fruit—something that Mia herself underscores later in the episode when she says, "Besides it's more exciting when you don't have permission"—and it's this taboo aspect of the meeting that makes Mia and Vincent so desirable to one another.

Furthermore, this white man's—or in this case—white woman's soul music helps to establish the ersatz quality that will pervade the rest of the episode. Mia's choice of a restaurant is Jack Rabbit Slim's, a faux-fifties' diner, complete with Ed Sullivan, Marilyn Monroe, and Buddy Holly impersonators and tables inside Chrysler convertibles. Though this environment creates a superficial sense of wholesomeness (the soundtrack for much of this segment is by that most clean-cut of fifties' pop idols, Ricky Nelson), the seaminess of Tarantino's pulp fiction is never far beneath the surface. For example, when Mia excuses herself—in good fifties' fashion—to go "powder my nose," Tarantino perversely literalizes this seemingly decorous euphemism by showing her snorting coke in the bathroom. Once they return to Mia's house— euphoric over their victory in the Jack Rabbit Slim's dance contest—the sexual subtext becomes overt. Now, when Vincent goes off to "take a piss," Mia puts on some mood music—which, in one further knowing anachronism, she plays on a reel-to-reel tape recorder. This time her choice is somewhat more contemporary—Urge Overkill's cover version of Neil Diamond's "Girl, You'll Be a Woman Soon"—and here, again, Tarantino seems to be constructing a largely unreadable irony. On one level, this song serves as the flip side of "Son of a Preacher Man." Just as Vincent is clearly no preacher's kid, Mia—with her Cleopatraesque hairdo, her vampish makeup, and sex-kitten manner—is clearly already a woman. Still, the irony does not work through simple inversion or kitsch. Tarantino doesn't appear to be ridiculing this silly love song, and, as we might expect by now, he claims even to like the original version: "Well, I love Neil Diamond, and I have always loved Neil Diamond's version of that song, but [Urge Overkill's] version is even better." Here, however, we think Tarantino is being somewhat disingenuous as there is no way that the scene would have worked if he had used the Neil Diamond version: the irony would be overdetermined, and we would laugh out loud as we do at "My Sharona" in *Reality Bites* or "Dream Weaver" in *Wayne's World*. On the other hand, by using this bass-heavy, flamenco version, Tarantino defamiliarizes Neil Diamond's cheesy ballad so that—in spite of its pedigree—the song succeeds in heightening the intensity of the scene. In this case, rock 'n' roll really does have "the beat of sexual intercourse"[16]—and so while we may be aware that this is a Neil Diamond song, we don't let that intrude on the mounting sexual tension until the scene yields a final grim irony. Mistaking Vincent's heroin for a bag of cocaine, Mia snorts it, with the result that it seems this girl will be a corpse soon.

Perhaps, though, the best way to demonstrate what makes Tarantino's use of music so distinctive is by viewing it in direct comparison with Ben Stiller's more conventional handling of his films' soundtracks. In a key scene from Stiller's recent directorial effort, *The Cable Guy,* Jim Carrey's Chip Douglas, the title character, performs a thoroughly over-the-top karaoke version of Jefferson Airplane's "Somebody to Love." Gyrating in front of a TV screen swirling with psychedelic colors and patterns, he flaps the ridiculously long fringes of his sixties' leather jacket while grotesquely exaggerating the vibrato of Grace Slick's original vocal. Clearly, the song is being ironized as we are asked to participate in this knowing send-up of Bay Area psychedelia, but, at the same time, we are also intended to recognize how revealing this character's choice of songs is. After all, the entire narrative of the film revolves around the attempts of this TV-obsessed cable guy to achieve some real human contact by befriending a customer: he truly does want someone to love. Thus Stiller's basic strategy is to make fun of the song's surface features while using its lyrical content to further the plot and provide reliable insight into his character's psyche.[17] As his use of "Son of a Preacher Man" and "Girl, You'll Be a Woman Soon" indicates, Tarantino's modus operandi is the exact opposite. Unlike Stiller, he never openly parodies the music he selects, and—rather than using the soundtrack to underscore the film's narrative line—he often creates a highly unstable, even contradictory relationship between the song lyrics of the soundtrack and the action taking place on the screen.

A second example comes from what is for us a very fortuitous coincidence. At one point, Tarantino considered using "My Sharona" for the "sodomy rape sequence" during the later "Gold Watch" episode in *Pulp Fiction* because, as he explains, " 'My Sharona' has a really good sodomy beat to it." The plan eventually fell through because the Knack objected to this appropriation of their song and decided to let Stiller use it in *Reality Bites* instead. Thinking back on his original plan, Tarantino is now pleased that he had to use "Comanche," another surf music cut: "I like using stuff for comic effect, but I don't want it to be har, har, wink, wink, nudge, nudge, you know?"[18] Once again, this kind of irony is for Tarantino too broad and easily decipherable, and so he sets up a far more complex and demanding scenario for his viewers. He expects us to recognize the songs he selects and to acknowledge their cheesiness, but, by using them in unexpected and unfamiliar contexts, he alters our experience of them. As a result, we start to hear them in something like the way Tarantino himself does, a man who boasts of liking "certain music that nobody else on the planet has an appreciation for."

From this last comment, it seems to us, a whole new problematic arises because here Tarantino appears to take a perverse pride in his sense of taste, a stance that appears to conflict with his usual self-representation as an aesthetic man of the people. In a recent *New York Times* interview, for instance, he dismissed the idea that he is a "collector" of pop culture by saying, "I don't believe in elitism. I don't think the audience is this dumb person lower than me. I am the audience."[19] But, as in the above quotation, Tarantino does on occasion appear to congratulate himself for having a more highly evolved sensibility, an aesthetic sense so acute that he can find beauty in things that most people see as having no socially redeeming value. It may be something of a Bizarro standard of taste, but it's a standard of taste nonetheless. Such a statement, then, reveals how difficult it is to maintain the kind of instability and undecidability that we see as the hallmarks of cheese and how tenuous the distinction between camp and cheese really is. Cheese may be, finally, all about self-consciousness, but, paradoxically, cheese that betrays its self-consciousness, its aesthetic investments, quickly spoils and loses its ability to delight and instruct.

Notes

1. Susan Sontag, "Notes on Camp," in *A Susan Sontag Reader* (New York: Vintage, 1983), p. 107.
2. Since cheese is of relatively recent vintage, there have been few academic or theoretical treatments of it. To our knowledge, the fullest discussion is in Michiko Kakutani's August 7, 1992, *New York Times* article, "Having Fun by Poking Pun: A New Esthetic Called Cheese" (B1, B6). Here, Kakutani usefully compares cheese to camp, noting very accurately that cheese "willfully focuses on the vulgar, the meretricious, the bogus"; she goes on to argue that, unlike the "generous" spirit of camp, "cheese tends to be judgmental, cynical, and detached" (B6). This—as the following examples we hope will demonstrate—is a severe misrepresentation of how genuine cheese functions. No less than camp, cheese "relishes, rather than judges" (Sontag, "Notes," 119), but it takes this process one step further, effectively obliterating or at least ignoring the distinctions between good and bad art, high and popular culture that underlie most standards of aesthetic judgment.
3. For other analyses of rock music soundtracks, see Claudia Gorbham, *Unheard Music: Narrative Film Music* (London: BFI, 1987); R. Serge Denisoff, *Risky Business: Rock in Film* (New Brunswick, NJ: Transaction, 1991); Lawrence Grossberg, "The Media Economy of Rock Culture: Cinema, Post-Modernity, and Authenticity" in *Sound and Vision: The Music Video Reader,* ed. Simon Frith, Andrew Goodwin, and Lawrence Grossberg (London: Routledge, 1993), pp. 185–209.
4. Fredric Jameson, *Postmodernism: or, The Cultural Logic of Late Capitalism* (Durham, NC: Duke University Press, 1991), pp. x, 17.
5. The Knack, "My Sharona," *Reality Bites* (RCA 44364, 1994).

6. Peter Frampton, "Baby I Love Your Way," *Frampton Comes Alive* (A&M 540930, 1976; reissue, 1998).
7. Ethan Hawke, "I'm Nuthin'," *Reality Bites.*
8. The Rolling Stones, "Street Fighting Man," *Beggar's Banquet* (ABKCO 7539, 1968).
9. Jameson, *Postmodernism,* p. 9.
10. U2, "Even Better than the Real Thing," *Achtung Baby* (Island 314–510 347-2, 1991).
11. Bret Easton Ellis, *American Psycho* (New York: Vintage, 1991).
12. Linda Hutcheon, "The Power of Postmodern Irony," in *Genre, Trope, Gender: Critical Essays by Northrop Frye, Linda Hutcheon, and Shirley Neuman* (Ottawa: Carelton University Press, 1992), p. 35.
13. "Truth and Fiction," liner notes to *Pulp Fiction/Reservoir Dogs* (MCACD 11188, 1994), p. 7.
14. Stealer's Wheel's "Stuck in the Middle with You," *Reservoir Dogs* (MCA 10541, 1992).
15. "Truth and Fiction," pp. 5–7.
16. This infamous quotation is, of course, from Allan Bloom, *The Closing of the American Mind* (New York: Simon and Schuster, 1987), p. 73. Bloom continues with a comment that sheds an interesting light on the flamenco feel of Urge Overkill's cover: "That is why Ravel's *Bolero* is the one piece of classical music that is commonly known and liked by them ["young people"]."
17. As in *Reality Bites,* Stiller's use of music may not be as enigmatic as Tarantino's, but it is by no means simplistic. This scene works on an additional level as well because Carrey's performance is intercut with the foreplay of Steven—the Cable Guy's would-be friend—and a young woman whom we later learn is a prostitute hired by the Cable Guy. The song thus also applies to Steven—especially when we consider that he only subscribes to cable because he has just broken up with his girlfriend. This may only be a pay-per-screw version of the Summer of Love, but Steven, too, is seeking someone to love.
18. "Truth and Fiction," p. 16.
19. Lynn Hirschberg, "The Man Who Changed Everything," *New York Times Magazine,* 16 November 1997, p. 116.

READING WRITING

This Text: Reading

1. What value do Dettmar and Richey place on the intelligent use of music in movies? How do we know this? Do you have similar values?
2. Review the authors' definition of cheese. Is it a positive definition or a negative one? Name something else that is "cheesy."
3. How often do you pay attention to the music in movies? Or do you try to avoid paying attention?
4. Like other forms of expression, music necessarily reflects a variety of factors, some of them beyond the control of the musician. What do you think of Quentin Tarantino's ideas about using music in movies? Do you think they are consistent with the musician's intent?

Your Text: Writing

1. Do your own examination of cheese in a popular text. What other popular culture form contains its share of cheese?
2. Music soundtracks are notorious for being manipulative. Watch—and listen to—a movie and document where the director uses music to indicate mood. Write a short paper examining this idea.
3. How does "seeing" a favorite song change your view of it? Write a short paper examining your response to a favorite song in a movie.

The Rock Lexicon

Chuck Klosterman

Chuck Klosterman is one of America's most prominent commentators on popular culture. The author of four books, *Fargo Rock City*; *Sex, Drugs, and Cocoa Puffs*; *Killing Yourself to Live*; and the recently released *Chuck Klosterman IV*, Klosterman has written for *Spin*, *Esquire*, and *ESPN.com*, among many outlets. Here (2005) he writes about the arcane definitions of genres he encountered as a writer for *Spin*.

"I DON'T READ YOUR MAGAZINE ANYMORE," says my 36-year-old sister as we ride in a rental car. "I don't read your magazine anymore because all you guys ever write about is emo, and I don't get it."

Now, for a moment, I find myself very interested in what my sister is saying. I absolutely cannot fathom what she could possibly hate about emo, and (I suspect) this subject might create an interesting ten minutes of rental-car discussion. Does she find emo too phallocentric? Do the simplistic chord progressions strike her as derivative? Why can't she relate to emo? I ask her these questions, and I await her answer. But her answer is not what I expect.

"No, no," she says. "When I say I don't get emo, I mean I literally don't know what it is. The word may as well be Latin. But I keep seeing jokes about emo in your magazine, and they're never funny, because I have no idea what's supposed to be funny about something I've never heard of."

This, of course, leads to a spirited dialogue in which I say things like "'Emo' is short for emotional," and she says things like "But all pop music is about emotions," and I respond by saying, "It's technically a style of punk rock, but it's actually more of a personal, introspective attitude," and she counters with "That sounds boring," and then I mention Andy Greenwald (author of *Nothing Feels Good: Punk Rock, Teenagers, and Emo*), and she asks, "Wasn't Andy Greenwald a defensive end for the Pittsburgh Steelers in the late '70s?" and I say, "No, that was L.C. Greenwood, and I'm pretty sure he doesn't know any of the members of Senses Fail."

But anyway, I learned something important from this discussion: that reading rock magazines must be very confusing to people who only listen to rock music casually. Whenever journalists write about music, we always operate under the assumption that certain genres are self-evident and that placing a given band into one of those categories serves an expository purpose. Just as often, an artist will be described as a synthesis of two equally obscure subgenres, and we're all supposed to do the sonic math ourselves. However, this only helps the informed; that kind of description is useful to those who have already conquered the rock lexicon. What we need is a glossary of terms so we can all share an equal playing field.

I will do my best.

DISCO METAL: This is up-tempo, semiheavy guitar rock that someone (usually a stripper) could feasibly dance to. White Zombie made a lot of songs in this style. Weirdly, it does not seem to apply to straightforward metal bands (Kiss, Van Halen) who overtly write disco songs ("I Was Made for Lovin' You," "Dance the Night Away"). No one knows why.

SHOEGAZE: Music by artists who stare at their feet while performing—presumably because they are ashamed to be playing such shambolic music to an audience of weirdos.

POST-ROCK: This is when a group of rock musicians employ traditional rock instrumentation to perform music for people who traditionally listen to rock—except these musicians don't play rock and the songs don't have any vocals. I don't get it either. The premier band of this genre is Tortoise, and the kind of people who like post-rock are the same kind of people who think it's a good idea to name a band Tortoise.

PSYCH: (as in "psychedelic") The modifier psych has only recently come back in vogue, which is interesting. You have possibly heard the terms "psych folk" (sometimes applied to artists in the vein of Devendra Banhart) or "psych country" (which is vaguely similar to what used to be called "outlaw country") or "psych rock" (which is what Courtney Taylor of the Dandy Warhols calls his band's sound in the documentary *DIG!*). I've made a great effort to try to find the unifying principle among these permutations of psych music, and the answer is probably what you'd expect: This is music for drug addicts, made by drug addicts. If you are in a Tejano quartet and all four of you start taking mescaline (and if all the kids who come to your shows drop acid in the parking lot before entering the venue), you now play "psych Tejano." That's the whole equation.

GRIME: Almost two years ago, I asked two learned people at *Spin* to explain to me what grime is. They both said, "Don't worry about it. You will never need to know. It's completely unnecessary knowledge." Then, over the next few weeks, grime came up in conversation on three separate occasions. And it would always come up in the same manner: Someone would mention either Dizzee Rascal or the Streets, refer to them as grime artists, and immediately be told, "Those aren't real grime artists. That's not real grime." As such, this is all I know about grime—it's British rap (but not really) that is kind of "like garage and 2-step" (but the word garage is pronounced like marriage), and it's supposedly a reflection of life in lower-class London neighborhoods like Brixton. If anyone out there knows what grime is, e-mail me at cklosterman@spin.com. But make sure you write "This is about grime" in the subject line so I will know to ignore it completely.

FASHION ROCK: The concept of fashion rock revolves around (a) appearing to be impoverished while (b) spending whatever little money you possess on stylish clothing (and possibly cocaine). In short, fashion rockers aspire to look like superfancy hobos, which is obviously nothing new (this look was called "gutter glam" by L.A. hair bands in the 1980s and "mod" by British goofballs in the late 1960s). What's curious, however, is that fashion rock—though defined by clothing—does seem to have an identifiable sound, which is a kind of self-conscious sloppiness that translates as a British version of the Strokes (this is best illustrated by the Libertines, but even more successfully by the Killers, possibly because they are not even British).

RAWK: This is how people who start bands in order to meet porn stars spell rock. It is also applied to long-haired guitar players who can't play solos.

PROG: There was a time when "progressive rock" was easy to define, and everybody knew who played it—Jethro Tull, ELP, Yes, and other peculiar, bombastic men who owned an inordinate number of Moog synthesizers during the mid-1970s. This was an extremely amusing era for rock; the single best example from the period was King Crimson's 1969 song "21st Century Schizoid Man," a track built on a spooky two-pronged premise: What would it be like to encounter a fellow who was not only from the distant future, but also suffering from an untreated mental illness? At the time, "21st Century Schizoid Man" was the definition of progginess. However, just about anything qualifies as prog in 2005. An artist can be referred to as "kind of proggy" if he or she does at least two of the following things: writes long songs, writes songs with solos, writes songs about mythical creatures, writes songs that girls hate, grows a beard, consistently declines interview requests, mentions Dream Theater as an influence, claims to be working on a double album, claims to be working on a rock opera, claims to have already released a rock opera, appears to be making heavy metal for people who don't like heavy metal, refuses to appear in his or her own videos, makes trippy music without the use of drugs, uses laser technology in any capacity, knows who Dream Theater is.

MUSK OX ROCK: Combining woolly '90s grunge with the ephemeral elasticity of Icelandic artists like Björk and Sigur Rós, so-called oxenheads deliver thick, nurturing power riffs that replicate the experience of melting glaciers, troll attacks, and political alienation. The genre includes bands such as Switchfoot, Radiohead, and Bettie Serveert.

IDM: This is an acronym for "Intelligent Dance Music." Really. No, really. I'm serious. This is what they call it. Really.

READING WRITING

This Text: Reading

1. How familiar are you with the genres that Klosterman writes about? Are there others that you know that are similarly obscure? Why do you think we categorize music this way?
2. In what ways does Klosterman use humor to make his point?
3. What purpose does the conversation with his sister serve?

Your Text: Writing

1. Write a short definitional paper about a particular genre, using examples to define it.
2. Write a persuasive paper arguing for abolishment of genre considerations. What would the musical world look like in such a scenario?
3. Invent your own genre and write a speculative piece defining it. What would it sound like? Who would listen to it?

We Are the Champions, Another One Bites the Dust

Daniel Nester

Daniel Nester wrote a poem in response to every Queen song, filling two volumes, *God Save the Queen* and *God Save the Queen II*. These are taken from his first collection. He is an assistant professor of English at the College of Saint Rose and he edits *Unpleasant Event Schedule,* an online literary journal.

We Are the Champions

In 1977, legend has it that the Sex Pistols were recording in a studio adjacent to Queen's. Pistols bassist Sid Vicious wanders into the wrong room, and bumps into Freddie Mercury, who sits at his piano with four fingers of vodka.

"Ah, Freddie Mercury," Sid says smugly, staggering.[1] "Bringing ballet to the masses then?" Freddie takes a sip, looks up from his instrument.

"Oh yes, Mister Ferocious," Freddie says. "Well, we're doing our best, my dear."[2]

---

[1] Liza Minelli's version of WATC, Freddie Mercury memorial concert, Wembley Arena (London, April 19, 1992). Billie Jean King and Freddie Mercury at Studio 54, *New York Post* reports rumor of "romance," 1978.

[2] "They were *both* afraid of each other, actually."—Jim Jenkins, Breakthru 2002 Fan Club Convention (Q&A session, August 17, 2002).

Another One Bites the Dust

Every man runs the same line, tries real hard to see how it would have all crashed down, which it most certainly does. Another defeated genre, another wide-eyed and wide-tied analyst.[3]

But this man completely hates metronomic duties as he fills another's coffers—*at least that's what I'm thinking right now,* the speaker thinks. So they go skiing together, and everything will be OK.

Another firearm-themed ditty, Michael Jackson's disco business advice.[4]

READING WRITING

This Text: Reading

1. What do you think of Nester's poems? How related to the Queen songs are they?
2. What qualities about music do Nester's poems demonstrate?
3. Why does Nester use footnotes here?

Your Text: Writing

1. Listen to a favorite album of yours and write responses to a few songs. Are you surprised by the associations that come up during listening?
2. Write a paper that compares Nester's poem to the actual lyrics of a Queen song. In what ways does Nester engage the lyrics?

Right on Target: Revisiting Elvis Costello's *My Aim Is True*

Sarah Hawkins

Student Essay

Sarah Hawkins wrote this review/re-evaluation for an advanced composition class at the University of San Francisco in 2001. A persuasive piece of sorts, she tries to reintroduce an artist (with whom many of her professors are familiar) to a younger audience.

ELVIS COSTELLO IN A NUTSHELL: a frustrated, neurotic, nonconformist who just so happens to be endlessly talented. With a song-writing capability second only to John Lennon and an Ani Difranco–esque tenacity, Elvis Costello is a pop music figure that cannot be ignored. *My Aim Is True* blends the personal with the political, shapes music to emotion, and captures moods ranging from stark depression to danceable

---

[3] Single released August 1980. "Disco? Queen ate it up and spit it out for breakfast"—Kal Rudman, editor of the Cherry Hill, NJ–based radio tip sheet *Friday Morning Quarterback* (1980). Chic, "Good Times" (single released June 1979, also on *Risqué,* 1979). Sugar Hill Gang, "Rapper's Delight" (single only, September 1979).

[4] Michael Jackson urges Roger Taylor to make AOBTD the next single (New York City, Studio 54, late 1979). Michael Jackson, *Off The Wall* (1979).

irony. Costello writes songs on edge, displaying the sensitivity and conceit of any true elitist. Ever feel a little at odds with society? Feel left out by the mainstream? Feel simultaneously rejected and superior? Well, Elvis Costello has and he is not going to take it lying down. Successfully, he throws all of these feelings in a bag with a dry sense of humor, adds more than a pinch of cynicism, and blends them with musical accuracy. The result? A musical masterpiece that deserves attention even twenty-four years after its release.

The underdog offbeat brilliance of *My Aim Is True* has aged like fine wine, creating a modern cult following much like that of actor John Cusack. Both speak a familiar language— that of the common man experiencing failure. Costello through his lyrics, Cusack through roles such as the down-trodden record store owner Rob in the movie *High Fidelity,* or the awkward teens he plays in both *Say Anything,* and *Better Off Dead.* Part of the attraction to figures such as Costello and Cusack is that people of an ordinary nature can relate to them. Everyone wants to see pop stars that are not perfect looking, perfectly graceful, or perfectly happy. And everyone likes to see the underdog represented in a way that is unique rather than stereotypical. Both Elvis Costello and John Cusack do this and do it well.

Take for example the opening song from Costello's *My Aim Is True.* He launches into the album singing, "Welcome to the Working Week," and reaching out to any unsatisfied employee. One of the album's simplest moments, this song places the chorus "Welcome to the working week, I know it don't thrill ya I hope it don't kill ya," against a fierce yet sing-along tune, automatically winning the hearts of all those disgruntled, tired and unsure. A manifesto of the working class, this song portrays the life of pre-fame Elvis. Just an average Joe working a passionless day job as a computer operator, straining his eyes day in and day out to the point where he needs those now infamous thick-rimmed glasses reminiscent of Buddy Holly and favored among members of his current cult following.

The glasses might have helped a man born Declan McManus to see, but they framed the style and stage presence of Elvis Costello, making Declan the computer operator look every bit Elvis's intellectual/outcast/critic of society. Yes, even the stage name, taken from "the King" of popular rock 'n roll, is an attack on the music industry. In the face of an emerging, dance-happy new wave, *My Aim Is True* threw a monkey wrench in the commercialized system. While pseudo-angry, underground, punk rock bands only managed to reinforce the traditional conventions of the music industry, Elvis Costello and his band the Attractions presented a vastly talented, deliriously fresh voice for stale angst. Only an album with such sophisticated musical influences—think British Rock classics: the Beatles, the Kinks, and the Who meet Motown—could possibly be taken seriously when fronted by such a funny looking guy. No glam rock. No gimmick. No apologies. No love songs.

Well—no love songs in the traditional sense, anyway. There is "Allison," the fifth track, and the reflective breath amidst a furious storm, the bluesy phantom that promises in its opening lines not "to get too sentimental like those other sticky Valentines." The music strikes a sorrowful chord, one any regretful lover could appreciate. Proving more elusive, the lyrics refuse the position of the heartbroken crooning for lost love. Instead, Costello once again widens the scope by reaching out for his more comfortable position as a keen observer, obscuring this obviously personal experience—so personal, in fact, that he no longer performs the song live. While affectionate and regretful, the song is also edgy and controlled. Using the encounter with a past flame to cynically portray marriage, Costello huskily vocalizes his disapproval, "Well I see you've got a husband now/did he leave your pretty fingers lying in the wedding cake/you used to hold him right in your hand/I bet it took all that he could take."

As quickly and comfortably as Elvis slipped into the introspective shoes of Allison, he ditches them for the furious funk of "Sneaky Feelings." One would get the impression that Mr. Costello must indeed have a closet full of shoes he fills quite perfectly. In "I'm Not Angry"—yeah, right—he sports a good pair of trainers. The first five seconds of fast guitar, intense keyboard and oddly timed cymbals are enough to get anyone running. No, Elvis Costello is not angry, he's irate. While some might mistake this as a chip on his embittered shoulder, the truth is that Elvis Costello's songs extend far beyond self-deprecation and personal failures. Take "Less Than Zero" for example—a song written in response to a disturbing broadcast he saw on T.V., the BBC segment on the supposed reform of Oswald Moseley, one of the British leaders of the fascist regime. Capturing what he sees as the ultimate decline of an already unraveling society, Costello creates a narrative in which Moseley is the main character, representing not only himself but consumer society at large. "Mr. Oswald has an understanding with the law/he said he heard about a couple living in the USA/they traded in their baby for a Chevrolet/let's talk about the future/we'll put the past away." This song shows that if London is welcoming the likes of Moseley back with open arms, it is no place for Elvis Costello.

Similar bitter irony is reflected in the songs "Waiting for the End of the World," "Cheap Reward," "No Dancing," and "Pay it Back." Okay, so Mr. Costello may never get the award for most happy camper. He *admits* in an interview that most of his songs are inspired by "regret and guilt." He *does* sing about failure and misunderstanding and bitterness and all the things people never want to talk about but feel all the time. He *really* used to keep a list—a blacklist—of all the record executives and industry bigwigs he saw as the root of musical evil. BUT. He managed to break the system. He got the last laugh. He made it. Unleashing his fury in the form of *My Aim Is True,* he broke musical ground. He blended jazz, funk, rock and new age with impeccable perfection. He said something that mattered at a time when no one was saying anything. He mastered language and music, introduced them, made them shake hands, then fight, then dance together and laugh about it all.

Most importantly, he didn't stop there. He went on to build a musical legacy. Not only did he record an expansive body of work showcasing his varying talents, he became a producer, guiding other brilliant bands. As a producer, Costello worked with bands as diverse as his own influences. One of these bands, the Specials, embodies the soul of two-tone ska, a musical genre emphasizing the importance of racial diversity and social consciousness. Another band that he worked with—The Clash—has been an instrumental part of the punk rock scene. Echoes of Costello can be heard in much of today's experimental indie rock. Elliot Smith, indie rock darling, cites Costello as a major influence. One of the most impressive contemporary songwriters, Smith wrote songs that while of a mellower and more melodic musical variety, echo the underdog sentiments popularized by Costello.

Perhaps his contribution to indie sensibilities of attitude and style are equal if less tangible than those he made in music. To be indie is to have a love of irony and embrace—on multiple levels—social awkwardness. In fact, indie owes much of this attitude to Costello. This "antiking" of pop was the first one to successfully bring these two elements into the spotlight. Traces of his fashion statement, namely the trademark glasses, can be seen among geek rock favorites like Weezer and on the faces of infinite "indie kids." And it all started twenty-four years ago. One little record untouchable in the eyes of major record labels. A record heralded by *Rolling Stone* as 1977's album of the year and remembered by VH1 as one of the best rock albums of all time. If the industry originally believed he had missed the mark, at least Elvis Costello knew he was right on target.

READING WRITING

Your Text: Reading

1. How would you describe the tone of this piece? Does it work for you? Why or why not? Is it appropriate for the type of writing she's doing?
2. How would you classify this piece? Is it a review? An essay? A paper? What makes you think so?
3. Why does the writer like Elvis Costello? How does she try to make others like him? Who does she think will like him? Look at specific places in the text where she does this work.
4. What other albums of a certain age deserve this type of revisiting? Name a few and talk about them in class.

Your Text: Writing

1. Do an assignment similar to Hawkins: Find an older album and re-introduce it to a younger crowd. What things might you have to consider about "youth" and "age" when doing this assignment?
2. Think about your criteria when choosing to listen to an album. How does that change when looking at an older album? Write a short paper about why you choose what you listen to.
3. If it's possible, go to the record collection of an older friend or relative and interview them about the experience with one of their favorite albums. Now go back and listen to it on your own and write a paper about your experience.

"Smells Like Teen Spirit"

Matt Compton

Student Essay

Matt Compton wrote this analysis of Nirvana's "Smells Like Teen Spirit" for English 101 class at Virginia Commonwealth University.

IN 1991 A SONG BURST FORTH onto the music scene that articulated so perfectly the emotions of America's youth that the song's writer was later labeled the voice of a generation (Moon). That song was Nirvana's "Smells Like Teen Spirit," and the writer was Kurt Cobain; one of the most common complaints of the song's critics was that the lyrics were unintelligible (Rawlins). But while some considered the song to be unintelligible, to many youth in the early 90s, it was exactly what they needed to hear. Had the song been presented differently, then the raw emotions that it presented would have been tamed. If the lyrics had been perfectly articulated, then the feelings that the lyrics express would have been less articulate, because the feelings that he was getting across were not clear in themselves. One would know exactly what Kurt Cobain was saying, but not exactly what he was feeling. The perfect articulation of those raw emotions, shared by so many of America's youth, was conveyed with perfect inarticulation.

1991 was a year when the music scene had become a dilute, lukewarm concoction being spoonfed to the masses by corporations (Cohen). The charts and the radio were being dominated by "hair bands" and pop ballads; popular music at the time was making a lot of noise without saying anything (Cohen). Behind the scenes "underground" music had been thriving since the early eighties. Much of this underground music was making a meaningful statement, but these musicians shied away from the public eye. The general public knew little about them, because they had adopted the ideology that going public was selling out (Dettmar). Nirvana was a part of this "underground" music scene.

In 1991 Nirvana broke the credo, signing with a major label, DGC, under which they released the chart-smashing *Nevermind*. "Smells Like Teen Spirit" was the first single from the record, and it became a huge hit quickly (Cohen). Nirvana stepped up and spoke for the twenty-something generation, which wasn't exactly sure what it wanted to say (Azerrad 223–233). A huge part of America's youth felt exactly what Cobain was able to convey through not just "Smells Like Teen Spirit" but all of his music. Nirvana shot into superstar status and paved the way for an entire "grunge" movement (Moon). No one complained that they could not hear Cobain, but many did complain that they could not understand what he was saying.

Kurt Cobain did not want his music to just be heard and appreciated; he wanted it to be "felt" (Moon). His music often showed a contrast of emotions; it would change from a soft lull, to a screaming rage suddenly. And few could scream with rage as could Cobain (Cohen). There is a Gaelic word, "yarrrrragh," which ". . . refers to that rare quality that some voices have, an edge, an ability to say something about the human condition that goes far beyond merely singing the right lyrics and hitting the right notes." This word was once used to describe Cobain's voice by Ralph J. Gleason, *Rolling Stone* critic (Azerrad 231). It was that voice, that uncanny ability to show emotions that Cobain demonstrated in "Smells Like Teen Spirit."

Cobain's raging performance spoke to young Americans in a way that no one had in a long while (Moon). Michael Azerrad wrote in his 1993 book, *Come as You Are: The Story of Nirvana*, "Ultimately it wasn't so much that Nirvana was saying anything new about growing up in America; it was the way they said it" (Azerrad 226). Cobain's music was conveying a feeling through the way that he performed. It was a feeling shared by many of America's youth, but it was also a feeling that could not have been articulated any way other than the way that Cobain did it (Cohen).

"Smells Like Teen Spirit" starts out with one of the most well-known guitar riffs of the 90s. The four chord progression was certainly nothing new, nothing uncommon. The chords are played with a single guitar with no distortion, and then suddenly the bass and drums come in. When the drums and bass come in the guitar is suddenly distorted, and the pace and sound of the song changes. The song's introduction, with its sudden change, forms a rhythmic "poppy" chord progression to a raging, thrashing of the band's instruments (Moon), sets the pace for the rest of the song.

The chaos from the introduction fades, and it leads in to the first verse, which gives the listener a confused feeling (Azerrad 213). In the first verse the tune of the song is carried by the drums and bass alone, and a seemingly lonely two-note guitar part that fades in and out of the song. The bass, drums and eerie guitar give the listener a "hazy" feeling. Here Cobain's lack of articulation aids in the confused feeling, because as he sings, one can catch articulate phrases here and there. The words that the listener can discern allow them to draw their own connections. Cobain's lyrics do in fact carry a confused message, "It's fun to lose, and to pretend" (Azerrad 213).

The pre-chorus offers up clear articulation of a single word, but this articulation is the perfect precursor to the coming chorus. As the first verse ends, the pre-chorus comes in; Cobain repeats the word "Hello" fifteen times. The repetition of the word Hello draws the confusion that he implicates in the first verse to a close, and in a way reflects on it. As the tone and inflection of his voice changes each time he quotes "Hello," one is not sure whether he is asking a question or making a statement, or both. It is like he is saying, "Hello? Is anybody at home?" while at the same time he exclaims, "Wake up and answer the door!"

The reflection that he implicates in the pre-chorus builds to the raw raging emotions that he expresses in the chorus, as the guitar suddenly becomes distorted, and he begins to scream (Azerrad 214, 226). In the chorus he screams, but somehow the words in the chorus are actually more articulate than those in the verse. As Cobain sings, "I feel stupid, and contagious," anyone who has ever felt like a social outcast understands exactly what Cobain is saying (Cohen), and they understand exactly why he must scream it.

I remember the first time that I heard that line and thinking about it; I was about thirteen, and I thought that there was no better word than "contagious" to describe the way it feels being in a social situation and not being accepted. Because no one wants to be around that person, they will look at the person with disgust, as if they have some highly *contagious* disease. There is certainly a lot of anger and confusion surrounding those feelings. People needed to hear Cobain scream; they knew how he felt, because they knew how they felt.

People who were experiencing what Cobain was expressing understood what he was saying, because they understood how he felt. In much the same way when someone hits their hand with a hammer that person does not lay down the hammer and calmly say, "Ouch, man that really hurt." They throw the hammer down, and simultaneously yell an obscenity, or make an inarticulate roar, and one knows that they are going to lose a fingernail. Anyone who has smashed their finger with a hammer understands why that person is yelling; in the same way anyone who has felt "contagious" or confused about society knows why Cobain is screaming about feeling "stupid and contagious." Cobain is not examining society. He is experiencing the same things as his audience (Moon); he is "going to lose a fingernail." As the chorus draws to a close, the music still rages, but it changes tempo and rhythm slightly.

The chorus is the most moving part of the song; it is a display of pure emotion. In the chorus Cobain demonstrates what it was that connected with so many; his lyrics said what he meant (Moon). But what he said had been said before, and whether he was articulate or not, people felt what he meant. It was the articulation of that feeling that gained the song such high praise (Moon).

The chorus ends with the phrase, "A mulatto, an albino, a mosquito, my libido"; this line is a reference to social conformity. Cobain is referring to things, or the ideas associated with them that are "outside" of social conformity, and then relating those things back to himself with the phrase "my libido" (Azerrad 210–215). This end to the chorus again goes back to reflect on the feelings expressed in the chorus, and ties them together with a return to the confusion expressed in the verses.

The articulation of the lyrics in the second verse gives the confusion more focus than in the first verse. He begins the second verse with the lyric, "I'm worse at what I do best, and for this gift I feel blessed." Although the lyrics are more articulate in the second verse, the feelings of confusion are still there, due to the tempo and rhythm of the music. After Cobain has sung the second verse he returns to the pre-chorus, the repetition of the word Hello. The cycle begins anew.

"Smells Like Teen Spirit" in its entirety gives the listener a complete feeling after listening to it, especially if that listener is feeling confused and frustrated. The song carries one through an entire cycle of emotions, from confusion, to reflection, to frustration. Tom Moon, a Knight-Ridder Newspaper writer, described Nirvana's music as having moments of "tension and release." Being carried through those emotions allows the listener to "vent" their own feelings of confusion and frustration, and at the same time know that someone else feels the same way (Azerrad 226–227). Despite the connection that Cobain made with many there were still many who did not "get" the song; these people often complained about the inarticulation of the lyrics (Azerrad 210).

Weird Al Yankovic utilized the common criticism of the song in his parody "Smells Like Nirvana"; Yankovic parodied "Smells Like Teen Spirit," based entirely on Cobain's obscure articulation. Yankovic is known for parodying popular music, and with lines such as, "And I'm yellin' and I'm screamin', but I don't know what I'm saying," Yankovic stated exactly what so many of the song's critiques had, though he did it with a genuine respect for the song, and its impact (Rawlins).

Weird Al Yankovic's version struck a note with many who liked Cobain's music but could not understand his lyrics (Rawlins). There were many people who did not understand the feelings of confusion, frustration, and apathy that Cobain was getting across. In 1991 when "Smells Like Teen Spirit" first came out I was only 9, and I did not like that kind of music at all. I remember my brother, who is nine years older than me, and who listened to a lot of "heavy metal," bought Yankovic's *Off the Deep End,* with his parody "Smells Like Nirvana" on it. He thought it was funny because he did not like Nirvana. He never really connected with Cobain's message; even though he did not get what Cobain was saying, he could still enjoy the music. When I became older I did connect with Cobain's music, and Nirvana was one of my favorite bands. My brother never did understand, like many people who never did understand what it was that Cobain was saying (Azerrad 210).

Nirvana made the generation gap clear. It was Nirvana that spoke for a large part of that generation (Moon), where no one else had ever really addressed the confusion and frustration about growing up in America at that time, or at least no one had expressed it in the same way that Nirvana did. They were not the first to vocalize a problem with corporate America, but they were the first *popular* band to convey the feelings that many were feeling *because* of growing up in corporate America, in the way that they did. Cobain did not just show that he has experienced those feelings, but that he was still *experiencing* them, and many young people connected with that (Moon).

In 1992 singer-songwriter Tori Amos illustrated why Cobain's "Smells Like Teen Spirit" had connected with so many by making a cover of the song that was a clear contrast to the original. She rendered the song with a piano, and a clear articulate voice. Her cover of the song became fairly popular, because it was different, and because many people could now understand the lyrics that Cobain had already popularized (Rawlins). The cover was interesting, to say the least; however, it would have been impossible for her version ever to have had the same impact as Cobain's (Rawlins). The lyrics to the song have meaning, and depth, but the emotions that the song conveyed were in and of themselves abstract.

Amos's version of the song articulated each word clearly, her clear voice hit each note on key; her song was comparable to a ballad. Cobain's "Smells Like Teen Spirit" could be described as "sloppy," his guitar distorted through much of the song; he either screamed or mumbled most of the song (Azerrad 214). The two versions of the song illustrate a clear contrast: it is as if Cobain is "angry about being confused" (Azerrad 213), while Amos sings the song to lament Cobain's feelings.

Amos's version of the song became popular for the same reason that it could never have paved the way as Cobain's version did. It was like a ballad, and after everyone heard what Cobain was saying, about society, about America, about growing up, there is one clear emotion that follows the confusion and frustration: sadness. Her "ballad-like" cover of "Smells Like Teen Spirit" exemplified that sadness. But at the same time, people had written ballads about being confused or frustrated, and performed them as Amos performed "Smells Like Teen Spirit"; that was nothing new. However, no one had yet *demonstrated* such clear and yet abstract confused, frustrated emotions as Cobain did, and at that moment in time that was exactly what America needed to hear (Azerrad 224–225).

Cobain had written and performed a song about his own confusion, and in the process he had connected with young people all over the United States (Moon). He had helped those people to understand their own confusion better. The problem with "Smells Like Teen Spirit" was not that Cobain was not articulate; he could not have articulated his point more clearly than he did. The problem was that not everyone knew what he was talking about, just like not everyone knows what it is like to strike their finger with a hammer. And in the same way, if someone doesn't know what it is like they might say something foolish like, "That couldn't hurt *that* bad," or "What's *his* problem?" when someone else hits their finger with a hammer, and they make an inarticulate roar. That roar expresses exactly what that person is feeling, but only those who know that feeling can really understand it. As Michael Azerrad, author of *Come as You Are: The Story of Nirvana* put it, "you either get it, or you don't" (Azerrad 227). Thus was the case with Cobain's music. "Smells Like Teen Spirit" was his inarticulate roar; it was articulate in that it expressed exactly what he was trying to point out; however, not everyone could grasp what that was.

Works Cited

Azerrad, Michael. *Come as You Are*. New York: Doubleday, 1993.

Cohen, Howard and Leonard Pitts. "Kurt Cobain Made Rock for Everyone but Kurt Cobain." *Knight Ridder/Tribune*. 8 April 1994: Infotrac.

Dettmar, Kevin. "Uneasy Listening, Uneasy Commerce." *The Chronicle of Higher Education*. 14 Sept. 2001: 18. Lexis-Nexis.

Moon, Tom. "Reluctant Spokesman for Generation Became the Rock Star He Abhorred." *KnightRidder/Tribune*. 9 April 1994. Infotrac.

Nirvana. *Nevermind*. David Geffen Company, 1991.

Rawlins, Melissa. "From Bad to Verse." *Entertainment Weekly*. 5 June 1992: 57. Infotrac.

READING WRITING

This Text: Reading

1. In what ways does the music of "Smells Like Teen Spirit" reflect the lyrics?
2. Some critics think songs such as "Like a Rolling Stone" and "Smells Like Teen Spirit" are the "song of a generation"—do you agree? If so, who makes up these generations—who was Bob Dylan and Nirvana speaking to (and for)? Do you think these songwriters would think they were speaking for anyone?
3. Notice how Compton uses comparison to make his points. What work does comparison do in his piece?

Your Text: Writing

1. Choose a song you think is poetic. Write about the poetic aspect of it. Now write about how music either enhances or detracts from the poetic intent.
2. Choose a song that you think symbolizes what some people in your generation (age group) believe. Examine how well this song addresses this idea.
3. Compare two songs like "Smells Like Teen Spirit" and "Like a Rolling Stone" that some critics have labeled as songs that represent a particular generation.
4. Mirroring Matt Compton's approach, look at how the lyrics and sounds of the song work together.

"Coal Miner's Daughter"

Alessandro Portelli

Alessandro Portelli teaches American Literature at the University of Rome–La Sapienza. Noted for his work on oral history, Portelli has written a number of books, including his landmark work, *The Text and the Voice* (1994), and his most recent book, *The Order Has Been Carried Out: History, Memory, and Meaning of a Nazi Massacre in Rome* (2007).

When I state myself, as the Representative of the Verse—it does not mean me—but a supposed person.

—*Emily Dickinson*

1.

There is a scene in Robert Altman's *Nashville,* in which a singer with long wavy black hair steps on the stage at Opryland, sings a song and then, as the band starts vamping for the next number, breaks into a rambling speech, which soon turns into a loose reminiscence of childhood:

> I think there's a storm a-brewing. That's what my granddaddy used to say before he lost his hearin' and sometimes he'd say, "Oh gosh," or "Durn it," or "My word" ... My granny, she'd go round the house clickin' her false teeth to the radio all day. She was a lot of fun, and always cooked my favorite roast beef and she was a sweetheart. She raised chickens, too. She, uh—in fact, did ya ever hear a chicken sound?[1]

This scene is a fictionalized account of the most famous crackup in country-music history: that of Loretta Lynn in the early '70s. An authorized version of the same episode appears in a later film, Michael Apted's *Coal Miner's Daughter,* based on Loretta Lynn's autobiographical book by the same title (the episode, however, is not discussed in the book). Both films concur in showing the breakdown as an eruption of private memories: a compulsive autobiographical act.

2.

The book takes its title, in turn, from Loretta Lynn's best and most successful song, "Coal Miner's Daughter." The song appears at first hearing as another autobiographical act, containing many features of Lynn's later descriptions of her own life: the sentimental cliché ("We were poor but we had love"), the precise description of background details, the relish in the sound of vernacular speech. In her book, Lynn says:

> I'd always wanted to write a song about growing up, but I never believed anybody would care about it. One day I was sitting around the television studio at WSIX, waiting to rehearse a show

. . . I went off to the dressing room and just wrote the first words that came into my head. It started: "Well, I was borned a coal miner's daughter . . .", which was nothing but the truth.[2]

Before we go on to examine her autobiographies, let us take a quick look at Loretta Lynn's life. She was in fact born a coal miner's daughter in the mid-Thirties in Western Kentucky; she barely learned to read and write, married at thirteen, followed her husband to Washington state, worked hard, lived poor, had four children by the time she was eighteen (was a grandmother at twenty-nine), and never thought of a career in music until she was twenty-four. Since then, she has moved to Nashville, had two twin daughters, and worked her way up to be the most successful female country singer and one of the most successful entertainers in the history of show business.

It was more than a year before Lynn and her entourage could bring themselves to issue "Coal Miner's Daughter" as a record. The time in which the song was "kept . . . in the can" seems like a metaphor for a repressed autobiographical urge. Lynn says that she did not think that people would be interested in a song about her life; in fact, the first important decision in autobiography is always accepting that one's life is worth telling in public. Once the song hit the charts, however, all doubts were removed, and the floodgates of autobiography were thrown open. In further songs, interviews, ceremonies, and finally in a book and a film, the story of the coal miner's daughter, the Washington housewife, the Nashville Opry star was told over and over, in a variety of media but with remarkable consistency.

> I was given up when I was a baby. I came close to drowning near my ranch a few years ago. I never told anybody about that until now. And the doctors told me that my heart stopped on the operating table when I had chest surgery in 1972. Ever since then, I've wanted to tell my life story (p. 18).

Autobiography as a response to a death threat is a standard concept not necessarily to be taken at face value. In fact, the song "Coal Miner's Daughter" was composed before Lynn's surgery. It is a fact, however, that telling her life story means more to Loretta Lynn than the public relations gesture it is for many other public figures.

In 1974, an interviewer asked her how country music had changed since she came to Nashville. Most musicians would be content to give a professional answer to this professional question. But terms like "change" and memories of coming to a new place start a whole other chain of associations in Loretta Lynn's mind:

> I didn't live in Nashville. Of course I had never been any place except I went to the state of Washington—my husband sent for me and I went on the train. I was pregnant. . . .[3]

The interviewer comes back to the original question shortly afterwards, asking "How has country music changed?"—and again Lynn digresses freely, associating autobiographical thoughts:

> It seems like everything has changed. When I was growing up . . . like for me to see a loaf of bread [. . .] There ain't many people live the way we did in Butcher Holler, and Butcher Holler has changed.

When asked about career and business, Lynn almost compulsively responds in terms of her early life, of before she became a professional musician. There is an undeniable degree of authenticity in this urge, as the episode of the breakdown confirms, an inner need. On the other hand, the autobiographical urge also sells. Within a year after "Coal Miner's Daughter," she had three more singles out with songs of an autobiographical nature, signaling both the open floodgates of autobiography and the sequels to a commercial hit—from coal mine to gold mine, as it were. "Coal Miner's Daughter" becomes a trademark, designating a song, a best-selling book, a major movie, a publishing company (Coal Miner Music), a band (Lynn's backup group changed names, from Western—Trailblazers—to Appalachian—Coal Miners).

On the other hand, some members of the band did come from coal mining families, and all were supposed to have been factory workers at one time (at least, this is the point she was making at the time her autobiography was written). The same sign, then, designates a commercial gimmick, and a factual truth: the constant tension in all of Loretta Lynn's autobiographical image-making and soul-searching. The most obvious example of this process is, of course, her name. Contrary to the practice of many stars, she did not change her name (which happens to possess the feature of alliteration, highly prized in advertising); on the other hand, her name increasingly designates objects other than her person—her voice, her image, her records, all the way to Crisco shortening and franchised western wear stores.

3.

If we look at the front and back cover of a paperback edition of *Coal Miner's Daughter* (in this case, the 1977 Warner paperback), we find there one of the most concise statements of the nature of autobiography anywhere. The two pictures—the glamorous star on the front, the bucktoothed little girl on the back—are the same person, and yet two different people. The contrast shows the distinction between past and present selves, public and private lives, which creates the inner tension in the autobiographical genre; and it also underlies that this contrast takes place within what remains, after all, one and the same person.

Structurally, this means that autobiography has much in common with metaphor. A metaphor is the discovery of similarity in a context of difference: "Achilles is a lion" makes sense as a metaphor precisely because Achilles is not a lion. Jean Starobinski has pointed out that in order for autobiography to exist, there must have been a change, a dramatic development in the subject; I would stress the fact that the change is only significant because the subject remains the same. The difference between the narrating and the narrated self is worthy of our attention because these two selves happen to belong to the same person.

This is true also at another level. Autobiography is a public performance; but the story teller is expected to reveal the private self in it. On one level, the autobiographer is supposed to abolish the difference between public and private self; on another, this act is only relevant inasmuch as the reader is constantly reminded that the two selves are logically distinct. "One does not dress for private company as for a public ball," says Benjamin Franklin, the founding father of modern autobiography; and Nathaniel Hawthorne muses that "it is scarcely decorous to speak all."

This double metaphorical structure is best expressed in the autobiographies of stars. Their success story enhances difference and change, but they always strive to prove continuity and identity insisting that success has not changed them; they build an elaborate public image, but must persuade their fans that it also coincides with their private selves. Country music as a genre claims sincerity to a very high degree, linking it closely with autobiography: "A hillbilly is more sincere than most entertainers," Hank Williams used to say, "because a hillbilly was raised rougher."

In fact, the ideal country star must be born in a cabin and live in a mansion, like Loretta Lynn; and, as she does, must travel back and forth between them, at least in imagination. Most importantly, they are expected to live in a mansion as they would in a cabin. Stars must look dazzlingly glamorous on the stage, declaring distance; but must open their homes to visiting fans and tourists, stressing familiarity. No wonder autobiography is also a thematic staple in so many country songs.

> My fans and writers—says Lynn—are always making a big deal about me acting natural, right from the country. That's because I come from Butcher Holler, Kentucky, and I ain't never forgot it. [. . .] We're country musicians; I don't think we could play our kind of music if we didn't come from little places like Butcher Holler (p. 59).

In her book, Lynn presents herself as a regular housewife (an image doubled by her Crisco commercials), who has some problems with her husband but still understands and loves him, who hangs drapes and even worries about where the money for the children's braces is coming from. "When you're lookin' at me, you're lookin' at country," she sings; "I was Loretta Lynn, a mother and a wife and a daughter, who had feelings just like other women," she says (p. 151). And yet—if she were just another housewife, mother, and daughter, who would buy her book and see her movie? But then—*who* is she? As in most autobiographies, the answer is blowing somewhere along the continuum of past and present, public and private.

4.

Let us begin with public and private. *Coal Miner's Daughter* opens in the bedroom; there's another bedroom scene two pages later, and early in the book Lynn describes her wedding night in detail. These, however, are not love scenes. In the opening episode, she has a nightmare and winds up bloodying her husband's nose with her wedding ring; the next thing she mentions is the gun her husband keeps on the night table. The wedding night scene, though ostensibly humorous, describes a rape: "He finally more or less had to rip off my panties. The rest of it was kind of a blur" (p. 78).

On one level, Lynn is grappling with inner dreams and deepseated fears; on another, she is casting herself in the folksy role of the country girl whose mother never told her about the facts of life and who—"just like other women"—had to find out the hard way. The autobiographical urge merges with the commercial image-making: Lynn takes her fans into her bedroom, but then resents the invasion and hides.

This is true also literally. When she was in the hospital, "the fans heard I was in bed [and] they trooped right into my room and started taking pictures" (p. 163). Every year, Loretta Lynn opens her house to thousands of fans, in a ritual of reunion between the star and her social constituency that blurs the line where the public ends and the private begins. Fans "just pop into my kitchen when we're sitting around. It sounds terrible, but I can't relax in my own home," she complains. So she winds up checking in at a motel—leaving her private residence to seek shelter in public places. The same process functions in the autobiographies: the need to show and the need to hide establish a constant tension. She displays her inner self to the public, but when the public gets there she has retired somewhere else—and regrets it, and thinks "it's terrible."

A similar contradiction occurs in the relationship between past and present. Being a coal miner's daughter is both an inner identity actively sought and a mask imposed by business associates and fans. Fidelity to roots is an authentic part of herself as well as a role imposed from outside. Thus, in order to play up continuity she is forced to repress the changes that make her what she is. She speaks dialect freely and spontaneously, but a critic has noticed that "from time to time, she will repeat a word which she has pronounced correctly, only to repeat it *incorrectly* (as *born* to *borned*), almost as though she were reminding herself."[4]

Thus, the same sets of signs designate truth and fiction, spontaneity and manipulation. Loretta Lynn does artificially what comes naturally—like speaking dialect—and does naturally what comes artificially—like wearing a mask.

5.

All the theory and practice of autobiography revolve around the first person pronoun, "I." The question is, what does Loretta Lynn mean, to what exactly does she refer, when she uses that word?

Let us consider the songs first. When she sings "I was borned a coal miner's daughter," she is using the autobiographical first person; but when she sings "I'm a honky tonk girl," her first hit, she is using the fictional-lyrical first person of popular song. These two meanings of "I" interact intensively in her work. Because she uses autobiography so much, many songs that are not about herself have been taken for autobiography: an exchange favored by the fact that in all her repertoire Lynn consistently projects a character based very much upon herself, the spunky woman who does not question the system but won't take no nonsense from nobody—"Don't Come Home a-Drinkin' with Lovin' on Your Mind" because "Your Squaw's on the Warpath Tonight."

The interaction of autobiographical and fictional–lyrical "I" generates intermediate forms: first-person songs, written by herself, but not autobiographical; first-person songs, written by others, but based on aspects of her life. She wrote "The Pill," a song about contraceptives which was one of her most controversial hits, though she says she hardly ever used it herself (it would have been harder to write, and sell, a song about her husband's vasectomy, which she talks about in the book). On the other hand, "One's On the Way"— a vivid description of a housewife with four kids, a careless husband, maybe twins on the way, the pot boiling over, and the doorbell ringing—is based on recollections of her early married life, but was written by Shel Silverstein. There is even another Shel Silverstein song, called "Hey, Loretta," in which Lynn sings to herself as if she were somebody else.

To further confuse matters, there is the problem of performance. Singers—like all oral performers—present even the most impersonal material through their body and their voice, thus making it intrinsically personal. Even when she performs someone else's songs, Lynn steps closer to an autobiographical act, although it might not be technically described as such. On the other hand, when Emmylou Harris records Lynn's "Blue Kentucky Girl," the autobiographical overtones are lost.

In conclusion, there are at least four meanings of the word "I" as used in Lynn's repertoire and performances, going from the purely autobiographical to the purely fictional lyrical, through at least two intermediate forms. Each of these forms shades or may turn into another through the processes of performance and reception.

Much the same can be said about the book. A capsule definition of autobiography is based on the coincidence between the hero and the narrator inside the book's covers and the author outside: they all have the same name. But if we look at the cover of *Coal Miner's Daughter,* we see that the names on the cover are split: "by Loretta Lynn with George Vecsey." *Coal Miner's Daughter* is one of those "as told to" autobiographies in which famous people delegate the writing to a professional when they are too busy or unable to take care of it themselves. Although these books are billed as autobiographies, the person who says "I" in them is not the same person that does the actual writing. Loretta Lynn makes no pretense about it: George Vecsey is frequently mentioned in the text as "my writer," in the third person. In quite a postmodern fashion, Vecsey writes about himself in the third person, about somebody else in the first, and enters his own text as a character in someone else's story: while he writes his own name, he pretends that this is Loretta Lynn talking about him. One assumes that, when the "I" character is different from the author, we are dealing with fiction; *Coal Miner's Daughter,* however, is supposed to be factually straight. The only fiction about it has to do with the uses of the first person.

With the film, we take another step. By definition, there can be no autobiographical film in the strict formal sense. When a book is turned into a film, the first consequence is the disappearance of the first-person narrator: films are always in the third person. In the movie *Coal Miner's Daughter* (whose credits are reproduced on the back cover of the paperback) the "author's" name on the cover is Michael Apted, filming a screenplay by Tom Rickman based on the book written by George Vecsey as told by Loretta Lynn. The face and voice on the screen belong to Sissy Spacek. Yet, the name is still Loretta Lynn: the film is clearly intended as a "true" statement, largely meant to "set the record straight" after *Nashville.* Many side characters in *Coal Miner's Daughter* actually play themselves, reinforcing the "documentary" overtones.

We come full circle when we turn to the paperback and discover that the film has been incorporated into the book. First of all, as we have already pointed out, the book displays the film credits, making it look as if the book was a novelization of the film: the written autobiography is somehow validated by having been the subject of a fictional movie. In the second place, the images from the film are also included in the book.

In the book, indeed, Loretta Lynn tells her story not one, but three times: with words, with photographs from her family album, with stills from the movie. The two sets of photographs are almost interchangeable: the family album's captions, however, are in the first person, while those of the movie stills are in the third. But the pictures themselves are sometimes hard to tell apart. The picture of Loretta Lynn in her first stage outfit is so similar to the one of Sissy Spacek wearing the replica of it that they perform a sort of reversal of the autobiographical process: while the pictures on the cover portray two different people who are yet the same person, those two photographs inside portray one character who is in fact two different persons. It may not be irrelevant, in the book's rhetorical structure, that the film stills come before the family album: it looks as though Loretta Lynn's photos were patterned after Sissy Spacek's. Which, of course, has been the problem all along: which of the two, the image or the person, is the real one, which one comes first.

6.

In a passage in *The Day of the Locust,* Nathanael West describes the main female character, Faye Greener, as she tries out one identity after another:

> She would get some music on the radio, then lie down on her bed and shut her eyes. She had a large assortment of stories to choose from. After getting herself in the right mood, she would go over them in her mind, as though they were a pack of cards, discarding one after another until she found one that suited. On some days, she would run through the whole pack without making a choice [. . .] While she admitted that her method was too mechanical for best results [. . .] she said that any dream was better than no dream.[5]

Let us compare this passage to one from *Coal Miner's Daughter,* in which Lynn describes her belief in reincarnation—a subject clearly related to the question of the mutable and multiple self.

> I once read that you could feel your past lives if you concentrated real hard. So I tried it in my hotel room. I wasn't asleep but kind of in a trance. I lay down quiet and let my mind drift. All of a sudden I was an Indian woman wearing moccasins and a long buckskin dress and I had

my hair in pigtails. Even the sound and smell were vivid to me. All around me there was a huge field with Indians riding horseback. I was standing next to a mounted Indian. I sensed that he was about to go off into battle, and I was saying good-bye to him. Then a shot rang out, and my husband fell off his horse [...] In the second such experience, I saw myself dressed up in an Irish costume, doing an Irish dance down a country lane in front of a big white house (p. 98).

Loretta Lynn is part Cherokee, and almost as proud of her Indian blood as she is to be a coal miner's daughter. The rest of her ancestry is the Scots–Irish stock prevalent in Appalachia. As she thumbs through her past lives, she meets her ancestors: the idea that one's past lives are those our ancestors lived is not as flat a banality as one would expect in the autobiography of a star. Like Faye Greener's second-hand dreams, however, Loretta Lynn's earlier selves are fashioned after artificial patterns. The Indian warrior chief on horseback is more reminiscent of plains Indians, of Western movie Sioux, that of a mountain Cherokee. The "big white house" is a plantation house, and in anybody's book an Irish girl in front of a Southern plantation house is named Scarlett O'Hara. "I never picture myself after Scarlett O'Hara," says Lynn later in the book—but she makes this claim in the context of buying her new house because its "huge white columns" remind her of Tara (p. 136). The more she seeks inside to find her true self, the more she encounters someone else's fictions.

The paradox in *The Day of the Locust* is that, by having only masks and no face, Faye Greener achieves a sort of purity: she hides nothing, because there is nothing to hide. She is incapable of deceit because she lives in a world (Hollywood, which is to her what Nashville is to Loretta Lynn) in which deceit is real life and fiction is the only truth.

The Day of the Locust anticipates many developments which would later be labelled as "postmodern"; it concerns the relationship between mass culture, the fragmentation of the self, the erasure of distinctions between image and substance, sign and referent, truth and fiction in a universe in which image is the only substance and signs are the only referents of signs.

"In country music," Lynn complains, "we're always singing about home and family. But because I was in country music, I had to neglect my home and my family" (p. 140). Let us not be deceived by the sentimental wording: these are the only words she has, but her problem is serious. She is dealing with the disappearance of reality in a sign-dominated universe. Success in country music is based on foregrounding the autobiographical ingredient (one need only think of the early Dolly Parton and Merle Haggard); but the more an artist achieves success, the less "life" there is to talk about. In many cases, this erosion of reality turns the autobiographical urge of country music toward the writing of songs about being a country-music singer—metasongs like self-reflexive postmodern metanovels about novels, composed much for the same causes.

In Loretta Lynn, we can see the autobiographical impulse grow stronger while her career develops, as if she were groping back toward a time when she was a nobody but knew who she was (or now thinks she did). She lives through some of the basic problems with which many contemporary intellectuals are concerned, and deals with them with her limited means and ambitions, in the most direct way there is: by trying her level best, over and over again, to tell the story of her life.

Notes

1. *Nashville,* screenplay by Joan Tewkesbury (New York: Bantam Books, 1976), no page numbers.
2. Loretta Lynn with George Vecsey, *Coal Miner's Daughter* (New York: Warner Books, 1980), p. 201. All further quotations will be indicated in the text with page numbers.

3. Rick Broan and Sue Thrasher, "Interview with Loretta Lynn," February 25, 1974, typescript (courtesy of Sue Thrasher). The interview appeared in *The Great Speckled Bird;* Lynn refers approvingly to it in *Coal Miner's Daughter,* p. 91.
4. Dorothy A. Horstman, "Loretta Lynn," in Bill C. Malone and Judith McCulloch, eds., *Stars of Country Music* (Urbana: University of Illinois Press, 1975), p. 32.
5. Nathanael West, *The Day of the Locust,* in *The Collected Works of Nathanael West* (Harmondsworth, Midds.: Penguin, 1975), pp. 60–61.

READING WRITING

This Text: Reading

1. How important is biography in understanding an artist? Does Portelli make a case one way or another?
2. How can one describe a song as an "autobiography"? Does Portelli make a good case?
3. Listen to "Coal Miner's Daughter." How do you think reading Portelli's piece affected your listening?

Your Text: Writing

1. Listen to a rap or country song in which the artist speaks in the first person about their experiences. Now go to an electronic database or a newspaper or magazine archive and find out something about the artist. Write a paper about what differences emerge and why or whether that matters.
2. Do an examination of an autobiographical song (or one that sounds like one). Do a literary analysis of the way the artist constructs the self.
3. In one of the two papers above, see how structuring the paper in multiple pieces in the way Portelli does affects your writing and might affect the reader's response to it.

The Authenticity Suite

One of the dominant issues in American musical culture is the concept of **authenticity,** especially how it relates to musical taste. Critics often judge artists' quality and stature by how well they seem to reflect criteria seemingly unchanged since the 1960s, when rock and roll emerged as a dominant music genre. Music that is generated by artists rather than professional song-writers, music whose production seems organic, bands at the early stages of their career before they "sell out," and music that seems thematically sophisticated rather than simple is generally taken more seriously by music critics—and probably your friends and classmates as well. Indeed, there is a certain cachet in college to knowing, liking, and listening to alternative bands and singers on the fringe. Ironically, the most popular musical act in the culture at large is rarely the most popular on college campuses. Often, budding critics, DJs at college radio stations, and club owners tend to prioritize musical acts that go out of their way to sound different than mainstream music heard on Clear Channel radio stations or promoted in Wal-Mart.

Of course, this is not the only way to judge music, as Britney Spears, Justin Timberlake, and Kelly Clarkson fans have demonstrated. Most of the music by these artists goes through extensive production and is not written by the artists themselves. Not surprisingly, their music is also immensely popular, and such popularity is often taken as a sign of being fake— after all, those concerned with authenticity ask, how can something that is any good be liked by so many people? Or, phrased in the lingo of authenticity, how can anything popular be *real*? Arguably these fans are judging the music by how it sounds, even if the associated phenomena—videos, interviews, media incidents—affects their opinions. Moreover, how a song sounds is an inherently emotional reaction whereas judging via authenticity is an intellectual one. We could argue that in fact hearing songs is much more organic than thinking them. While these distinctions are still in place, things are changing—witness the four stars given to Timberlake's *Justified* album by *Rolling Stone*.

At the heart of any discussion of musical authenticity lies a complicated mix of race, class, autonomy, and sincerity. For example, Amy Winehouse gets points on the authenticity scale because songs about being a tortured, troubled woman mirror her life as a troubled, tortured woman. Critics consider classic performers such as Johnny Cash and Hank Williams models of authenticity because they stuck to a sound and to themes that seemed to reflect their personalities. On the other hand, bands like R.E.M. lost many fans when they moved from their independent label IRS to the more mainstream Warner Brothers, despite the fact that some of their most interesting and edgy music has come in the Warner Brothers years. Similarly, critics tend to lionize blues singers and jazz players for their adherence to traditional and innovative forms.

In this suite, we print several essays about authenticity. David Sanjek, the director of research and archives at BMI, writes about the use of authenticity as a trope in *Ghost World*, as well as the implications for listeners generally. Carrie Brownstein, of the late great band Sleater-Kinney, writes about the authenticity of live music versus recorded music. Keena Sanfeh, a music critic with *The New York Times*, writes about authenticity's music cousin, "rockism," a phenomenon that places rock music at the apotheosis of popular music expression. Finally, Stephen Metcalf writes about Bruce Springsteen's use of authenticity as a marketing tool.

All the Memories Money Can Buy: Marketing Authenticity and Manufacturing Authorship

David Sanjek

A Bargain at $1.75

THE CRITICAL PLAUDITS EARNED by Terry Zwigoff's 2001 motion picture *Ghost World* have focused for the most part upon its astute depiction of adolescent life and the difficult transition into the precarious independence of adulthood. Few notices, however, commented upon the important role music plays in the film unlike the source material, Daniel Clowes's 1998 graphic novel. There, one of the central female protagonists, Enid, is drawn back to the comforting support of her childhood by the 45RPM recording of a ditty entitled "A Smile and a Ribbon." ("A smile is something special, A ribbon is something rare/ So I'll be special and I'll be rare, with a smile and a ribbon in my hair.")[1] The appeal of the material is altogether retrospective, for its presence in the plotline of the graphic novel underscores the disparity between the cloying sentiments of the song and the incomprehensible entanglements of Enid's day-to-day life.

Zwigoff jettisons this episode altogether, for his interest in the influence of music exceeds simply the invocation of lost innocence. He is drawn instead to the manner in which music can function as a foundation for the establishment of personal identity, particularly when the material under consideration lies outside the commercial mainstream. Think in this context of the opening shot of *Ghost World*. As the camera pans by a variety of windows of an urban apartment complex, we see one resident after another engaged in some manner of mind-numbing behavior. [Kind of an homage to Hitchcock's *Rear Window* (1954), in that Zwigoff emulates that film's voyeuristic engagement with human behavior, particularly in the subsequent moments when Enid (Thora Birch) and her girlfriend Rebecca (Scarlet Johansson) gaze with sarcastic wonder at a variety of subsidiary characters, like the Satanist couple at the diner.] Then, we discover Enid, bopping away happily to Ted Lyons and his Cubs' rendition of "Jaan Pehechaan Ho" in the Bollywood vehicle *Gumnaam* (1965). Not only is she alone and enraptured, but she also appears to be the sole viewer of some television channel one imagines does not appear in the common cable guide. Unlike the other figures shown in the sequence, she fails to come across as weighed down by anomie, but, instead, buoyed up by her uncommon cultural sensibility.

This scene is elaborated upon by the introduction of the character of Seymour (Steve Buscemi), the sad sack record collector whom Enid befriends. Seymour does not appear in the graphic novel, and while he first enters the narrative as simply an object of the girls' contempt, he soon thereafter comes to embody Enid's access to the musical culture upon which she begins to determine her path in life. They first encounter one another face-to-face when Seymour sells Enid a vinyl reissue collection that contains Skip James's 1932 recording "Devil Got My Woman" for the bargain basement price of $1.75. If Enid initially buys the LP as a lark, once it begins to play on her stereo, the music affects a transformation upon her. As Zwigoff comments, "She's trying to find her identity in the world, and then she plays this weird eerie thing, and thinks maybe there *is* something this guy has to offer."[2] The singer's otherworldly falsetto and evocative depiction of the torments of affection amount to the farthest possible thing from the au courant material Enid's peers live by. Moreover, the manner in which James strips his material of any form of false sentiment parallels Enid's seemingly affectless approach to her own feelings. You can imagine she would be drawn by Stephen

Calt's description of James's material: "His songs were expressions of his own bleak temperament. He was an aloof person who begrudged banter and mistrusted merriment."[3] Even if the song is played only once in the film, its influence upon Enid and the fact that Seymour has been her access to it resonates throughout the rest of the narrative. For through "Devil Got My Woman" and him, Enid has sampled the most tantalizing of cultural categories: authenticity. All for just $1.75.

Enid may not use this term specifically nor does Zwigoff draw it into the film, yet the notion of authenticity resonates from beginning to end. Enid defines it, or at least one version of the phenomenon, when she explains to Rebecca why she is attracted to Seymour: the fact that he's so square that he transcends the sphere of hip. However, what Seymour has to offer the young woman is as much a form of negation as any kind of affirmation or indication of what Enid should do with her life. Even though the consequences of his behavior make Seymour alienated and unhappy, he has deliberately and energetically erased any interest in or connection to the vast majority of contemporary life. (We'll leave unanswered the question of exactly when *Ghost World* takes place. The film seems at one and the same time set in the present day and a near-distant past. Why a stereo and not a CD player?) He epitomizes a state of disaffiliation whose only sense of meaning emerges when in contact with music or other forms of culture related to the 1930s or earlier. Seymour does not indicate that access to this body of material satisfies his life—he dismisses his hobbies with the most melancholy declaration, "Go ahead and kill me. You think it's healthy to obsessively collect things?"—yet he fails to give one the sense that he could live without either his vintage disks or memorabilia. Enid in turn does not take up his obsessive dedication to collecting nor listen intently to another historic piece of material other than Skip James. No matter, the one song and the interaction with Seymour have made an indelible impact. Both offer her access to something substantial and satisfying that neither her peers nor the society about her embody. They each have triggered in Enid a need to retain her independence, whatever the cost.

Zwigoff's fascination with the authentic as embodied by a certain sphere of musical culture resonates through his other two pictures, the 1985 documentary on the string musician Howard Armstrong, *Louie Bluie*, and the 1994 portrait of the artist Robert Crumb. In the first case, Zwigoff not only pays tribute to a rare and unforgettable character but also a form of performance—the African American string band—that has by and large been written out of most history books for being, it appears, unfashionable and somehow unaffiliated with customary notions of racially-determined forms of performance.[4] Armstrong therefore is made heroic by Zwigoff because he stuck to his guns in the face of arbitrary definitions of how and what he should play. In effect, Armstrong and his fiddle come across as being more authentic than what we are accustomed to hearing of music at that time, for the material simultaneously breaks with our very notion of what it meant to be black and musically inclined in the period before and during the Depression. In the case of *Crumb*, Zwigoff illustrates how for the cartoonist, as for the filmmaker, the sphere of the 78 constitutes one of the precious few precincts untouched and undefiled by the crass influence of present-day culture. Zwigoff at one point interpolates a telling, if misguided strip by Crumb that condemns technology for replacing live performance with sterile copies.[5] This position fails to take into account Crumb's own fetishizing of certain select recordings as well as uncritically valorizes a simplified notion of vernacular culture. Nonetheless, both the set of drawings and the memorable sequence in which the artist's collection is packed for shipping to his new home in France vividly conjure up the defense of authenticity that Zwigoff dramatizes in *Ghost World*.

The conviction shared with equal vigor by Enid, Seymour, Crumb and Zwigoff that certain kinds of music are authentic and others ersatz encapsulates the fundamental parameters of a familiar debate. This tussle of perspectives all too often reduces the discussion of music to nothing more or less than a collision of incompatible and absolute categories. Each time one encounters a performance, it becomes appraised as if one were examining raw ore in search of rare metals. The frequency with which the object is determined to be bogus therefore leads to interminable cycles of despair, as if the vast majority of recording artists engage in a deliberate exercise in deceit, pawning off fool's gold for the real thing. Moreover, the propensity on the part of many people to assume that most music fails the test of authenticity by virtue of its institutionalization at the hands of commercial interests unnecessarily complicates the matter. Where can one go with such an *ad hominem*, and therefore debateable, proposition such as that made by Charles Keil: "Everything mediated is spurious until proven genuine."[6] This kind of absolutism equates all manner of packaging with desecration. From my perspective, I do not know of any commercial music that lacks dirty hands, so to speak. Rather than a cut-and-dried category, authenticity amounts in my mind to a constructed determination that must encompass the commodified with the non-commercial, the immediate with the mediated, the raw with the cooked. Seldom are we in a position to isolate these domains from one another. The circumstances under which we assess recorded music for its quantity of authenticity parallels the proposition that the character actor Walter Brennan would put before directors: did they want him to play a particular part with or without his dentures. Same man, with or without the incisors. Same music, with or without the apparatus that we associate with the mass media.

I wish therefore to proceed in this discussion by assenting to the proposition put forth by Simon Frith some time ago that

> Because it cannot be denied that rock and pop [or any other musical genre, in my mind] are indeed "commodities," [the] problem is to show that there is, nevertheless, something "authentic" to that commodity . . . My starting point is that what is possible for us as consumers—what is available to us, what we can do with it—is a result of decision made in production, made by musicians, entrepreneurs, and corporate bureaucrats, made according to governments' and lawyers' rulings, in response to technological opportunities. The key to "creative consumption" remains an understanding of those decisions, the constraints under which they are made, and the ideologies that account for them. Such understanding depends on both industrial research and the intelligence revealed in single songs.[7]

It does us no good to proceed as if we were Dorothy on the emerald road and find out, time and again, that the Mighty Oz has rigged the machinery behind the scenes, thereby clamping down upon any undiluted access to self-expression. Should we proceed down this path, we can only end up as dyspeptic as Seymour, Crumb and Zwigoff, convinced that we are surrounded by charlatans who operate at the behest of confidence men. We can come to some understanding of the forces against which musicians must contend and regardless of which they occasionally remain true to some value system only by examining individual instances of cultural production.

As even *Ghost World* indicates , the definition of authenticity has to be as flexible as the material to which it applies. No master template of characteristics exists that can be checked off and tallied up so as to determine where on the scale a particular piece of music lies.

The Authenticity Suite

Much as many of us scorn the rating practices typified by the weekly analysis conducted on Dick Clark's *American Bandstand*, the fixation upon authenticity is, to me, only a slightly more sophisticated version of that enterprise. Our reasons for preferring one piece of music or another or one genre above all else may be an interesting arena of investigation, but, in the end, the exercise amounts to a pissing contest over taste. Not an activity I prefer to engage in, for, as compelling as it might be, someone simply acquires a wet shoe in the end.

Even more to the point, debates over authenticity really come down to distinctions about repertoire, which person's list is superior to another's. It's nothing short of a collector's reflex, a conviction that catalog outweighs content. Whenever the mainstream taste of the wider public descends into a pattern that the cognoscenti consider debased, the obsession with repertoire emerges in full force. Preserving material that blows the current Top Ten out of the water bears a less than appetizing analogy to the educated classes in the Middle Ages barricading themselves against the barbarians at the gates. Gina Arnold's metaphor comes to mind in this context: "That, after all, is my generation's symbol of a roving mind: great record collections in cardboard boxes, kept the way monks hoarded literature from marauding pagan masses."[8] I cannot share her, and others', conviction that the world could be transformed by a better playlist. When she argues that the presence of Nirvana on the radio meant that "my own values are winning: I'm no longer in the opposition," my rejoinder is that I never really wanted to start a fight over what's on the jukebox in the first place.[9] Taste is transitory, and the belief that when someone shares my preferences, the chance of better things emerging on the horizon increases does not parallel my sense of social transformation. In the end, I'm more interested in what music people like and the role it plays in their lives than whether or not I get off on the same material. Their authenticity could easily be my ersatz.

Therefore, I have to concede that, in the end, I share Nick Tosches's admonition that "meaning is the biggest sucker's-racket of all; and any regard for it, no matter how fleeting, befits a middle-aged fool like me."[10] Seeking out this elusive category may be a quixotic crusade, yet, to return to Enid in *Ghost World*, otherwise how can I make sense out of why Bollywood soundtracks make a young girl dance and the scratchy vocalizing of a long-dead delta cynic nearly drive her to tears?

Notes

1. Daniel Clowes, *Ghost World* (Seattle: Fantagraphic Books, 1998), p. 62.
2. Simon Reynolds, "In Between Days," *Village Voice,* July 18–24, 2001 http:www.villvoice.com (access April 3, 2002).
3. Stephen Calt, *I'd Rather Be The Devil. Skip James and the Blues* (New York: Da Capo Press, 1994), p. 18.
4. It is a mistake to correlate what we can hear on recordings and what was played concurrently in the sphere of daily life. The kind of string-based dance music that Armstrong and others created was judged by A&R men of the period as being somehow not sufficiently parallel with what they determined "race" music to be. As the blues scholar Paul Oliver has stated, "the phases of recording black music do not correspond in all details with the changing nature of the music itself. . . . Few attempts have been made to make a comprehensive analysis of all the forms of black song (let alone of instrumental music) which appeared on disc through all these phases. Nor has there been adequate consideration of how representative these were of the music in both the urban and the rural contexts of the times, nor whether their appearance or absence from record was a reflection of their popularity within the black community." Paul Oliver, *Songsters and Saints. Vocal Traditions on Race Records* (Cambridge: Cambridge University Press, 1984), pp. 11–12.

The Authenticity Suite

5. Crumb's piece "Where Has It Gone, All the Beautiful Music of Our Grandparents" appears in *R. Crumb Draws the Blues* (London: Crack Editions, 1992). It is also reproduced in the tandem collection by Charles Keil and Steve Feld, *Music Grooves* (Chicago: University of Chicago Press 1994), pp. 233–37. As he states in one panel, "Wherever technology invades a culture, you find the youth embracing it, going for it, disdaining the old ways. They want the goodies, the shiny toys, the promise of all that glitter, the comfort and, the convenience, the sophistication ... it's only natural ..."

6. Charles Keil and Steven Field, *Music Grooves: Essays and Dialogues* (Chicago: University of Chicago Press, 1995), 313.

7. Simon Frith, *Music for Pleasure. Essays in the Sociology of Pop* (New York: Routledge, 1988), 6–7.

8. Gina Arnold, *Route 666. On the Road to Nirvana* (New York: St. Martin's Press, 1991), p. 6.

9. Arnold, p. 4.

10. Nick Tosches, *Where Dead Voices Gather* (New York: Little Brown, 2002), p. 6.

More Rock, Less Talk: Live Music Turns Off the Voices in Our Heads

Carrie Brownstein

AS AN ARTIST, IT IS MOST FRIGHTENING to feel that the meaning in your work is slipping away from you. I think that this is a natural by-product of placing art into the world. But it's especially true in a medium like music, one that is populist—where the audience naturally adopts it as their own. In some ways it should belong to them. Listeners are each allowed their own interpretation, without the need for any kind of theoretical or technical understanding.

Their belief that they can have a unique response or a visceral relationship to the art is what removes it from an elitist, academic realm. However, for every individual vision of the art there is also an individual definition of who the artists are and what they represent. If the audience for the work is large, you wind up with a multitude of definitions, and these are likely to vary enormously. Eventually there comes to exist, separate from the artist, an entity that is externally defined, one that embodies the expectations inhabited by the outside world. This external entity, a veritable artistic doppelgänger, is difficult to ignore. It can feel like a demanding evil twin, and artists can begin to ignore or lose sight of their own motivations.

Since my own goals in music lie in forging a connection with people, with an audience, it's disheartening to feel as though my message is misinterpreted or no longer of my own design. I struggle to tune out the external expectations and definitions. At the same time, I cannot wholly ignore those to whom I am trying to relate, who are sharing the experience along with me. It is a precarious position.

Recorded music, by fixing the sound in a specific time and place, can't help but form a definitive sonic blueprint for a band. The recorded medium is much more likely to be categorized and posited within the ever-growing and ever-limiting list of genres. We can hear the same instance replayed over and over, and though the listeners bring their own experience to the songs, and may hear new textures with each pass, the sonic nature of the song is fixed.

In contrast, the context of playing live allows for fluidity and continuity between the otherwise disparate past and present, the fixed (recorded) and the ephemeral, and the artist's private and public identities. The live experience elevates the art of music by making it permeable and improvisational. To me, the dialogue in a live context exists in the sonic and visceral relationship between the artist and the song and between the artist and the audience.

The Authenticity Suite

Essentially, the live show is nothing more than an impromptu conversation. It's a moment that lets us connect on a level free from the restraints of everyday discourse. It welcomes as opposed to shuns lexical ambiguities. Our translation of the experience is not reliant on our intellectual grasp of the moment; it operates more spontaneously, as an intuitive and physical response. In addition, the language of any given live show is unique, a spontaneous and instantaneous negotiation of sound, utterance, and gesture. It is useful only in this moment. Few other forms of communication or art achieve this evanescent beauty.

For myself, the moment when the live aspect became the most crucial was when the identity of my band, Sleater-Kinney, became uncertain, when there became a joint ownership between us and the audience. We had been split into two: there were two distinct definitions of the band, our own and that of the audience. Often, the dichotomy felt irreconcilable.

To us, Sleater-Kinney was a dialogue among three people. It was our source of salvation, escape, strength, and joy. Sleater-Kinney was nothing more than the sounds that traveled from our mouths, fingers, hands, and our hearts. It traveled no further than the walls of our practice space. All of the meaning was both surrounding us and inside of us; there existed little disparity between the internal and external worlds of the band. Whatever sounds came out of us at that moment, that was who we were, we owned it. Yet the moment we left the practice space, recorded the songs, and placed them into the world, our formerly insular identity, or lack of conscious identity, became public and therefore open to debate.

Though we had no intention of remaining obscure, we also had no way of preparing for the outside definitions and expectations. Suddenly, we were defined by specific songs, albums, photographs, quotes, politics, and genders. We were a "girl group," a "feminist band," we had "risen from the riot grrrl ghetto," we were Call the Doctor, we were Dig Me Out. We went from mutable to fixed identities.

But live we remained and remain nothing except the moment itself. The audience, hearing it brought together in front of them, senses the congruencies in the music. Two seemingly disparate songs suddenly come off as unified. People tend to fear growth and change in artists, but live performance has a way of proving that this evolution contains a common thread, a core that is true to the original artistic vision.

My early relationship to performing live music is best described in the song "I Wanna Be Your Joey Ramone," which we wrote in 1995. Joey Ramone was a performer who embodied both diffidence and grandiosity. To me, he was a man who was simultaneously awkward, with his spindly legs and his hair falling into his face, and also larger than life. This contradiction seemed to be an ideal metaphor for my own relationship to performing and music. Part of me wanted to own the stage while the other part of me remained uncomfortable with such power. The song was also about stepping into someone else's shoes (in this case Joey's) as a means of exploring my own fears and dreams.

When Sleater-Kinney first began, it seemed to me that the only way to get a sense of rock 'n' roll was to experience it vicariously. At least that was the message coming to us from the outside world: the archetypes, the stage moves, the representations of rebellion and debauchery were all male. The song has us exploring a role typically associated with male performers. By doing so, we get a glimpse of the absurdity, the privilege, and the decadence that wasn't inherently afforded to us.

Some people are born with the certainty that they own sound or volume; that the lexicon of rock music is theirs to borrow from, to employ, to interpret. For them, it might be nothing to move around on stage, to swagger, to sing in front of people, to pick up a guitar, to make records. I set out from a place where I never assumed that those were acceptable choices or that

I could be anything but an accessory to rock 'n' roll. Coming out of a tradition that historically didn't allow women much of a voice, then finding myself helping to create a sound that filled an entire room, that reached into every person in that room, that is a power that I had to learn. I needed to try it on before I could call it mine. I had to find a means to make it my own.

The transition from a vicarious exploration of power to empowerment could happen only in live environments. There one faces not only the audience's expectations of what it means to be a performer on stage but also one's own mental catalog of the archetypal images of rock, which are often affirmations of adolescent male sexual identity. Playing live felt like battling history, icons, images. It is hard not to be reduced to the category of "women in rock." I didn't feel like I could be rock 'n' roll.

Instead, we were women imitating and participating in rock 'n roll, something we didn't create. To feel comfortable with the power, I couldn't feel like it was being lent to me, and certainly no one was passing it to me. I had to claim it. I had to carve a space for myself in my own imagination and in the imagination of the audience.

Because the live moment is fluid, so too is the identity: it passes back and forth from audience to performer; it presents a form and then turns that form on its head. On stage, questions of identity, gender, or categorical indexing begin to feel obsolete. They are obliterated by the visceral. The live performance allows gender to take on an ambiguous or even androgyne role; it smashes the historical assumptions about who owns rock 'n' roll. Whoever is on stage at that moment owns the music; whoever is watching and hearing it at that moment owns it as well.

Live music also frees me from the restraints of the rhetorical. Art historian Anne Middleton Wagner writes: "It is a necessary consequence for working 'as a woman.' Making art from such a position is inevitably rhetorical; it must often be strategic, must often employ assertion, denial, tactical evasion, subterfuge, deception, refusal." I certainly feel that this is the case with Sleater-Kinney: talking about the experience has become part of the experience itself. In interviews, we are constantly asked the question, "What is it like to be a woman playing rock?" More than anything, I feel that this metadiscourse, talking about the talk, is part of how it feels to be a "woman playing rock."

There is the music itself, and then there is the ongoing dialogue about how it feels. The two seem to be intertwined and also inescapable. This dialogue also began to appear in our own songwriting. The songs responded to and addressed the fans, the critics, and even our own work: the new songs (such as "Male Model" or "#1 Must Have") explaining the old ("I Wanna Be Your Joey Ramone," "Little Babies"), discussing what we had already done and why we had done it.

The metadiscourse and the rhetorical form a disconnect; a psychological, linguistic, and identity fissure. However, these elements are made congruent and whole in the live context. Here the rhetoric ceased; there is no explanation but the sound itself. I am not talking about the music, I am the music.

For all the freeing possibilities that live performance opens up, it also introduces another dynamic that is more problematic: the inherent hierarchy assumed between performer and audience. There are few moments when this imbalance is effectively dismantled. Recently, however, I experienced a disruption of this dynamic. It was at an outdoor show, at the moment when night fell upon the stage, when the sky was fixed for an instant, holding elements of both night and day in its hues. This was a moment that could never happen indoors, a straddling of two contrasting environments and moods. It came to me that you could see it as nature's way of illustrating how a concert is simultaneously a public and a private experience.

Whatever form it takes, live music draws on both individual and collective elements, for performer and audience alike. Outdoors, however, the dichotomy is exaggerated. During the day,

The Authenticity Suite

everyone is made much more aware of just how public and shared the experience really is. Not only can you sense how close you are to the strangers in front of or next to you, but after a few hours you know every detail of their faces, every whisker, every blemish, every twitch. In the midst of a song, you can watch their faces change in response to the lyrics and the music; you know how they look with their eyes closed, mouthing the words. In the light of day, the private experience is exposed and the collective experience is no longer merely visceral—it is also visible.

When I play outside I am constantly aware of this visibility. I like the way the environment lends itself to demystifying the performer and removes some of the artifice. Aside from the stage itself, there exists less of the performer-fan hierarchy perpetuated by elements such as elaborate lighting. Everyone is under the same indiscriminate glare of the sun. I can look out into the crowd and see individual faces and expressions, I can see the dimensions of the space, where the crowd begins, where it ends; there is nowhere to hide for me or for them.

Naturally, there is a drawback to a heightened awareness of one another and the fact that the private has been made public. Many people come to rock 'n' roll and punk out of desperation. They like the anonymity provided by a dark room, where emotions are less transparent, where appearances can be obfuscated. Thus, there is often a feeling of reservation at a summer concert, a reluctance to allow oneself to be exposed. And this brings me back to my favorite moment, which is when the spotlight of the sun begins to fade.

Often, by the time night falls, we have been participants long enough to be acutely aware of the collective nature of the event. By this time we are yearning for a moment that is our own, a moment that goes unseen. The onset of darkness is that moment, the one where the private and public experience converge. We at last have the privacy to feel and express ourselves without anyone watching. At the same time, there is a relief in knowing that we're not alone.

In general, I feel that live performance is the truest and most organic way to experience the tradition of music, for the listener and for the artist. It frees us from our own intellectual restraints—the kind of analytical discourse that we use on a daily basis that distances us from an interior emotional landscape. Appearing live is also a way for artists to ward off static or reductive definitions. The moment relies on movement, connection, continuity, spontaneity. We are reminded that music is an experience, not merely an object, and thus it becomes difficult to separate it from our own bodies. It feels crucial to form connections with one another, to be aware of how our private and public selves intertwine. Lastly, live music is about breaking free of restraints, of tradition, of roles. This is possible because the live moment is ephemeral, it leaves no singular residue. All that exists once it is over is the potential in ourselves to be transformed.

The Rap Against Rockism

Kelefa Sanneh

BAD NEWS TRAVELS FAST, and an embarrassing video travels even faster. By last Sunday morning, one of the Internet's most popular downloads was the hours-old 60-second .wmv file of Ashlee Simpson on "Saturday Night Live." As she and her band stood onstage, her own prerecorded vocals—from the wrong song—came blaring through the speakers, and it was too late to start mouthing the words. So she performed a now-infamous little jig, then skulked offstage, while the band (were a few members smirking?) played on. One of 2004's most popular new stars had been exposed as.

As what, exactly? The online verdict came fast and harsh, the way online verdicts usually do. A typical post on her Web site bore the headline, "Ashlee you are a no talent fraud!" After that night, everyone knew that Jessica Simpson's telegenic sister was no rock 'n' roll hero—she wasn't even a rock 'n' roll also-ran. She was merely a lip-synching pop star.

Music critics have a word for this kind of verdict, this knee-jerk backlash against producer-powered idols who didn't spend years touring dive bars. Not a very elegant word, but a useful one. The word is rockism, and among the small but extraordinarily pesky group of people who obsess over this stuff, rockism is a word meant to start fights. The rockism debate began in earnest in the early 1980s, but over the past few years it has heated up, and today, in certain impassioned circles, there is simply nothing worse than a rockist.

A rockist isn't just someone who loves rock 'n' roll, who goes on and on about Bruce Springsteen, who champions ragged-voiced singer–songwriters no one has ever heard of. A rockist is someone who reduces rock 'n' roll to a caricature, then uses that caricature as a weapon. Rockism means idolizing the authentic old legend (or underground hero) while mocking the latest pop star; lionizing punk while barely tolerating disco; loving the live show and hating the music video; extolling the growling performer while hating the lip-syncher.

Over the past decades, these tendencies have congealed into an ugly sort of common sense. Rock bands record classic albums, while pop stars create "guilty pleasure" singles. It's supposed to be self-evident: U2's entire oeuvre deserves respectful consideration, while a spookily seductive song by an R&B singer named Tweet can only be, in the smug words of a recent VH1 special, "awesomely bad."

Like rock 'n' roll itself, rockism is full of contradictions: it could mean loving the Strokes (a scruffy guitar band!) or hating them (image-conscious poseurs!) or ignoring them entirely (since everyone knows that music isn't as good as it used to be). But it almost certainly means disdaining not just Ms. Simpson but also Christina Aguilera and Usher and most of the rest of them, grousing about a pop landscape dominated by big-budget spectacles and high-concept photo shoots, reminiscing about a time when the charts were packed with people who had something to say, and meant it, even if that time never actually existed. If this sounds like you, then take a long look in the mirror: you might be a rockist.

Countless critics assail pop stars for not being rock 'n' roll enough, without stopping to wonder why that should be everybody's goal. Or they reward them disproportionately for making rock 'n' roll gestures. Writing in *The Chicago Sun-Times* this summer, Jim DeRogatis grudgingly praised Ms. Lavigne as "a teen-pop phenom that discerning adult rock fans can actually admire without feeling (too) guilty," partly because Ms. Lavigne "plays a passable rhythm guitar" and "has a hand in writing" her songs.

Rockism isn't unrelated to older, more familiar prejudices—that's part of why it's so powerful, and so worth arguing about. The pop star, the disco diva, the lip-syncher, the "awesomely bad" hit maker: could it really be a coincidence that rockist complaints often pit straight white men against the rest of the world? Like the anti-disco backlash of 25 years ago, the current rockist consensus seems to reflect not just an idea of how music should be made but also an idea about who should be making it.

If you're interested in—O.K., mildly obsessed with—rockism, you can find traces of it just about everywhere. Notice how those tributes to "Women Who Rock" sneakily transform "rock" from a genre to a verb to a catch-all term of praise. Ever wonder why OutKast and the Roots and Mos Def and the Beastie Boys get taken so much more seriously than other rappers? Maybe because rockist critics love it when hip-hop acts impersonate rock 'n' roll bands. (A recent Rolling Stone review praised the Beastie Boys for scruffily resisting "the gold-plated phooey currently passing for gangsta.")

From punk-rock rags to handsomely illustrated journals, rockism permeates the way we think about music. This summer, the literary zine The Believer published a music issue devoted to almost nothing but indie-rock. Two weeks ago, in *The New York Times Book Review*, Sarah Vowell approvingly recalled Nirvana's rise: "a group with loud guitars and louder drums knocking the whimpering Mariah Carey off the top of the charts." Why did the changing of the guard sound so much like a sexual assault? And when did we all agree that Nirvana's neo-punk was more respectable than Ms. Carey's neo-disco?

Rockism is imperial: it claims the entire musical world as its own. Rock 'n' roll is the unmarked section in the record store, a vague pop-music category that swallows all the others. If you write about music, you're presumed to be a rock critic. There's a place in the Rock and Roll Hall of Fame for doo-wop groups and folk singers and disco queens and even rappers— just so long as they, y'know, rock.

Rockism just won't go away. The rockism debate began when British bands questioned whether the search for raw, guitar-driven authenticity wasn't part of rock 'n' roll's problem, instead of its solution; some new-wave bands emphasized synthesizers and drum machines and makeup and hairspray, instead. "Rockist" became for them a term of abuse, and the anti-rockists embraced the inclusive possibilities of a once-derided term: pop. Americans found other terms, but "rockist" seems the best way to describe the ugly anti-disco backlash of the late 1970's, which culminated in a full-blown anti-disco rally and the burning of thousands of disco records at Comiskey Park in Chicago in 1979: the Boston Tea Party of rockism.

That was a quarter of a century and many genres ago. By the 1990's, the American musical landscape was no longer a battleground between Nirvana and Mariah (if indeed it ever was); it was a fractured, hyper-vivid fantasy of teen-pop stars and R&B pillow-talkers and arena-filling country singers and, above all, rappers. Rock 'n' roll was just one more genre alongside the rest.

Yet many critics failed to notice. Rock 'n' roll doesn't rule the world anymore, but lots of writers still act as if it does. The rules, even today, are: concentrate on making albums, not singles; portray yourself as a rebellious individualist, not an industry pro; give listeners the uncomfortable truth, instead of pandering to their tastes. Overnight celebrities, one-hit-wonders and lip-synchers, step aside.

And just as the anti-disco partisans of a quarter-century ago railed against a bewildering new pop order (partly because disco was so closely associated with black culture and gay culture), current critics rail against a world hopelessly corrupted by hip-hop excess. Since before Sean Combs became Puff Daddy, we've been hearing that mainstream hip-hop was too flashy, too crass, too violent, too ridiculous, unlike those hard-working rock 'n' roll stars we used to have. (This, of course, is one of the most pernicious things about rockism: it finds a way to make rock 'n' roll seem boring.)

Much of the most energetic resistance to rockism can be found online, in blogs and on critic-infested sites like ilovemusic.com, where debates about rockism have become so common that the term itself is something of a running joke. When the editors of a blog called Rockcritics Daily noted that rockism was "all the rage again," they posted dozens of contradictory citations, proving that no one really agrees on what the term means. (By the time you read this article, a slew of indignant refutations and addenda will probably be available online.)

But as more than one online ranter has discovered, it's easier to complain about rockism than it is to get rid of it. You literally can't fight rockism, because the language of righteous struggle is the language of rockism itself. You can argue that the shape-shifting feminist hip-pop of Ms. Aguilera is every bit as radical as the punk rock of the 1970s (and it is), but then you haven't challenged any of the old rockist questions (starting with: Who's more radical?), you've just scribbled in some new answers.

The challenge isn't merely to replace the old list of Great Rock Albums with a new list of Great Pop Songs—although that would, at the very least, be a nice change of pace. It's to find a way to think about a fluid musical world where it's impossible to separate classics from guilty pleasures. The challenge is to acknowledge that music videos and reality shows and glamorous layouts can be as interesting—and as influential—as an old-fashioned album.

In the end, the problem with rockism isn't that it's wrong: all critics are wrong sometimes, and some critics (now doesn't seem like the right time to name names) are wrong almost all the time. The problem with rockism is that it seems increasingly far removed from the way most people actually listen to music.

Are you really pondering the phony distinction between "great art" and a "guilty pleasure" when you're humming along to the radio? In an era when listeners routinely—and fearlessly—pick music by putting a 40-gig iPod on shuffle, surely we have more interesting things to worry about than that someone might be lip-synching on "Saturday Night Live" or that some rappers gild their phooey. Good critics are good listeners, and the problem with rockism is that it gets in the way of listening. If you're waiting for some song that conjures up soul or honesty or grit or rebellion, you might miss out on Ciara's ecstatic electro-pop, or Alan Jackson's sly country ballads, or Lloyd Banks's felonious purr.

Rockism makes it hard to hear the glorious, incoherent, corporate-financed, audience-tested mess that passes for popular music these days. To glorify only performers who write their own songs and play their own guitars is to ignore the marketplace that helps create the music we hear in the first place, with its checkbook-chasing superproducers, its audience-obsessed executives and its cred-hungry performers. To obsess over old-fashioned stand-alone geniuses is to forget that lots of the most memorable music is created despite multimillion-dollar deals and spur-of-the-moment collaborations and murky commercial forces. In fact, a lot of great music is created because of those things. And let's stop pretending that serious rock songs will last forever, as if anything could, and that shiny pop songs are inherently disposable, as if that were necessarily a bad thing. Van Morrison's "Into the Music" was released the same year as the Sugarhill Gang's "Rapper's Delight"; which do you hear more often?

That doesn't mean we should stop arguing about Ms. Simpson, or even that we should stop sharing the 60-second clip that may just be this year's best music video. But it does mean we should stop taking it for granted that music isn't as good as it used to be, and it means we should stop being shocked that the rock rules of the 1970s are no longer the law of the land. No doubt our current obsessions and comparisons will come to seem hopelessly blinkered as popular music mutates some more—listeners and critics alike can't do much more than struggle to keep up. But let's stop trying to hammer young stars into old categories. We have lots of new music to choose from—we deserve some new prejudices, too.

Faux Americana: Why I Still Love Bruce Springsteen

Stephen Metcalf

IN HIS EARLY LIVE SHOWS, Bruce Springsteen had a habit of rattling off, while the band vamped softly in the background, some thoroughly implausible story from his youth. This he punctuated with a shy, wheezing laugh that let you know he didn't for a second buy into his own bullshit. Back then, in the early 1970s, Bruce was still a regional act, touring the dive bars and dive colleges of the Atlantic coast, playing any venue that would have him. As a matter of routine, a Springsteen show would kick off with audience members throwing gifts onto the stage. Not bras and panties, mind you, but gifts—something thoughtful, not too expensive. Bruce was one of their own, after all, a scrawny little dirtbag from the shore, a minor celebrity of what the great George Trow once called "the disappearing middle distance." By 1978, and the release of *Darkness on the Edge of Town*, the endearing Jersey wharf rat in Springsteen had been refined away. In its place was a majestic American simpleton with a generic heartland twang, obsessed with cars, Mary, the Man, and the bitterness between fathers and sons. Springsteen has been augmenting and refining that persona for so long now that it's hard to recall its status, not only as an invention, but an invention whose origin wasn't even Bruce Springsteen. For all the po-faced mythic resonance that now accompanies Bruce's every move, we can thank Jon Landau, the ex-*Rolling Stone* critic who, after catching a typically seismic Springsteen set in 1974, famously wrote, "I saw rock and roll future, and its name is Bruce Springsteen."

Well, Bruce Springsteen was Jon Landau's future. Over the next couple of years, Landau insinuated himself into Bruce's artistic life and consciousness (while remaining on the *Rolling Stone* masthead) until he became Springsteen's producer, manager, and full-service Svengali. Unlike the down-on-their-luck Springsteens of Freehold, N.J., Landau hailed from the well-appointed suburbs of Boston and had earned an honors degree in history from Brandeis. He filled his new protégé's head with an American Studies syllabus heavy on John Ford, Steinbeck, and Flannery O'Connor. At the same time that he intellectualized Bruce, he anti-intellectualized him. Rock music was transcendent, Landau believed, because it was primitive, not because it could be avant-garde. *The White Album* and Hendrix and the Velvet Underground had robbed rock of its power, which lay buried in the pre-Beatles era with Del Shannon and the Ronettes. Bruce's musical vocabulary accordingly shrank. By *Darkness on the Edge of Town*, gone were the *West Side Story*–esque jazz suites of *The Wild, the Innocent, and the E Street Shuffle*. In their place were tight, guitar-driven intro-verse-chorus-verse-bridge-chorus songs. Springsteen's image similarly transformed. On the cover of *Darkness*, he looks strangely like the sallower cousin of Pacino's Sonny Wortzik, the already quite sallow anti-hero of *Dog Day Afternoon*. The message was clear: Springsteen himself was one of the unbeautiful losers, flitting along the ghostly fringes of suburban respectability.

Thirty years later, and largely thanks to Landau, Springsteen is no longer a musician. He's a belief system. And, like any belief system worth its salt, he brooks no in-between. You're either in or you're out. This has solidified Bruce's standing with his base, for whom he remains a god of total rock authenticity. But it's killed him with everyone else. To a legion of devout non-believers—they're not saying Bruuuce, they're booing—Bruce is more a phenomenon akin to Dianetics or Tinkerbell than "the new Dylan," as the Columbia Records promotions machine once hyped him. And so we've reached a strange juncture. About America's last rock star, it's either Pentecostal enthusiasm or total disdain.

To walk back from this impasse, we need to see Springsteen's persona for what it really is: Jon Landau's middle-class fantasy of white, working-class authenticity. Does it derogate Springsteen to claim that he is, in essence, a white minstrel act? Not at all. Only by peeling back all the layers of awful heartland authenticity and rediscovering the old Jersey bullshitter underneath can we begin to grasp the actual charms of the man and his music. A glimpse of this old bullshitter was recently on display when Springsteen inducted U2 into the Rock 'n' Roll Hall of Fame on March 14. Springsteen had recently caught the new iPod commercial featuring the Irish rockers. "Now personally, I live an insanely expensive lifestyle that my wife barely tolerates," the old BSer confided to the audience of industry heavyweights, adding,

> Now, I burn money, and that calls for huge amounts of cash flow. But, I also have a ludicrous image of myself that keeps me from truly cashing in. You can see my problem. Woe is me. So the next morning, I call up Jon Landau . . . and I say, "Did you see that iPod thing?" and he says, "Yes." And he says, "And I hear they didn't take any money." And I said, "They didn't take any money?" and he says, "No." I said, "Smart, wily Irish guys. Anybody—anybody—can do an ad and take the money. But to do the ad and not take the money . . . that's smart. That's wily." I say, "Jon, I want you to call up Bill Gates or whoever is behind this thing and float this: a red, white and blue iPod signed by Bruce 'The Boss' Springsteen. Now remember, no matter how much money he offers, don't take it!"

Every now and again, the majestic simpleton breaks character, and winks; and about as often, he works his way back to subtlety and a human scale and cuts a pretty great song or album. From the post-Landau period, the harrowing masterpiece *Nebraska* is the only record you can push on the nonbelievers, followed by the grossly underrated *Tunnel of Love*. The Oscar-winning "Streets of Philadelphia," an account of a man with AIDS slowly fading into his own living ghost, is the equal of any song he's written. In 1995 Springsteen produced *The Ghost of Tom Joad*, the culmination of a 15-year obsession with Woody Guthrie, whose biography he had been handed the night after Reagan defeated Carter, in 1980. The album is stronger than its popular reception might lead one to believe. "Across the Border" and "Galveston Bay" are lovely and understated and bring home the fact that Springsteen—a man who wrote monster hits for acts as diverse as Manfred Mann, the Pointer Sisters, and Patti Smith—remains a skilled melodist. Nonetheless, the record is a little distant in its sympathies, as if Springsteen had thumbed through back issues of *The Utne Reader* before sitting down to compose.

His new album, *Devils & Dust*, is a sequel to *The Ghost of Tom Joad*. It's mostly acoustic and intimate in scale; but Springsteen appears to have taken criticism of Tom Joad to heart, and *Devils & Dust* is warmer, and in patches, fully up-tempo. It's hard to describe how good the good songs are. The title song is classic Springsteen—"a dirty wind's blowing," and a young soldier may "kill the things he loves" to survive. And on "Black Cowboys," Springsteen unites a visionary concision of detail with long lines in a way that channels William Blake:

> Come the fall the rain flooded these homes, here in Ezekiel's valley of dry bones, it fell hard and dark to the ground. It fell without a sound. Lynette took up with a man whose business was the boulevard, whose smile was fixed in a face that was never off guard.

Though initially signed as a folkie, Springsteen has never been much of a technician on the acoustic guitar, compared to, say, the infinitely nimble Richard Thompson. But on *Devils & Dust* there's a new comfort with the instrument; and he decorates many of the songs with a lovely, understated filigree. Ah, but how hard the lapses in taste! The strings and vocal choruses used to punch up the sound are—what other word is there?—corny. Next to, say, *Iron and Wine*, *Devils & Dust* too often sounds like a chain store selling faux Americana bric-a-brac. One always suspects with Springsteen that, in addition to a blonde Telecaster and "the Big Man," a focus group lies close at hand. The album is suspiciously tuned in to two recent trends, the exploding population of the Arizona and New Mexico exurbs; and the growing religiosity of the country as a whole. *Devils & Dust* is very South by Southwest—Mary is now Maria, there's a lot of mesquite and scrub pine, and one song even comes with a handy key to its regional terminology (Mustaneros: Mustangers; Pradera: Prairie; Riata: Rope). It's also crammed with Biblical imagery, from a modern re-telling of the story of Leah to Christ's final solacing of his mother. The first is a silly throwaway; the second is a fetching, Dylan-inspired hymn that ends with the teasing rumination, "Well Jesus kissed his mother's hands/ Whispered, 'Mother, still your tears,/ For remember the soul of the universe/Willed a world and it appeared.'"

The high watermark for Springsteen commercially, of course, was 1984, when "Born in the USA" somehow caught both the feelings of social dislocation and the euphoric jingoism of the Reagan era. Landau's mythic creation, the blue-collar, rock 'n' roll naif, has never held such broad appeal since. In recent years, Springsteen has settled into a pattern of selling a couple million albums (*Born in the USA* sold 15 million) to the Bruce die-hards. A clue to who these people are can be found in Springsteen's evolving persona, which is no longer as structured around his own working-class roots. On a short DV film on the CD's flip side, Springsteen says he tries to "disappear" into the voices of the migrant workers and ghetto prisoners whose stories make up *Devils & Dust:* "What would they do, what wouldn't they do, how would they behave in this circumstance, the rhythm of their speech, that's sort of where the music comes in." With Landau nowhere in evidence (he's thanked, but excluded from the album's formal credits), it is up to Springsteen alone to impersonate the voices of the dispossessed. The pupil has finally surpassed the master.

Nonetheless, here I am, starting to hum its tunes, growing a little devil's patch, hitting the gym, and adding a distant heartland twang to my speech. (My wife, meanwhile, curls up on the sofa in shame.) You old bullshitter, you got me again.

READING WRITING

This Text: Reading

1. How do all the authors define authenticity? Where do they differ?
2. Do you agree with any of the definitions of authenticity? More importantly, do you agree with the concept of authenticity—or do you know people who do?
3. What do you think the criteria for judging music should be?
4. Write down ten people or things you think are authentic. Now look at the list and think about what are the common links between them. Then compare your definition with those of the writers.
5. Which demographic do you think is most vulnerable to the authenticity argument?
6. What is the relationship between authenticity and cool?

Your Text: Reading

1. Write a persuasive paper about why authenticity should be the guiding principle in choosing which art to view or buy.
2. Or take the opposite tack—write about why authenticity is overrated.
3. Write a definitional paper about the criteria people use to judge art. (You might refer to the "Is It Art?" suite in the visual art chapter.)
4. Write a paper about the future of the use of authenticity.

Classroom Activities

1. Compare your experiences listening to songs and reading the lyrics. First listen to a song, then read its lyrics. For a different song, reverse the procedure. What differences in understanding the song does this make?

2. If possible, listen to a song, then watch a video. What differences in understanding the song does this make?

3. Before listening to its content, read its album/CD cover. What symbols and themes does the band use in designing the cover? What do they suggest about the album's content? About the nature of the band? Now listen to some of the music. How do your preconceived ideas about the music compare to those presented by the music itself?

4. Watch a section of a movie with a soundtrack. What emotions does the soundtrack try to convey? Now watch the same movie with the sound lowered. Do you get the same ideas without the music? Does the music enhance your understanding of the movie? Detract from it?

5. Come up with some sample band names. Name genres for which the band's name would be appropriate. What does this exercise say about the way we view a band's name?

Essay Ideas

1. Pick a song. What is the mood of the music compared to its lyrics? Do they work well together? Why or why not? Are the lyrics more sophisticated than the music or vice versa? Write a paper that makes an argument about the compatibility of music and lyrics.

2. Find a CD you do not know well. Study its cover, making notes on what the cover is "saying" to a potential listener. Now listen to the songs (reading the lyrics if you wish). Does the message behind the cover reflect the music? Why or why not? You can also do similar work with the band's name.

3. Find a well-known song you like. How would you find out information about the song? What sources might be appropriate? How might you approach writing a paper if you had this information? As you think about this question, look for information on the song. When you have gathered enough information, think of arguments or ideas about the song about which you could write.

4. Take a band you like that has produced more than one album. Trace its critical history. What elements of the band's work do the critics pick up on on a consistent basis? What is their general opinion of the band? How do they classify its genre? Now sit and think about whether you agree or disagree with these critics—and why.

5. Find two songs that have similar subjects. Compare and contrast their approaches to the subject, through both their music and lyrics. What approach do you favor, and why?

6. Find a band or bands with an explicitly political approach. Do you know their politics through their music or outside of it? Does their outside behavior argee with their music? How do critics and other members of the media approach their relationship between politics and music? What do their fans think?

7. Find a movie or television show with a prominent soundtrack—does the music work well with the movie or TV series? What are your criteria? Is there a specific moment in the movie or television show that embodies the success or failure of the director's use of music?

The Authenticity Suite

Though this technology does not exist yet, it undoubtedly is on its way.

HEY, WHERE DID THE CHAPTER GO?

In the table of contents, you were promised a technology chapter, and we're going to give you one—just not here. For years, we wanted to put our technology chapter entirely on the Web. Part of the reason was that so many of our essays in previous versions were actually a pretty even mix of material gathered from printed and electronic sources. But we noticed that more and more of the printed sources we like, including those from *The New York Times, The Washington Post,* and other more traditional media outlets, are investing as much (or more) energy in their Web portals as their printed versions. A big change came from Time Warner, who decided in recent years to foreground their Web presence. Now *The New York Times* has followed suit. In fact, two of the most important cultural magazines in the United States— *Slate* and *Salon*—exist solely in cyberspace. So now, when doing a chapter on "technology," it makes more sense to place readings on that topic within the space that has changed that term forever.

THE HISTORY OF OUR PRESENCE ON THE WEB

For our first edition, we had a Web companion site that focused on the authors of our material. Last time, we changed the form to a more interactive site that supplemented an edition that was much more visual in nature and added a blog, where we added (admittedly a little haphazardly) new links as we came about them. This time, we are striving to be a larger presence on the Web by placing an entire chapter there. Additionally, by placing an entire chapter and readings that link to our other chapters on the Web, it will facilitate jumping from reading to reading, Web site to Web site.

BUT THAT'S NOT ALL

One of the more academic reasons for placing material on the Web is that it also mirrors how we increasingly interact with academic material. Although professors and students consult books routinely for studying, so much of our reading comes through the Web or electronic databases. Many teachers and students also use programs like Blackboard and WebCt to respond to work on discussion boards or hand in assignments. In many classes, these sites become a clearinghouse of information. But not only that—we increasingly see the Web as our first place to find information, whether it be academic, trivia, entertainment, or geographic. In fact, we often are upset when we cannot find information we want on the Web.

HOW THIS WORKS WITH OUR BOOK

Much if not most of the material we have gathered here has appeared either online in a periodical or electronic database. We already have material on technology in our book, including a new suite directly engaging the battle between bloggers and journalists, and individual articles about technology as well. What this Web-based chapter allows us to do is expand the book beyond its printed pages, giving us a chance to link you to resources we could not fit here, including media outlets, writing resources, and material like photo essays. It also allows us to be more precise in our use of technology. In a literal sense, technology is the subchapter behind all of our chapters—it is various forms of technology that allow artists and companies to create and us to read or watch and buy. In the chapter on the Web, we have made more specific links between the idea of technology and our individual chapters, hoping to broaden our use of technology.

In order to get to our website, please go to www.prenhall.com/silverman <http://www.prenhall.com/silverman>. That will bring you to a page with further explanation on how to access the articles.

TEXT CREDITS

PHOTO CREDITS

Leonardo da Vinci (1452–1519). "Mona Lisa." Oil on canvas, 77 x 53 cm. Inv. 779. Photo: R.G. Ojeda. Louvre, Paris, Reunion des Musees Nationaux/Art Resource, NY.

Photo of San Francisco State University sign. © Courtesy of Professor Dean Rader.

Photo of San Francisco State University sign, close-up: © Courtesy of Professor Dean Rader.

Photo of City College sign (Fall Classes). © Courtesy of Professor Dean Rader.

City College of San Francisco Student Parking sign. © Courtesy of Professor Dean Rader.

City College of San Francisco, front. © Courtesy of Professor Dean Rader.

University of San Francisco, stairs. © Courtesy of Professor Dean Rader.

USF shrubs (University of San Francisco). © Courtesy of Professor Dean Rader.

Moon Pie wrapper. © Courtesy of Professor Jonathan Silverman.

Rest Stop, Route 66. © Courtesy of Professor Jonathan Silverman.

Gatorade bottles. © Courtesy of Professor Jonathan Silverman.

Kansas road, sky, landscape. © Courtesy of Professor Jonathan Silverman.

Arkansas landscape. © Courtesy of Professor Jonathan Silverman.

Wrong Way Road Signs. © Courtesy of Professor Jonathan Silverman.

"Hell Is Real" billboard. © Courtesy of Professor Jonathan Silverman.

Homeland Security threat level (sign). © Courtesy of Professor Jonathan Silverman.

Road Signs, Albuquerque to Phoenix/LA. © Courtesy of Professor Jonathan Silverman.

Restrooms. © Courtesy of Professor Jonathan Silverman.

Bear (outside gas station). © Courtesy of Professor Jonathan Silverman.

Fixie Graffiti, Downtown San Francisco. Photo: Jonathan Hunt.

Bike Race. © Steve Velvo/Jonathan Hunt.

Scene Still of *Judge Dredd*, year 1995, Sylvester Stallone. Cinergi Pictures/Richard Blanshard/The Kobal Collection.

Pink Fixie bike in San Francisco. Photo: Jean Davis.

People sitting on lawn with bikes. © Randy Reddig/Jonathan Hunt.

Movie still from *The Impossible Hour* (1974). Photo: Jonathan Hunt.

Bike chained to car meter. Photo: Jonathan Hunt.

Your Fixie Makes You Look Fat–Sign painted on sidewalk. © Franco Folini/Jonathan Hunt.

Washington, United States: This image taken 18 December 2006 shows the 25 December/ 01 January cover of *Time* Magazine featuring the "Person of the Year" cover. Time magazine named "You" as its person of the year 16 December, with a mirror cover design. Karen Bleier/Agence France Presse/Getty Images.

Woman with skateboard in dorm room. Photo: Getty Images/Digital Vision.

24–US TV Series–2002–Currie Graham, Kiefer Sutherland. Photo: Fox-TV/Picture Desk, Inc./Kobal Collection.

Heroes–US TV Series–2006–Adair Tishler, Ali Larter, Gray-Cabey Noah, Leonard Roberts. Photo: NBC/Universal TV/Picture Desk, Inc./Kobal Collection slightly.

Seinfeld–US TV Series–1990–1998–Jerry Seinfeld and Jason Alexander. Photo: NBC TV/Picture Desk, Inc./Kobal Collection.

Wearing Black pride, Black Bart teeshirt, New York, NY. Photo: © Beryl Goldberg, Photographer.

Sex and the City–US TV Series–1998–2004–Sarah Jessica Parker and Kim Cattrall. Photo: DarrenStar Productions/Picture Desk, Inc./Kobal Collection.

American Idol. American Idol Productions/19 Television/Fox TV Network/Fremantle Media North America/The Kobal Collection.

The Apprentice–US TV Series. Photo: Trump Productions/Mark Burnett Productions/ Picture Desk, Inc./Kobal Collection.

05 Jan 2003, Coppel, Texas, USA—Sheila Wessenberg's son watches *Blue's Clues* on a portable television in the family minivan while she works. © Ed Kashi/CORBIS. All Rights Reserved.

Cassius Marcellus Coolidge (Dogs at table playing cards). Source: Time & Life Pictures/Getty Images, Inc.

Two dogs dressed up at a table called Jack Sprat, 1996. Source: William Wegman.

Grant Wood, "American Gothic." 1930. Oil on Beaver Board. 29 7/8″ x 24 7/8″. Friends of American Art. Source: The Art Institute of Chicago. Photograph © 2005 The Art Institute of Chicago. All Rights Reserved.

American Gothic t-shirt. Source: Imagination Photo Design.

American Gothic tie. Source: Imagination Photo Design.

An American Gothic illustration with Sadam in the background. Source: Abu Mahjoob Creative Production.

"American Gothic," made from balloons. Photo: Larry Moss/Airigami.

American Gothic–Beavis Butt-head magnet. Source: Imagination Photo Design.

American Gothic–Spongebob & Patrick. Source: Imagination Photo Design.

American Gothic–goth couple by Leo Abbett. © Leo Abbett/artoons@comcast.net.

Washington, DC: The AIDS memorial quilt is spread out near the White House, forming an ellipse. Photo: Agency France Presse/Getty Images.

Volunteers and others walk on the 21,000 panel Names Project AIDS Memorial Quilt in Washington. Organizers anticipated more than 300,000 people would view the quilt during the weekend. Photo: AP Wide World Photos.

AIDS quilt–overhead shot. Photo: Vanessa Vick/Photo Researchers, Inc.

Graffiti L.A.: Street Styles and Art by Steve Grody/The Anatomy of a Piece–Diagram–How two images should look with the illustrating arrows and text. © Graffita L.A.: Street Styles and Art by Steve Grody, Abrams, 1007. pp. 64–65.

Andy Warhol, "Marilyn Monroe," 1962. Oil on canvas. 81″ x 66–3/4″. TM 2002 Marilyn Monroe LLC by CMG Worldwide Inc. www.MarilynMonroe.com. © 2003 Andy Warhol Foundation for the Visual Arts/ARS, New York.

Warhol, Andy. One Hundred Cans, 1962. Oil on canvas, 72 x 52 in. © Copyright The Andy Warhol Foundation for the Visual Arts/ARS, NY.

Pages 63–69, 164–169 from UNDERSTANDING COMICS by SCOTT MCCLOUD. Copyright © 1993, 1994 by Scott McCloud. Reprinted by permission of HarperCollins Publishers Inc.

World Trade Center buildings burning from 9-11 attack. People sitting in Brooklyn at park–talking. Photo: Thomas Hoepker/Magnum Photos, Inc.

Beirut Residents Continue to Flock to Southern Neighborhoods. Affluent Lebanese drive down the street to look at destroyed neighborhood August 15, 2006 in southern Beirut, Lebanon. As the United Nations brokered cease fire between Israel and Hezbollah. Photo: Spencer Platt/Getty Images Inc.

Reporter Gert Van Langendonk located the subjects of Spencer Platt's prize-winning photo from the Lebanon War. From left to right: Bissan Marou, 29, Noor Nasser, 21, Jad Maroun, 22, Lana El Khalil, 25 (the owner of the car, not seen in Platt's photograph). Karium Ben Khelifa/OEIL PUBLIC.

Errol Morris as a boy sitting on a wall. Courtesy of Errol Morris, Fourth Floor Productions, Inc. c/o Wylie Agency.

Errol Morris as a boy with a dog in a backyard. Courtesy of Errol Morris, Fourth Floor Productions, Inc. c/o Wylie Agency.

Photo of the *Lusitania*, a British ship launched 1907. Michael W. Pocock Collection provided by www.maritimequest.com.

Poster subject relates to the victims from the sinking of the passenger liner *Lusitania* by a German U-boat on May 7, 1915. The sinking contributed to the United States' eventual involvement in World War I. ca. 1915. Creator Name: Fred Spear. © David Pollack/CORBIS. All Rights Reserved.

130 victims of *Lusitania* disaster buried in one large grave at Queenstown, Ireland, May 10, 1915. Source: Underwood & Underwood / Courtesy National Archives, photo no. 165-WW-537.10.

Newspaper Article titled Watch's Fixed Hands Record Lusitania's Last 30 Minutes. Source: *Toronto Star*.

Piss Christ. © A. Serrano. Courtesy of the artist and the Paula Cooper Gallery, New York.

Art exhibit display called "What is the proper way to display the US flag?" Photo: Scott Tyler (AKA Dread Scott).

Welcome to America's finest tourist plantation. Courtesy of Louis Hock, David Avalos and Elizabeth Sisco.

Kissing Doesn't Kill. Source: Gran Fury Records, Manuscripts and Archives Division, The New York Public Library, Astor, Lenox, and Tilden Foundation.

Klanswoman (Grand Klaliff II) 1990. © A. Serrano. Courtesy of the artist and the Paula Cooper Gallery, New York.

Kurt Cobain Citybank poster. Source: Andy Cox.

Arnold Swarzenegger Citybank poster. Source: Andy Cox.

Chris Ofili's "The Holy Virgin Mary," a controversial painting of the Virgin Mary embellished with a clump of elephant dung and two dozen cutouts of buttocks from pornographic magazine, is shown at the Brooklyn Museum of Art Monday, Sep. 27, 1999, in New York. Photo: Diane Bondareff/AP Wide World Photos.

Our Lady. © 1999 Alma Lopez.

Yo Mama's Last Supper, 1996. Courtesy Robert Miller Gallery.

Marnie Spencer, "Between the Devil and the Deep Blue Sea," 2003 acrylic, ink, pencil on canvas, 60 x 60 inches. Collection of Howard and Judy Tullman. Image courtesy of Julie Baker Fine Art, Grass Valley, CA.

Stupid Comics © 1998 by Jim Mahfood. "true tales of amerikkkan history Part II: the true Thanksgiving . . ." Stupid comics. © 1998 Jim Mahfood.

Indians fan Jim Stamper shows a Chief Wahoo sign prior to game 3 of the AL Division Series at Jacobs Field in Cleveland, Saturday Oct. 4, 1997. The series between the Indians and the New York Yankees stands at 1–1. Photo: AP Wide World Photos.

Jets vs Washington. A fan holds up a sign. Photo: Joe Rogate/AI Photo Service/Newscom.

Fans hold up Chief Wahoo logo signs as they celebrate the Cleveland Indians' opening win over the Minnesota Twins in Cleveland, Ohio, Monday, April 8, 2002. Photo: AP Wide World Photos.

Cartoon: "Which one is the mascot?" Thomas Little Moon.

BUT I'M HONORING YOU, DUDE! © 2002 Lalo Alcaraz/Universal Press Syndicate.

Pow Wow Cartoon. Richard Crowson Illustration.

1968—American sprinters Tommie Smith and John Carlos raise their fists and give the Black Power Salute at the 1968 Olympic Games in Mexico City. The move was a symbolic protest against racism in the United States. Bettmann/CORBIS. All Rights Reserved.

John Wayne in "The Telegraph Trail." Photo: Photofest.

MTV Movie Awards 1999 Ceremony. The actor Jackie Chan with his award. Photo: Trapper Frank/Corbis/Sigma.

Leonardo daVinci (1452–1519), "Mona Lisa," oil on canvas, 77 x 53 cm. Inv. 779. Photo R.G. Ojeda. Louvre, Paris. Reunion des Musees Nationaux/Art Resource, NY.

Britney Spears at the Super Bowl Party hosted by Britney Spears and Justin Timberlake to benefit their individual foundations. Planet Hollywood, New York, NY. Photo: Fashion Wire Daily/AP Wide World Photos.

Exterior of the Parthenon and surrounding ruins, Athens, Greece. Photo: Bill Bachman/PhotoEdit Inc.

State Capitol Building designed in Greek architectural style with unfluted Ionic columns, Richmond, VA. Photo: Dennis MacDonald/PhotoEdit Inc.

Evelyn Street Laundry. Photo: Cheryl Aaron.

Teddy bears hanging on clothesline. Photo: David Graham.

Mexican flag hangs on white block wall. Photo: Tony Freeman/PhotoEdit Inc.

American flag. Photo: © Joseph Nettis/Photo Researchers, Inc.

Rundown Street in Washington DC. Boarded-up windows, overrun grass, and litter fill a rundown street. © Shepard Sherbell/CORBIS SABA Press Photos, Inc. Photographer: Shepard Sherbell. Date Photographed: May 24, 1996.

"City: SINKING SPRING. State/Prov: PA. Create Date: 9/27/2004. Caption: A sign advertising a model home stands in a housing development of new homes. Sinking Spring, Pennsylvania on Monday, September 27, 2004. Photographer: Bradley C Bower/Bloomberg News/Landov.

1979 Pontiac Firebird Trans Am 6.6 litre special edition. Photo: Alvey & Towers.

Ford 1948 yellow pick up truck. © Randy Reddig/Transtock/CORBIS. All Rights Reserved.

Pedestrian crossing sign. Roy Morsch/AGE/SuperStock, Inc.

Drinking Road Crossing Sign. Photo: Rick Lopez.

Deer Crossing Sign. New Britain, PA. Photo: William Thomas Cain/Getty/Newscom.

Dear Crossing Sign. Photo: Eunice Harris/Jupiter Images–FoodPix–Creatas–Brand X–Banana Stock–PictureQuest.

Our Lady of Guadalupe on side of a building. Photo: Kim Karpeles, Life Through The Lens.

Mural of Our Lady of Guadalupe. Photo: Richard Puchalsky.

The Salem Diner. www.roadsidearchitecture.com

Exterior of Denny's Classic Diner. Copyright © Ronald C. Saari.

Exterior of Diner called Halfway Diner in Village. Copyright © 1997 Ronald C. Saari.

Rigo 1995, One Tree. Photo: RIGO/Gallery Paule Anglim.

Birds and Cars (Acrylic on wood 40′ x 80′). Courtesy of Rigo23 and Gallery Paule Anglim.

Pages 114, 117, 118, 119, 120, 123, 126, 127, 128, & 129 from American Signs by Lisa Mahar. Courtesy of Lisa Mahar from her book, *American Signs*.

Glurpo, World's only underwater clown–Aquarena–San Marcos, Texas postcard. Source: The Greater Beaumont Chamber of Commerce.

El Jardin Hotel postcard. Source: The Greater Beaumont Chamber of Commerce.

Title: Romeo Must Die, year 2000. Kharen J. Hill/Warner Brothers/The Kobal Collection.

Still Scene–Title: The Fast and the Furious, 2001. Actors: Paul Walker, Jordana Brewster, Vin Diesel. Bob Marshak/Original Films/The Kobal Collection.

Scene Still from I, Robot, 2004 with Will Smith and Bridget Moynahan. 20th Century Fox/The Kobal Collection/Digital Domain.

Scene Still from Waiting to Exhale, 1995, Loretta Devine, Lela Rocchion, Angela Bassett and Whitney Houston. 20th Century Fox/The Kobal Collection.

Scene still of Star Wars Episode IV: A New Hope–Year 1977. Lucas Film/20th Century Fox/The Kobal Collection.

Cinderella TV/DVD Player. A special "Cinderella" themed television DVD player combo. Reuters/CORBIS.

Scene still from SICKO 2007. Dog Eat Dog Films/Weinstein Company/The Kobal Collection.

Movie, The Searchers, with John Wayne and a Native American. Photo: Photofest.

Scene still from X-Men The Last Standing–X-MEN 3. 2006. 20th Century Fox/The Kobal Collection.

Scene still from Buffy the Vampire Slayer. 20th Century Fox Television/The Kobal Collection.

Scene still from Marie Antoinette (2006). Columbia/Pathe/Sony/The Kobal Collection.

Scene still from Grey's Anatomy 2005. ABC-TV/The Kobal Collection.

Scene still from Veronica Mars 2004, personality Kristen Bell. Warner Brothers TV/The Kobal Collection.

RuPaul Poses on New York Sidewalk. © Mitchell Gerber/CORBIS.

RuPaul as a man at the 2000 Soul Train Lady of Soul Awards. Photo: Getty Images Entertainment, Inc.

Gurule–Memorial cross road sign with flowers and beads. Photo: Bob Bednar.

Padilla–Memorial cross road sign–Wreath, flowers, rocks, fence. Photo: Bob Bednar.

Memorial cross road sign–road, guardrail, cross with flowers set against sky (silhouette). Photo: Bob Bednar.

Memorial cross road sign–cross with flowers under Burger King billboard sign. Photo: Bob Bednar.

Memorial cross road sign–Two engraved wooden crosses surrounded by stuffed bears and some flowers. Photo: Bob Bednar.

Memorial cross road sign–Ricky & Karen–Two engraved crosses with flowers and sunflowers growing on the fence. Photo: Bob Bednar.

Memorial cross road sign–Ricky & Karen–Two engraved white crosses with flowers on a curve. Photo: Bob Bednar.

Memorial cross road sign–Engraved wooden cross attached to wire fence covered in imitation floral vine. Photo: Bob Bednar.

Sandoval/Memorial cross road sign–Engraved wooden cross and marker below highway. Photo: Bob Bednar.

Horey–Memorial cross road sign–State Police car in background. Photo: Bob Bednar.

Memorial road sign with a photograph of the person who died. Sign says, "Please Don't Drink and Drive In Memory of Barbara Howell." Photo: Bob Bednar.

Memorial road sign with a photograph of the person who died. The cross (looks like totem pole) is in memory of a young girl and is covered with rosary beads, necklaces of flowers and beads. Photo: Bob Bednar.

Memorial cross road sign with the MOM in flowers. Photo: Bob Bednar.

Memorial cross road sign–two wooden crosses with flowers on the side of a hill off a highway. Photo: Bob Bednar.

Memorial Star of David Road Sign with rock and flowers, mountains in distance. Photo: Bob Bednar.

Memorial Star of David Road Sign–wooden with flowers. Photo: Bob Bednar.

Memorial cross road sign with the words MOM in flowers. The cross carries the name Martah Martinez. Photo: Bob Bednar.

Memorial cross road sign–Concrete holding up the road sign that says mom. A child's hand print is surrounded by several names and a man's hand with a wedding ring is pressed against the concrete. Photo: Bob Bednar.

Las Vegas' NYC replica. Photo © www.danheller.com/Dan Heller Photography.

27 Jul 2007, Washington DC, USA—Comedy Central's Stephen Colbert meets the White House Press Corps while awaiting a meeting with White House Press Secretary Tony Snow in the Brady Press Briefing Room. Martin H. Simon/CORBIS. All Rights Reserved.

Katty Ostapowicz, 26 year old female, whose image is on the Internet. Photo: Alyson Aliano Photography.

A young man in his home. Photo: Alyson Aliano Photography.

A young Asian woman in her home. Photo: Alyson Aliano Photography.

Caitlin–myspace.com–On line site. Photo: Imagination Photo Design. © Caitlin/IRC/Pearson.

Caitlin's Blurbs and Interests–myspace.com–On line site. Photo: Imagination Photo Design. © Caitlin/IRC/Pearson.

Caitlin–Vimeo–Videos & Clips–myspace.com–On line site. Photo: Imagination Photo Design. © Caitlin/IRC/Pearson.

Caitlin–flickr–Various photos posted–myspace.com–On line site. Photo: Imagination Photo Design. © Caitlin/IRC/Pearson.

Caitlin's Profile–facebook–filled with facts and pictures–myspace.com–On line site. Photo: Imagination Photo Design. © Caitlin/IRC/Pearson.

Couple using mobile phone standing on a busy street in Mumbai, India. Photo: Zubin Shroff/Image Bank/Getty Images.

Johnny Cash (1969) flipping off the photographer. Photo: Jim Marshall.

Businessman standing in front of television screens displaying technology. Photo: Colin Anderson/Getty Images, Inc.–Blend Images.

INDEX

A

Ad hominem fallacy, 47

Advertisements, citing, 70

Advertising. *See also* Media
  analysis of, 558–560
  artistic components and, 544
  case studies, 113–115
  code words and, 560–570
  communication through images
    and, 544
  criticisms of, 540
  effects on consumers, 544
  influences on, 543
  of movies, 343–344
  pathos and, 43
  race and ethnicity and, 552–557

"Advertising and People of Color,"
    552–557

African American culture, 155–157. *See
    also* Race and ethnicity

Age
  depiction on television, 126
  perspective and, 28–29

Alexie, Sherman, 373–376

"All the Memories Money Can Buy:
    Marketing Authenticity and
    Manufacturing Authorship," 689–692

American culture, race and, 273–282

American Gothic, 201–205

American Psychological Association
    (APA), 65

*American Signs: Form and Meaning on
    Route 66,* 412–423

Analogies, 45

"Andy Warhol: The Most Controversial
    Artist of the Twentieth Century?",
    221–224

Annotated student essay (sample), 57–65

Antagonistic audiences, 53

The Apprentice, 185–189

Arab American experience post-9/11,
    304–306

Arboleda, Teja, 300–303

Architectural decisions. *See* Public and
    private space

Arguments, 41–53
  avoiding fallacies and, 47
  common sense and, 53
  credible information and sources and, 46
  differing opinions and, 46
  emotional, 43
  establishing credibility and authority
    and, 46–47
  inductive or deductive reasoning and,
    47–48
  knowing audience and, 51–53
  knowing your arguments, 41–44
  logical, 42–43
  making claims and, 44–45
  meaning of, 42
  purpose of, 42
  sense of credibility and, 43–44
  synthesis and, 49–51
  thinking like a lawyer and, 48–49
  Toulmin system and, 48–49
  using claims and support in, 45

Aristotle, 9–10

Articles, citing of, 69

Art works, citing of, 70

Asian American culture, 307–312. *See also*
    Race and ethnicity

Assignments, understanding, 299

Atwood, Margaret, 611–613

Audience
  knowledge of, 51–53
  manipulation of and movies, 344

Aura, 202

Authenticity, musical, 688–702. *See also*
    Music

Q

"Quallunaat 101: Inuits Study White Folks in This New Academic Field," 298–300
Queen (rock group) songs, 671–672
Quoting, 50

R

Race and ethnicity, 28–29. *See also* Stereotyping
  advertising exploitation of, 552–557
  biological traits and, 267–268
  changing definitions and, 269–270
  class and, 272
  discriminatory practices and, 270
  ignorant absolutes and, 175
  individual views and, 272
  movies and, 349–358
  "otherness" and, 269
  as political and social constructions, 270–271
  reality television and, 185–189
  self-perception and, 268
  social construction and, 268
  stereotyping and, 271
  television and, 122, 126
  visual construction and, 268–269
"Race Is a Four-Letter Word," 300–303
Racelessness, movies and, 349–358
Racial identity development, 288–290
Rader, Dean, 76–82, 113–116
Radio programs, citing, 70
"The Rap Against Rockism," 696–699
Reader's Guide to Periodicals, 57
Reading backward, 40
"Reading Cindy Sherman and Gender," 224–226
Reading systems, 6–7
"Reading the Nautical Star," 514–516
Reality television, 177–189. *See also* Television
  commercialization and, 183–185
  explosion of, 177
  phenomenon of, 177
  point-counterpoint regarding, 178–179
  reality of, 182–183
  situating, 180–182
  television culture and, 179–185
"Reality Television: American Myths and Racial Ideology," 185–189
"Reality TV: Remaking Television Culture," 179–185
"Reality TV Bites– or Does It? The New Soap Opera or the End of Civilization; A Point-Counterpoint," 178–179
Reasons
  argument building and, 49
  building good paragraphs and, 38
"Red State, Blue State: Hometown News," 597–602
Regions, perspective and, 28–29
Relationships. *See also* College relationships
  blogging and, 623–635
  college relationships, 636–650
  as fluid texts, 608
  friendships, 613–617
  mothers, 618–622
  objectivity and, 608–609
  personal experiences and, 607–608
  romantic, 611–613
  societal expectations and, 607–608
  what constitutes "good relationships," 609
Research
  guerilla research, 57
  nontraditional texts and, 53–57
  nuts and bolts, 56–57
Revising and editing, 40–41
Rhetoric, 9–10
Rich, Frank, 242–244
Richey, William, 658–667
"Right on Target: Revisiting Elvis Costello's *My Aim Is True*," 672–675
Rinehart, Fave, 165–174
Roadside car crash memorials, 497–507
Road stories, 82–90
Rockism, 696–699
"The Rock Lexicon," 669–671
"Rolling the Dice," 578–581
Romantic relationships, 611–613
Romeo Must Die, 349–358